Islam
ART AND ARCHITECTURE

The Kaaba in the Great Mosque of Mecca is the focal point of the Islamic religion and the destination for every muslim pilgrim.

Islam
ART AND ARCHITECTURE

Edited by
Markus Hattstein and Peter Delius

KÖNEMANN

Contents

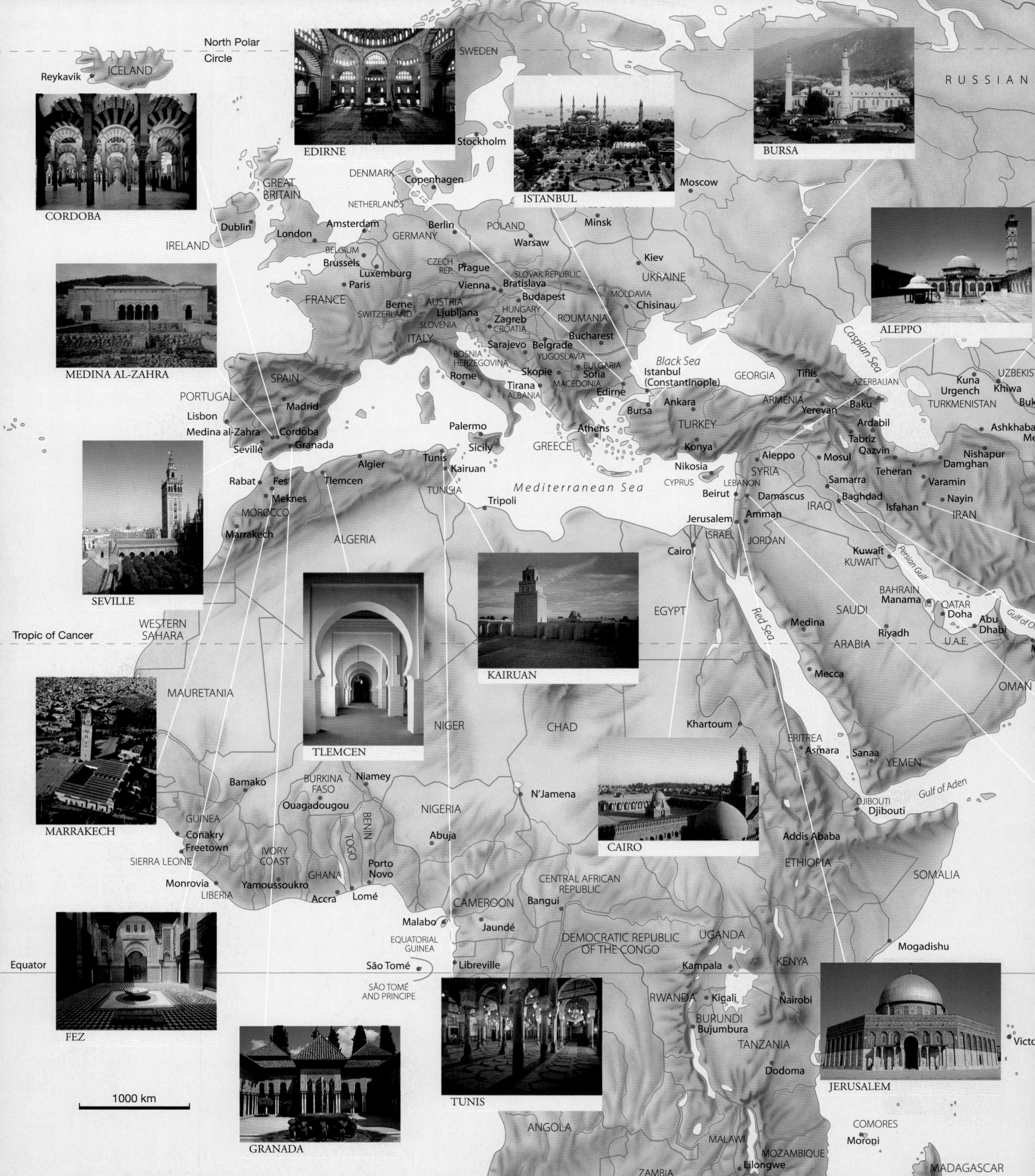

CORDOBA

EDIRNE

ISTANBUL

BURSA

MEDINA AL-ZAHRA

ALEPPO

SEVILLE

KAIRUAN

MARRAKECH

TLEMCEN

CAIRO

FEZ

TUNIS

GRANADA

JERUSALEM

North Polar Circle

Tropic of Cancer

Equator

1000 km

ICELAND
Reykavik

GREAT BRITAIN
IRELAND
Dublin
London

SWEDEN
Stockholm
DENMARK
Copenhagen
NETHERLANDS
Amsterdam
Berlin
GERMANY
BELGIUM
Brussels
Luxemburg
Paris
FRANCE
CZECH REP.
Prague
Vienna
Berne
AUSTRIA
SWITZERLAND
Ljubljana
SLOVENIA
Zagreb
CROATIA

POLAND
Warsaw
Minsk
Kiev
UKRAINE
MOLDAVIA
Chisinau
SLOVAK REPUBLIC
Bratislava
Budapest
HUNGARY
ROUMANIA
Bucharest
Belgrade
BOSNIA HERZEGOVINA
Sarajevo
YUGOSLAVIA
Skopie
BULGARIA
Sofia
MACEDONIA
Tirana
ALBANIA
Edirne

Moscow

RUSSIAN

SPAIN
PORTUGAL
Lisbon
Madrid
Medina al-Zahra
Cordoba
Seville
Granada

ITALY
Rome
Palermo
Sicily

Black Sea
Istanbul (Constantinople)
Bursa
Ankara
Athens
GREECE
TURKEY
Konya
Nikosia
CYPRUS

GEORGIA
Tiflis
ARMENIA
Yerevan
AZERBAIJAN
Baku
Ardabil
Tabriz
Qazvin

Caspian Sea

UZBEKIST
Kuna Urgench
Khiwa
Buk
TURKMENISTAN
Ashkhaba
Me
Nishapur
Damghan
Teheran
Varamin
IRAN
Baghdad
Isfahan
Nayin

Algier
Tlemcen
Rabat
Fes
Meknes
MOROCCO
Marrakech
ALGERIA

Tunis
Kairuan
TUNISIA
Tripoli

Mediterranean Sea

Aleppo
SYRIA
Beirut
LEBANON
Damascus
Jerusalem
ISRAEL
Amman
JORDAN
Cairo
Mosul
Samarra
IRAQ

Kuwait
KUWAIT
BAHRAIN
Manama
QATAR
Doha
Abu Dhabi
U.A.E.
OMAN
Gulf of O

Persian Gulf

WESTERN SAHARA

MAURETANIA

EGYPT
Red Sea
Medina
SAUDI
ARABIA
Riyadh
Mecca

Bamako
BURKINA FASO
Niamey
Ouagadougou
NIGER
CHAD
N'Jamena
GUINEA
Conakry
Freetown
SIERRA LEONE
IVORY COAST
GHANA
Monrovia
Yamoussoukro
LIBERIA
Accra
TOGO
BENIN
Porto Novo
Lomé
NIGERIA
Abuja
CAMEROON
Jaundé
Malabo
EQUATORIAL GUINEA
São Tomé
SÃO TOMÉ AND PRINCIPE
Libreville

Khartoum
ERITREA
Asmara
Sanaa
YEMEN
DJIBOUTI
Djibouti
Gulf of Aden
Addis Ababa
ETHIOPIA
SOMALIA

CENTRAL AFRICAN REPUBLIC
Bangui
DEMOCRATIC REPUBLIC OF THE CONGO
UGANDA
Kampala
RWANDA
Kigali
BURUNDI
Bujumbura
TANZANIA
Dodoma
KENYA
Nairobi
Mogadishu

Victo

ANGOLA
ZAMBIA
MALAWI
Lilongwe
MOZAMBIQUE
COMORES
Moroni
MADAGASCAR

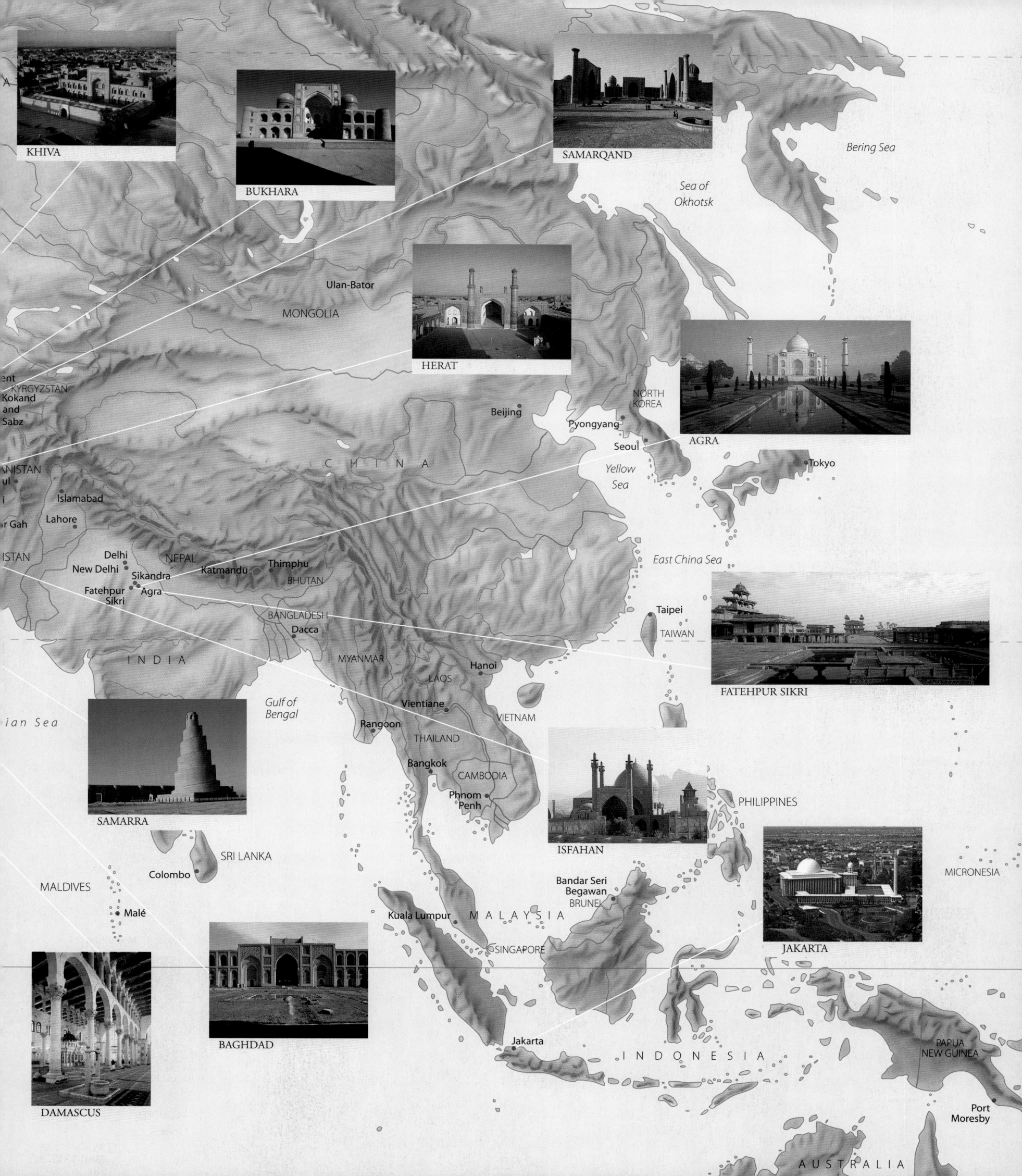

KHIVA

BUKHARA

SAMARQAND

Bering Sea

Sea of Okhotsk

Ulan-Bator

MONGOLIA

HERAT

ent

KYRGYZSTAN
Kokand
and
Sabz

ANISTAN
ul
i
r Gah

Islamabad

Lahore

ISTAN

Beijing

NORTH
KOREA

Pyongyang

Seoul

*Yellow
Sea*

Tokyo

AGRA

C H I N A

Delhi

New Delhi

Sikandra

Fatehpur
Sikri

Agra

NEPAL

Katmandu

Thimphu

BHUTAN

East China Sea

Taipei

TAIWAN

FATEHPUR SIKRI

BANGLADESH

Dacca

I N D I A

MYANMAR

Hanoi

LAOS

VIETNAM

*Gulf of
Bengal*

Vientiane

Rangoon

THAILAND

ian Sea

SAMARRA

Bangkok

CAMBODIA

Phnom
Penh

ISFAHAN

PHILIPPINES

SRI LANKA

MALDIVES

Colombo

Malé

Bandar Seri
Begawan

BRUNEI

MICRONESIA

JAKARTA

Kuala Lumpur

M A L A Y S I A

SINGAPORE

DAMASCUS

BAGHDAD

Jakarta

I N D O N E S I A

PAPUA
NEW GUINEA

Port
Moresby

A U S T R A L I A

Islam – World Religion and Cultural Power

Markus Hattstein

Literally, Islam means "devotion to God," more specifically to Allah, the One God. Those who practice such devotion and submit themselves to the will of Allah, are Muslims.

The profession of belief in the One God and in Muhammad as his Prophet, to whom God has revealed his message for mankind – as it is described in the Koran, the holy book of Islam – unites Muslims throughout the world. Obedience to the five main duties, or "pillars" of Islam, and the use of classical Arabic for all religious purposes, form the religious bond of the Muslim community. Islam means being aware of the omnipresence of God, in whose hands human beings place themselves and in whose mercy they trust, knowing God to be just and compassionate. Mankind is capable of acting for itself only if God wills or allows such action. Islam is the youngest world religion (although it actually regards itself as a revival of an ancient monotheistic religion that had existed from very ancient times). Its early success and the speed with which it spread even to non-Arab cultures immediately after the death of Muhammad, make it unique in religious history.

Within the bond of a common religion, many distinctive local, cultural and ethnic features developed quite early, since Islam constantly absorbed elements of the cultures it had conquered or converted. There were also recurrent episodes of religious schism, the most important and far-reaching being the split between Shiites and Sunnis. To that extent, Islam may be described as "diversity within unity." Between the Maghreb in the west, parts of China and Southeast Asia in the east, the entire Arab and Persian area, and parts of northern Africa in the south, as well as an increasingly strong presence in Europe, Islamic culture is a combination of unity and variety, which keeps it dynamic and alive, giving it a prominent position among the religions and cultures of the world.

The Arab cultural area – ancient Arabia and its cultural development

The Arabian Peninsula has a long tradition of settlement, although research into the subject has only just begun, since archeologists have excavated relatively few sites. Ancient Arabian culture is best documented in the Hadramawt and the rest of the Yemen, and in the south Arabian Peninsula, where mighty buildings or their ruins and the sites of fortresses testify to the splendor of the ancient Arabian Mina kingdom (4th–1st centuries B.C.) with its center of Qarnawu, Qatabanian kingdom (5th–1st centuries B.C.), and Sabaean kingdom (10th century B.C.–3rd century A.D.). Traces of early civilizations can also be found in the Arabian Peninsula that reveal influences from the Fertile Crescent.

The Arabian Peninsula comprises an area of 1.2 million square miles (3 million square kilometers), but it was, and still is, only sparsely populated because of its vast areas of desert. In the north, ancient Arabia shared a border with Mesopotamia (modern Iraq), and in the south it met the Indian Ocean. Monsoon rain from the sea fell on the mountain ranges in the south of the peninsula, making the Yemen and Oman fertile regions which have been permanently settled since very early times: the mountain slopes here were terraced and supplied with water by highly developed irrigation systems, and as a result extensive arable farming could develop. In the desert, on the other hand, there are only a few isolated fertile oases with date palms and sparse grazing for the nomads' herds. Rainfall is also very irregular above the mountains in the south, and there are prolonged periods of drought.

From early times, consequently, there was a great gulf between the sedentary, prosperous Arabs of the south and the impoverished seminomads of the desert, although the latter profited by the through traffic of caravans. The prosperous southern Arabs fitted out merchant ships, made good use of the mon-

Opposite: **The Kaaba in Mecca**, Saudi Arabia
The Kaaba, a gray stone building 36 ft (11 m) in height, is the main shrine of Islam. Only Muslims are permitted to enter it. The term *kaaba* (Arabic: "cube") describes the shape of the building. It is covered with a black veil of silk and cotton, which is replaced by draperies of white fabric during the pilgrimage season. The Kaaba contains the sacred Black Stone, which, according to tradition, was brought down to earth by the angel Gabriel. Even in pre-Islamic times, the Kaaba in Mecca was an important shrine.

Tarin in Hadramawt, Yemen
Already dating back to the Ancient Arabian Empire (10th century B.C.), Yemen's favorable climate conditions contributed to the development of a high culture with a powerful irrigation system. The city enjoyed a significant role in the trading along the "Incense Road."

Tarim is one of the most important cities of Hadramawt, a region in southern Yemen, which, owing to intensive irrigation was especially fertile, and through its diverse agriculture had a high standard of living. Today, the city still shows the ancient Arabian style of narrow dwellings of five to nine stories.

The rock tombs of Petra, Jordan
Petra was one of the most important regions in the ancient Arabian cultural area, and from the 4th century B.C. was at the center of the old Arabian kingdom of the Nabataeans, who made it a flourishing commercial market, and controlled a large part of the "Incense Road." They thus profited from the trade between the Greeks, Medes, Persians, and Egyptians, and set up many depositories to protect their goods. In the 2nd century B.C. they extended their rule to Syria and Palestine, but were defeated in A.D. 106 by the emperor Trajan, and the area became a province of the Roman Empire. Characteristic evidence of Nabataean culture exists in the multistory temples and tombs built into the rock walls of Petra, and in Aramaic inscriptions on stones. Petra lay forgotten for a long time, and was not rediscovered by archeologists until the beginning of the 19th century.

soon winds, and engaged in flourishing foreign trade, particularly with the Malabar coast of India, the Mesopotamian kingdoms to the northeast, and the kingdom of Egypt in the northwest (first mentioned in the records in 2100 B.C.). The goods traded were chiefly spices and incense. The camel caravans of the "Incense Road," as it is called, which had trading intersections distributed over the entire Arabian Peninsula, also brought a certain prosperity to the semi-nomadic caravan traders, certain desert cities and oases, and so to the northern regions. Arabia thus became the hub of trade between east and west at an early period, and exerted significant influence on the cultural development of the Mediterranean area.

In the 6th century B.C., Arabia was regarded as part of the Persian kingdom of the Achaemenid dynasty, which founded the province of Arabiya in 539 B.C. Thereafter, southern Arabia saw the rise of a great number of kingdoms, most of them on the western coast. On the border with Palestine lay the kingdom of the Nabataeans of Petra, whose cultural wealth was founded on trade; art was in its prime there between the 4th century B.C. and the 1st century A.D. When the region was annexed by the Roman Empire in 106, it achieved great prosperity under the relatively mild rule of its Roman overlords. The best-known example is probably the semi-independent kingdom of Palmyra, although it overestimated its power when in the 3rd century, under Queen Zenobia, it challenged Rome and was crushed by the emperor Aurelian. After profiting from the extension and improvement of the trade routes carried out by the Roman administration, Arabia found itself increasingly positioned between two hostile fronts, as the great powers of Rome, and later Byzantium, opposed their adversaries, the newly strengthened Persian kingdoms of the Sassanians and Parthians.

After the 4th and 5th centuries A.D. a certain military stalemate set in. Both great powers – Byzantium and the Sassanian Persians – were anxious to create buffer states ruled by Arab vassals, who were bound to perform military service for their overlords, in exchange for cultural independence under their protection. On the Persian side, those involved were the Lakhmids, with Hira, their capital, near Kufa, and on the Byzantine side, the Christian Ghassanids, with their capital Basra. The Arab tribes on both sides learned a great deal about the techniques of warfare and fortification from these great powers, and acquired knowledge that would be of significance later on for the military successes of Muhammad and early Islam.

"Oriental despotism" – forms of government in the region

The "irrigation states," a term used for the early advanced civilizations of Egypt and Mesopotamia, had in common, as the earliest development of a logical concept of the state, the form of government described by K. A. Wittfogel as "Oriental despotism." Many institutions found in early Islamic kingdoms can be interpreted as descended from and succeeding ancient oriental forms of government and administration. This is especially true of the centralized rule of the caliphs, more particularly in the caliphate of the Abbasids.

These states shared a common interest in the extensive exploitation of water and the local inundations that left the fertile mud of the Nile, the Euphrates, and the Tigris behind when they receded. Artificial irrigation by canals rivers and the system left behind of dam-building under the centralized administration, were pre-conditions of the prosperous agrarian culture that went hand in hand with such methods. The basis of the economy of these states was self-

Stela of an ancient Arabian deity
Tunis, Bardo Museum
The period in which the population of Arabia was polytheistic, in Islam, is called the "time of ignorance." The ancient Arabian pantheon contained a great number of gods and goddesses, and worship of the heavenly bodies – the sun, moon, and evening star – was originally a major part of the religion. In Mecca, the moon god Hubal was venerated as the god of the city, as a tribal god, and as "lord of the house" (that is, the Kaaba). Three female deities were also worshipped: al-Uzza (Venus, or the evening star), al-Lat (the moon goddess), and Manat (the goddess of fate). They were also called "daughters of Allah," that is, the greatest god. Muhammad's struggle against ancient Arabian polytheism went through several phases.

Great Colonnade and Tetrapylon, Palmyra in Syria
Palmyra acquired great wealth from its excellent situation on the caravan route between the central Euphrates and Damascus. It was important as a buffer state between the Iranian Parthians and the Roman Empire, of which it became part in the 2nd century. In the 3rd century it proclaimed independence under its queen Zenobia, defying Rome, whereupon it was destroyed by the emperor Aurelian in 273. The magnificent buildings of the city, its gates and temples, the towers of its tombs, and its squares, as well as this street lined with pillars, bear witness to the former wealth and short-lived power of Palmyra.

sufficiency, social division of labor and the performance of compulsory services, and technical progress, rapid at first, later stagnating to an increasing extent, particularly in the development of tools.

Within these states, the outcome was the construction of central cities, protected by the army, with strict urban administration, and large markets in which to trade goods such as pottery and craft products were bought and sold, while rigorous police supervision guaranteed public order and the security of commercial dealings. Class societies developed on the basis of small patriarchal family and professional distinctions, and thus urban and middle classes and upper classes formed. Urban administration was the task of professional civil servants organized in a strict and official hierarchy of well-defined areas of responsibility: in essence a fully fledged bureaucracy. Administration and legislation were centralized and a precisely adjusted system of taxation governed the distribution of goods, and there was constant expansion of the supply and exploitation of cultivated plants, although the keeping of livestock was hardly practiced at all, and was essentially the prerogative of the ruling class.

Political rule was based on theocratic foundations: the sovereign was sacrosanct because of his supposed function of mediating with the divine powers, which he demonstrated at the celebration of urban religious events, through the ceremonial calendar, and as a leader in war. He was usually regarded as the son in the divine hierarchy, and in line with ideas of religious absolutism, his rule was considered cosmic law. God-kings or priest-kings ruled the Egyptians and Sumerians. Divine worship in temples and the presence of palaces made the capitals of these kingdoms national centers. The temples also served as granaries for the storage of provisions, and goods were often directly distributed by the administrative staff of the temple, an office which increased their power. Luxury surrounded rulers, magnificent buildings, and an increasingly complex court ceremonial. As a result, they became more and more

Ceramic tile showing the shrine of the Kaaba in Mecca, Turkey, 16th century, Cairo, Islamic Museum

This tile is decorated with a stylized representation of the Kaaba in the Great Mosque of Mecca. The pillared ambulatory of the mosque forms the inner framework of the design. Such depictions, also found in book illustration, were less concerned with topographical accuracy than with presenting the most important elements of the shrine. This tile, for instance, shows the six minarets of the mosque, the *minbar*, and the Well of Zamzam, which God caused to spring from the desert when Abraham's concubine Hagar and her son Ismail were close to dying of thirst.

Key of the Kaaba, Ottoman, Paris, Musée du Louvre

While supervision of the Kaaba and the performance by pilgrims of their ritual obligations is the hereditary privilege of the Banu Shaiban clan, sovereignty over Mecca and Medina bestowed religious prestige on many dynasties, including the Fatimids, the Seljuks, and the Ayyubids. From 1517 the Ottomans held sovereignty, and thus the symbolical "power of the key." Since 1924, the control of Mecca and the pilgrimage industry has been in the hands of the Saudi Arabian royal family. In 1986 the ruling King Fahd officially abandoned his royal title, instead calling himself "Protector of the Two Holy Places" (Mecca and Medina).

remote from the common people, while their bodyguards and close advisers gained increasing political power. A strictly organized army, quartered in barracks and divided into infantry and cavalry (or the drivers of war chariots), provided the ruler with a military fighting power that could be mobilized at any time to enforce his claims to dominion.

Early ideas and innovations in the sciences inclined strongly toward their practical and technological aspects: hydraulic engineering, the development of weapons of war, mathematics, geometry, astronomy, medicine, and magic were the subjects of predominant or sole interest. Common features of the states ruled by oriental despotism were economic prosperity, usually considerable, together with ever-increasing stagnation in the field of social policy.

The prophet Muhammad in his world
The milieu of Muhammad

The extreme climatic and natural conditions of Arabia meant that, before Muhammad, it was only on the periphery of the great cultural centers of the age. Those centers regarded it as a barbaric place inhabited by Bedouin (nomadic Arabs of the desert), and sought to exploit its meager resources for their own advantage. With the spread of the cultures of Iraq, Palestine, and Syria, however, intellectual and spiritual life – particularly Judaism and Christianity – made an impact on the Arab area.

A considerable number of Jewish family groups emigrated to Arabia after the capture of Jerusalem by the Romans in A.D. 70, and again after the Bar Kochba rebellion of A.D. 135. They formed a culture of their own there, and in some cities they were strongly represented. Before the advent of Muhammad, for instance, half the inhabitants of Medina (still known as Yathrib at the time) were Jews. They became assimilated to the Arab lifestyle, but remained exclusive in their religion, holding fast to their monotheism and their unshakeable awareness of their identity as a chosen people even in a polytheistic environment. Both these beliefs made a great impression on Muhammad, and molded his later attitude to the Jews.

The influence of Christianity was felt even more strongly in the Arab area, more particularly through the sovereignty of Byzantium over Syria, Palestine, and Egypt. Abyssinia, and the trading nomadic tribes of central Arabia, were Christian too. This oriental Christianity was under the authority of the Syrian church, and several characteristic features distinguished it from western Christianity. Many of Muhammad's later utterances can be seen as evidence that he became acquainted with Christianity through the Copts of Egypt and other monophysites (adherents of the doctrine of the single nature of Christ). A number of apocryphal writings were current in the area at the time, and examples were known in Arabia of the often extremist forms of desert monasticism practiced by the anchorites. Since the ancient Arabian polytheistic faith had already lost its hold, during Muhammad's youth Arabia looked like it was becoming mainly Christian.

The ancient Arabian faith, and the pilgrimage to Mecca

The period of the ancient Arabian polytheistic faith is described in Islam as the "time of ignorance" (jahiliya). The Arabs originally seemed to have a cult of nature and the heavenly bodies, centering on the sun, the moon, and the evening star, and the meteorite known as the Black Stone, still in the Kaaba in Mecca, may be regarded as a part of this cult. The male god Hubal was worshipped in Mecca, the center of the ancient Arabian religion, but there were also

three female divinities – Uzza, Lat, and Manat – somewhat later regarded as the "daughters of Allah."

The Arabic generic term for "god" was *ilah*; when described as "the god" the term was *al-ilah*, and even before Muhammad the two words were often contracted to *al-lah* (Allah): god in general, the One God in particular. As the One God, he was often addressed as "master of the house," meaning the Kaaba in Mecca. But initially Allah, "the God," was primarily used as a title for a tribal god. Although the early Arabs cannot be described as definitely monotheistic, they already showed tendencies in that direction, and several passages in the Koran suggest that Muhammad himself, in his youth, wrestled extensively with ideas of the divinity. Ancient Arabia thought highly of the "seekers after God" (Hanafis) who had given up polytheism and declared themselves monotheists. It is accurate to say that the ancient Arabian faith had largely lost its ability to carry conviction, even before the emergence of Muhammad. What remained of it, however, particularly in Mecca, was religious custom, much of which, including the pilgrimage to Mecca, Muhammad adopted and Islamicized. Certain details of the "great pilgrimage" clearly show ancient Arabian influence. One example of this is the idea of the "peace of God" ruling the shrine and its surroundings as a kind of religious right of sanctuary and guarantee of immunity.

The Kaaba, in the Great Mosque of Mecca by night
During the pilgrimage to Mecca, which all Muslims are required to make, the faithful perform the *tawaf*, circling the Kaaba seven times. Tradition says that when Muhammad arrived in Mecca his enemies spread a rumor that the Muslims were weakened by fever. The Prophet therefore told his supporters to run around the Kaaba for the first three times, to show how strong they were, and the custom is a part of the pilgrimage to this day. At the end of their pilgrimage, the faithful then perform another farewell *tawaf* of the Kaaba. The Koran states: "It is the duty of all men towards God to come to the House a pilgrim, if he is able to make his way there (sura 3. 97)."

In 630 Muhammad "cleansed" the Kaaba, by having all its idols removed. Countless cult objects had been venerated in ancient Mecca, and a considerable number of magical and ritual practices were celebrated. The statements made in the Koran about the world of spirits, and angels and jinn, also derive from the ancient Arabian tradition. Muhammad's efforts in the Koran to distinguish between the prophets and those mere soothsayers, seers, and magicians who used the world of spirits for their own ends, suggest that ancient Arab practices survived into the Islamic period.

The life of Muhammad

Muhammad was born in Mecca around the year 570. His father had died before the boy's birth, and his mother died when he was six. Muhammad was brought up first by his grandfather, and then (around 578) by his uncle, Abu Talib, who was his protector until Abu died in 619. Muhammad became a caravan driver, and at the age of about 25 married the prosperous widow Khadija, 20 years his senior, to whom he was a faithful and loving husband, until her death in 619. The couple had three sons and four daughters, but all the sons died in infancy.

Around the year 610, at the age of 40, Muhammad had his first experience of religious vocation. This dramatic event is featured in sura 96 of the Koran, the oldest of the suras, and in this passage he is commanded by the angel of the Lord to "Read!" (or "Recite!" – *iqra!*). After a period of introspection, accompanied by self-doubt and depression, Muhammad accepted his mission as the "messenger of God" (*rasul allah*). He preached to the Meccans on his visions, warning mankind against social indifference, and against making material aims the main object of life. He also opposed the polytheism of the ancient Arabian religion, in particular the idea of the association with the One God Allah of subsidiary gods, or God's children (the concept known as *shirk*).

Muhammad's position was increasingly difficult in Mecca after 620, since he became more and more intolerant in his opposition to heathen polytheism, and his enemies mocked and derided him for his beliefs. In this situation, Muhammad and his followers decided to emigrate (the *hegira*) to Medina in 622, a date that marks the beginning of the Islamic calendar. On arriving in Medina, Muhammad was transformed from an admonitory preacher into a farsighted statesman and political arbitrator: he drew up a system of government for the new Muslim community in 623, and made contact with the large Jewish community of Medina. Although at first the two religious communities coexisted by agreement, the final outcome was the expulsion of the Jews from Medina. When his attempts to convert them failed, Muhammad became increasingly embittered and intolerant toward Judaism, although he adopted a great many of its religious ideas – in particular interpreting Abraham as an early Muslim, a prototype of the prophet and monotheistic seeker after God (Hanaf), and crediting him with building the Kaaba in Mecca as a place devoted to the worship of the One God (Allah). However, in 624 Muhammad changed the traditional direction toward which the devout turned in prayer from Jerusalem to Mecca.

Between 625 and 630 there were a number of armed conflicts with the Meccans, with both sides attacking each other's caravans, and Muhammad also proved himself a gifted military commander, particularly in what was known as the "War of the Trench." The suras of the Koran from the Medina period testify to the self-confidence felt at this time by Muhammad and the Muslims, who naturally assumed their success in warfare to be God's work. More particularly, however, Muhammad consolidated his community by skilfully smoothing over the dangerous tensions between the "old believers" from Mecca, his first adherents, and the "new believers" from Medina and its surroundings.

Finally, in January 630, he entered his native city of Mecca victorious, and on the whole showed clemency to his former opponents. He "cleansed" the Kaaba of the worship of idols and declared the pilgrimage to Mecca a Muslim institution. On June 8, 632, shortly after his "farewell pilgrimage" to Mecca in March of the same year, and still planning expeditions to conquer Byzantium and Persia, Muhammad, after a short illness, died in Medina.

Muhammad's view of himself – the "Seal of the Prophets"

It is indisputable that, after a brief phrase of self-doubt immediately after his first experience of vocation, Muhammad was utterly convinced of the truth of his revelations, and from that conviction he developed his sense of mission, which became particularly strong after the *hegira* to Medina. The Prophet's position, as leader of the Muslim community, was based on the authority of divine revelation, and his own personality. From the first, he understood the Muslim faith, not primarily as an introspective religion, but one with a socio-

The Prophet Abraham, Ottoman miniature, 1583. Istanbul, Museum of Turkish and Islamic Art
Abraham is regarded by Muslims as the earliest of the prophets, and the first *Hanaf* (seeker after God), and is closely linked to the shrine in Mecca. According to the Koran, Abraham prayed to God to make Mecca a safe place, and give it to him and his descendants as their home. He and his son, Ismail, then erected the Kaaba there as a shrine of the One God (Allah). Abraham is the prototype of the Hanaf, monotheists who seek God in a polytheistic environment. In this tradition, Islam looks back to the time before ancient Arabian polytheism, and relates Mecca to an original monotheism.

Muhammad preaching in the mosque of Medina, Arab miniature, 14th century

In Medina, to which the young Muslim community emigrated in 622, the Prophet, as its leader, came to concentrate more and more on political tasks. He was active, among other things, as an arbitrator in disputes and as leader of negotiations with the Jewish community. In 623 he proclaimed the first constitution of the Muslim community. He also led ritual prayers in the courtyard of his house in Medina, on which the design of the Islamic mosque is based, and preached to his congregation. In 628/629 Muhammad had a pulpit built, three floors high, since the community had become so large that not all the faithful could see or hear him.

Below: **The Prophets Moses and Muhammad with the angel Gabriel**

Berlin, Museum of Islamic Art

Muhammad's visit to heaven is a favorite theme of Islamic miniature painting. The motif derives from the visions of the Prophet described in the Koran in which messengers from God appear to him. According to the Hadiths handed down by Ibn Ishaq, Muhammad said that the angel Gabriel had led him through seven heavens, where he saw Adam dividing good souls from evil souls, and met Moses. Moses asked him how many prayers he was supposed to say, to which Muhammad replied that the number was 50 daily. Moses said: "Prayer is a difficult thing, and your people are weak." Then Moses allowed Muhammad to petition God for a reduction in the prayers, until at last he had reached the number of five prayers; which is still binding today.

Muhammad's wet nurse Halima breast-feeds the orphaned child, miniature from the *Siyer-i Nabi* Istanbul, Istanbul, 2nd half of the 16th century

Muhammad was born in Mecca in 570, a member of the Hashimite tribe. His father, Abdallah, died before his birth, and his mother, Amina, died when he was six. He was then brought up by his paternal grandfather, and after his grandfather's death in 578, was taken into the house of his uncle, Abu Talib, his father's brother, who remained faithful to Muhammad until his own death in 619, and protected him from attacks.

political (and later a "national") mission, so that religion and politics were inseparable in the early Islamic period, an attitude still evident today. Muhammad made treaties, but did not shrink from waging religious wars. He acted as an arbitrator in disputes, punished enemies and apostates ("the hypocrites"), and claimed political power for himself and his community.

To understand Islam's awareness of itself and the cultural sense of superiority felt by Muslims, particularly during the Middle Ages, we must remember that Muhammad did not think he was founding a new religion, but simply restoring the original monotheistic faith that had existed since ancient times, and that he saw himself as the last in a long line of prophets who had all borne witness to the same religion of the One God.

In the Islamic mind, God made his covenant with Adam's progeny, particularly Noah; Abraham was regarded as the first prophet, testifying to the unity and sole existence of the One God, Moses was considered the lawgiver and bringer of the Torah, and Jesus was seen as a great preacher and outstanding prophet who spread the gospel and was Muhammad's direct precursor. With Muhammad, the "Seal of the Prophets," the series reached its end, and the revelation of God through the prophets was complete.

In Muhammad's opinion, the One Truth had been revealed to Jews and Christians, but they had distorted or ignored it. Through him, it would now appear in a new and radiant light. Setting out from this view of himself, Muhammad really seems to have believed at first that Jews and Christians would have no difficulty in converting to Islam.

The pillars of Islamic life
The Koran: structure and message

The Koran (*al-qur'an*) is comprised of the collected revelations made to Muhammad, and became the holy scriptures of Islam; the Arabic word *qur'an* means reading or recitation. To the Muslim mind, the original text of the Koran (from Arab. *umm al-kitab*, "mother of the book") was recorded in the heavens from the beginning of time, and the revealed Koran corresponds to it word for word. Consequently, it was a matter of controversy for a long time, whether the Koran could be translated from its original language of revelation, classical Arabic, into any other language at all.

In its present form, the Koran has 114 sections (called suras), written in rhyming prose, and of different lengths. The longest sura (sura 2) has 286 verses, the shortest sura, only three. They are not given in chronological order of their composition, and most are not complete units in themselves but consist of several fragments of text. The suras are arranged in decreasing order of length, and, as a rule, are called after their main, or opening theme. Furthermore, with the exception of sura 9, they all begin with the *basmala*, the opening invocation: "In the Name of God, the Merciful, the Compassionate ...." The brief first sura, "The Opening" (*al-Fatiha*), occupies a special position of its own, placed like a prayer at the beginning of the Koran.

Directly after the death of Muhammad, the first caliph, Abu Bakr, had the suras of the Koran collected and placed on record; previously, they had been passed on by oral tradition from one of the Prophet's companions to another. The present standard version of the Koran – there were several in the early period – dates back to the time of the third caliph, Uthman, who had the revised version distributed by a committee of scholars, and suppressed all others. Therefore, this version finally became the canonical Koran, and established the order of the suras as they stand today. Since the suras generally contain a direct address by God to Muhammad, Islam sets

Muhammad's Night Journey to heaven on his mount, Buraq, Persian miniature, 1458, Istanbul, Museum of Turkish and Islamic Art
The incident shown here is the Prophet's night journey, described in sura 17, when God took him from Mecca to Jerusalem and back again. It stresses the links between these two holy places. Although Muhammad changed the prayer direction from Jerusalem to Mecca in 624, Jerusalem remained a holy city of Islam.

The mount Buraq, a creature like a sphinx or centaur with wings and a human head, is a popular theme of Islamic painting. The story of the night journey looks back to such ancient oriental and biblical themes as Jacob's vision of the ladder to heaven (Genesis 28: 10–22).

Muhammad and his followers on their way to Mecca, miniature from the *Siyer-i Nabi*, Istanbul, 2nd half of the 16th century. In the years after the emigration to Medina in 622, relations between the young Muslim community, and its native city of Mecca, were extremely strained. The Muslims were involved in warfare with the Meccans until 630, beginning with attacks on caravans, and eventually going on to pitched battles. Early in 630, Muhammad and his followers were able to enter Mecca almost without opposition, since he had promised beforehand to spare all who did not resist him. When he had removed the idols from the Kaaba, which now became the chief shrine of Islam, Muhammad's benevolent government quickly won over the Meccans to the new teachings.

special value on oral recitation. Linguistically and formally, the art of reciting the Koran is very difficult. One must observe strict rules that often requires thorough training.

In terms of its content and in its times of composition, the Koran is roughly divided into three Meccan phases and one Medina phase. The earliest writings of what is described as the first Meccan period are concerned with the experiences of Muhammad's vocation (in particular in suras 96 and 74), and emphasizes the connection with the traditional scriptures of the "peoples of the book" (in particular Jews and Christians). The suras of the early Meccan period (for instance suras 77, 79, 86, 91, and 100) contain the oldest revelations, and with their emotional language bring the shattering experience of the Prophet's vocation vividly to life. Muhammad is usually addressed directly in these brief suras with their short verses (and is often commanded to "Speak!"). They also contain formulas of adjuration naming God as the creator of mankind, to reinforce their message. God watches over human beings during their lives and calls them to account for themselves after death; hence the necessity of a way of life that will be pleasing to him. Some of the suras (for instance 69, 81, 82, 84, 99, and 101) invoke the apocalypse or Day of Judgment. Those suras (for instance 21 and 37) in which Muhammad defends himself against his enemies' accusations of being a mere poet or soothsayer, or even possessed by demons, also fall into this early phase. The suras of the later Meccan period are long and more explanatory in style, demonstrating the omnipotence of God through examples. Some of the suras refer to events and figures of the Old Testament (Abraham and Noah, Moses in suras 18 and 28, Joseph in Egypt in sura 12, and instances of Old Testament judgments). These characters and incidents are interpreted as precursors of Islam.

The suras from the Medina phase are didactic in tone and concern themselves with everyday problems of the young community; for example charity and the giving of alms, the concluding of agreements, and conduct during and after battle (for instance suras 8 and 48). These express the Muslim struggle for independence, particularly from the Jews of Medina, and opposition to the waverers within their own ranks. There is a strong element of legislation in the foreground.

The image of God and man in the Koran

First and foremost, like the Jewish Bible and the Christian Gospels, the Koran emphasizes the position of God as free creator and preserver of the world and of mankind. The Koran has no explicit creation story comparable to that in the Book of Genesis, but there are strong parallels. The creation of the world is depicted as the making of heaven and earth separately out of an original coherent mass, and man is made of earth or mud, but several times the process of creation is also expressed by the divine command "Be!" (and it was so). Again and again, the Koran stresses the

Muhammad borne up by the angels of God, Ottoman miniature, 1583. Istanbul, Museum of Turkish and Islamic Art
The journey to heaven described in suras 53 and 81 is considered a special proof of God's favor, a moment when Muhammad was close to the Lord and his faith was reinforced. According to sura 81 he saw the "noble messenger" of the Lord, the angel Gabriel. In sura 53, we are told: "He (God) drew near and suspended hung, two bows'-length away, or nearer, then revealed to his servant that [which] he revealed." Muslims celebrate this journey to heaven on the night of the 27th day of Radjab, the month of the moon, by reflecting on the firmness of their faith and their role in the Muslim community as a whole.

Guardian angels record the deeds of men in their scrolls, miniature from *The Wonders of Creation*, Wasit, Iraq, 1280
As companions and protectors of mankind, guardian angels have the special task of recording the works of men in books and reciting their deeds on the Day of Judgment. With God's permission, the angels may then intercede for humanity, asking God to be merciful. The Koran refers to the guardian angels in sura 82.10–12: "There are guardians set over you, noble writers, who know whatever you do."

Sura 27, "The Ant," verses 36–39, manuscript of the Koran, North Africa, 12th century, written in the Maghrebi style, London, Spink College
Sura 27, al-Naml ("The Ant"), deals with the meeting of Solomon and the Queen of Sheba, who submits to Allah as "Lord of the Worlds" when she has seen how rich and powerful he has made King Solomon. This sura is an example of the Koran's frequent reference to Old Testament stories, with Islam placing itself in line of descent from the old monotheistic religions. Figures like Noah, Abraham, Moses, and Solomon feature prominently in Muslim tradition, and show that, as the "Seal of the Prophets," Muhammad is the last prophet of all.

goodness and mercy of God, showing how well he has ordered everything. The creation appears to be designed for man, who is distinguished from the rest of created beings; God will forgive his sins if he truly repents, and will reward him if he lives a virtuous life. As the judge of mankind, God assesses human beings according to their deeds, and after death, he divides the just from the unjust (as in sura 78, verses 1–40, and 80. 17–42). The Last Judgment figures as a "Great Catastrophe" (sura 79. 34) that no one can escape. Both the torments of the damned and the joys of paradise are described in very vivid and sensuous terms in the Koran (as in sura 39. 60–75). Unbelief is regarded as ingratitude to God and his proven favors to man, and intercession through the prophets is possible only if God himself allows it.

Emphasis on the sole and unique nature of God lies at the heart of the Islamic faith. The Koran represents radical monotheism and an uncompromisingly theocentric view of the world: God is the One God, has taken no child to him (sura 21. 25–36), and has certainly not founded a family. The "association" with him of other divine persons (*shirk*) is regarded as the worst of sins against the One and Only God. This point is stressed by Islam in opposition not only to ancient Arabian polytheism, but also, and with increasing frequency, to the Christian understanding of Jesus. Jesus (Isa) was called to be a prophet (see the "Mary" sura 19. 16–40, and sura 3. 45–55), and he is regarded as the direct precursor of Muhammad. He will return at the end of time and rule as a righteous Muslim, but his identification as the son of God is regarded in Islam as Christian exaggeration and misrepresentation. Islam emphasizes the radical transcendence of God, something that man cannot grasp, and yet God reveals himself to man through the prophets. The world is given to man only for his use; it is not his property. On earth, he acts as "God's trustee," and his assistant in establishing the divine order of creation.

The Koran sets out from the assumption that man was created good and is in a position to lead a life which is pleasing to God, citing the example of such virtues as concern for other people, compassion, and giving charity to the needy (see suras 2. 21–39, and 57. 1–29). The idea of original sin is alien to Islam. But men are often hesitant, timid, or idle, allowing pugnacity, pride, and avarice the upper hand, and in times of prosperity they incline to be thoughtless and ungrateful.

Since Adam – that is to say, since the first revelation of the original monotheistic religion – man has often been shown the right path to tread, but almost as often has failed to follow it. Again and again, prophets emerged to spread the divine message and warn mankind to change its ways. Examples from the Old Testament (for instance sura 2. 40–61) and the Gospels are often quoted in the Koran to demonstrate the consequences of forgetting or distorting God's original message. Forgetfulness of God leads to sin, for which man can, in most cases, make amends by penance, although polytheists and idolaters will face particularly severe punishment.

Osmanic decorative tile with the inscription "ma sha'a Allah", 19th century
The declaration "ma sha'a Allah" literally means "What God wants." It is meant in the sense of "What God does, is done well." It appears in many suras of the Koran and has become a part of the daily language usage of the Muslims as an exclamation of surprise or awe, as well as one of recognition. "Ma sha'a Allah" expresses that everything that occurs does so as part of God's will, and that humans should except things in faith as God's intention; in some regions, the declaration is also used as a protection from bad luck and danger.

Man is free, and fully responsible for his actions on earth (compare to sura 89. 15–30). While the Koran recognizes a number of temptations at large in the world, which are constantly trying to seduce mankind away from the faith (in particular Iblis or Satan, a fallen angel), it stresses that man is free to choose between good and evil, so therefore, human beings are individually responsible for their salvation. Those who turn fully to God, and are "Muslims" in the original sense of the word, can live their lives without doing evil; the Muslim, according to tradition, is the true seeker after God, and knows that he is correctly guided by the creator and his commandments. It is the Muslim's own duty to show his faith in words and deeds, and to fight for his faith.

Islam teaches that the mind is mankind's greatest gift, enabling humanity to recognize God's order of creation clearly. In Islam, there is no contradiction between faith and understanding, or reason, since the world was made subject to such rational divine laws, as the laws of nature, and can thus be perceived and imitated by the reasoning mind; the insight of reason into the world order necessarily, as it were, leads to belief. As a result, great emphasis is placed on rationality in Islamic theology and jurisprudence. Reason or understanding leads man to God, and God is venerated – at least in classical Islam – in accordance with the criteria of reason. Islam is the world order desired and pre-ordained by God, and leads mankind to salvation.

The Five Pillars of Islam

Muslim religious practice is based on the principles known as the Five Pillars. These pillars (*arkan*), place their chief emphasis on the cohesion of the Islamic community (*umma*), and the general duties of Muslims toward God and their fellow men.

The first pillar is the public profession of faith (*shahada*, "confirmation"), which represents the simplest and most important religious act, and consists of the passage: "There is no god but God, and Muhammad is the messenger of God." This confirmation of the sole existence and unique nature of God, and the righteous mission of Muhammad, regarded as the prerequisite of the Muslim way of life, is thought to repeat the archangel Gabriel's opening words to the Prophet, words that not only accompany every Muslim throughout life, but are also the most popular motif of Islamic calligraphic art.

The *shahada* must be spoken only with serious intent and after intensive self-examination, for its pronunciation before witnesses is a condition of acceptance into the Muslim community. Once someone has been accepted in this way there can be no going back, and since apostasy is punishable by death, Islamic teachers of law stress the momentous nature of the step, which can be taken only freely and without compulsion. There are considerable differences of opinion in Islamic schools of law on the relationship of the profession of faith to the performance of the good works incumbent on believers, and the question of whether it is solely the profession of faith or primarily the good works that make them true Muslims.

The second pillar, and the one that has become most strictly ritualized, is the obligatory liturgical prayer (*salat*) which must be recited five times a day at fixed times. First – as before all religious acts – the believer must perform a series of precisely laid down ritual ablutions, from the face to the feet. These ablutions create a state of ritual purity, and illustrate the believer's rejection of sin and inner readiness to approach God. From the minaret, or tower of the mosque, the muezzin (more precisely transliterated: *mu'adhdhin*) calls the community to join in prayer. The liturgical prayer is very important because the Koran explicitly defines believers as "those praying."

The *salat* can be performed anywhere a Muslim happens to be, but at least some of the faithful should pray in the mosque. The turning toward Mecca of all who pray (the direction is indicated by the *qibla* wall in the mosque) demonstrates the community of Muslims all over the world, since their religious center is the Kaaba in Mecca. The congregation, in which men and women are separated, stands in rows behind the imam, or prayer leader, who takes his place before the prayer niche (*mihrab*). The course of the prayer and the attitudes adopted in it are precisely ordained: first, all the believers bow several times while standing, and then they immediately kneel and touch the ground or the

prayer mat twice with their foreheads, in token of their reverence and submission to the will of Allah.

Each of the five daily prayers ends with the panegyric *Allahu akbar* (God is Most Great), and the recitation of the first sura of the Koran, followed by the peace greeting *salamu alaykum* (peace be with you!), spoken by each worshipper to his or her neighbors.

The most important time of prayer is the midday prayer on Friday, when the *salat* is preceded by a sermon (*khutba*) delivered by a preacher either speaking from the pulpit (*minbar*) or standing in front of the congregation. To Muslims, Friday is not considered to be a holiday like the Jewish sabbath or the Christian Sunday, but in many Islamic countries no work is done that day. The important feature is the communal and obligatory nature of the *salat*, which is to be distinguished from personal petitions or prayers of thanks offered by a believer on certain occasions (*du'a*).

The third pillar, the giving of alms (*zakat*), was originally a voluntary pious exercise, but even in the early Islamic period it was extended to become an established and legally prescribed system of dues (a "poor tax"). It is derived from the duty that all Muslims should share their wealth with those fellow believers who are less prosperous, or who may have fallen on hard times. The *zakat* is therefore a religious duty, and is distinct from the making of additional voluntary contributions (the *sadaqa*), a charitable act regarded as meritorious but not obligatory. The Koran itself says nothing precise about the amount and frequency of these dues, but dwells on the value of charity and the frame of mind of those who give; the most highly regarded manner of giving is free from any taint of self-righteousness and does not shame the recipient.

During this time, an established system of social dues arose, which were levied on all kinds of different goods, such as crops, cattle, and precious metals, as well as merchandise and capital yields, and were each assessed at different lev-

The Islamic profession of faith (*shahada*)
The Muslim profession of faith states: "I bear witness that there is no God but God, and Muhammad is the messenger of God." A person becomes a Muslim by making this profession of faith before witnesses – an act that can be performed only of the convert's own free will, and not under coercion. In the teaching of Sunni orthodoxy, "profession with the tongue" is only a prerequisite of faith; the core of faith is inner conviction, and belief in the truth of divine revelation is at its very heart.

Muezzin on the Shah-i Mardan minaret,
Afghanistan
The muezzin calls the faithful to ritual prayers
five times a day. A Hadith recounts that the
Prophet said: "When the call to prayer is
heard, the Devil takes flight, to avoid hearing
the words of the call." In reminding the
faithful of their duties, the muezzin utters the
words of the *allahu akbar* (God is Most Great),
and the Muslim profession of faith. The Koran
says: "When proclamation is made for prayer
on the Day of Congregation [Friday], hasten
to God's remembrance (sura 62. 9)."

The muezzin, Indian miniature, 1502,
Delhi, National Museum
According to tradition, the young community
in Medina wondered how the faithful should
be summoned to prayer. Umar, later to be
caliph, was against adopting the traditional
use by Jews and Christians of a wind or per-
cussion instrument, and suggested: "Why do
we not appoint a man to call us to prayer?"
The Prophet agreed to this proposition, and
the Ethiopian slave Bilal was immediately
appointed to call the faithful to prayer
because he had a loud and carrying voice.

Muslims at prayer
Performing the *salat*, the inclusive term for
the five prayers, is one of the daily duties of
Islam. Both the prayer by an individual (above,
a Mughal miniature, India, 19th century) and
the ritual community prayer (right, Muslims at
Friday prayers in the Great Mosque of Balkh)
go through several stages, also expressed in
various changes of the worshippers' physical
positions. At the prayer assembly in the
mosque, a prayer leader (imam) leads the
community.

els. Various groups were identified as recipients of these dues. First and foremost, the poor and needy, but orphans, the sick, pilgrims and travelers, debtors, and those voluntarily fighting for the faith, were also remembered. In the early Islamic period, a part of this money was also used to buy the freedom of slaves and prisoners. Today, the *zakat* is a cross between a religious duty and a carefully calculated kind of social legislation. Politically minded Muslims see the *zakat* as a successful way of institutionalizing social responsibility, one that anticipated the arrangements of the modern welfare state.

The fourth pillar of Islam, ritual fasting (*saum*) in the holy month of Ramadan (the ninth month in the Islamic calendar), was also originally a matter of voluntary self-denial (as laid down in sura 2. 185) but later became a religious duty. From sunrise to sunset, the believer abstains from eating and drinking, smoking, and sexual intercourse. All adult Muslims are bound by this duty, although exceptions are made for certain groups, such as the sick, travelers, pregnant women, nursing mothers, and laborers engaged in very heavy work, who must either compensate in some other way or observe the fast later. The general and flexible principle is that fasting is mandatory only if it represents no danger to health.

Physical self-discipline serves the cause of inner purification. In the month of Ramadan, Muslims commune with themselves, are reconciled with their fellow believers, thank God through their abstention for the gifts of daily life, and as a rule make special donations to the needy. Many Muslims spend long periods of the month in the mosque, and to some extent the whole pace of public life slows down in Islamic countries, while in certain regions the nights are full of special parties and social gatherings. According to a saying of Muhammad, God regards fasting as the best form of prayer, because only He sees it. The 27th night of Ramadan is of great significance; this is the "Night of Destiny" (*laylat al-qadr*), in which Muhammad received his first divine revelation, and the descent from heaven of the Koran is commemorated with great festivities and public gifts of food to the poor.

The fifth pillar of Islam is the pilgrimage to Mecca and its surroundings (the *hajj*), which all adult Muslims, according to sura 3. 97, are required to make at least once in their lives, as long as their health, means, and the safety of the journey allow. The pilgrimage leads them through the holy places of Islam. Through their center, inside the Great Mosque of Mecca, stands the Kaaba, cubic in shape and draped in black, with the sacred Black Stone set in it. A visit to Muhammad's house in Medina is often combined with the pilgrimage to Mecca. According to the Koran, the Kaaba was erected by Abraham and his son Ismail as a token of their veneration of Allah. The Great Pilgrimage takes place mainly between the 8th and 12th of the month of pilgrimage Dhu l-hijja (the 12th month of the Islamic calendar), when hundreds of thousands of Muslims flock to Mecca from all over the world.

Before making the journey, believers must ensure that they are in a state of consecration (*ihram*), and must have a clear idea in mind of the aim of their pilgrimage. The wearing of a simple white garment defines them as pilgrims, and as such, they enjoy particular respect and protection. During the pilgrimage they abstain from shaving, cutting their hair, sexual intercourse, hunting, and the wearing of perfume. When they arrive in Mecca they circle the Kaaba seven times (the *tawaf*, and then walk back and forth seven times between the hills of al-Safa and al-Marwa (now leveled), in memory of the hardships suffered in the desert by Abraham's concubine Hagar, and her son, Ismail. Believers drink the water of the Well of Zamzam, caused by God to rise from the desert sands to save Hagar and Ismail, and supposed to have miraculous powers. Arrival at the well marks the end of the individual part of the pilgrimage and the beginning of the collective phase, which must take place between the 8th and 12th days of the month Dhu l-hijja.

Minbar of the Qaitbai Mosque in Cairo, 1472/73, engraving from a drawing of 1877
The pulpit (*minbar*) of the mosque where prayers are held on Fridays, usually wooden and made in the form of a flight of steps, originally served not only as a place for the preacher to stand but as a throne or judgement seat for Muhammad and the caliphs, who were political as well as religious leaders of the community. As the number of the faithful increased, and mosques grew larger, higher *minbar* were necessary. They also became more and more elaborately and artistically ornamented. Today the *minbar* is exclusively used as a pulpit for the sermon (*khutba*) at Friday prayers.

The climax of the pilgrimage comes on the 9th of the month on Mount Arafat, which is 16 miles (25 kilometers) from Mecca, where the pilgrims stand in meditation, abandoning themselves entirely to the omnipotence of God, and praying from noon until sunset. After sunset they set out for nearby Mina, breaking their journey overnight in Muzdalifa, where each of the faithful collects seven small pebbles that they will later add to the towering heaps of stones in Mina on the morning of the 10th day of the month. This custom is supposed to refer to Abraham's temptation by the Devil to go mad when faced by God's command to sacrifice his son, and also to symbolize resistance to evil. Next begins a feast of sacrifice lasting several days (*tashriq* days) in memory of this event. During this time sheep are slaughtered and most of the meat is given to the poor. Muslims all over the world celebrate this festival. On the 12th of the month, the pilgrims return

Islamic law, its sources, and its law schools

Islam is both a "lay religion" in that it has no priestly caste, and a religion of law. Muslims therefore receive assistance in their daily life and conduct, not from a priest, but from a jurist (*faqih*, pl. *fuqaha*). The Five Pillars and Islamic law (*sharia*) are the most important elements in the life of the Muslim community. Consequently, Islamic scholars (*ulama*) have always studied both religion and the law.

When the Medina phase of Islam began, the individual's need for salvation was set within the framework of a well-regulated community, and Islam became "God's law" on earth. Muhammad also confronted features of ancient Arabian customary law, and after the late Meccan period the suras of the Koran concerned themselves with such questions of the community code as the payment of dues and giving of alms (see suras 6 and 58), the terms of marriage contracts (suras 60. 10–13, and 33. 50–52), divorce (sura 65), and the guardianship of orphaned children (sura 4). The Koran also deals with matters of inheritance and family law, ritual acts, and physical punishments (*hadd*) such as stoning or the amputation of limbs (sura 5. 33–40). The provisions of the law are presented as God's commandments, so that transgression of them becomes an offense against the divine order of creation. Since human beings are too weak and thoughtless to find the right path for themselves, they need divine guidance. It is a general principle that God in his mercy wishes to make that path easy and not difficult for mankind, and consequently almost all the commandments of Islam have alternative forms providing types of relief, making exceptions, or suggesting substitute acts to atone for failure to observe them. The Koran presents the law as a light that makes men wise, and enables them to make correct judgments.

From the first, and although it developed considerable casuistries and instances of subtle hairsplitting, the Islamic *sharia* was on the whole very practical in character, oriented toward legal matters concerning the family, inheritance, guardianship, and the payment of dues. It distinguishes between divine and human law, as it also discriminates between the duty of Muslims to God and their duty to their fellow men; it is not the human judge (*qadi*) but God himself who will pass sentence on various transgressions of the commandments, particularly those relating to man's duty to God. Only denial of the binding nature of the requirements of the *sharia*, not an isolated instance of failing to observe a law, makes the offender an unbeliever.

Since man can tell the difference between good and evil, and can choose one or the other (the dominant Sunni orthodoxy sets out from the assumption that only divine authority, not the innate quality of an action, determines what is good and what is evil), the actions of mankind in relation to divine law are divided into five categories:

a) obligatory or compulsory acts: those who perform them are rewarded by God, those who neglect them are condemned and punished;

b) recommended or desirable acts, of benefit to religion or to the community: to perform them brings a reward, but to neglect them does not entail punishment or condemnation;

c) permissible acts of a morally neutral character: those who perform them are not rewarded, nor are those who neglect them punished – they are left to the will of the individual;

d) undesirable or reprehensible acts which are disadvantageous to religious obedience or the customs of the community: abstention from them brings its reward, but those who perform them are not punished;

e) forbidden acts (originally described as *tabu*): avoiding them is a duty and is rewarded, and those who perform them are condemned and punished.

A Muslim giving alms, Persian miniature from the *Bustan* (garden) of Sadi, Bihzad, 15th century, Cairo, National Library
The legally imposed alms tax (*zakat*) turned what was originally the voluntary giving of alms into a religious duty, also called the "tax for the poor." The *zakat* serves the practical object of promoting solidarity among Muslims, and is regarded by believers as an early form of social legislation. Over and beyond the alms tax, the believer gives other voluntary dues or alms to the needy, particularly during the fasting month of Ramadan and on great Muslim feast days. Giving in this way is considered especially meritorious. Since non-Muslims are not obliged to pay the *zakat* in Muslim states, they have a special poll tax imposed on them, and thus become *dhimmi* ("protected citizens") of the state.

to Mecca to perform a farewell *tawaf* seven times around the Kaaba. The pilgrimage, and some of the ceremonies, probably derive from pre-Islamic times and were adopted by Muhammad, just as the places near Mecca were probably shrines in ancient Arabia. The annual organization of the Great Pilgrimage, and care of the holy places since their conquest by Ibn Saud in the year 1924, is the royal family of Saudi Arabia's responsibility. Thus King Fahd abandoned his official royal title in 1986, and has called himself "Protector of the two Holy Places" (Mecca and Medina).

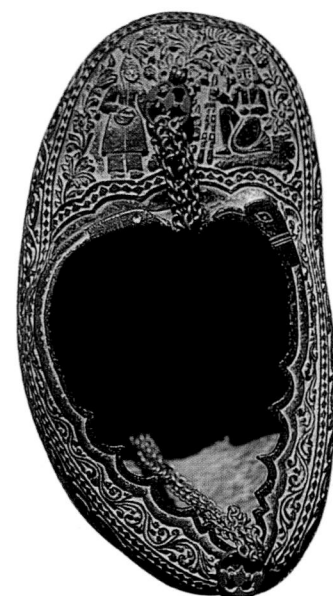

Right: **A dervish's begging bowl**, made from an Indian fruit, Tehran, Malek Collection

The religious duty of alms-giving also provides the beggar with an honorable place in Islamic society, since he gives the prosperous, or indeed any Muslim, a chance to do his duty and give to charity. It is one of the rules of courtesy to thank a beggar for being allowed to give him something, in order to avoid humiliating him.

Left: **White-clad pilgrims**, miniature

The pilgrimage to Mecca *(hajj)* is a religious duty to be undertaken by all Muslims at least once in their lives, so long as their health and financial means allow. Pilgrims consecrate themselves by wearing white garments, allowing their hair, beards, and nails to grow, and refraining from sexual intercourse, as well as wearing perfume, and hunting. Pilgrims are protected and enjoy special respect wherever they go. Their state of dedication shows that they are set apart from the secular world and wish to approach God. If for some valid reason a Muslim cannot make the pilgrimage to Mecca in person, it is permissible to equip and send a substitute.

Human sins are classified: the worst are sins against God and the faith, then come sins against other human beings, those calculated to do others harm, and finally such sins against the proper conduct of everyday life such as offenses against property, slander, and bearing false witness.

According to the Koran, God can forgive all human sins – if he wants to – with the exception of unbelief.

The *sharia* recognizes four sources or "roots" (*usul*) of the law, two material and two procedural. The first and supreme source of the law is, of course, the Koran; however, as there are many matters on which it makes no specific pronouncement, the so-called Hadiths (*hadith*, literally "communication") are adduced as the second source. The Hadiths are the traditional sayings and acts of Muhammad and his intimate circle, also described as the *sunna* ("usual way of action", or "custom"). A vast and contradictory number of hadiths came down from the early Islamic period; in the 9th century scholars began examining them and drew up the six orthodox collections (*sahih*, literally, "authentic") still accepted today. They are used chiefly to provide precedents in actual legal cases. The general criterion of their authenticity is an unbroken chain of people who have handed them down (*isnad*), going back to the Prophet Muhammad and his circle.

Festive procession at the end of Ramadan, Arab miniature from the *Maqamat* of Hariri, Baghdad, 1237, Paris, Bibliothèque Nationale

Since fasting is a religious duty, Muslims abstain from eating, drinking, smoking, and sexual intercourse between sunrise and sunset in the fasting month of Ramadan. During this time they pay particular attention to their religious duties, are reconciled with their enemies, do good works, and remember the fellowship between all Muslims. The climax of Ramadan is the night of its 27th day, when the first revelation of the Koran is said to have been made to the Prophet. Since public life slows down during Ramadan, the end of the fast is celebrated with great festivities in all Islamic countries.

The understanding (*ra'i*, "reason") of legal scholars is taken as a methodological source of the law. It derives from consistency between the laws with reason and the general rationality of the order of creation, as described above, and leads to the drawing of analogies (*qiyas*) between an earlier case and one that is similar. The second methodological source is the principle of "consensus" (*ijma*), that is, the consensus of scholars on any question. This principle derives from the idea that God may allow an individual to go astray, but in his loving kindness will never permit the whole community to be in error. A Hadith of the Prophet is quoted to this effect: "My community will never agree upon an error."

Islamic schools of law (*madhahib*, sing. *madhab*) were formed in the Abbasid period (after 750), during the phase of the internal stabilization of Islam. At first they were chiefly concerned with the interpretation of canonical texts dealing with the proper conduct of human life. In the course of time, four Sunni schools and one Shiite school became firmly established. The "closing of the gate" of independent reasoning by individuals (*ijtihad*), even if those individuals are scholars, was an idea current among the Sunnis from the 11th and 12th centuries onward. It helped them to consolidate their schools, and led to a certain rigidity in the Sunni legal canon. The Shiites do not recognize the closing of the gate of *ijtihad*, a quality that must be constantly exercised by a Shiite legal scholar, who is therefore known as a *mujtahid*, one who is independently "struggling for himself."

In practice, in doubtful cases, the individual believer, a community, or a government appoints a scholar to give an expert legal opinion (a fatwa); the individual or person commissioning this opinion then exercises "imitation" (*taqlid*), that is to say, he complies with the judgment and acts according to it, and if he does so in good faith he is not, as a rule, held responsible for erroneous decisions.

There are four Sunni schools of thought. The first school, the Hanafi school, named after their founder Abu Hanifa (699–767), is the oldest and largest school of law. It is considered flexible and comparatively liberal, since it leaves much scope for personal evaluation (*ra'i*) and reason. Its tendency to split legal hairs and dwell on niceties is much criticized by its opponents, but it has introduced into Islamic law a great many principles of conduct and thought that are generally current today. As the established state school of the Abbasids and Ottomans, its main modern distribution is in their successor states, and in Central Asia, Pakistan, and India. About a third of all Muslims follow the teachings of the Hanafi school.

The Maliki school, named after Malik ibn Anas (715–795). This school is comparatively conservative, and strongly oriented toward the customary law that prevailed in Medina in the time of the Prophet. It emphasizes the principle of *maslaha*, the general good of the Muslim community. As the established school of Islamic Spain and the Maghrebi states, it is still predominant in northern Africa, in the Maghreb, Mauritania, Nigeria, and Sudan, as well as Kuwait.

In many respects, the Shafii school, named after al-Shafii, a scholar who had studied with the two preceding schools, occupies a position midway between them. It is the most systematic and subtle of the legal schools, and endeavours to eliminate any "arbitrary" legal findings.

Al-Shafii can therefore be regarded as the real founder of Islamic jurisprudence. As the established state school of the Ayyubids and Mamluks, it is still predominant today in Jordan, Palestine, parts of Egypt, and the Lebanon, and also in Southeast Asia (Indonesia, Malaysia, Sri Lanka).

The Hanbali school, named after Ahmad ibn Hanbal (780–855), is the smallest and most conservative of the Sunni schools of law. It represents a rigorous and uncompromising traditionalism of great piety, and is also philosophically opposed to rationalism in Islam. Because of its rigidity, it has not found very wide distribution, but it has always been cited as the intellectual basis of puritanical reform movements, particularly by Abd al-Wahhab (1703–1792), founder of the Wahhabi movement in present Saudi Arabia, where it has been the established state school ever since his time. However, there are also small communities in other countries, for instance Syria, Algeria, Iraq, and Afghanistan.

The Shiite school of legal interpretation is known as the Jafari school, after the sixth Shiite imam, Jafar al-Sadiq (d. 765). It differs from the other schools in a number of ways, for instance, the retention of the *ijtihad* and early Islamic rationalism, the legal institution of fixed-term marriage, and the establishment

of an additional obligatory tax, the "fifth" (*al-khums*), for the return of the "imam in hiding." The Jafari school has been the established school of Iran since the beginning of Safavid rule in 1501, but also has many adherents in Iraq, Lebanon, and on the Indian subcontinent.

Normally every Muslim follows the teachings of the school of law dominant in his country, but he can turn to others, or in certain cases can even combine the decisions of different schools. In many matters, the often violent disputes of the past between the various Sunni schools have now largely been eliminated, or pragmatic solutions have been found.

Early history:
The period of the "Four Rightly Guided Caliphs" (632–661)

The time between the death of Muhammad and the accession to power of the Ummayad dynasty in 661, was of great significance for Islam's understanding of its identity. Sunni tradition regards the time of the "Four Rightly Guided Caliphs" as a golden age in which the community (*umma*) was governed with justice and piety, living according to the laws of the Prophet, and in this time the power of Islam began to unfold. The Shiites, on the other hand, see the first three caliphs as mere usurpers, and concede the right of succession only to the imam Ali, the fourth Sunni caliph, and his direct descendants. We shall be looking at this point more closely. To this day, in fact, the period of the Rightly Guided Caliphs features prominently in Islamic discussion of a just social order.

The immediate reaction in the young community to Muhammad's demise was one of shock. The Prophet's death, following after a short illness, had been sudden and surprising, and he had not nominated a successor to lead the *umma*. The first caliph (from Arabic *khalifa*, "representative"), Abu Bakr (632–634), who was elected by the elders of the community, came from a highly esteemed family of Meccan merchants. As the father of Muhammad's favorite and much younger wife Aisha, Abu had been the Prophet's father-in-law and close friend, one of the first to follow him and join him in the *hegira* of 622. He secured himself as the successor by his saying, "Muhammad is dead, but Allah lives!" for he had already led prayers in the community during Muhammad's sickness, and was regarded by many as the Prophet's *alter ego*. His authority enabled him to keep any tribal rivalries that broke out under control, sometimes by the use of military force, and he thus forged a loosely connected group of tribes into a community. The Sunnis regard Abu Bakr as the greatest of all Muslims after the Prophet's immediate family.

The second caliph, Umar ibn al-Khattab (634–644), was also a father-in-law and friend of the Prophet, and had risen to become one of Muhammad's chief advisers in Medina. Unanimously chosen caliph in 634, Umar may be regarded as the most forceful personality among the Rightly Guided Caliphs. There are innumerable tales of his courage and strength of will, his exemplary piety, and his humility. Together with his outstanding generals Khalid ibn al-Walid, Amr ibn al-As, and Sad ibn Abu Waqqas, Umar can be seen as the true

Muhammad and Abu Bakr in a cave
Turkish miniature, 17th century. Dresden, Sächsische Landesbibliothek
Abu Bakr (c. 570–634) was one of Muhammad's first followers in Mecca, and in Medina he became one of his most important political and military advisers. He accompanied Muhammad on his flight from Medina, during which they are supposed to have hidden from their enemies in a cave. When Muhammad married his daughter Aisha, he was highly esteemed as the Prophet's father-in-law. In 632 Muhammad appointed him leader of his farewell pilgrimage to Mecca, and prayer leader during his last illness. The Sunnis regard this as evidence that he had been designated Muhammad's successor as leader of the community, and on those grounds he was chosen as the first caliph in 632. The Shiites, however, regard him as a usurper, who deprived Ali and his descendants of leadership of the community.

In Sunni Islam, the time of the Four Rightly Guided Caliphs is thought of as a period when God's commandments were faithfully kept, and it is still cited today as a golden age. The first two caliphs, Abu Bakr (632–634) and Umar (634–644), were fathers-in-law of the Prophet, and the caliphs Uthman (644–656) and Ali (656–661) were his sons-in-law. While Abu Bakr succeeded in consolidating the community, and Umar distinguished himself as an organizer in the early triumphal progress of Islam, the unity of the early community finally crumbled under Uthman and Ali.

Jesus on a donkey and Muhammad on a camel, riding together, Persian miniature from a work by al-Biruni, 18th century, Tehran, Parliamentary Library
This miniature illustrates the high esteem that was felt for Jesus in Islam (Isa). He is regarded as one of the great prophets, and the direct precursor of Muhammad. He proclaimed the Gospels, as Moses before him proclaimed the Torah, and as Muhammad proclaimed the Koran after him. In the Koran he is called the "Word of God" and "Messiah," but he is considered only a man free of sin and beloved by God, *not* the son of God or God himself. He will return at the end of time, rule as a righteous Muslim, and restore unity to mankind.

founder of the Islamic empire. He planned the wars of conquest, organized the powerful Islamic military camps, and possessed the vision of a statesman, which gave him great authority over the proud clan chieftains. In 637, he consolidated the organization of the Islamic empire by measures including land distribution, the introduction of a pension system, a poll tax on non-Muslims (*dhimmi* taxes), and various other agreements. He also added the title of "Commander of the Faithful" (*amir al-muminin*) to that of Caliph. In 644, on his way to the mosque, he was murdered by a Christian.

The third caliph, Uthman ibn Affan (644–656), one of the richest merchants in Mecca, had joined Muhammad very early and became his son-in-law. The traditional idea of his character is ambivalent: profoundly virtuous and pious, but yielding and rather unworldly, he was not a natural leader, and had no personal ambition. His choice as caliph was surprising, and was probably made with the intention of appointing an outstandingly religious man to that position, but political authority eluded him from the first. Autocratic governors opposed his orders, and he indulgently filled the central administrative posts in Mecca and Medina with family members, thus earning a reputation for

nepotism. He became increasingly unpopular, and in the end, even Muhammad's widow Aisha turned against him. When he refused to comply with demands for him to step down, although by then he was 80 years old, a mob stormed his house and murdered him. Uthman died bending over the Koran. (Later, several mosques displayed bloodstained pages from the Koran as relics, claiming that the blood was Uthman's.) His outstanding achievement was to have completed the collection of the suras of the Koran, thus giving the scriptures their present form.

The fourth caliph, Ali ibn Abu Talib (656–661) was Muhammad's cousin, and also his son-in-law through his marriage to Muhammad's daughter Fatima. He was one of the first people to become a Muslim – indeed, the Shiites claim that he was the very first after Muhammad's wife Khadija – and after Muhammad's death had a considerable following which was anxious to ensure that the imamate (or caliphate) went to him. These people described themselves as the "Shiat Ali", the party of Ali, a description from which the term "Shiite" derives. Ali was chosen caliph in 656, although Uthman's family as well as Aisha and her supporters, whom Ali defeated in 656 at the Battle of the Camel,

Muhammad and Ali cleanse the Kaaba of idols, miniature from the *Raudat ai-Safa* of Mir Havand, Shiraz, Iran, 1585–1595
This miniature depicts Ali as the Prophet's right-hand man in the year 630, when the Muslims took Mecca and removed the red stone idol of the god Hubal from the Kaaba, which since then has contained only the Black Stone. The Shiites regard Ali (602–661), the Prophet's cousin and son-in-law, as the only

legitimate successor of Muhammad, and as leader (imam) of the community. He is said to have adopted Islam as a boy, and was the first to become a Muslim after Muhammad's wife Khadija. To the Shiite way of thinking, Muhammad imparted the inner meaning of the Koran to Ali, making him the greatest of experts in its interpretation. His piety and justice made him the prototype of the Muslim who leads a life pleasing to God.

refused to recognize him. His caliphate therefore marked a very difficult situation for the young Islamic community.

Ali is described as personally courageous and pious, just and generous. He had poetic talent and a considerable gift for oratory that sprang from deep ethical feeling. Many of his sayings are part of Muslim didactic literature.

However, Ali did not have great political or military talents, and he proved both overscrupulous and hesitant. He was confronted by a serious opponent in the person of the governor of Syria, Muawiya, a cousin of Uthman, who forced a tribunal of arbitration on the question of legitimate rule over the community. Ali agreed to arbitration, fearing a Muslim civil war, and thereby himself contributed to the first serious Islamic schism: part of the community, the Kharijites ("those going out") thought it beneath the dignity of the caliphate for a caliph to meet a governor on equal terms. Disappointed in Ali, they chose a rival caliph, and moved toward open rebellion. Ali defeated the Kharijites in battle in 658, but then, in January 661, on his way to the mosque he was stabbed and killed by a Kharijite.

Sunnis and Shiites – caliphs against imams

The majority of Muslims (about 88–90%) describe themselves as Sunnis; the word is derived from the Arabic word *sunna*, meaning "usual practice, custom", and initially meant the conduct of Muhammad and his companions as described in the Hadiths. The Koran and the *sunna* of the Prophet are equally important as guidelines to the Muslim's conduct and way of life. The majority of Muslims, who followed the historical tradition of the Four Rightly Guided Caliphs and their successors, called themselves "the people of the *sunna* and the community," in contrast to those with non-conformist tendencies, particularly the Kharijites and Shiites.

The rise of the Shiites falls into the period of dispute over the legitimate succession of the Prophet. The "Shiat Ali" ("party of Ali") defended the principle that the sole legitimate successors were the Prophet's cousin and son-in-law and his direct descendants from his marriage to Muhammad's daughter Fatima. In this way the succession would remain in Muhammad's family. The Shiites are a minority in Islam, but have always had a very strong influence on Islamic intellectual and political life. They regard Ali and his descendants as infallible imams (leaders of the community of the faithful), and revere them almost as much as the Prophet himself. The history of the Shia is very complicated, and involves various schisms, persecutions, and rebellions. In the course of its development, the Shia has always been the spiritual home of apocalyptic, socio-revolutionary, and enthusiastically mystical tendencies in opposition to traditional orthodoxy, and the actions of Shiite fighters for the faith are often marked by a yearning for salvation and by revolutionary impatience.

A positive cult of martyrdom is linked to the death and downfall of the third imam, Ali's son Husain, at Kerbela on the 10th of Muharram (October) in 680, when he was abandoned by his allies in the course of a revolt against Ummayad

rule. Especially in Iran and Iraq, this event is commemorated by processions of flagellants and the acting of scenes from the story on the appropriate days, and it marked the real birth of the Shia, being central to the sense of identity of the Shiites, who see themselves as subjected to persecution for the sake of Ali and the true succession of the Prophet.

Leaving aside various extremist movements, known as *ghaliya*, "those who exaggerate," three Shiite groups can be distinguished. They are described, from the number of the imams they venerate, as Fivers, Seveners, and Twelvers.

The Fivers, or Zaydis (named after Zayd ibn Ali, a son of the fourth imam, who was killed around 740 in a rebellion against the Umayyads), are the smallest and most moderate Shiite group. They have absorbed much of the rationalist tradition of early Islam. They recognize no strict succession in the

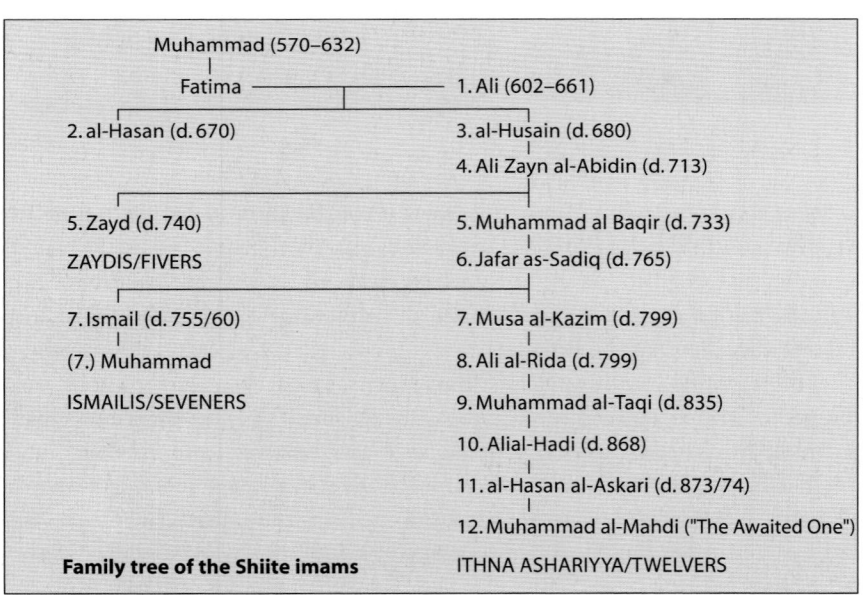

Ya Ali – the ax of Ali, Ottoman battle-ax, 16th century. Istanbul, Museum of Turkish and Islamic Art
At the time of the Crusades, Ali's courage and moderate treatment of his enemies made him a model of the righteous Muslim fighting for his faith. This chivalric ideal, as represented, for instance, by Saladin, the greatest Islamic hero of the period of the Crusades, became famous in the West as well.

series of imams, but believe in the appointment of the ablest (and most warlike) of Ali's descendants. They do not share the belief of other Shiites in the "imam in hiding." Zaydi dynasties ruled the Yemen (where they are still strongly represented) between 901 and 1962, and the Zaydis also ruled the regions by the Caspian Sea (modern Iran) between 864 and 1126.

The Seveners, or Ismailis (named after Ismail ibn Jafar, a son of the sixth imam, who was nominated by his father to succeed him but died around the year 760, before Jafar himself) are the most splintered and mysterious group of Shiites; their philosophy is largely speculative, and has ancient Persian and Neoplatonic Gnostic aspects. Some tendencies are marked by esoteric features, such as operating with an "inner" doctrine (secret or concealed) and an "outer" doctrine (for the masses). Throughout their history, the Ismailis have always shown socio-revolutionary tendencies, and are enthusiastic proponents of the *mahdi*, or messiah doctrine. They became historically significant with the countercaliphate of the Fatimids in Cairo (909–1171), which in 1094 split into two religious groups (the Mustalians and Nizaris). The Qaramita (Carmathians, 9th–11th centuries) on the Persian Gulf were also Ismailis, as were the much-feared assassins of the time of the Crusades, who were Nizaris. Today Nizaris live in Syria, Yemen, Afghanistan, Turkestan,

and above all in India, where they are called "hodjas." Their leader is the Agha Khan. Mustalians live in Yemen and India, where they are called "bohras."

The Twelvers (*ithna ashariyya*) or Imamis are the largest and most organized of the Shiite groups, and theirs has been the established state religion of Iran since the beginning of Safavid rule in the area. They recognize a series of 12 imams in direct succession from father to son, the last of whom, Muhammad al-Mahdi, "went into hiding" for his own safety as a boy in 873/874 after his father's death. He will return at the end of time as "the Awaited One" (*al-mahdi*, "he who is under divine guidance"). The *ithna ashariyya* have a highly developed theology and rationalist legal doctrines. They regard the sayings of the imams as important Hadiths, and in their tradition the 12 imams, Muhammad, and Fatima are "the 14 infallible ones." In Iran, the Twelvers adopted both powerful and popular Islamic practices, such as the Muharrain processions and pilgrimages to the graves of the imams. There are also large groups of Ismailis in Iraq (where they make up the majority of the population), Syria, Lebanon, Turkey, Afghanistan, and the Indian subcontinent. In Iran, the legal scholars (mullahs, from Arabic *maula*, "lord, master") occupy a special position through their prerogative of exercising *ijtihad*, independent judgment, and can be described as Shiite clergy. There are different ranks among them, access to these qualifications being acquired by intensive study and recognition of the expert legal judgments they have given. At the head of the hierarchy are the ayatollahs (from *ayatu'llah*, "sign of God"), among whom the few recognized Grand Ayatollahs like Ayatollah Khomeini – are considered important spiritual leaders and "authorities for imitation" (*marja al-taqlid*).

A major difference between Sunnis and Shiites is in the political area. The Sunnis recognize the caliphs as successors to Muhammad, even when government by dynastic kingship was introduced by the families of the Umayyads (661–750) and Abbasids (750–1258). The caliph bore the title of "Commander of the Faithful," but from the Abbasids onward caliphs thought of themselves more as "the shadow of God on earth" than as mere followers of Muhammad in the leadership of the Muslim community, and direct divine legitimation of the monarchy moved to the forefront of their thinking.

In contrast, the Shiites not only do not recognize the caliphs who ruled after the murder of Ali in 661, but despise them as usurpers, and regard the direct descendants of Ali as imams, although they were largely excluded from actual power. The Shiites understand the imamate as the source of spiritual and charismatic guidance through the agency of an exemplary life.

In fact, in all Islamic systems of government there was an increasing tendency toward the institution of monarchy. After the rule of the Umayyads, who were notable for their organization of Arab tribal groups, the caliphate of

Family tree of the Shiite imams

```
                Muhammad (570–632)
         Fatima ─────────────── 1. Ali (602–661)
   2. al-Hasan (d. 670)        3. al-Husain (d. 680)
                               4. Ali Zayn al-Abidin (d. 713)
   5. Zayd (d. 740)            5. Muhammad al Baqir (d. 733)
   ZAYDIS/FIVERS               6. Jafar as-Sadiq (d. 765)
   7. Ismail (d. 755/60)       7. Musa al-Kazim (d. 799)
   (7.) Muhammad               8. Ali al-Rida (d. 799)
   ISMAILIS/SEVENERS           9. Muhammad al-Taqi (d. 835)
                               10. Alial-Hadi (d. 868)
                               11. al-Hasan al-Askari (d. 873/74)
                               12. Muhammad al-Mahdi ("The Awaited One")
                               ITHNA ASHARIYYA/TWELVERS
```

the Abbasids assumed the form of a power structure on the old Oriental (and particularly Persian) model, in the shape of "Oriental despotism." With the Turkomans and Mongols, features of tribal and warrior elites were initially reintroduced into Islam, but the Ottoman, Safavid, and Moghul dynasties that were descended from these peoples created an elaborate cult of sovereignty on a legitimate religious basis, with a complex court ceremonial of previously unknown form.

Islam's early triumphal progress

The swift and comprehensive spread of Islam in its early period is unique and unparalleled as a historical phenomenon. This success reinforced the self-confidence and sense of mission of the young Muslim community, and to this day it is regarded by Muslims as a kind of historical and empirical proof of the irresistible force of Islam, and of Allah's will to see his restored religion spread swiftly over the whole face of the earth.

From the first, the Muslim troops were swept along by their religious zeal and fighting force, and they were also historically fortunate in that the death of

the Prophet coincided with the military exhaustion of the great powers of Byzantium and the Sassanian empire of Persia, which had been wearing each other down in murderous battles since 610.

The death of the Prophet did not interrupt the process of Islamic expansion. Yemen, which had already partially come over to Islam in 628, came fully under its control in 634, while Abu Bakr was still caliph. In 633, Islam began its inexorable and victorious advance on the provinces of the Byzantine Empire. The campaign was organized by the man who was to succeed Abu Bakr, Umar, and was carried out by his outstanding generals Khalid ibn al-Walid and Amr ibn al-As: Damascus fell to the desert warriors in 635, Jerusalem in 636, and the

Kerbela in Iraq
In 690, a tragic event in Kerbela gave birth to the Shia movement. After the death of the Umayyad caliph Muawiya, the people of Kufa persuaded Ali's son Husain, the Prophet's grandson and the third Shiite imam, to take power as the rightful leader of the Muslims. On their way to Iraq, Husain's clan was surrounded by the caliph Yazid's troops and defeated after days in which its besiegers starved it out. The help that was promised from Kufa never arrived. The incident is at the root of the Shiites' concept of themselves as a group persecuted for the true faith. The tomb of Husain in Kerbela was surmounted by a golden dome, and became a major place of Shiite pilgrimage.

Below: The ruins of Carthage in Tunisia
As capital of the Punic empire, Carthage was the outstanding trading force and greatest sea power of classical antiquity. Until the 6th century B.C. it had colonies in southern Europe and Africa. The city was taken by the Romans in 146 B.C., and was destroyed. Rebuilt as a Roman colony in 44 B.C. onward, it again became (with Alexandria) the most important city of northern Africa. When the Arabs conquered the territory of modern Tunisia in 698 during their triumphant campaigns, they destroyed the city again, but used many of its classical columns and capitals as material for building mosques, particularly in Tunis and for the Great Mosque of Kairouan.

Above: The holy city of Qum in Iran, with the mausoleum of Fatima al-Masuma
The city of Qum, where Arab Shiites began to settle in 712, is one of the most famous places of pilgrimage in Iran. The sister of the 8th Shiite imam, Fatima al-Masuma ("the sinless one"), died here in 817 on her way to meet her brother. Her shrine, with its great golden dome, dominates the city, which has been one of the most important centers of training for Shiite scholars since the 9th century. The Persian Safavid and Qajar shahs, who chose Qum as their own burial place, favored the city, and since the 19th century it has again become a center of Shiite intellectual life.

The Shiite al-Kazimain mosque in Baghdad
Before the Shia became established in Iran, Iraq was the center of Shiite movements. Most Shiite imams lived there, either in honorable custody or under the supervision of the Abbasid caliphs – a time of martyrdom in the eyes of the Shiites. The two gilded domes of the Kazimain mosque mark the tombs of the seventh imam Musa al-Kazim and his grandson, the ninth imam Muhammad al-Taqi (d. 835), and consequently the building housing the double shrine is called after the "two Kazims" (al-Kazimain). Today, the majority of the population of Iraq, particularly in the south of the country, is still of the Shiite faith.

whole of Syria and Palestine by 637. At the same time a campaign against the Sassanian Empire of Persia began in 634, under Sad ibn Abu Waqqas, the third great general of early Islam. The Sassanian royal residence, Ctesiphon, and the whole of Mesopotamia were conquered in 637.

Caliph Umar immediately set up military camps and military garrisons in the occupied countries, where he could better discipline his warriors and keep the region under control. He thereby created an Arab military aristocracy as a political ruling class in those areas – a problem with which Islamic culture was to be concerned for a long time to come. Between 639 and 641, Amr subdued the whole of Egypt, and between 640 and 644 Muslim warriors, with Hira, Basra, and Kufa as their bases, conquered the rest of Iraq and the south of Persia. Muslims successfully advanced from Egypt on Tripolitania (Libya) in 647, and then extended their conquests to the whole of the Maghrebi coastline: Carthage in Tunisia fell to them in 667, Algeria in 680, and Morocco all the way to the Atlantic Ocean in 681/682. In 711, the general Tariq went on by way of Gibraltar to Spain, which he conquered for Islam, except for small areas in the north of the country. Arab troops pressed on to the south of France, and were halted only by Charles Martel and the Franks at the Battle of Tours and Poitiers in 732.

As early as 673, Muslim troops had laid siege by land and water to Constantinople, the capital of the Byzantine Empire, but they had to withdraw in 678 after a defeat. In 717, they were at the gates of the city again, and were driven away only with difficulty. However, they brought a great part of the Byzantine long-distance trading routes under their control, and severely damaged the economy of the empire. Internal confusion during the caliphates of Uthman and Ali, and the necessity of internal consolidation under the first Umayyad caliphs, temporarily slowed down Islamic expansion, but the new world religion turned east at the end of the 7th century. The governor of Iraq, al-Hajaj (d. 714), was the driving force behind this eastward expansion, and he

Ruins of the palace of Ctesiphon in Iraq
Ctesiphon, on the left bank of the Tigris, was the capital city of the Persian Empire of the Parthians (3rd century B.C.–A.D. 224) and Sassanians (A.D. 224–651). The Great Kings of Persia built a magnificent palace here, and constantly extended it. With Byzantium, the Sassanian Empire was the major adversary of the Muslims as they embarked on their victorious campaigns. Ctesiphon was conquered by the Arabs in 637, and subsequently fell into decay, since the early Muslims did not wish to use the city because of its excessive splendor. In Arabic poetry of the Middle Ages, Ctesiphon was a symbol of the transience of earthly glories.

mounted a campaign to Central Asia and India in 694. By 711, his troops had taken first Afghanistan and parts of modern Pakistan, and after 704, the governors of Khorasan went on from there to conquer Bukhara and Samarqand as well as parts of Turkestan, while other contingents of troops moved over the Oxus into Baluchistan and established themselves in the delta of the Indus. It seemed as if nothing could stop the Muslim advance into Central Asia: Tashkent and Transoxania also fell to Islam after 724. The eastern Islamic world was born.

The early success of Islam would not have been possible without the energy, excellent tactics, and fanaticism of a whole series of outstanding generals. The fact that at first many regions were Islamicized only superficially, and only through the agency of garrisons, favored the particularism of local states and cultures that soon began to develop within the vast area of Islamic territory, bringing with it dissolution of the central authority of the international Islamic empire. Indications soon suggested that, to an increasing extent, the sworn unity of Islam and the central figure of the caliph were acquiring merely symbolic significance.

Art and Culture in the Islamic World

Oleg Grabar

The presence of art – that is to say, of techniques beautifying man's surroundings and of the evaluation of things made or built by and for society or individuals – is generally assumed for all cultures. And in each place this art has been affected by ideological, social, religious, historical, or geographical constraints; this explains why individual civilizations have artistic traditions which differ from each other. Islamic culture is, of course, no exception, and this chapter will elaborate on a few of these constraints.

Firstly, there are the complex ways in which Islamic culture recognized, accepted, or rejected the historical past in inherited or conquered regions. A second constraint consists of features imposed or implied by the new faith; although interpreted differently over the centuries, these are altogether permanent and constant characteristics of Islamic civilization. The special case of the mosque, which was not technically a requirement of the faith at its inception but which became a constantly evolving requirement and sign of Muslim presence, is a third example of a particularly Islamic development and constraint. The last two constraints that developed derived from particularly original features of Islamic culture. One is the encounter of the new faith with the ancient philosophy of classical Greece, and with the mathematics, technology, and natural sciences available in the Mediterranean world in late antiquity, in Iran, in India, and even in China. This occurred first in Baghdad, the center of Muslim thought and rule, and then expanded slowly and eventually, nearly everywhere in the region. The other is the character of the literature created in the Islamic world. Like all literatures of this time, it was meant both to edify and to please. In the forms it developed in Iran from the 12th century onwards, it was a literature of universally effective lyricism and had a considerable impact on the arts.

Muslim thought and the literature of Muslim lands are but two of several social and cultural constraints influencing the arts: possibly the only ones which have affected the whole Muslim world. Other constraints, for instance the mix of ethnic and social communities or religious diversity within Islam itself, vary in importance and impact from area to area and period to period, and do not lend themselves as easily to broad definitions. But it is important to remain aware of their existence.

Early Arabian art

Islam was revealed to the Prophet Muhammad in western Arabia in the early 7th century. Later Muslim historiography defined this period as a "time of ignorance" (the *jahiliya*), in the primary sense of a spiritually unenlightened period, but also as a time of relatively limited cultural achievement. This was always, however, with the exception of poetry, which became an exemplar both for its themes and for its forms. Whether western Arabia was indeed at this time in a state of cultural and artistic poverty is a matter of some debate. Few artistic remains are directly connected with the area, and only the site of al-Faw in Saudi Arabia has been excavated, partly at least. Luxury and other manufactured items, such as they existed, were, for the most part, imported from elsewhere, primarily Egypt and the Mediterranean, but also India, which was much involved in the Arabian trade. Architecture was hardly present in terms of major monuments, but the societies of western Arabia, nomadic and settled, did possess spatial concepts, as illustrated by a rich vocabulary dealing with boundaries between different kinds of places and with permanent or ephemeral sacred enclosures. And the Kaaba in Mecca, which became the holiest spot in Islam, the direction (*qibla*) towards which all Muslims pray and the goal of the pilgrimage (*hajj*) is a pre-Islamic sanctuary that had been used for centuries by pagan tribes. Although occasionally modified, its basic shape was the same; before Islam, the practice of covering it with an expensive cloth accent its use as a shrine for idols and a focus for all the religions of the Arabian Peninsula.

Left: **Holy man in pavilion**, 1553, illustration from Jami's *Rose Garden of the Pious*, Washington, Arthur Sackler Gallery
Text and image combine to form a handsome ensemble reminiscent of a theatrical stage. A Sufi holy man seems imprisoned in a richly decorated pavilion. A figure is trying to make contact with him through a closed door while, above, angels pour down inspiration and rewards. The two inquisitive characters in a window, the doubting smile on the face of the hero, and the contradiction between ascetic mysticism and luxurious surroundings introduce a slightly satirical note to the miniature.

Wild cat relief, Qasr al-Hair al-Gharbi, 8th century, Palmyra, Archaeological Museum
Palaces such as Qasr al-Hair al-Gharbi, which the Umayyads built in the Syrian desert, are prominent examples of the secular art that flourished around the Mediterranean in late antiquity. Their decoration of paintings, mosaics, and sculptures is striking for the wealth of its subject matter. There are hundreds of representations of people and of animals, typical of the ancient world, as well as rich geometric ornamentation, expressing the new Islamic decorative style.

Other parts of the vast Arabian world had an often brilliant artistic history. Not much is left of it in Yemen, except for remote temples and spectacular irrigation works used to control the flow of an often unpredictable water supply. Medieval sources often described the tall buildings of that land, and the memory of their sculpted decoration, for instance roaring lions on top of buildings, entered the realm of myth and fantasy. The most spectacular and best-known pre-Islamic Arabian cultures were those of the Nabataeans, centered on Petra in Jordan, and of Palmyra, farther north; both are now celebrated tourist attractions.

These Arab kingdoms left a major architectural tradition, strongly influenced by Hellenistic and Roman imperial models and practices, and, especially in Palmyra, impressive sculpture in temples and, above all, necropolises. Even though the remains of Nabataean and Palmyran art must have been even more spectacular in the Middle Ages than they are today, there is practically no acknowledgment of the existence of that art in medieval Islamic written sources and very little in artistic remains. Here and there – for instance in the sculpture of the Umayyad palace of Qasr al-Hair al-Gharbi in the Syrian steppe – the impact of neighboring Palmyra is clear and some have argued that certain features of early Islamic representational art – deeply drilled eyes in sculpture and lack of facial expression in paintings – should be related to the styles and techniques of these early Arabian kingdoms. But, outside of the obvious example of Qasr al-Hair al-Gharbi, the relationship, while not impossible, is difficult to demonstrate. It seems, then, proper to conclude that the great and original Arabian cultures that developed in the north of the Arabian Peninsula, between Syria and Iraq, under the aegis of the Hellenistic and Roman empires, were indeed barely present, if not wilfully obliterated, in the collective memory of traditional Islam.

This is not so in the instance of two tribal Arabian kingdoms, those of the Lakhmids and the Ghassanids, which flourished during the centuries before Islam in the steppe borderlands of Iraq, Syria, and Palestine, respectively.

Palmyra, Syria
This oasis, halfway between Damascus and the Euphrates, was an important center for east-west trade until the 3rd century: Chinese silks were discovered in its ruins. Its enormous temple complex and colonnaded streets, now in ruins, owe much to Hellenistic and Roman urban architecture, but the religion and culture of Palmyra belonged to the Semitic world of the Arab tribes of the desert. The rich sculpture of Palmyra demonstrates a magnificent synthesis of several traditions of representation from all over the Mediterranean and Iran.

They are usually remembered for their role as client states of Byzantium and Sassanian Iran, protecting each empire from the other. However they were also significant cultural entities of their own with a considerable impact on the following centuries, if not necessarily during their flowering in the 5th and 6th centuries. The Lakhmid palace of Khawarnaq in southern Iraq remained as a monument of fabled luxury even in much later Persian poetry. The first steps towards a differentiated Arabic script took place under the aegis of the same dynasty, while the Ghassanids sponsored the construction of many buildings in Syria, one of which, an audience hall, still stands in Rusafa, in the northern Syrian steppe, and includes an inscription in Greek celebrating the king al-Mundhir.

Altogether, the Arabian past seems to have played a relatively small role in the development of Islamic art, especially if forms are considered exclusively. Its importance was greater in the collective memories it created and in the Arabic vocabulary for visual identification it provided for future generations. It is, of course, true that the vast peninsula has not been as well investigated as it should be and that surprises may well await archeologists in the future. At this stage of scholarly knowledge, however, it is probably fair to say that Islam's Arabian past, essential for understanding the faith and its practices, and the Arabic language and its literature, is not as important for the forms used by Islamic art as the immensely richer

Mountain village in South Yemen
Many towns in the mountains of Yemen are still characterized by tall, narrow houses, with the main living quarters in the upper parts of the buildings and the lower parts devoted to storage or services. Such buildings were easy to defend against attacks by nomads or rival families. Medieval texts describe, before the appearance of Islam, quasi-legendary palaces built in this fashion, crowned with statues of lions that roared as the wind blew through them. It is unclear how much in these descriptions is mythological and how much corresponds to some 7th-century reality.

world, from the Atlantic Ocean to Central Asia, taken over by Islam in the 7th and 8th centuries. Even later, after centuries of independent growth, new conquests in Anatolia or India continued to bring new local themes and ideas into the mainstream of Islamic art. It is only today, in line with national aspirations for traditions related to a land as much as to a culture, that interest in the pre-Islamic monuments of Arabian history has increased.

Stucco decoration from a house in Samarra, Iraq, 9th-century
During several decades of the 9th century, the Abbasid caliphs ruled from a newly created city, about 100 kilometers north of Baghdad. There the army and the administration could operate without interference from an often unruly urban population. An enormous and rapid program of construction created palaces, mosques, houses, and all the amenities of luxury living. The decoration on this particular building is remarkable for its transformation of vegetal motifs into abstract designs covering a large surface. The term *horror vacui* ("fear of emptiness") can be used to describe much nonrepresentational Islamic art.

Islamic attitudes to art

Over the centuries, many different attitudes toward the arts came to light within the vast Islamic world and it is altogether impossible to talk of a single set of principles that determined the course of artistic development. But it is possible to argue that Islam's initial revelation, the Koran, contains passages and points of view on which attitudes to the arts could be, and often were, based. Many of them acquired different interpretations over the centuries and it should some day be possible to sketch out a history of their use.

There are, first of all, references to categories of manufacture and of construction. One set of examples involves concrete and unique items, all of which relate to Solomon, the King-Prophet whose patronage of works of art was legendary and whose artisans were usually the no less legendary jinns. He ordered the making of a fountain of molten brass, a Muslim adaptation of the celebrated Brazen Sea in Solomon's Temple in Jerusalem, as described in the Old Testament (Koran 34. 12). Then, the jinns manufactured for him *maharib* (pl. of *mihrab*), statues, cooking vessels, and tableware (34. 13). The word *mihrab* reappears several times in the Koran; it had several meanings before becoming attached primarily to a niche in the back of the mosque, about which more will be said further on. Essentially it means a place of honor, but it is difficult to know exactly what was meant in the context of this passage. The interesting point about some of these items made by the jinns is that they are very practical, almost of daily use, and could be related to the great originality of later Islamic art which developed a devotion to the beautification of common objects: plates, ewers, candlesticks, pen boxes, and so forth. Just as Solomon had done, it was proper to give attention to one's man-made surroundings.

Another passage dealing with Solomon is more complicated. In order to test the Queen of Sheba, and ultimately to demonstrate his superiority over her, Solomon orders the construction of a *sarh* covered with or built of slabs of glass or of crystal (27. 45). The exact meaning of the word *sarh* is the subject of much controversy and it may be easier to think of it as some sort of constructed space, without trying to be more precise. The peculiarity of whatever it is that Solomon built is that it is supposed to be interpreted by the Queen of Sheba as a body of water, as something different from what it really is. The pious implications of the story need not concern us here, but what is important is that a work is manufactured in order to create an illusion of reality. Two aspects of the story are pertinent to Islamic attitudes toward the arts, in partial contradiction with each other. One is that a work of art is something to wonder about, to be amazed by; it belongs to the category of wondrous things that became known as the *ajaib* (pl. of *ajib*, "wonderful" or "astonishing"), a term used constantly to praise manufactured items of all sorts. The other implication is that a work of art is a falsehood, a lie, because it gives you the impression of something that it is not. It can be

Wooden plaque, Egypt, 9th century
Paris, Musée du Louvre
It is not known how this strikingly shaped wooden plaque would have fitted on a wall, a door, or a piece of furniture. It is mostly celebrated for its design, usually interpreted as the depiction or evocation of a bird. Yet, as one looks at the details of the design, there is almost nothing bird-like about them. Most of the elements are leaves and other derivatives from vegetal ornament. It is one of the most obvious examples of an early Islamic ambivalence, perhaps even a willed ambiguity, regarding representational art.

ART AND CULTURE IN THE ISLAMIC WORLD

seen, therefore, as reprehensible, and some Muslim thinkers, even in our own time, continue to argue this point.

Individual passages such as this one will continue to be studied and discussed for various interpretations regarding the values, and even the validity, of art in Islamic culture. But one issue dominates all discussions of Muslim attitudes toward the arts: the representation of living beings. In the Koran itself, there is no formal statement opposing such representations and there is a general consensus that what can be called the Muslim "aniconism" (as opposed to "iconoclasm," implying the violent destruction of images, something which happened only rarely, and mostly in later times) was a reluctance to use such images in the face of the rich religious imagery found in the Mediterranean area and Iran or, later, India and Central Asia. Initially this reluctance was social and psychological rather than ideological, but, over the centuries, it acquired intellectual and theological justification, and used various Koranic passages and doctrines to do so. There was, in particular, the passage which relates how Jesus gave life to the effigy of a bird as a miracle showing that God alone has the power to bestow life (3. 47–49). The unique omnipotence of God is an essential feature of Islam and one of its corollaries is the absolute opposition to idols (for instance 6. 74). The artistic representation of life was seen as idolatry and eventually considered sinful by most theologians. According to many traditions, artists would be expected, on the day of the Last Judgment, to put life into their creation and to be tossed into the fire of hell when they fail to do so.

This prohibition was, of course, loosely applied, and many a treatise argued matters differently. Yet, it did affect Islamic art in several ways. The faith itself could not be expressed through images and, thus, piety had to find other ways to be shown visually, at least in more formal art; one way, as has been argued by many, was through writing and the promotion of calligraphy to a sort of sacred art form. Another effect may well have been the importance taken by secular arts, especially artisanal ones, during centuries when, almost everywhere else, religious art dominated. And, perhaps more importantly, sacred writings did not become a continuous source of inspiration for artists. There are exceptions, no doubt, especially after the 13th century and in the Iran-influenced world, or in folk art. But they are, for the most part, rare, and the expression of the faith did not form a major aspect of Islamic art outside architecture and calligraphy.

Two last themes affecting Islamic art from the very beginning deserve mention. One is the very vivid, visual, and often very precise, descriptions of Paradise, with its gardens, fountains, and pavilions. It is possible that these descriptions and evocations had an almost immediate impact on the decorative arts of the Muslims and some have argued that the mosaic decoration of the Great Mosque in Damascus of the early 8th century included a representation of that Muslim Paradise. And Paradise is forcefully evoked in the gardens of 17th-century Mughal India. Whether or not the theme has always been present when scholars saw it is a matter of debate, but its existence throughout Islamic art is certain. Then, more recently, some architects and urban designers from the Muslim world have argued that, by making man his vice-regent on earth, a central theme of the Koran, God has entrusted the earth to man. As a result, the preservation of nature in a healthy state is part of the Muslim message, and several attempts have been made in recent years to design houses, urban complexes, even whole cities in terms of respect for the environment as inspired by the faith.

Fantastic landcape, anthology of literary and mystical texts, Iran, late 14th century, Istanbul, Museum of Turkish and Islamic Art
This is a rare image of an ideal landscape showing mountains in the background, a brook winding through a meadow in the center, and trees in the foreground. It is not clear whether it should be interpreted as the illustration of a specific text (possibly the Koranic description of Paradise), the evocation of an idyllic landscape on earth, or simply a decorative design.

The mosque

The building known as a mosque is permanently and appropriately associated with the presence of Islam. But it is not possible to simply transfer whatever meaning churches, temples, or synagogues have in other religions, into the Islamic context.

The Arabic word *masjid*, from which all forms of "mosque" derive, appears frequently in the Koran. Technically it means "place of prostration," that is to say, the place where believers bow their heads to the ground in veneration of God and as part of a well-defined ritual of prayer, the main action required every day of all Muslims in order to express their faith. In a passage which was frequently used in inscriptions (Koran 9. 18), it is said that "Only he shall inhabit God's places of worship who believes in God and the Last Day, and performs the prayer, and pays the alms, and fears none but God alone." What is implied here is not a specific and new kind of building, something which did not really exist at the time of the Prophet, but a space reserved for the community of believers in which they can gather to pray, and to deal with communal affairs. Such spaces could be anywhere, for example in a private house (as with the house of the Prophet in Medina, which later became the Mosque of Medina), or in an open space, where most rudimentary elements like stones served as symbolic more than real boundaries, as was the case for many centuries with the *musallas* (literally "places for prayer") found on the edges of many traditional cities. It was during the first century of Islam that the mosque emerged as a separate and individualized building with an architectural typology of its own and with a set of technical requirements peculiar to it. This was the result of the conquest of so many different lands where Muslims had to find or build their own restricted spaces, and of the

foundation, especially in Iraq, of new cities primarily for Arabs emigrating from the Arabian Peninsula. Kufa and Basra were the main early examples of the latter, but Baghdad, Fustat (Cairo's predecessor), and Kairouan, in Tunisia, were also new cities created primarily for Muslims. These developments, as well as the Muslim encounter with the sanctuaries of many other religions, led eventually (the developmental details are not always clear) to a functional typology of Muslim religious spaces which is reflected, as late as the 14th century, in the North African polymath Ibn Khaldun's (1332–1406) celebrated *Muqaddima* (Preface) to his chronicle of the Muslim west.

The three pan-Islamic sanctuaries

Simplifying matters slightly, one should distinguish between what we can call "sanctuaries" and mosques, even though the term *masjid* is used for both. Sanctuaries are true holy places, divinely endowed with some special sanctity; their pious meaning or meanings are known and significant to all Muslims and extend much beyond their own space. Three of them are truly pan-Islamic. One is the Haram (meaning "sacred enclosure") in Mecca itself. It is not only the direction of prayer for Muslims wherever they are, but is also associated with Abraham, venerated as a holy man (*hanaf*) and the first Muslim, who is

Namazgah in Goa, India
Namazgahs, mosques consisting only of an enclosed space and a *qibla* wall, but which could accommodate large numbers of people who gathered for prayer, were frequently built near towns. Here can be seen the most important features of a mosque – the *mihrab* and the *minbar* – as well as low-lying conical towers. These, however, did not function as minarets, from which the call to prayer was issued, but marked the boundaries of the mosque in relation to the surrounding space.

The third pan-Islamic sanctuary is the Haram al-Sharif ("Noble Sanctuary") in Jerusalem, also known as the Mosque of the City. Its huge space had been determined by the size of the Jewish Temple built by Herod the Great and destroyed by the Romans. A mosque was built there shortly after the conquest of Palestine by the Muslims and then in 691 Abd al-Malik (685–705) erected the spectacular Dome of the Rock which still dominates the city. Dozens of other buildings were constructed over the centuries, most of them of very high quality, and several themes were associated with the site according to a rhythmic evolution which is still poorly understood. These echo in part the current situation between Jerusalem and the sanctuary in Mecca, and also the relationship with the Jewish tradition. There was also the theme of the miraculous Night Journey of the Prophet and his Ascension to the heavens (which he started with his foot on the rock for which the building

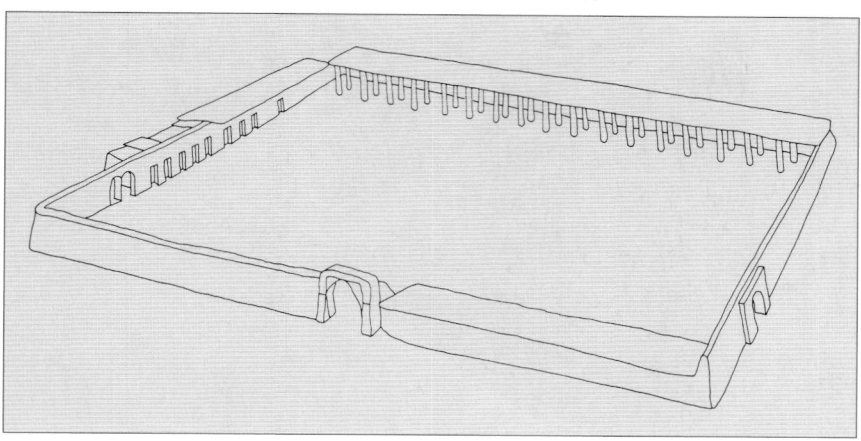

Reconstruction of the house of the Prophet, in Medina
In 622, Muhammad fled from Mecca to Medina, where he established the center for his preaching, and later the capital of the new Muslim state. His house can be reconstructed to some extent from written sources; it became the model for the earliest hypostyle mosques of Iraq and elsewhere. The house was very large, so it could serve at the same time as a public space for meetings of the entire Muslim community and as a private space for the family of the Prophet. Colonnades of various depths indicated the direction of prayer, as would be the case in later mosques, or else served simply as shelters against the elements. The gates, initially functional, all acquired symbolic meaning.

believed to have first built the Kaaba, and the site of several sacred spots directly linked with Abraham's son Ismail, and with the Prophet Muhammad. It is also the place to which all Muslims must come as pilgrims at least once in their lifetime. All sorts of complex liturgical practices have developed around the pilgrimage (*hajj*), just as, in the transformation of Mecca from an ancient Arabian to an Islamic holy place, many different influences have come, gone, or been added to the space of the Haram; these changes may have found a physical expression in the site itself – in the form of buildings, donated treasure, accumulated booty – thus clearly making the Meccan Haram a model example for the study of sanctuaries.

The second pan-Islamic sanctuary is that of the Mosque (known as al-Munawwara, "The Illuminated One") of Medina, the city of the Prophet located in western Arabia, north of Mecca. It had been Muhammad's house, which was transformed shortly after his death into a mosque and rebuilt in the early 8th century as a typical courtyard mosque, on a rectangular ground plan and its courtyard surrounded by hypostyle halls. The tomb of the Prophet, enclosed as a separate entity, is located in the southeastern area of the covered part of the mosque. Over the centuries different views have been expressed about the importance of this tomb in a Muslim context, given that Islam's strict monotheism forbids the veneration of saints, and some particularly rigorous theologians have wanted to remove it from the mosque. But there is no doubt that it is the life of the Prophet that created and still dominates the holiness of this mosque, which is an expected, if not required, stopping place for pilgrims.

Ottoman miniature with a representation of the Haram in Mecca, 16th century
At some time in the Middle Ages, there developed the practice of obtaining pious "souvenirs" from the obligatory pilgrimage to Mecca (the *hajj*). Eventually, especially from the 16th century, these took the form of large or small decorative tiles that were set in the walls of mosques, sanctuaries, or house. Here, in a schematic picture combining several different viewpoints, one can see the Kaaba and all the major commemorative or functional structures enclosed within the holy space, which is surrounded by a colonnade.

is named), the celebrated *miraj* often illustrated by later Persian painters. There are various Old Testament themes associated with this place, known as the tomb of Adam, as well as as the spot where Abraham prepared to sacrifice Isaac. Jerusalem also has eschatological significance, as the appointed place for the Last Judgment. The Haram al-Sharif in Jerusalem inspired a far more remarkable architecture than the other two sanctuaries, especially in the 14th and 15th centuries, when it became a showplace for Mamluk patronage, but, although a significant pilgrimage site, it never acquired the universal visitation obligation of the two Arabian sanctuaries. Its importance within the Muslim world as a whole varied a great deal over the centuries.

In addition to these three pan-Islamic holy places, more restricted or limited sanctuaries also developed. These were usually associated with funerary cults and always transformed into places of pilgrimage. They are often called *mashahid* (pl. of *mashhad*, "place of witnessing"). Important examples are the major Shiite *mashahid* in Meshed and Qum in Iran, and in Najaf and Kerbela in Iraq. Smaller funerary sanctuaries, often commemorating the place of burial of a holy man or the presence of a prophet from pre-Islamic times, are found in many places from Morocco to Indonesia. Fundamentalist leaders have always objected to the existence of these sanctuaries on the grounds that Islam does not formally recognize the existence of inter mediaries or intercessors other than the Prophet, or, in Shiism, the imams descending from Ali, but popular piety often overwhelmed these theological objections.

The Haram al-Sharifi in the Old City of Jerusalem
The Dome of the Rock on the Temple Mount – the "Noble Sanctuary" and the third holiest shrine of Islam – is associated with the mystical Night Journey and Ascension of the Prophet Muhammad, with many biblical figures (Abraham, Jacob, Jesus, David, and Solomon, among others) accepted as prophets by Islam, and with the Last Judgment. The shape of the sanctuary was determined by the platform created by Herod the Great for the Jewish Temple and destroyed by the Romans in A.D. 70. The most important buildings in the holy enclosure are the Dome of the Rock in the center and the Aqsa Mosque to the left.

Structure and function of the mosque

Turning now to the mosque itself, it should be recalled that to a Muslim any place suitable for prayer, even a temporary one, is a mosque, and thousands of small mosques exist, restricted to a family, a quarter, or a corporation of some sort. But from the very beginning, when the Prophet gathered the community into his house in Medina, the notion arose of a location which is not so much a religious space as one restricted to the Muslim community. It was originally meant for prayer, especially for the collective prayer suggested, if not required, of all Muslims on Fridays, but also for swearing of allegiance to princes and their representatives, as well as for teaching, tax collection, announcements of all sorts, and most aspects of social and political life. This space for the collective, ideally all male Muslims in a given settlement, was called a *masjid al-jami*, "the mosque of the community," sometimes expressed

ART AND CULTURE IN THE ISLAMIC WORLD

as the "Friday mosque." By the end of the Middle Ages the word *jami* (Turkish: *cami*) became a common equivalent to *masjid*. The only initial requirement of a mosque was a space large enough to contain the whole population of a given settlement. A wall, (at the beginning simply a ditch), separated it from other parts of the city. This space was oriented toward the *qibla* (direction for prayer, towards Mecca) by being provided with a deep covered area on the appropriate side. Little by little, other requirements were introduced: a *mihrab* or niche on the *qibla* wall to emphasize the direction of prayer and to commemorate the presence of the Prophet in the midst of his followers; a *minbar* or pulpit from which the sermon (*khutba*) was given; at times, a *maqsura*, a space reserved for the ruler and his entourage; various platforms for readers of the Koran and of other pious works; a minaret, which served to denote the presence of a Muslim center and eventually to call the faithful to prayer. Some of these features, like the *mihrab*, are found in all mosques. Others, like the *minbar*, were initially restricted to mosques in cities with governors appointed by the caliphs, whereas a feature like the minaret, grew into the most visible feature of Islamic architecture anywhere. For, as Ibn Khaldun emphasized in his great theoretical work, the building and upkeep of mosques was the responsibility of the state, because its primary purpose was the maintenance of

the cohesion of the community of the faithful. Purely religious and pious considerations of a more spiritual nature followed in a more uneven manner. In a general way, it is fair to say that the history of the mosque's evolution is revealed in its shape, in the parts it contains, in the decoration it generates, in the needs it reflects, and in the attitudes and behavior it fosters. This evolution is still continuing today.

Interior of the Dome of the Rock, Jerusalem Built in 691 by the Umayyad ruler Abd al-Malik, this is the earliest, and one of the most beautiful, monuments of Islamic architecture: a near-perfect octagon around a cylinder with a high dome, originally gilded, visible from afar. There is much discussion about the meaning of the building, whose name derives from the rock visible here in the foreground. Today it is a shrine to the mystical Ascension of the Prophet into heaven. More simply, it may serve to symbolize Muslim rule over the Christian city of Jerusalem.

The Mosque
Oleg Grabar

A fountain in the courtyard of the Sehzade Complex, Istanbul

By the end of the 7th century, only two or three generations after the appearance of Islam, the basic functions and the formal typology of the Friday (congregational) mosque (masjid al-jami) had been established. Meant for use by the whole community of the faithful in any one city, it required space. The earliest mosques were of the hypostyle type, with a large number of single and relatively small supports (usually columns) over a potentially infinite space. This type, with many variations, has remained to this day the most common in Arab countries and also whenever, for instance in Southeast Asia, patrons wished to recall, for ideological or other reasons, the beginnings of Islam. In Iran, after the 11th century, and in India, a different solution was found to provide space: a large central courtyard with four vaulted halls (known technically as iwans) opening onto the court. The Ottomans developed the single central dome into the generator of a huge internal space, another response to the community requirements of a Friday mosque. Small private mosques (simply called masjids) always existed as well and could take many forms.

But the mosque is not only a large space. It contains symbolic or functional features, each one of which has its own history. The *minbar* (stepped pulpit) dates back to the time of the Prophet. Originally a somewhat high, three-stepped stool, it was used for sermons, proclamations, and readings. Very rapidly it acquired additional steps and, in many cases, a seat at the top, covered by a canopy; elaborate examples with decorated side walls of carved wood or sculpted stone have been constructed, but the simple ones still remain.

In early Islam, the treasury of the Muslim community was kept in the mosque; a few examples have survived, for instance in Damascus, where the treasury is a domed octagon, set on columns. On a more practical level, the requirement for ablutions before prayer led to the installation of fountains, sometimes of considerable artistic merit, either in the courtyard of the mosque, or at the side.

Two features of a mosque are as symbolic as they are functional. One is the *mihrab*, a niche indicating the *qibla*, the direction of prayer, which also commemorates the presence of the Prophet. Developed around 700, the *mihrab* is found in all mosques, and has become the most decorated part of the building, often with lamps, symbolizing the divine presence and the universality of the Muslim message. The other such feature is the minaret, usually considered to be the place from which the faithful are called to prayer. However, especially during the first centuries of Islam, the minaret was primarily a visual beacon indicating a Muslim community or, as in the Arabian sanctuaries of Mecca and Medina, broadcasting as far as possible the location of a holy place.

An arcade in the courtyard of the mosque in the Citadel of Cairo

Minbar and reading podium in the Great Mosque in Mandu

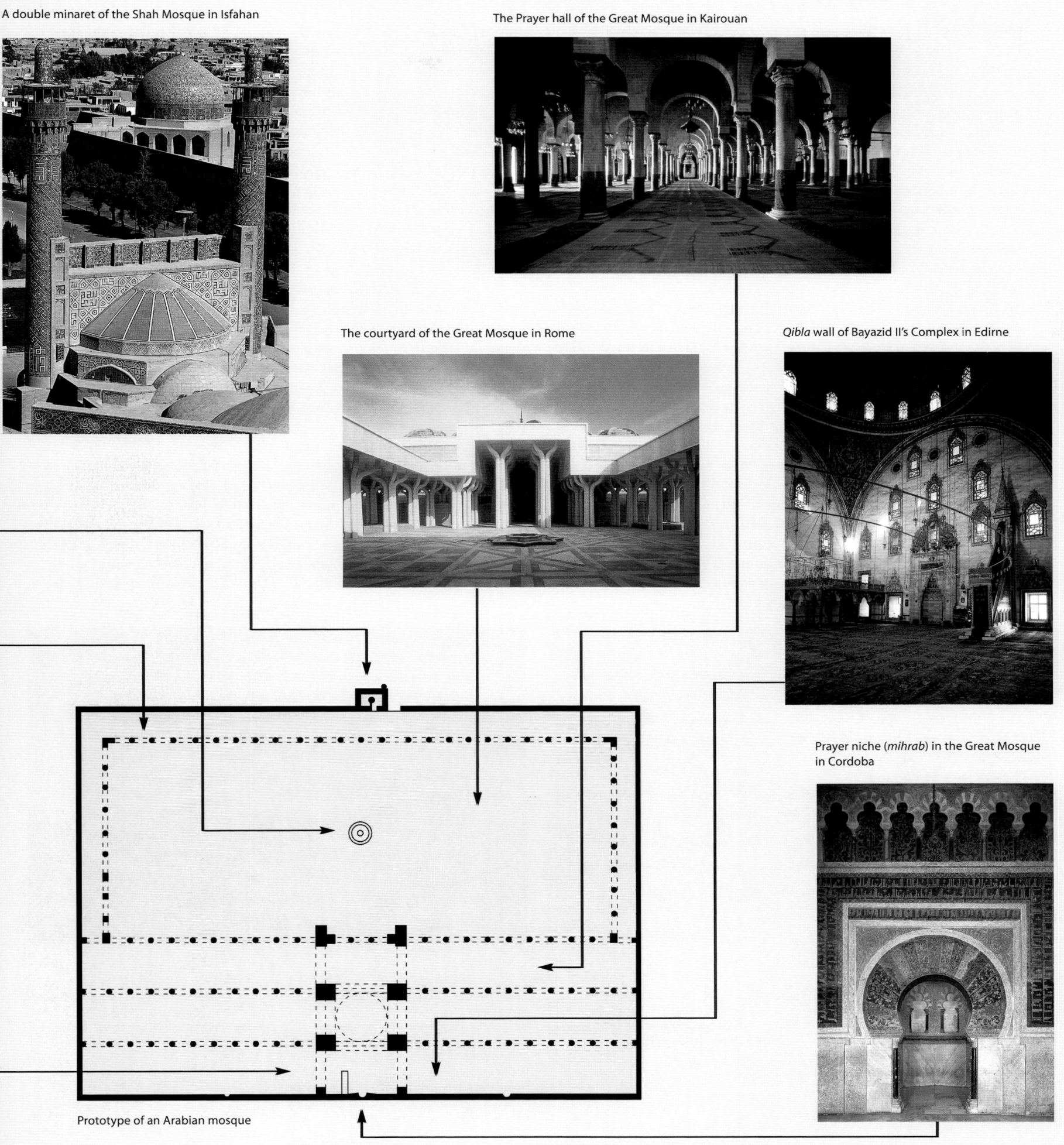

A double minaret of the Shah Mosque in Isfahan

The Prayer hall of the Great Mosque in Kairouan

The courtyard of the Great Mosque in Rome

Qibla wall of Bayazid II's Complex in Edirne

Prayer niche (*mihrab*) in the Great Mosque in Cordoba

Prototype of an Arabian mosque

Philosophy and science

It is difficult today to reconstruct, or even to imagine, the results of the encounter, primarily in and around 9th-century Baghdad, between the science and philosophy of antiquity and the new faith, confident in its physical power and eager to include all knowledge in its systems of thought. Two aspects of this encounter are pertinent to the arts. One is that it was not restricted to Baghdad. In the provinces of northeastern Iran – Khorasan and Transoxiana – and in al-Andalus at the other extreme of the Muslim world, local schools of philosophy, theology, law, and sciences developed quite rapidly, and often with much originality as early as in the 10th century. Later on, northern Iraq, Azerbaijan, and, of course, all the imperial capitals like Cairo, Istanbul, Samarqand, Delhi, to a lesser degree Isfahan, and religious capitals like Madhiya, Mashhad, or Qum in Iran acquired more or less significant scientific and philosophical schools.

For, just as with the arts, it was a proper function of rulers to support learning and the scholars engaged in its search. At times, rulers themselves or the ruling establishment were tempted to impose some views and intellectual attitudes at the expense of others and alternate positions, sometimes highly heterodox ones, developed, more or less openly, in most major centers. These various antagonisms were often displayed in urban confrontations which could become riots, but their impact, if any, on the arts is still unclear. Another aspect of this growth of science and philosophy within Muslim civilization is the identification of areas where a relationship with the arts can be established. Examples are aesthetic theory and geometry.

In the past, a few scholars tried to identify an "Islamic" aesthetic theory, and a vague consensus had been established around two philosophical themes and the arts. One is "atomism." This is the notion that all things, living or not, are made up of combinations of exactly identical atoms. The composition of atoms into "things," it is argued, is a divine prerogative, but artists or artisans, who must not compete with God, are allowed to organize these atoms in any arbitrary way they wish. Thus the free and imaginative variations of Islamic ornament or unusual combinations of motifs were seen as reflections of a philosophical doctrine on the nature of reality. The other theme pertinent to the arts was detected in the contrast between outer and inner meaning. Much used in mysticism, this is a belief in the simultaneous existence of two meanings for any form – an exterior meaning easily accessible to everyone, and a hidden one available only to the "enlightened" few. This particular theory brought to the fore a variety of mystical interpretations of Islamic art, which may well be justified by the significance of mystical movements in Islamic history and by the special role they have played in the realms of culture, symbolism, and taste. But these interpretations must be used with care, as they do not apply to all times and in all places.

In general, the difficulties with all these explanations is that they are too broad to be really useful in understanding works of art, and they are therefore unlikely to have been consistently effective artistically. More recent investigations and reflections tend to suggest that there were many aesthetic theories operating in the Islamic world, each influenced by its temporal, regional, or intellectual origins. There were, for instance, aesthetic theories connected to the philosophy found in the essays written by the Brethren of Purity, a fascinating group of texts from 10th-century Baghdad, or to the writings of Ibn Hazm (994–1064), the sophisticated philosopher and writer of Muslim Spain, a determined opponent of the concept of allegorical interpretation. The Aristotelian concept of mimesis – the practice of imitating nature or reality – appears in the philosophical treatises of al-Farabi (c.870–950), Ibn Sina (Avicenna; 980–1037), and Ibn Rushd (Averroes; 1126–1198), without, however, direct references to works of art. Al-Ghazzali (1058–1111), the great eclectic, frequently expressed his personal pleasure at seeing or feeling beautiful things, without, apparently, venturing beyond platitudes to explain his feelings. It was

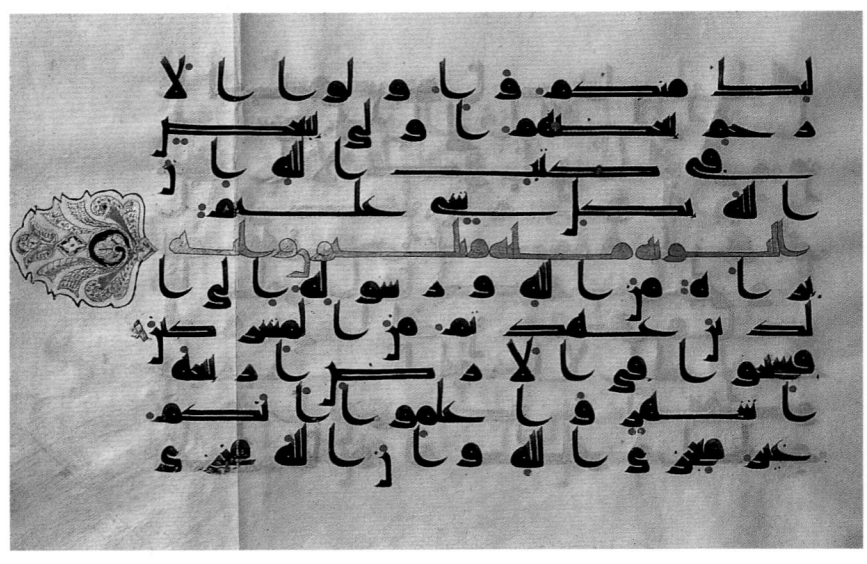

Page from a manuscript of the Koran,
Kairouan, 10th century, Tunis, National Library
This manuscript was written on parchment, an expensive material that in early Islamic times was generally used only for the Koran. The script is known as "Kufic," from the southern Iraqi town of Kufa, where it originated. The individual letters have been stylized and positioned on the page to make a harmonious arrangement of horizontal and vertical shapes. There are few diacritical marks so the text is difficult to read without prior knowledge of its words (and their pronunciation).

Page from the "Blue" Koran manuscript,
Kairouan, probably end of the 10th or beginning of the 11th century. Tunis, National Library
This celebrated manuscript, pages from which are found in many collections, was written in Ifriqiya (modern Tunisia) or in Egypt for the rulers of the Fatimid dynasty. It is stylistically different from the somewhat earlier example to the left (fewer curved lines, more angularity). It is especially remarkable for the color of its parchment, possibly imitating the purple of Byzantine imperial manuscripts.

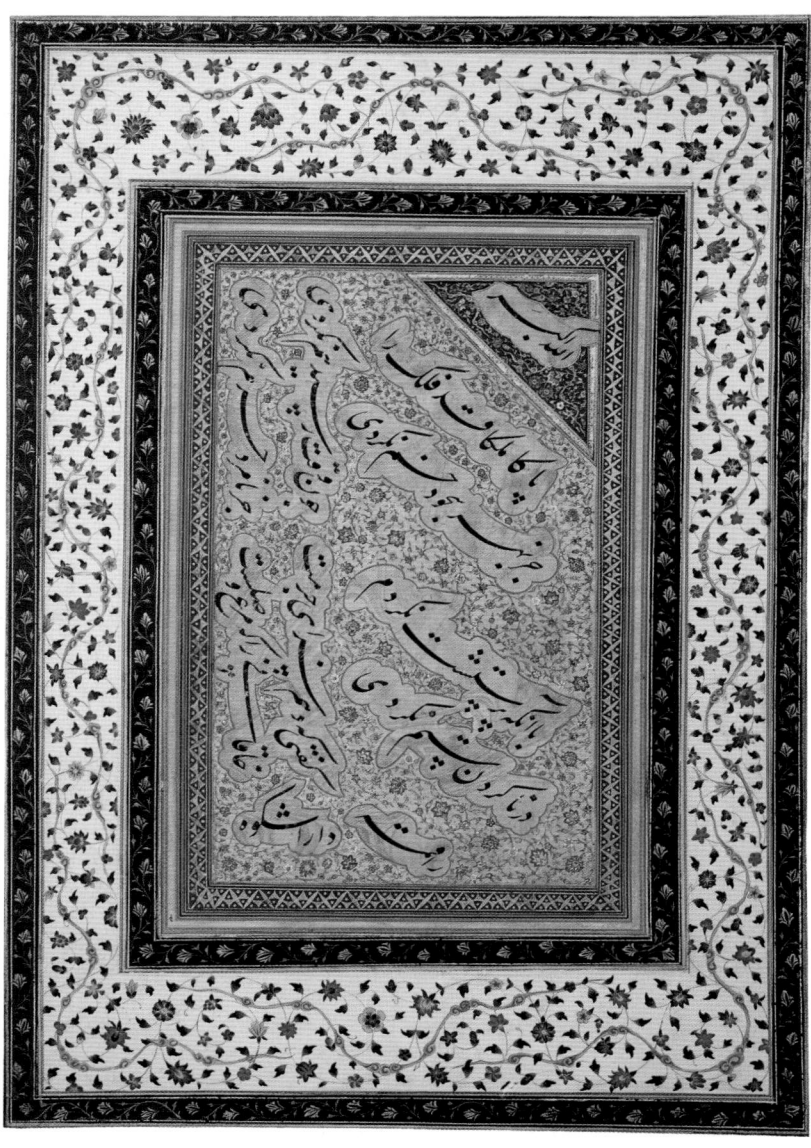

Calligraphy of the Mughal prince Dara Shikoh, 17th century,
Berlin, Islamic Art Museum
The form of cursive writing known as *nastaliq* was developed in Iran in the 14th century and was a revolution in writing technique. The lines, graciously curved, spread out diagonally or horizontally like so many springs from a fountain. Elegance dominates legibility, and most of these pages were composed to be ends in themselves, works of calligraphic art as much as, if not more than, written texts.

Ceramic bowl, Nishapur, Iran, 10th century, Berlin, Islamic Art Museum
Calligraphy on a practical object did not always convey a message but was often purely decorative. If a general blessing was expressed, this usually referred to the owner, but also frequently to all the company present.

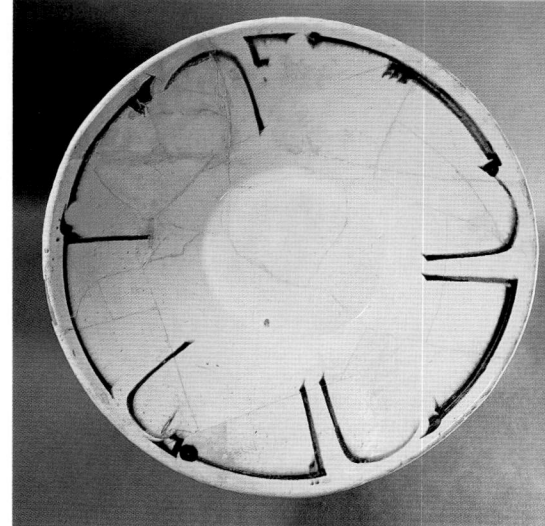

Luster tile, Iran, 13th or 14th century. Rome, Museo d'Arte Oriental
The few words on this tile are from a text too fragmentary to identify. Inscriptions, often religious in character, were ordered for public buildings or for private houses, made into panels and eventually attached to clay-brick walls. They endowed architectural surfaces with a superficial brilliance, and could also serve the piety of the beholder. At times, these inscriptions contained verses from secular, lyrical, or epic poetry. Objects like these demonstrate the importance of the written word in Islamic culture.

within these milieus that the distinction began to be made between significance (*maana*) and form (*sura*, which also used to "picture").

A more interesting and a more fruitful approach was provided by Ibn al-Haitam (Alhazen; 965–1039), a scientist from Basra who set the study of optics on a totally new track. He developed a theory of beauty on the basis of his almost empirical theory of perception, emphasizing, in particular, the very contemporary notion of "visual meaning" as well as more traditional concepts like "proportion" and "harmony." The 14th-century philosopher and historian, Ibn Khaldun, discussed the arts in more sociological terms and was very conscious of their importance to the functioning of society. He emphasized, among other things, the social position of artists – from architects to silk weavers and calligraphers – which he regarded as more than artisans.

It is, therefore, more appropriate to conclude that, beyond the few general tendencies established by the Koranic revelation at the very beginning of Islamic history, many aesthetic theories arose throughout the classical centuries of Islam. Their rise, growth, and interrelationships are still too little understood to be successfully utilized by art historians. An interesting case, the source of an abundance of theories, is that of geometry, where two cultural phenomena met. Firstly, from the 10th century onward, sophisticated geometrical ornamentation became one of the major modes of decorating the walls of buildings and objects of all sorts; it also affected the composition and design of buildings. The other phenomenon was the appearance, at the same time, not only of new theoretical mathematics at the highest level but also of applied mathematics which could use novel and complex ideas for the solution of practical, everyday problems of construction and measurement.

Above: **Section of wall in the Court of the Myrtles in the Alhambra**, Granada, 14th century
In the Spanish palaces (both Muslim ones like the Alhambra in Granada or Christian ones like the Alcazar in Seville), the lower part of the wall was covered with tiled mosaics with elaborate compositional patterns. At eye level, there was often a running inscription, and above the script was geometric or vegetal ornamentation in stucco. The overall effect was one of rich and sensuous luxury.

Below: **Detail of a Timurid Koran binding with *shamsa* (sun) rosettes**, 15th century, Istanbul, Museum of Turkish and Islamic Art
This simple design features an eight-pointed star enclosed in eight petals. The design is a closed one which would be subsequently repeated rather than transformed in order to completely cover a surface.

Above: **Door panel**, Syria or Egypt, 14th century
One of the most common motifs used in decoration was the star, in many variations. The carving of this door panel features a 12-pointed star that can be extended almost indefinitely via an elaborate geometric growth pattern, and thus be applied to surfaces of any area. Small panels in ivory or mother-of-pearl have been fitted into the pattern, and their light color creates an interesting contrast with the darker wood.

ART AND CULTURE IN THE ISLAMIC WORLD

It is easy enough to relate the two phenomena and to argue that, in order to avoid representational art and to satisfy the needs of any culture for the replicability of its finest creations, geometric order, at times in its purest form, at other times diluted with vegetal or calligraphic additions, became the norm for Islamic art, reflecting a Muslim preference for an art of pure abstraction. It does not seem that Islamic thought ever developed the notion of the Creator as a geometrician, but many attempts have been made to explain the social and artistic implications of such cultural phenomena as the poet Omar Khayyam's major contribution to geometry. Some have even argued that there must have existed discussion groups, akin to the "think tanks" of today, devoted to the exploration of geometric principles and their applicability to real life. Geometry is still a favorite pursuit of many contemporary architects and designers in the Islamic world, who, thanks to the computer, can continue to investigate the rational and irrational proportions of classical times or the ways in which harmonic theories may be used to explain historic buildings, and to design new ones.

Main hall of Qusair Amra, Jordan, 1st half of the 8th century
The remarkable feature of this Umayyad bath house, located in the semi-arid steppe of central Jordan, is that its walls were entirely covered with mural paintings exhibiting motifs from classical or late antiquity in the Mediterranean, from Iran, perhaps even from India, and certainly from the observation of Umayyad life. The quality of the paintings varies a great deal, but the finest have a unique vivacity and liveliness in their depiction of the leisure and imagination of the ruling class. The paintings of Qusair Amra are a rare example – in any culture – of private secular art preserved for posterity.

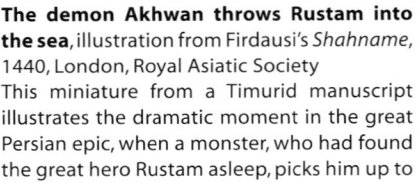

The demon Akhwan throws Rustam into the sea, illustration from Firdausi's *Shahname*, 1440, London, Royal Asiatic Society
This miniature from a Timurid manuscript illustrates the dramatic moment in the great Persian epic, when a monster, who had found the great hero Rustam asleep, picks him up to throw him into a sea full of horrible creatures. The composition of gleaming mountains and the brilliance of colorful details with a minimum of emotional involvement are characteristic of the mainstream of Persian painting.

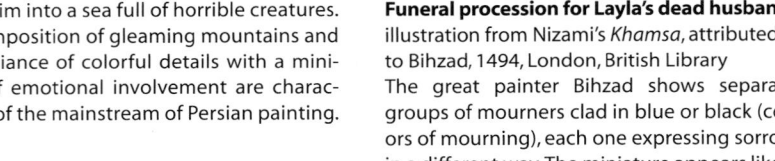

Funeral procession for Layla's dead husband, illustration from Nizami's *Khamsa*, attributed to Bihzad, 1494, London, British Library
The great painter Bihzad shows separate groups of mourners clad in blue or black (colors of mourning), each one expressing sorrow in a different way. The miniature appears like a *tableau vivant* of which the effect is of the sadness and pain caused by the death rather than of the depiction of an event.

Literature

As in many cultures, literature, in the classical centuries of Islam, mostly in Arabic and Persian, was a major source of inspiration for the arts. Most of it was highly secular in mood and subject matter, although, especially in the case of Persian lyrical poetry, mystical thoughts and attitudes can be clearly detected, just as poetry itself had an impact on the symbolism of mystical writing. The ways in which literature inspired the arts can be discussed in three different ways.

The first, and most obvious one, is iconographic. Literary subjects inspired artists working in many different media (ceramics, wall painting, metalwork, even textiles), while, from the 12th century onward, book illustration became a significant artistic activity. The variety of genres illustrated was considerable and only a few of the most significant examples follow. The *Maqamat* (Assemblies) of al-Hariri of Basra (1054–1122), is remarkable for brilliant use of the

Arabic language to recount the adventures of its cunning hero, Abu Zaid. The illustrations of the various manuscripts, executed over a period of a century and a half, aimed to depict the stories involved, and, through them, the urban milieu in which they were supposed to have taken place. The epic *Shahname* (King's Book), composed by the Persian poet Firdausi (d. 1020) around the year 1000, consists of a heroic and largely mythical history of Iran from the time of Creation to the beginning of Islam. Its many stories of kings, warriors, battles, feasts, and love lent themselves to illustrations, of which hundreds have survived from the end of the 13th century onward. Most of them exhibit a dramatic mood and a highly symbolic rendering. The Indian animal fables *Kalila wa-Dimna* (Kalila and Dimna), translated in the 8th century from Persian into Arabic by Ibn al-Muqaffa, are in fact a "Mirror of Princes" used for the moral and political edification of rulers, but they contain wonderful anecdotes, which are illustrated in Persian as well as Arabic manuscripts. And,

Majnun and Salim in the palm grove, illustration from Nizami's *Khamsa*, 1462, Istanbul, Topkapi Palace Museum
This Iranian miniature depicts one of the most touching episodes in the tale of how Majnun, Layla's "mad" lover, becomes alienated from society. He is visited by his only friend, Salim, in a grove of palm trees artfully arranged to emphasize Majnun's isolation. Only pairs of animals have befriended him and seem to stand in an admiring guard around him. Everything, even the contrast between Majnun's and Salim's outward appearances, emphasizes Majnun's loneliness.

Jackal and lion, illustration from *Kalila and Dimna*, Herat, 1429, Istanbul, Topkapi Palace Museum
The book *Kalila and Dimna* is of Indian origin and tells the tale of two jackals who create riot and discord in the animal kingdom. The individual tales, with both people and animals as heroes, usually serve to illustrate a moral precept to guide kings to rule ethically and successfully. Here, one of the jackals is trying to lead a rather dull-looking lion astray, in a setting of pure colorful fantasy.

as a final example, one must mention Persian lyrical poetry, especially the beautiful romances known as the *Khamsa* (Quintet) composed c. 1200 by the poet Nizami (d. 1209). From the end of the 14th century, these were often illustrated, as were also, but more rarely, the poems of the Persian Hafez (d. 1389). Histories were occasionally illustrated, although, for the most part, they hardly qualify as literature; several examples exist of illustrations provided for the moralizing stories of the mystic poet Saadi (1219–1292). Enormous variations exist between these texts and the ways in which they were illustrated. As a general rule, imagery was created which directly reflected the written content but, over the centuries, complex relationships developed between images relating to different texts. Most of this iconography was restricted to books until fairly late in the 17th century, and, except for the epic stories of the *Shahname*, there is little evidence that it was used in wall painting or in other forms of decoration. Altogether, although not as varied nor as huge as the repertoires found in Christian, Buddhist, or Hindu art, the primarily secular vocabulary of Islamic painting provides examples illustrating a vast range of historical, legendary, and romantic events.

The second way in which literature inspired the arts is more interesting than a simple recital of topics. As early as the last decade of the 12th century (at least insofar as preserved examples are concerned), literary works were used to express messages other than simply the illustration of a story. Many manuscripts were provided with frontispieces and dedications intended to reflect the glory of ruling princes. They could also be used as lessons in statesmanship, and, in many instances, served as ways to recollect, and to interpret, contemporary events through references to past heroes. Satire could also be a feature, as in 13th-century Arabic, some 15th-century Iranian manuscripts, and, especially, from the 17th century onward, in the depiction of individuals. It is possible to argue that, as literature inspired paintings, it also used paintings to make itself more im-

Opposite: **Tortoise and two cranes**, illustration from *Kalila and Dimna*, late 13th or early 14th century, Paris, Bibliothèque Nationale

Three people making conventional gestures indicating amazement (note in particular the one to the left with his hand to his mouth) observe with wonder an instance of cooperation between animals, as two cranes help a tortoise cross a river. The composition is two-dimensional, with individual labels identifying each protagonist, similar to a comic script. There is a naive charm to such simple and direct images, which have no significant ornamental effect, yet make clever use of artistic conventions.

Illustration from the *Babur-name*, India, Mughal era, Delhi, Museum of Fine Arts

Indian miniatures of the Mughal era are remarkable for their depiction of the secular life of princes and heroes. Often, they manage to crowd an amazing number of features into a single picture: collections of buildings from various perspectives; details of walls, towers, and gates; and, especially, a procession of imperial attendants marching toward the ruler, who is seated under a canopy. Poses and features are differentiated: perhaps there are portraits of individuals. Animals, especially elephants, are painted with full knowledge of their anatomy and behaviour.

Poet in the garden, Mughal style, 1605–1615, Boston, Museum of Fine Arts
From the 16th century onwards, Persian painting began to represent individuals separately from narratives. Youthful men and women predominate, but an interesting category of such images is that of elderly men presented as poets, teachers, or holy men.

mediately responsive to the pressures of any one time. Painting permitted constant *aggiornamento*, and thus the continuing relevance of literature.

The deep involvement of both Persian and Arabic speakers in their literature affected art in yet another way. As early as the 9th century, debates and discussions arose on literatary topics, the qualities of poets or writers, and the hierarchy of the genres they used. Literary criticism became the subject of theoretical analysis, and, of endless debates. Some of this analysis, such as that of al-Jurjani in the 11th century dealing with semantics or with metaphors and their psychological effect, or of Ibn al-Rami in the 15th century aiming to define beauty by describing ideal women, can be used to understand art. Just as with philosophy and the natural sciences, it is unlikely that many of these often abstruse theories of literature were commonly held or even known to the general public. Their existence in written works is, however, certain, and through them it is possible to imagine the critical climate within which art was created.

A word should, finally, be added about a literary genre which, mostly, emerged after the 15th century, and, apparently, was restricted to the Iranian world. As exemplified by Safavid artists like Qadi Ahmad, Dust Muhammad, and Sadiqi Beg, the artist's autobiography is the most important factor for understanding Persian painting. Such personal artistic statements became particularly common in the Moghul period in India, where the memoirs of rulers, like the *Babur-name* (Book of Babur), in which the emperor Babur recounts the story of his life and his opinions on nearly everything, are essential in constructing the framework within which the arts can be understood.

Science in Islam

Markus Hattstein

Islamic science was in its prime during the European Middle Ages, between the 9th and the 13th centuries, particularly in the brilliant period of the Abbasid caliphate from the 9th century to the 11th. A considerable degree of education and scientific knowledge existed on many levels of Islamic society. At the time of the Crusades, for instance, the Islamic knights could read and write, skills which were exceptional among their Western opponents. However, the encouragement of science and art was mainly the province of the courts, from the caliphate in Baghdad down to the residences of local governors and minor regional potentates. Many a second-tiered ruler made his court an important center of science and art, the best example being the Spanish *taifa* rulers of the 11th century. All the major philosophers and scientists of the Islamic world spent at least some time at such a court. They not only received money from open-minded and interested rulers, but were often appointed as their political advisers.

The sciences of Islam, particularly the so-called exact or natural sciences in the widest sense, had from time immemorial taken as their unquestioned authorities (together with the religious sources of the Koran and the Hadiths) the writers of Greek antiquity, more particularly the philosophers Socrates, Plato, and Aristotle, to whom every scientist referred in one way or another. Another authority was the physician Galen. Contrary to what is generally thought in the West, where the achievements of Arab and Persian science are seen as consisting almost exclusively in the preservation and transmission of the inheritance of classical antiquity, these scholars adopted an intellectually original and independent approach to the texts of antiquity; the Greek inheritance was not simply copied and read, but revised, brought into line with the requirements of Islamic culture (and religion), supplemented, and expanded.

A striking feature is the universal erudition of Islamic scientists. The thinkers of the early period were almost all trained physicians and recognized medical authorities. They were also skilled astronomers, and developed complex philosophical systems based largely on the natural sciences, but they also tried to reconcile

Socrates in discussion with his pupils, Seljuk manuscript, 13th century, Istanbul, Topkapi Palace Library

Treatise on alchemy, 18th century, London, British Library

and interrelate religion and science, not a contradiction in terms in the Islamic concept of reason. Many of them also produced travel writings and autobiographies, and experimented with alchemy, particularly in the manufacturing of precious metals. In each of these areas they wrote a great deal and compiled extensive collections, taught students, gave lectures, and enriched the libraries of their princely patrons. Many scientific terms and names of plants and spices reached the European languages by way of Arabic or Persian. These words include alchemy, algebra, alcohol, amulet, caliber, carat, chemistry, cipher, elixir, magazine, mummy, sugar, talisman, and zenith. Expansion of the trade and travel routes of the Islamic world also ensured the extensive distribution of scholarship and written works.

Philosophy and the caliph's dream

Philosophy and all the other sciences received their first major boost under the scholarly Caliph al-Mamun (813–833) and his direct successors. Al-Mamun made the rationalistic faith of the Mutazilites the state religion, allowing philosophy to free itself from its subservience to theology. This encouraged an interest in the thinking of classical antiquity by announcing that a dignified old man had appeared to him in a dream, identified himself as Aristotle, and that he had expounded the nature of good on a basis of philosophical doctrine (rather than divine revelation). The first major philosopher of Islam was al-Kindi (c. 800–870), a descendant of a distinguished family, who took Platonic thinking as his point of departure, argued for the acceptance of causality, and also wrote over 200 works on subjects ranging from philosophy, medicine, mathematics, physics, chemistry, astronomy, and music. He was also politically influential as the tutor of princes at the court of Caliph al-Mutasim, where he introduced arithmetic using Indian numerals. Al-Farabi (c. 870–950), who bore the honorific title of "second teacher" (that is to say, second only to Aristotle) and was active at the court of the Hamdanids of Aleppo, combined Aristotelian thinking with neo-Platonism, and confidently stated that philosophy held the primacy over theology. In his book, *The Model State*, he sets out the pattern of an ethical and rational ideal state, ruled by a philosopher king who also has some of the characteristics of an Islamic prophet.

One of the most important Islamic polymaths was Ibn Sina of Bukhara (c. 980–1037), known in the West as Avicenna. He worked to compile a detailed collection of all the knowledge of his time, wrote works on philosophy, astronomy, grammar, and poetry, and was regarded as one of the most outstanding physicians of his day. He also wrote a remarkable autobiography, and held important political offices at various princely courts. In his major work, *The Book of the Cure (of the Soul)*, he combines metaphysics and medicine with logic, physics, and mathematics. His compendium of medicine was regarded as a standard work in Europe as well as the Islamic countries until the early modern period. Avicenna's contemporary al-Biruni (973–1048), who came by adventurous ways to the court of the Ghaznavids Mahmud and Masud, and remained bound to it for the rest of his life in a curious love-hate relationship, proposed strong links between philosophy and astronomy in his book *Gardens of Science*. He accompanied

Mahmud of Ghazna on Indian military campaigns, and wrote a cultural history of the Indian world.

Ibn Tufail (c. 1115–1185), who enjoyed the protection of the Almohads, was an original thinker. His work, *The Living One, Son of the Watcher* (God), tells the story of an Islamic Robinson Crusoe who is cast up on a desert island, where he comes to an understanding of the world and the nature of the One God through natural reason alone.

Philosophy in Islam reached its peak with Ibn Rushd (c. 1126–1198), who was also under the protection of the Almohads, and became known in the West as Averroes. As an uncompromising champion of Aristotle, he supported the idea of the eternal existence of the world and the cosmos, which had no beginning; in his doctrine they were created by God, but developed according to their own laws. The intuitive mind, Aristotle's *nous*, was a purely intellectual entity to Averroes, operating on the souls of men from outside, and he therefore rejected ideas of the continued existence and immortality of individual souls. He came into violent conflict with Islamic orthodoxy, had to face many tribunals and hearings, and often survived only because he enjoyed the protection of the Almohad rulers. The doctrine of the eternity of

Elephant clock, al-Jazari, north Syrian manuscript, 13th century, 33.8 × 22.5 cm, Istanbul, Topkapi Palace

the world and its existence without beginning reached the West as "Latin Averroism" (its outstanding proponent was Siger of Brabant at the Sorbonne in Paris), and it was contested by the most important European thinker of the Middle Ages, Thomas Aquinas, who himself was strongly influenced by Aristotelianism of the kind proposed by Averroes. In the Islamic world, however, orthodox and dogmatic theology clearly gained the upper hand over philosophy.

The natural sciences: astronomy, physics, and medicine

Islamic science's special interest in astronomy was derived from the traditions inherited from old oriental religious communities, such as the Parsees, and in particular the Sabaeans of ancient Mesopotamia, whose center was in the north of Iraq and who were largely absorbed by Islam in the 11th century. Under Hellenistic influence their original Babylonian cult of the heavenly bodies had given way to monotheism, but they still retained ancient oriental knowledge of the mathematical calculation of the course of the planets. Such calculations fascinated Islamic scientists because, under Greek influence, they developed a concept of the divine architect of the universe as a great mathematician and geometrician who kept

Jai Sing Observatory, Delhi, 18th century

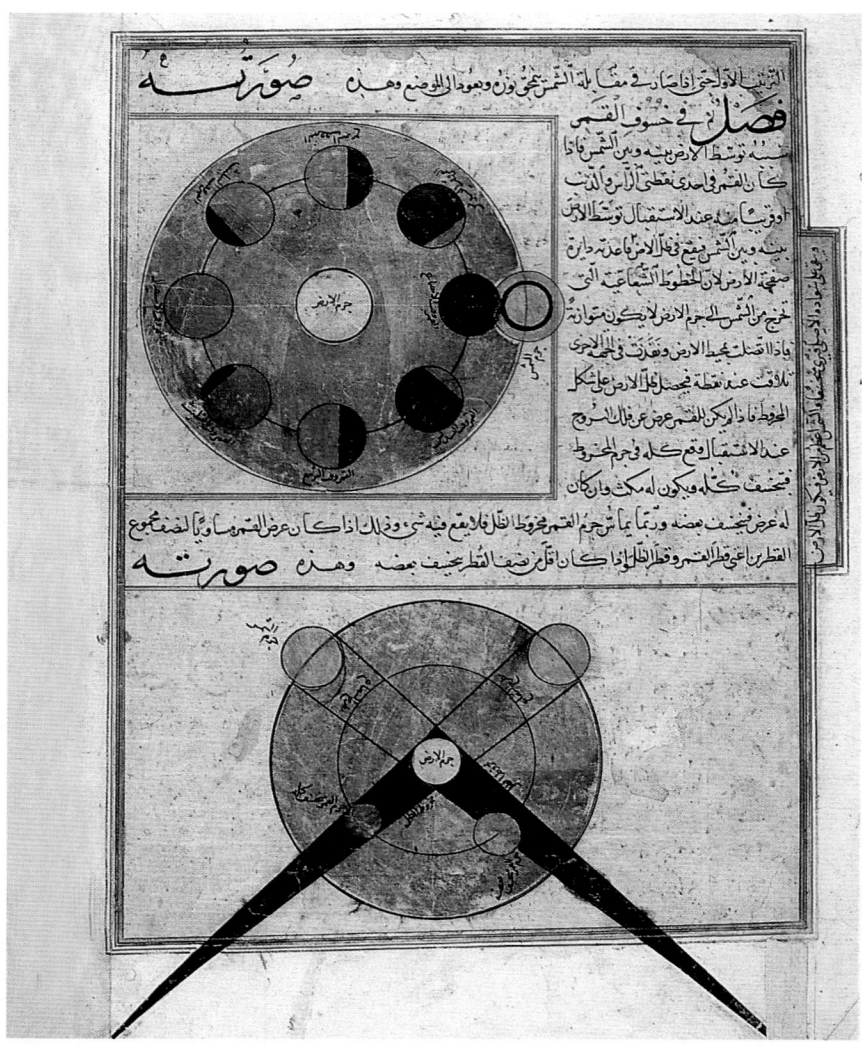

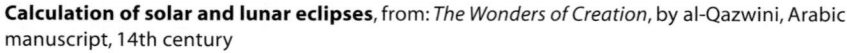

Calculation of solar and lunar eclipses, from: *The Wonders of Creation*, by al-Qazwini, Arabic manuscript, 14th century

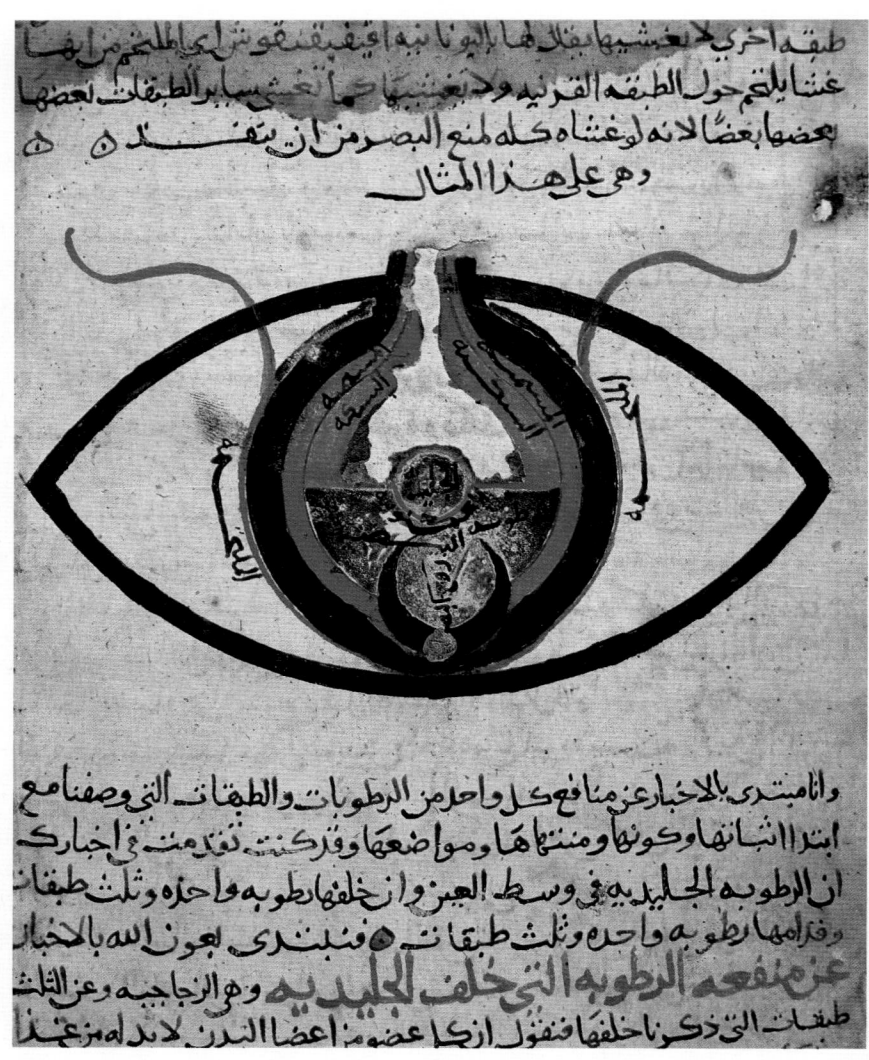

Anatomy of the Eye, by al-Mutadibih, Arabic manuscript, c. 1200, Cairo, National Library

everything in order by the operation of precisely calculable laws. Astronomy and astrology were closely connected in this system of thought, and the calculation of favorable conjunctions became a politically influential field of knowledge. All the important philosophers, and many rulers, took an interest in astronomy, calculated the courses of the stars and the dimensions of the earth, forecast the weather, and predicted the state of the water supply – calculations that served very practical purposes.

The Fatimid caliph al-Hakim, for instance, made use of the knowledge of the astronomer and physicist Ibn al-Haitham or Alhazen (965–after 1040), who was required to calculate the amount of water in the Nile for agricultural purposes. Alhazen is regarded as the greatest physicist of the Middle Ages, and was outstanding for his work on optics, in which he described refractions of light in calculating the earth's distance from the stars. Al-Biruni, mentioned above, drew up very

precise measurements of the earth, constructed a great globe, and made remarkable progress in the understanding of the rotation of the earth and the force of gravity. The phenomena of solar and lunar eclipses could be very precisely calculated at this time. Many astrolabes and astronomical charts, once the property of rulers well versed in astronomy, have been preserved. Outstanding among such rulers was Ulugh Beg (1394–1449), the grandson of Timur, whose residence was in Samarqand. In 1428/29 he had a huge observatory built with a sextant for calculating the height of the sun, and with the aid of expert astronomers, drew up the most precise astronomical charts of the Middle Ages.

Medicine was at first very closely linked to philosophy, and every Islamic thinker who was also a doctor developed theories about mankind from both a medical and a philosophical viewpoint. Hunayn ibn Ishaq (808–873), an Arab Christian, had studied with Arab and Byzantine

scholars and doctors, and became the most important translator into Arabic of the medical writings of classical antiquity, particularly the works of Galen. Everywhere he went on his long journeys he collected the texts of classical authors, translated them, compared them, and then wrote commentaries on them. His meticulous methodology allowed for the compilation of a medical canon with a standardized vocabulary that became the basis of medical training in the Arab countries; he himself was an excellent eye specialist, and wrote compendia describing his own medical methods. The independent-minded Persian, Muhammad ibn Zakariya al-Razi (865–925), also known as Rhazes in the West, organized hospitals in Baghdad and Rayy, compiled a collection of clinical cases, and thus created a great medical encyclopedia. He communicated the knowledge that it contained in his own extensive teaching activities. He championed

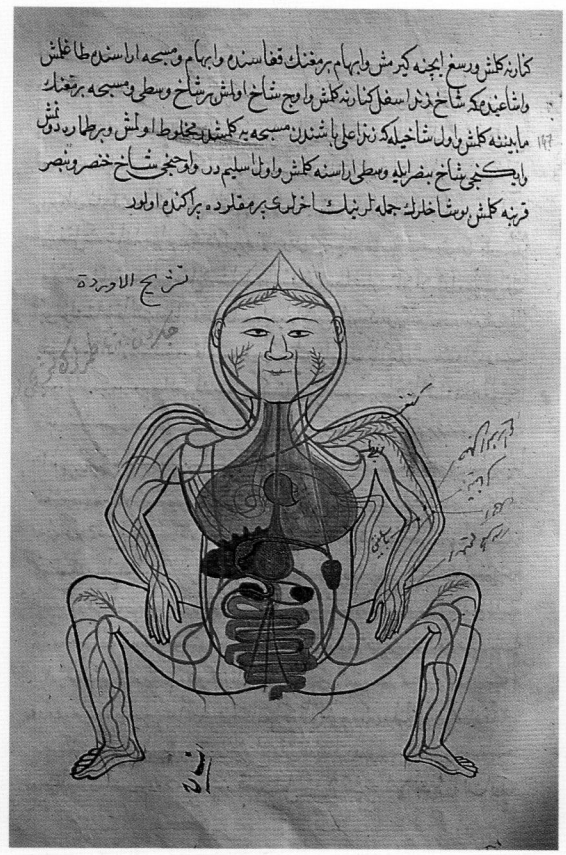

Circulation of the blood, medical manuscript, 15th century, Topkapi Palace Museum

Canon Medicinae **of Avicenna** (990–1037), Damascus, National Museum

the liberation of medical and scientific thinking from the dogmas of religion, made many experiments in alchemy, and described the symptoms of smallpox. Interestingly, he called the philosopher Socrates the "true imam" of reason, since so far, to his way of thinking, the prophets had done nothing but sow discord among mankind.

The medical schools in the Islamic world made great progress in the fields of pharmacology, infectious disease, therapeutics, and above all the treatment of eye disorders; around the year 1000 they were already successfully operating on cataracts, and also knew a great deal about the circulation of the blood, which is shown in many illustrations. Finally, the physician Ibn an-Nafis discovered pulmonary circulation through his understanding of the impermeability of the membrane of the heart. Many Islamic rulers founded large hospitals that took patients from all

walks of life and nursed them around the clock. There were also special hospitals for the "care of lunatics," with trained staff.

The compendia of Ibn Ishaq, Rhazes, Avicenna, and other scholars reached Europe by way of southern Italy and Andalusia. Avicenna's *Canon Medicinae*, in particular, became a major textbook of Western medical schools. Arab physicians thus not only handed on the knowledge of classical antiquity, but were the direct forerunners of medical progress in Europe from the Renaissance.

Blood-letting machine, al-Jazari, north Syrian manuscript, 13th century, 33.5 × 22.5 cm, Istanbul, Topkapi Palace

Syria and Palestine: The Umayyad caliphate

The small "bathhouse palace" of Qusair Amra in Jordan, early 8th century
This rear view of the complex makes its design clear: the entrance hall and throne room, roofed by three barrel vaults, face the baths, which consisted of a number of smaller rooms. These small rooms were furnished for the alternate enjoyment of hot and cold baths. In its exterior structure, the palace is an ashlar building with barrel vaults and domes. Of the interior decoration, some frescoes and the remains of mosaic floor decoration are still extant.

History
Volkmar Enderlein

The foundations of Umayyad rule were laid during the reign of Caliph Umar (634–644), when Muawiya, a member of the Umayyad family, was appointed governor of Syria in 639. The influence of the dynasty grew with the reign of the Umayyad Caliph Uthman (644–656). His assassination led to civil war, waged like an Arab family feud by Muawiya, who emerged victorious in 658 after the Battle of Siffin. After three years under two rulers, during which Ali, the Prophet Muhammad's son-in-law, also held the title of caliph, Umayyad supremacy became definitive in 661.

The power center of the Umayyads was always Syria, with Damascus as their capital. They were outstandingly efficient in maintaining a balance between the two major Arab tribal federations of Syria, the Qais – to whom they themselves belonged – and their deadly enemies the Kalb. The bitter hatred with which individual members of the Umayyad family pursued each other can be understood only if one bears in mind the fact that some of their mothers belonged to the Kalb tribe. Such links did not bring reconciliation between the tribes; instead, hostility made its way into the ruling family itself. Cousins avenged themselves on one another in acts of terrifying cruelty.

Detail from the western ambulatory of the Great Mosque of Damascus, c. 715
The exterior wall of the ambulatory, which encircles the courtyard of the Great Mosque of Damascus, has mosaic decoration showing a series of monumental trees depicted in a relaxed style, with buildings arranged in picturesque groups among them. They are standing on the banks of a stretch of water that holds the composition together. This huge mosaic is also known as the Barada Mosaic, after the name of the river Barada that flows through Damascus.

mosque at Kufa, and bring him back to the capital by camel within the space of 12 days and nights.

Ali-Walid II ibn Yazid, nephew of Caliph Hisham, had plenty of time and opportunity to follow his inclinations during his long years as crown prince (724–743). He was a true connoisseur of Arabic poetry, and wrote verses himself on the subjects of love and wine. He loved horses, enjoyed life in the desert, and hunted lions and gazelles. On his visits to monasteries, where he indulged himself in the forbidden enjoyment of wine, he came to know Christian architecture and Christian churches, an experience that certainly influenced his own building projects. He was not a man of whom orthodox Muslims approved, and it is hardly surprising that he fell victim to a rebellion in orthodox circles.

There are traces of Iranian Sassanian influence here and there in the castles built by Caliph al-Walid. The lifestyle of the Sassanian Great Kings was considered an exemplary model, and was deliberately imitated. When al-Walid II succeeded to power, he told his governor in Iraq, to whom he had also entrusted the administration of Khorasan, to procure from Iran slaves and slave girls, gold and silver pitchers, lutes, guitars, and women musicians.

Under the Umayyads, Arab armies steadily extended the territorial borders of the caliphate. In 711 they crossed the Straits of Gibraltar and the Indus at about the same time,

The caliphs of the Umayyad house led the lives of Arab aristocrats. They avoided the great city of Damascus, with its frequent epidemic outbreaks of disease, and spent most of their time in their castles on the outskirts of the desert. Since the caliphs were all well versed in traditional Arab music and poetry, they were generous patrons to poets and singers. It has also been said that Caliph al-Walid II (743–744) gave a singer, who had performed several songs costly garments that he himself had worn, as well as a thousand dinars (gold pieces) and a string of jewels.

Caliph Hisham (724–743), who with Muawiya and Abd al-Malik is regarded as one of the outstanding Umayyad caliphs, had the reputation of being a particularly able administrator. Money flowed into his hands in vast quantities, and he spent it on public works. He had canals and water reservoirs dug, hostelries built along the pilgrim road; he secured his borders and reformed the armies. The police force was so effectively built up that when an alleged enemy of the state fled Damascus by night, it could easily pick him up in the

making their way into both Spain and India. Their invasion of France was halted only by the Battle of Tours, where they were defeated by Charles Martel in 732. In 712 they conquered Samarqand, and in 717/718 they were outside the walls of Constantinople. The expansion of the Islamic world as it would be for the next few centuries was now complete.

The territory conquered by the Arabs extended from parts of the Byzantine Empire to the entire area once ruled by the Sassanians and comprising modern Iran and Iraq. Since their administration relied on the governmental structure of the peoples they had conquered, the administrative language in Damascus was Greek, in Kufa in southern Iraq it was Central Iranian Pahlavi, and in Egypt it was Coptic. Only toward the end of the 7th century did Arabic become more common as an administrative language. Taxes were still collected by the native authorities, and the minting of coins followed local traditions. In Syria, the coinage was still on the Byzantine model, in Iraq it was in the Sassanian style. Both Muslims and unbelievers were taxed, but at different levels.

While Muslims were bound to pay the tax for the poor (*zakat*), and a tithe if they were landowners, non-Muslims had a poll tax and property tax imposed on them. Since conversion to Islam would mean exemption from the poll tax, and thus a decrease in the revenue from taxation, Arab rulers could not really wish for mass conversions. The precise amounts of these taxes are not known, but must have been considerable. For instance, as early as the time of the second of the "Rightly Guided Caliphs," Caliph Umar (634–644), the province of Sawad in Iraq paid 120 million dirhams (12 million dinars) a year, and one of the governors of Iraq amassed a state treasury of 100 million dirhams during his time in office in that province. Under Hisham, tax administration was tightened up; it was taken out of the hands of the governors themselves, and organized by tax officials assigned to assist them. As well as the revenue from taxation, throughout the period of Arab conquests, huge amounts of money flowed into the state coffers from the loot taken in victorious military campaigns. It was only thanks to this vast influx of wealth that the caliphs were able to finance costly building projects such as the construction of the Great Mosque in Damascus, on which a sum of 56 million dirhams was spent.

A special form of taxation consisted of the labor dues imposed on provinces, towns, or smaller communities. The inscription found on the castle of Qasr al-Hair al-Sharqi in the east of Syria provides information about the way in which individual communities were obliged to provide labor services of this kind. It reads: "In the name of God the Merciful, the Compassionate. There is no God but Allah, the One God, who has no companions. Muhammad is the messenger of God. God's servant Hisham, Commander of the Faithful, ordered the building of this town, and the work was done by the people of Homs under Sulaiman ibn Ubaid. Dated this year 110 (728/729)."

Gateway of the Umayyad palace on the Citadel of Amman,
1st half of the 8th century
The cubic structure of the building was originally roofed by a dome. Halls arranged in a cruciform design opened into the domed area. The walls were divided up by blind arches, and filled in with abstract tree designs. Their draftsman-like reproduction of flowers and leaves is reminiscent of the relief decoration of the Qasr Kharana, dating from before 710/711.

Southern precinct of the palace in Anjar,
Lebanon, begun c. 715
The town of Anjar, on the Beqa plain in the foothills of the Anti-Lebanon mountain range, was excavated in 1957. This relatively small town, built on the Roman model, was laid out on an area of 370 × 310 m. It was divided into quarters by two main streets, and a structure, consisting of four archways, rose on 16 pillars above their intersection. The main streets were lined with colonnades; shops and workshops lay behind them. The mosque was in the southeast quarter of the town, next to the palace. According to inscriptions found there, work on the building of Anjar began in 714/715.

The interesting point about this inscription is the evidence it provides that the builders came from Homs in Syria, and constructed this building east of Palmyra, 125 miles (200 kilometers) away from their home town. It also names the patron who commissioned the work, the site foreman, and the date.

Such a commission entailed the provision of building materials and expert builders, including stonemasons, carpenters, bricklayers, and plasterers, all bound to provide labor on certain sites, and they all needed board and lodging too. The presence of ancient columns and capitals in Umayyad buildings is evidence of the practice of taking building materials from sites of classical antiquity and reusing them. Sometimes communities might actually be ordered to plunder classical cemeteries for their lead sarcophagi, since lead was an important material for covering roofs and plugging the gaps between blocks of stone.

Provision of these labor dues was incumbent on subjects from anywhere in the entire caliphate. It is not surprising, then, to find stonemasons from Egypt and bricklayers from Iraq working on buildings in Syria. Linguistically, the building sites of the Umayyads must have been like the Tower of Babel. Even Byzantine craftsmen were called upon for their services. We are told repeatedly that the caliphs turned to the emperors of Byzantium asking to have building workers made available to them.

Information about the organization of such building projects comes from the historian Ibn al-Muqaffa, writing on the architectural achievements of Caliph al-Walid II: "Since the people hated him, however, he began building a city named after him, for he gave his name to it. But the water was 15 miles (24 kilometers) away. He gathered together craftsmen from all parts, and built the city with forced labor. And because there were so many laborers, a great number of them died daily for lack of water, for the water was brought by 1200 camels. The camels were divided into two groups. Six hundred brought the water one day, and six hundred brought it the next day. Then al-Walid was attacked by a man called Ibrahim, who killed him and deprived him of the caliphate. Ibrahim freed the enslaved craftsmen and they went away, each to his own home."

The accession speech of Yazid ibn al-Walid in 744, after the assassination of al-Walid II, clearly illustrates the extent of the people's sufferings in connection with the building projects of the caliphs: "O people! You have my word that I will not set stone upon stone, nor will I set brick upon brick. I will dig no canals. I will accumulate no treasures..." It is obvious that even civil engineering works for the common good, such as the digging of canals, were felt to be a burden.

Even before the rule of the Umayyads came to an end, many of their buildings were destroyed in an earthquake that devastated large regions of the Middle East in 746. In the castle of Mshatta, the stones of the vaulting were found lying where they had fallen to the ground in the earthquake.

The Umayyads were weakened not only by tension between the Arab tribes

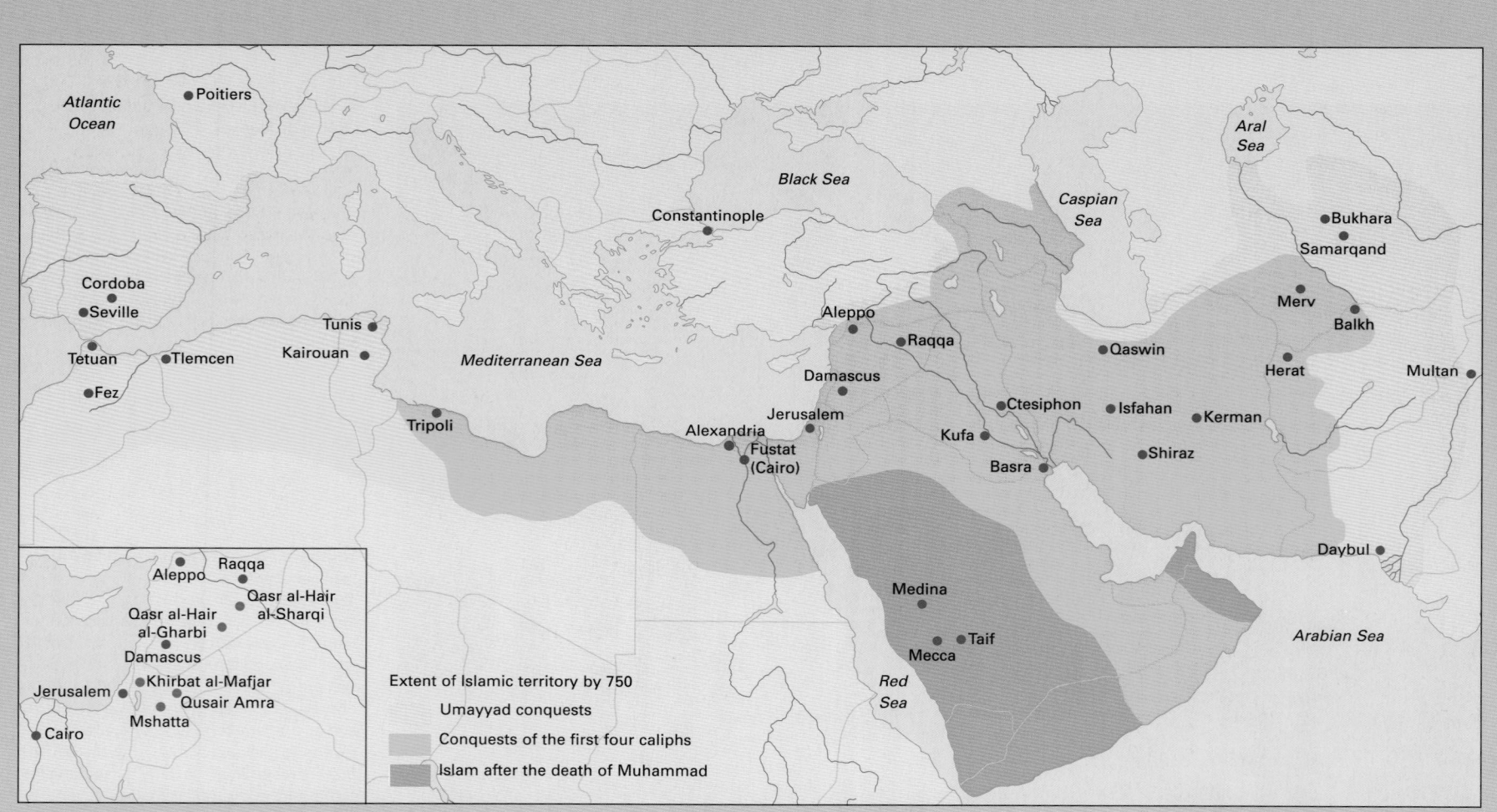

Extent of Islamic territory by 750

Umayyad conquests

Conquests of the first four caliphs

Islam after the death of Muhammad

of Syria, but also by the recurrent quarrels over the succession to the caliphate that were constantly breaking out. The caliphate was conducted like a family firm in which all family members wanted a share. Naturally, there were frequent attempts to settle the question of the succession in advance. Hisham tried to eliminate from the running his brother's son, who had been designated his successor, and replace him with his own. Al-Walid II had been barely three months in power when he had homage paid to his two under age sons al-Hakim and Uthman, in an attempt to secure them the succession. Nonetheless, he himself was subsequently murdered, and in 744 was succeeded by his cousin Yazid al-Walid, who led a rebellion against him.

However, the internal disputes in the vast state structure were certainly the deciding factor in bringing about the end of Umayyad rule. There had been unrest and revolts throughout the period. As early as 680 there was a rebellion by the supporters of Ali under the leadership of his son Husain, but it was suppressed at Kerbela. The death of Husain on the battlefield gave the Shiites a martyr whose violent death is commemorated annually to this day.

Finally, the Abbasid movement brought Umayyad rule to an end. The Abbasids, who traced their claims from an uncle of the Prophet Muhammad, were against the "godless" regime of the Umayyads in questions of faith, and recruited their supporters chiefly from the recent converts of Iran and Central Asia. In 750, after his victory over the last Umayyad caliph Marwan in the Battle of the Great Zab, a tributary of the Tigris, the Abbasid general Abu Muslim dealt ruthlessly with the survivors of the dynasty. Eighty Umayyad princes, along with their wives and children, were murdered at a banquet in Jaffa. One prince escaped into the Maghreb, and later founded a caliphate in Andalusia. In Syria, the Arab Bedouin continued to rise in support of the Umayyads; the last such revolt was in 810. Historians writing in the period of their Abbasid successors undoubtedly did the Umayyads less than justice, and their memory lingered on chiefly in Arabic poetry.

661	After the assassination of the fourth of the Rightly Guided Caliphs, Ali, and his son Hasan's refusal to accept the position of caliph, Muawiya ibn Sufyan, governor of Syria, becomes the next caliph (661–680)
670	Uqba ibn Nafi conquers northwest Africa and founds Kairouan
674–678	First attempt to capture Constantinople
680–683	Reign of Yazid
680	Alid rebellion: the Battle of Kerbela, in which Husain, grandson of the Prophet, is killed
683–684	Caliphate of Muawiya II
683–692	Civil war: Abdallah ibn al-Zubair claims the caliphate
684–685	Caliphate of Marwan
684	Battle of Marg Rahit between the Qais and Kalb tribes
685–705	Reign of Abd al-Malik
685–687	Alid rebellion in Iraq, led by Muhtar
694	Abd al-Malik makes Hajjaj ibn Yusuf governor of Iraq (694–714); he stabilizes Umayyad rule and reforms the administration and the economy
698	Arabic becomes the new administrative language; coins bearing Arabic script are minted; Carthage is taken
701	Unrest in southern Persia and Iraq
705–715	Caliphate of al-Walid
711–712	The Umayyad governor, Musa ibn Nusair, begins the conquest of Spain; Sind and Transoxiania are taken in the east
715–717	Caliphate of Sulaiman
717–720	Caliphate of Umar II
717–718	Constantinople is besieged again
720–724	Reign of Yazid II
724–743	Caliphate of Hisham; frequent revolts; Coptic rebellion against taxation in Egypt (725); campaign for fair pay for non-Arab Muslim converts (mawali) under Harith ibn Suraij in Khorasan (734–746); rebellion under Zaid ibn Ali in Kufa; Kharijite-led Berber uprising in North Africa (740)
743–744	Disputes over the official succession mark the caliphate of al-Walid II; beginning of the fall of the Umayyad dynasty
744	Caliphate of Yazid II, later succeeded by his brother Ibrahim (744); Abu Muslim begins his pro-Abbasid propaganda program in Khorasan
744–750	Reign of the last Umayyad caliph, Marwan II
744–747	Abdallah ibn Muawiya leads a revolt against the Umayyads
749–750	The rule of the Umayyads in the Middle East ends with the Abbasid revolution; the Umayyad family is wiped out. Abd al-Rahman, the only survivor, flees to Spain, where he founds the emirate of Cordoba in 756.

Architecture

Volkmar Enderlein

The holy city of Jerusalem: the Dome of the Rock

The traditional story of the life of Muhammad tells how he turned and prayed toward Mecca instead of Jerusalem during divine service in Medina. With this act he finally established that the prayer direction, the *qibla*, which determines the layout of all Islamic places of prayer, was toward the ancient Arabian shrine of the Kaaba. The change of direction was the result of internal political problems with the Jewish tribes of Medina, but after its conquest in 638 Jerusalem remained a religious center to the Muslims. The Kaaba in Mecca and the site of the Temple in Jerusalem are closely linked by the tale of Muhammad's ascension into heaven. According to a passage in the Koran (sura 17. 1), Muhammad was taken from the "Holy Mosque," the Kaaba, to the "Further Mosque," the Temple in Jerusalem. Muslim commentators see this as a reference to the story of the Prophet's mysterious Night Journey from Mecca to Jerusalem, riding his fantastic mount, the winged creature Buraq. He is said to have set out from the Rock in Jerusalem on his journey to appear before the throne of God in heaven, and consequently, the Rock enjoys special veneration.

The two shrines are linked by a series of connections, and play an important part in the story of Abraham, tribal patriarch of the Arabs and Jews alike. The original Kaaba in Mecca is said to have been built by Abraham himself, and the Dome of the Rock in Jerusalem, the successor to the Temple destroyed by Herod, was erected above Mount Moriah, where Abraham was to have sacrificed his son Isaac (or, in the Islamic version of the story, his son Ismail). Circumambulation of the shrines was a central religious act in both Mecca and Jerusalem.

According to a historical tradition, the site of the Temple was extended for reasons of internal politics. In using the Temple Mount in Jerusalem, Caliph

Dome of the Rock in Jerusalem
691/692
The ground plan of the Dome of the Rock is strictly octagonal in outline, with four gateways in its two main axes opening onto the Temple square. The great dome is supported by four pillars, with four arches over the three columns set between each pair of pillars. The section through the building shows the impressive height of the dome, rising 30 meters above the rock. The many windows allow daylight to enter the interior.

Abd al-Malik wanted to create a sanctuary that would be a counterweight to the shrine in Mecca. It is alleged that his aim was to reduce the influence of the ruling cliques in Mecca and Medina, with whom he was in dispute over the succession to the caliphate. The historian al-Yaqubi states that Abd al-Malik forbade the Syrians to make the obligatory pilgrimage to Mecca that is incumbent on all Muslims; instead, they were to go on pilgrimage to the "mosque of the Holy City," and walk around the sacred Rock instead of the Kaaba.

A visitor approaching Jerusalem will see that the Dome of the Rock, set on the Temple Mount terrace, occupies a dominant position, although from a distance it looks more like a decorative jewel, a reliquary for the shapeless Rock within it. Together with the Kaaba, the Dome of the Rock is the oldest Islamic work of architecture, and even after 13 centuries it retains its original function. Its maintenance, like that of the holy places in Mecca and Medina, was always the task of the central government. After the conquest of Palestine and Egypt by the Ottoman sultan Selim I in 1516/17, that responsibility was in Ottoman hands. The exterior facing of the building, with its tiles in the Ottoman style, dates from this period; Sultan Suleyman the Magnificent had the tiling fitted in 1552, and it has been regularly restored up to the present day.

Situated at the center of the Temple Mount terrace, the Dome itself rises some 100 feet (30 meters) above the Rock. It is set above a cylindrical drum resting on four pillars, with arcades between them, the sections of each arcade rising above three columns. There is an octagonal lower story around the Dome building, which is divided into two aisles by a circle of eight pillars, again linked by arcades. Four gateways, one at each point of the compass, give access to the building. Light falls in through 16 windows in the drum, and 40 windows in the exterior of the octagonal lower story, five to each section of the wall.

The interior decoration, which has been largely maintained in its original state, is impressive. The lower sections of the walls are faced with costly and attractively patterned stone slabs, similar to those in Hagia Sophia in Istanbul. Above that point, the walls are covered with mosaics on a gold background, representing a fantastic garden. The trees, made up of acanthus and other vegetative motifs, bear various kinds of fruits and jewels. The supporting bars also have their original bronze facing, which follows models of classical antiquity in its patterning of palmettes, acanthus leaves, and vine tendrils.

For the first time in an Islamic building, the Dome contains a monumental Arabic inscription in what is known as Kufic script, running in a band of mosaic above the arcades around the inner ambulatory. The various sections of text all come from the Koran. The selection is unusual, and may be linked to the special function of the Dome of the Rock in Jerusalem, located as it is in the immediate vicinity of the major Christian shrines. A brief quotation describes Allah as the creator, the One God, who has no family; in making this point Islam distanced itself from the Christian doctrine of the Trinity. Next come texts describing Muhammad as the successor to the Jewish prophets and to Jesus, and as the last of the line, the "Seal of the Prophets." An unusually extensive part of the text is concerned with Jesus and Mary from the Islamic viewpoint, and requires believers to submit themselves to this concept, and to Islam in general. These texts provide a good indication of the real function of the building: the Dome of the Rock was intended to emphasize the superiority of Islam in the Christian environment of Jerusalem, and to lead unbelievers – even those who were "Peoples of the Book" – to the true faith. The inscription ends with a date: "This dome was built by the servant of God Abdallah, the Imam al-Mamun, Commander of the Faithful, in the year 72. May it be pleasing to Allah!" There are some puzzling elements in this part of the inscription, since the date and the name of the caliph do not match. Here we are dealing with a "*damnatio memoriae*," a deliberate suppression of memory: in 831 the Abbasid caliph al-Mamun had some alterations carried out on the Dome of the

Dome of the Rock in Jerusalem, 691/692
The domed structure of the Dome of the Rock (Qubbat al-Sakhra) rises above the central square of the Temple Mount. According to Islamic tradition, it shelters the rock upon which Abraham, the original ancestor of the Jews and the Arabs, was to have sacrificed his son, and from which the Prophet Muhammad embarked on his Night Journey. It is thus one of Islam's holiest shrines. Caliph Abd al-Malik made the building a place of pilgrimage, which had to be circumambulated, like the Kaaba. Centrally planned Christian buildings were therefore used as models, their proportions strictly adhered to. This jewel was completed in year 72 of the *hegira* (691/692).

Rock, and did not shrink from using this opportunity to have the name of Abd al-Malik removed from the inscription on the building and replaced by his own. However, he did not change the date of the building, year 72 of the *hegira* (691/692), which was bound to give him away.

The furnishing and decoration of the Dome of the Rock correspond in every detail to the forms of Christian art usual in Syria and Palestine. The same is true of its architectonic design, which follows the model of Christian buildings in groundplan and structure. A building very close to the mosque was the Church of the Holy Sepulchre, built by the Emperor Constantine, and in fact, the diameters of the domes of both buildings are almost identical, at 67 feet (20.44 and 20.46 meters) respectively. The Dome of the Rock is also closely related to the Church of the Ascension on the Mount of Olives, which is similarly built on a rectangular ground plan, with the length of the exterior walls identical to those of the inner octagon of the Dome of the Rock. Visitors to the Church of the Ascension were shown the footsteps of Jesus, visitors to the Dome of the Rock saw the footsteps of the Prophet Muhammad.

In its ground plan, the Dome of the Rock is very closely related to yet another building of late antiquity, the Cathedral of Bosra in the south of Syria, built in 512/513. The dome of this cathedral, too, rested on four pillars, with three columns in each of the spaces between them. The two circular aisles surrounding the area beneath the dome are separated by pillars and columns

Tiled panels on the exterior wall of the Dome of the Rock
Originally, the upper part of the Dome of the Rock was covered outside as well as inside with mosaics on a gold background. Under Sultan Suleyman the Magnificent, however, the exterior was faced with colored tilework, which needed constant replacement. The last thorough repairs, before the renovations of 1959–1964, were carried out in 1874.

65

Below: **View of the ambulatory arches in the Dome of the Rock**
The octagonal design was laid out in two aisles surrounding the sacred rock at the center of the building. The supporting bars above the columns dividing these ambulatories still have their original bronze facing, ornamented with motifs from classical antiquity. The arched wall above the bars is covered with gleaming gold mosaic. The decoration of the ceiling of the ambulatories dates from the Mamluk and Ottoman periods.

Above: **Interior view of the dome of the Dome of the Rock**
The wooden dome of the Dome of the Rock has required frequent renovation. Inscriptions give information about its restoration under Sultan Saladin in 1187, the Mamluk Sultan al-Nasir Muhammad in 1318–1320, and the Ottoman Sultan Mehmed II in 1818. The interior of the dome is decorated with concentric circles of painted and gilded arabesques made of applied stucco, which in its present form probably dates back to the restoration of 1818.

Left: **View from the outer ambulatory into the domed area of the Dome of the Rock**
The Dome of the Rock was lavishly decorated, to reflect its importance. The lower areas of the walls are faced with specially selected stone slabs, and mosaics adorn the walls above the pillars and columns. Their patterns are either Byzantine or at least designed on Byzantine models. The reused classical columns are exquisitely beautiful, and the gilding gives the Corinthian capitals an impression of great magnificence.

alternating in the same way as in Jerusalem. This relationship with Bosra may be no coincidence, for according to tradition, it was in that city that Muhammad met the monk Bahira, who foretold his future as Prophet of the Arabs. Both Bosra and Jerusalem were thus closely connected with the life and work of Muhammad.

Courtyard mosques in the early Islamic period

The usual type of mosque in the Umayyad period was represented by the courtyard mosque or the garrison mosque of the newly founded cities of Iraq, also known, after the Mosque of Kufa, as mosques of the Kufa type. According to tradition, they were designed on the model of Muhammad's house in Medina, and consisted of a large square courtyard with a clay brick wall around it. The wives' living quarters were on the eastern side of the courtyard, and their number grew with each additional wife, so that, in the end, there were nine apartments arranged side by side. This was where Muhammad received his guests, who left their camels in the courtyard. It was only gradually that the courtyard became a special place where the faithful assembled for prayer. An open hall was erected on the south side of the courtyard in front of the *qibla* wall to give shade, and consisted of two rows of palm tree trunks with a roof of palm fronds above them. The basic design of the mosque, consisting of a courtyard and a prayer hall, was thus established. The Arab conquerors of new territory laid out military or garrison mosques in the centers of their new towns, which had begun life as army camps. Their walls measured 200 ells along the sides, twice the length of the walls of the Mosque of Medina, so that the area was four times as great. They consisted of a roofed prayer hall on one side of a wide courtyard, surrounded by covered ambulatories on its other three sides. The long exterior wall of the prayer hall was also the *qibla* wall, marking the prayer direction.

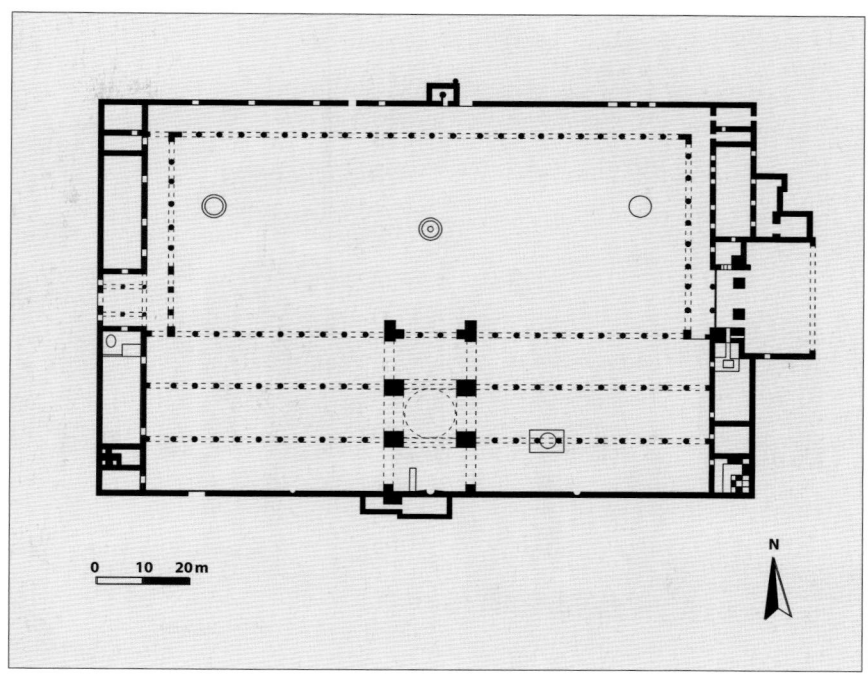

The Great Mosque of Damascus,
706–714/715
After seven decades of common usage by both Muslim an Christian alike, the Basilica of John the Baptist, in the center of Damascus, was razed by the new rulers in 706, and the Great Mosque was then built on the same site. However, the Christian relic of the head of John the Baptist is still venerated today in a tabernacle integrated into the building. A dome over the crossing lends prominence to the area in front of the prayer niche. Two-storied ambulatories encircle three sides of the wide courtyard.

View of the prayer hall with the transept,
Great Mosque of Damascus, 707–714/715
The prayer hall originally opened into the courtyard in a rhythmic arrangement of archways. Instead of the present row of pillars, there was a series of pillars interspersed with columns, like the arrangement still standing on the eastern and western sides of the ambulatory. The wall of the prayer hall facing the courtyard is dominated by the projecting facade of the transept.

Garrison mosques had to be very large in order to accommodate the entire Islamic community of a town. The mosque in Kufa, erected as soon as the place had been conquered in 638, was therefore replaced only three decades later by another building, more lavishly designed, and built by local non-Muslim laborers. While the palace of the governor of Kufa has been excavated, our knowledge of the nearby mosque depends entirely on literary sources, according to which it covered a square surface area with sides measuring 340 feet (104 meters). The roof of the prayer hall was supported by a veritable forest of columns, 17 yokes in width, in five rows running parallel to the *qibla* wall. These columns, 50 feet (15 meters) high, were made of stone and rose to just below the roof, where teak rafters rested on them. The columns were spaced at regular intervals, so that no part of the prayer hall stood out from any other; the mosque of Kufa had no *mihrab*. The ambulatories ran in two aisles around the other three sides of the courtyard.

The 1942 excavations in Wasit brought to light confirmation of the literary evidence for the design of the early Islamic courtyard mosque. Caliph Abd-al-Malik's governor of Iraq, al-Hajjaj ibn Yusuf, began laying out his new administrative center in year 83 of the *hegira* (702). As was so often the case, when new cities were founded in the Islamic world, the reason lay in internal politics. In this case, the viceroy hoped that the new order would overcome existing tensions between the various Arab groups. The Mosque of Wasit was also built on a square site, and had walls measuring 340 feet (104 meters),

View of the Great Mosque's courtyard, looking toward the eastern side of the ambulatory
On the eastern side of the courtyard, the arrangement of pillars and columns retains its original form. The alternating rhythm of a pillar and two columns resembles that of the ambulatory of the Dome of the Rock in Jerusalem. In the upper story of the facade, the wall is pierced by a double number of archways.

Mosaic on courtyard side of ambulatory,
Great Mosque of Damascus, 706–714/715
While large areas of mosaic work have been preserved in the interior of the ambulatories, the mosaics in the courtyard were exposed to worse damage. Only a small part of the mosaic surfaces, which once covered some 43,000 square feet, has been preserved. Plant and tree motifs were depicted on the spandrels above the columns, in a range of color variation that even imitates the effects of light and shade in the trees.

Western side of courtyard with treasury,
Great Mosque of Damascus, 706–714/715
The old treasury (*Bait al-Mal*) at the northwest corner of the courtyard has been preserved. The small domed annex stands on eight classical columns that have no foundations and have simply been sunk into the ground. The facing of mosaic work on a gold background dates from the last decades of the 20th century.

apparently in imitation of the Mosque of Kufa. The prayer hall was again divided up by five rows of columns running parallel to the *qibla* wall, but unlike those in the Mosque of Kufa they formed 19 aisles. The site in the middle of the hall for the *maqsura*, the royal precinct occupied by the viceroy, was marked by heavily ornamented pillars bearing relief decoration of palmettes, leaves, and bunches of grapes.

An innovation in the design of the courtyard mosque came with the introduction of a *mihrab*, an apsidal prayer niche, in the Mosque of Medina. In 707, Caliph al-Walid I had demolished the old Mosque of Medina and replaced it with another more magnificent building on the same layout as the garrison mosques of Iraq. The prayer niche in the *qibla* wall was new. However, it was not placed at the central axis of the hall, nor was it given any particular emphasis by the placing of the columns. To traditionally-minded Muslims, who rejected this innovation, the prayer niche suggested the apses of Christian churches, and it is true that the form of the niche goes back to the Coptic craftsmen whom al-Walid I had brought to Medina from Egypt and Syria. The date of the first prayer niche of which we have a record is 709 – a year of great significance for the dating of mosques in the palaces of the Umayyads.

The great mosques of Iraq were built in newly founded cities. When Arabs moved into old and fully functioning towns, they usually began by using the buildings that were already there for community prayers and sermons. Such was the case in Damascus, the Umayyad capital, where the building of a central mosque did not begin until the reign of Caliph al-Walid I (705–715). The site chosen was the Basilica of John the Baptist, in the precincts of the former classical Temple of Jupiter in the city center. The necessity of tearing the church down first must have met with resistance on the part of the predominantly Christian population, and consequently, the caliph began the demolition work in person. Dressed in yellow robes, he struck the first blow with a golden pick.

Supervision of the building work was left in the hands of his brother, Sulaiman ibn Abd al-Malik, who succeeded him as caliph.

The inscription marking the start of the building has not been preserved, but it is said that work on it began in year 87 of the *hegira* (706), and was concluded in the year of the caliph's death. It was constructed by the labor service system: papyri from Upper Egypt record the fact that craftsmen were summoned to Damascus to build the Great Mosque in 709. Al-Walid I apparently wrote asking the emperor of Byzantium: "Send me 200 Greek laborers, for I mean to build a mosque the like of which my predecessors never constructed, nor will my successors ever raise such a building."

The Great Mosque of Damascus

The design and decoration of the Great Mosque of Damascus, built in just under a decade, surpassed anything previously created, and was regarded by the Arabs as one of the wonders of the world. The temenos wall of the Temple of Jupiter – the original exterior wall of the temple precinct – now formed the outer wall of the mosque, determining its external measurements of 33×52 feet (100 × 157.5 meters). Its area was one and a half times as large as the great garrison mosques of Iraq. The four watchtowers at the corners were used as minarets for use in the call to prayer; the number of four was borrowed from the mosque in Medina, under construction at the same time. A few decades ago the outer walls of the mosque, now in the bazaar quarter, were excavated, and their connections with classical antiquity became even clearer when the entrances were exposed.

A prayer hall consisting of three aisles was built almost all the way along the south side of the ancient temenos wall, and had two rows of monumental columns with Corinthian capitals running parallel to the *qibla* wall. The wall

SYRIA AND PALESTINE: THE UMAYYAD CALIPHATE

Left: View of the prayer hall of the Great Mosque of Damascus, 706–714/715
The three aisles of the prayer hall, with their mighty columns and the arches vaulting above them, are reminiscent of Christian ecclesiastical architecture, except for the difference of orientation between church and mosque. While the long aisles of a basilica point forward to an apse, the rows of columns in a mosque stand in front of the *qibla* wall, and worshippers stand parallel with them. The wide arches above the columns make it possible for them to be set further apart, giving worshippers a better view of the prayer leader. Some of the columns of this mosque, originally dating from classical antiquity, were destroyed in the fire of 1893, and have been replaced by modern columns during the renovation of the building.

Right: *Mihrab* and *minbar* of the Great Mosque of Damascus, 706–714/715
The mighty transept dominating the prayer hall of the Great Mosque leads straight to the prayer niche (*mihrab*), which is further emphasized by the great dome in front of it. When the mosque was first built, under Caliph al-Walid I, the prayer niche must have been in the same place as the new niche built toward the end of the 13th century by order of the Mamluks, and encrusted with precious stones. That prayer niche was destroyed in the fire of 1893, together with the rest of the interior furnishings of the Great Mosque. The present prayer niche and the *minbar* or pulpit rising beside it date from the restoration that began in 1894.

above the columns was originally broken by smooth arched openings, two of them above each of the arches between the columns. In its three-aisle layout, the Great Mosque imitated the church architecture of late antiquity. This was the first prayer hall to have walls containing supporting arches, with the columns spaced wide apart, so that worshippers could orient themselves more easily and have a good view of the prayer niche. A great transept intersects the three aisles, towering high above their roofs. A vaulted dome stands above the crossing and in front of the prayer niche. It was here, in the *maqsura* or ruler's precinct, that the imam prayed; during the period of Umayyad rule the caliph himself often led prayers. The special prominence that a dome imparted to the place occupied by the ruler or imam emphasized its significance: the dome was obviously an attribute of sovereigns, and domes also roofed the throne rooms of Umayyad palaces. Light enters through a series of windows in the drum and in the aisle walls, as it does in the Dome of the Rock in Jerusalem.

There is an ambulatory consisting of a single aisle around the other three sides of the courtyard. It has two stories of archways matching the double story in the prayer hall. The lower story of arches consists of an alternating series of one pillar and two columns, and in the upper story a double arch supported on a delicate column stands above each of the archways below.

The interior decoration of the Great Mosque resembled that of the Dome of the Rock. The lower area of the walls, which followed classical tradition in being faced with specially selected stone slabs, rose to a broad band of mosaic on a gold background running round the walls at a height of over 23 feet (7 meters). The Great Mosque of Damascus is thought to have had the largest surface area of gold mosaic to be found in any building in the world, covering some 43,000 square feet (4000 square meters).

Today, only part of the original mosaic is extant, since much of it was destroyed in the great fire of 1893 and had to be replaced. The polygonal treasury resting on columns in the courtyard of the mosque has similar mosaic decoration.

The full magnificence of the design and decoration of the mosque is evident to visitors only when they have entered the courtyard, since the exterior walls of the building are relatively plain. Like the oriental dwelling house and other types of Islamic buildings, the mosque turns its most striking features toward the inner courtyard, and the facade of the transept assumes special importance.

The architecture of the Great Mosque of Damascus set an example. For the first time, the prayer niche in the *qibla* wall within the prayer hall was given prominence by its setting in the transept and the building of a dome in front of it. The builders of later courtyard mosques took up and modified these ideas.

The desert palaces of the Umayyads

The palaces built by the Umayyads make demands on the viewer other than those made by the Dome of the Rock in Jerusalem and the Great Mosque of Damascus, where, in spite of later alterations, it is reasonably easy to imagine their original appearance. Thanks to the Islamic institution of the religious foundation, the *waqf*, they have been constantly maintained.

The urban palaces of the Umayyad period, however, can be reconstructed only with the aid of archeological excavations, and much the same may be said of the buildings known as desert palaces, which have survived only as ruins. An exception is the small "bathhouse palace" of Qusair Amra, a building preserved almost complete, although its colored decoration has suffered in the course of 13 centuries. Later on, the desert palaces were visited only by Arab Bedouin with their herds, and no one lived there but owls. If they did not collapse in the earthquake of 746, they became dilapidated over the next few centuries. However, they are often in an incomplete state because the original buildings were never actually finished.

When the caliphs were in Damascus they inhabited the city palace south of the Great Mosque. In Islamic cities, the main mosque and the palace were always very close to each other, so that the caliph or governor had as short a way as possible to go in order to reach the mosque. We are told that the city palace of Damascus had a striking green-colored dome, and that there was a pool of water inside it.

Excavations have been carried out on the site of the city palace in Kufa. The governor's residence was a building resembling a castle, built on a square ground plan with walls about 230 feet (70 meters) long. The measurements of the building, constructed at the end of the 7th century, corresponded to those of the Umayyad desert palaces. The outer wall was reinforced with towers, and special prominence was given to the great gate. Opposite the gateway stood a three-aisled hall, leading to an area with a dome over it. This arrangement of rooms is also found in the mightiest of the desert palaces, Mshatta. In Kufa, both the hall and the domed area would certainly have been used for councils and audiences, while the purposes and function of the rooms and groups of rooms on the other side of the courtyard are not perfectly clear.

The desert palaces convey a more graphic idea of palace buildings in the Umayyad period than can be gained from the archeological excavations at Kufa. The term "desert palace" is in fact a misnomer, since these buildings are not actually located in the desert but in the steppes, or even in fertile country. They form a chain running from the palaces of Qasr al-Mshatta, Qasr al-Tuba, and Qusair Amra in Jordan, to the complex of Khirbat al-Mafjar at Jericho in Palestine, Khirbat Minya on the Sea of Genesareth in Israel, and so on to the palaces of Usais, Qasr al-Hair al-Gharbi, and Qasr al-Hair al-Sharqi in Syria. Apart from the small "bathhouse palace" of Qusair Amra, mentioned above, all these palaces were built in the form of citadels with defensive towers, to which other buildings might be added, as they were at Khirbat al-Mafjar. The normal length of the walls of

Qasr al-Tuba, Jordan, mid-8th century
This small palace, a double complex, was probably intended for the two sons of Caliph al-Walid II, to whom he had homage paid soon after he succeeded to the throne in 743. The closest parallels to such technical details as its brickwork and vaulting are to be found in the palace of Mshatta. The bricklaying technique, unusual in Syria, can be explained as the result of labor service done on the caliph's buildings by Iraqi brickmakers and bricklayers.

View through a row of doorways
Qasr al-Tuba, Jordan, mid-8th century
The lower parts of the walls at Qasr al-Tuba are built of stone, with brickwork rising above them. The two layers of vaulting are still clearly visible today. The indentations in the walls originally accommodated the wooden lintels, which were presumably used for firewood by the Bedouin soon after work on the building was abandoned.

such palaces was about 230 feet (70 meters) long. At the double complex of Qasr al-Tuba, two such palaces were constructed next to each other. At Mshatta, as well as Qasr al-Hair al-Sharqi, the walls are double the usual length, and consequently these buildings have four times the usual surface area. In each of these palaces the rooms were arranged around a wide courtyard, surrounded in the smaller palaces by roofed colonnades.

The desert palaces as pseudo-citadels: basic architectural concept

A glance at the ground plans of Umayyad palaces show that they were designed on a basis of two intersecting diagonals on which the dimensions were based. If the diagonals did not intersect exactly at a right angle, adjustments were made to the ground plan. Mshatta provides a particularly good example of the development of such a ground plan. As early as 1932, it was suggested that the complex had been built to a plan based on diagonals. These diagonals

Above: **Qasr Kharana**, Jordan, early 8th century
Like the Umayyad palaces, Qasr Kharana was designed as a pseudo-citadel. Semicircular and three-quarter circular towers project from the walls, and the portal is set in a "broken" tower. The site, however, is only a quarter the size of the smaller Umayyad palaces. The roughcast rubble masonry technique also indicates a need to use building materials sparingly. The two-story building must date from the early years of the 8th century, since a graffito inscription of 710 gives the name of a visitor. It has been suggested that the building, which had stabling on the lower floor and living accommodation on the upper floor, was a rest house for pilgrims.

Right: **Internal view of Qasr Kharana**, Jordan, early 8th century
The interior of Qasr Kharana was also executed with minimum expenditure. The walls are smoothly plastered, and architectural elements like the half-columns supporting the wall arches shown here bore no ornamentation. The only decorations consist of rows of rosettes with vegetal motifs on the ceilings of some of the rooms.

run to the corners of the great courtyard, dividing up the central area of the palace precinct so that the entrance area and mosque site are the same size as the residential area with the throne room.

New investigations at Mshatta have led to further discoveries about the design and planning of such a palace. It proved possible to relate the measurements of the portal facade to the main ground plan. The standard measurement of about 1.9 feet (57.66 centimeters) found in the facade and the gateway opening, termed an "ell" in the following account, were checked at various intervals inside Mshatta. The diagonals of the courtyard came to exactly 140 ells, giving a measurement of 99 ells for the side of the courtyard. A glance at the way the complex of rooms beyond the courtyard is divided into three makes such a measurement seem particularly appropriate. The three aisles of the hall leading to the throne room were constructed on a site with a ratio of 30 to 40 ells. The diagonals of the throne room itself measured exactly 24 ells. All these distances match the ell measurement used at Mshatta perfectly, to within a millimeter.

The exterior appearance of the palaces, which give the impression of being fortresses, arises from the high walls reinforced with towers. However, they were not really fortresses, since they did not contain the devices necessary for defense during a siege of any length. The towers were either filled up with rubble, or (as at Mshatta) served as latrines.

The wide portals were given particular prominence. They were either framed by two towers, or might be placed in a "broken" semicircular gate tower,

Palace precinct of Mshatta, Jordan, 743–744
Mshatta is the most lavishly constructed of the Umayyad palaces. It had a wide courtyard at the center, with groups of rooms built (or planned) around it. The three arches of the residence building also opened out on the courtyard. There were living rooms on both sides of the hall, with brickwork walls into which the openings of the arches were fitted.

as at Khirbat Minya and Usais. An idea of the great height of such portal towers is conveyed by the portal of Qasr al-Hair al-Sharqi, which has been preserved with its semicircular towers. They remained undecorated; the only ornamentation to this portal facade was part of a reused Roman portal. At Qasr al-Hair al-Gharbi, the upper two-thirds of the gateway towers bore stucco decoration. The portal towers of Mshatta were built on a square ground plan, and the outer wall of the lower parts of the towers was filled in with relief work. The incomplete state of Mshatta casts doubt on any attempt to reconstruct the probable height of the entrance facade. Portal buildings always contained benches where visitors could sit while they waited to be admitted for an audience. Traditionally, justice was often administered in such gateway buildings, as the Bible records (see, for instance, Amos 5: 15, Zachariah 8: 16). The portal buildings of the Umayyad palaces may have had a similar function.

Portal facade of Mshatta,
Berlin, Islamic Art Museum
The main entrance to the palace was on the south side of the exterior wall. It was given prominence by polygonal towers and lavishly worked relief decoration extending to the next towers on both sides. A zigzag band over the surface of the wall divided it up into triangles containing large rosettes. The remaining background of the wall was densely covered with delicate reliefs. Groups of animals and fabulous beings are placed among twining vine tendrils. On the right half of the facade, facing the interior of the mosque, the ornamentation was confined to vine tendrils and showed no living creatures. On the left side of the facade, however, animals or fabulous creatures are repeatedly depicted on both sides of a vessel.

The various complexes of rooms

The center of these palaces, as mentioned above, was the wide inner courtyard. In this they had adopted a feature already typical of the oriental courtyard dwelling house and the courtyard mosque. All such buildings turned inward, not outward. As in the Great Mosque of Damascus, where the side of the courtyard was marked off by the facade of the transept in the prayer hall, the courtyard facade at Mshatta was dominated by the three arches opening into the hall which lead to the throne room. The three aisles of this hall led to a room which, in its own turn, was extended by three apses. The formal design of the hall, ending in a triconch, was adopted from early Christian church architecture, and the only new feature was its north-south direction. When the caliph sat on his throne in this room with its three apses, he could look down the hall to the inner courtyard and was facing the *qibla*, the prayer direction, on which the layout of the entire palace complex was designed. The site of the mosque was planned to be on the right of the main portal. The *mihrab*, a semicircular niche, was set into the surrounding wall. The inclusion of a mosque within the square ground plan of the palace was a special feature that Mshatta shared with the palaces of Khirbat Minya and Qasr al-Hair al-Sharqi. As at Khirbat Minya, the prayer hall might have a second entrance, so that believers from outside could enter to take part in prayers without having to use the ceremonial palace gateway. If the site of the mosque was not within the square of the walls, as for instance at Usais and Khirbat al-Mafjar, a small mosque building was constructed next to them. This smaller mosque shared a wall with the palace, so that it too faced in the *qibla* direction. The palace mosques were plain buildings on a rectangular ground plan with two or three rows of pillars in front of the *qibla* wall. They all had a *mihrab* in the shape of a niche. The *mihrab* in this form was first introduced in the Great Mosque of Medina in the year 709, so the palaces mentioned above must have been built after that date.

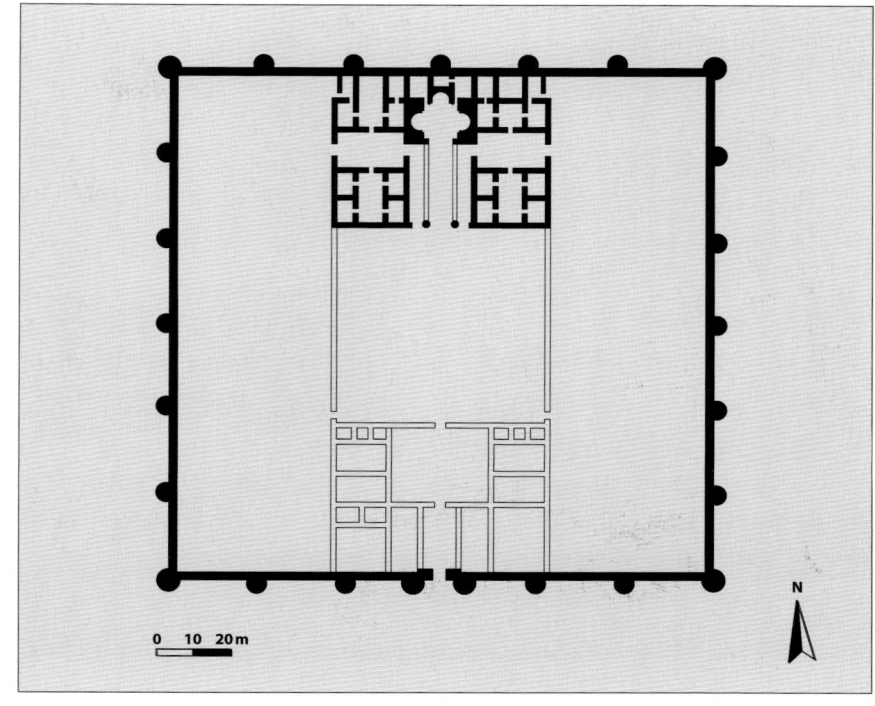

Mshatta: ground plan and throne room entrance, Jordan, 743–744
Mshatta is built on a square ground plan with sides measuring 144 meters, and is one of the larger Umayyad palaces. Only part of the central precinct behind the facade was actually built. Visitors entered the courtyard through the portal, with the site of the mosque on the right and a planned bathhouse on the left. Here they would have faced the three aisles of the hall (which collapsed in the earthquake of 746) leading to the throne room. The throne room at the end of the hall, of which visitors had a view on the diagonal, ended in three apses.

Qasr al-Hair al-Sharqi, Syria, 2nd quarter of the 8th century
This building too is a pseudo-citadel with a mighty enclosing wall reinforced by towers on the exterior. The portal lies between two semicircular towers. The articulation of the wall is restricted to plain contours. In the Iraqi tradition, the brickwork is roughcast. According to an inscription, the building was constructed under Caliph Hisham in 728/729.

Below: **Mosque of Qasr al-Hair al-Sharqi**, Syria, 2nd quarter of the 8th century
The remains of a mosque were found in the southeast corner of the great enclosure, which is of dimensions suggesting the design of a whole town. In its architectural detail, the mosque is a small-scale replica of the Great Mosque of Damascus.

Above: **Interior view of the enclosure wall of Qasr al-Hair al-Sharqi**, Syria, 2nd quarter of the 8th century
To the west of the small complex of Qasr al-Hair al-Sharqi lies the great rampart, enclosing an area with sides of double the usual length and four times the usual area. It surrounded what was almost a town, with mosque, houses, and workshops within its walls.

Architectural standardization of forms in the Umayyad period extended to the prayer niches themselves. The *mihrabs* in Mshatta and Khirbat Minya were both 5.31 feet (1.62 meters) wide, although there are obvious differences in other respects between the various palace complexes and their decoration.

As a rule, Umayyad palaces contained a bathhouse. Situated as they were on the edge of the steppes, the question of the water supply was especially crucial. The complications that might arise were illustrated by the building of the "city of al-Walid." Water was brought either by an aqueduct or through underground pipes. This probably explains the choice of a former Byzantine building complex as the site of a palace, for instance, at Qasr al-Hair al-Gharbi, where facilities for a water supply already existed and could be brought back into working order or adapted. The requisite water might also be brought up from a well by a mechanical device, as at Qusair Amra. A bathhouse needed heating, provided by hypocausts or hot air shafts. The sequence of rooms for steam, hot and cold baths followed the example of the baths of classical antiquity. Qusair Amra is a "bathhouse palace," consisting of separate baths and an audience hall. Even the view from outside shows that in this building rooms of different shapes and sizes were placed side by side purely in accordance with their function. If large gatherings of people ever visited the place, they would have had to be accommodated in the tents usual among the Bedouin. All the rooms were ornamented with wall paintings, and the floors with mosaics.

At Khirbat al-Mafjar, a single large building, served as both bathhouse and reception hall. An indication of the number of people for whom it was planned is given by the 23 latrines annex. The audience hall, where the master of the palace received his guests, was a building constructed in the 16 multiple-ribbed pillars, with costly mosaic floors in patterns of great diversity. The excavator of Khirbat al-Mafjar thought this room was intended for musical performances, and it may have been commissioned by al-Walid ibn Yazid, whose love of music and poetry was mentioned above, in a time when he was still crown prince. The size and the decorative themes of these audience halls, which were placed in front of bathhouses and descended from the changing rooms and rest rooms of the baths of classical antiquity, was mainly ceremonial in function. There was also to have been a bathhouse at Mshatta, as we may deduce from the sequence of small rooms in the entrance area, but only its foundations were ever built.

The actual living quarters within the palaces are often arranged in groups of five rooms, and the term *bait* (house) has come into general use for such a group. Mshatta has four groups of rooms, two on each side of the throne room. They are tall halls with barrel vaulting, and in this case, are relatively well preserved. They received cool air-conditioning through narrow air channels. The number of four groups of five rooms at Mshatta probably goes back to a ruling in the Koran (sura 4. 3) allowing a Muslim to be married to four wives at once, but at the same time obliging him to treat them all equally.

The dating and function of the desert palaces

The dating of the palace buildings in Jordan, Palestine, and Syria was a source of heated controversy for decades, since it involved such unfinished buildings as Mshatta, where there are no inscriptions recording its construction. Today, however, a number of the palaces have been thoroughly studied, and excavations have disclosed a great many facts: building inscriptions have been found giving the names of the men who commissioned them. Excavations at Khirbat Minya in the 1930s brought to light an inscription naming the man for whom it was built as al-Walid, and the master builder as Abdallah. Near the palace of Usais, inscriptions were discovered bearing the names of sons of al-Walid I (705–715), which indicates that Usais, too, was built during his reign. The same conclusion was drawn from a depiction of the caliph enthroned at Qusair Amra. The kings

Roman watchtower, Qasr al-Hair al-Gharbi, Syria, 3rd century
Parts of buildings dating from classical antiquity were frequently incorporated into new buildings during the Islamic period, including watchtowers from Roman and Byzantine fortifications on the eastern borders of the empire. Building materials from antiquity were reused in the frame of the portal and the northeast tower of the palace of Qasr al-Hair al-Gharbi.

of the world are paying him homage, and are identified in inscriptions in Arabic and Greek; they include Roderick, king of the Visigoths and a contemporary of Caliph al-Walid I. The building inscription of 728/729 at Qasr al-Hair al-Sharqi, naming Caliph Hisham as the man for whom it was built, has already been mentioned, and graffiti from Hisham's time have also been found at Khirbat al-Mafjar. Even at Mshatta, the dating of which entailed the most problems, cleaning work in 1964 uncovered a tile with a five-line Arabic inscription in Kufic script, the draft of a letter written by one Sulaiman ibn Kaisan. This man held a series of important offices under Caliphs Hisham, al-Walid I, and Yazid III (reigned 744), and he is known to have been killed in

View of audience hall of Khirbat al-Mafjar, Palestine, 2nd quarter of the 8th century
The reception hall of the bathhouse tract contained a whole forest of ribbed pillars. They remained preserved up to a considerable height, and it was therefore possible to excavate them. Lavish mosaic floors were found among them, their composition reflecting the form of the vaulting above.

Brickwork measurements and bricklaying technique in the residential area at Mshatta are of Iraqi origin, while the ashlar masonry in the entrance area is reminiscent of Syrian and Egyptian stonemasonry. The Umayyads were able to bring building workers from the distant provinces of their empire together in one and the same place, to work in a variety of techniques.

The function of these palaces, distant as they are from the great cities of Syria and Palestine, is still a matter of dispute. Recently it has been suggested that they should be regarded as manor houses at the center of extensively landed estates, built for members of the Arab aristocracy so that they could administer their lands from such centers. Today, agriculture can no longer produce a good yield near most of them because of the water shortage, but conditions for productive farming may have changed in the course of over a millennium. Their existence has also been explained in relation to the tendency of the Umayyad princes to avoid cities, instead preferring to lead the life of their southern Arabian forefathers in the steppes of Syria, hunting, enjoying social gatherings, wine and food. Another possible explanation depends on power politics: from these palaces on the outskirts of fertile land, the Umayyads could have maintained their special relationship with the Arab Bedouin, whose grazing grounds were in the immediate vicinity.

Enough of the art ornamenting the mosques and palaces of the Umayyads has been preserved to enable us to form an impression of the sculpture and painting of the period. The sculptural art and large-scale figural paintings found in the palaces have exerted great influence on our ideas of early Islamic art, and have corrected a number of prejudices that were once generally held.

750, with his brothers, when the Abbasid army took Damascus. The tile must therefore have been inscribed toward the end of the Umayyad period, probably under al-Walid II, who is also, for other reasons, regarded as the man for whom Mshatta was built. Qasr al-Tuba was probably built in his time as well. Technically, for instance in its bricklaying and vaulting methods, this building greatly resembles Mshatta. The reason for its double layout may be that al-Walid II wished to build a house for his two sons al-Hakim and Uthman, to whom he had homage paid after his accession.

The very different building techniques employed also indicate that the palaces were erected in the Umayyad period, since they can be explained by the labor service system of conscripting craftsmen from different traditions.

Opposite: **View of the gateway hall in the palace complex of Khirbat al-Mafjar**, Palestine, 2nd quarter of the 8th century
The gateway area contained a number of benches on which visitors could sit to rest. Through the gateway, they would have looked straight into the courtyard, which had pillars set around it. The rose window, opposite the entrance, consists of a complete guilloche pattern.

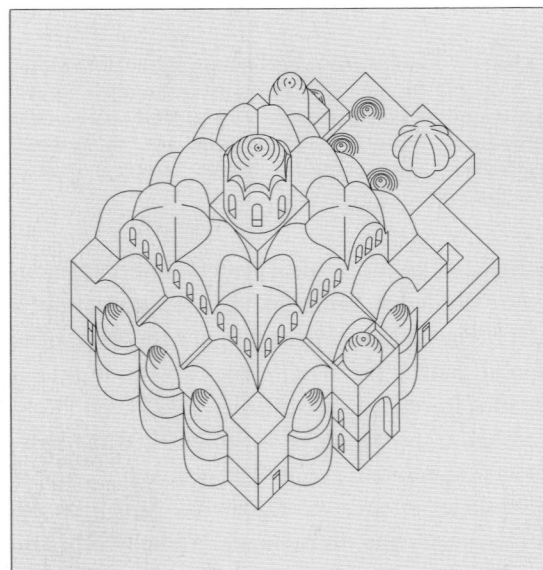

The audience hall of Khirbat al-Mafjar, Palestine, 2nd quarter of the 8th century
The audience hall, next to the bathhouse, was a highly organized building. It had its own entry building. The reception room, which also served as a concert hall, was surrounded by rooms with cupolas and vaulted rooms. A room at the side functioned as a place for the caliph to receive guests.

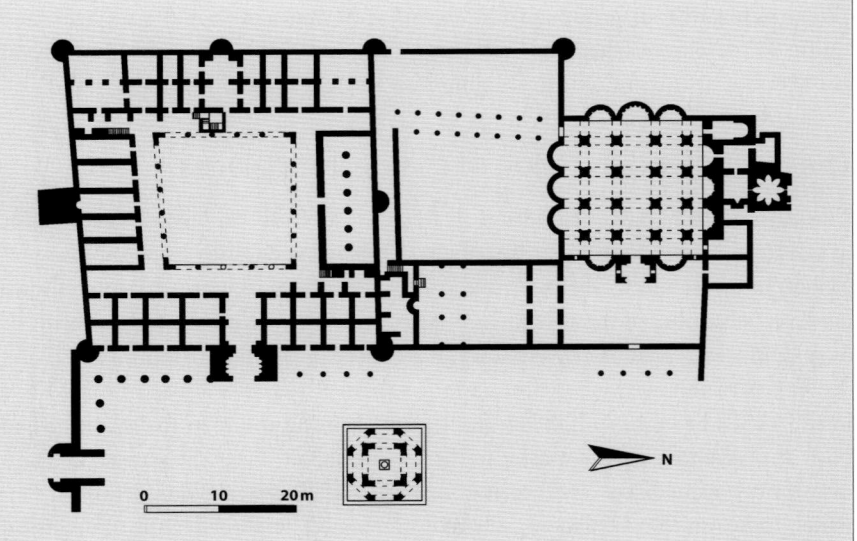

0   10   20m   N

Building Decoration
Volkmar Enderlein

Wall mosaics

Large mosaics of breathtaking magnificence cover many of the wall surfaces in the Dome of the Rock in Jerusalem and the Great Mosque of Damascus, yet the various theories put forward for their interpretation have not solved the problem of their significance beyond all doubt. The walls of the Dome of the Rock depict a fantastic garden against a background of gleaming gold, although real trees such as palms and olives appear relatively seldom. The rectangular or triangular spaces are usually filled in with spiralling bands of the luxuriant foliage known as acanthus. The foliage emerges from a rosette of leaves or from precious vessels. It is not surprising to see dates growing on the palms, but when fruits such as pomegranates and bunches of grapes are placed among the leafy tendrils, the fantastic character of the garden is obvious.

Special kinds of fruits are the royal crowns integrated into the tendrils of the trees, together with other precious items of metalwork. In their variety of forms they are reminiscent of Byzantine and Iranian Sassanian models. The crowns of several of the Sassanian Great Kings were indicated by stylized

double wings or winged palmettes, and they appear in that form again in the mosaics of the Dome of the Rock. The defeated rulers, represented by their crowns, thus paid homage to the sacred Rock. In using this decorative feature, the Dome of the Rock referred back to a custom also mentioned in connection with the Kaaba in Mecca: during their campaigns of conquest, Arabs had sent valuable gifts in the form of thrones and crowns from all over the world they had conquered back to Mecca, where they were displayed in the Kaaba. The homage implied in these depictions was perhaps intended to underline the competing claims of the Dome of the Rock as against the Kaaba.

The trees adorned with precious stones in the Dome of the Rock have also been interpreted as signifying Paradise for, in his 30-volume commentary on the Koran, al-Tabari, a polymath of the Abbasid period, described the lotus tree growing in Paradise as being richly decked with jewels.

The style of the mosaics in the Dome of the Rock is reminiscent in many details of the mosaic ornamentation of Christian churches. Similar trees, made of fleshy acanthus tendrils, appear on the mosaic facings in the Church of the Nativity, in Bethlehem. However, the stylized features of many of the trees, showing palmette flowers and winged palmettes, also indicate the influence of the Sassanian art of Iran, evident again in the Umayyad palaces.

The mosaic decoration of the Great Mosque of Damascus is unique. A wide band of mosaic depicting a landscape runs over the walls of the ambulatories, and originally covered the wall of the prayer hall as well. Its lower area represents a stream of water, with mighty fruit-bearing trees up to 23 feet (7 meters) high against a golden background growing on its banks. Their trunks, branches, and leaves are depicted with such richness and variety of design that it looks as if the light were playing on them. Groups of buildings stand among the trees. These buildings are extraordinarily diverse in form: cubic houses tower above each other like mountain ranges; colonnaded halls open out in a semicircle, surrounding open expanses; pavilions are disposed in picturesque groups. The general impression is that contrasting architectural elements have been combined into fantastic compositions. On close inspection, the viewer will see that these mosaics show a world where no birds perch in the branches of the trees, no fish play in the waters of the river. When we remember that they were intended to adorn a mosque, it is clear that we have here an early example of obedience to the Islamic prohibition of images.

That prohibition cannot be traced back directly to any of Muhammad's statements in the Koran; indeed, the Hadiths (oral traditions relating to the Prophet) referring to it were not collected until long after his death, in the 8th and 9th centuries. His attitude was expressed obviously enough, however, in his cleansing the Kaaba of idols after the conquest of Mecca in the year 630. The ban on images becomes even clearer in the coinage reform of Caliph Abd al-Malik in 696/697, when pictorial depictions on coins were replaced by religious texts. In the art of the Umayyads, the prohibition is confined to the interior decoration of mosques.

Various attempts have also been made to interpret the mosaics in Damascus. The theory that the water flowing through the city is the river Barada, and the buildings represent Damascus itself, sounds very plausible. Another hypothesis assumes that, in imitation of depictions of cities in late antiquity, the various groups of buildings represent the cities of the Islamic world, gathered together

Detail of the courtyard side of the western ambulatory, Great Mosque of Damascus, 706–714/715
While the spandrels of the walls above the columns of the ambulatory are adorned with tree motifs, the rather larger surfaces above the pillars bear architectural themes. This example could be a catalog of patterns comprising Corinthian columns, archways, a parapet, and various forms of roofs. The mosaics on the inside of the archways all follow the same pattern.

Left: **Courtyard facade of the transept**, Great Mosque of Damascus, 706–714/715

Left: **Courtyard facade of the transept**,
Great Mosque of Damascus, 706–714/715
The three great archways of the transept
open into the courtyard. Only small parts of
the original mosaic facing survived the great
fire of 1893. Large areas have now been
restored, and convey some idea of the former
magnificent mosaic decoration of the Great
Mosque. Caliph al-Walid I asked the emperor
of Byzantium to send him skilled craftsmen
to help with its building.

Above: **Detail of the mosaic in the western ambulatory**, Great Mosque of Damascus, 706–714/715
The architectural features standing between
the mighty trees on the Barada mosaic, like
those found in early Christian churches in
Syria and Jordan, seem to be abbreviated references to characteristic buildings in certain
actual places, and it has been thought that
the mosaics are intended to show the world
and its major cities.

here as a great urban panorama in the central mosque of the Umayyad empire. This theory is supported by the representations of series of cities on the mosaic floors of late antiquity Syrian churches. They, too, differ from each other in the shapes of the buildings shown, but as a rule, they are clearly identified by Greek inscriptions. Perhaps the first people to see the mosaics in the Great Mosque of Damascus were so familiar with the characteristic groups of buildings denoting certain cities that they could name them unprompted.

Figural ornamentation in Umayyad buildings

While the prohibition on images was obviously observed in the decoration of the Dome of the Rock in Jerusalem and the Great Mosque of Damascus, no such restrictions were placed on the decoration of the Umayyad palaces. At the beginning of the 20th century, the figural representations on the facade of Mshatta and the sculptural finds in the residential area of the palace were so far from reflecting prevalent ideas of Islamic art that doubt was cast on the dating of the building: did it belong to the Umayyad period at all? However, excavations in Qasr al-Hair al-Gharbi in Syria and Khirbat al-Mafjar in Palestine brought to light such a number of figural depictions clearly originating from the Islamic period that ideas of early Islamic art had to be fundamentally revised. These three palaces all had sculptural ornamentation. While Caliph Hisham (724–743) is thought to have commissioned the building of Qasr al-Hair al-Gharbi, Khirbat al-Mafjar and Mshatta are connected with al-Walid II ibn Yazid (743–744). These two caliphs,

Lion from Mshatta, Jordan, 743/744, Berlin, Islamic Art Museum
Fragments of sculpture were found in the residential precinct of Mshatta, including this statue of a recumbent lion. Various details of the animal's mighty body, for instance the spiral curls of the mane, were traced on the statue after it was made. Intolerant visitors to the ruins have mutilated the lion's head. Originally, it must have been meant to stand near the throne as a symbol of royal power. Caliph al-Walid II, who had Mshatta built, was known as an enthusiastic lion hunter.

also uncle and nephew, were obviously very different characters, for Hisham was considered pious, while al-Walid had the reputation of a godless man. None the less, their attitudes regarding art and the prohibition on images were very similar. The robe given by Caliph al-Walid II to a singer, mentioned previously, was adorned with figures. Textiles with figural decoration were made in the Umayyad empire, both in the former Byzantine provinces and in Iraq. Given the caliph's predilection for the products of Sassanian Iran, it seems quite likely that his robe was made of valuable Persian silk with a figured pattern. Silks of this kind have been preserved as wrappings for Christian relics, so that we can form some idea of them, and the story of the caliph's robe shows that in all areas of life the Umayyads were surrounded by depictions of living creatures.

Right: **Door lunette from Qasr al-Hair al-Gharbi**, Syria, 2nd quarter of the 8th century, Damascus, National Museum
The palace of Qasr al-Hair al-Gharbi was richly decorated with stucco carvings, both on the interior and on the portal facade of the exterior. The motif shown here, a fruit tree entwined by a vine, is so fashioned, that the plants depicted stand out in contrast to the deep dark background. The Umayyads imported the stucco technique from Sassanian Iraq, where it had been commonly used for hundreds of years, to adorn palace buildings in Syria as well.

Left: **Dome ornamentation from Khirbat al-Mafjar**, Palestine, 2nd quarter of the 8th century, Jerusalem, Rockefeller Archaeological Museum
This large rosette adorned the central domed area of the reception hall in the bathhouse precinct. The heads of youths and maidens, framed by leafy tendrils, grow from acanthus leaves in its six-lobed center. The comparatively unsophisticated style of the faces corresponds to figural representation elsewhere in the decoration of the palace. This rosette has also been interpreted as an illustration of Paradise.

Sculptural decoration

The sculptural decoration of Qasr al-Hair al-Gharbi was made of carved and painted stucco. Stucco technique was foreign to the Hellenistic art of Syria, but common in Sassanian Iran. Stylistic and iconographic features indicate that not only the technique, but many Sassanian decorative motifs were also adopted for the decoration of the palace. Above the entrance portal itself, the caliph is depicted in a manner very like a representation on a silver dish of the Sassanian Great King: he wears on his head a Sassanian type of crown – a winged diadem – and is clad in wide trousers and an upper garment reaching to the knees. He is shown from the front, with his knees bent slightly outward – an attitude typical of the seated ruler shown enthroned. Inside the palace, the caliph is shown again, this time seated on a chair with posts, and with his feet resting on a footstool. Not only does the throne derive from Byzantine models, the extant parts of the caliph's flowing robe are reminiscent of the clothing of Roman emperors. In these two depictions of the ruler enthroned, the caliph was stating his claims as heir to both the Roman and the Sassanian Empires. He was, quite simply, lord of the whole world.

In the relief of a mounted archer, the similarity between the decorative style at Qasr al-Hair al-Gharbi and earlier Sassanian models is astonishing. The modeling of the horse's body and the draftsman-like reproduction of details of its bridle, mane, and tail are so like the Iranian depiction of a horseman, now in the Berlin Museum, that the two pieces could almost be confused with each other. On the other hand, figures and figural groups which continue the Hellenistic tradition, in their attitudes and the representation of their garments, were found in the same palace.

A visitor to Khirbat, al-Mafjar, also saw an image of the caliph over the entrance to the large assembly hall in the bathhouse area. He stood erect on a base consisting of two lions. Although these lions look rather more like small dogs, they are to be understood to be symbols of sovereign power. The caliph wears a long, belted robe and has his left hand on the hilt of his sword; his eyes, wide open, are looking straight ahead of him. This pictorial type – a standing caliph, bare-headed and with a hand on his sword – had already been used decades earlier on the coinage by Caliph Abd al-Malik (685–705), before he introduced nonpictorial coins bearing only lines of written text as the standard, binding on the whole Islamic world.

The dome above the entrance was supported by atlantes: powerful male figures clad only in a loincloth, their raised hands pressing against the entablature above. Statues of opulent female forms, wide-eyed and looking straight at the viewer, were found in the palace area and the bathhouse. The modeling of these figures is relatively crude, but the effect is enhanced by heavy painting of their luxuriant hairstyles and their faces. The reliefs of winged horses, rams, and partridges in the throne room are also from Sassanian imagery. Winged horses bearing up the Great King's throne, and rams symbolizing the glories of royal power, were deliberately used by al-Walid II to underline his claim to the throne.

During the excavation of Mshatta by a group of German archeologists in 1903, a whole series of sculptural fragments was found, including parts of life-sized figures of men and women. In 1962, when further excavation was undertaken on behalf of the Jordanian government, another fragment came to light: part of the statue of a woman carrying a basket of flowers. A second female figure, now in the Berlin Museum, is holding a baby in her arms. Her name is given in an inscription on her thigh. Both female figures are shown naked, letting their garments slip down over their hips. Girls dancing with veils on items of Sassanian metalwork are of the same figural type. There were also statues of male figures, but these were damaged beyond recognition. Better preserved is the sculpture of a recumbent lion, also intended for the throne room area.

Statue of a woman with a basket of fruit, Khirbat al-Mafjar, Palestine, 2nd quarter of the 8th century, Jerusalem, Rockefeller Archaeological Museum
Statues of women were found both in the palace and in the reception hall of the bath-house precinct. They are opulent figures clad only in a skirt, with details traced on their naked upper bodies dividing up the basic shape. Their lavish hairstyles and features such as their eyes are picked out in color.

Section of a floor fresco, Qasr al-Hair al-Gharbi, Syria, 2nd quarter of the 8th century, Damascus, National Museum
Two huge floor frescoes found in the palace of Qasr al-Hair al-Gharbi are unique: their delicacy makes their location on the floor seem wholly inappropriate. The center of this circle contains the head and shoulders of a youthful figure holding a cloth full of fruits. The picture is thought to show a fertility deity of antiquity, and draws on Hellenistic tradition.

There is no doubt that this lion, too, was intended to be seen as a symbol of royal power, but it should also be noted that the caliph who commissioned the building was an enthusiastic lion hunter; there were still lions in the steppes of Syria in the early 8th century, although today they have been eradicated by the Bedouin in order to protect their herds. A single extant fragment of a lion's paw shows that there must have been another lion at Mshatta, shown with its forepaws braced. The style of the sculptures, like those at Khirbat al-Mafjar, is unsophisticated, and details like the lion's mane were traced on them later.

Relief decoration

The real importance of Mshatta for Umayyad art lies in the relief decoration preserved on the facade of the portal. The surfaces above the gateway towers and the sections of wall beside them, as far as the next two towers, are densely covered with relief work. It has often been pointed out that this wall ornamentation resembles a textile design. A zigzag band extends over a length of about 187 feet (57 meters) between base and cornice, and monumental rosettes project from the wall surfaces in the triangles it creates. The wall between the zigzag line and the rosettes is the surface for the carving of the relief work, which depicts a great vineyard. There is a wealth of artistry in the twining tendrils alone as they rise from acanthus leaves, circles of pearls, or vessels of various shapes, or from the rosettes of leaves also found in the Dome of the Rock. On the left half of the

Ceiling painting in the reception hall of Qusair Amra, Jordan, early 8th century
A number of craft activities are shown in a series of rectangular fields in the vaulting of the reception hall. The huge wall surfaces below contain hunting and bathing scenes populated by many figures, and obviously relating to the function of the building.

facade, the vineyard is populated by animals, fabulous creatures, and even human beings, with birds perched everywhere pecking at the bunches of grapes. Griffins paired with peacock-dragon hybrids, lions paired with cattle, centaurs paired with griffins, and more and more lions are grouped on either side of basins of water. Close to the entrance portal, a small child, a Cupid-like figure, bears a basket or dish of grapes. The alternation between the various depictions shows that a leading architect was responsible for the design executed on the facade of Mshatta.

At the portal itself, there is a conspicuous change in the decoration of the facade. From the gateway tower on the right, and on the section of wall beside it, there are no depictions of animals or fabulous beings at all. The vine tendrils grow from small vessels, or straight out of the ground, and are executed as regular spiral shapes with delicately depicted leaves and bunches of grapes. This change in the ornamentation of the facade at Mshatta has been interpreted in various ways. It has been suggested that the artists and craftsmen employed on the relief of the facade converted to Islam during their work, and from that point on portrayed no living creatures. But a more likely explanation seems to be that the site of the mosque lies behind the facade at this point. Within the palace, the prayer niche would have been built into this part of the masonry of the wall, and it could well have been with the mosque in mind that the caliph who commissioned the work would have no living creatures shown here. Yet the part of the facade adorned with living beings and fabulous animals presents problems of its own. Hellenistic and Sassanian Iranian traditions of the world of fabulous animals mingle. The griffin and centaur descend from Hellenistic imagery, while the peacock-dragon or *senmurv* was taken from Sassanian art. On many of the pictorial fields of the Mshatta facade, animals and fabulous creatures are shown one on each side of a vessel. When a lion and an ox face one another amicably across a basin of water, we are reminded of the passage in Isaiah (65: 25) which says that in the age of eternal peace "the lion shall eat straw like the bullock." Lions and oxen are shown several times meeting beside the Tree of Life in the early Christian mosaics in of Madaba, east of the Dead Sea and close to Mshatta. This Old Testament theme became part of Christian imagery, and thus eventually reached the Mshatta facade. In this case, it probably also suggested, that Islam, under the rule of the caliph, had ushered in an age of peace. The many basins of water, and the pairs of animals drinking from them, have parallels in

the depictions of fountains and Trees of Life in early Christian art. They could also refer to Paradise.

Fresco painting

Specimens of large-scale paintings have also been preserved in the Umayyad palaces. The most extensive pictorial program is in the small "bath house palace" of Qusair Amra, mentioned several times above. Both the reception hall and the rooms in the baths are covered with frescoes. On entering the reception hall, the visitor faces a likeness of the caliph, enthroned in Byzantine style on a chair with posts. A boat is passing through the water at his feet, and the birds of the air fly around his head. The same room contains depictions of six kings and emperors paying homage to the caliph. They are named in inscriptions, so that even today we can still distinguish between the emperor of Byzantium, the Great King Khusraw of Iran, the Negus of Abyssinia, and Roderick, king of the Visigoths. The other walls of the reception hall contain hunting and bathing scenes, and depictions of various craft activities, while a number of animals such as donkeys, camels, and gazelles, with a musician and a dancing girl, a

Wall painting in the bathhouse area of Qusair Amra, Jordan, early 8th century
The walls and domes of the bathhouse area of the small palace were also ornamented with paintings. There is an early depiction of the night sky in one of the domes. The detail here shows a flute player and a dancing girl in a leafy framework of diamond shapes. Gazelles and birds can be seen in the diamond-shaped fields next to the human figures. The painting is relaxed and lively, and clearly looks back to traditions of classical antiquity.

dancing ape, and a bear playing the flute, adorn the walls of the baths themselves. The sky of the northern hemisphere, with its constellations, was reproduced inside the dome of the *caldarium,* or steam bath. This painting is thought to be the oldest extant spherical representation of the northern sky. The outlines of all the paintings in Qusair Amra display confident draftsmanship, and the color is delicately graduated. These works may be described as the last Hellenistic paintings.

In the paintings from Qasr al-Hair al-Gharbi, which lies southwest of Palmyra, western and eastern traditions meet in a particularly striking way. The floors of two rooms in this palace were decorated with fresco painting, an extremely unusual technique for floors, since the frescoes would never have survived much wear and tear. Perhaps the paintings were meant to be a quick substitute for mosaics – not too outlandish an idea in view of the fact that the border of one of these floor frescoes has exact parallels in the mosaic floors of Khirbat al-Mafjar. It has also been thought that both rooms had a flight of stairs to an upper story, from which viewers could look down on the frescoes.

The floor of one room is divided into three horizontal pictorial zones. In the upper area, two musicians, one playing a lute with a turned-back pegbox and the other a flute, stand facing each other beneath a double arch. In the central area, a young horseman is shown hunting gazelle. While Sassanian counterparts for the musicians can be cited, the depiction of the horseman is inconceivable without Sassanian models. His clothing is Sassanian, with the flowing ends of the band around his diadem and belt, and so is the way in which the horse is bridled. Its tail is wound into an elaborate knot and colored with henna. The use of stirrups and a composite bow derives from Iranian and Central Asian examples. The depiction of the prey animal twice, once during its pursuit and the second time dead, also follows Sassanian models. The lower pictorial area is preserved only in a fragmentary state, but seems to have continued the hunting scenes.

In the other room with a floor fresco, the center of the design shows the head and shoulders of a fertility deity inside a circle of pearls, with a snake wound around its neck. The figure is holding a cloth filled with fruits. The upper corners of the pictorial area are occupied by fabulous creatures of classical antiquity: sea centaurs, hybrids of humans and horses, humans and fish, etc. It is difficult to imagine what ideas the lord of the palace connected with such an image; in a Christian environment its heathen nature would also have given offense.

Only written accounts survive of the movable interior furnishings of the Umayyad palaces. However, we may assume that many of the rooms were carpeted. A poet who visited al-Walid ibn Yazid, later to be caliph, found him sitting in a room surrounded by Armenian carpets and wall tapestries. When a carpet was required in Samarra a century after the end of the Umayyad period, a suitable one was found among the booty taken from the Umayyads. The carpet selected was 100 ells long and 20 ells wide, about 177 × 36 feet (54 × 11 meters), and was estimated to be worth 10,000 dinars. It had originally belonged to Caliph Hisham (724–743). Several of the accounts of this caliph mention his particular liking for carpets as well as costly clothing and perfumes. He kept such a lavish household that he needed 600 camels to transport his household goods even on the pilgrimage to Mecca.

Mosaic floors

As a rule, the floors in the Umayyad palaces were paved with mosaic. More of these mosaics were preserved in the small palace of Khirbat Minya and in Khirbat al-Mafjar than elsewhere, but there are also some specimens in Qusair Amra. The mosaics of Khirbat Minya are patterned like a carpet, with a central area and a border. The central area contains an interlacing design of varying complexity, with the interlacing band usually following a meandering rectangular or diagonal pattern. This center is surrounded by a border consisting of rows of rosettes, or of another meandering band. Divisions are marked off by an area of artistically twining knot patterns. Over the centuries, these knots were credited with the ability to avert evil; as late as Goethe's *Faust,* the Devil is unable to leave Faust's study because the pentagram traced on the threshold holds him back. Since the mosaic floors still extant in Khirbat Minya are very like carpets, we may picture Caliph Hisham's

carpet as having a complex pattern of interlacing bands at the center, with a separate border executed in bright colors.

The mosaics in the ceremonial hall of the bathhouse of Khirbat al-Mafjar are more artistically designed than those at Khirbat Minya. Here the meandering bands create a spatial illusion of the kind found in the mosaic art of the Hellenistic world. In other respects, the composition of the mosaics always follows the form of the ceiling of the room. Mosaic floors under domes and semidomes have scale-like patterns built around a central circular movement, while those on the floors of barrel-vaulted halls are rectangular in composition. The mosaics in Khirbat al-Mafjar include the depiction of a knife and a fruit, a theme interpreted by the excavator of the palace as a pictorial riddle alluding to the name of the man who commissioned the building.

None of the mosaics described above contain figures, and the only mosaic floor with figural depictions was found in the throne room of the ceremonial hall of the bathhouse in Khirbat al-Mafjar, which al-Walid II probably used as an audience chamber. This room also contained a copy of the caliph's headdress hanging from the ceiling by a stone chain, in imitation of the crown of the Sassanian king Khusraw in the palace of Ctesiphon, the capital of his empire.

The statement of the mosaic floor here relates to the special functions of the caliph. It shows a tree with luxuriant foliage, bearing 15 fruits among its branches. The design of the tree, with the different colors used in its leaves, trunk, and branches, is reminiscent of the trees in the mosaic of the Great Mosque of Damascus. There are groups of animals to the right and left of it. On the left-hand side, a pair of gazelles are plucking leaves from the twigs; on the right a gazelle is falling as a lion pounces on it. Until recently, the depiction of the gazelle was romantically linked with a love story in the caliph's life: al-Walid II, so the tale goes, fell in love with a girl called Salma, who was as beautiful as a gazelle. But his happiness with Salma did not last long, for she died after only a few months of harmonious marriage. The theory was that the figures of the gazelles under the fruit tree reflect this story. However, any serious attempt to decode the meaning of the picture requires us to imagine the caliph enthroned above the crown of the tree. Just as the sheep and the goats are divided and sent to the right or left hand of the Divine Judge on the Last Day, an image of peace was set beneath the caliph's right hand, an image of war beneath his left hand. To the Islamic way of thinking, peace ruled the world of Islam (*dar al-islam*) and war dominated the world of unbelievers (*dar al-harb*). Peace was the guarantee of the caliph's government, and art was pressed into service to propagate this idea.

Mosaic floor in Kirbat al-Mafjar, Palestine, 2nd quarter of the 8th century
An unusual mosaic floor was found in a room ending in an apse in the bathhouse precinct of the palace. It shows a fruit tree: on one side of the tree, two gazelles beneath its branches are nibbling leaves, while a lion is killing a gazelle on the other side. To understand its meaning, we may imagine the caliph enthroned above the tree: the uninjured gazelles are shown beneath his right hand, the injured gazelle beneath his left hand. These scenes have been interpreted as showing the world of peace and the world of war.

Iraq, Iran, and Egypt: The Abbasids

View of the Great Mosque of al-Mutawwakil in Samarra, 848–852
The Great Mosque of Samarra, built by Caliph al-Mutawwakil in Samarra, was for centuries the largest mosque in the world. The enormous, 50-meter minaret (the Malwiya) stands outside the enclosure wall and is famous for its spiral form. The smooth brickwork is characteristic of Abbasid architecture.

History

Sheila Blair, Jonathan Bloom

The architecture and arts of the Abbasid period cover an enormous range of material in terms of geography, medium, and style. From their capitals in Iraq (the Mesopotamia of ancient times), the Abbasids controlled an empire which stretched between North Africa and western Central Asia. In addition to constructing brick buildings decorated in carved wood, stone, stucco, and paint, the Abbasids patronized the arts of textiles, metalwork, glassware, and pottery. The capital served as a magnet for artisans and ideas, and the imperial style created in the center was then disseminated to the provinces. Because so much of the art produced in Abbasid Iraq has perished, it is necessary to look at the arts of the provinces as reflections of what is now lost from the center. Until the 10th century, these provincial arts still reflect the tastes and techniques of the central lands; afterward, however, they increasingly reflect local and regional concerns.

Part of the inscription on the bridge over the Tigris River at Harba, 1232
Harba, a town in the Tigris River Valley about 30 kilometers south of Samarra, became more important in the late Abbasid period, when Caliph al-Mustansir carried out a great irrigation project. A canal was constructed running parallel to the Tigris River which supplied water to the northern part of Baghdad. The caliph also had this great stone multi-arched bridge built; its 90-meter-long inscription gives details of its construction in 1232, and heaps praise on its builder.

The long period of Abbasid rule was coincidental with the classical age of Islamic civilization, when the Arabic language and its associated culture spread from the Atlantic to the Indian Ocean, and from Central Asia to the Sahara, and people from all over the Muslim world looked to Baghdad and the culture of Iraq for artistic inspiration. Under al-Mansur, his son al-Mahdi (775–785), and his nephew Harun al-Rashid (786–809) – caliph of the *Thousand and One Nights* – theology, law, historiography, poetry, and architecture developed. When Harun's son, al-Mamun (813–833), became caliph, after defeating his brother Amin (809–813), the Abbasid empire enjoyed a cultural apogee. Al-Mamun was a highly educated caliph, and in 833 he established the "House of the Sciences" (*bait al-hikma*) in Baghdad as a scientific library and center for learning.

The spiritual climate

A serious theological dispute, which dated back to the origins of Islam, came to a head during this period. Philosophers and theologians had argued over such questions as man's free will, divine predestination, and God and his attributes. One of the most important controversies was whether God's attributes, especially his Word as revealed in the Koran, are created, or are as eternal as he is.

History of the Abbasids

The Abbasid line of caliphs, the longest-lived dynasty of the medieval Islamic world, ruled from 749, when they seized power from the Umayyads, to 1258, when their capital Baghdad fell to the Mongols. After Abu I-Abbas al-Saffah (749–754), his brother al-Mansur (754–775) was the first important Abbasid caliph, who secured the dynasty's claims to power against all enemies both internal and external.

Abbasid rule from Iraq can be divided neatly into two periods. The first begins with the foundation of the dynasty and lasts until approximately 945, when the Buyids of northern Iran, notably under Adud al-Daula (949–983), rose to power, entered Baghdad, and finally reduced the caliphs to puppet status. In the second period, which lasted until the fall of Baghdad, real power in Iraq and Iran was transferred from a series of nominal caliphs into the hands of first the Buyids (945–1055), and then the Seljuks (1055–1194), Persian and Turkish dynasties, respectively. By this time, provinces such as Egypt and Syria had become independent. The Abbasid caliphate ended after the Mongol invasion, though it continued in name only under the Mamluk rulers of Egypt (1250–1517) until the Ottoman conquest of the Mamluk.

Some theologians, known as Mutazilites ("those who keep themselves apart"), took a rational approach and upheld God's unity and transcendance, but believed that the Koran was not part of God's actual essence. Rather, they deemed it a created message which God had inspired in Muhammad. Others, including the Sunni legal scholar and traditionalist Ahmad ibn Hanbal (780–855), took the opposing view that man could not use reason to comprehend God, and that the Koran was God's word, uncreated and eternal. Caliph al-Mamun came down on the side of the Mutazilite rationalists and tried to impose their views over those of the traditionalists. At first, jurists were forced to swear to the createdness of the Koran, but this inquisition soon foundered, and by 848 the authority of the *sunna* of the Prophet and the doctrine of the eternality of the Koran had been firmly reestablished.

The *ulama*, or class of religious and legal scholars, developed into a major institution in Abbasid times. The *ulama* developed various methods of interpreting the two fundamental sources of Islam: the Koran and the Hadith, the traditional words and deeds ascribed to the Prophet Muhammad. The *ulama* believed that they alone should formulate legal and theological doctrines, which the caliphs should be responsible for executing. The caliphs thereby came to be regarded not as Muhammad's spiritual heirs, but only as his political successors, charged with holding the Islamic community together. By the middle of the 9th century, the *ulama's* doctines began to coalesce into "schools of law." At first, many such schools coexisted, but by the beginning of the 11th century only four remained: the Hanafites, who predominated in Abbasid Iraq, the Malikites, the Shafiites, and the Hanbalites.

The Golden Age and the decline of the Abbasids

The Abbasid dynasty traced its origins to al-Abbas ibn Abd al-Muttalib ibn Hashim (d.653), the uncle of the Prophet Muhammad. As the Prophet had left no male heirs, the Abbasids' claim of descent from the Prophet's uncle was a closer relationship than any that their predecessors, the Umayyads, had been able to muster. The Abbasid family came to power by channeling general dissatisfaction with Umayyad rule, gathering support from disparate groups in a bloody revolution. Although dissatisfaction with Umayyad rule was widespread in the first half of the 8th century, it was especially strong among converts to Islam in northeastern Iran, who resented the privileges that had been granted to new Arab settlers in the region.

The Abbasids had initially enjoyed and encouraged the support of the Shiites (those who claimed that power had passed from the Prophet through his son-in-law Ali to his grandchildren Hasan and Husain), but once in power the Abbasids quickly distanced themselves from their erstwhile allies to become the champions of orthodoxy. For the first 50 years of Abbasid rule, numerous revolutionary movements developed in support of members of Ali's family.

Above: Julian Köchert, **Harun al-Rashid Receives the Delegation of Charlemagne, 786**, 1864, oil on canvas, Munich, Maximilianeum Foundation.
From 797 there was a frequent exchange of delegations between Harun al-Rashid and Charlemagne, who recognized and appreciated each other as the most powerful men of their respective cultures. Diplomatic contacts between their domains also helped to encourage trade relations.

Below: **Bab al-Wastani**, Baghdad, 1221
In 1221, the Abbasid caliph al-Nasir reconstructed the walls around the eastern sector of Baghdad, on the east bank of the Tigris River. The new walls were pierced by four gateways. The most famous is that on the northeast, once called the Bab al-Zafariya, but is known today as the Bab al-Wastani. The large, round corner tower and parts of the adjacent walls still stand, but the gateway itself was blown up in 1918.

Al-Mamun was forced to react to these groupings politically and ideologically, in order to underpin his claim to power, and in 817 named Ali al-Rida (d. 818), the eighth imam of the Shiites, as his successor.

To separate themselves from their predecessors and place themselves amid their supporters, the Abbasids chose to move the capital from Syria, where it had remained throughout the Umayyad period, to Iraq. Since much support for the early Abbasids had come from the east, Iran – and particularly the northeastern province of Khorasan – also remained important. Cities there, such as Nishapur and Merv, flourished under Abbasid patronage and maintained close commercial links with Central Asia and the Far East.

At first the Abbasids made their capital in the region around Kufa, the tempestuous garrison city that had been founded a century earlier by the first Muslim armies to conquer Iraq. But in 762 Caliph al-Mansur began construction of a new capital, named Medina al-Salam, "City of Peace," near the ruins of Ctesiphon, the Sassanian capital on the Tigris. Baghdad, as it was commonly known, not only became the political center of the empire, but also quickly assumed a preeminence in the sciences, literature, and the arts that it would maintain long after the city had lost its political power.

The Abbasids proceeded to create a new governing elite. Some of its members were new converts drawn from old Iranian families that had traditionally served the state. For example, the Barmakids, a family of former Buddhist aristocrats from Central Asia, played an enormous role in the development of new administrative systems to unite the empire. Other bureaucrats belonged to the ruler's entourage and might include freed slaves brought from Africa or Central Asia and trained to serve in the caliph's household or army. Power was therefore concentrated in the hands of a small group and orchestrated by the Abbasid caliph, who often appointed his relatives or supporters to govern the provinces in his name.

During the 9th century, the Abbasid caliphs increasingly adopted Persian models for government and the court. The rulers became increasingly remote from the ruled, withdrawing into immense palaces guarded by Turkish troops imported from the steppes of Central Asia. As the troops evolved into a dominant military cadre, the native population became restive, and in 836, Caliph al-Mutasim (833–842) moved the capital – and his guard – upriver to the new city of Samarra, where it remained for the next 56 years until the caliph returned his court to Baghdad.

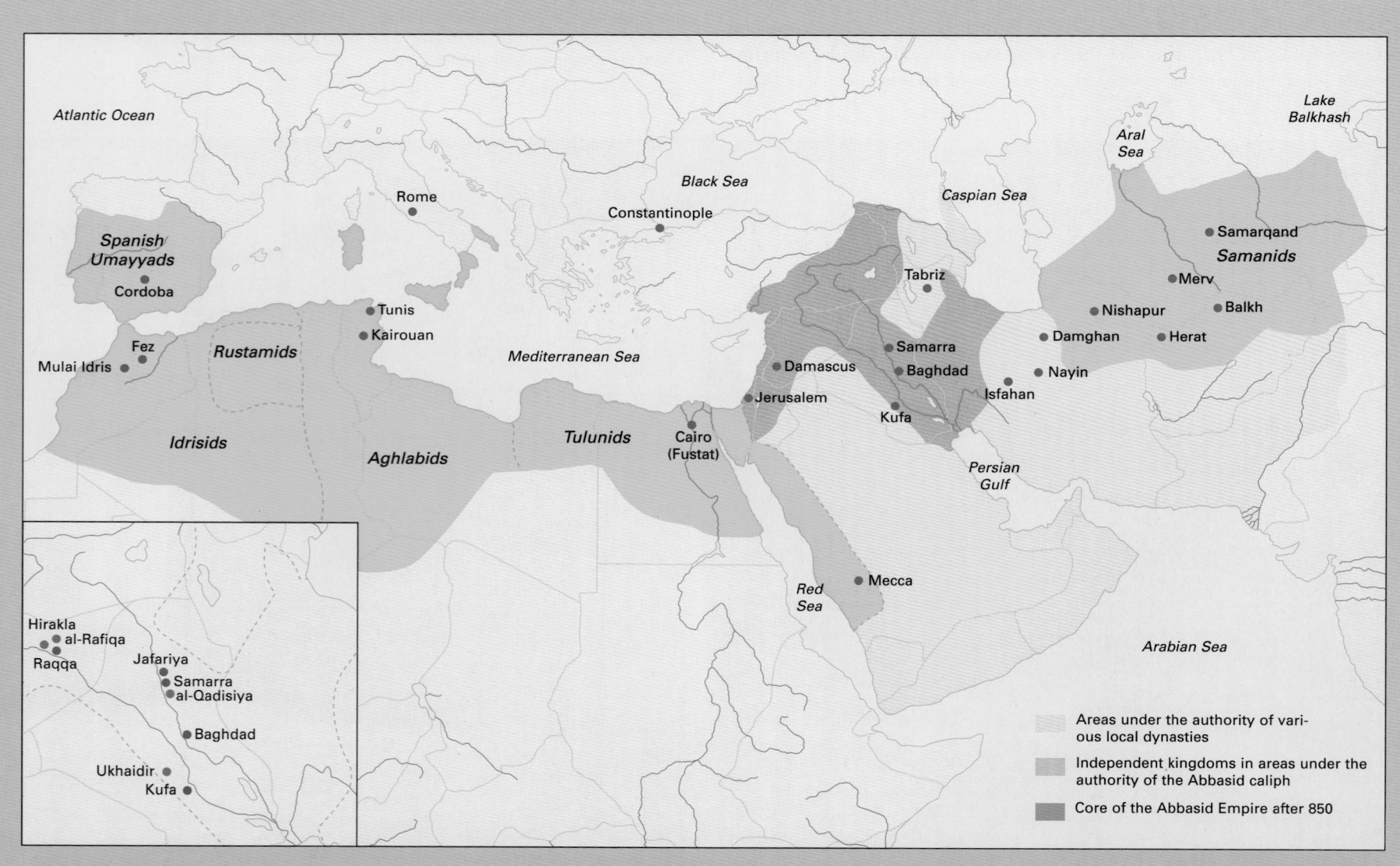

IRAQ, IRAN, AND EGYPT: THE ABBASIDS

Under the Umayyads, the borders of the Islamic empire had nearly reached their fullest extent; the early Abbasids were too absorbed in consolidating their own power to successfully extend the empire. The only active frontier was between Syria and Anatolia, where, for centuries, the caliphs continued to wage an inconclusive campaign against the Byzantines. Indeed, much of the newly conquered west fell from Abbasid hands: by 756 the only Umayyad prince to survive the Abbasid massacre of his family had established an independent princedom in Spain; and much of North Africa refused to recognize anything more than nominal Abbasid rule, which, in any event, was too distant to be effective. In the 9th century, both North Africa and Egypt became effectively independent under the Aghlabid (800–909) and Tulunid (868–905) governors, respectively, although both regimes continued to profess nominal allegiance to the caliph in Baghdad.

In the 10th century, the Shiite Fatimid dynasty (909–1171) challenged the caliphate itself by establishing a rival one, based first in North Africa and, after 969, in Egypt. In response, the Umayyads of Spain, who had until then been content with the modest title of emir (prince), also claimed to be caliphs. In the east, the Samanid (819–1005) and Saffarid (861–1003) dynasties established similar semi-independent princedoms. By the middle of the 10th century, therefore, the Abbasids controlled a much-reduced empire. Their prestige was further lessened when the caliphs themselves came under the tutelage of the Shiite Buyids (932–1062), condottieri who, originally hired as troops by the Abbasids, had come from the mountains of Dailam in northern Iran and brought extensive areas of Iran and Iraq under their influence.

749/750	Abu l-Abbas al-Saffah is made caliph in Kufa	811–813	When Amin designates his son as heir to the throne, civil war breaks out between Amin and al-Mamun
750	Battle of the Great Zab leads to the final triumph of the Abbasids over the Umayyads	813–833	Caliphate of al-Mamun
754–775	Caliphate of al-Mansur	817	Al-Mamun names as his successor the Shiite imam Ali al-Rida, who dies in the following year
755	The caliph has Abu Muslim, one of the organizers of the Abbasid revolution, murdered, for his attempt at power	817–819	Rival caliphate of Ibrahim ibn al-Mahdi in Baghdad
762/763	Baghdad founded	819	Al-Mamun moves from Khorasan to Baghdad, defeats Ibrahim ibn al-Mahdi, and appoints military leaderTahir ibn al-Husain governor of Khorasan
775–785	Reign of al-Mahdi; he introduced that the caliph himself should appoint officials	821–873	The Tahirids establish a *de facto* independent kingdom
780	Hostilities with Byzantium	833	Al-Mamun introduces the teachings of Mutazila via the Inquisition (*mihna*) as state doctrine
783	Prince Harun enforces a cease-fire with the Byzantine empress Irene	833–842	Reign of al-Mutasim
785–786	Reign of al-Hadi	836	Samarra founded
786–809	Caliphate of Harun al-Rashid	837	Conspiracy against the caliph in Khorasan
786–803	The Barmakids take over the vizier's office and actual political authority	842–847	Caliphate of al-Wathiq
802	Harun al-Rashid names his son Amin as first in line and al-Mamun as second, endowing al-Mamun with governorship for life of the eastern empire	847–861	The Inquisition ends under Caliph al-Mutawakkil; from then on the *ahl al-hadith* teaching is accepted as orthodox
809–813	Reign of Amin		

861	Murder of al-Mutawakkil by a Turkish military commander	991–1031	Caliphate of al-Qadir
861–945	Period of decaying power for the caliphate, during which the provincial governors assert their independence and local dynasties arise - the Saffarids (867–911), the Samanids (819–1005), the Tulunids (868–905), and the Buyids (945–1055)	999	Mahmud of Ghazna (998–1030) captures Khorasan
		1031–1075	Caliphate of al-Qaim
		1036–1037	The Seljuks, under Tughril Beg and Chaghri Beg, capture Khorasan
869–883	Slave rebellion in Iraq	1055	Tughril Beg takes over rulership of the Buyids; the Seljuks become the new guardians of the caliphate of Baghdad
873	Yaqub al-Saffar takes Nishapur and ends the rule of the Tahirids		
875	The Samanid Nasr I ibn Ahmad (864–892) takes Transoxiana from the caliph	1180–1225	Caliphate of al-Nasir
		1242–1258	Reign of al-Mustasim, last Abbasid caliph in Baghdad
877–899	Revolts by Shiite Carmathians in Iraq	1258	The Mongol invasions, under Hülägü Khan, ends the rule of the Abbasids with the murder of the last caliph
877	Ahmad ibn Tulun, governor of Egypt, occupies Syria		
909	Rival caliphate of the Fatimids in North Africa	1260–1517	Abbasid shadow caliphate in Cairo under Mamluk authority
929	The Spanish Umayyads also proclaim a caliphate		
945	The Buyids march into Baghdad		
977	The Buyid Adud al-Daula (949–983) becomes emir of Baghdad		

Mihrab
Baghdad, Islamic Museum
Most mosques built in the Abbasid period had a *mihrab*, a niche in the wall facing Mecca. This marble mihrab has been removed from its original mosque and is now in the Baghdad Islamic Museum.

Architecture
Sheila Blair, Jonathan Bloom

The "imperial style" and the cultural unity of the caliphate

In the time of the Prophet and his immediate successors, the mosque had combined several functions. It was, of course, a place of worship, but it was also the social and political center of the nascent Muslim community. Under the Abbasids, the mosque developed a new character as an exclusively religious institution. In early Islamic times, there had been no architectural uniformity, as mosques were made out of older structures or constructed in local vernacular styles. Under the Umayyads, the great Friday (congregational) mosques of the major cities such as Damascus, Jerusalem, and Medina had been monumentalized with the panoply of late antique architectural forms and decoration, but the effective confinement of Umayyad power to greater Syria meant that the "imperial style," such as it was, was limited to the core Umayyad region. All this changed in the Abbasid period. The great power of the early Abbasid caliphate, combined with the growing role of the *ulama*, meant that a standard type of Friday mosque evolved over a wide geographical area, although individual examples might differ in the use of local materials and techniques of construction.

The typical Friday mosque in the Abbasid period was a rectangular structure, somewhat longer than it was wide, with a rectangular courtyard in its center. The courtyard was surrounded by hypostyle halls, in which many stone columns or brick piers supported a flat wooden roof. The hall was wider on the side of the *qibla* wall, which faced Mecca, and had in its middle a *mihrab*, or niche. In order to emphasize the *mihrab*, builders might add a small dome directly in front of it or a wider aisle leading from the courtyard. To the right of the *mihrab* stood a stepped *minbar*, or pulpit, from which the imam (prayer leader) gave the Friday sermon (*khutba*). In the Umayyad period, the caliph himself had often given the sermon, but by Abbasid times the caliph rarely, if ever, attended worship in the Friday mosque, and the job of leading prayers was taken over by a member of the *ulama*.

On the opposite side of the courtyard from the *mihrab* stood a tower. This, usually called a minaret (from the Arabic *manara*, "place of or thing that gives light"), is often associated with the call to prayer, but there is little contemporary evidence that Abbasid towers were used for this purpose. Rather, their monumental size and prominent placement suggest that they were erected to advertise the presence of the Friday mosque from afar and symbolize the preeminent role of the mosque in Abbasid society.

In the same way that a standard mosque style was spread throughout the Abbasid domains, many other forms and techniques that had been developed in the capital were disseminated to the provinces. In contrast to the Umayyads, who in Syria had built stone structures, Abbasid builders favored mud brick and baked brick covered with a rendering of gypsum plaster, often painted, carved, or molded with geometric and vegetal designs. In part, this choice of materials may have been due to the lack of suitable building stone in the heartland of Abbasid power, but in practical terms it meant that Abbasid-style buildings could be erected wherever the raw materials – clay, lime, and gypsum – were found, in effect everywhere. Similarly, the Abbasid style of molded stucco decoration, which combined late antique Mediterranean motifs with materials and techniques used in Sassanian Iran, could hide indifferent construction under a showy but inexpensive revetment. Again, what might have been just a

IRAQ, IRAN, AND EGYPT: THE ABBASIDS

practical innovation was transformed into an aesthetic one, as builders throughout the Abbasid lands adopted this type of stucco revetment.

Baghdad, the imperial metropolis of a far-flung empire, exerted a magnetic attraction on people and ideas. The capital also served as a kind of clearing house, as people and ideas returned to the provinces with new ideas and experiences. For example, it now seems that in the 8th century Syrian glassmakers invented the decorative technique of using metallic oxides to give their wares a lustrous sheen after they had been fired a second time in a reducing, low-oxygen kiln. This unique technique of luster decoration was adapted by potters in Abbasid Iraq, who used it to decorate their earthenware ceramics. From Iraq, Abbasid potters introduced the technique to Egypt, where it took on a new life of its own.

Baghdad also set the style for cultural norms in the Abbasid period, even for rival powers. For example, the Umayyads of Spain, who challenged the Abbasids' political legitimacy, nevertheless emulated their art and culture. The musician Ziryab (789–857), an émigré from Baghdad, became the arbiter of fine taste in 9th-century Cordoba, where he set the standards for dress, table manners, protocol, etiquette, and even the coiffures of men and women.

Similarly, Abbasid elegance was emulated by their religious and political rivals in Byzantium. In 830 a Byzantine envoy went to Baghdad, where he was so impressed by the splendor of Abbasid architecture that on his return to Constantinople he persuaded Emperor Theophilos (829–842) to build a palace exactly like the ones he had seen. Theophilos complied, and a palace was built at Bryas, now Maltepe, an Asiatic suburb of Constantinople on the Sea of Marmara. Only the substructure remains, but it shows a large rectangular enclosure that calls to mind Umayyad and Abbasid palaces. The only departure from the Abbasid model was a chapel added next to the imperial chamber and a triconch church set in the middle of the courtyard.

Virtually nothing but memories remains of Abbasid Baghdad, which has been rebuilt over the centuries, and the vast palaces of Samarra have long since fallen into ruin. Much Abbasid art was ephemeral, made of materials such as cloth, plaster, and wood, which have not survived the ravages of time. Fragile ceramics and glassware were broken, but their shards have remained to give an unusually clear picture of the tableware of the Abbasid elites. Since what remains does not necessarily reflect what was made, the historian needs to combine the artistic remains with the many textual sources for the period and the archeological evidence to recreate a picture of the splendors and glories of Abbasid art.

The search for a capital

Building large new cities was the major architectural activity of the Abbasid caliphs. In terms of function, these cities were logical successors to the garrison cities that the Umayyads had built in newly conquered regions. In terms of architecture, however, these new cities were the continuation of a long Mesopotamian and Iranian tradition of rulers building administrative capitals. These range from Durr Sharrukin, the city founded by the Assyrian ruler Sargon II (721–705 B.C.) northwest of Mosul at Khorsabad, to the round city founded by the Sassanian emperor Ardashir I (224–241) at Gur (modern Firuzabad) in the province of Fars in southwest Iran.

During the first decade of Abbasid rule, the caliphs erected several administrative centers in the vicinity of Kufa, in southern Iraq. They were known as al-Hashimiya (in reference to the family from which both the Prophet and the Abbasids descended), but nothing remains of them and the sources provide little additional information. These centers must have been royal residences, since at least one of them had a throne room, called a *khadra*, the same word that had been used in the Umayyad period for a throne room.

Stucco decoration from room four in house one in Samarra
Berlin, Museum of Islamic Art
The clay brick buildings constructed in Samarra were frequently decorated with stucco reliefs. The artisans developed three different styles, differentiated by the level of stylization of the vegetal motifs. The decoration of this panel exemplifies the first Samarra style, in which the field is divided by decorated bands into compartments, here hexagonal, which contain recognizable leaves growing from vines. The leaves often have four "eyes" and veins.

The Abbasid throne room was on an upper floor, for the 9th-century historian al-Tabari reported that, when the Rawandiya rebels, members of an extremist Shiite sect, approached Caliph al-Mansur (754–775) in his *khadra*, they attempted to escape out the window and fell to their deaths. Al-Tabari's report indicates that even the earliest Abbasid administrative centers were substantial multistory buildings.

The construction of Baghdad

The residences near Kufa proved unsuitable, so on August 1, 762, the second Abbasid caliph, al-Mansur, decided to move the capital to Medina al-Salam (Baghdad). The site, near Ctesiphon, was chosen for its easy riparian communication with Mesopotamia, the Persian Gulf, and northern Syria, as well as its important land routes to the Iranian plateau, southern Syria, and the Hijaz. Work on the new capital was completed four years later in 766/767. As with the first Abbasid capitals near Kufa, nothing remains of Abbasid Baghdad, which is entirely covered by the modern city. Extensive descriptions in medieval texts, however, have allowed scholars in modern times to reconstruct the city's general plan. About 1.7 miles (2.7 kilometers), the Round City was surrounded by a double set of sturdy, mud-brick walls, and a broad moat fed by the Tigris River. The walls were pierced at the intercardinal points by four gates – the Khorasan Gate on the northeast, the Basra Gate on the southeast, the Kufa Gate on the southwest, and the Damascus Gate on the northwest – from which roads led to the four quarters of the empire.

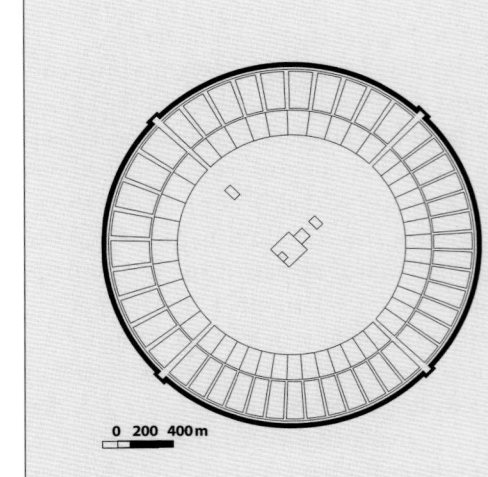

Round City of Baghdad,
begun 762
In 762 the Abbasid caliph al-Mansur began construction of his new capital Baghdad. It has been completely covered by modern construction, but scholars have reconstructed the round plan. Two sets of mud-brick walls and four axial gates protected a ring of residences and government offices. In the open space in the center stood the caliph's palace and the adjacent mosque.

0 200 400 m

Each of the four gates to al-Mansur's Round City possessed a complex, bent entrance passage designed to guard it against violent attack. Each gate was surmounted by an elevated chamber reached by staircases or ramps. Each of the chambers was crowned by a dome, and the whole 50-cubit (82 foot, 25 meter) structure was topped by a weathervane in the shape of a human figure. The caliph used these rooms as audience halls when he wished to view anyone who might be approaching or whatever lay beyond the city walls. The audience halls

Air view of Firuzabad, Iran, c. 224–241
The Sassanian emperor, Ardashir I, founded the city of Gur (modern Firuzabad) in southwestern Iran. Round cities of this type may have inspired the Abbasid caliph al-Mansur, in the 8th century, to build his capital Baghdad as a round city.

Above: Courtyard and minaret of the Great Mosque of al-Rafiqa, late 8th century

The Great Mosque of al-Rafiqa, the companion city to Raqqa, was constructed under the early Abbasids to serve the garrison of soliders from Khorasan. It has massive mud-brick walls strengthened by baked brick facing and encircled by a chain of semicircular towers. The central courtyard was surrounded on three sides by a double arcade and on the fourth by a hypostyle prayer hall with a triple arcade carried on brick piers. This mosque is the first known example of piers used to support the roof and served as the model for mosques at Baghdad, Samarra, and Cairo.

Below: **Bab al-Amma in Samarra**, 836/837

The Bab al-Amma, built of baked brick, is the only major section of the Abbasid palace at Samarra to survive. Designed in the form of a triple *iwan*, the gate stood at the top of an impressive flight of steps rising up from the banks of the Tigris River to the enormous (70 acre, 175 hectacre) palace known as the Dar al-Khalifa ("House of the Caliphate"). This was a complex with numerous courtyards and gardens, enclosed within a high wall.

Qasr al-Banut in al-Rafiqa, 8–12th century

Like the Great Mosque, this palace – known as the "Girls' Palace" – is located within the city wall, built at the end of the 8th century. The baked-brick building has a paved courtyard, which is enclosed on four sides by open halls, and thus resembles a type of four-*iwan* layout. The northern hall has a three-aisle porch, the same width as the central courtyard. The four-*iwan* layout and the three-aisle porch could be attributed to Persian influence, blended with local building traditions. Although the palace in its present form for the most part dates to the 12th century, some features and details of the Abbasid palace are clearly recognizable.

also marked the extension of his personal domain and authority over the extremities of the city.

Four major avenues lined with shopping arcades and other buildings led from the gates into the interior of the city. Abutting the wall on the interior was an outer ring of residences for the caliph's family, staff, and servants. An inner ring of residences housed the arsenal, the treasury, and government offices. The innermost zone of the city was a broad esplanade in which stood the police station, the Friday mosque, and the caliph's palace.

The mosque was a square hypostyle structure measuring 200 cubits (approximately 330 feet, 100 meters) on each side, with an open interior courtyard. Adjacent to the mosque was the palace; located in the exact center of the city, it covered four times the area of the mosque. At the back of the palace, a reception hall (*iwan*) measuring 30 × 20 cubits (50 × 33 feet, 15 × 10 meters) led to a domed audience chamber 20 cubits (33 feet, 10 meters) on each side. Above it was another domed audience hall, known to contemporaries as the "Qubbat al-Khadra," often translated as the "Green Dome" but more accurately rendered as the "Dome of Heaven," thereby making reference to an ancient tradition of associating the ruler with the heavens. The top of this dome stood 80 cubits (130 feet, 40 meters) above the ground and was itself crowned by a weathervane in

Palace of Ukhaidir, Iraq, second half of the 8th century
The desert palace of Ukhaidir was probably built by a wealthy individual (either the uncle or the nephew of Caliph al-Mansur), as a private retreat enclosed within a massive outer wall. The best-preserved of the early Abbasid palaces, it was built of rubble and brick masonry and originally stood three stories high.

the shape of a horseman. Contemporaries considered the horseman the crown of Baghdad, a symbol of the region, and a monument to the Abbasids. The revolving horseman was also a convenient metaphor for the caliph's power and authority. It was said that, if the sultan saw the figure with its lance pointing toward a given direction, he knew that rebels would appear, before word had reached him. Like a weathervane, the horseman was supposed to predict storms before they blew in. The collapse of the Qubbat al-Khadra and its horseman during a storm in 941 was indeed an omen: within four years the Buyids entered Baghdad and established themselves as "protectors" of the Abbasid caliphs.

The Round City was built to separate the caliph from his subjects. Several settlements stood outside the walls: a great army camp stood at Harbiya, markets were located in al-Karkh, and al-Mansur's son al-Mahdi built a subsidiary camp for his troops on the east bank of the Tigris at Rusafa. The Round City soon failed to achieve its original purpose, as the population settled thickly around it, and even the administrative core was quickly transformed into a normal urban entity. This was particularly apparent following the siege of 812/813 during the civil war between Harun al-Rashid's sons, when the original Khorasani army was replaced by new units. The victorious Caliph al-Mamun moved his palace from the Round City to a suburban estate on the east bank of the Tigris, and the Round City was swallowed up by the new metropolis developing on the west bank. Sections of the original city wall remained visible for centuries, but no trace of the Round City has been found in modern times.

Its circular form and centralized planning, with the caliph's palace in the exact center of the city and the mosque adjacent to it, invite speculation about the city's intended cosmic significance as the center of a universal empire. It has been speculated, for example, that al-Mansur modeled his city on such earlier round-shaped royal foundations as Firuzabad, in Fars. As attractive as this hypothesis and others may be, there is no contemporary evidence to either support or disprove them. In any event, within a few decades, if not years, of its foundation, the administrative center had been transformed from a large-scale palace into a rich and vibrant industrial and commercial center.

Palace of Ukhaidir
Ukhaidir is the best-preserved palace from the early Abbasid period. The exterior is protected by a large wall built of limestone rubble in heavy mortar, with round towers at the corners, semicircular towers along the sides, and quarter-round towers protecting the axial gates. In the center, a courtyard opens onto a *iwan*, with a square hall behind it. On each side is a self-contained residence arranged around a smaller court, and to the east is a bath complex.

0 10 20m

Other Abbasid cities and residences

Baghdad was not the only city founded by Caliph al-Mansur. He also developed a site in northern Syria on the east bank of the Euphrates River. The area had been settled in classical times, but in 772, as part of a program of border fortification, al-Mansur founded a settlement known as al-Rafiqa, or "the Companion" (of the older settlement Raqqa). According to medieval texts, al-Rafiqa was modeled after the Round City of Baghdad, and the surviving fortifications confirm this statement. In plan, al-Rafiqa consists of a horseshoe-shaped area 0.8 mile (1.3 kilometers) wide, but contemporaries might have considered this shape to have been "almost" round. It was protected by a massive wall, nearly 3.1 miles (5 kilometers) long and fortified by 132 defensive round towers, as well as an advance wall and a moat. Three gates led to the interior. In the center of al-Rafiqa stood a large (350 × 300 feet, 108 × 93 meters) Friday mosque, built to serve the garrison of soldiers from Khorasan. Its massive mud-brick walls were faced with baked brick and buttressed by a series of semicircular towers. The interior courtyard was surrounded by hypostyle halls carried on brick piers. The prayer hall on the *qibla* side was three bays deep, while those on the other three sides of the court were only two bays deep.

Raqqa, together with al-Rafiqa, formed the largest urban entity in Syria, and it was surpassed in all of Mesopotamia only by Baghdad. It is hardly surprising, therefore, that Harun al-Rashid, who disliked Baghdad, transferred his residence there in 796, and it was to remain his base until 808. During his 12 years of residence, he not only added to the city's fortifications, but also constructed an impressive palace quarter to the north. Covering almost 1 square mile (10 square kilometers), it included 20 large palace complexes. The largest of them, set in the center, measured about 1150 × 980 feet (350 × 300 meters). It can be identified with Harun's residence, which was mentioned in the sources as the Qasr al-Salam ("Palace of Peace"). Surrounding structures housed the caliph's family, his court, and his troops. Constructed of mud brick occasionally strengthened by baked brick, the complexes were carefully laid out. The mud-brick walls were covered with white plaster carved in deep relief, particularly with designs of vine scrolls.

Harun also began construction of several other circular or octagonal establishments. Hirakla, located between Raqqa and Balis in northern Syria, was a walled circular enclosure with axial gates and a square building in the center. Al-Qadisiya, located at the entrance to the Qatul canal at Samarra in Iraq, was a huge octagonal enclosure, 0.9 mile (1.5 kilometers) across, with axial gates and a road leading to a central square structure. The outer walls were built of mud brick, and foundations were set out for a mosque, a palace, a central square, and three avenues. Neither establishment seems to have been completed, and they are known only through archeological excavations, which scholars have attempted to match with the equivocal and brief mentions in medieval texts.

The best-preserved of the early Abbasid palaces is, paradoxically, the one about which contemporary texts have the least to say: Ukhaidir, located almost 125 miles (200 kilometers) south of Baghdad on the steppe to the northwest of Kufa. It consists of a large outer enclosure 575 × 555 feet (175 × 169 meters), built of limestone rubble in heavy mortar to a height of about 62 feet, (19 meters). Each corner had a round tower, and semicircular towers were spaced regularly between them. Quarter-round towers in the center of each side flanked gates, except on the north side, where a projecting block marks the main entrance. It leads to the palace proper (365 × 270 feet, 112 × 82 meters), which is next to the outer enclosure on the north. Along the central tract of the rectangular palace an entrance complex with a small mosque to the right leads to a large open court; onto this opens a great vaulted *iwan*, behind which stands a square hall, flanked by apartments. On either side of the central tract are two

View of the upper gallery of the Palace of Ukhaidir
One of the remarkable features of this palace is that many of the upper story rooms are still intact, whereas in the case of most Abbasid palaces only the outline could be uncovered. The open gallery, with the round columns characteristic of Ukhaidir, forms the eastern section of the group of rooms above the entrance-*iwan*.

self-contained residential units arranged around smaller courts. To the southeast of the palace is a bath complex constructed of baked brick.

Ukhaidir is remarkable for its state of preservation, particularly of the vaults and upper stories, for most other early Abbasid buildings are known only in plan. Some of the vaults were built of bricks, which are occasionally laid in complex decorative patterns. In other palaces, the vaults are decorated with plaster elaborately carved to imitate brick patterns. Particularly noteworthy is the use of transverse vaulting to cover rectangular spaces. Many of these features will reappear in later Iranian architecture, suggesting that they were probably used in many buildings that no longer survive. The scale and quality of

construction and decoration suggest that this structure was built by an important person, probably someone closely connected to the Abbasid court. Some scholars have ascribed its construction to Caliph al-Mansur's powerful nephew, Isa ibn Musa (d. 784), while others have suggested that it was the palace of al-Mansur's uncle, Isa ibn Ali, built some two decades earlier. As no inscriptions were discovered at the site, the state of the evidence does not allow a decision one way or the other. In any case, the palace at Ukhaidir gives some substance to textual descriptions and archeological excavations of better-known sites.

Some of these features can be seen on a more modest scale at the site of Uskaf Bani Junaid, also known as Sumaka, on the banks of the Nahrawan Canal, in southern Iraq. In early Islamic times, it was the largest city in the Diyala basin, apart from the capital. Excavations in the 1950s uncovered a rectangular palace 213 × 180 feet (65 × 55 meters) which was divided into three tracts. In the center, a courtyard opened onto an axial *iwan* flanked by rooms leading to a reception hall with apartments on either side. The mosque, measuring 165 × 150 feet (50 × 45 meters), had a central courtyard surrounded by arcades, two bays deep on three sides and five bays deep for the prayer hall. The *mihrab* is to the left of center in the *qibla* wall. The exterior walls of the mosque were built of baked brick, but the columns were of walnut wood. Since the mosque is undated, it must be dated by comparison to other, dated structures; these suggest a building date in the late 8th or the 9th century, probably before Samarra.

adopted a new military policy. They appointed several chiefs in Transoxiana, Armenia, and North Africa as hereditary governors and hired regiments of Turkish slaves from Central Asia to serve in the army. This new institution strengthened the hand of the caliph but was also a major source of trouble, for bloody clashes broke out in Baghdad between the foreign Turkish soldiers and the local Arab soldiers and populace.

To separate the feuding groups, al-Mutasim, like his father Harun al-Rashid, decided to establish a new administrative capital. In 836, after trying several sites, he settled on Samarra, located 78 miles (125 kilometers) north of Baghdad on the east bank of the Tigris River, where his father had begun to build a palace some decades earlier. Unlike the Round City of Baghdad, which has been built over continuously since medieval times, the enormous area of ruins at Samarra was largely abandoned in medieval times and remained that way until the 20th century. When archeologists rediscovered it in the early 1900s, the site stretched for 30 miles (50 kilometers) along the bank of the Tigris and covered more than 60 square miles (150 square kilometers).

Palaces and mosques

In contrast to the self-contained and block-like palaces of al-Mansur and Harun al-Rashid, the one al-Mutasim built at Samarra covered more than 175 acres (70 hectares) and was enclosed by high blank walls. Al-Mutasim's vast palace, which was occupied by nearly all the caliphs who resided at Samarra, is known in the sources as the Dar al-Khalafa ("House of the Caliphate"), although archeologists initially misidentified it as another palace called the Jausaq al-Khaqani ("Pavilion of the Emperor"). A complex of interconnected courts and gardens, the Dar al-Khilafa measured 0.9 mile (1.4 kilometers), from the riverbank on the west to the viewing stand that overlooked a gargantuan cloverleaf race track on the east. A vast flight of broad steps ascended from the Tigris to the Bab al-Amma, the great public entranceway, still marked by its three large brick arches. Beyond the gate lay a string of courtyards and chambers, which eventually led to a central domed hall, surrounded by four vaulted *iwans*, presumably the caliph's throne room. In adjacent areas, sunken apartments arranged around pools provided the inhabitants relief from the torrid climate.

Although it was the largest palace at Samarra, the Dar al-Khilafa was only one of many. Adjacent to it were several lesser palaces and grand houses, and other palaces and gardens, such as al-Mutasim's Qasr al-Jis ("Stucco Palace") and the one built by his successor al-Wathiq (842–847) on the floodplain, stood on the west bank of the Tigris. There were also camps for the army, each comprising a palace for the commander, lesser residences, a ceremonial avenue, and a grid of streets along which stood quarters for the troops.

Al-Mutasim's son, Caliph al-Mutawakkil (847–861), was the greatest builder at Samarra. He doubled the size of the city and at the beginning of his reign gave it a colossal new Friday mosque. Measuring 784 × 512 feet (239 × 156 meters), the building has the 3:2 proportions of many mosques of this period. It stood within an outer enclosure of 1,456 × 1,233 feet (444 × 376 meters), enclosing a total area of 41 acres (17 hectares). For many centuries it

Samarra, the new imperial capital

Harun al-Rashid's long and glorious reign left many problems. After his death in 809, civil war broke out between his sons: Amin, who had inherited the caliphate, and Amin's younger brother al-Mamun, who had been given only the governorship of Khorasan. The Abbasid army of Baghdad supported Amin, the local candidate, so al-Mamun was forced to turn for support to independent warlords from his power base in eastern Iran. Al-Mamun emerged as the victor, but, during the bitter civil war, Baghdad was severely damaged, and the Abbasid army and Iraqi population, who had suffered most, were totally alienated from their new rulers.

To strengthen their control over a rebellious population, al-Mamun and al-Mutasim, another of his brothers and his eventual successor (833–842),

IRAQ, IRAN, AND EGYPT: THE ABBASIDS

was the largest mosque in the world. The mosque's exterior walls of baked brick were buttressed with semicircular towers and decorated with a brick-and-stucco frieze along the top. Sixteen doors led into the interior, where a central courtyard was surrounded by hypostyle halls. Hundreds of square piers of brick and stone supported a flat wooden roof. The interior was decorated with glass mosaics and cut marble panels. The *mihrab*, flanked by two pairs of rose-colored marble columns, was rectangular in plan and decorated with gold glass mosaic. Openings on either side of the *mihrab* provided access for the imam on the left and storage for a movable *minbar* on the right. Opposite the *mihrab*, within the walls of the outer enclosure but outside the mosque proper and connected to it by a bridge, stands a tower known as the Malwiya (spiral). The tower is a great helicoidal ramp ascending counterclockwise to a pavilion more than 165 feet (50 meters) above the ground. The ramp gets steeper as it rises so that each story is the same height, an aesthetically pleasing but impractical solution for anyone charged with climbing to the top. The unusual form of the tower has often been linked to the Mesopotamian ziggurat, but it is more likely to be the other way around. For example, spiral ziggurats, particularly the

View of whole structure and Malwiya,
Great Mosque of al-Mutawakkil at Samarra, 848–852
The Friday mosque built by Caliph al-Mutawakkil was for centuries the largest mosque in the Muslim world. The walls of the outer enclosure are largely ruined, but those of the mosque itself, which were built of baked

brick and buttressed by semicircular towers, are better preserved. The enormous, 50 meter minaret (called the Malwiya), belongs to the Great Mosque complex, which Caliph al-Mutawakkil had built and is especially celebrated for its spiral shape.

Tower of Babel in European depictions by Brueghel and others, seem to have been inspired by travelers' accounts of the Malwiya.

In the 850s, al-Mutawakkil built a new palace quarter for his son, the future al-Mutazz (866–869), at Balkuwara to the south of Samarra. The rectangular palace was set inside a square enclosure measuring more than 0.6 mile (1 kilometer) each side and facing the river. As at the Dar al-Khalafa, the reception halls form a square block, with a central domed chamber surrounded by four *iwans* arranged in a cross shape. Later in the decade, al-Mutawakkil began a new city to the north of Samarra, which was known as Jafariya (from

Exterior walls of the Great Mosque of al-Mutawakkil at Samarra
Although the exterior walls of al-Mutawakkil's mosque have been heavily restored, they give a good idea of the size and scale of Abbasid imperial construction. The upper part of the brick wall was decorated with a frieze of recessed squares.

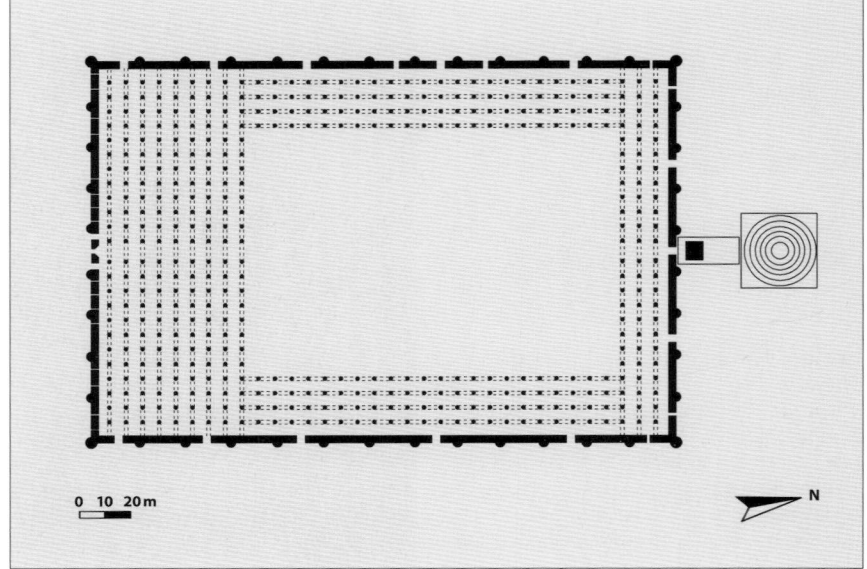

the caliph's given name Jafar) or al-Mutawakkiliya. A grand avenue flanked by smaller palaces and houses led to the main palace, known as the Jafari, which had reception halls at the junction of the Tigris River and the Kisrawi Canal. The rest of this immense palace spread for over a mile (1.7 kilometers) to the east. The Friday mosque for the new city is now known as the Mosque of Abu Dulaf. Measuring 700 × 443 feet (213 × 135 meters), it is a smaller replica of al-Mutawakkil's earlier Friday mosque. Rectangular piers of fired brick supported arcades perpendicular to the *qibla* wall and a flat wooden roof. The spiral minaret, which reaches its height of 52 feet (16 meters) with three turns, was also modeled on the earlier prototype, the Malwiya.

Like earlier Abbasid foundations, the architecture of Samarra uses local materials such as brick and stucco to achieve its dramatic effects. The great wealth of the patrons, however, allowed them to enhance these humble materials with expensive wood and marble panels and glass mosaics. Nevertheless, the buildings at Samarra differ from what we know of earlier Abbasid foundations in several significant ways. Earlier palaces had tended to be high and to have domes over elevated thronerooms, which made the buildings seem even higher, while mosques were generally low affairs. In Samarra, by contrast, the palaces made their impact of impressive grandeur by covering huge areas, while the mosques were marked by enormous towers. Unlike the palace at Baghdad, where the ruler was literally and figuratively at the center of his realm, at Samarra, the caliph was removed from the populace behind blank walls. At this time, the towers and elaborate portals that had earlier been used in palaces began to be used in mosques.

View from minaret of courtyard and ground plan, Great Mosque of al-Mutawakkil. This view of the whole layout 239 × 156 meters of al-Mutawakkil's mosque shows the courtyard, originally surrounded by hypostyle halls. In the distance are the remains of the covered prayer hall, which had a *mihrab* decorated with gold and glass mosaics. The halls around the courtyard would have also been covered, and the entire interior was lavishly decorated with marble revetments and mosaic.

The mosque tower, known today as a minaret, in fact, became the most distinguishing feature of mosques from the Abbasid period.

Although the contemporary texts are silent about why this change in architectural form occurred, it seems likely that it reflects the evolution from the more egalitarian society of early Islamic times into the more hierarchical society of the Abbasid period, where Persian ideas of kingship were increasingly adopted by Islamic rulers. Another reason for these architectural changes may be that the mosque was becoming an institution less attached to the ruler and increasingly associated with the *ulama*. Although theoretically there was in Islam no distinction between religious and secular authority, by the Abbasid period the two had begun to diverge in practice. The Friday mosque, for all its magnificence provided by the caliph's purse, served as the center of a self-perpetuating class of religiously minded people, while the ever more splendid palaces became the centers of secular power in which the caliphs and their governors were increasingly removed from the people they ruled.

Building decoration

Most, if not all, of the buildings at Samarra were constructed of mud brick which was protected and embellished with a covering of carved or painted plaster. Baked brick, rammed earth, and an unusual brick made of gypsum were also used, and some particularly important areas were revetted with stone or wood. To enliven the large expanses of stucco, carvers developed three increasingly abstract styles of decoration, which show how both technique and subject matter evolved over the course of time.

The first style is a carved technique that was clearly derived from the geometricized vegetal decoration that had been widely used in the Umayyad period. The decorative field is divided by pearl bands into compartments filled with vines, which, unlike the vines at Raqqa, have no grapes. The vine

Minaret of the Mosque of Abu Dulaf in Samarra, 860/861
The Mosque of Abu Dulaf, like the older Mosque of al-Mutawakkil, has a spiral minaret opposite the *mihrab*, but it stands only 16 meters high, about one-third the height of the Malwiya.

Arcades in the Mosque of Abu Dulaf in Samarra
The Mosque of Abu Dulaf, the second Friday mosque built by al-Mutawakkil in Samarra, was intended to serve the needs of a new district to the city's north. Somewhat smaller in scale than the earlier mosque, it is also distinguished by its use of arcades to support the roof (now destroyed).

leaves have five lobes separated by four eye-like holes, and stand out against a dark, deeply carved ground. The second style, also carved, is characterized by the use of cross-hatching for surface details. Subjects are somewhat simplified but are still distinguished from the background and enclosed within compartments. The leaves do not "grow" naturalistically from a vine but have become abstract forms. The third style, also known as the "beveled" style, is a molded technique especially suitable for covering large wall surfaces quickly. It uses a distinctively slanted but relatively shallow cut, which allowed the plaster to be released easily from the mold. Decoration in the beveled style is distinguished by rhythmic and symmetrical repetitions of curved lines ending in spirals that form abstract patterns – including bottle-shaped motifs, trefoils, palmettes, and spirals – in which the traditional distinction between the subject and background of the decoration has been dissolved. The beveled style was undoubtedly developed for stucco, but it was also applied to wood, which was used for doors and other architectural fittings. It is perhaps the most original contribution of Samarra decorators to the development of Islamic art, for the geometricized vegetal subjects and the quality of infinite extendibility are key elements in the arabesque decorative scheme.

Thousands of fragments of paintings found in the palaces at Samarra show that figural decoration, as in the Umayyad period, continued to be acceptable for private interiors, especially in palaces. Some of the scenes included cornucopia scrolls inhabited by wild animals and naked women, as well as hunting scenes. One reconstructed mural shows a pair of dancing girls with interlocked arms. While they dance, each figure pours wine

Wall decoration of a house in Samarra
Abbasid builders developed special techniques to construct and decorate the enormous palaces and other buildings in Samarra. Buildings were usually made of mud brick, which was readily available and cheap. The rough walls were protected and embellished with a covering of carved or painted plaster. Scholars have discerned three styles of decoration. The first two styles involved cutting the wet plaster with a straight vertical cut, but the third style was a molded technique with a distinctive slanted or beveled cut which allowed the plaster to be released easily from the mold. This technique was especially suitable for covering large wall surfaces quickly and became a hallmark of Abbasid decoration.

from a long-necked bottle into a cup held by the other. Fragments of broken wine bottles, identified by their painted labels and smashed in bouts of revelry, littered parts of the palace, suggesting that some of the mural decoration evoked the kind of activities that took place in the palace's more private rooms.

Above: **Stucco decoration from room 23, in house three, in Samarra**, Berlin, Museum of Islamic Art

The decoration of this panel exemplifies the first Samarra style, in which the field is divided by decorated bands into compartments, here polylobed, which contain recognizable leaves growing from vines. The leaves often have four "eyes" and veins.

Right: **Stucco decoration from room 16, in house three, in Samarra**, Berlin, Museum of Islamic Art

The decoration of this panel exemplifies the second Samarra style, in which the field is divided by plain bands into compartments, here polylobed, which contain abstracted leaves. It produces a flatter and more abstract effect than in the first style.

Below: **Stucco decoration from room one in house one, in Samarra**, Berlin, Museum of Islamic Art

The decoration of this panel exemplifies the third Samarra style, in which the decorative field is filled with rhythmic and symmetrical repetitions of curved lines with spiral endings which create patterns of abstracted leaves. The technique is distinguished from the first and second styles by the use of a slanted, but shallow, cut, which gives rise to its other name, the beveled style. The slanted cut allowed large areas to be covered quickly with molded decoration.

Above: **Wall painting from the "Harem,"** Dar al-Khilifa in Samarra, Reconstruction by Ernst Herzfeld

The interiors of the palaces at Samarra were lavishly decorated with carved stucco and paintings. Many of these paintings faded immediately upon exposure to air and light during excavation and are known best from the excavators' reconstructions. This painting shows two dancers with interlaced arms pouring wine into each other's cups. The subject of the decoration suggests the kinds of activities that took place in the private areas of the Abbasid palaces.

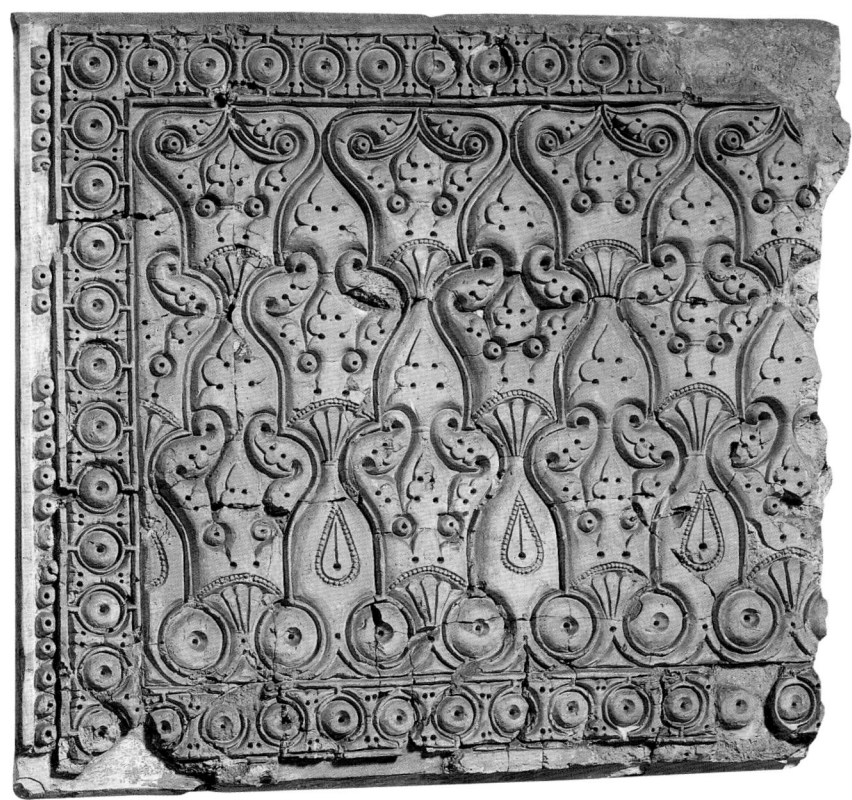

Qubbat al-Sulaibiya in Samarra, 862
The Qubbat al-Sulaybiya, an octagonal structure surrounded by an ambulatory, has been identified as the tomb built for Caliph al-Muntasir (861–862) by his Greek mother. Although the Prophet had disapproved of marking graves with such massive structures, by the 9th century many Muslims were having tombs built over their final resting places.

Elevation and ground plan: the tomb, near the Abbasid palace Dar al-Khalifa, with an octagonal ground plan and a diameter of 19 meters, has a surrounding ambulatory, whose high external walls are pierced by large windows. The burial chamber is sunk deep in the ground.

Tombs

The site of Samarra also yielded another type of building. The Qubbat al-Sulaibiya, standing on the west bank of the Tigris, opposite the Dar al-Khilafa, is an octagonal domed structure 62 feet (19 meters) in diameter surrounded by an ambulatory. It is raised on an open platform approached by four ramps. Ernst Herzfeld, who discovered the building, identified it as the mausoleum of al-Mutawakkil's son, Caliph al-Muntasir (861/862), built by his mother, who was a Greek slave. Two other caliphs, al-Mutazz (d. 869), and al-Muhtadi (d. 870), were also buried there. Although the Prophet Muhammad had disapproved of building monumental tombs, literary references establish that tombs were soon erected over the graves of prophets as well as of Muhammad's descendants. The Abbasid caliphs had initially been buried in their palaces, but as the Alids increasingly venerated the grave sites of Muhammad's descendants, the Abbasids attempted to divert attention by monumentalizing their own tombs. By the early 10th century, they had built a magnificent dynastic tomb, later destroyed, on the east bank of the Tigris at Baghdad. The Qubbat al-Sulaibiya seems to be the first monumental example of this type to survive.

In the decade that followed al-Mutawakkil's murder in 861, the Turkish troops made and unmade four caliphs. The importance of these troops declined in the 870s when they were drafted to fight the Zanj (African slave) revolt in southern Iraq. Al-Mutawakkil's son, Caliph al-Mutamid (870–892), continued to live at Samarra; his nephew al-Mutadid (892–902) reestablished residence in Baghdad. Samarra declined in importance, although it was not, as used to be thought, entirely abandoned. Innovations introduced there continued to reverberate throughout the empire as local governors from North Africa to Central Asia emulated their masters in Iraq.

Abbasid architecture in the provinces

The Abbasids' predecessors, the Umayyads, had conquered the enormous region between the Atlantic Ocean and the Oxus River, but their culture was concentrated in Syria and Palestine, the heartland of their empire. Because of its limited geographical and chronological scope, Umayyad architecture displays a clear and coherent style, but it would be impossible to describe – or even imagine – an "Umayyad" architecture in Iran or North Africa. In contrast, the Abbasids were able to extend their culture over a vast territory, and it is possible to speak of Abbasid architecture and art in such provinces as Transoxiana or Egypt. Abbasid culture was also emulated in Ifriqiya, the province corresponding to modern Tunisia, and even in Spain, which was governed by descendants of the Umayyad rulers that the Abbasids had displaced.

The evidence delineating the Abbasid imperial style in the provinces is widely scattered, making it difficult to paint a coherent picture. Only a few buildings have survived from such distant times, and many of these have been transformed or remodeled as fashions and political allegiances changed. Mosques, which have continued to be used and respected over the centuries, have survived better than palaces, which were normally abandoned once the original patron was no longer in power. Knowing this, builders tended to use more durable materials, such as baked brick, to construct mosques, while using materials that might quickly disintegrate, such as mud brick or plaster, for palaces. Thus, our knowledge of provincial Abbasid palace architecture is almost entirely based on scanty textual or archeological material.

The Abbasid type of hypostyle mosque, known archeologically from Uskaf Bani Junaid and Samarra, seems to have been the most common type erected throughout the empire because its plan could be built in different sizes with virtually whatever materials were at hand and expanded without difficulty when the Muslim population of a given city increased.

The Great Mosque of Isfahan

The largest provincial mosque known is the Abbasid mosque at Isfahan, whose plan was uncovered in the 1970s during the course of excavating the present Friday mosque. The Abbasid mosque measured 226 × 338 feet (69 × 103 meters), virtually the same size as the Friday mosque erected in 836 at the other end of the Abbasid empire, at Kairouan in Tunisia, and one quarter the

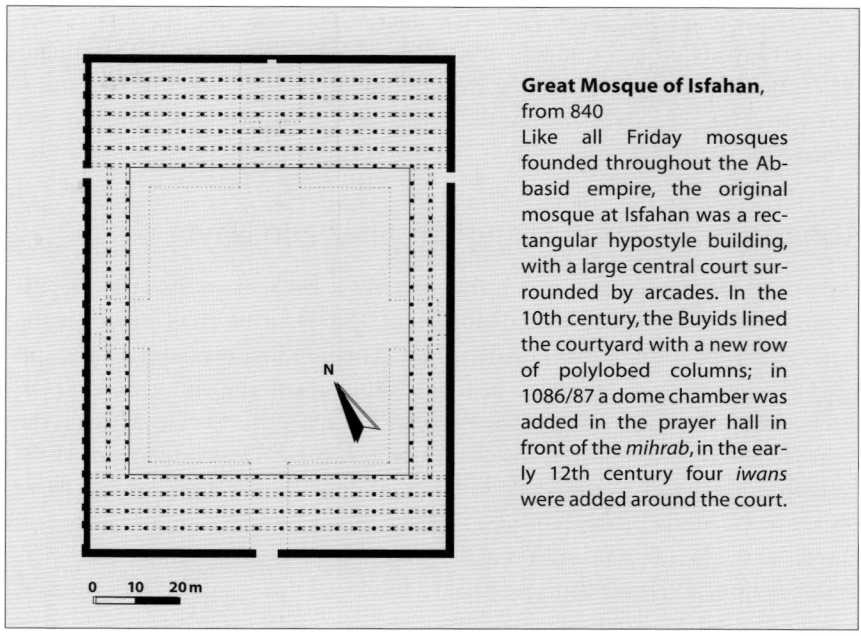

Great Mosque of Isfahan, from 840
Like all Friday mosques founded throughout the Abbasid empire, the original mosque at Isfahan was a rectangular hypostyle building, with a large central court surrounded by arcades. In the 10th century, the Buyids lined the courtyard with a new row of polylobed columns; in 1086/87 a dome chamber was added in the prayer hall in front of the *mihrab*, in the early 12th century four *iwans* were added around the court.

size of al-Mutawakkil's mosque at Samarra. The exterior mud-brick walls of the Isfahan mosque were decorated with a blind arcade. A central court was surrounded by brick piers supporting arcades and roof, presumably covered with brick vaults. The arcades on the sides of the court were two bays deep, those opposite the *qibla* was four bays deep, and the prayer hall was six bays deep. The center aisle from the courtyard to the *mihrab* was slightly wider than the others, suggesting that its roof was also somewhat higher. According to textual sources, this mosque was founded in 840/841 during the reign of the Abbasid caliph al-Mutasim. The apparent absence of a minaret opposite the *mihrab* is remarkable for this period, since one formed part of the mosques erected at Samarra and Kairouan.

The Abbasid mosque at Isfahan was soon remodeled. Archeologists discovered that a line of polylobed brick piers was added around the courtyard. These columns would have given the building a new look at a relatively low cost. The piers were decorated with small bricks laid in relief patterns of circles,

Tariq-khana Mosque at Damghan, 9th century
The mosque at Damghan is the only Abbasid mosque in Iran that preserves something of its original aspect. Like most mosques of the period, it was a rectangular hypostyle building, with a central courtyard surrounded by arcades, but its techniques of construction are traditional. The piers are constructed of alternate courses of baked bricks set horizontally and vertically, a technique known since Sassanian times. The barrel vaults covering the prayer hall are elliptical, a profile also used in Sassanian times, but since the mud-brick vaults have been rebuilt, it is difficult to be sure what the original profile might have been.

diamonds, zigzags, and other geometric shapes. This style of brickwork can be associated with other buildings erected under the patronage of the Buyids (932–1062), although it is difficult to pinpoint exactly when this restoration was done. The Isfahan mosque shows how mosques were founded and remodeled.

Abbasid mosques in Damghan, Siraf, and Nayin

Only one mosque survives in Iran that presents some sense of its original 9th-century aspect: the Tariq-khana Mosque at Damghan, a small town on the major east-west route across northern Iran. The building measures 128 × 150 feet (39 × 46 meters), and has a central courtyard surrounded by arcades. On three sides the arcade is but one bay deep, while on the fourth side, which is the prayer hall of the mosque, the arcade is three bays deep. The central aisle, which leads from the court to the *qibla* wall, is slightly wider than the others. There are no inscriptions in the mosque, and it is not mentioned in any historical source, so the building must by dated by the style of its construction. The piers are made up of alternate courses of baked bricks set horizontally and vertically, a technique known from Sassanian times and used until the 10th century, as at the octagonal pavilion at Natanz, dated 998. The elliptical barrel vaults covering the prayer hall of the mosque at Damghan were built of mud-brick, but since they were probably rebuilt several times over the centuries, it is difficult to draw any conclusions from their profiles. The *mihrab*, which is rectangular in plan, is slightly to the left of center, perhaps to make room for the integral brick *minbar* built to its right in the *qibla* wall. There seems to have been no minaret in the original plan, although a tall cylindrical tower, decorated with brick patterns, was added to the north of the building by a local notable in

1026. Putting together these pieces of information, we can attribute the mosque at Damghan to the 9th century.

Another Abbasid Friday mosque has been excavated at Siraf, a site lying 150 miles (240 kilometers) southeast of Bushire on the Iranian coast of the Persian Gulf. Between the 9th and the 11th centuries, Siraf was the largest and finest port in Iran, but the city declined when maritime trade shifted in the 12th century. The original mosque measured 167 × 144 feet (51 × 44 meters) and comprised a courtyard surrounded by a single arcade on three sides and by a prayer hall three bays deep on the fourth side. A square minaret was added opposite the *mihrab*. The walls were built of rubble held together with gypsum mortar and faced with stone. The floors were paved with sandstone blocks. Coins and other finds suggest that the mosque was begun after 815 and completed some 10 years later. Probably as a result of increasing prosperity and population, the mosque was enlarged and rebuilt by 850. The rebuilt mosque had more covered space and a large area for ablutions outside the east corner.

The Friday Mosque of Nayin, a small town in central Iran on the caravan route skirting the western edge of the great salt desert, provides the best example of how an Abbasid mosque in Iran was decorated. Measuring 154 × 121 feet (47 × 37 meters), the building is unusual among Abbasid mosques in being broader (12 bays) than it is deep (nine bays). The central courtyard has been reduced in size (5 × 4 bays) and is now surrounded by deep halls on three sides and a shallow raised arcade on the fourth side opposite the *qibla*. A variety of piers supports a barrel-vaulted ceiling. A minaret with a square base and a tapering octagonal shaft has been set in the southeast corner. Irregularities in the plan, supports, and vaulting suggest that the original mosque might have been only nine bays wide, which would have given the original building more typical proportions and a symmetrical layout.

Even more remarkable than the plan, however, is the superbly carved stucco decoration of the six bays directly in front of and on either side of the *mihrab*. The cylindrical piers are decorated with the first style of Samarra ornament, in which geometric pearl bands separate compartments filled with leaves. The spandrels and soffits of the arches are decorated with vines, rosettes, and acanthus leaves in a variant of the second Samarra style, crowned by a superb Koranic inscription in foliated Kufic script. The *mihrab* itself comprises three

Mosque of Nayin, mid-10th century
Like Damghan, the central Iranian town of Nayin was an important trading point in the Abbasid empire, so a Friday mosque was built here. Constructed by the Buyids, it has a central courtyard, surrounded by vaulted halls, well-preserved stucco decoration, and one of Iran's earliest surviving minarets.

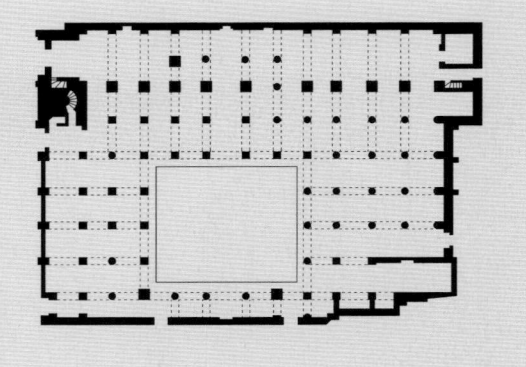

Mosque of Nayin, mid-10th century
The Friday mosque at Nayin is a good example of a provincial Abbasid mosque: it was a rectangular hypostyle building, with a central courtyard surrounded by arcades. The deepest arcade is on the *qibla* side, where a wider aisle leads to the *mihrab*.

Opposite: **Interior looking towards the minbar**, Mosque of Nayin
The walls, piers, and arches directly in front and on either side of the *mihrab* in the Mosque of Nayin are lavishly decorated with stucco carved in a variant of the Samarra styles. Although the mosque is undated, the style of carving suggests a date in the early 10th century, and shows how the metropolitan style was adapted in the provinces.

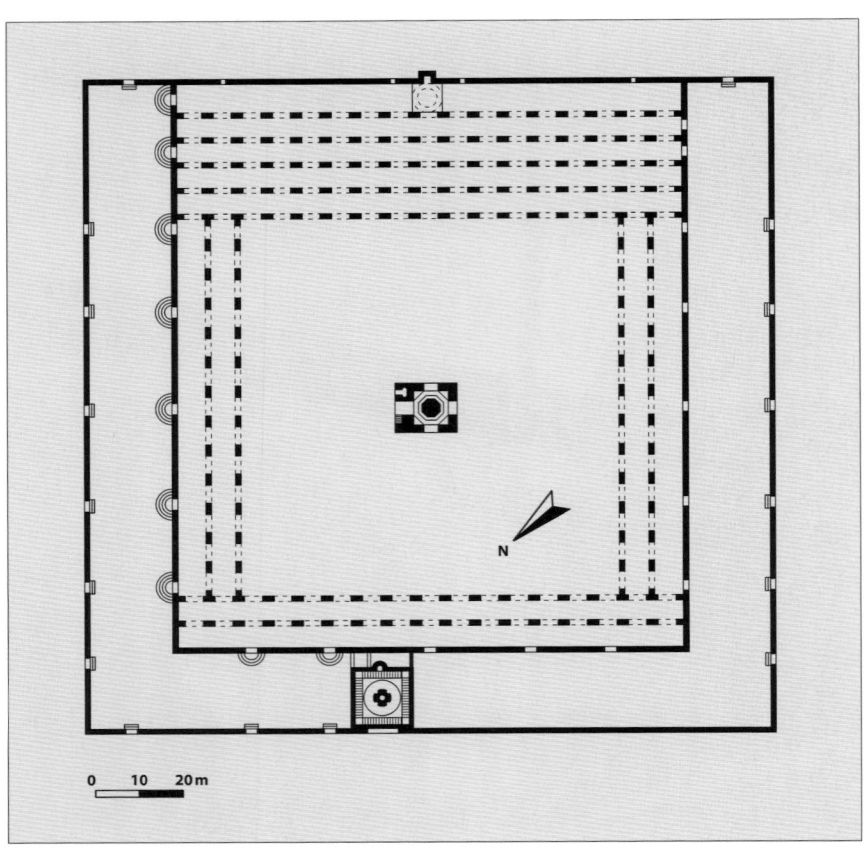

nested niches, beautifully decorated with carved stucco. The innermost niche is destroyed, and the outermost niche is decorated in the first Samarra style, but the hood of the middle niche is the finest, having luscious three-dimensional decoration in high relief. All of these features would suggest a date in the mid-10th century.

Another style of decoration is visible on the piers facing the courtyard. They are decorated with small bricks laid in relief patterns of diamonds, zigzags, and other geometric shapes. This style of brickwork is also found in other buildings in the area associated with the Buyids, suggesting that the court facade of the mosque at Nayin, like that at Isfahan, was remodeled at that time.

Mosque of Ibn Tulun in Cairo, 876-879
The mosque built by Ahmad ibn Tulun, the semi-independent governor of Egypt for the Abbasids, is the best example of how the architectural style of the Mesopotamian capital was received in the provinces. In large part, it retains its original form. The spiral minaret, modeled on those of Samarra, was rebuilt in the late 13th century. In ground plan, it also resembles the mosques in Samarra, but the square proportions and arcades parallel to the *qibla* are local adaptations to foreign specifications.

Courtyard, Mosque of Ibn Tulun, Cairo
Egyptian builders, who had previously supported their mosques with stone columns reused from older buildings, here employed the Mesopotamian system of brick piers covered with a rendering of stucco. The soffits of the arches, as well as their outlines, are decorated with carvings in the Samarra style. The domed building in the background belongs to an adjacent *madrasa*, or theological college, built in the Mamluk period.

Interior, Mosque of Ibn Tulun, Cairo
Rows of massive piers supporting arches carry the timber roof of the mosque's prayer hall. The flat *mihrab* on the pier in the foreground was added by the Fatimid vizier al-Afdal in the late 11th century. The raised platform (*dikka*) between the central arches, also added at a later date, was used by a man with a loud voice to repeat certain invocations of the prayer leader during Friday worship.

The Ibn Tulun Mosque in Cairo

Hypostyle mosques were also built in other areas of the Abbasid realm. Perhaps the finest example is the mosque in Cairo built by Ahmad ibn Tulun (835–884), which preserves much of its original aspect. The son of a Turkish slave who had been sent from Bukhara as tribute to the Abbasid court at Samarra, Ibn Tulun received military training there. Coming to the notice of the caliph, he was sent to Egypt, becoming governor of Egypt and Syria in 869. The following year Ibn Tulun established a new district in Cairo named al-Qatai' ("The Plots of Land") in an area previously used as a cemetery. He built an aqueduct there to bring water from the Nile, as well as a palace, a hippodrome, a mosque, offices, and housing for his troops, all probably based on his experiences at Samarra.

The Ibn Tulun Mosque (876–879) bears many superficial resemblances to the mosques of Samarra, although it is clearly the product of local craftsmen working to the specifications of a foreigner. The building measures 400 × 460 feet (47 × 37 meters), unusually square proportions for an Abbasid mosque. The whole is enclosed on three sides in a *ziyada* (walled precinct) measuring 530 feet (162 meters) each side. This outer enclosure served to separate the mosque from the bustling city outside, and seems once to have contained latrines, ablution areas, and the like. The interior of the mosque comprises a vast courtyard 202 feet (92 meters) each side, surrounded by rectangular brick piers supporting arcades that support a flat wooden roof. The arcades are five bays deep on the *qibla* side and two bays deep on each of the other sides. A limestone minaret, dating from the late 13th century, stands on a square base opposite the *mihrab* in the *ziyada*. Although it now shows some similarities to the Samarra type of helicoidal tower, the present minaret seems to have replaced the original minaret, which was also of a similar type, perhaps even more closely modeled on the Samarra example. The present fountain pavilion in the center of the court, also dating to the late 13th century, replaces the original two-storied structure, which was also used for the call to prayer.

The mosque is built of red brick plastered with white stucco. The plain walls were enlivened with carved plaster bands and friezes which run along the arcades and line the soffits of the arches around the court. They are worked in a great variety of motifs in the first and second Samarra styles. Wooden lintels and door panels were carved in the third Samarra, or beveled, style, and narrow wooden friezes of Koranic inscriptions in Kufic script, reputed to contain the entire text of the Koran, decorated the interior. The new style of decoration seems to have set a precedent throughout Egypt at this time, for similar work is found in the carved wood and plaster decorations of the Christian monastery known as Dair al-Suryani (914) in the Wadi Natrun.

The Ibn Tulun Mosque is often nowadays seen as an Egyptian imitation of the imperial Abbasid style seen at Samarra. The mosque and its accompanying minaret are normally interpreted by modern scholars as architectural expressions of the power of a central authority over the provinces through the imposition of distinctive, foreign forms.

We are fortunate, however, to have several medieval Egyptian sources that describe the mosque, and none of them supports this hypothesis. For example, the geographer al-Yaqubi (d. 897), who had lived both at Samarra and in Egypt, explained that the mosque's form was the product of a dream of Ibn Tulun's.

The historian al-Qudai (d. 1062) explained the unusual use of brick as a precaution against fire or flood, while the bureaucrat al-Qalqashandi (c. 1412) said that piers had been used to eliminate columns, which were tainted by having been used before in Christian chapels and churches.

One may therefore conclude, that, if Ibn Tulun had intended that his contemporaries see his mosque as an imitation of Samarra, he failed, for contemporary viewers did not understand the reference. The relationship between architectural form and political message was, therefore, more complicated than it might appear at first sight.

Nine-domed mosque in Balkh,
late 9th century
Small, square mosques with four supports and nine domes were built throughout the Abbasid lands from Spain to Central Asia. In this ruined example from Balkh (in present day Afghanistan), the brick domes, now fallen, were once supported on heavy brick piers covered with carved stucco.

Small mosques and tombs

Although widely popular, the hypostyle mosque was not the only type of mosque built in this period. At Nayriz in Iran, for example, the prayer hall of the mosque consists of a single barrel vault, open at one end, a type of space known as an *iwan*. *Iwans* had been used for centuries in Iranian architecture, but no earlier mosques incorporating them are known. The early date of the Nayriz Mosque is suggested by an inscription in the *mihrab* which mentions that the mosque had been built in 973/974, repaired in 1067/68, and repaired again in 1164/65. Some scholars believe that small, domed cubes also served as mosques in early Islamic Iran, although the evidence for them is less clear. The undated domed mosques at Yazd-i Khwast and Qurwa, for example, may be older buildings that have been converted into mosques.

In addition to Friday mosques meant to serve the entire community, there were also smaller mosques built to serve smaller segments. At Siraf, for example, at least 10 small mosques, ranging in size between 320 and 1,100 square feet (30 and 100 square meters), were found in the residential quarters of the site. Most of these were simple rectangular structures entered through a yard and divided by an arcade that supported the roof. Three of them had a staircase minaret, an early type known from the Umayyad period.

From archeological evidence, the most widespread type of small mosque was a square structure with four internal columns or piers supporting nine domes. This type is found from Spain (Toledo, Mosque of Bab Mardum, 999/1000) to Central Asia (Hazara, undated), suggesting that the mosque

Above: **Tomb of the Samanids in Bukhara**, early 10th century
The tomb of the Samanids is an exquisite, jewel-like cube surmounted by a dome ringed by four small cupolas at the corners. Once the center of a large cemetery, the building now stands in splendid isolation. Built as a mausoleum for members of the Persian family who ruled Transoxiana for the Abbasids, it was probably inspired by the tombs of the Abbasid caliphs (long destroyed) in Baghdad. Although the building is the first of its type to survive in the region, the fine quality of its construction and decoration show that it could not have been the first built.

Left: **Interior squinch, tomb of the Samanids at Bukhara**
The interior is as masterfully decorated with brick patterns as the exterior. Particular emphasis was given to the zone of transition between the square walls and the round base of the dome. Builders here used the typical Iranian solution of a squinch, or arch thrown across the corner. As the interior of the squinch arch carries no load, builders displayed their inventiveness by piercing it with windows and decorating the area with elaborate brick patterns. This tendency to break up the squinch into smaller parts would eventually culminate in the muqarnas.

of this type, like its bigger brother, the hypostyle mosque, diffused from some central source. One of the best-studied examples of a nine-domed mosque is found at Balkh, a town in northern Afghanistan, once the capital of ancient Bactria and a major city in Khorasan during the Abbasid period. The building is approximately square, and measures about 66 feet (20 meters) on each side. The walls and piers are built of baked brick, but all of the nine domes they originally supported have fallen. The glory of the building is its decoration, for the piers and arches are superbly decorated with deeply carved stucco. The style of the carving, combining the first and second Samarra styles with several new elements, suggests that the building was constructed toward the end of the 9th century.

Other buildings erected in the provinces during this period were tombs, which are known from textual sources and monumental remains. Texts indicate that members of the Alid family were venerated at Najaf, Kerbala, Qum, Mashhad, and other sites, but their sanctity precludes archeological investigation of these complexes, which have been repeatedly restored and enlarged over the centuries. Other figures were also venerated. The Abbasid ruling family appears to have encouraged the veneration of their ancestor Qutham ibn Abbas, a cousin and companion of the Prophet who accompanied the caliph's army in the invasion of Transoxiana in 676. Qutham died at Samarqand – it is unclear whether in battle or of natural causes – and his grave site was subsequently developed as a shrine and place of pilgrimage. Most of the extant complex dates from the 14th and 15th centuries, when many members of the Timurid elite, especially princesses, were buried there, but fragments of patterned brickwork and carved wood suggest that the complex was founded in the 10th or 11th century. The remains of a cylindrical brick minaret from the 11th century suggest that the tomb was accompanied by a mosque as well.

Tombs were also built for local rulers. The earliest complete example to survive is the tomb of the Samanids at Bukhara. The Samanids (819–1005), who descended from an old Persian noble family, had served as the Abbasids' governors in Transoxiana. Ismail ibn Ahmad (892–907), the most successful member of the family, came to control much of the land between Baghdad and India, although he always acknowledged the caliph's suzerainty. Popular tradition ascribes the mausoleum in Bukhara to Ismail, but it is more likely to be a family tomb erected after his death. Constructed and decorated with baked brick, it is a small cube with sloped walls supporting a central dome with small domes at the corners. Despite the simple forms, the interior and exterior are elaborately decorated with patterns worked in the cream colored brick. The quality and harmony of construction and decoration show that this building

could not have been the first of its type to have been built. This tradition, perhaps inspired by the Abbasid tombs in Iraq, only grew stronger in the 10th century. The Buyid rulers, for example, built their dynastic tombs at Rayy, one of their capitals, south of modern Tehran. According to the geographer al-Muqaddasi, writing in 985, the rulers erected high and solid tombs over their graves and lesser princes erected smaller tombs.

Even lesser rulers sought immortality by building grandiose tombs, and a striking group of tomb towers survives from the 11th century in northern Iran. Some of them are located in the mountains, others on the plain; some are domed cubes, while others are cylinders with conical or domed roofs. The most extraordinary example of this ambitious structure is the Gunbad-i Qabus, a brick tower built by Qabus ibn Wushmgir (978–1012), the ruler of the local Ziyarid dynasty. It stands 170 feet (52 meters) high and gains an additional 33 feet (10 meters) from an artificial hill that makes it look even taller. With its soaring verticality and simple form of a flanged cylinder topped by a conical cap, the tower dominates the surrounding plain. The undecorated exterior is broken only by two identical inscriptions which encircle the tower and state that Qabus himself ordered the tomb in 1006/07. Qabus' attempt to attain immortality succeeded in part, for this minor ruler has thus achieved a place in the history of architecture.

Tombs were also erected in Egypt. The geographer al-Muqaddasi mentioned that the beautiful tombs in the cemeteries of Egypt were equaled only by those of the kings of Dailam at Rayy. Many thousands of dated tombstones survive from the period before the Fatimid conquest of Egypt in 969. Most were formerly to be found in the great Muslim cemeteries at Aswan and Cairo, but at the end of the 19th century they were removed from their original contexts in order to be preserved in museums, since scholars at that time were mainly interested in studying the evolution of the Arabic script on them.

Above: **Court of the Mustansiriya Madrasa in Baghdad**, founded 1233
The Mustansiriya Madrasa, founded in the Abbasid capital by Caliph al-Mustansir, was the first theological school specifically established to house all four of the main schools of jurisprudence. The huge building, measuring 106 × 48 meters, has a large central court with *iwans* on three sides connnected by halls and smaller rooms. Its large size demonstrates the strength of a Sunni Islam reinvigorated in the early 13th century under a strong caliph, after centuries of foreign domination and religious schism. This brief resurgence was soon destroyed by the Mongol invasions, however.

Right: **Muqarnas vault, Bishiriya Madrasa in Baghdad**, 1255
This building, formerly thought to be an Abbasid palace, was probably a *madrasa* founded at the end of al-Mustansir's reign. The central courtyard is encircled by a portico covered with *muqarnas* vaults. The *muqarnas* elements are formed of terracotta panels decorated with arabesques. This building and the contemporary Mustansiriya Madrasa are among the very few vestiges of this extraordinary finale to the glories of Abbasid architecture before they were destroyed by the Mongols.

Left: **Tomb of Sitt Zubaida in Baghdad**, 1179–1225

The Abbasid caliph al-Nasir is said to have built this octagonal tomb over the grave of his mother. Its glory is the *muqarnas* dome, consisting of ever-smaller tiers of super-imposed niches. Ths type of dome was common in hot and dry regions like lower Iraq, but elsewhere, as in Iran or Syria, similar domes were usually protected from rain and snow by conical roofs.

Many, however, had originally been attached to buildings, of which several dozen survived in whole or in part. They range from simple structures comprising a single-domed room or canopy to more elaborate, multichambered edifices comparable to the nine-bay mosque type. As these buildings now lack any inscriptions, they can be dated only on stylistic and historical grounds. The nine-bay *mashhad*, or martyrium, of the Sharif Tabataba outside Cairo, for example, has plausibly been dated to the middle of the 10th century because it is identified by later sources as the tomb of a descendant of the Prophet who died in 943. Similarly, some of the simplest mausoleums in the cemetery at Aswan have been dated to the 10th century on the basis of the type of squinch used to support the dome. These structures suggest that by the 10th century the construction of tombs was not only a royal prerogative but was also carried out by a broader segment of society.

Above: *Muqarnas* **dome, tomb of Sitt Zubaida, in Baghdad,**

The interior of the tomb is covered with a *muqarnas* vault, in which tiers of niches are superimposed, apparently defying the laws of gravity, to form a dome. The effect is often likened to a honeycomb, or to stalactictes. The *muqarnas*, the most distinctive feature of Islamic architecture, was used in buildings across the Islamic lands from Spain to Central Asia.

Left: **Gunbad-i Kabus in Jurjan,** 1006/07

Rising like a rocket pointed to the sky, this tall brick tower was built by Qabus ibn Wushmgir, the ruler of the local Ziyarid dynasty ruling the area round the Caspian Sea, to mark his own grave. At 52 meters high, it is the tallest and most extraordinary of a series of tomb towers built in northern Iran in the 11th century and presents a striking contrast to the smaller domed cubes used as tombs by other rulers such as the Samanids. The decoration, too, stands in sharp contrast, for Qabus' tomb is decorated only with two simple inscribed bands giving his name and the date of construction.

Decorative Arts

Sheila Blair, Jonathan Bloom

As rulers of the largest empire that the world had seen to date, the Abbasids patronized a rich panoply of decorative arts. Most objects are remarkable for their exuberant use of color, as inherently cheap materials such as clay and sand were fashioned into elegant wares, which were made all the more appealing by all-over decoration and patterning. Many also had inscriptions that proclaimed the name of the patron or invoked God's good wishes on him. Museums and collectors have amassed some of the finest and best-preserved specimens, but to judge from textual descriptions and archeological excavations, many more types were made.

Textile art

Most important was the art of textiles. The production of dyes, fibers, mordants, and other goods needed to weave textiles, along with the transport of finished fabrics, was the heavy industry of medieval times, comparable to the iron and steel industries of modern times. The importance of textiles in medieval Islamic society is clear from the number of words for textiles that have passed from Arabic and Persian into European languages. Some terms derive from the site where a specific fabric was thought to have been woven. Thus, damask derives from Damascus, the capital of Syria; muslin from Mosul, a city on the upper Euphrates; and organdy from Urgench in Central Asia. Other terms are modifications of Arabic or Persian words: mohair, for example, comes from the Arabic word *mukhayyir*, "choice, select"; and taffeta comes from the Persian verb *taftan*, "to spin."

Left: **Woman at a spinning wheel**, page from a manuscript of the *Maqamat* by Hariri, Yahya al-Wasiti, 1237, Paris, Bibliothèque Nationale. On the right are the hero Abu Said and his friend al-Harith, while in the center is a woman at a spinning wheel, one of the few contemporary depictions of the important art of weaving.

Above: **Dioscorides and a student,** illustration from a translation of Dioscorides' *De materia medica,* 1229, Istanbul, Topkapi Library
This painting depicts Dioscorides, the physician showing his pupil a mandrake root, regarded as one of the most effective medicines.

Fragment of a *tiraz* textile, silk and undyed cotton, 932, Iran or Iraq. Washington, Textile Museum
The most prestigious textiles made under the Abbasids were those decorated with the name of the Abbasid caliph and distributed by him. They are known as *tiraz* (from Persian: "embroidery". This *tiraz* fragment is inscribed with blessings to God and the date, year 320 of the *hegira*, correponding to 932. The middle part of the inscription is missing, but it must have contained the name of the reigning caliph, al-Muqtadir. The text is embroidered in dark-blue silk on yellow *mulham*, a type of cloth woven with silk warps and cotton wefts. Both the type of fabric and the technique and style of decoration suggest that it was made in the eastern Islamic lands, either Iraq or Iran. Its value meant that it was saved and probably used as a shroud in Egypt.

Different regions produced different fibers and fabrics. Linen, for example, was the favored fabric of the Nile Delta, whereas cotton was woven in Mesopotamia, Iran, the Yemen, and India. The most expensive fiber was silk. Knowledge of silk production had been brought from China to Iran and Syria in pre-Islamic times and, under the Abbasids, production increased dramatically. More unusual fabrics were also produced during this period, such as the delicate *mulham*, which combines fine, raw silk floss with heavier cotton and was a specialty of Iraq and Iran. Under the centralized Abbasid state, techniques of weaving were also disseminated widely. The production of silk was spread westward across the Mediterranean to Spain. Similarly, Z-spinning, characteristic of Iraq and Iran, was introduced to Egypt in the mid-9th century, and for a century this technique replaced the S-spinning that was traditional there.

Textiles served various functions in Abbasid society. As elsewhere, textiles were used for clothing, and dress was an important marker of social status. The caliphs and most of the upper classes wore long, loose robes that wrapped around the body. Such a robe is often called a caftan (from Persian *khaftan*), but this was only one of many, many different terms used for these robes, which differed in length, cut, type of sleeves, lapels, and other details. Almost all men wore a turban, which earned the nickname "the crown of the Arabs." Judges and other Abbasid officials wore a special high hat called a *qalansuwa*. Under Caliph al-Mansur, it is said to have become so tall that it resembled a long tapering wine jar, and illustrations in 13th-century copies of al-Hariri's *Maqamat* show figures wearing cone-shaped hats. These garments were often covered by various mantles and scarves, which could be draped around the body and head in many ways. In short, the Abbasids favored the layered look, particularly suitable in a hot and dry desert climate where the temperature drops at night.

Textiles also served as furnishings in Abbasid society. In much of the Middle East, where wooden furniture such as tables and chairs is basically unknown, textiles were used as floor coverings, curtains, sacks, pillows, and spreads. The estate left by Caliph Harun al-Rashid shows how textiles pervaded Abbasid life. At his death, he is said to have owned 8,000 coats, half of them lined with sable or other fur, 10,000 shirts and tunics, 10,000 caftans, 2,000 pairs of drawers, 4,000 turbans, 1,000 hooded cloaks, 1,000 outer wraps, and 5,000 kerchiefs. In addition to the clothing, his estate included 1,000 Armenian carpets, 4,000 draperies, 5,000 cushions, 5,000 pillows, 1,500 silk pile carpets, 100 silk spreads, 1,000 silk cushions, 300 carpets from Maysan, 1,000 carpets from Darabjirid, 1,000 brocade cushions, 1,000 cushions of striped silk, 1,000 pure-silk drapes, 300 brocade drapes, 500 carpets and 1,000 cushions from Tabaristan, 1,000 small bolsters, and 1,000 pillows. The caliph traditionally provided seasonal outfits for his enormous retinue, and other members of court also stockpiled vast quantities of textiles.

Fabrics inscribed with the caliph's name are known as *tiraz* (from Persian. *tirazidan*, "to embroider"), though by the Abbasid period weavers had figured out how to incorporate long and complex texts while weaving. *Tiraz* fabrics were produced in state factories established throughout the empire. The institution of the *tiraz* had already existed in Umayyad times, but it reached its heyday under the Abbasids in the 9th and 10th centuries, with state factories spread across North Africa, Egypt, Yemen, Syria, Iraq, Iran, and Transoxiana.

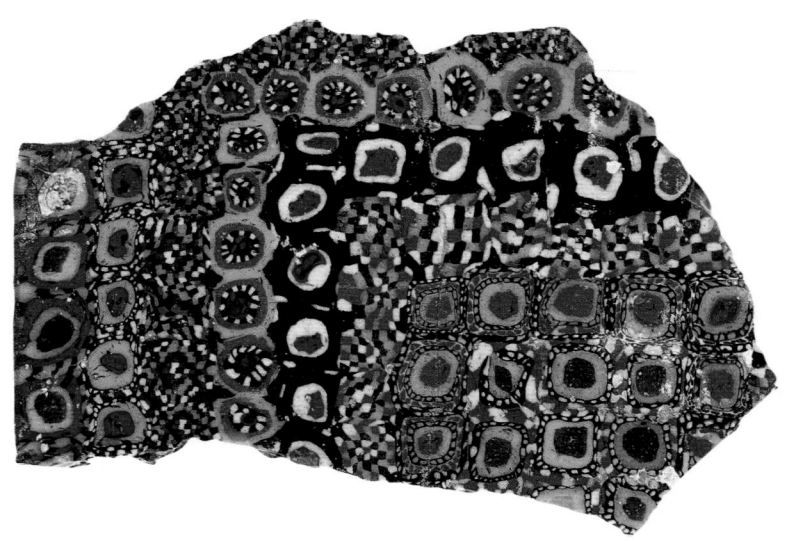

Tile from Samarra, 1st half of the 9th century, glass, maximum width 22 cm, Berlin, Museum of Islamic Art
This brightly colored tile of black, blue, green, yellow, red, and white glass was made using the ancient millefiori technique, in which bundles of colored glass rods are assembled in patterns, fused together by heat, sliced, and reassembled into tiles or vessels. Excavators discovered this fragment in the Dar al-Khalifa Palace in Samarra along with lapis lazuli and mother-of-pearl elements, presumably part of the wall decoration.

Very few of these garments have been preserved intact. Most were literally worn to shreds, and the linen and cotton rags were recycled into paper. Sometimes, the textile was cut up, and the inscribed part, which was deemed to have talismanic properties, was saved. Several thousand inscribed fragments have been preserved, mostly in the burial grounds at Fustat (Old Cairo) or in Central Asia, for these prized textiles were often used for shrouds. Most surviving *tiraz* are linens and other lightweight fabrics, probably fragments from mantles, summer outfits, undergarments, turbans, shawls, sashes, napkins, presentation towels, curtains, and other furnishing fabrics. Surviving fragments, however, give only a bare hint of the full range of materials, for the many literary texts that describe court vestments and furnishings speak primarily of silks, and illustrations from 13th-century manuscripts show rulers and courtiers wearing striped and patterned robes with inscribed armbands, presumably meant to represent elaborate and expensive fabrics like brocade and watered silk.

The typical surviving *tiraz* fragment is inscribed with a single line of Arabic text that offers good wishes and blessings (Arabic: *baraka*) to the caliph. Sometimes, the text also names the vizier who ordered the piece, the place of production, and the date. Over time, both the script and the text evolved. *Tiraz* from the 9th century have shorter texts in angular Kufic letters, whereas those from the 10th century have more elaborately decorated letters and longer texts with fuller titles and more information, such as the name of the factory supervisor. These inscribed fabrics were used as signs of Abbasid prestige and, when the Fatimids conquered Egypt in 969, they had their names inserted in the *tiraz* produced there.

In addition to the many thousands of *tiraz* fragments, a few pieces of silk have been preserved in European church treasuries. These rich and fancy fabrics were brought home by merchants and Crusaders who sold or gave them to monasteries and churches, where they were used to wrap the bones of saints. The most famous is the Shroud of St. Josse, so called because it was used to wrap the bones of Saint Josse in the Abbey of Saint Josse-sur-Mer, near Caen in northern France. It is a weft-faced compound twill with a red warp and seven colors of weft: plum, yellow, ivory, sky blue, light brown, copper, and golden brown. The border shows a train of two-humped, or Bactrian, camels, with a rooster set in the corner, and the rectangular field shows two facing elephants with dragons between their feet. An inscription underneath the elephants' feet, although written upside down, invokes glory and prosperity for the commander, Abu Mansur Bakhtikin, and asks God to prolong his existence. Although the textile bears no date or place of manufacture, the person named in the inscription can be identified as a Turkish commander in the province of Khorasan in northeastern Iran who was executed by order of his Samanid sovereign in 961, so the textile must have been woven before that date. Several elements of the design confirm the Iranian or Central Asian origin of the textile. The roosters and flying scarves on the camels, for example, are motifs that had been used extensively in pre-Islamic Sassanian art; dragons are a Chinese motif; and Bactrian camels are indigenous to Central Asia. We can only guess how this cloth was used. Such pieces were certainly woven in multiples, for setting up the loom was a time-consuming process. The contemporary Persian traveler Nasir-i Khusrau, who came from this part of the world, mentioned that he saw the retinue of the Fatimid caliph in Cairo lined up on horses decked with magnificent saddlecloths inscribed with the name of the ruler. This cloth might have been used similarly, with the elephants upright to the audience and the inscription readable to the Samanid cavalryman seated on the horse.

Shroud of St. Josse, Iran or Central Asia, before 961, two fragments of silk, 52 × 94 and 24 × 62 cm, Paris, Louvre
Silks were the most expensive and most prized textiles produced in the Islamic lands. This silk cloth is inscribed with the name of a Turkish commander in Central Asia, who died in 961. Such silks, probably intended as elegant saddlecloths, were also prized by Europeans, and this example was probably brought by Crusaders to Europe, where it was used to wrap the bones of St. Josse in his tomb near Caen, in northern France.

Below: **Bowl**, Iraq, 9th century, earthenware painted in luster, diameter 27 cm, Berlin, Museum of Islamic Art
Painting in luster was the most expensive way that potters could add color to their ceramics because it required costly materials and a second firing in a special kiln. This bowl, which was discovered in the course of the 1911–1913 German excavations at the Abbasid capital of Samarra, is painted in polychrome luster with a motif halfway between a bird and an abstract design. The ambiguity is intentional and is a hallmark of many of the works of art produced under the Abbasids.

Below: **Bowl**, Iran or Transoxiana, 10th century, glazed earthenware, diameter 22 cm, Berlin, Museum of Islamic Art
Alongside the elegant inscribed wares, contemporary potters also produced bowls decorated with figural scenes of a decidedly "folkish" character. This example shows a mounted rider carrying a sword, while others show animals and birds. In contrast to the spare quality of the decoration on the inscribed bowls, these figural ceramics are filled with ornament, including little birds, flowers, contour panels, and bits of inscription.

Above: **Bowl**, Iraq, 9th century, earthenware painted in blue on a white glaze, diameter 23.5 cm, Munich, Staatliches Museum für Völkerkunde
Wealthy people in the Abbasid capitals coveted the fine, hard porcelains imported from China, but local potters did not know how to reproduce the porcelain of the Chinese originals and made earthenware imitations instead. They covered the coarse body with a thick white glaze opacified with lead or tin. During firing, the color used for decoration often ran, producing a blotted effect.

Above: **Dish**, Iran or Transoxiana, 10th century, glazed earthenware, diameter 44 cm. Tehran, National Museum
This large dish is decorated with two bands of inscriptions in brown and red slip on a white background.

Left: **Dish**, Iran or Transoxiana, 10th century, glazed earthenware, diameter 37.5 cm, Paris, Louvre
This beautiful dish's elegant inscription, in a blackish brown slip on a white background, says: "Knowledge is bitter to the taste at first but sweeter than honey at the end. Blessings (to the owner)."

Ceramics

People in Abbasid times also used fine, brightly colored tableware. Excavators have uncovered fragments of Chinese stoneware and porcelain at many sites, confirming textual reports that these imported wares were available throughout the Abbasid empire. Chinese ceramics were prized for their thin and hard body, made from special clays and minerals fired at high temperatures. Lacking both the materials and the technology, local potters in the Abbasid lands could not reproduce this porcelain body. Instead, they produced imitation Chinese wares by using local clays to make a cream-colored earthenware body, which they covered with a thick opaque glaze and decorated to look like Chinese wares. The open shapes copy Chinese models, but the Arabic inscriptions painted in cobalt across the surface immediately reveal these shallow bowls as Islamic. During firing, the cobalt runs into the glaze, creating a blurry outline to the letters and decorative motifs.

Glass bottle, Iran or Iraq, 9th or 10th century, height 15 cm, Copenhagen, David Collection

Glassworkers in the Islamic lands inherited many of the decorative glassmaking techniques of antiquity and used them to add color to their wares. To make this cameo glass bottle, for example, the glassmaker encased a colorless bottle in an outer layer of green glass. He then cut away most of the outer layer to reveal a design of stylized birds facing a central vase. The curvilinear design also recalls the beveled style of decoration which was popular at Samarra.

Potters in the provinces devised their own methods of imitating Abbasid ceramics with inscriptions. Some of the most striking pieces were produced under the patronage of the Samanids, in Iran and Transoxiana. Made of buff-colored earthenware covered with a fine white slip, these bowls and plates are painted with inscriptions under a colorless transparent glaze. Written in an elegant Kufic script with many interlaced letters, the inscriptions are very difficult to decipher. They must have been valued for their decorative as well as their literary merits. In contrast to the rather casual script on earlier ceramics made in the Abbasid heartlands, the script on these Samanid slipwares is truly calligraphic, suggesting a different method and aesthetic of production. On the earlier wares the potter worked out the text by painting directly on the surface, often running out of space before he completed the final word or syllable. By contrast, the calligraphy on these Samanid earthenwares is carefully planned and must have been worked out beforehand on paper. This use of paper makes sense, for by the 10th century paper was widely available in the eastern Islamic lands, where it had been introduced from Central Asia at least two centuries earlier.

Potters in Abbasid times also developed other ingenious ways of adding color to their ceramics. The most famous – and the most expensive – was the luster technique, in which an already glazed and fired ceramic was painted with metallic oxides and then fired again in a special reducing kiln. During firing, the oxygen from the metallic oxides was removed, leaving a thin film of metal on the surface, which was made shiny by polishing. Lusterwares were extremely expensive because of the additional fuel and labor, special kiln, double firing, and technical know-how needed to make them. The luster technique seems to have been invented by glassmakers in Egypt and Syria at the beginning of the Abbasid period. The earliest dated example is a broken glass beaker inscribed with the name of an Abbasid governor of Egypt who served for only a month in 773, and another inscribed piece was made at Damascus sometime in the 8th century. Although a few complete beakers and goblets are known, most pieces are fragmentary. Both polychrome and monochrome decoration were produced. Potters seem to have taken up the technique from glassmakers in the 9th century. At first, potters seem to have applied several tones of luster in complex designs that covered the surface of the vessel with intricate designs, but in the late 9th century the palette was restricted to one or two tones which were often used to silhouette large figures of animals or people.

Like potters, glassmakers experimented with a range of techniques to enhance the colors and enliven the surface decoration. The technique of wheel-cutting, already known in pre-Islamic times, was expanded, and Abbasid glassmakers achieved particularly spectacular effects by using blanks made in the cameo technique, in which patches or a layer of glass of one color would be applied to an object of a different color. When the glassmaker cut away the outer layer, he left a design in relief on a ground of another color.

Metalwork

Metalworkers, too, devised ways of enhancing their wares with color and pattern. In Sassanian Iran, metalworkers produced many silver plates with hunting scenes in relief. These hunting plates continued to be made in Iran for several centuries after the Islamic conquest, but the designs became more convention-alized and the relief was increasingly flattened. Such stylization is clear on a gilt silver dish decorated with mythical lion-headed birds called *senmurvs*. The earlier scenes of royal hunting and feasting have been changed into a pattern of interlaced bands forming circular compartments filled with stylized flowers and animals. The shape has evolved, too, as the round shape of pre-Islamic dishes has become octagonal. The octagonal shape, however, was not very suitable for the beating and chasing necessary to produce the design, so at some later date crude metal strips had to be added on the outside to support the rim.

Most of the metalwares that survived the Abbasid period are made of bronze or brass. Conservative Muslims frowned on the use of precious metals for personal adornment or tableware. Nevertheless, this prohibition, like the one against wearing silk, was rarely observed, and texts often describe the gold and silver vessels used by the caliph and other rich people. Most of these objects of precious metals were melted down in times of need, and the only ones that have

Dish, Iran, 9th or 10th century, gilt silver, diameter 36 cm, Berlin, Museum of Islamic Art
This dish is a variant of the type of silver dish decorated with hunting scenes that had been produced for the Sassanian rulers of Iran in pre-Islamic times, but the typical round form has been modified into an octagonal dish, the high relief has been flattened, and the realistic scene has been abstracted into a symmetrical design of stylized *senmurvs*. Similar depictions of *senmurvs*, the lion-headed birds from Iranian myth, are found on contemporary textiles and architectural decoration.

survived were buried and forgotten, to be dug up only in modern times. One such example is a silver hoard now in the Iranian National Museum in Tehran. It comprises three bowls, two small dishes, a large dish, an ewer, two jars, a bottle, and a cup. Seven of the pieces are inscribed with the owner's name, the emir Valgin ibn Harun, who is identified as a client of the Abbasid caliph. Based on the style of the Kufic script and the mir's titles, the set is usually dated c. 1000. It served as the emir's personal wine service. Made for an otherwise unknown emir somewhere in the greater Iranian world, it is a provincial reflection of the rich court life that went on in Baghdad and Samarra under the Abbasid caliphs.

Islamic Ornament

Sheila Blair, Jonathan Bloom

Since figural imagery was unnecessary in Islamic religious art, other themes of decoration, such as writing, geometry, and the arabesque, became important. Several of these themes, including geometric elements and vegetal designs, had been subsidiary elements in the figural arts of pre-Islamic times.

In Byzantine art, for example, depictions of people had been set off, framed, or linked by geometric and vegetal designs. In Islamic times, these subsidiary elements were transformed into major artistic themes. Thus, the mosaics decorating the Dome of the Rock in Jerusalem, erected by the Umayyad caliph Abd al-Malik in the late 7th century, are clearly derived from the traditions of late antiquity in both technique and subject matter. In classical and Byzantine art, the vines issuing from vases decorated with crowns and jewels would have been subordinate to larger figural compositions showing Christ and the saints, but in the mosaics inside the Dome of the Rock the vines,

vases, jewels, and plants themselves form the main subject of the decoration. It must be admitted, however, that modern observers find it difficult to determine what, if anything, these vines and vases were originally meant to signify.

In the Jerusalem mosaics, vines, fruit, and flowers are still readily recognizable, but such specific representations were quickly supplanted by increasingly stylized, abstracted, and geometricized motifs as Muslims became increasingly reluctant to depict anything in their religious art. While the arts in secular contexts continued to employ representation, the broad taste for increasingly abstract ornament permeated many other types of art. For example, when the Abbasids transferred their capital to Samarra in the 9th century, the palace walls were covered with large expanses of carved and molded stucco. At first, the artisans employed recognizable foliate and floral elements within geometric frames, as at the Dome of the Rock, but eventually these

Above: **Stucco decoration from room four, in house one, in Samarra**, 9th century. Berlin, Museum of Islamic Art

Below: **Arcades in the ambulatory of the Dome of the Rock** Jerusalem, 1091

craftsmen developed a new type of ornament in which simple vegetal elements, such as tendrils and leaf-shapes, were subjected not to the laws of nature but to the rules of geometry. These elements were combined to create patterns which not only filled the surface to be decorated, but also did not distinguish between the ostensible subject of the decoration and the background. In many cases, this ornament is not constricted by framing elements as in early types of decoration, but it can be extended infinitely in any direction, suggesting that what the viewer sees is just part of a continuous whole.

This type of ornament, known in the West as the arabesque, appeared in its fully, geometrized form by the middle of the 10th century, when such foliate motifs as the vine or acanthus scroll began to be interlaced with geometric frameworks, which themselves were also transformed into vegetal stems. In this manner, vegetal scroll patterns were assimilated to geometric frameworks: stems and leaves were given geometric shape and geometric frameworks sprouted stems and leaves. It seems most likely that this approach to ornament was developed in and around Baghdad, the cultural capital of the Islamic world in the 10th century, but it was quickly disseminated to all the Islamic lands because of the cultural prestige radiated by the Abbasid capital. For example,

the beautiful carved marble panels flanking the *mihrab* of the Great Mosque of Cordoba, installed in 965, are the earliest datable instances of this distinctive and original development. They show how quickly artisans began to adopt this new approach to ornament. A central stem, itself patterned, has tendrils growing unnaturally from its base and tip; the stem provides the armature for a symmetrical interlacing of tendrils, leaves, and flowers that seems to press out against the confines of the similarly patterned frame.

Arabesque elements are found in the thousands of small carved wooden panels decorating the *minbar* from the Kutubiya Mosque in Marrakesh, which was begun in Cordoba in 1137. The individual wooden panels, which were made in four basic shapes, were exquisitely carved with consummate detail by the descendants of the ivory-carvers who had worked for the Umayyad caliphs 150 years earlier. Unlike the ivory caskets, the individual panels of the *mihrab* were combined within a geometric strapwork pattern executed in marquetry of precious wood and bone.

In the *mihrab*, the basic organizing principles of the design are the subtle contrasts between the techniques of carving and

Attarin Madrasa, in Fez, 1323–1325

Main portal of the Ulu Cami in Divrigi, 1228/29

marquetry, the textures of smooth and patterned surfaces, the subjects of geometric and vegetal ornament, and the colors of monochrome wood and vibrantly colored marquetry. Viewed from a distance, the colorful tile-like patterns seem to take precedence, but from close up the viewer is beckoned to explore the intricacies of each individual element. At the same time, as in much Islamic art, there is a strong sense of ambiguity between what is meant to be the subject and what is meant to be the background of the decoration. It is unclear, for example, whether the carved panels are meant to be seen as the background between the strapwork bands. Within this fairly narrow repertory of forms and techniques, which in the hands of lesser masters might have approached monotony, all of these elements are played off against one another in a series of subtle variations, an equilibrium between static and dynamic.

This type of geometric ornament, with or without the arabesque infill, became extremely popular in the western Islamic lands. It seems to have been developed first by woodworkers, who were attempting to make the most of a valuable commodity by combining little bits of wood and ivory, and then applied to other materials such as tile, where such patterns were extensively used to cover the lower surfaces of walls the upper surfaces of which would have been decorated with carved stucco and

wood. One of the finest ensembles of this type of decoration is found at the Attarin Madrasa, erected in Fez, in 1323–1325, where the interior of the building is enveloped in a web of intricate decoration. Glazed tiles ar-ranged in geometric – often strapwork – patterns cover the floor and lower walls. They are separated by a band of writing from the low-relief carved plaster arabesques covering the middle register of the walls. Above, carved wooden beams and brackets support the roof. Each medium has its own typical geometric, vegetal, or epigraphic ornament, and each is intricately worked on several planes. This in-tricacy is often seen as a characteristic feature of Islamic art, and the great 14th-century philosopher and historian, Ibn Khaldun, seems to indicate that the degree of "refinement" in a work of craft, by which he probably meant this kind of complexity, is directly related to the degree of civilization in a given society. Thus, the complexity of design and execution seen in much Islamic art in this period can be understood as a symbol of civilized life.

Using many of the same materials, such as molded brick, glazed tile, and carved plaster, artisans in the eastern Islamic lands developed quite different types of ornament. In Iran, for example, under Seljuk rule in the 11th and 12th

Dome of the Shah Mosque in Isfahan, 1611–1630

were translated into stone. The north portal, which consists of a rectangular frame enclosing a pointed and a "broken" arch, is embellished with a bewildering and exuberant array of fantastic vegetal, arabesque, and geometric motifs, some of which project from the wall in high and even undercut relief. The geometric decoration executed in low relief immediately within the rectangular frame, as well as that just within the pointed arch, was inspired by tile patterns. The Divrigi portal illustrates an important feature of Islamic ornament, namely the portability of motifs from between mediums.

The gallery vaults, surrounding the mausoleum, built between 1305 and 1315, for the Ilkhanid sultan Üljaitü at Sultaniya in Iran, illustrate a new approach to the transfer of motifs in Islamic ornament, once paper had become widely available to craftsmen. The sophisticated designs of the vaults display a wide variety of carved and plaster motifs painted in red, yellow, green, and white. Many of the strapwork panels closely resemble the designs seen in contemporary manuscript illumination, indicating, not that stucco workers looked at manuscript frontispieces, but that in the Ilkhanid period professional designers at some central location began to make pattern books or scrolls, presumably on paper, which artisans could then use on different scales in such varying media as architecture and manuscripts. The new role of the pattern and the pattern book indicates the emergence of the designer as a new type of artist in the Islamic lands, and his role would only grow in the following centuries.

In Islamic art, the arabesque's popularity lasted until the 14th century, when it began to be displaced by Chinese-inspired designs incorporating chrysanthemum, peony, and lotus flowers and cloud bands, but even these new designs retain some of the arabesque's geometric underpinnings. Although some of these chinoiserie designs were disseminated through direct knowledge of works of art, paper patterns were increasingly used in the Timurid period to create designs which could then be applied to textiles, manuscripts, leatherwork, metalwork, ceramics, wall painting and even carved stone. The wide circulation of these designs in the 15th century created a Timurid "international style" which was appreciated from Central Asia and India to Egypt and the Balkans.

Simultaneity and counterpoint of motifs were favorite concepts of Islamic designers.

centuries, plasterers covered brick walls with increasingly three-dimensional and sculptural ornament, particularly in important, but protected, interior areas of the mosque such as the *mihrab*. In more exposed parts of the building, such as exterior portals, artisans used more durable materials, mainly tile and brick. When new mosques were built in Anatolia, after the Seljuks opened the area to Muslim settlement, artisans combined and integrated the traditions of Iranian plasterwork with

indigenous Anatolian, Georgian, and Armenian traditions of fine stonemasonry and carving. The results were often astounding, as in the north portal of the Great Mosque of Divrigi (1228/29), part of a complex which includes a hospital and tomb built by the Mengujak prince Ahmad Shah and his wife, Turan Malik.

The mosque at Divrigi is remarkable for the exuberant, high-relief stone decoration of its portals and *mihrab* in which the themes developed in Iranian stuccowork and tilework

Gallery underneath the dome, tomb of the Ilkhanid ruler, Üljaitü, in Sultaniya, 1307–1313

At the Shah Mosque in Isfahan, for example, two superposed networks of tiles envelop the swelling, bulbous dome. The first is a network of yellowish-gold curved lines that form ogival panels of decreasing size; a second network of white spirals bordered in blue is overlaid. The designer has created a sense of ambiguity and dynamism by interweaving the gold network with the blue-and-white one. Furthermore, the decoration becomes denser as the surface diminishes towards the top of the dome. The blue arabesques are joined with gold floral elements, and the gold ones are joined with blue and gold symmetrical leaf-like elements.

Ottoman artists transformed the Timurid chinoiserie style into a more naturalistic style known as the *saz* (reed) style, which combined long, feathery, sawtoothed leaves with composite blossoms, as well as Chinese-inspired dragons, in a much freer, less geometrical design. The *saz* style, whose name perhaps derives from the reed pen used for drawing it, was applied to such media as textiles, carpets, tiles, and ceramics. This style, which was associated with the Ottoman court, was itself transformed into a more popular variant as 16th-century artists, particularly painters of Iznik pottery, accurately rendered botanically distinguishable flowers such as dianthus, hyacinth, carnation, and tulip, along with cypress trees and more abstract elements in a vibrant palette of blue, green, black, and red on a brilliant white background.

Artists in the Islamic lands had only sporadically looked directly to nature as a source for their art, but Ottoman naturalism was

Spiral tendril plate, Iznik, c. 1540, Kuwait, National Museum

paralleled by quite a different sort of naturalism which developed in 17th-century India. Whereas earlier Moghul decorators had worked in a Persian-inspired style of vegetal arabesque, the decorators of such buildings as the Taj Mahal at Agra, built as a tomb by Shah Jahan in the 17th century, introduced an entirely new type of vegetal decoration. Both interior and exterior of the tomb are decorated with a continuous dado in low relief showing flowering plants growing naturally from a stem in the ground; the same motif is repeated in pietra dura inlay on the two cenotaphs for Shah Jahan and his wife and in red sand-stone on the structures surrounding the tomb itself. This type of naturalistic depiction was quite foreign to the Islamic tradition of conventionalized representation and arabesque. It was inspired by engraved illustrations found in European herbals that had been brought by Jesuit missionaries to India in the early 17th century. From this time the growing plant motif became ubiquitous in all the arts produced for the Moghuls and shows how the principles of Islamic vegetal ornament were always open to new inspirations.

Detail of a panel, Taj Mahal in Agra, 17th century

Tunisia and Egypt: the Aghlabids and Fatimids

The Great Mosque of Sousse, founded in 850
The Aghlabids did not confine the building of magnificent structures to their capital city of Kairouan. Other cities in their territories also experienced a cultural revival, as the Great Mosque of Sousse shows. It was founded by Emir Muhammad I.

128

History of the Aghlabids

Sibylle Mazot

In 647 the Arabs began advancing into Ifriqiya, the former Roman province of Africa, a rich area but weakened by the confusion following the fall of the Byzantine Empire. Inadequate local defenses facilitated Arab aggression, but it was not until 23 years later, with the campaign of conquest led by Sidi Uqba ibn Nafi (d. 683), that the Muslims succeeded in establishing themselves permanently in the area. At first the province was ruled by the Umayyads (until 749), and then by the Abbasid dynasty. At the beginning of the 8th century, when Berber tribes threatened the governors sent from Baghdad and unrest spread through the whole of Ifriqiya, the Abbasid caliph Harun al-Rashid (786–809) entrusted Ibrahim ibn al-Aghlab of Khorasan, one of his generals, with the delicate task of putting down these revolts and restoring order. In return, Harun al-Rashid transferred Ifriqiya to Ibrahim as a hereditary emirate, although on condition of annual payments of tribute and the recognition of the Abbasids as its overlords. Nonetheless, Ibrahim and his successors – the Aghlabids – enjoyed a wide degree of autonomy.

During the century of rule by the Aghlabid dynasty, it was represented by 11 emirs who tried, with varying success, to restore the region to prosperity. Trade and craftsmanship revived the economy of the cities. Ibrahim ibn al-Aghlab (800–812) made his capital in Kairouan, which had been founded in 671 by Sidi Uqba ibn Nafi, and set up an efficient administration there, so that within a few decades Ifriqiya had regained something of its former glory.

The population was extremely heterogeneous, consisting of the original inhabitants – Berbers, Romans, and Africans – and the descendants of the Arab and non-Arab conquerors of Ifriqiya. Many of the influences that left a perceptible mark on Aghlabid culture arose from this ethnic and religious mixture. The ruling class, however, remained true to its oriental roots in its way of life and its system of government.

Internal troubles were endemic to the whole region; the Aghlabids had to put down several rebellions fomented by the Arab army. In 802 and 810 the Arab troops stationed in Tunis rose, and the city was entirely out of Aghlabid control for a time. A period of about 13 years in the reign of Ziyadat Allah (817–838) saw almost constant Arab revolts that weakened the Aghlabid regime, and finally contributed to its fall. The Berber tribes had resisted Arab occupation of the province ever since the 7th century. They belonged to the Kharijite sect, and regarded rebellion as an appropriate way of opposing an unjust or despotic government.

Especially in the capital of Kairouan, the most important cultural and spiritual center of the Maghreb, the emirs regularly had to deal with violent resistance from the population, which, like the local theologians and lawyers, publicly criticized the attitude of the ruling class. As a clever politician, Ziyadat Allah recognized the necessity of directing the warlike potential of the rebellious Arab troops into other channels and distracting the Berbers from their seditious

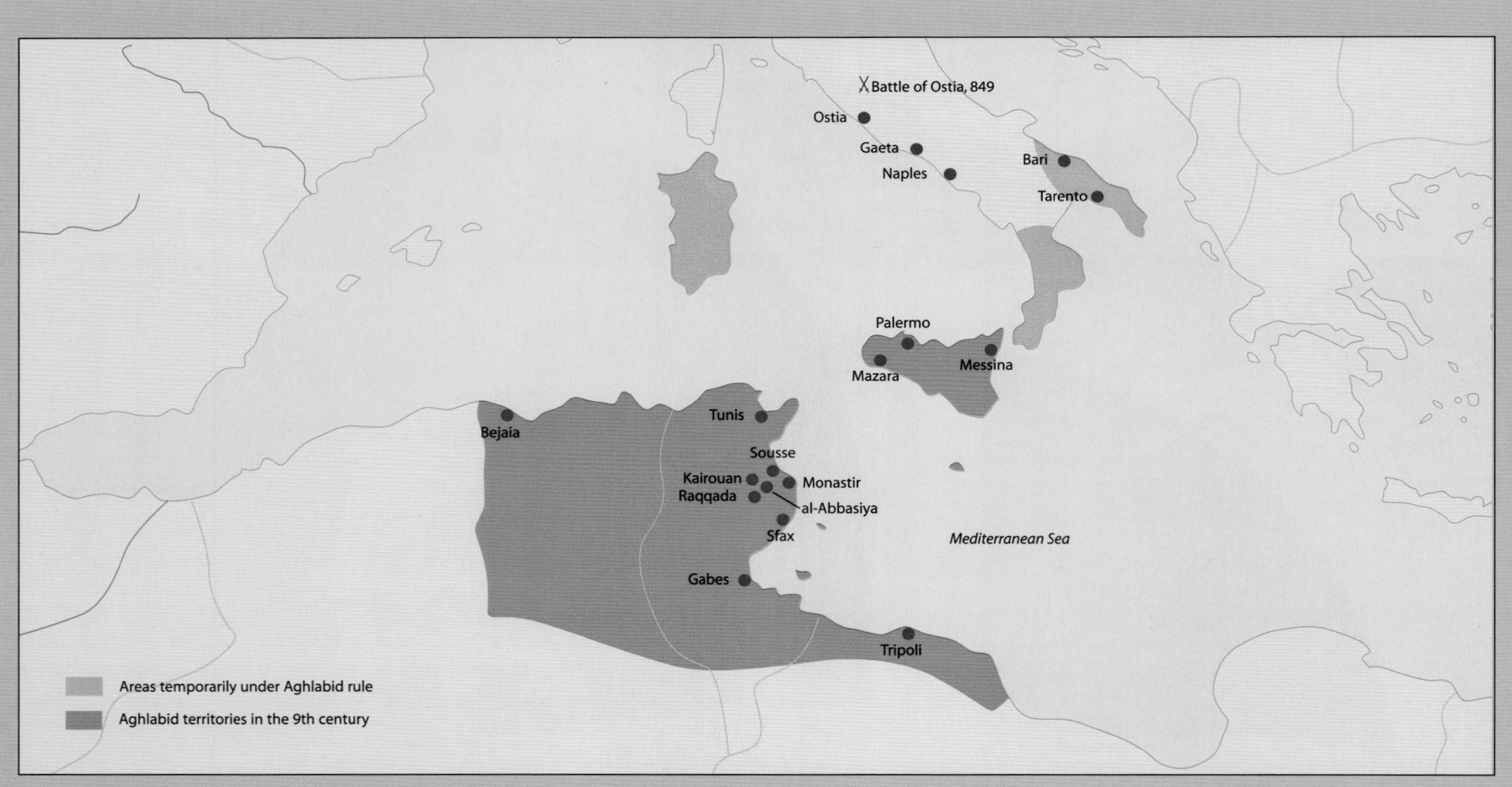

Areas temporarily under Aghlabid rule

Aghlabid territories in the 9th century

TUNISIA AND EGYPT

Medina and Great Mosque of Sfax, second half of the 9th century

Not only the capital, Kairouan, but other Tunisian cities such as Sfax experienced a revival during the Aghlabid period: a Great Mosque with two domes was built here in 849. It was reconstructed in 988. The kadi of Sfax ordered and financed the building of the city wall and the Great Mosque. A few decades later, the Great Mosque was partly destroyed. Dwelling houses and shops were erected on a portion of the site.

ideas. It was with this end in view that he prepared for the conquest of Sicily, a move that also pleased the religious leaders, who approved of the campaign as a holy war.

Sicily was famous for its wealth, which had made the island a profitable target for would-be conquerors since the 7th century. The Aghlabid troops landed in Mazara in 827, subsequently taking Palermo in 832, and Messina in 842. When they had also taken Sardinia and Malta, the Aghlabids controlled the whole western Mediterranean area, and were in an extremely good strategic position. At the same time they also tried to bring continental Italy under Muslim rule. In 840 the Aghlabid troop destroyed the Venetian fleet at Tarento and laid siege to Naples, before advancing to Rome in 846 and sacking St. Peter's. The advance of Islam through the continent was halted only by the destruction of their fleet at Ostia in 849. As a general consequence, these Italian campaigns brought fruitful and lasting cultural exchanges to the entire Mediterranean area.

The Muslims were now uncontested rulers of North Africa, although they had to repel repeated attacks from the Christian kingdoms of Europe. However, apart from the invasion of the Egyptian Tulunids in 880, the borders of Ifriqiya were never exposed to serious danger. The political, economic, and religious fortunes of the Ifriqiya region thrived under the Aghlabids, accompanied by an intellectual and artistic flowering which found its finest expression in the impressive architecture.

800	The Abbasid caliph, Harun al-Rashid, appoints his general Ibrahim ibn al-Aghlab, who was commander of the Khorasan army, to be emir of the province of Ifriqiya (800–812)
802	First rebellion of the Arab armies against Aghlabid rule; the mutineers are led by Hamdis ibn Abd al-Rahman al-Kindi
809/810	Another revolt of the Arab armies, under Imran ibn Mukhallad
817–838	Reign of Emir Ziyadat Allah
824–836	Rebellion of the Arab armies under Mansur ibn Nasr al-Tunbudhi; destruction of Tunis
827	Beginning of the campaign against Sicily, led by the kadi of Kairouan, Asad ibn Furat
832	Conquest of Palermo by the Aghlabids
835	A pact of mutual assistance with Duke Andreas of Naples enables the Aghlabids to establish a permanent foothold on the Italian mainland
840–842	The Aghlabids conquer Tarento, Brindisi, Bari, and Messina
841–856	Emirate of Muhammad I
846	The sacking of Rome
846–860	Tarento under Arab rule
847–870	Emirate of Bari
849	Aghlabid expansion on the European mainland ends with the naval battle of Ostia
856–863	Emirate of Abu Ibrahim Ahmad
863–875	Reign of Emir Abu l-Gharaniq Muhammad II
868	The Aghlabids take Malta
876	Emir Ibrahim II (875–902) founds the new palace city of al-Raqqada
876	Syracuse taken and destroyed by the Aghlabids
879–880	The Aghlabids successfully repel invasions by the Egyptian Tulunids and the northern African Ibadites
881/882	Berber unrest in the North African Zab region is suppressed by the Aghlabids
893	Abu Abdallah al-Shii begins spreading Fatimid propaganda in the northwest of Ifriqiya
896	Unsuccessful Aghlabid campaign to Egypt
902	Death of Ibrahim II at Cosenza; the Aghlabids withdraw from the Italian mainland
904	Emir Ziyadat Allah III (903–909) calls for a *jihad* against the Fatimids
906/907	The Fatimids take the Zab region
909	The Fatimids occupy Kairouan; flight of the Aghlabid emir to Syria

The Architecture of the Aghlabids

Sibylle Mazot

Kairouan – the capital of the Muslim west

At the time of the conquest, Kairouan was a military base for operations in North Africa. Sidi Uqba ibn Nafi, a general of the Umayyad caliph of Baghdad, made it his capital and began enlarging it in 670. Kairouan did not arise, as legend would have it, from inhospitable terrain populated only by beasts of prey and reptiles, but was close to the ruins of a city of classical antiquity. It became the model for a new kind of urban development, and could soon boast magnificent buildings in line with its new role. The Great Mosque and the governmental palace of Dar al-Imara stood at the center of the city; the palace, however, was destroyed in 801 by the first Aghlabid ruler. Ziyadat Allah had the ring of defenses that had been built around Kairouan in 762 razed to the ground after the rebellion of the Arab troops in 824, but it was rebuilt by the Zirids (972–1152).

The population was increasing at such a rate that the Great Mosque, called the Sidi Uqba Mosque after its founder, soon proved too small. It had to be renovated in 703, and then enlarged in 724 by order of the Umayyad caliph Hisham. During the period of Aghlabid rule the mosque underwent three further phases of rebuilding, and it was completely renovated under Ziyadat Allah in 836. In 862 Abu Ibrahim Ahmad (856–863) had the prayer niche remodeled and the prayer hall enlarged, and the gallery in front of the prayer

The Great Mosque of Kairouan,
late 9th century
The Great Mosque of Kairouan was founded by Sidi Uqba in the 7th century, but in its present form dates principally from the 9th century, when the minaret of three superimposed towers was built in imitation of the lighthouses and watchtowers of classical antiquity. It became the model for many North African mosques. The Qubbat Bab al-Bahu dome, built under Ibrahim II (875–902), rises above the porch leading to the courtyard, a prolongation of the central aisle. It rests on an octagonal drum, and concludes the raised center section of the facade, consisting of a central arch flanked by two smaller arches. Its tripartite structure is reminiscent of classical architecture.

Below: _Mihrab_ of the Great Mosque of Kairouan
The interior of the prayer niche, built during renovations in the time of Ziyadat Allah, is adorned with perforated wall panels, and the vaulting is painted with beautiful tendril ornamentation. The side walls and the front of the arch are faced with shimmering metallic luster tiles, some of them from Baghdad.

hall was roofed with a dome. Nothing is now left of the original sanctuary; the monumental ensemble as it stands today dates in essence from the 9th century. The brick walls, reinforced with buttresses, have eight gates in their long sides. The hypostyle prayer hall has 17 aisles seven bays deep laid out vertically in the direction of the *qibla* wall and Mecca. There is a rectangular courtyard in front of it. Twin columns mark off the center aisle, which is larger and taller than the others, forming a T with the transept of roughly the same size and height in front of the *qibla* wall, so that the design is a T-shaped plan. Horseshoe arches rest on the columns, which together number 414 and, since they all come from various different ancient buildings, are of varying height and diameter. Only two of the columns bear cartouches with Kufic inscriptions which indicate medieval origin. The prayer hall has a painted wooden ceiling.

The geographer al-Bakri tells us that, when Ziyadat Allah ordered the complete destruction of the Umayyad mosque, all possible persuasions were brought to bear to induce him to leave the *mihrab* alone. Apparently it was preserved by a ruse: it was left standing between two of the walls of the new building, so that at least it could still be seen through openings in those walls. In view of the perforated decoration of the niche, this anecdote could have a grain of truth in it, but it really derives from a legend testifying to the great religious veneration in which Sidi Uqba's building was held. The present *mihrab* is in the architectural style of the 9th century, and consists of a semicircular niche between two red marble columns. The interior of the prayer niche is lined with 28 perforated marble panels. Its vault is painted with ornamental tendrils, and the front of the arch and the walls next to it are covered with more than 100

Prayer hall of the Great Mosque of Kairouan
The prayer hall is divided into arcades, with round arches resting on columns of Roman or Byzantine origin. Imposts of wood or carved stone were fitted to the columns to compensate for the differences in their height. The wooden ceilings were plastered or decorated with painting, as the remnants in the curve of the vault of the *mihrab* demonstrate.

luster tiles. Some of these come from Baghdad, and were installed in the mosque during the improvements made to it in 862. The *minbar* stands in its usual position to the right of the *mihrab*, and is notable not only for its beautiful ornamentation but also for its age. Its two outer sides consist of 90 finely perforated wooden panels with geometric and floral patterns. Traditionally, these wooden panels and the luster tiles were supposed to have come from Mesopotamia: the tiles from Baghdad, according to this story, were originally intended for the emir's palace, and the wooden panels were to have been used to make lutes, but after a night spent carousing the repentant ruler made the Great Mosque a present of them. However, the nature of the ornamentation, and in particular its execution, leave no room for doubt that the carving was done locally. Two domes emphasize the central axis of the prayer hall, one of them a ribbed dome over the bay in front of the *mihrab*, the other, known as the Qubbat Bab al-Bahu, over the middle of the arcade just outside the hall.

The minaret is placed roughly at the center of the northeast side of the courtyard and emphasizes the long axis of the building, although it does not stand exactly in line with the central aisle. Three superimposed towers rise above a square ground plan with sides measuring 36 feet (11 meters). The towers are linked by an interior stairway, and their total height is 102 feet (31 meters).

Prayer hall of the Great Mosque of Tunis, rebuilt 856–863

As in the Great Mosque of Kairouan, which served as the model for all the Aghlabid mosques, the round arches of the prayer hall in the mosque in Tunis rest on columns.

The aisle parallel to the *qibla* wall is lined by a double row of columns, emphasizing the T-shaped ground plan imitated from Kairouan. Again, columns from buildings of classical antiquity were reused.

The top tower, which resembles a pavilion, has a fluted dome and a horseshoe arch flanked by two blind niches on each side. This sequence of three recurs on the second story, where three blind niches are recessed into each of the sides.

The mosque is captivating in its simple elegance, and represents a synthesis of the typical architectural forms of Ifriqiya in the 9th century. The decoration of the dome and the perforated marble panels of the *mihrab* derive from Romano-Byzantine and Umayyad ornamentation, while the minaret is a reflection of the watchtowers of its time, in particular the two-story Khalaf tower in Sousse. Oriental influences are clearly perceptible in the ornamentation of the principal architectural elements, presenting Umayyad, Abbasid, and Tulunid ideas. Both inside and outside their buildings the architects of Kairouan had a fondness for blind niches with either flat or semicircular walls, surmounted by horseshoe or round arches. Such niches were used as ornamental design elements in the Abbasid east from Raqqa to Ukhaidir, as well as Cairo. The use of luster tiles, at first imported from Baghdad and then made locally, confirms that there was increasing exchange between east and west. However, perhaps the adoption of these decorative forms should also be seen as evidence that the Aghlabid rulers were still dependent on the Abbasid caliphate in Baghdad and its cultural influence, which extended throughout the Islamic world. The Great Mosque of Kairouan represents the synthesis of a number of different tendencies, and became the model for western Islamic religious architecture.

Medina and Great Mosque of Tunis

The city of Tunis was not a very important place in the time of the Carthaginian empire, although it already had a large seaport. With the arrival of the Muslims, however, the fortunes of Tunis began to revive, but it did not become a capital city until the 13th century, under the Hafsids. The building of the first Great Mosque, al-Zaituna, goes back to the time of the Umayyads. Like the Kairouan mosque, it was completely rebuilt under the Aghlabids, and was redesigned in the late 10th century.

An architectural revival – the cities of Tunis, Sousse, and Sfax

Like Kairouan, the capital of the Aghlabid state, Tunis, Sousse, and Sfax experienced a marked revival of their fortunes during this time. All these cities were first founded in the age of classical antiquity. Ancient Tunis had a modest role when the power of its neighbor Carthage was at its height, but after the Arab conquest it grew enormously in importance, while the influence of Carthage decreased. Sousse was built on the site of ancient Hadrumetum, and became the seaport of Kairouan. Typical architectural features of these cities were their massive walls, which in some cases, for instance in Sousse, followed the same course as the walls of antiquity. Urban planning was based on the classic design of an oriental city, consisting of a citadel and a *medina* (town) with its markets and mosques. Sousse and Tunis also had arsenals, since both cities were important as bases for maritime trade, and later on for attacks on Christian countries.

The great religious buildings of Tunis, Sousse, and Sfax all followed the model of the Sidi Uqba Mosque of Kairouan, with some variations, but were more modestly laid out. The Great Mosque of Tunis, also called the Jami al-Zaituna (the "Olive Tree Mosque"), was founded by the Umayyads and later entirely renovated by Abu Ibrahim Ahmad. It has a courtyard surrounded by arcades in front of the prayer hall, which comprises 15 aisles and six bays. The columns, taken for reuse from older buildings, support horseshoe arches. The center aisle and the transept in front of the *qibla* wall are taller and broader than the other aisles, on the T-shaped plan first introduced in Kairouan. There is a fluted dome above the bay in front of the *mihrab*, which rests on an octagonal substructure with shell-shaped squinches at the corners. The round drum is decorated with blind arches and pierced with window openings. All these features derive from the Kairouan mosque, and the fine *minbar* is also very similar to its equivalent in Kairouan, again confirming the important status of the Sidi Uqba Mosque as an architectural model. Above the lower edge of the dome a Kufic inscription states that the building was commissioned in 864 by the Abbasid caliph al-Mustain (862–866), showing that, in spite of the autonomy he allowed the governors of Ifriqiya, the caliph continued to take an interest in his provinces.

The Great Mosque of Sousse, founded in 850 by Emir Muhammad I (841–856), is in the northeast of the city. Its hypostyle prayer hall has 13 aisles and is three bays deep. There is a dome over the bay in front of the site of the original *mihrab*, which was destroyed during enlargement of the mosque in the 11th century. The building displays one major innovation: it has groin vaulting instead of a wooden ceiling. The usual rectangular courtyard surrounded on three sides by arcades lies outside the prayer hall, and an elegant band of calligraphy carved into the stone runs above the outer walls of the prayer hall and the courtyard arcades. There is a round tower with a domed octagonal superstructure in the northeast corner.

The T-shaped plan and the dome in front of the *mihrab* are characteristic of Aghlabid architecture, and the Great Mosque of Sfax, originally of the year 849 and rebuilt in 988, follows this architectural design. The minaret, like the minaret in Kairouan, rises above the central axis of the prayer hall.

As well as these great mosques, more modest places of worship were built, not necessarily to the same plan. Two smaller mosques deserve particular attention. One of them is in Sousse, and was built by a freed slave called Bu Fatata during the reign of Emir Abu Iqbal (838–841). The building, which bears the name of the man who commissioned it, consists of a prayer hall with three aisles and three bays, roofed with barrel vaulting. In front of it, following the model of the Great Mosque of Kairouan, there is an open porch with three

View from the *ribat* of the Great Mosque of Sousse, 850
As in the Great Mosque of Kairouan, there are terraces above the prayer hall, and the slightly raised center aisle is surmounted by two domes. The arches of the portico in front of the prayer hall are less massive, and must therefore date from a later phase of rebuilding. The parapets have battlements as well as loopholes.

Prayer hall, the Great Mosque of Sousse, 850
In the Tunisian part of the Sahel region, architects did not make use of ancient columns, although there were plenty available, but built masonry pillars. The mosque has stone vaulting instead of wooden ceilings. The massive masonry pillars do not produce the light, spacious effect that distinguishes the prayer halls of Kairouan and Tunis.

Cistern in Carthage
Cisterns were part of the irrigation systems found *in situ* and used by the Arabs when they conquered the sites of ancient settlements. An aqueduct brought water from the Zaghouan Mountains to the cisterns of Carthage, and in the Roman period supplied all the houses in the city as well as two sets of baths. Of the 24 cisterns, which are each 95 meters in length, 15 are still extant today.

Mosque of the Three Doors in Kairouan, 866
The Mosque of the Three Doors was founded by a religious scholar from Andalusia who taught at the university in Kairouan. The facade above the three doorways is covered with unique ornamentation, showing the influence of typically lavish Andalusian design. Stone and stucco from the 9th century bear a proliferation of plant motifs, chiseled ornamentation, tendrils, and rosettes, as well as ancient Arabic inscriptions in Kufic script. The minaret, on the other hand, is plain and undecorated.

arcades of horseshoe arches on massive supporting columns. The small Mosque of the Three Doors in Kairouan, built in 866 and particularly notable for its exterior decoration, also has its interior structure divided into three parts. Inscriptions were a particularly important part of the decorative scheme and confirm the increasing popularity of this ornamental element, first used in the Great Mosque of Sousse. Three horseshoe arches stand above the doorways, their spandrels lavishly filled with tendril ornamentation. The upper section of the facade consists of three cornices, two of them bearing inscriptions naming the former Andalusian slave Muhammad ibn Khairan al-Maafar as the man who built the mosque. A frieze of vegetative and geometric motifs runs between them. The building is surmounted by an upper cornice resting on 25 ornamental brackets. By comparison with the sober buildings typical of its period, the Mosque of the Three Doors is striking for the ornamental articulation of its facade, which makes it a unique monument of its kind.

The splendor of the Aghlabid court – the royal cities of al-Abbasiya and Raqqada

Like the caliphs of Baghdad, the Aghlabids built their royal residences just outside their capital. The situation was chosen partly on the grounds of oriental tradition, and partly because of the open hostility of the population of Kairouan to its rulers. Two palatial complexes were therefore built to the south of the city itself: al-Abbasiya (or Qasr al-Qadim) in 801, and Raqqada in 876. Ibrahim I built a complex with a palace at its center known as Qasr al-Abyad ("White Palace"), later called Qasr al-Qadim ("Old Palace"), to distinguish it from more recent buildings. In honor of his feudal overlord, Ibrahim gave the city the name of al-Abbasiya. Initially it was surrounded only by a trench, soon to be superseded by a fortified wall with five gates. At first, only the emir's intimates, including his bodyguard, lived in al-Abbasiya. The place also contained storehouses for provisions and weapons, as well as baths, markets, and a mosque of which we know only what al-Bakri tells us. His description of the minaret – he says it was "cylindrical in form, built of brick, and adorned with seven-story columns" – indicates that it was modeled on the oriental type of minaret. An irrigation system enabled flower gardens and orchards to flourish, and meant that al-Abbasiya was never short of water, which if necessary could be supplied to Kairouan. Not far from this palatial city the Aghlabids build their delightful summer palace of Munya al-Rusafa, where the emir could relax or hunt cranes.

On his accession to the emirate in 876, Ibrahim II ordered the building of a second city, Raqqada ("The Beguiling"), six miles (nine kilometers) south of Kairouan. Originally intended as a summer residence, the complex soon developed into a walled city with a Great Mosque, baths, storehouses for goods, and a hippodrome. Inspired by oriental custom, each of the emirs now built a new residence on coming to power. The Qasr al-Futuh ("Palace of Victory") was built to celebrate the victories won in Sicily, and was succeeded by the Qasr al-Sahn ("Palace of the Court"), the Qasr al-Bahr ("Palace of the Sea"), the Qasr al-Baghdad, and so forth. Under Ibrahim II, Raqqada became so important that for a while it cast its troublesome neighbor Kairouan into the shade. After the fall of the Aghlabids, in 909, the people of Kairouan destroyed Raqqada, and according to al-Bakri the Fatimid caliph al-Muizz (953–975), finally sealed its fate by issuing an order to destroy "whatever is left of the city, and plow it into the ground." This report is certainly an exaggeration, since Raqqada, like al-Abbasiya, was still inhabited at the end of the 10th century.

However, the perishable building materials – clay bricks and stamped earth – could not survive long periods of neglect, and the destruction of the ruins by the people of Kairouan, in search of building material to use themselves, obliterated the last traces of these once magnificent Aghlabid cities. In spite of several archeological excavations carried out since the beginning of the 20th century – although so far confined to a tiny part of al-Abbasiya and Raqqada – it is very difficult to form any picture of the splendid residences of Ibrahim I's successors. However, investigations have brought to light the remains of certain buildings and fragments of stucco decoration, which convey some idea of the lives of the rulers. For instance, the retaining walls of a large water cistern have been found; it was constructed on a trapezoid ground plan measuring 292 and 396 feet (89 and 130 meters) on the shorter sides and 561 and 597 feet (171 and 182 meters) on the longer sides. In true oriental tradition, this artificial lake was intended for princely pleasures, and was the scene of such favorite leisure pursuits as aquatic jousting and boating parties. The reflection of the palace facade in the water would have added greatly to the general aesthetic effect of the whole complex. In all probability, the foundations of walls extending from the middle of the short, northwest side of this pool were part of the Qasr al-Bahr palace built by Ziyadat Allah III in the year 906. Mosaic floors are still extant in three rooms of this palace, one with a pattern of squares and stars containing diamond-shaped, interlaced, and spiral ornamentation. The mosaic in another room consists of juxtaposed diamonds and squares.

Hydraulic engineering – the Aghlabid cistern

The great cistern at Raqqada is evidence of the high technical standards of Muslim architects in the field of hydraulic engineering. Water is undoubtedly a very important feature of Islamic civilization. Not only is it the ruler's duty to provide his people with water to drink, it is also essential for the observance of the Muslim religion, for the faithful are obliged to perform a process of ritual cleansing before prayer, and a source of water near the prayer hall is a necessity.

Many ancient works of hydraulic engineering such as aqueducts, grottoes, and cisterns dating from the Roman and Byzantine period of occupation were still in existence in Ifriqiya, and no doubt inspired the Arab engineers. We know, for instance, that water was brought to Kairouan by way of an ancient aqueduct, which had been put in working order and brought back into use under the Umayyads and Aghlabids. Demographic growth in the cities of Ifriqiya, however, called for the construction of new systems for water catchment, drainage, and supply. Al-Bakri tells us that the Umayyad caliph Hisham ordered the construction of 15 water reservoirs to supply the population of Kairouan. The water supply network was complemented by water towers and a number of cisterns to collect the water from rivers and drainage systems. There is a fine cistern, known as the Sofra, in the center of Sousse. This building, possibly of pre-Islamic times, is said to have been restored by Ibrahim II, but the dating is rather uncertain.

Aghlabid cisterns, Kairouan, 9th-century
Impressive works of hydraulic engineering from the Aghlabid period are still extant near Kairouan and the neighboring royal city of Raqqada. Water was an extremely valuable commodity in this steppeland region, and the engineers of classical antiquity had already begun to build systems that would ensure a supply. A series of extraordinary 9th-century structures has been preserved, including these two circular pools. They served not only as water reservoirs and filtration cisterns, but as places where the rulers could enjoy leisure pursuits such as aquatic jousts and boating parties.

Inner courtyard of the *ribat* of Monastir, 796
Living quarters, prayer rooms and domestic offices, bedchambers and casemates were arranged on several floors around the inner courtyard of the *ribat*. On the south side of the courtyard of this *ribat* for men, which now houses a museum, there is access to the smaller *ribat* for women, which had its own gateway to the world outside.

The cistern, constructed on a rectangular ground plan, is covered with a barrel vault which rests on 12 square pillars and is sub-divided into 20 sections. The apex of the vaulting contains rectangular openings through which the water could be brought in from outside. In addition, there is a small, round settling tank which is situated on the south side of the cistern.

The Aghlabids became masters of the building of outdoor cisterns – not all of them, of course, as large as the lake at Raqqada. Massive rectangular water reservoirs have been preserved near the two palatial cities. With round buttresses at their corners and along the longer sides, they resemble fortifications. However, the most spectacular examples of such reservoirs were undoubtedly those built about a half mile north of Kairouan, and known as the "Aghlabid cisterns." They are two linked circular pools, the smaller of which has a diameter of 123 feet (37.4 meters) and a depth of about 16 feet (5 meters); it was designed to collect the water of a nearby river and act as a settling tank. The filtered water flowed through a small opening linking this pool to the larger one, which has a diameter of over 430 feet (131 meters). The actual reservoir was a vaulted cistern, which also received pure water brought along the Roman aqueduct from springs some 25 miles (40 kilometers) from Kairouan. Water pipes ran from this reservoir and finally carried the water to various points in the city. These two cisterns are impressive for their construction, and not just for their considerable size. As with the artificial lake at Raqqada, the walls were strengthened inside and outside by semicircular buttresses, and like that lake the larger basin must also have been used for leisure pursuits, for there was an octagonal tower in the middle of it, surmounted by a top floor resembling a pavilion with four doors which would have given access to a boat.

Prayer and fighting – the construction and function of the Islamic *ribat*

Far removed from the magnificence of the palaces, a special kind of military architecture developed, owing much to the traditional Romano-Byzantine art of building the kinds of fortifications with which it is sometimes confused. The period during which Ifriqiya was exposed to many and various threats from the European powers led to the building of a series of fortified structures along the coast. They were described by the term *ribat*, and acted principally as bases from which naval expeditions set out to make conquests in Sicily and the other islands of the western Mediterranean.

Closely connected with the *ribat* are the concepts of meditation and of a holy war (*jihad fi sabil allah*), for not only did the faithful seek peace and seclusion in them, but they were also meeting places for a holy war's warriors (*al-murabitun*). To fight for the faith is a sacred Islamic duty, incumbent on every Muslim depending on his age and his physical constitution; the battle may also take the form of an intellectual or even a spiritual struggle. Finally, the *ribat* represented a place of refuge in times of danger for the inhabitants of local villages, and could sometimes be used to store such treasures as the 30 consignments of gold that Ziyadat Allah III left in the *ribat* of Sousse when he escaped from the Fatimids in 909.

The institution of the *ribat* implied not only a certain way of life but also a special architectural style, with some similarity to a number of the caravanserais located in Central Asia and Anatolia. Typical features of the Aghlabid *ribat* are a square ground plan, and a fortified wall with a round tower at each corner and semicircular towers in the middle of the curtain walls. The rooms were grouped around a courtyard and distributed over several floors. They consisted of living rooms, a prayer hall, as well as storerooms for provisions and weapons.

South side of the *ribat* of Sousse,
early 9th century
The porch is placed in the middle of the curtain wall. The rectangular bastion at the southeast corner is surmounted by a tower in the shape of a truncated cone, which served the *ribat* as a minaret. There is an inscription on the tower doorway (not shown here) stating that Ziyadat Allah built the *ribat* in 821. However, soil analysis does not support his claim to be its founder, and clearly shows that it was originally built earlier, in the 8th century.

Since there were also reservoirs of water, the inhabitants were well equipped to resist a siege.

The *ribat* of Monastir, founded in 796, underwent a great deal of rebuilding, particularly during its enlargement in the 10th century, so that it is difficult to establish the original ground plan. The square fortified wall, with sides measuring 130 feet (40 meters), had round or polygonal bastions along it. The various parts of the building were arranged on several floors around the large inner courtyard, and included two prayer halls of different sizes, one of them for women. There was a *mihrab* on the terrace, so that the inhabitants could pray in the open air. A tall tower in the southeast corner fulfilled two functions, acting as both watchtower and minaret. Monastir had not only its "great *ribat*" but also several smaller buildings, although the traces of some of them have now disappeared. Their building was justified by the enormous influx of people coming into Monastir, a place of great importance in the politics of the holy war. It enjoyed such prestige that it was said a visit to Monastir opened up the way to Paradise.

As the inscription on the door of the tower tells us, the *ribat* of Sousse was built by Ziyadat Allah in 821, to the north of the city, and slightly removed from it. The building, of quarry stone, is comparable in size with the *ribat* of Monastir. Vaulted, windowless living areas are grouped around the inner courtyard on two levels. On the ground floor, a mosque occupies the whole south side, with a portal in front of its center. A rather exaggeratedly high dome rises in front of the *mihrab*, which is among the oldest in Ifriqiya and is surprisingly rustic in character, a feature no doubt explained by its great age. The ceilings of the rooms resemble those in the Great Mosque and the Bu Fatata Mosque in Sousse. Access to the terraces, which have a parapet around them, once fortified by battlements, is by way of a staircase in the southwest corner. As in Monastir, a tower shaped like a truncated cone rises to a height of 50 feet (15 meters) above the eastern corner. The *ribat* of Sousse is probably older than the inscription suggests. Soil analysis has clearly distinguished two phases of

The ribat of Monastir, founded 796
The original plain ground plan had a square exterior wall fortified with bastions. During the 10th century, however, the place was enlarged, and became a huge complex of buildings consisting of a number of *ribats* fitted together. The ribat also gave the city its name, which derives from the Greek word for a monastery, *monasterion*.

construction: the original building of the 8th century, and its reconstruction under Ziyadat Allah. There is also evidence that the site was occupied in classical antiquity. Many *ribats* in Ifriqiya were constructed on the sites of earlier military buildings, for instance Younga to the south of Sfax, where medieval walls rest on the foundations of a Byzantine fort. Not only *ribats* but smaller fortifications, too, were built as coastal defenses, and consisted of walled complexes which could accommodate a small garrison.

While some examples of the Ifriqiyan *ribat* were built in preparation for a holy war and as a defense against the threat from Christian countries, they could not halt the Shiites, who came overland from the east, the source of all the Muslim invasions of Ifriqiya. This time they came to crush the Aghlabids and, in 909, to raise a new dynasty to power, the Fatimids.

The Fatimids

History
Sibylle Mazot

The origin of the Fatimids is obscure, and is still a controversial subject to this day. The Fatimids themselves claimed descent from the Prophet's daughter Fatima and her husband Ali, Muhammad's cousin. The dynasty arose in Khuzistan in southern Iraq in the middle of the 9th century. Its members belonged to the Shiite Ismaili sect, which disputed the legitimacy of both the Umayyad and Abbasid caliphs, recognizing as Muhammad's successors (the imams) only the descendants of the Prophet's cousin Ali. Their aim was to bring down the Sunni caliphate of Baghdad, since, in their view, it had usurped power. They believed that a "hidden" imam, the Mahdi ("the Rightly Guided One"), would at last appear, depose the caliph, and reunite the Islamic world. Alarmed by this revolutionary prophecy, the Abbasids persecuted those who proclaimed it. The Fatimids, now obliged to leave Khuzistan, went to Salamiya in Syria, where they continued to proselytize, sending missionaries out all over the Islamic countries. One of these missionaries was Abu Abdallah al-Shii, who settled in Ifriqiya in the early 10th century and won useful support from the Berber tribes. Meanwhile, the leader of the Fatimids, Ubaidallah, had to flee from Salamiya to escape the Abbasid governor, going first to Palestine and Egypt, and then to North Africa. When he was arrested for his active propaganda operations in Sijilmasa in southeast Morocco, he was freed by Abu Abdallahal-Shii, by now the master of Ifriqiya. In 910 Ubaidallah entered Raqqada in triumph, had himself proclaimed the Mahdi, and founded the Shiite Fatimid caliphate in Tunisia. His real ambition, however, was to move east and conquer Egypt, Baghdad, and Constantinople.

Like their predecessors, the Fatimids had to contend with many internal political crises, confronting the Berber tribes as well as the Rustumids and Idrisids, who feared for the independence of their rule in Morocco and consequently refused to recognize the caliphate. There was also much dissension in the Mahdi's own circles, coming to a head in the banishment of Abu Abdallah al-Shii and finally his execution in 911. Efficient policies, particularly in the fiscal sector, filled the Fatimid coffers and allowed the ruler a luxurious lifestyle. Ubaidallah's dream of ruling Egypt, however, was not yet to be fulfilled. His son al-Qaim, who later succeeded him as caliph (940–946), failed in two campaigns, and a third in 925 was no more successful. However, the Fatimids were able to assert their dominion over the Muslims of Sicily, which was now ruled by an energetic emir, Hasan ibn Ali al-Kalbi.

Fatimid doctrine was at odds with the Sunni beliefs still dominant locally, and also with Kharijism; the Kharijites, under the Berber leader Abu Yazid, hoped to put an end to Shiite rule. In 943/944 Abu Yazid and his men represented a threat to the government of al-Mansur (946–953), who had succeeded al-Qaim. (Abu Yazid was also known as "the man with the donkey," since for several years he chose that animal as his mount.) They managed to gain control of major cities such as Raqqada, Kairouan, and Sousse, but they had to abandon their attempt to take Mahdiya after laying siege to it for several months. The cruel atrocities committed by Abu Yazid's men quickly robbed them of popular support, and when their leader was taken prisoner in 947 the movement petered out. The Fatimids, on the other hand, consolidated their power in Ifriqiya after this

Courtyard facade of the Azhar Mosque Cairo, founded 970–972
When Cairo was founded, the Azhar Mosque was the religious center of the city. The lavish design of the facade is inspired by the older Ibn Tulun Mosque, with an alternating sequence of blind niches and rosettes in the spandrels and over the apexes of the arches. The pointed arches were added during renovations under Caliph al-Hafiz (1129–1149), while the stepped battlements are typical of the early Fatimid style.

Woman flute player, Egypt or Tunisia, 10th century, marble. Bardo Museum, Tunis
Although the Koran itself does not forbid the depiction of living beings, a tradition to that effect developed. Figural decoration was especially common in the early Islamic period for secular buildings such as the palaces and houses of persons of high rank. It conveys an idea of the everyday life and amusements of the Fatimid court.

crisis, and all the western provinces were finally pacified under al-Muizz (953–975). After half a century of strained relations with Byzantium, the Fatimids and the Roman emperor of the east, Nicephoros Phocas, finally signed a peace treaty in 967.

Ubaidallah's dream became reality under al-Muizz, when he ventured on the invasion of Egypt, a country which had considerable resources but was facing a severe recession after several poor harvests. The Fatimids waited for a favorable moment before the campaign was entrusted to a Slav officer named Jauhar. Active propaganda paved the way for his arrival, and negotiations with the population over religious liberty and reforms began. In 969 Jauhar conquered Fustat, where he showed a tolerant attitude toward Sunnis, Christians, and Jews. This climate of peaceful coexistence was characteristic of the two centuries of Shiite rule of Egypt, and was broken only by a period under the temperamental and violent Caliph al-Hakim (996–1021), when Christians and Jews were persecuted. It was after al-Hakim's reign that the religious community of Druses who revered him as a divine incarnation arose. The autonomy allowed to the various religious communities contributed to the remarkable revival of Egypt's economic fortunes. Jauhar had a new city built near Fustat, where he had pitched his field camp: it was called al-Qahira (Cairo), "the victorious." Cairo became the capital of the state in 973 when al-Muizz transferred the ruler's seat from Ifriqiya to Egypt, transferring responsibility for Ifriqiya to Buluggin (d. 984), a Zirid of Berber origin whom he appointed emir.

In 970 Mecca and Medina placed themselves under the protection of the Fatimids, who also extended their dominion to Yemen, but met with fierce resistance when they tried to move on into Syria and Palestine. Ubaidallah's aim appeared to have been achieved in 1058 when the Abbasid caliph fled and Baghdad was briefly occupied. However, the occupation of Baghdad and the recognition of Caliph al-Mustansir (1036–1094) represented both the culmination and the turning point of Fatimid rule, for their border provinces were slipping away from the Fatimids again.

In the west, in 1048 the Zirids of North Africa refused to recognize the supremacy of Cairo, made common cause with the Abbasids, and returned to the Sunni fold. Thereupon al-Mustansir sent troops of Upper Egyptian Arab nomads, the Banu Hilal and Banu Sulaiman, to the Maghreb, where they laid waste to the country and the cities. The political equilibrium of the region was permanently disturbed, and the old centers began falling into decay. The situation was no better in the northern provinces, and Syria was lost once and for all in 1076. As a result, there were economic problems, for the Fatimids had lost an important source of income, and the border regions were also weakened, a particularly crucial factor when the Christian threat was increasing at a considerable rate.

Bad harvests, famines, and anarchy dogged the failing regime. In 1068 the state coffers were empty, and the caliph's guards and administrative functionaries, who had not been paid, sacked the palace. To halt the process of decline, al-Mustansir appealed for aid to an Armenian general, Badr al-Jamali, who had distinguished himself as governor of Syria and Palestine. His reforms revived the fortunes of Egypt. The income from agricultural produce, crafts, and the spice trade was immense, and a strong, gold-based

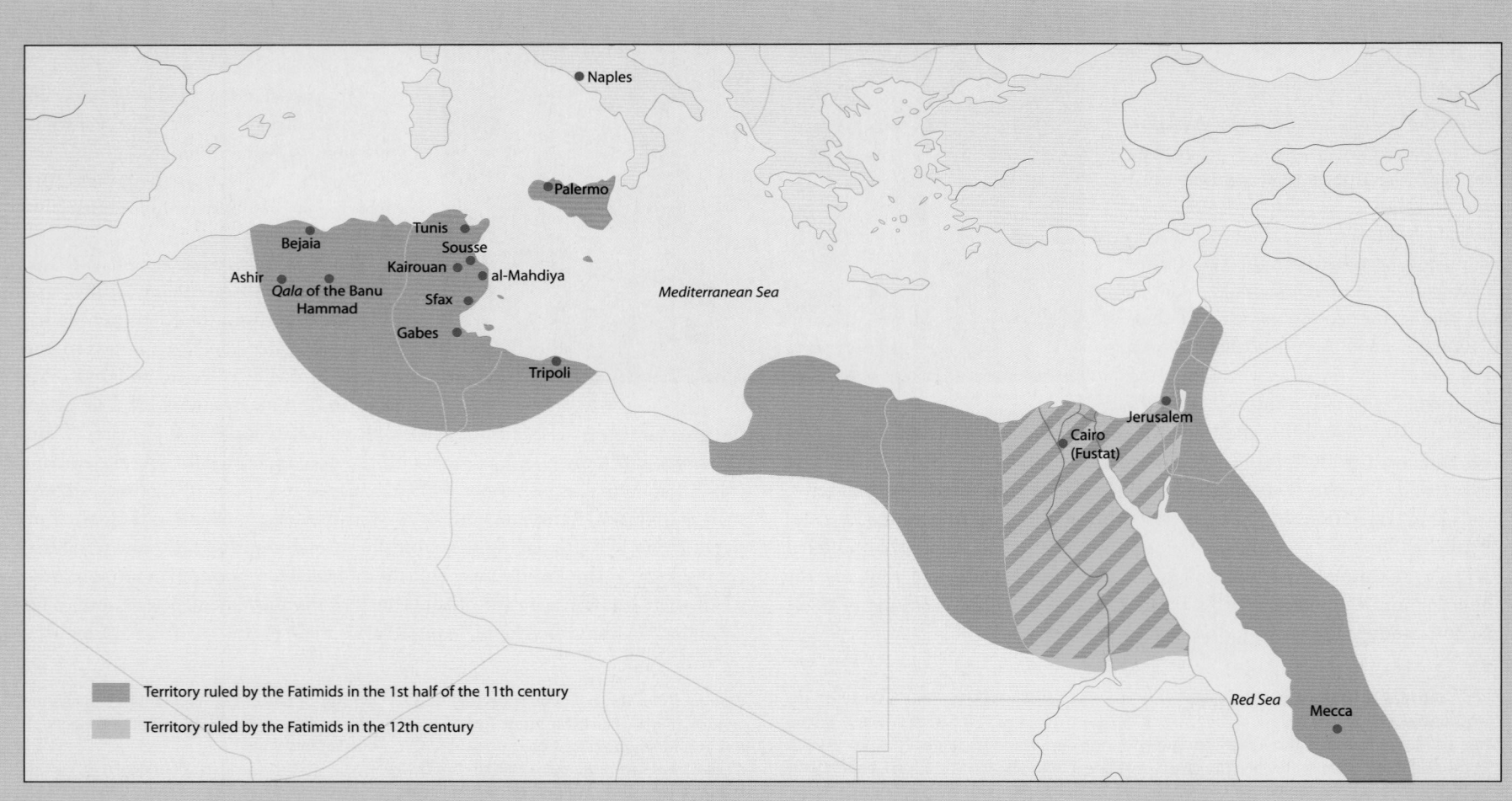

Territory ruled by the Fatimids in the 1st half of the 11th century

Territory ruled by the Fatimids in the 12th century

currency boosted the economy. Nonetheless, economic crises and quarrels over the succession, palace intrigues, and the outside threat from Christendom, finally spelled doom for the rule of the Fatimids. In 1159, Saladin, a general in the service of the Syrian ruler Nur al-Din, took Cairo, overthrew the Fatimid caliphate, and in 1171 restored supreme power to the Abbasids.

Drawing of two warriors, Fustat, 11th century. Ink on paper, (14 × 14 cm). Cairo, Museum of Islamic Art
This drawing is from a manuscript, and shows two warriors, in magnificent garments, to the right and, to the left of a highly stylized tree. The warrior on the left is holding a spear in his right hand, and is wearing a sword at his belt.

The execution of the warriors' robes and faces is of high artistic quality, showing obvious oriental influence. The Kufic inscription reads: "Fame and riches to the commander Abu Mansur."

909	Abu Abdallah al-Shii succeeds in expelling the Aghlabids from Ifriqiya	1017–1021	Rise of the new Druse religious community, venerating the Fatimid caliph al-Hakim (996–1021) as an incarnation of God	1095	The Fatimids take southern Palestine
910	Ubaidallah al-Mahdi becomes caliph in al-Raqqada (909–934)	1021–1036	Caliphate of al-Zahir	1098	Siege of Jerusalem by the Fatimid vizier al-Afdal
917	Hasan ibn Ali al-Kalbi becomes governor of Sicily (917–936)	1036–1094	Caliphate of al-Mustansir	1099	The Fatimid armies are defeated by the Crusaders at Acre; the First Crusade (1096–1099) ends with the conquest of Jerusalem
921	Mahdiya becomes the new palace city of the Fatimid caliphate	1043–1076	The Fatimids lose control of Syria		
		1048/49	The Zirids make themselves independent in Kairouan	1101–1130	Caliphate of Amir
944–947	The Ibadites, led by Abu Yazid, rebel against the Shiite Fatimids	1057/58	The Fatimids incite the Banu Hilal ("Huns of Islam") to invade and lay waste to the Zirid regions of Ifriqiya	1102	King Baldwin I of Jerusalem (1100–1118) defeats the Fatimids at Ramla
934–946	Caliphate of al-Qaim				
953–975	Caliphate of al-Muizz			1153	King Baldwin III of Jerusalem takes the city of Ascalon on the Syrian coast from the Fatimids
967	Peace treaty with Byzantium	1058/59	With the aid of the Mamluk officer Arslan al-Basasiri, the Fatimids conquer Baghdad		
969	The Fatimids conquer Egypt and found Cairo			1163–1168	The Fatimid empire is downgraded to something like the status of a Frankish protectorate by an alliance with the kingdom of Jerusalem
970	Mecca and Medina recognize the Fatimid caliphate	1073–1094	The Fatimid empire is governed by the emir and vizier Badr al-Jamali		
973	Cairo becomes the capital of the Fatimid empire; Ifriqiya is now governed by the Zirid Buluggin	1089	Acre, Tyre, and other Palestinian seaport towns are occupied by the Fatimids	1164	First military operation in Egypt by Nur al-Din al-Zangi, emir of Aleppo; his army, led by the Kurdish officer Shirkuh, reinstates the former Fatimid vizier Shawar in office
		1094	Religious schism dividing the Fatimids into Nizarites and Mustalites		
975–996	Caliphate of al-Aziz				

1167	Second attempt by Nur al-Din al-Zangi to take Egypt
1168–1169	The Franks, under King Amalric, attempt to conquer Egypt; Caliph al-Adid (1160–1171) asks Nur al-Din al-Zangi for help, and he orders the third Egyptian campaign, led by the Ayyubid generals Sirkuh and Saladin
1169	Saladin becomes vizier of the Fatimids
1171	Saladin (1169–1193) brings down the Fatimid caliphate, makes Egypt part of the Abbasid empire again, and himself founds the Ayyubid dynasty in Egypt and Syria

Architecture

Sibylle Mazot

The long period of Fatimid rule, lasting almost three centuries, and the dynasty's political and ideological principles brought with them a major architectural revival. Clear evidence of change is provided by the monuments of the period, with their many new or additional features deriving from the traditions and cultures of the locations where they were distributed.

Mahdiya and al-Mansuriya

When Ubaidallah seized power in Ifriqiya in 910, at first he moved into the Aghlabid palace city of Raqqada, but political turmoil induced him to look for somewhere else. His choice fell on Mahdiya. No doubt the decision was made for strategic reasons, together with the wish to create a new capital – involving the replacement of the entire ruling class – but it was also in line with Ubaidallah's ambition to make his young state a great naval power.

The 9-mile (14-kilometer) peninsula on which the city lay was surrounded by massive fortifications, with access from the landward side secured by two strong gateways. Ubaidallah laid out a harbor and built an arsenal, a palace, and a Great Mosque. Remains of the fortifications and one of the two city gates, the Sqifa al-Kahla, are still extant. The gatehouse consists of a vaulted anteroom 108 feet (33 meters) long and 16 feet (5 meters) wide, and a series of six doors, which, according to medieval written sources, were adorned "with bronze lions, modeled in relief, and facing each other." These doors reinforced the defenses. Light fell into the Sqifa al-Kahla through two small openings on its narrow sides, and there were benches for the guards in the niches. According to the Iraqi geographer Ibn Hauqal, the gates of Mahdiya surpassed

The Sqifa al-Kahla gatehouse in Mahdiya,
10th century
This gatehouse controlled access to the peninsula, linking the royal city to its suburbs on the mainland. The Sqifa al-Kahla ("Black Entrance") is flanked by two bastions. A horseshoe arch leads into the vaulted gatehouse, once protected by a heavy iron door. A stairway in the south bastion led up to the terraces and into the tower, which contained a hall.

Porch and courtyard of the Great Mosque of Mahdiya, 916
The tripartite design of the facade of the Great Mosque of Mahdiya, with its porch built out in front and its two corner towers, was an innovation, although it faintly echoes the triumphal arch of classical antiquity and certain Abbasid and Umayyad military buildings. Colonnades with horseshoe arches surrounded the inner courtyard. The central arch of the facade of the prayer hall is noticeably taller and broader than the other arches, corresponding to the central aisle. This building was the model for the al-Hakim Mosque in Cairo.

"in form and function all [others] with the exception of the two gates of Raqqa, on the model of which they were built."

Ubaidallah's palace rose in the east of the city, and the palace of his son al-Qaim stood opposite it, with a large open space between them. Excavations have brought to light the ruins of a building which is probably al-Qaim's palace. A curving entrance leads from an anteroom into the courtyard, with the various living areas grouped around it. They consisted of four small rooms around a larger one. A mosaic has been uncovered in one of the palace halls, showing a geometric pattern of interlacing bands which is reminiscent in style and motif of the mosaic floors of Raqqada.

The most important building in the whole complex is the Great Mosque, which is to the south of the peninsula. It was built in 916 on an artificial terrace, and modifications were made on several subsequent occasions. During the excavations of the 1960s, archeologists managed to reconstruct the plans of the first phase of building, and brought some original fragments to light. The Great Mosque covers a large rectangular area, consisting of a prayer hall and a courtyard surrounded on three sides by arcades of columns. A monumental portico, flanked by smaller entrances, stands in front of the middle of the north facade, which has massive, rectangular towers. The prayer hall consists of nine aisles and three bays, divided by eight rows of twin pillars, and the center aisle is taller and broader than the others; there is a dome above the bay in front of the *mihrab*. The semicircular *mihrab* niche recessed into the *qibla* wall is flanked by two small columns, and is divided into nine narrow niches with shell-shaped semicircular domes above them.

In its structure, the Great Mosque of Mahdiya is reminiscent of Aghlabid buildings, but there are some striking innovations in the design of its facade. As in the al-Qaim palace, the entrance is built out in front of the facade, and so becomes a striking architectural element of decoration. A large central porch is surmounted by a horseshoe arch. On both sides of this porch there are two niches with horseshoe arches, one above the other, the lower niche with a flat back wall and the upper niche with a semicircular wall. Two similar vertical sets of niches also ornament the side walls of the porch, which is surmounted by an attic story between cornices. With its tripartite decoration and its niches, it resembles the monumental city gates of classical antiquity, but also shows some similarity with the military buildings of the Abbasid and Umayyad periods, and represents a further stage of development, as Ibn Hauqal suggests in his comparison of the porches of Mahdiya and Raqqa. The model of this mosque was followed in many religious buildings of North Africa, and later of Egypt.

When al-Mansur came to power in 946, he decided, for strategic and political reasons, to move his capital. The geographical position of Mahdiya had certainly proved advantageous when Abu Yazid unsuccessfully besieged it, but its situation on a peninsula could equally well have led to disaster. Al-Mansur also felt drawn to the vicinity of Kairouan, where he built a third royal city near al-Abbasiya and Raqqada, calling it al-Mansuriya. The founding of this city should probably be seen as both a sign of reconciliation with a citadel of the Sunni faith, and an ostentatious demonstration of Shiite power.

Al-Mansuriya was built south of Kairouan and within a very short space of time (like all the cities of the period). It was surrounded by a circular defensive wall of fired and unfired brickwork, and medieval illustrations show four gates in it. The curtain walls, 13 feet (4 meters) thick, were flanked by massive semicircular and rectangular towers. A large mosque, called al-Azhar ("The Resplendent"), was built, and the markets of Kairouan were moved to al-Mansuriya. Many baths – 300 such establishments, according to the geographer al-Idrisi – and many cisterns were built. Water was brought along the aqueduct restored by the Aghlabids, making it possible to control the water supply to neighboring Kairouan. Many of the palaces are known to us by name:

Gallery of the inner courtyard of the Great Mosque of Mahdiya, 916
Like most of the rest of the building, the inner courtyard was restored in the 1960s. A colonnade runs around all four sides of the courtyard. The cross-vaulted north portico has mighty masonry pillars bearing the load of the wall arches. The pillars standing considerably closer together on the courtyard side give the structure a massive appearance. The horseshoe arches are set on console-like projections from the imposts.

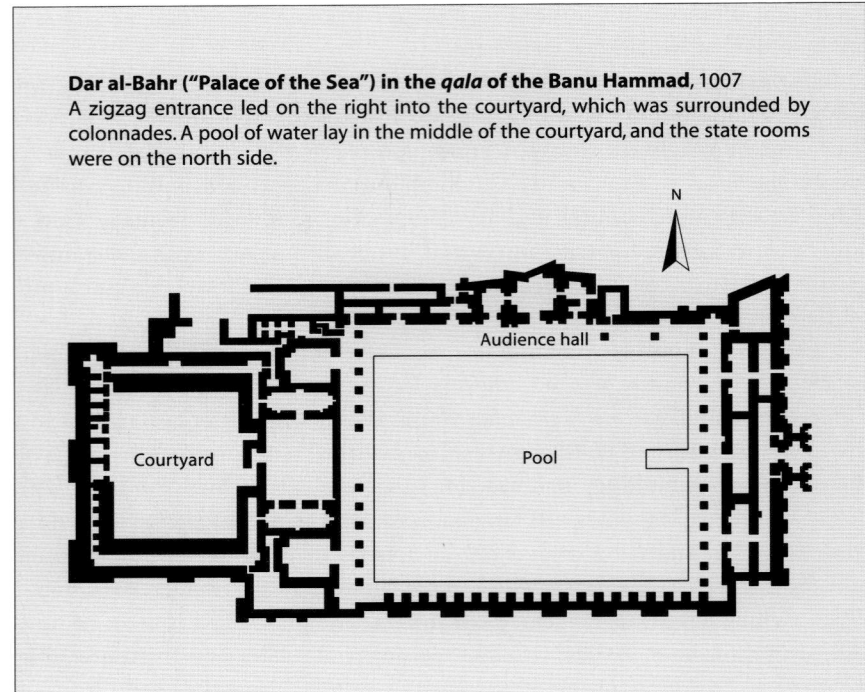

Dar al-Bahr ("Palace of the Sea") in the *qala* of the Banu Hammad, 1007
A zigzag entrance led on the right into the courtyard, which was surrounded by colonnades. A pool of water lay in the middle of the courtyard, and the state rooms were on the north side.

Audience hall

Courtyard

Pool

N

South side of the minaret of the Great Mosque in the *qala* of the Banu Hammad, early 11th century
The Banu Hammad built a *qala*, a fortified city complex, on the Hodna plateau. It contained dwelling houses and palaces, and a Great Mosque. The minaret has tripartite decoration of the south facade only. The central arch, which runs all the way up the height of the minaret, is flanked on both sides by three superimposed blind niches.

Qasr al-Bahr, Qasr al-Iwan, Qasr al-Kafur, the Camphor Palace, the Crown Palace, the Myrtle Palace, the Khawarnaq (after a pre-Islamic palace near Hisa), and so on. The ruler's intimate circle participated in the building of this vast site within its fortified walls, and had their own magnificently furnished houses erected here.

Contemporary authors record the beauty and luxury of the buildings, and their accounts have been confirmed by archeological excavations. A huge building measuring 295 × 66 feet (90 × 20 meters) stood in the south of the city, with a series of three long halls at its center and a building in front of them forming a reversed T-shape – an arrangement suggesting an audience room, with living areas off both sides of it. In front of the building there was a huge pool of water measuring 460 × 230 feet (140 × 70 meters), comparable with the pool in Raqqada, and again it had a large open space in front of it. The walls of the palace were adorned with tiles and stucco panels, either white or painted, and sometimes decorated with geometrical and floral or calligraphic patterns. Ceramic plaques and plaster sculptures of human beings and animals show oriental influence in the features of the human figures and the details of their clothing. Al-Mansuriya seems to have enjoyed very high prestige. We know, for instance, that Caliph al-Muizz gave his general Jauhar precise instructions for the founding of the new imperial city of Cairo, and one can well imagine that the plans were modeled on the buildings of al-Mansuriya. According to medieval sources, the caliph even took many items from al-Mansuriya itself to Egypt with him, transporting them by ship or on camel-back.

The buildings of the Zirids and Hammadids

The tradition of Fatimid secular architecture continued in the buildings of their vassals, the Zirids and Hammadids. Shortly before moving to Cairo in 973, Caliph al-Muizz had transferred the government of North Africa to the Zirid Buluggin. The Zirids and the Hammadids alike belonged to the great Berber family of the Sanhaja. Buluggin's father, Ziri, founder of the dynasty, had already founded the city of Ashir in 935 with the permission of Caliph al-Qaim, who sent him laborers and an architect from Mahdiya. The city, built on a rectangular ground plan, was surrounded by a strong fortified wall of quarry stone.

The ruins so far excavated include the remains of a large, well-fortified palace measuring 236 × 131 feet (72 × 40 meters). Its enclosing wall has square towers at the corners, and rectangular bastions placed at regular intervals. A massive porch protects the entrance, which follows a double bend and leads to the courtyard. The individual buildings are symmetrically distributed on both sides of the north-south axis, and on the side opposite the entrance there is a large, rectangular hall with three alcoves and an anteroom area in front of it. This arrangement – anteroom and hall – echoes the reverse T-shaped plan first introduced at al-Mansuriya, and usefully served its purpose, which was ostentation. Four groups of apartments, also arranged around a rectangular inner courtyard, flank the main courtyard. Of the many decorative elements found, a frieze with a row of intersecting round arches is particularly notable. This ornamental motif is rather unusual in Islamic architecture, although not entirely unknown, as the two minarets of Biskra and al-Oued show. At Benia, the circular city near Ashir founded by Buluggin when he took office as governor, it is clear that al-Mansuriya was not only the model for individual buildings but influenced the plan of the city as a whole.

Like the Fatimids and Zirids, the Hammadids left impressive traces behind them. In 1007 they founded a *qala* (fortress) on the Hodna plateau. This city, surrounded by a polygonal wall 4 miles (7 kilometers) long, contained among other buildings a Great Mosque and some magnificent palaces – the Government Palace, the Lighthouse Palace, the Palaces of the Stars, of Salvation, and of the Sea – all of them surrounded by beautiful gardens. The Qasr al-Manar, or Lighthouse Palace, is a particularly interesting building. Its interior structure, with two halls one above the other, and its lavish ornamentation show that it had an important position in the city. The tower, on a square ground plan with sides measuring 66 feet (20 meters), has deep vertical niches on three sides. The square hall on the ground floor contains three alcoves and almost certainly once had a dome, as the remains of squinches found among the rubble would seem to suggest. Its ground plan is reminiscent of the hall at Ashir. Some way from Qasr al-Manar lay the largest palace complex in the *qala*, the Dar al-Bahr or Palace of the Sea. It forms a huge rectangle with walls which, like those at Ashir, were reinforced by rectangular bastions, while a porch protected the double bend of the entrance in the center of the eastern facade. There was a pool of water in the middle of the large courtyard, which was surrounded by arcades, and a reception building containing three rooms was laid out along its northern side. The lavish decoration – *muqarnas* cornices, calligraphic friezes, small marble domes, the remains of marble fountains, ceramics with figural motifs, animal sculptures, and coins – bears witness to the splendor and wealth characteristic of life at the Hammadid court.

Religious life centered on the Great Mosque, a rectangular building measuring 184 × 210 feet (56 × 64 meters) along the sides. The *maqsura*, the area close to the *mihrab* reserved for the ruler, is a striking feature. The minaret rises in the center of the north wall, on the axis of the central aisle of the mosque. Only its south side is ornamented, with a tripartite design. A deep niche with round arches is recessed into this south facade, running all the way up it and flanked by three superimposed blind niches on each side. The decoration of this minaret is reminiscent of the entrance to the Mahdiya Mosque, particularly in the tripartite arrangement of the niches.

Prayer hall of the al-Azhar Mosque in Cairo, 972
In this first Fatimid building, the prayer hall was constructed in the North African tradition of the mosques of Kairouan and Tunis as a hypostyle hall. The stucco ornamentation, however, is not at all like these Mediterranean models, but shows strong oriental influence. The prayer hall consisted of five aisles running parallel to the *qibla* wall. After the fall of the Fatimids, however, the *qibla* wall was demolished, and further aisles were added.

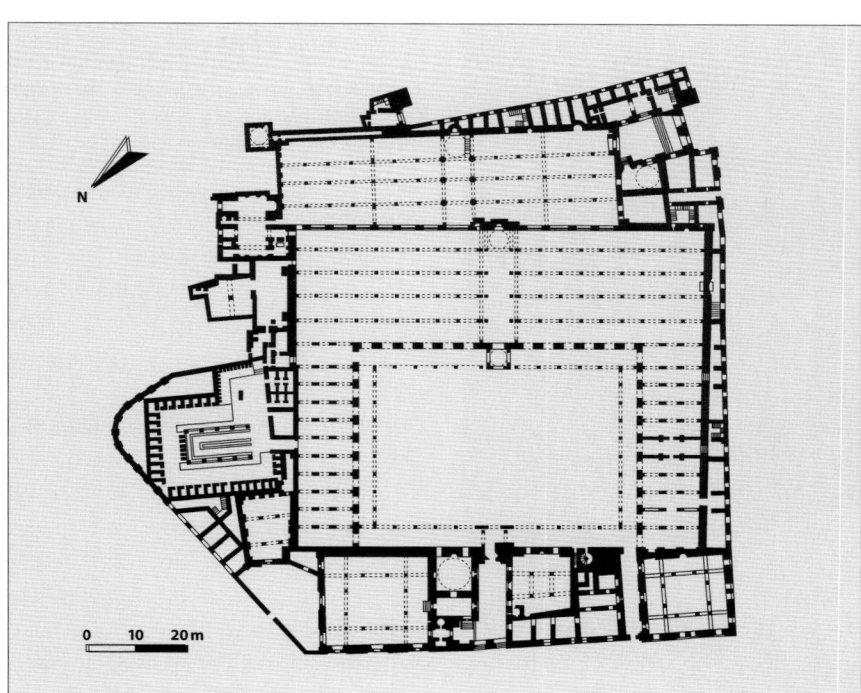

Courtyard layout and ground plan of the al-Azhar Mosque in Cairo, 972
Soon after the conquest of Fustat, the victorious general Jauhar began building the al-Azhar Mosque, which subsequently became a center of Shiite Islam and was one of the most important universities of the Islamic world during the Ottoman period. Because of its prominence it underwent much rebuilding, but the ground plan still shows traces of the original rectangular building with its five aisles in front of the *qibla*. In 1469 the Mamluk sultan Qaitbai added the dome and minaret seen on the right.

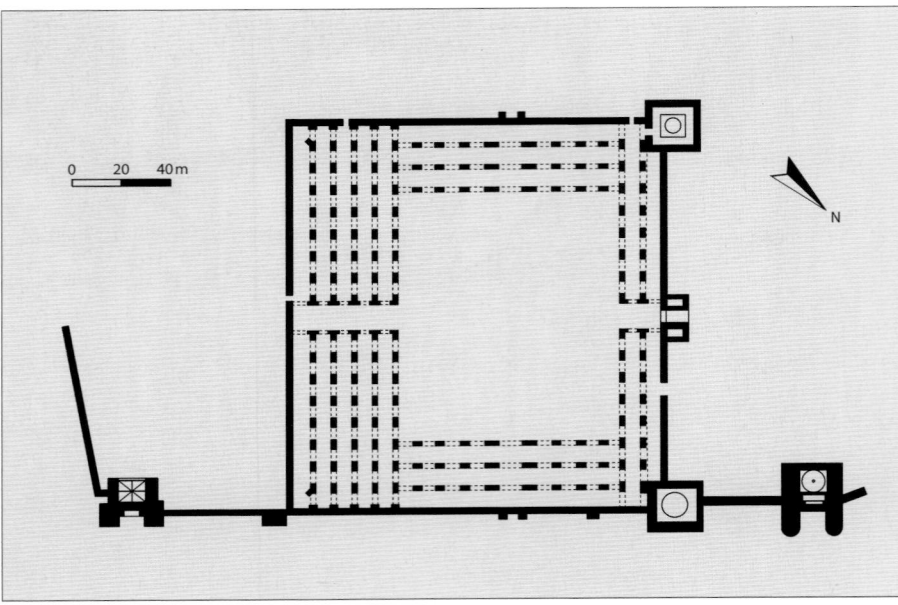

Below and above: **Courtyard and ground plan of the al-Hakim Mosque in Cairo**, 990–1013
The al-Hakim Mosque stood outside the old city wall before al-Jamali had the fortifications renovated. The five-aisled prayer hall has a wide, raised central aisle. The old courtyard, which was allowed to fall into dilapidation and is largely destroyed, was sometimes used as a military barracks in the past, and later as a sports ground. At the beginning of the 20th century it was decided to found the first Museum of Islamic Art in Cairo here. Only in recent years was the mosque completely restored by the Bohras, and resumed its original function.

Above: **Northern corner of the al-Hakim Mosque in Cairo**, 990–1013
The two minarets framing the northwest wall of the al-Hakim Mosque were the oldest extant minarets of the Fatimid period. Unfortunately, their original appearance has been concealed by the later addition of a square, massive base structure which greatly modifies it. The northern minaret, for instance, was once cylindrical. The conversion of its upper part was the work of the Mamluk period.

Opposite: **Outer ambulatory of the courtyard of the al-Hakim Mosque in Cairo**, 990–1013
The arches of the arcade surrounding the courtyard rest on pillars with flanking columns. The style of Fatimid Egypt is clearly recognizable, and derives from Ifriqiyan concepts. The windows of the exterior walls were arranged to match the bays of the arcades.

However, the prosperity of the Hammadids after the fall of the Zirid dynasty (as a result of the Banu Hilal invasion) was short-lived. In 1067 they began looking for a new, less vulnerable residence with access to the sea, and chose Bejaia. Thirty years later they finally abandoned the *qala*, and its palaces fell into decay. They constructed magnificent buildings in Bejaia, but in spite of archeological research very little is known of the palaces there, or indeed of the *qala* of Ashir, or the palace of al-Mansuriya. It is to the palaces of Sicily that we must look for more information about the sophisticated art of the princely palaces of North Africa.

Cairo – the Fatimid capital

In 970, on the instructions of Caliph al-Muizz and at the foot of the hill of al-Muqattam, his general Jauhar laid the foundation stone of the new capital city, Misr al-Qahira, "The Victorious," 3 miles (5 kilometers) north of Fustat. According to legend, astrologers were summoned to determine the most propitious moment for the building to begin. A rope with little bells attached to it was stretched around the perimeter of the future city, so that work could begin everywhere at the same time when the astrologers gave the signal, but a bird set the chime of bells ringing by mistake.

Cairo was a palace city reserved exclusively for the caliph and his court, although it also contained army quarters. Its clay brick walls were built to an almost square plan, measuring 3,600 × 3,770 feet (1,100 × 1,150 meters), and had eight gateways in them. According to the Persian poet Nasr-i Khusrau, who visited the city in 1048, storehouses for provisions and other items, markets, and baths had to be built within the city walls to supply the needs of the inhabitants. A great street called al-Shari al-Azam ran along the north-south axis, and the palace of Caliph al-Muizz, later known as the Great Palace or Eastern Palace, stood in the city center, together with the Great Mosque. During the reign of al-Aziz (975–996), another palace, the Western Palace, was built opposite the palace of al-Muizz. There was a wide, open space between them, called Bain al-Qasrain ("Between the Two Palaces"). It was the scene of the great events staged by the Fatimids.

These palaces, abandoned after the fall of the caliphate, were destroyed in the 15th century, but old texts provide valuable information about them. The Eastern Palace was the caliph's residence, and accommodated various government departments such as the treasury and the army office. Its rectangular enclosing wall had nine gateways and also contained the gardens and the hippodrome built under the Ikhshidid ruler Kafur (966–968). Access to it from the large open place between the palaces was through the Bab ad-Dhabab ("Golden Gate"), which was surmounted by a pavilion where the caliph presided over parades, and could show himself to his people on festive occasions. Nasr-i Khusrau mentions "a series of buildings, terraces, and halls" belonging to the palace, and the Mamluk historian al-Maqrizi (d. 1442) describes some 10 halls or pavilions of different periods, standing in fine gardens and furnished with open porches (or *iwans*). Their names – Khawarnaq, Camphor Hall, Crown Hall, Myrtle Hall – are reminiscent of al-Mansuriya. The ground plans of the caliph's palaces were sometimes adopted by private individuals, with slight modifications. Fustat contains some fine residences with square inner courtyards, and a main hall reached through a porch in front of the building and flanked by one or two other rooms.

The dwelling apartments, as literary sources tell us, were magnificently ornamented. The chronicler William of Tyre, whom the king of Jerusalem sent as his envoy to the caliph in 1167, describes "a vast, open courtyard, surrounded by porticoes borne on columns, all paved with marble in different hues, with unusually rich gilding … the hall was closed by a curtain of gold and silk in

every color, upon which one might see wild animals, birds, and human beings, shining with rubies, emeralds, and a thousand other precious stones." Nasr-i Khusrau writes of the Qaat al-Dhabab throne room in similar terms: "In one [of the halls] there stood a throne occupying the whole breadth of the room. Three sides of it were made of gold, and adorned with hunting scenes showing galloping horsemen and other subjects.... The throne was surrounded by a golden balustrade of surpassing beauty, and behind it there was a silver stairway." This magnificence is confirmed by the discovery of several wooden friezes showing figural scenes in the Maristan al-Qalawun, the hospital founded near the Western Palace by the Mamluk sultan who reigned from 1279 to 1290. An inventory of the caliph's treasury also conveys some idea of the luxury in which the princes lived, mentioning the caliph's library, which comprised 40 rooms and, in the words of the 11th-century historian al-Mushabbihi, contained "volumes dealing with all areas of science, including ... the knowledge of antiquity." Sources of the Ayyubid period give the number of works in this library as between 200,000 and 600,000.

When Cairo was founded, the al-Azhar Mosque, built to the south of the palace in 970–972, was the focal point of the city's religious life. It quickly developed into a center of Shiite teaching, and to this day is prominent in the Islamic educational world. Little is left of the original building, since the mosque has undergone frequent renovation over the centuries, for instance in the first half of the 12th century when Caliph al-Hafiz (1131–1149) had a domed porch erected in front of it. The building, measuring 279 × 226 feet (85 × 69 meters), has brick walls with stucco decoration. The prayer hall originally had 5 bays and 19 aisles, with a broad middle aisle and a dome over the bay in front of the *mihrab*. The *mihrab* itself is ornamented with calligraphic bands and friezes of highly stylized interlacing tendrils. The hypostyle halls around the courtyard are also richly ornamented, in a style related to that of the Amr and Ibn Tulun Mosques. The columns are surmounted by blind niches with rosettes above the apexes of the arches, and the courtyard facades end in striking stepped battlements.

In 990 al-Aziz had a new mosque built outside the city walls; it took the name of Caliph al-Hakim, under whose rule it was completed in 1012. It resembles the al-Azhar Mosque in having five bays, but there are 17 aisles, and not only is the bay leading to the *mihrab* domed, so are the two corner bays in front of the *qibla* wall. The pointed arches of the prayer hall, like those of the other colonnades, rest on masonry pillars, and the outer walls of the courtyard galleries are divided by niches and surmounted by battlements, as in the al-Azhar Mosque. The main facade of the al-Hakim Mosque has a tripartite

Opposite: **Bab al-Futuh in Cairo**, late 11th century
Bab al-Futuh lies close to Bab al-Nasr, and like Bab Zuwaila in the south of the city, has round flying buttresses. There are rooms above the gatehouse to accommodate the men on guard duty. Although it was a functional military building, Bab al-Futuh was rather more elaborately designed than Bab al-Nasr, for instance in the radiating arrangement of the voussoirs of the arches in the arcades. There are machicolations above the gate, and the parapet has battlements.

Right: **Bab al-Nasr in Cairo**, late 11th century
Remains of ruined Pharaonic temples were used during the reconstruction of the fortifications by Vizier Badr al-Jamali in 1087–1092. The city walls and gates of Cairo, erected for purposes of defense, never had to stand up to a single siege over the centuries. Bab al-Nasr might have been turned into an observatory if the vizier in charge of its conversion had not fallen out of favor, whereupon Caliph Amir (1101–1130) put an end to the project.

structure, and is also reminiscent of the Great Mosque of Mahdiya. There is a monumental porch at the center of the facade, and rectangular towers with minarets, one cylindrical and the other rectangular, rise above the corners.

During the period when the power of the Fatimid caliphs was beginning to wane, and Egypt was mainly ruled by strong viziers, a new architectural revival began under the patronage of these men.

Badr al-Jamali (d. 1094), vizier of Caliph al-Mustansir, ordered an extension of the fortified walls; demographic growth made it necessary to enlarge the city boundaries, and the old defenses were in poor repair. He entrusted the building of the fortifications around the city to Armenian architects from Odessa, who – as usual in Syria – used quarry stone and reinforced the walls with columns from older buildings. The ring of walls, surmounted by round-arched battlements, was fortified at regular intervals by massive square bastions. The gatehouses of three of them are still extant: Bab al-Futuh and Bab al-Nasr in the north, and Bab Zuwaila in the south. Bab al-Futuh has a straight entrance about 16 feet (5 meters) long, set between two round towers 26 feet (8 meters) high. The plain decoration of this gateway consists of large arched areas framed by rectangles, and a cornice pierced by loopholes. The two towers of Bab al-Nasr are on a square groundplan, and are ornamented only by a horizontal cornice.

Bab Zuwaila is in some respects a synthesis of the other two gateways.

Two unusual mosques founded by viziers adopted (and reinterpreted) the architectural style and decoration of the al-Hakim Mosque: the Aqmar and Salih Talai Mosques testify to a new delicate, almost Baroque aesthetic. The first of these two mosques was built in 1125 for Vizier Mamum al-Bataibi. The prayer hall has five aisles and three bays, the bay in front of the *mihrab* being much wider than the others. As in the arcades surrounding the courtyard, the pointed arches rest on elegant marble columns. On the exterior, a continuous calligraphic band runs around the extrados of the arches, and their spandrels are decorated with rosettes. A notable feature is the unusual decoration of the facade, which follows the course of the street and does not run parallel to the *qibla* wall. As in the al-Hakim Mosque, the porch projects slightly from the surface of the wall, and is tripartite in its structural design. The central arch, which extends all the way up the height of the building and is flanked by two narrower niches, not so tall, has a ribbed, shell-like intrados with a medallion bearing decorative inscriptions at its center. Rectangular areas filled with *muqarnas* appear above the small lateral niches, and there are two blind niches with shell-shaped vaulting and small inset columns above these rectangles, echoing the shell-shaped intrados of the main arch. The individual elements are

Above: **Upper lateral niche in the facade of the Aqmar Mosque, Cairo**, 1125
This niche is one of the decorative architectural elements rediscovered about 30 years ago, when the facade, which had been entirely concealed by residential buildings, was uncovered. With its small inset columns and the curve of the wall, it can be regarded as one of the last architectural references back to Tulunid designs.

Below: **Medallion in the tympanum of the Aqmar Mosque, Cairo**, 1125
The ribbed, upper part of the arch, over the gateway, contains a circular area with an inscription repeating the name of Muhammad. The name of Ali, the Prophet's cousin, is at the center. These inscriptions are evidence that the Fatimid dynasty adhered to Shiite doctrine.

Above: **Facade of the Aqmar Mosque, Cairo**, 1125
The Aqmar Mosque marks the change, at the beginning of the 12th century, from brick masonry to stone, in the construction of sacred buildings. The decoration is worked, not in stucco, but in stone. The tripartite structure of the design is interesting, with the central portal being clearly broader and higher than the two blind portals that flank it and carry projections adorned with *muqarnas*. Above each of these blind portals is a blind niche, and the facade ends with an inscription in stone running all the way across the top of it.

decorated with friezes of interlacing patterns, floral motifs, and calligraphic bands. There is a calligraphic frieze at the top of the facade. The mosque, which was built in 1160 by Vizier Salih Talai and was the last of the Fatimid buildings, resembles the Aqmar Mosque in its interior design. It was constructed above a barrel-vaulted basement floor where shops were housed, and is the oldest mosque of this type in Egypt.

At the time of the viziers, new elements were appearing in Fatimid architecture – memorial monuments and tombs, funerary mosques, mausoleums. Shiite doctrine contributed to this development with its veneration of the descendants of Ali. When al-Muizz came to power in Cairo, he sent to Ifriqiya for the remains of his ancestors and had a mausoleum built for them inside the palace precincts. From then on funerary mosques became a widely distributed type of building in Egypt. In 1085 Badr al-Jamali had a funerary mosque known as the Mashhad al-Juyushi built on the hill of al-Muqattam, but it contained no tomb. It has a minaret over the entrance with a domed octagonal area on top, and the porch leads to a courtyard adjoining the prayer hall. The bay in front of the *mihrab* and the room intended as a burial chamber are covered by squinch domes. The building contains the oldest *muqarnas* in Egypt. Many mausoleums of this type have been preserved in Cairo and Aswan.

Two funerary mosques, Sayida Atiqa (1120) and Sayida Ruqaya (1133), dedicated to members of the family of the Prophet, were built outside the city wall. Sayida Ruqaya has three rooms, with five *mihrabs* in all, richly ornamented with stucco decoration. The central room is covered by a dome with *muqarnas* pendentives. In general, the mausoleums are simpler in design. They are built of brick or stone, with a squinch or pendentive dome, and usually on a square ground plan, with one, two, or three of the sides designed as open arcades. Four buildings of this kind are still extant in the south of Cairo, known by the name Saba Banat, "The Seven Maidens," and there are similar mausoleums in less important cities, for instance in Aswan, where about 60 funerary mosques have been preserved.

A striking feature of the Fatimid buildings in Cairo is the new and extremely lavish decoration of both interior and exterior walls, in materials as different as stucco and stone. The pointed arches, *muqarnas*, and ribbed niches derive from the ornamentation of the Iranian provinces, and are very different from those earlier decorative elements where the link with Ifriqiya is still clearly perceptible. This remarkable synthesis of extremely different tendencies is characteristic of the new artistic style, which from now on can be properly called Egyptian. Fatimid art came to its peak in Cairo, but the Fatimids were also active in Mecca, Syria, and Palestine, although they did not leave their mark so strongly on those places. However, the fine mosaics in the spandrels of the great arch of the al-Aqsa Mosque are undoubtedly significant evidence of their presence in Jerusalem.

Tombs in the Aswan necropolis, 12th century
The construction of these tombs is reminiscent of the domed buildings of Ifriqiya. For instance, the square drums are surmounted by raised domes, like similar structures in Cairo and Sousse. The amount of stucco decoration varies from tomb to tomb.

Decorative Arts

Sibylle Mazot

The Fatimid period was a golden age of arts and crafts. Cairo became a major center for the production of valuable artifacts, superseding Baghdad and Constantinople. The Egyptian capital ably exploited the considerable economic and artistic potential of its geographical situation on the Mediterranean coast, where brisk commercial and cultural exchange had been going on for centuries. In addition, Cairo not only satisfied the desire of the ruling classes for luxury, but also (as we know from the *Geniza*, the records of the synagogue of old Cairo) supplied the more everyday needs of a prosperous sector of the population. Furniture and textiles made in Cairo had a particularly high reputation, and were exported to the entire Mediterranean area.

The political, religious, and social conditions in which Fatimid art developed undoubtedly exerted a crucial influence on its revival of the decorative repertory. Toward the end of the 11th century, figural depictions were especially popular. Representations of hunters, musicians, dancing girls, wrestlers, acrobats, and drinkers illustrate the daily life and pleasures of the Fatimid court. There was also a wide variety of animal depictions, from now on including not only "classic" (that is, Sassanian and Byzantine) subjects, showing lions or gazelles as symbols of power, but also more naturalistic images, especially of giraffes and elephants, deer, leopards, and hares, whose long ears were characteristic of the new style. There were also, however, depictions of fabulous creatures such as griffins, sphinxes, and harpies. Vegetative motifs were notable for a high degree of stylization in the tradition of Samarra. The importance of the Coptic community in Cairo is clear in depictions of Christ, monks, pilgrims, and some Jewish subjects also featured. Figural depictions in general had lost the stiffness of their predecessors, and displayed greater artistic freedom.

Ceramics and glass

A particularly large number of ceramic items is extant, including some dating from the period of the caliphate in Ifriqiya, when Mediterranean elements merged with the Mesopotamian tradition. They provide evidence of the wide distribution of the lusterware technique, colorful ornamentation suggesting the gleam of gold and the shimmer of silk. The technique was invented during the 8th century in Syria or Egypt, reached Samarra around 850, was then introduced into Kairouan, and came to its full flowering in Cairo. Finds from the *qala* of the Banu Hammad show that lusterware continued to be made in Ifriqiya. Although most ceramic products were plain, unglazed pots for everyday use, the pieces commissioned by the wealthy are particularly interesting, since almost the entire surfaces of such items are covered by ornamentation. These ceramics were much sought after in Italy, where Fatimid bowls – *bacini* – were used to decorate facades or as liturgical vessels.

Glass as well as ceramics was ornamented with shimmering metallic luster decoration, and colored glass vessels were also made. This technique had been known in Egypt since late antiquity. Glass flasks, cups, and jugs were blown and cut in the workshops of Cairo, which developed forms making higher productivity possible. The surfaces of such vessels were decorated with plant motifs or graphic patterns, sometimes in several colors; reliefwork might be carved, imprinted with a stamp, or incised. Such items as vases and lampstands, trays, and perfume burners were made of metal. Large, round objects – water containers of the aquamanile type, parts of fountains – were made for the court, usually in cast bronze. Fatimid craftsmen were the first to make purely decorative objects of this kind in such a size. The inventories drawn up when the caliph's treasury was looted in the year 1068 mention luxury items adorned with jewels and precious metals: a gold peacock with ruby eyes, a large cockerel decorated with pearls and jewels, a date palm with fruits made of pearls. Only the written records have survived, however, and none of the pieces themselves are extant. Gold and silver were also used in jewelry, particularly for filigree work.

Blue glass cup, Egypt, 9–11th century, height 11.4 cm, diameter 11.5 cm, London, Victoria and Albert Museum
The upper part of the cup is decorated with oval motifs made in the glass with pliers while it was still hot. Fatimid glassware is distinguished by its strikingly wide range of forms and colors. The technique of shaping glass in this way developed in Egypt, spread through the whole Middle East, and was known in the Mesopotamian area from the 9th century onward.

Glass cup with luster ornamentation, Egypt, 10th century, height 8.5 cm, diameter 13.3 cm, Berlin, Museum for Islamic Art
The luster ornamentation on the inside of the vessel consists of four cartouches with rounded edges, each containing a drop shape, while the spaces between the cartouches are decorated with superimposed spirals. Two sets of horizontal lines mark off the decorated area. The luster decoration technique, using silver oxide and copper oxide, is the same as on ceramic lusterware items.

Carvings – wood and ivory

Items made of wood, ivory, and rock crystal are undoubtedly among the most attractive artifacts of the Fatimid period. These pieces are astounding in the delicacy of their workmanship and the craftsmen's perfect mastery of the materials. Since Egypt has little timber of its own, the various woods – pine and ebony, cypress, teak, box, and acacia – had to be imported. Most of the carving was done in Coptic workshops, which had maintained the skills of the Tulunid period. Depictions of human beings and animals are surrounded by tendrils or densely interlacing patterns through which plant motifs and calligraphic bands wind their way, as they do, for instance, on the gatehouses of the Western Palace and the *mihrabs* of the Sayida Nafisa and Sayida Ruqaya Mosques. Carving adorned rafters for the ceilings of palaces and mosques, panels for doors, *minbars*, and caskets, and small portable *mihrabs* were also made and ornamented with carving. The work was done with a cant chisel, and once carved the panels were sometimes inlaid with ivory. The patterns and themes used for wood carving are identical with those found in the work on ivories.

Rock crystal

Rock crystal artifacts and textiles are probably the most emblematic of all craft products of the Fatimid period. They had wide distribution as luxury goods regularly sold and exported, or as loot taken in war. Techniques that had originated in Mesopotamia were used to carve rock crystal. The pure quartz blocks were initially shaped with a saw and drill before the surface was carved with animal or plant reliefs. Some remarkable pieces – pitchers, cups, chessmen – were made in the royal workshops, and sometimes bore the name of the ruling caliph. The incomparable purity of the crystal made them suitable gifts for guests of high rank. Since they were treasured in the Christian West, some especially fine examples of rock crystal artifacts came to the treasuries of churches, where they were used as reliquaries. It is possible that some of these rock crystal artifacts

Ceramic bowl, al-Baitar, Fustat, 10th–11th century, height 8.5 cm, diameter 27.5 cm, Berlin, Museum for Islamic Art
The bowl has characteristic Fatimid motifs in luster. The central medallion contains a hare with long ears, and the sides are decorated with four palm leaves divided by stylized plant motifs. The palm leaf under the hare's feet has the signature of the artist, al-Baitar, concealed in it.

Ceramic bowl, al-Saad, Egypt, 11th century, height 10.4 cm, diameter 23.5 cm, London, Victoria and Albert Museum
The center of this dish, decorated with luster, shows the figure of a monk, sometimes described as a "Coptic priest." He is holding a lamp or a censer. Beside him there is a motif that is either a stylized tree or a Coptic cross of life. Presumably this piece was either made by Coptic potters or was intended for sale at a Christian market.

Ceramic bowl, Egypt, 11th century, height 7.5 cm, diameter 27.2 cm, Cairo, Museum of Islamic Art
The luster decoration of this bowl shows two harpies with interlocking wings and a stylized tree between them. The background is decorated with small spiral ornaments. The stylized features, the details of the geometric decorative motif with its circles, and the depictions of plants are all descended from a long ornamental tradition inherited from the Abbasid period.

Frieze of figures, fragment from the Fatimid Western Palace, Cairo, 11th century, 30 × 430 cm, Cairo, Museum of Islamic Art
Restoration work on the mausoleum in the Maristan al-Qalawun brought to light several wooden friezes of this kind. They were very probably from the Western Palace in Cairo, which was abandoned after the fall of the dynasty. The old parts of the building were reused, but fitted into their new locations in such a way that the decorated areas were not visible. The frieze shows members of the royal family enjoying music, hunting, and dancing.

were originally from the caliph's treasury, and were sold after it was looted in 1068. The historian al-Maqrizi tells us that approximately 18,000 items of rock crystal and glassware were stolen at the time, and subsequently were taken to Byzantium and Christian Europe.

Textiles

Fatimid textiles also made their way to the treasure chambers of Western churches, and some of them, for instance the veil of St. Anne from Apt and the shroud of Cadouin, were the object of special veneration by pilgrims. Egypt has a very ancient tradition of linen weaving, and the first textile production centers in the east were set up here under the Fatimids, with several workshops in the Nile Delta. As with the wood carving workshops, this branch of craftsmanship was a Coptic monopoly under the control of the caliph. It had its own administrative system, known as the *tiraz* (Persian, "embroidery") and the workshops were divided into *tiraz khass* ("private *tiraz*") and *tiraz amm* ("public *tiraz*"). The fabrics were ornamented with decorative bands, embroidered in wool or silk, or with gold thread worked into them. They bore Kufic inscriptions which, like the rock crystal artifacts, bore the names of the ruling caliph and the workshop where they had been made. The bands sometimes showed figural scenes or plant motifs. Robes for the caliph and his court were made from the most valuable of these textiles, and so were hangings of the kind described by William of Tyre in his account of the caliph's palace in Cairo. As with pottery and glassware, plainer fabrics must certainly have been made as well. We know of other workshops in outlying regions, including one in Palermo, where the splendid mantle of King Roger II of Sicily was made in the 1130s. Sicily was also a major center of the craft of wood and ivory carving, and its carved or painted caskets and ivory horns were particularly famous.

Because the palace library was broken up after the fall of the caliphate we cannot now, unfortunately, form any good idea of Fatimid painting in general. Only a few copies of the Koran and of secular texts survived, and excavations in Fustat have brought to light only drawings on paper, done in black ink and sometimes in color. These sketches show much the same stylistic features as the ceramics. The ceiling of the Cappella Palatina in Palermo, executed at a time when the decline of the Fatimid caliphate was already far advanced, is a kind of pictorial inventory of Fatimid themes in the variety of scenes it shows, testifying to the consistently high creativity of such a center, even though it was a long way from Cairo, and in addition was Christian.

Inlaid panel, Edfu, 10th century, lacquered wood, wood and ivory or bone intarsia work, 22×41 cm. Cairo, Museum of Islamic Art
This fragment of intarsia paneling is evidence of the great skill of Fatimid culture. The middle of the medallion shows an animal scene, with a hare being attacked by a hawk. The bodies of the animals are adorned with ivory intarsia work. The remains of an inscription can be seen above left. The pseudo-Kufic script on the right, however, is purely decorative in nature.

Gold pendant, Egypt, 11th century, diameter 3 cm, London, Ancient Art and Architecture Collection
The pendant is worked in the shape of a crescent moon. On the other side, the center contains a bird in translucent blue, green, red, and white cloisonné enamel, with the separate areas marked off from each other by golden lines. It seems likely that such cloisonné items were not made by the goldsmiths themselves, but bought and then fixed in place in the middle of the finished piece of jewelry.

Fragment of fabric, Egypt, 12th century, linen and silk, 48 × 28 cm. Cairo, Museum of Islamic Art
This fabric comes from the Coptic linen weaving workshops established under the control of the caliph in the Fatimid period.

Some parts are adorned with flower motifs, while the lower part has two bands containing a white inscription on a red ground, referring to "fortune and prosperity."

Figure of lion, Egypt, 11 –12th century, height 21 cm, length 20 cm, Cairo, Museum of Islamic Art
This bronze figure was probably made as a functional item – perhaps a jet for a fountain. The whole body is covered with engraved

reliefwork, and the small holes were hammered in. The tail is worked like a dragon's head. The metal casting technique derives from a long tradition of metalworking in the eastern Mediterranean area.

Fatimid Influences in Sicily and Southern Italy

History
Sibylle Mazot

There can be no doubt that the coming of the Kalbid emirs in 917 was a turning point in the history of Sicily. Their drastic reallocation of land boosted the region's economy, and within a few decades the former granary of Rome was restored to its old prosperity. The capital of the emirate was Palermo, which became one of the great metropolitan centers of the Mediterranean area. The last years of Kalbid rule, however, were marked by palace intrigues and disputes between regional emirs. Roger de Hauteville, a Norman condottiere who had settled in southern Italy, exploited the prevalent atmosphere of anarchy and conquered Sicily in 1060. His son, Roger II, made the island a monarchy in 1130. The Normans launched campaigns against the coastal cities of North Africa, and occupied Jerba, Tripoli, Mahdiya, Sousse, Sfax, Gabes, and Bona (now Annaba). Finally, in 1174, William II of Sicily sent military reinforcements to the Fatimids to halt the advance of Saladin. Under the rule of Roger II (1130–1154), William I (1154–1166), and William II (1166–1189) there was peaceful coexistence between religions, and their places of worship were maintained.

The death of William II in 1189 marked the beginning of fierce disputes over the succession, resolved only six years later with the accession to the throne of Constance, daughter of Roger II and wife of Emperor Henry VI. The island was now in the hands of the Hohenstaufen dynasty, and the couple's son Frederick II, who became king of Sicily at the age of four, was later crowned emperor. In 1225 he acquired the title of king of Jerusalem through his marriage, and he became friendly with Fakhr al-Din, envoy of the Ayyubid sultan of Cairo, al-Malik al-Kamil (1218–1238), with whom he concluded a pact of mutual assistance in 1226. This good understanding had a positive effect on diplomatic relations between Egypt and the Holy Roman Empire, but Frederick's policy toward the Muslim population of Sicily was notoriously harsh. He suppressed a Muslim revolt in 1224 with great severity, and deported approximately 16,000 of the rebels to Lucera in Apulia. When another rebellion broke out in 1243, those who were involved were exiled, and Islamic life in Sicily ended.

It is not easy to form an impression of Islamic art in southern Italy, and it is impossible to define precisely the contribution made by Islamic civilization, both Aghlabid and Fatimid. Although Sicily was under Muslim rule for over 200 years during the Kalbid period, almost none of the buildings from that time have survived. The exceptions are a small mosque in Palermo and the substructure of the Favara Palace, the residence built by the Emir Jafar around 1000. Even less of the architecture of the period is extant outside the capital. This absence of remaining Islamic buildings is in marked contrast to the wealth of textual sources, the traditional place names, and the large and varied number of objects now preserved in museums. Paradoxically, it is the buildings commissioned from Islamic architects by the Normans that tell us most about the tradition of Islamic architecture on the island.

Detail of the coronation mantle of Roger II, 1133/34, silk, Vienna, Kunsthistorisches Museum
The coronation mantle of the Norman ruler of Sicily, Roger II, was made of red silk interwoven with gold and silver thread, and consisted of three layers. The illustration shows a detail from the oldest layer of fabric, very probably originating from a Sicilian workshop. The embroidery around the edge, visible when the mantle was worn open, shows scenes reminiscent of Christian iconography, with the theme of the Tree of Life. The two figures standing one on each side of a stylized tree are usually interpreted as Adam and Eve.

Fountain Hall in La Zisa, Palermo, 1166
The Fountain Hall with its beautiful indoor fountain lies at the heart of the Norman summer residence of La Zisa. The ornamentation of the hall is remarkable: the vaulted upper parts above the communicating doors are decorated with *muqarnas*, and there are marble panels and mosaics. The three medallions side by side in the central alcove show scenes of hunting, the favorite leisure pursuit of the Norman rulers. The stepped basin of the fountain, built in the medieval Islamic style, is in the middle of the alcove. This is the oldest extant example of such a structure.

Architecture and Art

Sibylle Mazot

Eastern myth – the brilliance of a multicultural court

The emirs whose made Palermo their residence in the 10th century moved into the former citadel and turned the basilica into a Great Mosque. In 937, for strategic reasons, the Kalbids founded a second city not far from the harbor. It was called al-Khalisa ("The Chosen"), and was abandoned after the Norman conquest of Sicily, when the new rulers of the island moved into the old palace, converted it, and reinforced its defenses. The royal palace accommodated the most important administrative offices, and also a number of workshops including the textile manufacturing workshop, which was famous far beyond the island itself. Like the emirs before them, the Norman princes surrounded themselves with scholars and intellectuals, including such men as al-Idrisi, who made a map of the world for Roger II and wrote a geographical work, the Kitab *Nuzhat al-Mushtaq.* A few decades later Fakhr al-Din, a respected dialectician and astronomer, introduced Emperor Frederick II to the sport of falconry. Frederick, who took an interest in poetry and the natural sciences, commissioned translations of Arabic works.

In 1140 Roger II had the magnificent Cappella Palatina built as an extension of the royal palace. In addition to its beautiful floors and magnificent mosaics, the chapel is particularly notable for its unique wooden ceiling, ornamented with *muqarnas.* Each individual *muqarna* bears a picture painted in tempera, with beaded edging and inscriptions mentioning such blessings as felicity, charity, perfection, power, fame, and well-being. The pictures show scenes of everyday life and the life of the court, sometimes in front of an architectural setting of domes or arcades. There are also depictions of plants and animals (hares, birds, beasts of prey, stags, and elephants), and of fabulous creatures such as sphinxes, griffins, and sirens. The rigid attitude of the human figures, shown full front or in three-quarter profile, their powerfully contoured faces, the women's hairstyles, clothing, and jewelry, the folds of the garments, and the beaded edgings all show similarities to the frescoes of the Umayyad Qasr al-Hair al-Gharbi and the palaces of Samarra, Cairo, and Fustat. Analysis of the inscriptions confirms that the ceiling is related to the Fatimid art of Ifriqiya and the Middle East, but the problem of the symbolic interpretation of the design has not been solved. Does it depict Paradise? Did it glorify the ruler? Did the iconography have a didactic function, or was it indeed purely allegorical?

The rooms in the palace, like those in the Cappella Palatina, were magnificently furnished. The Roger Hall (so called although it was completed only by Roger's successors) has fine mosaics on the walls showing highly stylized scenes of palm trees, lions, leopards, swans, and peacocks, and reminiscent of the beautiful mosaics in the Umayyad palace of Khirbat al-Mafjar.

Adopting the customs of their predecessors, the Norman princes restored the old hunting grounds at the foot of the city wall which had originally been laid out by the Kalbids, and added some new buildings. The name of this huge park, Jannat al-Ardh ("Paradise of the Earth"), is in the tradition of Muslim terms denoting luxury and extravagance. In their love of exotic things, the Norman kings gave Arab names to their palaces, which as Ibn Jubair picturesquely

San Cataldo in Palermo, 1161, with the Martorana Church in the background, 1143
Both churches were built by Norman dignitaries, on a terrace, but their ground plans are very different. While the first is laid out like a basilica, the foundation walls of the second are in the shape of a Greek cross. Neither church has a central dome; instead, there are three small and unusually tall domes over the nave of San Cataldo. The domes, the large blind arcades, and the protuberant friezes dividing up the facades all show similarities to the architectural style found in North Africa and Egypt.

Principal facade of the palace of La Zisa in Palermo, 1166
Like their predecessors the Kalbid emirs, the Norman rulers of Sicily had a series of summer residences built around Palermo, including the palace of La Zisa in the middle of the Genoardo park. It was not just a residence for princely pleasures but also – in the tradition of the *munyas* of Ifriqiya – an agricultural estate. Pools of water were laid out in front of the palaces, or around them, as in the Muslim palaces of North Africa. The foreground contains the remains of a small pool and the pavilion that once adorned its center.

Paradise Cloisters of Amalfi Cathedral,
1255–1268
The Paradise Cloisters are perhaps the most elegant example of the interlacing arches widely distributed in Campania during the Norman period. The origin of this feature is obscure. Comparable forms are found all along the Mediterranean coast, and there are many (and often older) examples of this type of arch in Normandy and in England, the northern home of the Normans. Here the very slender columns supporting the ornately intertwined arches lend the courtyard a unique atmosphere.

put it were distributed around the city "like pearls on a young girl's necklace." These palaces were built as summer residences, but like the Umayyad palaces, or the Aghlabid palace of al-Rusafa, they were surrounded by fields and orchards where citrus fruits, date palms, sugarcane, olives, and other agricultural products grew. In the second half of the 12th century, the summer residences were generally built to a rectangular ground plan with a building projecting in front of it. Inside, they were perfectly symmetrical, comprising a cross-shaped main hall with three alcoves. The existence of an anteroom in the palaces of La Zisa (1166) and Scibene suggests a T-shaped ground plan. The plan of La Cuba (1180) is interesting because, since it was designed as a residence for use all the year round, this palace does not open onto the surrounding gardens but looks out on its interior courtyard. Elaborate ventilation systems had to be built into these Sicilian palaces as protection from the heat, and their floors and walls were insulated. The interior decoration, too, was very sophisticated. *Muqarnas* decoration of stucco or stone adorned the palace alcoves and corridors.

Water was important both inside and outside these buildings. A fine example of an internal fountain (*shadirwan*) has been preserved at La Zisa. It not only served an ornamental purpose but also improved air quality. The water gushes from the wall of the main room, and flows over the steps of a *salsabil* before passing through a narrow channel and into the small pool outside the palace. In Muslim tradition, there was always a source of water outside a building. La Cuba was even laid out in the middle of a pool, like an island.

Chapels and bath houses were built near the palaces, as we know mainly from the archeological excavations around La Zisa. Literary sources confirm that there were a great many baths in Sicily. A small bathhouse in Cefalù Diana, about 13 miles (20 kilometers) from Palermo, deserves mention: the

Bell tower of Amalfi Cathedral, 12th century
In spite of much rebuilding, the 12th-century bell tower has remained unmodified. The intertwining arches of multicolored voussoirs on the gable wall are evidence of the stylistic syncretism of the region, and represent a decorative element widely distributed through Campania in Norman times.

building has only one room, but it contains three pools fed by the water from hot springs. The exterior still bears traces of a Kufic inscription, which might seem to suggest Islamic origin but for the late Norman shape of the arches in the building. The calligraphic band is therefore evidence that some architectural elements were deliberately orientalized.

The symmetrical arrangement of the interiors of these palaces and the use of a cross-shaped ground plan is reminiscent of the palaces of al-Mansuriya and Ashir, and of the *qalas*, although the Sicilian buildings must not be regarded as copies of any particular prototype, but rather as adaptations. The modest dimensions of the buildings in Palermo, and the fountains placed in the middle of cross-shaped areas, made any kind of court ceremonial impossible, and in fact these palaces were not designed as a setting for official events, but served private purposes – and even then for only part of the year. Frederick II did not have any notable changes made to the little palaces built by his predecessors. Instead, he built many fortresses in Sicily and Apulia, in general corresponding to the European designs of the time but also reminiscent in their structure of the *ribats* of Ifriqiya. A more unusual example is the Castel del Monte, built by Frederick II in Apulia in 1240. It has an octagonal ground plan, with all eight corners reinforced in turn by octagonal bastions. The exterior decoration of this building, which has a central courtyard, is confined to a continuous line of molding halfway up the walls, linking the towers together. Inside, an ingenious visual and acoustic communications system

Glove, Palermo, 1220, Vienna, Kunsthistorisches Museum
This magnificent glove of red silk embroidered with gold thread, and ornamented with pearls, rubies, sapphires, and cloisonné enamel, was made for the coronation of Emperor Frederick II in the royal workshops of Palermo. Like the robe known as the coronation mantle of Roger II, it reflects the great skill of the craftsmen in the Sicilian workshops. The *tiraz* workshop, as in Cairo, was under the control of the ruler, and supplied the court with magnificent textiles. The reputation of Sicilian weaving obviously went far beyond the island, and the textiles produced in Sicily were in demand all over Europe.

Liturgical robe (or alb), Palermo, 1181, Vienna, Kunsthistorisches Museum
This silk-lined yellow taffeta robe has magnificent wide bands of silk embroidered in gold and set with pearls and precious stones. It bears two inscriptions – in Arabic and Latin – recording that it was made in 1181 in the royal *tiraz* workshops of Palermo for King William II. It was worn as a coronation robe by both Frederick II in 1120 and Charles V in 1520.

allowed visitors to be supervised. There were also cleverly designed ventilation systems, like those in La Zisa, and water pipes running from cisterns in which rainwater was collected to be piped to the palace baths and other sanitary installations. These arrangements have their analogies in Islamic architecture, particularly in Umayyad buildings, which clearly influenced the gatehouse of Castel del Monte. As in the military buildings and residences of North Africa and the Middle East, the way through its entrance follows a bend.

Sicilian domed buildings – the legacy of Ifriqiya

The domed churches of Palermo, Mazara, and the surroundings of Messina are astonishingly similar to buildings in Ifriqiya. Their domes have hemispherical calottes of dressed stone, resting on a drum and squinches. The church of San Giovanni degli Eremiti in Palermo has a cross-shaped ground plan and is divided into five bays, all roofed with domes of different sizes. The nave of the church of San Cataldo, built in 1161 in the last years of Norman rule, is unique in the arrangement of its three unusually tall domes. Smaller domes originally surmounted the towers of San Giovanni dei Lebbrosi (1155) and the Martorana Church (1143). The domes in the area around Messina are more sophisticated, with a network of superimposed honeycomb cells. Finally, there was a small pavilion on a rectangular ground plan in the park of La Cuba; with four arcades running through it and a tall dome; it was inspired by the mausoleums of Ifriqiya and Egypt.

Ifriqiyan models were followed in secular as well as sacred buildings. Facades are structured by tall blind arcades with single, double, or triple arches, and wide niches with either flat or semicircular walls, sometimes with shell-shaped fluting at the top. Very often doors and windows are framed by protuberant decorative bosses in two colors, like those in buildings of the same period in Fatimid Cairo, Christian Palestine, and Ayyubid Syria. These decorative elements, however, did not originally come from North Africa or the Middle East, but are also found in the ornamental repertory of other regions under Norman rule, from southern Italy to England. The various different forms of battlements in Palermo show some similarity to fragments excavated at al-Mansuriya and in the *qala* of the Banu Hammad. The same applies to the bands of script, very popular in Norman architecture, and which usually give the date of the laying of a foundation stone and the name of the patron who commissioned the building, and were directly inspired by the mosques of North Africa and Egypt.

The architecture of Ifriqiya was undoubtedly the model for the Sicilian buildings of the 12th century, but the question of the origin of the architects and craftsmen themselves remains open. Roger II's coronation mantle is among the few pieces that clearly indicate Islamic and Sicilian origin. Apart from the *tiraz* of Palermo, we know nothing of the existence of native or imported workshops, but it may be assumed that craft schools had been founded and artists and craftsmen trained in them during the two centuries when Islam had a strong presence on the island.

Stag, Egypt, c. 1000, height 46 cm, length 30 cm, Munich, Staatliches Museum für Völkerkunde

The size and artistic execution of this stag make it a rare piece. Its body is covered with tendril ornamentation, and there are inscriptions on the throat and stomach, one of which appears to name the craftsman as a man called Ghasan. If medieval accounts are to be believed, such sculptures were created as independent works of art. Many are said to have been set with jewels, although no such piece has been preserved.

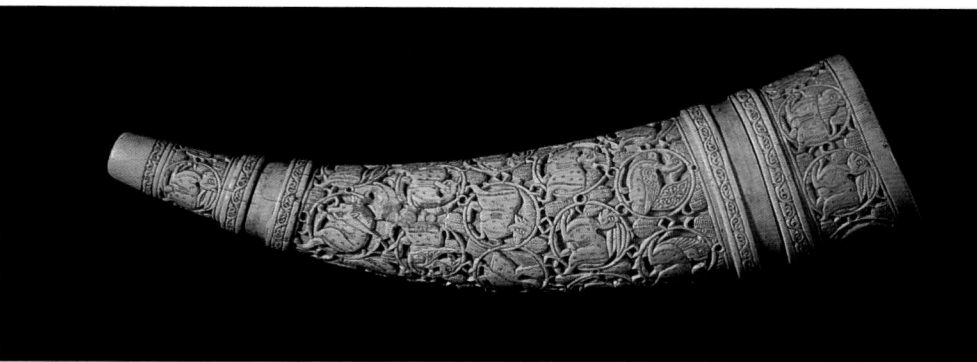

Above: **Ivory horn**, southern Italy or Sicily, 11–12th century, carved ivory, length 50 cm, diameter 11.5 cm, Berlin, Museum für Islamische Kunst

Ivory horns from southern Italy were used as both hunting horns and drinking vessels, and were exported all over Europe. Their secular function left the artist free to use a wide range of motifs. This ivory horn is ornamented with a tendril pattern containing animals – hares, gazelles, and birds – and fantastic creatures.

Below: **Casket,** southern Italy or Sicily, 11–12th century, carved ivory, 17.3 × 39.5 × 22.8 cm, Berlin, Museum für Islamische Kunst

This casket, its edges ornamented with elegant palm leaves, displays the classic repertory of animal subjects, and adds human figures in the hunting scenes. The sides of the lid show two lions, one attacking a gazelle and the other a hare. Unlike some other examples, this casket is not naturalistic in style, and does not preserve the relationship of size between the animals.

Above: **Griffin**, Spain, 11–12th century, 107 × 87 × 43 cm, Pisa, Museo dell'Opera del Duomo

This sculpture seems to have been part of a fountain, and its exact place of origin is unknown. For a long time it was believed to have come from a Fatimid workshop in Egypt, but its striking similarity to sculptures from Spain suggest that this griffin, too, was made on the Iberian Peninsula. The inscription reads: "Blessings, good fortune, joy, eternal peace, health and happiness be to the owner."

Syria, Palestine, and Egypt: Ayyubids, Mamluks, and Crusaders

Sultan Barsbai's Complex in the Eastern Cemetery of Cairo, 1432
Egypt's rulers built great harmonic complexes of buildings linked to their mausoleums in the cemeteries of Cairo, which extend from the south of the city to the northeast. The impressive domes of these buildings were symbols of their power and were decorated with great skill by the Mamluk stonemasons.

History

Almut von Gladiss

The Ayyubids
Saladin – Hero of Islam

The Crusades devastated the eastern Mediterranean during the 12th century. Following their occupation of Jerusalem in 1099, the Crusaders, whom the Arabs referred to indiscriminately as "Franks," occupied almost all the coastal cities of Palestine. The historian Ibn al-Athir from Mosul (today in northern Iraq) followed events from a certain distance and classified the Crusades as an important episode in the great cultural conflict between Islam and Christianity. Although phases of Holy War (*jihad*) alternated with periods of peaceful coexistence, he warned his contemporaries urgently of the decline of Islam and Islamic culture.

Nur al-Din ibn Zangi of Aleppo (1146–1174) built up a broad power base by unifying the minor Syrian states with Egypt. During his reign the idea of Holy War began to grip the whole of the eastern Mediterranean region. The main priority was Jerusalem, the Holy City venerated equally by Jews, Christians, and Muslims that had been the capital of the Frankish Kingdom of Jerusalem since 1099. The Muslims saw their shrines on the Temple Mount being desecrated under Christian rule. Their outrage was reflected in the propaganda literature praising Jerusalem and the Holy Land read out in the mosques in order to create a climate of opinion that would support action to reclaim the holy sites. In this literature it was emphasized that the Dome of the Rock, which the Crusaders incorrectly called the Templum Domini (Temple of the Lord), had been built by one of the early Umayyad rulers, and reference was made to its significance as a memorial to the Prophet Muhammad, who began his Night Journey to heaven there (Koran 17. 1).

As early as 1168/69, the general mood of revolt had prompted Nur al-Din, in a gesture of confidence in the ultimate Muslim victory, to order a wooden *minbar* for the Aqsa Mosque on the Temple Mount from four master craftsmen in Aleppo. However, it was only possible for this symbol of faith to be installed

Map of Jerusalem, The Hague, Koninklijke Bibliotheek
The maps of Jerusalem dating from the time of the Crusades reduce the city to a schematic circle divided into four sections. The upper half shows the Cathedral of the Rock and the Aqsa Mosque as the "Templum Domini" and "Templum Salomonis." The main goal of Christian pilgrimage, the Holy Sepulchre, is depicted as a round building in the bottom left corner. The picture beneath the map shows a legend about St. George, who was claimed to have assisted the Crusaders in battle against a Muslim army, and refers to the conquest of Jerusalem by the Crusaders in 1099.

after Saladin captured Jerusalem in 1187. This *minbar*, which was destroyed in the 20th century, bore an inscription that proclaimed the victory of Islam and the destruction of its religious enemies.

Saladin (Salah al-Din al-Ayyub), the founder of the Ayyubid dynasty, came from a high-ranking Kurdish military family and spent his youth in Baalbek, the city in the mountains of Lebanon famous around the world for its Roman temple. From 1152, he served in the retinue of Nur al-Din, the ruler of Damascus, Aleppo, and Mosul. With his uncle Sirkuh, a capable general, he took part in the conquest of Egypt. In 1169, after Sirkuh's death, he rose to become the supreme commander of the army. At the same time he was appointed vizier to the Fatimids who ruled in Egypt, only to overthrow them two years later. Sunnis regarded the Shiite caliphate of the Fatimids as heretical, and Saladin's actions in bringing it to an end assured him great acclaim among his contemporaries, who celebrated him as a champion of orthodoxy. In 1174, when Nur al-Din died in Damascus, Saladin was accepted as his successor in Syria and as the Muslims leader in the war against the Christians.

Saladin's plans for territorial expansion received backing from the caliph of Baghdad. Basing himself in Damascus, which was then a stronghold of Islam with more than 240 mosques and over 20 *madrasas*, he planned the great offensive against the Crusaders. The First Crusade had been a success for the Christians thanks to divisions between the Muslim powers. Now the Muslims were gathering their forces in the eastern Mediterranean under a unified leadership at a time when the Frankish states were being shaken by internal crises. Saladin had always denounced the treaties between his Muslim rivals and the Crusaders as treason against the principle of *jihad*, although he had agreed truces with them himself. However, when Muslim traders and pilgrims continued to face attacks, despite the conclusion of a peace treaty, and even the coasts of the Red Sea were being ravaged, he decided to turn to arms. As "Protector of the Holy Sites of Mecca and Medina," a title given to Saladin by the caliph of Baghdad, it was his duty to ensure that the pilgrims were able to travel in safety, and, as a politician, he had to guaran-

Reception hall at Shaubak (Montreal), Jordan, from 1115
The Frankish castles, Shaubak and Kerak, were both built in steep and rocky positions. They were crucial links in a security cordon running between the Dead Sea and the Red Sea that was used to close the Frankish defensive line when necessary. They were captured by Saladin in 1188/89, and were of enormous strategic significance to the Ayyubid state, helping it to maintain control of the southern end of the Dead Sea and the network of roads between Egypt, Syria, and the Arabian Peninsula.

tee secure trading routes. After years of propaganda about the Holy War, it eventually broke out as a result of a provocative act on the part of the Crusaders, who robbed a caravan on its way from Cairo to Damascus while it passed the Frankish castle at Kerak in Transjordan (now Jordan). Saladin won a famous victory over the Christian army at Hattin in the summer of 1187, and then went on to capture many of the cities and fortresses in Palestine, until Jerusalem finally surrendered as well. The city was retaken by the Muslims on the anniversary of the Prophet's ascension to heaven, which was interpreted as a sign of divine providence. In the course of the restoration of Islam, Christian images were removed from the Dome of the Rock, the dome was regilded, and the cross removed and replaced with the Islamic crescent. In the Aqsa Mosque, the Templum Salomonis (Solomon's Temple) used by the Crusaders as a royal palace, Nur al-Din's *minbar* was put in its rightful place and the *mihrab* repaired.

Preparations were begun for a new Crusade following the fall of Jerusalem. On the journey to the Holy Land, the German emperor, Frederick Barbarossa, drowned in the river Halys (Kizil Irmak) close to the Cilician Gates, a pass through the Taurus mountains. Although his army disintegrated, Philip II, King of France, and Richard Coeur de Lion, King of England, reached the important port of Acre. This city had been occupied by the Crusaders in 1104 and now, following its reconquest by Saladin, was besieged by them until it surrendered. With its magnificent buildings and a widely famed scriptorium, Acre was to be

Above: **Krak des Chevaliers**, Syria, from 1110
Krak des Chevaliers, in the Syrian mountains about 30 km away from the coast, was built during the Crusades. It was strengthened by the Knights Hospitaller and played an important role as a base for attacks on Arab-controlled areas until it was captured in 1271 by the Mamluk Sultan Baibars. On the western side the two concentric defensive walls are separated by a wide moat. The inner castle dominates the view from the south with its circular towers (right). The towers built by the Mamluk sultans and the aqueduct that supplied the castle with water can be seen below.

Right: **The Dome of the Rock**, Jerusalem, 691–692
The Dome of the Rock dominates the Temple Mount in Jerusalem. It was used by the Crusaders as a cathedral, but was later converted back into a mosque by Saladin.

Latin inscriptions and Christian devotional images were removed and the Islamic crescent returned to the dome. Saladin used many other Christian buildings in Jerusalem for the foundation of madrasas and other important institutions.

the *de facto* capital of the Kingdom of Jerusalem for the next 100 years. Alerted by the defeat at Acre to the possibility of further invasion attempts, Saladin concentrated on the defense of Jerusalem. However, as both Muslims and Christians recognized the hopelessness of their plans to drive out and destroy the enemy, they reached agreement on another peace treaty, in which Saladin conceded Richard Coeur de Lion free access to the holy sites in Jerusalem for Christian pilgrims. The Holy War came to an end after Saladin's death in 1193. The Crusaders continued to be viewed as enemies, but Saladin's successors no longer sought out conflict with these foreigners. They had been living in Palestine for 100 years, and the population had now become accustomed to them. As the contemporary historian Ibn Jubair emphasized, everyday business between Christians and Muslims usually ran smoothly.

The Ayyubid possessions were ruled by members of the dynasty under the emperor's overall control. When Saladin died, his brother, al-Adil (1200–1218), ascended to the throne, sending his three sons as regents to Egypt, Syria, and the Jazira (northern Mesopotamia). A number of small principalities in Syria and the Jazira were also ruled by members of the Ayyubid dynasty or allied local princes. In order to consolidate their power in these territories, they kept peace with the Crusaders, even though the Europeans refused to abandon their aim of restoring the Kingdom of Jerusalem. After 25 years of relative peace, they launched a crusade against Egypt in order to weaken Ayyubid power with an attack on Damietta, an important trading center. After the capture of this city in the Nile Delta and the accompanying massacres of the population, the Egypt-

ian Ayyubid sultan al-Malik al-Kamil (1218–1238), who feared for his own position, showed himself ready to grant concessions to the Crusaders. In 1219 he offered to cede Jerusalem in exchange for the return of Damietta. After a century of military conflict and innumerable proclamations of Holy War, he accepted a negotiated solution, even though this was by no means the only option open to him. However, the Crusaders failed to make full use of the chance this offered them to end their campaign successfully.

At his coronation as Holy Roman Emperor, Frederick II (1215–1250), Barbarossa's grandson, spoke out in favor of a new crusade. He gained a dynastic claim to the Holy City in 1225 by his marriage to Isabella, the daughter of the King of Jerusalem, and hoped to improve his standing and unite west and east under his rule by regaining Jerusalem. He engaged in long negotiations with al-Kamil, during which he professed his great respect for the scholarship and theology of Islam, and exchanged valuable gifts with the Arabs before finally concluding a peace treaty in 1229. This sealed the return of Jerusalem and the areas once conquered by Saladin to the Crusaders, who promised, in return, to refrain from crusades against Egypt in future. In March, of the year 1229, Frederick II had himself crowned King of Jerusalem in the Church of the Holy Sepulchre, an act that later caused dismay and outrage throughout the Muslim world. Although al-Kamil sought to justify his actions by pointing out that he had retained control of the Islamic shrines in the city, this hardly calmed the general uproar. Just 15 years later the city was won back again for good when it was occupied by the Khwarazmian Turks, who were allied with al-Salih, one of

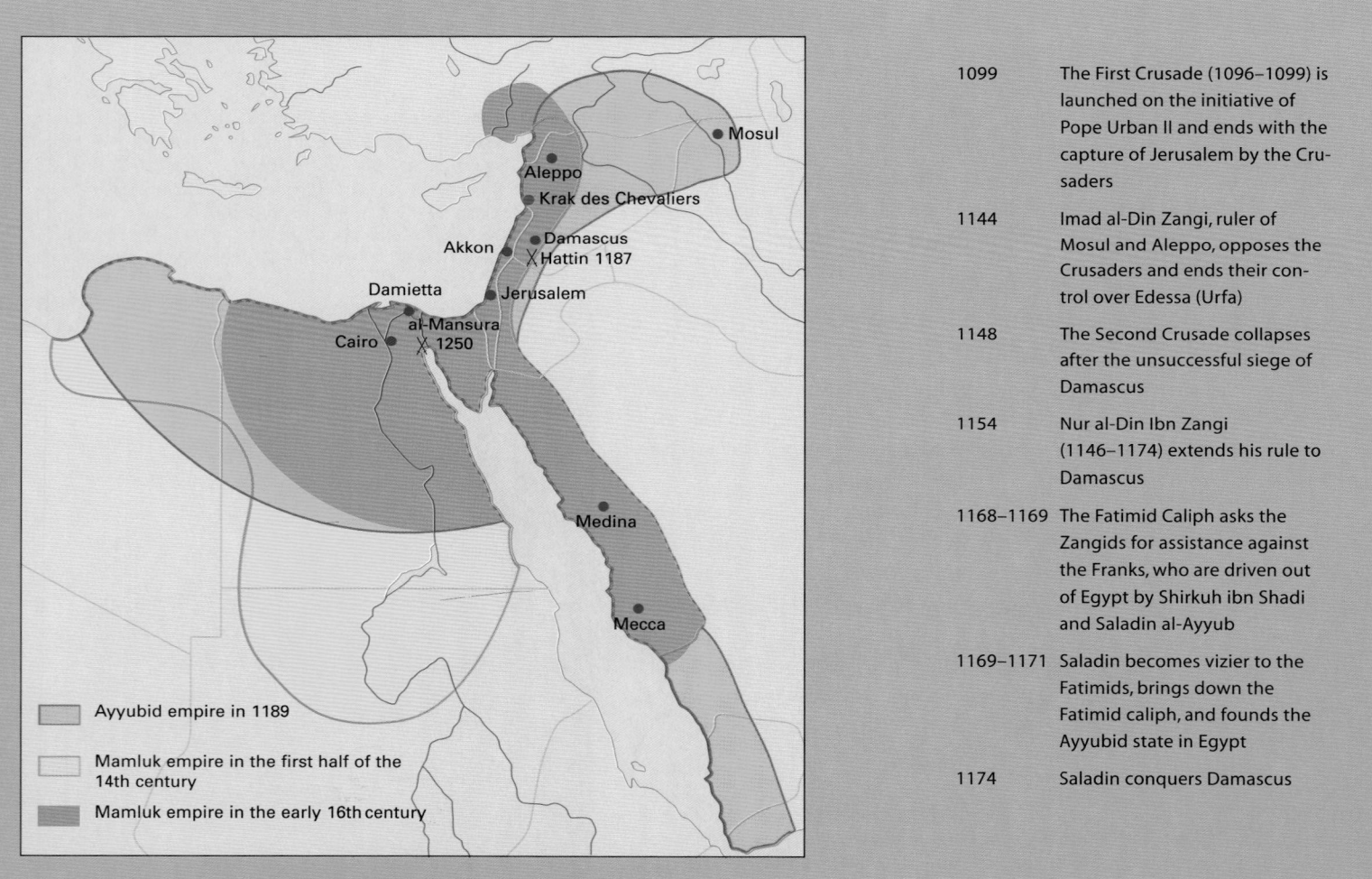

1099	The First Crusade (1096–1099) is launched on the initiative of Pope Urban II and ends with the capture of Jerusalem by the Crusaders
1144	Imad al-Din Zangi, ruler of Mosul and Aleppo, opposes the Crusaders and ends their control over Edessa (Urfa)
1148	The Second Crusade collapses after the unsuccessful siege of Damascus
1154	Nur al-Din Ibn Zangi (1146–1174) extends his rule to Damascus
1168–1169	The Fatimid Caliph asks the Zangids for assistance against the Franks, who are driven out of Egypt by Shirkuh ibn Shadi and Saladin al-Ayyub
1169–1171	Saladin becomes vizier to the Fatimids, brings down the Fatimid caliph, and founds the Ayyubid state in Egypt
1174	Saladin conquers Damascus

Ayyubid empire in 1189

Mamluk empire in the first half of the 14th century

Mamluk empire in the early 16th century

al-Kamil's sons. Not only did saving Jerusalem from the hands of the Christian infidels earn Saladin great prestige among his contemporaries, it also secured his reputation with the following generations. In the west, his fame as the "noble heathen" was based on his generous treatment of the population of Jerusalem. When the city capitulated in 1187, he spared the local Christians and gave them free passage in exchange for a ransom. This contrasted with Christian actions on taking the city in 1099, when they massacred the population in a bloodbath that created outrage even among their own ranks. Saladin willingly allowed Christian pilgrims access to the holy sites in Jerusalem under the peace agreement concluded in 1192.

Western literature created the image of the "noble heathen" as early as the 13th century. There seemed little to choose between the virtues of the Muslim prince and the Christian Crusader, and their tragic conflict was viewed as a result of a historical situation that forced the two to meet in battle. In this context, Saladin became transfigured into an unrivaled statesman above all religious fanaticism. Despite this, the Mamluk sultan, Baibars (1260–1277), who inflicted decisive defeats on the Crusaders, enjoyed greater fame among Muslims as the courageous, vigorous hero of the Arabic *Sirat Baibars*, an epic piece of folk poetry that recounted his life and exploits.

Saladin, Gustave Doré, woodcut, 1884
Saladin's heroic reputation in Europe was reflected in Gustave Doré's book illustration, which featured in Otto Henne am Rhyn's monumental historical work on the Crusades, *Die Kreuzzüge und die Kultur ihrer Zeit* (The Crusades and the Culture of their Time), published in 1884.

1187	Saladin defeats the Crusaders at Hattin and drives them from Jerusalem	1248–1254	The Seventh Crusade ends with the Crusaders' defeat in Egypt
1189–1192	The Third Crusade; the Crusaders take Acre and make it the capital of the Kingdom of Jerusalem	1250	Mamluk officers of Kipchak Turkish origin take power in Egypt
1192	The Ayyubids and the Crusaders conclude a peace treaty; Saladin guarantees Christians free access to the holy sites in Jerusalem	1258	The Mongols led by Hülägü topple the Abbasid caliph in Baghdad
1202–1204	The Fourth Crusade ends with the capture of Constantinople	1260–1277	Reign of the Mamluk Baibars
1217–1219	The Fifth Crusade culminates in the capture of Damietta in the Nile Delta	1260	The Mamluks defeat the Mongols in Palestine and extend their rule to Syria
1225	Frederick II gains a claim to Jerusalem by his marriage to Isabella, the daughter of the King of Jerusalem	1270	Another Crusade collapses in Tunis
1228/29	The Sixth Crusade ends with a peace treaty between al-Kamil, the ruler of Egypt, and Frederick II: Jerusalem is returned to the Crusaders	1279–1290	Sultanate of Qalawun
		1291	Sultan al-Ashraf Khalil, one of Qalawun's sons, conquers Acre and drives the Crusaders out of Palestine for good
1244	The Khwarazmian Turks bring the Crusaders' rule over Jerusalem to an end	1323	Sultan al-Nasir Muhammad (1293–1294, 1299–1309, 1310–1341), another of Qalawun's sons, drives the Mongols back in Syria and concludes a peace treaty with Il-Khan Abu Said
		1382	Sultan Barquq (1382–1389, 1390–1399) takes power,

	bringing Caucasian Mamluks of Circassian origin to power
1400–1401	Timur's armies lay waste to Syria
1426	Sultan Barsbai (1422–1438), who had served as a Mamluk under Barquq, drives the Crusaders out of Cyprus
1485–1496	Conflicts begin to flare up with the Ottomans during the reign of Sultan Qaitbai (1468–1496), who had served as a Mamluk under Barsbai
1516/17	Under Sultan Selim I the Ottomans conquer Syria and Egypt, which now become provinces of the Ottoman Empire

The Aqsa Mosque, Jerusalem, 707–709
The Aqsa Mosque is situated on the southern side of the Temple Mount. This longitudinally-oriented building has seven aisles and a dome over the *mihrab* bay dating back to the early Islamic period. It was rebuilt after the capture of Jerusalem. The Ayyubids saw parallels between the restoration of Islam in the Holy Land and the original conquest of the area by the Umayyads.

The Mamluks

The last Ayyubid, al-Salih Najm al-Din, a great-nephew of Saladin, imported a large number of Turkish military slaves from southern Russia into the empire. After his death and the murder of his young successor to the throne, they took control of Egypt in 1250 and Syria in 1260. The Ayyubids had involved members of the dynasty in the business of government, but now political power was vested in an officer caste composed exclusively of slaves of non-Arab origin (*mamluk* means "owned"). Muslim by upbringing, they were entrusted with all military functions and formed an elite faithful to the government. They were integrated into state institutions via the person of the sultan, who was chosen from among their ranks and acted as supreme commander of the army and head of the state administration. From 1250 to 1390 the empire was ruled by Kipchak Turks known as the Bahri Mamluks, and from 1390 to 1517 by Circassians from the Caucasus known as the Burji Mamluks, whose rule came to an end with the conquest of Syria and Egypt by the Ottoman sultan Selim I.

The real founder of the Mamluk sultanate was Baibars (1260–1277), who, by contrast with Saladin, was a cunning, level-headed general, whose triumphs over the Mongols and the Crusaders were commemorated in Arabic folk poetry. He had played a decisive role in the defeat of King Louis IX of France (St. Louis) in 1250 at the fortress of al-Mansura in the Nile Delta, and when he became sultan he decided immediately to abandon the policy of promoting coexistence between Christians and Muslims that had brought the Ayyubids al-Adil and al-Kamil so little respect among their Muslim contemporaries. The constant military campaigns in Syria and Palestine that came to an end in 1291 with the expulsion of the Crusaders and the fall of Acre, the capital of the Kingdom of Jerusalem, were accompanied by a clever policy of alliance-building. Thanks to his good relationships with Byzantium and the Khan of the Mongol Golden Horde, a convert to Islam, Baibars was able to gain access to the areas from which new Mamluks continued to be recruited. He won great respect in the Islamic world, as well as gaining control over the holy cities Mecca and Medina, by welcoming an Abbasid prince who had escaped from the murderous

Mongols in Baghdad and installing him as caliph in Cairo. In this way, the Mamluks exploited the power vacuum left behind by the Mongol onslaught to promote themselves as protectors and defenders of Islam.

Baibars was succeeded by Qalawun (1279–1290), who had also served under the Ayyubids and founded a dynasty that was to preside over a golden age. The almost 50-year reign of his son, al-Nasir Muhammad, in the first decades of the 14th century was particularly glorious. The sultan expanded the royal estates until they made up almost half of all the feudal land in Egypt. As a result, thanks to his regular income from taxes, he had unbelievable sums at his disposal for building and luxurious living. After the long, drawn-out conflict with the Mongols had been brought to an end by a peace treaty with Il-Khan Abu Said, trade with Asia began to expand rapidly. Caravans from Aleppo traveled out across Iran on the famous Central Asian Silk Road, bringing back silk, jade, porcelain, technical procedures, and artistic motifs as they returned to the eastern Mediterranean. There was a long history of highly prized luxury goods, such as drugs, spices, perfumes, pearls, and precious stones, being transported to Cairo across the Red Sea and the Indian Ocean, and the sea trade profited from the good relations established with the Rasulids in Yemen. This dynasty descended from a branch of the Ayyubids and had created excellent conditions for commerce by opening the port at Aden and developing direct

Minbar **of the Aqsa Mosque**, Jerusalem
This *minbar* was destroyed in 1969 by arson. The Zangid prince, Nur al-Din, commissioned it from four woodcutters in Aleppo for the Aqsa Mosque in Jerusalem, and it was finally put in place to the right of the restored prayer niche after Saladin captured the city in 1187. The *minbar* is richly carved and its side walls are decorated with paneling and intarsia work. A gate gives access to the steps that lead up to the canopied pulpit.

contacts with India and China. Mamluk officers, known as emirs, gained influence and power under the sons and grandsons of al-Nasir Muhammad, and there were constant struggles for dominance between the rival factions at court. Eventually, Qalawun's great-grandson, the young Sultan Hajji II, was deposed in 1382 by the Mamluk commander in chief, Barquq, who established the rule of the Circassian Burji Mamluks. With a few exceptions, future sultans were chosen from among their supporters, and had to court their favor. The emirs now formed a self-serving ruling caste torn apart by internecine feuding.

The internal disturbances that flared up after Barquq's death were exploited by the Mongol ruler Timur. In a single campaign he destroyed the flourishing cities Aleppo, Hama, Homs, and Damascus, and carried off the best artisans to his capital Samarqand. Repeated plague epidemics accelerated the empire's decline. They decimated the population, and weakened craft production and agriculture to the point of collapse. The state tried to compensate for its lost income by tightening controls on commerce. Under Barsbai (1422–1438), who had served under Barquq and came to prominence as the governor of the trading city Tripoli, new sources of income were developed by the institution of a state monopoly on sugar and spices, and the diversion of trade with India via the port of Jidda. However, the duties levied at every stage affected the major merchants, who had previously drawn high profits from trade and not infrequently acted as patrons of the arts. The Mamluk empire lost what importance it still

David Roberts, **Cairo Looking West**, lithograph This view of Cairo by the English artist David Roberts was based on sketches made on his journey through the Orient. It shows the palaces, mosques, and mausoleums of the Mamluk quarter Tabbana in the foreground. The city skyline is dominated by the minarets of a late Mamluk mausoleum and the Mosque of the Emir Aqsunqur, which was built in 1347 and can be seen close to the Citadel (right).

retained as a link between the economies of India and the Mediterranean in 1498, when the Portuguese discovered the direct sea route from Europe to India around the Cape of Good Hope.

Efforts were made to recreate the glories of the past by targeted support for artisanal industries during the long reign of Qaitbai (1468–1496). The regime also sought to strengthen the power of the army by doubling military expenditures. However, the recruitment of the Mamluks and their integration into the system were increasingly a source of difficulties, as many of them refused to live in barracks, where there was rough treatment and violence. It was not possible to modernize the army's weaponry by introducing the firearms with which the Ottomans had achieved their military successes because the cavalry considered them dishonorable and refused to use them. Following Qaitbai's decision to grant asylum to a brother of the Ottoman sultan Bayazid II, the Egyptian regime began to come into conflict with this rising great power, leading to a decline in Mamluk fortunes under Qaitbai's successors. After the capture of Jerusalem and Cairo, the Mamluks became part of the Ottoman Empire in 1517.

The Mediterranean between East and West

Almut von Gladiß

The geographical proximity between the Islamic world and the countries of Europe gave rise to many relationships between the two, leading to vigorous trading across the Mediterranean in spite of the religious reser-vations on either side. After victories over their religious enemies both Muslims and Christians tended to recycle artworks plundered during times of war in their own religious buildings. In Morocco, bells from Christian churches on the Iberian Peninsula were changed into mosque lamps, while the portal of a Crusader church in Acre was incorporated into a newly constructed *madrasa* in Cairo.

These trophies were insignificant, however, compared to the flood of goods that passed across the Mediterranean. The growth in the vol-ume of trade was encouraged by improve-ments in navigation. The Italian maritime cities founded trade missions in the ports of the eastern Mediterranean and organized regular sea passages between these ports and Europe. The crossing between Ifriqiya (modern Tunisia) and Sicily became a matter of routine early on. The first ceramic bowls from the Islamic potteries of Majorca, Ifriqiya and Egypt arrived in Italy by this route as early as the 11th century. They were set into the facades of newly built Romanesque churches. In Pisa alone there are hundreds of these *bacini,* as they are known, decorating churches built between the 11th and 13th

Rock crystal water ewer, from the treasury of the Cathedral of Saint-Denis (Paris), Egypt, late 10th-early 11th century, height: 24 cm, Paris, Musée du Louvre

centuries. While these ceramic goods mainly provide information about trade in the western Mediterranean, the cargo carried by a merchant ship that sank off the Turkish coast at Serce Liman (near Bodrum) has provided valuable informa-tion about activities in the eastern Mediter-ranean. Apart from tons of glass cullet, 80 intact pieces of glassware from Fatimid glassworks were discovered on the seabed. Copper coins of the Byzantine emperor Basil II (976–1025) were found with quarter dinars of the Fatimid caliph al-Hakim (996–1021), suggesting that the goods were meant for Byzantium.

In Europe, the Islamic countries of the Mediterranean had gained access to a huge sales market for consumer goods made of pottery and glass, as well as rare luxury products made of precious materials, such as ivory and rock crystal. In particular, the wonderful objects made of rock crystal from the treasure houses of the Fatimid caliphs enjoyed a fabulous reputation. Many pieces were taken to Italy and came to be owned by the churches of Europe. Local goldsmiths would prepare them for ecclesiastical use by setting them in metal mounts, and they found a

place in Christian culture as liturgical vessels and reliquaries. It is even possible to reconstruct the route by which a Fatimid rock crystal ewer from the treasury of the Cathedral of Saint-Denis (Paris) found its way across the Mediterranean. From the caliph's court in Cairo it probably passed via Arab merchants into the possession of the Norman king Roger II of Sicily (1130–1154). He then gave it to Count Theobold of Blois-Champagne, who, in his turn, donated it to Saint-Denis.

Sicily was the hub of Mediterranean trade. The island was integrated into the Mediter-ranean commercial world in the 10th century under Fatimid rule, and the Arab community continued to play a leading role in many sectors of the economy there even after it had been con-quered by the Normans. The island's main city, Palermo, had been a great center of Islam, with over 300 mosques, and the construction projects undertaken by the Norman kings bene-fited from the achievements of Arab architects there. The textile industry was largely dom-inated by Arabs. A magnificent ceremonial cloak used by Roger II bears an Arabic inscription, according to which it was made in 1133/34 in the court workshops of Palermo, evidently by Arab artisans. The motif of a lion triumphing over a prone camel was probably a symbol of the Chris-tian *reconquista,* which forced the Muslims out of Sicily in the 13th century.

Small numbers of products from Europe were taken to the eastern Mediterranean coun-tries during the Crusades. Many were vessels that the Crusaders carried with them for liturgical purposes. A hoard discovered in the main church of the northern Syrian town of Rusafa includes an oriental incense burner, a silver paten, and a silver goblet engraved with the arms of Raoul I de Couzy of Picardy, who went to Syria with the Third Crusade. According to inscriptions added at a later date, the goblet had been presented to the church of a fortress on the Euphrates, while the paten was donated directly to the church in Rusafa by a citizen of the Crusader city Edessa. Candlesticks from southern France deco-rated with colored *émail champlevé* (sunken enamel), a technique unknown in the Orient, have been excavated in Bethlehem. During their almost 200-year rule over the Kingdom of

***Baptistère* (baptismal basin) of St. Louis,** Muhammad ibn al-Zain, Syria, late 13th century, brass inlaid with gold and silver, diameter 50 cm, Paris, Musée du Louvre

Jerusalem (1099–1291), however, the Crusaders established their own workshops, in which a unique artistic style was developed with the help of local artisans.

Many medieval sources describe gifts exchanged between the princes of the Islamic world and Europe at this time. Despite the constant tensions, relations with foreign states were promoted by the presentation of costly gifts, which symbolized the giver's immeasurable riches and ensured a friendly welcome for emissaries. The medieval texts, *Royal Chronicles of Cologne*, refer to a mission from Jerusalem dispatched by the leprous King Baldwin IV (1174–1185) with numerous gifts for Emperor Frederick Barbarossa in order to draw his attention to the seriousness of the situation in the Holy Land. Barbarossa, who was to die on the Third Crusade while crossing the river Saleph (Göksu) in Turkey, accepted many treasures from Saladin, who also sent Henry of Champagne a ceremonial cloak and matching turban in order to introduce him to oriental customs when he became the ruler of the Kingdom of Jerusalem in 1192. Frederick II, Barbarossa's grandson, won the sympathy of the Ayyubid court in Cairo by presenting several noble horses, one of which came from his own stables and wore a golden saddle set with precious stones. On the other side, Sultan al-Kamil, reciprocated with gifts from all parts of his empire that were more than twice as valuable, as far as the Arabs were concerned, at least. They included a saddle decorated with gold and precious stones, an Indian lute, and a silver tree

with little birds that twittered when the leaves moved. Louis IX, King of France and Regent in Acre from 1250 to 1254, also received numerous precious gifts from his Levantine counterparts, among them animal figurines made of rock crystal, amber apples, and a chess set of rock crystal figures perfumed with ambergris fastened to golden threads.

One of the most wonderful pieces of Islamic inlaid work is the *Baptistère* of St. Louis (Louis IX). This brass basin was included in the inventory of the treasury of the Sainte Chapelle, which was founded in the 14th century at the Château de Vincennes. As it is not decorated with the usual Arabic inscriptions, there can be no doubt that it was made for a Crusader prince. It is lavishly inlaid with gold and silver, and decorated with a repeated fleur-de-lys motif, which, like the whole concept of heraldry, was first introduced to the east by the Crusaders. The basin also depicts royal audiences, hunting trips, battles, and processions of the royal household. These were themes that reflected a chivalrous culture that was of equal importance in both east and west.

Mediterranean commerce gained new impetus in the 14th century as internal trade between the Islamic states collapsed and quality products came increasingly to be manufactured for export. In earlier times, a great deal of Syrian glass decorated with enamel or gilding had been taken to Europe, often in the baggage of returning Crusaders, who would usually give it to the church. Syrian glass was now being copied with great success at Murano (Venice), but the

Hans Holbein the Younger, **The Merchant Georg Gisze**, 1532. Berlin, Gemäldegalerie

brilliant metalwork from Damascus continued to find its way across the Mediterranean. Apart from export products, the luxurious household wares used by the Islamic upper classes were also purchased on the oriental markets. Brass balls emitting incense were considered the epitome of luxury in Italy.

Perfumes and spices were exported from Damascus in lavishly painted ceramic jars. These attractive containers, which have been found at Trapani and other locations in Sicily, were not seen as mere packaging at their destination but valued as works of art and cared for accordingly. Many of these jars were bulbous in form, but cylindrical shapes were also in use. They were described as *albarelli* (normally used to denote medicinal jars) in the Italian commercial contracts and inventories of the 14th and 15th centuries and spurred local Italian potters to make imitations. The "golden" lusterware from Islamic Malaga was made principally for export. No other product in the countries of the eastern Mediterranean could compete with this cheap, mass-produced pottery, and it was of great importance on many European markets, such as those of the Netherlands, England, and Italy.

Italian merchants also recognized at an early date the value of exported oriental carpets. Some of the exquisite wool carpets of the period have survived the centuries in churches and palaces, while the extent of the trade is reflected in many old master paintings of the 15th and 16th centuries, in which they appear as prestigious possessions and symbols of cosmopolitanism.

Cloak of the Norman king Roger II, later used as the coronation robe of the Holy Roman Emperor, Palermo, 1133/34, width 3.5 m, Vienna, Kunsthistorisches Museum

Architecture

Aleppo
Julia Gonnella

"The city is as old as eternity, but still young, and it has never ceased to exist. Its days and nights have been long; it has survived its rulers and commoners. These are its houses and dwellings, but where are their former residents and the people who visited them? These are its palaces and chambers of court, but where are the Hamdanid princes and their poets? They have all passed away, but the city is still here. City of wonders! It endures. Its kings fall; they disappear, but its destruction has not been ordered...."

Like most introductions to the history of Aleppo, the description of the city by the Andalusian traveler Ibn Jubair, who visited Aleppo in 1184, begins with a reference to its great age. It is said, he writes, that Abraham passed through Aleppo on his way from Ur to the Holy Land, milked his cows on the mound that is now crowned by the Citadel, and distributed the milk as alms. Legend has it that Aleppo's name goes back to the patriarch's visit. In Arabic, the city is known as Halab, which is interpreted popularly as being derived from the word *halib* (milk). Many holy sites in the city are associated with Abraham's visit, including the small mosque on the Citadel, where the rock on which he supposedly sat was preserved for many years.

Historical and archeological records also point to a long tradition of settlements on this site, and there can be no doubt that Aleppo has profited from its advantageous geographical location. The city lies on a small river, the Quwaik, in a fertile valley on the western edge of the plains of northern Syria, about halfway between the Euphrates and the Mediterranean. The river guaranteed basic water supplies, while the easily defended rocky mound to the east of the river offered protection from hostile incursions. The site's closeness to the northen plains of Syrian and the fertile hinterland were favorable conditions for a city that has thrived for thousands of years on the interaction between city dwellers, farmers, and nomads. Aleppo's most prosperous periods coincided with the development of trade routes extending beyond the immediate region to the Mediterranean or Mesopotamia. The city has repeatedly shown itself to be an important commercial center, provided that political conditions were favorable and allowed it to be integrated into long-distance trading networks.

Great Mosque of Aleppo, early 8th century, view of the courtyard and minaret
The Great Mosque is still the most important religious site in the city. It was founded in the early 8th century, probably by Sulaiman ibn Abd al-Malik shortly after the Muslim conquest of Aleppo. Its slim, square minaret, which was built in 1094 during the reign of the Seljuk prince, Tutush, on the orders of the judge Abu I-Hasan Ibn al-Khashshab, is one of the architectural gems of northern Syria. This six-story structure is divided by Kufic and *naskhi* inscriptions, and "classicizing" architectural details, such as continuous moldings, pilasters, and elaborate trefoil and polyfoil arches. The architect of this minaret was Hasan ibn Mufarraj al-Sarmini, who was also responsible for the minaret at Maarrat al-Numan.

Mihrab in the Great Mosque of Aleppo
After the sacking of Aleppo by the Mongols, the Mamluk sultan Qalawun ordered his governor Qaransunqur to rebuild the city's Great Mosque on its early Islamic foundations. This major project was undertaken under the supervision of Muhammad ibn Uthman al-Haddad. By 1285 the original colonnades of the prayer-hall and the arcades around the courtyard had been replaced with cross-vaults on pillars, an imitation of elements found in Crusader architecture. The same governor also donated to the mosque a valuable *minbar* made by the craftsman Muammad ibn Ali al-Mausili.

The pre-Islamic period

Our knowledge of ancient Aleppo comes mainly from cuneiform texts that prove the existence of the city dates back to 2000 years B.C. Even at this early stage the city bore the name by which it is still known in Arabic: Halab. Aleppo flourished politically and economically during the 18th century B.C. as the capital of the kingdom of Yamkhad, which during its hieght extended from northern Mesopotamia to the Mediterranean. This magnificent period ended with the Hittite invasion. From this time on the city was a center of only local importance. It was, however, prominent as the site of a temple to the Hittite weather god Teshub, which must have played a significant role across the region until the 1st millennium B.C. The remains of this extraordinarily large religious site are currently being excavated on the Citadel mound. This is the first major archaeological investigation carried out in Aleppo itself and findings have suggested that the mound was used as the *acropolis* of the ancient settlement.

Aleppo was refounded by Seleucus Nicator between 301 and 281 B.C. under the name Beroia. It is still possible to trace the grid system of the ancient city, with its regular blocks of houses, in the modern pattern of streets in the souk. Later, Aleppo came to be ruled by the Romans, and then the Byzantines, under whose rule it was once again known as Halab. In 540, the city was attacked by the Sassanian king Khusrau I, and all its buildings razed to the ground, including the Citadel. Emperor Justinian (518–565) had the city walls rebuilt during a period of peace between the Persians and the Byzantines. He also built a cathedral, the remains of which can still be viewed today in the Madrasa al-Hallawiya.

Islamic Aleppo

Aleppo's capture by Muslim troops in 636, under the command of the Umayyad general Khalid ibn al-Walid, was an event with far-reaching consequences for the city. The first mosque was built in the west of Aleppo, where it was easily accessible to the Arab troops who had set up camp outside the Bab Antakiya, one of the gates to the city. The Great Mosque, which still serves as Aleppo's main place of worship, was founded about 80 years later, probably by the Umayyad caliph Sulaiman (715–717). If we are to believe the medieval historians, it was built in the former garden of the Byzantine cathedral. Sulaiman evidently wanted this building to rival the Umayyad mosque built by his brother Walid in his new capital Damascus. According to the historian Ibn al-Adim, the mosque was decorated with marble and mosaics, which were probably destroyed when the Byzantine emperor Nicephorus Phocas sacked the city in 962. There is now little about the Great Mosque to suggest comparisons with its precursor in Damascus, except its layout as a rectangular mosque with a three-aisle prayer hall (*haram*) and a courtyard surrounded by arcades (*riwaq*). The direction of prayer towards Mecca (*qibla*) is emphasized by a nave leading to the *mihrab*. It is wider than the aisles and is given additional prominence by the dome in front of the prayer niche.

In 750, Aleppo came under the rule of the Abbasid caliphs, who consciously shifted the region's political center to the east with the founding of their new capital Baghdad. Aleppo – no longer a medium-sized provincial city – now

Ground plan of the Great Mosque of Aleppo
The Great Mosque of Aleppo has been rebuilt and renovated many times over the centuries, and only its basic layout still goes back to the early Islamic period. With its rectangular courtyard, which has a three-aisle prayer hall on the southern side and is surrounded by arcades, it is based on the Umayyad mosque in Damascus. The Zangid ruler Nur al-Din restored the mosque in 1174 after a fire and extended it to the southeast.

0   10   20 m

found itself on the border between Mesopotamia and Egypt. Indeed, it was ruled from Egypt for a while by the Tulinids (877) and the Ikhshids (936–37).

Aleppo enjoyed a cultural revival thanks to the Hamdanid prince Saif al-Daula, who conquered the city in 944 and made it the capital of his empire. Saif al-Daula has been recorded in history as a great patron of literature. It was his magnificent court for which the writer Ibn Jubair mourned in the passage quoted above, and it has been celebrated in verse throughout the Islamic world. The greatest poets of the age, such as al-Mutanabbi and Abu Firas al-Hamdani, met there. The flowering of culture that took place under the Hamdanids ended suddenly in 962 with the conquest and destruction of the city by the Byzantines. The looting was so systematic that nothing has remained of Hamdanid architecture, not even Saif al-Daula's famous palace by the river. The city suffered further years of unrest as a result of constant attacks by the Byzantines and regular raids by Bedouin tribes. For a time, Aleppo was controlled by the Egyptian Fatimids but then came under the rule of two nomadic Arab dynasties, the Mirdasids and the Uqailids. It is said that the Mirdasids converted the two churches they found on the Citadel mound into mosques.

For the next two centuries the city's fortunes were dominated completely by the conflict with the Crusaders. As an important staging post on the land route to Jerusalem, Aleppo was attacked by the Franks not long after they took Antioch (in 1100 and 1103). They succeeded in forcing the Seljuk prince, Ridwan ibn Taj al-Daula Tutush, to pay tribute to them, and it was probably only thanks to the committed judge Abu l-Hasan Ibn al-Khashshab that Aleppo was not taken by the Crusaders. The judge took the administration of the city into his own hands and entreated Atabeg Aksunqur al-Bursuqi to become its new ruler, a step taken with the full support of the population. Bursuqi's famous

The Citadel at Aleppo

The most imposing building in Aleppo is the medieval Citadel, which rises high above the city. This natural, flat-topped mound was used in pre-Islamic times as a settlement and place of worship. The Ayyubid ruler al-Malik al-Zahir Ghazi (1186–1216) strengthened it into one of the best fortified military bases in Syria. He had a deep moat dug round the mound and filled with water, and built an imposing new entrance, which was flanked by two massive rectangular towers and could only be reached over a multiple-arch bridge. The Citadel was heavily renovated during the Mamluk period. The most significant addition was a sumptuous ceremonial hall, which the Mamluk governor Jakam min Iwad had built above the Ayyubid gate in 1406/07.

descendants, Imad al-Din Zangi and Nur al-Din, were to build the city up into one of the most important military bases in the struggle against the Crusaders. After a heavy attack by the Crusaders, Ibn al-Khashshab ordered four of the Christian churches in the city to be converted into mosques, including the Cathedral, which was situated next to the Great Mosque.

Imad al-Din Zangi (1127–1146) and his son, Nur al-Din (1146–1173), were both feared generals and determined politicians who enthusiastically propagated ideas about Holy War (jihad) and the unification of the Islamic world among the Muslim population. For the first time in many years, Nur al-Din succeeded in bringing Damascus and Aleppo together under one ruler. Like Damascus, Aleppo was also refortified under his reign. He had the city walls, the Citadel, and aqueducts repaired. He also rebuilt the markets and renovated the Great Mosque, which had suffered heavy damage following a fire.

Nur al-Din believed that the Muslim world should be unified under the banner of Sunni Islam, and promoted himself as its zealous champion. Following the example of the Seljuks, he founded a large number of new legal schools (*madrasas*), which were intended to counter the Shiite influence on the

SYRIA, PALESTINE, AND EGYPT: AYYUBIDS, MAMLUKS, AND CRUSADERS urban population in Syria. The remains of the Madrasa al-Muqaddamiya, the Madrasa al-Shuaibiya, and the Madrasa al-Hallawiya can still be seen in Aleppo. The Madrasa al-Hallawiya is a former cathedral converted into a mosque. This was an example of the care with which Nur al-Din selected sites for the legal schools he built: there can be no doubt that the foundation of a *madrasa* on this site was intended to demonstrate the triumph of Islam over Christianity. The establishment of the Madrasa al-Shuaibiya, on the site of the first mosque in Aleppo at Bab Antakiya, was also highly symbolic, because this mosque was associated more than any other with the capture of the city by the Muslims.

Nur al-Din also gave orders for several monastic institutions (*khanqas*) to be founded. These were places where Islamic mystics (Sufis) lived, taught, and held religious ceremonies. This mystical movement had become influential in Syria under the Zangids, and Nur al-Din himself supported work at several popular places of pilgrimage. For example, he built a new mosque over the site where Abraham milked his cows. This mosque was equipped with a beautiful wooden *mihrab*, which unfortunately, has been lost during the intervening centuries.

The Ayyubid Golden Age

In 1183, Aleppo was conquered by the legendary Ayyubid ruler Saladin, who installed first his brother, al-Adil, then his son, al-Malik al-Zahir Ghazi, as regents. Ghazi's descendants ruled the city until 1260 and were to have a lasting influence there. Ghazi had Aleppo refortified, a large project, much of which had to be completed by his successors. The focus of his work on the defenses was the Citadel, which he had strengthened into one of the most powerful fortresses in the medieval Islamic world. He reinforced the ramparts, regraded the sides of the mound, and had them revetted with stone. The moat round the Citadel was deepened, filled with water, and spanned with a multiple-arch bridge. Visitors still have to cross this bridge to reach the Citadel's entrance, a massive barbican that leads into the center of the fortress through a "bent" passage that turns five times and is protected by three heavy iron gates.

The work executed by Ghazi is fully documented in Arabic sources. Thus we know that in the Citadel he built a large water reservoir, an arsenal, a grain store, and a deep well (*satura*), which was probably intended to function as a secret escape route to the city. The Citadel, however, was not just a military garrison; it was also the ruler's residence, with several palaces, bathhouses and gardens. One of the palaces, a complex with several courtyards, has been excavated. Its center was a main courtyard surrounded by four *iwans* (vaulted halls open on one side) with an octagonal fountain in the middle. The courtyard was paved with marble slabs, and an ornamental pool with water running over a small weir (*shadirwan*) was built in the niche of the northern *iwan*. This palace was probably the much-vaunted Palace of Glory (*dar al-izz*), which burnt down on Ghazi's wedding night. Ghazi also renovated the small Mosque of Abraham in the Citadel and built a second mosque further up the hill with a square minaret that can supposedly be seen from throughout the whole city.

In many respects, Ghazi was continuing the work started by Nur al-Din. Like his predecessor, he had a new courthouse built to the south of the Citadel, from which it could be reached via a secret covered passage. Not only that, he also invested heavily in the foundation of Sunni legal schools, which he considered an important tool in the campaign against the Shiites. Like Nur al-Din, Ghazi also supported the various sites of pilgrimage in Aleppo.

The sultan was not the only person to encourage architecture on a grand scale. Other patrons included state officials, such as Ghazi's closest adviser, Tughril Beg, who completed the Madrasa al-Sultaniya, which had originally been commissioned by the sultan, and patrician families living in Aleppo.

Ramparts of the Aleppo Citadel
Little of the original Ayyubid masonry has survived in the towers and curtain walls making up the defenses of the Aleppo Citadel, particularly as large parts of the fortress had to be reconstructed after the city was sacked by the Mongols in 1260 and by Timur's troops in 1400. A major program of construction work began under Sultan Qalawun and was completed under Sultan Ashraf Khalil. After the destruction inflicted by Timur, the governor Jakam min Iwad made great efforts to rebuild the Citadel. A huge amount of renovation work was also done under the last Mamluk sultan, al-Ghauri, who tried – unsuccessfully – to prepare the Citadel to repel the Ottoman troops.

Archivolt over the first gateway of the Aleppo Citadel
The three huge Ayyubid gateways to the Citadel are decorated with figurative reliefs to which were attributed the power to ward off misfortune. The archivolt over the first gateway shows two double-headed winged dragons with gaping jaws and entwined serpent bodies – a motif traditionally used in the art of the Anatolian Seljuks and Artuqids, who decorated many citadels, city walls, and caravanserais with similar figurative images.

View of the upper and lower mosques in the Aleppo Citadel
Under the Zangids and Ayyubids the Citadel was more than just a heavily fortified military base, it was also used by Aleppo's rulers as their residence and had several palaces, gardens, and bathhouses. The two mosques on the Citadel were originally churches, but were converted under the Mirdasids in the 11th century. The lower mosque, which is associated with the patriarch Abraham, is regarded as the most important shrine in the city. The upper mosque's slim, square minaret was built by Ghazi and is modeled on that of the Great Mosque. It was probably used as a lookout post – in good weather the view from the Citadel extends 130 km north to the Taurus Mountains and eastward to the hills around the river Euphrates.

For example, the al-Agami family founded three schools in the city. Parts of their palace have survived, including a courtyard with an octagonal fountain surrounded by four *iwans*. Ghazi's wife, Daifa Khatun, was also an important patron. She was responsible for the most famous legal school in Aleppo, the Madrasa al-Firdaus (School of Paradise). This *madrasa*, which was used simultaneously as a mosque, mausoleum, and Sufi monastery, is laid out around a courtyard with an octagonal fountain flanked on three sides by arcades. On the northern side there is a wide *iwan*, behind which the living quarters of the students are located. A mosque roofed with three domes is found on the southern side of the courtyard and is flanked by mausoleums to the east and west. In addition to this, Daifa Khatun founded a Sufi monastery

that can probably be identified as the Khanqah al-Farafra. This building is also laid out around a courtyard with an octagonal fountain, and houses a mosque, an *iwan*, and monks' cells arranged on two floors.

Ayyubid architecture has survived comparatively well in Aleppo, including some wonderful buildings constructed with regular blocks of finely dressed stone. Since they are largely unadorned, the appearance of these buildings is determined by the quality of the stone. Usually, the only decoration is a richly ornamented *muqarnas* portal marking the entrance. The heart of the building, whatever its function, is always a courtyard with an ornamental fountain. The courtyard may be surrounded by one or more *iwans*, or by arcades with rooms opening out behind them. In religious complexes, the mosque, with its dome over the *mihrab bay*, is located on the southern side of the courtyard. The four-*iwan* layout was evidently preferred for palaces, but there was no set pattern for Aleppo's legal schools.

One of the most characteristic elements of Ayyubid architectural ornamentation is the stone *muqarnas*, also known as stalactite or honeycomb decoration. This feature dominates the portals found in Aleppo – most of which have shell-shaped vaults – and was also used on squinches. A *muqarnas* dome has survived in the Madrasa al-Sharafiya. Another typical feature is the use of different types of stone in the same structure. Attractive horizontal stripes were created by laying courses of stone of contrasting colors (the *ablaq* technique). The ornamental motifs later applied on a monumental scale under the Mamluks and Ottomans also appeared for the first time during the Ayyubid period, and were used to decorate portals and other features. The most perfect examples are the designs that decorate the *mihrabs* of Aleppo's mosques with their artfully curved and intertwined knot patterns.

Aleppo's cultural life flourished under the rule of the Zangids and the Ayyubids. At the same time, the conflict with the Crusaders had very positive consequences for the city. The lively trading relations established with the Crusader states of the Levantine littoral were a profitable source of income, and the first commercial treaties were concluded with the Venetians in 1207/08. Goods were also exchanged with North Africa and Spain. In addition to this, the city was an important center of artisanal production. Aleppo was famous for its textiles, excellent enameled glass, exquisite ceramics, and, of course, for its metalwork. High-quality woodwork had also been produced in Aleppo since the Zangid period. One of the most brilliant examples of the craft was the *minbar* ordered by Nur al-Din for the Aqsa Mosque in Jerusalem (now destroyed). It was made in Aleppo by members of the Ibn Maali family, a family of woodcarvers who were also responsible for the *mihrab* in the Mosque of Abraham on the Citadel, another treasure that has since been lost. The *mihrab* in the Madrasa al-Hallawiya, which was made in 1245 and is still in place, is a late Ayyubid masterpiece.

The last Ayyubid ruler of Aleppo, al-Nasir Yusuf II (1250–1260), managed to unite Damascus and Aleppo under a single regime, the last time that this happened. However, when the Mongol armies attacked Syria in 1260, Aleppo and Damascus were both captured and sacked. Al-Nasir Yusuf II was taken prisoner by the Mongols, carried off to Tabriz, and subsequently, murdered there.

The Mamluk period

Aleppo came under the rule of the Mamluks and now lay on the northern edge of their empire, which was governed from Cairo. At first, the reconstruction of the city was neglected. Sultan Baibars (1260–1277) merely financed the restoration of two sites of pilgrimage in the west of the city. Only under Sultan Qalawun (1279–1290) was the city rebuilt again. He entrusted his governor,

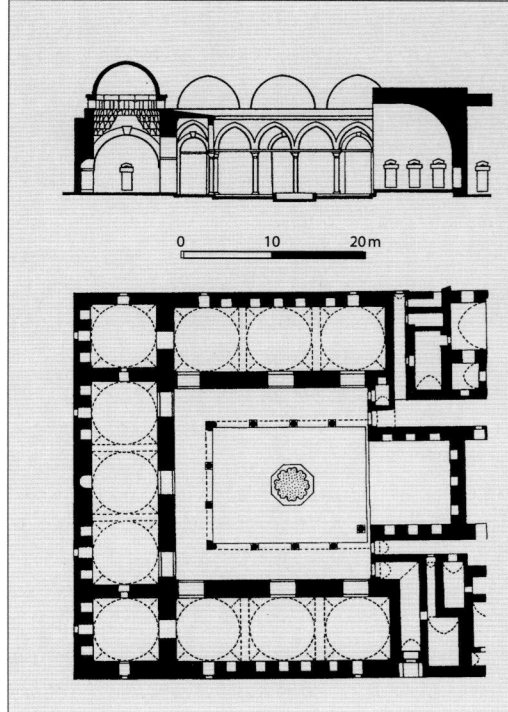

Ground plan of the Madrasa al-Firdaus in Aleppo,
1235–1241
The Madrasa al-Firdaus combines a legal school as well as mausoleums, and monastery in one complex. The courtyard measures approximately 55 x 45 m, with a triple-domed mosque flanked by two mausoleums on its southern side. The halls along the eastern and western sides were probably used for teaching and meetings. Passages lead through past the *iwan* on the northern side to separate residential wings. There was originally a garden in the north of the *madrasa* with a second *iwan* opening off it. Access to the complex was through a narrow corridor from the east.

Courtyard of the Madrasa al-Firdaus in Aleppo, 1235–1241
The Madrasa al-Firdaus (School of Paradise) was founded by Daifa Khatun, the widow of the Ayyubid Sultan al-Malik al-Zahir Ghazi. It is probably the most beautiful Ayyubid building to have survived in Aleppo. The rectangular courtyard of this elegant complex is flanked on three sides by arcades. Their slim marble columns are crowned with a variety of *muqarnas* capitals. A wide *iwan* opens out off the northern side of the courtyard. The octagonal pool with cloverleaf inner walls in the middle of the courtyard is typical.

Qarasunqur, with the repair of the Citadel. This work was completed under his son, Sultan Ashraf Khalil (1290–1293), as is recorded by a monumental band of inscription over the entrance. When the Great Mosque was restored, the original flat roof was replaced with cross-vaults on pillars, a feature that shows the building's links with the architecture of the Crusaders. The use of cross-vaulted halls supported on pillars is typical of many later religious buildings. The Mosque of Governor Altinbugha al-Salihi (1318–1319) is also modeled on the Great Mosque. It was the second Friday (congregational) mosque in Aleppo and was built outside the city walls in the southeast of the city, an indication of the increasing importance of this district.

It only becomes possible to trace a real revival in the city's fortunes, however, in the second half of the 14th century. The traveler Ibn Battuta, who visited Aleppo in 1355, was impressed by the city and praised its bazaar, which was covered with wooden roofing. The records show that there was increased building activity in Aleppo during this period. The best-preserved buildings in the city include the Maristan of Governor Arghun al-Kamili, a palace converted into a hospital, which was founded in 1354/55. It had a large main courtyard and several small courtyards with fountains, each one laid out differently. Another building from this period is the Mosque of Governor Mankalibugha al-Shamsi, which commemorates his victory over the Crusaders near Ayas. This mosque also largely follows the pattern set by the Great Mosque.

In general, the buildings of this period show a strong relationship to Ayyubid architecture. The direct predecessor of the main courtyard of the *maristan*, with its *iwan* and arcades, was the Ayyubid Madrasa al-Kamiliya, while the *mihrab* of the Mankalibugha ash-Shamsi Mosque, with its polychrome knot design, is based on the *mihrab* at the Madrasa al-Firdaus. The rectangular stone reliefs with interlaced patterns that became popular in the late 14th century are also quotations from Ayyubid ornamental masonry. They are features of the Maristan (Hospital) of Argun al-Kamili and the Mosque of

***Mihrab* of the Madrasa al-Firdaus in Aleppo**
This magnificent *mihrab* is constructed of marble of various colors and forms, a point of contrast in an otherwise sober building. The interlaced patterns framing the semicircular prayer niche, which is also flanked by slim columns, are particularly lavish. This *mihrab* is the most perfect example among a number of Ayyubid prayer niches, mostly in Aleppo, that are decorated with the complex, polychrome, interlaced patterns that were particularly influential on Mamluk decorative architecture.

***Mihrab* of the Khanqah al-Farafra**, 1237/38
The *mihrab* of the al-Farafra Sufi convent is one of Aleppo's simpler Ayyubid prayer niches. It is flanked by columns with foliate capitals and framed with a simple interlaced pattern. Like the Madrasa al-Firdaus, the convent is believed to have been founded by Daifa Khatun, the widow of the Ayyubid ruler al-Malik al-Zahir Ghazi. It has an almost square courtyard with cells on the eastern and western sides and an *iwan* on the northern side.

Mankalibugha al-Shamsi. By contrast, another building, the Madrasa of Ishiqtimur al-Maridani, dating from 1371/72, shows foreign influences. Its facade is divided by recessed windows, a feature of the new architecture of the imperial capital Cairo.

This brief boom was rudely interrupted by Timur's troops. The Central Asian army took the city in 1400 and plundered it for three whole days. This was the period of the greatest instability for the Mamluk empire. Additional challenges threatened in the form of natural catastrophes: Aleppo suffered an earthquake in 1403, and there was a severe famine in 1422, followed by an epidemic. However, the city was rebuilt again immediately on account of its strategically important situation on the northern borders of the empire. Its entire defenses were repaired, and the city walls were extended to the east. At the same time, there was a revival of religious building in the shape of a great program of construction, for which additional craftsmen were summoned to Aleppo. One of the first buildings completed was the Utrush Mosque (1410) to the south of the Citadel. This had been begun before Timur's attack and replaced the Altinbugha al-Salihi Mosque as the governor's Friday mosque.

In the meantime, the conflict between the Timurids and the increasingly assertive Ottoman Empire was having positive consequences for Aleppo. The trading routes between Europe and Iran, through Asia Minor, were interrupted, and a great deal of traffic moved to the south. Aleppo was now able to attract the profitable silk trade between Persia and the Italian city-states. The importance of this business to the city is shown by the fact that the most significant buildings erected in Aleppo during the 15th century were caravanserais. There were originally at least seven, but only four have survived. Most of these two-story complexes covered greater areas than the city's religious buildings.

Even if Aleppo profited economically from its proximity to the Ottomans, the expanding empire to the north also represented a threat to the Mamluks, and the large amount of work done on the fortifications shows how seriously this danger was taken. Sultan al-Ashraf Qaitbai (1468–1496) had a great deal of renovation work carried out on the Citadel and the city defenses, and part of the eastern wall was repaired under his son, al-Nasir Muhammad (1496–1498). The most extensive fortification measures were ordered by the last sultan, Qansuh al-Ghauri (1501–1516). He had the Citadel completely rebuilt and strengthened with two massive towers in the north and south. Much repair work was done on the city walls, and the city's northern gate, Bab al-Hadid, was completely rebuilt.

Khusrau Pasha's Mosque Complex,
1537/38–1546
This complex of buildings, which includes a mosque and a *madrasa*, was built for the Ottoman governor Khusrau Pasha in the southwest of the Citadel. It was designed by the famous Ottoman court architect, Sinan. The central building is made up of a square prayer hall with a squinch dome raised above it and a wide hall at the front. It stands in the Ottoman architectural tradition and therefore represents a contrast to mosques built at the same time in Damascus and Cairo, which are much more deeply indebted to the Mamluk legacy.

The Ottoman period

The measures taken by the sultan to fortify the city were not enough to prevent its capture by the Ottomans, who were welcomed warmly by the population. It now became possible for Aleppo to be integrated into the large empire's trading network, and the city was soon able to exploit its favorable geographical situation between the Mediterranean and the Euphrates. In the 16th and 17th centuries Aleppo developed into one of the most prosperous international trading centers in the Middle East. Raw silk from Persia, spices, pepper, indigo, coffee, and other luxury goods were traded there. The range of goods on offer attracted merchants from throughout the world, including the great mercantile nations of Europe, which were allowed to establish trade legations with the permission of the sultan. The magnificence of the city is described in detail in the accounts written by Ottoman and European travelers. There was much admiration for the souks, in which an abundance of goods was to be found, but there are also descriptions of other buildings, such as mosques, *madrasas*, bathhouses, private residences, and the newly-introduced coffee houses, which were very popular.

In fact, most of the monuments in Aleppo that have survived to the present date from the Ottoman period, including the residential houses built of grayish stone, still dominate the appearance of the Old City. These rich courtyard

houses were always built with an *iwan* and a *qa'a*, a domed reception room that was usually paneled with wood. Above all, however, the caravanserais testify to the city's thriving commercial life. One of the most impressive of these complexes is the Khan al-Gumruk, which was built in 1574. During the 17th century it housed the customs authorities, the money changers, the commercial court, and the English, French, and Dutch consulates. Many mosques have also been preserved. The first mosques to be built after the Ottomans took Aleppo, such as the al-Tawashi Mosque and the Takiya al-Maulawiya, were still based on Mamluk models, but by the middle of the 16th century mosques were being built in the classic Ottoman style. The domed, centered buildings with their slim minarets dominate Aleppo's skyline to this day. The new mosques were mainly founded by provincial governors posted to Aleppo and high-ranking Ottoman dignitaries as a way in which they could erect a memorial to themselves. At the same time they also succeeded in using the foundations (*waqf*) they established to finance the mosques as a means of gaining ownership over valuable parts of the city center. Aleppo's last period of prosperity ended with the collapse of the Iranian Safavid dynasty in 1722. The flow of Persian silk came to an end, and the trading routes shifted further to the south.

Altinbugha Mosque in Aleppo, 1318–1323
The mosque of the Mamluk governor Altinbugha al-Salihi was the first Friday mosque built in addition to the Great Mosque. The almost square layout of the Altinbugha Mosque, with its vaulted aisles, was copied from the Great Mosque as it was rebuilt in 1285, when its arcades were replaced with cross-vaults supported on pillars. The octagonal minaret rises from a square base, has a slim shaft divided into three tiers, and is regarded as the earliest example of its type.

Cairo – the changing face of a capital city

Viktoria Meinecke-Berg

The political ambitions and wealth of the Ayyubids (1169–1260) and, above all, the Mamluks (1250–1517), under whom Cairo developed into the center of the medieval Islamic world, were clearly expressed in their urban architecture. Even today, the streets of Cairo's Old City are dominated by the many Mamluk ashlar buildings, with their richly decorated facades, domes, and minarets. However, the basic shape of the city, and the essential features of these complexes, date back to the Fatimids, as does the name Cairo (al-Qahira), which originally denoted their royal capital situated to the north of al-Fustat, the garrison town built by the Arabs when they conquered Egypt.

Cairo's development under the Ayyubids and Mamluks

As the two cities grew together, the main lines of urban development were laid down by the Ayyubids. After taking power in Egypt, the successful general, Salah al-Din (Saladin) attempted to unite al-Qahira and al-Fustat by extending the city walls. Although this ambitious project, which was begun in 1171, was never completed, the whole orientation of the double city was altered by the construction of a citadel, which was integrated into the ring of fortifications on a spur of the Muqattam Hills in the southwest of the Fatimid capital.

The transfer of the center of political power from al-Qahira to the Citadel had major consequences for the former Fatimid capital. There were far-reaching changes to the shape of the city as the royal palaces and their grounds were gradually redeveloped. The process by which al-Qahira and al-Fustat grew together took hundreds of years and only ended in the course of Mamluk rule. However, the two cities never truly merged. Al-Fustat still remained a vibrant center of trade and artisan production, but parts of it were abandoned to decay architecturally during the frequent periods of crisis, while

View of the Sultan Hasan Mosque in Cairo from the south, 1356–1362
This is the largest of the Mamluk mosque and *madrasa* complexes, and houses the sultan's monumental mausoleum. It rises like a massive fortress above the sea of houses in the quarter around the old "Cross Street" (al-Saliba), which leads from the Ibn Tulun Mosque to the Citadel (right). The course of al-Saliba can be traced by following the domes and minarets of the Mamluk complexes that run along the street one after the other.

most of the new building was concentrated in al-Qahira and the areas radiating out to the north, west, and, above all, the south toward the Citadel.

The central district where the Fatimid palaces had been situated became a fashionable area among the upper classes. It was here that the Ayyubid and Mamluk sultans competed for the most prominent locations on which to raise their personal memorial monuments within large complexes of religious buildings. Of course, the most prestigious site was the central area on either side of the main street (Quasaba) where it ran through Bain al-Qasrain, the square between the two great Fatimid palaces. At first, the palace complexes here remained in the hands of Ayyubid and, later, Mamluk aristocrats. They resided in the various palaces and renovated them, but very few major changes were made. For example, the large palace of the Mamluk emir Bashtak (1334–1339) was based on an earlier building dating back to the Fatimid period and still includes a Fatimid mosque.

The first significant alteration to the substance of the Fatimid Eastern Palace came towards the end of Ayyubid rule, when parts of it were torn down to make room for the construction of a large double *madrasa* by Sultan al-Salih Najm al-Din Ayyub (1240–1249). *Madrasas* were introduced to Egypt from Syria by the Ayyubids. There were, therefore, no local models for this type of complex, and the *madrasas* built in Cairo, with their long courtyards, two *iwans* at either end, and several floors of cells at the sides, were based on examples in Syria and Asia Minor.

The Ayyubid sultan, al-Kamil, had built a *madrasa* (al-Kamiliya) already on the opposite side of the road, on the site of the Fatimid Western Palace and the open square situated in front of it (Bain al-Qasrain). All that remains of this

Right: Reception hall in the Palace of Bashtak,
Cairo, 1334–1339
The heart of every Mamluk palace is a reception hall rising
the height of at least two stories. The high central section is
lit by windows in the upper gallery. It opens at each end into
an *iwan* with a flat ceiling, while galleries run along the sides
supported on colonnades. The high lattice screens of the
galleries were intended to allow the female members of the
household to remain unseen and they observed festivities
in this hall, which was reserved for men. The reception hall
was kept at a pleasant temperature by a simple system: the
external screened windows allowed air to penetrate the
building, while the fountain set into the floor in the center
of the hall helped to cool it as it circulated.

Palace of Bashtak, Cairo, 1334–1339
This was once an extensive complex of buildings, but only
the central wing facing onto the main street and housing
the reception hall still survives today. On account of its
location on a busy street, the ground floor of this large,
almost unadorned building accommodates shops that sold
sweets during the Middle Ages. The floors above are almost
completely taken up by the reception hall, the central
section of which rises over two stories in height. Its upper
gallery can be identified from the outside by the group of
high, round-arched windows. The other windows are
covered with wooden lattices.

Lattice window in the Palace of Bashtak,
Cairo, 1334–1339
The traditional, artfully turned and joined
wooden lattices placed over windows provide
effective protection against the heat of the
sun, particularly during the summer months,
and bathing rooms in a pleasantly diffuse
light. They play an important role in secular
buildings, particularly for female residents,
since they allow women to observe life on the
street without themselves being exposed to
the gaze of strangers.

madrasa, however, is a large, ruined *iwan* hidden behind an Ottoman facade. It was probably at this time – at least by the time the Mamluk Sultans erected their large complexes – that the square between the two Fatimid palaces was narrowed and turned into a section of mainstreet or Qasba. The richly embellished ashlar facades of the religious buildings built by Sultan Qalawun (1284–1285), his son al-Nasir Muhammad (1295–1304), and Sultan Barquq (1384–1386) run continuously as far as the Madrasa al-Kamiliya, while on the other side of the street the ruins of a corner of wall and two windows decorated with the lion blazon of Sultan Baibars are all that remains of the large *madrasa* built by the first Mamluk sultan immediately next to the mausoleum of the Ayyubid Madrasa al-Salihiya (1262–1263).

Other royal buildings were erected by sultans to the south of al-Saliba. For example, there is the Madrasa of Sultan Barsbai (1242), which houses his mausoleum and also accommodated in its frontage a public drinking fountain, combined with a

school for orphans called a *sabil-kuttab*, in the loggia above. Next follow two complexes of *madrasas* and the Madrasa and Mausoleum of Sultan al-Ghauri (1501–1504), with their related portals, face each other across the road. Finally, the great courtyard Mosque of Sultan al-Muaiyad was founded next to the southern city wall (1415–1420). Al-Muaiyad made the most of the special advantages offered by this prominent location when he triumphantly placed the minaret of his mosque on top of Bab Zuwaila, the Fatimid city gate that stood next to it.

The expansion of the city beyond the Fatimid city walls mainly took place during the Mamluk period. At this time a series of important foundations connected with the royal family were established along the main road leading to the Citadel (*darb al-ahmar*), raising its status markedly. It is lined by a succession of impressive buildings: the courtyard Mosque of Emir Altunbugha al-Maridani (1338–1340), a favorite and son-in-law of Sultan al-Nasir

Mausoleum of Emir Hairbak, Cairo, 1502
This mausoleum abuts directly onto the early Mamluk palace in which the emir lived and was built to match the monumental proportions of this building, which is now completely ruined (right). The axes of the mausoleum rotate between the main facade, which is aligned with the street, whereas the inner hall is oriented towards Mecca and followed by the side facade. Through this rotation of axes, the building presents itself in an interesting series of steps. The arabesque dome towers over the mosque and *madrasa* which Hairbak later built together with the minaret.

Facade, mausoleum, and minaret of Sultan Qalawun's Complex, 1284/85
This complex consists of a *madrasa* and mausoleum, and once included a hospital. It was built very quickly – in just 13 months – due partly to the use of slaves captured during military campaigns, and partly to the availability of building materials salvaged from the demolished Fatimid palaces. The unusual plastic treatment of the pointed-arch recesses in the facade and the form of the three-light windows let into them suggest Western influences probably introduced by the Crusaders.

Muhammad; the *madrasa* built by the mother of Sultan Shaban (1368/69); the Mosque of Emir Aqsunqur (the "Blue Mosque"), incorporating the Mausoleum of Sultan Kujuk (1346/47); and next to it the Mosque of Emir Hairbak (1502), who was appointed governor of Egypt by the Ottomans. The early Mamluk palaces of the most powerful emirs, impressive ruins of what were once very extensive complexes, are to be found directly at the foot of the Citadel. It was here that Sultan Hasan built his monumental mosque and *madrasa*, which, to a certain extent, forms a counterweight to the Citadel in the urban landscape.

The buildings of the Ayyubid and Mamluk periods

The examples mentioned above represent only a fraction of the Ayyubid and Mamluk building activities in Cairo. Not only were the sultans enthusiastic builders, every emir who achieved high office and rank sought to gain God's blessing (*baraka*) and keep his name alive by building religious and charitable institutions connected to his mausoleum.

These complexes are usually made up of several buildings, bringing together religious and social institutions, and, according to location, commercial premises. An examination of the layout of these complexes and the way they are situated in the streets shows that, when construction work was undertaken in areas beyond the city walls that were becoming increasingly built up, the new buildings continued to be integrated carefully into the urban landscape by the same methods as were applied during the Fatimid period. The fact that land and property were increasingly protected by the establishments of pious endowments called *auqaf* (sing. *waqf*) had a stabilizing influence on the structure of the city because these holdings could not easily be interfered with or extended at will.

Dome of Qalawun's Mausoleum, 1284/85
In Qalawun's Mausoleum the usual square plan of Cairene mausoleums was adapted to create an octagon formed of four colossal columns and four piers that rise higher than the outer walls, supporting a circle of windows and, above them, the dome. One of the outstanding achievements of early Islamic architecture, the Dome of the Rock in Jerusalem (691/92), provided the model for this exceptional double construction. The interior decoration is also remarkable, in particular the colorful marble incrustation of the dado and the rich stucco work in the arches of the octagon and the windows.

Building land was becoming increasingly difficult to obtain, and it often required great skill to accommodate a complex with several structures effectively into a limited amount of space. On the whole, the architects' approach was based on the principle of adapting their buildings as advantageously as possible to the existing environment and optimizing the size of the plot available.

Mausoleums

Apart from some Friday mosques, almost all the religious buildings in Cairo are characterized by the incorporation of one or more mausoleums (known as either *turba* or *qubba*). These domed buildings are usually square in plan, their domes resting on zones of transition that became more and more lavishly decorated over the centuries. The only exception to this pattern is the Mausoleum of Sultan Qalawun (1284/85) next to his *madrasa* and hospital (*maristan*) in Bain al-Qasrain. Like the whole complex built by this important sultan, the architecture of this building is unique. The dome is supported by four columns and four piers forming an octagon within the square construction of the chamber – an arrangement that draws on the ideal model provided by the early Islamic Dome of the Rock in Jerusalem. By contrast, the equally as large

Monastery of Sultan Faraj ibn Barquq, Eastern Cemetery of Cairo
Exterior view of the *qibla* side and the inner courtyard with arcades in front of the entrance, 1400–1411
On the *qibla* side, the prayer hall is topped with a small, ribbed dome, while the corners are occupied by comparatively large mausoleums. By contrast with the brick dome in the center, they are built completely of stone and decorated with the chevron pattern commonly used on domes from this period until the mid-15th century. On the opposite side of the complex there are two minarets corresponding to the mausoleum domes on the entrance side. These towers are also decorated with rich ornamental masonry.

Mausoleum of Sultan Hasan (1356), with its square construction, impresses the visitor by its size alone.

It would appear that the Mamluk patrons saw the erection of their own mausoleums as the main reason for establishing foundations, as within the city walls such monuments were only built in connection with religious institutions, usually a *madrasa*, mosque, or monastery (*khanqa*). This tendency can be traced back to the late Ayyubid period, when the Mausoleum of al-Salih Ayyub (1250) was added posthumously to the Salihiya Madrasa by the first woman to rule the Mamluk state.

The importance that the Mamluks attributed to their mausoleums is also shown by the fact that the mausoleum was usually the first part of a complex to be built, as is evident from inscriptions on the buildings and written sources. Contemporary documents relating to building work show that the aristocracy preferred to build their mausoleums close to their own residences, would buy up continuous plots of land over a long period, and collect the necessary structural and decorative materials. The mausoleum would then be given a prominent place in the complex. Within the heavily built-up central district it was, without exception, placed on the street. Where a complex was built on a corner plot, the mausoleum would be placed on the more important street, so that the dome

would be seen by as many passers-by as possible. Often the exterior appearance was more important than the interior design of a mausoleum, and, since the domes would be set on the roof at an imposing height, the interior chambers were often very high – as in the complex of Emir Janibak (1426/27) on al-Saliba.

This deliberate placing of mausoleums on the streets within the urban area of Cairo is all the more remarkable since the tombs in the cemeteries, which extend from the south to the north-east of the city, were traditionally placed in the south-east of the complexes of which they are part, the side facing Mecca. Since, in addition to this, no restrictive limits on the size of plots had to be taken into account in the cemeteries, the large funerary complexes built in these locations are more balanced in their layout, and sometimes completely symmetrical. For example, the monastery (*khanqa*) of Sultan Faraj ibn Barquq (1400–1411) is designed symmetrically on a square plan with two mausoleums flanking the prayer hall and two minarets corresponding to them on either side of the entrance.

The religious character of the mausoleums is also underlined by the presence of prayer niches. These sacral endowments were intended by the donors for regular Koranic recitations and therefore involved a mausoleum to a certain extent in the regular activities undertaken in mosques and *madrasas*. The tombs themselves would be placed in a vault under the chamber.

Courtyard mosques

At the heart of each complex there stands a mosque, *madrasa*, or Sufi monastery established in association with the patron's mausoleum. Under the Mamluks, these buildings, which had initially been clearly differentiated in their function and architectural form, developed into multifunctional institutions that could be used equally as mosques or *madrasas*, regardless of how they were built. The Ayyubids did not leave any notable mosque architecture. Rather, where necessary, they would extend, restore, and renovate the mosque buildings that were already in place, such as the old Amr Mosque in al-Fustat. The Fatimid Hakim Mosque became the main mosque in the center of Cairo, while al-Azhar was closed, only to be reopened under the Mamluks.

Al-Zahir Baibars, one of the most active patrons of architecture among the Mamluk sultans, built a large courtyard mosque in 1267–1269 in the newly developed district of al-Husainiya just outside the gates of the northern wall, the first of a great many new mosques founded by the Mamluks. It is an example of the traditional Arab courtyard mosque, which is characterized by *riwaqs* (arcades) running around an open courtyard, and therefore stands in the tradition of the preceeding main mosques of Cairo (Amr, Ibn Tulun, al-Azhar, al-Hakim).

In fact, it is said that Baibars consciously based the monumental dimensions of his building on the first mosque in Cairo, the Amr Mosque. However,

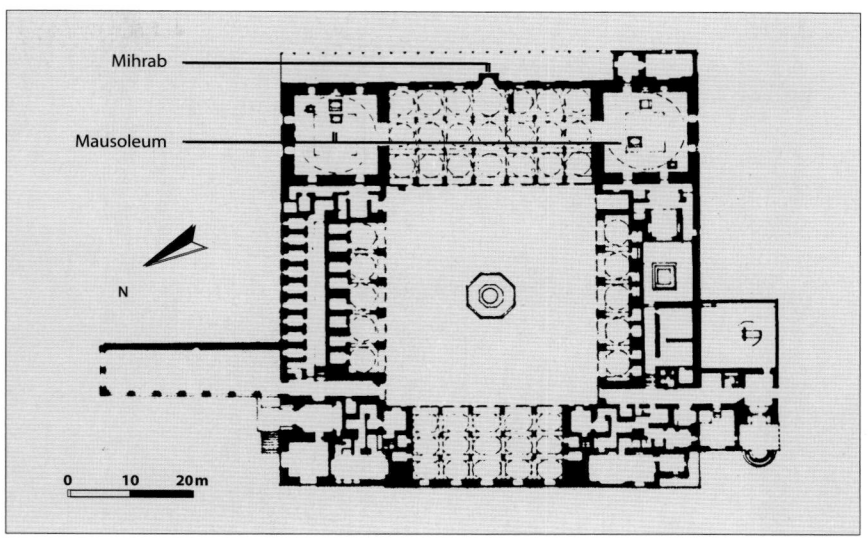

Monastery of Sultan Faraj ibn Barquq
Plan and dome of the women's mausoleum, Cairo, 1400–1411
This funerary complex accommodated a Sufi monastery. It was founded for Faraj's father, Sultan Barquq (d. 1399), and his family. Conse-quently, the two mausoleums dominate the complex, rising in the corners of the building on either side of the prayer hall. The mausoleum on the left was intended for the sultan and the male members of the royal family, the one on the right, for the women.

Mausoleum and plan of the Sultan Hasan Mosque in Cairo, 1356–1362

This complex is about 150 meters long and 70 meters wide, with walls that rise to a height of 38 meters. It is oriented with Mecca, combines a mosque and *madrasa* in its central four-*iwan* complex, and is said to have been larger than any previous building in Cairo. The sultan's mausoleum, which adjoins the main *iwan*, forms a huge salient projecting from the southeast face of this colossal building.

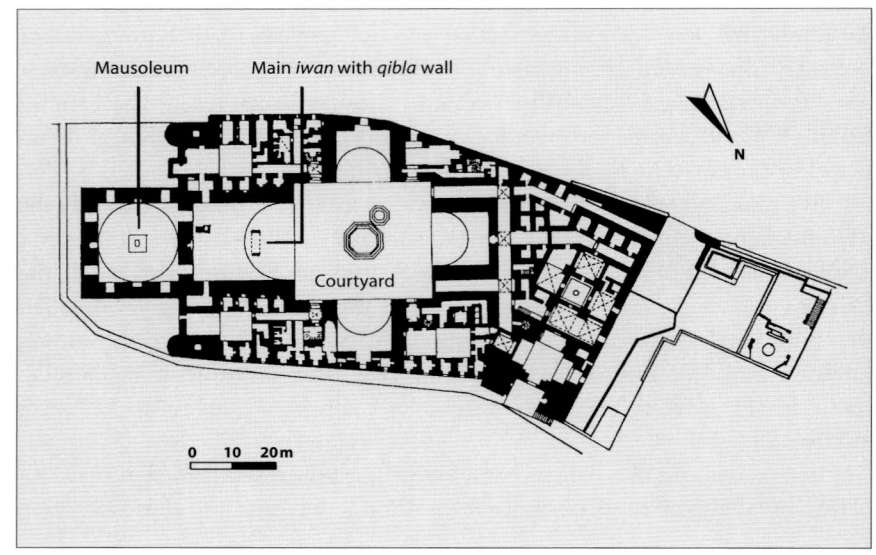

Below: **Prayer niche in the main *iwan* of the Sultan Hasan Mosque**, Cairo

In the Sultan Hasan Mosque, the typical Mamluk-period marble incrustations cover the *qibla* wall of the main *iwan* in its fulll height. The panels were cut from ancient columns and are set in stone frames, most of them of white marble, some bearing fine floral reliefs. The jamb-shelf columns of the prayer niche with their foliate capitals were looted from Crusader buildings in Syria.

Below: **Courtyard of the Sultan Hasa Mosque**, 1356–1362

All four classical Islamic law schools were allotted, and taught in, one of the four *iwans* that open off the courtyard of this complex. The large main *iwan* on the *qibla* side was also used as a prayer hall. The doorways situated at the sides of the *iwan* are highlighted by a type of decoration normally reserved for outer facades. They lead to the corner annexes housing the schools, in which the living quarters and communal spaces used by teachers and students are grouped around courtyards on several stories.

significant stylistic features, such as the decorated projecting portals, were derived from the Hakim Mosque, the proportions of which had also been based on the Amr Mosque. Contemporary sources explicitly state that the unusually large dome in front of the prayer niche (*maqsura*, i.e. the Sultan's prayer place), was modeled on the largest mausoleum built up until this time and was considered one of the holiest sites in Cairo after the reintroduction of Sunni orthodoxy: the Mausoleum of Imam al-Shafii (d. 820), which was built by Sultan al-Kamil in 1211 over the grave of the founder of the Shafii legal school. Such quotations from earlier monuments of the greatest historical and religious significance always played a role for the Mamluk builders as they attempted to reflect their masters' political ambitions in monumental form.

Magnificent courtyard mosques were built after the Baibars Mosque during the reign of Sultan al-Nasir Muhammad, who was also an enthusiastic builder. In these buildings, the dome of the *maqsura* tends to be particularly prominent because, although they were designed on a smaller scale – as is true of the Sultan's Mosque in the Citadel (1335/36) or the Mosque of Altunbugha al-Maridani (1338–1340) – their domes are just as large as those of earlier buildings. As a symbol of power, the dome dominates the interior of a prayer hall and the view of a mosque in the city skyline. The last large courtyard mosque was built by Sultan al-Muaiyad Shaikh inside the south wall next to Bab Zuwaila (1415–1420). It functions as al-Muaiyad's memorial and with two mausoleums flanking the prayer hall.

Four-*iwan* complexes

Apart from the courtyard mosque, another type of building proved practical for mosque architecture at an early date: the cruciform four-*iwan* complex, which was introduced to Cairo when *madrasas* began to be built there. One of the buildings commissioned by Sultan Baibars set the pattern for this type of architecture: his *madrasa* on Bain al-Qasrain (1262/63). Almost nothing is left of this building today, but some idea of how the early cruciform complexes were laid out can be gained from the Madrasa of Sultan al-Nasir Muhammad, which was modeled on the Madrasa of Baibars and stands on the opposite side of the street. Such complexes consisted of four barrel-vaulted *iwans*, grouped around a courtyard to form a cross-shaped ensemble, with accommodation on several stories at the corners, which included cells for the teachers and students. Like the Ayyubid variant with two *iwans*, this type of layout, which first originated in Iran, was introduced to Egypt from Syria. The four-*iwan* complex had become the preferred form for all kinds of religious institutions by the time the Mosque and Madrasa of Sultan Hasan (1356–1362), which combined a Friday mosque and teaching facilities for all four of the classical schools of Islamic law, was built beneath the Citadel. The mosque and *madrasa* complexes built by the late Mamluk sultans Qaitbai (1486–1496) and al-Ghauri (1501–1516) are almost all constructed on a four-*iwan* plan.

The basic four-*iwan* pattern was constantly varied, adapted, and combined with elements derived from arcaded courtyard complexes. Of the early examples, the Madrasa of Sultan Qalawun (1284/85) is outstanding. Like his mausoleum, its main *iwan* is articulated by interior arcades. The qibla *iwan* in the nearby Madrasa of Sultan Barquq (1384–1386) was built on a similar, if simplified, pattern with a three-aisle colonnaded hall.

From the mid-14th century, the layout of the four-*iwan* scheme changed significantly due to the increasing density of building in the city. The cramped plots available made it impossible to build on a large scale. This meant that the side *iwans* sometimes had to be reduced to niches, while the barrel-vaulted *iwan* – itself a monumental architectural feature – was replaced by structures with flat ceilings. Eventually, a roof was placed on the center court as well. This

Mausoleum Complex of Sultan Qaitbai in the Eastern Cemetery of Cairo, 1472–1474
A room housing a drinking fountain with the loggia of an orphans' school above it is situated to the left of the entrance. The portal leads into a four-*iwan madrasa*, from which there is access to the sultan's mausoleum. This chamber forms a salient projecting from the qibla facade, and rises above the rest of the complex with a stepped zone of trans-ition, on top of which a drum supports the dome. The architectural ornamentation, in particular the exquisite masonry of the portal, minaret, and dome, is matched by the lavish interior decor with its marble incrustations, and carved and gilded woodwork.

created comparatively intimate interior spaces, the appearance of which was not dissimilar from the secular buildings that provided models for these flat-roofed constructions. On account of their exquisite decorations, the mosque and madrasas of Qajmas al-Ishaqi (1480) and the mosque *madrasa* of Sultan Qaitbai (1472/73) are among the most impressive of these late Mamluk four-*iwan* complexes.

The *sabil-kuttab*, a public drinking fountain with a Koranic school for orphans above it, is an integral component of many complexes. The drinking fountain was placed on the ground floor at the front of the building. It often forms a salient, and there was a preference for it to be placed on street corners, so it is accessible from several directions. The upper story was an obvious place to accommodate a school. This was usually designed as a loggia shielded by wooden lattices (*mashrabiya*). During the late Mamluk period, public fountains were also established as separate foundations, usually as relatively large buildings. Several were founded by Sultan Qaitbai. The connection between the fountain and the orphans' school, which had been combined in complexes for practical reasons, was maintained in these independent "fountain schools."

Shops are often built into the facades of these buildings, according to their location, on busy streets that were occupied by markets. The mosque or *madrasa* would be moved up to the first floor due to the inclusion of shops or, as in the case of the Madrasa of Sultan Ghauri (1501–1504), a market hall (*qaisariya*). These hanging mosques (*al-muallaqa*), are entered through portals placed at the top of projecting flights of steps. Mixed usage of buildings is also a feature of secular architecture located on public sites. There is a row of ten shops

that incorporate the front of the Palace of Emir Bashtak (1334–1339) in the center of Cairo. Significantly, the large palaces built close to the Citadel by some of the most powerful emirs do not include examples of this kind of urban building. The lower stories of these complexes were used to accommodate stables. The mixture of business and residential developments, typical of the city center, is also found in the city's caravanserais (*wakala*), of which the example built by Sultan-al-Ghauri (1508) is still the best preserved. Storage rooms, offices, and other commercial facilities are found only in the two lower stories, while the floors above are reserved for rented accommodation (*rab*).

Architectural ornament

The preferred material for large public buildings under the Ayyubids and Mamluks was ashlar, mostly combined with brickwork, which was used for vaultings and less exposed sections without a structural function. Brick had traditionally been used for building in Cairo, and ashlar first became important during the Fatimid period, when it became common as a dressing for external facades. Master builders from northern Syria, a region with a long tradition of masonry, were entrusted with the three Fatimid city gates, vaulted buildings constructed with great precision. Syrian craftsmen also played a major role in the further development of stone building under the Ayyubids and Mamluks, while materials for decorative dressings with alternating courses of colored stone (*ablaq*) were imported from Syria. New forms of architectural ornamentation, such as *muqarnas* formations on vaulted portals, niches, and zones of transition

Prayer niche detail, Mausoleum of Qalawun, 1284/85
Colored marble incrustations were used for the first time in the dado of this mausoleum. This subsequently became an established part of the repertoire of Mamluk architectural ornamentation. This lavishly designed prayer niche is embellished with pillars and three layers of small arches.

Portal of the Mosque of Sultan al-Muaiyad Saih, 1415–1420
This recessed portal, which rises above from the facade of the building with its frame, is additionally marked out by its contrasting black-and-white layers of stone and rich decorative masonry – the *muqarnas* vault, floral reliefs on the vaulted zone, and the stone intarsia elements around the door.

Mausoleum of Qaitbai, 1472–1474
This high Mamluk minaret springs from a square base. The lower tier is octagonal, while the upper tiers are round and culminate in a finial. The structure follows a common pattern, but the ornamentation added by the stonemasons is unique in every detail.

Stucco details above the entrance to the Mausoleum of Sultan Qalawun, 1284/85

Ornamental stucco work has a long local tradition. In the early Mamluk period it was mainly applied to the upper zones of walls where they were built of brick. On the high recessed portal of Qalawun's Mausoleum it forms a frame for two bands of windows. The multi-layered interwoven floral patterns on the walls, intrados sections, and spandrels contrast with the geometrical star patterns of the stucco lattice windows.

found their way to Cairo by way of predecessors in Aleppo and Damascus. But, it was in the empire's capital, that they were raised to their greatest heights.

These monuments are lavishly decorated, inside and out. The facades of religious buildings are articulated with recesses – a typical feature in Cairo from the Fatimid period on. Freestanding buildings are dressed with facades running along all their exterior walls. The richest decoration is reserved for the wall around the entrance, where the portal projects from the facade, and is covered by a *muqarnas* vault. The height and depth of these portals vary, as is also the case in secular architecture. The facades of secular buildings were not, however, divided by recesses, and the only adornment was provided by decorative groups of windows. The standard repertoire of ornamental masonry included calligraphic friezes that decorate the walls of portals and run horizontally along facades, *muqarnas* vaults in niches and windows, alternating courses of different-colored stones (*ablaq*), intarsia panels with geometrical patterns, and stone carvings with floral patterns. These decorations were varied, enriched, and became increasingly refined as time went by.

Apart from decoration added in stone, to which the rich marble incrustations typical for Mamluk architecture belong, stucco, the traditional ornament for brick architecture, still played a significant role long into the Mamluk period. Lavish stucco work is found on many buildings of the 13th and early 14th centuries. It was attached to sections built of brick, such as the areas above stone facades, the zones of transition and domes of mausoleums, inside and out, as well as minarets. Stucco ornament was also used in prominent locations inside buildings, such as prayer niches, *qibla* walls, intrados sections, and the frames around windows. From the

Mausoleum of Sultan Qaitbai, 1472–1474

This dome is regarded, justifiably, as the masterpiece of the increasingly refined, elaborate masonry of the late Mamluk period. On earlier decorated domes, one pattern had always given way to another. In this case, however, two types of pattern – an interlaced geometric star pattern and a floral arabesque – are combined, forming a sharp contrast, yet complementing each other perfectly. The star pattern is made up of smooth lines that divide up the surface of the dome. It is laid over a delicate arabesque consisting of hollow-molded double lines that create interesting textures and effects.

mid-14th century, however, domes and minarets were increasingly constructed of solid stone and decorated with great delicacy by stonemasons. In particular, the ornamentation of the mausoleum domes is characterized by a great deal of inventiveness. At first, forms taken from brick architecture, such as ribs, were simply translated into stone. Later, the ribs would be extended down over *muqarnas* consoles, knotted in great loops, or sometimes twisted. Eventually these patterns developed into chevrons, interlaced star patterns that lay over domes like fine nets, and finally – the height of refinement – filigree floral arabesques. This same variety of ornamental motifs decorated the tall and slender minarets.

This rich architectural ornamentation was complemented by the carved, painted and gilded wooden ceilings, cupboards, and turned wooden lattices (*mashrabiya*) found inside the buildings. In order to have some idea of how richly and luxuriously decorated medieval mosques in Cairo were, we also need to keep in mind the movable fittings donated by the founders of the religious institutions, such as glass lamps decorated with luster painting, bronze candlesticks and Koran boxes inlaid with silver, fine fabrics, and many other masterpieces of the decorative arts that are now preserved in international museums.

Damascus – the development of an ancient cultural center

After the fall of the Umayyad dynasty (750), Damascus had become a minor provincial city. It only regained its regional importance when the Zangid Nur al-Din Mahmud occupied it in 1154 and used it as a base in the campaign of resistance against the Crusaders. As in other Syrian cities, the modernization of the fortifications was the main priority during the over 100 years of armed hostilities. The ancient city walls were repaired and strengthened partly incorporating old sections of walling and reusing ancient blocks of stone. The gates of the city were also gradually replaced with new structures. The Citadel, which was located in the northwest of the city on the site of an ancient military camp, was enlarged by the Ayyubids to its current size (starting in 1207) and established as the seat of the government. In the course of construction work in the city center, the main axes of the ancient road network were maintained – such as the Decumanus Maximus, the modern "Straight Street," which cuts through the city from west to east.

For centuries the Umayyad Great Mosque had been a center of religious veneration and a site of pilgrimage. Now, the area between it and the Citadel developed into the main Muslim district in the city, which had a Christian quarter in the northeast and a Jewish quarter in the southeast. It was here that Nur al-Din founded his famous hospital, the Maristan al-Nuri (today a museum of the history of medicine) in the year in which he took power (1154). This was followed by a series of religious and civic institutions founded by Nur al-Din and the succeeding Ayyubids (from 1186): the Madrasa al-Nuriya al-Kubra, which included Nur al-Din's Mausoleum (1167–1172); a bathhouse that is still in use today, the Hammam al-Buzuriya (pre-1172); and the Madrasa al-Adiliya, which was begun by Nur al-Din, but only completed by the Ayyubids in 1223/24.

During this period of cultural prosperity, the city began to expand to the northwest, beyond its fortified walls. Further to the north, on the slopes of Mount Kassioun, a new, independent district, al-Salihiya, was created in the years after 1159 for Palestinians who had fled from the Crusaders when they invaded Jerusalem. With its places of pilgrimage and holy sepulcher's graves, this area had had strong religious associations since ancient times. Now it became the home to new religious institutions, such as the Madrasa al-Umariya (founded in the early 13th century) and the al-Muzaffari Mosque (1202/03), the district's main mosque. The district began to attract both the religious clerical caste and Ayyubid princes and their families, who erected mausoleums in combination with mosques, madrasas, and smaller educational institutions (dar al-hadith, dar al-Quran).

Under the Mamluks, who subjected Syria to Egyptian rule in 1260, Damascus asserted its status as the capital of the empire's Syrian province and enjoyed a degree of economic prosperity, but obviously it lacked the commitment of royal patrons. Sultan Baibars (1260–1277) was the only Mamluk to be buried in Damascus. The proportions and artistic ambitions of the mausoleum, built by his son immediately after his death, derive from the Ayyubid Madrasa al-Adiliya (1223/24), which it faces across the street.

Nur al-Din's Hospital, Damascus, 1154
The local tradition of masonry and eastern brickwork techniques meet in this portal. The building is a stone structure to which a stucco and brick *muqarnas* half-vault has been added over the doorway, which is also spanned by an antique pediment. This new type of decorative portal is derived from the *muqarnas* domes of other buildings built by Nur al-Din, such as the domes over the hospital's vestibule, which draw on Iraqi precedents. Translated into stone, this feature, initially intended purely as additional ornamentation, became the recessed *muqarnas* portal.

Mausoleum of Baibars in Damascus, 1277–1281
The interior of the mausoleum is decorated with a wide frieze of golden mosaics depicting elaborate buildings in a landscape of trees and ornamental plants. It was based on the early Islamic mosaics in the nearby Great Mosque. Later, in the early Mamluk period, mosaics were used occasionally to decorate prayer niches, but their rather clumsy finish suggests that there were no longer specialists available with a mastery of this complicated decorative technique.

The public buildings of Damascus were traditionally built of stone. The technically perfect finishing of the stone and decorative details point to a constant, sometimes strong, influence exerted by builders from Aleppo. It is probable that craftsmen from Aleppo were recruited specifically for particular projects. The Ayyubid and early Mamluk buildings represent a high point. Their smooth, sparingly decorated facades are made up of large blocks of tightly jointed ashlar.

The development of 18 recessed portals are of some significance in historical terms. They extend almost the entire height of the building and are decorated with *muqarnas* formations – intricate patterns of overlapping niches. The earliest example of this new form of decoration, the *muqarnas* vault, is the portal of Nur al-Din's Hospital (1154). Ayyubid stonemasons developed a virtuoso mastery of the technique and passed it on to Mamluk builders. Two outstanding examples of different types of portal vaults are across the street: the entrances to the Madrasa al-Adiliya (completed 1223/24) and the Mausoleum of Sultan Baibars (1227). The Madrasa al-Adiliya has a recessed portal with a pair of small twin *muqarna* domes, while the portal of the Mausoleum of Sultan Baibars consists of a ribbed half-dome built up of *muqarnas* niches.

Architectural ornamentation began to become more lavish under the Mamluks (1260–1517). By comparison with the impressively solid buildings of the Ayyubid and early Mamluk periods, those constructed during the middle and late Mamluk period generally look much lighter thanks to their construction out of small blocks of ashlar and the addition of intricate decorative elements, particularly as they are comparatively modest complexes. They are finely dressed with ornamental facades consisting of courses of stone of alternating colors (*ablaq*), round and diamond-shaped medallions, decorative voussoirs, and cuneiform inscriptions. The use of recesses to articulate facades, a typical feature of Cairo architecture during this period, was only adopted in exceptional cases, such as the Madrasa Afriduniya (1343/44), while motifs common in the highly developed ornamental masonry of Damascus spread to Cairo.

A new type of construction was introduced with Nur al-Din's great public foundations: the cruciform four-*iwan* complex imported from Persia via Iraq. Nur al-Din's Hospital (1154) is the purest incarnation of this style. It was the model for a second important Ayyubid hospital at al-Salihiya, the Maristan al-Qaimari (1248/49). *Madrasas* were built using an adapted form of this scheme in which the *qibla iwan* was replaced by a closed prayer room running along one side of the courtyard, as at Nur al-Din's Mausoleum and Madrasa (1167–1172) and in the Madrasa al-Adiliya (1172/73), which was also founded by Nur al-Din. Nevertheless, the classic four-*iwan* layout was preferred for the mausoleum and *madrasa* of the Ayyubid princess Rabia Khatun in al-Salihiya (c. 1245). During the Mamluk period, the mausoleum and *madrasa* complexes in Damascus became smaller: a large recessed portal led to a corridor flanked on either side by domed chambers – one serving as a mausoleum, the other as a *madrasa* and prayer hall. These halls were yoked together by a continuous facade lining the street. The majority of these small complexes line along the main street of the Midan district, a southern suburb on the road leading into the Hijaz. From the beginning of the 14th century the area developed into a prospering suburban center of Damascus.

***Madrasa* of the Emir Jaqmaq**, Damascus, 1421
The founders of religious institutions preferred corner plots in the narrow alleyways of the Old City. This meant that their presence was emphasized by facades facing in two directions. The street corners were dominated by the domes of the mausoleums incorporated into these complexes. This *madrasa*, which was close to the northern portal of the Great Mosque, was based on a school begun in 1361 by Sultan Hasan. Only parts of this building had been completed, such as the beautifully decorated side facade.

Decorative Arts

Almut von Gladiss

The arts under the Ayyubids and the princes of the Jazira

The countries of the eastern Mediterranean formed a single political unit which was held together by related ruling dynasties and unified by a common culture. From the point of view of contemporary chroniclers, the most noble characteristic of the Ayyubids was the fact that although they fought among themselves, they refrained from murdering one another at a time when it was common for defeated opponents to be cut in two with a sword or strangled with a bowstring. As a result, the number of male members in the family soon grew to a dozen. They were joined by allied or dependent princes, the Zangids and Artuqids, who ruled the Jazira, the upper reaches of the Euphrates and Tigris.

As Saladin's biographers point out with approval, the great prince exercised restraint in personal matters. However, his successors and the princes with whom they were allied spent lavishly on their households, proving to be great patrons of the arts and scholarship. The engineer al-Jazari worked at the Artuqid court in Diyarbakir (now in southeast Turkey) in the late 12th century. In the introduction to his *Treatise on Automata*, he writes at great length about the kings and philosophers of the time who bestowed their attention upon him, and how their interest spurred him on to hard work and ever greater successes.

Al-Jazari explains about 50 inventions, giving detailed descriptions of their design, including illustrations and intricate diagrams. For the most part, the machines he created were intended for the entertainment of court society, which naturally showed not the slightest interest in the laws of mechanics, but was excited by fountains, clocks with moving figures that indicated the time, and the *hydraulis*, an early forerunner of the modern organ that used water to create the air pressure needed to play it. They took pleasure in al-Jazari's mechanical cupbearer, which held a glass tumbler in its right hand and a fish in its left hand. When the glass was filled

with wine from the fish, the machine extended it for the drinker to take. Al-Jazari developed these luxury toys exclusively for royal clients who had the resources to pay for such things. They also included a combination lock for the safekeeping of valuables. Other machines built by the inventor were of more widespread and practical use, such as pumps and devices for drawing water from wells.

Miniature painting

In this period, miniature painting developed as an offshoot of the art of book illustration, which was based on the models offered by ancient manuscripts. The popular theories of the Greek physician Pseudo-Galen, particularly his *Book of Antidotes*, were decorated with miniatures. They show famous doctors preparing the famous universal panacea known as theriaca from honey, gentians, myrrh, cotus root, bay leaves, white pepper, cinnamon, and saffron, or a selection of these ingredients. Islamic medicine began to rely increasingly on the efficacy of magical treatments from the 12th century on. How power could be gained over natural phenomena was a central question. Mysterious deaths were not infrequently explained by the mixing or administration of poisons, and collections of remedies were an essential part of any ruler's library. Two books about poisons have survived, one dating from 1199 and one from the 1320s. Like many copies of the Arabic translation of the *Materia medica*, an ancient work on medicinal herbs by Dioscorides, these books were copied in the scriptoria of the Jazira. Their figurative illustrations retain the sensuousness of their models, which dated from late antiquity, and some of them display the lengthened proportions and treatment of clothing typical of Byzantine art, which was flourishing beyond the borders of the Islamic world at this time.

In the 13th century, works of fine literature also began to be illustrated. A multi-volume copy of the *Kitab al-Aghani*, a 10th-century collection of lyrics, was made in 1218/19 for Badr al-Din Lulu, who was later to become the ruler of Mosul. The title pages of its 20 volumes do not illustrate the text but, like the court scenes in the *Book of Antidotes*, depict the patron who commissioned the work with his retinue. Three of the six title pages to survive have *tiraz* bands, ornamental strips decorated with inscriptions that mention the prince by name, an unusual feature that identifies their owner beyond all doubt.

Ivory box with combination lock
Syria, c. 1200, Maastricht, Sint Servaas
This ivory box, which was probably presented to the church of Sint Servaas by a Crusader, was one of the many treasures transported to Europe from the East during the Crusades.

The combination lock on the front of the box has four dials with Arabic letters representing numerals. The design of a combination lock of this type had been described by al-Jazari.

Metalwork, glass, and ceramics

Like the ruler of Mosul, the Ayyubids wanted their surroundings to be impressive. The great amount of work they ordered contributed to the growth of metalwork and the glass industry. The brass vessels inlaid with silver and glass objects decorated with enamel and gilt testify to the refinement of the dynasty's life style. The inscriptions on these vessels name the rulers who commissioned them: al-Aziz (1216–1237), the grandson of the legendary leader Saladin and Lord of Aleppo; his son Salah al-Din Yusuf (1236–1260), who reigned in Aleppo and Damascus; al-Kamil (1218–1238), a nephew of Saladin who ruled Damascus and Egypt; and his sons al-Adil II (1238–1240) and al-Salih (1240–1249). In all, 16 metal objects bear the names of Ayyubid rulers. The deep-brass basins with diameters of up to 20 inches (50 centimeters) made for the brothers al-Adil II and al-Salih Najm al-Din are particularly impressive. It would appear that the two brothers competed with each other, not just for political influence, but also to see who could collect the most lavish ornamental metalwork. Apart from washing sets consisting of basins and jugs that were handed around at court banquets, containers for soap or aromatic substances, incense burners, candlestick holders, and pen boxes were among the most common objects made. Inspired by the thriving art of making and decorating books, these objects began to be decorated with figurative representations. The great clarity of these pictures was a result of the use of polychrome inlays. They

Left: **Servant with water ewer**,
Miniature from al-Jazari's *Treatise* on
Automata, 1206, Istanbul, Topkapi Palace
The earliest surviving copy of al-Jazari's
work dates back to 1206, and includes more
than 120 illustrations. This design for a
hand-washing machine shows a mechanical
servant with a water ewer. Water flows from
the breast of the figure into the jug. When
the bird on top of the ewer sings, the water
is poured out and sets the arm carrying the
hand towel and mirror in motion. The arm
returns back to its original position when
the towel and mirror are put down after use.

Right: **Title page of the *Book of Antidotes***,
northern Iraq, mid-13th century, Vienna,
Österreichische Nationalbibliothek
The title page of this copy of the *Book of
Antidotes*, by Pseudo-Galen, shows the
patron who commissioned it at a festive
meal of grilled meat with his household. A
wild hunt unfolds in the upper panel, while
the women of the court approach on
camels in the lower panel. The women are
heavily veiled, but dare to glance at the
festivities with their black almond eyes. The
arrangement of these scenes in horizontal
friezes is derived from ancient models.

Below: **Water ewer**, Damascus, 1259, height
34 cm, Paris, Musée du Louvre
This water ewer bears the name of the last
Ayyubid, Salah al-Din Yusuf of Damascus. It was
made in 1259 by the master craftsman Husain
ibn Muhammad of Mosul, who emphasized its
inscriptions by adding friezes of animal motifs,
as well as its arabesque medallions by inlaid in
silver.

were made by carving or incising a motif on the background metal, then
inlaying it with sheet silver that was thick enough to allow detailed chasing to
be added afterwards.

The most important theme is the ruler, who is always shown in iconic,
unapproachable pre-eminence on his throne. He appears in the company of his
guard of honor or in the society of musicians and drinkers, and disregards the
Islamic prohibition of wine with his raised goblet. He is seen riding on
horseback, hunting, killing game, and fighting with dangerous beasts of prey or
even sometimes, legendary monsters. The adventures depicted suggested the
supernatural powers to which rulers laid claim, while the symbols of the planets
and the zodiac were used to emphasize the legitimacy of monarchs who claimed
to rule in complete harmony with the divine order of the world. There were
many water basins, including examples owned by the brothers al-Adil II and
al-Salih Najm al-Din, on which the zodiac was depicted in concentric circles
inside the bowl to create the illusion that the firmament was reflected in the
water they held.

A celestial globe, inlaid in silver with 48 constellations that was made for
al-Kamil in 1225, is preserved at the Museo di Capodimonte in Naples. It bears
witness to the great medieval interest in astrology, with which rulers sought to
gain control over the constant crises they faced. When al-Kamil was engaged in
negotiations with the Crusaders, his brother, al-Ashraf, presented Frederick II
with a golden planetarium – the Holy Roman Emperor's belief in astronomy
was just as strong as that of his Islamic contemporaries.

The master inlayers who made ornamental vessels and tableware for the
court in Damascus came from the city of Mosul, which is situated on the Tigris
River. The economy of Mosul enjoyed vigorous growth under the Zangid
prince Badr al-Din Lulu. As it was his habit to carry the luxurious tableware
used by his household with him at all times, even when he went on military
campaigns, much of it was plundered or destroyed, as we know from
contemporary accounts. Nevertheless, five pieces bearing his name have
survived to the present, including a magnificent serving plate made for the

trousseau of one of his daughters. Its 36 figurative medallions depict royal audiences, court entertainments, the symbols of planets, and the signs of the zodiac. This assortment of subjects was probably meant to cover all aspects of court life and display the traditional virtues of the ruler.

The plate was made in the same workshop as a ewer that is now exhibited in the British Museum and bears inscriptions that not only state the year of its manufacture (1232) and the place where it was made (Mosul), but also name Shuja ibn Manaa as the master craftsman responsible. Within a short time, the metalwork of Mosul gained a reputation that extended far beyond the borders of the Jazira. Inlaid vessels were supplied to the princely courts of the entire eastern Mediterranean, as the geographer, Ibn Said, noted in the mid-13th century. At the same time, the number of master craftsmen was soon growing faster than demand, forcing some to emigrate to other cities in search of work. They laid great emphasis on the byname *al-Mausili*, which indicated that they originated from Mosul and had been trained there. The signatures of about 30 master craftsmen working over a period of 100 years have been identified.

Apart from Damascus, Cairo gained importance as a center of artisanal production, and even Jerusalem is thought to have had workshops – one chalice that has been found bears an inscription saying it was ordered by a priest at the Church of the Holy Sepulchre. The Christian themes on some pieces of metalwork suggest that some of the master craftsmen were also Christians, who constituted influential minorities in northern Iraq and northern Syria. A large pilgrim's flask in the Freer Gallery in Washington shows a series of saints, some of whom are identified by the objects they carry, such as an incense burner, a reliquary, a copy of the Gospels, a Madonna and Child, and depictions of Christ's birth, Christ and the elders in the Temple, and Christ's entry into Jerusalem. The same flask also bears a chivalric frieze designed to appeal to the taste of the Muslim upper classes. The magnificent water basin of the Ayyubid sultan Najm al-Din, who was killed during the Crusade led by Louis IX in 1249, is also marked by the juxtaposition of chivalric scenes and motifs from the New Testament.

The glass industry now began to thrive in the countries of the eastern Mediterranean, drawing on ancient traditions of glassblowing in the region. Ancient decorative techniques were also revived in the 12th century, such as marvering, in which threads of opaque glass were wound round a glass vessel, then pressed into its surface with a special tool. Sometimes the threads were "dragged" or "combed" to create curving or feather-like patterns. Where contrasting colors, such as white and dark red or black, were used this simple technique lent a refined appearance to tumblers, spherical vases, and perfume bottles. The coastal city of Tyre, which was ruled by the Crusaders from 1124, was known for its glasswork, which was made by the Jewish craftsmen who were well established there. These widely famed products were exported in large quantities. In the northern Syrian city

Clay sphinx, Syria, early 13th century, glazed clay, height 38 cm, Copenhagen, David Collection
This clay sphinx, which was pressed in a mold and decorated with a polychrome glaze, comes from the northern Syrian city of Raqqa, which was renowned for its potteries. The wings and the tail are connected to the main body only with small pins. Like figures of a cock and rider also discovered in Raqqa, it was used as a gargoyle.

Glass goblet, Aleppo, late 13th century, height 19 cm, New York, Metropolitan Museum
This glass goblet was used for drinking. Festive scenes with drinkers toasting each other alternate with eulogistic inscriptions. Names and titles are only rarely given on glassware, since it was not considered prestigious on account of its negligible material value. For this reason it is not certain whether this goblet dates from the late Ayyubid or Mamluk period.

Ceramic bowl, Syria, 13th-century, Copenhagen, David Collection
This ceramic bowl depicts a centaur, a mythical beast with the body of a horse and the head and shoulders of a man. This beautiful artifact is an example of the elegance with which ceramic containers were painted during the Ayyubid period. Polychrome ceramics were made in the northern Syrian city of Raqqa, until the Mongol invasion of 1259 completely destroyed it as a center of production.

Ceramic bowl, Syria, c. 1200, Copenhagen, David Collection
This ceramic bowl is one of the few examples extant depicting a human form: a prince sitting on his throne and surrounded by elegant arabesques. This piece must have been very precious on account of the metallic pigments used. Tell Minis ceramics, as they are known, are named after the site of their discovery in central Syria, where about 100 bowls were found hidden in a cave. It is presumed this was made somewhere in the region.

of Aleppo they were sometimes decorated using the elaborate techniques developed in the Islamic world around 1200: enameling and gilding.

The Ayyubid Salah al-Din Yusuf of Aleppo and Damascus was an important patron of the arts who gave decisive encouragement to artisanal production. His name appears in gilded script on an elegant wine carafe that is now in the Museum of Arabic Art at Cairo. The body of this 32 cm (10 in.) high vessel bears a row of red enamel medallions decorated with gilt arabesques. Early Ayyubid ornamentation tends to be sparing, and figurative depictions begin to occur only towards the end of the Ayyubid period. They depict court scenes in thick, colored enamel, while the accompanying arabesque and animal friezes are examples of very delicate gilding. For the enamel, a colored glass paste was applied to the surface of a colorless or honey-colored glass vessel and fixed by firing. Next, gold was ground to a powder, then applied as paint. This gilt was fused to the glass at low temperatures. Various enterprises could be involved in this manufacturing process, mainly a glassworks and the workshop of the artisan who decorated the vessels.

It is possible to demonstrate a similar division of labor in the production of inlaid goods, as the master craftsmen responsible would sometimes sign with their own names. A candlestick in the Museum of Islamic Art at Cairo was signed by the coppersmith Hajji Ismail and the inlayer Muhammad ibn Futtuh, who describes himself as an employee of the Mosul master craftsman Suga. Among other achievements, Suga is famous for a ewer made in Mosul in 1232.

The ceramics of the Ayyubid period are well known thanks to finds at Syrian sites such as Raqqa, Aleppo, Hama, and Tell Minis. Artificially composed ceramic bodies were an innovation of the islamic potters. Apart from white clay, they

contained large quantities of finely ground quartz and alkaline frit, which made the shards similar to Chinese hard paste porcelain in color, delicacy, and hardness. The exorbitantly expensive imports from China had been used as models by Muslim craftsmen for a long time before this imitation was invented. Decorative methods were also changing. Expensive lusterware was decorated with metallic pigments that created a unique golden shine after firing. It began to spread in Syria in the late 12th century after flourishing for two centuries in Egypt. At the same time, underglaze painting began to become common and was to dominate fine Islamic ceramics from this time on. The northern Syrian city of Raqqa was home to a unique style of painting characterized by flowing lines in rich shades of blue, green, black, and, occasionally, red. The brilliance of the colors was intensified by colorless glazes. Alternatively, transparent blue or turquoise-green glazes were used to give black underglaze painting even greater depth.

After a stormy political career, the North African scholar Ibn Khaldun (1332–1406) composed the theoretical introduction to his universal history at a lonely castle near Oran. He described the rise of cities and markets in terms that prove to be highly applicable to the development of craftsmanship under the Ayyubids and the princes of the Jazira. He described a stratum of society that had recently attained prosperity and its desire for luxurious lifestyles that imitated those of the upper classes. These *nouveaux riches* townspeople did not limit themselves to spending on the necessities of life, but increasingly devoted their expenditure to the purchase of beautiful vessels and tableware, refined clothing, exquisite jewelry, and servants. Craftsmen and artists won respect with their quality products, which became increasingly prized and expensive. It is not surprising to us that their growing confidence was expressed in the signatures that were found not just on metal vessels, but also on other artisanal goods.

Left: **Abu Zaid in the pulpit of the Samarqand Mosque**, miniature from Hariri's *Maqamat*, Cairo. Vienna, Österreichische Nationalbibliothek
This miniature, from the *Maqamat*, shows Abu Zaid in the pulpit of the Samarqand Mosque, the dome rises above the picture frame. His hand is raised in a gesture as he lectures the congregation. The black clothes and black flag refer to the Abassid Caliph, resident in Cairo since 1261. This magnificent manuscript was made at the Mamluk court in Cairo.

Above: **Woman playing the lute**, miniature from Hariri's Maqamat. Vienna, Österreichische Nationalbibliothek
This miniature shows a tavern with men courting a woman who plays the lute. On the left, we see Abu Zaid, who, like his companions, is shown with a wine goblet raised in his hand. The consumption of wine was closely associated with prostitution at this period. It is the stiff composition of the figures and the brilliant colors in this painting that make it so expressive.

Decorative arts under the Mamluks

In contrast to the loose association of principalities under Ayyubid rule, the Mamluk empire was a centralized state governed from Cairo, and the sultan's court was the most important patron of the arts and crafts. The early Mamluks also took possession of the treasures previously owned by the Ayyubids, such as a magnificent storage jar made for Salah al-Din Yusuf that, according to a later inscription, was appropriated for Baibar's cellars. After the victories over the Mongols and the Crusaders, great efforts were devoted to demonstrations of power and splendor, as well as the promotion of craft industries that would be capable of producing top-quality artifacts and satisfying the upper classes' desire for ostentatious decor.

The art of the book

On account of their education, most of the Mamluks were fervent defenders of Islam. As the founders of mosques, *madrasas*, and monasteries, they made available large amounts of money to fit out the new buildings appropriately. During the Ayyubid period, the demand for copies of the Koran increased as new *madrasas* were founded. However, many of the library stocks inherited from earlier generations were destroyed during this period. For example, the famous library of Tripoli, where a Christian priest had discovered early Koranic manuscripts, went up in flames. When they made endowments to religious institutions, the Mamluks included editions of the Koran in one or several volumes for use during ceremonial recitations. These manuscripts and the accompanying ornamental boxes, stands, and cases inlaid with gold and silver transformed religious buildings into real treasure troves. The leading scriptoria in Cairo and Damascus were assisted by wandering illustrators and calligraphers from Mesopotamia. The Baghdad school enjoyed the greatest respect, going back as it did to Yaqut al-Mustasimi, the secretary of the last caliph of Baghdad. Magnificent ornamental pages were inserted at the beginning of the Koran or even at the beginning of each sura. The specialized nature of this work is shown by the names of the calligraphers and ornamental painters, which have been recorded in many cases. The most famous painters, often known as "gilders," came from the school of the master Sandal, who had perfected interlaced geometrical patterns, with great central stars surrounded by polygonal fields, intended to reflect the underlying order of the cosmos.

Later there was competition between Cairo and Damascus as to which center could produce the most magnificent Koranic manuscripts. In Syria, Korans were made for Sultan al-Ashraf Shaban (1363–1376), his mother Khwand Barakah, and his most powerful emirs. Many of these Korans are outstanding for their lavish gilded illuminations, among them some enormous books with pages up to three feet wide. Their size emphasized the significance of the Holy Book, as well as underlining the status of the patrons who commissioned these manuscripts. Literary works were also decorated with colorful miniature paintings for the royal court. Two magnificent editions of a work by Hariri, the head of the Iraqi secret service in the early 12th century, have survived. His *Maqamat* (Assemblies) was highly prized for its entertainment value and its popularity spread thanks to the richly illustrated copies of it that were made. The *Maqamat* describes the adventures of a wily man of the world, Abu Zaid, who always knows how to get his own way, no matter where he may be. One manuscript produced at the royal court in Cairo in 1334 is illustrated with 70 miniatures. The wide variations in its figurative style suggest it was produced by a team of artists, while a version made in 1337, all the illustrations included, was the sole work of the Damascus calligrapher Ghazi ibn Abd al-Rahman.

The richly illustrated copy of the *Treatise on the Uses of Animals*, now kept in the Royal Library of the Escorial, was made in Damascus. The author was the scholar Ibn al-Duraihim al-Mausili, who came from Mosul and spent most of his life in Syria, finally teaching at the Umayyad mosque in Damascus. In his work of 1354, which is based on Aristotle's *Historia animalium* (*History of Animals*), he classifies animals as either tame or wild four-legged beasts, birds, fishes, or insects. The special value placed on the horse is also reflected in numerous monographs on the art of riding and fighting on horseback. A book by the veterinarian and royal master of the horse, Abu Bakr ibn Badr, who worked at the court of Sultan al-Nasir Muhammad, contains instructions on exercises for military riders and shows dressage routines for exercising with lance, saber, and bow and arrow, parading in battle formation, and playing polo.

The Mamluks were great lovers of weapons. And the helmets, swords, axes, and standards that have survived from the late Mamluk period show this. Inscriptions picked out in gold leaf run along the visor and the neck protector of a conical iron helmet used by Sultan Barsbai. The silvery shimmering steel surfaces of battle axes were decorated with gold, among them some bearing the name of Sultan Qaitbai. As traditional symbols of power, swords were decorated with the greatest attention to detail. Sultan Tumanbai, who ruled for just four

months in 1501, owned a sword with a horn handle, silver cross-guard, and steel blade. It is still not clear whether the legendary blades with glittering patterned surfaces renowned as "damascene steel" were actually smithed in Damascus, or whether the city was just an important center for the trade in these products. The entire blade of Tumunbai's sword is covered with a gilded inscription that ends with the conventional blessing for the sultans: "may his victory be glorious."

Glassware and metalwork

The great building projects of the Mamluk upper classes ushered in a golden era for the decorative arts. Mosques were illuminated with dozens of metal candlesticks and lamps, and glass hanging lamps. The hanging lamps had round bodies and funnel-shaped necks, and were usually about 14 in. (35 cm) high. They would be decorated with gilt and enamel designs. Often the Light Verse (Koran 24. 35) appears on the neck, while the patron who established the foundation might be named on the body, or even tribute paid to his high standing with a reproduction of his coat of arms. The use of heraldry had become widespread as a result of the impression made by the coats of arms carried by the Crusaders, from whom the lion of England, the fleur-de-lys of France, and the eagle of the German Empire were adopted. The Mamluk sultan had a calligraphic blazon incorporating the ruler's name from the 14th century on, while his officers bore emblems that referred to the functions that they had once performed in the royal corps of pages: weapon carrier (saber/bow), cup bearer (cup), taster (napkin), secretary (pen box), or polo-stick carrier (polo sticks).

There was also great competition between Damascus and Cairo in the field of glassmaking. According to the historian al-Umari, the gilded luxury goods from Damascus were greeted with great interest not just in Syria, but also in Mesopotamia and Asia Minor. Under Sultan Qalawun, many craftsmen settled in the new capital, Cairo, to work on the development of the stereotyped form of the mosque lamp. Just as in the Ayyubid period, costly glassware was used in rich private households as well as public buildings. A perfume bottle with gilt

Left: **Glass bottle**, Syria, c. 1300, Berlin, Museum for Islamic Art
The reputation of enameled and gilded glass spread far beyond the areas where it was produced. With its precise engraving and rich colors, this bottle with 12 galloping riders, one of them holding a polo stick, marks a high point of Mamluk glassmaking. It was made for one of the Rasulid rulers of Yemen, to whom the repeated five-leafed rosette refers. The blazon of the Yemeni banner was a red rose on a white background.

Right: **Hanging lamp**, Cairo, early 14th century, Berlin, Museum for Islamic Art
This mosque lamp bears the name of the Sultan al-Nasir Muhammad and, on its neck, the Light Verse (sura 24. 35): "God is the light of the heavens and the earth; his light may be compared to a niche that enshrines a lamp, the lamp within a crystal of a star-like brilliance …" The lamp is decorated with a blue enamel calligraphic frieze on a gilt background, and a gilded eulogistic inscription on a background of blue enamel.

Incense burner, Cairo, c. 1320–1330, height 36 cm, London, Nuhad El-Said Collection
This ornamental incense burner bears an inscription eulogizing Sultan al-Nasir Muhammad and is richly inlaid with gold and silver. It was designed to have a removable lid which allowed it to be filled with the exotic perfumes that were burnt at court festivities.

Koran box, Cairo, early 14th century, Berlin, Museum for Islamic Art
This wooden box held a 30-volume edition of the Koran. It is paneled with brass sheets decorated with verses from the Koran and arabesques inlaid in gold and silver. The lock bears the names of two master craftsmen, Muhammad ibn Sunqur al-Baghdadi and Hagg Yusuf, who carried out many commissions for Sultan al-Nasir Muhammad.

Steel mirror, Syria, c. 1330, Istanbul, Topkapi Palace
This unusually large steel mirror is decorated with the 12 signs of the zodiac, which give this practical object a higher significance. The gilt inscription that radiates out from the center includes the title of a high dignitary, whose name, Ala al-Din, appears in the central medallion. This is probably Altinbugha, who governed Aleppo until 1338. The fine detail of the engraving on the inlaid silver identifies it as the work of a master known as Muhammad.

and enamel decoration, found in the Upper Egyptian provincial town of Qus, bears the name of a local governor, whose coat of arms is placed between figurative scenes depicting musicians and drinkers. The themes used in the decoration of these vessels – perfume bottles, bottles for beverages, and drinking cups – clearly show how the upper class liked to spend their free time. Arabesques and interlaced patterns became popular at this time, and fish might be woven into these patterns to mark a vessel as a water holder. An extraordinarily large stem glass in the Gulbenkian Collection in Lisbon stands out from the mass of glassware on account of its expert decoration. Numerous birds are depicted in vivid colors flying over a waterfall, among them an eagle fighting with a duck. Above them all sweeps a phoenix, a motif indicative of Mongolian influences.

Metalware was another area in which Damascus and Cairo competed. Inlaying was highly developed in the two cities thanks to master craftsmen from Mosul. The artisans in Cairo were strongly influenced by the brothers Ali and Ahmad, the sons of Husain ibn Muhammad al-Mausili, who had once worked for the Ayyubid court at Damascus. Ibn al-Zain is said to have been the supreme master of the art. The only examples of his work to have survived are a small dish and a large basin decorated with court scenes. The entire inner surface of the basin is covered with inscriptions of fish and aquatic animals, such as sea snakes and ducks, which turn the basin into a fairy-tale lake, its vitality promising riches and abundance. Apart from this new water symbolism, the astrological signs lost none of their appeal. Indeed, astrological magic became more widespread as esoteric studies flourished. The zodiac appears on the unpretentious brass bowls used for tending to the sick and the ostentatious export goods made for the rulers of Yemen and the kings of Cyprus.

A large hand mirror made of steel, now kept at the Topkapi Palace, is decorated with personifications of the 12 signs of the zodiac, and richly inlaid in silver and gold.

A new, nonfigurative style can be seen on the large water basins made for al-Nasir Muhammad. About 30 pieces of metalwork refer to the sultan, among them a magnificent incense burner with a eulogy inlaid in gold radiating out from a central medallion to create a graphic image of the charismatic power of the royal court. The designs of the ceremonial objects used at court were based on the fittings found in mosques, which were dominated by calligraphy as required by Islamic law. Apart from written friezes, the gracious lotus flowers, and fantastic arabesques are typical of the Egyptian work produced under the successors of al-Nasir Muhammad, though the pen box of the historian and geographer Abu l-Fida Ismail, the last Ayyubid ruler, who governed the principality of Hama in the early 14th century, is distinguished by its clear geometrical patterning. In the 15th century inlaying was abandoned due to an economic crisis and shortages of precious metals. In its place, metal goods were decorated using techniques of engraving, which combined calligraphic friezes with arabesque or interlaced patterns. The candlesticks that were donated by the pious Sultan Qaitbai to the mosque in Medina in 1482 are dominated by wide calligraphic bands running on a spiral background with occasional leaf motifs. Other brass products bearing his name provide evidence of attempts to revive the techniques. A magnificent water basin with gold and silver inlay fell into the hands of the Ottomans when they conquered Egypt and was taken to Istanbul as part of their rich booty.

Textiles

The drawloom, with which complicated patterns could be produced, was introduced to the weaving shops of Syria and Egypt in the 13th century. The Ayyubid luxury fabrics from Damascus mentioned in contemporary literature were decorated with pairs of animals surrounded by elaborately varied arabesques, but went out of fashion under the Mamluks. Heraldically stylized motifs disappeared from the arabesques, and a system of oval medallions developed, such as those on a fragment of a child's robe at the Museum for Islamic Art in Berlin. Damask silk, which dates back to the 14th century, can be identified by inscriptions woven into the fabric with common honorifics and, sometimes, the names of sultans. It was named after the Syrian capital, though it is thought that it may have also been produced in Cairo and Alexandria. Damask weaving was probably stimulated by imports from China. In the eastern Islamic weaving shops of the Mongolian empire, fabric patterns were adapted to the taste of Muslim customers each with Islamic ornamentation and fragments of Arabic script, while the weavers of Syria and Egypt made use of Chinese motifs, such as complex wreaths of leaves and lush lotus blossoms. Some weaves incorporate the honorific al-Malik al-Nasir, which was assumed by many Mamluk rulers, as a decorative element, repeating it endlessly. According to the literature, al-Nasir Muhammad was given 700 pieces of silk woven with his honorific when he concluded a peace treaty with the Mongolian ruler Abu Said. They were shipped to Cairo by camel caravan. It is not clear whether the numerous striped fabrics bearing this formula were actually made in Mongolian centers of silk production for the Mamluk market.

The weaving shops of Syria and Egypt profited from a privilege enjoyed by civil servants, who, according to old-established custom, received a ceremonial robe each year from the sultan in person as a mark of favor. Belts set with precious stones were given as accessories, and served as badges of rank. While the silk industry stagnated during the 15th century, carpet knotting developed into a lucrative economic sector. Three knotted carpets have survived marked with the official blazon used by Sultan Qaitbai (1468–1496). This emblem combined the symbols of various offices: a napkin in the upper field, a cup topped with a pen box and flanked by powder horns in the central field, and another cup in the bottom field. The sultan's official blazon and the impressive dimensions of some pieces, such as the Bardini carpet, which was originally 30 feet (9 meters) long, and a 36-foot (11-meter) carpet that belonged to

Wool carpet, Cairo, c. 1500, 3.34 m x 5 m, Vienna, Österreichisches Museum für angewandte Kunst
This wool carpet comes from the late period of the Mamluk empire. A kaleidoscopic pattern radiates out over the whole width of the carpet from the central octagon, which is echoed at each end by pairs of smaller octagons. Heavily stylized plant motifs are combined in the ornamental fields.

the Medicis and was mentioned in the catalog of the Palazzo Vecchio of 1571, point to a court workshop in Cairo. These carpets were built up of thousands of asymmetric knots and are characterized by soft, shiny wool and colorful patterns. The dominant colors are cherry red and varying shades of green, yellow, and blue. These patterns were constructed on geometrical principles and were often decorated with a central octagonal motif framed by straight fields containing strongly stylized leaves, bushes, and cypresses. The Mamluk carpet manufacturers enjoyed great respect among the new rulers following the Ottoman conquest of Syria and Egypt. In 1585, the Ottoman Sultan Murad III ordered 11 master carpetmakers from Cairo to come to Istanbul, along with more than a ton (1,000 kilograms) of dyed wool, in order to employ them in the Ottoman court workshop.

Islamic Metalwork

Almut von Gladiss

Metalwork has always enjoyed great prestige in the Islamic world. The beautifully shaped metal wares used at meals and banquets were regarded as status symbols and tokens of a family's prosperity. As in ancient times, bronze household goods were prized for their durability and natural beauty. The exact appearance of the metal's shimmering or shining surfaces and nuances of color depended on the specific alloy used. The invention of bronze was sometimes attributed to persons of rank and name, such as the Moghul ruler Akbar during the 16th century, though it was also claimed to be the work of legendary artisans of the distant past, such as Gushtasp the Smith, who was said to have labored to perfect the craft of metalwork. Apart from a variety of different bronzes, alloys based on copper (70–80%) and large proportions of tin, lead, or zinc were particularly widely found.

The early Islamic vessels were based on ancient models. They were mostly cast, and their timeless forms were embellished only with simple grooves or bosses. On a ewer signed and dated by the master craftsman Ibn Yazid with an inscription saying that it was produced in Basra (Iraq), the need for ornament felt in Islamic art is satisfied in the engraved arabesques and the leaf-shaped thumb-rest that rises up from its handle. A 19 inch (49 cm) tall bronze jug expresses the ornamental tendencies of Islamic art with its arabesque garlands, which cover the whole surface, following one another in an ordered, recurring pattern adapted to the diameter of the vessel, the form of which reflects pre-Islamic traditions. Some vessels from the 8th and 9th centuries even have raised arabesques inlaid with red copper. This metalware is usually characterized by balanced, practical forms. For example, oil lamps were not only made with a single spout, but also with up to four wick holes, so that they gave off more light. The early hanging mosque lamps were spherical vessels with funnel-shaped necks. Their sides were perforated with fine honeycomb patterns, which often surround unpierced Koranic inscriptions. When the lamps were lit, these inscriptions stood out in expressive starkness to inspire the faithful. Piercing reached its highest level of development in the eastern Islamic lands, where lampshades and large incense

Door knocker, probably Diyarbakir, c. 1200, bronze, Berlin, Museum of Islamic Art

Incense burner in the shape of a lion, Iran, bronze, New York, Metropolitan Museum of Art

burners were manufactured. Some of these goods even reached Scandinavia along the extended trading routes that followed the River Volga. Incense burners were used to burn expensive perfumes from India or the Arabian Peninsula. They were designed with domes, or in the shape of birds or wild cats. The examples that have survived are evidence of the refined life style enjoyed by the prosperous stratum of the population that lived on trade. Merchants liked to have incense burners decorated with their own names. One of the earliest examples of this is a piece in the Hermitage: an incense burner in the shape of a lion that is inlaid with silver. One lion incense burner in the New York Metropolitan Museum is particularly remarkable on account of its great height of 3 feet (91 centimeters). Its head can be removed in order to fill it with aromatic substances and light them easily.

The heavy door knockers made in the 12th and 13th centuries in the area around the Euphrates and the Tigris stand out from the mass of functionally designed products. They were mounted in pairs and formed the focus of the huge doors made of wood and completely covered with bronze panels that were installed in palaces and mosques. Stylized dragons were believed to scare off evil spirits and prevent them from crossing the threshold. They were Loosely attached with pins that ended in lions' heads. Solid casting with the aid of a reusable wooden mold made it possible to produce them in pairs. Al-Jazari, who made a door for the Artuqid palace in the late 12th century that was 15 feet (4.5 meters) high and completely covered with cast bronze stars, describes this process, which opened the way to mass production.

Al-Jazari also provides an exposition of inlaying techniques, in which various metals were combined together. The design would first be cut out of the background metal and its surface roughened. Then sheet copper, silver, or gold would be hammered into it, sometimes using a black resin as an adhesive. This particularly labor-intensive technique established the fame of Islamic metalwork, the reputation of which had spread beyond the bounds of the Islamic world at the latest by the 14th century.

Bronze ewer, Iran or Iraq, 7th century, New York, Metropolitan Museum of Art

Golden pitcher, Iran or Iraq, 10th century, Washington, Freer Gallery of Art

Golden ewer, Istanbul, mid-16th century, Istanbul, Topkapi Palace

The Arabs plundered large quantities of precious metals on their campaigns of conquest in the 7th and 8th centuries. They developed a taste for luxury tableware, with which they would display their wealth at festive banquets, even if this was frowned on by Islamic tradition. The powerful hoarded fine metal goods and saw them as both a symbol and the basis of political and economic power. Collections of gold and silver were always affected by the ups and downs of history. In times of crisis they were used as the raw materials for minting gold and silver coins. As a result, very little medieval metalwork has survived. A jug with inscriptions blessing the Buyid prince Izz al-Daula Bahtiyar (967–978) was beaten from a pound of high-carat gold. It is decorated with reliefs that include arabesques and animal symbols of happiness, including a peacock, ibex, and sphinx, that stand out against a background with a matte finish achieved by pounding with round punches. The foliate pattern shows the influence of earlier Sassanian work. A golden water jug in the treasury of the Topkapi Palace that was borne behind the Ottoman sultans on their official appearances is identified as a royal

accessory by the lavish jewels set into it. The golden crown of the Volga Tartars, a symbol of absolute power created in the 14th century, is preserved in the Armory of the Kremlin. It was used in the coronation ceremonies of the Russian czars from the 16th century on. With its rich filigree and granulation, in which the finest golden threads and tiny golden grains are fused to create a superb network, it is an example of a particularly costly technique practiced by Islamic goldsmiths that was almost exclusively used for the decoration of jewelry.

In the east of the Islamic world, which was rich in silver, table silver remained an essential accessory for the court banquets described in chronicles until the 10th or 11th century. A few vessels bear the name of princes or viziers. In the west, silverware had to compete against carved ivory for the favor of the rulers in the 10th and 11th centuries. The box ordered by Caliph Hisham of Cordoba and the perfume bottle owned by a princess from one of the *taifa* states established in Spain after the fall of the caliphate are examples of the luxurious goods popular with the upper classes. We find large amounts of silverware preserved only from the

time of the Ottomans, whose capital, Istanbul, was never invaded. Of these pieces, the 4 foot (118 centimeter) high candlesticks from the Mausoleum of Sultan Ahmed I (1603–1617) are remarkable on account of their sheer size.

Many silver vessels were given a polychrome finish by gilding or niello work. In fire gilding an amalgam of gold and mercury was applied to the vessel. When it was heated, the gold was fused to the surface, and the mercury evaporated. In niello work, lines and grooves cut out of the background metal were filled with black silver sulfide, which was then fused to the surface by means of heating. For awhile, silverware was inlaid with copper, while some craftsmen experimented with inlaying on bronze. Whether as a result of the revival of ancient methods or the transfer technology encouraged by the growth of trade with India and the Far East, the mercantile cities in the eastern part of the Islamic world, where there was plenty of copper and silver, offered perfect conditions for the widespread application of these techniques.

A pen box dating from 1148 and a basin from the year 1163 belonged to figures who moved in affluent commercial and financial

circles. These artifacts bear the names of business people with international contacts who had already made the expensive pilgrimage to Mecca. Inlaid pen boxes and inkwells had recently become accessories carried by any educated citizen. The contrasting decorations of inlaid copper or silver added to these goods naturally included images that reflected the scholarly life, such as the game of chess, or the signs of the zodiac and the symbols of the planets. The inkwell in the Keir Collection depicts the signs of the zodiac in groups of four medallions inlaid in copper and silver on a dark bronze. On the left are Cancer and Gemini, on the right Capricorn and Taurus (with human figures). The three contrasting colors used in this design give these symbols great clarity and are typical of the early period of eastern Islamic inlaying. Planetary symbols are also found on

the magnificent water pitchers made for the Ghurids, who were the first to see inlaid bronze and tin goods as alternatives to traditional court tableware made of precious metals. One 12-inch (30 centimeter) high candlestick is decorated with an endlessly recurring pattern of fighting animals – a common symbol of victory. The silver inlaid inscription on this artifact not only states the year of production, but also the patron for whom it was made, the Ghurid prince Abu I-Fath Muhammad. He had captured the flourishing trading city of Herat, where specialists worked on elaborately decorated goods. A different example of work from Herat is a bucket dating from 1163, which is inscribed with the names of the craftsman who cast it and the "decorator" who did the inlaying work, Masud ibn Ahmad. Another master inlayer named Mahmud ibn Muhammad left behind a poem

on a water pitcher that he made in Herat in 1181/82. He emphasized the uniqueness of his work and extolled the astrological symbols represented as tokens of happiness, claiming their benign power on his own behalf. In order to advertise their mastery, some artists signed their work with the byname *al-Herawi*, which indicated that they came from Herat.

The eastern Islamic refugees from the Mongols had a wealth of experience in these techniques, and inlaying began to flourish in the Jazira and in Syria when they arrived in the 13th century. The Armenian Badr al-Din Lulu (1218–1259), who rose from being the vizier to the Zangids to become an independent prince, supported the crafts of his capital Mosul by placing many commissions, including one for a serving plate with a diameter of 2 feet (62 centimeters). He also created the best possible conditions for artisans exporting

Hookah bottle, India, 18th century, Bidar, Munich, Staatliches Museum für Völkerkunde

Inkwell, eastern Iran, c. 1160–1180, bronze inlaid with copper and silver, Ham (Surrey), Keir Collection

Candlestick, western Iran, c. 1300, bronze inlaid with silver and gold, Berlin, Museum of Islamic Art

Pilgrim's flask, Syria, mid-13th century, bronze inlaid with silver, Washington, Smithsonian Institution, Freer Gallery of Art

Column-shaped candlestick, Iran, c. 1600, brass, Berlin, Museum for Islamic Arts

to neighboring principalities. Many craftsmen worked to perfect the techniques of inlaying in this traditional trading center under the supervision of the masters Shuja ibn Mana and Ahmad al-Dhaki. There was now a trend for the inlaying of complex figurative scenes. The masters of Mosul signed their work and indicated their own origins with the byname *al-Mausili*, which was recognized as a quality mark for over a century. Indeed, it was still used by some craftsmen whose families had moved their businesses to cities such as Damascus or Cairo two or three generations earlier. Under the Mamluks and Mongols, figurative representation was increasingly neglected in favor of majestic calligraphic designs with gold and silver inlays.

Inlaid wares were now no longer exclusively reserved for the upper classes. However, as the Mamluk historian, al-Maqrizi, reported in the early 15th century, they were still luxury goods for the rich. They filled the gap between undecorated bronze and costly silver vessels in the trousseaux of the daughters of emirs, viziers, secretaries, and rich merchants. The superb goods in the bazaars filled travelers from Europe with enthusiasm and, as the economy declined, they eventually came to be manufactured exclusively for export across the Mediterranean.

In the 15th century, copper and brass goods began to be decorated with intricate patterns of unprecedented virtuosity. Late Mamluk, Timurid, and Safavid products are covered in spirals of leaves and tendrils to form networks and ordered symmetrical patterns. One 13 inch (34 centimeter) high candlestick, made around 1600 in Iran, is decorated with entwined bifurcating tendrils that extend over the edges of the shaft and are ordered in a network that is subject to the principles of eternal repetition. Just as typical as these virtuoso patterns are the mystical verses from Saadi's *Bustan* quoted on the foot of the candlestick.

Products with a zinc content of more than 80% came into fashion in India under the Mughal rulers. They were known as "Bidri-ware" after the city of Bidar in the Deccan where they were made. Most of these cast pieces were bell-shaped or spherical water bottles for hookahs (*huqqa*), which the miniatures of the Mughal period show as essential accessories to a luxurious lifestyle. They bear deeply incised floral patterns, which glitter with inlaid sheet silver, gold, or brass. The inlaying was carried out by Muslim workshops, while the vessels were cast by Hindu craftsmen.

Ewer, Herat, 1180–1200, brass inlaid with silver, London, British Museum

Spain and Morocco

Prayer hall of the Great Mosque of Cordoba, 785–988
Since the 8th century the Great Mosque of Cordoba, known as the Mezquita, has always
been – and still is – the major landmark of the city, forming the religious focal point of the
500-plus mosques which Cordoba apparently possessed in the years of the caliphate. The
beauty of the architecture can be appreciated fully only from the inside, where one can see
the symmetry of innumerable pillars with their capitals, as well as red-and-white striped
arches. These constitute some of the most famous motifs of Islamic art and have been
praised by leading literary and cultural figures throughout history. In the 16th century a
Christian cathedral was built into the Mezquita's central nave. When Emperor Charles V saw
this, he remarked in consternation: "You have built something that already exists
elsewhere and to do so you have destroyed something that was unique in the world."

207

History

Markus Hattstein

The conquest of Spain for Islam and the early years (711–756)

After the year 670, from their base in Kairouan, the North African governors of the Umayyad caliphs had brought the whole of the Maghreb as far as the Atlantic Ocean under Islamic rule. In the early 8th century they looked beyond Morocco to Spain and thus to Europe. At this period the Visigothic kingdom of Spain was in a deplorable state. In 710, the Visigothic king, Witiza, who sought to strengthen royal power against the church and the nobility, was overthrown and murdered. Many of the empire's nobles were openly opposed to his successor, the usurper Roderick.

No doubt informed of this situation, Musa ibn Nusair, the governor of Ifriqiya (North Africa and the Maghreb) planned to invade Spain. In April, 711, he entrusted his subordinate, General Tariq ibn Ziyad, with conquering Spain. With some 7,000 Berbers, Tariq landed in Gibraltar (derived from the Arabic *jebel-al-tariq*, "Rock of Tariq") and pushed on without major resistance. He captured Malaga, Granada, and Cordoba, and on July 19, 711, at the Rio Barbate, he defeated the Christian army led by Roderick. The king was killed in battle, the Christians flooded back to the North, and Tariq

Narrow street in the Old Town of Cordoba, 8th century
In the days of the Spanish Umayyads Cordoba was a labyrinth of alleys, houses, and palaces. It was a multicultural city housing Muslims, Jews, and Christians, and, from the 8th century onwards, it grew into Europe's unofficial capital, perhaps comparable with Constantinople. A census al-Mansur conducted in the late 10th century lists the following properties in Cordoba: 213,007 middle-class and working-class houses, 60,300 palaces or villas belonging to the aristocracy and prominent officials, 600 public baths, and 80,455 shops.

These included new Islamic converts (the *muwalladun*), those Christians who lived under Arab rule (the Mozarabs, from the Arabic word *mustarib*, "Arabized"), and – especially in later centuries – those Muslims who lived under Christian rule (the Mudejar). The territory of Islamic Spain was known as al-Andalus, which (according to Heinz Halm) is derived from the Gothic word for "landless," *landahlauts*.

In the early years, therefore, the main task was to compensate for the numerical disadvantage of the Muslim ruling class. Several waves of settlers and soldiers were brought to Spain from Islamic countries. Once in Spain, they were given the lands vacated by Christians who had fled to the North, and were generally settled according to their tribal groups. Nevertheless, Musa and Tariq were already in open conflict about the distribution of land, because those Arabs who were considered privileged (mostly Yemenites) were settled in the fertile, well-protected South, whereas the poorer Berbers had to make do with central Spain and areas near the frontier with the Christian North.

This contrast determined much of the history of al-Andalus, and between 741 and 746 resulted in a devastating civil war, as the under-privileged Berbers in Spain joined forces with a Berber revolt in the Maghreb. The rebellion spread like wildfire through all areas of the population in Spain, especially the new converts and the Christians in those cities where the process of Islamization or Arabization was

occupied the royal city of Toledo, from which he took vast treasures. In June, 712, Musa himself landed in Spain with about 18,000 Arabs, conquered Seville and Mérida, and joined forces with Tariq outside Toledo.

Meanwhile, it proved difficult to secure the conquered regions. This was because the Christian fighters under Count Pelayo attacked the numerically inferior Muslims from mountains in the province of Murcia, thus entangling them in a continuous guerrilla war, and retaining those territories which later became the Christian kingdoms of northern Spain. After their victory in the battle of Covadonga in 722, they established themselves firmly in Asturias and were able to go on extending the area of Christian rule. Over the next few years, constantly shifting boundaries between the Christian North and the Islamic South led to the creation of independent cultural entities.

advancing only slowly. Attempts at new settlement and the resettlement of whole tribal groups had only limited success, since the fertile South was still controlled by the southern Arabs and Yemenites. In other ways, too, the political situation proved very unstable – in the 30 years between 716 and 747 a total of 19 different governors ruled Cordoba.

Around the year 719 the Arabs undertook their first campaign across the Pyrenees, to invade and plunder the Frankish Empire. A few years later they conquered Carcassonne and invaded territory beyond the Rhône as far as Autun, Burgundy, where they seized rich booty. Governor Abd-al-Rahman al-Ghafiqi (730–732) won victories up to the Loire and sacked Tours. In October, 732, however, in the famous Battle of Tours and Poitiers, he was defeated by the Franks under Charles Martel, and perished.

Left: **Puerta del Sol in Toledo**, 14th century
Toledo vied with Cordoba to be the most
important city in Spain. In the 9th century this
center of trade, science, and the arts, which had
sizable Jewish and Christian communities,
acquired a quasi-Republican status. In 1085, the
year the Christians recaptured Toledo, marked
the real beginning of the Reconquista and the
Moors' expulsion from Spain.

Above: **View of the Great Mosque of Cordoba
above the Guadalquivir**
This depicts the Great Mosque, with the 16th-
century Christian cathedral towering up out of
it. Originally, the whole city was enclosed by
city walls with several gates. In the course of
time, 21 suburbs, each provided with its own
walls, marketplaces, and mosques, grew up
around the Old Town.

This battle, which the Christians later dubbed the "salvation of the
West," was only one among many. Frontier disputes continued for several more
years, and after 791 Islamic troops again penetrated as far as Carcassonne and
Narbonne. It is not historically proven whether Islamic armies really wanted
to conquer parts of the Frankish Empire permanently or whether they were
content to raid and seize booty, thus exacting tribute from Christians who lived
beyond the Pyrenees and out of the control of the Islamic rulers in Spain.

Under Governor Yusuf al-Fihri (747–756), who succeeded in installing
his family in key positions in the leading cities within Spain, the situation in
al-Andalus became much more stable. Yusuf expanded roads as well as cities,
traveled through the country's provinces, and won the frontier war against
the Christians in the North. Striving after self-sufficiency from the very outset,
he exploited the power vacuum left after 750, once the Umayyad family
had been eliminated, to achieve real independence. Even so, the struggles for
the caliphate in the Orient also reached Spain. The discontented southern
Arabs, who were hostile to Yusuf's rule, demanded that the Umayyad prince
Abd al-Rahman ibn Muawiya assume power in Spain.

The Cordoba emirate (756–912)

Prince Abd al-Rahman, grandson of the Umayyad caliph Hisham, survived the extermination of his family by the Abbasids and, after an adventurous life as a refugee, landed on the southern coast of Spain in August, 755. In May, 756, he defeated Yusuf outside the walls of Cordoba and took the capital, which he saved from being sacked. This action persuaded other cities to submit to his authority, and Abd al-Rahman I (756–788) proclaimed himself emir of al-Andalus.

Although he had to suppress various regional rebellions, Abd al-Rahman's domestic politics strove to settle differences and cooperate with his enemies, so that one can see him as the great creator of Islamic Spain. He was also a successful general, created a standing army of 40,000 men, consisting mostly of foreign mercenaries, and also began establishing a navy. He provided many cities with fortifications and controlled the country by dividing it into military provinces. The civil administration he introduced, based on an oriental pattern, split the territory north of Cordoba, which was governed by client noblemen, into three Marches: the "Lower March" around Mérida, the "Central March" around Toledo, and the "Northern March" around Zaragoza.

Both in commerce and in culture, Abd al-Rahman established close links between Islamic Spain and his former homeland, and was especially anxious to extend agriculture through accurate land surveying and efficient irrigation canals. Proficient technical expertise led to small- and medium-sized farms steadily increasing in number. Sugarcane, cotton, rice, and several varieties of

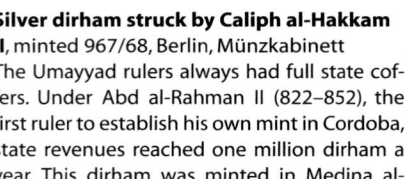

Silver dirham struck by Caliph al-Hakkam II, minted 967/68, Berlin, Münzkabinett
The Umayyad rulers always had full state coffers. Under Abd al-Rahman II (822–852), the first ruler to establish his own mint in Cordoba, state revenues reached one million dirham a year. This dirham was minted in Medina al-Zahra in Year 357 of the hegira. Apart from quoting the Islamic profession of faith and a verse from the Koran (9. 33), it also names Caliph al-Hakkam II as "ruler of the faithful."

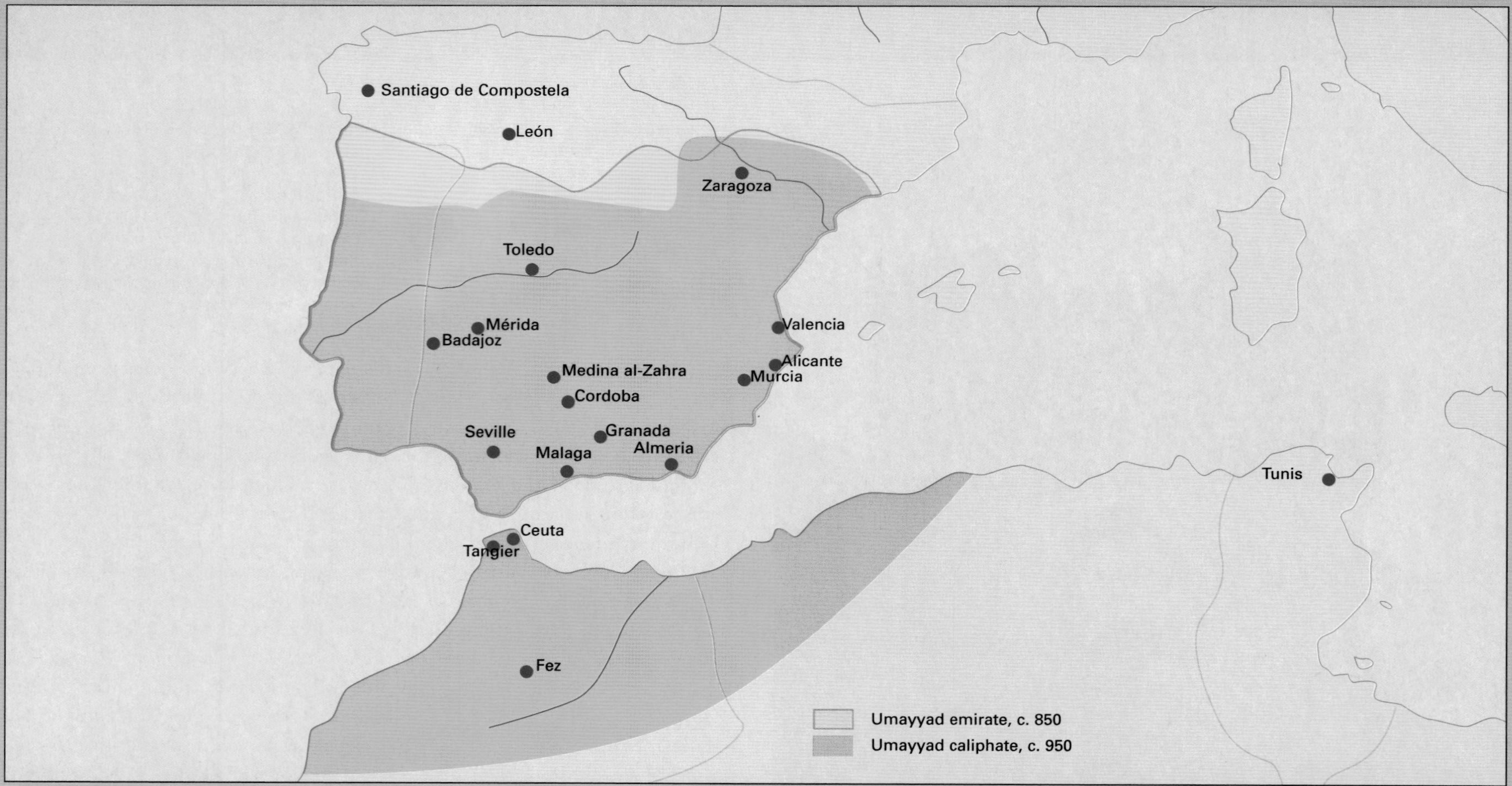

fruit, vegetables, and spices were imported from the Orient, and all over the country granaries were constructed for times of shortage. Certain regions and cities became famous for their products: along the whole Mediterranean coast sugarcane and cotton were planted, in the south mainly figs and olives, and in the provinces of Malaga and Granada, oranges and wine. Artificial irrigation made the area around Valencia fertile: primarily oranges, palm trees, and rice

[Map of the Iberian Peninsula and North Africa showing cities: Santiago de Compostela, León, Zaragoza, Toledo, Mérida, Badajoz, Valencia, Alicante, Murcia, Medina al-Zahra, Cordoba, Seville, Granada, Almeria, Malaga, Ceuta, Tangier, Fez, Tunis]

Umayyad emirate, c. 850
Umayyad caliphate, c. 950

were cultivated here. In the Murcia region, mulberry trees were planted for silkworms, and as a result an important textile center grew up. Overall, the most important industries in al-Andalus were silk and wool manufacture, as well as dyeing and leatherwork in the area around Cordoba. Toledo became famous for its ordnance industry and the Almeria region became a center for ceramics.

In time, the cities assumed an increasingly oriental character. The mosque was always central, and near it one always found the market (bazaar). The market districts consisted of narrow alleys (souks), in which various tradespeople and merchants settled. The cities on the trade routes generally had large caravanserais (*funduqs*) which accommodated and looked after travelers. The living quarters were divided along ethnic, religious, or professional lines, and houses were built in oriental style. They had walls closed to the outside, and the living quarters were usually arranged around a rectangular inner courtyard with a fountain (a patio). This was not visible from the entrance; the private sphere was considered sacred and needed protection.

Waterwheel near Cordoba
In Umayyad-ruled Spain, agriculture achieved enormous success, establishing the country's prosperity. This was achieved by highly developed and precisely regulated soil irrigation. In the caliphate, water use was monitored by an independent "water court," which extracted and distributed this precious resource. On land, most irrigation was achieved by underground water channels. The colossal waterwheels, of which only this one near Cordoba has survived, regulated how much water was extracted from rivers.

711	At the request of the governor of North Africa, Musa ibn Nusair, the Moorish conquest of Spain begins under Tariq ibn Ziyad	751	Loss of Narbonne; the Pyrenees form the province of al-Andalus' northern frontier	900	In a defensive treaty Emir Abdallah recognizes the supreme authority of King Alfonso III over all Spain
720	Barcelona and Narbonne are both conquered. Furthest ever expansion northwards of the province of al-Andalus	754–756	The Umayyad prince Abd al-Rahman I successfully flees to Spain; after his victory over Yusuf al-Fihri, he establishes an independent emirate	929	Abd al-Rahman III proclaims himself caliph
				931	The Umayyads conquer Ceuta and Tangier
722	In the Battle of Covandonga, a Muslim expeditionary force is defeated by the Visigoths under Count Pelayo	785	In Barcelona province, the Franks establish the "Spanish March"	932	Abd al-Rahman II is proclaimed overlord of Fez and Mauritania
		788–796	Emirate of Hisham I	939	Battle of Simancas: the Umayyads suffer heavy defeats against León
732	At Tours and Poitiers the Muslim armies are beaten by the Franks under Charles Martel	805	An unsuccessful conspiracy against al-Hakam I in Cordoba	961–976	Caliphate of al-Hakam II
		818	While suppressing a rebellion, al-Hakam destroys the suburbs of Cordoba	976	The 11-year-old Hisham II becomes caliph. The *de facto* ruler is the chamberlain, Muhammad ibn Abi Amir, known as al-Mansur
741–746	Disputes between Arabic and Berber population groups in Spain	822–852	Reign of Abd al-Rahman II		
747–756	Governorship of Yusuf al-Fihri	844	The Normans overrun Spain	997	Al-Mansur takes control of the Christian pilgrimage site Santiago de Compostela
		850–852	Christian martyr movement unleashes religious disturbances in Cordoba	1002–1008	Abd al-Malik, son of al-Mansur, assumes power
750	In Damascus the Umayyad caliphate is overthrown by the Abbasids	852–886	Rule of Muhammad I	1008–1009	Abd al-Rahman, brother of Abd al-Malik, assumes
		884–927	Rebellion led by Umar ibn Hafsun		

	power. In 1009 there are rebellions in Cordoba, forcing Hisham II to abdicate as caliph
1010–1013	Cordoba is besieged by Berber troops
1016–1030	Hammadids and Umayyads struggle for supremacy in al-Andalus
1031	Reign of Hisham III, the last Umayyad caliph, ends with the breakup of al-Andalus into a mass of minor kingdoms (the *taifas*)

A configuration dangerous to Abd al-Rahman started to develop when the rebellious governor of Zaragoza went to Paderborn to persuade Charlemagne, to fight the emir. In 778, Charlemagne marched on northern Spain with two divisions, conquering Pamplona and Zaragoza, though he had to return to Germany to quell a revolt in Saxony. Even though Abd al-Rahman succeeded in reconquering most of the territories occupied by the Franks, they reappeared in Spain in 785, and in Barcelona province they established the Franks' "Spanish March."

Abd al-Rahman's son Hisham I (788–796), who followed his father's wish that he should succeed him, first had to defeat his turncoat brothers, whom he sent into exile only after several battles. The highly educated Hisham, a poet and scientist, laid the foundations for scientific study in Islamic Spain, instituted much new building, and increased the country's economic prosperity. As a strictly devout Muslim he prepared the ground for the conservative Malik law school, which triumphed in al-Andalus and in the Maghreb.

Hisham's son, al-Hakam I (796–822), had a very unsettled reign. In 803, new converts in Toledo rebelled. Al-Hakam, who was a brave general and effective regent, was also severe to the point of cruelty, and at a banquet supposed to be a feast of reconciliation he had 5,000 Toledo nobles massacred. Consequently, over the next few years several cities and tribes openly rebelled. In 805 a conspiracy to replace al-Hakam with a cousin was crushed. The conspirators, leading Cordoba nobles, were punished by crucifixion. Soon afterwards al-Hakam gathered a bodyguard consisting of about 5,000 Slavic slave-mercenaries (*saqaliba*), who played a major role as the caliphate declined. He also vastly increased the navy, which often harried and plundered Italian coasts. When, in 818, the densely populated suburbs of Cordoba violently rebelled against crippling taxes, al-Hakam had his Slavic mercenaries raze it to

The ruins of the Fort Bobastro
Between 884 and 928, Fort Bobastro near Ardales was where the rebellious Ibn Hafsun clan gathered the country's social malcontents and some aristocrats about him, forming a de facto independent kingdom in southern Spain. At times he exerted such power that he could restrict the emir's hegemony to Greater Cordoba. In about 900, he converted to Christianity, and died as "Count Samuel" in 917. Caliph Abd al-Rahman III, who restored central rule, failed to expel his successors until 928.

the ground. A total of 25,000 inhabitants, whom the emir first planned to kill, were exiled to Africa. Such brutal measures enabled al-Hakam to impose political unity on the emirate.

Culturally, the reign of his son Abd al-Rahman II (822–852) was a high point of the early emirate. He reorganized the country's internal administration and reinforced his father's initiatives to make Spanish court life more oriental and culturally sophisticated – by bringing influences from Baghdad and Samarra to bear. New fashions in clothes established themselves in al-Andalus, as did refined eating habits, chess, intensive preoccupation with poetry and scholarship, and a school of music. Artists, musicians, and poets set the tone for society at large. Discussing how highly the emirate's citizens regarded clothes, a chronicler wrote: "Of all nations, the Moors care most about their clothes, fabric cushions, and so forth. Those who have no other resources beyond a daily allowance would rather fast and use the money saved to buy some soap to wash their clothes. Not even for one hour would they wear them in a state not pleasing to the eye."

The emir himself, who was a well-read man with a keen interest in natural science, began to purchase learned texts as well as translations from Greek and Sanskrit. However, this extra refinement also multiplied court intriguers and harem conspirators. Abd al-Rahman amply demonstrated his own claims to power with many monumental public buildings. He maintained good diplomatic relations with the imperial Byzantine court in Constantinople and also protected several minor North African states against the Aghlabids of Kairouan, inducing the Spanish Umayyads to become more directly involved in North Africa. Towards the end of his reign, a strange phenomenon emerged. Inspired by Mozarabian rebellions in Cordoba and Toledo since 850, Christians increasingly developed a "lust for the martyr's crown," publicly reviled Islam, and allowed themselves to be executed; while their fellow believers fought over their corpses as cult relics. After great waves of executions, the Muslim administration – working in tandem with Catholic bishops – managed to dampen this movement, but after 859 it flared up again.

Under Abd al-Rahman's son, Muhammad I (852–886), central authority rapidly weakened. Governor-organized rebellions led to several years of *de facto* independence in Toledo (in 852) and Mérida (in 868) while, until his death in 862, the Mozarabian general, Musa al-Qasi, who had been reigning independently in Tudela since 842, also gained Zaragoza's and Toledo's loyalty. King Alfonso III of León (866–910) exploited this pressure on Muhammad to extend his empire vastly, and he led a campaign deep into the heart of al-Andalus. In 883 the emir was obliged to ask Alfonso for peace. Yet the greatest threat to continued Umayyad hegemony came from the uprising, centered on Fort Bobastro, of *muwalladun* Umar ibn Hafsun and his family. From 884 to

917 – with the support of rebellious Berbers and Mozarabs – they extended their power between Cordoba and the Mediterranean, and undermined the emirate's authority through treaties made with rich Christians and the Fatimids.

The warlike al-Mundir (886–888) had already shown himself to be his father's leading general and, during his last years, had ruled as regent. Highly irascible and a thoroughgoing warrior, the emir immediately attacked Ibn Hafsun, besieging him in Fort Bobastro, where, in July, 888 he was killed fighting in the vanguard. His younger brother, Abdallah (888–912), succeeded under the worst possible conditions. Apart from the activities of various troublemakers, the country suffered religious disturbances. In addition, in southern Spain several members of the ruling family rebelled, captured Ronda, and established a foothold in Seville and Jaén, leaving Abdallah's emirate temporarily limited to the Cordoba province. In 889 the emir also lost Murcia and Valencia to the rebels.

Alcazaba and Medina from Almeria
Caliph Abd al-Rahman III (912–961) extended the northern port of Almeria, – the Arabic name means "mirror of the sea" – protected by a mountain range, into the territory's most important seaport. At times of danger, this fortress (Alcazaba), which is situated on a slope, allegedly sheltered 20,000 people. This vantage point allowed occupiers to check ships sailing in and out, while protecting the countryside with an extensive rampart. In 1489 Catholic kings captured the city.

Right: **Bronze candelabrum and oil lamp**, caliphate period, 10th century, Copenhagen, David Collection

Below: **Brass oil lamp with a stag's head handle**, emirate period, 9th century, Granada, Museum of the Alhambra

The bronze candelabrum depicted here shows how symbolic motifs were assimilated into Islamic art in Spain. Several similar objects originated at this period, heavily influenced in form and decoration by Islamic ideas about Paradise. Elaborate ornamentation and inventive form made even functional objects decoratively beautiful, while remaining functional. This candelabrum is a good example: on its foot an Arabic blessing is inscribed, and the central section comprises a small pavilion with six pillars. The arches above are covered with plant designs, and around the top ring sit a number of doves with breasts raised.

Abdallah was under such pressure that he renewed the peace treaty – valid until 900 – with Alfonso III of León by signing a treaty of protection, whereby the emirate recognized King Alfonso, now calling himself "Rex Hispanorum Regum," as *de facto* ruler of Spain. Alfonso attacked Ibn Hafsun, who had challenged him, and inflicted several devastating defeats on him. Simultaneously, some members of the Orthodox *ulama*, or religious council, accused the emir of becoming a vassal of the Christian king. In many mosques, sermons were preached against Abdallah, poets wrote derisive verses, and the emir's status had reached its nadir.

The caliphate of Cordoba – glory and decline (912–1031)

Abd al-Rahman III (912-961), the great recreator of Umayyad rule in Spain, his predecessor's grandson, succeeded at the age of 22. He reconquered Seville by 913 and, after Ibn Hafsun died in 917, Hafsun's sons back towards the east. In 928 he finally managed to storm Fort Bobastro and capture Mérida, thereby permanently expelling the Hafsun clan from al-Andalus.

The power struggle between Alfonso III's sons gave Abd al-Rahman breathing space on the northern frontier; though after 916, the kings of León conquered several cities and frequently sacked al-Andalus. Eventually, Abd al-Rahman led an enormous army against the Christians, but in August, 939, near Simancas, he was heavily defeated, wounded, and almost captured. Nevertheless, in the following years, he forced León into an armistice. The caliph exploited the ensuing political weakness in the Christian lands to conclude a treaty of protection with León and Navarre, recognizing Abd al-Rahman as *de*

facto ruler and arbiter in all Spain. Even Castile and Barcelona were compelled to pay him tribute. After intense battles, Abd al-Rahman's North African campaigns were also successful. Traditionally, relations with the Maghreb had been good but these were endangered when the Shiite Fatimids rapidly spread out from Tunisia after 920 and conquered all the western Maghreb as far as the Atlantic, also subjecting Fez to their rule. Abd al-Rahman then occupied Majorca to protect his forces from a possible seaborne attack, and in 931 he conquered Ceuta and Tangier.

On January 16, 929, mainly to demonstrate his power against the Shiite Fatimids, Abd al-Rahman III named himself caliph. Cordoba became the third caliphate to be ranged against Baghdad (where Abbasids predominated) and Mahdiya – later Cairo – (a Fatimid stronghold). The new caliph wanted to show the Spanish and North African Sunnis he was both protector and supreme authority. In 932 he was proclaimed ruler of Fez and all Mauritania. In North Africa he established Umayyad governors, who later besieged Tunis, a city they ransomed for an enormous sum, but late in his reign the Fatimids inflicted heavy losses on him. Internationally, Abd al-Rahman III fostered good relations with the Byzantine imperial court and various European rulers. After tortuous negotiations, he established diplomatic relations with Otto the Great's imperial court in Germany, and in 959 the caliph received Imperial Ambassador Abbot Johann von Gorze.

Abd al-Rahman III instituted a strictly centralized internal administration, ensuring the country rapid prosperity – thanks mostly to extensive irrigation and efficient agriculture. A skillful tax system, overflowing state coffers, trade concessions for Jews, and sound municipal administration made al-Andalus the most populous country in Europe at this time. Cordoba, its capital, was a lively economic and cultural center, and as a European metropolis could almost be compared to Constantinople. A significant symbol of al-Rahman's power was the palace city of Medina al-Zahra, begun in 936, and known as the "10th-century Versailles," where he surrounded himself with poets and scholars. The caliph thoroughly inspected the whole country, exploited mineral resources and commerce, protected domestic manufacturers through a customs and forwarding system, and trained an efficient bureaucracy.

Abd al-Rahman also reorganized the country's military administration, favoring those soldiers, namely Berbers and Slavs, which were directly under his command. During his decades-long rule, tensions between individual population groups largely disappeared, and mass conversions to Islam helped the culture to acquire a strongly Arabic character. Abd al Rahman III was considered a leading Islamic ruler, and by his death in October, 961, al-Andalus was at the height of its power.

The Andalusian poet, historian, and statesman Ibn al-Khatib (1313–1375) confirmed this: "Abd al-Rahman III represents the best of the Umayyad dynasty. His life was long, his luck constant, his government famous, his renown wide-spread… When Abd al-Rahman came to power, al-Andalus was a coal which flared, / a fire which blazed; / in both open and secret opposition / driven nearly to perdition. / Through his happy hand / and strong grip God brought peace to all the land. / The third Abd al-Rahman was often compared with the first: For he tamed the rebels (as they came); / built castles, established culture, and perpetuated his name. / He bled the unbelievers' veins; he freed al-Andalus of enemies, / and rid it of all rivalries. / Nations paid him tribute gladly, / – they all needed peace terms badly!"

Fragment of fabric from the Pyrenees, caliphate period, 10th century, Madrid, Instituto Valencia de Don Juan
The exquisite fabrics and textiles produced by Spanish workshops during the caliphate were a precious commodity in Europe, North Africa, and the Near East. This fragment was discovered in a Christian church in the Pyrenees. It was probably an ornamental band for a piece of fabric underneath – a bishop's cope, perhaps. It depicts linked colored medallions, with a central peacock, whose plumage comprises overlapping scales. The bordering flower pattern is probably based on plant stucco ornaments in the palace city of Medina al-Zahra. In 971, similar fabrics are mentioned in Caliph al-Hakam II's court chronicles.

Above: **Stone relief on a basin from the Palace of Medina al-Zahira**, c. 980, Granada, Hispano-Islamic Museum
Powerful lions overwhelming their prey (antelopes) symbolize the triumph of Islam over its enemies: General al-Mansur is remembered primarily as victor in allegedly over 50 campaigns against Christian kingdoms in northern Spain.

Below: **Ivory box belonging to the daughter of Abd ar-Rahmans III**, after 961, 4.5 x 9.5 x 7 cm London, Victoria and Albert Museum
This very small box with metal clasps shows a rich ornamentation, indicating that is was made in Medina az-Zahara. An inscription provides information about the patron and expresses blessings for the ruler Abd ar-Rahman III.

As crown prince, Caliph al-Hakam II (961–976) shared in government from the age of 40, and he developed his father's achievements. A peace-loving character, during a long period as crown prince he surrounded himself with scientists and scholars, also amassing many books. Helped by several agents, he purchased newly compiled books and compendia in the Orient and spent vast sums on scholars and scribes. In Cordoba he deposited a library of 400,000 books, indexed in 44 catalogues, adding his own commentaries to most volumes. Sciences like geography, agriculture and irrigation, astronomy, medicine, and mathematics were encouraged; as was philosophy, based mainly on classical Greek thought. Caliph Al-Hakam commissioned works on ethics and statecraft, concentrating on history, which at that time was largely genealogy. In establishing schools and centers of learning for all social strata, he took a personal interest in popular literacy and education. His reign is regarded as the apotheosis of science, scholarship, and poetry in al-Andalus. Maintaining his father's astute commercial policy enabled him to increase the country's prosperity, and he began extensive public building.

Politically, Hakam retained his father's successes. The caliph compelled the kingdom of León to extend the peace treaty. He also arbitrated in disputes in Navarre and Galicia, and in both cases the Christian kingdoms had to acknowledge his *de facto* supremacy. In North Africa, too, he temporarily upheld the Umayyads' predominance. However, after establishing themselves in Cairo (in 969), the Fatimids successfully attempted to conquer the Maghreb. By offering bribes, Hakam re-established friendship with the Berber tribes of Morocco, which helped him reconquer Fez.

When al-Hakam II died in October, 976, Crown Prince Hisham II (976–1009 and 1010–1013) was only 11 years old. Two other people initially reigned for him. First, his mother, the Basque Sultana Subh (real name Aurora), and secondly, Hajib (Prime Minister) Jafar al-Mushafi. This period includes the meteoric rise of the ambitious Muhammad ibn Abu Amir, originally a Yemenite noble, who, favored by the sultana, swiftly rose from mint overseer to *de facto* ruler of Spain. First, he stripped Mushafi of power; then, known as al-Mansur, his *nom de guerre* in his military campaigns (978–1002), he succeeded Mushafi as *hajib*. On the banks of the Guadalquivir he built his own palace city, Medina al-Zahira, which became the empire's new center of power.

Supported by the military, to whom he declared personal loyalty, al-Mansur kept Caliph Hisham prisoner in a "golden cage" in Hisham's palace. Screened off from the outside world, the caliph was shown to the populace only on certain public occasions. Al-Mansur used the seal of state, had himself named immediately after the caliph at public prayers, and in 996 assumed a king-like title. Ruling with severity tempered by justice, after securing power, he showed himself as a firm supporter of the arts and sciences just as the previous caliphs had been. He also gave the most important state offices to members of his family. Both gifted generals, Al-Mansur and his eldest son, Abd al-Malik, who succeeded al-Mansur as *hajib*, swelled the army's ranks with many Berbers from Africa.

Al-Mansur is mainly remembered as allegedly winning over 50 campaigns against the Christian kingdoms of North Spain. His first military campaign, in 977, was directed mainly against Castile; in 988, he plundered and destroyed the capital of León; and then, in 995, defeated the Christian armies on the river Douro. In August, 997, he even captured Santiago de Compostela, the national shrine of Spanish Christians, destroying the city and the church built above the tomb of St. James. In 1000, al-Mansur marched deep into Castilian territory and sacked Burgos. In Africa, too, he extended his predecessor's triumphs. A peace treaty he concluded with the king of the Maghreb protected his rear for campaigns against the Christians. When, in 983, the Fatimids conquered Morocco and Mauretania, al-Mansur sent his son, Abd al-Malik, to reconquer these territories; then, in 997, he captured Fez, and raised a large contingent of Berbers to serve his father. After al-Mansur died in Medinaceli in August, 1002, returning from a campaign against Castile, Abd al-Malik (1002–1008) naturally succeeded his father, establishing the Almoravids as a legitimate line. Like his father, Abd al-Malik was an able king who ruled with courage and psychological finesse. He attacked Navarre and Barcelona, again sacked the city of León in 1004, and severely tested Christian frontier defenses. Abd al-Malik's unexpected death in October, 1008 ended not only the al-Mansur family's most glorious period but also that of the caliphate of Cordoba. By completely excluding the caliph, the Almoravids had held the power of Islamic Spain in check, but undermined the idea of central control.

While the Almoravids initially remained powerful, Abd al-Malik's younger brother, Abd al-Rahman (1008–1009), became the *de facto* ruler; but he was so badly advised that he secretly risked his family's honor by trying to make himself caliph. He persuaded Hisham II, who was childless, to make him crown prince. Shortly thereafter, Abd al-Rahman fell victim to popular fury in the streets of Cordoba. In subsequent years, however, two Umayyad pretenders opposed one another, unleashing a bloody civil war. In consequence, real power passed increasingly to military cadres and mercenary armies. In May, 1013 Berbers sacked and burnt the capital, Cordoba, and during the fire the legitimate caliph, Hisham II, perished.

After 1016, various Umayyad princes battled for the caliphate against the Hammadids, led by Banu Hammad, who ruled from Malaga in southern Spain, while al-Andalus sank into ever-deepening chaos and anarchy. After his expulsion from Cordoba on November 30, 1031, the last caliph, Hisham III (1027–1031), abdicated. This marked the end of the caliphate of Cordoba, and also of an important epoch in Islamic and European history.

Ivory casket with a portrait of Abd al-Malik, 1004

Pamplona, Museo di Navarra

The medallion on the front side of this ivory casket depicts Abd al-Malik as defender of the faith, defeating the enemies of Islam. Al-Mansur's eldest son had proved to be an able general and grand vizier even during his father's lifetime. In 1002 he succeeded al-Mansur as administrator, and again campaigned against Christians in northern Spain. After his sudden death in October, 1008, the caliphate in Spain collapsed, and devastating civil wars followed. During these, in 1013, Cordoba and the palace city of Medina al-Zahra were plundered and largely destroyed.

Architecture
Natascha Kubisch

Architecture of the Spanish Umayyads and the *taifa* kingdoms

In 27 B.C., under Emperor Augustus, Cordoba became the capital of the Roman province Baetica, roughly the area of present-day Andalusia. Later, especially in Visigothic times (6-7th centuries), steady population growth necessitated the city's frequent expansion. When, in 711 A.D., the Muslims advanced towards al-Andalus from the Maghreb, they occupied not only Malaga and Granada but also Cordoba with its Visigothic character. Here, they initially decided against building a mosque, sharing San Vicente, a church situated in the south of the city, with the Christian community. The situation changed when Abd al-Rahman I, grandson of the Umayyad caliph, Hisham, was proclaimed emir in 756, and made Cordoba capital of his then small and insecure kingdom. Cordoba's new status demanded not merely a new administrative system but also implied extensive municipal rebuilding. Accordingly, Abd al-Rahman built new structures onto many ancient buildings, so that in time the city acquired an increasingly oriental character. Above all, however, he commissioned a major mosque, to represent Islamic power in Spain. Around 785, work began on the Great Mosque of Cordoba (*La Mezquita*), completed in several building phases over the next two centuries. When, in the 9th century, the city's population expanded further Emir Abd al-Rahman II undertook the first expansion, from 833 to 848. Yet the increasing political strength of the emirate of Cordoba cannot be measured simply by the mosque's size, but indirectly also by its construction. Whereas Roman and Visigothic ruins, which reveal the city's Roman and Visigothic origins, were mainly used for the basic structure, in the mid-9th century we see the first signs of an independent artistic style. This is called the "emirate style," and is expressed mainly in the capitals, revealing an almost inexhaustible variety of forms.

When, in 929, Abd al-Rahman III proclaimed himself caliph, and, in 936, founded the palace city of Medina al-Zahra near Cordoba, the building work in Medina was so demanding that in the Great Mosque in Cordoba he concentrated on less important aspects, such as extending the mosque courtyard and replacing Hisham I's old minaret. Not until the mid-10th century (962–966) did his son and successor, al-Hakam II, inaugurate a new building phase. With its magnificent arch constructions, its domes, and its gold mosaics, which adorn, for instance, the *mihrab* facade, this phase created the Great Mosque's greatest splendors. The mosque even reflects the caliphate of Cordoba's decline. This we see in the last building phase (987–988), supervised by al-Mansur, regent for young Caliph Hisham II, who merely "copied" the forms of previous building phases, without creating an individual style.

More than any other building in al-Andalus, the Great Mosque of Cordoba accurately documents the history of early Islamic architecture in Spain, with its different stylistic features.

Cordoba's expansion during the caliphate

In the 10th century the caliphate was centered in Cordoba, making it the capital of the western Islamic empire, stretching over al-Andalus and the Maghreb. Ibn Hazm, a contemporary Spanish-Arab scholar, reports that in the 10th century Cordoba had a diameter of about 6 miles (10 kilometers). Contemporary records also confirm that Cordoba had many mosques – the chronicler, al-Bakri, counted 471, but another scholar totaled 1,600. Al-Bakri also mentions that Cordoba was greatly enlarged under al-Mansur. He mentions 213,077 working-class and middle-class houses, 60,300 residences for aristocrats and high officials, and 80,455 shops – excluding numerous lodgings for travelers. These figures are less an expression of exact figures than of amazement at Cordoba's vast size. Ibn Hauqal, a Baghdad scholar, wrote that in the 10th century no city in the Maghreb, Egypt, or Syria was as large as Cordoba.

Cordoba's social center lay in the South City, by the Guadalquivir (Spanish for "large river"), near the Roman Bridge, alongside which the Great Mosque was built. Around the mosque there grew up numerous markets – so-called *zocos* (from Arabic *suk*). The government district with the fortress-like residence, the Alcázar (from Arabic *qasr*, "imposing house") lay alongside the main mosque. On the opposite riverbank was a suburb whose diameter al-Maqqari calculated at 47,500 ells, which is about 1 mile (1.5 kilometers). From these data, the French scholar, Lévi-Provençal, deduces that the whole city was 14 miles (22 kilometers) in diameter with a surface area of over 12,350 acres (5,000 hectares) – much larger than present-day Cordoba.

In the northwest, the city stretched to the foot of the Sierra Morena mountain range. Even during the emirate its appealing climate made the area popular for country estates, so-called *al-munyas*. In the west, suburbs nearly reached the residence of Medina al-Zahra, which, in 936, Caliph Abd al-Rahman III built as his empire's administrative and government headquarters. In the east, Cordoba extended to the similarly named residence of Medina al-Zahira, which al-Mansur, the first ruler of the Amirid dynasty, had

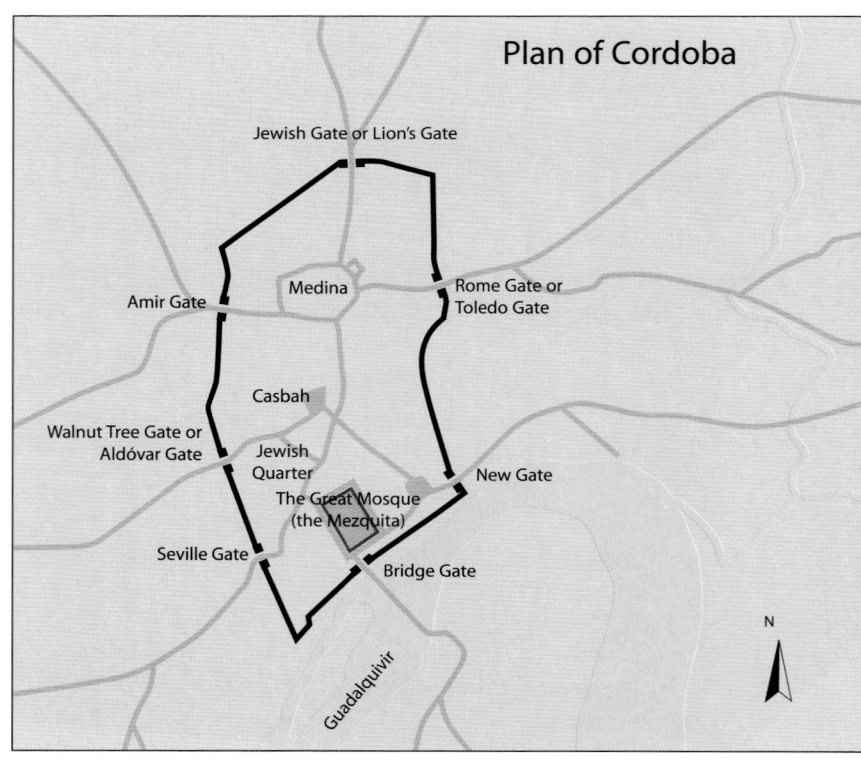

built during the late 10th century. Contemporary Arabic authors determined the Cordoba city limits on the basis of estates and residences, a method which enables us to conclude that a fertile belt of gardens and parks enclosed the city.

In the northern area of Cordoba Old Town sections have survived of the massive city wall – frequently repaired and extended over the centuries. This wall, which enclosed the city, had several portals. The first portal, near the Alcázar and the Great Mosque, was called the Bridge Gate because it lay within the extension of the old Roman bridge. The second gate was not built until Caliph al-Hakam II's reign, and in its day, supposedly sealed off the southern suburb. The River Gate stood near the Guadalquivir at a city intersection where roads led to Seville and the rest of southern Andalusia. The city wall extended along the Guadalquivir, where another gate, erected during Caliph al-Hakam II's rule, was probably built rather late – and is thus called the New Gate. About 660 yards (600 meters) northeast was another portal – over the Roman road, the Via Augusta. According to Ibn Bashkuval (1101–1183), a historian from Cordoba, the Via Augusta started in Cadiz and went through Cordoba to the interior, Zaragoza, and thence far across the Pyrenees to Narbonne. Originally called the Rome Gate, this portal was renamed the Toledo Gate after the road to Toledo – about 190 miles (300 kilometers) away – had gained importance as a commercial and transport link. Finally, yet another City Gate is mentioned: in the northern city, near the central traffic axis. Called the Talavera Gate, this led to the main road toward Talavera. The name Lion's

Cordoba city wall with the Almódovar Gate
The medieval Cordoba city wall dates back to the time of the caliphate of Cordoba (929–1031), though in subsequent centuries it was often rebuilt and restored. Projecting from the well-preserved western section near the Jewish Quarter is the Almódovar Gate – so-named after the main road to Almódovar del Rio, which was an important route during the caliphate of Cordoba.

Gate, which it is sometimes given, presumably alludes to some power symbolism connected with Abd al-Rahman I and his residence, "Rusafa." One also finds the name Jewish Gate or Portal of Good Direction. This portal led across an old Roman necropolis, later also used as a burial place by Jews and Muslims: mindful of their future death, people passing through this portal should steer their life in a "good direction." Formerly, the western city had three more portals in the city wall running from the northwest to the southwest.

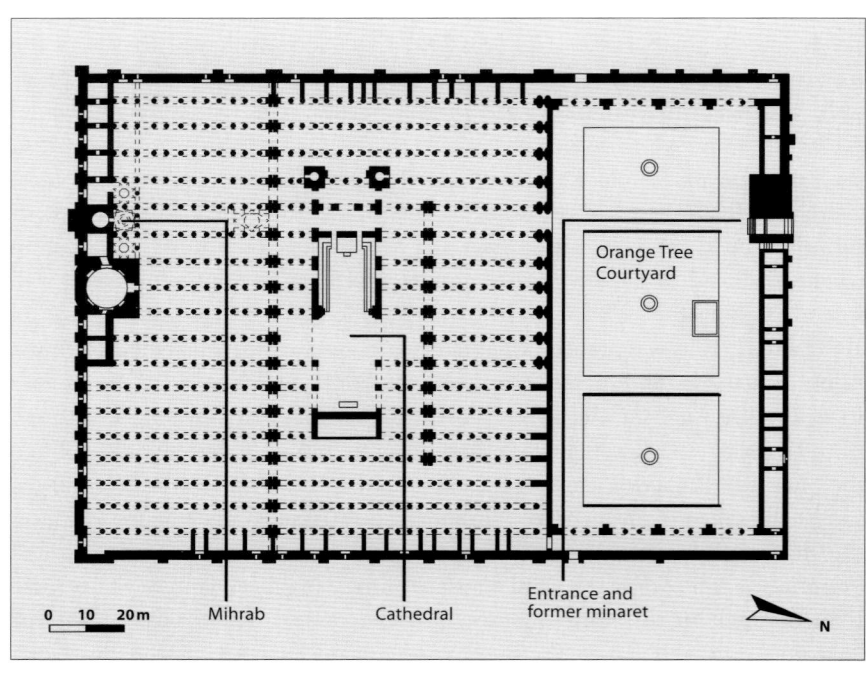

Decline of Cordoba after the fall of the caliphate

The Berber rebellion of 1010, and the expulsion of the last legitimate caliph in 1031, spelled the end of the Cordoba caliphate. The territory fragmented into so-called minor states, called *taifa* kingdoms in Spanish. This period of *taifa* rulers, or *fitna* (strife), was a time of internal turmoil for Spain. No single ruler could gain political control over the country. Cordoba lost not only its political and artistic importance but also declined noticeably. Then, in the 12th century, under the Almohads, the city increased in importance and was enlarged, even if scant archeological evidence of this period has survived. After Cordoba's conquest by the Christians (in 1235), under King Fernando III of Castile and León, most Islamic estates and palaces were abandoned, and individual districts repeatedly rebuilt over the years. Nevertheless, even today, a walk through the Old Town's alleyways gives one a taste of its Moorish character and former glory and splendor.

Great Mosque of Cordoba, 785–988
The aerial view, above, and ground plan, right, show the mosque's construction. The southern exterior wall in the foreground is identical with the *qibla* wall, facing Mecca. The octagonal superstructure with its pointed tent roof surmounts the *mihrab* in al-Hakam II's extension (962–966). The prayer hall comprises 19 aisles running from the *qibla* wall, each with a saddleback roof. Within the mosque's center lies the massive cathedral structure, begun in the 16th century, and not completed until the 18th. Facing north, the former mosque courtyard abutted the prayer hall. The freestanding former minaret, dismantled then completely restructured in the 16–17th century, now functions as the cathedral's bell tower.

Orange Tree Courtyard

0 10 20m Mihrab Cathedral Entrance and former minaret N

The Great Mosque of Cordoba's original construction under Abd al-Rahman I

Cordoba's most magnificent structure, the Great Mosque, was commissioned in 785 by Emir Abd al-Rahman I after he had chosen Cordoba as his kingdom's capital. It was built on the site occupied by the Christian church San Vicente, whose foundations were found in excavations during the 1930s. Work began on building the mosque around 785. Its position near the Guadalquivir, at the end of the (now restored) bridge, not only exploited existing traffic links, but also demonstrated its connections with the city's Visigothic heritage. Reports suggest that near the mosque, immediately abutting the San Vicente Church district, stood a Visigothic palace, which Abd al-Rahman I made his residence. Thus, the spiritual and secular centers of the new emirate lay close together and were inseparably linked. Construction on the basic structure of the Great Mosque of Cordoba supposedly took a year (785–786). One reason was Abd al-Rahman's personal wish and ambition to make this mosque worthy of Cordoba, a metropolitan city. The other reason was that Roman and Visigothic remnants were used in the construction of the mosque.

The Great Mosque of Cordoba comprises a rectangular prayer hall, with a mosque courtyard in front. This courtyard is nearly as large as the prayer hall because originally believers also assembled for prayers in the courtyard – if the prayer hall were already full. Initially, the prayer hall in the original mosque building was designed with dimensions of about 260 × 138 feet (79.02 × 42.21 meters), and 11 aisles arranged perpendicular to the *qibla* wall. The center aisle, leading to the prayer niche or *mihrab*, which indicates the direction of prayers to Mecca, is 26 feet (7.85 meters) wide. This is about three feet broader than the other aisles, which are only 23 feet (6.86 meters) across. Accentuating the center aisle also gives the central axis, oriented on the *mihrab*, greater emphasis, and there-fore this type of mosque is called "directional." However, the center aisle is not only slightly broader but also higher than the other aisles – something particu-larly obvious when you look at the mosque from the nearby cathedral.

The al-Aqsa Mosque, Jerusalem, is built similarly to the Great Mosque of Cordoba. Begun in 715, the al-Aqsa is exactly 70 years older than the original Cordoba building. It also has a basilica-like structure with the central aisle markedly broader and leading axially to the *mihrab*. Abd al-Rahman might have encountered this or a similar form of mosque during his youth in the east. It is therefore not surprising that he adapted this pattern to distant Cordoba, espe-cially as his ambitions were predicated on his glorious East Umayyad ancestry. The prayer hall's size is due not merely to the mosque's importance as a spiritual center for the western Islamic empire, but also to the size of the city, with its massive population, necessitating a large prayer hall with many aisles.

The original building (dating from 785–786) did not include a minaret. Arabic sources state that calls to prayer were made from the tower of the nearby Visigothic palace, which was also used as a government palace. Originally, the mosque supposedly had four entrances, of which the Bab al-Wuzara (Ministers' Gate) in the west facade has survived to this day almost unchanged. According to an inscription over the lintel, it dates back to 786. Through this gate – now called the Stephen Gate after the Chapel of St. Stephen which stands behind it – high-ranking officials would enter the mosque from the government palace located opposite.

Entering the Mezquita today, one is amazed to find that a cathedral exists within it. In 1523, the cathedral chapter of Cordoba commissioned the cathe-dral building when, after the Reconquista, the cathedral had regained the mosque territory. Accordingly, 63 pillars were removed from the mosque, so that the cathedral could stand exactly in the mosque's center. It took over three cen-turies to build and decorate because construction work was often interrupted.

Ministers' Gate, Great Mosque of Cordoba, 785–988
In the west facade of the Great Mosque of Cordoba, the mosque's oldest portal (dating from 786–787), called the Bab al-Wuzara (Min-isters' Gate), still exists.

View into the Orange Tree Courtyard
The mosque courtyard was designed to be very large, so that if the prayer hall were full more believers could participate in prayers. Orange trees were planted only later.

Apparently, construction workers downed their tools as soon as building work began, refusing to wreak havoc on the mosque's fabric. Although this incident is not historically proven, it is often happily quoted in books, and it shows how strongly Cordobans still identified with their city's Islamic roots, even in the 16th century. Apparently, workers, city council and cathedral chapter reached agreement only after Emperor Charles V, consulted as ultimate arbiter, had intervened. He endorsed the cathedral's construction, so that it could be built with a clear conscience – on the emperor's authority, as it were. When the emperor later visited Cordoba he apparently said in consternation, on seeing the inserted cathedral: "Had I known what was here I would never have dared touch the old structure. You have destroyed something that was unique in the world and added something one can see anywhere!" These or similar thoughts may strike a visitor entering the cathedral today. One must remember, however, that the mosque might have survived precisely because a cathedral was built inside it. Any building frequented for worship would be maintained, whereas one left empty is exposed to decay – a fate which, after Jews and Muslims had been expelled from Spain in 1492, would undoubtedly have befallen the Great Mosque of Cordoba.

The mosque itself beguiles viewers with its solemnly austere, almost mysterious impression of space and its numerous views through two-story arcades, making the space seem nearly weightless. The Spanish art historian, Manuel Gómez-Moreno, compared the two-story arcades of the Great Mosque of Cordoba with the Roman aqueduct of Merida, whose entresol is also supported by brick arches, and therefore reveals distant similarities in construction. However, one is now more likely to find possible influences in mosques which have not fully survived. A good comparison is the Umayyad Great Mosque of Damascus (begun in 707), which also has a two-story arcade structure. There, though,

unlike in the Cordoba mosque, the arcades are not lateral but run parallel to the *qibla* wall. The lower arches reveal large, supporting round arches, resting on tall, capital-crowned columns. The upper arches are characterized by several small, shallow round arches, so arranged that one arcade division below matches two divisions above. Even if the positioning of the arches in the Ummayad Great Mosque of Damascus does not exactly match the Cordoba model, it is still incontestable that two-story arcades were a common feature of eastern Umayyad sacred architecture. Christian Ewert cites early North African mosques to explain the arch arrangement. In the Amr Mosque of Fustat, (situated in present-day Cairo and dated 827), and in the Zaituna Mosque, Tunis (9th century), the capital-crowned arcade columns are surmounted by inverted pyramid bases with shallow, cubiform blocks, on which the mosque's arches rest. These blocks distantly recall the pillars of the upper arches at the Great Mosque of Cordoba, and are similarly supporting. We can thus suppose that they have adapted and extended systems first developed in North Africa. The combination of horseshoe and round arches in the Great Mosque of Cordoba is unusual, nevertheless. Horseshoe arches have precursors in local Visigothic buildings, but can also be found in pre-Islamic structures in the Middle East. However, combining horseshoe arches with alternating ashlar and brick in different colors must be considered a Cordoba invention, which in succeeding centuries remained a stylistic peculiarity of the Mezquita.

Though not the case originally, at the present times light determines the impression of space conveyed by the Great Mosque of Cordoba. Originally, the courtyard facade arcades were open, so that light from the mosque courtyard would fall into the prayer hall, bathing it in a warm glow that made the colored carpets on its floor shine radiantly. Because the floor was carpeted it did not seem strange that some taller columns – they were all reclaimed remnants of

Relief emblem, Great Mosque of Cordoba
Above the Puerta de Santa Catalina there is a 16th-century relief emblem, showing a historical view of the minaret built by Abd al-Rahman III. We can see the stepped main body of the minaret becoming smaller as it rises, the prominent ashlars, and the typical horseshoe-shaped window openings.

Visigothic capital, 7th century
In the original Great Mosque (dating from 785–786) both Roman and Visigothic capitals were used. This one can be classified as one inspired by the Corinthian order. Above a relief wreath of acanthus leaves, the capital is decorated with a flat, highly stylized calyx. The abacus has geometric adornment.

Emirate period capital, between 833 and 848
The first extension (833–848) of the Great Mosque produced a unique, purely Islamic type of capital. This example is a Mosque masterpiece: particularly striking is the delicacy of the acanthus leaves, achieved by deep chiseling which produces relief effects and the fleshy character of leaf forms.

Roman and Visigothic buildings – had to be embedded more deeply in the floor. A striking feature is that only reddish columns appear in the center aisle, re-emphasizing that the central axis is oriented on the *mihrab*; while the side aisles have alternating black and red marble columns. The mosque's capitals warrant special attention. The original building mainly used Roman capitals of the Corinthian order. However, one also sees Visigothic capitals and even isolated pieces from the eastern Mediterranean. The Visigothic capitals differ from the Roman ones in terms of their flat reliefwork and a schematic, at times even geometric simplification of the vegetal decoration. The center aisle has the finest capitals, and these reused capitals further accentuate the central axis.

In 793 Hisham I, Abd al-Rahman I's son, first had a minaret built. This supposedly stood against the mosque's north wall, but no archeological traces have survived to show this. Major rebuilding did not commence until the mid-9th century.

The unique importance of the Great Mosque of Cordoba is not due solely to the fact that it was the city's main mosque, but also to the close connection between secular and spiritual power that made it the empire's religious and cultural center. Inside, people not only met to pray, but also discussed the religious and secular laws that were irrevocably determined here for the whole western Islamic world. Every ruler whose claim to rule originated from Abd al-Rahman I, founder of the Spanish Umayyad dynasty, also gave the mosque he founded special respect. This might be shown in generous gifts – the building of a minaret, for example – or in constructing an extension. This also explains why over the centuries – almost to the end of the caliphate – work continued on the mosque.

Extension by al-Hakam II, 962-966
This extension to the Great Mosque was built under the highly cultivated Caliph al-Hakam II. Its most impressive features are the numerous columns which convey an impression of expansiveness. Together with a constant flow of views through the building, the two-story arcades with their voussoirs in alternating colors provide a unique rhythm. The restrained lighting evokes a mystical mood which creates this architecture's true charm.

The first mosque extension under Abd al-Rahman II

Due to the city's increasing population, Abd al-Rahman II ordered the Great Mosque of Cordoba to be extended over the years 833–848 – which resulted mainly in the prayer hall being enlarged to the south. As work progressed, the *mihrab* was demolished, and the masonry of the *qibla* wall removed, so that eight more bays could be added in an extension to the original building, comprising 11 aisles and 12 bays; as a result, the prayer hall covered a nearly square area of 260 × 227 feet (79.29 × 69.09 meters).

Here, we should also mention the capitals, exhaustively examined by Christian Ewert and Patrice Cressier. According to them, not only Roman and Visigothic, but now also Islamic capitals are apparent. These embody a new form, that, in keeping with their epoch, we shall call "emirate period" capitals. Just as with all medieval capitals, those of the emirate period capitals are based on the classical Corinthian type, distinguished by subtle ornamentation that leads one to conclude deep chiseling. One can also detect a search for new forms and expressive possibilities, resulting in a formal richness almost unique to this period. Nor is the distribution of these capitals here arbitrary. The central aisle and last bay before the no longer visible *qibla* wall contain the best capitals – though the 16th-century construction of the cathedral and its buttresses have greatly impaired their visibility.

Within the original building's center aisle, the area of the *mihrab* is given great emphasis. Whereas the prayer hall normally has the usual red and black alternating marble columns, in the central aisle directly in front of the *mihrab*, two white, chamfered marble columns have been placed. Moreover, the columns in the last bay of arcades, ending immediately before the *qibla* wall, are adorned with especially splendid capitals. Together with the mosque's central axis, oriented on the *mihrab*, this emphatically lateral *qibla* wall, indicating the direction of prayers, forms the shape of a "T" – which explains why commentators refer to it as a "T-type" here.

Building work on the Great Mosque of Cordoba by Abd al-Rahman III

When, in 929, Abd al-Rahman III proclaimed himself caliph, he was mainly interested in the palace city, Medina al-Zahra (built 936–1010) which is only 8 miles (13 kilometers) northwest of Cordoba, and which he founded as his empire's administrative and government headquarters in 936. Preoccupied by supervising building work in Medina al-Zahra, the caliph undertook only relatively unimportant work on the Great Mosque of Cordoba. Thus, he mainly enlarged the mosque's courtyard, which also meant extending the women's galleries. Moreover, Abd al-Rahman III demolished Hisham I's minaret, which no longer fulfilled its purpose, and presumably, now failed to meet the community's needs, and built a new minaret. Abd al-Rahman III's minaret was built on the courtyard's southern side. Today it no longer exists, for in the 16th century the cathedral's belltower was erected in its place, and in the 17th century this acquired a Baroque tower. We get a view of Abd al-Rahman III's caliphate period minaret in a 16th-century relief emblem found outside on the Great Mosque's eastern facade, where it adorns a spandrel on the mosque courtyard's eastern entrance portal. The minaret stood on a square surface and comprised two building structures. The lower structure was cubic, and about 75 feet (23 meters) high. The upper building was shorter and more narrow and was used for the muezzin summoning the faithful to prayer. Atop this was a little dome with an arched opening on either side. Al-Maqqari (d.1631), a text compiler from the Maghreb, saw the original minaret. He memorably describes the minaret's sum-

Cross-section through the *maqsura* area with dome constructions,
al-Hakam II's extension, 962–966
The *maqsura* area is directly in front of the *mihrab*. Originally, it was the caliph's private domain, emphasized architecturally by three large domes. The central dome, directly abutting the *mihrab*, is somewhat higher than the lateral ribbed domes, and also larger in diameter. These three domes are an ensemble unique to the Islamic world.

mit (*yamur*) as a vertical pole on which two golden and one silver balls were balanced, a small pomegranate crowning them. The minaret and its crown also served other Andalusian mosques as a model.

The extension under al-Hakam II

Immediately after being enthroned (in 961), al-Hakam II, Abd al-Rahman III's son and successor, started work on the Great Mosque of Cordoba. His extension (962–966) also reflects the caliphate of Cordoba's artistic apogee. In keeping with earlier buildings, the mosque was extended southwards by 12 more bays, until it totaled 376 feet (114.6 meters) in length, though the mosque stayed the same breadth – 260 feet (79.29 meters). When the building work was finished, the prayer hall had an area of 260 × 376 feet (79.29 × 114.60 meters) – in other words, it was far larger than the courtyard. Extending the mosque necessitated demolishing the original building's *qibla* wall and *mihrab*. As a mark of respect to the emirate's heritage, the original *mihrab*'s capitals and columns were relocated to the new *mihrab* in the caliphate extension (dating from 962–966). At the start of the center aisle, architects created a complex two-story structure of interlacing multifoil arches, crowned by a massive ribbed dome. In Christian times this section of the mosque was named the "Capilla de Villaviciosa."

The center aisle of al-Hakam II's extension of the Great Mosque is accentuated by the use of uniform red marble columns. In the side aisles we see alternating red and black columns, which are diagonally connected and lead toward the *mihrab*. As is typical, capitals crown the columns. While in previous versions of the mosque building different forms of capital could be admired, we now see uniform boss capitals everywhere. Only in the center aisle, on the upper arcade, do we find elaborate stucco reliefs on the smooth pillars. These are crowned by Islamic-style composite stucco capitals and serve to highlight the central aisle.

The *mihrab* facade makes a striking impact, and its effect is made even more overwhelming by the brilliant golden mosaics and the transverse arcade with its interlacing multifoil arches. In front of the *mihrab* lay the *maqsura* area, the place reserved for the caliph's private prayer alone. We can assume that the two

Central aisle with *mihrab* and *maqsura* area,
al-Hakam II's extension, 962-966
The central aisle leads to the *mihrab*, the enclosure before which is effectively accentuated by a complex, two-story structure of interlacing multifoil arches; this directs the eye to the *mihrab* facade, the mosque's most important area.

last southern bays of the five center aisles formed part of the *maqsura*. The *maqsura* area is accentuated by a transverse arcade running parallel to the *qibla* wall, to distinguish the caliph's from the people's sphere. The arches of the transverse arcade replace the traditional railing which originally separated the ruler from his people; the arches were also sufficiently decorated to further accentuate the importance of the *maqsura* area and the *mihrab*. The transverse arcade, which extended laterally across the central *maqsura* area, was later demolished to make room for Christian chapels and tombs in this area.

The *mihrab* itself reveals a familiar pattern: a base area with a central horseshoe arch, an arch field with a rectangular frame (the *alfiz*) and topped by an arcade of blind arches. The horseshoe arch opens into an octagonal prayer recess, which, for acoustic reasons, is surmounted by a large shell. The shell's curve magnified the prayer leader (*imam*)'s voice so effectively that it could be heard all over the mosque. As mentioned, the *mihrab*'s horseshoe arch is flanked by the two marble columns and capitals of the preceding emirate period building. On either side of the *mihrab*'s base area are affixed large marble plaques, adorned with plant motifs. They are among the most beautiful and magnificent decorative reliefs created during the Cordoba caliphate. The spandrels of the *mihrab*'s arch area are decorated by large gold stucco creepers. The arches are then enclosed by a rectangular *alfiz* frame, bearing a Koranic inscription of gold mosaic on a blue ground. Above the inscription, an arcade of blind arches extends, their fields decorated with Trees of Life, executed in mosaics. Above these are the support structures of the large melon dome, which rises above the enclosure before the *mihrab*, and, like the *mihrab* proper, is adorned with small golden mosaic stones. Some texts report that al-Hakam II asked the Byzantine emperor to send him a mosaicist able to reproduce the gold mosaics of the Great Mosque of Damascus. The master who supervised the mosaicists in Cordoba had learned Byzantine traditions, however the gold mosaics also retain formal links with Spanish-Islamic art, which show influences from local workshops.

In the *maqsura* area, the central melon dome is flanked by two ribbed domes, similar in form to the dome of the Capilla de Villaviciosa. Precursors of these domes presumably come from the Middle East. As yet, however, they have been inadequately examined and, for lack of convincing models, we

Mihrab of the Great Mosque of Cordoba,
al-Hakam II's extension, 962–966
The *mihrab* is among the most precious achievements of Cordoba's caliphate-period art. Its facade opens through a horseshoe arch to the *mihrab* recess. The arch face is adorned with voussoirs, decorated with gold mosaics and foliage motifs. The arch's rectangular *alfiz* frame is decorated by golden letters on a blue ground. In the *mihrab*'s base area there are large marble plaques which are adorned with Trees of Life.

SPAIN AND MOROCCO

Opposite: **Melon dome of the enclosure before the *mihrab***, al-Hakam II's extension (962–966)

From the almost square ground plan of the enclosure before the *mihrab*, graduated arch structures lead to the complex dome vault. Its interlacing ribs form an octagonal star, its center crowned by a flat dome. Masters from Constantinople completed the magnificent golden mosaics with floral and calligraphic elements.

The last extension under al-Mansur

The last extension of the Great Mosque of Cordoba (987–988) was commissioned by al-Mansur (Spanish: Almanzor), Caliph Hisham II's prime minister and regent. While the caliph, still a minor, lived a virtual prisoner in his palace at Medina al-Zahra, al-Mansur obtained his mother Subh's agreement to take over government duties. In this high office, as the caliph's representative, he was able to commission an extension of the Great Mosque. Because al-Mansur was regent – not official ruler – he was not the equal of emirs and caliphs, and, had he extended the mosque southwards, his action might have been so interpreted. An added structural problem was that in the south the mosque terrain sloped down to the river. Earlier, al-Hakam II, during his mosque extension (962–966), had to shore up and level the mosque's substructure, making it structurally impossible to enlarge the mosque further southwards. Extending westwards was also impossible, since government and administrative palaces stood there; in the north stood the mosque courtyard, which had to be retained to accommodate believers. Consequently, plans were made to extend the mosque eastwards. As always, al-Mansur was very concerned that Mecca should lie in the right direction – a geographical detail that previous architects had hardly heeded. Considering the scientific expertise then available, especially in astronomy, geometry, and mathematics, we can be virtually certain that the original building was not simply misaligned. We must therefore assume that Abd al-Rahman I sentimentally made the original building face his old homeland, Syria, and in particular, Damascus. With his extension, however, al-Mansur makes the Great Mosque face Mecca.

This last mosque extension was also the largest ever undertaken in Cordoba. Allegedly, by this means al-Mansur wanted to justify to the people the vast amount of state finance he had expended. He had eight side aisles added, extending the mosque eastwards by about 164 feet (50 meters). The portals on the eastern facade of al-Hakam II's previous building were walled up and 11 large arch openings created, through which one could enter the mosque's new area. Because the rooms adjoining the *mihrab* were not continued, the aisles became longer by two bays, and thus reached the southern surrounding wall. The principle – in al-Hakam II's extension – of a line of transverse arches to accentuate the *maqsura* area was abandoned. However, the arcade structure that distinguishes Abd al-Rahman II's part of the building from that of al-Hakam II did proceed.

The Great Mosque of Cordoba now had 19 aisles. The southern wall, identical with the *qibla* wall, had increased to a length of 421 feet (128.41 meters). The prayer hall now had an area of 376 × 421 feet (114.60 × 128.41 meters), and the courtyard 198 × 421 feet (60.42 × 128.41 meters). Including the projecting mosque courtyard, the mosque now had a total area of 574 × 421 feet (175.02 × 128.41 meters), or 251,550 square feet (23,400 square meters). If one discounts later Christian insertions, Al-Mansur's extension gives the Great Mosque of Cordoba the appearance it has to this day.

Dome of the Capilla de Villaviciosa, al-Hakam II's extension, (962–966)

At the entrance to the central aisle, the massive ribbed dome of the Capilla de Villaviciosa towers up over a complex, two-tier arch structure. Similar dome constructions can be seen near the prayer hall's *maqsura* area on both sides of the central main dome, decorated by gold mosaics. These elaborate, complex ribbed domes seem typical of the period when al-Hakam II was caliph – as a patron, he greatly encouraged the arts and sciences.

must regard the Cordoba ribbed domes as an original idea. Their existence is intimately linked to the arch structures in the mosque's *maqsura* area, reserved solely for the caliph, and not present in this form in any other mosque anywhere. Thus, the uniqueness of the Great Mosque of Cordoba partly derives from the caliph's unique position – for his presence first inspired these architectural solutions in the *maqsura* area. On either side of the *mihrab* there are five square rooms, not accessible to mosque visitors. The caliph used the western rooms as a secret, secure passageway (the *sahn*), leading from the adjacent palace direct to the mosque's *maqsura* area, while the eastern rooms were apparently for storing treasure. Above these ten rooms was an upper story of 11 chambers, whose central room was placed directly over the *mihrab*. Today, its function is still not entirely certain. Perhaps the mosque's innumerable manuscripts were kept there.

Other caliphate period mosques in al-Andalus

The most magnificent caliphate period mosque is undoubtedly the Great Mosque of Cordoba, also a model for other mosques. All the more regrettable, then, that of the 500 mosques apparently in Cordoba in the 10th century, no other has survived in its entirety.

We should mention, however, the Great Mosque of Almeria, built in the second half of the 10th century and extended as early as the 11th century. Almeria, a city that lies on the Mediterranean coast some 210 miles (330 kilometers) southeast of Cordoba, is important because of the nearby harbor of Pechina, where, during the caliphate of Cordoba, Abd al-Rahman III's fleet was anchored. Today, we find the church of San Juan where the Great Mosque of Almeria used to be. A few years ago traces were discovered on its south wall, identical with the former mosque's *qibla* wall, of the *mihrab* facade from late in the caliphate period – as well as the *mihrab* itself, which had been restored under the rule of the Almohads in the late 12th century.

Another important mosque of the caliphate period stood in Zaragoza, a city on the Ebro about 440 miles (700 kilometers) northwest of Cordoba, and formerly an important traffic intersection. According to documentary sources, the Great Mosque of Zaragoza was built in the mid-9th century, and was extended in the early 11th century. Today, in its place we find the old cathedral, which Spaniards call the "Parroquita" (small parish church). From excavations in the cathedral cloister it is estimated that the mosque was square with sides about 165 feet (50 meters) long – the total area was about 27,200 square feet (2,500 square meters). Many capitals and fragments of building decoration were also found. Recent investigations have also permitted the reconstruction of the caliphate period minaret, whose partly preserved ornamentation clearly owes a

formal debt to Cordoba and Medina al-Zahra, even if the motifs are much more crudely executed. We can therefore presuppose the existence of a provincial workshop which, in the early 11th century, continued working in the tradition of the caliphate of Cordoba, but without the perfection of court workshops.

A special case among mosques of the caliphate period is the "La Rabit"a complex of buildings at Guardamar, near Alicante, which is about 375 miles (600 kilometers) northeast of Cordoba on Spain's Mediterranean coast. The Spanish name "La Rabita" is derived from the Arabic word *ribat*, generally meaning a fortified place for praying. Unlike a traditional *ribat* – usually like a fortress – the Andalusian versions were mainly pious, often private, institutions, regarded as centers of meditation, to which believers temporarily withdrew to pray. The "La Rabita" complex in Guardamar comprises three rows of buildings made of tamped clay and connected by a road. Oddly, these buildings usually comprise only one room, with a prayer niche clearly formed in the masonry – and this confirms that these are small-scale mosques. On Friday, the Islamic holy day, it was customary to meet in the locality's main mosque, centrally located in the middle row of buildings. Its size, 77 × 18 feet (23.5 × 5.4 meters), and its ground plan, which reveals two side aisles, distinguish it from the other buildings. Within the mosque, in the area near the *qibla* wall, vestiges of geometric murals, accentuating this section of the mosque, were found. The smaller mosques in "La Rabita" at Guardamar served for private prayer, while the main mosque was principally attended for solemn communal Friday prayers. An inscription found near the settlement attests to a date of 944, although architectural features on most of the buildings suggest the second half or even end of the 10th century. Still other buildings indicate the early 11th century; these would then date from the late period of "La Rabita", and therefore also from the late years of the caliphate of Cordoba.

Toledo, the former Visigothic capital, lies in Spain's interior, around 190 miles (300 kilometers) north of Cordoba, in a loop of the Tajo River. The city

Above: San Juan de Caballeros in Cordoba, 930
This belltower is a former minaret, erected by Caliph Abd al-Rahman III. Of over 500 mosques originally in Cordoba, only two other caliphate period minarets have survived.

Bab al-Mardum Mosque in Toledo, 999–1000
The blind arches in the mosque at the Bab al-Mardum Gate, Toledo, recall similar arch constructions at the Great Mosque of Cordoba, while the brick lattice pattern above them is a western Islamic innovation.

Mosque of the Casa de las Tornerías, Toledo, 2nd half of the 12th century
The Mosque of the Casa de las Tornerías is a direct descendent of the Bab al-Mardum Mosque. Its division into nine sections with a square ground plan, and its horseshoe arches on low columns, crowned by archaic-looking capitals, follow the usual pattern, even though the architects eschewed an entresol tier with crowning domes, which makes the space seem lower.

was captured soon after the Muslims seized the Iberian Peninsula in 711, after which they stayed, until repulsed by Alfonso VI's Christian troops in 1085. In a city district north of the cathedral, near the ancient Bab al-Mardum Gate, a mosque named after this gate has survived. The Spaniards also call it "Cristo de la Luz," since, a few years after the Christians conquered Toledo, it was turned into a church with this name. To help the building meet the needs of Christian worship, before the church was consecrated (in 1097), a semicircular apse was added. This is among the most striking examples anywhere of Spanish Mudejar style, a distinctive mingling of Christian and Islamic architectural forms.

The original mosque was built in 999–1000 as a private institution, according to an inscription on the facade. The small, nearly cubiform structure is about 26 feet (8 meters) high, and, judging by its interlaced and horseshoe arches, is a "copy" of the Great Mosque of Cordoba. Four centered columns, crowned by capitals, divide the interior space into nine bays. Above the ground level horseshoe arches an entresol story starts, with small multifoil and horseshoe arches, which form the supporting structures for the nine ribbed domes, all of which are constructed differently. A particularly fine dome in the form of a star vault can be seen in the very center of the mosque. It is slightly raised, and can therefore be called a "crowning feature" of the otherwise very small prayer hall.

The Bab al-Mardum Mosque is directly emulated in Toledo. The Mosque of the Casa de las Tornerías, near the cathedral, has an almost identical structure, for the interior is also divided into nine bays. As in the Bab al-Mardum Mosque, here, too, a ribbed dome gives the central bay special emphasis. It reproduces in miniature the schema of the whole mosque's ground plan, and copies the model of one of the nine domes in the Bab al-Mardum Mosque. The Casa de las Tornerías was built at a time when Toledo was already under

Christian rule, but Jewish and Islamic communities still lived in the city. Today, the mosque is unanimously dated to the 12th century, which demonstrated that the art and architecture of the Cordoban caliphate period had a powerful influence for many decades.

The palace city of Medina al-Zahra near Cordoba

By 929, when Abd al-Rahman III proclaimed himself caliph, the Spanish Umayyads had reached the zenith of their power. The caliph demonstrated his new status by building – only 8 miles (13 kilometers) northwest of Cordoba – the palace city of Medina al-Zahra (in existence 936–1010), making it his empire's administrative and governmental headquarters. The construction work in Medina al-Zahra proceeded apace, especially since Abd al-Rahman III invested a third of all state revenues in it. Thus, he pursued the largest and most ambitious building project of his epoch, which remained unsurpassed by the foundation of other cities in succeeding centuries.

Medina al-Zahra exploits its position on a terrace-like slope below the Sierra Moreno. According to al-Idrisi, a cultivated traveler and historian who visited the ruins of the palace city in the 12th century, the complex divided into three terraces. At the highest point stood the caliph's palace, distinguished from other buildings by its isolated position. It strikingly symbolized the power of the caliph, who, from this vantage point, could see far across city and countryside. Presumably, this palace was one of the first buildings to be finished in Medina al-Zahra. On the middle terrace stood the government buildings and palaces, as well as the reception halls and accommodation for important individuals. Between the middle and lower terraces, on an artificially created mound, stood the mosque, which connected the court-related area on the middle terrace with more simple dwellings. In 941 the first solemn Friday prayers were held in this mosque, which was apparently built by 1,000 cratsmen in just 48 days. The first grand reception took place in the palace city in 945. A short time later, the caliph must have moved his family household and mint there. Later, but while the caliph was still alive, his son and successor al-Hakam II was asked to supervise the building works.

Historical sources report that the construction work in Medina al-Zahra took 40 years – 25 years under Abd al-Rahman III's rule (from the founding of the palace city in 936 or 937 to his death in 961), and 15 years under al-Hakam II – from 961 to 976. As well as the extension of the Great Mosque of Cordoba, which al-Hakam II undertook 962–966, he must have strongly influenced some palace buildings in Medina al-Zahra. The reception halls, gardens, bathhouses, and fountains, in particular, show his personal involvement. With the death of al-Hakam II, in 976, construction work on official buildings in Medinaal-Zahra probably stopped, though work on the lower terrace buildings – not immediately linked to the palace area – may have continued. That is where the city proper lay – with its simple houses, garrisons, gardens, and markets. Historical sources mention state factories and even a subterranean prison.

The importance of Medina al-Zahra as a palace city and the caliph's headquarters decreased when al-Mansur, the first minister and regent for Caliph Hisham II – who was still a minor – founded the similarly named residence of Medina al-Zahira near Cordoba in 978–980. However, Medina al-Zahra was not destroyed until 1010, when rebellious Berber groups ransacked this erstwhile symbol of the caliphate of Cordoba. Even so, the palace city ruins were still inhabited up to the 12th century.

The complex of buildings

The fortified area of Medina al-Zahra comprises a rectangle that is about one mile (1.52 kilometers) long and 815 yards (745 meters) wide, of which to date about 10 percent has been excavated: as yet, only the upper and middle terraces, that is, the palace area proper. Buildings on the lower terrace – the plain – have not yet been excavated, though the position of other buildings has been pinpointed by infrared photography. Eventually, as excavations increase, these in particular should reveal more details of everyday life in the palace city.

At Medina al-Zahra's highest point stands Caliph Abd al-Rahman III's palace, called Dar al-Mulk (in Arabic) or Casa Real (in Spanish). The palace is striking for its decoration, including parts of ornamented wall spaces and mosaic-like floor covering. Conservation measures in this area have so far made the palace inaccessible to visitors.

Near the palace there is a row of buildings mainly notable for their large, almost square inner courtyards. These are administration and government buildings. Not far from the palace there is a group of buildings with a trapezoid-shaped courtyard, around which partly ruined suites of rooms are grouped. This accommodation complex lies about 7 feet (2 meters) below the caliph's palace, the only upper terrace building that survives; though it projects about 23 feet (7 meters) beyond the other middle terrace buildings, so the division between terraces is not nearly as definite as historical sources suggest. The building situated in the northwestern corner of the middle terrace was presumably reserved for servants, or possibly the caliph's bodyguards. There is also another complex of houses, with two very similar courtyards, separated by a ramp. Because the courtyards are almost identical, this complex, lying about 26 feet (8 meters) lower than the caliph's palace, is called the "twin esplanade." The left – namely, western – esplanade has a large, rectangular courtyard, whose north-south axis is about 66 feet (20 meters) long, while its east-west axis is about 46 feet (14 meters) long. It is surrounded by suites of rooms on three sides, of which the northern, front-facing suite is best preserved. The central room in the

Medina al-Zahra near Cordoba, 936–1010
The palace city of Caliph Abd al-Rahman III is divided into three terraces, with the caliph's palace on the highest plateau. The middle terrace accommodated administrative buildings, reception halls, and the houses of high-ranking officials and their families, while the lower terrace was reserved for working-class citizens. Especially striking is the High Garden, arising out of the plain like a podium, and enclosed by a massive wall. Its central transverse axis points directly to the Ornate Hall, which suggests that this was the palace city's main ceremonial hall.

northern suite measures 11.5 × 32.2 feet (3.5 × 9.82 meters), and is the building's main hall. The adjoining rooms are somewhat smaller, with a uniform depth of about 11.5 feet (3.5 meters). The western esplanade of this twin layout contained the complex's imposing living quarters, while the eastern esplanade was devoted to financial matters.

Immediately beneath the twin esplanade – about 23 feet (7 meters) lower – lies a trapezoid-shaped courtyard, 90 feet (27.4 meters) long and, at the center, about 26 feet (8 meters) wide. Several of the palace city's paths intersect here, which is why this area was very carefully guarded – explaining why it is often called the "guard complex." This area not only gave access to the twin esplanade above, but also offered access to buildings further south in the palace city. Here, presumably, were the houses of important people, including members of the caliph's family, as well as his ministers, viziers, and high-ranking officials.

In the south, the guard complex leads on to further city palaces. One complex deserves special mention, the one that a building inscription calls the House of Prime Minister Yafar al-Mushafi. In 961 Caliph al-Hakam II appointed Yafar prime minister, which made him a highly influential figure at court. His house is divided into three sections: a public area for official receptions, the minister's living quarters, and the staff rooms. The public area is notable for a three-aisle, basilican hall with a projecting portico, through which one enters a large, square courtyard. Behind the basilican hall is Yafar's private apartment, with numerous rooms leading into one another, and the servants' quarters leading off them. The house's large courtyard led to a small private bath, which was referred to as the House with Basins, which could also be entered from an adjoining palace building. This complex of buildings comprises two almost identical structures, whose once ornately decorated porticoes give access to the courtyard's narrow side. Archeological finds and stylistic indications from the remaining fragmentary decoration enable us to date this palace to the early phase of Medina al-Zahra. Abd al-Rahman III presumably built it for his son and successor al-Hakam II. The slightly higher Pillar Courtyard, so called because its central courtyard is surrounded by pillars, adjoins the palace on the north side. Fragments of a Roman sarcophagus that had clearly been reused as a basin for a fountain were found in this nearly square courtyard, with an area totaling 4.700 square feet (440 square meters).

Strictly speaking, it is possible to identify a building only if architectural inscriptions or historical sources have survived to provide information about its function. In Medina al-Zahra, however, it is striking that we have two types of building. One has large inner courtyards with surrounding suites of rooms – a pattern that has come down to us from ancient times and is widespread throughout the Mediterranean. The other type has basilican halls that fulfill a public function. The mosque and reception halls in Medina al-Zahra fall into this second category.

The Medina al-Zahra Mosque was built in 941 in the eastern palace city. Those of its foundations that have been excavated reveal a five-aisle hall, with aisles extending vertically to the *qibla* wall. As also in the Great Mosque of Cordoba, the two outermost aisles were extended beyond the building front and then continued as a semicircular ambulatory around the projecting mosque courtyard. Very probably, the Great Mosque of Cordoba was the inspiration behind the palace mosque. Today, only the foundation walls of the Medina al-Zahra Mosque survive. This was certainly not the only mosque in the palace city, however, but merely one whose immediate proximity to the palace area makes it particularly prominent. Directly outside the mosque is a house that was used for ritual washing – or so we assume from the numerous well shafts in this complex of buildings.

Medina al-Zahra, 936–1010
Above: The ruins of Medina al-Zahra were discovered in the late 19th century, and have meanwhile been exposed in various excavations. By now, some 10 percent of the fortified area of Medina al-Zahra has been excavated – mainly the public buildings on the upper and middle terraces. Extensive halls with projecting porticoes adorned with magnificent horseshoe arches are char-acteristic features of palace architecture in Medina al-Zahra.

Dionisio Baixeras, **Reception with Caliph Abd al-Rahman III in Medina al-Zahra**, late 19th century
This painting depicts the historically documented reception held for the monk Johannes von Gorze, who visited Caliph Abd al-Rahman III as ambassador of Emperor Otto I (962–973).

Looking across the High Garden to the reception hall, Medina al-Zahra, 936–1010
The reception hall lies directly on the main axis of the palace city, a position which emphasizes its importance as the main ceremonial hall. In front of this there used to lie a large pool, in whose surface reflected the building's facade with its distinctive red and white arches.

Interior view of the reception hall, Medina al-Zahra, 936–1010
Visitors enter the five-aisle reception hall through a projecting portico. Both sides of the center aisle are bordered by horseshoe arches, supported by columns of alternating colors. On the far wall we can see a blind horseshoe arch, before which the caliph presumably sat for formal audiences.

The great reception halls of Medina al-Zahra

The two, now extensively reconstructed, great reception halls in the palace city follow a pattern of space division similar to that adopted in the Medina al-Zahra Mosque. Both these reception halls date back to Caliph al-Hakam II – they were thus built a good ten years after the mosque. A striking feature of the middle terrace is a large, five-aisle hall with a portico, outside which there is a colossal square courtyard, with an area of 26,900 square feet (2,500 square meters). This palace lies in the eastern sector of Medina al-Zahra's palace area, and up to now has been called Dar al-Jund ("House of the Army"). Because basilican halls have had various different functions, one cannot be sure how exactly to identify this building. Nevertheless, it is likely that it fulfilled public tasks, which is why older research books often called its major rooms reception halls. Since meetings were also held in these great halls, this building is now increasingly associated with Medina al-Zahra's administrative apparatus. We now call this the "House of the Viziers" (Dar al-Wuzara), and assume that viziers held conferences here – issuing orders, signing purchase and tenancy contracts, completing documents, and clarifying legal questions.

The Ornate Hall – its name comes from its ornate decoration – has a ground plan like that of the House of the Viziers. Lying in the very center of the city, it comprises five aisles with a longitudinally projecting portico, and flanking corner bays. Its exterior dimensions are about 125 × 92 feet (38 × 28 meters). A large garden, called the "High Garden," lies in front of the palace. From this garden, through the Ornate Hall's access arcade, one could enter the portico, in which a building inscription dates the structure to between 953/954 and 956/957. Access to the center aisle is through a three-arch opening, flanked on either side by a two-arch opening at the same height as the two adjacent side aisles. The three central aisles form the structural core of the reception hall, which is flanked by two outer aisles, running parallel and divided into two chambers, separated from the main room by a massive wall. Large portals, with horseshoe arches, connect the outer aisles with the three-aisle core building and the southern corner bays that flank the portico. The main room is divided by two longitudinal arcades of six, large horseshoe arches. On the wall at the end of the central aisle there is a large, blind horseshoe arch, before which the caliph would sit during receptions or other court ceremonies.

The architectural decoration of the Ornate Hall

The reception hall is striking, mainly for its architectural decoration. On the lower walls of the three-aisle core building, for instance, there are large relief plaques with plant motifs. The plants are Trees of Life whose composition is based on a central trunk, from which a thick-stemmed creeper splits off, then twists and winds upwards to a large, circular crown of leaves and blossoms. The leaf crowns of these Tree of Life motifs distantly recall 6th-century Sassanian palmette crowns; having first featured in 8th-century eastern Umayyad art, these found new forms in Medina al-Zahra a good two centuries later. These wall panels' individual leaf and blossom designs suggest that Abbasid art in 9th-century Samarra has also found new life here. Apparently, the craftsmen working in Medina al-Zahra knew these models from the east and adapted them to local taste – a process that led ultimately to the final forms we now consider typical of caliphate art in Cordoba and Medina al-Zahra.

Outside the reception hall runs a broad path, giving access to the High Garden and the palace buildings further west. Directly outside the hall is a large pool, in which the surface once reflected the building's facade, accentuating

House of the Viziers, front and side views, Medina al-Zahra, 939–1010
The five-aisle hall of the "House of the Viziers" gives access to a broad, elevated walkway, from which steps lead down to a colossal, equal-sided square, now laid out as a garden. There are different views about this building's

use. For a long time it was called the House of the Army, since the dimensions of its hall and forecourt suggest public functions. But now the complex of buildings is assumed to have had an administrative purpose.

Middle terrace arcades in Medina al-Zahra, 936–1010
A massive arcade of horseshoe arches block off the middle terrace administrative area in Medina al-Zahra. Above the central, somewhat larger horseshoe arch, there was originally a small, pavilion-like superstructure, from

which the caliph – or other high dignitaries – could watch military parades taking place immediately in front of the arcade, on Weapons Square.

its importance. Moreover, in the center of the High Garden, on the central axis leading to the hall, stands a garden pavilion designed as a three-aisle hall – which refelcts the reception hall in miniature. All that has survived of this pavilion are the foundation walls, the flanking pool, and the pillar foundations.

The reception hall occupies a central position in the palace city's overall plan and also forms the focal point of the middle terrace. The central axis of the "High Garden," positioned outside the hall, and the centrally placed garden pavilion, only emphasize its importance. The "High Garden" measures about 213 × 253 feet (65 × 77 meters) – over 54,000 square feet (5,000 square

meters) in total area. It is enclosed by a massive wall, which raises the ensemble comprising the reception hall and "High Garden" like a podium above the buildings on the lower terrace – sometimes called the plain – overcoming a 40 foot (12 meter) difference in height. This also explains the name "High Garden." West of this, on the lower terrace, lies another garden in similar style, called the Low Garden. Seeing the palace buildings must have deeply impressed visitors originally approaching Medina al-Zahra from the plain. This would have gratified the caliph, who wanted Medina al-Zahra to give everyone visible proof of his power.

The architecture of the *taifa* kingdoms

After the caliphate of Cordoba had collapsed (in 1030/31), and the last legitimate caliph had been expelled, the empire fragmented into numerous minor states, called *taifa* kingdoms. Among these were the kingdoms – equally important artistically and politically – of Malaga, Toledo, and Zaragoza. *Taifa* art followed several caliphate precedents, though it also adopted autonomous decorative forms. In the Aljafería of Zaragoza, the leading royal seat in the 11th century, for instance, new arch forms were developed that are still clearly influenced by caliphate precursors. Simultaneously, new decorative forms emerged in stucco decoration. Plant designs became smaller in scale, finer, and more abstract. Also, the acanthus leaf, which had been very common in caliphate art, was increasingly replaced by finely segmented, frayed leaflets, typical of 11th-century *taifa* art. Caliphate wall panels of the 10th century were often still of marble or stone, as we see, for example, on the walls of the reception hall at Medina al-Zahra, while *taifa* art has almost exclusively

Wall panel in the Ornate Hall, Medina al-Zahra, 936–1010
The magnificent marble wall panels in the reception Hall feature plant imagery whose composition is based on a central trunk from which stems branch off symmetrically. They carry finely wrought clusters of leaves and blossoms that intertwine in orderly yet endlessly repeated complexity. Thus, despite enormous formal variety and delight in decoration, these panels also demonstrate that *horror vacui* – "fear of emptiness" – often typical of Islamic art.

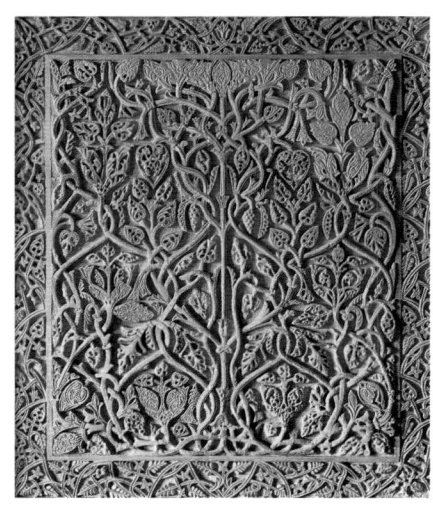

stucco panels. Molds allowed rapid execution and unlimited reproductions; this technique was further developed in succeeding centuries. Thus, the importance of *taifa* art in developing Spanish-Islamic art cannot be overstressed. As yet, its importance has been underestimated, since only a few *taifa* kingdom buildings have survived, and even these, only recently, have attracted research interest. Moreover, palaces and mosques of this period did not attain the spectacular dimensions of, say, the Great Mosque of Cordoba or the palace city of Medina al-Zahra, which, in its day, housed the government not just of a minor kingdom but a world empire.

The Alcazaba of Malaga

The Alcazaba of Malaga represents one of the most important fortified complexes in al-Andalus; its significance is inseparable from the nearby harbor. To protect the harbor more fully, a fort was built on the nearby hill, as well as a lighthouse – after which the mountain was named Gibralfaro ("Lighthouse Mountain") – that was visible for miles. The fortified complex built on the Gibralfaro was founded in the 9th century and was extended in the 11th century, after the Hammadids (1023–1058) had established themselves in Malaga. They immediately constructed a residence in the Alcazaba area, later extended by the Berber potentate Badis (1058–1075), who came from Granada. Repeatedly extended in subsequent centuries, it was almost completely renovated and rebuilt by the Nasrid ruler Yusuf I (1333–1354). By the 14th century the Alcazaba was one of Islam's last bastions in al-Andalus. The Catholic kings did not seize it until 1487, only five years before the capitulation of Granada, which signaled the end of Islamic hegemony in Spain.

The Alcazaba complex is enclosed by a double circle of walls, densely lined

The Alcazaba of Malaga, 9–14th century
The Alcazaba dominates the whole cityscape of Malaga. On the mountain peak are the fortifications of the 11th-century palace complex. This residence, enclosed by a double ring of walls, was one of the last bastions of Islam in al-Andalus; it was captured during the Spanish Reconquista only five years before the fall of Cordoba (in 1492).

with towers. Within the inner wall, on the mountain peak, are the Chambers of Granada, which originate from the 11th century and form the real core of the palace area. Presumably, these buildings were lodgings for high-ranking palace servants, but, after being attacked, they were abandoned. The Chambers of Granada comprise five inner courtyards with surrounding suites of chambers – a pattern that we have already encountered in the Medina al-Zahra palace complex. Only in the most westerly of the five inner courtyards – all of which have now been restored – has original 11th-century fabric survived. A large, rectangular hall, with a projecting portico, extends along the whole building. This portico's three-bay arcade was not built until the 13th, or even 14th century, and it reveals a division typical of Nasrid architecture: a large, tall round arch, with an alternating curved and jagged outer shape, is flanked by two low horseshoe arches sharpened to a point. The central arch gives a clear view of the entrance to the main chamber, whose three horseshoe arches, all standing close together, are characteristic of 11th-century *taifa* architecture. Even faces and soffits are sometimes adorned with smooth, stuccoed panels, which were originally painted. The arches' articulation and their ornamentation – slender, intertwining leaf tendrils – follows caliphate tradition. A small pavilion adjoins the side of the portico, giving access to another small hall. This pavilion's side facades are formed by interlacing multifoil arches, recalling the arch constructions in the *maqsura* area of the Great Mosque of Cordoba. This pavilion's stucco work resembles caliphate creations, even if the plant motifs are less varied. Instead, the leaf tendrils are more slender and more finely segmented. Moreover, the thin stems show a greater tendency to roll up and entwine – creating constantly repeated ornamentation. The erstwhile variety of forms employed under the caliphate of Cordoba – evident, for instance, in the decorated wall spaces of the reception hall of Medina al-Zahra – was now in danger of disappearing.

The al-Mamun's Palace in Toledo

Despite its original political importance, nothing of the palace built by al-Mamun (1043–1075), the most powerful of Toledo's *taifa* rulers – has survived. However, the Museum of Santa Cruz, Toledo, houses several capitals and relief plaques associated with al-Mamun's Palace. Their ornamentation shows that artists working in Toledo followed caliphate period formal patterns, while also developing plant designs further. Another example of this development is the stuccoed arch of a private house on the Plaza del Seco in Toledo, dating from the late 11th or even early 12th century. The arch's horseshoe structure, the decoration of the narrow voussoirs, the *alfiz* frames, and the spandrel decoration indicate adoption of caliphate period creative principles, while the buildings' plant motifs unequivocally suggest *taifa* art, which reached its apogee in Toledo.

Relief plaque from Toledo, 11th century
From the palace built by al-Mamum, Toledo's most powerful *taifa* ruler, some relief plaques with plant motifs have survived. Depicted here are intertwined branches, striking for their strict symmetry, delicate execution, and astonishing formal variety. The ornamentation of this relief plaque confirms that, while following caliphate period forms, Toledo artists further developed plant motifs.

The Aljafería of Zaragoza

In the second half of the 11th century, Abu Yafar Ahmad I ibn Suleiman al-Muqtadir billah (1049/1050–1082/1083), second ruler of the Banu Hud dynasty, built the Aljafería of Zaragoza. The Aljafería, named after him (it is derived from the Arab name Yafar), is the most important *taifa period* palace complex and has survived almost intact. In 1118, King Alfonso I of Aragon reconquered Zaragoza and immediately chose the city as his kingdom's capital. In succeeding centuries, kings of Aragon continued to use the Aljafería as a royal residence, and frequently remodeled it – following the contemporary taste.

The Aljafería is a triangular, nearly square complex, its sides measuring about 260 feet (80 meters), and outer walls are interspersed by round towers. Inside the enclosure are three sections running north-south in an axially symmetrical way, with only the central zone built upon. This constitutes the palace area proper, in the center of which is a large, rectangular courtyard, bordered on its two narrow sides by building complexes called the palace's northern and southern wings. The southern wing comprises a long hall (the South Hall), outside which stands a portico with flanking corner bays. A striking feature of this portico is the arcade consisting of six large, interlacing round arches, whose faces are uniquely ornamented. Crossing the courtyard provides access to the northern wing, comprising three extended halls, flanked by two side sections, with alcoves and adjoining rooms, that are stylistically

Southern palace wing of the Aljafería of Zaragoza, 2nd half of the 11th century
Outside the southern wing of the palace stands a portico, whose arcade comprises six wide-spanned, interlaced semicircular arches with uniquely ornamented faces. The orna-mentation is constructed from a repeated framing of the basic elements forming the arches, and is a typical *taifa* period innovation.

Opposite: **Exterior view of the Aljafería of Zaragoza with the Tower of the Troubadors**, 2nd half of the 11th century

The Aljafería of Zaragoza is the best-preserved *taifa* period palace in Spain. The whole complex, with its almost square ground plan (sides of about 80 meters), and its projecting round towers, resembles the design of 8th-century eastern Umayyad desert palaces. The massive rectangular tower on the northern side dates from the 9th century. In the palace's eastern section there is a small, though ornately adorned mosque.

similar to Medina al-Zahra's reception halls. These days there is a pool in the first hall of the northern wing of the palace, installed during a later Christian extension. Formerly, its surface reflected the arcade of the adjoining northern portico, whose massive, interlacing multifoil arches recall comparable arches in the Great Mosque of Cordoba. Through the portico one can look at the magnificent access arcade of the adjoining main room (the northern hall), called the Golden Hall (Salón del Oro, in Spanish), or the Throne Room (Salón del Trono, in Spanish). Today, hardly any of its original architectural decoration survives. The Throne Room's central position on the castle's main axis, the graduation of both preceding halls, and its design also suggest that this has always been the palace's most important location.

The Aljafería also contains a small palace mosque, located in the eastern side section of the northern palace wing, and can easily be found within the Aljafería complex because of its octagonal ground plan. Inside, the small mosque, which is about 16 feet (5 meters) across and, including the dome, about 33 feet (10 meters) high, is remarkable for its highly ornate stucco decoration, extending along the walls on either side of the *mihrab*. The stucco plant designs show the caliphate's influence, even though the leaf tendrils are now smaller, slimmer, and more finely segmented. The leaf stems also reveal a strong tendency to roll up, which helps establish the rhythm and articulation of the plant decoration – both features that are very typical of *taifa* architecture.

Ground plan of the Aljafería of Zaragoza
The complex is divided into three, almost equal zones, running from north to south, of which only the central one is built upon. This zone, measuring 16 × 80 feet (50 × 24 meters), contains the palace area proper.

***Mihrab* and dome of the palace mosque**, Aljafería of Zaragoza

The small palace mosque of the Aljafería has an octagonal ground plan, above which an arcade of eight semicircular arches, interlaced at the corners, form a ribbed dome, in whose center an octagon is inscribed. The whole mosque, including the ornately decorated *mihrab*, was extensively restored in the 20th century.

Decorative Arts

Almut von Gladiss

Art under the Umayyads of Cordoba and the *taifa* princes

With the rise of the Umayyads, who had been ruling from their capital Cordoba since the 8th century, art began to flourish in al-Andalus, and, by combining various traditions, gained its own autonomous character. The Islamic conquerors had assimilated part of Christian Europe. Now, they needed to take further measures, apart from religion, which would integrate society – Muslims as well as the indigenous population.

The Great Mosque of Cordoba housed a massive Koran, which contained several pages from the caliphal copy of the Holy Scripture above which the Rightly Guided Caliph Uthman was murdered in 656. Preserved as a sacred relic, the blood-spattered pages became an easily identified symbol, fascinating for many people of different backgrounds. This Koran was the focal point of an unusual ceremony corresponding to Christian rites. In a solemn procession, led by a ministrant carrying a candle, it was shown to the community before the imam read an extract from it at Friday prayers.

After modest beginnings, art and scholarship soon entered the mainstream of state patronage. The first caliph of the western empire, Abd al-Rahman III, was one of the Islamic world's richest rulers. After his defeat at Simancas-Alhandega in 939, where he only just escaped capture by the Christians, he gave relations with northern Christian princes and the Byzantine emperor top priority. Though himself modest, as confirmed posthumously by Ibn Arabi from Seville, a critic of the ostentation practiced by eastern Islamic religious leaders, he sought the recognition of the mighty; and, like the caliphs of Baghdad, he hoped to achieve this by monumental buildings and costly public show. In his memoir, Ibn Haiyan, the historian who lived to see the collapse of the caliphate of Cordoba in the 11th century, confirms that the empire's power expressed itself primarily in the splendor of court life.

The palace city of Medina al-Zahra, whose architecture included extensive gardens with magnificent fountains, was the apogee of these efforts. Such showpieces realized the rulers' claims to dominate not merely people, but also nature. Stone or metal fountain statues helped dramatize water games. One marble basin in the palace's main hall had ten of these waterspouts in the form of animal bronzes, whose variety suggests a workshop of gifted and adventurous bronze founders. A 20-inch (50-centimeter) tall statue of a stag, found in the palace city, standing on a hollow rectangular plate, over which water was pumped into the body, has a strikingly timeless simplicity. A typical Islamic art forms developed out of late classical and oriental traditions. At court a new elite grew up, recruited from erstwhile slaves who had become familiar with Islamic ways, and who had integrated themselves perfectly into court life, were now controlling important areas. The calligrapher Mutarrif ibn Abd al-Rahman, named in the wall texts at the great Mosque of Cordoba, was a former slave of Abd al-Rahman III. In time, Arabic script also made fresh conquests. It appears as a striking main motif on functional objects made of ordinary, very common material. Numerous ceramic plates and bottles from the palace city have inscriptions redolent of Islamic hegemony: not only *baraka* ("blessing"), but especially *al-mulk* ("authority"). As an abbreviated form of the popular formula *al-mulk lillah* ("authority is with God"), this constant refrain presumably evoked not only the Almighty's power but also that of the caliph, whom many saw as God's representative on earth. The ceramic ware was manufactured, not merely in Medina al-Zahra, but also in numerous southern Spanish localities for unrestricted use.

In the mid-10th century, not only the exchequer and the mint but also the textile workshop and the production of high-quality artifacts were transferred

Marble basin, Cordoba, length: 1.4 m, Granada, Museo del Alhambra.
This marble basin comes from a Cordoba palace, probably from that of al-Mansur, and was later brought to Granada to be used again in the Alhambra gardens. For this, the original inscription was replaced by a dedication, dated 1305, to Emir Abu Abdallah. The basin's long sides depict lions fighting ibexes and stags; while the short sides show heraldically depicted eagles with their prey.

Marble basin, Medina al-Zahra, 987/988, length: 1 m, Madrid,
Museo Arqueológico Nacional
The arcade decoration on this marble basin refers to the palace architecture, while the motif of the eagle with its prey (shown with its mirror image) indicates the patron's power.

An inscription names al-Mansur (978–1002), who managed government business for Caliph Hisham. The basin's long side, now replaced, formerly depicted a fight between a lion and either a bull or goat.

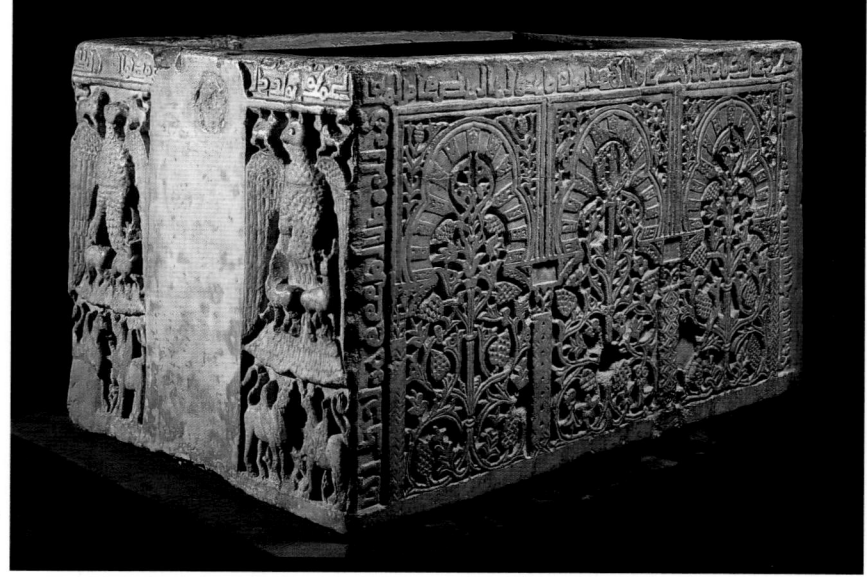

Left: **Ceramic bottle**, Medina al-Zahra, late 10th century, Cordoba, Museo Arqueológico Provincial

This bottle from Medina al-Zahra shows the striking script decoration used by the Umayyad court. Fine ceramics, painted in green or manganese, were produced not only in Cordoba but also in several other areas of southern Spain; they were society's "best" china for the most prosperous. Vessel decorators used applied leaf motifs as well as script designs.

Right: **Ceramic plate**, Medina Elvira, 2nd half of the 10th century, diameter 35 cm, Granada, Museo Arqueológico Ethnológico

This unusually large ceramic plate was found in Medina Elvira, Granada's early Islamic settlement. Its animal painting, albeit mechanical, distinguishes it from mass-produced articles. This is an impressive depiction of the horse that always had to stand saddled and bridled for the ruler at every royal court.

Left: **Marble fountain relief**, East Andalusia, 11th century, length 1.7 m, Játiva, Museo del Almudin

This marble fountain relief depicts a stylish gathering entertained by musicians and acrobats. The procession, bringing gifts of a fruit bowl, chicken, and goats, originates from a pre-Islamic motif used to honor kings and proclaim happy times. Ornamental line strongly reduces the physicality of these richly varied figure scenes. With their relaxed postures, they are unique in Islamic relief work, as opposed to sculpture.

Right: **Animal bronze**, Cordoba, 2nd half of the 10th century, height including base 61 cm, Cordoba, Museo Arqueológico Provincial

Animal bronzes, manufactured as fountain figures in the newly established metal factories in Cordoba, were made by the molten wax method. The form is simple and self-contained. The surface features uniform plant arabesques, intensifying the abstract decorative effect. Another animal bronze from a different tradition (housed in the Archeological Museum, Madrid), is even gilded.

Ivory container, Medina al-Zahra, 964, height 18 cm, Madrid, Museo Arqueológico Nacional

This box, carved out of an elephant's tusk, was a gift from al-Hakam II to his Basque concubine. It depicts plants with ibexes, and birds, including peacocks, which were considered a symbol of female beauty. In classical tradition, foliage animated by animals symbolized joy and abundance. The relief stands out sharply against the receding background.

Ivory box, Medina al-Zahra, dated 968, height 15 cm, Paris, Louvre

The throne scene and fighting animals on Prince Mughira's ivory container represent the dynasty's power. Rich in figures, the composition also has the unfamiliar motifs of princes harvesting the fruit of a date palm, and stealing stealing eggs from brooding birds. These evoke the "golden age" that Abd al-Rahman III, Prince Mughira's father, ushered in.

to the palace city. The weaving mill was managed by Jafar, formerly a slave of Abd al-Rahman, who had earned his spurs as architect of the Ornate Hall. The luxury goods atelier was supervised by Durri al-Sagir – also a non-Arab former slave. Presumably it was their task to grade and manage the precious materials.

Works in ivory

Relocating to the palace city inspired and obliged firms to achieve great things creatively. The caliph's family and top functionaries invested in precious ivory and silver artifacts. Among the surviving ivory works, eight have inscriptions dedicating them to members of the dynasty, mostly women at the caliph's court. The oldest article is a case for game pieces, dedicated to one of Abd al-Rahman III's daughters, name unknown. The caskets and boxes manufactured under al-Hakam II include three gifts to his Basque concubine, Subh, who bore him sons in 962 and 966. The ivory pieces, mentioning her role as mother, show rampant arabesques, perhaps suggesting female fertility and, thus, happiness. Turbulent foliage arabesques are found on another ivory box, presumably also for a woman, accompanied by verses in Arabic: "I look upon the loveliest things, like a maid's firm breasts. Beauty has furnished me with raiment finer than a show of jewels. I am a vessel holding musk, camphor and amber."

A container for aromatic substances did not necessarily belong to a woman at court. A contemporary book of etiquette from Baghdad, to which Cordoban aristocrats presumably adhered, states that men also used perfume, preferring a mixture of amber, musk, and aloe. Al-Hakam's personal physician, Abu l-Qasim al-Zahrawi, whom medieval Europe knew as Abulcasis, author of *Chirurgia* and designer of numerous surgical instruments, popularized aromatic preparations in his thesis on medicines, inspired by eastern Islamic science.

The containers, which, the inscriptions suggest, were carved for male dynastic members and leading functionaries, are generally adorned with rich imagery. A pyxis or box bearing al-Hakam's name, from the mid-960s, also bears arabesques, but the lid displays a heraldic eagle in quadruple reflection, emphasizing legitimate authority. Retaining classical symbols, also visible on Byzantine silks available in Spain, this tradition confirmed state orderliness.

Later, the pyxes for Mughira, al-Hakam's brother and rival, and for Abd al-Malik ibn al-Mansur, chancellor under Hisham, al-Hakam's son and successor, featured figure scenes. Human figures, reaching for fruit from trees, give the arabesques characteristic intensity. The inscription, beginning: "God's blessing, well-being, happiness, and prosperity for al-Mughira," also mentions the year of manufacture, 968, when Mughira might have dreamt of succeeding, as both the caliph's sons were still children. When Hisham ascended the throne in 976, he was murdered.

Al-Hakam's son and successor was kept away from government by the chancellor, Ibn Abi Amir, who later adopted the title al-Mansur, and his son, Abd al-Malik, chancellor from 1002. On the Pamplona Museum ivory casket, Hisham appears in a side medallion in iconic isolation with the distinctive caliph's seal ring. The most dramatic scenes feature his chancellor Abd al-Malik, who, after the conquest of León, was given the title, confirmed by an inscription, *saif al-daula* (sword of faith). The central medallion depicts him fighting a lion. This motif varies a pictorial theme common on late classical sarcophagi, that of Daniel in the lions' den, and confirms the hero's invincibility. Wearing the short tunic and bound sandals of a typical classical hero, he holds a large round shield bearing the good luck message "God's blessing, happiness, and well-being."

The workshop's signature on the inside of the lid dedicates it to "Faraj and his pupils." Master and pupils have identified their work on individual ivory

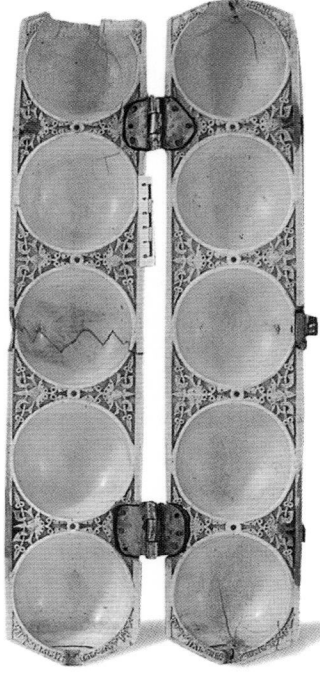

Silver casket, Medina al-Zahra, 976, length 38 cm, Gerona Cathedral
The black niello inlay strongly accentuates this silver casket's relief inscription, which nominates Hisham as the caliph's heir. The rows of palmettes – also niello-work – adapt architectural motifs, and are likewise executed as reliefs. Monotone motifs contrast with versatile execution that combines repoussé embossing with gilding and niello work. The casket has a wooden core.

Ivory containers, Medina al-Zahra, mid-10th century, Burgos, Museum
Among shell-like hollows to hold game pieces, this container, made for one of Caliph Abd al-Rahman III's daughters, has arabesques inspired by the relief decoration on the major new buildings. Apart from a dedication, a rectangular ivory casket owned by the princess bears nothing but arabesque decoration, evoking Paradise. These two ivory pieces represent the first fruit of Medina al-Zahra's court workshop.

relief plaques. Otherwise, there is no proof that several carvers collaborated. This suggests that the project had a deadline – a new anti-Christian campaign, perhaps. It also indicates a workshop that, given sufficient staff, regularly completed large-scale contracts. The project was supervised by a confidant of Abd al-Malik, called Zuhair ibn Muhammad al-Amiri, who is also mentioned on the chancellor's slightly later ivory pyx. The building boom and the proliferation of crafts made court firms' master signatures increasingly common. Like stonemasons inscribing their names on structures in the Great Mosque of Cordoba or the reception hall in Medina al-Zahra, ivory artists advertised themselves along with their priceless material. Khalaf was the first master to name himself on a casket for Subh and a box for the court. With these he established new quality criteria.

Ivory vessels have survived in the greatest numbers in northern Spanish churches and monasteries. In 997, al-Mansur, Abd al-Malik's father, had plundered the shrine of Santiago de Compostela and had the church bells brought to Cordoba on Christian prisoners' shoulders. Similarly, Christians used Muslim defeats to collect valuable booty in their church treasuries, where ivory boxes made highly prized reliquaries. With its arcade pattern and vaulted lid, the pyxis in Braga Cathedral's treasury resembles a miniature building, a quality shared by some Christian liturgical vessels. From medieval times onward, it has been used to house a suitably sized chalice or a small paten – both gifts of the Portuguese count, Mendo Goncalves, who died the same year as Abd al-Malik.

These exquisite Islamic ivory artifacts inspired carvings from Mozarabic artists in Christian northern Spain. Mid-9th century executions of Christian fanatics in Cordoba had caused many Christians to move north, to pursue their traditions in remote monasteries. Featuring arabesques and symbolic beasts such as the eagle, griffin, and lion, the processional crucifix and the altar of San Millán de la Cogolla – known as a center of book production far beyond Castile since the 10th century, document the undimmed attraction of Islamic originals.

Metalwork

Some silver caskets from Cordoba and *taifa* centers have survived among the treasures of Christian churches and monasteries. Hisham's casket in Gerona Cathedral, and two caskets from the church of San Isidoro, León, exemplify the once countless silver pieces inventoried, for instance, in St. Foy Church, Conques, southern France. Even churches that guarded their treasures often failed to stop their precious metal artifacts from being melted down. Hisham's casket, made in 976, is distinctive for the open palmettes that appear in regular rows, reflecting elements of the caliphate period palace. Implausibly tucked away behind the tongue of the clasp are the signatures of the masters Badr and Tarif, identified as servants who – like ivory artists – presumably worked for the Medina al-Zahra court workshop. The casket probably fell into Christian hands in the disturbances of the summer of 1010, while Hisham was still alive.

Even during the emirate, metalwork increased in importance. Bronze lamps from Medina Elvira, an Islamic settlement in the Vega region of Granada, follow the Byzantine polycandelon type that was modified in the Islamic Mediterranean – Kairouan, for instance – for use in mosques. An incense burner with an openwork domed lid, kept in Cordoba, resembles early Islamic objects excavated in Syria and Jordan. Another incense burner, from the Plaza de Chirinos, exemplifies local artifacts. The lid, crowned by a blossom-pommel, has familiar arabesques in the arcade divisions, executed as openwork, in keeping with the item's function. Perfume flasks with cylindrical necks, closed by a lid or stopper, came from a hoard discovered in Lucena, 44 miles (70 kilometers) east of Cordoba. Dated by the 1,500 silver coins also found there, the treasure included ten rings, four silver bracelets, and some exceptionally fine gold earrings. Along with the free-standing wire palmettes in the form of lilies, they indicate the artistic style of the capital, whose gold goldsmithing was initiated and influenced in the 9th century by the famous serpent collar worn by Zubaida, wife of the Abbasid caliph Harun al-Rashid.

After the collapse of the caliphate, the creation of gold, silver, and ivory art works took place in the *taifa* residences. For financial reasons, probably only a few kings could commission such luxury articles regularly. The Cuenca ivory carving workshop thrived again solely because *taifa* rulers in Toledo supported it. The only silver article that can be definitely traced back to the court of Albarracín is a perfume flask. This minor kingdom, sited on the road from Valencia to Zaragoza, was well known for its wealth, which probably temporarily financed goldsmiths and silversmiths; though the nearest city, Zaragoza, which, under Abu Jafar, could afford a magnificent castle, must have offered the craft better long-term prospects.

The kingdom of León, which certainly kept two silver caskets in the treasury of San Isidoro, exacted heavy tribute from the *taifa* states of Badajoz, Toledo, Seville, Granada, and Zaragoza to spare them from Christian attack. These high charges might be paid in kind with luxuries such as silk and silver. Similar arabesques on the oval box from San Isidoro, now exhibited in the National Archeological Museum in Madrid, reflect some details of Zaragoza's architecture. The *taifa* kings endured continuous Christian demands, and al-Mutatid of Seville was even prepared to surrender St. Isidore's remains for a rebate. Bishop of Seville in the early 7th century, and author of religious works, St. Isidore was celebrated in al-Andalus for the *Origines*. On surrendering the remains of the

saint, the *taifa* king recited verses honoring the scholar, and covered his remains with an ornately embroidered fabric.

Textile art

After the Arabs had introduced silkworms and established a court workshop in Cordoba, silks quickly acquired an excellent reputation and, by the 9th century, had appeared in papal inventories. Following Syrian Umayyad practice, silk products bore the name of the current ruler. Abd al-Rahman III had his clothes made from woven silks that bore his name and which were so unique that his contemporaries claimed the quality was unmatched among the Abbasynian manufacturers. As was customary at the caliph's court in Baghdad, deserving officials and friendly potentates were distinguished by other textiles. A silk fragment, long stored in a Pyrenean church, shows medallions with peacock motifs that were inspired by eastern, maybe Byzantine, textiles. The first textile item that we can reliably attribute to the court workshop is a veil, into which the name Hisham has been woven. Although Hisham relinquished real power to his chancellor, al-Mansur, he retained the right merely to put his name on coins and Tiraz textiles. The 43-inch (109-centimeter) long veil, or shawl, which probably served as the caliph's head-covering, was found in a container beneath the altar in the church of San Estebán de Gormáz in Soría.

Gold statuette, Andalusia, 11th century, height 6 cm, Lugo (Orense), Museo Provincial
This unusual gold statuette of a winged ram, found in northwestern Spain, is an elaborate gold artifact, decorated with ornate filigree and granulation. Winged rams also appear on the ivory casket, owned by Abd al-Malik (1002–1008), complementing the winged griffins, and similarly symbolic beasts suggestive of the owner's supernatural powers. The fine, subtle workmanship of this miniature statue confirms that *taifa* kingdom metalwork was highly sophisticated.

Silver perfume flask, c. 1044/45, Teruel, Museo Provincial
This silver perfume flask belonged to the wife of the *taifa* prince, Muaiyad al-Daula, of Albarracín. The widely swirling arabesques of highly decorative foliage surround two ibexes, centralized as the focal point. The decoration is accentuated by niello inlays, and both the handles and the base are gilded.

Silk shawl, Medina al-Zahra, late 10th century, Madrid, Real Academia de la Historia
Distinctive Kufic borders identify this shawl, originally from the palace city's Tiraz workshop as an accessory of the caliph Hisham.

Between the inscriptions, arranged as mirror images, runs a medallion strip, depicting two people – identified as Hisham and his mother, Subh.

An embroidered cloth of the same date, from the parish church of San Salvador, Ona, shows animals like the peacock, eagle, lion, elephant, horse, gazelle, and hare representing the variety of nature, and leaving the human figure who appears in one medallion to be interpreted as the caliph, lord of the universe. The reburial of St. Isidore's remains dates the embroidery to the mid-11th century. On this we find quadrupeds – rams and deer – alternating with birds: eagles and peacocks.

When, in the mid-10th century, Ibn Hauqal traveled through Spain, he was astonished by the numerous textile mills, whose linen and silk fabrics constituted the regional bazaars' luxury articles, and were also exported to the eastern Mediterranean. Various quality items, including wool, hemp, and cotton material, were famous for their brilliant natural colors, originating from plants common throughout the territory. Textile weaving significantly helped urban crafts and commerce to thrive. Some *taifa* kings' generous gifts to Fatimid caliphs in Cairo helped exports develop. In the Egyptian port of Tinnis, whole boatloads of Spanish raw silk were transported by ship, and then sold at top prices. By contrast, Egyptian luster ceramics were imported before Spanish potteries themselves began manufacturing these luxurious golden articles, to meet eastern Mediterranean demand.

Almoravids and Almohads

History
Markus Hattstein

Spain under the *taifa* rulers

With the dissolution of the caliphate of Cordoba in 1031, the religious and cultural unity of Islam in al-Andalus also went into decline. As early as 1009, political and military cohesion was failing, with bloody struggles around the throne of the caliph. In the developing power vacuum individualist and unscrupulous adventurers seized the opportunity and created a number of small regional states, often very short-lived, known as the *taifa* kingdoms. There arose 26 chief *taifa* kingdoms and a plethora of tiny states. These were formed by members of the three Islamic ethnic groups in al-Andalus: the Spanish Arabs, the Berbers, and the Islamized Slavs (*saqaliba*). Since the Berbers and the Slavs had been the original auxiliary troops for the caliph of Cordoba, they set up what were, primarily speaking, military states.

Principal representatives of the Spanish Arabs were the Abbadids in Seville (1013–1091), whose court became the center of refined Andalusian culture under al-Mutadid (1042–1069) and al-Mutamid (1069–1091). These kings were just as outstanding as poets and equally unscrupulous as politicians. The province of Saragossa was also an independent petty kingdom under the Banu Hud dynasty (Hudids, 1039–1110), who registered their claim to power by building the defensive castle of Aljafería in Saragossa. The most important Berber dynasties were the Banu Hammud (Hammudids) in Malaga and Algeciras (1016–1058), the Dhun-Nunids in Toledo (1028/29–1085), and most significant of all the Zirids in Granada (1012–1090), who in 1058 extended their power to include Malaga and Algeciras. The Slav rulers controlled Almeria, Valencia, Murcia, Tortosa, and the Balearic Islands, thus the east of Spain.

Political conditions in the *taifa* period were characterized by incessant minor wars. Alliances were formed merely for some individual advantage. Court intrigue, acts of violence, and tyranny were just as typical of this period as was the blossoming of science, the fine arts, and literature. Conditions in al-Andalus were useful mainly to the Christian rulers in northern Spain, giving them the opportunity to steadily build up their power. The most important of them was the overbearing King Alfonso VI of Léon and Castile (1065/72–1109), who made the *taifa* rulers of Badajoz, Toledo, Saragossa, and Seville pay tribute to him. After a long siege he conquered Toledo for Christianity in 1085. This event gave renewed impetus to the Christian Reconquista, the effect of which could hardly be over estimated. Roused by the successes of Alfonso VI, the remaining *taifa* rulers abandoned their squabbles and formed an emergency alliance against the Christians, calling on the Almoravids in North Africa for help.

The Almoravids (1060–1147)

The Almoravids came from the western Sahara. They emerged as the dominant force of the Sanhaja, the great nomadic Berber association of tribes. A chieftain of the Lamtuna tribe, which belonged to this association, had endeavored while on a pilgrimage to Kairouan in 1035 to persuade a Muslim legal scholar to work with members of his tribe as a teacher in questions of faith. The strictly Malikite legal professor Ali ibn Yasin took on this task and immediately went to work with great enthusiasm, introducing a strict tax for the benefit of the poor and the duty to pray, also reducing unlimited polygamy. As a frontier fortress against the interior of Africa he founded a *ribat*, a fortified monastery for the training of future religious warriors. The severe discipline imposed there, together with the idealization of the Berbers' meager life-style, stressed unquestioning obedience of the religious leader (*sheikh*).

This community of warlike ascetics called themselves *al-murabitun* ("the men of the ribat"), whence the name Almoravids. It was composed mainly of members of the Berber tribes of the Lamtuna, the Juddala, and the Massufa. While Berber women were unveiled, the men of the Lamtuna tribe wore the dark-colored mouth veil (*litam*), which covered the lower part of the face, as a sign of their aristocracy, which is why they became known as the "veiled ones"

Opposite: **Kutubiya Mosque in Marrakech**, 1158
The Great Mosque of Marrakech, known as Kutubiya, is the most important Almohad building in all of Morocco. When the first Almohad ruler, Abd al-Mumin, captured Marrakech in 1147, he had a mosque erected on the site of the former palace of the Almoravids, a symbolic erasure of all memory of his hated predecessors. His successor replaced the original building with the present mosque, whose minaret rises high over the city and shows striking similarities to the Giralda in Seville.

Above: **King Alfonso X, the Wise**, *azulejos* (tile) picture of the *Cantiques a Santa Maria*, Seville, Plaza d'Espagna
King Alfonso X of Léon and Castile (1221–1284) succeeded his father Ferdinand III to the throne in 1252. He continued the Reconquista launched by his father, but at the same time reigned with great religious tolerance. He received his epithet "the Wise" (el Sabio) on account of his extraordinary learning. Apart from the world of Christian thought, Islamic and Jewish knowledge also influenced him and he knew how to combine them into an intellectual symbiosis.

(*al-mulattimun*). The Almoravids first proved themselves in combat against heathen tribes in the south, but their attention soon turned towards the north. After the religious leader Ali ibn Yasin had been killed in combat in 1059, Yusuf ibn Tashfin (1060–1106), who was to lead the Almoravids on their triumphal march, took over. The spiritual leadership, on the other hand, passed to the Malikite *ulama* ("learned ones"), who played an important role in the material form and the legitimization of Almoravid power. Seldom were Islamic legal opinions (*fatwas*), which were obtained and meticulously obeyed by Yusuf as the basis of dynastic rule, as important as they were with the Almoravids.

The new regime brought the whole of Morocco under its control within a few years. In 1062 Yusuf founded the city of Marrakech (from which Morocco derives its name) as the capital of the Almoravid movement and headed north from here with his warriors. In 1069 they took Fez, in 1077 Tangier, and 1082 Algiers, thus bringing under their dominion a unified region as far to the east as Little Kabylia (Algeria). Wherever they gained power the Almoravids abolished "illegitimate" taxes, destroyed all the wine, and suppressed worldly pleasures such as dance and music. In the process, however, many things remained limited just to members of the ruling class. In the south, too, the Almoravids rapidly enlarged their territory. They destroyed the African ("heathen") kingdom of Ghana and Islamized the northern part of the interior of Africa, which remains Islamic to this day.

The *taifa* rulers in Spain were fully aware of the rapid and resolute rise of the Almoravids. When Alfonso VI conquered Toledo in 1085 and advanced further to the south, the *taifa* kings recognized the danger that lay in their disunity, formed an alliance, and called on the Almoravids to come from Africa to help. In June 1086 Yusuf crossed over to Algeciras with his army, marched to Seville, and defeated Alfonso VI in October 1086 in the Battle of Zallaka (Sacralias, northeast of Badajoz). Afterwards he returned to Morocco with most of his army, but left Berber contingents behind in Spain. Angered by the contradictory political stance of the *taifa* princes and supported by Spanish legal scholars, who quite openly denied their rulers the moral justification to rule, Yusuf landed in Spain once more in 1089 and deposed most of the *taifa* rulers over the next few years. By 1094 the Almoravids had brought the whole of the south of Spain under their rule as a united region. Only Valencia, which fell in 1102, and Saragossa, which was able to stay independent right up to 1110, were still capable of putting up any prolonged resistance. In the end, the Almoravids controlled the whole Muslim region of al-Andalus, as well as the African interior as far as the border with Sudan, and were even able to expel the Pisans from the Balearic Islands. In 1098 Yusuf ibn Tashfin adopted the title of Amir al-muslimin ("Ruler of the Muslims"), following the title Amir al-muminin ("Ruler of the Believers") of the Caliph of Baghdad.

Almoravid rule was not exactly popular with the native Muslims of Spain. The cultivated inhabitants of Andalusia, particularly in the towns, traditionally regarded the Berbers as semibarbaric auxiliaries, while the Almoravids faced the fertile land, the courtly customs, and the highly developed commercial life with a mixture of contempt and reverence. Although most of the Almoravid elite and

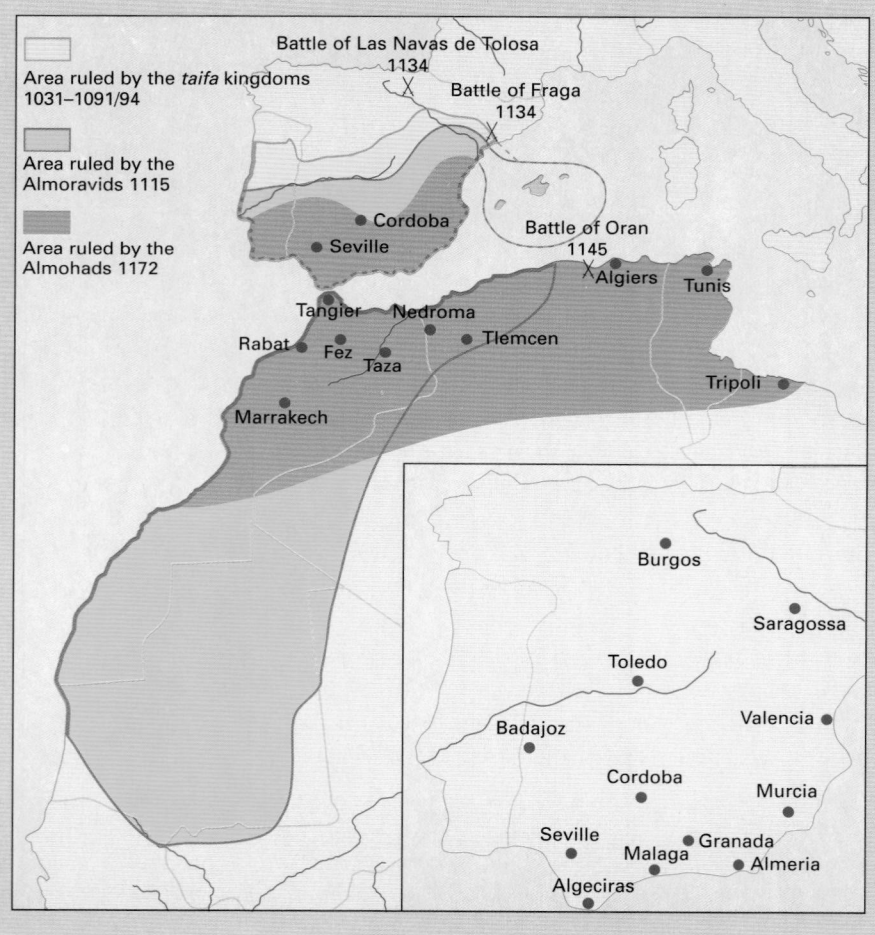

1031–1090/94	After the end of the Omayyad caliphate in Cordoba, various taifa dynasties spring up in Andalusia, among which are the Abbadids (1013–1091) in Seville, the Hudids (1039–1110) in Saragossa, the Hammudids (1016–1058) in Malaga and Algeciras, the Dhun-Nuniden (1028/29–1085) in Toledo, and the Zirids (1012–1090) in Granada
1030/35–1059	The Almoravid movement comes into being in the Maghreb under the leadership of Abdallah ibn Yasin
1060	Yusuf ibn Tashfin (1060–1106) assumes the leadership of the Almoravids
1062/1070	Foundation of the city of Marrakech
1069	The Almoravids take Fez
1077	Tangier falls to the Almoravids
1082	The Almoravids take possession of Algiers
1085	Alfonso VI of Léon and Castile (1065/72–1109) captures Toledo

Almoravid clay seal, 11th–12th century. Almeria, Museo Arqueológico
This clay seal was probably used for the authentication of documents and was either spread with ink and then pressed on the relevant paper or (more likely) pressed as a negative into the wax used to seal the document.

al-Ghazzali (1058–1111) in Cordoba. On the other hand, Ali had a more open mind than his father as regards the urban culture of al-Andalus. The lowering or abolition of taxes, which had earned the Almoravids a certain amount of popularity, had to be revoked in favor of military expenditure under pressure from the military strength of the Christians, which led to unrest in the cities. Yusuf's successor could no longer maintain the political unity of the Almoravid empire.

There arose a resolute opponent to the Almoravids in the person of King Alfonso I of Aragon and Navarre (1104–1134), known as El Batallador ("The Warrior"), who assumed the title of Emperor of Spain. In 1118 he won back Saragossa, which had only just been captured, for the Christians, together with the Ebro basin, and then progressed inexorably southwards until in 1126 he arrived at Guadix. Ali's son Tashfin opposed him as Almoravid governor in Spain, using troops hastily levied in Africa, and in July 1134 was able to gain a victory over Alfonso at Fraga, which once again stabilized Almoravid rule. In 1139 the earldom of Portugal raised itself to become an independent Christian kingdom, which continued to expand. Alfonso VII of Castile (1126–1157), after the death of the warrior "Emperor of Spain," had by 1133 already besieged Seville and was able to take Almeria, the most important Muslim naval base. In the context of Crusade propaganda, several Christian military orders were established in Spain which were fully dedicated to the "Moorish struggle."

While this was happening, the Almoravids also found themselves on the retreat before the powerful forces of the Almohads in Morocco and generally in the African interior. Tashfin ibn Ali (1143–1145), who had complete control

administration in Spain began very soon to adapt themselves to local conditions, they remained by and large strangers to the Spanish Muslims. While the whole Almoravid leadership stayed in Morocco most of the time, the cities and provinces of al-Andalus were administered by governors or princes of the ruling house operating relatively independently.

Under Yusuf's son and successor Ali ibn Yusuf (1106–1143) the rift in Spain became totally apparent. His religious intolerance, under the influence of the theologians, and the power of the traditionally minded Malikite legal scholars (*fuqaha*), which was becoming ever more rigid, led in 1109 to the public burning of the works of the most important Islamic theologian and philosopher

1086	Battle of Zallaka: the Almoravids provide military aid to the taifa kings against Alfonso VI	1133	Alfonso VII of Castile (1126–1157) besieges Seville
1090–1094	The Almoravids depose the taifa kings and send them into exile in Morocco; Andalusia becomes an Almoravid province	1134	Victory of Almoravid troops under Tashfin ibn Ali over Alfonso I of Aragon and Navarre (1104–1134) at Fraga
1098	Yusuf ibn Tashfin assumes the title of "Ruler of the Muslims"	1139	An autonomous Christian kingdom is established in Portugal
1106–1143	Rule of the Almoravid Ali ibn Yusuf	1143–1145	Rule of the Almoravid Tashfin ibn Ali
1118	Alfonso I of Aragon and Navarre (1104–1134) brings Saragossa under his control	1144	Anti-Almoravid unrest in Andalusia; reestablishment of taifa kingdoms
1121	In North Africa the scholar Ibn Tumart (c.1080–1130) proclaims himself Mahdi and founds the Almohad movement	1145	Defeat of the Almoravids by the Almohads at Oran
		1146	Beginning of the conquest of Andalusia by the Almohads
1124	Ibn Tumart establishes himself in Tinmal with his followers	1147	The Almohads take Marrakech by storm and put to death the last of the Almoravids, Ishaq ibn Ali (1146–1147). In Spain they take Seville
1130	First attempt by the Almohads to capture Marrakech		
1130/33	Abd al-Mumin (1130/33–1163) assumes the leadership of the Almohads	1148	Almeria falls to Alfonso VII of Castile
		1157	The Almohads conquer Granada and Almeria

1163–1184	Rule of the Almoravid Abu Yaqub Yusuf		against Almohad supremacy
1184	Almohad campaign against Portugal (Santarém)	1232	Arjona becomes autonomous under the governorship of Muhammad ibn Nasr, who founds his own state in 1238 after the conquest of Granada
1195	Victory of the Almohads under Yusuf Yaqub al-Mansur (1184–1199) over Alfonso VIII of Castile (1158–1214) at Alarcos		
1199–1213	Rule of Muhammad al-Nasir	1269	The Merinids take Marrakech; end of Almoravid rule
1212	Battle of Las Navas de Tolosa: Almohads defeated by Christian armies		
1216	In Morocco the Banu Marin gain autonomy		
1217	Conquest of the Algarve by the kingdom of Portugal		
1217–1252	Ferdinand III of Castile succeeds in taking the cities of Cordoba (1236), Murcia (1243), Jaén (1245), and Seville (1248)		
1226	Valencia becomes tributary to Aragon and finally falls to Aragon in 1238		
1229/30	Mallorca falls under the dominion of Aragon		
1228–1237	Rebellion of Muhammad ibn Hud al-Mutawakkil (governor of Murcia)		

after his father's death, suffered a crushing defeat at Oran (Algeria) in 1145 at the hands of the Almohads and met with a fatal accident. His successor, Ibrahim (1145–1146), was ruler for only a short while, and the last overall ruler of the Almoravids, Ishaq ibn Ali (1146–1147) was killed by the Almohads in the capture of the city of Marrakech in April 1147. The disintegration of the Almoravid empire in the interior of Africa also led to a general revolt in Spain from 1144, which began in the small towns and rapidly spread to the cities. Called to help one of the short-lived new regional rulers, the Almohads crossed over to Spain in May 1146 and conquered al-Andalus.

The Almohads (1133–1269)

The origin of the Almohad movement can be traced back to the theological sense of mission and aggressive energy of one man, who is among the most important charismatic leaders of political Islam: the theologian and preacher Ibn Tumart (c. 1080–1130). Born into the settled Berber tribe of the Masmuda in south Morocco, he went to study in Cordoba sometime around 1106 but soon after that traveled to the east of the Islamic world. Nothing definite is known about his early years, but it is certain that Ibn Tumart was in contact with the dominant theological school of the Asharites, from which he adopted measured rationalism and the use of Islamic scholasticism (*kalam*). The Malakites, who were predominant in his homeland, together with the Almoravids, were too literal for him, understanding the statements of God in the Koran word for word, describing God, for example, as hearing, seeing, sitting on his throne, and so on. Their adversaries, like Ibn Tumart, reproached them for this "humanization of God" (*tajsim*) – attributing human characteris-

tics to Him. This was regarded as the actual heresy – the "humanizers" of the indivisible unity of God (*tauhid*) added features which broke up this unity.

Early schools of Islam had already put forward an allegorical and metaphorical interpretation to counter this "humanizing" tendency, since the strict emphasis on the unity and indivisibility of God permitted no hypothesizing about God's characteristics. Not only the political struggle but also, and principally, the fanatical religious hatred of Ibn Tumart for the Almoravids increased to the point where, for Ibn Tumart, the Malikites and the Almoravids, with their literal understanding of the "unification" (*shirk*) – in this case that of the (separated) attributes brought together to form the one and only, simply stated unity of God – incriminated themselves and were strictly speaking "polytheists." This was regarded as one of the worst theological crimes in Islam.

Sometime in the year 1118 Ibn Tumart returned from the East and traveled via Egypt and Libya to Tunisia and Algeria. Moving from town to town, he preached against the decline in morals and the lavish life-style and laxity of the ruling Almoravids, calling for a holy war against the "humanizers of God" (*mujassimun*), whom he accused of "godlessness" (*kufr*). Greeted with approval in some places and opposed by the local authorities in others, his crowd of supporters grew steadily. The community became known as *al-muwahhidun*

City gate and wall of Niebla, 12th century
The massive city wall of Niebla is one of the most important examples of defensive architecture in al-Andalus. It is 3 km long and was constructed using the Moorish shell construction technique. This consisted of an inner wall of cut stone and clay surrounded by an outer fortified ring. The city belongs to the emirate or caliphate of Cordoba and became the capital of an independent *taifa* state in the 11th century. In 1257 Alfonso X of Castile succeeded in conquering the city for Christendom but only after a six-month siege.

Ibn Tumart Mosque at Tinmal, Morocco, 1153/54
Tinmal in the High Atlas Mountains was the inaccessible fortress of the founder of the Almohads, Ibn Tumart (c. 1080–1130), who withdrew here with his followers after 1118 in order to be safe from the attacks of the Almoravid government in Marrakech. Here he proclaimed himself Mahdi in 1121 and planned the organization of his community. His successor, Abd al-Mumin (1130/33–1163), had a memorial mosque erected to Ibn Tumart, who was buried here.

("confessors of the unity of God"), whence the name Almohads. Having arrived in Morocco, and in order to avoid being waylaid, Ibn Tumart withdrew with his supporters to Tinmal in the High Atlas, where later the famous mosque was built in his memory. There in his native country he started the systematic organization of a community that was both religious and politico-military. By giving a strong nationalist feel to his teachings – the call to prayer was expressed in the Berber language, as were all his works – the community became extremely popular among those Berber tribes that felt excluded from Almoravid power. Ibn Tumart stressed the legitimate prophetic tradition of his teachings and advocated uncompromising and direct compliance with Islamic law.

His sense of mission increased to such an extent that he acquired familial descent from the Prophet and assumed the name Muhammad. He gave himself the title of Mahdi, "The Expected One," who as imam was infallible, who was to restore Islamic righteousness, and who demanded unquestioning obedience and self-sacrifice from his followers. Thus he said about himself as the Mahdi: "There is no one like him among Mankind, there is no one who can resist him or speak against him … To no one can he remain unknown, no one can ignore his command. Whosoever opposes him as an enemy recklessly hurls himself into destruction and has no prospect of salvation. One can approach him only with something with which he is in agreement; all things come from his command. All things happen according to his wish, but this is also the wish of his Lord (God). To recognize him is an imperative duty of religion, obedience and humility towards him are imperative duties of religion, just as one follows him and complies with his actions … The commandment of the Mahdi is the commandment of God …"

Ibn Tumart established a strictly hierarchically structured governmental and administrative apparatus. The constitution of the community was arranged rigidly according to the example of the Prophet and original Islam. The Mahdi at the head surrounded himself with a council of 10 tribal chiefs, with 40 delegates of the affiliated Berber tribes. A band of wandering preachers ensured that his teachings were propagated, while muezzins, censors, and Koran readers were assigned to the units for the supervision of morals. The Mahdi had his own name mentioned in prayers from the pulpit and thus put all claims of the caliph of Baghdad to one side. He renewed his call for a holy war against the "godless states" of the Almoravids; all attempts to penetrate his mountain lair failed.

Shortly before his death in 1130, the Almohads felt strong enough to attack Marrakech but they were repulsed. Ibn Tumart was buried in Tinmal, yet those who had been closest to him, the Council of Ten, were allegedly able to keep the death of the Mahdi secret from the community for three years, until Abd al-Mumin had secured his authority as successor in 1133. The Algerian Abd al-Mumin (1130/33–1163), who had followed Ibn Tumart from 1118, was an important and brave army commander and had a great talent for organization. It is thanks to him above all that the Almohad community expanded its power structures to become a major political empire. He unified the great Berber tribal associations of the Masmuda, the Zanata, and the Sanhada and launched a systematic war against the Almoravids, whose empire quickly collapsed after 1143.

From Fez, Abd al-Mumin eliminated the central power of the Almoravids in Marrakech, where he had the Kutubiya Mosque erected as an emblem of his victory, and annihilated the independent Berber states in the Maghreb in quick succession. By about 1160 he had extended his empire eastwards as far as Tunisia and Libya. At first, the roots of Almohad power were principally among the settled, agricultural Masmuda Berbers, and later mainly among the Arab army contingents. Abd al-Mumin had the mosque at Tinmal erected to the memory of Ibn Tumart in 1153/54. He transformed the more prophetic charismatic leadership of Ibn Tumart, however, into a dynastic principle, though he was careful to tie the leading tribes into his power structure by means of a council. He had already assumed the title of Amir al-muminin, "Ruler of the Believers," following his entry into Marrakech, whereby he officially put himself on the same level as the caliph of Baghdad, whose spiritual leadership he thus contested. Through their moral rigor and cultural puritanism, as well as their highly organized military strength, the Almohads established a tight administration for their empire, while at the same time allowing the economy and trade to flourish.

Since the Almohads acquired the whole of the Almoravid dominions, they also kept a watchful eye on conditions in Islamic Spain, where with the collapse of Almoravid rule *taifa* states began once again to establish themselves. In May, 1146, the first Almohad contingents landed in Spain and took most of the southern cities. In 1147 they expelled the last Almoravids from Seville and Cordoba and in 1157 again took Almeria from Alfonso VII after a siege. Only the province of Murcia was able to retain its independence until 1172.

The rigid rule of the Almohads was at first not as popular in al-Andalus as that of the Almoravids. However, the Almohads were successful in stopping the first phase of the Reconquista, even though they were unable to win back any of the great cities (Toledo, Lisbon, Saragossa) for Islam. Internally, the Almohads, in contrast to their predecessors, acted intolerantly in Spain against the Jews and Christians under their jurisdiction (who enjoyed the *dhimmi* status of "protected ones"), yet they retained the Christian mercenary troops they had inherited. So as not to fall into the same trap as the Almoravids, who

Grave stela of Ibrahim ibn Jalil, Lerena, 12th century. Madrid, Museo Arqueológico Nacional
So that they would not be taken for foreign rulers in Spain like their Almoravid predecessors, the Almohads in al-Andalus enlisted extra local officials and judges. These were taken from the class of Hispanic Arabs who had been resident in Spain to a certain extent since the 8th century. They thus assured themselves of an efficient and well-controlled government apparatus, which also provided the high standard of public safety in the cities and on the trade routes of the empire. This grave stela of the Almohad vizier Ibrahim ibn Jalil, who died in August 1152, was found on the estate of the ruler of Lerena near Badajoz.

had remained in Spain as foreign rulers, the Almohads in their administration relied on the educated Muslims of al-Andalus. Abd al-Mumin himself, who was occupied with the consolidation of his territory in the Maghreb, made his way to Spain for a short while to supervise the fortification of Gibraltar but installed his sons as governors in the cities of al-Andalus.

His son and successor Abu Yaqub Yusuf (1163–1184) spent most of his time in Marrakech like his father, but was obliged on several occasions to intervene in wars in Spain, since the kings of Castile, Portugal, and Léon were constantly extending their domains towards al-Andalus. Internally, Yaqub Yusuf endeavored to develop culture and science. Thus he sponsored the most important Islamic philosopher, Averroes (Ibn Rushd, 1126–1198), who was treated with

City walls of Seville
In the 11th century, Seville, under the Abbadids, became the most important and the richest city in al-Andalus. In 1170 the Almohad rulers made Seville the capital of their Spanish realm.

Right: **Interior of the Mosque of Almonaster la Real**
The *mihrab* of the five-aisled Mosque of Almonaster la Real in the province of Huelva is a clear example of the simple, plain, almost fortified style of Almohad building.

SPAIN AND MOROCCO

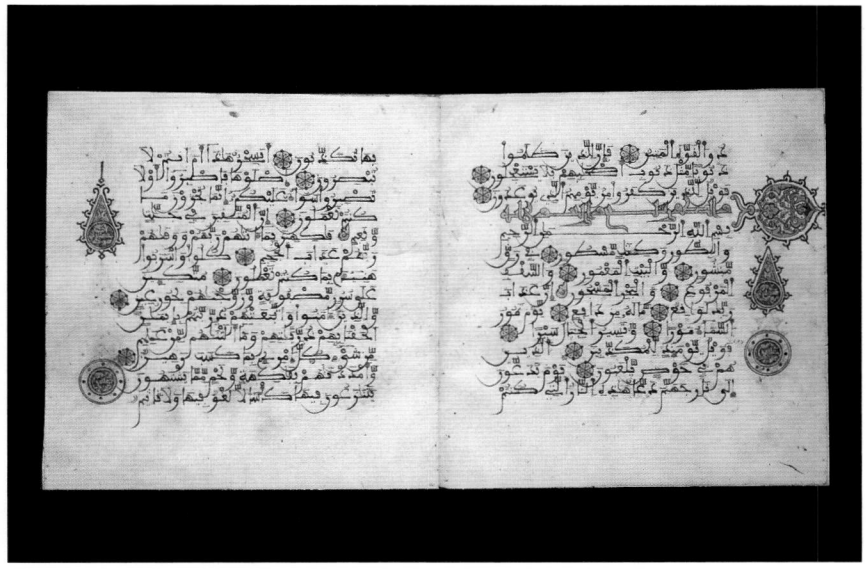

severe hostility by the orthodox *ulama*, mainly because of his thesis on the immutability of the world, and appointed him high court judge of Cordoba. He made the polymath Ibn Tufail (d. 1185), who tried to reconcile good sense and revelation theology, his personal physician and vizier in Marrakech. In the spring of 1184, Yaqub Yusuf landed in Spain with a powerful army, marched into Portugal, and besieged the Christian city of Santarém, where he was fatally wounded when the king of Léon intervened in July 1184. His sons transported the ruler's body to Seville.

He was succeeded by his son Yusuf Yaqub al-Mansur (1184–1199). The new ruler had first of all to undergo a dangerous trial of strength, when hostile Berber tribes led a rebellion in the interior of Africa, which embroiled the Almohads in a civil war involving heavy casualties and led for a while to the secession of Tunisia. Under Yaqub al-Mansur (from 1170) the magnificent conversion of Seville into the capital of the Spanish Almohad empire, begun under his father, took place. The Seville region had achieved a considerable degree of prosperity, mainly through its olive oil processing developed by the rulers. In strict Almohad style, Yaqub commissioned the Great Mosque in the new capital, which with its minaret towers (Giralda) was similar to the Kutubiya in Marrakech. At that time, it was one of the largest mosques in the Islamic world.

This magnificent manifestation of Islam progressed under Yaqub al-Mansur, along with a perceptible intensification of government measures against Christians and Jews, including compulsory conversions in the Maghreb. The ruler subjected the Jews to a strict code of dress. Since he did not wish to tolerate any more local Christians in Muslim Spain, the Mozarabs were forced through excessively high taxes to migrate to the Christian north. Cultural diversity in al-Andalus was impoverished. When Yaqub needed the support of the professors of law, he was forced to banish Averroes to Morocco and to authorize the burning of his philosophical writings. After his victory at Alarcos in 1195, however, the ruler summoned him to return to his court in Marrakech.

On the whole, within the cultural development of the Almohad empire in the 12–13th centuries there emerged a general tendency for Islam to abandon philosophical speculation and research in favor of a rigid orthodox dogmatism in theology and jurisprudence ("closing the gate" on the *ijtihad*, on the independent search for conclusions). At the same time, in the Christian West there developed a great thirst for knowledge and a passion for ancient philosophy, which also led to extensive adoption of the ideas of Islamic thinkers.

Under Yusuf Yaqub and Yaqub al-Mansur, Almohad rule reached its zenith. Their strict organization led to a significant increase in trade, the development of cities, and the protection of trade routes. Almohad government provided above all for an effective financial and tax regime, which orientated itself strictly by the contributions laid down in the Koran. Through the forced construction of ships in Alicante and Algeciras they were successful in building up an extremely powerful naval fleet, which fought the north Italian cities for domination of the Mediterranean. The navy was even called to the Syrian coast to help Sultan Saladin in his struggle against the Crusaders. Yaqub himself suffered a defeat by the Crusaders in 1190, but was able to advance against Christian Portugal in the following year. On July 19, 1195, Yusuf Yaqub al-Mansur ("The Victorious") won a brilliant victory at Alarcos, northeast of Cordoba, over the united Christian armies of Castile and Léon, and was able to advance as far as Toledo. The victory made the ruler the hero of Islam, while it led the Christians to regroup for a new phase in the Reconquista. Finally, Yaqub

returned to Morocco, where he had to accept the loss of the greater part of Tunisia to the rebels. In January, 1199, he died in Marrakech.

He was succeeded by his son Muhammad al-Nasir (1199–1213). Stung by the defeat at Alarcos, Pope Innocent III (1198–1216) called on the Christian kings of the Iberian Peninsula to launch a joint "Crusade" against the Almohads, a call which almost all the rulers obeyed. Al-Nasir had now succeeded to a large degree in reconquering the regions of Tunisia lost to the rebels. In Spain, in the meantime, a Christian army was formed for the struggle under the leadership of Alfonso VIII of Castile (1158–1214). In order to meet the impending threat, al-Nasir landed in Spain with his army in 1211 and marched from Cordoba against the Christians. On July 16, 1212, the Almohad army suffered a devastating defeat by the Christian troops at Las Navas de Tolosa, a little to the south of Alarcos, and was completely annihilated. Ten thousand Muslims were killed and the Christians captured rich booty. Las Navas de Tolosa was, for European Christianity, the signal for an invigorated Reconquista.

The end of the Almohads and the Christian Reconquista in Spain

In December, 1213, al-Nasir, the last significant Almohad ruler died. His youthful son Abu Yaqub Yusuf II al-Mustansir (1213–1224) was dominated by the tribal chiefs (sheikhs) and hastened to conclude an armistice with Castile and Aragon. He had to watch helplessly in 1217 as the kingdom of Portugal annexed the whole of the Algarve and colonized it with Christians. In Morocco, the Banu Marin tribe, later the Merinids, declared themselves independent in the Muluya-Tal in 1216. Following the death of al-Mustansir in January 1224, the power initiative passed to the Almohad sheikhs, who were, however, divided among themselves. So, between 1224 and 1236 two branches of the Almohad ruling house were in rivalry in Morocco and Spain. They exhausted their strength in fighting each other, while more and more regions of the empire became independent. The last Almohad caliphs in Morocco, who governed until 1269, were to a large extent powerless and managed to remain in Marrakech only with considerable difficulty. Authority in the country had already largely passed over to the Merinids, who from 1248 ruled over the north of Morocco from Fez.

In Spain, the government administration had very quickly slipped away from the Almohads. In the province of Murcia the governor Muhammad ibn Hud rose up in revolt and declared himself ruler under the name of al-Mutawakkil (1228–1237). He was able to achieve recognition in Granada, Cordoba, Malaga and a series of other cities, and also took Seville in 1229. In the following years he had the whole of al-Andalus under his control except for the province of Valencia. In 1232 Seville made itself independent of al-Mutawakkil's rule and later a series of other cities followed suit. The governor of Arjona, Muhammad ibn Nasr from the Banu l-Ahmar tribe, also gained his independence in 1232 and was able to conquer Granada in 1238, where he established the Nasrid dynasty, which was to hold on as the last Islamic power in southern Spain until 1492.

The leaders of the Reconquista took advantage of these symptoms of the collapse of Islamic power in Spain. The warlike and clever Jaime I of Aragon (1213–1276), El Conquistador ("The Conqueror"), made Valencia a tribute state in 1226, took Merida, and blockaded Mallorca with his fleet in 1229/30, forcing all the Balearic Islands to recognize him as their overlord. Valencia succumbed in September 1238.

The leading personality on the Christian side was Ferdinand III of Castile (1217–1252), El Santo ("The Holy"), who also inherited the kingdom of Léon in 1230 and united it with Castile. A courageous army commander and a gifted politician, he had dedicated himself to the victory of Christendom, but he always treated the defeated Muslims with leniency and did not attempt to destroy either Islamic or Jewish culture. In 1233 Ferdinand began to annex various minor cities and made the ruler al-Mutawakkil tributary to him. He advanced inexorably towards Cordoba: the city surrendered at the end of June 1236 after a siege. In April, 1243, Murcia was also forced to open its gates to the Christians and in August 1245 Ferdinand seized Jaén from the Nasrids,

A Muslim and a Christian playing chess, 13th century, Madrid, Bibliotheca del Monasterio de El Escorial
Relations between the Islamic south and the Christian north of Spain were not characterized by war and strife in every respect, but also included flourishing commercial and cultural exchanges. This miniature painting shows a Muslim and a Christian knight playing chess, a game which the Europeans learned from the Arabs.

The Conquest of Mallorca by Jaime I of Aragon, fresco (detail), c.1280, Barcelona, Museo d'Art de Catalunya
One of the most important leaders of the Christian Reconquista, apart from the kings of Castile, was King Jaime I of Aragon with his epithet El Conquistador ("The Conqueror"), who constructed a powerful fleet. In 1229 he started the blockade of Mallorca, which continued until the Muslims surrendered in 1230 and had to give up the island to Jaime, who also imposed his sovereignty on the other Balearic Islands.

thus opening the road to Seville. The king took possession of all the fortifications between Cordoba and Seville and besieged Seville itself, which had to capitulate in November 1248. The last important center of Spanish Islam was therefore in Christian hands.

Ferdinand's well-educated son and successor Alfonso X (1252–1284), El Sabio ("The Learned"), settled Christians throughout the Seville region, and yet his court was tolerant and Arab science had influenced him to such a degree that he was to his contemporaries just as much "a Christian Arab on the throne" as was the Hohenstaufen emperor Frederick II. Alfonso X firmly supported the Toledo translation schools, which again matched on the Christian side the splendor of the caliph's Cordoba as a center for the meeting of East and West in art and science. The king attracted to his court many Islamic thinkers and scientists, who were under pressure from Islamic orthodoxy.

Alfonso had to quell several revolts by the Mudejars in the newly conquered cities and from 1260 sought to break the power of the Merinids by invading Morocco. From 1275, however, there was a counterattack and he had to face several successful Merinid landings in Spain. However, this changed nothing as regards the developing predominance of Christian culture in Spain, which was being molded by the spirit of the Reconquista. The Nasrid empire of Granada was soon to become tributary to the Christian rulers, who at first treated it with considerable tolerance but eventually abandoned this policy.

F.P. van Halen, **The Battle of Las Navas de Tolosa, 1212**
Oil on canvas, Madrid, Palacio del Senado
In the Christian history of Spain, the Battle of Las Navas de Tolosa on July 16, 1212, is considered to have been the decisive victory of the Reconquista. After the Almohads had inflicted a severe defeat on the Christian armies at Alarcos in 1195, the pope in Rome called on Christendom to mount a Crusade in Spain. In 1212, an army composed of troops from all the Christian states in Spain, under the leadership of Alfonso VIII of Castile, marched south from Toledo. The Almohad ruler al-Nasir set out from Cordoba to meet them. The Battle of Las Navas ended with a clear victory for the Christians over the Muslims.

Architecture
Natascha Kubisch

Almoravid architecture in the Maghreb

The Almoravids, Berbers from the Sahara, established control over the western Maghreb within a few years and in 1062 founded Marrakech as the capital of their new empire. The city was, according to contemporary writings, very imposing, and of such great importance that the whole country was named after it (from the Arabic Marakush, through the Spanish Marruecos, to the English Morocco). When discussing early Almoravid buildings we are in many cases really talking about fortifications, such as the fortresses of Banu Tuada and Amargu in the Riff Mountains and the fortifications at Tasghimut, which lies some 19 miles (30 kilometers) southeast of Marrakech on a plateau. However, much building activity began under the charismatic ruler Yusuf ibn Tashfin (1060–1106) and was concentrated mainly on the capital. Yusuf ibn Tashfin had

a fortified palace built in Marrakech, which in Arabic sources is described as "Dar al-Hajar," ("House of Stone"). Because ordinary buildings were generally built of compressed clay, we can conclude that the palace was a prestigious structure. After Yusuf ibn Tashfin had given up the palace, the three succeeding Almohad rulers actually went on to use it as a residence and also carried out extensive building alterations. At a later period there was a graveyard on this site, which covered over the combined heritage of the Almoravids and the Almohads.

Almoravid religious buildings in the Maghreb

The political and military reputation of Yusuf ibn Tashfin continued to grow. In 1080/81 the Almoravids conquered the central Maghreb and took the city of Tlemcen, which lies in Algeria on the border with Morocco. The very next year the leader ordered the construction of the Great Mosque of Tlemcen (1082) and shortly after that had built the Great Mosque of Nedroma (1086) close to Tlemcen, which in its turn was to exert a considerable influence on the Great Mosque of Algiers (1096), whose foundation also belongs to the Almoravid period. In 1086 Yusuf ibn Tashfin penetrated into al-Andalus with a well-equipped army and took the cities of Granada and Seville in southern Spain, before returning to the Maghreb and capturing the important city of Fez. Through these conquests he had decisively consolidated his power on both sides of the Straits of Gibraltar, establishing himself as ruler in equal measure over the Maghreb and al-Andalus.

A view over Marrakech
Yusuf ibn Tashfin, the first Almoravid ruler, founded the city of Marrakech in 1062 and laid out the great palm grove, but then handed over the further development of the city to his son. Marrakech remained the capital of the empire under the Almohads and is one of the four royal cities of Morocco, alongside Rabat, Fez, and Meknes. It is still a fascinating city today because of its African character and its surviving medieval buildings.

View up the long nave in the prayer hall of the Great Mosque of Tlemcen, founded 1082
The foundation of the mosque dates back to a Yusuf ibn Tashfin and was completed a few years later by his son and successor Ali ibn Yusuf. The stereoscopic alignment of the horseshoe arches gives the narrow prayer hall an impression of depth and breadth, an effect typical not only of 12th-century Almoravid mosques but one which is still popular in the architecture of the Maghreb today.

Dome of the Great Mosque of Tlemcen
The construction of the ribbed dome rests on a series of multiple arches, which can be seen at the foot of the dome base. The three-way arches in the corners conceal squinches, which lead up from the rectangular ground plan of the area before the *mihrab* to the polygonal base of the dome. The squinches are crowned with little stalactite vaults, their first recorded use in the Maghreb. The slender ribs, which begin from the side over the triple arches, intersect many times, creating a large many-pointed star at the apex of the dome.

The Great Mosque of Tlemcen

Despite the political importance of the Almoravids, which was very closely linked to the personality of Yusuf ibn Tashfin (1060–1106), only a small number of buildings from their era have survived. The foundation of the Great Mosque of Tlemcen (1082) demonstrably dates back to that period, even though it underwent substantial alterations under his son and successor Ali ibn Yusuf (1106–1143). Today it is situated beside a splendid boulevard and catches the eye because of its minaret, whose facades are richly decorated. Immediately next to the minaret lies the entrance to the mosque courtyard, which is surrounded on all sides by arcades and where the visitor is tempted to linger in its stillness. In the prayer hall, the central aisle leading to the *mihrab* is somewhat wider than the other side aisles. This emphasis on the central aisle serves primarily to direct the eye towards the *mihrab*, which gives the direction of prayer to Mecca and thus constitutes the most important element of the mosque. By the time the Great Mosque of Cordoba, the most important mosque in western Islam, was built (785/786), the concept of emphasizing the central aisle to the *mihrab* through its width and decoration was already well established, and so the "oriented" mosque, which became obligatory for all later mosques in both al-Andalus and the Maghreb, came into being. The *mihrab* of the Great Mosque of Tlemcen is in fact inspired on that of the Great Mosque of Cordoba (in al-Hakam II's extension of 962–966), with its horseshoe-shaped opening and its polygonal niche. The *mihrab* facade also takes after the same model, with its central horseshoe arches, a rectangular *alfiz* frame, a decorative frieze to finish it off, and an arcade suggested by the use of false arches, even though stucco alone was used for decoration in Tlemcen. The vegetal shapes here, however, are smaller and more delicate, as is the case with comparable works for the caliph in Cordoba, and, moreover, they are carved in a rich variety of forms. The great dome above the area before the *mihrab*, which also quite specifically emphasizes the location of the *mihrab* area, is another

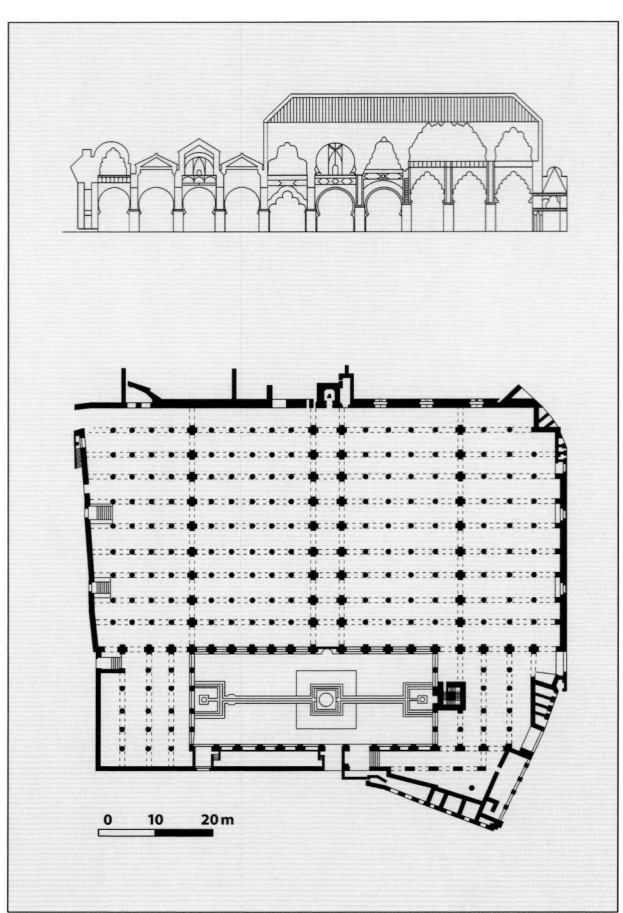

parallel with the Great Mosque of Cordoba. Another dome at the height of the second span of the central aisle serves the same purpose, accentuating the longitudinal axis of the mosque oriented towards the *mihrab*. While the area before the *mihrab* in the Great Mosque of Cordoba (in al-Hakam II's extension) is vaulted with a large dome decorated with gold mosaic, in Tlemcen there is a somewhat higher ribbed dome, covered with stucco. The ribs of this dome intersect, forming areas filled with openwork stucco decoration, whose vegetal ornamentation shows a clearly Andalusian influence. The fine leaf and flower paintings are reminiscent of comparable motifs on the stucco panels of the Aljafería of Saragossa (1049/50–1082/83), that famous palace which, with its outstanding artistic decoration, is an exceptional example of 11th-century Spanish *taifa* art. The building of the Aljafería of Saragossa was completed at roughly the time when work on the Great Mosque of Tlemcen was begun. As a result of this, we can infer that Andalusian artists moved into the Maghreb after the local *taifa* courts could offer them no further appropriate commissions. This way, Spanish-Islamic art forms were conveyed to the Maghreb, where they met with an immediate echo in Almoravid art.

The Qarawiyin Mosque in Fez

When Ali ibn Yusuf (1106–1143) succeeded to the throne in Marrakech on the death of his father, he ordered to be built not just a palace but also a Great Mosque in the capital, which, however, was razed to the ground with the invasion of the Almohads (1147). It was different in Fez: in the complex maze of the Souk stands the venerable Qarawiyin Mosque, which was founded as early as the middle of the 9th century by immigrants from Kairouan and for that reason was named after them. But, to concentrate on the Almoravid period of

View of the courtyard, ground plan, and cross section of the Qarawiyin Mosque in Fez, started mid-9th century
In the middle of the 12th century, the Qarawiyin Mosque was extended by the Almoravids into one of the largest mosques of its time and developed into one of the most important universities of the Maghreb. Its ground plan dates essentially from the Almoravid building period (1135–1142). The elongated prayer hall has 21 aisles, which run at right angles to the *qibla* wall. The central aisle is somewhat higher and wider than the side aisles and is, in addition, adorned with a whole series of domes. One exceptional feature is the variety of the dome designs, which are shown on the cross section.

building (1135–1142), Ali ibn Yusuf ordered that the prayer hall, which already contained 18 aisles, be extended to 21 aisles, so that it measured 270 × 145 feet (83 × 44.2 meters) and increased its surface area to 39,000 square feet (3,668 square meters). Thus the Qarawiyin Mosque in Fez became one of the largest contemporary mosques in the Maghreb. What is more, the enormous impression of space within the mosque is emphasized by the slender architecture and the light coloring of the prayer hall. The central aisle, raised in height during the Almoravid building phase, is decorated with five *muqarnas* vaults, which accentuate the longitudinal axis of the mosque and draw the eye of the visitor towards the *mihrab*. The *muqarnas* or stalactite vaults constitute a real innovation in building decoration for the Almoravid period. Apart from the Qarawiyin Mosque in Fez, Almoravid *muqarnas* domes can only be found in the squinches of the great ribbed dome over the area before the *mihrab* in the Great Mosque of Tlemcen (founded 1082), and also in the Banu Hammad settlement in Algeria, which experienced its most flourishing period during the Almoravid era. The *muqarnas* vaults are not only fascinating for their fine handcrafted design but also for the refraction of light at their edges. So the visitor wanders along under numerous domes as far as the *mihrab*, the niche of which was adorned with new stucco decoration under Ali ibn Yusuf. It survived the

Almohad attack (1147) thanks to later temporary covering and has therefore remained largely unscathed to this day. The *mihrab* facade, on the other hand, was reworked several times in the following centuries.

The Almoravid pulpits

In connection with Almoravid mosques, mention should be made of the large wooden pulpits (*minbars*), which originally stood next to the *mihrab* and were used by the preacher of the mosque (the imam) for the Friday sermon. The *minbars* are in the form of a staircase, on which the imam would stand during the sermon, so that the believers could see him and his voice could be heard in a full prayer hall. The importance of the pulpits is shown by the fact that they were generally beautifully decorated. Apart from the pulpits of the Great Mosques of Tlemcen, Nedroma, and Algiers, those of the Great Mosque of Marrakech and the Qarawiyin Mosque of Fez are also notable. The *minbar* of the Great Mosque of Marrakech was commissioned by Ali ibn Yusuf between 1125 and 1130 from the workshops at Cordoba, which were already famous for their outstanding wood carving in the time of the caliphs of Cordoba (929–1031). This reputation was presumably based on the *minbar* of the Great Mosque at Cordoba, which has not survived. The *minbar* was known beyond the borders of the empire and admired for its exquisite marquetry work. Just as the Great Mosque of Cordoba had once been the spiritual center of the western Islamic empire, the Great Mosque of Marrakech was now to become the spiritual center of the Almoravid empire. It is therefore not surprising that the mosque was destroyed in the Almohad invasion (1147). The Almohads were, however, so impressed with the pulpit that they transferred it – perhaps out of respect for the heritage of the caliphs of Cordoba – into the Kutubiya Mosque they had erected in Marrakech (1146–1164), which now served as the principal mosque of the city.

The main attraction of this 13-foot (4-meter) high *minbar* is its fine marquetry work. The inlaid wooden panels show a pattern of intertwining bands, which is based on a framework of squares, in the center of which there are eight-pointed stars. The steps are decorated with arches, on the ground of which can be seen symmetrically arranged tendril patterns. The variety of these vegetal patterns suggests a whole school of wood carvers, who have together created this masterpiece. Some 1,000 wooden panels, which are decorated with exquisite carvings, have been fitted together in the pulpit to make a harmonious masterpiece. The tiny leafy tendrils on the individual panels recall the vegetal motifs on the marble dado panels of the Great Mosque of Cordoba's *mihrab*, dating from 956, so here one can observe the Cordoba caliphs' legacy in every detail.

A similar *minbar* is situated in the Qarawiyin Mosque in Fez. It is dated to the year 1144 by an inscription on one of its lateral arches and was therefore constructed a good 20 years later than the pulpit in Marrakech. Evidently numerous pulpits were commissioned in the 12th century, which have survived almost intact to the present day, thanks to the high esteem in which they were held and also to their extremely artistic handcrafted finish.

The Almoravid domed building in Marrakech

An unusual building dating from the Almoravid era stands in Marrakech. This is not, however, a palace or a mosque, but a domed building rather unprepossessing in size, which, presumably, was erected close to the former Almoravid principal mosque which no longer survives. Today it is situated in the Ibn Yusuf Madrasa quarter, which was erected in the middle of the 16th century by the Sadites. Since this Almoravid domed building was constructed over a well, it is assumed that it originally served as a hall for ritual ablutions. The Qubba al-

Barudiyin, named after its founder, dates from the reign of Ali ibn Yusuf (1106–1143). It is a cube-shaped building barely 26 feet (8 meters) high. The surfaces of the sides of the building are broken up on the two floors by differently shaped arches, whose models are to be seen in Spanish-Islamic art. So the multifoil arches derive their shapes from arches in the Great Mosque of Cordoba, while the arches with alternate concave and convex curved outlines – known as composite arches – refer to the lower arrangement of arches in the palace-mosque of the Aljafería in Saragossa (1049/50–1082/83). The effects of Spanish-Islamic *taifa* art is unmistakable in these "borrowings." On the other hand, the slightly heightened and pointed horseshoe arches may be described as typically Almoravid.

The building is surmounted by a dome, whose shell is decorated at the base with a ring of crossed horseshoe arches. Above them can be seen the outlines of stars, which, starting at the center of the dome, continue to the outside. The internal construction of the dome is interesting. From the rectangular ground plan of the building the spandrels, decorated with conspicuously large stucco

***Minbar* of the Kutubiya Mosque**, c. 1120, Marrakech, Badi Palace Museum
This Almoravid pulpit dates back to the time of Ali ibn Yusuf. It was produced in the workshops of Cordoba and installed by the Almohads in the Kutubiya Mosque, which they had built. During the Friday sermon, the imam would position himself halfway up the steps. This *minbar* is distinguished by its fine marquetry and represents a masterpiece of 12th-century Andalusian wood carving.

open arches in varied shapes, and its exquisite interior decoration. It has long been
presumed that the building served as a place
for ritual ablutions.

shells, lead up to the dome base, from which rise a series of crisscrossed arches forming the actual dome, which in turn is surmounted by a drum. The arches are vaguely reminiscent of comparable methods of dome construction at the Great Mosque of Cordoba (particularly in the Capilla de Villaviciosa), which were developed there in the 12th century. Stucco decoration, in addition, became more and more important. Thus the spandrels of the dome base are decorated internally with a ground of delicate leafy tendrils, which are reminiscent of comparable decorative stucco motifs on the Aljafería of Saragossa (second half of the 11th century), so that here also the Spanish-Islamic heritage is unmistakable. Ali ibn Yusuf demonstrably not only maintained commercial contacts with al-Andalus, but also engaged Andalusian craftsmen, through whom the traditions of the caliphate of Cordoba (929–1031) and the *taifa* kingdoms (1031–1091) continued to be passed on.

Almoravid architecture in Spain

Apart from a few stucco fragments in Cordoba, Granada, and Almeria, no buildings of the Almoravid period have survived in Spain itself. Based on this, one may assume that they were all destroyed during the conquest by the Almohads (1146). Also, the Almoravids had never become as important in al-Andalus as they were in the Maghreb, so one would expect less building activity.

Closely bound up with the Almoravid era is the loss of power of the *taifa* dynasties and the ending of this artistic period in Spain. The continual power struggles between the Almoravids and the *taifa* rulers caused a power vacuum to develop in the eastern part of Andalusia, which Muhammad ibn Mardanis

crisscrossed arches, which bear a large dome reminiscent in its form of the large dome of the area in front of the *mihrab* in the Great Mosque of Cordoba (in al-Hakam II's extension).

(1147–1172), who was descended from a Muwallad family, turned to his advantage by conquering the coastal city of Murcia and founding a self-governing state. This extended as far as the Atlantic coast towards Cadiz and expanded to include that city in the middle of the 12th century, making his territory larger by far than today's Andalusia. His rule only came to an end in 1172 with the advance of the Almohads.

The best-known building of this period is the Castillejo de Monteagudo outside Murcia, which rises from a fertile plain on a high plateau. This edifice, of which today only the foundations have survived, had been built of compressed clay and has a rectangular ground plan of about 200 × 124 feet (61 × 38 meters). It is presumed to have been some kind of country residence *(al-munya)* of Muhammad ibn Mardanis. If one approaches the site from the north, one enters a garden subdivided into the shape of a cross. On the short sides of the garden are two pools of water, aligned axially one to the other. The garden and the spaces it surrounds are enclosed within an outer wall, which is divided up by numerous towers. The models for this central garden site can clearly be seen in the architecture of the former caliphal residence at Medina al-Zahra (936–1010) near Cordoba, for example in the palace complex known as the "House with Pools." The ground plan, with its straight spaces and rectangular towers, refers to the palace of La Zisa at Palermo in the south of Italy, which has a comparable underlying division of space. La Zisa in Palermo was constructed in the middle of the 12th century by the Normans, who ruled southern Italy at the time. They maintained a trading relationship with Spain and were also very heavily influenced by Islamic art and culture.

With the excavation of the monastery of Santa Clara la Real in Murcia it was possible to uncover the foundations of a palace comparable to the Castillejo de Monteagudo. These permitted the reconstruction of a cruciform site with a central pavilion, which has been dated to the middle of the 12th century. It is regarded as a town residence of Muhammad ibn Mardanis, which, according to historical sources, was called Dar al-Sugra ("Small Palace"). The site of this urban palace was entirely covered in buildings in the first half of the 13th century. It was possibly Emir Hud al-Mutawakkil (1228–1238) who carried out this construction: he successfully resisted the Almohads in Murcia. In the course of the excavation, a considerable number of stucco fragments with geometric, vegetal, and calligraphic motifs were found. The finding of some painted stucco fragments, which evidently belonged to a *muqarnas* dome that has not survived, caused a particular sensation. Especially well known is the representation of a female flautist, which is captivating as much through its elegantly curved lines as through its vivid coloring. Since up to now no further similar figural wall paintings from al-Andalus or the Maghreb are known, this stucco fragment represents a unique find in spite of its modest size. With the female flautist, the stylistic similarities are striking with the figural motifs of a *muqarnas* dome in the Cappella Palatina in Palermo, which originated from about the same time. Evidently there were not only flourishing commercial contacts between al-Andalus and Sicily in the middle of the 12th century: besides the export of silks there were also cultural exchanges.

The Almohads in the Maghreb

With the victory of the Almohads in the Maghreb (Marrakech was captured in 1147) a new cultural era began. In Tinmal in the High Atlas Mountains, the Berber leader Ibn Tumart had founded the Almohad movement, which was important in both religious and political terms and within a few years spread throughout the Maghreb and into al-Andalus. It was characterized by a particularly strict and ascetic interpretation of Islam, which not only determined their politics but was also expressed in their sacred buildings, which in accordance with their religious doctrine were very simple. Behind the great Almohad mosques lay a standard architectural plan, which provided for a multiple-aisled prayer hall and a rectangular forecourt. The central aisle oriented towards the *mihrab* (in the "oriented" type of mosque) was given a higher status than the

other side aisles of the mosque by being wider and having special decoration. The transept running parallel to the *qibla* wall, where the believers stood in rows for prayer, is distinctive because of its decorative form, as for example the use of special arch shapes in this area or the elaboration of domes in chosen places in the transept. This transept joins the central aisle to form a T, and is thus referred to as a T-plan. It is characteristic of all Almohad mosques. Since the Almohad doctrine was regarded as "inviolable," it tolerated no deviations. This also explains why they adhered strictly to a standard architectural plan, which remained obligatory for all Almohad mosques. Apart from mosques, the Almohads also founded various Islamic fortified monasteries, such as the Ribat of Tit, which lies some 7.5 miles (12 kilometers) southeast of Mazagan (today's Mulai Abdallah), or the important Almohad *ribat* from which developed the city of Rabat, the modern capital of Morocco. Fortifications were added by the Almohads to the most important cities, and can still be seen at least in part in Fez, Marrakech, and Rabat, as well as in Taza (Algeria) and Seville. Reference should also be made to the monumental Almohad city gates at Fez and Marrakech, which have survived in all their simplicity to the present day.

Mosque of Tinmal, founded 1153/54
The mosque lies 100 km (60 miles) southeast of Marrakech in the High Atlas Mountains and was established in memory of Muhammad ibn Tumart, founder of the Almohad movement, which started from Tinmal. This simple mosque, which survives today as little more than a ruin, may be viewed as the forerunner of all Almohad mosques, with its multiple-aisled hall oriented towards the *qibla* wall and the mosque forecourt.

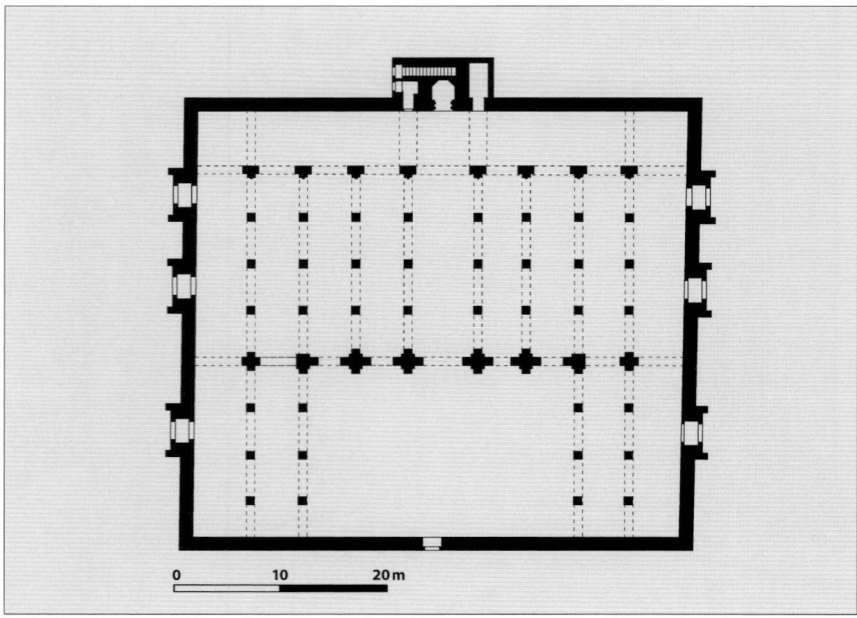

View from the forecourt and ground plan of the Mosque of Tinmal, founded 1153/54
The prayer hall of the mosque consists of nine aisles, which all run at right angles to the qibla wall. The longitudinal axis oriented towards the mihrab is accentuated by the large horseshoe arch over the central entrance, while there are somewhat smaller pointed arches which runs over the side entrances. The transept parallel to the qibla wall forms a T with the widened central aisle, and is the basis for the so-called T-plan.

The Mosque of Tinmal – the prototype of all Almohad mosques

One of the oldest mosques of the Almohad era is the Mosque of Taza (Algeria), which was founded in 1142 by Abd al-Mumin, a follower of and later the successor to Ibn Tumart. This mosque, which covers an area of 200 × 137 feet (61 × 42 meters), consists of a rectangular prayer hall and forecourt. Within the prayer hall the simple architecture is impressive, with its elegantly curved horseshoe arches combined with the subdued lighting, giving the space a warm glow. The central aisle, directed towards the *mihrab,* is somewhat wider than the other aisles and is, in addition, distinguished by special stucco decoration, some of the pillars being adorned with friezes of geometric ornamentation. Apart from the *mihrab* facade this is the only decoration in an otherwise very simple prayer hall. The tendency, already mentioned briefly here, to favor abstract geometric decoration was to develop in Almohad art, becoming a feature that left its mark on the style.

Comparable to the Mosque of Taza is the basic construction of the Mosque of Tinmal, which was founded in 1153/54 in memory of the work of Muhammad ibn Tumart (d. 1130), leader and founder of the Almohads. Set in the High Atlas Mountains some 63 miles (100 kilometers) southeast of the capital Marrakech, the village of Tinmal originally formed the spiritual center of the early Almohad movement. The memorial mosque which survives today simply as a ruin is captivating for its unique setting in the High Atlas. Covering an area 150 × 141 feet (46.4 × 43.5 meters), the mosque has a rectangular prayer hall, which in turn has a similarly shaped forecourt, enclosed on three sides by arcades. The prayer hall and forecourt are surrounded by a crenellated wall as fortification. The main entrance to the mosque is located on the northern side of the surrounding wall and there are other smaller side entrances to the west and east. A single minaret, relatively short and shaped like a tower, rises from the center of the south-oriented *qibla* wall directly behind the *mihrab* and further underlines the defensive character of this ruined mosque, which has now been extensively restored.

The prayer hall of the mosque is divided into nine aisles, the central one of which is oriented towards the *mihrab* and is clearly wider than the other side aisles (this is an "oriented" type of mosque). A transept runs parallel to the *qibla* wall, which is accentuated by an arcade consisting of multifoil arches. The central area in front of the *mihrab* and both the outer corner areas of the transept are adorned with suspended conical arches and surmounted by *muqarnas* vaults, which further accentuate the transept. The central aisle forms a T with the transept, a characteristic feature of the T-plan, which is typical of the whole of 12th-century Almohad religious architecture.

Even if the Mosque of Tinmal exists today merely as a ruin, the building is still impressive for the austerity of its construction and the simple elegance of its arches, whose shadows are cast onto the light sand floor in the gleaming sunlight, while the multifoil arches that still survive today make an impressive reference to the magnificent *mihrab* facade. The Mosque of Tinmal was to be regarded as a sure model for the character of other mosques, as much in its ground plan and outline as in its architectural style. In this context, reference should be made to the two Kutubiya Mosques built in Marrakech. These were erected in what was at that time the souk (market) of the booksellers and are therefore named after them.

The two Kutubiya Mosques in Marrakech

The model of a nine-aisle mosque following the prototype in Tinmal, with an obviously wider central aisle directed towards the *mihrab*, a distinct transept at right angles to the *qibla* wall, and outer aisles opening onto the shorter sides of the forecourt, was adopted and extended here in the Kutubiya Mosques. This was already evident in the initial building phase of the "first" Kutubiya Mosque (1147), surviving today only in its foundations, which the Almohads chose to be the principal mosque of the city. This edifice was over 293 feet (90 meters)

Colonnade of the Kutubiya Mosque in Marrakech, from 1147
The simple interior design of the so called "second" Kutubiya Mosque is striking in its simple elegance and the numerous views it offers through its horseshoe arches. The only ornamentation to be seen is the large multifoil arch at the beginning of the courtyard arcade, which impressively frames the seemingly unendless row of arches. The silhouettes of the arches appear especially beautiful when they are accentuated by the sunlight falling through the courtyard.

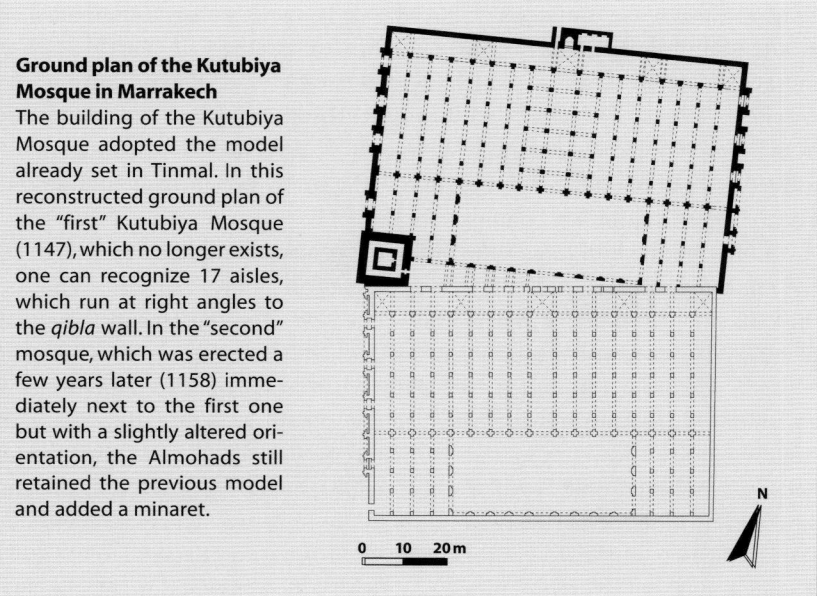

Ground plan of the Kutubiya Mosque in Marrakech
The building of the Kutubiya Mosque adopted the model already set in Tinmal. In this reconstructed ground plan of the "first" Kutubiya Mosque (1147), which no longer exists, one can recognize 17 aisles, which run at right angles to the *qibla* wall. In the "second" mosque, which was erected a few years later (1158) immediately next to the first one but with a slightly altered orientation, the Almohads still retained the previous model and added a minaret.

0   10   20m

N

long and nearly 188 feet (58 meters) deep, and consisted of 17 aisles, the outer four of which were extended beyond the north arcade, which is angled towards the courtyard. This "first" Kutubiya Mosque was razed to the ground by the Almohads. It is possible that they were unable to make the necessary small correction to the orientation of the mosque towards Mecca in accordance with their strict religious understanding and therefore decided to demolish the building. All the same, the Kutubiya Mosque is the principal mosque in Marrakech representing the Almohad empire. A few years later (1158) a "second" Kutubiya Mosque was constructed next to the "first". By this time, the orientation towards Mecca had now been slightly adjusted and a minaret added. This "second" mosque has since then become a symbol of the city.

Great Almohad minarets

The minaret of the Kutubiya Mosque of Marrakech stands on a (40-foot) 12.5-meter square base and reaches a height of 67.5 meters (220 feet). A ramp inside leads up over seven domed floors to the platform. The square body of the minaret is surmounted by a lantern-shaped upper section, on which there is a dome decorated with a minaret crown *(yamur)* in the form of three golden spheres. The sides of the minaret are broken at most floors with pairs of windows, which are framed with blind arches. An arcade of blind arches forms the upper section of the minaret, the curves of which are elongated beyond the points of the arches so that they intersect to form a grid, which is described as a *sebka* ornament. Over the *sebka* pattern stretches a broad band of masonry, which was once adorned with glazed Turkish tiles, some of which have survived to this day. They form a colorful focus to the otherwise very simple minaret.

Two further great Almohad minarets with comparable design are particularly worthy of mention. They are the minaret, known today as the Giralda, of the former principal mosque of Seville (1172–1198), and the Hasan Tower (1195–1196) of Rabat. While the minaret of the Kutubiya Mosque of Marrakech is chiefly remarkable for its elegance and simplicity, the decoration of the 260-foot (80-meter) Giralda is extended to the point where the *sebka* ornament, which was seen as the uppermost band of ornamentation at the top of the Kutubiya minaret. Here it stands out as a pattern covering the whole surface. Inside the Giralda, there are ramps instead of stairs leading up so that, during construction, stones, columns, and capitals could be carried up by mule. Apart from that, the ramps also made the climb up much easier. In the late 16th century a baroque belfry was added to the former minaret, which today serves as bell tower for the Cathedral of Seville. The balcony-like balustrades in front of the arched openings to the minaret also date from this time. The Giralda has on its summit a bronze figure of Fides almost 13 feet (4 meters) high, now looking out over Seville with a self-confident smile as a symbol of the Christian faith.

The third important great Almohad minaret is the Hasan Tower in Rabat (1195–1196) – the unfinished minaret of the equally incomplete Hasan Mosque, which was built under the rule of Yaqub al-Mansur on the outskirts of the city. The minaret stands on a 52-foot (16-meter) square base and it is thought that it could have been intended to reach a height of 260 feet (80 meters). Today's building is impressive because of the coloring of its weathered cut stone and its discreet molded embellishments. While the ground level is intended just to be a base for the minaret and has a horseshoe arch entrance as its only decoration, the second section is adorned with inset blind arches. In the third section of the minaret as it survives today, one can see a triangular blind arcade of multifoil arches, over which is an area covered with a braided pattern, the geometric structure of which is reminiscent of the *sebka* pattern of the Giralda in Seville. This can be confirmed by comparison with the decoration on numerous Moroccan minarets, so that it is possible to conclude that the influence on minaret construction in the Maghreb of the ornamentation on the Hasan Tower should not be underestimated.

Although the building of the mosque was never completed and, apart from the imposing minaret, only the stone pillars of the prayer hall still stand today, these seemingly endless rows are still impressive. Was the mosque never completed perhaps because this building project had been too ambitious? The Great Mosque of Cordoba (founded 755–756), which was extended many times over a period of three centuries and provided the sole spiritual center for the western Islamic empire and its thousands of believers, after its last and most comprehensive extension under al-Mansur (987–988), including prayer hall and courtyard, attained 569 × 417 feet (175.02 × 128.41 meters). The Hasan Mosque in Rabat, however, surpassed even these measurements with its 585 × 453 feet (180 × 139.4 meters)! Did the Almohads, with the construction of the Hasan

Kutubiya Mosque of Marrakech, from 1158
The Kutubiya Mosque was chosen by the Almohads to be the principal mosque of the city, the spiritual and administrative center of their empire, transferring its outstanding importance to the Almohad dynasty. Its slender yet still visible minaret is 67.6 meters high, 12.5 meters square, and has since its construction become a symbol of Marrakech. This square edifice is surmounted by a lantern-shaped top section. The minaret has pairs of windows on most floors. Particularly striking are the intersecting arches, described as *sebka* ornamentation, on the top section.

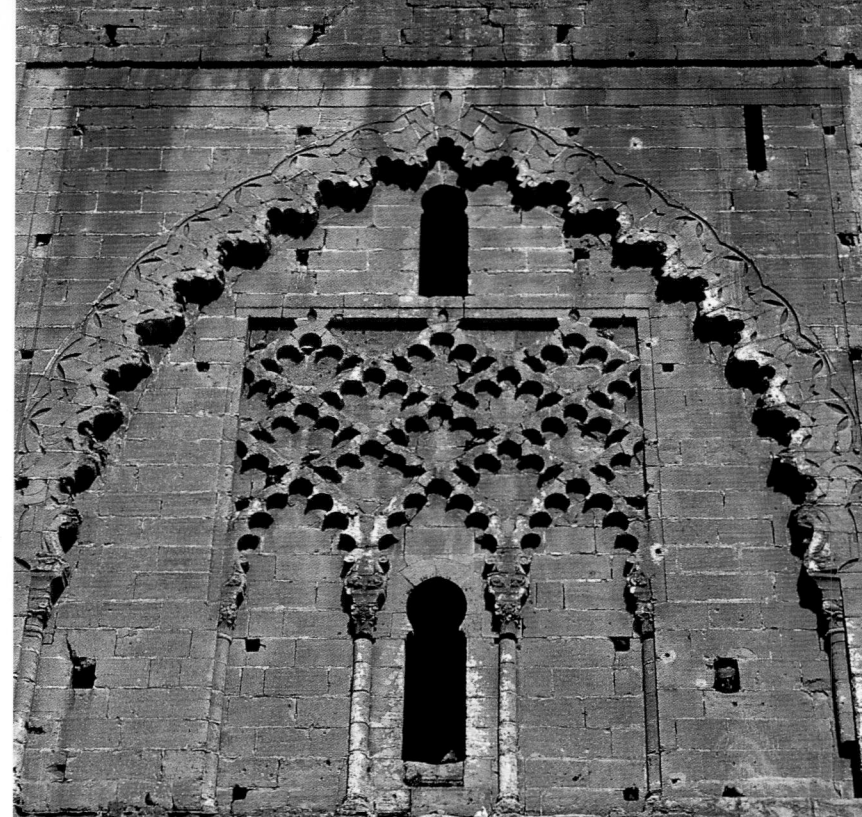

View and detail of the Hasan Tower in Rabat, 1195/96

The Hasan Tower in Rabat is the unfinished minaret of the equally incomplete Hasan Mosque in Rabat, which is impressive mainly because of its imposing dimensions and its seemingly endless rows of stone pillars. The minaret itself has a 16-meter square base and might have been intended to reach a height of about 80 meters. The blind arcades (above) that adorn the facade of the minaret show a particularly fine example of intersecting multifoil arches. This filigree decoration contrasts with the solid form of the building.

Mosque, want to outshine even the Great Mosque of Cordoba, which was itself still viewed in the 12th century as a powerful symbol of the Spanish Umayyad caliphate which had by then come to an end? Had the Almohads not claimed the title of caliph just like the Spanish Umayyads and thus given notice that they sought to assume their power or even attempt to surpass them? It is obvious that the colossal dimensions of the Hasan Mosque in Rabat were out of all proportion to the population density of the city at that time and that this colossal unfinished mosque may perhaps be interpreted as exceptional evidence of the power of a single, extremely ambitious ruler, Yaqub al-Mansur (d. 1199).

The Almohad settlement of Cieza

Apart from mosques and palaces, the Almohads also built numerous fortified installations, such as the fortresses of Badajoz and Cacéres in Extremadura or the Alcazar of Jerez de la Frontera in Andalusia. Research on settlements which might give information about the daily lives of their inhabitants has begun in the last few years, and excavations in the Andalusian villages of Saltés, Sénes and Cieza bear testament to this. The settlement of Cieza was founded by the Almohads towards the end of the 12th century in the region of Murcia and was abandoned in the middle of the 13th century with the conquest of the city by the Christians (1243). The walls exposed by Julio Navarro Palazon in the 1980s during excavations show a site with dwellings separated from each other by alleyways. Up to the present, 18 houses have been excavated, which are all alike as regards their layout. Built of compressed clay and subsequently plastered with lime, they usually have a large inner courtyard, around which are grouped the living quarters and workrooms, as had been customary in the whole of the Mediterranean area since ancient times. These traditional ways of living continued in Islamic culture over a period of centuries, as is confirmed at Cieza. The courtyard formed the center of family life. Almost every house in Cieza had a kitchen and a well; in addition, considerable finds of domestic pottery were made, which confirms the use of these buildings as dwellings. It is noticeable that each house had stucco decoration, even if it was perhaps only a matter of a single beautiful archway, which in many cases can be assigned to the Almohad era. There are, however, other houses in the same settlement, whose stucco and arch shapes refer to the early Nasrid period of the 13th century, which reached its peak of perfection with the building of the Alhambra in Granada.

Almohad mosques and palaces in Spain

Within a few years the religious movement of the strictly devout Almohads seized not only the whole of Morocco but also al-Andalus, where Seville was chosen as the capital city and as the preferred residence of Yaqub al-Mansur, all of which is demonstrated by, among other things, the amount of construction work in the city. The principal Almohad mosque, on the site of which the city's cathedral stands today, was the most important building: its minaret has not only stood the test of time but has become a symbol of Seville. Two arcades have survived from the old mosque courtyard, which is known today as the "Orange Tree Courtyard" on account of the planting there. Other than this, the Almohad city wall, which in the 12th century encircled the whole city, is worthy of note. The line of the wall can still be traced today, since its route is followed by a major ring road.

In front of the gates of the city, on the banks of the Guadalquivir ("Great River"), lay the harbor, where there is still a fortified tower, dating from Almohad times, which was originally linked to the city walls. Because it was formerly decorated with gleaming golden-glazed tiles, this is known as the "Golden Tower" (Spanish: Torre del Oro). Similarly to the Giralda, it has become a symbol of the city. On the opposite bank of the Guadalquivir stood a tower similar in construction and known as the "Silver Tower" (Spanish: Torre del la Plata). It was originally connected to the "Golden Tower" by a chain, in order to control the entry of ships into the harbor.

Near the "Golden Tower" the residential quarter with its palaces extended towards the center of the city. The only one of all the Almohad city palaces to survive to the present day is that known as the "Patio de Yeso" ("Plaster or Stucco Courtyard") in the district of the Christian Alcazar, which, standing in its own grounds, dates back mainly to the time of King Pedro III, "The Cruel," of Aragon (1276–1285). This monarch was a great admirer of Islamic architecture, so it is not surprising that not only did he spare the Almohad palace but was even able deliberately to integrate it into his new residence. The "Patio de Yeso" occupies an elongated site with a central pond and palace buildings at the sides, one wing of which has survived. This has a long rectangular hall with a portico in front, whose tripartite facade is richly decorated with arches. The design of the palace facade is impressive because of the austerity of its structure and also the elegance of the open leaf-shaped arches.

Another palace dating from the Almohad era has survived in the neighborhood of the Alcazar in one of the city's administrative buildings, whose inner courtyard is known as the "Patio de Contratación." The name "Casa de Contratación" (Commercial Exchange) is found in documents of the 16th

century, when goods for trade with the "New World" were handled in the building. Within the courtyard are parts of an Almohad palace, which date from the end of the 12th century. The central part of the site forms a cruciform garden with a raised footpath and a fountain in the middle. The garden is flanked on the shorter sides by palace buildings, which are relatively well preserved on the south side. There is an elongated hall with a portico in front, the facade of which is richly adorned with arches. A portico with similar decoration has survived on the northern courtyard facade opposite.

The cruciform courtyard and garden site of the "Patio de Contratación" is reminiscent of the High Garden of the palace-city of Medina al-Zahra at Cordoba, the caliph's residence (936–1010), which has left its mark on the architecture in al-Andalus throughout the centuries. The palace buildings flanking the garden, on the other hand, refer in their design to the Aljafería of Saragossa (1049/50–1082/83), that *taifa* palace cited as representative of 11th-century Spanish Islamic architecture, while the facade decoration of the "Patio de Contratación" resembles the nearby "Patio de Yeso". It appears that the Almohad rulers not only followed the model of Medina al-Zahra with their palace buildings but consciously developed the Spanish Islamic architectural tradition. Like the Spanish Umayyads of Cordoba they had also claimed the title of caliph for themselves and sought to adopt the heritage of the caliphs of Cordoba, which, among other things, also accounts for their adoption of the caliph's principles of design in palace architecture. This allowed more artistic freedom in decoration based on their private, frequently intimate, character than the strictly regimented religious architecture.

The influence of Almohad art on the Spanish Mudéjar style

The art of the Almohads exerted an influence on the art in the Christian north of Spain. The Castilian King Alfonso VIII (1158–1214) had chosen the Monastery of "Las Huelgas" near Burgos, founded in 1187, as the mausoleum for himself and his successors, whereby it became necessary to make numerous modifications. While the church and cloister are in the Cistercian style, the little cloister chapel, known as the "Capilla de las Claustrillas" (earlier: "Capilla de la Asunción") has stucco decoration that is close to Almohad art. Obviously this stucco work was carried out by craftsmen who had been trained in Almohad workshops. The population referred to them as Mudejars (from the Arabic *mudayyan*, "authorized to remain"), Moors who, from the 13th century, lived under Christian rule in Spain. This is all the more surprising when one bears in mind that King Alfonso VIII was a bitter opponent of the Almohads. He fought them in numerous battles, but consciously protected their art forms and even understood how to integrate them into Christian religious architecture in the Royal Monastery of "Las Huelgas."

The "Capilla de las Claustrillas" near the cloister has many Almohad stucco features. Among these are the large suspended conical arches in the entrance area and the small *muqarnas* vaults and the fine stucco decoration on both sides of it. The main room of the chapel is vaulted with a large ribbed dome of plaster, whose models in the caliph's buildings are self-evident. This very rare dome construction is all the more surprising since *muqarnas* domes are almost exclusively found in Almohad buildings. Perhaps it can be explained by the cooperation of various schools of craftsmen, who, among other things, also carried out the stucco work on the arches of the nearby cloister of San Fernando.

The influence of Almoravid and Almohad decorative styles can also be detected in the former synagogue in Toledo which is today the Church of Santa Maria la Blanca. The synagogue was built at the beginning of the 13th century in the Jewish quarter of the city and was subsequently converted into a Christian church at the beginning of the 15th century. From the original site it is not entirely clear whether this synagogue is identical with the New Synagogue which was built at the beginning of the 13th century by Yosef ben Salomon ben Susan (d. 1203 or 1205). He was "Patriarch of the Castilian Jews" and senior tax collector for King Alfonso VIII. This building may also possibly be the Great Synagogue of Toledo, which was built by a certain Abraham ben al-Fahar, who held a senior position at Alfonso VIII's court. Neither of these hypotheses has been able to be confirmed convincingly via research on only partly surviving documents, but a reference to the government of Alfonso VIII, who had had such a distinct influence on the design of the Capilla de las Claustrillas in the Royal Monastery of "Las Huelgas" near Burgos, is common to them both.

With an unprepossessing exterior, the Toledo synagogue's interior is surprising, with its light and wide impression of space. Five parallel longitudinal aisles indicate a basilica structure, inspired by Christian religious architecture, since a similar division of space can be found in various Mudejar churches in Toledo, as for instance in the 12th-century Church of Santiago del Arrabel. The simple architecture of Santa Maria la Blanca with its wide horseshoe arches is enriched with some fine stucco decoration, which extends right up to the roof and clearly betrays its Islamic character.

The stucco work sprouts above the capitals into the arcade spandrels, where there are medallions adorned with geometrical ornaments flanked by elegantly curved arabesques. Over them stretches a frieze with elongated rectangular and square fields, in which appears a molded Venus shell, placed immediately above

Patio de Yeso, Seville, 2nd half of the 12th century
In the precincts of the Christian Alcázar of Seville is the Almohad palace called the Patio de Yeso ("Plaster or Stucco Courtyard"), one wing of which with a portico entrance still survives.

The facade of the courtyard is richly decorated with arches. In the center one can see a large pointed arch, whose archivolt is made up of little branches with leaves, which show the characteristic arch profile of Almohad art, hence the description "suspended equilateral arch."

Alcázar, Seville
Built by Peter I, "The Cruel" of Castile (1530 –1369) as a royal residence, the Alcázar is considered today to be one of the most beautiful Mudéjar palaces in Spain. The arches of its large courtyard, which dates back to

the 14th century display clear islamic forms of decoration, while the gallery above was constructed during the 16th century and therefore exhibits the style of the Renaissance.

Right: **Interior of the Church of Santa Maria la Blanca in Toledo**, 1st half of the 13th century
This former synagogue, which was transformed into a church in the 15th century, is fascinating because of its impression of wide space and its fine stucco decoration, whose geometric ornamentation and curved arabesques clearly betray an Almohad character. The capitals, on the other hand, refer to the Mudejar style, which reached its height of perfection in Toledo.

the medallions. In both the side aisles there is a gallery with blind multifoil arches over the frieze, while in the central aisle the decoration, because of the height of the space, becomes somewhat more extensive. There one can see a broad band with network ornamentation, over which extends a further, narrower frieze, on which is a gallery of blind multifoil arches. This broad band of the central aisle with its geometric decoration can in particular be classified stylistically in the tradition of the Almohads, while the elegantly curved arabesques on the sides of the medallions hint at a somewhat further advanced stage of development, which already appears to refer to the Nasrid art of Granada. It is evident that there existed at the court of Alfonso VIII at the beginning of the 13th century an artistic workshop which brought Almohad art forms from Andalusia and North Africa to Castile, where they were to find an echo over the centuries in Mudejar art. Strangely enough, both of these masterpieces of Almohad stucco work are not situated in a mosque, but in a chapel and a synagogue – a fact which bears witness to the former artistic and cultural interchange between Christians, Jews, and Muslims in the Iberian Peninsula.

Decorative Arts
Almut von Gladiss

Art under the Almoravids and the Almohads

Under the Almoravids and the Almohads, the western Mediterranean countries formed a unified economic area, which benefited from a strong gold standard. The dynasties controlled the trade routes to the famous gold mines in the western Sudan and the Andalusian port cities developed to become popular

Banner, 1st half of the 13th century, 3.3 × 2.2 meters, Burgos, Monasterio de S. Maria la Real de Huelgas, Museo de Telas Medievales
This banner is associated with the decisive Battle of Las Navas de Tolosa, where in 1212 the Muslim armies suffered a crushing defeat by the armies of Castile, Navarre, and Aragon under Alfonso VIII of Castile. The star pattern uses ideas from contemporary Koran illumination. Quotations from the Koran (Sura 16. 10–12) promote the holy war and promise Paradise to the warrior-believers.

trade centers for the gold trade to western and central Europe. As we learn from literary sources, the merchants traveled unhindered between the Christian north and the Islamic south, from Santiago de Compostela and Léon to Valencia and Seville. The most important trade was in Andalusian silk, which, in spite of competition from Byzantine products, proved itself to be a reliable mainstay of Andalusian economic power. Almeria, Murcia, Malaga, Valencia, and Seville all flourished to become famous centers for silk. According to a description by the geographer al-Idrisi, who traveled around Spain in the middle of the 12th century, the leading silk city of Almeria had 800 weaving mills, which to some extent at least used fully equipped drawlooms with sufficient leading frames to create a variable weave using field and pattern.

Textiles

Al-Idrisi mentions complicated patterns with figured medallions, which have precursors in the time of the caliphs. They competed with medallion fabrics from Baghdad, as is shown by an inscription on a silk fragment from the grave of San Pedro de Osma: "This was made in Baghdad. May God protect the city." The falsification of inscriptions was apparently common practice, in order to raise the value of an article, because we hear about a ban on them from a market inspector, al-Saqati of Malaga. In the case of the silk fragment, the type of weaving and the style of the sphinx medallions definitely indicate al-Andalus as the manufacturing area. An eastern Islamic mirror-image forms the basis of the principal motif, as this design was widely distributed in the 12th century, perhaps as far as the western Islamic countries. Other medallion fabrics show pairs of griffins or lions, which, like the pair of sphinxes, appear as mirror-images beside a Tree of Life, which more often than not is reduced to a palm leaf motif.

The cloak of San Juan de Ortega (d. 1163), from the parish church of Qintanaortuno, forms the basis for dating. This relic bears an Arabic inscription with the name of the Almoravid Ali ibn Yusuf (1106–1143). The artists were evidently entrusted with the traditional power symbols, for pairs of lions appear, with small prey animals, probably gazelles, under their front legs. The sultan suffered several severe defeats by Alfonso VII of Castile, who temporarily occupied Almeria in 1147 and donated to the Cathedral of Sigüenza two silk fabrics taken from there as booty, one with griffin and the other with eagle medallions. From this same period also comes the tunic of his son Don García, who died young, which features large double-headed eagles with lines of Arabic writing.

Under the Almohads, art began to reflect on the spiritual principles of Islam, and the figured patterns with their symbolic references were increasingly superseded by abstract systems of ornamentation. Geometric patterns on bands and fields, and the principle of composition involving the endless repetition of patterns corresponded to and explained the orderliness with which the world was arranged by Allah. Sultan Abu Yusuf Yaqub (1184–1199) had the gold and silver garments from the state wardrobe sold off and forbade women to wear silks or richly embroidered garments, since, according to the teachings of the Koran, luxury was only to be permitted in Paradise. Gold threads, which in Andalusia up to that time had consisted of thin strips of leather painted gold, began to be replaced by yellow silk. Gold, on the other hand, was hoarded in large quantities, as is shown by a find of treasure on Mallorca with countless items of jewelry. The golden earrings from the hoard prove their orthodoxy through the prominent *basmala* ("In the Name of God, the Merciful, the Compassionate"), and the silver bracelets by the Hand of Fatima engraved as a symbol of belief.

The 10.7 × 7.2 foot (3.3 × 2.2 meter) banner from Las Navas de Tolosa, one of the most famous trophies of the Reconquista, which Fernando III donated to the Royal Monastery of Las Huelgas, displays a powerful eight-pointed star as its central ornament, which, together with the continually repeated set phrase *al-mulk* ("The Power") appears to be a national emblem with some magical symbolic force. In the borders are quoted encouraging Koranic verses applying to the desperate situation.

Under the Almoravids and the Almohads, who founded numerous religious buildings in Andalusia, religion formed a special source of power to support governmental order. Koran production was thus afforded correspondingly great importance. One of the earliest Koran manuscripts, originating in Malaga in 1106, has been preserved in the Royal Library of the Escorial as a unique example surviving on the Iberian Peninsula.

Manuscripts

The Koran manuscripts of the 12th and 13th centuries are almost without exception parchments of approximately square format, hardly any larger than 8 inches (20 centimeters) in size. The calligraphers wrote in the elegant miniature handwriting of the *andalusi*, in order to make economic use of the expensive parchment (which had been replaced by paper in the eastern Islamic countries). Besides the regularly recurring golden palmette leaves on the borders, magnificent ornamental pages at the beginning and end of the text emphasize the preciousness of the Holy Scripture. Among the standard motifs of the illuminators were star motifs surrounded by polygonal patterns. These were also converted into meticulous inlay work on the wooden boxes which served for holding writing materials. Cordoba, Malaga, Valencia, and Seville were the leading places for manuscript production, as mentioned in the colophons, often combined with a blessing for the Prophet Muhammad and his family.

At that time, the first Latin translation of the Koran was made on the orders of the Abbot of Cluny, Petrus Venerabilis. Books about the life of the Prophet, about the first Caliphs, and a discussion between a Muslim and a Christian (*al-kindi*) were also translated, so that the basic tenets of Islamic doctrine could be discussed by "unbelievers."

Via the Reconquista, Christians came into possession of complete Islamic libraries. In Toledo, the first city taken by the Christians, as early as 1085, because of the Convivencia, the friendly coexistence of Muslims, Jews, and Christians, there developed the famous Translation School. Scholars from all over Europe would meet there to translate Arabic texts from all parts of the Islamic world, philosophical works from antiquity and their interpretations, as well as the medical, mathematical, scientific, and esoteric literature of Islam, including many scientific works from al-Andalus, where medicine, mathematics, and astronomy flourished. First and foremost astronomers, who had come from the school of the mathematician Maslama al-Maghriti in Cordoba, earned a high reputation. The astrolabe makers Muhammad ibn al-Saffar and Ibrahim ibn Said al-Sahli were known for their numerous measuring instruments, al-Sahli also for globes of the heavens, while Ibn al-Zarqallu made his name with the astronomical tables of Toledo, later translated into Latin translations and available for all.

As in the other Islamic countries, manuscripts of miniature paintings were produced in al-Andalus, yet they were apparently particularly affected by the continual burning of books by Muslim fanatics, the final occurrence under the Almohads. The *Book of Bayad and Riyad*, presumably originating in Seville, with its 14 surviving miniatures, is one of the very earliest examples of Islamic

Medallion fabric, probably Andalusian, c.1100, Boston, Museum of Fine Arts
This medallion fabric, taken from the grave of Bishop Pedro de Osma (d. 1109) in the Cathedral of Burgo de Osma, shows two sphinxes as the principal motif, and a human figure between two griffins in the borders. In the intersecting circles that unite the pattern appears a Kufic inscription, calling Baghdad the place of production of the silk. The structure of the weave and the gold thread made from gilded leather wound around a silk core indicates, however, production in Andalusia, which copied imported fabrics from Baghdad.

In Andalusia and Morocco the Koran was written on expensive parchment up to the 14th century. The comparatively small manuscripts often contain magnificent decorative pages with braidwork developed from stars, its geometric rules mirroring the order of the cosmos. At the end of the manuscript there are details of the time and place the copy was made. Many Korans owe their survival solely to the fact that they were gathered together immediately after the collapse of the last Muslim state on the Iberian Peninsula. Two Koranic manuscripts in the possession of the statesman Johann Albrecht Widmanstetter (1507–1557), among them this copy made in 1227 in Seville, were passed to the Bayerische Staatsbibliotek.

book illumination. The love story between the merchant Bayad and the maid-servant Riyad contains numerous scenes with figures, which are reminiscent of the expressive painting of late antiquity. This was continued on the Iberian Peninsula at the level of folk art in the famous apocalypse commentaries of various Mozarabic artists.

In the Arabic manuscript the figures appear in a context reflecting the idyll of Islamic Spain with a surprising proximity to reality: the blooming gardens and the evergreen trees, the babbling brooks and the rivers lined with water wheels, and finally the lookout towers (*miradóres*) with their window grilles and horseshoe arches, which allow views over the fertile landscape.

Left: *Bayad on the riverbank*, Andalusian manuscript of *Bayad and Riyad*, Seville, c.1200, Rome, Biblioteca Apostolica Vaticana
The love story of Bayad and Riyad, known from this copy from Andalusia, takes place in the eastern Mediterranean. The painter adopted important elements of composition from the contemporary art of the book of Syria and Mesopotamia, but also presented some of his ideas in an environment familiar to upper-class readers from al-Andalus. This miniature painting featuring Bayad, who has collapsed on the riverbank from grief over his unfulfilled love for Riyad, shows the typical lookout towers with window grilles, and irrigation technology with wooden water wheels.

Opposite: **Astrolabe**, Toledo, 1029/30, Berlin, Staatsbibliotek
The astrolabe, a portable instrument for sighting the fixed stars and planets, can be used for measuring time at places with known geographical coordinates, for determining the direction for prayer towards Mecca, and the daily times for prayer. Manufactured in Toledo by the Cordoba scholar Muhammad ibn al-Saffar, this astrolabe comprises nine inset disks with 16 registered places, from Cordoba, Toledo, and Saragossa, to the holy cities of Mecca and Medina, as far as the "Ruby Island" of Ceylon and the "limits of the known world." The grid on the front of the astrolabe indicates 29 stars with the curved star pointers. On the back there are additional scales for the zodiac and the solar year, a Spanish innovation. The instrument makers of al-Andalus not only paid attention to perfect astronomical workability but also to artistic styling.

The Nasrids of Granada

History

Markus Hattstein

The last Islamic kingdom in Western Europe and the rise of the Nasrids

The last Islamic kingdom in Western Europe, the Nasrid kingdom of Granada, has always fascinated historians and, since the Romantic period, has inspired European interest in the Orient. Forced onto the defensive at an early stage, and always having to struggle for its continued existence, the kingdom not only successfully held its own for 250 years, but also became the last bastion of sophisticated Andalusian-Arab culture, despite infighting and various attacks from the outside world.

The Nasrid family, who until this time had been insignificant provincial princes, took advantage of the fall of the Almohads in Spain after 1229, when a series of local rulers and governors again started to set up small, albeit very short-lived, kingdoms. One of these was Muhammad ibn Yusuf ibn Nasr, from Arjona, in the province of Jaén, who, as head of the Banu l-Ahmar, could trace his ancestry directly to one of the Prophet Muhammad's comrades-in-arms. On April 18, 1232, he proclaimed himself Muhammad I, Sultan of Arjona, thereby rapidly extending his rule to Jaén, Guadix, and Baza, and in May of 1237, he conquered Granada, making it the capital of his kingdom.

Through a tactically adept policy of alliances with the Christian kingdoms as well as the Merinids in Morocco, Muhammad I extended his kingdom, forcing some towns to submit to him, and conquering others. Displaying astute judgment of the existing power relationships, he accepted King Fernando III of Castile as his sovereign and in 1248 even helped him, as his vassal, to conquer

Seville. While still on the throne himself, Muhammad I named his sons as his successors, to ensure the continued existence of his kingdom in the face of the Christian Reconquista. By the time he died in January of 1273, he had eliminated his enemies and rivals within his kingdom and brought the power of the rebellious nobility under his control.

Power and government were further consolidated in Granada under Muhammad II (1273–1302), the eldest son of the kingdom's founder. Muhammad II first terminated the policy of alliances with the Christians, and then entered into a pact with the Merinids of Morocco, who also had bases in Andalusia and ruled jointly in several cities in southern Spain. His original objective was to unite all Muslims in Spain and North Africa in battle against the Reconquista.

However, this alliance with the Merinids fell apart during the fight for Malaga, which, after a prolonged siege, reverted to the Nasrids in 1279, after an interim period under Merinid vassals. Muhammad II was thus faced with a major alliance between the Merinids and the Christian kings, but was able to counteract it by skillfully exploiting the internal quarrels among his enemies. After 1290, he created an alliance with the Christian kingdoms against the Merinids. The Christian king, Alfonso XI, successfully drove the Merinids from the south coast and forced them to relinquish all their bases in Spain.

Muhammad II was as politically astute and farsighted as his father and entered into various alliances to strengthen the kingdom of Granada. He had also extended the region under his control to parts of Castile. Muhammad II was succeeded by his intellectual but politically inept son, Muhammad III

Opposite: **The Court of the Lions' arcades in the Alhambra**, Granada, 14th century.
The Court of the Palace of the Lions built under Muhammad V has to be the most famous part of the Alhambra. The lavish ornamentation on the arcades and the pavilion situated immediately in front are even more impressive than the beauty of the symmetry that underlies the Court of the Lions. The foliage and geometric decoration created using minute mosaic tiles includes calligraphic bands and medallions containing dedications, quotes from the Koran, and prayers to Allah. Applying rich decoration to buildings that are themselves quite plain is a typical feature of Islamic architecture.

Above: **Moorish ruler**, detail of a ceiling painting on leather in the Sala de la Justicia in the Alhambra
The pictures on the oval ceiling painting were for a long time thought to represent the first ten Nasrid rulers of Granada. In the 13th century, the first two sultans, Muhammad I and his son Muhammad II, laid the foundations for the kingdom of Granada, which lasted for over 250 years. The dynasty reached its cultural zenith in the 14th century with Yusuf I and Muhammad V, both of whom were artistic architects and designers of the Alhambra.

(1302–1309). The father's achievements were all but lost when, in 1304, Muhammad III and his troops occupied the Moroccan port of Ceuta, used by the Merinids as a springboard to Spain, and which the king therefore wanted to conquer. The enterprise ended in disaster, because the kingdom of Granada was suddenly surrounded on three sides by an alliance between the Merinids, Aragon, and Castile. Muhammad III was thus deposed and replaced by his younger brother, Nasr (1309–1314), who tried to save the situation by making major concessions to his opponents, especially the Merinids.

His successor, Ismail I (1314–1325), made another alliance with the Merinids. In 1319, with the help of Moroccan Berber contingents, he won an important victory over Castile in the battle of the Vega, which temporarily halted the advance of the Christians. However, after Ismail's assassination, Granada was once again forced on the defensive and had to accept heavy land losses under the rule of the child sultan Muhammad IV (1325–1333).

The kingdom of Granada at its zenith

Under the rule of the sultans Yusuf I and Muhammad V, who are most famous as architects of the Alhambra, the kingdom of Granada was at its peak. The extremely diverse countryside between the coast on the one side and the high mountains of the Sierra Nevada on the other meant that the kingdom had to be cultivated in a very organized fashion. Andalusia was famed by its contemporaries for its agriculture. The fertile land around Granada, the Vega, was artificially irrigated in summer, so that it was possible to cultivate a wide variety of vegetables, grafted fruit trees, olives, vines, citrus fruits, and dates. Corn, wheat and barley were grown and processed as staple foods, while, on the coast, fishing and sea trade with northern Africa were particularly important.

The domain of the sultan, who also demanded a major part of the produce of the Vega for his own personal use, was very extensive, whereas private land ownership and leased land formed increasingly small parcels. Larger tracts of land were managed on the basis of a joint lease or a system of shared ownership. Increasingly, the many small villages and hamlets in the countryside developed in line with the example of the cities – with the mosque and marketplace forming the center. It would be wrong to speak of general prosperity, however, because the high tribute payments to Castile were a constant burden on the population. Nevertheless, the splendid buildings of this period bear witness to the life of luxury enjoyed by the ruling classes. The lower echelons must also have been able to earn a reasonable living, because the kingdom of Granada experienced no social unrest.

Yusuf I (1333–1354) concluded various peace treaties so that he could devote himself to cultural activities within his kingdom and to his passion for building. At the very start of his reign, he negotiated a peace treaty with Castile and Morocco, and from 1336 he maintained close diplomatic relations with Aragon. In 1340, however, Castile and Portugal formed an alliance and defeated him at Tarifa. In 1342, the fortress at Algeciras, on the southern tip of the kingdom, was besieged by the Castilians and was forced to capitulate two years

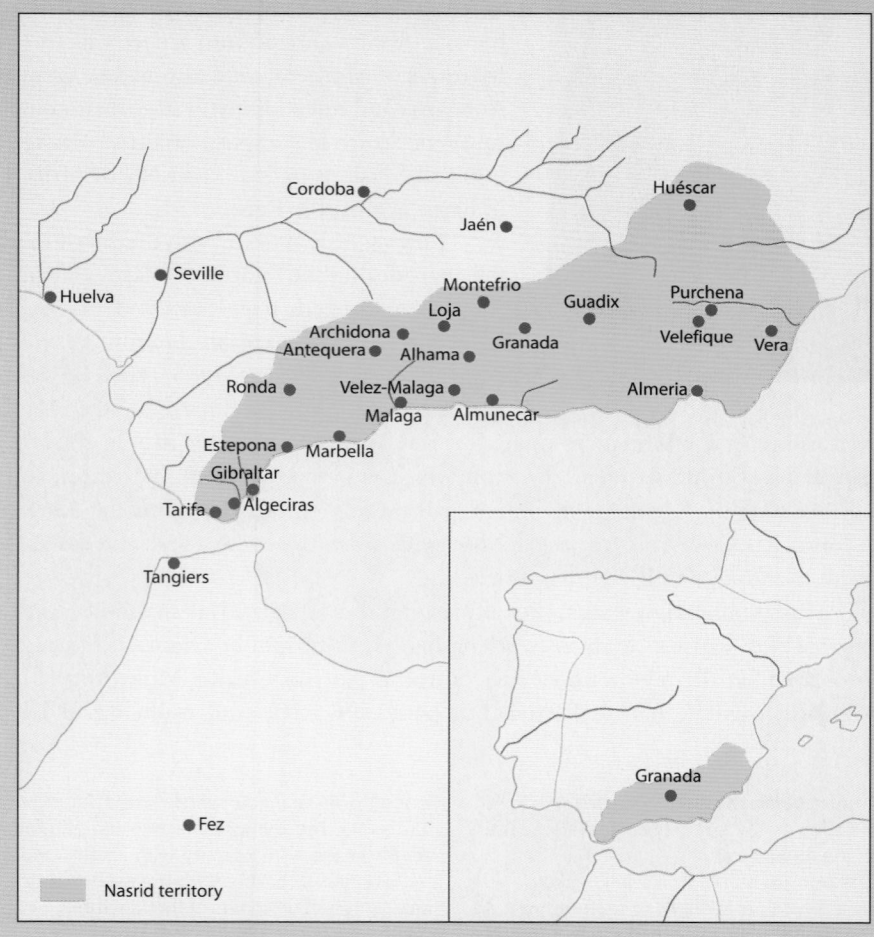

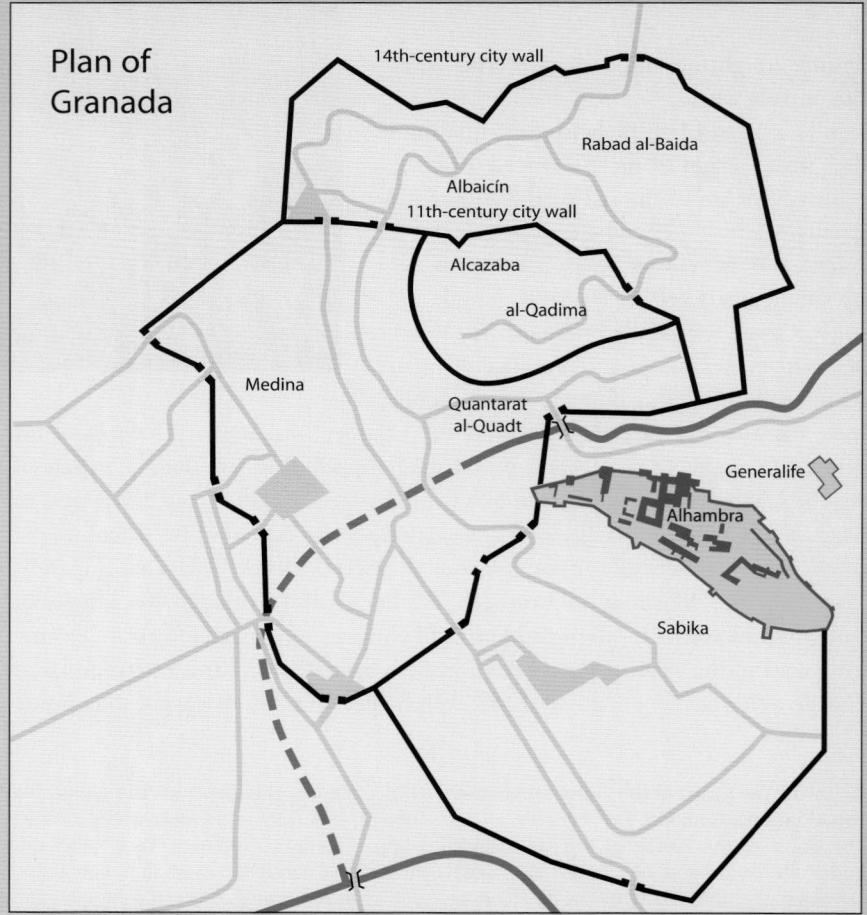

Vase from the Alhambra, 14–15th century. Granada, Museo Nacional de Arte Hispanomusulmán
The production of valuable objets d'art enriched not only the court of the ruler, but also enlivened Granada's busy trade in merchandise with the Islamic kingdoms of the East and northern Africa, particularly with the Merinids in Morocco. This winged vase is based on classical amphorae and shows two exaggeratedly thin golden gazelles on a blue background, moving while facing each other, surrounded by foliage and geometric motifs. The Muslim blessing of "Happiness and Prosperity" is inscribed on the central band that goes right round the vase.

later. Despite this, in the same year (1344), Yusuf concluded a ten-year peace treaty with Castile and used this period to carry out his major building plans. In 1348, he started the major works to extend the Alhambra, and opened the Madrasa of Granada, which became the kingdom's greatest mosque school.

When Yusuf was assassinated by a bodyguard in October 1354, his son, Muhammad V (1354–1359 and 1362–1391), came to the throne. In 1359 the port of Malaga was lost to the Christian fleet, and Muhammad V was overthrown in a palace uprising, and exiled to Morocco. It was another three years before he regained the throne of Granada. He was able to ensure a longer period of peace after 1370 by means of a policy of close alliances with Morocco and Christian Spain, and he also developed good diplomatic relations with the Mamluks in Cairo, which also benefited trade.

Muhammad V developed his keen interest in building and carried out most of his extensive construction work mainly in the second period of his reign, creating the Alhambra complex in the form we know it today, with verses carved in the stone walls in praise of its ruler. The reign of Muhammad V saw Nasrid art and culture reach its peak. In terms of religion, Granada was a bastion of conservative-orthodox Malikite Islam. The kingdom's theology schools produced many outstanding orthodox jurists, and, with the works of the world traveler Ibn Battuta, who spent some time in Granada, and of Vizier Ibn al-Khatib, literature also reached a high point in Granada.

The sciences received a particular boost when the Madrasa was founded in Granada and it produced a great number of commentaries, historical works,

1232	Muhammad ibn Yusuf ibn Nasr proclaims himself Sultan Muhammad I in Arjona	
1237	Conquest of Granada; Granada becomes the capital of the Nasrid kingdom	
1246	The Nasrids place themselves under the supreme power of Fernando III of Castile	
1246	Muhammad I helps King Fernando III conquer Seville	
1273–1302	Sultanate of Muhammad II	
1274–1275	Alliance between the Nasrids and the Merinids; the Merinids conquer Tarifa and Algeciras	
1278	The Banu Ashqilula in Malaga come under Merinid rule	
1279	The Nasrids win back Malaga	
1280–1281	Alliance of the Banu Ashqilula, the Castilians, and the Merinids against Granada	
1288	The Banu Ashqilula lose Guadix to the Nasrids and retreat to North Africa	
1295	Nasrid offensive against Castile	
1304	The Nasrids take Ceuta	

1309	A palace uprising overthrows Muhammad III (1302–1309), succeeded by his brother Nasr (1309–1314); the Merinids recapture Ceuta
1319	Under Ismail I (1314–1325), the Nasrids defeat the Castilians (Battle of the Vega around Granada)
1325–1333	Reign of Muhammad IV
1333–1391	Cultural golden age under Yusuf I (1333–1354) and Muhammad V (1354–1359 and 1362–1391)
1340	The Nasrids defeated by Castilian-Portuguese troops at Tarifa
1344	Algeciras falls to Castile; the Nasrids conclude ten-year peace treaty with Castile
1362	With the help of the Castilian king, Muhammad V succeeds in recapturing Granada
1369	Algeciras recaptured by the Nasrids
1392–1408	Reign of Muhammad VII
1408–417	Reign of Yusuf III
1421	Pope's call for Crusades against the Nasrids

1431	Battle "de la Higueruela" in the Vega around Grenada: Nasrids besiege troops of Juan II
1464–1482	Reign of Abu l-Hasan Ali
1483–485	(known as Mulai Hasan)
1469	Marriage of Ferdinand of Aragon and Isabella of Castile paves the way for the unification of Christian Spain
1470	In Malaga, Muhammad al-Zaghal rises up against Abu l-Hasan Ali
1483	The Nasrids are defeated by Castile. Muhammad XII (1482, 1486–1492), known as Boabdil, taken prisoner; on his release, he rules as vassal of the Catholic king in Guadix
1485	Muhammad al-Zaghal seizes power for himself, as Muhammad XIII; the Castilians conquer Ronda; further conquests follow: Malaga (1487), Guadix, Almeria (1489)
1486	Muhammad XII returns to Granada
1492	Muhammad XII capitulates and hands Granada over to the Christian kings

Filippo Baratti, **The Sultana**, 1872, oil on canvas, Private collection
After having been forgotten and neglected, the nearly ruined Alhambra was rediscovered in the Romantic era and became a focal point for European longings for the exotic and the supposed sensuality of the Orient. No work contributed more to this feeling than the travelogs and tales of the American author Washington Irving. In *The Alhambra*, written in 1832, he combined historical records with motifs from oriental and romantic legends and sentimentally transfigured the Granada of the Moors. Many historic paintings and book illustrations were based on his stories.

Poetry was particularly encouraged from the time of Muhammad III, who, like his vizier Ibn al-Hakim al-Rundi, was a distinguished poet. Yusuf I surrounded himself constantly with poets, and under Muhammad V, established literary circles grew up in the court. As well as hymns of praise to the ruler, particularly Muhammad V, there were also satirical poems and poems in the traditional Arabic style (*tawriya*). Some more significant poets, such as Ibn Zamrak (1333–1393), whose poems also adorn the walls of the Alhambra, set the style for the Madrasa of Granada. Many members of the Nasrid dynasty, such as Sultan Yusuf III, were famous for their poems. There was an active cultural and intellectual exchange with Morocco and the Mamluks of Egypt. Many scholars and poets visited the various courts, thus reinforcing this cultural symbiosis.

Political decline and the end

After the death of Muhammad V, Castilian armies again invaded the Nasrid kingdom in April 1394, but were decisively beaten by the bellicose Sultan Muhammad VII (1392–1408), the last politically powerful Nasrid ruler. Under Yusuf III (1408–1417), the constant pressure from Castile further increased, and after 1410, Granada faced a relatively strong alliance of the Christian princes.

After 1417, the kingdom sank into a lasting crisis in terms of domestic politics, when a succession of short-lived emirs fought against each other, drove each other out, and then returned to the throne time and again with the help of Christians and changing alliances. One of these emirs, Muhammad IX, ruled a total of four times between 1419 and 1447. The Christian kingdoms' help with alliances did not come cheap, and they constantly wrought further concessions from the weakened kingdom. The Muslim troops suffered a heavy defeat in 1431, after which the Christian kings began their systematic advance into the region of Granada. In June of the year 1431, Juan II of Castile even managed to advance briefly as far as Elvira at the foot of Granada's city walls. As early as 1421, the pope in Rome had called Christendom to launch Crusades against Granada. The end of Nasrid rule was only a matter of time.

In the 1440s, the anarchy in Muhammad IX's struggles for the throne came to a peak. This period also saw uprisings by the Andalusian nobility and the bloody end of the powerful Abencerrajes dynasty within the Alhambra's walls. In the 1450s, several equally powerful sultans of the now divided ruling dynasty were at this moment fighting for power, and the situation was becoming rapidly more chaotic. Granada owed its survival solely to the anarchy that also prevailed in Castile at this period. Only the penultimate Nasrid emir, Abu l-Hasan Ali, known as Mulai Hasan (1464–1482 and 1483–1485), managed to bring some semblance of order back to the situation within Granada. In particular, he reorganized military affairs, thus for one final time establishing the borders of the kingdom, and he also suppressed the rebellion led by his brother, Muhammad al-Zaghal, who had settled in Malaga in 1470. Starting fresh negotiations with the Christian kingdoms, he set up permanent legations and recognized the risk posed by the unification of the two Christian kingdoms as a result of the marriage of the "Catholic Monarchs," Ferdinand of Aragon and Isabella of Castile, in 1469.

The end of the kingdom, or sultanate, of Granada became a favorite subject of 19th-century Romantic literature, particularly as a result of Washington Irving's stories, and it is difficult to separate historical facts from romantic embellishments. Authors have liked to attribute the end of Moorish Granada to Mulai Hasan's love for an aristocratic Christian woman.

In actual fact, there was a power struggle in the palace between the Sultana Fatima and the Christian favorite, Turaiya. Moreover, with regard to the succession to the throne, Mulai Hasan intended to overlook his elder sons in favor of Turaiya's children. Taking advantage of Mulai Hasan's campaign at Loja

and anthologies. Forced out by the Reconquista, important and traditional schools of medicine and astrology also settled in Granada. Alongside commentaries on Hippocrates and Galen, these schools also produced new compendia of surgery and pharmacology. Attempts were also made to investigate in greater depth the natural causes of the great plague, which struck Granada in several waves after 1348.

Ibn al-Khatib (1313–1375) was a prominent historian who entered the service of Yusuf I as secretary in 1340 and was quickly promoted. In 1359, he accompanied Muhammad V when he was exiled to Morocco, and on his return, held the highest office, that of vizier, between 1362 and 1371. He knew the major scholars of his time, such as Ibn Khaldun, and left a legacy of over 60 works.

in July 1482, his eldest son, Muhammad XII, whom the Spaniards called Boabdil (a corruption of his real name, Abu Abdallah) or El Rey Chico, ("The Little King"), seized the throne with the help of the Christians and some noble Arab families. This resulted in a civil war between father and son, which sapped the kingdom of its last vestiges of strength. At the battle of Lucena, in April 1483, the Christians took the inexperienced Boabdil prisoner, and Mulai Hasan returned to the throne. When he died two years later, his brother, al-Zaghal, seized power as Muhammad XIII in Almeria.

This created an opportunity for the extremely cunning King Ferdinand of Aragon, who was holding Boabdil prisoner, and who, since 1484, had been steadily advancing on the land surrounding Granada. Boabdil was released in return for concessions, under which he became a vassal of the Catholic Monarchs and large sums of money were paid. In March of the year 1486 he was once again in Granada, from where he conducted the fight against his uncle. The Catholic Monarchs had in the meantime been advancing towards Granada: Ronda fell into Christian hands in 1485, Malaga in 1487, and Guadix in 1489. In December of 1489, the courageous, bellicose al-Zaghal was forced to hand over Almeria in return for free passage. Many Andalusian Muslims, especially members of the nobility, were exiled to Morocco and Egypt.

In 1491, the siege closed around the city of Granada, and Boabdil capitulated in return for free passage. On January 2, 1492, Ferdinand and Isabella entered Granada without a struggle at the head of their army. A cultural epoch and an era had come to an end. The tragic figure of the last king of Granada, who, after 1527, fell in battle in the service of the Sultan of Morocco, has particularly attracted the attention of historians and writers, especially those of the 19th century. Whereas all sorts of cruelties and excesses used to be attributed to him, he is now viewed more as an inept ruler whose actions were unfortunate and who could no longer defend himself against his enemies.

The Catholic Monarchs, incidentally, revoked the agreements they had generously sworn for the right of the Muslims and Jews remaining in Granada to practice their religions and unleashed a wave of compulsory baptisms. But that really belongs to the history of Christian Spain.

Nasrid sword, 15th century, Cassel, Staatliche Kunstsammlung
This sword, made for the Nasrid court, with its richly ornamented blade showing the heads of two fabulous creatures, must have been used for ceremonial purposes rather than for fighting. From the very beginning, the rulers of Granada recognized the military supremacy of Castile on the Iberian Peninsula and assumed the status of vassals to the Christian kingdom. The internal strife of the 15th century led to a gradual loss of territory for Granada. Even though the bellicose Sultan Mulai Hasan, and his courageous brother Muhammad al-Zaghal, co-ruler of Malaga, did manage to achieve further military successes against the Christians, the last sultan Boabdil was taken prisoner by the Christians in 1483. He regained his freedom only by making major concessions that led, just a few years later – in January 1492 – to Granada being taken by the Catholic Monarchs.

The Alhambra

Jesús Bermúdez López

Architectural history

The Alhambra, the palace complex of the Nasrid dynasty in Granada, can perhaps be considered as one of the most famous examples of Islamic art overall, but is certainly the culmination and grand finale of medieval Islamic culture on the Iberian Peninsula. Our idea of the Alhambra is defined by the buildings of its apogee in the 14th century, which were constructed at the same time as York Minster, Cologne and Milan Cathedrals, the Strasbourg Cathedral, Westminster Abbey, the Pope's Palace at Avignon, the Signorie of Florence and the town halls of Bruges and Prague. The history of the Alhambra building complex, however, stretches right back in Islamic times to the 9th century. We first learn of the existence of the "Red Fort" – for that is what *al-hamra* means – around 860, though nothing remains of this today. The earliest buildings of the Alhambra that can be dated are from the 11th century, from the time of the Zirid dynasty, under which a forerunner of the Alcazaba came into being. The present area of the Alhambra, with its wall and its earliest towers in position, began to take shape under the Nasrids, the last Islamic sultanate on the Iberian Peninsula, in the first few decades of the 13th century. The dynasty had made the southern Spanish city of Granada the capital of its kingdom. For a long time, the sultanate was able to exist alongside the Christian rules by means of a skillful policy of treaties, vassalage, and military campaigns, while at the same time being adept at furthering its own cultural development. Construction of the Generalife, a summer palace near the Alhambra that underwent many alterations by subsequent sultans, probably started at the beginning of Nasrid rule. At the beginning of the 14th century, Muhammad III (1302–1309)

The Alhambra viewed from the east and from the northwest

The Alhambra is a fortress enclosed by a wall, containing palaces, houses, streets, and towers of various sizes and functions. It is a city – unique in its design, chronology, and present condition. The sultan lived in the palace complex, making the Alhambra the kingdom's seat of government throughout the rule of the Nasrid dynasty (1238–1492)
Above: The fortress viewed from the east
Below: The palace complex of the Alhambra viewed from the hill of the Albaicín

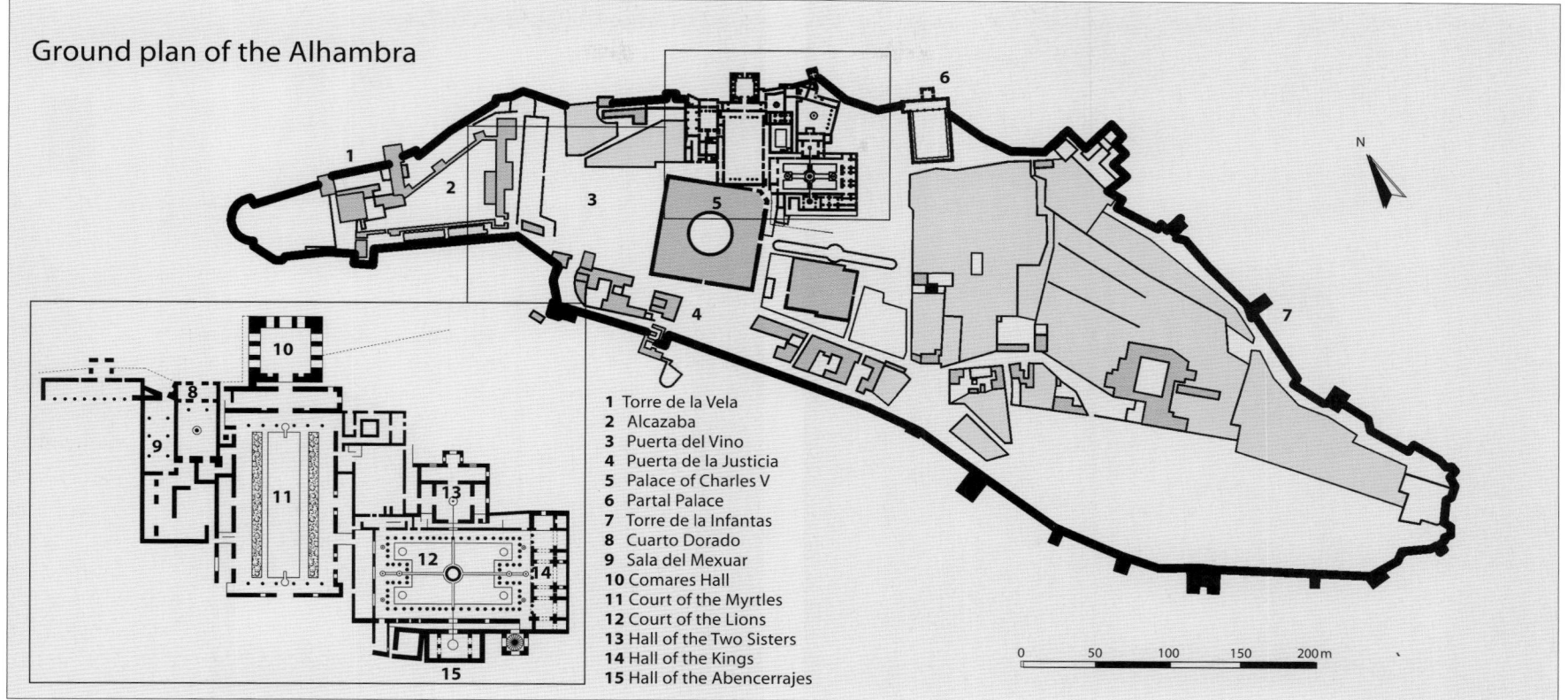

Ground plan of the Alhambra

1 Torre de la Vela
2 Alcazaba
3 Puerta del Vino
4 Puerta de la Justicia
5 Palace of Charles V
6 Partal Palace
7 Torre de la Infantas
8 Cuarto Dorado
9 Sala del Mexuar
10 Comares Hall
11 Court of the Myrtles
12 Court of the Lions
13 Hall of the Two Sisters
14 Hall of the Kings
15 Hall of the Abencerrajes

contributed to the infrastructure of the city center, the Medina, with the construction of the mosque, the adjoining baths, the *rauda* (the sultan's mausoleum), and the Puerta del Vino ("Wine Gate"), where the main street, the Calle Real, left the city. The actual palace area of the Nasrids was first developed under Ismail I (1314–1325). There are still significant remains of his palace, hidden among the palaces of the second half of the 14th century. The middle of the 14th century saw the sultanate's most fertile period under Yusuf I (1333–1354). He built the Palacio de Comares ("Comares Palace"), the city gates of the Puerta de la Justicia ("Gate of Justice") and the Puerta de los Siete Suelos ("Gate of the Seven Stories"), and, among other things, the wonderful Torre de la Cautiva ("Tower of the Captives"). The golden age of the Nasrid dynasty was undoubtedly that of Muhammad V in his second reign (1362–1391). The Riyad Palace – also known as the Patio or Palacio de los Leones ("Court of the Lions" or "Palace of the Lions") – owes its existence to him. In terms of architecture and wall decoration, this is one of the masterpieces of Islamic culture. The present appearance of the Alhambra is the work of Muhammad V, for it was in his reign that buildings were decorated and many more were erected. During the 15th century, the sultan's time was increasingly taken up with the advancing Christian armies rather than artistic creativity. As a result, this was a period of decline, with no significant construction work and with no innovation in terms of building ornamentation. Before that, however, Muhammad VII (1392–1408) built the Torre de las Infantas ("Towers of the Infantas") on the city wall, and Yusuf III (1408–1417) made alterations to the Generalife and built his own palace in the part of the palace area called the "Partal." When the Christians captured the city at the end of the 15th century, they reinforced the city wall and the major gateways with circular bastions, so that they could better withstand an artillery attack. The Christian governors made alterations primarily to the houses and the urban structure, adapting them to their own requirements. These works also affected the palaces, as the Patio de la Reja and the Patio de Lindaraja illustrate. The Palace of Charles V, a jewel of the European Renaissance, is the

16th century's major contribution to the Alhambra, and represents a counterpoint to the Moorish buildings. Planned in 1526 as an imperial palace on the Alhambra, it was never actually completed. The Convento de San Francisco ("Monastery of St. Francis"), the beautiful Charles V fountain at the Puerta de la Justicia, and the Puerta de las Granadas ("Pomegranate Gate") on the ascent to the palace complex, are also Renaissance contributions to the Alhambra. In 1576, the Friday Mosque was demolished and replaced by the Church of S. María de la Alhambra, which was completed in 1617.

The palace complex

From a geographically favorable position on a high plateau, the Alhambra kept watch over the kingdom's capital city situated at its feet. It acted as the administrative and power center of Granada and as such is in line with the typical Islamic palace complex containing the sultan's residence and seat of government. It developed following the municipal architectural ideas of medieval Islamic culture. It was laid out as an independent fortified town, separate from Granada, its *medina* and suburbs, with a city wall approximately 1,900 yards (1,730 meters) long, which had about 30 towers, varying in size and function. Granada and the Alhambra were two cities that complemented each other, but were autonomous, and their sole point of direct contact was at the Puerta de las Armas ("Arms Gate"). This gateway, which was situated between the Albaicín – the town district on the hill opposite the Alhambra – and the lower city, represented the most important connection between the two. Through it the subjects entered the palace complex to seek an audience with the court, to sort out administrative matters, to pay dues, or to undertake other such tasks. Gradually, and especially after the last few decades of the 15th century, the population of Granada increased considerably due to the arrival of Muslim refugees from other cities conquered by the Christian armies. This created a new town area with its own walls, which in the end almost surrounded the Alhambra.

Puerta de la Justicia
Built in 1348 by Sultan Yusuf I, the Gate of Justice is the largest of the Alhambra's four outer gates. A hand is carved in the keystone of the outer horseshoe arch, which, like the key in the inner arch, is one of the symbols used by the Nasrids in facade decoration. The large foundation inscription is above the entrance, to which, in the 16th century, the Christian kings added a statue of the Virgin Mary by Roberto Alemán. The vaults inside the gate, which has to negotiate a great difference in height, are lavishly painted.

Puerta del Vino
The Wine Gate was one of the first gates erected in the inner area of the Alhambra. Built between 1303 and 1309, it was the entrance to the Medina, the area of town within the fortress where the administrative and court officials lived. The Puerta del Vino had a dual protective function, in that its strong doors could be locked to protect against attack from enemies outside the city and also if the inhabitants of the Medina rose up against the sultan. Despite its function as a fortification, the gate looks like a public pavilion.

The city wall of the Alhambra has four large gateways at roughly equal intervals – two to the north and two to the south – that served to defend the city. The Puerta de las Armas was one of the first gates to be built, probably one of the very first buildings built by the Nasrids in the Alhambra in the 13th century. The gateway exhibits a distinctive feature of Spanish-Islamic fortress construction: the passageway is not straight, but is deflected once or twice for more effective defense, thus making it more difficult to lay siege to the city and easier to establish a firm, defensible position. In addition to the elegant structure and successful proportions, the simple, yet beautiful portal of the Puerta de las Armas also merits attention. A pointed Moorish archway, the top of which is decorated with a frieze of interlacing bands with different colored luster inlay, is surrounded by a rectangular frame (*alfiz*) with guilloche ornament. The arch imposts are made of stone, a building material that, unlike tiles and stamped clay, was hardly used in the Alhambra, with the exception of the outer gates. In the passageway, a series of three rooms in the middle has a reflective vault and umbrella domes on the sides. The plaster on this type of vault is painted to imitate a red brick wall, typical of Nasrid architectural decoration. Niches with benches for the sentries are found on the sides and at the back of the passageway. At the eastern continuation of the wall lies the Puerta del Arrabal ("Suburban Gate") below the Torre de los Picos ("Points' Tower"), which owes its name to the remains of the battlements. The stone gateway leads to a sunken path used by the sultan and his escorts on their way to the ornamental and kitchen gardens of the Generalife on the other side. On the southern flank of the city wall to the east is the Puerta de los Siete Suelos, which was probably built in the mid-14th century. It was close to the Medina of the Alhambra, and chronicles state that jousting tournaments and military parades were held in front of it, so that it had a certain ceremonial character. When Napoleon's armies retreated in 1812, it was almost totally destroyed, but it was possible to reconstruct it fairly reliably from old engravings of the gate. The final outer gate of the Alhambra is the large Puerta de la Justicia, which the foundation inscription above the entrance arch dates to the year 1348. The key carved into the keystone is an iconographic symbol often found on Nasrid gates, just like the hand in the large outer arch that provides such a magnificent frame for this entrance. The passage to the interior of the gate is interrupted repeatedly, and the rooms have the obligatory benches for the sentries. Again, the paintings on the various vaults imitate ordinary red brickwork.

Within the city walls, the Alhambra extends over an area of about 26 acres (10.5 hectares) It lies about 2,300 feet (700 meters) above sea level on a foothill of the Sierra Nevada called Sabika, which extends into the fertile Vega. In medieval times, the agriculture and cattle farming of the Vega were, and in some cases still are, important economic pillars of the town. The builders did not alter the landscape in order to erect the city's buildings, for they were constructed without the need for major earth moving and were adapted to, and sometimes cleverly exploited, the differences in height and the irregularities of the terrain.

The palace complex comprised three sectors that, although protected by a shared city wall, had independent functions. One was a citadel, or barracks area, reserved for an elite troop whose task it was to be on constant guard over the whole complex and who were always ready to leap quickly and effectively into action any time and any place. Another was a palace area, the residential apartments of the sultan and his close family, where the daily life of the court unfolded. And finally, there was the Medina, a small town for court and administrative officials, and for artisans who were meant to meet the sultan's immediate wishes. These three parts of the town were linked by a complex system of streets and gateways, but could at the same time also be cut off from each other if the safety of the ruler so required. Streets and gateways thus had an ambivalent function. Under normal circumstances, they made it possible to pass from one part of the town to another; in the event of a siege or of an uprising, however, the gates could be shut, thus transforming the streets into securely blocked, and barely accessible, sections. Unlike the outer gates, these gates were straight, and were closed from the inside by means of large wooden doors. The best example of the construction of such an inner gateway is the Puerta del Vino, which leads from the outer entrances to the Medina. Built at the turn of the 14th century, its facades were decorated at various times. The western facade was made of sandstone, and the symbolic key typical of a portal adorns the top of the arch. The decoration of the eastern portal – the *cuerda seca* tiles framing the archway and the stucco panels to both sides of the window in the upper story – dates from the second half of the 14th century.

The Alcazaba

Opposite the Puerta del Vino, towers and walls majestically enclose one of the three areas of the Alhambra: the citadel, or Alcazaba. It looked like a separate small town within the royal city and had accommodation for an admittedly small, but elite, contingent of specialized soldiers. This was where the permanent guard for the whole complex lived, and from here the sentries swooped down to their positions on the battlements of the city wall and at the inner gates. Like all military establishments, the Alcazaba was also built at a strategically favorable position from which the lower town and its surrounding area could be observed and controlled. It actually lies on a long, protruding spur from the Alhambra hill. A long, narrow street divides the inner Alcazaba into two zones. To the north, irregularly arranged remains of walls and brick floors give an indication of ten houses of varying size but similar construction in the guards' quarter.s They are in keeping with the typical layout of Spanish-Islamic houses. As with fortress construction, there is the typical entrance area with its many protrusions, which in this case protects the privacy of the inhabitants from prying eyes, and there is a small patio that always has a water feature in the middle. This can be a small bubble fountain, a stone trough, or a small basin set in the ground, known as an *alberca*. Depending on the size of the house, one to

The Alcazaba
From the terrace of the Torre de la Vela, there is a fine view over the inner area of the Alcazaba. The remains of the foundation walls still give an impression of this small quarter, which contained the homes and barracks of the guard. Depending on size, the two-story houses had one to three rooms on each floor.

The public facilities included a steam bath, cistern, and communal kitchen. As you would expect for a military district, there were also prisons – underground rooms accessible only by ladders or ropes.

three ground floor rooms open onto the patio, from which narrow steps lead to the upper story. Hidden in a corner, each house had its own toilet complete with flushing cistern. As can be clearly seen, the entrance to the houses opened out directly onto the street, to secondary alleys or to passageways.

To the south of the main street, the remaining walls indicate houses with similar features, but more uniformly and regularly distributed. This was where storehouses and probably communal accommodation for young sentries were found. Other buildings complete the urban area of the Alcazaba: a steam bath as an established integral part of Spanish-Islamic towns, a cistern to ensure the water supply, and a communal kitchen where food prepared at home was cooked. Of course, no military district would be complete without its dungeons, the *mazmorras*, which were notorious under the Christians. After working all day as agricultural or manual laborers, at night the prisoners were lowered down into subterranean dome-shaped rooms, similar in cross section to a bell. Inside, they were usually divided into small sleeping areas by brick walls radiating from the center. These caverns could also be used as silos, i.e. as stores for wheat, spices, or tools. The dungeons were of fundamental importance, especially in the last few years of Nasrid rule, the prisoners had a considerable exchange value since during the ten-year war with Castile, particularly if they belonged to the upper echelons of the Christian army, or even to the royal family. The most important prisoners were probably accommodated in the dungeons of the Alcazab, literally under the feet of the elite troops.

The Alhambra is dominated by a large building, square in outline, that can be seen from afar and that seems to be a focal point: the Torre de la Vela ("Guard Tower"). In the ground beneath the tower there is a silo, above which rise four stories, although the connecting stairway from the Nasrid period no longer

El Mexuar audience chamber
This chamber was altered repeatedly over time and was in fact the first throne room in the palace of Sultan Ismail I. When the palaces were extended, from the 1330s onwards, it became the reception and meeting hall of the Nasrid court. It was particularly suitable for this function because of its rich tile and stucco decoration. After the Christian con-quest, a chapel was installed here.

survives. The impressive roof terrace of the tower, which originally had battlements, offers perhaps the best view of the city of Granada. There in a wall is the famous bell that, after the Christian conquest, set the rhythm of life in the town and the surrounding area and which for centuries sounded the alarm. The bell was also rung at particular times during the day and night and on important days of remembrance, such as the "Day of Conquest," which commemorated the town's surrender to Christian troops on January 2, 1492.

The largest tower of the Alhambra, however, is the Torre del Homanaje ("Tribute Tower"), which was probably one of the first buildings erected by the Nasrids in the 13th century. This probably accommodated the military staff who directed and controlled the Alhambra's defense system from this elevated point. The tower's five floors display a wide variety of vaults. An additional storage bin on the ground floor of the tower and a terrace with a small podium are also worth noting. From here, visual signals could be exchanged with the fortresses and watchtowers which occupied geographically strategic positions in the mountains around Granada.

The royal palaces

The Alhambra is held in such high esteem primarily because of the Comares Palace and the Palace of the Lions, both dating from the 14th century. Since the 16th century, these two buildings together have been called the Casa Real Vieja ("Old Royal Palace"), to distinguish them from the large Renaissance palace of Emperor Charles V, the Casa Real Nueva ("New Royal Palace"), built at that time. The Catholic Monarchs retained the medieval Nasrid palaces as private residences to enjoy their magnificent decor and – as they stipulated in their will – "so that they may never be forgotten." Although partly altered in shape, neglected, sacked, and left to the mercy of nature over the centuries, most of their structure and decoration have survived.

In all the domestic architecture of the Spanish-Islamic culture – including the palaces – the plain exterior is in stark contrast with the interior patio around which the rooms are arranged. When you enter the patio, all your senses are captured by a profusion of colors, scents, light, and imagination. The roots of this dynamic probably lie in the *jaima*, the nomads' desert tent and cradle of Arab civilization. There the inhabitants gathered on the narrowest space around the open circle in the middle. Around this main tent, more tents were pitched in no apparent order, thus producing a camp. On a different scale, this principle underlies towns, houses, and even the palaces of the Alhambra: buildings were added on or overlapped each other as long as there was sufficient space within the walls.

The administrative function of the palaces can be seen from the way they are divided into rooms. This design began with a series of courtyards, grouped in hierarchical order, and restricting the movements from courtyard to courtyard of those with access. It culminated in the Sala del Mexuar, where the Council of Viziers would take the important decisions for the kingdom, and

which was the Alhambra's first throne room, probably at the beginning of the 14th century. After the Christian conquest, it was used as a chapel. The various decorative styles express power and supremacy and must have instilled awe in anyone entering the room.

Behind this zone of officialdom, the imposing Comares facade forms a boundary between the semipublic administrative area and the private residential area, although this boundary was in general flexible. The facade, built in 1370, epitomizes the ornamentation of the Nasrids of Granada superbly: geometry, inscriptions and ornamental foliage (*ataurique*) are carved into the stucco panels of the facade, dividing it into harmonious proportions. It is crowned with a projecting roof, a masterpiece of the carpenter's art in the Alhambra. This facade signified a high point in the development of building decoration. Although the glowing colors have now almost totally disappeared, its majestic character is still clearly apparent. On the steps in front of the facade, which gave him an air of authority, the sultan sat, as though before an imaginary royal canopy, and administered justice to his subjects. Behind this splendor lies first a dark, winding corridor leading to the dazzling side wing of the patio, now called the Court of the Myrtles. Its focal point is formed by a long pool, which becomes an essential architectural element, as the surrounding buildings are reflected in the tranquil surface of the water, thus producing an impression of spaciousness. On the narrow sides of the patio, water flows from two fountains, and drains away through small overflows in the corners. The water is circulated in such a way as to produce a water surface that is as smooth as a mirror, called "the sea" by Arab poets. There, where the myrtle bushes now stand, some of the water was led off into the long flower beds, originally sunk lower, on the long sides of the pool, thus serving as irrigation: a complex and beautiful water system. This courtyard arrangement is typical of Nasrid architecture, with the buildings always arranged around an inner courtyard with a

Main facade of the Comares Palace
In 1370, Muhammad V commissioned the decoration of the Comares Palace facade, which faced the Cuarto Dorado. The door to the right gave access to the private apartments of the palace, while the ones to the left led to the official halls of the Comares complex. An inscription over the doorways reading "My gateway is a fork in the ways" summarizes this arrangement. A projecting roof that used to be painted in bright colors deserves special mention, as it is a gem of Islamic carpentry. The colored tiled panels (illustration above), which also adorn other courts and halls, are a recurrent motif. In front of this impressive background, the sultan of the 14th century would grant his subjects an audience.

Opposite: **Court of the Myrtles in the Comares Palace**
The Comares Palace, built under Yusuf I, is in line with typical Nasrid building design, with all the important rooms arranged around a splendid inner courtyard. The residential apartments are on the long sides of the Court of the Myrtles, while at each narrow end a portico leads onto the public reception and administrative halls. In the background rises the Torre de Comares, the highest tower of the Alhambra, which houses the Throne Room.

Detail of the central arch of the portico on the northern side of the Court of the Myrtles
Behind the richly decorated arch of the portico you can see the beautiful *muqarnas* arch, immediately in front of the entrance to the throne room. It is decorated throughout in carved stucco, originally painted in many colors. The arches are purely decorative and have no supporting function.

Southern side of the Court of the Myrtles
Two stories are built onto the portico on the southern side of the patio and are usually called the harem. The upper story has an open gallery looking out over the courtyard. The central opening has a flattened arch instead of the usual rounded arch. The myrtle hedges that give the court its name can be seen on both sides of the pool.

water source at its center, thus setting the proportions of the building's ground plan and elevation.

The most elegant apartments, most of which were in the northern part, were lit from the south. These rooms also occasionally open onto the north. In the Alhambra palaces, this occurred where the steep slope of the hill offered them some protection. In general, the desire for privacy and intimacy meant that the rooms did not open onto the outer walls but onto the patio, where a portico marked the beginning of the most elegant rooms, almost always situated on the narrow sides of the patio. The walls usually had a dado lavishly decorated in mosaic tiles (*alicatado*).

The patio thus includes water, gardens, light, and heavenly vaults, and can be seen as a return to the nomad tent, shutting out the outside world – creating a feeling of ambivalence ever present in the old civilization of the crescent of Islam. This is just as true of the modest, sometimes tiny houses of the Moriscos (Moors forcibly christened after 1500) that can still be seen in the Albaicín, as it is for the royal palaces of the Alhambra. The porticoes of the Comares Palace, with their seven great arches, have retained two further important decorative elements of Nasrid architecture: slender marble columns with delicate *muqarnas* capitals and, above the arches, magnificent, filigree stucco panels,

carved with lozenges, known as *sebka* ornamentation. These pillars and panels are purely decorative and have no supporting function.

In Spanish-Islamic culture, rooms had no specific function and could be used as sitting rooms during the day and bedrooms (alcoves) at night. An example is the Sala de la Barca, which was simultaneously the sultan's sitting room and bedroom. Above the tiles and stucco slabs, splendid wall carpets or tapestries probably adorned the walls, reaching right up to the intricately worked wooden vaults, whose star motifs would originally have been gilded. The sultan here wanted for nothing. His hygiene needs were met by a toilet with running water in an adjoining room with wonderful wall pictures, and for religious duties there was a small prayer room with a prayer niche (*mihrab*). The one in Granada points as accurately as possible towards Mecca. Other prayer rooms that still exist today, such as those of the Mexuar, are somewhat larger. Here the open arcades on the northern side look out onto the countryside as though the architect wanted to give believers sitting on the ground reading the Koran the opportunity to contemplate the wonder of the Creation. A separate, pavilion-like building in the Partal gardens houses a third, smaller prayer room for the sultan. The most impressive room in this palace, which seems to summarize all the ideas underlying Nasrid art and architecture of

Wall niche on the northern side of the Court of the Myrtles

On both sides of the portico galleries on the narrow sides of the patio are small rooms, known as *albamíes*. These illustrate the full range of Nasrid decorative art. Above the ceramic decorative tiling in the dado area rise *muqarnas* vaults and intricate polychrome plasterwork, with epigraphic borders.

Ceiling of the Sala de la Barca in the Comares Palace

The name of this room, the sultan's sitting room and bedroom, is derived from the Arab word *baraka*, meaning "Happiness" and "Blessing." The magnificent timber ceiling has strip ornamentation and intricate star-shaped designs. Some parts had to be restored after a devastating fire in 1890. Above their tiled dados, the walls are lavishly decorated with carved plasterwork, with spaces being left for wall hangings and wall carpets.

Detail of an inscription

As well as various other decorative elements, all the palace rooms display a large number of epigraphic embellishments, mostly poems or *qasidas* that refer to the place or to the sultan who commissioned the construction work. Other writings praise and glorify Allah, or quote from the Koran.

Baño de Comares

At the lower level, one of the few remaining medieval steam baths is attached to the Comares Palace. This photograph shows one of the two water tanks of the actual steam bath, which is similar to the caldarium of classical warm-water baths. Although this 14th-century bath, which is of great significance structurally, has undergone many changes, the most important decorative elements have survived.

Relaxation room of the Baño de Comares

The Sala de las Camas (Room of Couches), is the most important room in the baths. It is named after its two spacious alcoves, situated on the sides and slightly raised behind twin arches. The room, which has no side windows, was lit from above by a lantern structure, around which the upper-story rooms are arranged. The entire area was repainted at the end of the 19th century.

the mid-14th century, is the Comares Hall, also called the Throne Room. It looks like a gigantic cube filling the entire interior of the largest tower of the Alhambra. With the exception of the entrance wall, each side of its strong outer walls contains a small alcove, two of which are exactly the same. The one opposite the entrance, which was reserved for the sultan, is different, and outshines the others in terms of embellishment. All the walls are richly decorated. The dado has remarkable *alicatado* decoration with various geometric patterns, and is topped by stucco panels with carved decoration on vertical and horizontal sheets. Everything is based on a geometric arrangement, in the context of which foliage motifs (*atauriques*) and inscriptions in rounded (*naskhi*) and straight (*kufi*) versions develop. Close examination is required to appreciate the diversity of coloring and the intricate details displayed by the stucco work in the past, as these are now reduced to mere soft pastel tones. The ornamental high point of the chamber is, however, the roof timbering, a genuine masterpiece of Islamic carpentry. Numerous polygonal wooden panels are nailed to the timber roofing, which is propped-up on the walls and itself has no supporting function. Following geometric principles, these panels unite to form star shapes that fill the three-timbered roof areas, one after the other, finishing with a small *muqarnas* dome. The timbered roof is also based on the cosmic and eschatological representation of the eight heavens of the Muslim Paradise. Here, as in no other room in the palace, the sultan would appear in his full power in this life and the life to come, and be surrounded by the symbolism of lawfulness and magnificence.

Throne Room of the Comares Palace
Also known as the Salón de Comares, or Hall of the Ambassadors, this is probably the most impressive room in the Alhambra, as its interior exhibits the entire range of Nasrid decorative arts and architecture. The room is in the largest tower of the Alhambra complex. Its walls are covered with expensive carved plasterwork, which was originally painted in glowing colors. Details of miniatures can be found in many places. As was customary, the lower wall area is tiled in the Moorish style, but the tilework is particularly lavish here.

Tunnels for the guards run under the main rooms of the palaces. They are part of a tangle of crooked passages, corridors, and stairs, invisible from the elegant rooms, that relate to the different levels of life within the palaces. In one of these systems of passageways, at the point where the two large palaces of the Alhambra meet in the north on the city wall, there is a steam bath, an essential part of Islamic communal life. Of the several baths within the palace complex, that of the Comares Palace is the best preserved, although here, too, structural alterations have been carried out over time. Although the Christians generally found Arab baths strange, and in the 16th century even banned their use, the installations were retained as an exotic element or as evidence of a sophisticated lifestyle. Access to the royal bath was gained via the central patio of the palace, the Court of the Myrtles. There was a changing room and a toilet next to the northern portico. A narrow stairway led to the lower story and the most magnificent room of the baths, the Sala de las Camas ("Room of Couches"). This part of the baths owes its name to the two slightly raised alcoves which are behind two twin arcades. The room is lit and ventilated by a lantern structure, a typical feature of Nasrid architecture, surrounded by a gallery of service rooms. Most of the decoration – fountains, walls, floor coverings, columns, tiles, and stucco – is original, although the stucco slabs were repaired and repainted in glowing colors in the second half of the 19th century. Next to the relaxation room is the actual steam bath, the vault of which has conical star-shaped skylights. The servants could open or close the movable glass covers from outside to regulate the amount of steam in the baths. It is the largest and warmest room, with a central, almost square-shaped section that opens onto galleries on two sides. Pipes of varying sizes run underneath the marble floors and in the walls, bringing hot air and steam from the water boilers to produce the required temperature and humidity. The last room, with its two water troughs, which could be filled with hot or cold water as desired, lies above the baths' hypocausts. Boiler, timber store, and the servants' entrance complete the site. The tiled dado of these rooms was disturbed in parts during renovation work carried out in the 16th century, as can be seen from the abbreviated imperial motto "Plus Ultra" on some tiles.

The Palace of the Lions was built onto the Comares Palace as an independent building with its own entrance. There was no direct link between the two until Christian times. This building displays the geometry and proportions of Nasrid architecture and ornamentation of the second half of the 14th century at their peak. Here, a marble fountain at the intersection of two water channels replaces the central pool. Twelve verses carved into the outer edge use poetic imagery to praise the intricacies of its hydraulic system. They are among the most beautiful poems to be integrated into the decor of the Alhambra. Twelve lions, all slightly different and arranged male and female alternately, support the bowl and, with their many and sometimes contrasting symbols of power, courage, strength and justice, they emphasize an iconographic duality, the forerunners of which can be found in antiquity. In Islamic art, animal-shaped water dispensers are frequently around fountains, pools, aquamaniles, etc., and are used to link two aesthetic points of reference: the representation of animals, and water.

The apartments are arranged around the patio, which is framed by its famous colonnade. The arcades give the effect of a portico around and directly in front of the apartments. Two ornamental pavilions with a square ground plan, situated on the narrow sides of the patio, seem to highlight the royal apartments that lie behind them.

One of these apartments is the Sala de los Mocárabes ("Muqarnas Chamber"), which is situated on the western side right by the original entrance to the palace and has the feel of an antechamber. The rectangular room opens onto the courtyard with three large *muqarnas* arches. It owes its name to a

Above: Ceiling of the Throne Room
The splendidly decorated ceiling of the Throne Room is made up of small, geometric pieces of inlaid wood that were once painted in glowing colors. They are applied in ascending order of size and form different levels that refer to the seven heavens of Islam, over which the eighth heaven, the throne of Allah, forms a dome.

Right: Recess in the Throne Room
Nine recesses are made into the thick walls of the Comares Tower, two each of four different designs. The ninth recess opposite the entrance is the odd one out, obviously more lavishly decorated because it was reserved for the sultan.

Left: Arch in the Throne Room
In the entrance areas of the various apartments there are small recesses (known as *taqas*) to hold jars of liquid.

muqarnas vault, which has to be one of the most beautiful in the entire Alhambra. It was badly damaged when a nearby gunpowder store exploded in 1590, and was replaced by a stucco vault designed in 1614. Beneath this, only part of the original vault base on the back wall has survived, with the remains of its paintwork. The wall decoration, which must have had a dado area with the traditional *alicatado* and wall carpets or stucco in the upper section, has also disappeared. The Sala de los Reyes ("Hall of the Kings") on the eastern side of the courtyard deserves its special status. In structural terms, it is a room with no specific purpose and has five, instead of nine, alcoves at the side. It is reminiscent of the Throne Room of the Comares Palace, where a rectangular, not square, structure dominates the ground plan. Here too, alcoves – five in this case – are arranged around a multipurpose room. The alcoves also emphasize

the central axis, whose dome gave the room its name. Here ten people are depicted deep in conversation. This used to be interpreted as representing the most important kings (sultans) of the Nasrid dynasty, but this has now been rejected. The two outer domes show court scenes and are of great interest in terms of iconography and design. Attitudes to depictions of living creatures have been very varied in the Islamic world, although this work is thought to have been commissioned from Christian artists, probably from the Italian city of Genoa. The distinctive features and technique of the decoration of these domes is unique in a medieval Islamic palace. They were painted in egg tempera on a ground of several layers of plaster, in which the initial sketch was chiseled out, and were varnished with wax. The ground was made of tanned sheepskins, which were stretched over the wooden roof struts and joined at the seams with small bamboo nails.

Two separate residential apartments on the northern and southern sides, each arranged around a square-shaped room, complete the layout of the palace: the Sala de las Dos Hermanas ("Hall of the Two Sisters") and the Hall of the Abencerrajes. The scale here is smaller and the decor more sumptuous, without in the least diverging from the general intimate scheme. The two rooms display the most beautiful *muqarnas* domes. Based on a geometric plan and working outwards from a star motif in the center of the dome, colored stucco prisms were jointed together and mounted on top and underneath each other to form concentric circles. Both residential apartments are slightly elevated from the patio and each open onto it – exactly at the coordinate axes – through a large, rounded arch. They can be shut off with timber doors, decorated with geometric arrangements of richly carved panels. In the upper floor, there are also rooms, which look out over the rooftops like small pavilions. On the garden side, the great Mirador de Lindaraja lies directly in front of the Hall of the Two Sisters. This is an elegant area of the apartment, where the palace's finest decor is to be found: small-tiled *alicatado* dadoes, a twin window, and the stucco decoration that surrounds it, as well as the unique small roofing pieces, made of timber latticework inlaid with colored glass.

The palace buildings of the Alhambra open only hesitantly to the outside, to the city below, and onto the river valley, and seem to want to climb over the city wall. The Palacio del Partal, or del Pórtico ("Portico Palace"), provides a graphic example of this. It was probably built in the first part of the 14th century and thus represents the oldest palace architecture on the site. The front part of a patio house, the Torre de las Damas ("Ladies' Tower"), whose roofing can be admired in the Museum for Islamic Art in Berlin, has survived as part of the city wall. The arcades of this portico, which gave the palace its name, project from this section. In front of it is the usual, elongated pool. These set pieces are now surrounded by luscious gardens. Until practically the end of the 19th century, this sector of the Alhambra was divided up into small, private plots that were gradually acquired by the local authority to group the land into a memorial complex. During several decades of archeological research, walls, floor coverings, and *albercas* came to light, giving an idea of the original layout of the town. Visitors today will be able to see them in the context of later gardens laid out in the soil terraces (*paratas*) that date back to the time of the Nasrids. These stretch up the slope from the wall to the Medina.

Palacio de los Leones
Apart from the Comares Palace, the Palace of the Lions is the only palace in the Alhambra to have survived from the 14th century. It is made up of a system of separate private residential areas, grouped around a patio. The famous Court of the Lions is bordered on all sides by a gallery of columns, with the individual apartments behind. The whole courtyard area is intersected by four water channels in the shape of a cross, alluding to the points of the compass, and fed by the fountain in the center of the courtyard.

SPAIN AND MOROCCO

Capital of columns in the Court of the Lions

The slender marble columns of the galleries that surround the courtyard are particularly impressive. The symmetrical, cube-shaped capitals, with their moldings decorated with inscriptions praising the architect, Sultan Muhammad V, deserve particular attention.

The fountain in the Court of the Lions

Even in the 14th century, a complex hydraulic system provided sufficient water pressure and a constant water level in the fountain. The 12 lions, from whose jaws the water flows down, symbolize all 12 signs of the zodiac and thus the entirety of time, eternity. Verses written by the vizier and poet Ibn Zamrak adorn the dodecagonal rim of the fountain.

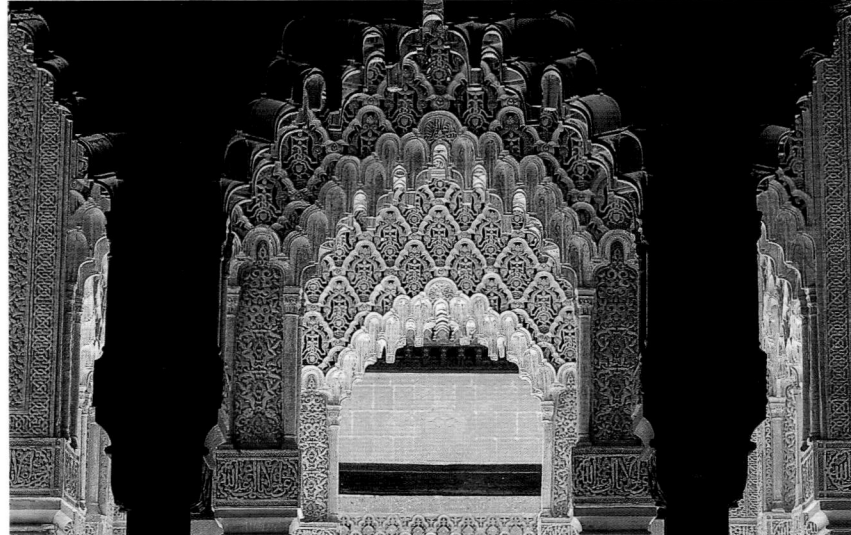

The portal pavilion in the Court of the Lions

The geometric design of the architecture of the Court of the Lions is particularly emphasized by the two square-shaped pavilions that project into the east and west axis of the courtyard. The architecture of the Alhambra is distinctive for the ephemeral nature of the materials used: as most of the columns and arches are purely decorative and have no supporting function, they could be made of soft stone and plaster. The masterly arrangement of projections and recesses, the modulation of exterior surfaces, and the gradation of richly decorated *muqarnas* arches help to create the particular aesthetic effects of the Alhambra with the play of light and shadow.

Hall of the Kings

The Sala de los Reyes is an elongated chamber, divided into several rooms by a series of *muqarnas* arches. The alcoves in the back wall give an unrestricted view onto the courtyard. The three alcoves that open onto the Sala de los Reyes have vaults that are among the Alhambra's most important decorative treasures. They are adorned with pictures painted on tanned sheepskins using miniature techniques and then attached to the vault ceiling. The paintings depict scenes of court life, and the central picture, which shows a group of noblemen in the style of the time, is particularly impressive.

Hall of the Two Sisters

Within the Palace of the Lions, there are various, separate residential areas. One of these is the Sala de Dos Hermanas, the Hall of the Two Sisters, which opens onto the Court of the Lions. The architecture and decor of this hall are particularly impressive. Perhaps the most surprising element of this section of the building is the splendid *muqarnas* dome that rises over the entire central part of the room. It is made of plaster and is based on a central star motif, developed by overlaying individual, multicolored prisms at different levels. The hall derives its name from the two large marble slabs (the sisters) on the floor by the central fountain.

Ceiling decoration in the portico gallery of the Partal Palace
Portico galleries, either between the open courtyard and the most important, roofed residential areas or separating them from each other, are a distinctive feature of the architecture of the Alhambra palaces. The interior of the galleries is usually decorated with timber constructions assembled in a geometric pattern, as illustrated by the colonnade of the Palacio del Partal.

The Medina

The Medina, which rises gently from west to east, was a proper little town in its own right, set apart, to maintain and supply the palace. Its main artery was the Calle Real. It had public baths, a mosque, and stores, and by the mosque it had a *rauda*, the sultans' mausoleum. Texts from the 14th century indicate that nearby there was also a *madrasa*. The remains of two large sites point to the existence of further palaces: the Palace of Abencerrajes and a palace that subsequently became part of the Franciscan monastery. The upper part of the town was made up of a network of small industries, including kilns and water wheels for making ceramics and glass, a tannery, and a mint. Water was vital for the whole town and was drawn from the river almost four miles (six kilometers) upstream, reaching the Alhambra by means of a water pipe, the Acequia del Sultán. This became an aqueduct when it entered the walled area and ran downhill parallel to the street, then branched off into a network of pipelines, forming part of a complex hydraulic system that also regulated the water levels in the pools. Cisterns and public squares completed the cityscape, with the houses being reached by small streets, alleyways, and arcades. The largest houses served as homes for court officials and servants.

Ceiling of the Hall of the Abencerrajes
On the southern side of the Court of the Lions is the Sala de los Abencerrajes, which also has an impressive dome rising above it. It, too, is based on a central star motif, which is made up of *muqarnas* prisms, and merges into the square-shaped ground plan of the room with the help of hanging *muqarnas* spandrels.

Palacio del Partal
The Partal (or Portico) Palace is the oldest palace in the Alhambra. It was probably built at the beginning of the 14th century, but all that remains from its original form are the large central pool and the five-arched portico that gave the palace its name.

The maze garden between the Alhambra and the Generalife
Next to the walled palace complex is the Generalife estate, with its many vegetable gardens and palace with ornamental gardens. The foreground of the photograph shows a section of the maze garden in the Jardines Nuevos del Generalife, the new gardens, which were laid out around 1930 to link the Alhambra with the Generalife. The background shows the outer wall of the Alhambra and the Torre de las Infantas.

Two towers on the Medina section of the town wall illustrate what these houses may have looked like: the Torre de la Cautiva, or the Tower of the Captives, is one of the examples of the golden age of Nasrid art in the mid-14th century. Like the other houses, the main room was entered from a small patio with arches resting on pilasters behind a partitioned entrance area. Small, axial recesses with twin windows are let into the three outer walls. The most remarkable are the wonderfully shaped, multicolored *alicatado* dadoes, where the color purple is particularly striking, as it was rarely used in architectural ceramics. A frieze of inscriptions adds the finishing touch to the bases. Stucco panels cover the remaining sections of the walls. These were originally painted and gave the effect of wall hangings or carpets. Following the traditional scheme of residential architecture, the tower also has living rooms on the upper floor, and is topped with a terrace. The Torre de las Infantas was designed in a similar way, but was not built until the end of the 14th or beginning of the 15th century. Features of the building decoration, such as a cruder painting technique or more simple proportions, indicate the beginning of the decline in Nasrid art. The interior follows the traditional pattern, but the three main rooms are grouped around a roofed space with a fountain in the middle, and not around a patio. They give the effect of alcoves and have windows that open in the outer walls. The lantern structure was originally topped with a *muqarnas* vault, but this was lost and replaced in the last century by an ornamental roof. In the upper floor, there is a gallery on two sides, and it opens onto the terrace.

The Generalife

The Nasrid sultans also had many estates to provide for them or where they could build outside the city walls of the Alhambra. Some of these lay in the area surrounding the palace district. By far the best preserved is the Generalife (*jannat al-arifa*), which is directly adjacent. In contrast to the past, the Generalife is now linked to the Alhambra by a series of gardens created in the first three decades of the 20th century and based on a free interpretation of the Spanish-Muslim garden. The "*jannat*" prefix means "the gardens" in the comprehensive sense of the word as a place of vegetation, of cultivation. Surrounded by almost 500 acres (220 hectares) of meadowland, the four large vegetable gardens form the Generalife, which is dominated by a palace building with ornamental gardens. Most of the vegetable gardens are still cultivated today and so the site of the Generalife is also of major ecological and even anthropological, not just historical, significance.

The central building in the Generalife displays the same architectonic structure as the Alhambra palaces: a patio with a water source – in this case part of the canal that used to irrigate the estate by means of four watercourses – forms the central point of the residential buildings. The most elegant room lies on the northern side and opens onto the countryside via a *mirador*, or observation tower. The patio has coordinate axes inlaid with four large, lower-lying beds on the edge of the water channel, which is bordered by narrow paths. Despite the decidedly rural nature of this complex, which is particularly striking in the entrance courtyards, the building is decorated like a palace. It is embellished throughout with *alicatado* dadoes, stucco panels that

Opposite: **Interior view of the Torre de las Infantas**
Roughly 30 towers of varying size and shape punctuate the outer wall of the Alhambra. In addition to the towers, which are an integral part of specific palaces, there are also so-called palace towers, which differ from the others in their decor and building features. The Torre de las Infantas was built between 1392 and 1408, and comprises a roofed courtyard with various alcoves and adjoining apartments, which are arranged around it creating two stories.

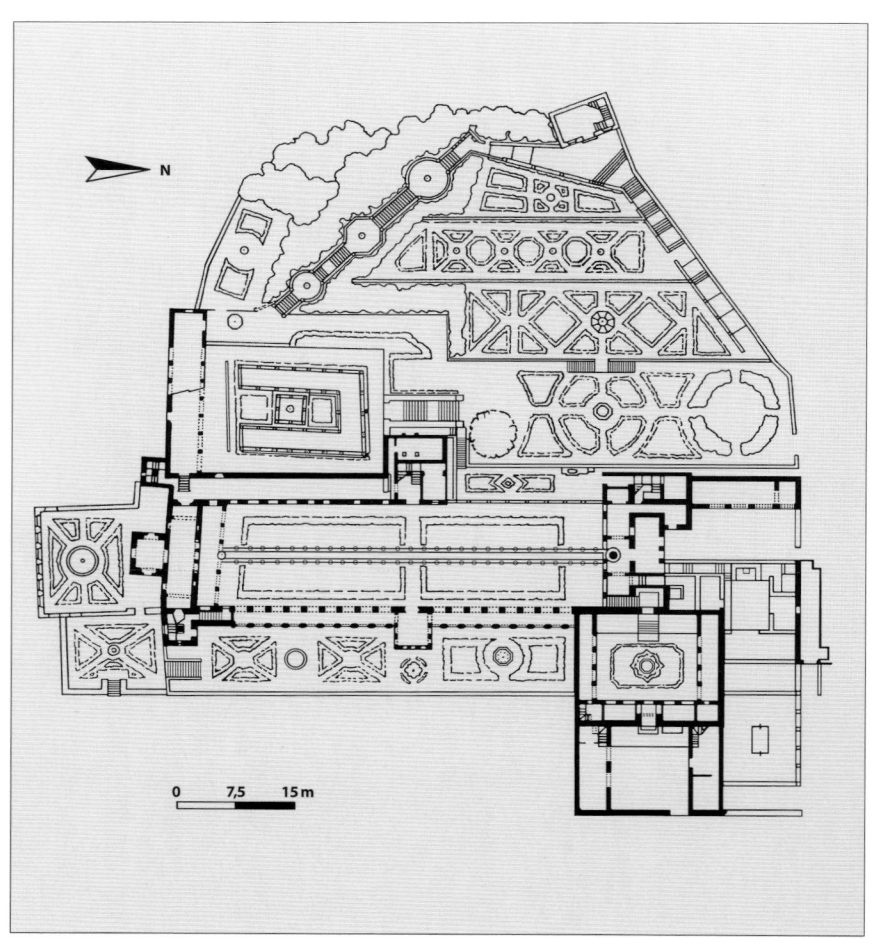

Palace of the Generalife

The Generalife includes not only seven vegetable gardens but also an elegant palace, similar to the Alhambra palaces in terms of construction and decoration. Here, too, an elongated patio with a water source forms the focal point around which the palace was built.

Instead of the usual fountain, the Generalife has a canal, known as the Acequia, surrounded by gardens that gave the courtyard its name. Here, too, the ingenious hydro-technology provides convincing evidence of the great significance and symbolism of water throughout Islamic cultures.

covered the walls right up to the timber ceilings and roof struts, geometric decor, calligraphy, *muqarnas* and *atauriques*, marble columns, arches, and latticework, etc. The small *mirador* projecting from the patio is particularly remarkable with its magnificent view over the vegetable gardens and the Alhambra behind.

The cityscape of Granada

Through many openings in the walls, windows, and open loggias, especially in the magnificent halls of the Alhambra, there is an unrestricted view directly onto the town of Granada situated at the foot of the hill.

The Islamic town of Granada developed in the Darro valley in the period between the Zirid (11th century) and the Nasrid dynasties and looked out on the fertile landscape of the Vega. Some bridges, such as the Tableros bridge, and a few gates, including the Elvira, Monaita, and Bibrambla Gates, still survive from this period of the town's development. They formed landmarks along the town walls which rose up the hill of Cerro de San Miguel and which protected extensive cemeteries and large areas of the town, such as the Albaicín, the Realejo, and the Antequeruela. These parts of the town still reveal their medieval Islamic roots: the irregular layout of the streets, the emphasis, in town planning terms, on private as opposed to public spaces, and stark topographical contrasts.

Some of the surviving buildings have retained their original appearance totally or partially intact. Examples are: the El Bañuelo steam bath; a *funduq* (trade center with accommodation and warehouses), the Corral del Carbón; schools such as Yusuf I's Madrasa; commercial areas such as the Alcaicería; mosques turned into Christian churches such as San José, El Salvador, San Juan de los Reyes, or the Ermita de San Sebastián; palace buildings such as the Dar al-Horra, the Cuarto Real de Santo Domingo, the Alcázar Genil, the Casa de los Giornes; and Morisco houses such as the Casa de Zafra, the Case del Chapiz, or the Casa de Horno de Oro. Remains of the excellent water supply system, such as the Aynadamar canal and numerous cisterns in the Albaicín, have also survived.

Patio de la Sultana, in the Generalife
Although the medieval structure of the Generalife has for the most part survived, it has seen some changes over the centuries. Thus the baroque garden, for example, was laid out where the palace baths used to be.

The garden with its many ornamental water fountains is now called the Patio de la Sultana.

View of the El Albaicín district of Granada
Opposite the Alhambra, on its northern side, lies Granada's other great medieval building complex: the Moorish quarter of El Albaicín. With its narrow, steep alleyways, white-washed houses set at random, varying angles to each other, and tree-filled squares, this quarter has retained much of its character as a medieval Moorish settlement. The Albaicín was a place of refuge for the Moors driven out by the Christians from other parts of Andalusia. They occupied the district until 1568. The Alhambra and the Albaicín present an unusual unity of town and country, confirmed by UNESCO declaring them a World Heritage Site.

The Maghreb: From Morocco to Tunisia

Attarin Madrasa in Fez
After taking Morocco from the Almohads, the Berber Merinids made Fez their capital. It became the center of their strictly orthodox, traditional Islam in the Maghreb, and they built many *madrasas* (Islamic law schools) there in a refined Moorish style. The young theologians of the entire region were trained in these institutions. Of more than 30 *madrasas* that the Merinids constructed in Fez during the 14th century alone, the Attarin *Madrasa* is one of the most beautiful. It was built between 1323 and 1325, and is laid out in a fashion typical of Maghrebi *madrasas,* which usually have cells, prayer halls, and classrooms arranged around a courtyard with a fountain or pool at its center.

History
Markus Hattstein

The 13th–16th centuries
The Berber dynasties

When the Almohad regime collapsed, the political ties between North Africa and Spain were loosened, and Berber dynasties inherited the legacy of the great empire throughout the Maghreb. The Merinid dynasty from the south of Morocco conquered much of the country after capturing Meknes (1244) and Fez (1248). In 1269 they deposed the last Almohad ruler in Marrakech, and made Fez their capital. At first their rule remained unstable, as they had to defend themselves simultaneously against their neighbors to the east and several Crusades by the Christian kingdoms of the Iberian Peninsula.

The Merinids could not legitimize their rule by claiming descent from the Arab family of the Prophet, and did not share the reformist fervor of the Almohads, so made themselves defenders of conservative Islamic orthodoxy, which was cultivated in the many *madrasas* they built in the cities of Morocco. They began with a harsh campaign against the many regional cults and local saints (*marabouts*), but were finally forced to compromise and permit the masses to practice an emotionalized form of Islam, particularly in the south of the country. This accommodation stabilized the religious landscape of Morocco, which has subsequently remained practically unchanged.

The Dyers' Souk in Fez, Morocco
To the present day the cities of the Maghreb are dominated by lively bazaars and souks, which are not just centers of economic activity, but also key loci of public life. The open places and alleys are named after the trades of the craftsmen and merchants who worked in them. This photograph shows the dyeing process taking place. Fabrics are dyed traditionally, using natural and artificial dyes in stone tubs.

There was a brief period of political consolidation during the reigns of the two most important Merinid rulers. The rule of Abu l-Hasan Ali (1331–1335) was marked by great cultural and economic confidence in the country, and this popular leader began ambitious public building programs, creating many of the cities in Morocco as we know them today. Fez profited most from this work. Abu l-Hasan Ali secured peace for his country by means of a clever policy of building alliances, particularly with Tunisia and Egypt. He also occupied Algeria (Tlemcen) in 1347, and even reached Tunis, but was not able to hold onto the areas he had gained, as he suffered painful defeats at the hands of the Spanish. His son, Abu Inan Faris (1351–1358), who removed his father from the throne in a civil war, continued both his policies and his building activities. He invaded Algeria and parts of Tunisia again in 1352, though his ambitious attempt to reestablish the Almohad empire failed. The rapid decline of the

dynasty began with his murder. The rulers who succeeded him were either too young or too weak to impose their will, and came permanently under the aegis of the Wattasids, a related family. For a while they also fell under the sway of the Nasrids of Granada. The last in the line of Merinid rulers, Abd al-Haqq (1421–1465), tried to break the dominance of the Wattisids in 1458 by slaughtering the entire family (except for two brothers who escaped), but was killed himself during a popular revolt that took place in Fez in 1465.

Under the Merinids, the Wattasids from the east of Morocco rose to assume the highest offices of state and finally took complete control of the government in 1358 as regents and viziers. Muhammad al-Shaikh al-Mahdi (1472–1505), one of the two brothers to survive the massacre of 1458, fought his way to power over Morocco in 1472, from his base in Arzila, but the Wattasid regime remained on the defensive. The Portuguese had begun occupying extensive tracts of land along the country's coastline in 1471, capturing Agadir in 1504, and besieging Marrakech in 1515. They tried to cut the Wattasids off from sea trade and sold captured Moroccans into slavery. In 1497 the Spanish established a permanent base in Melilla. Whole areas of the country, such as the Rif region, remained completely independent, and after 1524, southern Morocco was lost to the Saadis, while the Wattasid dynasty wore itself out in bloody power struggles. A flexible policy of pragmatic alliances and attempts to gain the support of Ottoman Algeria were not sufficient to prevent the fall of the dynasty. The last Wattasid ruler was driven out of Fez by the Saadis in 1554.

The area that is now modern Algeria was politically divided. Western Algeria (the Oran region) was under the control of the Abd al-Wadids, who ruled from Tlemcen. They had originally been local governors for the Almohads, but asserted their independence in 1236. They had to hold off the Christian powers while maintaining a constant balancing act between their stronger neighbors to the west and east (the Merinids and Hafsids), whose superior power they were forced to recognize. They suffered many invasions and expulsions, yet, despite their military weakness and the complete autonomy of the tribes in their territory, created a functioning administration. Court life flourished, particularly under the highly educated Abu Hammu II Musa (1359–1389), whose close friend, the great scholar Ibn Khaldun, worked as his private secretary. Tlemcen became an important center for caravans trading between sub-Saharan Africa and the Mediterranean. In the early 16th century, the Abd al-Wadids found themselves threatened ever more frequently by the Spanish and the Turkish Corsairs, and in 1540, they placed themselves under the protection of the Ottomans, who occupied Tlemcen in 1552, in order to use it as a base for attacks on the Spanish. This signaled the end of the Abd al-Wadid's rule.

The Hafsids took power in Tunisia, eastern Algeria (the Algiers region), and Tripolitania (modern Libya). They became independent in 1236, after being the Almohads' governors in Tunis. They were descended from, and named after, Abu Hafs Umar, one of the first followers of Ibn Tumart, who founded the Almohad dynasty. This gave them immense religious prestige. After the fall of Baghdad (1258) they claimed the caliphate, and their title was accepted by several Islamic states. The first hundred years of their rule were troubled, and the dynasty split into several lines. Independent emirates were founded in Bougie and Constantine, and a number of city-states sprang up. Despite this, in 1270 they managed to repel the Crusade led by Louis IX of France, and extended their territory gradually to the west. After 1311 the court at Tunis also became a center of theological studies where Islamic scholars debated philosophical and religious questions with Christian missionaries, such as Ramón Lull.

Abu l-Abbas Ahmad (1357–1349) first came to power in Constantine. He established his family as the ruling line in Tunis in 1370, and was succeeded by a series of capable rulers. His success in combating sea piracy secured trade with the eastern Islamic world, Central Africa, and Europe, particularly with the Italian princely courts, and made Tunis the richest and most important trading center in the Maghreb. The resulting stabilization of conditions coincided with a long period of peace under his successors Abu Faris Azzuz (1393–1434) and Abu Amr Uthman (1435–1488). Azzuz conducted diplomatic policy with great

Marabout on the beach at Safi

The religion of the Maghreb has a character quite distinct from that of the rest of the Islamic world. The region has a large Berber population, which was subjugated and Islamized by the Arab invaders who constituted the ruling classes. As a result of Berber influences, the region's "popular Islam," as it is known, is dominated by magical and mystical practices manifested above all in the worship of local wise men, preachers, and mystics as saints. These figures are venerated for their piety and asceticism, and regarded as mediators between the people and the divine power. The word marabout is actually murabit, and is related to ribat, the term for a (fortified) monastery. It originally denoted a saint, but with time, came to be applied to a saint's tomb. There are many of these monuments throughout North Africa, and most of them are popular places of pilgrimage.

View of Fez

The city of Fez was founded in 807 by the Idrisid ruler, Idris II, and settlers from Kairouan. The Fatimids and the Spanish Umayyads fought over Fez in the 10th century. Under the Almohads it became one of the most significant cities in the Maghreb. The Merinids captured Fez in 1248 and made it the capital of their empire. Under their rule it enjoyed a golden age, and became the center of western Islam. The city is said to have had 200,000 inhabitants and 785 mosques in the 13th and 14th centuries. Between 1666 and 1912, Fez was also the capital of the Alawite sultans.

astuteness, strengthened the public finances by levying profitable customs duties, improved the infrastructure of the cities and ports, and allowed Europeans to establish trade legations. The central power of the state was strengthened by undermining the influence of the clans.

After 1494 the state became increasingly powerless. Many areas were lost to independent tribal leaders, and the Spanish began establishing permanent military bases on the coast in 1505. When an appeal for help was made to the Ottomans, all real power in the Hafsid empire soon slipped into the hands of pirates (Corsairs), who were supported and armed by the Turkish government. The most notable Corsairs were the legendary brothers Aruj and Khair al-Din Barbarossa from the Greek island of Lesbos. In 1516 Aruj occupied Algiers and Tlemcen, where he established his own rule, but fell in 1518 fighting against the Spanish. His younger brother, Khair al-Din, an audacious military strategist and later supreme commander of the Ottoman fleet, occupied and fortified Algiers and Tunis. He inflicted devastating defeats on the Spanish, provoking the intervention of Emperor Charles V.

In 1535 the emperor occupied parts of the Tunisian coast and Tunis with a fleet of Spaniards and Genoese (while Khair al-Din was plundering Menorca in retaliation). However, he was only able to hold on to some of the territory he had taken. The daring Corsair Dragut took up the fight from the island of Jerba, became the Ottoman governor of Tripolitania in 1553, and inflicted a heavy defeat on the Spanish fleet in 1560. He was killed in 1565 attempting to occupy Malta and expel the Order of the Knights of St. John. After 1505, the later Hafsid rulers became relatively impotent pawns in the power games played by the Spanish, Turks, and Corsairs. The reign of the last Hafsid puppet came to an end when the Ottomans occupied the Tunisian coast and Tunis as part of their strategy for establishing Turkish domination over the Mediterranean.

The 16th–19th centuries
Sharifs, Corsairs, and Turkish residents

In Morocco, power fell into the hands of Arab dynasties directly descended from the Prophet (Sharifs). The Sharif period, which has continued to this day, began when the Wattasids were overthrown by the Saadis, who came originally from southern Morocco. Their chief was the leader of a religious brotherhood and in the early 16th century assembled many *marabouts* and their supporters to wage holy war against the Portuguese and the weak Wattasid dynasty. Basing

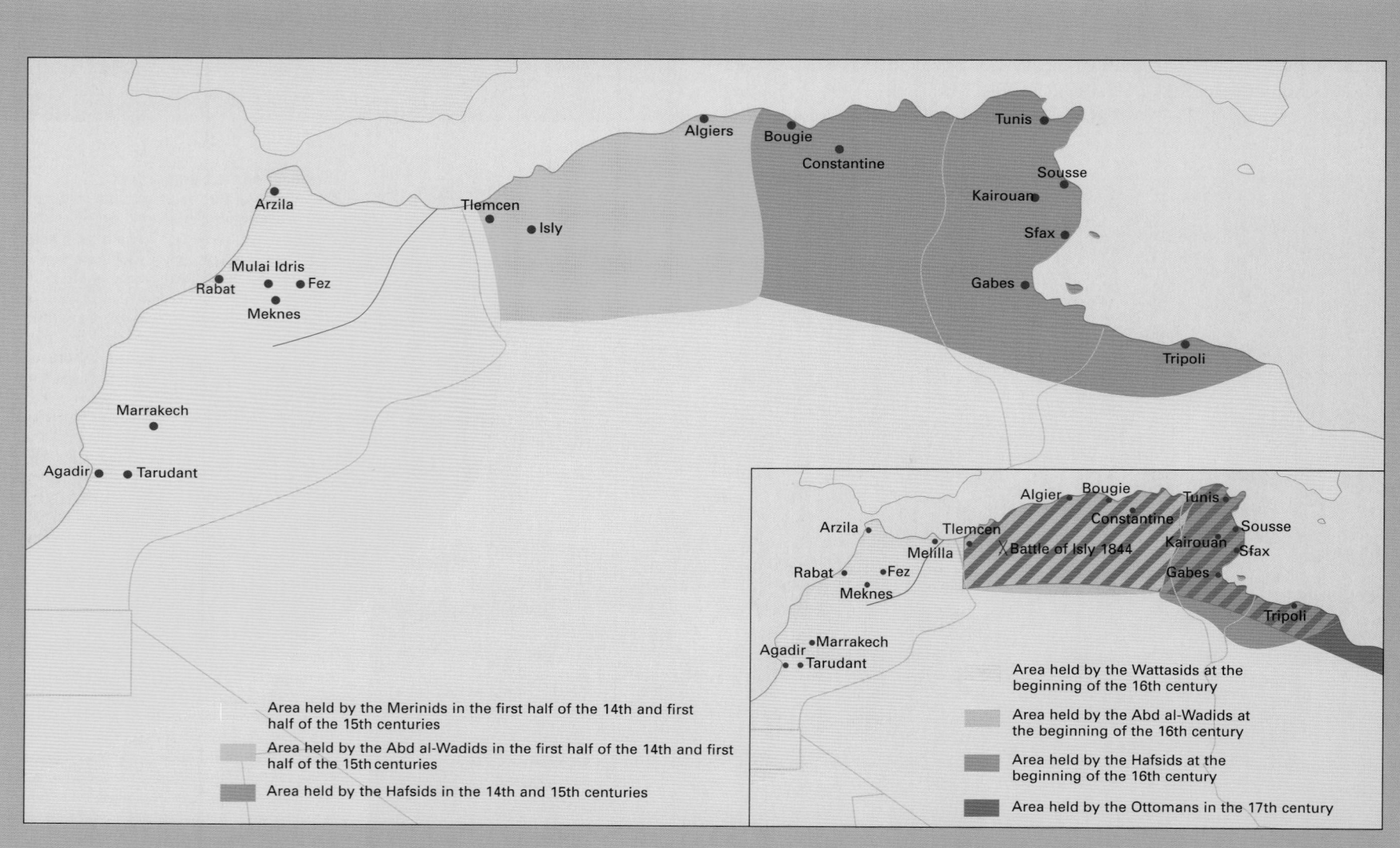

Area held by the Merinids in the first half of the 14th and first half of the 15th centuries

Area held by the Abd al-Wadids in the first half of the 14th and first half of the 15th centuries

Area held by the Hafsids in the 14th and 15th centuries

Area held by the Wattasids at the beginning of the 16th century

Area held by the Abd al-Wadids at the beginning of the 16th century

Area held by the Hafsids at the beginning of the 16th century

Area held by the Ottomans in the 17th century

Door knocker, Morocco

One of the typical features of popular Islam in the Maghreb, especially in the southern regions, is a strong belief in the protective powers of amulets and talismans. One of the most significant emblems is the "Hand of Fatima," as it is known. Its five fingers are associated with the healing power of Fatima, the Prophet's daughter, and are therefore regarded as lucky, as is the number five. Some commentators have interpreted this as a sign of the emancipation of the feminine in popular Islam. The Hand of Fatima is a favorite motif for pendants, door knockers, and door hinges, particularly in Morocco, and is believed to guard people and buildings from bad luck.

themselves in Taroudannt near Agadir, they occupied Marrakech in 1525 and drove the Portuguese out of Agadir in 1541, which, together with their religious prestige, brought them great popularity, and helped them to secure enthusiastic support among the population.

Muhammad al-Mahdi (1549/53–1557) drove the Wattasids out of Fez in 1554. He was able to gain acceptance as sultan in Morocco by allying himself with the Ottomans, and even took the title of caliph. He outmaneuvered his external enemies by agreeing to a series of temporary alliances, and conducted a bloody campaign of annihilation against the *marabouts* and their monasteries. His aims were to establish a strong central power and impose taxation on all sectors of the population. The Turks had him murdered in 1557 when he occupied Tlemcen, and his successors were forced to limit their ambitions to Morocco. They established an unprecedented cult around the ruling family and attempted to stem the increasing European influence, which was growing due to the activities of the trade legations. The Moroccan actions prompted the young king Dom Sebastian of Portugal to land in Morocco, where he suffered a crushing defeat and was killed in August of 1578, at al-Qasr al-Kabir.

Ahmad al-Mansur (1578–1603) ("the Victorious") was proclaimed sultan while still on the field of battle. He presided over a period of great economic

1236–37	The Abd al-Wadids (1236–1552/4) gain autonomy in Tlemcen, as do the Hafsids in eastern Algeria and Tripolitania (1228–1574)	1515	The Portuguese besiege Marrakech	1591	Military revolt in Tunisia	1832–1847	Emir Abd al-Qadir leads the Algerian struggle for independence from the French
		1516	The Corsair Aruj Barbarossa captures Algiers and Tlemcen	1640	Hammuda ibn Murad takes power in Tunisia and founds the Muradid dynasty (which rules until 1702)		
1244	The Merinids conquer Meknes	1525	The Saadis capture Marrakech			1837–1855	The first tax and administrative reforms take place in Tunisia under Ahmad Bey
1248	Capture of Fez by the Merinids	1535	Emperor Charles V (1519–1558) occupies Tunis and parts of the Tunisian coast	1659	End of Saadi rule		
1269	The Merinids (1269–1465) overthrow the Almohads in Marrakech			1666	The Alawite Mulai al-Rashid (1664–1672) takes power in Fez	1844	The Moroccan army is defeated by French troops
1270	A Crusade under the leadership of Louis IX of France is repelled by the Hafsids	1540	The Abd al-Wadids place themselves under Ottoman suzerainty	1669	Mulai al-Rashid conquers Marrakech and Morocco	1857–1861	Tunisian constitution proclaimed: Tunisia becomes a constitutional monarchy
1331–1351	Rule of the Merinid Abu l-Hasan Ali	1541	The Saadis succeed in driving the Portuguese out of Agadir	1671	Corsair rebellion in Algeria	1860	The Moroccan army is defeated by Spanish troops
1347	The Merinids occupy Tlemcen	1546	Death of the Corsair leader Khair al-Din Barbarossa	1671–1830	Algiers is ruled by deys, who are chosen by the Janissaries	1863	Béclard Convention: Morocco becomes a French protectorate
1351–1358	Renewed Moroccan attempt to conquer Algeria and Tunisia during the reign of the Merinid Abu Inan Faris	1552	The Ottomans occupy Tlemcen and bring Abd al-Wadid rule to an end	1672–1727	Reign of Mulai Ismail in Morocco		
		1553	The Corsair Dragut is appointed governor of Tripolitania by the Ottomans	1702	A conspiracy of Ottoman officers ends Muradid rule in Tunisia	1869	The Tunisian state goes bankrupt and is made subject to an international financial commission
1359–1389	Reign of the Abd al-Wadid Abu Hammu II Musa			1705	Husain ibn Ali (1705–1735) establishes himself as regent in Tunisia; political power remains in the hands of the Husainids until 1957		
1357–1394	Reign of the Hafsid Abu l-Abbas Ahmad	1554	The Saadis, led by Muhammad, al-Mahdi (1549/53–1557) overthrow the Wattasid dynasty in Fez			1870	Algeria is given a civil administration under French colonial control
1421–1465	Rule of Abd al-Haqq, the last Merinid			1727–1757	Civil war in Morocco under the sons of Mulai Ismail	1877	Fall of the Tunisian prime minister Khair al-Din (1873–1877)
1465	Revolt in Fez: the Wattasids (1465–1549) take power in Morocco	1574	The Ottomans establish control over the Tunisian coast and bring Hafsid rule to an end	1757–1790	Rule of Mulai Muhammad in Morocco		
1471	The Portuguese occupy the Moroccan coast			1792–1822	Rule of Mulai Sulaiman in Morocco	1881	Bardo Treaty: Tunisia becomes a French protectorate
1497	The Spanish occupy Melilla	1578	The Battle of al-Qasr al-Kabir: the Saadis defeat the Portuguese under King Dom Sebastian	1827	Algeria breaks off diplomatic relations with France	1883	The La Marsa Convention confirms Tunisia's status as a protectorate
1504	The Portuguese capture Agadir	1578–1603	Sultanate of Ahmad al-Mansur	1830	The French occupy Algeria		

prosperity and won immeasurable riches on his expeditions to the Sudan, where he gained control of the African gold trade. In Morocco he imposed a new administrative system called the *makhzan*, which continued to operate into the 20th century. The elites in the administration and the military were bound to the ruler by tax exemptions and gifts of land. This served to strengthen the central power of the state, and also resulted in the country's agriculture becoming highly productive thanks to the efficient management of the land by rich elite groups. With his restless energy, Ahmad reshaped Moroccan society in many areas and built Marrakech into a magnificent capital city.

His sons divided Morocco as the dynasty split into two lines, one based in Marrakech (until 1659), the other in Fez (until 1626). However, this did not weaken the country's economy, and trade with the European sea powers was intensified by the award of licenses. The later, rather weak, members of the dynasty found themselves exposed to strong pressure from the Europeans and various local independence movements, and the Saadi dynasty finally lost power in 1659.

Its legacy was inherited by the Alawites, a Sharif family who also led a religious brotherhood and had lived in the High Atlas in the south of the country since the 13th century. They have ruled Morocco ever since. After successful campaigns against various local rulers, Mulai al-Rashid (1664–1672) secured the support of the Ottomans in Algiers and invaded Fez in 1666, from where he conquered Marrakech and the rest of Morocco in 1669. His son, Mulai Ismail (1672–1727), was an extraordinary ruler: an intelligent, cruel man with a love of finery. He created a superbly disciplined army made up of 150,000 black slaves, broke the resistance of the religious brotherhoods and local rulers, and built the "Imperial City" of Meknes, one of the most formidable fortresses in the Maghreb. Since he placed the cities under military control, he was able

Al-Jadida Fortress in Morocco
This fortress, at the city of al-Jadida on the Moroccan coast, is a reminder of the defensive struggle of the sultans of Morocco against the incursions of the Portuguese, who, as the leading maritime power of the 15th and 16th centuries, established several naval bases in Morocco in order to control the sea trade along the African coast. The failure to repel this invasion eventually led to the fall of the Wattasid dynasty, who were replaced by the energetic Saadis.

to guarantee the security of trade and urban order, which he maintained with an iron fist. Although trade and diplomatic relations with Europe continued to be cultivated, he regained much of the territory that had been seized by the Europeans, and sought to secure the country wide-ranging independence from its neighbors in economic and political affairs.

As the system was tailored to Mulai Ismail's personality, it collapsed after his death. His seven sons, who all took the throne, plunged the country into a 30-year civil war, and order was only restored once his grandson, Mulai Muhammad (1757–1790), gained power. He reorganized the public finances and promoted foreign trade by awarding licenses, mainly to France and the recently independent USA. His son, Mulai Sulaiman (1792–1822), gave additional encouragement to commerce with reductions in customs duties for the European powers. At first he was tolerant in religious matters, but his attitude changed after 1810 under the influence of the puritanical Wahhabi movement from Saudi Arabia. He took a hard line against local religious customs and started a renewed persecution of the *marabouts*. These measures provoked religious unrest and revolts among various sectors of the population, and his successors were able to pacify the country only with difficulty. From the beginning of the 19th century, Morocco found itself an object of increasingly greedy interest in Europe, particularly France and Spain, and was unable to free itself from outside interference due to its traditional social structures.

Algeria and Tunisia initially experienced comparable political developments after the Turkish occupation in the mid-16th century, and both found themselves caught between the Turks and Spanish. Both powers placed particular emphasis on the military consolidation of their bases in the Maghreb as they struggled for dominance of the Mediterranean. The ruling class in both Algeria and Tunisia was a military oligarchy dominated by Turkish influence, with officers from the Janissaries, the Ottoman elite troops, sharing power with the Corsairs. The Janissaries, an outstandingly armed and disciplined force, competed with the Corsairs, who were mainly renegade Christians from southern Europe and the Mediterranean islands, for leadership in the region. When the two groups clashed, the better organization of the Janissaries usually gave them the upper hand. The Turkish garrisons forced the Corsairs, who were in charge of defensive measures along the coast, to share their booty with them.

At first, the Ottomans allowed Khair al-Din's son, Hasan Pasha, a relatively free hand in Algeria. However, in 1587 they began appointing governors with limited terms in office who bore the title of Pasha. The Ottomans also undertook a thorough reorganization of the Algerian administration, in effect creating the structures of modern Algeria. There was a short period when the province was ruled by the supreme commander of the Janissaries (the *agha*). However, following a Corsair rebellion in 1671, a series of deys ruled as regents in Algiers until the French occupation in 1830 (*dey* means "uncle," an honorary title in Turkish). The deys were chosen by the commanders of the Janissaries and held office for life. In reality, their authority was limited to the coastal region, as the tribes in the south retained their autonomy. On account of the endless flow of Christian slaves, trade flourished in the coastal cities, which developed into cultural melting pots, particularly as Christian monastic orders were permitted to minister to, or buy the freedom of, their fellow Christians in captivity. Algiers became one of the major trading centers in the Mediterranean,

and the decorative arts flourished, mainly thanks to the patronage of the city's rich Jewish merchants. In time, France managed to secure for itself the most important privileges in the Algerian sea trade, which was often not far removed from piracy. However, the increasing rigidity of the oligarchic administration meant that Algeria was unable to assert its interests in the modern global economy or resist the growing expansionist tendencies of the European powers.

In Tunisia, the Ottomans initially appointed *beylerbeys* or Pashas as regents with limited terms in office and a military council (*diwan*) to advise them. This system was overthrown by a bloody military revolt in 1591, following which the Ottomans were compelled to allow the Tunisian military aristocracy greater autonomy. Now the *diwan* elected a "head of state" for life with the title of dey, while the role of the Ottoman resident was limited to official functions, a system that was to stay in place until 1640. The Tunisian coastal cities also enjoyed great prosperity, thanks to their rich merchants and the trade in Christian slaves, from which the magnificently rebuilt city of Tunis profited greatly. After the Moors were driven out of Spain – following the Moresco rebellion of 1568–1571 – and finally expelled in 1609, most of them settled in Tunisia. The newcomers stimulated the economy by introducing advanced manufacturing techniques.

In 1640, a high government official, the energetic Hammuda ibn Murad (1640–1659), took power, pacified large areas of the country, and installed the Muradid dynasty, who relied on the Ottoman Empire in foreign policy, but remained largely autonomous as far as domestic matters were concerned. However, Hammuda's grandson and his whole family fell victim to a conspiracy of

Bab al-Khamis City Gate in Meknes, late 12th century
Mulai Ismail was the 2nd ruler of the Alawite dynasty, still in power in Morocco. During his reign he governed the country with an iron fist, secured its independence, and built the "Imperial City" of Meknes, one of the most impressive fortresses in the Maghreb. The capital, with its massive, impregnable city gates, were constructed by 30,000 slaves.

The most important building in Mulai Ismail's "Imperial City" is the ruler's magnificently decorated mausoleum, which consists of an antechamber, which non-Muslim tourists can visit, and the tomb chamber itself, reserved for Muslims. Mulai Ismail's love of self-interest, and his extravagant appearance made him famous far beyond Morocco.

Turkish officers in 1702. The Turkish cavalry commander Husain ibn Ali (1705–1735) emerged as the victor from the ensuing turbulence. After his recognition by the Ottomans, he founded the Husainid dynasty, which formally held power until the proclamation of the Republic, in 1957.

The rule of the Husainids was unstable at first, but they proved to be active builders. Conditions approached civil war when Husain was toppled in 1735 by his nephew, Ali Pasha, who had originally been designated to be the next in line to the throne, but was then demoted, and had to flee to Morocco with his family. In 1756 Husain's sons removed the enlightened regime of Ali Pasha (1735–1756) with Algerian help. Tunis was plundered by the Algerian troops, and the usurper executed. Under Ali Pasha's successors, Ali (1759–1782) and Hammuda (1782–1814), the country's economy was reorganized. The consequence of this was an era of such great prosperity that the reign of Hammuda Bey is known as "Tunisia's Golden Age." He aspired to extensive independence in cultural policy and put an end to Algerian dominance in the region, which had been a constant factor since 1756, when his troops won a decisive victory in 1807. Turkish influence declined rapidly, while the Husainids promoted the creation of a "Tunisian national state" within the Arabic-speaking world. Arabic replaced Turkish as the official language in 1830, and the government built up elite Arab army units (*mamluks*). However, Tunisia's debts to Europe became increasingly unmanageable, and eventually the country had to hand over all control of sea trade to the European powers.

The mid-19th century French intervention

The pretext for the direct French intervention in Algeria, which had been planned for some time, was provided by the high credits Jewish merchants had extended to France and the large amounts that the dey of Algiers had lent to earlier French governments. When France failed to react to repeated demands for repayment, Algeria broke off diplomatic relations in 1827. In response, the French bombarded Algerian ports until they were allowed access, and landed troops who occupied Algiers in July 1830 and conquered the country in the years that followed. Algeria thus became a French colony, but France would gain little happiness from it.

In 1834 the administration of Algeria was divided into *départements* on the French model. The number of European settlers rose rapidly, and the land was

Left: Agostino Veneziano, **Khair al-Din Barbarossa**, copperplate engraving, 1535, Berlin, Kupferstichkabinett
The pirate Barbarossa and his elder brother Aruj led the Corsairs at the beginning of 16th century.

Above: Eugène Delacroix, **Sultan Mulai Abd al-Rahman of Morocco, on horseback**, oil on canvas, 1845, Toulouse, Musée des Augustines
This painting depicts the sultan accompanied by his personal guardian in front of the gates of Meknes.

Left: **Interior at the Dar-Meluli Palace in Tunis**

The French occupation of Algeria, and the Protectorates imposed on Morocco (1863) and Tunisia (1881–1883), were accompanied by a Europeanization of taste and lifestyle in the countries of the Maghreb that was characteristic of the age of colonialism. It became fashionable among members of the upper and educated classes of these countries to decorate houses and palaces with French furniture and European historical paintings, though the traditional design of the buildings and the eastern approach to the division of living spaces were maintained. As it was common for people to obtain furniture on brief European tours or make regular purchases through intermediaries, many of these 19th-century living rooms simply look like overcrowded jumbles of the most disparate artistic styles.

Right: **Bardo Palace in Algiers**

The two Bardo Palaces on the outskirts of the cities Algiers and Tunis were the residences of senior local dignitaries. The Husainid beys lived in the Tunis Bardo. Both palaces, which combined oriental magnificence with French-influenced luxury, now house museums of national history. The representatives of the colonial powers in the 19th and 20th centuries did not interfere with the ceremonial functions of the domestic elites, but removed all political power from them by ensuring that the administration, army, and economy were firmly in the hands of European personnel.

placed under the rule of a governor-general with civil and military powers appointed by Paris. There was an aggressive program to requisition land and distribute it to French colonists, to whom large loans were extended. This ruined the native farmers, who were displaced to the coastal cities, where they lived as an impoverished proletariat. Trade and the exploitation of the recently discovered mineral deposits came firmly into French hands. The native elites were given a traditional French schooling, but kept well away from real power for a long time, while the colonists, the "Algerian French," exercised immense influence.

In the 19th century Morocco was led by a series of rulers who were eager to reform the country, but who came under increasing pressure due to the its economic dependence on Europe. In 1844 Morocco's military intervention in the struggle for the freedom of the Maghreb led to a defeat against the French at Isly, following which the country was forced to accept European interference, and in 1860 its army was crushed by the Spanish. On account of the high contributions demanded by Spain, Morocco found itself forced to sign the Béclard Convention with France in 1863. This made Morocco a French protectorate, and France eventually imposed a political, economic, and military administration based on a European model and run by French advisors. The local elites were supervised closely, and the most fertile land was given to European settlers, removing most of the control that the sultan and the *makhzan* still exercised over the economy. For a long time Morocco was only able to gain a hearing at European-dominated international conferences provided that this served the balance of power between the imperial regimes.

Tunisia resisted French intervention for longer than the other Maghrebi countries. The enthusiastic reformers Ahmad Bey (1837–1855) and Muhammad al-Saadiq (1859–1882) introduced many changes inspired by European ideas (abolition of slavery, reforms of the army, education system, and administration), but disastrous fiscal policies bankrupted the state in 1852. In

Interior of the Dar-Meluli Palace in Tunis
In the 19th century rooms lined with mirrors based on French models became popular, particularly in Algeria and Tunisia. The hall of mirrors in the Dar-Meluli Palace creates the optical illusion that it is much larger than it actually is. The stucco frames around the windows and mirrors are based on eastern forms, and are examples of an exceedingly elaborate Moorish style.

1861 agreement was reached on a constitution, and Tunisia became a constitutional monarchy. In 1869 natural catastrophes and failed harvests finally led to the country being placed under the supervision of the International Financial Commission on Tunisia, which was largely controlled by the French. The ambitious reformist policies launched in the late 1860s were sabotaged by the European powers. They were abandoned abruptly when the modernizing prime minister Khair al-Din was dismissed as a result of French pressure in 1877 because the Europeans were concerned about the possibility of Tunisia becoming more independent. In 1881 France imposed the Bardo Treaty, which made Tunisia – like Morocco – a French protectorate. France now controlled the country's foreign and military policy, the administration was restructured along the lines of French managemant style, and French and Italian colonists were settled in large numbers.

Like the other European colonies and protectorates in the Islamic world, the whole Maghreb experienced a radical transformation of its political and economic structures during the 19th century, at the end of which the urban population was increasing at an explosive rate, and the most profitable land was in the hands of European settlers, whose numbers were also growing rapidly. Rich mineral resources had now been discovered and were being systematically exploited by the European powers and the commercial enterprises to which they awarded licenses. After the Second World War all the countries of the region were faced with the challenge of managing the long-desired transition to independence from European rule at the same time as they carried out fundamental reforms of their traditionally structured social systems.

Architecture
Natascha Kubisch

Political power gradually slipped away from the last of the Almohad rulers of al-Andalus and the Maghreb in the first half of the 13th century. The central Maghreb still remained an Almohad province for the time being, but the western Maghreb, an area roughly equivalent to present day Morocco and inhabited by Berber tribes, fell to the Banu Marin, a clan from the western Sahara. Their descendants were to be the magnificent Merinid dynasty.

The Merinids conquered Fez in 1248 and made it their capital. In the year 1269 they took Marrakech, the former capital of the Almohad empire, which finally collapsed as a result. At the same time the Merinids attempted to extend their territory to the east, where the Banu l-Wad had taken power in Tlemcen. Tlemcen was an important military base on the way to Ifriqiya, where the Banu Hafs – the Hafsids – had come to power in 1230. They ruled over the eastern Maghreb – parts of present-day Algeria, including the cities Bougie, Constantine, and Biskra – and Tunisia, and chose Tunis to be the capital of their empire.

Courtyard of the Qarawiyin Mosque in Fez looking toward the minaret, 12th century
In the courtyard of the Qarawiyin Mosque are two remarkable pavilions decorated with stucco openwork. They were constructed opposite each other on the longitudinal axis of the courtyard, and extend out over basins of water, intended for ritual ablutions before worship in the prayer hall. The pavilions were built in the 14th century under the Merinids, and are laid out and decorated in a similar fashion to the pavilions in the Court of Lions at the Alhambra in Granada.

The Merinids of Fez

Fez was founded in 798 by Idris I, a descendant of Ali, the cousin and brother-in-law of the Prophet Muhammad. Today his grave at Mulai Idris is still the most venerated site of pilgrimage in Morocco. Fez experienced a flowering of culture in the 9th century thanks to immigrants from Kairouan, after whom the Qarawiyan Mosque is named, and from al-Andalus, who mainly came from Cordoba and founded the Andalusian Quarter that is named after them. The city's strong position as a trading center was achieved mainly thanks to its strategically favorable situation. The most important east-west route in Morocco ran from the Taza Gap in present-day Algeria to Fez and Meknes, and ended at Rabat or Salé. The most important north-south routes started from either Fez or Meknes. They ran to Marrakech and from there continued over the High Atlas to the oases of Tafilelt. A large proportion of the gold trade between al-Andalus, the Maghreb, and sub-Saharan Africa (Sudan and Ghana, in particular) was carried along this route, so that Fez also profited from it. At the same time the city was developing into a cultural center. The Qarawiyin Mosque in Fez was founded in 862 and chosen as the city's main mosque in 933. In the mid-12th century it was rebuilt by the Almohads. Not only was it one of the largest mosques of the age, it also became the home of one of the most important universities in the Maghreb. For a long time the Qarawiyin formed the city's intellectual and cultural center, around which the souk, the quarter of traders and craftsmen, developed. There was a special part of the souk, the "Kaisariya," which was reserved for trade in precious goods, such as silk and jewelry.

Fez however, enjoyed its greatest prosperity under the Merinids at the end of the 13th century. On the morning of March 27, 1276, the Merinid sultan Abu Yusuf rode along the valley of Wadi Fez to Fez al-Bali, where he had a horoscope drawn up by an astrologer for the new city that he had just founded. Fez al-Jadid, "New Fez," was now to become the center of his empire, hence his decision to surround the city with massive walls, which have been almost completely preserved to the present day. Here the sultan built a large palace, the Dar al-Makhzan, and ordered the construction of the Great Mosque (1276). Other projects undertaken during his reign included the building of barracks and administrative buildings. Christian traders were permitted to establish themselves in the city, and there was a Jewish quarter, the Mellah, on the outskirts of Fez al-Jadid, that has been preserved in its original state. The medieval Old City of Fez, Fez al-Bali, which is also known as the Medina, still forms the core of the city. The European settlement that was created during the French colonial era, "White Fez," rises on the highest ground in the area. It is separated from the Old City by open spaces, so the historic urban landscape of central Fez has hardly changed since the Middle Ages.

Merinid mosques

The Great Mosque of Fez al-Jadid was founded by Abu Yusuf in 1275, and rebuilt just over a hundred years later – in year 788 of the *hegira* (1393) – as a marble inscription inside the mosque informs the visitor. The mosque is a rectangular complex 177 feet (54 meters) long and 112 feet (34 meters) wide

that consists of an almost square prayer hall and a rectangular courtyard in front of it. The courtyard is surrounded on three sides by simple arcades, and there is a minaret in the northwestern corner of the mosque. In the center of the arcade that opens onto the courtyard at the front of the prayer hall there are two entrances. The entrance to the left was probably intended for women because it allowed direct access to the women's gallery, while the one to the right was the main entrance. Other entrances can be seen at the sides of the courtyard and the sides of the prayer hall. Visitors who go into the mosque through the main entrance find themselves standing directly on the mosque's longitudinal axis, which runs through the courtyard and the prayer hall, and leads to the *mihrab* or prayer niche. The prayer hall has seven aisles, each with six bays, which are decorated with elegantly curved horseshoe arches. In front of the *qibla* wall, which indicates the direction of Mecca, there is a long transverse aisle similar to those Almohad mosques. This forms a T-shape in combination with the central aisle leading to the *mihrab*. The T-type, as it is known, had become a common feature of Almoravid and Almohad mosques by the 12th century, and it was retained in the Merinid architecture of the late 13th century. This is hardly surprising, as the Merinids understood themselves as the direct successors of the Almohad caliphs, an attitude not only expressed in their religious doctrine and politics, but also in their architectural program. In addition to its magnificent *mihrab*, the prayer hall of the Great Mosque of Fez al-Jadid is notable for its large, richly decorated ribbed dome, which rises above the *mihrab* bay, intensifying the effect of the *mihrab* markedly. There is

another dome at the beginning of the central aisle, where it was placed to accentuate the building's longitudinal axis, which marks it out as an "axial" mosque. Both domes are reminiscent of the ribbed domes of the Great Mosque of Cordoba (as extended by al-Hakam II, 963–966), which rise to the side of the central dome over the *mihrab* bay and therefore accentuate the significance of the *maqsura* area that was reserved for the caliph.

Ribbed domes continued to be characteristic of the Almoravid mosques of the 12th century, as for example at the Great Mosque of Tlemcen (founded in 1182). At Fez, however, *muqarnas*, or stalactite, vaults were added above the central aisle of the Qarawiyin Mosque during the period of Almoravid building (1135–1142). The plan of this mosque, with its rectangular prayer hall and a courtyard surrounded by arcades, is similar to the great Almohad mosques of the 12th century, such as the Great Mosque of Taza (founded in 1142) in Algeria, the Mosque of Tinmal (1153/54) in the High Atlas, and the two Kutubiya Mosques in Marrakech, of which only the Second Kutubiya (1158) still exists. The courtyards of the Merinid mosques tended to become

Prayer hall and vault of the Qarawiyin Mosque in Fez, 12th century
The *muqarnas*, or stalactite, vaults of the Qarawiyin Mosque date back to the building work carried out by the Almoravids in the mid-12th century and were originally intended to accentuate the most important part of the building, the central aisle leading to the *mihrab*. These vaults have been restored many times in the following centuries in order to maintain their original beauty.

square with the passage of time. The interiors of the prayer halls are a surprising contrast to their plain exteriors. They are decorated with rich stucco work, which is mainly concentrated in the area around the *mihrab*. The large, interlaced geometrical patterns covering every surface, which had been typical of the Almohad period, now became less prominent. At the same time, the calligraphic inscriptions were finer and more elegant, and the foliate patterns, with their arabesques and flower motifs, grew increasingly delicate, multilayered, and rich. These ornamental features, with their rich variety of motifs, are among the most beautiful and influential elements of Merinid architecture which was to have a long-lasting influence on the artistic development of Morocco in the centuries that followed.

One of the most outstanding successes of Merinid architecture was the development of the *madrasa*, the religious law school. In contrast to the Koranic schools, the students at a *madrasa* did not study the Koran alone, but the whole range of Islamic law.

In the Maghreb, Islamic law (*fiqh*) is based closely on the Sunna and is opposed to the preaching of heterodox doctrines. Since civil servants were recruited from the *madrasas*, they functioned simultaneously as legal schools, universities, and training centers for high office, and the students who studied in them also received board and lodging. The concept of the *madrasa* developed in the east of the Islamic world and was introduced to the Maghreb in the 14th century, finding its highest development under the Merinids.

Merinid *madrasas*

The Merinids founded numerous *madrasas*, such as the Saffarin Madrasa (1271), which was built by Sultan Abu Yusuf on the banks of Wadi Fez at the beginning of the city's cultural and artistic ascendancy. The early Merinid *madrasas* in Fez include the Madrasa of Fez al-Jadid, which was built by Abu Said in 1320, and the al-Sahrij Madrasa (1321–1328), which prince Abu Hasan (1331–1351) built in memory of his father. Abu Hasan also ordered the construction of the Misbahiya Madrasa (1346), which is named after a scholar of the day and was built close to the Qarawiyin Mosque. The Misbahiya Madrasa was used as a hostel by the students of the University of Fez until the middle of the 20th century. The Sbaiiyin Madrasa stands in the same part of the city, and there is also, of course, the Attarin Madrasa (1323–1325), which was built in the middle of the spice traders' bazaar. It is the most elegant, and certainly the most impressive, *madrasa* in the city. An L-shaped entrance isolates the tranquility of the courtyard from the bustle of life on the street. Two doors open to the side of the vestibule, one leading to the bath for ritual ablutions (*midha*), the other to a staircase giving access to the student quarters on the upper story. The side galleries running along the courtyard are richly articulated with arches, wooden pillars, and decorative stucco. The real charm of this building resides in its combination of small and large arches, and the stuccoed wooden beams and piers, which alternate with onyx columns. The prayer hall itself is a simple, almost square space with attractive mosaic-tile dadoes and an exquisitely decorated *mihrab*. Surprisingly, the *mihrab* is not on the central axis of the mosque, but slightly to one side against the eastern wall, which faces Mecca. The *mihrab* axis runs at right angles to the axis of the courtyard and therefore forms an unusual, if ingenious, architectural solution.

The Madrasa of Salé (1341), which Abu Hasan built across the river from Rabat, stands out mainly for its fine decorative work. This is stylistically related to the Nasrid ornamentation of Granada, and therefore underlines the close artistic links between the two dynasties. Abu Hasan's son, Sultan Abu Inan (1351–1358), built the Bu Inaniya Madrasa named after him in Fez (1350–1355). This is certainly one of the largest Merinid buildings, and was provided by its founder with a pulpit from which the Friday sermon was preached, thus giving it the status of a Friday (congregational) mosque. Apart from this, Abu Inan had a minaret built and donated the money for a water clock. The Bu Inaniya has two entrances, of which one has a vestibule and leads through a long passage to the courtyard, while the other, the main entrance, lies directly on the central axis of the building. Its two doors are magnificently decorated with beautiful bronze hinges and massive door knockers. One door opens directly onto the courtyard, while the other leads to steps going up to the upper story, where there were lecture rooms for the students. Anyone who enters the courtyard immediately becomes aware of the peace and seclusion of this place. The rectangular courtyard is surrounded on three sides by two-story galleries, their facades richly decorated with colorful mosaic-tile dadoes, stucco

work, and the exquisitely carved wood of the beams and piers. There is another ring of students' cells behind these galleries. A pool in the center of the courtyard and a 6-foot (2-meter) wide channel at the rear were used for ritual ablutions. Two bridges lead across the channel to the prayer hall at the sides of the courtyard. The mosque was not used solely by the students, but also by the inhabitants of the quarter, many of whom still come to pray at the Bu Inaniya Madrasa today.

The facade of the prayer hall facing the courtyard is divided into two stories, of which the lower is articulated by five arches opening into the prayer hall. The central arch is slightly higher than the others. The prayer hall measures 57 × 43 feet (17.25 × 13 meters) and was built by Abu Said. The two transepts, which run parallel to the *qibla* wall, are divided by five arches supported on onyx columns with ornate capitals. The glorious *mihrab* itself, with its opulent carved stucco, makes the Bu Inaniya in Fez one of the most beautiful buildings of the Merinid period.

In the center of each of the galleries flanking the courtyard there is a large arch with heavy gates that leads into a lecture room. Both the lecture rooms are about 16 × 16 feet (5 x 5 meters), crowned with massive ribbed domes built of wood, and surrounded by passages that connected directly to the galleries above, so allowing the students to go directly from their cells to their lessons. The design of these two side classrooms is reminiscent of the Egyptian *madrasas*, such as the Hasan Mosque in Cairo, which was built 12 years later

Left: **Courtyard of the Attarin Madrasa in Fez**, 1323–1325
The Attarin Madrasa was built by the Merinids in the first quarter of the 14th century at one end of the spice bazaar, after which it is named. Today this building is still one of the most beautiful and magnificent *madrasas* in Fez. Its courtyard captivates the eye due to the spacious impression it creates, the regular articulation of the walls, and their colorful mosaic-tile dadoes, fine stucco panels, and exquisite wood carving. Apart from foliate and calligraphic motifs, the carved stucco on the walls is decorated with geometrical patterns and the infinitely repeating ornamental niches of *muqarnas* vaulting.

Above: **Carved stucco at the Attarin Madrasa in Fez**, 1323–1325
The courtyard of the Attarin Madrasa is lined with columns crowned by elaborate capitals supporting richly carved stucco arches. This heavily stylized capital bears a simplified acanthus wreath, while the abacus lying on top of it is decorated with delicate arabesques and volutes. The pillar dadoes are covered with glazed mosaic tiles, and are reminiscent of the decorative dadoes found in the Alhambra in Granada.

The al-Sahrij Madrasa is named after the courtyard fountain (*sahrij*), the waters of which flow into an unusually large pool. This courtyard is a showcase for the whole range of ornament used in Merinid architecture. The floor is tiled, the walls are decorated with a colorful mosaic-tile dado topped by a stucco frieze, and the finely carved portals are framed by richly decorated wooden panels.

Above: **Decorated facade at the al-Sahrij Madrasa in Fez**, 1321–1328
The al-Sahrij Madrasa is one of the oldest *madrasas* in Fez. The carved stucco panels and arches stand out particularly effectively against the smooth surface of the wall.

Above right: **Carillon at the Bu-Inaniya Madrasa in Fez**, 1350–1355
The carillon at the Bu-Inaniya Madrasa with 13 bronze hammer bells was donated by the Merinid ruler Abu Inan.

The kingdom of the Abd al-Wadids or Ziyanids of Tlemcen

The small kingdom of the Abd al-Wadids, who became the rulers of Tlemcen in 1236, consisted mainly of territory along the coastline, including the cities Oran and Algiers. In the 13th century Tlemcen was a significant economic center frequented equally by Muslim and Christian merchants. Its harbor, Honein, situated close to Oran, connected the kingdom to the countries on the other side of the Mediterranean, and its caravans made their way over the High Atlas to Tafilelt and sub-Saharan Africa. The founder of the dynasty, Emir Yaghmorasan ibn Zaiyan (1236–1283), had the Almoravid Great Mosque of Tlemcen extended to the north and added a courtyard surrounded by arcades to the prayer hall. The emir abandoned the old fortress, which stood next to the mosque, and built a new residence, the Mexuar, the perimeter walls of which are still standing.

The small Mosque of Sidi ibn Hasan in Tlemcen (1296) also dates from the same period and features a captivating, exquisitely decorated *mihrab*. However, the most impressive, and largest, buildings in the city were the work of Abu ibn Tashfin I (1318–1337), the fifth Abd al-Wadid ruler. According to Arabic chronicles, he constructed three palaces in Tlemcen. Only Muslim prisoners captured on his campaigns against the Merinids were allowed to work on his building projects, which explains their stylistic similarities to Merinid architecture.

In the 13th century the Merinids launched repeated attacks on Tlemcen. As a base for their siege of the city, they assembled their troops in the huge camp they founded nearby, Mansura. This fortress, which is now close to the border between Morocco and Algeria, was a massive military city heavily

than Bu Inaniya and therefore belongs to the same period. The Moroccan religious sensibility is expressed not only in its mosques and *madrasas*, but also in the memorials that were built at the tombs of revered figures. Many of the tombs of Sufi saints, who are known as *marabouts*, became sites of worship. In the Middle Ages, a form of mysticism involving elements of popular Islam developed and spread widely in the Maghreb. The ascetics and Sufis of the region were inspired by a passionate faith and sought ecstasy in the service of God. The Sufis established many religious foundations, including *ribats* (fortified monasteries) and *zawiyas* (places of reflection), in which recitations of the Koran were led by respected teachers. The Zawiya al-Nossak at Salé was built by Abu Inan and highlights the earlier importance of this city, which was founded by settlers who had moved the short distance from Almohad Ribat. At the beginning of the 14th century, the Zawiya al-Nossak at Salé was incorporated into the Challa (1310–1339), the Merinid royal mausoleum, which was soon abandoned. Abu l-Hasan (1331–1351), the last member of the family to be buried in the Challa, founded a *ribat* there just a few years before his death, as an inscription on the monumental entrance portal of the mausoleum tells us, but all that remains of this walled necropolis are the two small mosques with their richly decorated minarets and the hostels that were built for pious pilgrims.

fortified with towers and battlements. In addition to this, Mansura had a Great Mosque and numerous palaces, their decorative and architectural opulence bearing witness to the Merinids' love of luxury, even in times of war.

The Saadis of Marrakech

In the mid-16th century, the Merinid dynasty that ruled Morocco was replaced by Sharif families who claimed descent from the Prophet, while the other Maghrebi countries, Algeria and Tunisia, came nominally under the influence of the Ottoman Empire. The first important Sharif dynasty was that of the Saadis (1548–1659) in Marrakech. Only ruins remain of their residence, the famous Badi Palace (1578–1593), which was built by the legendary Sultan Ahmad al-Mansur (1578–1603). The building was demolished in the 18th century by the Alawite ruler Mulai Ismail (1672–1727), who wanted to eliminate all traces of his great predecessor. Despite this, it is possible to form an impression of its size and magnificence from the extensive site, with its abandoned gardens (*agdal*) and massive reservoir.

The most important Saadi buildings in Marrakech include the Bab-Dukkala Mosque (1557), the al-Muassin Mosque (1562), and the Ibn Yusuf Madrasa, which was extended by Mulai Abd Allah in the mid-16th century, making it one of the largest *madrasas* in the Maghreb. Its plan is reminiscent of the Great Mosque of Fez, and its magnificent stucco work and exquisite wood carvings make it just as captivating.

The best-known of the Saadi monuments are certainly the Saadi tombs of Marrakech, which are housed in two mausoleums built against the rear wall of the Casbah Mosque, from which they could originally be reached through a passage. The mausoleums are situated within a necropolis surrounded by a high wall. This site is known to have been used as a graveyard (*rauda*) by the Almohads and the Merinids, and hundreds of tombs have been preserved there, most of them prismatic in form, and many decorated with tiles. About 100 fallen funerary steles have also survived.

The two Saadi mausoleums stand in the middle of the graveyard. The smaller houses the tomb of Muhammad al-Shaikh (d. 1557). It was built by his son Mulai Abd-Allah (d. 1574), and later extended by Ahmad al-Mansur, and has a simple dome construction decorated with richly carved stucco. The mausoleum of Ahmad al-Mansur is much more magnificent.

It is divided into a prayer hall at the front and the actual mausoleum at the rear. The prayer hall, which is rectangular in plan, is divided by four columns into three aisles that run parallel to the *qibla* wall. The *mihrab* niche, with its small *muqarnas* dome, can be seen in the center of the *qibla* wall. The entrance to the mausoleum is directly on the *mihrab* axis. This mausoleum is an almost-square hall, about 33 feet (10 meters) in length divided into nine bays by twelve columns of Italian marble. The side bays are crowned with small *muqarnas* vaults, while there is a wooden ceiling over the central, slightly higher, bay, which is square and flanked by arches resting on columns crowned with capitals. On each side there is a group of three arches supported on columns with opulent capitals. The walls above are decorated with stucco fields. Their ornamentation is based on a *sebka* pattern of adjacent rhombuses, which are built up of crossing tendrils and decorated with delicate arabesques. The side walls of the mausoleum bear a high dado of mosaic tiling, above which

Above: **Mausoleum of Mulai Ismail in Meknes**

The mausoleum of Mulai Ismail (1672–1727) stands close to the Great Mosque in the center of the Imperial City of Meknes, which the sultan built in the late 17th and early 18th centuries as his royal residence. Mulai Isamil's iron rule reorganized Morocco and he presided over a period of great economic prosperity. The rich decoration of the mausoleum reflects the importance of this ruler, though its modern appearance is now very different from its original state due to additions and restoration work.

Interior of a Saadi mausoleum in Marrakech, 2nd half of the 16th century
The Saadi mausoleums of Marrakech house the family tombs of the Saadi dynasty, one of the two Sharif families that have ruled Morocco since the mid-16th century. Notable features of this mausoleum include the prismatic tombs in the foreground and the colorful mosaic-tile dadoes with their geometrical motifs. The plain wall above provides an effective background to the carved stucco of the arch.

Bab al-Mansur in Meknes
The massive Bab al-Mansur Gate leads to the Mausoleum of Mulai Ismail (the interior of which is pictured on the opposite page), the great second sultan of the Alawite dynasty. The facade of this symmetrical structure is covered with lavish decorations and articulated by three deep recesses. The massive central gateway is constructed as a horseshoe arch.

there is a narrow stucco frieze with bands of calligraphic decoration. Above this, extensive fields of stucco with geometrical and foliate motifs rise up to the ceiling, which is 8 feet (11.5 meter) high. The contrast between the height of the hall and the restricted floor space creates a unique effect.

Above the center of the mausoleum there is an artesonado ceiling, an elaborately joined and paneled cedarwood construction. The wooden beams and panels are brightly painted and gilded to create a complex geometrical pattern based on star shapes. Ahmed al-Mansur rests under this "starry sky," surrounded by the tombs of his children and relatives. Even though the Saadis were not great innovators in architecture and interior decor compared to the Merinids, this building captivates the viewer with its rich carved stucco and the magnificent colors of its mosaic-tile dadoes. The seclusion of this place in the center of the city's lively bustle leaves an unforgettable impression on the visitor.

The Alawite dynasty

Saadi rule was brought to an end in the mid-17th century by the Alawites, Morocco's second great Sharif dynasty, which still rules the country today. The Alawites trace their descent back to al-Hasan, the grandson of the prophet. They originated in the mountains south of the High Atlas and the oases of Tafilelt. The founder of the dynasty, Sultan Mulai al-Rashid (1664–1672), kept Fez as his capital. He had the city walls fortified as soon as he took power and built the Sherratine Madrasa (1670) close to the Qarawiyin Mosque, the intellectual and cultural center of the city. His son Mulai Ismail (1672–1727) later moved the court to Meknes.

Mausoleum of King Muhammad V, in Rabat
In Rabat, the Royal Capital of Morocco, King Hassan II (1961–1999) built a mausoleum for his father, Muhammad V, close to the ruins of the massive, unfinished Almohad Hasan Mosque. The almost cube-shaped mausoleum is visible from some distance far away, and the tomb chamber is crowned by a tent roof covered with green tiles.

Meknes, the Imperial City

Meknes is divided into the ancient, traditional Medina, the fabric of which dates mainly from the Merinid period (14–16th centuries), and the Imperial City, which is quite distinct and was built as a royal residence on the orders of Mulai Ismail in the late 17th and early 18th centuries. The core of this huge complex, with its triple ring of walls, is formed by the Dar al-Kabira, the palace compound known as the "Great House," in which the city's main mosque (1670) is to be found. This mosque is named after Lalla Auda, a pious woman of the time. Nearby stands the Mausoleum of Mulai Ismail, which is topped with a green tiled roof. The mausoleum is now open to all visitors, though only Muslims are permitted to enter the tomb chamber. Other palatial buildings, including living quarters, reception rooms, small prayer halls, and *hammams* (traditional Arab bathhouses), are grouped around the mausoleum. A huge network of covered narrow streets runs beneath the Imperial City, a labyrinth in which tourists have been known to get terribly lost. The inner palace compound of the Imperial City, Dar al-Kabira, is surrounded by a double ring of walls, beyond which are extensive residential areas, reception rooms, barracks and warehouses of the most varied kinds. The adjacent gardens, a huge palace complex measuring 2 × 1 miles (3 × 2 kilometers), were built by thousands of slaves. The garden's most interesting features are the ornamental pavilions and the large water reservoir (the Agdal Basin).

After Mulai Ismail's death, some of the Alawite sultans ruled from Fez, and some from Marrakech. As a result, Meknes soon went into decline, and many of the buildings erected by Mulai Ismail fell into disrepair. From the 18th century onwards, the Alawites shared their building activity equally between the cities Fez, Marrakech, Rabat, Meknes, and Tetouan, but the most magnificent palaces are to be found in Marrakech. Mention should be made of the heavily restored Dar al-Baida Palace, which was built by Mulai Muhammad Abd Allah (1757–1789), and the Dar al-Makhzan Palace, which was completed in the 19th century. The Alawite palaces are characterized by their comfortable living spaces and their generously laid out inner courtyards, which are designed as ornamental gardens (*riads*) with fountains, beds of flowers, and fragrant orange and lemon trees. The most beautiful garden is at the Bahia Palace (1894–1900) in Marrakech. This complex was built at the end of the 19th century by a former slave who had risen to become a vizier. As many senior officials and affluent merchants were involved in the construction of these palaces, there is a sense in which these buildings genuinely represented the citizenry of the Maghrebi cities. The palace architecture of the Alawites was strongly bound to Andalusian and North African traditions, but there is often a European touch to the interior design that is to be attributed to the period of the French protectorate (1912–1956).

Rabat, Morocco's Royal Capital

King Hassan II (1961–1999) built a mausoleum in memory of his father, Muhammad V, in Rabat, the modern capital of Morocco. This building was erected opposite the Hasan Tower, the minaret of the Almohad Hasan Mosque (1195–1196), a massive complex that was never completed. Apart from this, Rabat is the site of the Royal Palace, the magnificent interior decoration of which is a masterpiece of Moroccan craftsmanship. However, there can be no doubt that the most important modern building in the country is the Great Mosque of Casablanca, with its 660 foot (200 meter) high minaret, which was built by Hassan II as a symbol of modern Morocco.

The Hafsids of Tunis

In the 13th century the Hafsid dynasty (1229–1574) established control over the eastern Maghreb. Sultan Abu Zakariya I was the Almohad governor of Ifriqiya (1228–1237), who eventually became an independent emir (1237–1249). Soon after coming to power, he built a mosque and minaret (1233) in the Tunis Casbah, which had been founded by the Almohads. With the simple pillars of its prayer hall, the architecture of this mosque is firmly in the local tradition, but the *mihrab* bay, with its stalactite vault, appears to have been based on models in Andalusia and the Maghreb, such as the Qarawiyin Mosque in Fez. The Sammaiya (1249), the oldest *madrasa* in Tunis, was also founded by Abu Zakariya. The magnificently colorful mosaic tiling, rich stucco work, and exquisite wood carvings of this building are strongly reminiscent of Merinid *madrasas*.

The souk, the Arab market devoted mainly to the sale of costly spices and fabrics, was built directly next to the Great Mosque of Tunis, which was established by the Almohads during the first half of the 12th century. The souk is entered through a great arched gateway flanked by columns with acanthus capitals. The simple treatment of the acanthus leaves identifies these capitals as typically Hafsid. The three streets in the souk, of which the central one is slightly wider than the others, are lined with colonnades and covered with vaults. Large wooden doors lead into the shops on either side. These shops were built on two stories, with goods on sale in the lower story and storage space

Right: Mosque of Sidi Mahrez in Tunis, 1675

The Sidi Mahrez Mosque is the only mosque in Tunis to have been built in the Ottoman-Turkish style. Typical for this type of mosque is the nearly square plan of the central building, which is surrounded by arcades on three sides. The prayer hall is dominated by four huge pillars supporting a pendentive and a drum, on which the massive central dome rests. This is flanked by four small half-domes, while more domes can be seen at the corners of the building. However, this mosque also shows features of the Tunisian architectural tradition. For example, it has two prayer halls, one on top of the other. The lower prayer hall dates from the time of Abu Muhammad, one of the last Hafsid rulers, while the upper one, which is reached from the street by a flight of steps, is typically Ottoman.

Below: Saber Mosque in Kairouan, 1860

Kairouan has three important *zawiyas,* or places of spiritual reflection. The activities and functions of these institutions are comparable to those of *madrasas.* The Zawiya of Sidi Amor Abbada was built in 1860 as a mausoleum for a blacksmith venerated as a saint. It contains an enormous tobacco pipe and several sabers made by him that give the mosque its name. The Saber Mosque is distinguished by its five fluted domes, which can be seen from all over Kairouan. Distant precursors of these domes can be found in the east, though the construction of domes has a tradition which goes back to the 9th century in Tunisia.

upstairs. Tunis was an important commercial center under the Hafsids (13–16th centuries) and has retained its commercial vitality to this day.

Unfortunately, the gardens that Caliph al-Mustansir (1249–1277) laid out close to his capital no longer exist, but we know about them from the descriptions left by the historian Ibn Khaldun (1322–1406). The scholar describes date, pomegranate, and olive trees, vines, tamarisks, orange and lemon trees, jasmine, and myrtle, all of which were planted in the now lost park of Abu Fihr not far from Tunis. According to Ibn Khaldun the park had a massive pool as "large as a sea" flanked on each side by pavilions decorated with colonnades. The French archeologist Marcel Solignac investigated this site in 1936 and measured the pool with greater precision, finding it to be 686 × 264 feet (209 × 80.5 meters). The Bardo Palace (1420) was founded by the Hafsids as a garden pavilion. It was extended in the 16th century by the Ottomans, who did a great deal of construction on it in the following centuries. In the gardens of Ras al-Tabya (which were close to the site of the Bardo Palace), Ibn Khaldun was most taken with a pavilion called Qubba Asarak, the entrance of which was decorated with magnificent doors. A Flemish traveler visited the park in the 15th century and described its cruciform plan with a central fountain and many pavilions. These extensive gardens must have been the grounds of a large palace, of which only a few traces have been uncovered by archeologists, including the remains of the drainage system and foundations of walls.

Entrance of the Kachawa Mosque in Algiers, 1794
The Kachawa Mosque in Algiers was built in 1794 by Muhammad Pasha Hasan, in the Ottoman style. During the French Protectorate that was established in 1830, it was used as a cathedral by the French and minor alterations were carried out. Today, the building, which is dominated by Egyptian and Andalusian influences, is again in use as a mosque, and is one of the most important in Algiers.

area from Cordoba (ribbed dome of the *mihrab* bay in the extension in the Great Mosque of Cordoba built by Al-Hakam II, 962–966) and Taza (dome of the Great Mosque, 1142). The horseshoe arch and the blind arches are features that appear to point to Andalusian influences, which are probably to be attributed to immigrant Andalusian craftsmen. Many Muslims were forced to emigrate from Spain during the 13th century, when the Reconquista was gaining ground and one city after another fell into the hands of the Christians. The emigrants found new homes in the Maghreb, mainly in Tunis and the cities of Morocco, and were to have a decisive influence on Tunisian culture.

Large numbers of religious foundations were established during the 14th century, including mosques, *madrasas*, and *zawiyas*, though many of these buildings were rebuilt during the Ottoman period. Without doubt, the best known *madrasa* in Tunis is the Mustansiriya (1437), the construction of which was begun by Caliph al-Mustansir (1434–1435) and completed by his brother and successor Uthman. This *madrasa* consists of a small mosque and a central courtyard, which is surrounded on all sides by cells and long halls, In this respect, it is similar to the four-*iwan madrasas* built by the Ayyubids in Egypt, such as the Sultan Hasan Mosque (1362) in Cairo, and suggests that the architecture of the late Hafsid period was also influenced by the Ayyubids.

Ottoman influence in the Maghreb

In the 16th century, the rulers of the Maghreb came under great pressure from Christian Spain, which had become stronger after 1492. Their response was to place themselves under the suzerainty of the Ottomans. The Turkish dynasty built up its influence from then on, making Algeria and Tlemcen provinces of the Ottoman Empire. This continued to be their status until the French Protectorates were established (1830 in Algeria, 1881 in Tunisia). In consequence, the art and architecture of Algeria and Tunisia were to be heavily influenced by the Ottomans for the next three centuries.

The first Ottoman buildings in Algiers were constructed close to the harbor, including the Mosque on the Fish Market, also known as the Jami al-Jadid (the New Mosque), which was built in 1660. With its restored minaret and massive central dome, it came to be regarded as a symbol of Algiers. Not far away is the Mosque of Sidi Ali Bichin, which was founded in 1622 by an Italian, Biccini, who had converted to Islam. Its architecture is based on the same scheme as all the Ottoman mosques in Algiers. It has a square prayer hall surrounded on three sides by galleries and crowned with a large, elevated central dome flanked by smaller domes and vaults. The minaret fell down in the 19th century. Another fine building in this area is the Mausoleum and Mosque of Sidi Abd al-Rahman, which is named after the Algerian mystic Abd al-Rahman al-Thaalbi (d. 1470). In the same quarter there is the Kachawa Mosque (1794), which was built by Hasan, the successor Muhammad Pasha (1765–1791). In the 19th century the French used this building as a cathedral, but did not destroy its Ottoman character, and since 1962 the Kachawa Mosque has again been one of the most important mosques in the city. The minaret and the high central dome are noticeable features of the mosque's exterior. The central dome is flanked by barrel vaults running along the axes of the building and smaller domes set slightly to each side. In this respect, it is similar in plan to the Mosque of Sidi Ali Bichin. Finally, mention should be made of the Safir Mosque (1534). In its current form, this building goes back to the last dey, who had it rebuilt at the beginning of the 19th century.

The Casbah of Algiers is full of traditional houses with upper stories projecting out over the street below, wooden bay windows, and delicate stucco arches. There are only a few Ottoman buildings in the Casbah, such as the two Husain Mosques that date from the end of the 18th and early 19th century.

The successor of Caliph al-Mustansir, al-Warhiq, had fortifications built at Tunis for the first time in 1276, large parts of which are still preserved. The two city gates, Bab al-Jadid (New Gate), which is flanked by two formidable towers, and Bab al-Manara, which leads into the city through a horseshoe arch, date from this period.

The Hafsids did not, however, neglect Kairouan, the traditional religious center of the empire. At the end of the 13th century (1293/94) Caliph Abu Hafs Umar (d. 1295) undertook major reconstruction work at the Great Mosque of Kairouan, which had been founded by the Ayyubids in the 9th century. One of the biggest projects in the city was the Bab Laila Rihana Gate, which was named after a mystic of the time. This fortified gateway is constructed as a large horseshoe arch with blind arcades, and a ribbed dome, one of the first to be erected in the eastern Maghreb. Domes of this kind were introduced to the

The Ottomans mainly settled in the Lower City, the Janina, where they built government buildings, barracks, and palaces. The most beautiful palaces to have survived into the present include the Dar Hasan Pasha (18th century), the Dar Mustafa Pasha (1789–1799, now the National Library), the Dar al-Hamra (early 19th century), and Dar Aziza (first mentioned in 1712), and the Princesses' Palace (used as a residence until 1812 and now a museum).

All the Ottoman palaces in Algiers have an L-shaped entrance that leads into the square inner courtyard via a vestibule (*sqifa*). The courtyard is surrounded on four sides by arcades, which open onto the side chambers behind them. More living accommodation is found on the upper stories, to which access is gained from the vestibule via staircases. The inner courtyard is usually paved with marble and has a gently flowing fountain at its center. The colorful mosaic tiling of the dadoes and the two-story galleries, with their elegantly curved, pointed horseshoe arches resting on twisted columns crowned by magnificent capitals, are particularly beautiful. Often a strip of colored tiles runs between the ground floor and the first story, a feature that catches the eye in the otherwise plain courtyard facades.

The Ottomans built their summer residences on the outskirts of the region's major cities, such as the Bardo Palace (18th century) just outside Algiers. Magnificent palaces were also built at Bougie, Constantine, and Tunis. In Tunis particular mention must be made of the Dar Husain (18th century, restored 1876) and the Bardo Palace, which was situated on the edge of the city and built in the second half of the 18th century, though its grounds were only completed toward the end of the 19th century. The Ottoman legacy still continues to exert a strong influence in Tunisia. For example, when Habib Bourguiba (President of Tunisia 1956–1987), who replaced the Husainid dynasty (1705–1957) and finally lost power in 1987, built his mausoleum, a university, and a mosque at his birthplace in Monastir, the work was carried out in a neo-Ottoman style.

Pavilion and Mausoleum of Habib Bourguiba, in Monastir, 20th century
The former Tunisian president, Habib Bourguiba, (1956–1987) had a magnificent mausoleum built at his birthplace, Monastir. The central dome covered with golden luster tiles is flanked by two slim pencil minarets that frame the central building impressively. The pavilion (above), located on the road to the mausoleum, is laid out as an octagon, similar to Dome of the Rock in Jerusalem.

Decorative Arts

Natascha Kubisch

The crafts of the Maghreb and al-Andalus were dominated by the workshops of Cordoba for the whole of the Middle Ages. Even after the fall of the Caliphate of Cordoba (1031), a clear Andalusian influence continued to be felt, as is shown, for example, by the decoration of the Almoravid pulpit (1125–1130) in the Kutubiya Mosque at Marrakech. When the Almohads came to power, the political center of the region moved to Marrakech and then subsequently to Seville. This ensured that there was no weakening of the commercial links between al-Andalus and the Maghreb. The Almohads held ascetic religious beliefs and rejected excessively lavish decoration as sinful luxury. As a result, hardly any craftwork has survived from this period. The few exceptions include the famous Almohad golden jewelry at the Museum of Palma de Mallorca, and a number of bound Korans and religious manuscripts. The generally puritanical attitude to the arts and crafts did not change when the Merinids succeeded the Almohads in the mid-13th century. Like that of the Almohads, the art of the Merinids was dominated by a deep religious consciousness, which is why it is mainly religious manuscripts that have been preserved from this period. The artistic forms of the Merinid manuscripts are hardly any different from those of contemporary Andalusian examples. Moreover, in the 13th century the advancing Christian Reconquista in Spain, the subsequent capitulation of Granada (1492), and the final expulsion of Muslims and Jews, to which these events inevitably led, sent repeated waves of

immigration to the Maghreb, so that the artistic and cultural transfers continued. This process was certainly given new impetus by the final wave of migrants, who arrived in the 16th century. Their impact can be seen most clearly in the ceramic products of Tunis. For example, the Tunisian palaces of the period were decorated with magnificent ceramic tiles that are strikingly similar to contemporary Spanish work in their use of color and choice of motifs. Nevertheless, although there was a strong Andalusian influence, it was not as crucial to the development of the region's decorative style as is often assumed.

The culture of Morocco had always been strongly influenced by the Berber population. This can be traced not just in the language, but also in the country's arts and crafts. For example, the unglazed pottery of the Berbers features simple geometric patterns, which appear to be more characteristic of African than Islamic art. The golden jewelry of the Berber women was heavy and solid – it had great economic importance for them as a form of insurance in case they were ever divorced. By contrast, the metal wares produced by the goldsmiths and silversmiths of the Arab cities were much more finely worked. Exchange between the cultures took place in the urban centers, where farmers and nomads traded their agricultural produce and craft products, such as carpets, basketware, and unfired household ceramics, in return for metal goods, such as teapots, water cans, sugar hammers, and platters. The cities were also places where weapons could be bought and fine textiles purchased to make the costumes women wore for festivals. The constant cultural interaction encouraged by trade was of great significance for craft techniques. As a result, the trading cities Fez, Meknes, Marrakech, Rabat, and Tetouan developed into important centers of artisanal production. The work of skilled artisans can be seen in the architectural ornamentation of the palaces discussed previously.

Below: **Curved daggers and jewelry**, southern Morocco, 19th century
Curved silver daggers finely engraved with decorative motifs and inlaid with jewels were regarded among the Berbers as symbols of their bearer's dignity. One of the principal distinguishing characteristics of the heavy silver jewelry worn by Berber women is its combination of several silversmithing techniques in a single piece.

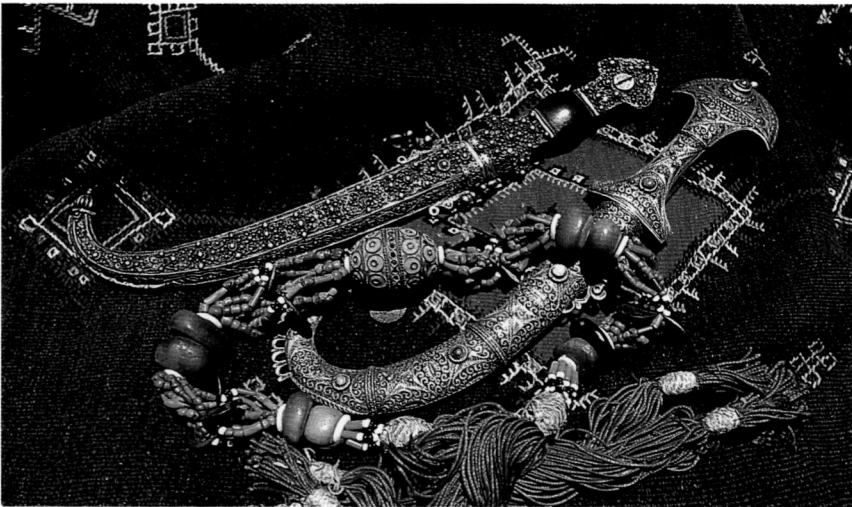

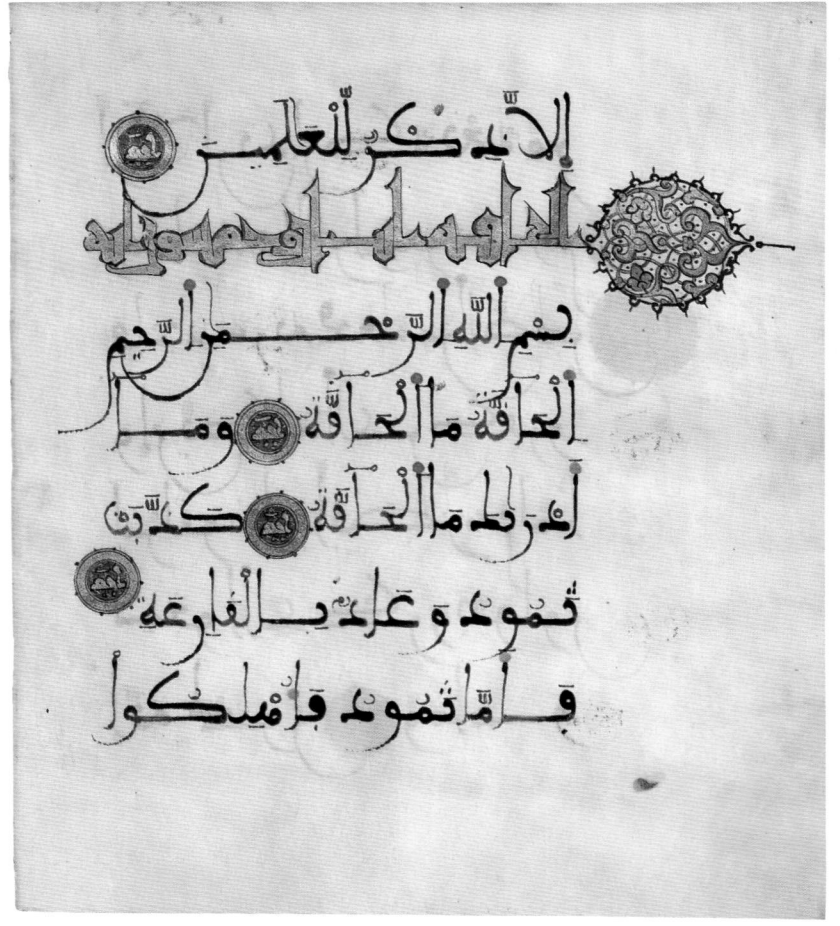

Right: **Koranic manuscript**, North Africa, 1304, black ink and gilt on parchment, Munich, Bayerische Staatsbibliothek
This Koran was commissioned in 1306 for the Merinid ruler Abu Yaqub Yusuf ibn Yaqub (1286–1307). The rounded bodies of the letters and the curved flourishes that lend the script its unique elegance are typical of "Maghribi" manuscripts, as they are known.

Left: **Glazed ceramic container**, Fez, 18th century, Paris, Musée des Arts d'Afrique et d'Océanie
Ceramics first became a major industry in Fez in the Middle Ages, though hardly any archeological evidence from this period has been found to confirm the accounts in the written sources. This *jobbana* is a traditional ceramic container, which would have originally been used to serve warm soups and stews. The *jobbana* shown here dates from the 18th century and is decorated with a fine foliate pattern.

Right: **Glazed ceramic plate**, Fez, early 19th century, Paris, Musée des Arts d'Afrique et d'Océanie
This plate bears a rare, if well-known, picture of a sailing boat on a white background surrounded by a border of small flowers. The colors are characteristic of pottery from Fez, but the picture of the sailing boat must be regarded as unusual, because figurative representations are very seldom found on Moroccan ceramics.

The colorful mosaic tiles (*zellijs*) that decorate the dadoes of many interior and external walls were cut to size from larger square tiles as required, then fitted together to create huge, geometric patterns, mostly with star motifs. The higher areas of the palace walls would be covered in magnificent stucco panels decorated with endless reciprocal patterns. They are composed of panels of stucco that were cast in large wooden molds, then carved with a knife or some other sharp implement while they were still damp, and finally painted. Apart from magnificent artesonado ceilings, Maghrebi wood carvers created beautiful gateways, doors, shutters, and chests that were used to store valuables, clothing, and household items. These chests were particularly beautifully decorated because they often formed part of a woman's trousseau. Many are carved and painted with horseshoe arches bearing rosettes and bouquets of flowers, and set with colored jewels. The shelves on which ceramic containers and spice jars were stored are examples of similarly bright, colorful paintwork. These pieces of furniture, which were more decorative than practical, must have been especially eye-catching in rooms that were traditionally sparsely decorated. Few households possessed cabinets, preferring instead to use small built-in wall cupboards. In addition to wooden furniture, many families also owned magnificently embroidered cushions and carpets, and walls were often decorated with beautiful wall hangings. The demand for such products contributed greatly to the success of the region's textile industry region.

Fabric with silk embroidery, Morocco, late 17th century, 224 × 126 cm, Private collection
This cochineal red linen, which probably comes from Azemmur in Morocco, is bordered with green silk and decorated with exceedingly rich silk embroidery. It is very uncommon for fabrics to be so well preserved. Pieces of this kind were originally used as wall hangings and formed an important component in the dowry of any bride. The selection of motifs, in particular the heavily stylized representation of birds, is reminiscent of Sassanian silks, though similar motifs are often found on carpets.

Trade and Trading Routes

Peter W. Schienerl

The Arabian Peninsula produced an exceedingly valuable commodity, incense, and was a vital part of the sea route between the Mediterranean world and India. In consequence, it was firmly integrated into the world trading network during ancient times. The biography of the Prophet makes it clear that he grew up in an environment pervaded by commerce. It was then only natural that when the Arabs succeeded in conquering a massive empire, trade should expand at an extraordinary rate and Muslim merchants find their way to the most remote areas of the then-known world. The extent of this activity is demonstrated by the great number of Islamic coins that have been found in excavations around the Baltic Sea, and the precious ceramics and valuable silks of far Eastern provenance that have been discovered in the burial sites of the Middle East, as well as many other pieces of archeological evidence. The desire for gold led Muslim traders from Morocco and the Libyan city of Tripoli straight across the Sahara to Timbuktu and Goa, while on the East African

Abbasid coin with Kufic inscription, Gotland, 751/752, Stockholm, Royal Coin Cabinet, National Museum of Economy

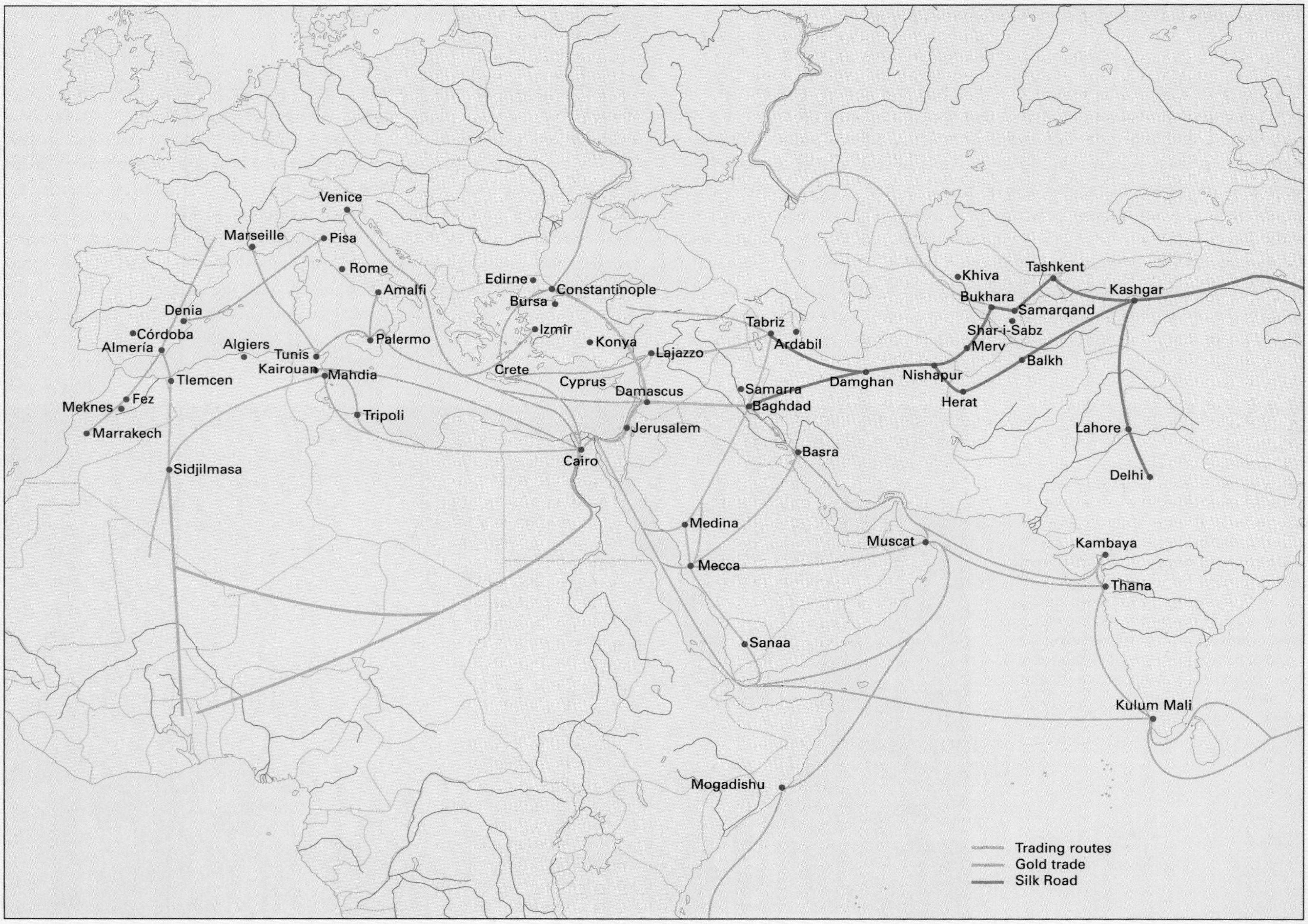

Trading routes
Gold trade
Silk Road

coast there were flourishing commercial centers, such as Sofala, Kilwa, Zanzibar, Malindi, and Mogadishu, which supplied the Islamic world with gold, slaves, ivory, rare woods, and precious stones.

After the foundation of his capital Baghdad, the Abbasid caliph al-Mansur (754–775) is credited with saying that now there was "nothing more to stop us between here and China." This demonstrated that trade could be sure of assistance from the state, for the courts and the leading strata of society relied mainly on commerce to satisfy their requirements for luxury goods. During the golden age of the Islamic empire trade was not subject to any restrictions. Customs duties were levied only on foreign merchants, who had to pay exactly the same rates as were imposed in their homelands on the goods of Muslim traders. A system of commercial law based on Islamic principles, and therefore uniform throughout the Muslim world, created a secure legal basis, without which many consortia of capital-rich merchants would not have been formed to finance particularly risky undertakings. The highly sophisticated business regulations, which differentiated between various types of partnership, joint-stock companies, and enterprises founded to carry out specific transactions for a limited period, offered merchants a sufficient range of opportunities to invest their capital profitably. There was also specialization within the merchant classes at an early date, which greatly improved the efficiency of commercial activities in many areas. A strongly developed and efficient banking and credit system – which also presupposed legal security – was highly beneficial to trade, because merchants were no longer forced to carry large amounts of gold with them on their travels.

Admittedly, these ideal circumstances were not to last very long, because the political fragmentation of the Islamic world and the economic decline with which it was associated forced many princes to augment their budgets by levying additional duties and taxes, or demanding more or less forcible contributions on the part of affluent merchants. Trade remained a very lucrative occupation, however, even under rather less-favorable conditions. The status of merchants within Islamic society was therefore very high, and their riches, their entrepreneurial spirit, and their adventurous way of life are reflected in many traditional stories, often romantically elaborated with wonderful occurrences, as in the famous tales of Sinbad the Sailor or the rhymed prose of Hariri's Assemblies, an episodic work that

Above: **Abu Zayd sailing, miniature from Hariri's** Assemblies, Baghdad, copied by Al-wasiti, 1236/37, Paris, Bibliothèque Nationale

Below: **Harith reads a message, from Hariri's** Assemblies, Baghdad, copied by Al-wasiti, 1236/37, Paris, Bibliothèque Nationale

was very influential, inspired several magnificently illustrated manuscripts.

Baghdad was not just a political center, it was also the economic heart of the empire during the golden age of the caliphate. It was here that the sea routes from China and Korea converged – via the city of Basra – bringing goods from India and the archipelagoes of South East Asia. The trading cities of the East African coast and the Arabian Peninsula were also integrated into this network of sea routes. The Silk Road, consisting of several routes that led through Central Asia, provided a land connection to the Far East. Trade with medieval Rus drew Muslim merchants to the Baltic and east-central Europe. To complete the picture, another trading route crossed the Syrian desert from Mesopotamia, connecting Baghdad with the Mediterranean.

Goods were taken up the Red Sea to Egypt, where the cities of Fustat, Cairo, and Alexandria became the most important marketplaces for the wholesale trade in the Mediterranean world – rivaled only by the Syrian coastal cities and the great trading center of Aleppo. Ships from the Italian maritime republics Venice and Genoa landed in Egypt, then returned to their home ports loaded with the luxury goods from the Orient that were so popular in Europe. Thus did the Italian maritime cities gain the riches that later made it possible for them to establish themselves as powerful forces in European politics.

By contrast with the Chinese, whose junks only rarely reached Arabia, the Muslim traders built up a network of foreign trading stations across the "Seven Seas" that had to be crossed on the way to China and the Indonesian archipelago. Silver and gold were accepted as payment practically everywhere, but the Arab ships also carried barter goods, principally worked iron and steel, as well as other metal products, carpets, and luxurious textiles. They returned westward laden with precious stones, spices, ivory, indigo, silks, the ceramic products of the Far East, ebony, and a variety of other precious woods. Some of these goods, including lead from India and paper from China, were shipped through the Persian Gulf to Basra. A second main trading route ran along the southern coast of Arabia via Muscat and Aden, where shipments also arrived from East Africa. This stream of imported goods continued through the Red Sea to Egypt, where they would be sold on for shipping to Europe or distribution throughout North Africa.

The land route to China branched out in several directions as it passed through the steppes and deserts of Central Asia. From Nishapur it was possible for the caravans to make for Kashgar, a flourishing oasis city in eastern Turkestan, either by traveling via Bukhara, Samarqand, and Tashkent, or by taking a more southerly route via Herat and Balkh. From Kashgar to Dunhuang, the "Gateway to China" situated in the Gobi desert, they either went along a northern route via Kucha or further to the south via Khotan. Within China, during this time, there was one main road that led to Peking (Khanbalik).

Furs, slaves, amber, breast plates, and swords made in central Europe were transported to Baghdad on a trading route that extended to the north and northwest. Traders followed this route to Itil, the capital of the Khazar empire on the northern coast of the Caspian Sea, and then

on to the Baltic, mostly making their way along the great river systems of Russia. This route also provided connections to eastern central Europe.

The position of superiority over the Christian West enjoyed by the Arabs and the other peoples of the Islamic world was based on this global trading network, and for many centuries the Middle East controlled the flow of goods to Europe. Only when the Portuguese rounded the Cape of Good Hope, and, a short while later, Vasco da Gama landed in India for the first time did the situation change. The first sign of a shift in the balance of power was the destruction of the Arab trading cities on the East African coast by European forces. Later, commercial monopolies were established with military backing in Oman and India, and finally the Arabs were forced out

of the profitable international trade in luxury goods and spices. South Asia became the stage on which the rivalries of the powerful European nations (the Portuguese, Dutch, British, and French) were acted out. They were soon interested in more than just trading monopolies, and eventually claimed the territories in which they held interests as colonial possessions.

In view of the international trading network developed by the Arabs, domestic commerce has often been ignored, though it was of no less significance, and routes often extended over long distances. In this respect, the annual pilgrimage was of particular importance. Many of the faithful who wanted to fulfill their religious duty paid for their accommodation along the way by selling desirable goods from their homelands. Merchants also joined the caravans of pilgrims coming from all over the world in order to sell their wares or barter them for other goods in the Hejaz. As in pre-Islamic times, Mecca was more than just a site of religious significance. Indeed, until very recently, it was also an exceedingly lively market for goods from all parts of the Islamic world.

The creation of regular stopping places for the caravans located along the important trading routes at intervals of approximately 19 miles (30 kilometers) – roughly a day's journey – was an essential precondition for the efficient transport of goods. Often caravanserais were established as religious foundations by private individuals, or built and maintained by the state. They offered the arriving caravans enough room to let their beasts of burden rest and store their goods securely, and protect travelers from thieves, robbers, and the rigors of the weather. Impressive buildings of this type have been preserved in Anatolia, where the Seljuk caravanserais are among the most remarkable achievements of Islamic architecture.

In the cities of the Islamic world, the destinations of the caravans, trade and craft production were concentrated in districts separated from residential areas. The economic center of an Islamic city, the bazaar, usually developed around the most important (usually the oldest) mosque. Here were to be found roofed-over streets of shops selling locally produced goods and wares imported from elsewhere in the Muslim world and beyond. The shops were grouped strictly by guild and the kind of goods sold, so that customers were able to compare prices and identify variations in quality. In addition to this,

Wakil Bazaar in Kerman, Iran, late 18th century

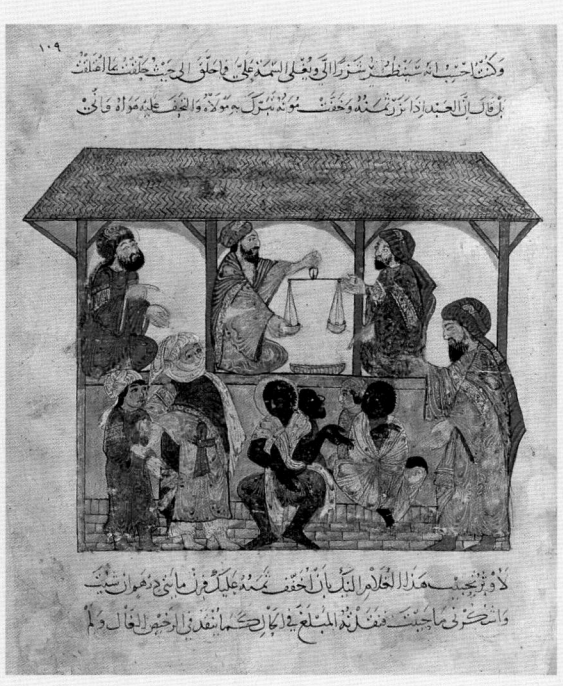

the market supervisors (*muhtasibs*) were given wide-ranging powers to prevent as much dishonest practice – such as the use of false weights and measures – as possible. Within the bazaar quarters there were complexes used mainly for wholesale trading, where traveling merchants were able to store and sell their goods. These enclosed courtyard complexes (*khans*, *wakalas*, and *funduqs*) would be entered from the street through a large gate. They housed stables for the animals used in transport, storerooms, business premises, and accommodation for merchants.

The gates to the bazaars were locked after trading stopped for the day, and additional precautions were taken at shops stocking particularly expensive goods in order to prevent theft and burglary.

The efficiency of the commercial system that developed in the areas under Arab rule made a highly significant contribution to the growth of Islamic culture.

Above: Enclosed courtyard of the Qansuh al-Ghuri Caravanserai, Cairo, 1504/05

Harith at the slave market, miniature from Hariri's *Assemblies*, Baghdad, copied by Al-wasiti, 1236/37, Paris, Bibliothèque Nationale

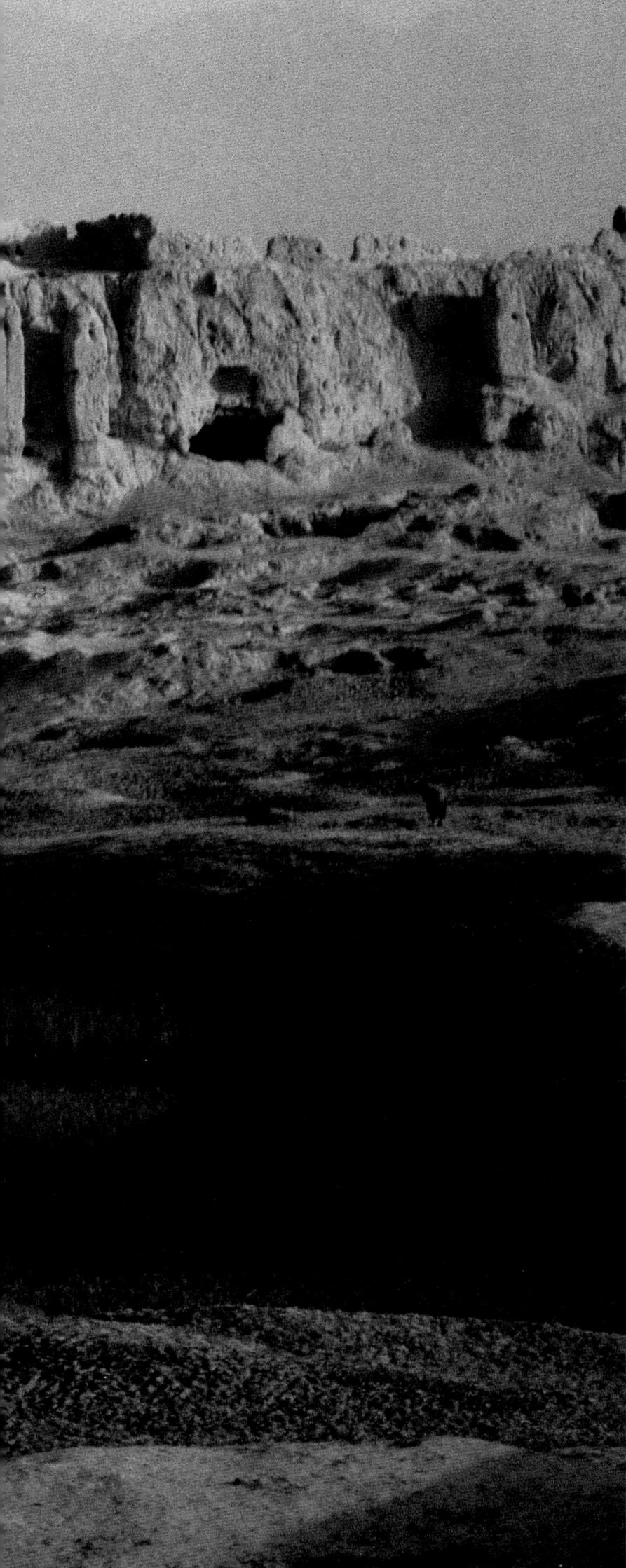

Early Empires of the East: Ghaznavids and Ghurids

The ruins of Farah, in Afghanistan
At the beginning of the 13th century, there were several flourishing city cultures on the banks of the Hilmend and the Farah Rud. The palace at Farah, long neglected by research, and possibly also the palace at Lashkar-i Bazar about 200 km to the south, were established by the 11th century.

History

Sheila Blair, Jonathan Bloom

In the 11th and 12th centuries the visual arts in the eastern Islamic lands reached an unusual level of inventiveness under the patronage of the Ghaznavid and Ghurid rulers of the region. They and their courtiers commissioned fine and varied buildings on a massive scale, which were constructed largely of mud brick and baked brick and decorated in carved stone and marble, painted and cut stucco, cut and glazed brick, and terracotta. Few of these buildings, however, have survived intact and, to imagine what these masterpieces might have been, one must extrapolate from a few tantalizing fragments of excavated remains. Writing was unusually important at these courts, whose rulers patronized poets and writers, many of whom used New Persian and transformed it from a vernacular into a literary language. The importance of writing is also reflected in the visual arts. Numerous buildings from the period carry multiple inscriptions executed in different styles and techniques, and the luxury book with fine illumination became one of the major art forms. Fine metalwork is another art form associated with this era, and many signed and/or dated pieces help us to reconstruct the nature of patronage and art in the eastern Islamic lands at this time.

Decorative panel on cenotaph of Mahmud of Ghazna, Ghazni, 12th century
This marble panel, with its horseshoe-shaped arch and intricate carving, is typical of the elaborate style of decoration developed in the 12th century under the Ghurids. It is possible that they reworked the cenotaph of the great Ghaznavid ruler Mahmud to reinforce their ties to his line.

9th and 10th centuries, had increasingly exercised their independence from the central authority. From the end of the 10th century, the outlying regions broke away almost entirely from Abbasid control as local strongmen established their own dynasties.

The first such dynasty was that of the Ghaznavids (977–1186), who descended from a Turkish military commander named Sebuktegin, a slave originally in service to the Samanids. From the mid-9th century, the Abbasids had come to depend on Turkish soldiers recruited from the steppes of Central Asia to prop up their government and maintain control over the population. The Abbasids' governors did the same, and in the 10th century the Samanid governor of Khorasan and Transoxiana had used the Turkish slave commander Alptegin to direct the army in Khorasan. In 961, when Alptegin was unable to secure succession in his own favor, he retired to the mountainous region around Ghazna in what is now eastern Afghanistan. There, on the periphery of the Samanid domains and facing the "pagan" Indian subcontinent, a series of Turkish commanders governed nominally for the Samanids for several decades until Sebuktegin (977–998) established an independent principality.

Sebuktegin's son Mahmud (998–1030) transformed this principality into a highly militarized empire. He not only challenged Islamic rulers to the west, such as the Samanids, Buyids and Quarakhanids, but initiated the era of Turkish eastwards expansion that changed the face of the Islamic world. The east, with India and Afghanistan, hitherto just an attachment to the Islamic cultural sphere, now became a political and cultural center in its own right. Having started as frontier warriors in the service of other rulers, the Turks were to create their own states and take charge of the military command of the Islamic world.

Mahmud's rule depended on his troops, which consisted mainly of slaves. They were paid a regular salary out of state funds and were also entitled to four-fifths of the booty recovered on campaign. To ensure their loyalty, Mahmud conducted constant campaigns, particularly against northern India. Sebuktegin had already begun invading the plains of India for slaves and loot, and Mahmud launched 17 attacks against the rich lands there. The most famous was his 1026–27 expedition in which he plundered the temple at Somnath, where he is said to have siezed over twenty million dinars' worth of spoil. Attracted by his success, plunder-seeking volunteers (*ghazis* or *mutatawwi'a*) swelled the rank of his already large armies. For the Somnath expedition, for example, he is said to have mustered 30,000 regular cavalry

History of Ghaznavids and Ghurids

The rich lands of the northeast had long been an important – and troublesome – area in the vast Abbasid caliphate. Large irrigation systems in Khorasan, the province of northeastern Iran, and Transoxiana, the land beyond the Oxus River, made these regions productive farmlands. The area was also rich in minerals, such as gold (found near Herat), silver (throughout Khorasan and near Balkh), copper (near Bukhara and in Farghana), lead (near Balkh), and mercury (Bamiyan). The Hindu Kush mountains are one of the few sources of lapis lazuli in the world, and the province of Badakhshan in northern Afghanistan, around the city of Balkh, is renowned for its rubies, garnets, and for asbestos.

Lying far from the Abbasid capitals in Iraq, these areas had also been centers of discontent for a long time. The Abbasids themselves had come to power in this area, and the Samanids, their governors in the region during the

plus volunteers. Mahmud and his armies returned to Ghanza with vast booty, which he used to transform the remote site into a world-famous metropolis and capital of an empire, and his ongoing *jihad* earned him a reputation as the "hammer of infidels."

Mahmud butteressed his authority by allying himself with the Abbasid caliph in Baghdad. The Ghanznavid ruler adopted a militant Sunni orthodoxy and took it upon himself to counter his rising threat of the Shiites, especially the Ismailis. In 999 Mahmud had restored the name of the Abbasid caliph to the Friday sermon, and in return was granted the title "Friend of the Commander of the Faithful and Right Hand of the State, the Faithful, and the Community." He often sent the caliph in Baghdad gifts from his plunder, and following his victory of Somnath, he was awardeded the title "Refuge of the State and Islam." Mahmud used religious orthodoxy to cement his vast empire which streched from northern India to the Caspian litoral.

Despite his Turkish heritage, Mahmud enthusiastically adopted the Perso-Islamic tradition of government inspired by Sassanian models. He tried to lure the leading intellectuals of the day to his court. Poets produced a stream of panegyrics in Mahmud's name, and the great poet Firdausi (d. 1025) dedicated his 60,000-verse epic, the *Shahname* ("Book of Kings"), to Mahmud.

Mahmud's successors were not so successful. They were unable to maintain the control in the west against the Seljuks, another group of Turks, who moved into the region in the first half of the 11th century. Defeating the Ghaznavids at the battle of Dandanqan in 1040, the Seljuks took control of Khwarazm, Khorasan, and northern Iran. After 20 years of intermittent warfare, the two Turkish dynasties worked out a modus vivendi, but the Ghaznavid empire was reduced to what is now eastern Afghanistan, Baluchistan, and nothwest India. Despite its eastward orientation, the Ghaznavid court con-

Interior of the tomb of Mahmud in Ghazni, 11th century and later
Mahmud (d. 1030), the most famous of the Ghaznavid rulers, transformed the Ghaznavid principality into a highly militarized Islamic empire. He used the booty from his campaigns into India to build his splendid capital at Ghazna. His grave is marked by a rectangular marble cenotaph, which has a rectangular base supporting a prismatic top inscribed with the date of his death. The cenotaph may have been added in the 12th century, and the surrounding tomb rebuilt at a later date.

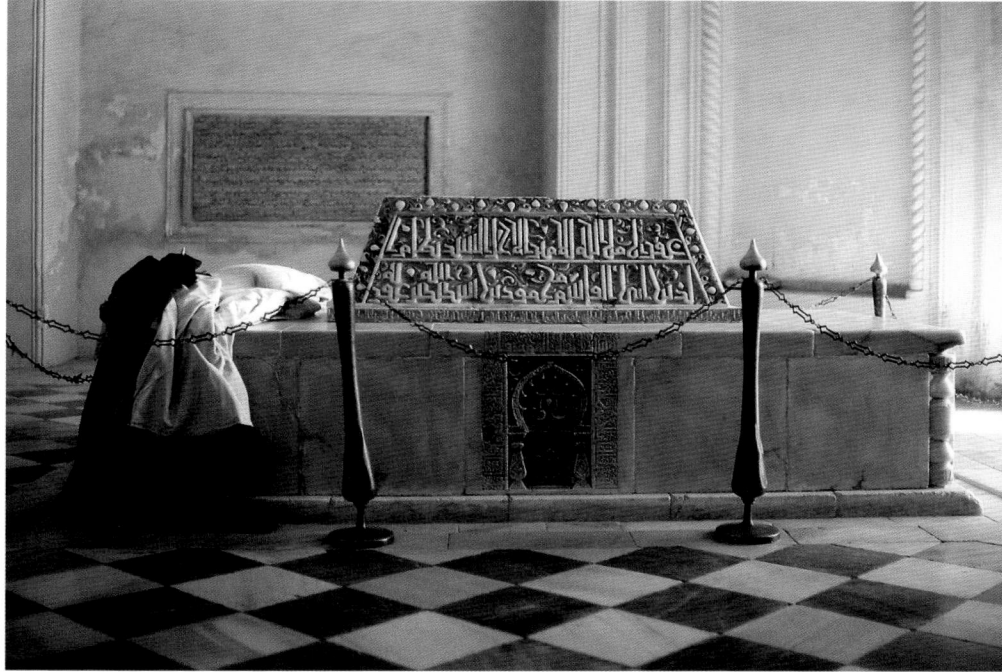

View of the city of Ghazna, built from the 10th century onwards
The Ghaznavids, a Turkish dynasty who established an independent principality on the eastern edge of the Abbasid empire, made their capital at Ghazna (modern Ghazni) in the mountainous area of what is now eastern Afghanistan. They built splendid palaces and mosques there, but the major buildings to survive from Ghaznavid times are two towers built by Masud III (d. 1114) and Bahram Shah (d. 1152). The citadel, which played an important role in the Anglo-Afghan War (1838–1842) stands in the distance.

tinued to be a center of Persian culture in the late 11th and early 12th centuries. The mystical poet Sanai (d. 1130), for example, worked at the court, and other poets produced laudatory poems in honor of the Ghaznavid rulers. Over the course of the 12th century, however, the Ghaznavids lost ground to a new dynasty that arose in the region, the Ghurids. Ghazna fell in 1161, and the Ghaznavids were pushed further eastward into the Punjab. They eventually surrendered their last Indian possession, which was their capital at Lahore, in 1186.

The Ghurids (c. 1000–1215) were bellicose chieftains of the Shansabani family who lived in Ghur, hence their name, a remote mountainous area in what is now central Afghanistan. The Shansabani remained pagans until well into the 11th century, when the Ghaznavids raided the area and made them their vassals. In the early 12th century, Ghaznavid influence in the region gave way to that of the Seljuks, and, when the Ghaznavid ruler Bahram Shah (1117–1152, with interruption) attempted to reassert Ghaznavid authority, the Ghurids retaliated. They sacked Ghazna in 1150, and the frightful orgy of devastation that ensued earned the Ghurid ruler leader Ala al-Din the epithet Jahan-suz ("World-burner").

Starting from this time, the Ghurids were no longer a small regional power but rulers of an empire. They eventually took over all the Ghaznavid territories on the Afghan plateau. At its height, the Ghurid empire, centered in their capital at Firuzkuh in Ghur, stretched nearly from the Caspian Sea to northern India. The two most important Ghurid rulers were brothers, both named Muhammad. Ghiyath al-Din Muhammad (1163–1203) was supreme

sultan in Firuzkuh and campaigned mainly in the west, while Muizz al-Din Muhammad (1173–1206) was ruler in Ghazna and campaigned in India. Another branch of the family controlled Bamiyan and the lands along the upper Oxus. Following the death of these two brothers, the dynasty was rent by internal squabbles, and the Ghurid empire was quickly absorbed by the Khwarazm-Shahs, in 1215. Khwarazmian domination, however, was short-lived, as all the eastern Islamic lands were soon engulfed by Mongol armies under the leadership of Genghis Khan.

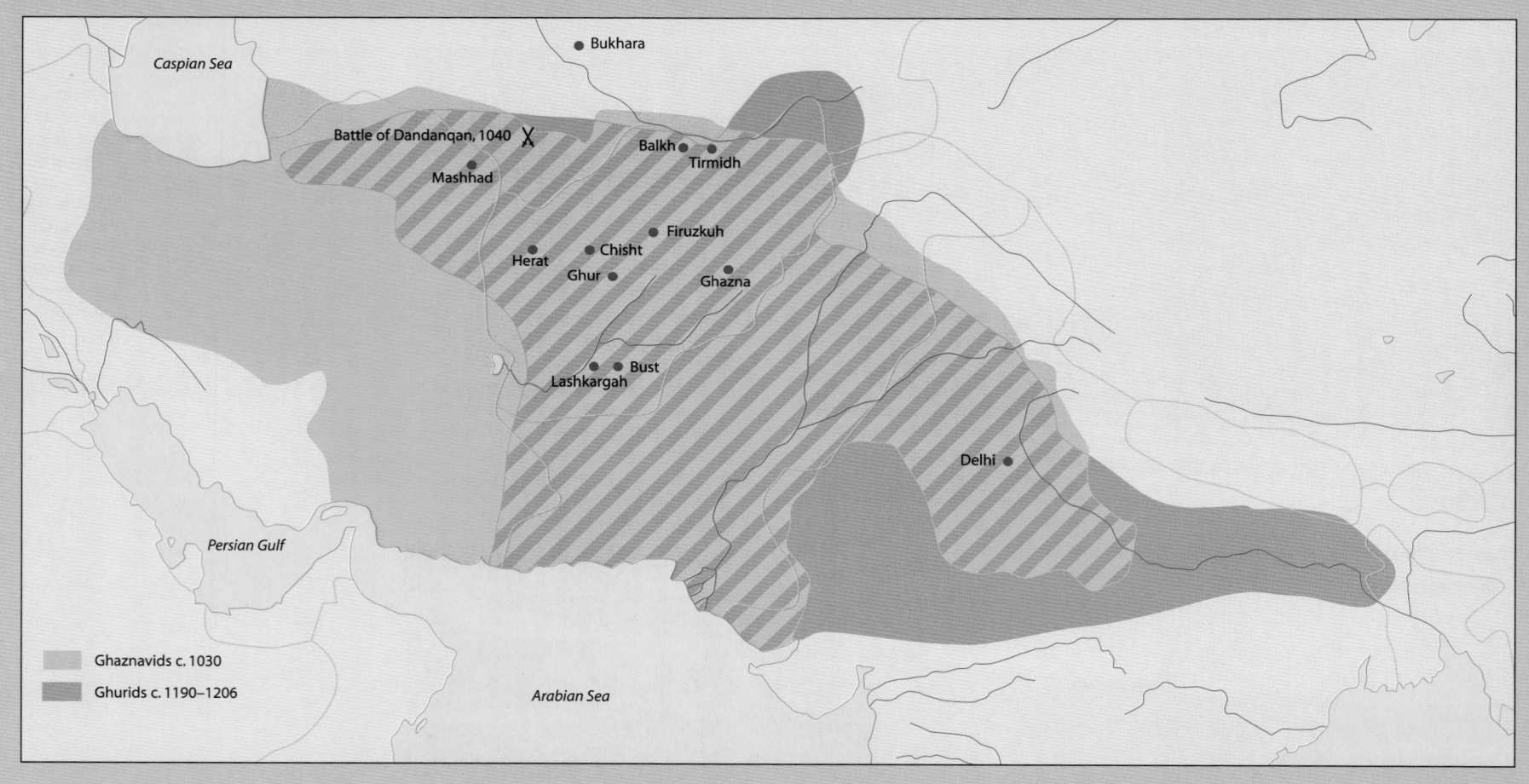

Marble panel from the palace at Ghazna,
11th century
Along the courtyard walls of the palace a long poetry inscription ran for about 250 m, above a dado with elaborately carved foliate decoration. It extols the virtues of the sultan and the glories of his palace. The palace, ruined since the fall of the Ghaznavids in 1161, was excavated at the beginning of the 20th century.

977	Sebuktegin (977–998), founder of the Ghaznavid dynasty, becomes governor of the Samanids in the Ghazna region of present-day Afghanistan		
998–1030	Rule of Mahmud of Ghazna, early Islam's most important conqueror		
999	Defeat of the Samanids by the Ghaznavids; Mahmud of Ghazna pays homage to the Abbasid caliph al-Qadir, who recognizes him as ruler of Khorasan		
1001–1024	Mahmud of Ghazna undertakes campaigns into India, thus preparing the way for the spread of Islam on the Indian subcontinent		
1030–1040	Rule of Masud I of Ghazna		

1040	Battle of Dandanqan: defeat of the Ghaznavids by the Seljuks under Tughril Beg		
1072–1076	Ibrahim ibn Masud I (1059–1099) extends the Ghaznavids' sphere of influence to the Punjab		
1088	Ibrahim puts down his son's rebellion		
1115–1118	Interdynastic struggles around the succession		
1117/18– 1152	Sultanate of the Ghaznavid Bahram Shah, recognizes the authority of the Seljuks		
1118	With the aid of the Seljuks under Sanjar, Bahram Shah suppresses an uprising by his brother Malik Arslan, ruler of the Punjab		
1118–1129	Bahram Shah establishes his rule in the Punjab		

1135/36	Unsuccessful attempt by Bahram Shah to shake off the authority of the Seljuks		
1149	Victory of the Ghaznavids over the Ghurids		
1150	The Ghurids under Ala al-Din plunder Ghazna		
1161	Ghazna falls to the Ghurids; Ghaznavid rule is restricted to the Punjab with its capital Lahore		
1163–1203	Reign of the Ghurid Ghiyath al-Din Muhammad in Firuzkuah		
1173–1206	Reign of the Ghurid Muizz al-Din Muhammad in Ghazna		
1186	Final defeat of the Ghaznavids; Lahore is taken by the Ghurids		
1198	Struggles between the Ghurids and the Khwarazmians in Khorasan		

1208	The Khwarazmians capture Herat, the Ghurids' capital
1215	The reign of the Ghurids ends with defeat at the end of the Khwarazmians

Architecture

Sheila Blair, Jonathan Bloom

The Ghaznavids and Ghurids emulated the Abbasids, their predecessors and overlords, by building large and splendid capitals dotted with magnificent structures. Many of the more remote sites have been destroyed, so that single buildings, particularly towers, stand in splendid isolation. This poetic image may be somewhat at odds with the more prosaic picture provided by texts and excavations. Nevertheless, they help us reconstruct something of the original splendor of these cities and establish the pattern of development, for, as at Samarra, the Abbasid capital in Iraq, successive Ghaznavid and Ghurid rulers added their own palaces and other buildings to their capitals in the eastern Islamic lands.

Palaces in the Ghaznavid capitals of al-Askar and Ghazna

The site we know best is the Ghaznavid winter capital known as al-Askar ("The Troop Quarters"), located in southern Afghanistan near the modern-day town of Lashkargah. Like Ghazna, the site was sacked by the Ghurids, but it was subsequently restored, and then destroyed again in the early 13th century under attacks from the Khwarazm-Shahs and the Mongols. Though constructed of mud brick, many of the abandoned buildings have survived in this area of low rainfall, and the ruins were excavated by a French team in the late 1940s and 1950s.

The site, at the confluence of the Helmand and Arghandab Rivers, had developed in the 10th century as a garden suburb of the nearby city of Bust after the restoration of an ancient canal supplying the city from the Helmand. The earliest construction, predating the Ghaznavid period, was a square garden with a formal entry to the east, a large pavilion in the center, and another large pavilion overlooking the river to the west. It probably served as a stand for reviewing troops, and it was soon replaced by a compact 115 × 170 feet (35 × 52 meters) two-story building. The living quarters were set on the second floor to take advantage of the breezes and river view. In plan, the second floor had four axial halls arranged in cruciform shape and converging on a central square area, possibly a lightwell. This is the same plan thought to have been used for the palace at Merv, built in the mid-8th century by Abu Muslim, leader of the Abbasid revolution. The building at al-Askar is usually known as the Central Palace as two other palaces were built adjacent to it.

The largest building on the site was the South Palace, generally attributed to the patronage of Mahmud and therefore datable to the early 11th century. Its plan and construction techniques followed models found in some of the Abbasid palaces in Samarra. Like them, it had a rectangular internal courtyard. An *iwan* flanked by rooms stood in the middle of each of the four sides, with a square throne room beyond the north *iwan*. The major adjustment to the site was another *iwan* beyond the throne room and opening north onto the river. The grandest

Lashkar-i Bazar, 11th century and later
The walls of the palaces were built of sun-dried brick, which was originally covered with a protective layer of plaster. The plaster was normally carved, and, in interior rooms, might be painted. In the late 1940s and 1950s, a team of French archeologists succeeded in excavating the ruins of at least three clay-brick palaces from the time of the Ghaznavids, which were well preserved thanks to the dry climate.

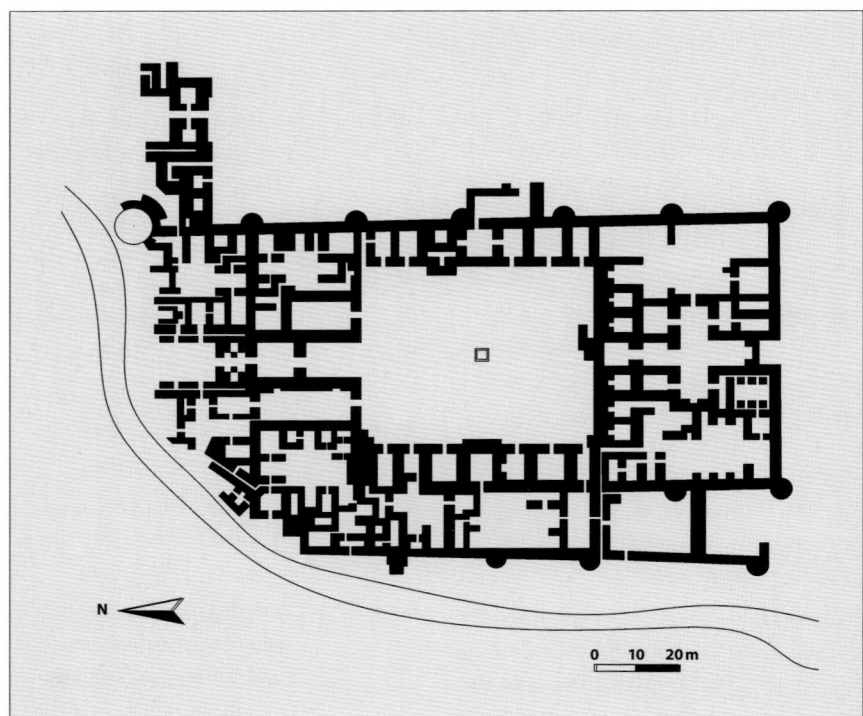

Ground plan of the South Palace at Lashkar-i Bazar, 11th century and later
The South Palace, which is assumed to have been built by the great Ghaznavid ruler Mahmud (d. 1030), is the largest of the palaces at Lashkar-i Bazar. In addition to the standard arrangement of a courtyard with four *iwans* on the sides and an audience hall beyond the main *iwan*, this palace had an additional *iwan* to the north, which overlooked the Helmand River and took advantage of the river's cool breezes.

reception room in the building, it was open to the breezes coming off the river and provided a view of the large river pavilion and the Central Palace.

Like the Abbasid palaces at Samarra, the *iwan* hall in the South Palace at al-Askar was richly revetted with stucco and brick decoration. In the Ghaznavid palace, however, the types of decoration were arranged in the reverse sequence from that used by the Abbasids, with a frescoed dado below and relief decoration above. The murals at both sites depicted the ruler's servants. The dado in the Dar al-Khalifa at Samarra had shown dancing women, but that in Mahmud's palace at al-Askar was painted with a frieze of attendants. They probably represented Mahmud's private guard, who would once have stood against the walls facing the enthroned monarch. On the back wall of the *iwan*, the dado was surmounted by geometric panels framed by bands of inscriptions. The one that survives contains Koran sura 27. 40–41. The verses describe Solomon receiving the Queen of Sheba, and were undoubtedly chosen to draw an analogy between the pre-Islamic hero who controlled the animals and spirits, and the patron of the palace, the great conqueror Mahmud.

As at Samarra, later rulers added to al-Askar, which eventually stretched for 4 miles (6 kilometers) along the east bank of the Helmand River. To the north of the earlier palaces is a sprawling third palace, with three courtyards surrounded by *iwans* and rooms. Other buildings on the site included barracks (perhaps designed for Mahmud's famous elephant corps), a bazaar, and a Friday (congregational) mosque. Other remains on the opposite bank of the Helmand River may represent a residential area associated with the palaces.

Because of its location in the warm Helmand basin, al-Askar served as the Ghaznavid summer capital. Their main capital, however, was at Ghazna (modern-day Ghazni) in the mountains to the northeast. Much of it, too, is in ruins, but Italian excavations there in the 1950s and 1960s have uncovered the remains of the palace built there by Mahmud's great-great-grandson, Masud III (1099–1115). It was a walled rectangle, with a long bazaar stretching along the north side. Like

earlier palaces, this one had an internal courtyard 164 × 105 feet (50 × 32 m), with an *iwan* flanked by rooms in the middle of each of its four sides. The throne-room lay beyond the south *iwan*. The courtyard was paved in marble and surrounded by 32 niches decorated with an extraordinary inscription in floriated Kufic script. The text, which runs for about 820 feet (250 meters) around the court, is a Persian poem extolling the virtues of the sultan and the glories of his palace. It was apparently composed specifically for the new construction.

Most contemporary palaces had *iwans* facing a courtyard, but decoration seems to have been determined by personal preference and availability of materials. The palace at Tirmidh, a site on the right bank of the Amu River near its confluence with the Surhan, for example, comprised several buildings arranged around a courtyard. The *iwan* opposite the entrance was decorated with three registers of carved plaster panels showing geometric patterns and zoomorphic motifs. One shows an extraordinary monster with a single head and two bodies. The isocephalic image may be traced to older Central Asian images, but here it has been abstracted and made symmetrical to conform to current ideas of decorative stylization.

Towers

Near the palace at Ghazna, Masud III built a magnificent flanged tower. Originally measuring about 144 feet (44 meters) in height, the tower comprised

Detail of the upper panels of the tower of Masud III at Ghazna, early 12th-century
The upper panels around the lower section of the tower are decorated with an inscription giving the name and titles of the patron, Masud III (1099–1114). The text is written in an elaborate, bordered Kufic script and set against a background of superbly carved terracotta scrolls. Explorers in the 19th century assumed that this was a victory tower built by the great Ghaznavid conqueror Mahmud to celebrate his conquests in India, and only with careful reading of the inscription in the 20th century was it possible to reassign this tower to his successor Masud III, and to question what its original use might have been.

two sections – an upper shaft with semicircular flanges atop a lower stellate base. The upper shaft tumbled in an earthquake in 1902, and only the lower one still stands, about 66 feet (20 meters) high. Built of baked brick, the remaining part is superbly decorated with brick patterns, stucco, and terracotta panels. The inscription band encircling the top gives the patron's name and titles. They are repeated in the second band from the bottom in the script known as square Kufic. This script was generated out of bricklaying techniques, as builders exploited the shadows created by spaces between bricks to spell out names or short phrases. The technique had already been used to create geometric patterns, but this is the first known example where it is used to spell out words. Bricklayers later developed this technique by spelling out words with glazed bricks whose surface and color contrasted with the matte baked bricks. This technique became a hallmark of Iranian architecture from the 12th century. Masud's son Bahram Shah (1117–1152) emulated his father and built a similar two-story tower about 660 yards (600 meters) to the west. It follows the shape of Masud's tower and has a similar foundation inscription encircling the top. Bahram Shah's tower is distinguished from the prototype by larger panels in which the bricks were laid in simpler geometric shapes, and by the absence of words.

Towers like these proliferated at this time, and about 70 others were erected throughout Iran and Afghanistan by the Ghaznavids and their contemporaries. By far the most spectacular is that erected by the Ghurids at their capital Firuzkuh. Located in such a remote mountain valley in central Afghanistan that it was only discovered by modern scholars in the 1950s, the tower soars an amazing 197 feet (60 meters). An octagonal base supports three cylindrical shafts of decreasing diameter crowned by a lantern. The exterior is encased in exuberant terracotta ornament, yet the endless ingenuity of the decorative details is always subordinated to the grander design of the whole. The lowest section is decorated with an interlacing band containing the entire text of sura 19 of the Koran, the "Mary Sura."

Tower of Masud III at Ghazna, beginning of the 12th century
This flanged section, 20 m tall and now covered by a metal cap, is the lower story for a much taller tower. The more slender upper shaft had semicircular flanges and measured another 24 m high; it fell in an earthquake in 1902. The tower is built of baked brick and beautifully decorated with six tiers of brickwork, stucco, and terracotta panels. It bears a Kufic inscription with the name and title of the patron, Masud III. This structure exemplifies the fine decorative style typical in Iranian architecture since the early 12th century.

It was undoubtedly chosen for a specific reason, which remains elusive to us today.

We can only speculate about why these towers were built. A few, such as the Kalan minaret in Bukhara, were erected adjacent to mosques and might have been used for the call to prayer, but most were not. Early travelers identified these constructions as victory towers, but this is unlikely, since there is no evidence that such a building type was used in Islamic lands. Some towers may have been political statements, erected to proclaim the power of a new ruler, for they often bear the name of the patron. One erected at Tirmidh, for example, is dated year 423 of the *hegira* (1031/32), the same year that the Ghaznavids appointed a new governor to the region. Some towers may have served as beacons or road markers, such as the one in the village of Kirat in eastern Iran near the modern border with Afghanistan. Set on a small hillock and visible from a great distance, it marked the pass through the chain of hills separating the cities of Mashhad in Iran from Herat in Afghanistan. Such beacons would have been important to the numerous caravans that traversed this area *en route* from India and Central Asia to Iran and Iraq. Gratifyingly visible from nearby, where they might indicate the mosque's location, or from afar, where they would indicate a town, these towers advertised the presence of Islam and demonstrated the piety of the founder.

Below: **Detail of the inscription around the lower shaft of the tower at Jam**, late 12th century
This tower is decorated with many inscriptions, some executed in brick, others in glazed ceramic. The lower shaft contains all of sura 19 of the Koran (the "Mary Sura"), as well as the name and titles of the Ghurid ruler Ghiyath al-Din Muhammad (1163–1203).

Right: **Tower at Jam**, late 12th century
The tower at Jam is the most striking of the group of some 40 towers erected in Iran, Afghanistan, and Central Asia between the 11th and the 13th centuries. It soars an amazing 197 ft (60 m) from the floor of a remote mountain valley in central Afghanistan. The site was so obscure that outsiders only discovered it in the 1950s, but it has since been identified as the medieval town of Firuzkuh, which served as the summer capital of the Ghurids and was destroyed by the Mongol khan Ügedei in 1222/23. The baked-brick tower comprises three tapering cylindrical shafts set atop each other, separated by *muqarnas* cornices, and crowned by a lantern.

Metalwork

The other important art form in this period was metalwork. Texts inform us that Herat was an important center for metalworking, and several superb bronzes from the period are signed by metalworkers bearing the epithet al-Harawi (from Herat). The most informative is a stunning bronze pail now in St. Petersburg, known as the Bobrinski bucket. Bought in Bukhara in 1885, it was later acquired by Count Bobrinski, from whom it gets its name. Its round body is cast of brass and inlaid in copper and silver with horizontal bands alternating Arabic inscriptions and figural scenes. The broad band at the top, which expresses good wishes to the owner, is written in an unusual script, one in which the upper parts of the letters are formed from human figures and some of the lower parts from animals. Below this band is a narrower one with scenes of entertainment, such as drinking, music-making, and playing such games as backgammon. The narrowest band in the middle has an elaborately knotted inscription expressing good wishes. The fourth band shows scenes of horsemen

hunting and fighting. The lowest band is another animated inscription bearing good wishes. The dedicatory inscription, clearly written in Persian along the rim, states that the bucket was inlaid by Muhammad ibn Abd al-Wahid, and designed by Masud ibn Ahmad, the engraver from Herat. It was ordered by Abd al-Rahman ibn Abdallah al-Rashidi for Rashid al-Din Azizi ibn Abul-Husain al-Zanjani, a merchant who bore the titles "pillar of the state," "pride of the merchants," and "ornament of the *hajj* and of the two shrines" (Mecca and Medina). The pail handle, connected to the bucket by two loops, both of which are formed by a fish and a leaping lion, is inscribed with the date Muharram 559 (December, 1163).

Although none of these individuals can otherwise be identified, the wealth of inscriptions tells much about both the piece and contemporary society. The bucket was made by a team of craftsmen who had specialized jobs within the workshop, one responsible for executing the other's design. The bucket was a specific commission, apparently by a dependent (he bears the epithet Rashidi, "of Rashid") for his master, Rashid al-Din, a merchant. The merchant's titles relating to the pilgrimage and

Title page of the *Kitab khalq al-nabi wa l-khuliq* by Abu Bakr Muhammad ibn Abdallah, copyist Abu Bakr Muhammad ibn Abi Rafi, Ghazna, c 1050, Leiden, University Library

This book concerning the physical and moral attributes of the Prophet Muhammad, is one of the earliest written in the eastern Islamic lands to survive. The manuscript, with its lavish use of gold, exemplifies the high quality of books prepared at the Ghaznavid court, whose rulers were especially distinguished as patrons of the literary arts.

Page from a manuscript of the Koran, 11th or 12th century, Munich, Bayerische Staatsbibliotek

A distinctive style of angular script developed in eastern Iran under the Ghaznavids and Ghurids. This "eastern" or "bent Kufic" script has little to do with the angular script used in early Islamic times. Rather, it was an elegant development by chancellery-scribes who sought to make their regular cursive hands suitable for copying the Word of God. In this particular manuscript, the letters have been surrounded by reserve panels and the background filled with small spirals, a decorative treatment also found on contemporary ceramics.

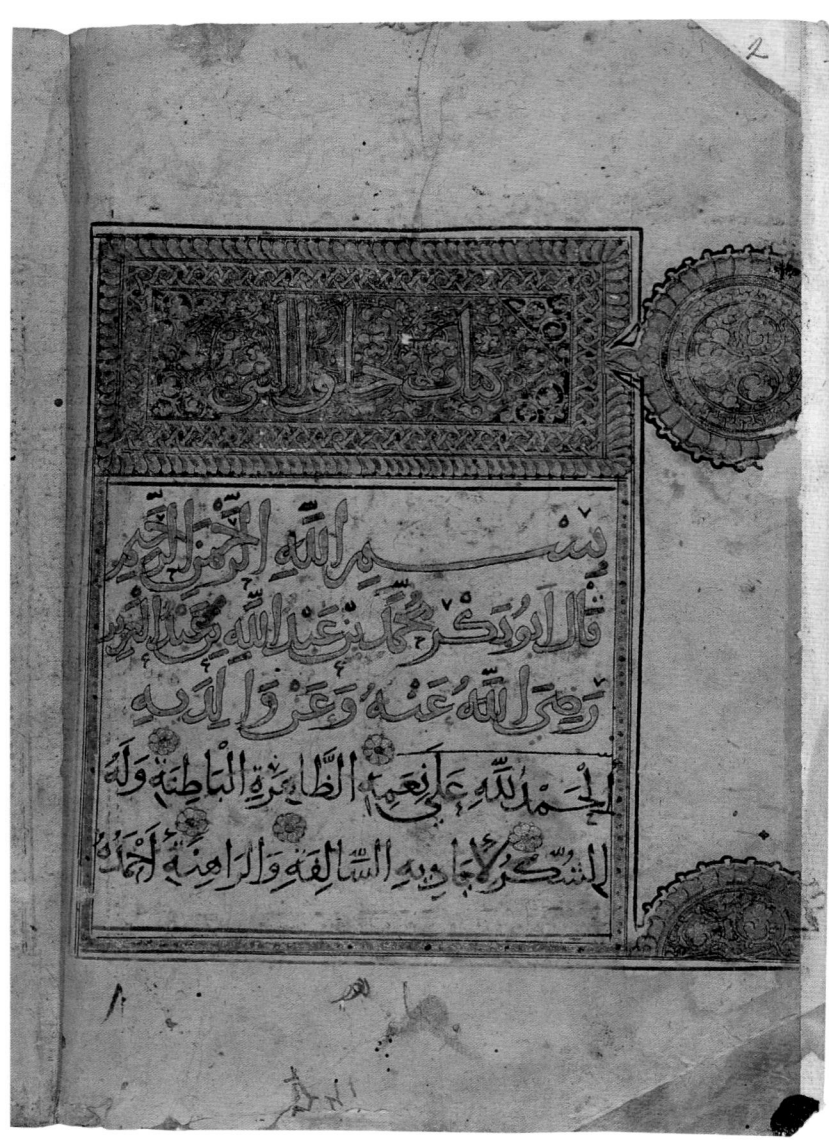

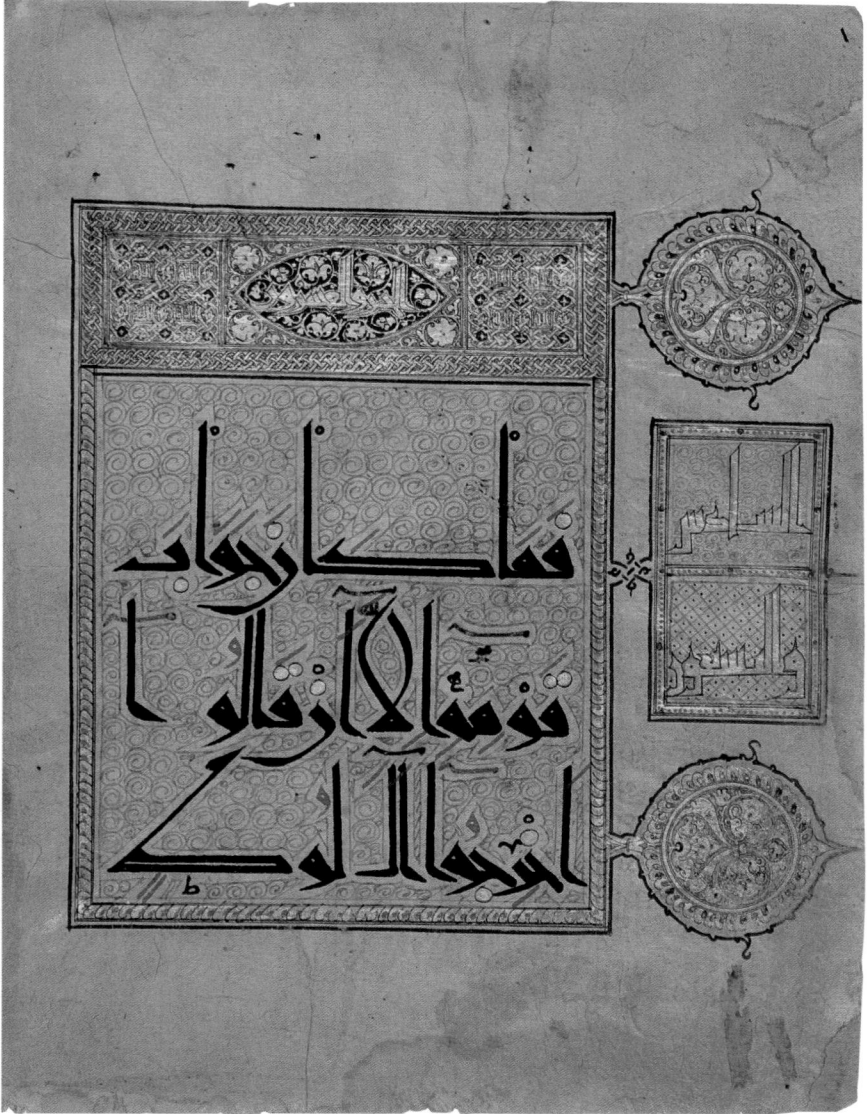

(1177/78). The same scribe penned another, similar copy of the Koran dated in Ramadan of the year 566 (June 1171), and now in the Dar al-Kutub, in Cairo. His *nisba*, or epithet of affiliation, al-Ghaznawi, shows that he was associated either with the Ghaznavids, who maintained control of some parts of the region until 1186, or with the city of Ghazna, which had been under Ghurid control since 1161. The distinctive broken cursive script had been used for large Koran manuscripts since the end of the 11th century. One of the earliest dated copies to survive (Mashhad, Astan-i Quds no. 4316) was completed by Uthman ibn Husain al-Warraq in the year 466 of the *hegira* (1073/74). The manuscripts by Abu Bakr are some of the latest known, for after this date broken cursive was relegated to headings and other incidentals. The high cost of these large manuscripts in broken cursive is conveyed by their spaciousness and rich illumination. The copies by Abu Bakr have only four lines of widely spaced text per page, an extravagant use of paper. Much of the illumination is painted in gold, and the background is laboriously filled with scrolling arabesques. These sumptuous and extravagant manuscripts must have been made for the court, since few could afford such luxury.

Decorative Arts

Sheila Blair, Jonathan Bloom

Many contemporary texts describe the rich furnishings and objects used by the Ghaznavid and Ghurid courts, but surviving finds give only a skewed sample. We know of no textiles that can be clearly associated with the period. Archaeologists working at Bust and Bamiyan have discovered a distinctive green-glazed pottery, and the palace at Ghazna yielded some monochrome glazed tiles decorated with animal motifs. Most of this pottery is second-rate, especially in comparison to the superb fritwares produced at Kashan in Iran at this time. The Ghaznavids and Ghurids certainly used fine ceramics, but they seem to have been content to import porcelains from China or luster-decorated fritwares from central Iran.

Art of the book

Two arts in particular flourished under the patronage of the Ghaznavids and Ghurids – the art of the book and metalwares. Sources indicate that some books were illustrated with pictures, but none survives. We do, however, have several examples of fine books illuminated with nonrepresentational decoration, especially headings and frontis- and finispieces. Some of these illuminated manuscripts were made for the court. All of these books are transcribed on paper. Papermaking, which had developed in China as early as the 2nd century B.C., had been introduced to Central Asia by the 8th century, when it was quickly adopted by the Abbasid bureaucracy in Iraq. The province of Khorasan was famous for its papermaking throughout this period.

One of the first dated books to survive from the eastern Islamic lands is a text about the physical and moral characteristics of the Prophet Muhammad, *Kitab khalq al-nabi wa l-khuliq*, composed by a certain Abu Bakr Muhammad ibn Abdallah. According to the colophon, it was transcribed in Ghazna by Abu Bakr Muhammad ibn Rafi' al-Warraq ("the copyist"). The gold ex-libris on the front names the Ghaznavid emir Abd al-Rashid (1049–1052), so the manuscript is datable to about 1050. It is a small volume with pages measuring 9.6 × 6.6 inches (24.5 × 16.7) centimeters and nine or ten lines of *Naskhi* script on each page. Titles and the last line of the colophon are done in *Thuluth*. This book is one of the earliest surviving manuscripts written in these round scripts, which had been used in the chancellery since early Islamic times but were only adopted for fine calligraphy in the 10th century. The text belongs to the Hadiths (traditions), reports about the words and deeds of the Prophet Muhammad as passed down through the generations, which would have been of great interest to the Ghaznavid rulers, who were pious Sunni Muslims.

The Ghaznavids and Ghurids also ordered fine presentation copies of the Koran made for the many mosques and *madrasas* they endowed. These Koran manuscripts were copied in several styles of script. The Bibliothèque Nationale in Paris, for example, owns part of a large manuscript transcribed at Bust in the year 505 of the *hegira* (1111). The 125-page section that has been preserved contains the fifth of a seven-part Koran. Each large page 8 × 6 inches (20 × 15 centimeters) has seven lines of text surrounded by cloud panels, with the background filled with scrolling arabesques. The Koranic text is transcribed in a fluid round hand with many connectors. It has been identified as a rare example of the script known as *tauqi*. Headings and other incidentals are written in another distinctive script, often known as "eastern" or "bent Kufic." This cursive script had been canonized by the Abbasid vizier Ibn Muqla (d. 940) and later became popular for large Koran manuscripts transcribed in the eastern Islamic lands.

One example of a large manuscript is a copy of the Koran transcribed by Abu Bakr ibn Ahmad ibn Ubaydallah al-Ghaznawi in year 573 of the *hegira*

Manuscript of the Koran, copied by Uthman ibn Muhammad, Bust, 1111/12, Paris, Bibliothèque Nationale
This manuscript of the Koran was a large presentation copy in seven parts, of which only one is known to have survived. The script, an unusual form of cursive with long sweeping tails and occasional unusual ligatures between letters, reflects the impact of chancellery scripts on the scribal tradition. The fine illumination used for chapter headings and sectional divisions indicates that this manuscript was probably made for the court.

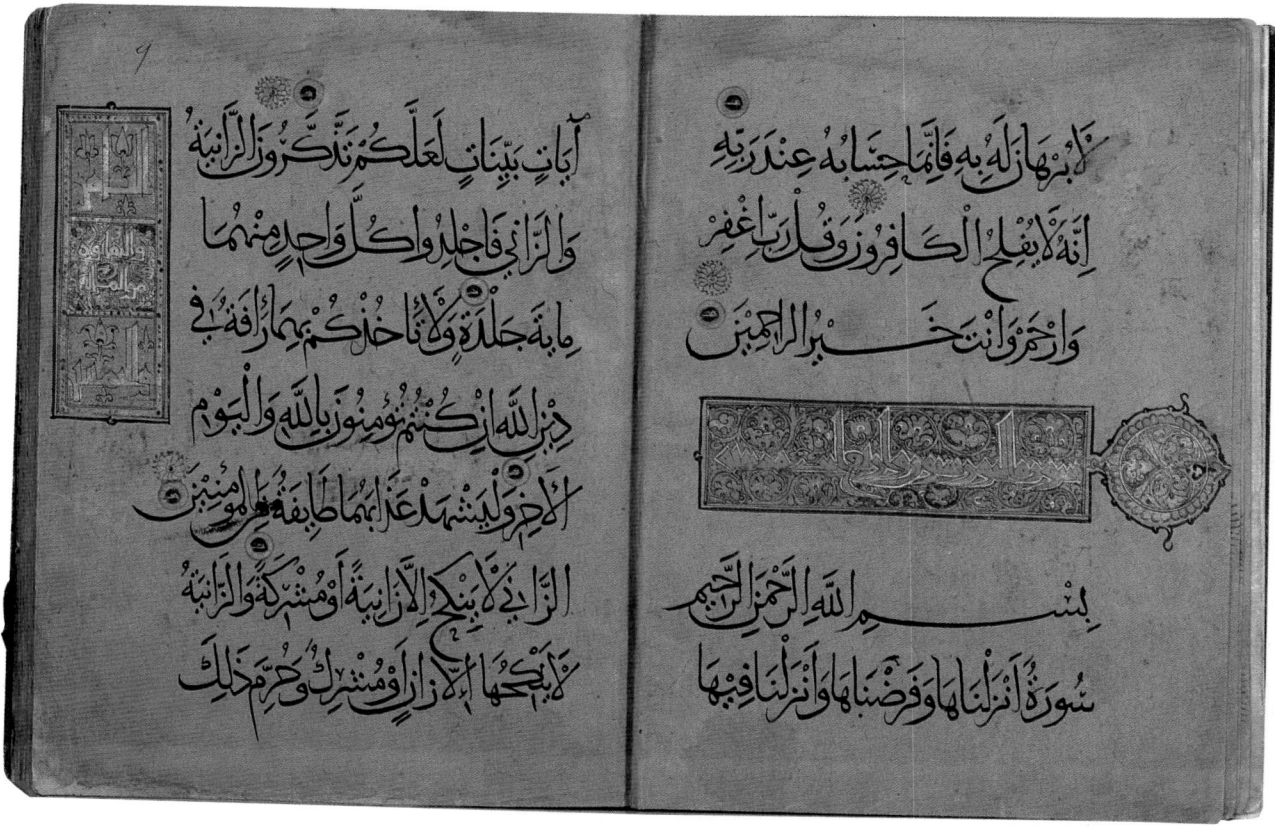

Below: Inscription on the lower story of the Qutb Minar, Delhi
The lower story of the Qutb Minar has 24 flanges, alternately semicylindrical and angular, and is encircled by several magnificent inscription bands set within complex arabesque borders. The cursive style of writing, with swelling vertical shafts, contrasts sharply with the angular Kufic script favored for Ghurid inscriptions in Afghanistan and shows the emergence of a distinctly Indian style of Arabic epigraphy.

Above: Southwest side of courtyard of the Quwwat al-Islam Mosque in Delhi, 1193 and later
Although the plan, with a large court surrounded by pillared halls, is modeled on Ghurid brick mosques in Afghanistan, the building was constructed from stone columns reused from local temples. Indigenous arch construction systems were used. The arched stone screen, added in 1199 by Qutb al-Din Aibak to give the mosque an "Islamic" appearance, is not made of true arches but is corbeled, unable to support any weight.

construction began on a huge sandstone tower known as the Qutb Minar. Like earlier towers erected by the Ghaznavids and Ghurids in Afghanistan, the Qutb Minar comprises several superposed flanged and cylindrical shafts decorated with inscriptions, and separated by balconies carried on muqarnas corbels. Later rulers added more stories to the tower, so that by the time the fifth story was completed in 1368, the tower soared an amazing 238 feet (72.5 meters).

Aibak had been the architect of the Ghurid conquests in India, but after his master Muizz al-Din Muhammad died in 1206, Abak assumed independent power, with the title of malik (king, ruler). His son-in-law and successor Iltutmish (1211–1236) severed the Indian provinces from the Ghurid domains and was the real founder of the dynasty of the Delhi sultans. To mark his authority and to meet the demands of the expanding Muslim population of Delhi, Sultan Iltutmish tripled the size of the Quwwat al-Islam Mosque so that it measured some 230 × 330 feet (70 × 100) meters, with the enormous Qutb minaret standing in the southeast corner of the courtyard. It took several decades to carry out this gargantuan project, which was completed only in 1229.

Qutb Minar in the Quwwat al-Islam Mosque, Delhi, 1199 and later
This extraordinary minaret was begun in 1199 by Qutb al-Din Aibak, the Turkish governor of the region for the Ghurids. Standing outside the southeast corner of the original mosque and rising about 263 ft (72 m) from the ground, the tower was clearly modeled on ear- lier Ghaznavid and Ghurid minarets at Ghazna and Jam. Like them, it is composed of superposed stories separated by *muqarnas* cornices, but unlike them it was built of rubble masonry faced with red sandstone. The upper stories, added at a later date, are faced in white marble.

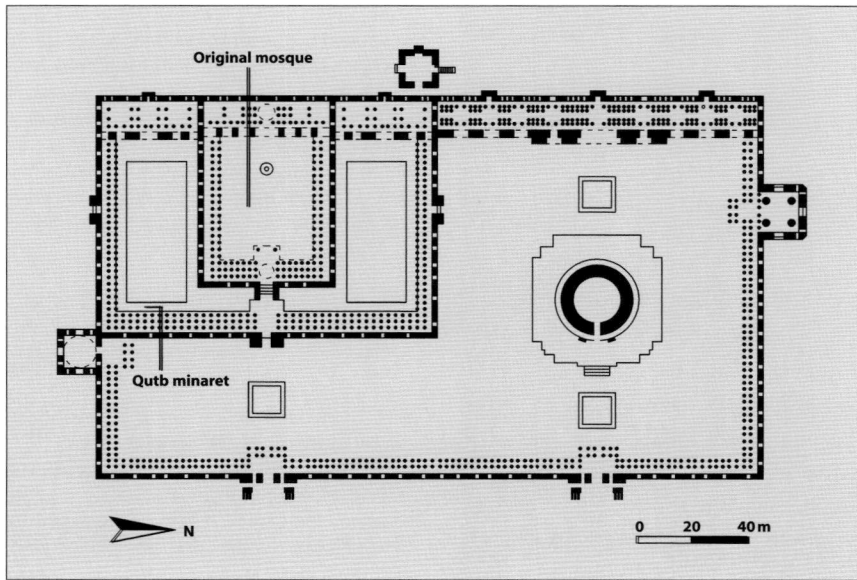

Ground plan of the Quwwat al-Islam Mosque, Delhi, 1190s and later
The mosque known as Quwwat al-Islam ("Might of Islam") was the first built in Delhi after the Islamic conquest of India. The original mosque was obviously unsatisfactory, and soon an arched screen was added in front of the prayer hall and a huge sandstone minaret known as the Qutb Minar built in the courtyard. Under Iltutmish, in the 13th century, the size of the mosque was tripled; it was later tripled again and a huge second minaret constructed.

of the 12th-century work. At least three other parts of the Friday Mosque of Herat also date to Ghurid times. The sanctuary *iwan*, near the *mihrab*, preserves a plaster inscription band written in stylized Kufic script and naming the Ghurid sultan. The Ghurids also erected a monumental portal on the southeast side of the mosque. It was completely covered by a Timurid vault until 1964, when it was discovered by restorers. Elaborately decorated in terracotta, the Ghurid portal is framed by a remarkable inscription band naming the Ghurid sultan and giving the date, Ramadan, in the year 597 of the *hegira* (June–July 1201). The sultan himself was buried in a tomb abutting the mosque to the north. A domed square, 56 feet (17 meters) on each side, it was decorated on the interior with plaster incised to resemble brick patterns. The main portal on the south side was decorated like the mosque portal with inscriptions and interlaced strips of cut terracotta. The building was destroyed in the 1940s.

The Great Mosque of Delhi

The best-surviving example of a Ghurid Friday mosque is that erected at Delhi by Qutb al-Din Aibak, Turkish slave commander of the region for Muizz al-Din Muhammad. Known as the Quwwat al-Islam ("Might of Islam"), it was the first mosque built in Delhi after the Islamic conquest of India. Construction began in the 1190s on the site of a Hindu temple. Like pre-Islamic temples in the region, the mosque is set on a raised platform reached by staircases on three sides. The mosque itself comprises a large open courtyard surrounded by halls supported by columns reused from ancient temples. The available columns were not tall enough to create a lofty space, so two or even three temple columns were set on top of each other to gain the necessary height. The columns supported beams, which in turn supported a flat roof, the traditional trabeated construction technique found in India. Because of the warm climate, the building was largely open to the elements.

This original mosque in Delhi was obviously unsatisfactory and was quickly modified. In 1198 Qutb al-Din Aibak ordered an arched wall added to screen the prayer hall in front of the courtyard. The screen consists of a high and wide central arch flanked by pairs of lower and narrower arches. Because the local masons did not know how to build true arches, which were unknown in India, they had to imitate them with corbelling, in which each course of stone is projected out slightly from the one below until the courses meet in the middle. A corbelled structure, however, cannot support any weight, so it could not serve as a support for a dome (as would have been the case elsewhere), and the arch serves only as a screen to mask what lies behind it. The Aibak screen is richly decorated with naturalistic vines and calligraphy. This carved decoration shows how native masons adapted local techniques to serve the needs of new Muslim patrons. Hindu and Jain architecture erected before the Muslim conquest was often decorated with exuberant figural sculpture, including gods and goddesses with multiple arms and legs. Muslims naturally found this idolatry horrific, so offending images were defaced on reused materials, and purely vegetal and geometric ornaments were carved on new construction. The mosque at Delhi was insufficient to meet either the size of the rapidly growing Muslim population of the city or the pretensions of the local rulers, who also saw public architecture as a fitting symbol of their expanding power. In 1199

struggle for succession among the Sufi disciples in the late 12th century, the order seems to have dispersed. The mystic Muin al-Din (1141–1236) took the order to India where he established a center at Ajmer; in later times it became one of the most popular and influential mystical orders in the Indian subcontinent. The tomb that Ghiyath al-Din ordered at Chisht is a domed square with elaborate decoration on the south facade. It stands near another, taller but similar tomb that must have been built at the same time. Those commemorated by these small tombs are not identified, but they may have been members of the Chishtiya order.

By contrast, the Ghaznavid rulers, from Sebuktegin onward, were buried at Ghazna, where their graves were marked by pyramidal cenotaphs inscribed with their names. These were sometimes reused in later times for other tombs. Doors bearing the name of Mahmud and purportedly from his tomb, for example, were taken to India, where they were installed centuries later at the Taj Mahal. Densely carved with stellar cartouches and even a stylized bull's head buried in the arabesques, they represent the finest of Ghaznavid wood carving.

The arch at Bust

A more monumental construction erected at this time by the Ghurids is the magnificent arch at Bust, with a span of about 82 feet (25 meters). Now standing in splendid isolation, it originally stood on the east side of the large square in front of the citadel, and was apparently part of a Ghurid redesign of the Ghaznavid *maidan* (town square). The arch, decorated on the front with a magnificent inscription in Kufic script with interlaced stems, is flanked by four-centered arches with a slight return at springing level, a type of arch typical of Ghurid work in the 12th century. The intrados of the arch was also elaborately decorated in terracotta with bricks in strapwork patterns enclosing stamped designs, but the back of the arch was relatively plain. The arch typifies Ghurid imperial architecture and shows that the Ghurids, who also redecorated some of the palaces at the nearby site of al-Askar, considered themselves successors to the Ghaznavids.

The Friday Mosque of Herat

In the last decade of Ghiyath al-Din Muhammad's life, the Ghurids undertook a major program of building mosques and related structures. In the year 597 of the *hegira* (1200/01), after a fire destroyed the Friday Mosque of Herat, Ghiyath al-Din ordered it to be rebuilt. The mosque, which retained its present plan until the 20th century, had four *iwans* arranged around a large central courtyard, with myriad vaulted spaces filling the corners. Much of the mosque was redecorated in Timurid times, but the massive piers carrying four-centered arches are typical

Above: **The courtyard and *qibla iwan* of the Great Mosque at Herat**, begun 1200/01
Built by the Ghurid sultan Ghiyath al-Din Muhammad on the site of an earlier mosque destroyed by fire, the Great Mosque of Herat has been restored many times, but preserves elements of its Ghurid plan. The main, or *qibla*, *iwan* lies to the west, as in the earlier mosque, which was built in the Hanafite tradition. Ghiyath al-Din respected this orientation, although he himself was a Shafii, who favored a southern orientation for the *qibla*.

Left: **Brick inscription on the southeast portal of the Great Mosque at Herat**
This inscription is one of the masterpieces of Ghurid architectural decoration. The rising shafts of the capital letters are grouped in twisted patterns and the ends decorated with floral arabesques.

Madrasa at Shah-i Mashhad, 1175/76
This *madrasa* ruin in Badgis province in north-western Afghanistan was unknown to out-siders until 1970. As is common in this region, it has a large open courtyard with *iwans*, of which two remain. An inscription identifies the building as a *madrasa* endowed by a high-ranking woman of the court of the Ghurid ruler Ghiyath al-Din Muhammad. It is elaborately decorated with brick, terracotta, and stucco, especially in the facade niches (below).

Religious buildings

The Ghaznavids were pious Sunni Muslims who supported the authority of the Abbasid caliphs in Baghdad. Mahmud himself was invested with a title and robe of honor by the caliph al Qadir in 1000, and the event was often recalled in later histories and depicted in miniatures. To promote their orthodoxy, Ghaznavid rulers built many mosques and *madrasas* in their capital cities. Mahmud, for example, is said to have embellished Ghazna with a fabulous mosque revetted in gold, alabaster, and marble, *madrasas*, libraries, aqueducts, and other public works. Some of the ruined buildings excavated at al-Askar and Ghazna have been identified as mosques or *madrasas* because they contain a *mihrab*, but these buildings are known only from their ground plans. We are better informed about examples of religious architecture built by the Ghurids.

Shah-i Mashshad

The only building that can definitively be identified as a *madrasa* is the ruined structure known as Shah-i Mashhad, located at a remote site on the west bank of the Murghab River, in Badgis province in northwestern Afghanistan. To judge from the ruins, it was a large (144 × 135 feet, 44 × 41 meters), almost square building with *iwans* and rooms arranged around a central court. *Iwans* surviving on the north and south may have been matched by two others on the east and west. To the right of the main entrance were two domed chambers, perhaps the precursors of the lecture room and assembly hall beside the main portal found in later Timurid *madrasas* in the region. As in those *madrasas*, the corners of the courtyard of Shah-i Mashhad were beveled with short walls set at an angle and connecting the sides.

Shah-i Mashhad is remarkable for its splendid decoration in brick, terracotta, and carved plaster. The most spectacular part to survive is the foundation inscrip-tion, which frames the portal. Executed in a magnificent Kufic script with plaited stems, it identifies the building as a *madrasa* erected by a woman in year 571 of the *hegira* (1175/76). Her name, given in the destroyed central part of the inscrip-tion, is missing, but, judging from the high rank and lofty benedictions, she can be identified as the wife of the reigning Ghurid ruler Ghiyath al-Din Muhammad.

Tombs

Ghiyath al-Din Muhammad, a devout follower of the Shafii school of law, was himself a great patron of architecture. In 1167, he ordered a small domed tomb at Chisht, a small settlement on the north bank of the Harirud about 95 miles (150 kilometers) upstream from Herat and downstream from the Ghurid capi-tal at Firuzkuh. The town had been the residence of the Syrian mystic Khoja Abu Ishaq (d. 941), founder of the Sufi order known as the Chishtiya. During the

Right: The arch at Bust,
late 12th century
Decorated in cut brick on the front and back, this large arch spans about 25 m. It led onto a vast square at the foot of the citadel and prob-ably had a ceremonial function. After the square was redesigned, it served to channel traffic through the citadel's main gate.

It was undoubtedly chosen for a specific reason, which remains elusive to us today.

We can only speculate about why these towers were built. A few, such as the Kalan minaret in Bukhara, were erected adjacent to mosques and might have been used for the call to prayer, but most were not. Early travelers identified these constructions as victory towers, but this is unlikely, since there is no evidence that such a building type was used in Islamic lands. Some towers may have been political statements, erected to proclaim the power of a new ruler, for they often bear the name of the patron. One erected at Tirmidh, for example, is dated year 423 of the *hegira* (1031/32), the same year that the Ghaznavids appointed a new governor to the region. Some towers may have served as beacons or road markers, such as the one in the village of Kirat in eastern Iran near the modern border with Afghanistan. Set on a small hillock and visible from a great distance, it marked the pass through the chain of hills separating the cities of Mashhad in Iran from Herat in Afghanistan. Such beacons would have been important to the numerous caravans that traversed this area *en route* from India and Central Asia to Iran and Iraq. Gratifyingly visible from nearby, where they might indicate the mosque's location, or from afar, where they would indicate a town, these towers advertised the presence of Islam and demonstrated the piety of the founder.

Below: **Detail of the inscription around the lower shaft of the tower at Jam**,
late 12th century
This tower is decorated with many inscriptions, some executed in brick, others in glazed ceramic. The lower shaft contains all of sura 19 of the Koran (the "Mary Sura"), as well as the name and titles of the Ghurid ruler Ghiyath al-Din Muhammad (1163–1203).

Right: **Tower at Jam**, late 12th century
The tower at Jam is the most striking of the group of some 40 towers erected in Iran, Afghanistan, and Central Asia between the 11th and the 13th centuries. It soars an amazing 197 ft (60 m) from the floor of a remote mountain valley in central Afghanistan. The site was so obscure that outsiders only discovered it in the 1950s, but it has since been identified as the medieval town of Firuzkuh, which served as the summer capital of the Ghurids and was destroyed by the Mongol khan Ügedei in 1222/23. The baked-brick tower comprises three tapering cylindrical shafts set atop each other, separated by *muqarnas* cornices, and crowned by a lantern.

the date of the commission, the first month of the Muslim year, together suggest that the bucket was intended as a New Year's gift after the merchant had performed the pilgrimage to Mecca, which he would have undertaken in the last month of the preceding year. Finally, the dedicatory inscription was written in Persian, showing that Persian was becoming increasingly accepted as a written language for everyday affairs. Arabic, still and forever the language of Islam, was used for the good wishes. The anthropomorphic inscriptions are extremely difficult to read, but the text is so banal – "glory and prosperity and power and tranquility and happiness … to its owner" – that any viewer could immediately guess its content. Important information that was meant to be read, such as the names of the donor, artisans, and recipient, and the date, was conveyed in more legible scripts. This same hierarchy of scripts was also used on the coinage, the most visible sign of a ruler's power, in the eastern Islamic lands. A ruler's name was often written in a flowing, legible cursive while the rest of the text was written in an old-fashioned angular script.

The function of the Bobrinski bucket is a puzzle. It was once called a "kettle" or "cauldron," but these are misnomers, for an inlaid object could not be used for cooking over a fire. Some scholars have hypothesized that the bucket was intended for carrying food or milk, but the copper interior would have had to have been covered with tin in order to avoid food poisoning from verdigris (corroded copper). Buckets and pails might be used to draw water from wells, but the luxurious decoration on this piece would have been subject to damage, and drinking water could equally have been tainted by verdigris. The most likely explanation is that the pail was intended to hold water for washing. Ritual ablution, which has been proposed by some scholars because of the recipient's pilgrimage titles, seems unlikely because of the figural imagery, which would have been inappropriate for use in or near a mosque. Furthermore, theologians condemned the game of backgammon, a game of chance (in contrast to chess, which relied on skill) as the Devil's temptation, so the bucket was unlikely to have been used in a religious context. The bucket was probably used when bathing in a bathhouse, and indeed, representations of bathhouses in Herat from a later period show similar buckets used to pour water over the bather's body. The luxurious inlay meant that it was unlikely that the bucket would have been left in the bathhouse; rather it was an exquisite version of an everyday object made as a commemorative gift. In short, the Bobrinski bucket was the present for the man who had everything.

Inlaying was not the only technique perfected by craftsmen from Herat, to judge from a group of extraordinary objects, such as ewers and candlesticks, hammered in high relief from sheet brass. One example is a truncated conical candlestick decorated with seven horizontal bands, alternately broad and narrow. The broad bands have lions and hexagons hammered in high relief; the narrow bands have inlaid arabesques and Arabic inscriptions with good wishes to an anonymous owner. The shoulder is further decorated with a row of ducks. The decoration was enhanced with copper and silver inlay. In contrast to the Bobrinski bucket, the function of this object – and others like it – is quite clear: it was set on the floor and held a large candle for interior lighting, whether in a house, mosque, or tomb. Many such candlesticks can be seen in later Persian paintings, and other examples, although not of this type, are inscribed with verses celebrating the candlestick.

Quite apart from the intricacy and beauty of this candlestick, it is technically extraordinary for – apart from the ducks – it was constructed from a single sheet of brass that was hammered from the front and the back. It has no seams at all and attests to the technical ability of the smith, who was able to transform a flat sheet into a large, truncated, conical base, ridged neck, and faceted socket, all decorated with elements in high relief. Several candlesticks and ewers were made in the same way. One of the ewers is signed by a Mahmud ibn Muhammad al-Harawi and dated year 567 of the *hegira* (1181/82); the whole group has been attributed to the province of Khorasan in northeast Iran and western Afghanistan in the

Candlestick, eastern Iran or Afghanistan, second half of the 12th century, height 40.3 cm, Washington, Freer Gallery of Art, Smithsonian Institution
This massive candlestick, hammered from a single sheet of brass and inlaid with copper, silver, and a black organic material, is one of a group of candlesticks and ewers made using this time-consuming technique. They clearly demonstrate the skill of metalsmiths in the region during the late 12th century.

late 12th and early 13th centuries. Together, they attest to the fine quality of metalwares known in the region at this time.

Central Asia and Asia Minor: The Great Seljuks, the Anatolian Seljuks, and the Khwarazm-Shahs

Mausoleums and palace ruins near Kuna Urgench, Uzbekistan, 12–13th centuries
Kuna Urgench was the capital of the Khwarazm-Shahs, who had initially been vassals of the
Seljuks, but had ultimately, from the middle of the 12th century onwards, taken over their
territory after pushing them further and further back. Many tombs and fragments of former
palace developments survive in both the city itself and in the surrounding area, such as the
Fakhr al-Din Razi mausoleum pictured here, which dates from the 12th century, and the so-
called mausoleum of the Khwarazm-Shah Tekesh, which is now thought to have been the
Great Khwarazm-Shah's audience chamber.

History
Markus Hattstein

Rise and glory of the Seljuk Empire

The Seljuks, who for a time ruled over one of Islam's largest empires, were originally nomadic Turkish shepherds from the steppes of Central Asia. They belonged to the great Oghuz federation of nine Turkish tribes that, since the 8th century, had been steadily spreading west as far as the Aral Sea. Deployed by the rulers of Central Asia from this time as defenders against invading Islamic Arabs, the Oghuz Turks had conquered their own territories and exerted pressure on the Samanids of Bukhara until the region finally fell to the Turkish Qarakhanids.

The clan adopted Islam c. 960 under one of its first leaders, Seljuk, from whom it took its name, and its members henceforth carried out their raids to the west and south as Islamic "frontier warriors" (*ghazi*) and religious fighters. After Seljuk's death, his three sons and ultimately two grandsons led the clan and spread further through Khorasan and the Oxus region. After being defeated by the region's ruler, Mahmud of Ghazna, in 1026, while in the service of the Qarakhanids, the Seljuks split into three groups. While one of them remained in the east, the two groups led by Seljuk's grandsons crossed Khorasan in a westerly direction to Afghanistan, where several cities succumbed to them: Merv in 1037, Herat and Nishapur in 1038. This was the beginning of the Seljuks' territorial rule.

The two brothers, Tughril Beg (1038–1063) and Chaghri Beg (1038–1060), then divided their territory into two: while the younger brother Chaghri, who bore the title "King of Kings," remained in the northern Afghanistan area as an independent ruler (with royal seats at Balkh and Merv), Tughril established himself in Nishapur with the more senior title "Most Honored Supreme Ruler" (sultan). He realized his political ambitions following a decisive victory over the Ghaznavids in 1040 with the consolidation of the state as an entity and an expansion towards the west: in 1042 he occupied western Iran including Rayy and also the provinces bordering the Caspian Sea, reached Shiraz in 1052, and in 1054 achieved recognition as sovereign of Azerbaijan and Khuzistan, having previously been acknowledged as supreme ruler of all the Oghuz tribes.

From 1050 Tughril led campaigns into Iraq, partly in order to liberate the caliph of Baghdad from the tutelage of the Shiite Buyids and, as a strict Sunni Muslim, to set himself up as the caliphate's new protector, but also to conduct a religious war against the Fatimids of Cairo. In 1055, when he marched into

Seljuk ruler on his throne, manuscript, 13th century
Because the Seljuks, being Turks, could not legitimize themselves by claiming to be related to the Prophet, they were careful to enhance their position through the acquisition of honorary titles, conferred upon them by the caliph of Baghdad.

Baghdad and overthrew the Buyids' rule, he had the caliph grant him certain honorary titles: in a document of 1062 Tughril is named as "Ruler of Rulers, King of the East and West, Restorer of Islam, Right Hand of the Caliph and Commander of the Faithful." Neither could the caliph refuse him the hand of his daughter in marriage in 1062, and it must have immediately been clear to him that he had simply exchanged one set of masters, the Buyids, for another. At the same time, new groups of Oghuz Turks were constantly streaming west, whom Tughril diverted into the border wars against the Christian empires of Byzantium, Georgia, and Armenia, while claiming the rich provinces of Iran for himself. He finally selected Isfahan as his seat, and this was also to remain the main capital under his two successors.

After the death of Tughril, who had no direct descendants, his nephew Alp Arslan (1063–1072), one of Chaghri's sons, became sultan and the tribal organization in existence up to that point, with its several local rulers, was replaced by centralized rule for the first time. Along with his vizier Nizam al-Mulk, Alp Arslan was the main founder of the Great Seljuk state. Strict control over the provinces was combined, in Persia primarily, with the fostering of trade and the life of the intellect. The sultan countered Turkish particularism by creating a standing army of military slaves, whose officers were placed under an obligation of courtly service to the ruler and thereupon dispatched as loyal administrators to distant provinces of the empire that had hitherto belonged to the Seljuk Empire in name only. Nizam al-Mulk had built up an efficient system (the *iqta* system) whereby provinces were given as fiefs to military commanders, who were only required to pay over a portion of the tax money to the government and could use the remainder to maintain themselves and their troops.

In 1064 Alp Arslan won supremacy over Kerman province and was able to safeguard the trade and pilgrim routes once the *sharifs* of Mecca had been subordinated to Seljuk sovereignty in 1070. The situation in Anatolia, where, along with the Oghuz Turks, other, rival, tribes of Turks had also settled, forced the sultan to intervene on several occasions. After the "frontier warriors" had laid waste to the Byzantine cities of Caesarea (Kayseri) in 1067, and Iconium (Konya) in 1069, Emperor Romanus IV Diogenes fortified the empire's cities as far south as Syria, and finally marched into Armenia with a large army. Alp Arslan realized that his tribesmen were in danger, and captured his opponent at Mantzikert (Malazgirt), where the Byzantines suffered a devastating defeat on August 26, 1071. From then on, the Anatolia region was open for settlement by the increasing number of Turkish tribespeople now flowing in. After this, Alp Arslan marched east and was crossing the Oxus River with a powerful army when he was assassinated in 1072.

His successor was his young son Malik-Shah (1072–1092), who had been named as heir to the throne in 1066 and who was completely under the influence of the towering Nizam al-Mulk. Although his reign represented a cultural golden age for the Seljuk Empire, it took place against a background of clashes with rival Turkish tribes in Anatolia and the Caucasus as well as attempts by individual branches of the family to gain their own independence. Malik was not able to prevent either the sons of his uncle Qawurt, (following the suppression of the latter's revolt), from creating the effectively independent Seljuk state of Kerman (which lasted until the end of the 12th century), or the rival family branch of Suleyman-Shah from making itself autonomous in Anatolia and later establishing its own rule with Konya as its capital.

In the east, Malik succeeded in extending his empire as far as Transoxiana, and in 1084 drove the Marvanids out of Diyarbakir. Following military successes in Syria in 1084, he intensified his engagement on the Arabian Peninsula, taking the island of Bahrain and occupying Yemen for a while. This meant that the Seljuk Empire now extended from the borders of China in the east all the way to Anatolia in the west, taking in the whole of Arabia in the south.

The internal structure of the Seljuk empire

The internal construction of the empire is closely associated with the name of one man, one of the most significant political architects of early Islam: Abu Ali Hassan ibn Ali Tussi (1018–1092), known by his name of honor, Nizam al-Mulk ("Order of the Empire"). The son of a Ghaznavid tax collector, he rapidly won high honors at the courts of Chaghri and Alp Arslan as a jurist and expert in administration. By 1060 he was already Alp Arslan's vizier for Khorasan, but in 1063 became vizier of the Great Seljuk Empire, when his

Rabat-i Sharaf Caravanserai, in Khorasan
In the 11th century the Seljuk Empire was the largest in the Islamic world. Divided into eastern and western halves for administrative purposes, its rulers attempted to assert their power even in the most remote of provinces. To this end they created an infrastructure of which caravanserais formed a part; these were used as stopping-off places for goods traffic and travelers, but also for the movements of troops and the well-developed postal and communications services.

Iranian landscape, near Natanz
After the Seljuks initially settled as nomads in Transoxiana in the east, Tughril Beg (1038–1063) pushed west in the years after 1040 as far as Anatolia and Iraq, where he placed the caliph under his protection. Iran formed the heartland of the western half of the empire, although Seljuk rule there deteriorated steadily after the assassination of Malik-Shah (1092), until the Seljuks were finally driven out by the Khwarazm-Shahs at the end of the 12th century.

master took over supreme leadership. Under Malik-Shah he was able to further increase his personal power further and establish the hegemony of his family in the political leadership of the empire.

Nizam developed this office into the most important political institution: as head of the Great Divan, the empire's government, he was, above all else, in charge of the finances and tax revenues, accompanied the sultan on his military campaigns, and controlled all the religious and juridical matters of the empire. In his *Siyasat-name* (*Book of Statecraft*), the most important political work of the early Islamic period, he set out the principles for efficient centralized government in a sober and pragmatic manner. As he considered the particularistic Turkish tribes to be unreliable, he appointed Arabic and Persian administrators, extended the Ghulam system of military slaves sworn to loyalty, and gave senior positions in the empire's administrative bodies to specialists he selected and trained himself. By standardizing the legal system, he was able to make the job of implementing the principles of Seljuk centralism easier for himself.

An important tool in the reorganization of Turkish tribal rule into a centralized state was the government's religious policy. Nizam and the sultans championed a strict Sunnism of a Shafiite and Hanafite character, which prefigured a bitter struggle against the Shiism of the Fatimids and other heterodoxies. In this, Nizam was motivated less by a love of *sunna* than by pragmatic political considerations: he was concerned with establishing a unified and centrally controlled state religion as a basis for the legitimation of Seljuk power. His rule was founded primarily upon the law rather than religion, which was why, in the Seljuk Empire, the *sunna* was applied more as a form of state or government ideology.

The most important instruments of this religiopolitical standardization were the *madrasas*, which, although not originally founded by Nizam, were nevertheless fundamentally fashioned by him. They were not simply Koran schools, but universities for the future juristic and administrative elite, and to this end tied religion and state together from day one. Theology, jurisprudence, languages, literature, the natural sciences, and political science were all taught in the *madrasas*; they were a platform for the propaganda battle against the Shia. The students, who needed approval from the state in order to study and whose upkeep was paid for by a monthly stipend from the government, all had their own rooms and attended lectures delivered from a chair or lectern by professors dressed in gown and turban. The professors' assistants, or *répétiteurs*, were responsible for developing these lectures with the students in depth.

Nizam created a dense network of *madrasas*, which he personally had built in all the important centers of the enormous empire, and which were known as "Nizamiya" in his honor. They provided the model for all later *madrasas*; Nizam's most significant foundations were the *madrasas* in Baghdad (1067), Nishapur, Herat, Damascus, Mosul, Balkh, Ghazna, Merv, and Basra. Nizam

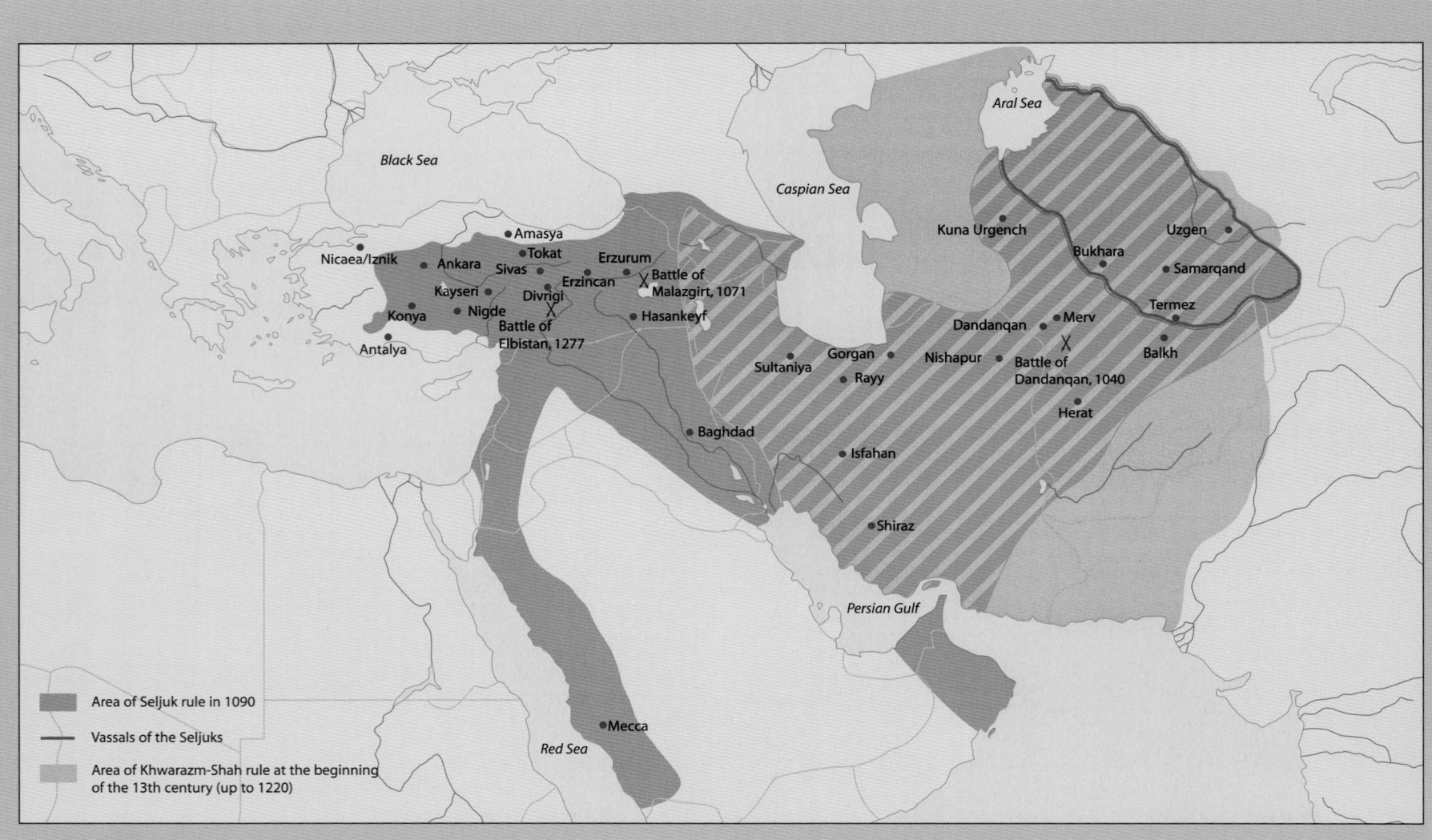

CENTRAL ASIA AND ASIA MINOR

Students being questioned in a mosque school, illustration from the *Maqamat* of al-Hariri by al-Wasiti, 1237, Paris, Bibliothèque Nationale

Whereas previously the most important places of learning in the Islamic world had been the mosque or Koran schools, where the Koran was taught, the Seljuk grand vizier Nizam al-Mulk founded numerous colleges or *madrasas*. This is where the future administrative elite were educated, which is why the curriculum included not only a strict Sunni Muslim content, but also political science, history, regional studies, languages, and literature.

chose the professors himself, and made sure the *madrasas* were equipped and furnished to the highest standards. In 1091 he summoned the most important scholar of the time, Muhammad al-Ghazzali (1058–1111), whose thinking on how to reconcile theology, philosophy, and mysticism was to prove revolutionary, to the Baghdad *madrasa*. By means of patronage and generous endowments, Nizam and the sultans sought to integrate Sufism and Islamic mysticism into the state theology in order to eliminate their spiritual closeness to the Shia.

Nizam al-Mulk as a man of action and al-Ghazzali as theoretician represented a collaboration between caliph and sultan, and together they undertook a serious reorientation of the concept of Islam rule which has been valid since that time. They gave the state a purely ethical-legal basis and neglected the divine legitimation of the caliphs. For al-Ghazzali, God has raised up two groups of men above all others: the prophets and the rulers; the caliph appears to be increasingly reduced to the role of symbolic unifying figure. The basis of

1037–1038	Merv, Herat, and Nishapur subordinated to Seljuk rule. Creation of the Great Seljuk Empire (1038–1157)	1078	The Seljuk Tutush becomes ruler of Syria and Palestine	1157	Disintegration of the Great Seljuk Empire following the death of Sanjar
1038–1063	Sultanate of Tughril Beg in Nishapur	1084	The Seljuks under Malik-Shah drive the Marvanids out of Diyarbakir	1176	Battle of Myriocephalon: Byzantines suffer devastating defeat at the hands of the Anatolian Seljuks
1038–1060	Rule of Chaghri Beg in Merv	1092–1105	Power struggle for the succession to Malik-Shah	1178	Anatolian Seljuks integrate the Danishmend principality in northeast Anatolia into their empire
1040–1054	Expansion of the sultanate west under Tughril Beg	1097–1128	Rule of the Khwarazm-Shah Qutb al-Din Muhammad		
1040	Battle of Dandanqan: the Seljuks, under Tughril Beg and Chaghri Beg, defeat the Ghaznavids	1097	Anatolian Seljuks defeated by the Crusaders under Godfrey of Bouillon, Nicaea falls to the Crusaders; Konya becomes capital of the Anatolian Seljuks	1156–1192	Rule of Qilic Arslan II in Anatolia
1042	Khwarazmia becomes a province of the Seljuk Empire			1190	Emperor Frederick Barbarossa of Germany conquers Konya
1055	The Seljuks replace the Buyids as protectors of the Abbasid caliphate	1117	End of Seljuk rule in Syria	1194	Khwarazmian Turks under Ala al-Din Tekish (1172–1200) end Seljuk rule in Persia
		1105–1118	Sultanate of the Seljuk Muhammad I		
1063–1072	Sultanate of Alp Arslan	1118–1157	Sultanate of the Seljuk Sanjar	1200–1220	Rule of the Khwarazm-Shah Ala al-Din Muhammad
1065–1092	Nizam al-Mulk vizier	1128–1156	Khwarazm-Shah Ala al-Din Atsiz rules in effect autonomously	1210	Khwarazmians victorious against the Qara-Khitai Mongols
1071	Defeat of the Byzantines at Malazgirt by the Seljuks under Alp Arslan	1138–1139	Battles between the Seljuks under Sanjar and the Khwarazm-Shahs under Ala al-Din Atsiz	1212	Samarqand destroyed by the Khwarazmians
1072	Assassination of Alp Arslan	1141	Defeat of the Seljuks under Sanjar by the Qara-Khitai Mongols	1215	Khwarazmians finally end Ghurid rule
1072–1092	Sultanate of Malik-Shah			1218	Execution of Mongol merchants by the Khwarazm-Shahs unleashes the Mongol assault on
1076	The Seljuks win Damascus from the Fatimids	1156–1172	Rule of Khwarazm-Shah Il-Arslan		
1077	Conquest of Konya				the west (1220)
				1219–1237	Rule of Ala al-Din Kaiqubad in Anatolia
				1220–1231	Rule of the last Khwarazm-Shah, Jalal al-Din
				1240–1242	Uprising, motivated by religion, of Baba Ishaq and his followers in Anatolia
				1243	Battle of the Kose Dagi: defeat of Anatolian Seljuks by the Mongols
				1258	Mongol assault ends the Abbasid caliphate in Baghdad
				1277	Battle of Elbistan: the Seljuks, supported by the Mamluks, push the Mongols back
				1279	Final Mongol victory over the Anatolian Seljuks
				1308	Anatolia subject to direct Mongol control

legitimation for Islamic rule is the exercising of justice (through the *sharia*) and the provision of political stability and general prosperity. These in turn allow the ruler to assert his authority, as all sections of the population are then willing to contribute to the general good. The state is held together by means of a unified state religion. This was a theoretical restatement of what powerful rulers such as Mahmud of Ghazna and Tughril Beg, or the early Buyids, who as Turks – just like the Mongols after them – were not able to claim religious legitimacy, had already managed to achieve in practice through the exercising of strength, through their cumulative successes, and through the dispensation of justice by the sovereign.

The decline of Seljuk rule and the Khwarazm-Shah Empire

Although having previously been exclusively directed against the Fatimids, the religiopolitical struggle of Nizam al-Mulk and Malik-Shah saw itself confronted by a new danger from 1090, when the Ismaili sect of Assassins, under their Grand Master Hasan-i-Sabbah ("the old man of the mountains") established itself in its Alamut mountain fortress and threatened to exert control over the north of Iran. In 1092 Nizam was stabbed to death in the middle of the street by a warrior for the faith (*fedain*) – the first prominent victim of the sect by whose hand kings, sultans, and caliphs were to perish too. In the same year, Sultan Malik-Shah also died the victim of assassination.

In the fratricidal war between Malik-Shah's sons that ensued, most of the empire's provinces degenerated into disorder; provincial governors and members of the Seljuk family declared their independence, and the advance of the Christian Crusaders into Syria and Palestine led to the loss of these regions. Once Berk-yaruq (1092–1105), who had the support of Nizam's family, had failed ultimately to win through against the other pretenders, the allied brothers Muhammad and Sanjar emerged victorious from the power struggle between Malik's sons.

Sultan Muhammad (1105–1118) restored order in the now smaller western part of the empire (Iran/Iraq) with the help of Nizam al-Mulk's sons, but was unable to drive the Assassins out of northern Iran. Following his death, the empire was divided. The western part came under the rule of Muhammad's sons and their descendants, whose power declined rapidly, particularly after the meteoric rise of the Zangids and Ayyubids in Syria and Egypt, and ended in 1194. Muhammad's brother Sanjar (1118–1157), who had been governor of Khorasan since 1097 and independent "King of the East" since 1105, was, however, able to secure the transfer of the title of sultan and senior member of the family to himself in the east. In 1119 he led a campaign against his nephews, who were henceforth compelled to bend to his will. From his seat in Merv, Sanjar led the Seljuk Empire, thanks to a well-filled state treasury, into a final golden age in the east; he managed to assert his sovereignty in Transoxiana and even dominated the area of influence of the Qarakhanids. In 1138 he occupied the province of Khwarazmia, but his luck ran out during the second half of his reign: severely defeated by the Qara-Khitai Mongols in 1141, he lost the Oxus region and twice even had to withdraw from Merv. When the Herat region became subordinated to the Ghurids in 1147, his rule was confined to Khorasan. Defeated and taken prisoner by the enemy Turkish Ghuzz tribe in 1153, he was only liberated with the help of the Khwarazm-Shahs. At the time of his death in 1157, total anarchy ruled in his empire, which was divided up between the Khwarazm-Shahs and various Turkish tribes. The empire that had at times during its history been the biggest in Islam, had finally met its end.

The Khwarazmia region, which had belonged to the Seljuk Empire as a province since 1042, had led an autonomous existence within eastern Islam. From 1065 the sultans started installing vassals of Turkish origin there as rulers

Painted stucco figure, Iran, 12th century, Berlin, Museum of Islamic Art
This fully three-dimensional plaster figure probably once belonged to a larger ensemble, possibly a reliefwork frieze made for the ruling court and serving a ceremonial purpose. It is assumed that this would have depicted real individuals from the court, which is interesting in the light of Islam's hostility towards representational images. The paintwork on this specimen has survived particularly well by comparison with other figures from the Seljuk period.

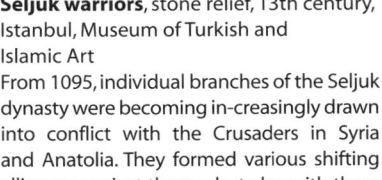

(the Khwarazm-Shahs), with the result that this area, which had hitherto been Iranian in character, received Seljuk administrative structures and became a flourishing oasis in the steppes over the following years.

The Khwarazm-Shah Qutb al-Din Muhammad (1097–1128) exploited civil war in the Seljuk Empire in order to achieve a far-reaching political autonomy which his son, Ala al-Din Atsiz (1128–1156), developed into *de facto* independence. He initially supported Sultan Sanjar, but his relationship with the Khwarazmians deteriorated rapidly after 1135. In 1138 Atsiz risked open rebellion and took advantage of Sanjar's defeat at the hands of the Mongols in 1141 to invade Khorasan. During the course of battles of varying fortunes, Atsiz managed to consolidate his position and advanced further and further into Khorasan from 1153 onwards. After 1157 his son Il-Arslan (1156–1172) appropriated a large part of Khorasan and thus turned the Khwarazmian Empire into the largest and most powerful in eastern Islam up to the invasion of the Mongols. By making tribute payments to the neighboring Qara-Khitai Mongols he secured the rear of his empire while occupying parts of western Iran including Nishapur.

His son Ala al-Din Tekish (1172–1200) advanced further west with his troops and won himself recognition not only as successor of the Seljuk sultans in Iran, pushing forward as far as Rayy in 1192, but also from the caliph of Baghdad as the caliphate's new protector. In 1199 the caliph also thought it wise to name Tekish sultan of Iraq, Khorasan, and Turkestan. Under Tekish's son Ala al-Din Muhammad (1200–1220) the Khwarazmian Empire experienced its greatest triumphs and its most dramatic fall. After 1206 he won the entire Ghurid territories (taking Herat in 1208), threw off the formal overlordship of the Qara-Khitai in 1210, and extended his empire in the following period at their expense as well as that of the Qarakhanids, making his territory for a short time the largest Islamic empire in history in terms of its surface area. When, after the fall of the Ghurids, the caliph was preparing to support even Shiite groups in order to remove himself from Khwarazmian hegemony,

Ala al-Din Muhammad marched on Baghdad in 1217 with a powerful army. Only the harsh winter of 1217/18 saved the caliph's city from a protracted siege.

Since 1215 diplomatic contact had existed between the Shah and the court of the Mongol ruler Genghis Khan, who had recently invaded China and was interested in opening up a trading route west through Khwarazmian territory. No agreement had yet been reached when, in 1218, the Khwarazmian governor of Utrar detained a Mongolian trading caravan consisting of several hundred merchants. He announced to the Shah that he had captured Mongol spies, and the Shah immediately ordered the prisoners' execution.

By arrogantly ignoring Mongol demands for amends, Ala al-Din Muhammad not only caused the downfall of his own empire, but also ultimately that of the entire early Islamic world in the east. Genghis Khan, to whom this incident represented a welcome cause for expansion in that direction, then marched west, overrunning Bukhara and Nishapur in 1220, continually driving the Khwarazm-Shah before him. The sultan was finally wounded in battle against the Mongols in Rayy and died in December 1220 while fleeing to Baghdad. The Mongol advance proceeded west, leaving in its wake thousands upon thousands dead and the devastation of whole areas, and bringing the Islamic east a period of unutterable suffering and depopulation; whole cities, such as Herat, were razed to the ground and their inhabitants massacred.

Muhammad's son, Jalal al-Din (1220–1231), the last Khwarazm-Shah, went into action several times against the Mongols, but was forced to flee time and time again. After a period of exile in India lasting several years, he engaged the Mongols in Iran and managed to occupy Georgia. Repeatedly driven out of his territories, he was finally murdered in Anatolia in 1231. He had been warning the Islamic rulers in vain about the Mongol threat and unsuccessfully attempting to unite the estranged empires in a joint defensive action.

Architecture

Sergej Chmelnizkij

While the Seljuk Empire was rapidly expanding from Transoxiana towards Iran, with the aim of bringing the caliphate of Baghdad under its protection, the Central Asian city of Merv remained its capital and artistic center. During this time, the Qarakhanids were erecting their impressive monumental buildings in Transoxiana in the flourishing cities of Bukhara and Samarqand.

The period from the 11th to the beginning of the 13th century is quite correctly considered the classical era of Central Asian architecture. The buildings dating from this time – public, sacred, and even memorial – are of an exquisite elegance and display a harmonious balance in construction and decoration.

Construction techniques as decoration

In this architecture there is no division between decorative adornment and construction technique, and consequently no continuous ornamental camouflage, as is the case with buildings of the 14–16th centuries. The main material for construction as well as decoration was brick, the bricks being usually square and combined in the most unusual ways, and carved terracotta of the same yellowish hue. In the 12th century, colored ceramic insertions – turquoise inscriptive bands, and decorative dark blue, white, and green elements – were used to break up the yellow ocher of the buildings, which was hardly distinguishable from the ground, but even at this time, the main decorative procedures were carried out in brick and terracotta: double brick bonds with or without carved ornaments, stepped bonds, and friezes and surfaces carved in brick. The effect of the brick bonds was achieved by a carpet-like overall structure with different elements clearly standing out, and by the play of light and shadow. Further decorative possibilities were offered by ornamental wall-painting and stucco (Persian: *gadj*) carving. This involved mixing pulverized alabaster with water and working it while still damp. It was sometimes also used to imitate brickwork. The manifold variety produced and consequent combining of technique and decoration is astonishing: during this period building techniques were the main source of decorative motif.

Space and dome solutions

As a major building material, brick also determined the form taken by the buildings' various types of vaulting and domed roofs. The round base of the dome, where it met the top of a square room, was determined by its ground plan; the transition between circle and square was achieved by means of squinches, i.e. arches spanning the corners of the square, forming the octagonal lower part of the dome. Console spandrels were also known, consisting of rows of superimposed brick brackets. These formed the basis of the stalactite structures (*muqarnas*) which had already appeared in the 11th century and which later became very widespread. The arches, and therefore the cross section of vault and dome too, were generally pointed. Here, a geometrical procedure allowed an infinite number of variations on the pointed arch to be developed.

In the 11th century, the first buildings – mausoleums – were built with double-shell domes, a technique that rapidly became widespread in monumental architecture. In this way the outer shell of the dome, resting on a drum, could be transformed into an impressive structure whose shape was independent of the building's interior. In the 12th, century the outer shell of the dome was sometimes given a steep pyramid or conical shape, which afforded the dome better protection against rain and snow.

The limitless variety of ground plan and interior designs in the architecture of Central Asia between the 11th and beginning of the 13th centuries can be reduced to two basic schemata: the courtyard-axis schema and the central dome structure. The first of these consists of a rectangular courtyard with two right-angular axes, the longitudinal axis being the main one, enclosed by buildings forming a rectangular outline. This schema was used for large buildings of both sacred and secular function, such as mosques, palaces, *madrasas*, and caravanserais. The simplest design was that of the courtyard mosque, where the space between the courtyard and windowless exterior wall was occupied by a continuous gallery. This consisted of several rows of brick piers forming continuous domed cells generally connected to each other by archways. Stone or brick columns were not used because of the frequent earthquakes in Central Asia.

Most of the surviving 11th- and 12th- century caravanserais, which served as inns for traveling merchants and their caravans, and often developed into trading centers themselves, stand out because of their combination of magnificence and functionality. They frequently had an impressive palace-like character. Here, too, the longitudinal axis dominates, beginning at a monumental entrance portal and continuing through one or two courtyards surrounded by various types of rooms (accommodation for the traders, storage for goods, stables) and ending in a suite of splendid halls. The numerous functions of the caravanserais explain the complexity of their design and the differences between the concrete forms they took.

Not much has been known about the architecture of the 11th- and 12th-century Central Asian *madrasa* for very long, the one definite example of it that has so far been discovered being the Khoja Mashhad *madrasa* in southern Tajikistan. This building shows that *madrasas* from this period already displayed the important features of *madrasa* design that were later to become the norm.

Central Asian palace complexes served on the one hand as the private residences of the rulers, but always, on the other, incorporated an official series of rooms that accommodated the authorities, and where officials carried out affairs of state. In the 11th and 12th centuries, these buildings were also as a rule constructed along the lines of the old courtyard-axis schema. Their starting point was the courtyard, whose primary axis led from a ceremonial portal through to a vaulted hall or *iwan*, completely open to the courtyard. This is where the ruler would hold his audiences, while the public was confined to the courtyard. While the architecture of the palaces was strongly influenced by the local building traditions, the courtyard principle, despite numerous variations, was common to all of them. Sometimes, however, the semantic and compositional center of the palace was not a vaulted throne *iwan*, but a domed hall. Whether the individual palaces and official residences of the 11th and 12th centuries known about as a result of excavations followed the axis principle or not, their layout, in keeping with their wider range of functions, was essentially more complicated than that of the courtyard mosques, *madrasas*, and even caravanserais.

This multifunctionality was typical of the complexes of the 11th and 12th centuries built according to the courtyard-axis schema; thus the courtyard mosques, for example, were also public, municipal centers and could additionally serve as fortresses at times of danger. The similar architectonic structure in each case permitted variations of function: caravanserais, *madrasas*, and even Friday (congregational) mosques could, under certain circumstances, undergo changes of basic function, or take on additional functions, without a fundamental alteration to their ground plan and room structure. Characteristic of the courtyard-axis structure, however, is its clear, rectangular basic shape and general symmetry with longitudinal and often transverse axis too.

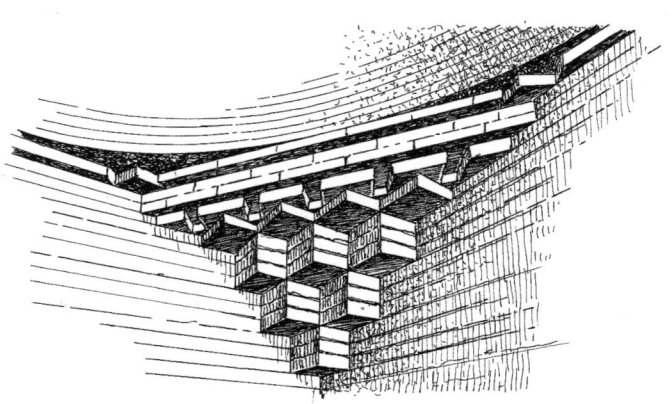

Left: **Squinch in the Kyz-Bibi Mausoleum in Merv**, 11-12th centuries
The squinches in this clay brick building take the form of the stepped, arched design previously widespread throughout Central Asia. This building represents one of the last examples of pre-Islamic architecture.

Below: **Stepped console spandrel in the Daya Khatun Caravanserai**, 11-12th centuries
Console supports of this type were the precursors of the weight-bearing as well as decorative *muqarnas* structures that were to become widely used in Islamic architecture in the following century.

The second design schema employed during this period, that of the central domed structure, found its realization in a design featuring identical, or near identical, symmetrical axes and a dominant dome-covered central building. In contrast to the dynamic courtyard-axis schema, this design was by its very nature static. Both schemata had their origins in antiquity and had been used in various different ways in pre-Islamic buildings.

The simplicity of the domed hall design allowed it to be used for a variety of purposes and also to be combined with other rooms. The domed hall could form a single building and as such serve as a domed mosque or mausoleum; it could form the nucleus of a centralized building with a number of rooms; it could be positioned at one end of the longitudinal axis of a courtyard complex; or form a constituent part of other combinations. The floor plan of a domed hall is seldom that of a simple square. In most cases, its space was increased by means of vaulted niches on the cross-axes, which rendered it cruciform. Its main axis would usually be accentuated by a portal or *pishtaq* (Persian: "fore-arch"). This consisted of a high, vaulted niche within a rectangular frame with an entranceway at the back of it.

Already in pre-Islam times, Central Asian buildings had followed a schema of proportions that firstly served a practical purpose and secondly guaranteed a harmony of architecture. Later on, in the 11th and 12th centuries, mathematical discoveries were exploited in order to extend this system, and thus opened up its possibilities. Widespread use was made of grid screens containing square

Detail of the interior decoration of the Hakim Termezi Mausoleum in Termez, 11–12th centuries
The Termez mausoleum is a rare example of a small, domed building decorated from top to bottom with carved stucco. The walls are covered with a "lily pattern," framed within a continuous interlaced design. This is topped by a wide Kufic script frieze with an ornamental in-fill between the letters. The dome decoration is based on round *gerich* medallions with a geometric star pattern.

Detail of portal of the Khoja Nakhshran Mausoleum near Regar, Tajikistan, 11–12th centuries
This is a particularly well-executed example of typical decorative brickwork arranged in double bonds with decorative elements of carved terracotta. The corner column is an example of the use of decorative elements to a structural end. The Kufic inscription and decorative embellishments alongside it are cut from specially baked pieces of clay.

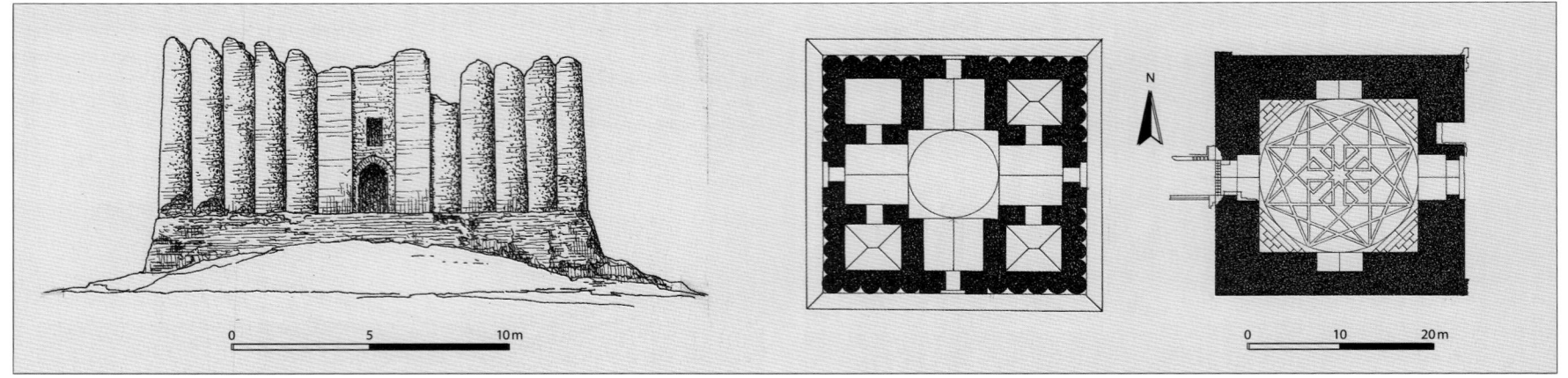

View and ground plan of a house in Kalta Minar, Merv oasis, 11th century
The main building in the Kalta Minar settlement was clearly no private dwelling, but was designed for public functions, as the courtyard-axis schema with central courtyard and *iwans* opening onto its suggests. The design of the facade, with its protuberant half-pillar brick walls, is typical of the Merv oasis, and was frequently used in pre-Islamic times for the walls of fortresses.

Above right: **Ground plan of Sultan Sanjar Mausoleum**, beginning of the 12th century
This enormous building, previously thought to be the mausoleum of Sultan Sanjar, was probably the audience chamber of the palace of the Great Seljuks, which no longer exists. The domed hall, which has survived, is a characteristic example of a monumental central building, a compositional principle widespread in Central Asia. The shell of the dome is embellished with decorative ribs forming a pattern in stone.

cells, the length of whose sides corresponded to the length of the arm from shoulder to fingertips. These grids were used to fix the measurements for the domed rooms and their axial niches, the thickness of the walls, the width of the entrance and so on.

The essential characteristics of Central Asian architecture from the 11th to the beginning of the 13th century, such as its unity of construction and decoration, its mathematical harmony of form, and its minimal number of basic design schemata which could be realized in endless variations, allow it to be seen as classical and thus comparable with that of classical Greek antiquity.

Mosques – the Arabian type

The large Friday mosques, where the faithful gathered for prayers on that day, formed the religious and social heart of the cities. None of the Friday mosques built in the 11–12th centuries using the model of the Arabian prototype, the courtyard mosque, have survived, except as ruins. The Samanid mosque built in Samarqand in the 10th century was originally square, but was transformed into a clay-brick rectangle oriented towards the southwest (the direction of Mecca) as the result of several alterations and additions. The long courtyard was enclosed on three sides by triple rows of wooden colonnades, resting on heavy pedestals, which extended back to a columned hall, seven rows of columns deep, with a forward-projecting *mihrab* in the middle of its back wall. With this plan, the Samarqand mosque is a typical example of the early Arabian mosque and bears a great similarity to the large Abbasid mosque in Samarra, built nearly 400 years earlier. This burnt down in 1220 during the Mongol invasion, and with it perished the inhabitants of the city, who had taken refuge behind its walls.

The mosque in Misrian, a rich trading city in the south of Turkmenistan, stood by the southern city gate on a street that led into the center of the city. The names of the building masters, Abd al-Husain ibn Muhammad al-Naka and Muhammad ibn al-Husain al-Naka – possibly father and son – and of the client, the Khwarazm-Shah Muhammad, have survived on the pillars of the portal, richly decorated with carved terracotta, so the building can be dated to 1200–1219. It is built of kiln-baked brick, like many of the city's buildings, which can be seen as evidence of the prosperity that prevailed there. The large mosque in Samarqand, for example, is only made of clay brick.

The mosque in Misrian unites two different concepts of space: the Arabian courtyard arrangement and the Iranian domed building. A dome-covered portal hall has been added to the area occupied by the Arabian mosque, a descendant of the ancient Iranian palace *iwan*, which forms the centerpiece of the whole.

Another completely different variant of the Arabian prototype is represented by the courtyard mosque in the city of Dandanqan in the Merv region, which also survives only as a ruin. Originally built in the 10th century, it was altered slightly in the 11th century to form a long rectangle surrounded by a wall, with its longitudinal axis running southwest in the direction of Mecca. The

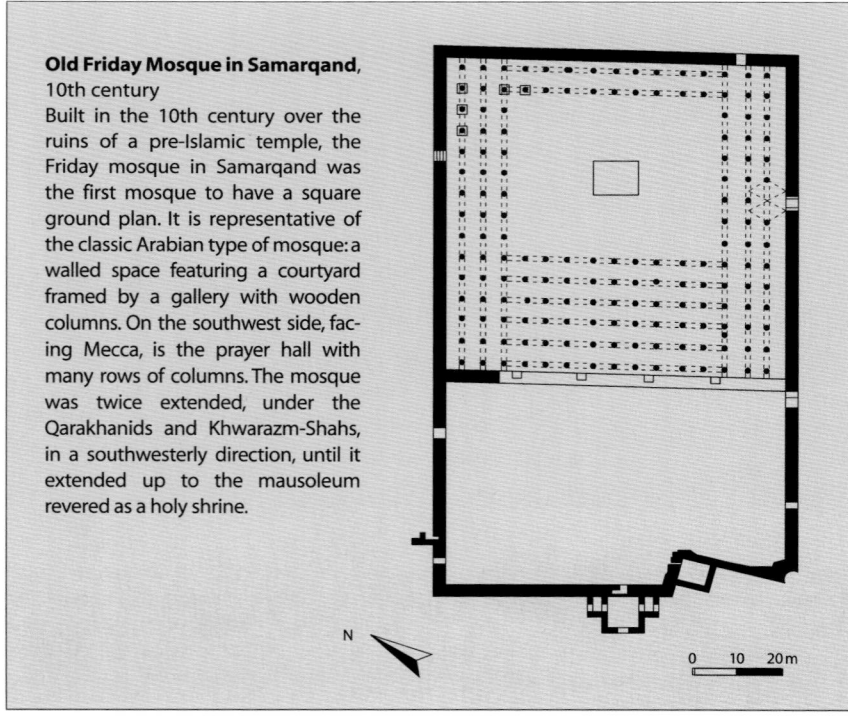

Old Friday Mosque in Samarqand, 10th century
Built in the 10th century over the ruins of a pre-Islamic temple, the Friday mosque in Samarqand was the first mosque to have a square ground plan. It is representative of the classic Arabian type of mosque: a walled space featuring a courtyard framed by a gallery with wooden columns. On the southwest side, facing Mecca, is the prayer hall with many rows of columns. The mosque was twice extended, under the Qarakhanids and Khwarazm-Shahs, in a southwesterly direction, until it extended up to the mausoleum revered as a holy shrine.

domed *khanqa* building was added on the eastern side, with its portal facing south (right), with the effect that, together with a further mausoleum and a courtyard between the mausoleum and the mosque, a whole complex developed, which was frequently altered and restored.

courtyard was surrounded by ambulatories formed by round brick pillars with carved alabaster elements. The corner pillars stand out because of their octagonal bases and round pillar design. The customary deep, pillared galleries of the Arabian mosque, with their many columns, are here reduced to one row of columns on three sides and two rows on the *qibla* side. When the building was altered, this modest prayer hall was closed off with a thin wall built between the columns on the courtyard side. A new prayer niche (*mihrab*), decorated with carved alabaster of rare splendor and refinement, was set into this wall. In the center of the courtyard was a water basin for ablutions, where the faithful washed their hands before entering the mosque. The similarities between the mosque in Dandanqan and the Arabian courtyard mosque are confined to the courtyard itself and the windowless outer walls.

The three-part type

The well-preserved and remarkably beautiful Seljuk Talkhatun Baba Mosque in the Merv oasis is an example of the "three-part" type. The building consists of a square central chamber, covered by a dome, with two narrow, domed side aisles, which are divided into two halves by a transverse arch. The wide, arched entrance to the middle part, along with the side entrances that flank it, are almost as wide as the space lying beyond them, giving the building the appearance of a triple-arched loggia. A similar composition, consisting of a wide middle arch and two narrower arches on either side, is also found in other Central Asian buildings from this time, but is more common in the Merv region, the ancient Margiana, than elsewhere. The main facade of the Talkhatun Baba Mosque brings together nearly all the artistic features of the architecture of this period, from its

harmonious proportions to its sublime symmetry and the richly varied splendor of its brick bonds. Just as beautiful is the rear facade of the mosque, with its four flat niches enclosed by rectangular relief frames, whose arches rest on round columns. The flat and reliefwork ornament in the tympana of these blind arcades, made of both simple and cut brick, is of an astonishing diversity. Putting aside its regional characteristics, the decorative brick bonds of the mosque form a virtual encyclopedia of the brick and terracotta decoration of Central Asian architecture from the 11th to the beginning of the 13th century.

Another surviving mosque of the three-part type dating from the 11–12th centuries is the memorial mosque in Termez next to the tomb of the city's "patron saint," the philosopher and poet, Hakim Termezi. Here we have a loggia opening to the east with three identical arches on solid pillars and three

Memorial mosque at the tomb of Muhammad ibn Zaid, Merv, Reconstruction of the side facade (G. Pugatschenkowa)
Although the building has a *mihrab* in its southwest wall, it was considered for a long time to be a mausoleum. The facade is formed by a sequence of wide and narrow arched niches in a style once popular in Merv. It represents one of the best-known examples of the artistic use of brick and terracotta decoration.

differentiated themselves from domed mausoleums through their obligatory *mihrab* niche, and often had a further *mihrab* in the middle of the main facade. A typical example of this type of mosque stands by the tomb of Muhammad ibn Zaid in Merv, and was until recently assumed to be a mausoleum. The building is enclosed by other buildings which were added during later periods; only a portion of the stone northwest facade escaped without added construction. This was decorated by two arched panels, of which the one on the right has now been walled up to form an entrance, with a narrow niche between them, the whole corresponding to the composition of the Talkhatun Baba Mosque. The fragment has retained a facing of polished brick. Also notable are portions of decorative panels of ornamental masonry reliefwork in its tympana. The *mihrab* niche, flanked by two entrances, can still be made out on the main northeast facade. The interior decoration is concentrated on the octagon forming the lower part of the dome and on a broad frieze decorated with a Kufic inscription above it. The inner *mihrab* in the middle of the southwest wall is of interest for its multifoil arch and shell-shaped niches, which have their parallels in the 12th and 13th century architecture of Cairo. This demonstrates that Central Asian architecture was not isolated, but part and parcel of the great Islamic architecture of the world.

Also worthy of mention among the other domed chamber mosques of the 11th and 12th centuries are the Yart-i Gumbad Mosque in southern Tukmenistan, notable for its interesting "three-part" spandrels, and the Shah Fadil Mosque in Kyrgyzstan, whose interior displays carved alabaster decoration of unusually complex design. The oldest mosque in Bukhara, the Magok-i Attari Mosque, lost its previous shape and form after alterations were carried out in the 12th century. A beautiful and unusual portal, transposed to the eastern corner of south facade of the west-facing mosque, was built on at that time.

dome-covered rooms. The middle room is emphasized by a *mihrab* surrounded by a wide rectangular frame and is unusual for its semicircular shape, rare in Central Asia. The domes rest on small console spandrels. The cube-shaped brick corbels have been coated in carved stucco and have the appearance of stalactite spandrels. Carved stucco, in the form of Arabic script and geometric and floral patterns, also covers the mosque's inner walls.

Musallas

Certain mosques, designed to accommodate very large numbers of the faithful, were specially built for the two most important Islamic feast days – the Breaking of the Fast (*id al-fitr*) and the Feast of the Sacrifice (*id al-adha*). For this reason, they were not buildings as such, but enclosed *piazzas* with a *qibla* wall facing Mecca and *mihrab* that were decorated in particularly resplendent fashion. Mosques of this type were called *namazgah* (Persian) or *musallas* (Arabic) and were generally located outside the city. The central part of the *qibla* wall has survived from a 12th-century *namazgah* in Bukhara onto which, in the 16th century, was built an enormous triple-domed extension.

Domed chamber mosques

Small mosques with domed chambers were primarily built as memorial mosques near the tombs of revered individuals. In Islam, there is no worshiping of saints, and prayer is not permitted at the tomb itself, which can merely be greeted, and only then with one's back to the *mihrab*. These memorial mosques

Central Asian minarets

Nothing survives of the old Friday mosque in Bukhara, but its minaret built in 1127, known as "Kalan" (the Great), remained undamaged, and became a symbol of the city visible from far around. Although it has survived in good condition, it lost the upper part of its crown-shaped summit in 1920, when Bukhara was stormed by the Red Army. The round, 150-foot (46-meter) high tower, which tapers upwards, stands on a 10-sided pedestal and is built of solid brick. This building is unique in the way it combines massive steadfastness with upward movement, and decorative splendor with the monolithic. Although the minaret stands in the city center, it seems isolated and detached in spirit from its surroundings; despite its exceptionally fine decoration it seems closed in on itself – Bukhara is unimaginable without the Kalan minaret, but the Kalan minaret has no need of Bukhara.

At a distance of 19 miles (30 kilometers) from the Kalan minaret stands the minaret of Wabkent. Built in the year 1141, this slightly younger contemporary looks like a scaled down but elongated copy of the Kalan minaret. The total height of this slim, strongly tapering tower is 135 feet (41 meters); it is crowned with a richly decorated arched rotunda, which provided a model for minarets built later. The mosque to which the minaret once belonged is no longer standing.

A remarkable minaret of another type survives – though not completely intact – in the Jarkurgan settlement in southern Uzbekistan. This gently tapering tower seems to be made of semicircular "ribs" projecting from a high octagonal pedestal. A frieze band containing a Kufic inscription in relief encircles the minaret just below where its summit once was. Above the frieze a continuation of the rib-like shaft is visible, which originally reached a height of 130 feet (40 meters). Minarets of this design are not found elsewhere in Central Asia; similar

Minaret in Wabkent, 1141

This tower in Wabkent is similar to the famous minaret in Bukhara, but has a more slender appearance and at 40 meters is not as high. The tower, which tapers upwards, is built of brick in double-width bonds with decorative insertions, and is segmented by narrow ornamental bands. The tower could be climbed, and was in fact used by the muezzin, who called the faithful to prayer from its exquisitely decorated lantern. The Wabkent minaret, along with the minaret in Bukhara, are the only ones to have survived, despite frequent earthquakes, and the narrow diameter of the upper part of the shafts, with their original height intact, and with no appreciable damage.

constructions, in Antalya (Turkey) and the Qutb-Minar in Delhi, were, however, built later than the Jarkurgan minaret, which we know – thanks to the date and name of the building master surviving on the shaft – to have been erected in 1108/09.

Mausoleums

The building of elaborate tombs was not permitted in early Islam, but this rule was soon to be broken. The first mausoleum in the Islamic world was built in the 8th century over the burial site of a Umayyad ruler. The fact that the memorial building thrived in Central Asia in the 11th and 12th centuries was directly related to the spread of Sufism and the honoring of its "saintly" teachers and their graves. The banning of prayer at the tombside remained, however, and in contrast to the Maghreb and Egypt, the Central Asian mausoleums have no *mihrab*. Neither do they face Mecca as a rule, unlike the mosques, but are aligned according to the points of the compass. In order to maintain the ritual of prayer a memorial mosque was normally built close to the tomb or mausoleum which was revered by the faithful.

A small group of mausoleums of the central building type, with four identical facades, goes back presumably to the *jartaq* (four-arch) plan. This ancient Iranian shrine design consisted of four pillars connected by archways to form a square, which was covered by a dome.

The austere centrally built Aisha Bibi Mausoleum in southern Kazakhstan, dating from the 11–12th centuries, opened outwards with portal niches on each of its four sides. Panels of carved terracotta ornament provide the lavish facing on its external walls. The corners of the building did not have cylindrical supports, as was usual, but were accentuated by high columns with pedestals and capitals. These were no doubt built to imitate the wooden columns characteristic of secular buildings in Central Asia.

Facade mausoleums

Facade mausoleums were widespread; these had an entire facade designed as a portal, which towered above the actual dimensions of the building and was accentuated by a large entrance niche. Some impressive examples of this type of tomb building have survived in Uzgen, which, at this time, was capital of the Qarakhanid dynasty. Here, two facade mausoleums from the 12th century flank a building positioned between them, which is now badly damaged. This building, constructed at the end of the 10th century, possibly served as a memorial mosque. The mausoleum on the left is somewhat older and larger than that on the right, but they each have the same plan, typical for their time: this consisted of a square room transposing into an octagonal, dome-bearing squinch area with niches on its cross-axes.

The wide portal facade of the left hand mausoleum is broken up in the middle by a small arched niche, set apparently in a massive, triple, rectangular frame. The outer strip of the frame is decorated with a large geometric pattern, the inner with a network of small crosses cut out of it. An Arabic inscription carved with exceptional virtuosity in terracotta occupies the archivolt of the portal arch. The back wall of the niche, above the entrance, sadly later destroyed, was decorated with a unique composition in carved stucco, consisting of blind arcading with a floral motif in-fill. Also unique is the well-preserved carved decoration of its vaulting, which has a masterfully executed ornamental motif.

The portal facade of the right-hand mausoleum is of the same type and is distinctive for its slender proportions and refined decoration featuring a multiplicity of narrow borders. An intricately carved pattern decorates the back wall of the portal niche, above the entrance, as well as the corner columns, composed of terracotta cylinders, and their capitals. The resplendent facade has thus been given a sober, graphic character not shared by the portal facade of the mausoleum on the left. Despite this, the right-hand mausoleum is a better example of the pre-Mongol memorial architecture that influenced the monumental buildings of the 14th and 15th centuries. If the carved terracotta were replaced with colored tiles, without changing anything else in the overall structure, the result would be an image of the decorative style that was to come later.

Also belonging to this type of facade mosque is the oldest surviving building of Kuna Urgench, the so-called "Fakhr al-Din Razi Mausoleum." This theologian was buried in Herat in 1208, and it is thought that the mausoleum was actually built over the mortal remains of the Khwarazm-Shah Il-Arslan II, who died in 1172. The building consists of a square, domed chamber with four niches, which probably originally opened outwards, on the cross-axes. The one, narrow entrance is today situated in the east niche. One of the unusual features

of this relatively small building is the pyramid roof, polygonal at its base, and which covers the inner dome. It stands on a drum of the same shape and gives the building tower-like proportions that do not correspond to the arrangement of the interior. The whitewashed interior of the mausoleum was either undecorated or else nothing of its decoration has survived. The main, east facade, on the other hand, is of exceptional splendor.

The monochrome of the bricks is broken up only by the blue-green glazed bricks that form a large geometric pattern on the 12-sided pyramid roof, and by a frieze around the base of the roof, of which a border composed of small blue-green glazed, and natural, yellowish bricks survives. Excavations have shown that the mausoleum was originally much higher.

Portal mausoleums

Another mausoleum type was the portal mausoleum, whose main entrance was accentuated by a portal jutting out from the facade, or *pishtaq*. The oldest surviving example of this type is the Alam-ber-dar Mausoleum, in which it is possible that Ismail, the last of the Samanids, who was murdered in 1005, lies buried. Each of the facades of the square, domed building is shaped by three flat arched niches in projecting rectangular frames, and small polygonal pillars occupy the corners. The central part of the east facade, that is to say the middle niche within its rectangular frame, is set forward from the facade, rises somewhat above it, and looks rather as if had been built on. The tripartite division of the facades is reflected inside, where pilasters accentuate the flat niches on the cross-axes and support the squinch arches.

The surface of the mausoleum walls consists of simple bricks with loam mortar. This rather rough finish is combined with fine decoration, which gives the decorative bonds, the double bond, the stepped bond, and the relief bond, widely used at the time, their special character. The modestly accentuated portal, which does not harmonize well with the rest of the building, and later ceased to be used in such a context, refers back to an earlier period of building.

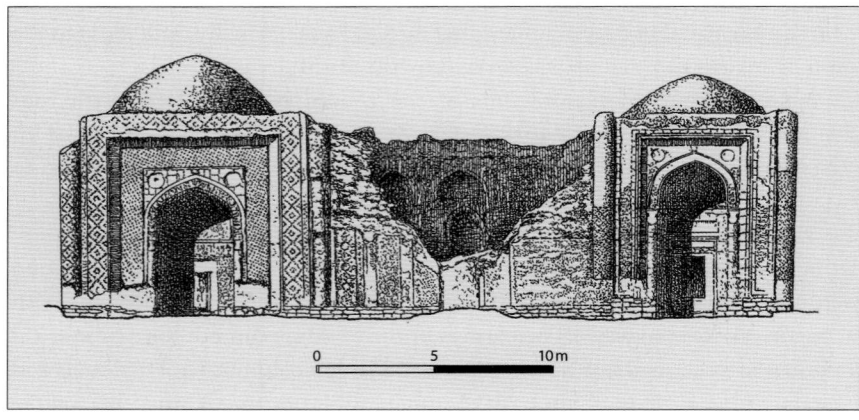

Three Qarakhanid dynasty mausoleums, Uzgen (Kyrgyzstan), 10th and 12th centuries
This ensemble consists of two mausoleums, dating from 1153 and 1186/87, bordering a third dating from the 10th century. The drawing illustrates their condition before restoration, while the photograph shows them afterwards. They can be seen as prototypes for the large tomb buildings in the Samarqand necropolis Shah-i Zinda.

Portal of the right-hand (south) Qarakhanid mausoleum, Uzgen, 1186/87
The right-hand mausoleum was smaller than the others, but is distinctive for its harmonious proportions and the intricate, almost seamless decoration of its main facade. The archivolt of the entrance arch, decorated with a carved Arabic inscription, rests on columns with elegant terracotta capitals composed of ceramic cylinders. The back wall of the arched niche is covered with terracotta panels containing ornamental carving.

Fakhr al-Din Razi Mausoleum, Kuna Urgench, end of the 12th century
This mausoleum is the oldest surviving building in Kuna Urgench, the capital of Khwarazmia in the Middle Ages. The theologian Fakhr al-Din Razi is, however, buried in Herat, and the mausoleum attributed to him may well have been built over the grave of the Khwarazm-Shah Arslan II, who ruled 1156–1172.

Abu l-Fadl Mausoleum, southern Tajikistan, 11th century
This large building, with facades in the shape of blind arcades their entire height, is one of the first buildings in Central Asia to have had a double-shell dome, with the outer shell forming a single entity with the drum. The inner dome rests, not on an octagon, as is customary, but on a 12-sided structure.

Further mausoleum types

A particular kind of mausoleum is represented by the Sultan Saadat necropolis, near Termez. At its heart are two mausoleums dating from the 11–12th centuries, which are connected to each other by a vaulted *iwan*. The three-arch facades of both mausoleums face northwest. The larger building on the right has entrances on each of its sides, but the main entrances of both mausoleums face each other inside the *iwan*.

Each wall of the chamber on the right, like its facades, is formed by three niches, whose arches rest on round columns – the triple-arch theme, as with the Alam-ber-dar Mausoleum, is taken up again on the inside. The interior of the left-hand mausoleum, and naturally its external proportions too, are smaller, because of a staircase in its thick back wall that leads up to the roof. In order to maintain a strict optical symmetry between the two buildings, however, the building master has slightly extended the northeast facade of the left-hand mausoleum.

The combination of two domed chambers positioned to the right and left of a vaulted *iwan* goes back to a tradition of simple domestic architecture that has been transposed to monumental architecture. It was widely used in the palace architecture of Central Asia and Asia Minor and that of the *madrasas* and the homes of the well-to-do, and is also to be found in country properties from the 11th century in Sistan (Afghanistan) and a few *madrasas* dating from the 13th century in Konya (Turkey). In terms of the memorial architecture of Central Asia, the two old mausoleums in the Sultan Saadat necropolis represent a rare example of this type of composition. They did, however, have an influence on tombs built nearby at a later date, between the 14th and 17th centuries.

The Shaburgan-ata tomb on the edge of the Bukhara oasis represents a polygonal type of mausoleum rare in Central Asia. The octagonal, dome-covered building has a massive, wide portal that faces south, and its oval dome has a large round opening at its apex. The interior of the mausoleum is less thoroughly decorated than is customary in the memorial architecture of the 11–12th centuries. The structure and shape of the building and its details render decoration of this type somewhat superfluous. The Khoja Isa Mausoleum, in southern Uzbekistan, provides an example of another unusual tomb type. This building consists of three domed rooms arranged in a row, and a narrow, domed vestibule, forming a common, elongated "shell." On the outside, the building is decorated by blind arcading with narrow arched niches set in the traditional rectangular framework and a recessed border that encircles the building. The square chamber of the mausoleum follows on behind the vestibule in the south, and contains a large tombstone. A brick grille separates it from the next two rooms, which would once have served as a mosque. The building's brick facades are adorned by their own rhythmic structure. The facade arcading, where the bricks out of which the arches are built are decorated in their middle with carved geometric figures, is the one exception to this. This procedure is also encountered in the Iranian architecture of the time.

Job's Spring

In Central Asia there are buildings similar to mausoleums, which were not, however, built over graves, but over legendary, traditionally revered places. One such building is the Jashma Aiyub, "Job's Spring," in Bukhara. It was built over a holy spring, which, according to legend, goes back to the time of the biblical Job, who was also revered in Islam and regarded in this context as a sorcerer with the power to bring forth water. According to tradition, this remarkable building dates back to the 12th century, but an inscription inside claims it was built on the instructions of the Mongolian ruler Tamerlane in the 14th century. There is nothing Timurid about its architecture, however; on the contrary, there are many indications of the Qarakhanid style, making it seem probable that the building was renovated or completed under Tamerlane and ascribed to him for reasons of flattery. The long and not especially high building is oriented toward the east along its longitudinal axis, and consists of three very distinct parts: the entrance on the eastern side, built in the 16th century, which is the latest part; a small middle portion dating from the 14th century; and the oldest, western part, which goes back to the 11–12th century. This is where the holy spring is located, in a dome-covered, east-facing *iwan*, with a mosque of the three-part type behind it. Above the middle part of the mosque, which has a polygonal, outward-projecting *mihrab*, rises a cylindrical drum. This is built in the characteristic Qarakhanid style with wide, deep cross-joints and is topped by a steep, conical roof. The building that dates from the 11–12th century occupies about half the area of the current floor plan. It is possible that the eastern half, added later, was originally a small, enclosed courtyard in front of the holy site.

Another "Job's Spring" was uncovered in 1985 near Wabkent. This consists of an elegantly proportioned portal, richly decorated with carved terracotta and tiles, along with an adjoining stretch of wall containing two narrow arched niches. Behind the portal there is no building, simply the "holy" spring itself and a wooden cenotaph. We are told the date of construction of 1208/09 in an inscription on the very impressive, symmetrical portal. The portal arch rests on elegant, delicate columns. The niche vaulting behind it is divided vertically by a wide half-arch, and the corners of the arched niche are filled with a stalactite and alabaster relief pattern. This composition is so similar to that of the Magok-i Attari Mosque that it could be assumeed that the same building master was responsible for both of the portals. The elongated proportions and intricate decoration of this portal, with its copious turquoise and dark blue tiles, give an impression of decadence.

Jashma Aiyub, Bukhara, 12th-century
This building, erected over a spring connected by legend to Job, is one of the most idiosyncratic in Bukhara. It took its present form over the course of several centuries. The oldest part, dating from the 12th century, with its tower-shaped structure – a conical roof resting on a cylindrical drum – can be seen in the background. In the foreground are the additions built on to the east in the 16th century, incorporating an entrance and the lower part of an unfinished portal facade with massive corner towers.

Madrasas

The colleges for Islamic theology, where Islamic law, but also worldly sciences such as astronomy and philology, were taught, came into being in Central Asia no later than the 9th century. From historical sources it can be concluded that the *madrasa* first saw light of day as an institution in Central Asia, having its origins in the Buddhist colleges. Among the many Central Asian *madrasas*, however, none dating from the 11–13th centuries were known until recently.

The Khoja Mashhad Madrasa, in southern Tajikistan, of which the remains were discovered in the 1940s, is still the oldest known example of a building with this particular form and function. The facade and longitudinal axis of the building face south. To the right and left of the vaulted *iwan*, with its portal niche, tower the domes of two halls. This part of the *madrasa* is built of brick, the remaining parts of clay bricks. The two halls appear alike, but the eastern one was built as a mausoleum back in the 9th century. The western hall served as a mosque and dates from the 11th century, along with the central *iwan* and spacious courtyard. A comparison between the halls shows how tastes had changed over the 200 years: there is no carved terracotta or patterned brick in-filling in the interior decoration of the eastern hall or mausoleum, and the arches above the corners of the octagon are of characteristic "Samanid" design, as was typical for the 9–10th centuries. In the western hall of the mosque the complicated variants of the stepped bond have been liberally applied. The design of the pointed arches is different here: it is typical of the 11–12th centuries, with an emphatic

Magok-i Attari Mosque, Bukhara, 9–10th centuries
The Magok-i Attari Mosque is one of the oldest buildings in Bukhara. The 12th-century portal was built onto the remains of a mosque that stood – legend has it – on the site of a pre-Islamic temple. The portal is one of the most beautiful in Central Asia. The arch of the inner entrance niche bears an inscription in blue tilework and rests on carved stone columns. The surviving vertical parts of the rectangular frame consist of terracotta "latticework" and panels decorated with stucco ornamentation.

curve in the lower part of the line of the arch and an almost straight line up to the point. Some impressive blind arcading decorated with brick, patterned panels, and carved terracotta adorns the southern main facade. The architects kept to the traditional design of domed hall and even repeated the large round aperture in the vertex of the dome. The two halls do, however, have a very different effect. While monumental sculptures dominate the mausoleum, the mosque has a sober, graphic character.

This oldest surviving *madrasa* already displays all the essential features of the *madrasas* which came afterwards: a courtyard with four *iwans* positioned on the cross-axes, courtyard perimeter buildings housing living chambers, and a resplendent portal with two large halls to its right and left. Here the symmetrical group of buildings at the front consists of the old mausoleum incorporated into the *madrasa*, and the new mosque. Even the corner towers of the south facade, whose foundations survive, were to keep their place in the *madrasas* of the 15–17th centuries. The building's ground plan is simpler than that of its successors, however. Here there is no vestibule behind the portal, as became customary later, and the entrance leads directly into the courtyard without branching off. The Central Asian type of *madrasa* had found its form by and large in the Khoja Mashhad Madrasa, but not yet its final canonical realization.

Caravanserais

Caravanserais were typically a form of accommodation along caravan routes, such as the Silk Road, between Europe and China or the trade routes running in a north-south direction between the southern parts of Central Asia and the Slavic empires in the north. They developed into trade centers where goods, such as furs from Russia, amber from the north, or spices from Central Asia, were traded. They were often reinforced as fortresses and could even incorporate palaces and mosques. Caravanserais were also to be found in towns and cities, where they then also accommodated shops and workshops. Characteristic of the caravanserais of the 11–12th centuries is a combination of pomp and functionality, at least for the majority of those so far examined.

South facade of the Khoja Mashhad Madrasa, Sajod, Tajikistan, 9–11th centuries
This *madrasa*, the oldest in Central Asia, which survives as a ruin, consisted of a large group of brick buildings in the south, along with a spacious courtyard bordered by buildings of clay brick. The southern group itself now comprises two domed halls which, in spite of their similar appearance, were built at different times: the eastern one was built as a mausoleum over a grave in the 9th century; the western one, serving as a mosque, dates back to the 11th century.

The increase in trade and crafts led to the building of more and more caravanserais, primarily by feudal rulers who wanted to give expression to their wealth and power. In their outward appearance, a fortress-like isolation was combined with extremely fine decoration. A courtyard built around with depots, lodging rooms, stables, guardrooms, and so on dictated their design, organized around two perpendicular axes bordered by *iwans*. The portal entrance lay on the longitudinal axis, and behind it the group of most splendid rooms. Space for freight and livestock ran the length of the walls. Until recently, the south wall of the great Rabat-i Malik ("Inn of the Ruler") Caravanserai, which stood on the road between Bukhara and Samarqand, was still standing, along with the portal and one corner tower. Now only the portal remains, but the design has been reconstructed as a result of excavations. On the majestic portal in the middle of the south facade survive an arch and archivolt bearing a Persian inscription in

Portal of the Rabat-i Malik Caravanserai, near Kermine, 11–12th centuries
The portal is the only surviving part of this caravanserai, whose main facade was fashioned from protruberant semicircular brick columns. The Persian inscription above the portal arch states that the building was erected by the "sultan of the whole world" and would, by the grace of God, resemble Paradise.

Ground plan of the Akcha Qala Caravanserai, 80 km northeast of Merv, 11th century.
This is a rare example in Central Asia of a caravanserai with two courtyards on a longitudinal axis. Its design follows the four-*iwan* schema common in courtyard mosques and *madrasas*. Living chambers were grouped around the northern courtyard, depots and stables around the southern one.

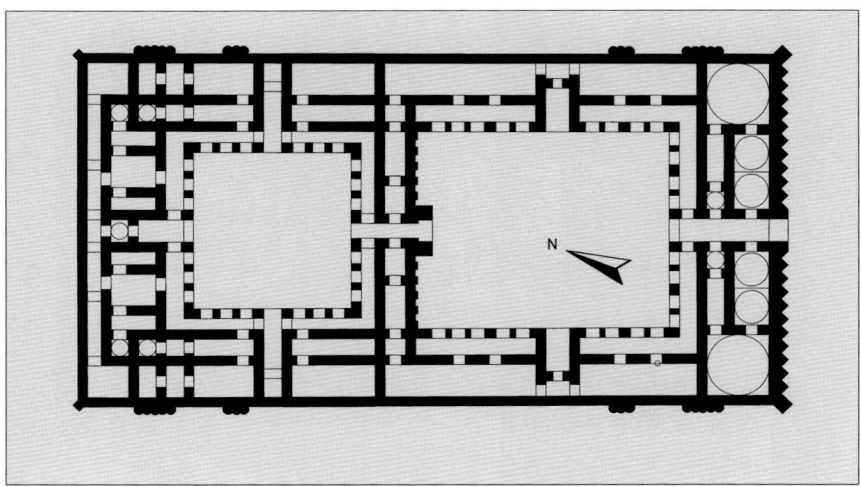

carved terracotta. The powerful design of the south facade of Rabat-i Malik is related to that of the minaret in Jarkurgan, and dates back to the old style of fortress architecture, in which round or rectangular brick columns protected the outer walls. In buildings of the 11–12th centuries, however, this technique is applied only for decorative effect.

The Akcha Qala, constructed in the 11th century near Merv, is representative of a type of caravanserai, rare for Central Asia, which has two courtyards lying on a longitudinal axis. As in the case of Rabat-i Malik, the main facade is decorated with brick columns, and even the side walls are decorated with semicircular brick columns of a similar kind. Both courtyards are bordered by galleries with pillars, and the cross-axes accentuated by *iwans*. The first, and more spacious courtyard, was reserved for livestock and goods, and the second was surrounded mainly by living accommodation. Particularly impressive here is the back wall of the front courtyard, which at the same time forms the entrance facade to the rear courtyard, and the row of buildings which form one of its sides. In the middle of this facade, whose central niche, giving access to the back courtyard, is flanked by two narrow, arch-shaped niches, rises a portal. This construction, encountered elsewhere, enjoyed a particular popularity in the Merv oasis.

Decorating the main facade with brick columns seems to have been peculiar to the Central Asian caravanserais of the 11–12th centuries. It is also a feature of the Chaldiwar Caravanserai, built in the 11th century or even as early as the 10th, which lies on the road leading out of the Farghana Valley in the Tien Shan Mountains of eastern Turkestan (Sinkiang), thus a very long way from the cultural centers of the time. The portal facade of this large, almost square building faces north. On the cross-axes of the inner courtyard are vaulted *iwans*, behind which, effectively extending them, lie rooms of the same width. The usual perimeter buildings of a caravanserai can be described as having two "zones": long spaces for freight and livestock the length of the perimeter walls, and, bordering these on the courtyard side, the living accommodation with a pillared arcade opening onto the courtyard. In the Chaldiwar Caravanserai there are three such zones. The inner zone, bordering the courtyard, consists of long rooms apparently used as utility rooms; the usual arcades around the courtyard are absent and it is enclosed by an almost continuous wall. Presumably this arrangement is the result of alterations entailing the traditional pillared gallery, which once ran around the courtyard, being walled up. The closed-off rooms that were created in this way became utility rooms that now formed the inner zone of the courtyard's perimeter buildings.

Khanqas

In spite of the fact that Sufism was widespread in Central Asia in the 11th and 12th centuries, only a few buildings survive from this time in which members of the Sufi brotherhood lived. This type of monastery and the later *khanqas* were both of the same type: at their center was a domed hall with niches on its cross-axes and cells providing accommodation occupying the corners. The entrance took the form of a monumental portal. The *khanqa* was often connected in some way to the tomb of an individual revered by the faithful, so that it became a place of pilgrimage. One such *khanqa*, dating from the 11–12th centuries,

Khanqa with the Hakim Termezi Mausoleum, Termez, 12th century
A khanqa is a building designed specifically for gatherings of the Sufi brotherhood. Most khanqas originated in the 11th and 12th centuries as Sufism spread through Central Asia. They were usually built in the vicinity of the tomb of a Sufi sheikh (elder), as is the case here with that of Hakim Termezi. At the center of the compact building is a domed hall for the meetings of the brotherhood, surrounded by rooms providing living accommodation.

stands next to the tomb of Hakim Termezi, and once played an important role in the cult of the highly revered Sufi philosopher. It consists of a spacious hall with niches on the cross-axes. Its high portal contains niches in its side-walls and faces south. The other niches in the hall also contain entranceways, and there are as many as three on the north side. These were probably the entrances to the living chambers, which have not survived; these formerly surrounded the hall used for mystic rituals on three sides.

One ancient and particularly mysterious building, which in all probability served as a living and meeting place for traveling Sufis, thus as a *khanqa*, dates from the turn of the 11th century and lies hidden away in the Tien Shan Mountains. The building is called Tash Rabat ("Stone Inn") and is constructed from roughly worked stone. Its entrance portal faces east, and the corners of the entrance facade are accentuated by round, tower-like projections. Tash Rabat consists of two parts connected by a corridor, which runs from the entrance into the depths of the building. The eastern half would have housed the living accommodation, and is divided into two groups of rooms opening onto side corridors. A square, domed hall with deep *iwans* positioned south, west, and north on its cross-axes forms the focus of the western half. This is evidently where the Sufis, who lived in the cells on the eastern side, held their ceremonies and gatherings. The long rooms to the south and north of this central area were probably utility rooms. Not only were the walls of Tash Rabat made of stone, but also the vaulting and domes, which are supported by console spandrels of a complex and unusual form. The modest decoration is confined to the 16-cornered space underneath the cupola in the central chamber. Above the corners of the squinch area there are small, three-sided niches, which are separated from each other by a panel of the same shape; each surface of the niche is decorated with flat carving on a thick layer of stucco. This large building, surmounted by a half-dilapidated dome, is like one big sculpture hewn from stone. Despite the sparseness of its decoration – perhaps even because of it – it is hugely impressive.

Palaces

Not a single Central Asian palace building, which generally housed both ruler's seat and administrative headquarters under the same roof, survives from the 11th or 12th centuries. But we do, however, have descriptions from historical sources and several ruins that have been exposed and examined. It is now clear that the general design principle – the combination of a courtyard with an *iwan* that opened onto it – was adapted endlessly and that a standard type cannot be identified. Until not too long ago, the excavated, and later destroyed, ruins of the palace of the ruler of Termez was the only example of Central Asian palace architecture from the 11th and 12th centuries. The palace stood in the eastern part of the city in what was effectively an aristocratic suburb. It was approximately 330 feet (100 meters) long and had a spacious inner courtyard with its longitudinal axis running east to west. This is where the ceremonial part of the palace was located, consisting of an *iwan* containing a throne surrounded down the sides and along the back by a gallery resting on heavy rectangular pillars. The *iwan* opened not directly onto the courtyard, but initially onto a wide, arched portico resting likewise on heavy pillars. The buildings that enclosed the courtyard, in the middle of which was a square water basin, remain unknown, as does the design of the entrance, which was situated opposite the *iwan* on the western side. The architectonic importance and decorative splendor of the audience chamber, however, lead us to assume that the less ceremonial parts of the palace must also have been extremely impressive.

Excavations carried out at Khulbuk, capital of Khuttalan province in southern Tajikistan, provide us with a fairly accurate idea of what the enormous palace there was like. Standing on a hill high above the city, its design was complex

Mausoleum of Sultan Sanjar, Merv, 12th century
The building known as the Mausoleum of Sultan Sanjar was probably the audience chamber of the Great Seljuks' palace. During the course of restoration, traces of buildings that would have been built onto its facades were discovered. Originally the structure had an exterior dome decorated with turquoise tiles, which, according to contemporary reports, could be seen from several days' traveling distance away. During the Middle Ages, "Sanjar's Mausoleum" was regarded, in the east, as the biggest building in existence.

and incorporated buildings from various different periods. High, brick-clad supporting walls with massive corner towers interspersed with projections, lent it a fortress-like character. The entrance on the western side consisted of a domed kiosk whose external frontage was shaped like a traditional portal, namely a broad rectangle containing an arched alcove. This led into the central courtyard where there was a large water basin. Two different groups of buildings can be distinguished from the courtyard: those on the south, including an audience chamber, formed the official, ceremonial part of the palace, while the ensemble to the north, judging by the smaller dimensions of the rooms, their positions, and the way they are grouped, were mainly residential. Two groups of rooms, in the northwestern corner and in the middle of the western wall, are of particular interest because of their design. They consist of small, square courtyards with a deep *iwan* on one of the cross-axes; this is flanked by two rooms whose entrances open onto the courtyard. Designs of this type, the so-called "courtyard-*iwan* design" look back to an old Iranian tradition, and were intended for holding large or small official ceremonies. They are represented here in almost perfect form.

The palace was decorated with gloriously colorful wall paintings and panels of carved and painted stucco which rivaled the decoration of the Termez palace in the variety and exquisite nature of their ornamental motifs. The palace at Khulbuk was frequently altered; many of its costituent parts underwent changes of form and function, but, at the beginning of the 13th century, it still retained its tripartite structure and clear division into official and everyday functions.

An enormous domed structure in the center of medieval Merv was long held to be the mausoleum of the Seljuk sultan, Sanjar, but it was later discovered that the building contained no grave and did not correspond to medieval descriptions of Sanjar's place of burial. Furthermore, traces of adjoining buildings have been discovered on its facades, indicating the one-time existence of a whole

Mausoleum of the Khwarazm-Shah Tekesh, Kuna Urgench, late12th to early 13th century This structure is actually the audience chamber of the palace of the Great Khwarazm-Shahs, the surrounding buildings of which have not survived. But their existence has been established by excavations, as in the case of the Mausoleum of Sultan Sanjar. Of particular interest, along with the tile decoration, is the unusual portal. The customary rectangular framework is absent here, but the arch-shaped niche is decorated on the inside with a complex stalactite structure.

complex of buildings. It is now clear that the spacious domed hall formed part of the palace of the Great Seljuks, indeed its most important, ceremonial part. In its present form, the large building, which is visible from a distance, comprises a square chamber more than 56 feet (17 meters) across with 16-foot (5-meter) thick walls. Two of the niches on the cross-axes – the western and eastern ones – contain entranceways. The dome, with a record diameter of 56 feet (17 meters), rests on an octagonal squinch. Traces of the decorative paintwork which covered the ribs, arches, and niches of the squinch as well as the walls, have survived. The back walls of the squinch house arched windows, each containing a wide window underneath and a narrow one above, which lead out onto a gallery running around the building and representing its most unusual feature. The upper part of the gallery has disappeared, as has the external dome, which, formerly covered with a blue glaze, could be seen at a distance of three days' journey away from Merv, or so, at least, contemporary chroniclers claimed. Many traces of the buildings that once surrounded the chamber have been destroyed during the course of "restoration work," but enough have survived or can be recognized from old photographs for us to know that the large, richly decorated domed chamber was enclosed by rooms all the way around, and that the whole entity formed a palace complex to which – in addition to the surviving audience chamber – a mosque, the tomb of Sultan Sanjar, and many other rooms belonged. Some of these have already been uncovered during the course of excavations.

A building in the Kuna Urgench settlement was also, for a long time, mistakenly thought to be a tomb, in this case, that of the Great Khwarazm-Shah Ala al-Din Tekish (1172–1200). Here, too, was a square chamber with thick walls, three cross-axial niches and a portal niche on the northern side. In the chamber there was no painting on the walls (or else it has not survived), but the variety of its sculptural ornament is remarkable. Above the traditional octagon is an area of semicircular niches containing shell-shaped decoration – a baroque form that is not readily associated with the art of Islam. The interior of the dome is decorated with small holes forming the shape of a regular star with 12 points. Above this rises a steep conical roof which is adorned with a large geometrical pattern made out of polished blue bricks. It sits on an impressively sculpted drum and, together with the conical roof, creates the impression of being a self-contained building. This impression is reinforced by the low body of the structure underneath it. This does not have any architectonic features at all, as the uneven walls of the facade were not designed to be looked at. The north facade, which is nearly twice as tall as the others and houses a very high and curious portal, is an exception. The portal itself contains a relatively shallow arched niche without the traditional rectangular frame, but instead having an unusual stalactite inner surface. In Central Asia, and Iran, there are no other examples of this kind of portal, but in the Seljuk architecture of Asia Minor they are well represented, with examples at the caravanserais of Konya (Sultan Khan) and Nevsehir, and at the Gok *madrasa* in Sivas, as well as many other places. It is possible that architects from Asia Minor played a part in the construction of the Kuna Urgench building. Recent excavations have revealed that this structure did not stand alone, but was part of a large complex which had an official rather than a memorial function, namely the palace of the Great Khwarazm-Shahs, of which this particular building was the audience chamber.

Private dwellings

Nothing survives of the private houses of ordinary people. Although they were built of the same material as the houses of the wealthy, that is to say, of clay bricks, they were not as solidly constructed. The typical 11th and 12th century houses of the wealthy were free-standing buildings and were directly descended from the compact pre-Islamic castle, or *kosk*, which stood on a high platform. This type of house would not just have been built by feudal lords, but also by rich city dwellers, tradesmen and craftsmen. They had abandoned their fortress-like quality, and the platform had been transformed into a lower story, but the basic features of their original interior layout had largely survived. At the center of the house was a domed, two-story hall connecting to the living accommodation and workrooms which surrounded it. The entrances normally had portals that either projected out from the facade or took the form of niches. The exterior wall of the upper floor, in which the living accommodation was located, was either ribbed with semicircular protuberances – the old three-dimensional building technique given a decorative function – or else was decorated with blind arcading. The ruins of one such aristocratic house can be seen in Merv, to the west of the central Sultan Qala district. The lower floor of this building, which has a more or less square ground plan, takes the form of a high platform with inclining sides. Two entrances on the main axis lead into the square central hall, which has niches on its cross-axes. Corridors connect the niches with rooms off to the sides, which were used for business and household purposes. In the eastern corner is a form of stairwell in which a ramp leads up around a square pillar. The walls of the upper floor are considerably thinner and incline less strongly from the outside than those of the lower floor. The square central room with a rectangular opening in the middle of the floor represents the continuation of the hall below and would have been covered by a dome. This room leads onto cross-axial *iwans*, which reach back to the external walls. The openings on this side are so wide that they have the appearance of loggias. The corner areas of the upper floor – except for the eastern corner where the ramp is situated – are occupied by similar groups of rooms consisting of one large room and one narrow one connecting to it. The symmetrical plan of the upper story, with its rooms stretching out in all directions, is an arrangement designed more for ceremonial purposes than for everyday living.

A house in the Kalta Minar settlement, which has "ribbed" walls and cross-axial portals on each of its four sides, and one in the "potters' district" of Merv are further buildings of this type. In each case, the layout is similarly characterized by a complete symmetry subordinated to the dome-covered central area. In Merv and the surrounding area, a good number of monumental buildings of this type have survived, but they are also to be found in other parts of Central Asia, for example in Khwarazmia. Here, however, the compact houses of the elite followed a tripartite design peculiar to the area. This consisted of three parallel parts, the middle of which featured an entrance niche on the outside and a central room on the inside that hints at a relationship with the "Merv" domed hall design. House no. 60, at the Kawat Qala oasis in Khwarazmia is a good example of this. The monumentality of buildings of this type stems from the symmetry of the facades and their internal organization.

A well-appointed house of another type, that of the wealthy landowner, has survived in the Shahriyar Ark administrative center of Seljuk Merv. It is aligned according to the four points of the compass and incorporates a square courtyard with the traditional *iwans* on the cross-axes. The walls of the courtyard to the sides of the *iwans* are decorated with blind arcading; the eastern *iwan* connects to the entrance portal via a vestibule situated between the two. Around the courtyard, which, in this case, takes on the role of the domed hall, are grouped a multitude of rooms, among which two in particular, matching dome-covered rooms in the southeastern corner, are distinctive for their unusual design. This manor house is made of clay bricks, and in various places the masonry bonds have a decorative function. The facades, which have been lost, were faced with brick and were richly and impressively decorated.

One large manor house in the Sajod settlement in southern Tajikistan has an almost fortress-like appearance due to its four corner towers. The figurative bonds of its brick floors in several of the rooms and in the gallery around the sunken central courtyard are extremely impressive, but of particular note is the unexpectedly magnificent carved and painted stucco with which this ordinary provincial manor house is decorated. Surviving wall panels, the grille in the southeast corner of the courtyard, and the walls of many of the rooms fully decorated with carving, all convey an impression of this splendor. This ornamentation, discovered far away from any cultural centers, is worthy of a palace and provides evidence of the widespread flourishing of the arts in Central Asia in the 11th and 12th centuries.

The discoveries made, and the research carried out over recent years have shown that from the 11th to the beginning of the 13th centuries there were no artistic differences in principle between the architectonic design and decoration of monumental buildings on the one hand, and private houses – naturally only those of the privileged classes – on the other. All in all, this culture, which did not survive the Mongol invasion, represents a high classicism remarkable for its perfection in comparison to both the periods that preceded it and, in particular, those that followed it.

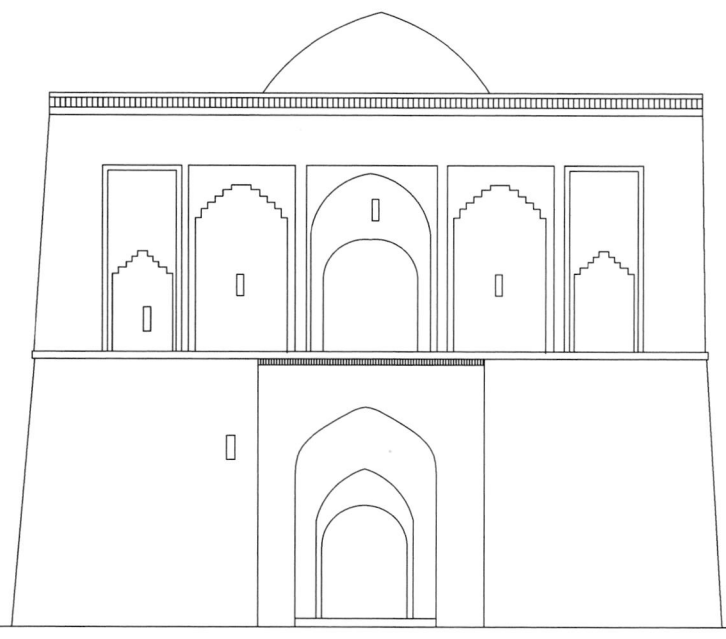

Reconstruction of the facade of a house to the west of Sultan Qala, Merv, 12th century
This house was the main building of a wealthy city property, and, to judge from its design, would have been used for ceremonial purposes rather than a private dwelling. The lower floor was occupied by utility rooms and living accommodations. On the upper story were spacious rooms and outward-facing *iwan* loggias grouped around a domed room. In its external design, the building imitates the pre-Islamic, early medieval fortresses, which were usually set atop a high platform with sloping walls. Here the lower floor takes the form of such a platform. It has virtually no windows, just two entrances framed by arches on two opposite facades. The upper floor displays curious blind arcading, which was probably designed to symbolize openness.

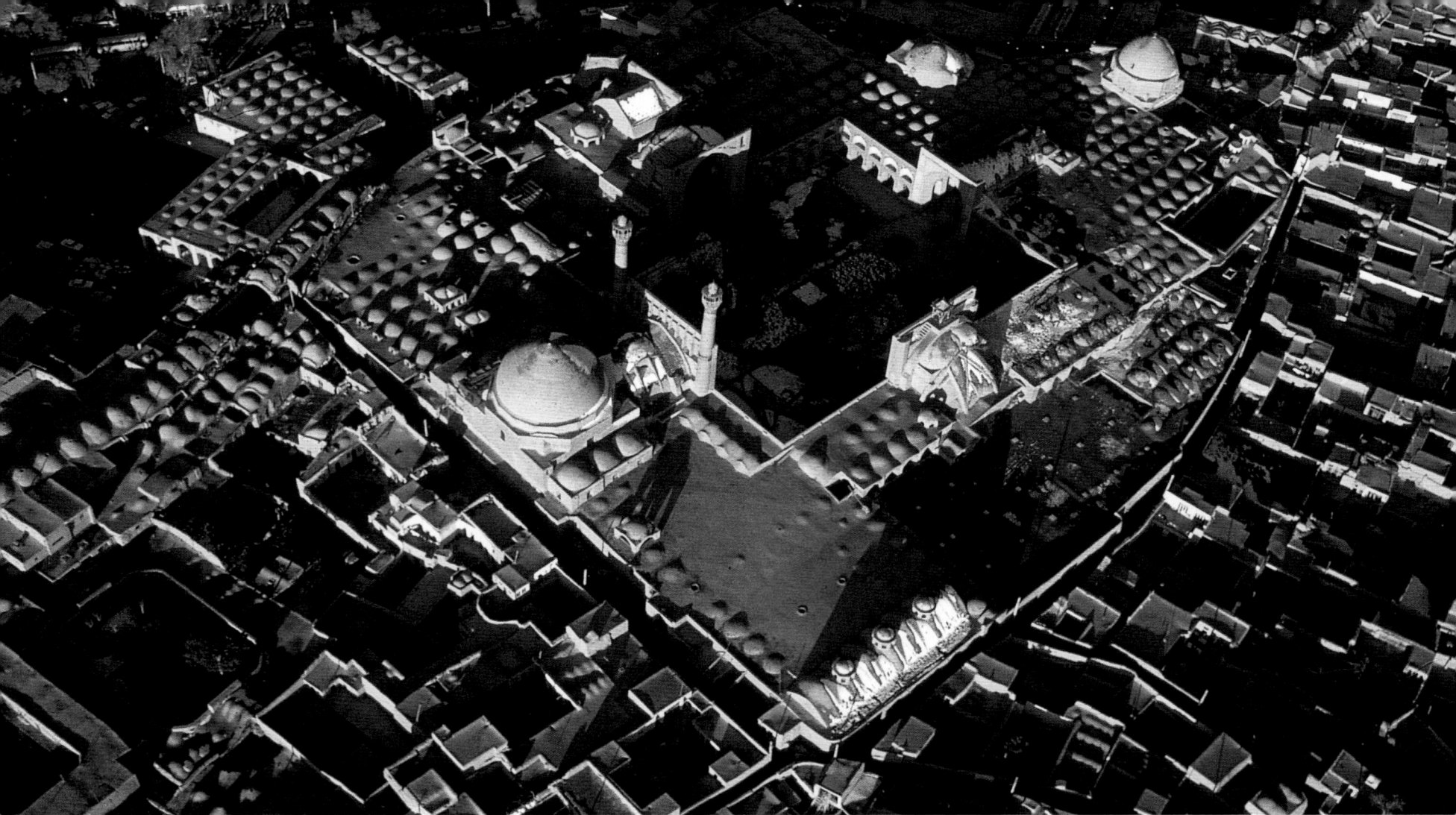

The Friday Mosque at Isfahan
Sheila Blair, Jonathan Bloom

Under the Seljuks, master builders developed a new ground plan, which became standard for Friday mosques in Iran. The evolution of this new plan is best seen in the Friday Mosque at Isfahan, capital of the Seljuk domains. In the 9th century the Abbasids had built a classic hypostyle mosque there, and in the 10th century the Buyids had relined the court facade with polylobed piers faced with small bricks. The Seljuks changed the relatively egalitarian space of the hypostyle building by demolishing the 24 columns corresponding to the 20 bays in front of and around the *mihrab* and inserting a free-standing domed pavilion supported on massive polylobed piers. An inscription band around the base of the dome states that this work was carried out under the patronage of Sultan Malik Shah and his vizier Nizam al-Mulk. The domed chamber was probably intended as a *maqsura*, or area reserved for the sultan and his court, and built in imitation of the great dome that the sultan had seen in the mosque at Damascus when he had visited in the autumn of 1086. On the basis of the titles used in the inscription and the historical situation, the work at Isfahan can be dated to the winter of 1086/87.

Two years later, in 1088/89, Nizam al-Mulk's archrival, Taj al-Mulk, ordered another domed pavilion to be added at the opposite end of the mosque in Isfahan. Slightly smaller than the south dome, the north dome has the same formal parts of the square room, tripartite squinch, 16-sided zone of transition, and hemispheric dome, but is considered more elegant as the parts are aligned vertically, as in Gothic architecture. Indeed, the north dome at Isfahan is sometimes considered the masterpiece of medieval Persian architecture. Despite its aesthetic merits, however, the north dome at Isfahan is an anomaly. It is

unclear what function it played, as it may well have been erected outside the mosque. Furthermore, the vertical alignment of its parts is unique.

The major transformation to the mosque took place within the rectangular space occupied by the original hypostyle mosque. The free-standing pavilion that had been inserted at the south end was neither visually nor structurally satisfactory, so Seljuk builders next demolished the 18 columns between the south dome chamber and the courtyard and inserted an *iwan*, or barrel-vaulted room open to the courtyard at one end and leading to the dome chamber at the other. To complement this *iwan*, in the center of the south, or *qibla*, side of the mosque, three other *iwans* were eventually inserted at the midpoints of the other sides of the courtyard. This work was probably carried out in the early 12th century, after a fire had damaged the mosque in 1121/22.

The combination of four *iwans* and a dome chamber evolved at Isfahan was soon repeated in Friday mosques in nearby towns. At Ardistan, for example, the hypostyle mosque was revamped between 1158 and 1160. From this point, the plan became the standard for Friday mosques erected all over Iran. Although the reasons for this change are not entirely clear, it may have been simple practicality and utility. This plan had already been used in many pre-Islamic buildings in Iraq and Iran, ranging from the Parthian palace at Ashur (1st century A.D.) to Sassanian houses at Ctesiphon (6th century A.D.). It provided a suitable setting of monumentality, without any rigid princely or cultic associations. The four-*iwan* plan is also ideally suited to the Iranian climate. The *qibla iwan*, which is used most frequently for prayer, opens to the north and is shaded from the sun most of the year. The other *iwans* get morning, noon, and afternoon sunlight and can be used accordingly for teaching, study, or rest, depending on the season and time of day. Although the plan inherently has no direction, builders can emphasize the *qibla iwan* in a mosque by

Opposite: **Aerial view of the Friday Mosque at Isfahan**, 9th century and later
The mosque displays the classic Iranian plan of four *iwans* arranged around a central courtyard. The courtyard was the organizing feature of the mosque and already served as the center of the hypostyle mosque established under the Abbasids. Under the Seljuks, the domed chamber in the south (foreground) was added, along with four *iwans* around the court. Today the mosque merges imperceptibly into the surrounding bazaars and cityscape.

Winter prayer hall of the Friday Mosque at Isfahan
The flexibility of the four-*iwan* plan meant that areas could be rebuilt and redecorated at different times to meet the changing needs of the community. This hall, for example, was added just north of the west *iwan* in the 14th century. It is remarkable for its transverse vaults used to cover the rectangular space. At the south end is the magnificent stucco *mihrab*, which was added by the Ilkhanid sultan Üljaitü in 1310.

Above: **Detail of the north dome chamber in the Friday Mosque at Isfahan**
The north dome chamber, added to the mosque in 1088/89, is often considered the masterpiece of medieval Persian architecture, as all of the separate parts – notably the blind panels on the walls and the squinches above – are aligned vertically. This vertical alignment leads the eye upward to the dome, superbly decorated with a pentagram. Though beautiful, this vertical alignment of parts is unique in Iranian architecture.

Below: **Qibla iwan of the Friday Mosque at Isfahan**
Under the Seljuks, the Friday Mosque at Isfahan was transformed from a hypostyle building into one with four *iwans* and a domed sanctuary beyond the south, or *qibla*, *iwans*. To emphasize the *qibla*, or direction of prayer, builders made the south *iwan* wider, and hence taller. Its width corresponds to five bays of the original hypostyle mosque, whereas the lateral *iwans* are only four bays wide. The tall, paired minarets atop the south *iwan* also show the worshipper that it marks the direction of prayer. In later times, the *iwan* was revetted in glazed tiles and covered with tiers of *muqarnas*.

making it bigger and by adding a domed chamber at its closed end. The practicality of the four-*iwan* plan made it popular for many other types of buildings. The Seljuks accelerated the program of founding *madrasas*, or theological colleges, to bolster their Sunni orthodoxy. To judge from later examples, these *madrasas* were probably built using the four-*iwan* plan, but no examples have survived intact from the Seljuk period. The four-*iwan* plan was also used for caravanserais, as in the superb example built by the Seljuk vizier, Sharaf al-Din Qummi, in 1114/15, on the old route north from Nishapur to Merv.

The changes made to the hypostyle mosque at Isfahan in the late 11th century also show the Iranian builders' inventiveness in manipulating domed spaces. The individual bays of the mosque are covered by about 200 different vaults. Although the exact chronology of the vaults has not been established, many may have been added at this period and, collectively, they attest to the superb mastery of building in baked brick, which evolved under the patronage of the Seljuks.

Anatolian Seljuks

Joachim Gierlichs

The Islamization of Anatolia (or Asia Minor), the Byzantine heartland, began in the second half of the 11th century. Following his death in 1063, the Great Seljuk Tughril was succeeded by Alp Arslan, who, like his uncle, was a capable military leader. He was organizing a campaign to Syria and Palestine in order to conquer Egypt, which was ruled by the Shiite Fatimids. In order to secure the rear, he annexed Armenia, which brought Byzantium into the plan. Romanus IV Diogenes went into battle against Alp Arslan on the Malazgirt (Manzikert) plain on August 26, 1071. The encounter ended with a decisive defeat for the Byzantines, and the Turkish tribes moving up behind the troops were able to penetrate far into Anatolia without meeting any resistance. Alp Arslan left Anatolia in the hands of a distant relative, Emir Suleyman, who advanced right into the west of Asia Minor. In 1078 he conquered Nicaea (Iznik), which he pronounced his first capital. With this action, Anatolia had become, at least formally, a province of the Great Seljuk Empire that had its capital at Merv in Turkmenistan.

After these swift initial successes, it took the Seljuks over 100 years more before they could consolidate their rule, following another victory over Byzantium (in 1176, at Myriocephalon and Niksar) and their annexation of the Danishmend Empire (1178) under Kilic Arslan II (1156–1192). During this time they were repeatedly involved in clashes with Byzantines and Crusaders, which saw all sides entering into changing alliances. Konya, whose outlying districts were conquered during the course of the Third Crusade by the German emperor Frederick Barbarossa in 1190, became the new capital. The division of the empire between the 12 sons of Kilic Arslan II, following the latter's death (1192) precipitated a new crisis, which was only resolved by Sultan Ghiyath al-Din Kaikhusrau I (1204–1211). He and his son Izz al-Din Kaikawus (1211–1219) laid the foundations of the new state and bequeathed a well-organized administration and powerful army to Ala al-Din Kaiqubad I (1219–1237), the Anatolian Seljuks' most capable ruler. Under his rule the empire experienced a short but impressive golden age. The general political climate, however, was already being determined by the beginnings of the Mongol wave of conquests, which had been unleashed by the murder of a Mongol envoy by a local Khwarazm-Shah commander in 1218. The Khwarazmian Empire, with its capital in Kuna Urgench (present-day

Qubadabad, central Anatolia, started 1227
Known to us from historical sources, the summer residence of Sultan Ala al-Din Kaiqubad (1219–1237), situated directly on the western shore of Lake Beysehir, is the most important palace building of the Anatolian Seljuks. It was built by the royal architect Sadr al-Din Kopek, on the instructions of, and with the active participation of, the sultan, and was started in 1227. It was only in use for a few years and fell into disrepair under Ala al-Din's successor Ghiyath al-Din Kaikhusrau (1236/37–1246/47). Among the various free-standing structures are two palace buildings, which were richly decorated inside with luster and underglaze-painted wall tiles.

Turkmenistan), fell to the Mongols, as did Iran, large areas of Central Asia and the Middle East, and finally the empire of the Anatolian Seljuks as well.

Ala al-Din Kaiqubad recognized the danger of the situation and attempted to strengthen and secure the state in every respect – militarily, politically, and economically. Among other things, he had a wall built around Konya and made all the emirs contribute to the cost of constructing and equipping it. After the death of Ala al-Din Kaiqubad, who was poisoned in 1237, his successor Ghiyath al-Din Kaikhusrau II (1237–1247) was not able to continue the work of his father adequately, even though he also achieved further (military) successes at first, for example over the Ayyubids. Internally, however, the empire was strongly shaken by the revolt of the Babai religious community. The state was so weakened by it that the Mongols were able to conquer Erzurum in 1242 and in 1243 managed to defeat the Seljuk troops at Kose Dagi near Ankara. Following this, the most important cities – Sivas, Erzincan, Tokat, and Kayseri – were occupied and plundered, while Sultan Kaikhusrau withdrew to Antalya in the south. The Konya sultanate continued to exist for over 60 more years, but became increasingly dependent upon the Mongols and their representatives. After the conquest and devastation of Baghdad by the Mongol Hülägü in 1258, which was the biggest catastrophe of the century, ending the caliphate of the Abbasids, the Seljuk Empire sufferings began to intensify. The capital, Konya, was plundered and the reigning sultan deposed – a event that occured with increasing frequency. The Seljuks survived, however, by adopting a markedly pragmatic policy towards Hülägü's successors, the Ilkhanids.

In 1277 an alliance of the Mamluks, under Sultan Baibars, and the Seljuks managed to defeat the Mongol armies at Elbistan (eastern Turkey). Out of fear of reprisals, however, Baibars retreated, and in 1279 the Seljuk army was easily defeated by the Ilkhanids, who now governed the state openly and appointed and deposed the Seljuk sultans as they saw fit, with the consequence that the power of the central authority continued to diminish steadily. In its late phase, the capital was moved to Sivas, and the Seljuk Empire eventually dissolved into individual principalities and emirates. After the death of Masud II (1281–1297 and 1302–1308) in Kayseri in 1308, the Ilkhanids, under Üljaitü (1304–1316), finally assumed direct control of the country: Anatolia had become a province of the Ilkhanid Empire with its capital in Sultaniya in northwest Iran.

Architecture

Joachim Gierlichs

Seljuk architecture in Anatolia was subject to a multitude of influences which have up until now only partially been examined in detail. Stimuli and borrowings can be detected from Central Asia, Iran, Mesopotamia, and Syria, as well as models from Anatolia itself. The latest research, however, emphasizes that Anatolian Seljuk architecture was not "merely a branch of the architecture of the Great Seljuk Empire," but a "new synthesis of Turkish-Islamic culture" (A. Kuran).

The number of Seljuk buildings that have survived in Anatolia is far greater than in Iran and Central Asia, not least because most monuments were made not of baked brick, but of carefully dressed stone. Apart from the main or Friday mosque (Turkish: *ulu cami*), the main buildings (Turkish terms given in parentheses) are: the high school or *madrasa* (*medrese*), the mausoleum (*turbe* or *kumbet*), and the inn, or caravanserai (*khan*), situated along trade routes. Along with these, examples of the palace building (*saray* or *kosk*), monastery (*zawiye*, *khanqa* or *ribat*), hospital (*sifahane* or *darussifa*), bathhouse (*hamam*), bridge (*kopru*), and a Seljuk shipyard (*tershane*) have also survived. The building complex (*kulliye*), which encompasses several buildings of differing functions that are characteristic of Ottoman architecture, can already be seen during the Seljuk period. The Huand Hatun complex in Kayseri, which alongside a mosque also contains a *madrasa*, a *turbe* and a double bathhouse, is one such instance.

Mosques

Anatolian Seljuk mosques differ substantially from those in southeast Anatolia, which are directly related to Arabic courtyard mosques. This hypostyle design did not manage to prevail in central Anatolia, even though a few buildings display comparable ground plans, such as the Sivas Ulu Cami (1196/97) and the Ulu Cami in Sinop (1267). It was more a case of several different ground

Ala ad-Din Cami, Nigde, 1223
The mosque situated on the castle hill at Nigde was constructed in the reign of Ala al-Din Kaiqubad (1219–1237). Its entrance portal, which does not lie on the *qibla* axis, towers above the facade and is the focus of all the exterior decoration. The very flat stone decoration also includes figurative reliefs (two human faces), which can now, however, be made out only with some difficulty. The minaret, stocky by comparison not only with Ottoman structures, is constructed completely of dressed stone, and stands on a square plinth that is transposed into the polygonal middle part on which the shaft rests by means of so-called "Turkish triangles."

plans, with a number of variants existing side by side, and until well into the 13th century no uniform mosque plan predominated.

In the first half of the 12th century, in a phase of experimentation, Friday mosques were built in Bitlis, Harput, Niksar, Sivas, Kayseri, and Konya. Surprisingly, the four-*iwan* schema developed by the Great Seljuks in Iran and Central Asia, consisting of a courtyard onto which open four barrel-vaulted halls, the so-called *iwans*, played no part in Anatolian mosque building; only in the Friday mosques of Harput and Malatya can faint echoes be found. In the 13th century a new type of ground plan appeared, known as "basilican" because of its linear alignment, and doubtlessly influenced by local church construction. While three different domes are situated in front of the *qibla* wall, which indicates the direction of prayer, in the Ala al-Din Cami in Nigde (1223), in the Burmali Minare Cami in Amasya (1237–1246) three domes are positioned above the length of the nave, thus very different inner spaces develop from similar ground plans. The Gok Madrasa Cami in Amasya (third quarter of the 13th century), with groups of three domes arranged both crosswise and length-

Interior of the Ala al-Din Cami, Nigde, 1228/29
The interior of the Ala al-Din Cami in Nigde is divided into 15 bays, whose vaults, in a variety of styles, are supported by strong, squat pillars. The three bays in front of the *qibla* wall, however, are domed, which strongly accentuates this part of the interior. The Ala al-Din Cami is one of a group of Anatolian mosques in which the ground plan is organized, not crosswise, but lengthwise, which is why it is also referred to as "basilican." There is a long tradition of covering the floor of the prayer hall with valuable carpets, which goes back to the Seljuk period, from which time the oldest surviving carpets date.

another building, in the Afyon Karahisar Ulu Cami (completed in 1272), they have contemporaneous wooden *muqarnas* capitals, which were originally painted. The Esrefoglu Cami in Beysehir (1298/99) has at its center an open, originally roofless air well, which is also referred to from time to time in literature as a "snow depository." It is not known for certain whether this is a relic of earlier courtyard mosques, a form of "shrunken inner courtyard," perhaps.

The internal furnishing of Anatolian mosques is dominated by the *mihrab* (prayer niche) and *minbar* (pulpit). The Mecca-orientated *mihrab*, which is often decorated with a mosaic of colored tiles, provides a contrast with the splendidly carved wooden *minbar*, whose side walls are decorated with geometric and vegetal designs. Prayer niches are sometimes made of stone, however, for example in the Kayseri Ulu Cami, and there are rare survivors made of wood, such that from the Damsa Koy Cami, which is housed in the Museum of Ethnography in Ankara.

The Anatolian Seljuk minaret is squatter than the typical narrow Ottoman "needle minaret," and the round or polygonal shaft generally sits on a stone plinth faced with brick. The shaft is frequently decorated with glazed turquoise or manganese-violet bricks up to the *sherefe* or balcony of the man who summons the faithful to prayer, or occasionally with mosaic tiles. In the case of the Yivli Minare in Antalya (1219), fan-like pendentives, so-called "Turkish triangles," lead up from a square plinth into an octagon on which the rounded, fluted shaft sits.

wise, represents a further development of this three-dome schema, which can be considered as a prototype of the early Ottoman mosques.

Particularly unusual are the "wooden-column mosques," which appeared in western central Anatolia in the 13th century, and which, from the point of view of their ground plan, are directly related to the hypostyle buildings. Among their characteristic features are slender wooden, rather than stone, columns, a flat, in part richly ornamented wooden-beamed ceiling, and simple walls of rendered, undressed stone. The oldest mosque of this type is the Sivrihisar Ulu Cami, which dates from 1232. While here, as in the Arslan Hane Cami in Ankara (1289/90), the wooden columns have marble capitals taken from

Madrasas

In order to counteract the growing influence of the Shiites, the Seljuk vizier Nizam al-Mulk (assassinated 1092) founded the institution of the *madrasa*, also called "Nizamiyas" after their founder, which were designed to be "well-organized, state-funded seats of learning of an advanced level." Following the construction of the inaugural *madrasa* in Baghdad (1066), numerous other *madrasas* were built which have not survived, but are known to us from historical sources. Their appearance as well as the question of their origins has therefore been disputed in academic writings right up to the present day. In contrast to the little-organized elementary education available in the mosque, the *madrasa* had a teaching curriculum that included law, philosophy,

Above: **Interior of the Afyon Karahisar Ulu Cami**, completed in 1272
The Afyon Ulu Cami is one of the wooden-column mosques that were widely constructed throughout western and central Anatolia between the 13th and 15th centuries. Wooden columns took the place of the usual stone columns or pillars. The flat wooden ceiling of the mosque in Afyon was originally painted in radiant colors, remnants of which can still be seen.

Esrefoglu Cami in Beysehir, 1298/99
The mosque in Esrefoglu dates from the later stages of the Anatolian Seljuk Empire and belongs firmly to the Seljuk tradition. The mosque, unspectacular from the outside, retains a large number of its original internal features, most notable of which are the slender columns and air well, originally open, in the center of the prayer hall, which was later covered by a polygonal wooden pyramid.

mathematics, astronomy, and medicine, alongside the study of the Koran. The terms which are often applied, "theological college" or "law school" are therefore only partially accurate.

Essentially, two types of *madrasa* developed on Anatolian soil: those with covered courtyards and those with open courtyards. The oldest covered *madrasas* are to be found in the Danishmend region in Niksar and Tokat. The Niksar Madrasa and the Cukur ("Sunken") Madrasa in Tokat were built in the middle of the 12th century by the Danishmend ruler Yagi-ba-san. The two buildings share a similar ground plan, which consists of a covered, domed court enclosed by two L-shaped wings of differing lengths, made up of several rooms. The students' living accommodation is situated along the front and left hand side, while the larger rooms occupy the space along the right-hand side and back. An *iwan* occupies the central area.

This plan was maintained, with certain adaptations, until the 13th century, achieving its "classical" expression in the second half of the century. An *iwan* was now positioned in the middle of the back wall (a one-*iwan madrasa*), flanked by a domed room on either side, while the cells lay along both sides of the courtyard. "Turkish triangles" lead from the walls up into the round dome. Examples of this type are the Karatay Madrasa (1251) and the Ince Minare Madrasa (around 1256) in Konya, as well as the Tas Madrasa in Cay (1278/79). A variation on this theme is provided by the Caca Bey Madrasa (1272/73) in Kirsehir, whose asymmetrical ground plan features four *iwans* of different sizes.

Along with the mostly smaller Anatolian Seljuk *madrasas* with a covered, domed court, there is also a second type, which is characterized by an open courtyard and either two or four *iwans*. Where there are only two *iwans*, these are situated opposite each other on the main axis, as for example in the Cifte Minare Madrasa in Erzurum (around 1250) or the Karatay Madrasa (1250/51) in Antalya. The external decoration of the building is concentrated on the entrance portal, which often has a vaulted, *muqarnas*-decorated niche towering above the ridge of the roof.

Turbes and kumbets

Originally located outside medieval settlements and cities, the tower-shaped (*turbes*) and domed (*kumbets* or, in Persian, *gumbads*) tombs were a prominent feature of the Anatolian landscape for centuries. During the last few decades, however, many of the tombs that once stood outside or on the edge of the cities have disappeared from view, hidden by the modern concrete buildings thrown up by the cities' boundless growth. *Turbes* and *kumbets* by no means always stood isolated in the landscape, however, but from the beginning of the 13th century were already frequently being integrated into other buildings or building complexes – hospitals, *madrasas*, mosques – or built onto them. In the case of the Izz al-Din Kaikawus I Sifaiye (hospital) in Sivas, dating from 1217/18, the founder's *turbe* was erected in the right hand *iwan* of the hospital after his death in 1219. In the complex of the powerful vizier Fakhr al-Din Ali, known as Sahip Ata, in Konya (1258–1279), which incorporates a mosque, cloisters, and baths, the *turbe* has even been given a spatial planning function: one of its antechambers connects the mosque with the cloisters. In the Huand Hatun Complex (1237/38) in Kayseri, the *turbe* is incorporated in the prayer hall, but is only accessible from the *madrasa*.

In contrast to the single-story mausoleums of the Great Seljuks in Persia and Central Asia, for example the Gumbad-i Qabus to the east of Jurjan, which has no crypt, the tombs of the Anatolian Seljuks are two-story buildings whose lower floor served as the burial vault and upper floor as a room for prayer and gatherings. Around a third of the mausoleums have a *mihrab* set into the wall, which is not, however, particularly conspicuous from the outside, as for example the Kilic Arslan II Turbe in Konya (1192/93).

The lower and upper floors possess separate entrances, with access to the upper floor usually via a double stone staircase. The mummified corpse would have been laid out in the crypt, which lies partly below floor level, while a cenotaph (dummy sarcophagus), as a rule richly decorated, would have stood on the upper floor. This two-floor design is a characteristic of the Anatolian

Left: Doner Kumbet in Kayseri, 1275
This tomb, popularly known as the "Doner Kumbet" (or rotating domed tomb), owes its name to the decoration of its conical cap, which gives the impression that the mausoleum is turning on its own axis. Like all Anatolian Seljuk tombs, the mausoleum has two floors, a largely underground lower floor serving as a burial vault, and an upper floor which held the cenotaph and was also designed to be used for gatherings and prayer. The cube of the upper floor, broken up into 12 parts, is articulated by flat, blind arcading that features some figurative reliefs although, unfortunately, these are now very badly damaged.

Right: Hudavent Hatun Turbe in Nigde
This *turbe* in Nigde was built in 1312 for Hudavand Khatun, daughter of the Seljuk sultan Qilic Arslan IV, and therefore already belongs to the post-Seljuk period. The mausoleum is still firmly within the Seljuk tradition, even though it displays certain new characteristics, such as the truly stocky proportions and the 16-sided projecting drum area. Worthy of note is the rich figurative decoration featuring eagles (some double-headed), sirens, and numerous human heads hidden away among the non-figurative ornamentation of the drum.

turbe and in all probability has its roots in old, pre-Islamic burial traditions. We know from Chinese chronicles that the Gok Turks initially kept mummified corpses for six months in a "tent of the dead" before burying them.

The earliest tombs, which in general had simple ground plans, date from the second half of the 12th century; they are all to be found in northeastern Anatolia, and were built under the Danishmend dynasty, whose territory was annexed by the Seljuks between 1176 and 1178. During the course of the 13th century, the number of *turbes* and *kumbets* increased significantly throughout the whole of the empire. The tombs can be divided into two types: structures whose square, polygonal, or round upper story is domed and covered on the outside by a pyramid or by multifaceted or conical roof are far more common than the second type, which has a square ground plan and a prayer room in the form of an *iwan*.

The rather meager decoration of the tombs, which were usually made of dressed stone instead of brick, is concentrated on the external walls, the majority of which are patterned with pointed-arch blind arcading, which shows an Armenian-Georgian influence related in particular to the dome drum of churches. The transition from the round or polygonal structure to the roof is often accentuated by a cornice that can sometimes project outwards in several stages. The surfaces within the blind arcades are sometimes filled in with geometric and/or floral ornamentation. A few buildings, mostly from the second half of the 13th and first quarter of the 14th centuries, also feature figurative

reliefs. Belonging to this type are the Doner Kumbet in Kayseri (around 1275), whose figurative reliefs, now badly damaged, belong, however, to a later period, and the already post-Seljuk Hudavent Hatun Turbe in Nigde (1312), with reliefs featuring birds, sirens, and double-headed eagles, which is still firmly rooted in the Seljuk tradition.

Monumental tombs were the preserve of the sultan, his wives, the highest officers of the empire, the viziers, and certain important "men of faith" (*sayids*), while "common mortals" were buried in cemeteries. In the courtyard of the Ala al-Din Cami on the castle hill in Konya is the Kilic Arslan II Turbe (1192/93), a kind of dynastic Seljuk burial vault.

The tomb of the most important mystic of the Middle Ages, Jalal al-Din Rumi, known as Mevlana (d. 1273) occupies a special position among the mausoleums. His *turbe*, covered with turquoise colored tiles and later altered, lies at the heart of the most important dervish monastery on Anatolian soil, which – as the recipient of precious gifts over the centuries – still attracts hordes of pilgrims and tourists today.

Khans/Caravanserais

The huge inns known as the "cathedrals of the steppes," which originally followed one another at regular intervals – roughly every 19 miles (30 kilometers) – along the trade routes, and provided the caravans with safe lodging, free of charge for up to three days, perhaps bear the most impressive testimony of all to Seljuk building activity in Anatolia.

Intensive research has enabled the history of the main trade routes, which crossed the Seljuk Empire from east to west and north to south, to be reconstructed. They provided the economic basis for the extraordinary cultural flowering that was reflected in numerous building projects, primarily during the reign

Cifte Minare Madrasa, Erzurum, c. 1250
In contrast to other *madrasas*, the Cifte Minare Madrasa in Erzurum is two-storied and has very high side *iwans* with star-shaped vaulting. The upper floor galleries are broken up by the side *iwans* so that the cells of the students are divided into four groups. The columns and arches of the arcades are

decorated with geometric and floral designs, the portal with unusual figurative reliefs (dragons, the Tree of Life, double-headed eagles), which have in part been left unfinished. The minarets that flank the portal are built of red brick with glazed ceramic ornament.

Sultan Khan near Aksaray, 1228/29
This *khan*, built by Sultan Ala al-Din Kaiqubad I on the road between Aksaray and Konya, is one of the biggest and best-furnished of the caravanserais. In the center of its courtyard is a *kosk*, a square, four-arched structure whose upper floor, reached via an external stone staircase, serves as a prayer room. The *khans* of he sultans stand out not only because of their size – their total area can measure around 4,500 square meters – but also because of their lavish decoration, based on geometric patterns and systems which are never directly repeated.

of Ala al-Din Kaiqubad (1219–1237). Although more recently the hitherto accepted typology has started to be questioned and many newly discovered *khans*, mainly in eastern Anatolia, are broadening our picture of them, detailed information on their positions, furnishings, and functions is nevertheless already available. Building activity started shortly after 1200 and ended around 1280. The majority of caravanserais were to be found in central Anatolia and were constructed during the reigns of Ala al-Din Kaiqubad I (1219–1237) and his successor Giyath al-Din Kaikhusrau II (1237–1247). Several viziers and a physician also appear as founders of *khans*.

Most of the surviving *khans* have a massive, multi-aisled, domed hall which incorporated storage room for goods, stables, and lodging for the merchants. Situated in front of the hall is a rectangular courtyard, slightly wider or the same width, which is surrounded either by galleries that open onto it, or smaller individual rooms. Some caravanserais have baths and a prayer hall or free-standing structure built on arches (*kosk*) with an upper floor providing a small room for prayers (*mescit*). The largest *khans* reach a total area of 48,400 square feet (4,500 square meters): the internal area of the domed hall of the Sultan Khan near Kayseri (1232–1236) alone measures 15,400 square feet (1,430 square meters).

The main areas of ornamentation, as with the *madrasas*, are located on the courtyard and hall portals, with the geometric and vegetal decoration of each portal being different in each case. There are no known cases of the patterns being exact copies of each other. Certain caravanserais, mainly the large ones built by the sultans, stand out because of their complex geometric systems of decoration and exceptionally exact stone cutting. Some *khans* are also remarkable for their figurative building decoration, which can take the form either of antique or Byzantine spoils, i.e. elements recycled from other buildings, or reliefs specifically created for them. The Karatay Khan (1241/42), on the road between Kayseri and Sivas, possesses the most comprehensive figurative repertoire, including gargoyles, and small animal and human heads within the nonfigurative decoration of the courtyard portal, an animal frieze on the cornice of the pump house, and large-scale stylized dragon figures on the reverse of the entrance *iwan*. By contrast, the figurative decoration on the hall portal of the Incir Khan (1238/39), on the way from Egridir to Antalya, is of an altogether different type. Here there are two striding lions placed one opposite the other with the sun emblem on their backs, an image that can be traced back to the builder, Giyath al-Din Kaikhusrau II, as can be seen from his coinage. Highly unusual is the figurative relief decoration on the *mescit* of the Sultan Khan (1232–1236) to the east of Kayseri. Two of its four archivolts are adorned with affronted dragons (i.e. facing each other), whose exaggeratedly elongated bodies, made up of a heart-shaped pattern, occupy the whole of the curve. The dragons, in elevation, are turning towards a little rosette positioned above their heads, raising the possibility that the relief has an astromythological meaning, depicting the sun threatened by the earthly powers.

One of the important overland routes connected the empire's two great ports: Sinop on the Black Sea and Alanya on the Mediterranean. In Alanya, not only the citadel and "Red Tower" have survived, but also a shipyard (Turkish: *tershane*). The five-berth, domed installation is partly built into the cliffside and permitted the building, maintenance, and repair of ships as well as offering a berth for a proportion of the fleet.

Saray and *Kosk*

Our knowledge of Seljuk palace building is very limited due to the paucity of physical remains. Apart from the two (earlier) Ghaznavid palaces, Lashkar-i Bazar and Ghazni (Afghanistan), Qasr al-Banat in Raqqa (Syria), Qara Sarai in Mosul (Iraq), and the palace buildings on the Takht-i Suleyman in northwestern Iran, built by Abaqa Khan (1265–1281) around 1270, our knowledge is primarily based on the palaces of the Anatolian Seljuks. With the exception of a few caliphs' palaces from the Abbasid period, the remainder, including the above mentioned, comprise a more or less uniform collection of individual buildings of rather modest proportions only indirectly connected to one another. In this respect, Islamic palace building is diametrically opposed to European palace building, which almost always involves a complex of buildings with a symmetrical ground plan.

While only the ruins of a pavilion (the *kosk*, 13th century) remain of the palace buildings on the castle hill in Konya that were once the seat of the Seljuks, researchers have succeeded in rediscovering the summer palace of Ala al-Din Kaiqubad, known from historical sources, which is situated directly on the western shore of Lake Beysehir. In 1965 and 1966 two palace-like buildings were uncovered there whose interiors were unusually richly furnished. In all likelihood, the structure was built for the sultan by his architect and master of the hunt, Saad al-Din Kopek, who started the project in 1227. At the same time, the ruler exerted a strong influence on the design of his palace. According to Ibn Bibi, "(he) sketched out the plan of the palace using his own ideas and decided upon the position of each and every room himself." After the death of Ala al-Din Kaiqubad in 1237, the palace was used for only a few years by his son and successor Giyath al-Din Kaikhusrau II. According to the latest research, the summer residence incorporated more than 18 very different, free-standing buildings on its grounds.

Among these, the "Great Palace" and "Little Palace" are particularly noteworthy, along with a structure divided into two parts, which was probably a small shipyard or boathouse. The remains can also be seen of the harbor moorings and harbor basin. Among the largely buried ruins of Saad al-Din Kopek's palace, mentioned by Ibn Bibi, must be the "vantage points that refresh the heart." These were the baths and a mosque whose inscription bearing the date 633 of the *hegira* (1235/36) was found in a nearby mosque, having found another use there. It is possible that the palace also had a zoological garden or "paradise," as the Umayyads and early Abbasids were known to have had, as for example in the Syrian desert palace Qasr al-Hair al-Gharbi. Only the two "palaces" have been fully excavated. These are lacking in any symmetry of design but, despite their

Kirkgoz Khan, middle of the 13th century
Kirkgoz Khan, constructed by Sultan Ghiyath al-Din Kaikhusrau, stands on the important road which leads southwards from the interior to the port of Antalya. The Anatolian Seljuk sultans embarked upon a systematic expansion and safeguarding of trade routes very soon after consolidating their empire in the second half of the 12th century. At the core of this economic policy was the construction of fortified caravanserais which provided merchants with secure accommodation, cost-free for up to three days. Animals could be stabled and goods stored in the two-bay deep courtyard arcades.

differing proportions and the different building materials used, share a common feature in their central set of two chambers, consisting of an *iwan* – presumably the throne room – and an arch-vaulted antechamber.

The interior surfaces of the initially unprepossessing rough stone walls of the Great Palace (165 × 115 feet, 50 × 35 meters) were richly decorated. No other palace in the whole of the Islamic world has the same kind of varied tile decoration, which has survived in places up to a height of about 7 feet (2 meters), that is found here. Some of the luster and underglaze-painted wall tiles in a star and cross pattern can today be seen in the Karatay Madrasa Museum in Konya. "The courtly program is reflected in the figurative hurly-burly: the enthroned prince sitting cross-legged, the double-headed eagle, his symbol of power, sphinxes and sirens as protective charms, peacocks and the Tree of Life, flanked by birds, to represent Paradise. But creatures of the hunt are also portrayed, with a pack of hounds, a falcon attacking a hare, a panther, a fox, a leaping mountain goat, a wild

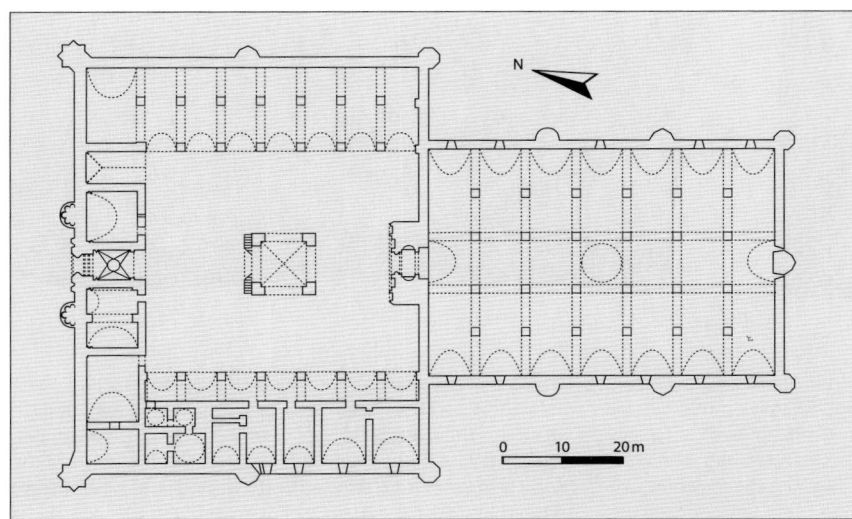

Ground plan of the Sultan Khan, in Tuzhisar, 1232-36
This *khan*, on the road between Sivas and Kayseri, belongs to the group of caravanserais found western and central Anatolia that feature a massive, vaulted hall with many bays, the central one of which is covered by a dome. In front of the hall is a large, rectangular courtyard, which is sometimes wider than the hall itself. In the middle of the courtyard stands a square *kosk*, the upper floor of which would have served as a small prayer room.

trotting ass, bears feasting on fruit, and birds such as wild geese and ducks flying heavenwards" (K. Otto-Dorn).

There are also a number of other palace-like structures, mainly in the countryside surrounding Kayseri, but also more recently discovered buildings in the coastal region around Alanya, which can perhaps best be described as fortified "manor houses" or palatial residences having various different functions. While the Haidar Bey Kosk in Argincik near Kayseri (c.1250) must in all likelihood, because of its emphatically defensive character and lack of decoration, have been more a sort of military station, it is possible to see the three-arched lakeside structures at Kaiqubadiye near Kayseri (c. 1224), which only survive in very fragmentary form, as the lakeside pavilion of a "royal retreat," complete with boathouse. In a prominent position in Erkilet, high above Kayseri, stands the Hizr Elias Kosk of 1241, which was without doubt used not only as a viewing pavilion but also as a watchtower.

Konya – capital of the Anatolian Seljuks

Following the rapid advance of the Turkish tribes into western Asia Minor under the leadership of Suleyman, Nicaea, or present-day Iznik, became the first capital of the slowly developing empire. Only under Sultan Kilic Arslan II (1155–1192) did Konya (previously Iconium) become the seat of the Seljuks, probably in 1181. At the center of the city was the castle hill (Ala al-Din Tepesi) on which the main mosque, the Ala al-Din Cami, was constructed in the 12th century. Its irregular ground plan alone gives some hint of its complicated building history, which no-one has been able to fully explain to this day. In close proximity stood the 13th-century palace, once richly decorated with ceramic tiles and wooden painted ceilings, of which only the ruined walls of one of its pavilions remain.

The palace and Friday mosque were, like the city, protected by two impressive rings of wall, of which nothing has survived today other than a row of figurative reliefs and marble inscription panels. The great importance attached to the fortification of the capital city, both in defensive and artistic terms, by Sultan Ala al-Din Kaiqubad (1219–1237) can be inferred from an account by the court chronicler Ibn Bibi: the sultan, accompanied by his emirs, rode through the city in person, stipulating where gates, towers, and curtain

Ince Minare Madrasa in Konya, 1256
The Ince Minare Madrasa in Konya, which stands right at the foot of the castle hill, as does the Karatay Madrasa, was built by Vizier Fakhr al-Din Ali. It was given its modern name, "Slender Minaret," after this part of the *madrasa*. Partially destroyed by lightning in 1900, the minaret's stump is decorated with turquoise brickwork. The building, which has a domed, covered courtyard, impresses with its massive portal featuring unusual stone decoration, whose ornament is worked in part from behind. Particularly striking are the ribbons covered with inscriptive friezes, which, crossing over and under each other, frame the actual entrance.

Reliefs from the castle wall and city wall, Konya, 1221/21
The Mongol threat, growing ever closer, provided the incentive for Sultan Ala al-Din Kaiqubad (1219–1237), shortly after coming to power, to secure the capital, Konya, by building a city wall. Like the castle wall, it has completely disappeared today. Numerous figurative marble reliefs have, however, survived, among them angels or spirits in "bent-knee mode" (a conventional depiction of the act of running), heraldic double-headed eagles, which can either be seen as a symbol of power of a general kind or related directly to Ala al-Din Kaiqubad who commissioned them, and reliefs depicting narrative scenes. One such relief, which must have belonged to a larger ensemble, depicts a winged unicorn pursuing an elephant trotting along ahead. This could be the illustration of a well-known fable, in which the rhinoceros/unicorn, mortal enemy of the elephant, gores him with his horn and kills him. As a result of some of the blood that flows from the elephant's wound landing in the eye of the rhinoceros, the latter is blinded and also dies.

walls were to be erected. He was attended by "his worthy building masters and draftsmen."

Today, around 20 large-format stone reliefs with figurative designs, which originally adorned the castle and city walls, are kept in the Ince Minare Madrasa. Among them are a seated prince holding a pomegranate in his hand, a pair of angels or spirits in "bent-knee mode," stylized heraldic eagles with the motto "*al-sultan*," various double-headed eagles and animals in chase, among them the scene, not illustrated anywhere else except in craftwork of this kind, of a rhinoceros/unicorn attempting to gore an elephant trotting along ahead, with his horn.

Two significant *madrasas* stand at the foot of the castle hill, the Karatay Madrasa of 1251 and the Ince Minare Madrasa, built around 1260, both of which are remarkable for their unusual facade decoration. While the Ince Minare Madrasa stands out because of its three-dimensional, almost "baroque" stone decoration, which incorporates wide, curving, inscription-bearing ribbons, the portal of the Karatay Madrasa uses a knotted motif brought to Anatolia by Syrian architects and stonemasons. This architectural ornament, known as the "Syrian knot motif," which is found on several *madrasas* of the 12th and 13th centuries, mainly in Aleppo and Damascus, is also found in almost identical form on the north wall portal of the Ala al-Din Cami in Konya, built under Ala al-Din Kaiqubad in 1221/22 by the Damascene architect Muhammad ibn Khaulan al-Dimashqi. Alongside this eye-catching form of stone decoration there is also, however, flat ornamentation in stone, for example on the portal of the Sircali Madrasa in Konya (1242/43). Here there is a contrast between the unremarkable stone decoration of the facade with the richly glazed decoration of the interior, which is executed using a variety of techniques. Aside from the brick mosaic technique, brought over from Iran and Central Asia, which involves a geometric pattern being created by the interplay between glazed and unglazed bricks, tile mosaics also dominate, a new technique which developed from the need to furnish stone and rough stone buildings, not just brick ones, with glazed decoration. As tile cladding using techniques developed in Persia was too costly and only suitable for relatively small surfaces, a technique was sought which would allow for a free application of ornament and a simple, affordable manufacturing process independent of building material.

Easy-to-manufacture monochrome tiles were cut into small pieces and fitted together on a flat underlay, glazed side down. The pieces were set with small gaps in-between and mortar was then applied, which forced its way into the spaces and held the whole firmly together. The white mortar appears on the finished front as a fine outline and forms a contrast to the turquoise, aubergine-violet, dark blue, and black pieces of tile. This new technique also enabled rounded surfaces such as pendentives and domes to be covered, and even prayer niches with miniature *muqarnas* dome cavities were decorated in this way.

The center for medieval tile decoration was Konya, where a total of 47 of the 120 buildings (in 42 places) known to have been decorated in this way are located. Of 40 medieval buildings in Kayseri, Nigde, and the surrounding area, on the other hand, where there is a strong local tradition of building in stone and a stonemasons' school, only two buildings display tile decoration.

The stone decoration of the Seljuks

The buildings of the Anatolian Seljuks impress less often with their dimensions than with their lavish architectural decoration, which is unique in a variety of ways. This is the main area where they differ from the buildings of the Great Seljuks in Iran and Central Asia, which were constructed mainly of baked brick and are dominated by tile and stucco decoration. Apart from a few exceptions,

North portal of the Divrigi Ulu Cami, 1228/29
The mosque and hospital complex in Divrigi was built by the Mengucekid ruler Ahmad Shah, vassal of the Seljuk sultan Ala-al-Din Kaiqubad, and his wife Turan Malik. It is remarkable for the unusual character and extremely high quality of its stone decoration, the north portal of the mosque being the most three-dimensional. Its decoration is dominated by self-contained vegetal motifs.

the latter plays no more than a very minor role. The stone decoration of both secular and sacred buildings represents a masterful achievement on the part of the Anatolian Seljuks. The ceremonial facades of mosques, *madrasas*, and *khans* were thus endowed with a special importance. Besides these, windows, lintels, vaulting, corbels, ledges, and *mihrabs* too, were decorated in this fashion.

Regional differences can be seen, as well as a chronological development. The stonework in the Divrigi, Sivas, and Erzurum regions exhibits markedly projecting ornamentation and therefore has a three-dimensional effect, while the buildings of Konya and Kayseri display delicate flat reliefs. A significant exception to this, however, is the portal facade of the Ince Minare Madrasa in Konya (around 1260) with its almost baroque ornamentation. Although it is difficult to establish general rules, a trend towards a complex, intertwining form of three-dimensional stonework can be detected in the 13th century. Whereas the stonework of the first half of the century was characterized by dense geometric interlacing, twisting motifs, Kufic inscriptions, rosettes, and *muqarnas* ornamentation, the decoration became more three-dimensional in the second half of the century, when the ornamentation often seemed self-important. Finally, towards the end of the century, the leaf design came to be the predominant feature in stone reliefwork. In its three portals of completely different design, however, the mosque-hospital complex in Divriği (1228/29), built by the Mengucekid ruler Ahmad Shah, unites all these different styles and forms of ornament.

The portal facades of the large *khans* founded by the sultans often display polished geometric systems of ornamentation, but it is their figurative architectural decoration that is worthy of special consideration. Figurative stone reliefs form part of the decoration of over 50 surviving buildings from pre-Ottoman times, i.e. from the 11th to the 15th centuries. In addition, more than two dozen reliefs which are attributable to Seljuk or Artuqid buildings to be found in various museums. Depictions of human beings, but mainly of animals and hybrid creatures, represent a rich repertoire deserving more attention than it generally receives. Further examples can be seen in other artistic media (wooden doors, stucco reliefs, and wall tiles in the summer palace at Qubadabad, metalwork, and so on).

By comparison with the heavily symbolic lions, double-headed eagles, sirens, sphinxes, and dragons, real creatures such as birds, hares, fish, bulls and gazelles have been given a rather subordinate role to play in all this. They are by no means confined to secular buildings, but are also in evidence on mosques, *madrasas*, and *turbes*, usually positioned on or near the portal. Small-scale figures are often well and truly hidden away among the nonfigurative decoration, while large-scale reliefs are strikingly positioned in prominent places. The purpose of this is certainly not just to indulge a love of decoration for its own sake, but in many cases to make a meaningful visual statement. The two double-eagle reliefs and the single-eagle relief on the west portal of the Divriği Ulu Cami (1228/29) both belong in this category. Viewed in conjunction with the inscription on the building, which clearly identifies Ahmad Shah as a local

prince feudally dependent upon the Seljuk sultan Ala al-Din Kaiqubad, the reliefs emphatically convey this dependent relationship, with the eagle symbolizing Ahmad Shah and the double-headed eagle symbolizing Ala al-Din Kaiqubad.

The unorthodox attitude held by the Anatolian Seljuks towards figurative representations of living things also ultimately expresses itself in the recycling of fragments of pre-Islamic buildings, in particular antique and Byzantine reliefs and sculptures of all kinds. Alongside newly made Seljuk reliefs, numerous "spoils," among them figures of lions and antique statues, were incorporated into Konya's city and castle walls.

Artuqid architecture

In the course of the Seljuk conquest of Anatolia, following their victory over the Byzantines at the battle of Malazgirt (Manzikert), the Artuqid dynasty, whose ancestor Artuq ibn Ekseb belonged to the confederation of Oghuz Turks, established itself in southeast Anatolia. His sons settled in this region, taking over the territories of the Great Seljuks. This gave rise to the Artuqid states of Diyarbakir and Hasankeyf (1098–1232), Mardin and Silvan (1104–1408) as well as the Harput line (1185–1233). The Artuqids erected numerous buildings in Mardin between the middle of the 12th and the end of the 14th centuries, developing an individual style of architecture showing predominantly Syrian influences. The overriding majority of these structures were mosques and *madrasas*, while the number of tombs and caravanserais was very small.

In contrast to the Anatolian Seljuk style of mosque building, the Artuqidic mosque with its transverse prayer hall, dominant dome in front of the *mihrab*, and large courtyard, represents a type that can be traced back indirectly, via the Diyabakir Ulu Cami to the courtyard mosques. Other than in southeast Anatolia there were no successors to this style in Asia Minor apart from a few exceptions such as the Sinop Ulu Cami (13th century), and the Isa Bey Cami in Seljuk (14th century). The minarets of Artuqid mosques, in contrast to the usually round brick minarets of the Seljuks, are square or octagonal and built of stone.

Courtyard facade of the Ulu Cami of Diyarbakir
The Ulu Cami (Friday mosque) of Diyarbakir (or Christian Amida) – with its complicated building history that remains unclear to this day, involving numerous alterations, extensions, and restorations – dates back in all probability to the 7th century. The mosque has a transverse, originally flat-roofed prayer hall, a large courtyard with a pump room, and is enclosed on three sides by *riwaqs* (halls) which were subsequently altered. The two courtyard facades of the smaller sides (picture shows a view from inside the courtyard) have a two-story columned front which cleverly combines late antique/Byzantine building elements with new Islamic elements to form a harmonious whole.

Bridge over the Tigris, near Cizre, before 1159
The great bridge over the Tigris, near Cizre, located today on Syrian soil in the Turkish-Syrian border area, was very probably built by Jamal al-Din Muhammad Isfahani, vizier of the Zangid ruler Qutb al-Din Maudud of Mosul. Five limestone reliefs, standing out very clearly against the dark basalt, are to be found on the surviving arch of the bridge. They show the seven planets known during the Middle Ages and the signs of the zodiac associated with each one, which give the planet its special powers and exalt and enhance it. The sun, however, is shown not at its zenith (Aries/the Ram), but in its own "house" (Leo/the Lion).

The Artuqid *madrasa* took the form of an open, courtyard *madrasa*, a design used by the Anatolian Seljuks too, whereas the *madrasa* design developed by the Anatolian Seljuks that featured a central, domed court, such as the Karatay Madrasa in Konya, does not occur in southeast Anatolia. The two-story Hatuiye *madrasa* in Mardin, founded by the wife of Artuqid Najm al-Din Alpi (1152–1176) in the final quarter of the 12th century, has an open courtyard with two *iwans*. The stone *mihrab* of the domed tomb chamber is richly decorated in a manner similar to the multifoil blind arch decoration of the Ulu Cami of Silvan. The Syrian influence mentioned earlier is evident in the Mesudiye Madrasa in Diyarbakir, which was started in 1193 and completed in 1223/24 using the plans of an architect from Aleppo. The original design of a central courtyard with rooms around it was abandoned and a further group of rooms built on to the west, which opened onto their own, second courtyard. This new design reached its high point and final realization with the Sultan Isa (Zinciriye) Madrasa in Mardin, dating from 1385, which resulted in a carefully planned complex of *madrasa*, *turbe*, and *masjid*, grouped around several courtyards on two levels.

Artuqid palaces are known to have existed in Diyarbakir, Harput, and Hasankeyf. Of these only the palace in the citadel at Diyarbakir has been partially uncovered and examined, though it was later completely built over. This richly furnished palace, laid out according to the four-*iwan* schema, is thought to have been built by Nasr al-Din Mahmud (1201–1222). Floor mosaics and a fountain were found, as well as baths close to the palace. Interestingly, no freestanding Artuqid mausoleums were constructed; the few known examples formed part of larger complexes, which usually had a *madrasa* at their center.

Along with caravanserais, which are almost exclusively known to us from historical sources, a series of bridges has survived, which are multi-arched and rise up towards the middle, where they sometimes also undertake a change of direction. One such bridge is that over the Batman Suyu near Malabadi on the road from Diyarbakir to Bitlis (1147), which has been fully renovated. Like the badly ruined Tigris bridge near Hasankeyf (1116 and 1155–1175), it was decorated with figurative reliefs which have today either disappeared or can no longer be made out because of their fragmentary condition. Both structures featured an astronomy or astrology related series of figures, as did the Cizre bridge over the Tigris (Jazirat ibn Umar), which dates from the same time.

The colossal basalt city walls of Diyarbakir, which date back to late antique times, have been constantly altered and reinforced under the various Islamic dynasties in power from the 10th century onwards. For example, the Artuqid sultan Nasir al-Din Mahmud (1201–1222) had the Ulu Badan (1208/09) and Yedi Kardes (c. 1208/09) bastions built, which featured symmetrically conceived figurative ensembles consisting of real animals and mythological creatures; double-headed eagles and winged sphinxes can still be identified. In the inscription the building master is named with the closing remark "following the plans of al-Malik al-Salih" (the then ruling Artuqid sultan), giving an insight into the nature of the influence exerted by the client and patron.

Detail of Tigris bridge near Cizre, c. 1160
To the seven planets on the bridge over the Tigris near Cizre is added an eighth in the form of a relief depicting the pseudo-planet al-Jawzahar in the sign of its zenith, i.e. in the zodiacal sign of Sagittarius (the Archer). The phenomenon of the solar eclipse has been portrayed as a giant dragon threatening the sun and moon and, in swallowing them, bringing forth darkness. The head and tail of the dragon embody the rising and falling "node of the moon."

Decorative Arts

Sheila Blair, Jonathan Bloom

Art under the Great Seljuks

Some of the finest and most inventive ceramics ever produced in the Islamic lands were made in Iran in the 12th and 13th centuries. Wealthy people in Islamic societies had long prized Chinese porcelains for their finely thrown, translucent body and their subtly carved or molded decoration under a thin transparent glaze. Local potters, however, could not reproduce these features using their traditional heavy clay body covered with thick and opaque tin glaze. So in the 12th century Iranian potters devised a method to overcome these difficulties by reviving an ancient Egyptian technique for producing an artificial body material made from ground quartz mixed with a small amount of white clay and ground glaze. This new body, usually known as "fritted" or "stone-paste," was white, hard, translucent (when thin), and readily covered with a thin, transparent alkaline glaze. By using this combination of materials, Iranian potters could exploit an extremely wide range of decorative techniques.

The introduction of this new fritted body was followed within half a century by a burst of creative energy unparalleled in the ceramic arts until the rise of the Wedgwood and Staffordshire potteries in 18th-century England. The extraordinary range of decorative techniques used in Iran in the 12th and 13th centuries included wares decorated with monochrome glazes, wares incised and carved before glazing, wares decorated with molded and applied ornament, and wares painted under and over the glaze. The last technique, overglaze painting, was the most expensive and produced the finest pieces.

Iranian potters in the 12th and 13th centuries produced two types of overglaze-painted ceramics. The first was lusterware, in which potters painted designs in silver or copper oxides on an already glazed piece, which was then refired in a special reducing kiln. The carefully regulated heat softened the glaze, and the oxygen-poor atmosphere took oxygen from the metallic oxides, leaving a thin film of metal on the surface of the glaze. The construction of a special kiln, the expense of the additional materials, particularly the metallic oxides, the extra fuel required for a double firing, and the difficulty of controlling all the possible variables made these ceramics the acme of the potter's art. Lusterwares had already been produced in Egypt and, like Fatimid lusterwares, Iranian lusterwares were decorated in one color of luster. In the Seljuk period, however, Iranian potters extended the traditional shapes (bowls, plates, and jars) to include such new ones as figurines, stands, and, most importantly, large expanses of wall tiles. Only one center of production has been identified: the city of Kashan in central Iran. Many of the lusterwares are signed, showing the high status of the craft. To judge from potters' signatures, many of the potters were related to each other. The names of some 17 potters are recorded, and at least two families of potters, that of Abu Tahir and al-Husain, can be established over several generations.

The second type of overglaze-painted ceramic developed in Iran in the late Seljuk period comprises enameled wares, often known in modern times as *minai* (from Persian: "enamel"). Unlike monochrome lusterwares, enameled wares were painted over the glaze in several colors, and occasionally gold,

Scalloped plate, Abu Zaid, Kashan, 1210, fritware overpainted with luster, diameter 35 cm, Washington, Freer Gallery of Art
This plate, which bears a long inscription saying that it was made by the famous potter Abu Zaid in year 607 of the *hegira* (1210) displays a complex scene of a horse, a sleeping groom, and five figures standing behind the horse. At the bottom is a naked woman swimming, surrounded by fishes.

Ceramic dish, Kashan, c. 1210, fritware overpainted with gold and polychrome, diameter 31 cm, Washington, Freer Gallery of Art
In addition to monochrome lusterwares, potters in Iran in the late 12th century developed a second technique of overglaze painting in which they decorated glazed ceramics with polychrome pigments and gold. These "minai" wares have elaborate scenes, often of royal motifs.

before being fired a second time at a relatively low temperature to fix the colors. Like lusterwares, many enameled pieces are bowls, and many are painted with scenes of enthroned figures and legendary scenes of hunting. These princely subjects, together with the high cost of the enameled objects, suggest that they were produced for an upper-class market.

Overglaze-painted wares are the showiest ceramics produced during this period, but another technique had more long-lasting significance for the history of ceramics, not only in Iran but also in China and Europe: underglaze painting. In comparison to overglaze painting, this technique was far cheaper, and the glaze protected the painting from abrasion. More importantly, the new alkaline glaze did not cause the pigments to run into each other during firing. This quality allowed the painter greater freedom of execution, and painters in the Seljuk period used the ceramic surface in the way that later painters used paper. To judge from the motifs used, many of the finest examples of underglaze painting were produced, like the luster and enameled wares, in Kashan.

In addition to these expensive wares painted over or under the glaze on a frit body, potters in the Seljuk period also continued to make traditional slip-covered earthenwares, covering the reddish body with a thin layer of white clay applied as a liquid slip. As the glaze was fluxed with lead, the pigments often flowed and blurred during firing. Potters in the Samanid period had already developed bold designs to counter this effect, and their successors in Seljuk times developed a carved or incised technique. Sometimes potters carved the slip so that the slip-coated carved areas contrasted with the dark body behind. In other cases, potters filled the areas outlined with incised lines, with green, yellowish brown and purple glazes.

In addition to pottery, other decorative arts also flourished in Iran during the period of Seljuk rule. Fine manuscripts of the Koran continued to be made, though few are signed or dated. One exception is a copy transcribed and illuminated by Mahmud ibn al-Husain, a scribe from Kerman in the city of Hamadan, at the end of Jumada in year 559 of the *hegira* (April 1164). Like most of the Koran manuscripts attributed to this period, it was transcribed on paper in the round hand called *naskhi*. It is also embellished with fine illumination, not only for chapter headings, verse markers, and marginal rosettes, but also for full pages at the beginning and end of the volume. These carpet pages of arabesques and geometric designs are some of the highlights of Seljuk decoration.

Contemporary texts state that illustrated manuscripts were also produced for the Seljuks. The Seljuk historian al-Rawandi, for example, reported that in 1184/85 the Seljuk sultan Tughril II ordered a poetic anthology with portraits of the poets. Only one illustrated manuscript, however, has survived from the period, a copy of Aiyuqi's *Warqa and Gulshah*. One painting in it is signed by Abd al-Mumin ibn Muhammad, a painter from Khoi, a town in northwest Iran. He was active at the court of the Anatolian Seljuks, and so this manuscript should be attributed to Konya, c. 1250. Other manuscripts produced for the Great Seljuks probably had similar paintings with small, moon-faced figures, like those seen on contemporary ceramics, especially luster and enameled wares, but none of these manuscripts has survived.

Fine textiles were undoubtedly made for the Great Seljuks, but we cannot be absolutely sure which ones they are. Many of the silks once associated with the Seljuk period have been shown to be modern forgeries, and the only contemporary silk bearing the name of a ruler was made for the Seljuk sultan Kaiqubad ibn Kaikhusrau (1219–1237). Splendidly woven in gold on a crimson ground, it has roundels enclosing two addorsed lions. Arabesques fill the spaces between the roundels.

Ewer, Iran, probably Kashan, early 13th century, underglaze-painted fritware, height 29.1 cm,
Washington, Freer Gallery of Art
This ewer, in the form of a cockerel, is a *tour de force* of the Seljuk potters' art. It shows how they expanded the traditional repertory of shapes to include zoomorphic vessels and even small pieces of furniture, and developed underglaze painting, which allowed great freedom of design.

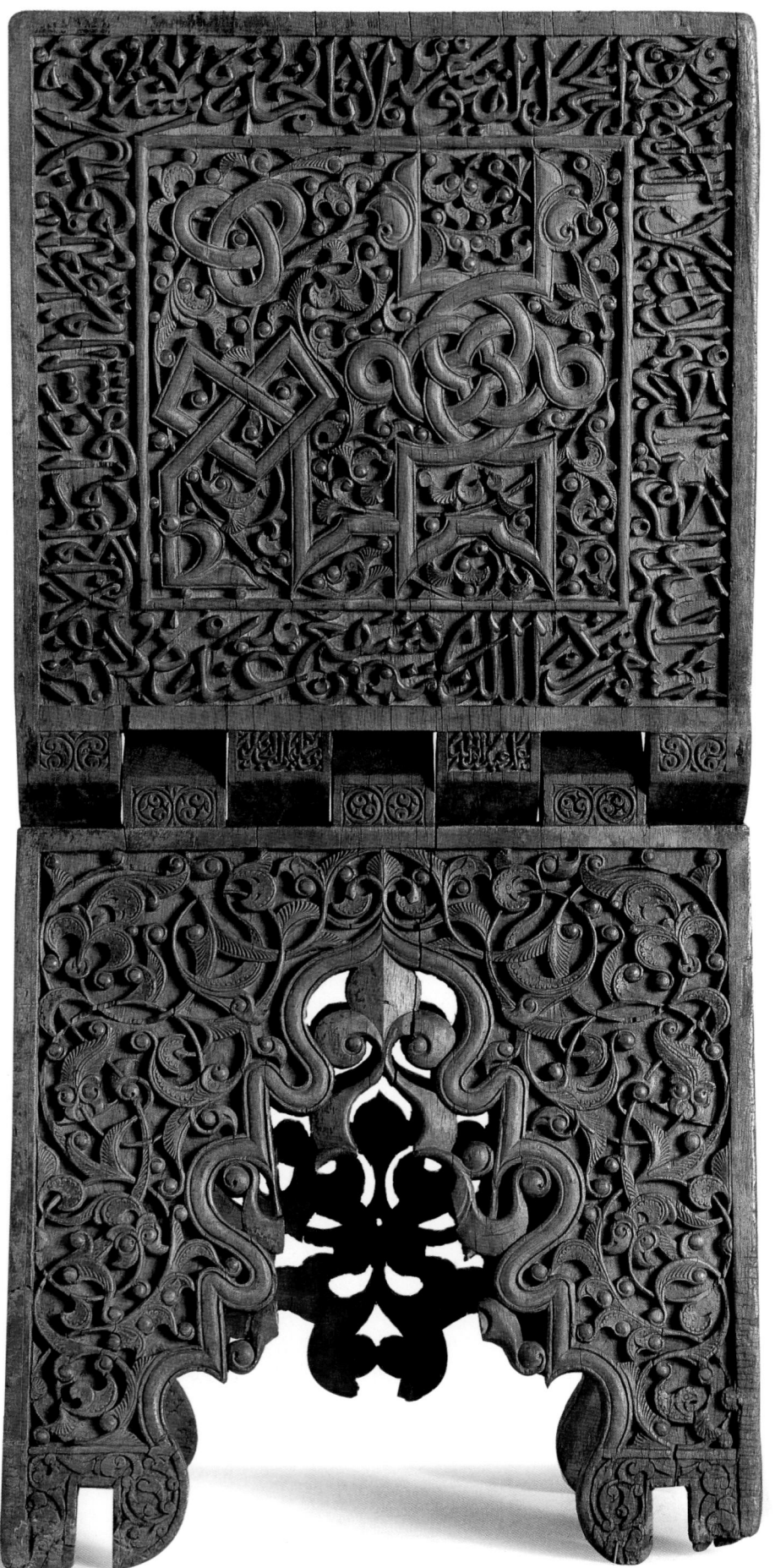

Decorative arts of the Anatolian Seljuks and Artuqids
Joachim Gierlichs

Architecture has a leading position in the art of the Anatolian Seljuks. Their decorative arts and their arts of the book appear as minor, in comparison. Contributing to this impression is the fact that many objects from the Seljuk period, but of no known provenance, have been almost automatically classified as Persian.

Despite the transitory nature of the material, numerous examples of Seljuk woodwork have survived, among them *minbars*, folding Koran stands (*rahle*), cenotaphs, doors, shutters, and a throne. Wood carving was already being executed in the "*kundekari* technique" by the middle of the 12th century, for example the *minbars* of the Ala al-Din Cami in Konya, which was made by Hajji Mengin Berti from Ahlat (eastern Turkey) in September 1155. Genuine *kundekari* consists of a framework holding in place polygonal, rhomboid, or star-shaped panels which are fixed together by means of tongue and groove construction without any additional form of fastening such as pins or glue. Apart from geometric and floral designs there is also evidence of a strong interest in the representation of living creatures. A series of wooden doors from the 12th or 13th centuries displays confronted or addorsed pairs of animals: lions, griffins, peacocks, and dragons. In the Mevlana Museum in Konya is a richly carved folding Koran stand (1279) which is unique for the lacquer painting on its inner surfaces: portrayed on a round medallion are a double eagle and 14 small lion figures springing from a web of tendrils.

In addition to the two major centers for metalwork in the 12th–13th centuries – Khorasan and northern Mesopotamia (Mosul) – a series of important metalware artifacts was also produced in Anatolia, which has its own ore deposits, in the 13th century. This includes round and polygonal brass candlesticks with silver inlays, heavy bronze mortars, incense burners, an openwork, gold-plated bronze lantern, a kettle drum, and bronze door knockers showing dragons facing each other and a lion head, which originally belonged to the doors of the Ulu Cami of Cizre. There are also numerous bronze mirrors, on the backs of which are depicted a pair of sphinxes with scorpion's tails, which can perhaps be interpreted as combining the characteristics of the neighboring astrological signs Leo, Virgo, and Scorpio. In addition, some of these mirrors feature talismanic signs and symbols on their fronts, suggesting some kind of magical function. Particularly interesting iconography is to be found on an iron mirror with gold inlays in the Topkapi Palace Museum. In the central medallion is a mounted prince, his head framed by a halo, with a hunting falcon in his hands. His horse is threatened by a snake-like dragon. In the border frieze, a pair of dragons with interlaced necks and gaping, backward-turning jaws form the centerpiece of a pair "animal processions," including two centaurs, with dragon-headed tails shooting arrows. On the front of another mirror, which was made in 1261/62 for the Artuqid Nur al-Din Artuq Shah of Harput, is the central motif of an eagle surrounded by the seven planets in the form of human busts, and outside these are the twelve signs of the zodiac.

Alongside Diyarbakir and Siirt in southeast Anatolia, Konya should be seen as a second center for metalworking. This is demonstrated, for example, by a hanging mosque lamp from the Esrefoglu Cami in Beysehir, which dates from

Folding Koran stand, 13th century, Berlin Museum für Islamische Kunst
This folding Koran stand (*rahle*), crafted from a single piece of wood, is one of relatively few examples from the Seljuk period. Its decoration is concentrated exclusively on the outer surfaces. The rich carving here skillfully combines geometric and floral motifs, and the central area is raised and decorated with an interlacing Kufic inscription.

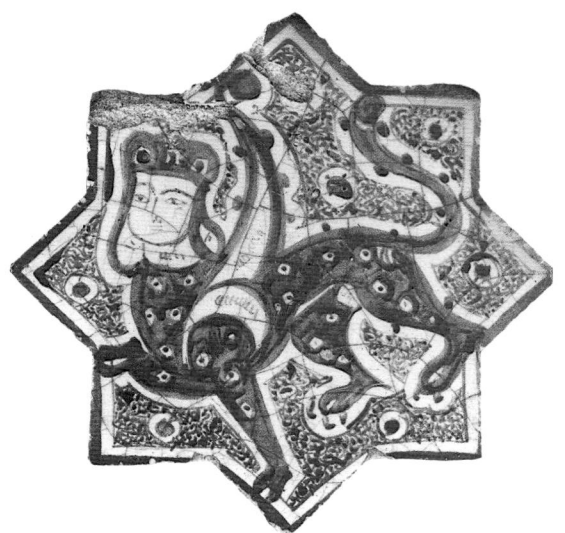

1280/81 and gives Konya as its place of manufacture and Ali ibn Muhammad from Nisibis (southeast Anatolia) as the craftsman who made it. It is noticeable that hardly any ceramic utensils have survived from the Seljuk period in Anatolia. Only from excavations have vases, bowls, plates, and jugs of white, unglazed clay been discovered, sometimes with figurative relief. Although a large number of luster tiles and also some using the *minai* technique have been found in the palaces, almost no Anatolian-manufactured lusterware pottery is known.

A lot of excitement has been generated by the large Seljuk carpets dating from the 13th century, the oldest knotted work of the Islamic period, which were discovered in the early 1900s in the Ala al-Din Cami in Konya and and the Esrefoglu Cami in Beysehir. Marco Polo, who journeyed through Asia Minor on his way to China, described them as "the finest in the world."

Illustrated manuscripts produced under, or commissioned by, the Anatolian Seljuks are extremely rare. One of these is the *Varqa and Gulshah* manuscript. This

Star-shaped tiles from the palace at Qubadabad, today mainly in the Karatay Museum in Konya
These luster and underglaze-painted wall tiles, discovered during the course of excavations at the summer palace of Ala al-Din Kaiqubad in Qubadabad during the 1960s, display a figurative repertoire not previously encountered. They are an impressive demonstration of the openness of the Anatolian Seljuks, in particular their rulers, towards figurative representation.

romance was written by Aiyuqi in the 11th century for the Ghaznavid sultan Mahmud. Manuscripts were also copied and illustrated at the Artuqid court of Nasir al-Din Mahmud (1201–1222) in Diyarbakir, as is demonstrated by the "Automata manuscript," a scientific work with over 150 drawings by al-Jazari in 1206, which concerns the construction of mechanical automata.

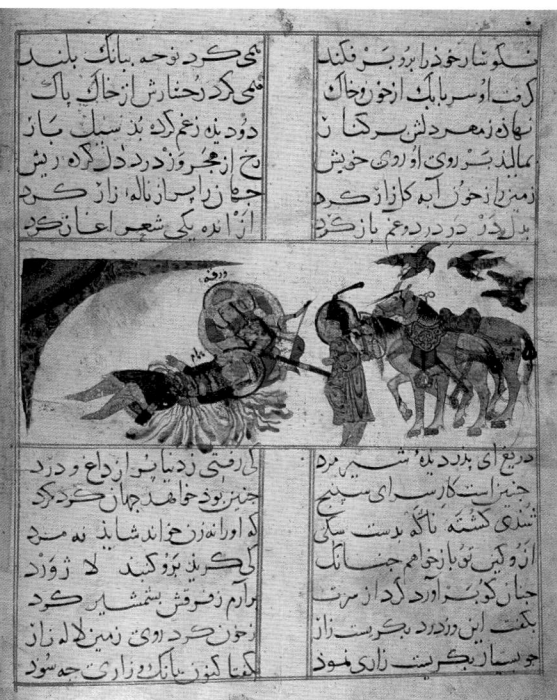

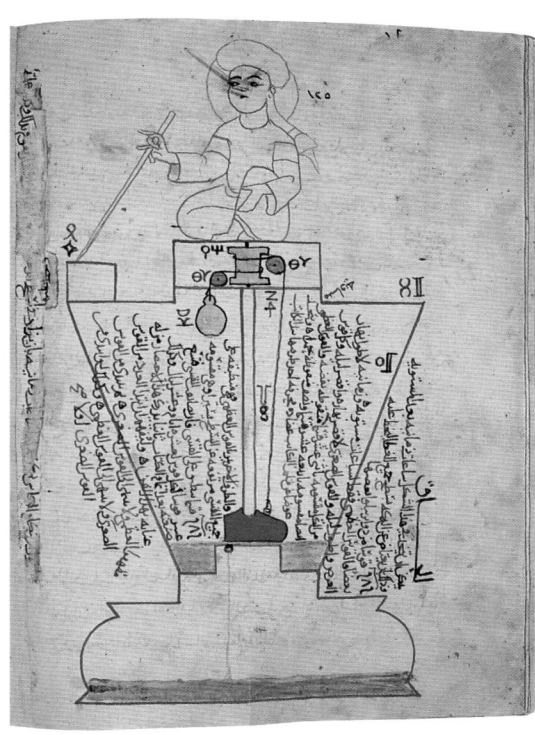

Two illustrated pages from the *Varqa and Gulshah* manuscript, mid-13th century, Istanbul, Topkapi Palace Museum
The *Varqa and Gulshah* manuscript, which may have been produced at the court at Konya, is a rare example of Anatolian Seljuk book illustration. Abd al-Mumim al-Khuwayi is named as the illustrator on one of its pages. The page-width miniatures,

interposed between the top and bottom halves of the two-column text, illustrate events from Aiyuqi's tragic love story. The page on the left shows Gulshah lying indisposed in her tent, being tended by her anxious mother, while on the right hand page, Varqa's father, Humam, lays dying in Varqa's arms.

Page from the "Automata manuscript" of al-Jazari, Muhammad ibn Yusuf ibn Uthman al-Haskafi, 1205, Istanbul, Topkapi Palace Museum
The page shown here explains and illustrates a beaker-shaped water clock activated by the changing water levels inside it.

Islamic Mongols: from the Mongol Invasions to the Ilkhanids

Alexander's Iron Cavalry, manuscsript of the *Shahname* by Firdausi, Tabriz, c. 1335, Cambridge, Mass., Harvard University Art Museums
The illustrations to the great Mongolian *Shahname* not only demonstrate the Mongols' arts of the book, but depict their whole epoch, as this miniature shows. Alexander had the inspired idea of confronting the huge elephants of the Indian cavalry with his own Iron Cavalry: horses and riders of metal and on wheels, filled with oil. The Cavalry rolled, with nostrils aflame, towards the Indian army, which took one look at this enemy and fled. In order to dramatize the scene, the illustrator has used expensive paints; silver for the iron soldiers and gold for the flames. The intensity, richness of color, and inventiveness of this painting give an enduring impression of the cosmopolitan and highly cultured world of the Persian Ilkhanids.

History
Sheila Blair, Jonathan Bloom

From the early 13th century, much of Asia was ruled by various descendants of the great Mongol conqueror Genghis Khan. In this new global empire, Europe was linked to China for the first time since the Romans. This Pax Mongolica fostered trade and communication between East and West, so that artists and artistic ideas, as well as merchants and merchandise, moved from China to the Mediterranean and vice versa. Unlike the Great Khans – the descendants of Genghis Khan who ruled China as the Yuan dynasty from 1279 until 1368 – most of his other descendants ruling in western Asia eventually converted to Islam, notably the Golden Horde in southern Russia, the Chaghatayids in Khwarazmia, and the Ilkhanids in Iran. Like the Great Khans, these three Mongol dynasties remained in power until the late 14th century, when Timur, the next great conqueror from the steppe, briefly and violently reunited much of South, West, and Central Asia under the revived banner of Genghisid legitimacy. Mongol prestige remained so strong that minor branches continued to rule in remote areas of the Islamic lands until the 17th century.

Capture of Baghdad by the Mongols, miniature probably from the *Compendium of Chronicles* of Rashid al-Din, Tabriz, early 14th century, Berlin, Staatsbibliothek In 1258 the Mongols captured Baghdad, the capital of the Abbasid Empire. In the foreground are the Mongols, recognizable by their feathered hats, who are catapulting missiles across the river. Above left three people are escaping from the palace in a boat. Their turbans denote that they are Muslims, perhaps the fleeing Abbasids.

Genghis Khan and his heirs

One of the very greatest conquerors of all times, Genghis Khan (c. 1167–1227) came from modest beginnings. His father was a minor chieftain, or khan, of a Mongol clan in the vast Asiatic steppe to the north and east of Central Asia.

Originally named Temujin ("Blacksmith"), the young warrior rose gradually to prominence by defeating other local chieftains in the region and, in so doing, gained the title of Chinggis (Turkish: "oceanic" or "universal") and later anglicized as Genghis. At an assembly, or *quriltai*, in 1206, Genghis Khan was proclaimed supreme chief (Great Khan) of all the Turko-Mongolian peoples. He and his armies soon expanded their conquests beyond Mongolia and vanquished most of Eurasia, from the China Sea to the banks of the Dnieper.

According to Mongol custom, after a leader's death his territory was divided among family members. Genghis Khan, though the most powerful Mongol leader, was no exception and, before he died in 1227, parceled out his territory among his four sons, allotting each of them a stretch of pasture ground, or *yurt*, for his followers and herds. Descendants of Genghis' sons, in turn, followed as rulers of the different territories, and descent from Genghis became the chief means of political legitimization in the region for several centuries. This era was

Some of the finest examples of Islamic architecture and art were produced under the patronage of these three great Mongol dynasties. Understandably, their art incorporates elements from many traditions – Islamic, Iranian, Central Asian, Chinese, and even European. Many of the building types such as mosques and tombs belong to the standard Islamic repertory. Indigenous Iranian features include the squinch and glazed tilework. Certain Mongol characteristics, such as the love of gold, were incorporated from the steppe tradition. Chinese motifs, such as the dragon, peony, and chrysanthemum, were combined with elements drawn from European traditions, such as an interest in developing pictorial space through the use of such devices as perspective and the repoussoir figure. These pictorial devices, which were probably introduced by European merchants traveling through Mongol domains, can be seen in illustrated manuscripts, especially in copies of the Persian national epic, the *Shahname* (Book of Kings), by the poet Firdausi (d. 1020), which became particularly important in this period. Altogether, the art of the Mongol period is marked by the blending of many diverse elements into an extremely sophisticated and colorful whole.

thus distinguished from most others in Islamic history, when legitimacy was determined by descent from the Prophet Muhammad.

Following steppe practice, the eldest son received the pasturelands farthest from the home camp. Genghis's eldest son Jöchi therefore received the territory of western Siberia and the Kipchak steppe, extending into southern Russia and Khwarazmia. Jöchi died before his father, and Jöchi's appanage was divided between his sons. The elder son, Orda (1226–1280), received the eastern part of his father's territories, or western Siberia, where he founded the line known as the White Horde. The younger son, Batu (1227–1255), received the western part of his father's lands, southern Russia, where he founded the Blue Horde, later known as the Golden Horde.

The Golden Horde ruled from two capitals on the Volga, both called Saray ("palace" or "court"). The first, known as Old Saray, was located 78 miles (125 kilometers) north of Astrakhan on the left bank of the Akhtuba, a tributary of the Volga. It served as capital until the 1340s, when Janibeg (1342–1357) moved the capital 78 miles (125 kilometers) further north to New Saray (modern Zarew), on the Akhtuba just below the great bend of the Volga. Muslim sources from the 14th and 15th centuries also mention a third city, Saray Berke, referring to a capital founded by Berke (1257–1266), the first ruler of the Golden Horde to embrace Islam. Berke's capital, however, was probably

no more than a pious fiction. From the time of Janibeg, all the khans of the Golden Horde were Muslims, although most of their subjects remained Orthodox Christians. The Golden Horde had important trade links with Anatolia and supplied slaves for the Mamluk rulers of Egypt and Syria but, with the expansion of the Ottomans in 15th-century Anatolia and Thrace, the Golden Horde was cut off from the Mediterranean and became a regional power in southern Russia alone.

In the late 14th century, one of Orda's more energetic descendants, Toqtamish (1377–1395), united the Golden Horde with the White Horde. He extended power further north into Russia, sacking Nizhni Novgorod and Moscow in 1382. After his death, however, the Golden Horde began to disintegrate. Foreign powers encroached from the north, and the khanates of Astrakhan, Kazan, Qasimov, and the Crimea split off. Finally, in 1502 the last

khan of the Golden Horde was defeated, and the Golden Horde was absorbed into the Crimean Tartar Horde.

Genghis's second son Chaghatai (1227–1241) received the Central Asian lands north of Transoxiana. As the eldest surviving son of Genghis and an expert in Mongol tribal law, the *yasa*, Chaghatai held great influence. The real founder of the Chaghatayid line, however, was his grandson Aluju (1260–1266), who took advantage of squabbling among other Genghisid heirs to seize Khwarazmia, western Turkestan, and Afghanistan. These territories became the nucleus of the Chaghatayid khanate. Because of its geographical position, the Chaghatayids preserved their tribal and nomadic ways longer than other branches of the Genghisids. Some Chaghatayid rulers converted to Islam; others did not. Like the Golden Horde, the Chaghatayids began to fall apart in the 14th century, when they fell prey to Timur, who conquered the western

Above: **The Mausoleum of Üljaitü at Sultaniya**, Iran, 1315–1325
The Ilkhanid ruler Arghun founded the city of Sultaniya ("The Imperial") in the grassy plain northwest of Qazvin, and his son Üljaitü made it the Ilkhanid capital. Contemporary descriptions mention the bustling markets, huge mosque, and powerful walls, but all that remains is Üljaitü's colossal tomb, which was once the center of a pious foundation comprising places for prayer and instruction as well as various social services.

Right: **The court of the Ilkhanids**, double-page frontispiece probably from the *Compendium of Chronicles* by Rashid al-Din, Tabriz, early 14th century, Berlin, Staatsbibliothek
This illustration shows the Mongol khan and his wife on the throne, with the courtiers arranged in serried ranks, always with women to the ruler's right. Members of the ruler's family are distinguished by clothing and headgear: women wear the *bughtaq*, the distinctive tall Mongol headdress, while men wear feathered hats, with the number of eagle feathers identifying their rank.

389

Chaghatayid khanate in 1363. However a branch of the Chaghatayids held on to power in eastern Central Asia until the 17th century.

Genghis's third son Ügedei had been his father's favorite. Genghis had wanted Ügedei to succeed him as Great Khan, and this position was confirmed by a *quriltai* in 1229. Within a generation, however, the Great Khanate had passed to descendants of Genghis's fourth and youngest son Tolui, who had initially received the heartland of the empire, Mongolia itself. Tolui's sons, Möngke (1251–1260) and Qubilai (1260–1294), and their descendants, ruled as Great Khans from their capitals, first at Qaraqorum in Mongolia and later at Beijing. In China, they ruled as the Yuan dynasty until 1368, when the native Ming overthrew them, but one branch of Tolui's descendants continued to rule in Mongolia until the 17th century. As the Great Khans and many of their followers became Buddhists, they came into conflict with the subordinate khans in western Asia and Russia, most of whom had adopted Islam.

The Ilkhanid Empire in Persia

In the autumn of 1253, the Great Khan Möngke sent his brother Hülägü to recover the territories in western Asia that had slipped from Mongol grasp after the death of Genghis. Moving westward across Iran, Hülägü took Baghdad, the capital of the Abbasid caliphate, in 1258. He assumed the title

Detail of a tapestry, China, c. 1330–1332, silk, width c. 38 cm, New York, Metropolitan Museum of Art
This portrait, which comes from a Buddhist mandala (representation of a magical and sacred realm), depicts the two donors, the brothers and Chinese emperors Wenzong and Mingzon. As members of the Yuan dynasty they could legitimize their rule via their ancestor Ghengis Khan.

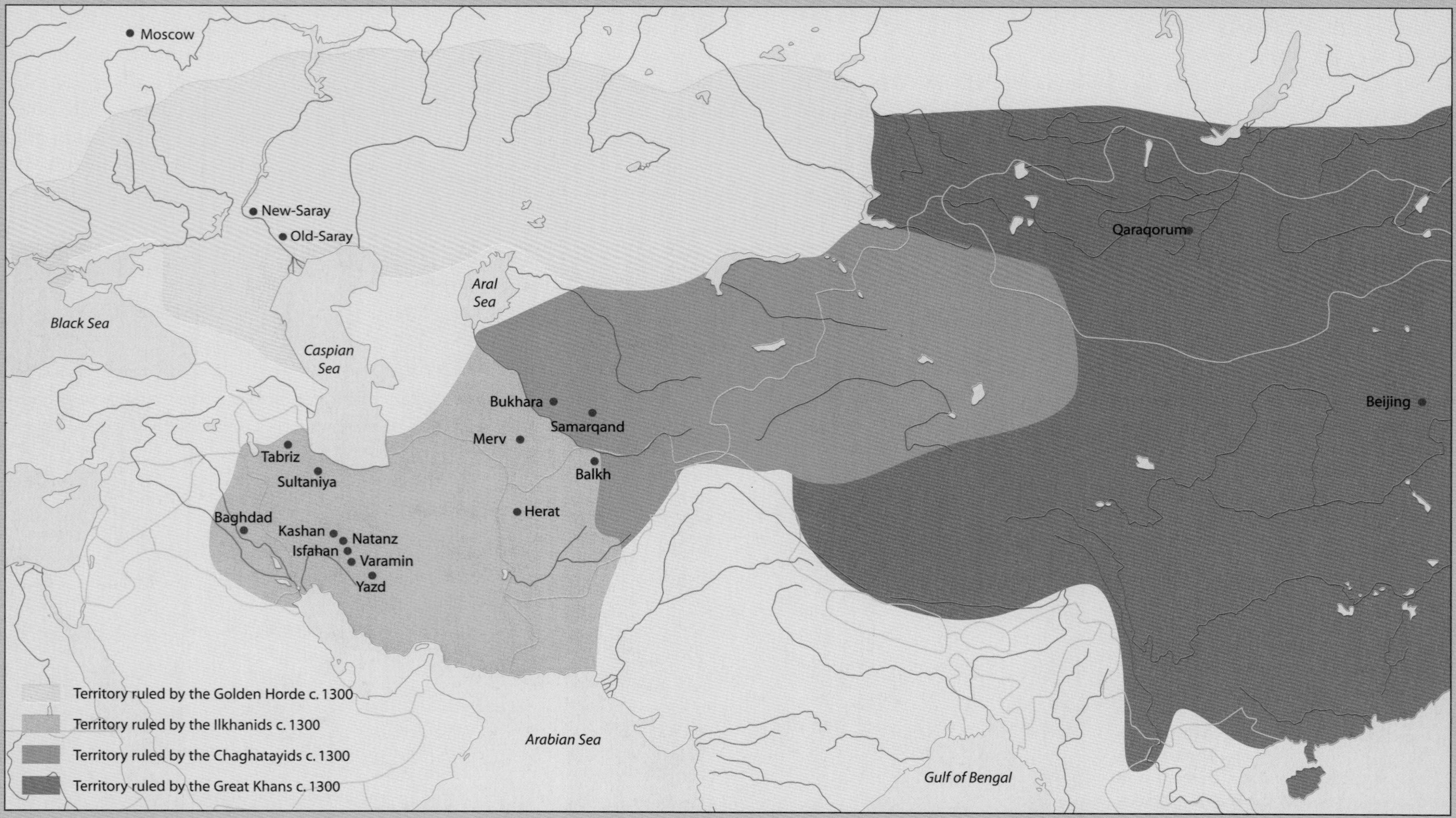

Moscow

New-Saray
Old-Saray

Aral Sea

Black Sea

Caspian Sea

Qaraqorum

Bukhara
Samarqand
Merv
Balkh

Beijing

Tabriz
Sultaniya

Herat

Baghdad
Kashan Natanz
Isfahan
Varamin
Yazd

Arabian Sea

Gulf of Bengal

Territory ruled by the Golden Horde c. 1300
Territory ruled by the Ilkhanids c. 1300
Territory ruled by the Chaghatayids c. 1300
Territory ruled by the Great Khans c. 1300

ilkhan, "subordinate or peaceful khan," in deference to his brother, the Great Khan in China, and ruled a territory similar in extent to that of the Sassanian empire of pre-Islamic times. Hülägü and his immediate successors remained dependent on the Great Khans in China but, after Qubilai died in 1294 and Hülägü's great-grandson Ghazan (1295–1304) converted to Islam, the close ties between the two branches of Mongols weakened.

The reigns of Ghazan, his brother and successor Üljaitü Muhammad Khudabanda (1304–1316), and his son Abu Said (1316–1335) marked the apogee of Ilkhanid power in Iran. Ghazan's conversion led to a reconciliation between the Turko-Mongolian elite and their Persian subjects, and the state evolved from a nomadic Central Asian regime into a sedentary Islamic polity. Despite warfare and internal strife, the economy prospered and cultural life flourished. Ilkhanid power was centered in northwestern Iran, where the fertile plains were a potent attraction to the seminomadic Mongols, and the capital cities at Tabriz and Sultaniya became entrepôts for an international trade connecting Europe and the Orient.

Soon after Abu Said's death in the year 1335, however, this cosmopolitan world fell apart. Although a series of Ilkhanid princes tried to maintain power for another 20 years, the outlying territories broke away, with local dynasts grabbing power until Timur reunited Iran under a single authority in the year 1370.

The Chinese khan visits the king, manuscript of the *Shahname* of Firdausi, Iran or Iraq, c. 1300, Paris, Louvre
The *Shahname* enjoyed great popularity under the Ilkhanids, who saw themselves as the heirs of the great line of Iranian kings. The illustrations of the text clothe events of the distant past in contemporary Mongol costumes.

1206	Genghis Khan (c. 1167–1227) is recognized as supreme leader (Great Khan) of all the Turko-Mongolian peoples
1215	The Mongols capture Beijing
1218	A Mongolian trade caravan is held up by the Khwarazmians; the merchants, at the command of the shah, are executed
1219–1220	Campaign of revenge by the Mongols: Khwarazmia and Transoxiana are conquered
!227	Death of Ghengis Khan and partition of the empire: the White Horde under Ordu (1226–1280) in west Siberia; the Golden Horde in southern Russia and Khwarazmia under Batu (1227–1255), the Chaghatayids under Chaghatai (1229–1241) in Transoxiana; Ügedei (1227–1241) established in northern China and Mongolia (Qaraqorum); and Tolui ruling in the heartland of Mongolia
1229	Ügedei is confirmed as Great Khan of the whole tribal group
1241	Battle of Liegnitz; Battle of Sajo River: the Golden Horde defeats a German-Polish army and a Hungarian army under Bela IV
1242/1243	Battle of Kose Dag, Anatolia: the Mongols defeat the Anatolian Seljuks
1253	Hülägü, commissioned by Möngke (1251–1260), begins campaigns into West Asia
1257–1266	Reign of Berke, first Muslim khan of the Golden Horde
1258	The Mongols under Hülägü capture Baghdad, terminate the Abbasid caliphate there, and found the Ilkhanid Empire in Persia (capital in Tabriz)
1260	Battle of Ain Jalut, Palestine: the defeat of the Mongols by Mamluks under Baibars checks the further westward expansion of the Ilkhanid Empire
1260–1266	The Chaghatayid Empire was reinforced during the reign of Aluju; Khwarazmia, western Turkestan, and Afghanistan were incorporated
1260–1294	Reign of the Great Khan Qubilai, who founded the Mongolian Yuan dynasty (1279–1368) in northern China
1295–1304	Reign of Ghazan, who converted to Sunni Islam
1307	The new capital Sultaniya is founded under the Ilkhanid Üljaitü Muhammad Khudabanda (1304–1316)
1310	Üljaitü adopts Shiite Islam
1316–1335	Reign of the Sunnite Ilkhanid Abu Said; end of Ilkhanid rule
1323	Mamluks and Ilkhanids agree a peace treaty
1342–1357	Reign of Janibeg; conversion of the khans of the Golden Horde to Islam
1360–1405	The Mongol Timur Lenk (1370–1405) declares himself the restorer of Mongol hegemony: he brings Transoxiana, Persia, Mesopotamia, part of Russia, India, and Anatolia under his rule and founds the Timurid dynasty (lasts until 1506)
1368	The Chinese Ming expel the Mongolian Yuan dynasty from Beijing
1377–1395	Reign of Toqtamish; he unites the White and the Golden Hordes (1378)
1382	The Mongols under Toqtamish plunder Moscow
1395	Death of Toqtamish, and the dissolution of the Golden Horde begins: the khanates of Astrakhan (1466–1556), Kazan (1445–1552), Qasimov (1452–1681), and the Crimea (1430–1783)
1502	Death of Sheikh Ahman (1481–1502), the last khan of the Golden Horde

Palace at Takht-i Sulaiman, c. 1275

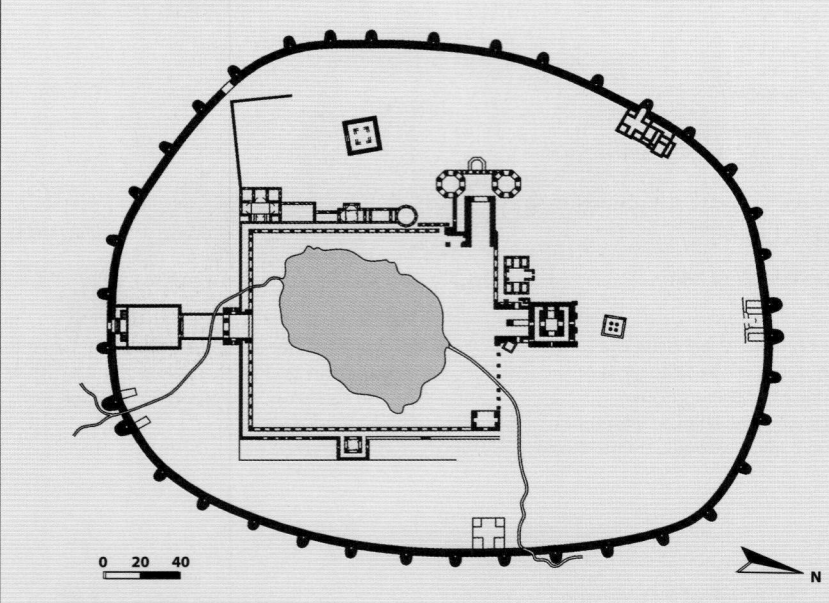

Palace at Takht-i Sulaiman, c. 1275
Like the mosque at Tabriz, the Ilkhanid summer palace at Takht-i Sulaiman was designed to connect the Mongol rulers with their pre-Islamic past. It was begun by the Ilkhanid ruler Abaqa (1265–1285) on the foundations of the sanctuary where the Sassanian emperors had been crowned. In the center, a huge courtyard encompassed an artificial lake. The court had an *iwan* on each of its four sides. The north *iwan* led to a domed room, which had been the site of the Sassanian fire temple and probably served as Abaqa's throne hall.

0   20   40

N

Architecture
Sheila Blair, Jonathan Bloom

Architecture in Iran under the Ilkhanids

The devastations caused by the Mongol invasions of Iran caused a hiatus in building, but construction soon resumed once the Ilkhanids were in power. Like their Mongol forebears in the steppes, the Ilkhanids continued the tradition of transhumance, moving between summer pastures in the grassy plains of northwest Iran and winter quarters around Baghdad in Mesopotamia. Hülägü's son Abaqa (1265–1282) began construction of a summer palace southeast of Lake Urmiya in Azarbaijan in northwestern Iran.

The palace was finished under his son Arghun (1284–1291). Now known as Takht-i Sulaiman ("Solomon's Throne"), it stands on the foundations of the Sassanian sanctuary of Shiz, the site where the Sassanian emperors had been crowned. By choosing this specific site, the Mongols connected themselves with the kings of pre-Islamic Iran. Enclosed within an oval wall protected by towers, the Ilkhanid palace had a huge central courtyard 410 × 490 feet (125 × 150 meters) oriented north-south and encompassing an artificial lake. The courtyard was surrounded by a portico and had an *iwan* on each of its four sides. The north *iwan* led to a domed room, which occupied the site of the Sassanian fire temple and probably served as Abaqa's audience hall. The west *iwan* led to a transverse hall flanked by two octagonal pavilions. Formerly the throne room of the Sassanian king Khusrau, it became the living quarters of the Ilkhanid ruler.

Abundant fragments of fine decoration from the palace at Takht-i Sulaiman show the high quality of construction. A *muqarnas* vault covered the southern pavilion, and the northern pavilion had a tiled dado. The lower tile courses were composed of star- and cross-shaped tiles, overglaze-painted in a technique known as *lajvardina* (from Persian: *lajvard*, "lapis lazuli,") because some of them are covered with a dark blue glaze. The dark blue tiles were set alternately with others glazed a light turquoise blue color. The star tiles, and some of the luster tiles above, were decorated with dragons and *senmurvs*, the human-headed birds of Iranian myth. Other luster tiles were decorated with verses and scenes illustrating the themes of the *Shahname*, the Persian national epic composed about 1010 at the court of Mahmud of Ghazna. By choosing such decoration for their palace, the Mongol Ilkhanids were making yet another connection between themselves and the glorious Iranian past.

Architectural patronage accelerated with the accession of Arghun's son Ghazan in 1295. Ghazan converted to Islam, and he and his Persian vizier Rashid al-Din (d. 1318), a convert from Judaism, inaugurated a vast program of economic reforms that provided a basis for significant amounts of new construction. Caravanserais were built along the main trade routes, and each

Decorated tiles from the palace at Takht-i Sulaiman, Iran, late 13th or 14th century, fritware, diameter 24.8 cm
The Mongols preferred monochrome turquoise or cobalt blue tiles, overglaze-painted in color and gold, to the luster-painted tiles that had been popular for wall-decoration in previous centuries. They are often known as *lajvardina* wares, after the Persian word for lapis lazuli. Many tiles feature dragons and other Chinese motifs.

Opposite: **External view of the *qibla* wall of the Mosque of Ali Shah**, Tabriz, 1315
Although the four-*iwan* plan had been standard for Friday mosques in Iran since the Seljuk period, other types were also constructed. One of the biggest was that built by the Ilkhanid vizier Ali Shah in the capital at Tabriz. It had one large *iwan* facing the courtyard, which was surrounded by walls 25 m high and 10 m thick, with a perimeter of 30 m. The *mihrab* was set in a huge semicylindrical bastion projecting behind the *qibla* wall and flanked by two large doorways. The mosque's walls were built of plain brick, but travelers to the city reported that the mosque's forecourt was paved with marble and the walls revetted with glittering tiles. A Sufi hospice and *madrasa* abutted the *iwan*. Apart from the *qibla* wall, the whole site has been the victim of the region's frequent earthquakes.

city in the realm was given a Friday (congregational) mosque and accompanying *hammam*, with the revenues from the bath used to support the mosque. The city of Tabriz became the capital, with a new wall measuring some 8 miles (12 kilometers) around, four times the perimeter of the old wall.

According to contemporary accounts by travelers and historians, Tabriz was a bustling entrepôt famed for its textiles (especially gold cloth), precious stones, and spices. It owed its commercial pre-eminence to its geographical position at the junction of several trade routes. The east-west route led across Khorasan to Central Asia, China, or northern India, or via the Black Sea to Constantinople. Another route led overland from Tabriz to Baghdad and then to the Mediterranean. Alternatively, one could head south from Tabriz to reach the Persian Gulf and then reach India and China by sea. The bustling bazaars of Tabriz indicated the commercial importance of the capital. Although they have been much rebuilt, they must have been spectacular at the time, and they probably served as the model for those built by the Safavid Shah Abbas (1588–1629) at Isfahan in the early 17th century.

Above: Caravanserai at Sing
The Mongol economy was based on overland trade, facilitated by Mongol domination of much of Eurasia. To encourage this trade, the Ilkhanids built caravanserais throughout their domains. Few, however, have survived, as the use they received was heavy and damaging. The typical caravanserai was built of brick or stone and had a single entrance that could be locked at night. Inside was a large courtyard with *iwans* connected by rooms around the four sides.

Ground plan of the Mosque of Ali Shah, Tabriz, c. 1315
In front of the colossal *iwan* was once a square courtyard with sides that were 150 ells long and in the middle of which was a pool.

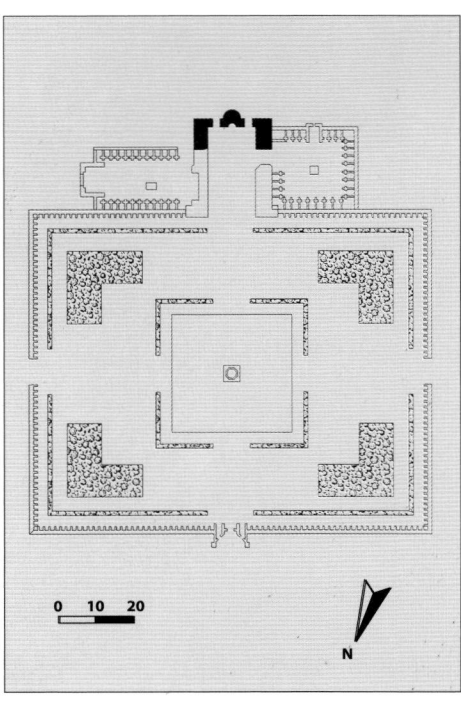

Qibla *iwan* and domed prayer hall, Varamin Mosque, 1322–1326

Mosques built under the Ilkhanids display many of the features that had been standard in Iranian mosques for several centuries. In plan, these mosques usually had large court-yards with four *iwans* and a domed prayer hall behind the *iwan* that faced Mecca. In elevation, the square dome chamber was transformed into an octagon, which in turn supported a 16-sided zone that supported the hemispheric base of the dome. All of these features can be found in the semi-ruined mosque at Varamin.

Below: **Squinch in the Varamin Mosque**

Squinches are used to bridge the corner of a square room and provide a base to support the dome above. From at least the 10th century it was realized that the back of the squinch carries no load and was thereby open to any decorative treatment. Here, in the 14th century, the back of the squinch was filled with *muqarnas*, projecting series of stucco niches, which, although not load bearing, provided visual support for the dome.

Below: **Dome above the prayer hall in the Varamin Mosque**, 1322–1326

As was usual in Iran for centuries, the four squinches alternate with four blind arches, each pieced by a window, to create an eight-sided zone of transition. This eight-sided zone, in turn, supports a 16-sided zone with eight windows alternating with eight blind panels. This dome support solution had been standard since the Seljuk period, but the elongated proportions, fine stucco carving, and intricate brick decoration here form a classic example of 14th-century Iranian architecture.

Mosques

Earthquakes and subsequent invasions have destroyed most of Tabriz. The major building to survive there from Ilkhanid times is the Friday mosque built by the vizier Ali Shah around 1315. It consisted of a large courtyard, 150 ells each side, with a central pool. On the *qibla* side was a gigantic brick *iwan*, once flanked by a *madrasa* and a hospice for Sufis. The vault of the *iwan*, which subsequently collapsed, originally spanned 98 feet (30 meters) and sprang from walls 33 feet (10 meters) thick and 82 feet (25 meters) high. In its own day, it was lauded as larger than the *iwan* at Ctesiphon, the Sassanian palace outside Baghdad, which was considered to be one of the wonders of the world. Visitors once marveled at its rich revetment in marble and tile, although only the baked brick walls remain. As at Takht-i Sulaiman, the Mongol rulers and their viziers used architecture to connect the Mongols with the pre-Islamic Iranian past.

In the Ilkhanid period, the standard type of Friday mosque had a courtyard with four *iwans* and a dome, a plan that had already become standard in the Seljuk period. The best-preserved example is the Friday mosque built between 1322 and 1326 at Varamin, 26 miles (42 kilometers) south of Tehran. The domed chamber shows the classic elevation developed in the Seljuk period, in which a square base supports a zone of transition with four squinches alternating with four blind arches. Above this a 16-sided zone supports the dome. The Varamin Mosque is distinguished from its Seljuk prototypes by its attenuated proportions, its small courtyard, and its extensive but routine use of tile mosaic.

A distinctive variant of this four-*iwan* plan developed in Yazd and its environs during the Ilkhanid period: Friday mosques have four *iwans* arranged around a courtyard, but the domed chamber is flanked by rectangular halls roofed with transverse vaults. This plan was used at the Friday Mosque in Yazd itself, which was rebuilt 1325–1334 by a local notable, Shams al-Din Nizami. One of the most prominent features of the mosque is its monumental tiled portal with two tall minarets. As Shams al-Din had married the daughter of the vizier Rashid al-Din, he had spent much time in Tabriz, and such new features of the Yazd Mosque as galleries on an upper floor and the easy flow of space between the sanctuary and the side halls were probably copied from now-lost buildings in the Ilkhanid capitals in northwest Iran.

Tombs

The greatest architectural projects from the Ilkhanid period are tomb complexes. The first Ilkhanids, like their Mongol forebears, had concealed their grave sites but when Ghazan converted to Islam he adopted Islamic burial traditions, as they had evolved in Iran, and ordered a charitable foundation to surround his "lofty" tomb in a western suburb of Tabriz. The complex included a hospice, hospital, library, observatory, academy of philosophy, fountain, pavillion, and two *madrasas*. Only vestiges remain at the site and at the analogous complex built by his vizier, Rashid al-Din, on the east side of Tabriz, but the high quality of the surviving tile decoration matches the fulsome descriptions given in the texts.

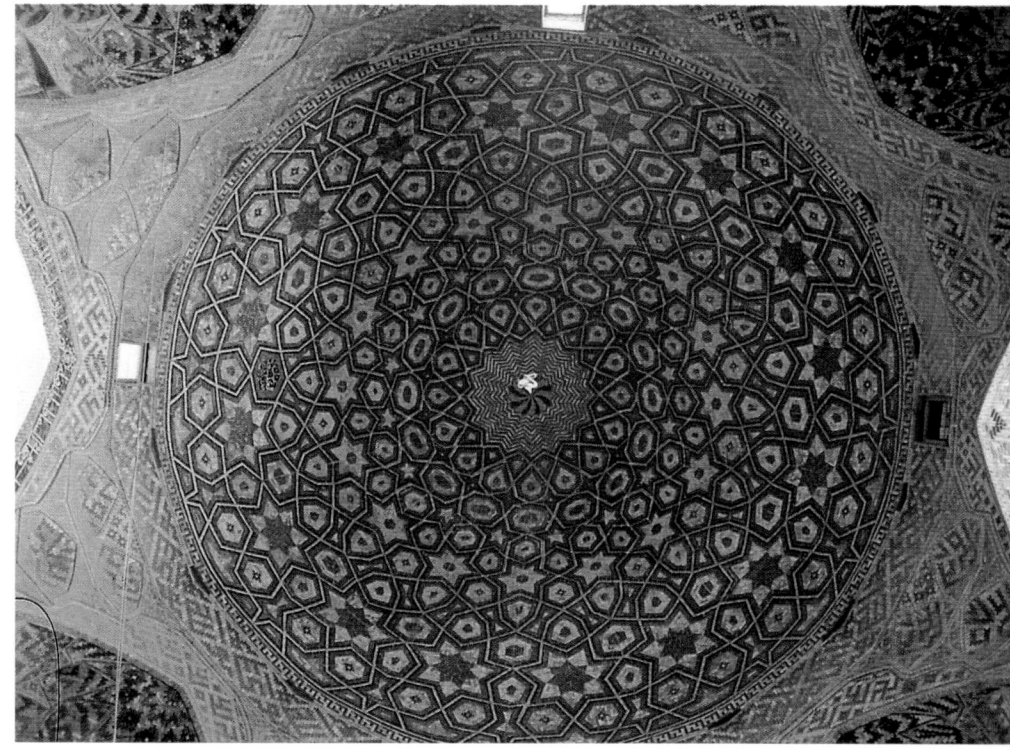

Portal and dome of the Friday Mosque of Yazd, 1325 and later
The Friday Mosque at Yazd in central Iran has one of the finest examples of the classic Iranian monumental portal surmounted by paired minarets. The fine decoration in colored tile and the tall and slender proportions make this portal a masterpiece. The portal was restored several times, and as its proportions became increasingly attenuated, buttresses had to be added on the sides to stop it from collapsing. This mosque also has the best tile decoration from the Ilkhanid period in Iran. The tile mosaic in the prayer hall, with radiating stars on a blue ground, was undoubtedly an allusion to the starry firmament and the almighty power of God.

Tomb of Üljaitü at Sultaniya, 1315–1325
The tomb of the Ilkhanid sultan Üljaitü at Sultaniya is one of the masterpieces of world architecture. Its enormous dome, spanning some 25 m, has often been compared to its contemporary one at the Duomo in Florence, though no relationship between the two has ever been established. The turquoise-tiled dome at Sultaniya, once encircled by eight minarets, seems to float above the surrounding plain. To the south (right) is a large hall that may have housed the cenotaph of the sultan.

Some idea of the magnificence and scale of these royal tomb complexes is given by the one built by Ghazan's brother and successor Üljaitü at Sultaniya. Arghun had chosen the site, some 75 miles (120 kilometers) northwest of Qazvin on the road to Tabriz, as his summer residence, and Üljaitü transformed it into the capital of his empire. The tomb is an enormous octagon, measuring some 125 feet (38 meters) in diameter and oriented almost cardinally, with a rectangular hall 50 × 66 feet (15 × 20 meters) appended on the south. Crowned by eight minarets and surmounted by a dome 165 feet (50 meters) high, the octagon contains a vast hall which has eight arched openings with balconies overlooking the interior. Hidden from the interior but above them on the exterior, a ring of galleries surveys the surrounding plain and provides a visual transition from the flat walls (which probably abutted subsidiary structures on

several sides) to the ethereal blue-glazed dome. This subtle design of interpenetrating volumes is complemented by the sophisticated treatment of the gallery vaults, which display a wide variety of carved and plaster motifs, painted in red, yellow, green, and white. Many of the strapwork designs closely resemble those found in contemporary manuscript illumination, suggesting that Ilkhanid designers were among the first to use paper patterns for realization on different scales in architecture and manuscripts. The lofty interior, one of the largest uninterrupted spaces of medieval times, comes as an awesome surprise after the stately exterior. The spatial sophistication and grandeur attest to the abilities of the designer(s), who were able to give physical form to the sultan's desire for monumentality with elegance and grace.

The tomb complexes of the Ilkhanid rulers and their viziers were the largest in the realm, but small complexes were built for other dignitaries and local notables. Many were constructed for Sufis. At Natanz in central Iran, for example, the grave of Abd al-Samad (d. 1299), the leading Suhrawardi sheikh (elder) of the day, was developed into a major shrine complex in the decade following his death. The vizier Zain al-Din Mastari refurbished the town's Friday mosque and built a tomb for the sheikh, a minaret, and a hospice for Sufis adjacent to it. The glory of the complex is the tomb, which is covered by a superb *muqarnas* vault, the finest to survive from the period. The interior was once revetted with luster tiles, often recognizable by a frieze of paired birds. The heads of the birds were later defaced by some zealous iconoclast who judged them in contravention of Islam's supposed ban on images. Large, specially ordered luster tiles also decorated the *mihrab* and the cenotaph marking the grave.

Detail of the dome of the Tomb of Üljaitü at Sultaniya,
In addition to tile mosaic, Ilkhanid builders used the *banna-i*, or "builders'" technique, in which rectangular glazed bricks were inset among the matte buff-colored bricks to make patterns or spell out sacred names and pious phrases. Here, for example, the base of the dome is encircled on the exterior with the words "God," "Muhammad," and "Ali," referring to the Shiite beliefs of the Ilkhanids.

Opposite: **Vaults in the outer gallery in the Tomb of Üljaitü at Sultaniya**
The massive tomb was encircled by an outer gallery which provides the transition between the base and the dome. On each of the eight sides of the building, the gallery had three vaults, decorated in carved and painted plaster. Many of these designs resemble those used in contemporary book illumination and suggest that both plasterers and illuminators were using paper patterns.

Tomb of Abd al-Samad at Natanz,
1299 and later
The tomb complex at Natanz in central Iran is a classic example of the "Little Cities of God" that flourished under the Ilkhanids. It honors the Sufi sheikh Abd al-Samad (d. 1299), who taught here. One of his disciples, an Ilkhanid vizier, honored his master by building a tomb over his grave in 1307, enlarging the adjacent Friday mosque, and building a hospice for Sufis. The tall and slender minaret was added in 1325 under the auspices of a local sheikh.

Portal of the *khanqa* of the Tomb of Abd al-Samad, Natanz, 1299 and later
The Ilkhanid vizier Zain al-Din Mastari ordered the construction of a *khanqa*, or hospice for Sufis, adjacent to the tomb of his master. The *khanqa* was a center of the Suhrawardi order. All that remains of the building is its portal, covered with glazed tiles and a magnificent *muqarnas* vault, but the portal and the facades of the adjacent buildings form a harmonious ensemble reminiscent of depictions of architecture in contemporary manuscript painting.

The decoration at Natanz epitomizes the work of the finest Ilkhanid craftsmen. The luster tiles were imported from Kashan, which continued to be the main source of lusterware. Some of the stucco work at Natanz, including a fine inscription band in the north *iwan* of the mosque, was designed by Haidar, the master artist who designed the finest sculptural achievement of the age, the *mihrab* added to the Friday Mosque at Isfahan in 1310. Haidar was one of the six followers of the master calligrapher Yaqut, and one of the notable artistic trends of the Ilkhanid period is that calligraphers branched out into other media as the arts of the book became the pre-eminent art form.

Not all Ilkhanid buildings were monumental in scale, and smaller freestanding tomb towers continued to be built. One example is the tomb known as Chelebi Oglu in Sultaniya, which was built to commemorate the Sufi sheikh Buraq (d. 1308). As it seems to have served as the model for the Imamzada Jafar in Isfahan, built to commemorate an Alid sheikh and descendant of the fifth imam, who died in 1325, the builders may have moved from Sultaniya to Isfahan. In the Ilkhanid period, teams of the finest artisans often moved from site to site. Tileworkers who decorated the shrine complex at Natanz in the first decade of the century, for example, moved in the second decade to Sultaniya, where they produced similar designs for the tomb of Üljaitü. The interior of these small Ilkhanid shrines was normally decorated with luster tiles made in Kashan, and pieces could be added by different patrons at different times. The Imamzada Yahya in Varamin, for example, was constructed in the early Ilkhanid period and decorated with luster tiles dating to 1261–1265. The tomb was redecorated in the first decade of the 14th century with luster tiles and carved stucco dated 1305 and 1307. Hundreds of these luster tiles survive, most of them now in museums. A survey of dated examples indicates that luster tiles ceased to be produced after the 1340s, when revetments of carved and painted plaster became popular.

Right: *Muqarnas* dome in the Tomb of Abd al-Samad at Natanz

The tomb is a square room with shallow recesses in each of its four walls, is covered with a spectacular *muqarnas* vault, in which 12 tiers of plaster niche-like elements are superposed under a pyramidal roof. Windows lighten up the interior and create the impression of a celestial dome. A magnificent inscription in carved plaster runs around the base of the vault, giving the names of the sheikh and the patron, as well as the date, year 707 of the *hegira*, corresponding to 1307–08.

Above: Tile decoration at the base of the minaret, Tomb of Abd al-Samad at Natanz

The shrine of Abd al-Samad at Natanz was decorated with some of the finest ornament of the period. In addition to the carved plaster in the mosque and tomb, there were several kinds of tile decoration. Here, at the base of the minaret, two tiers of shallow *muqarnas* elements are placed as a cornice over a majestic inscription in molded and glazed tile. The similarity of the tile patterns and techniques to those used in the following decade at Sultaniya suggest that talented artisans moved from site to site plying their trades for the wealthiest patrons of the day.

Right: Stucco *mihrab* in the winter prayer hall of the Friday Mosque at Isfahan,
Haidar, July 1310

The stucco *mihrab* in the winter prayer hall added to the Friday Mosque at Isfahan in the year 1310 is important not only for its artistic merits but also for its precise dating. Carved by Haidar, a renowned calligrapher of the period and the same artist who had designed the inscriptions at the Natanz Mosque a year earlier, the *mihrab* displays an extraordinary double-coiled arabesque and deeply undercut flowers beneath several types of calligraphy. It was ordered to mark the sultan's conversion to Shiism late in the previous year, an act that met with great hostility from the conservative Sunni population of Isfahan.

Decorative Arts
Jonathan Bloom, Sheila Blair

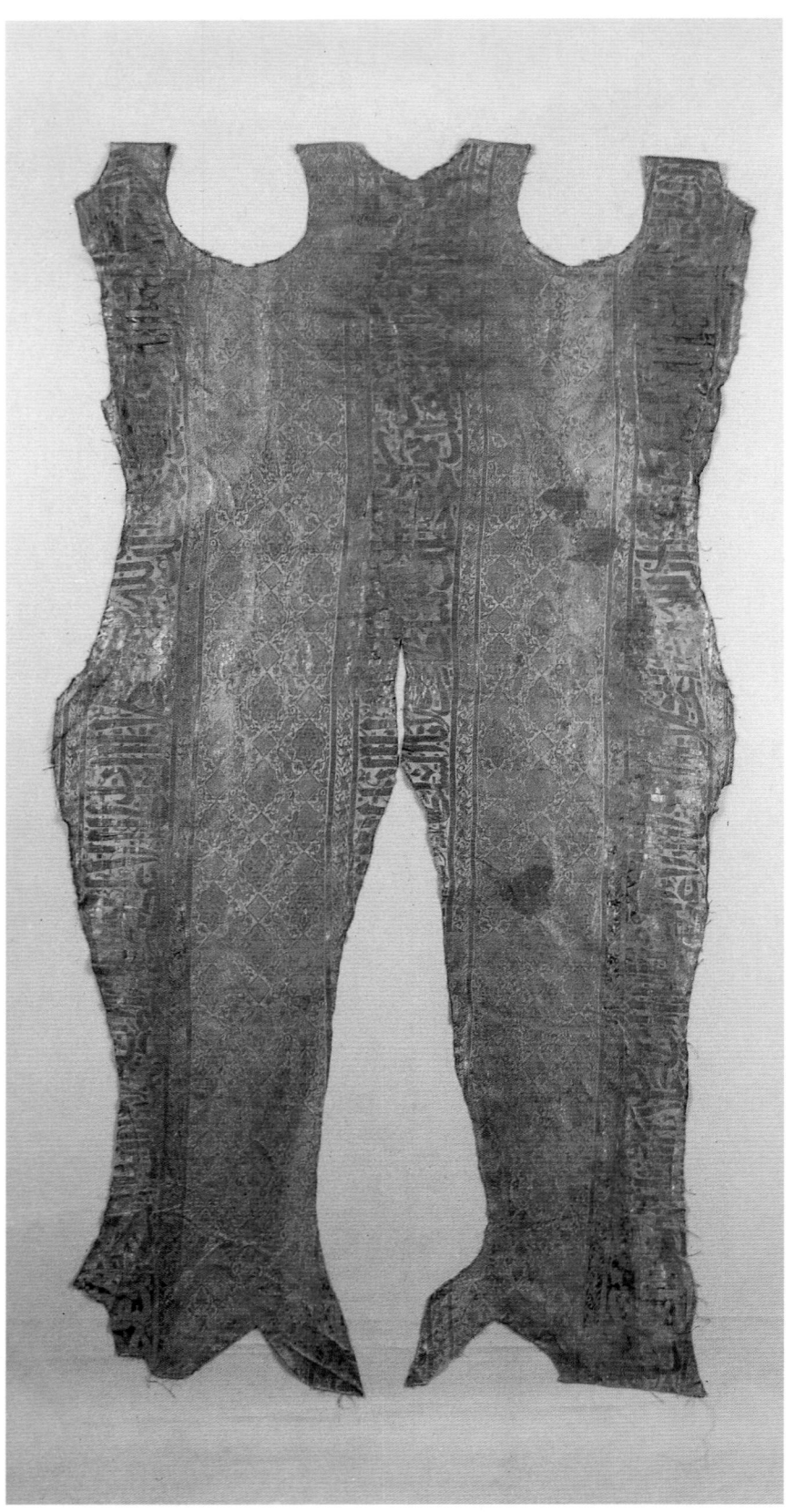

Silk fragment, Iran, c. 1335, 172 × 94 cm, Vienna, Erzbischöfliches Dom- und Diozesan Museum
This spectacular red and brown silk textile is woven through with strips of gilded silver wound around a yellow silk core. Its pattern consists of a wide band of alternately arranged polylobed medallions and rhombuses, with peacocks in between, bordered by narrow bands with running animals and wide bands of inscription. The silk is inscribed with the name and titles of the Ilkhanid sultan Abu Said, who died in 1335, but it was later taken to Europe.

Decorative arts under the Ilkhanids

Like the other Mongols rulers of China and Central Asia, the Ilkhanids in Iran had an impressive court and dedicated themselves to the patronage of the arts. Fine gold-and-silk textiles, for example, were also woven for the Ilkhanids. One fragment bears the name and the titles that the Ilkhanid sovereign Abu Said assumed after 1319. Woven in lampas with areas of compound weave in tan and red silk, this sumptuous textile has gold wefts made of strips of gilded silver wound around a yellow silk core. The striped pattern conists of a wide band of staggered polylobed medallions and ornamented rhomboids with peacocks in the intersices, flanked by narrow bands of running animals and wide epigraphic bands. The official inscription indicates that the textile was woven in a state factory, probably in Tabriz. Within a few years of its production, this precious textile was brought to Europe, perhaps by an Italian merchant, for it was made into the burial robe of Duke Rudolf IV of Austria, who died at Milan in 1365. Its use as a burial robe shows that in the 14th century, as in earlier times, Europeans considered Persian and Central Asian silks to the finest money could buy.

Some ceramics from Mongol Iran also share affinities with those made in Central Asia. The main type of pottery associated with the Ilkhanids is the underglaze-painted ware often called "Sultanabad" after the city on the road from Hamadan to Isfahan where many pieces were found in modern times. As the city was only founded only in 1808 and no kiln sites have been discovered there, the name is only a convenient, if misleading, label. Made of a soft white paste that precludes manufacture of the subtle shapes used in earlier periods, most pieces of Sultanabad ware are covered with a greenish or grayish-brown slip, which gives the surface a bumpy texture. The typical bowl is deep and conical, with a wide rim which overhangs the interior and exterior and is decorated with a pearl border. The interior displays animals or birds with spotted bodies on a ground of thick-leaved foliage. Vessels are covered with a thick glassy glaze which forms greenish pools and drops.

In addition to these rather clumsy, underglaze-painted wares, Ilkhanid potters also produced vessels decorated in the finer lajvardina technique, which had been used on tiles found at Takht-i Sulaiman. Made of the same grayish body as Sultanabad wares, *lajvardina* pieces were overglaze-painted in red, black, and white and gold. The costly materials and second firing made them expensive, and they may have replaced the *minai* and luster vessels that were produced at Kashan until the late 13th century. The latest dated lusterware vessel to survive was made in 1284, although luster tiles continued to be produced at Kashan until 1340. *Lajvardina* wares began to be produced in the 1270s or 1280s, to judge from the Takht-i-Sulaiman tiles, and production continued for at least a century, to judge from a bowl dated 1374. Like most lajvardina bowls, it is decorated with a radial pattern of scrolls, circles, and dots.

Gold and silver were as important to the Ilkhanids as to they were to the other Mongol rulers, but no vessels of these materials are known to survive. Ilkhanid metalworkers continued to make inlaid brasses but replaced the traditional copper inlay with gold in the finest pieces made for the court. Many of these objects are familiar types like penboxes, bowls and candlesticks, but Ilkhanid pieces are often larger or more elaborately decorated with figures and vegetal motifs than earlier ones. Large candelsticks, for example, were meant to stand on floor. The base of one given to the shrine of the Sufi Bayazid Bistami by a vizier

Ceramic bowl, Iran, 14th century, 9 × 21 cm, Los Angeles, Museum of Art
This bowl, typical of the fairly simple Sultanabad ware, has a deep, conical shape and a wide rim overhanging the interior and exterior. The interior usually (as in this example) features animals or birds with spotted bodies on a ground of thick foliage. The vessels are covered with a thick, transparent glaze, which develops greenish dots.

Ceramic bowl, Iran, late 13th or 14th century, diameter 17.7 cm, Washington, Freer Gallery of Art
This bowl, underglaze-painted in blue and green and overglaze-painted in red, dark green, white, and gold, was made by the expensive *lajvardina* technique. The radial pattern is comparable to patterns found on Kashan underglaze-painted wares of the 13th century, indicating that the Kashan potters continued to work in new techniques in the Ilkhanid period.

of Sultan Üljaitü in 1308–9 measures 13 inches (32.5 centimeters) high and is the largest candlestick to survive from Islamic Iran. A painting from a contemporary manuscript shows four of these candlesticks surrounding a bier, an arrangement perhaps derived from italian traditions. Inlaid brass was also used for architectural fittings, particularly ball joints for iron window grilles. Three such ball joints are inscribed with the name of Sultan Üljayitü and were probably made for his tomb in Sultaniya. A small example displays a roundel enclosing a mounted falconer set against arabesque scrolls and surrounded by a peony border. The rider typifies the Mongol figure, and the decoration mixes floral motifs from the Chinese tradition with geometric designs from the Islamic one.

Some of these inlaid brasses may have been made in northwestern Iran near the courts for which they were intended, but a center of inlaid metalwork also florished in Fars province in the southwestern Iran. The typical pieces made there were low, rounded bowls decorated with epigraphic cartouches alternating with polylobed medallions enclosing figures of hunters, riders or enthroned rulers. Many examples also have animals depicted in a band on the neck, a radiating sun on the exterior of the base, and a fish pond around a sun on the interior. These solar symbols were deliberately placed so that when the bowl was filled, the celestial light in the center was evident; when the bowl was tilted for drinking, the image of the sun in the heavens was visible to the viewer. Several are inscribed "heir to Solomon's kingdom," a title adopted by the rulers of Fars and referring to the Achaemenid monuments of Fars province, which were thought to be inhabited by Solomon's spirit. These bowls were made in substantial quantites over the course of the 14th century, and then, as in miniature painting, both the figurs and the script used to decorate them became taller and more attenuated.

Of all the arts produced under the Ilkhanids, the arts of the book were the most important. Illuminated and illustrated books had been produced for

Ball joint from window grille, Iran, early 14th century, diameter 9.7 cm, Ham (Surrey), Keir Collection
This brass ball, inlaid with the figure of a hunter, was probably used in a window grille to join horizontal and vertical iron bars. The rider, wearing a distinctive Mongol hat and holding a falcon on his right wrist, appears against a background filled with peony and lotus blossoms.

centuries in the Islamic world, but following the Mongol conquests in Iran, they became bigger and more numerous. The book was considered an integral unit, with transcription, illustration, illumination, and even binding united in a harmonious whole. The preminence of the arts of book is clear from the fact that famous calligraphers also designed inscriptions executed in other media such as carved stucco and that book designs were replicated in architecture, as on the carved and painted plaster vaults in Üljaitü's tomb in Sultaniya.

The most famous calligrapher of the period was Yaqut al-Mustasimi. As a boy, he had been brought to Baghdad to serve the last Abbasid caliph there, al-Mustasim billah (1242–58), thereby earning the sobriquet al-Musta'simi. Yaqut spent most of his life in Baghdad, where his career flourished under Mongol patronage until his death (c. 1298). By the 15th century, Yaqut's reputation had grown so that he was lauded as "qibla of writers" and credited with canonizing the six round scripts known as the Six Pens. Yaqut's prestige means that many manuscripts and individual specimens in various scripts bear his signature, authentic and otherwise. The most common are small single-volume mansucripts of the Koran in the small scripts of Rayhan or Naskh. Each copy has 200–300 folios with 13–19 lines of text to the page. Although small, the unmargined text in these manuscripts is eminently clear and readable, with gold rosettes separating individual verses in the text and marginal ornaments painted in gold outlined with blue marking groups of five and ten verses. These were fine and expensive copies of the Koran, and their value was appreciated by later owners. Several Qajar princes, for example, inscribed their names on the frist folio of a copy in Paris.

By contrast, manuscripts of the Koran penned by Yaqut's followers are much bigger. They were usually copied in 30 volumes on large sheets measuring 50 × 70 cm. One behemoth copy made for Üljaitü is twice the size, with bifolios measuring 40 × 28 inches (100 × 70 centimeters). These sheets correspond to what the 15th-century Mamluk chronicler al-Qalqashandi called the "full Baghdadi" size. It must have been a herculean task to lift these sheets from the mold, especially as over 1,000 were needed for these gigantic copies of the Koran.

The small, single-volume mansucripts penned by Yaqut were probably personal copies, whereas the large multi-volume manuscipts were presentation copies made for public recitation in the tomb complexes of the sultans and their court. Each page of the Üljaitü Koran is inscribed with five lines of *muhaqqaq* script, three in gold outlined with black alternating with two in black outlined with gold. The text was probably transcribed by Ahmad al-Suhrawardi, a follower of Yaqut and the scribe who signed the finest of these large manuscripts of the Koran made at Baghdad between 1302 and 1308. Like its counterpart, the manuscript was illuminated by Muhammad ibn Aybak ibn Abdallah. The text and vocalization are penned in a beautiful black muhaqqaq script, which contrasts with the polychrome and gold decoration in the margin. The balance between script and decoration makes this one of the finest manuscripts of the Koran ever produced.

The availability of large sheets of fine polished paper menat not only that scribes could tranbscribe beautiful calligraphy but also that illustrators had room to paint large and complex compositions. Several manuscripts of this large size were prepared for the vizier Rashid al-Din at the scriptorium attached to his tomb complex in Tabriz. According to the endwoment deed for the complex, the vizier stipulated that some of 220 slaves assigned to the complex had to copy several texts each year. All manuscripts had to be done on good Baghdadi paper in a neat hand, collated with the originals in the library, and bound in fine leather. The bound copies were displayed in the mosque, registered at the judiciary, and then sent to different cities through out the realm. The text copies included the Koran, a multi-volume commentary on it by Ibn al-Athir, and two copies, one in Arabic and another in Persian, of the vizier's own collected works, including his history, the *Compendium of Chronicles*. This was a multi-volume history of the world, covering the reigns of Ghazan and his forbears, the non-Mongol Eurasian peoples, the genealogy of ruling houses, and geography. The most famous example to survive is from an Arabic copy made about 1315. The surviving fragments form about one-half of the second volume concerning the Eurasian peoples. Originally, it comprised some three hundred folios (written surface 37 x 25 centimeters,

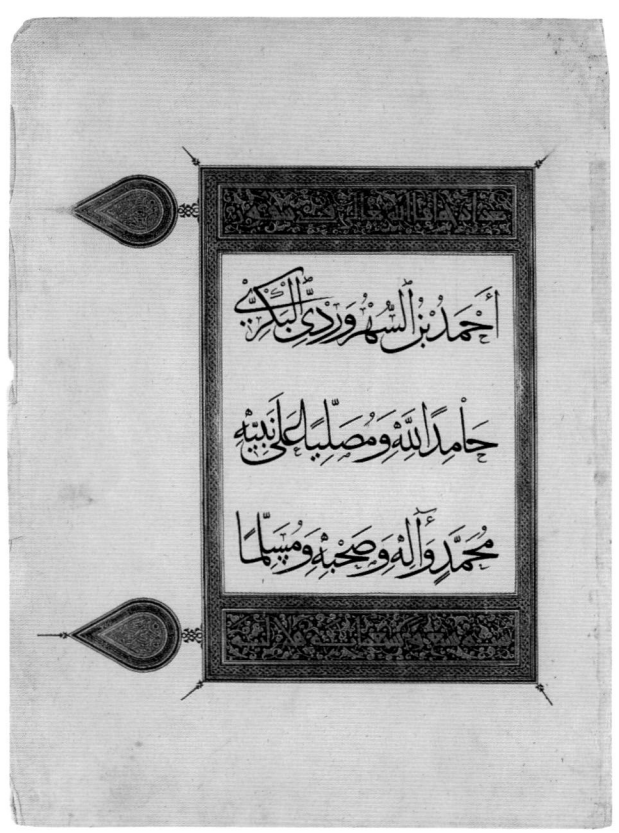

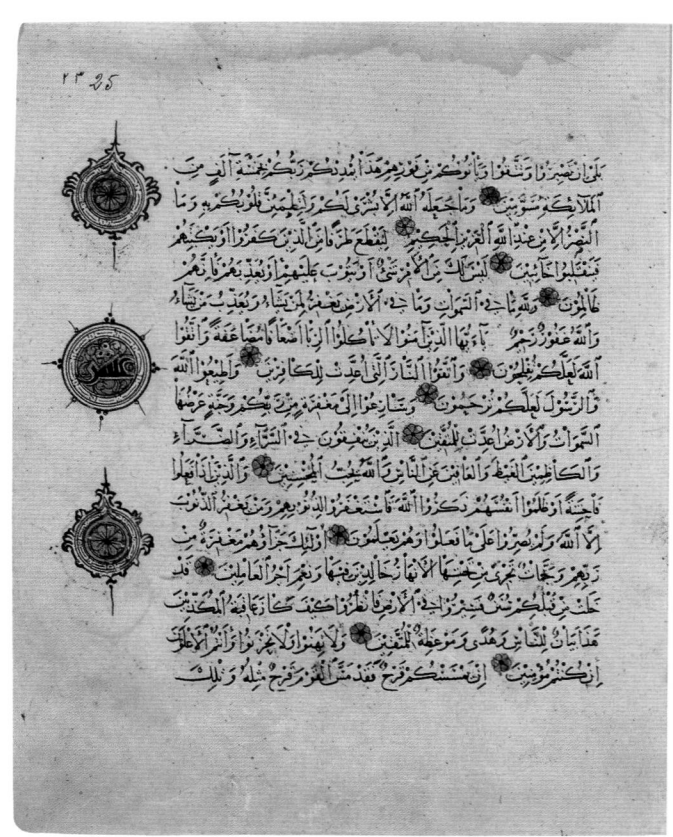

Right: **Koran manuscript**, Yaqut al-Mustasimi, Iraq, Muharran 688 (February 1289),
Paris, Bibliothèque Nationale
Yaqut is now considered the most famous calligrapher of the 13th century, and is said to have canonized the six classical styles of Arabic script. He began his career at the court of the last Abbasid caliph al-Mustasim, hence his epithet, and continued to work under the Mongols.

Left: **Koran manuscript**, calligraphy Ahmad al-Suhrawardi, illumination Muhammad ibn Aibak, Baghdad 1308, New York, Metropolitan Museum of Art
This page is the colophon to one of the 30 volumes of a magnificent Koran manuscript. Whereas Yaqut's manuscripts were usually of small format, his students' manuscripts were much larger. This one, measuring 50 × 35 cm, was written on extremely fine paper of the "half-Baghdadi" size in *muhaqqaq* script. The large format and the exquisite illumination indicate that this manuscript was a presentation copy used for public recitation in the mosque.

Alexander's Iron Cavalry, manuscript of the *Shahname* by Firdausi, Tabriz, c. 1335, Cambridge, Mass., Harvard University Art Museums
The most important project under Ghiyath al-Din was a two-volume, large-format copy of the *Shahname*, which was planned to include some 250 large and elaborate illustrations. By this point, Persian painters had integrated diverse elements into a coherent style. In this stunning scene the fire-spewing Iron Cavalry of Alexander the Great sends the enemy fleeing in terror.

The bier of Alexander the Great, manuscript of the *Shahname* by Firdausi, Tabriz, c. 1335, Washington, Freer Gallery of Art
This miniature also comes from the Great Mongol *Shahname*. The picture structure follows the traditional tripartite scheme, with the central space dominating the composition, which is completed by the circle of mourners gathered around the bier. Individuals like the veiled people in the foreground, and Alexander's mother throwing herself weeping over the coffin, are inspired by figures in Western depictions of the lamentation over the death of Christ.

15 × 10 inches) and 35 lines of text on each page with 110 illustrations and 80 portraits of Chinese emperors.

In contrast to illustrations in earlier manuscripts, which are generally square, most of the illustrations to the historical text are horizontal strips occupying about one-third of the written surface of each page. Indoor scenes are usually tripartite compositions, but outside scenes are more varied, as artists attempted to expand the pictorial space. Figures at the sides are often cropped, lances and hooves project beyond the frame into the text area, and figures occasionally turn directly toward or away from the viewer. Landscape elements such as clouds, trees, mountains, and water (depicted as imbrications), were modeled on Chinese prototypes, as the technique of black ink heightened with colored washes. Other features, however, were modeled on European, especially Italian painting, which Ilkhanid artists might have known from manuscripts and paintings brought by merchants to Iran. A scene such as the Birth of the Prophet Muhammad, for example, is loosley based on a depiction of Christ's Nativity, probably because such a scene was not part of the standard Islamic repertory. Another new feature of this manuscript is the selection of certain narrative cycles for illustration so that the paintings became a visual commentary on the text. The section on the Ghaznavids, for example, has the most, the largest, and some of the most inventive illustrations in the manuscript. By contrast, the long section dealing with the history of the Abbasid caliphate has no illustrations at all. The decided preference for the Ghaznavids, who in the larger scheme of the world history were less important than the Abbasids, was undoubtedly due to the way the Mongols saw themselves as heirs of the great Turkish tradition of military conquest, as exemplified by the Ghaznavids.

The important role of illustrations continues in the finest manuscript made by the next generation, a large copy of the Persian national epic made in the 1330s. Now dismembered and dispersed, the Great Mongol *Shahname* originally had some 300 illustrations and was bound in two volumes. The paintings are larger than those in the world history, sometimes taking up almost half the page, and the formats are more varied, sometimes with stepped frames. The compositions have been expanded to include more figures and deeper space. The greater size of the illustration seems to have encouraged artists to integrate larger figures into more developed landscapes than are found in earlier illustrations. For example, the scene showing the Bier of Alexander is still based on a tripartite scheme, but the central space dominates the composition, which is united by the circle of mourners clustered around the bier. Some of the figures, particularly the veiled mourners in the foreground and Alexander's mother lamenting over the coffin in the center, are inspired by figures in Western representations of the Lamentation, but the artist has combined individual elements to create a dramatic sense of pictorial space unknown in the earlier illustrations made at rashid al-Din's scriptorium.

Another scene from the Great Mongol *Shahname*, depicting Alexander's iron cavalry battling the indians, can be taken to exemplify not only the arts of the book, but also the Mongol period as a whole. To counter the huge elephants of the Indian army, Alexander devised the ingenious strategy of an iron cavalry, wheeled metal horses and riders filled with naphtha. He pushed these horseman, their nostrils aflame, down in the face of the Indian army, who turned tail and fled. The artist has dramatically depicted the scene with expensive pigments: the iron soldiers are painted in silver, their nostrils breathe flames of gold. Alexander's horsemen, dressed in laminated armor of chain-mail and casque-like helmets, bear down on the black-faced indians who wear striped tunics. The figure on the upper right glances backwards over his shoulder, leading the viewers to imagine pictorial space beyond the picture plane. The swirling clouds overhead, a type from Chinese painting, echo the swirling fire emanating from the horse. In its intensity, color and imagination, the painting exemplies the cosmopolitan and sophisticated world of Ilkhanid Iran.

Art and architecture in southern Russia and Central Asia at the time of the Golden Horde and the Chaghatayids

Old Saray served as the capital of the Golden Horde for about a century, from the 1240s to the 1340s. The Franciscan friar William of Rubruck, who visited in 1254 while en route from King Louis IX of France to the court of the Great Khan Möngke in Qaraqorum, was the first to mention the city by name. Other travelers and historians writing in the 1330s describe Old Saray as a large, populous city full of merchants and bustling markets. Russian archaeologists investigating the site confirmed these accounts. They uncovered a large city covering an area of nearly one square mile (10 square kilometers), with a network of streets defined by drainage ditches, cisterns, markets, and large districts where jewelers, metalsmiths, glassmakers, and potters worked. The city was both multiethnic and multireligious. Finds of metal icons show that the population remained Orthodox Christian, but the city took on a more Islamic character in the early 14th century. For example, Khan Uzbek (1311–1341), a convert to Islam, founded a *madrasa*, or theological college, there.

In the 1330s Uzbek began construction upstream of New Saray, and it became the capital in 1342 when his son Janibeg assumed power. Much smaller than the previous capital, it covered only one fifth of a square mile (a half of a square kilometer). A defensive embankment and trench were added around the city, probably in the 1360s. Timur destroyed the city in 1395, but Russian excavations since 1847 have uncovered its oval plan and a street network similar

Gold bowl with fish-shaped handles, New Saray, 1250–1350, diameter 17.8 cm, St. Petersburg, Hermitage
In 1847 the Russians began excavations at Zarevo Gorodische, the site near the Volga that has been identified as New Saray, the second capital of the Golden Horde since the reign of Janibeg (1342–1357). The excavators found many objects, including several large and spectacular gold bowls. Of the many gold objects that must have been made for the Mongols, few have survived, for most were later melted down to make coins.

to that of Old Saray. Artisans and the poorer classes lived in earthen dugouts in the center of New Saray, while richer inhabitants lived in wooden and brick houses or in tents. Russian excavations at New Saray also uncovered many objects, of which the most spectacular are several silver and gold cups with elaborate handles in the form of fish or dragons. Modeled on Chinese prototypes, these drinking vessels were made for the khans of the Golden Horde. For the Mongols, gold possessed many attributes and conveyed many meanings. It represented value, the primordial, the sun, and the heavens. Gold was the imperial color, just as purple was for the Byzantine emperors. Although many gold objects were made, only a few objects other than coins have survived from

Silver cup with dragon-shaped handle, Volga region, 1250–1350, diameter 11 cm, St. Petersburg, Hermitage
This cup is very similar to Iranian Mongol objects, but the dragon handle comes from the steppe tradition.

Ceramic bowl, Volga region, 1st half of the 14th century, diameter 19.4 cm, St. Petersburg, Hermitage
This bowl, from New Saray, resembles the slip-painted Iranian Sultanabad wares, though the execution and painting are somewhat coarser.

medieval times, because most were later melted down into coins in times of need or refashioned when tastes changed. Timur must have seized similar gold cups when he sacked New Saray in 1395, for wine cups of similar shape were made for the Timurid rulers. Those that survive are made not of gold, but of jade. This rare and precious material became available to the Timurids only after the Timurid prince Ulugh Beg (1447–1449) seized the jade mines in Mongolistan. The Timurids' descendants, the Moghul emperors of India, in turn, preserved these Timurid jade wine cups and reinscribed them with their own names, thereby neatly encapsulating the Moghuls' ancestry back to Genghis Khan. Similar silver objects have been discovered in the Ob river basin of northern Siberia. The hunters and trappers of the north sold their furs, walrus ivory, and birds of prey to Muslim merchants, and regular trade had been carried on since the 10th century, when the Volga Bulgars established their state near the confluence of the Kama and Volga Rivers. Instead of currency, which would have been useless in a tribal economy, these hunters and trappers often traded for silver objects, which they later hid in the Siberian forests. Some of these secreted objects have survived, whereas in the more civilized areas silver vessels were melted down to mint coins.

Russian excavators at New Saray also uncovered many ceramics, including unglazed and glazed vessels, glazed tiles, and fragments of tile mosaic panels resembling those used in contemporary buildings in Transoxiana. Some ceramics were imported, such as celadons from China and blue-and-white wares from Egypt, but the presence of kilns at the site shows that most pieces were made locally. The largest group comprises bowls with a thick white slip, blue spots, and black outline painting; they have bands filled with white leaf patterns or imitation Arabic inscriptions surrounding a central medallion containing animals or geometric designs. These slipwares are similar to the so-called Sultanabad wares made during the period of Ilkhanid rule in Iran but the bowls have a more rounded shape and the drawing is stiffer and more conventional.

The most important art during this period was textiles. A wide array of 13th- and 14th-century sources from Europe to China mention "Tartar cloth," known in Italian sources as *panni tartarici*. Scholars have recently identified these textiles as drawloom silks woven with gold, the *nasij* and *nakh* mentioned in Arabic and Persian texts. Under the Mongols, the technique for weaving these brocades was transferred from Central Asia to China. During their campaigns of 1219–1222 in Turkestan and Khorasan, the Mongols seized three colonies of artisans and moved them to China, where they were set up under the auspices of Genghis Khan and his son Ügedei and reorganized again under Qubilai in the 1270s. Silk-and-gold textiles woven in Central Asia during this period show an extraordinary degree of technical proficiency. Both ground and pattern are gold, with the design delineated by the silk foundation. These textiles combine Chinese and Iranian elements: single foundation warps, for example, are common in Chinese silks, while the binding of gold wefts in pairs is typical of silks from eastern Iran. These textiles are not inscribed, but their regal quality suggests that they must have been made for the court, presumably for the Chaghatayids, who controlled Transoxiana at this time. Many of the surviving pieces have only recently appeared on the art market. They are said to have been preserved in Tibet, perhaps given as royal gifts to monasteries there.

Cloth fragment, eastern Central Asia, c. 1250, gold and silk, width 49 cm, length 124 cm, Cleveland, Museum of Art
The Mongols' gold cloth demonstrates extraordinary technical ability, for both ground and pattern are woven in gold and the design is delineated merely by the silk foundation weave. This stunning example is woven in brilliant gold against a dark brown, nearly black, ground. The design of roundels enclosing an addorsed (back to back) pair of winged lions, with griffins filling the spaces between the roundels, derives from Iranian models. Frequently, the decoration, for example bands of clouds and animal tails running into dragon's heads, is borrowed from Chinese ornament.

Central Asia
The Timurids, the Shaybanids, and the Khan Princedoms

Khoja Ahmad Yasawi Mausoleum Complex, Turkestan (Jassy), 1389–1399
Both the architecture and politics of the Timurids were dominated by the forceful
personality of the conqueror Timur, who stamped his will on all areas of public life. The
Khoja Ahmad Yasawi Complex is a good example of the imperial style under Timur,
although, along with a mosque and the mausoleum of Sheikh Khoja Ahmad, this compact
development also includes an assembly room, a library, and a living area complete with
kitchen. Its exterior decoration is typical of Timurid building and consists of large-scale
geometric patterns made up of dark blue, turquoise, and white glazed bricks. Calligraphy,
legible from a considerable distance away, runs around the whole of the building and
decorates the drums of the domes.

History

Markus Hattstein

The history of the Timurids is dominated by the figure of the dynasty's founder, Timur, the paramount conqueror and "ruler of the world." History's verdict on him has been mostly negative: the mass murder of innocent people by his armies, the destruction of ancient cultural centers, and the laying to waste of whole geographical regions exceeded in their cruelty even the deeds of Genghis Khan and his like, and are far from counterbalanced by his artistic expansion of Samarqand and other cities in Transoxiana using deported artists and craftsmen. Furthermore, although he succeeded in conquering an enormous empire, he was not able to rule over it with a stable state administration. On the other hand, many Islamic historians, and Europeans since the Renaissance, when Timur was celebrated in plays and operas from Marlowe to Handel, admired in him the strong-willed man of action who rose from the position of minor prince to that of ruler of the Islamic world and the whole of Asia through a combination of ambition, energy, and cunning.

ride from Samarqand. The date of birth later widely cited, of April 8, 1336, stems from a "celestial conjunction" calculated subsequently. His right kneecap and upper thigh were malformed from birth, bringing him the nickname "Lenk" or "lame one," and resulted in him being able to move about only with the aid of crutches or later in life on horseback, and a deformation of his right shoulder, compounded by an arrow wound, restricted his use of his right hand. These deformities were confirmed by an examination of his skeleton, which was undertaken by Soviet scientists in 1941.

In the anarchic situation in Transoxiana during the period 1360–1370, Timur maneuvered and entered into pacts to his own advantage, proved himself to be an exceptional military leader at an early stage, and changed camps when it suited him. When Tughluq Temür invaded the Islamic region in 1360, Timur betrayed the leader of the Barlas tribe and placed himself at the service of the khan, receiving Kesh as a fief in return. In order to improve his social position, he formed an alliance with the powerful Emir Husein, who resided in Balkh, by marrying the emir's sister, and thus became his liege man. When Tughluq Temür had withdrawn again to Mongolistan, Timur and Husain got on together with the business of expanding their territories, and entered into alliances with different rulers until they gained possession of Samarqand in 1366. As they were both men of huge ambition, however, conflict inevitably broke out between them, climaxing in 1369, when Timur conquered Husain's seat of Balkh. On April 13, 1370, all the emirs and princes of southern Ulus pledged an oath of allegiance to Timur, who decided upon Samarqand as his capital.

The situation in Transoxiana and the rise of Timur

The campaign of conquest led by Genghis Khan and his successors had altered the whole situation in Eurasia, above all in the Islamic cultural region. The occupation of Persia and the fall of Baghdad in 1258 had unleashed terror and dejection in the Islamic world, although the Ilkhanids of Persia, who had converted to Islam, had undertaken a colossal program of reconstruction. Through their claim to lead the Islamic Mongols, they soon became embroiled in an ongoing conflict with the Ulus Chaghatai clan in Transoxiana, the tribal home of Genghis Khan's second son. When the Chaghatai khan Tarmashirin (1326–1334) converted to Islam, the Ulus split into an Islamic region between the Jaxartes and Oxus Rivers, and the "heathen" Mongolistan beyond the Jaxartes. During the following period, the Islamic part was ruled by various different military leaders. This lack of a central administration was exploited in 1360 by Tughluq Temür, the khan of Mongolistan, in order to reunite the Ulus Chaghatai under his leadership. Timur's rise occurred during this period of conflict.

Timur Lenk descended from the respected, but impoverished, Turkoman Barlas tribe, and was born around 1328 near Kesh (today Shahr-i Sabz), a day's

Timur's advance into Khwarazmia and Iran
The battle with Toqtamish

Timur actually spent his whole life on military campaigns, and crossed his conquered territories several times during the course of them. First of all, he took care to organize things throughout the whole of the Ulus Chaghatai exactly the way he wanted. In 1370, therefore, he marched north and installed a puppet khan there, who was descended from the house of Genghis Khan and who was loyal to him, and made repeated appearances in the role of protector and guardian. But Mongolistan remained an unsettled region, as many Chaghatai nobles regarded Timur as a parvenu and plotted against him. In 1372 he

Above: **Timur's memorial in Tashkent**
Timur (c.1328–1405) was considered to be the greatest conqueror the Islamic world has known. Through a combination of courage, cunning, and ruthlessness, he rose from the position of minor Transoxiana noble to that of ruler of a world empire that took in all the Islamic regions from Anatolia and Syria in the west to India and the borders of China in the east. He is still commemorated today, primarily in Central Asia.

Opposite: **Timur riding into Samarqand at the head of his troops**, Persian miniature from a *Zafarname*, 1486. Istanbul, Museum of Turkish and Islamic Art
Although Timur spent almost the whole of his life on campaigns of conquest, he chose Samarqand as his capital and used artists carried back from the conquered regions to help turn it into the magnificent "center of the world."

اقمقور بها درزد خنا یجه اسپ ازپای درآمد وسوار پیاده ماند واوج

successfully asserted the disputed Chaghatai claims to Mongolian Khwarazmia in the face of other, local branches of Genghis Khan's dynasty, occupied the territory, and married his son Jahangir to a local princess, which brought him an enormous increase in prestige. Over the following years he launched several campaigns into Khwarazmia as the region repeatedly reasserted its independence and formed alliances with Timur's enemies. When the Khwarazmians invaded Bukhara in 1376, Timur laid waste to Khwarazmia and in 1379 razed its capital Kuna Urgench to the ground.

Timur now decided to take over the Ilkhanid succession in Iran as well. When Ghiyath al-Din, ruler of the Kartids in Herat, refused to appear at Timur's court assembly in Samarqand in 1379, Timur was provided with an excuse to invade Afghanistan and Khorasan. In 1381 he occupied the whole of the Kartid territories and installed his second son, Miranshah, as governor of Khorasan. As he advanced west, Timur ran into resistance in the Persian regions of Mazandaran and Sistan from the Muzaffarids of Shiraz, who had been embroiled in internal power struggles since 1384 and who were finally removed by Timur in 1393. When he took Isfahan from them in 1387, he initially granted them a lenient occupation, but when the inhabitants of the city murdered his tax collectors he organized a terrible massacre in retribution.

Timur had decided to unite Iran politically and destroy the regional rule of the minor princes. By taking the title of sultan in 1388, he brought about, by force, the cultural unification of Iran and Transoxiana (Turan). The conflict between the two regions had already been the subject of the Persian national epic, the *Shahname*. Now Timur attempted to unite the cultural heritage of the Iranians, Mongols, and Turkomans in his own person.

In the meantime a new enemy had appeared in the battle for leadership of the Islamic Mongols. Toqtamish, khan of the Golden Horde since 1378, had invaded Iran in 1386 and pillaged Tabriz. Timur, who had taken Toqtamish in as a young refugee, regarded this action as breach of loyalty and invaded Georgia, which was Christian, and whose ruler then became Timur's vassal, in order to cut off the Golden Horde's route into Iran. Toqtamish, who in 1382 had burnt Moscow down and established his sovereignty over Russia, now claimed all the Mongolian territories. In 1387 he pillaged Timur's homeland and laid siege to Bukhara and Samarqand, but withdrew to his own territory ahead of the advancing Timur. In 1391 Timur followed him into the Urals and beyond, and defeated a Golden Horde army twice the strength of his. Toqtamish took flight and formed an alliance with the Mamluks in Cairo. Later on he was beaten in battle by Timur's troops several more times, before finally being murdered while on the run in 1405. For his part, Timur asserted his sovereignty over the Golden Horde, which extended far into Russia, and returned to Samarqand with substantial treasures in the form of war booty.

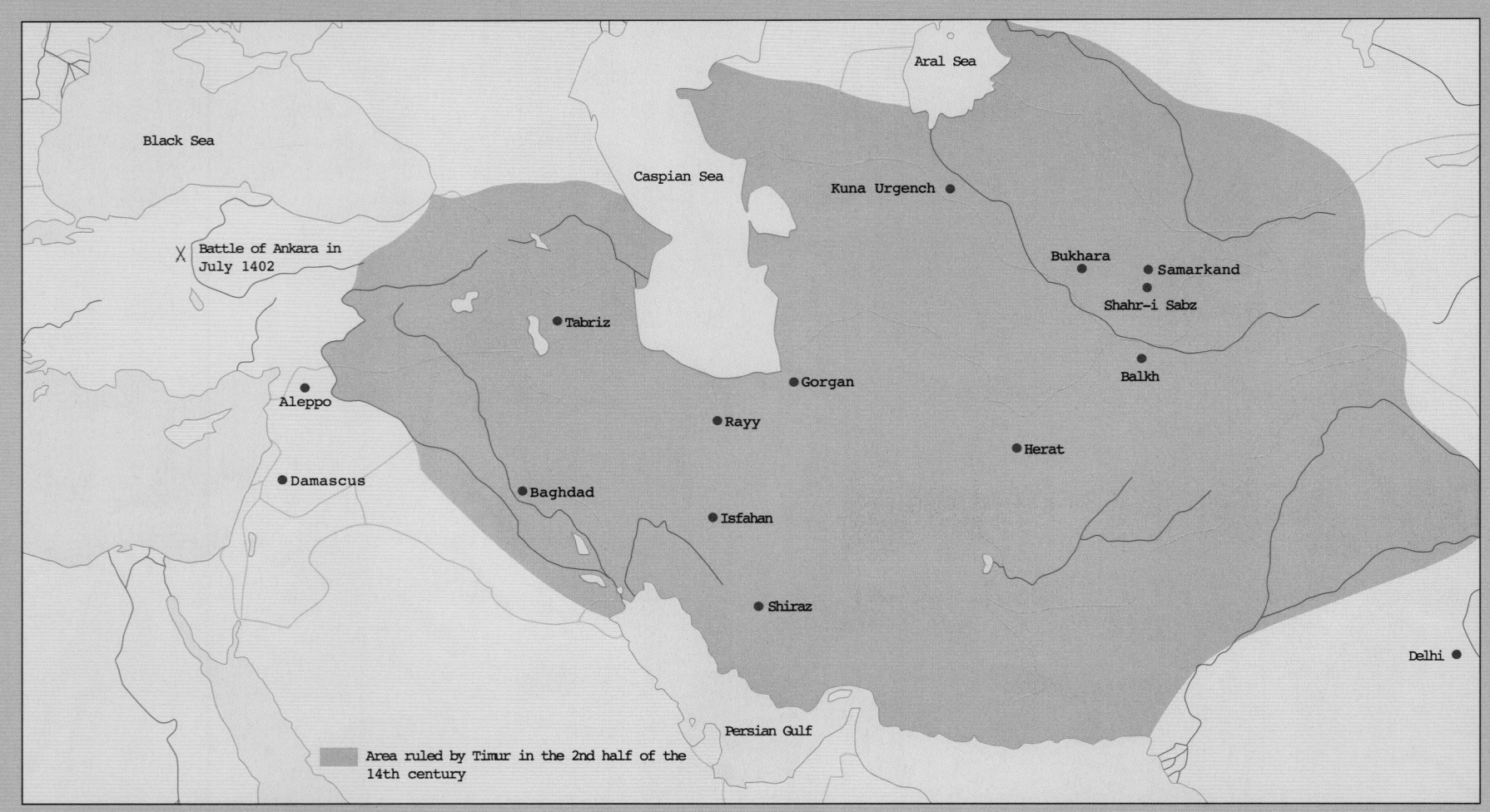

Pyramid of skulls from Timur's military campaigns, Indian miniature, Moghul period. Patna, Khuda Bakhsh Library
When Timur punished a city for its treachery, he took drastic measures and erected skull pyramids, constructed of the walled-up heads of those killed, outside the city, visible from far and wide. When, after their capitulation in 1387, the inhabitants of Isfahan murdered Timur's tax collectors, he had 70,000 people put to death and their heads stacked into 28 pyramids outside the city. He took similar action against the inhabitants of Baghdad in 1401, when they once more submitted to the enemies of Timur, who had conquered the city back in 1393.

Timur's advance into Syria, Iraq, and Anatolia
The battle with Bayazid

In 1392 Timur decided to push further west. After ousting the Muzaffarids from Shiraz, he invaded Iraq and in September 1393 drove the Jalayirids out of Baghdad. Here he showed himself to be a lenient upholder of Islamic *sharia* and purged the country of minor potentates and bands of robbers, for which the Baghdad tradespeople, whose trading routes he had secured, were grateful. An agreement with the Mamluks in Cairo foundered, however. The energetic Mamluk sultan, Barquq, who had taken over power in 1382, was determined to bring Timur's advance to a standstill, just as the Mamluks had managed to defeat the Mongols in 1260. In 1394 Barquq, in alliance with the Ottomans, the Golden Horde, and several Anatolian princes, had taken up position with his army outside Damascus, lying in wait for Timur's assault. But Timur avoided the confrontation at the last moment and turned towards Toqtamish in the north.

After Barquq died in 1399, Timur once more advanced west the following year, plundered Aleppo, and took up position outside Damascus, which was held by Barquq's son Faraj. When the two armies confronted each other, Faraj lost his nerve and fled to Egypt in January 1401. Although the city submitted to Timur, it was nevertheless sacked and pillaged. Timur then withdrew to Iraq, where the Jalayirids had once again taken possession of Baghdad and improved their position at Timur's expense. Enraged at the treachery of the city he had treated

Left: **Timur receives his grandson Pir Muhammad, in Multan**, miniature from a *Zafarname*, London, British Library
Timur made his grandson Pir Muhammad, who was governor of the Indian provinces, based in Kandahar, his heir. Pir Muhammad had already begun a campaign for Timur in India, but had laid siege to Multan in vain, whereupon, in 1398, his grandfather hurried to his assistance and subjugated India all the way to Delhi. After Timur's death, Pir Muhammad was not able to hold his own against Timur's other grandchildren and was assassinated by his own vizier in 1407, during an attempt to conquer Samarqand.

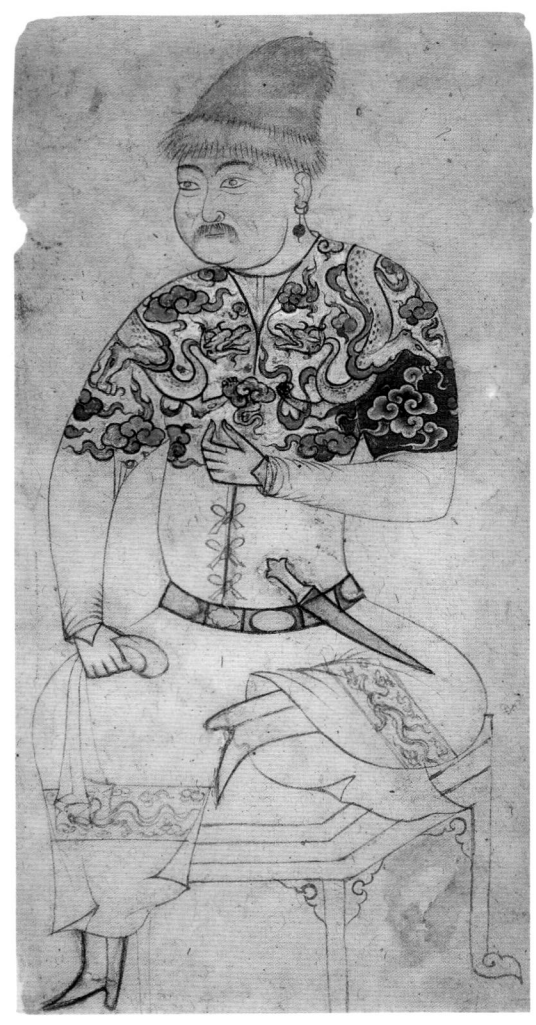

Right: **Timurid nobleman**, miniature. Berlin, Staatsbibliothek Preussischer Kulturbesitz
The ruling class under Timur consisted, to a large extent, of his sons and grandsons, who ruled the provinces of his empire as governors. But he also left defeated rulers in place in their conquered territory if they entered his league of peace, i.e. submitted to him as vassals and acknowledged his sovereignty over them. As he carried out all his actions in the name of the Ulus Chaghatai, the tribal clan of Genghis Khan's son, he appointed the Mongol members of the Genghis Khan dynasty who joined him to positions of high honor.

leniently, Timur took Baghdad by storm in July 1401 and butchered the population, sparing only the scholars, artists, and craftsmen.

Ibn Khaldun was one of the scholars who fell into Timur's hands in Baghdad. Timur treated him with extreme courtesy, and made him stay with him while he completed a description of the Maghreb lands. Ibn Khaldun also taught the ruler about the Islamic prophesies, which announced a "sultan of the world" who would attain this position through the intervention of nomadic shepherds. Ibn Khaldun saw in this a reference to the Turkoman tribes and thus made an association between Timur's rule and Muslim ideas concerning the apocalypse.

Anatolia now became the focus of conflict. The region's minor princes saw themselves as threatened in equal measure by the ambitions of the Mamluks on one hand and the Ottomans on the other, as each had appropriated various territories since 1397. Many of them regarded Timur, whose lands lay further away, as a possible guarantor of their independence, and subjugated themselves to his sovereignty. As Timur had also occupied various regions during the course of his march west in 1394 and had assumed the role of protector of Anatolia, this inevitably resulted in confrontations with the Ottomans, who were spreading east at that time.

In 1395 Timur had initially offered the Ottoman sultan Bayazid I (1389–1402) his friendship, praised him as a warrior for the faith, and asked him to join in with the battle against Toqtamish. This invitation also came with a warning, however: Bayazid was free to extend his territory into the Balkans, but the east – Iran and Anatolia – belonged to the Ulus Chaghatai clan. The restless Bayazid, however, not only appropriated territories in northern Syria and

Anatolia, but also granted refuge to the Jalayirids and Turkoman Qara Qoyunlu, sworn enemies of Timur, providing them with troops for the reconquest of their estates. As a result of this, Timur advanced into Anatolia in March 1402, crushing the Ottoman army near Ankara in July 1402. He took Bayazid prisoner and supposedly transported him around in an iron cage which he used as a stool to help him mount his horse. In announcing his victory to the rulers of Europe, Timur expressed the hope that the traffic in goods between Europe, the Orient, and Asia could now flow undisturbed. Liberation from the "Bayazid nightmare" contributed decisively to the positive image enjoyed by Timur in Europe.

Timur's campaign in India, the development of Samarqand, and Timur's death

Timur had already sent his grandson Pir Muhammad to India with troops, as he wanted to recreate the empire of Mahmud of Ghazna, whom he greatly admired, under his own leadership. In order to guarantee the eastern rear, he had been paying tribute money to the Chinese emperor since 1389. Pir Muhammad's advance had come to a halt outside Multan, and in 1398, Timur took over the military campaign himself. In September of that year he crossed the Indus, accepted the local princes' acts of submission and continued his advance in a southeasterly direction despite fierce resistance. During the course of this advance, his troops took many prisoners and plundered the cities. When he finally arrived outside Delhi in 1398, he had around 100,000 prisoners with him. Before the all-important battle he gave the order that all male prisoners were to be executed

Faramuz pursuing the army of the king of Kabul, miniature from the *Shahname*, Tabriz, Paris, Musée du Louvre
After having conquered Iran, Timur attempted to resolve the traditional enmity between the different cultural entities of Iran and Transoxiana, which had already been the main theme of the Persian national epic *Shahname*, by presenting himself as the Islamic unifier of the two worlds. The ruler's courtly art and literature increasingly depicted him in the guise of a mythical hero, warrior for the faith, and bringer of peace, whose power no one could withstand and whose laws had to be obeyed by all.

to prevent them going over to the enemy. By taking out the Indian war elephants, Timur achieved an overwhelming victory over the fleeing sultan of Delhi. The city surrendered and was largely spared, in spite of some pillaging by individual bands of troops. In 1399 the army pushed on further east, crossed the Ganges, and occupied Lahore. Timur was on the brink of subjugating the Hindu ruler of Kashmir, when bad news from Anatolia and Syria summoned him back west. In April 1399 he was back in Samarqand, laden with rich war spoils and accompanied by innumerable Indian artists and craftsmen.

After his victory over Bayazid, Timur also achieved his ambition of settling his differences with the Mamluks. In 1403 an exchange of ambassadors and precious gifts took place between Samarqand and Cairo, and Timur finally adopted Faraj as his "son," just as he did the king of Castile, whose ambassadors happened to be present at Timur's court. The ruler was finally able to devote himself to the embellishment of Samarqand – which was to become the "center of the world" and "threshold of paradise." Along with numerous splendid buildings, the ruler also endowed Samarqand with large gardens and surrounded the city with suburbs carrying the names of the other Islamic metropolises – Baghdad, Sultaniya, Shiraz, Cairo, and Damascus. Timur surrounded himself with artists and scholars whom he had transported back from just about everywhere. He had the scientific material that he had collected during the course of his campaigns of conquest investigated, while court poets disseminated the glory of the "lord of the celestial conjunction." To mark the rallying of the Islamic world under his "league of peace" banner, in 1404 Timur hosted a dazzling banquet, to which the envoys of both the conquered and allied countries were invited, as well

as those of China, and at which he married off five of his grandchildren, including Ulugh Beg, with great ceremony.

China took this opportunity to demand a resumption of the tribute payments that had stopped in 1396, and this inevitably led to tensions. As the Mongolian Yuan dynasty, descendants of Genghis Khan, had been driven out in 1388, Timur had been contemplating a plan to restore their rule in China. He organized a campaign that would involve firstly restoring peace in Mongolistan, which was restless once more, and from there advancing into China. In November, 1404, the army, under his leadership, left for the north and crossed the Jaxartes in January 1405. In Utrar, where the troops paused to assemble before the advance on Mongolistan, Timur was suddenly stricken with a severe fever and died there on February 18, 1405; his corpse was transported back to Samarqand.

It is not easy to evaluate Timur's rule. His extraordinary military gifts are beyond dispute, as are his skills as strategist and tactician, but so too are his ruthlessness and cruelty, which were able to recognize only subjugation or enmity. Far from being an uneducated barbarian, he had mastered Persian and knew and valued the scholars, scientists, historians, and poets of his time, with whom he surrounded himself and whose works he would discuss with them in depth. On the other hand, there is hardly any discernible concept of state administration, for all he focused his attention on certain cities and regions in particular. His original plan of reinstating the subjugated rulers as his vassals was abandoned in favor of installing governors from his own family, which effectively sowed the seeds for the later fragmenting of Timurid rule.

In religious matters, Timur retained the traditional tolerance of the Mongols, for whom the formalism of the Islamic jurists' schools remained foreign, thus giving a new impetus to the popular forms of Islam with their Sufis and devishes, cult of local saints, soothsayers, interpretation of dreams, and astrological calculations. He tried to combine the Mongolian *yasa*, or law of the steppes, with the Islamic *sharia* and, although Sunni Muslim himself, also acted as protector of the Shiites, to whose ideas some of his descendants were attracted. Although he actually led the life of a nomadic conqueror, he built Samarqand into the new "center of the world" and thus brought about a shift to the east of the center of the Persian-dominated Islamic world. He provided the old Iranian cultural region between eastern Anatolia and Transoxiana a sense of political unity before its ultimate collapse into Turkoman tribal divisions. As heir of the Mongols, Timur punished attacks on traders severely, thus guaranteeing himself an efficient post and news service.

For Europe, Timur's rule had some beneficial consequences: his victory over Bayazid and the ensuing turmoil in the Ottoman Empire provided the besieged Byzantium and Balkans with a breathing space, and the defeat of the Golden Horde permitted the rise of Christian Russia under the leadership of Moscow.

The heirs and successors of Timur: Herat and Samarqand

The two eldest of his sons, Jahangir and Umar Sheikh, were already dead at the time of his Timur's death, Miranshah was clearly unsuitable for the leadership due to mental problems caused by an accident, and even the youngest, Shah Rukh, appeared to be out of the question as a successor because of his godliness and love of peace. Timur had therefore named his grandson, Pir Muhammad, as

his heir. Pir Muhammad was the eldest son of Jahangir, and sat on Mahmud of Gazna's throne as governor in Kandahar. He was assassinated by his own vizier, however, in 1407. Of about 20 of Timur's grandsons holding the positions of governor, two of them now seized power in Samarqand, but their inexperienced and foolish rule led to a rebellion by the city. Shah Rukh, governor of Herat, was called in to help, thereupon occupied Samarqand, and finally became the Timurid's most important leader and head of the family (1405/09–1447).

Shah Rukh managed to hold on to his father's empire, albeit not in its entirety. Along with Transoxiana he brought Jurjan and Mazandaran in Iran under his control and occupied Kerman in 1416. Other regions also acknowledged his sovereignty and the Uzbeks, the Kipchak Empire (the Golden Horde), and the majority of the Indian princes sought alliances with him. But he ruled his empire largely from Herat, and made the Islamic *sharia* the only law, allowing the Mongol element to fade away into the background. By 1420 he had managed to extend his rule over central and southern Persia, but lost Mesopotamia to the Jalayirids and the Qala Qoyunlu, the old enemies of his father, who were also expanding their territories. After the Qara Qoyunlu ruler Qara Yusuf had driven the Jalayirids out of Baghdad in 1410, he became the Timurids' most dangerous opponent. After suppressing a number of revolts, in 1435 Shah Rukh was able to devote himself to the peaceful development of his empire, which benefited the arts and intellectual life, and to intensifying the trading relationships with China, India, and Egypt.

Of his seven sons, only Muhammad Taragai, known as Ulugh Beg, perhaps the most remarkable individual among the later Timurids, was still alive when Shah Rukh died in 1447. Ulugh Beg had been reigning in Samarqand since 1407 as a quasi-independent ruler, and his court, with its worldly

Above: ***Timur on his Throne***, Moghul painting. Paris, Bibliothèque Nationale
Timur officially began his rule in 1370, when the princes of Transoxiana were made to pay homage to him. Because of his successful rule, at the height of his power he was known as the "lord of the celestial conjunction."

Table of descent of Timur's Indian princes, Moghul miniature, 18th century, Jaipur, City Palace Museum
This idealized representation depicts Timur surrounded by the Moghul rulers of India, whose progenitor he was held to be.

character, perpetuated, in its intellectual openness, the Mongol traditions of his grandfather Timur. He was equally renowned as a patron of new building in Bukhara and Samarqand and as sponsor of Persian poetry and the natural sciences. He also emerged as an astronomer and mathematician in his own right, leaving behind a wealth of writings and star charts. Since 1407 he had ruled leniently during a long period of peace, but had a very tense relationship with the next generation, consisting of Timur's great-grandchildren.

Ulugh Beg's own son, Abd al-Latif, who had lived with his grandfather, Shah Rukh, in Herat since 1444, and who nurtured justified hopes of gaining the succession himself, took over supreme command of the army upon Shah Rukh's death in 1447, and others of the Shah Rukh's grandsons appropriated various territories and occupied the empire's cities as well. Ulugh Beg, who saw himself as the sole legitimate heir of his father, marched on the Oxus, but met with resistance from the assembled representatives of the younger generation; Ulugh Beg was not able to command the obedience that had been shown to his father. During the course of battles of varying fortunes fought out over the next two years, Ulugh Beg was able to hold on to Transoxiana, but lost all control over Khorasan. In the autumn of 1449 there was a military confrontation that resulted in Ulugh Beg being defeated by his son. Abd al-Latif granted him permission to make a pilgrimage to Mecca, but had him murdered on the way.

After Abd al-Latif was himself murdered by his emirs in May 1450, there was a period of political confusion out of which Abu Said (1451–1469), a great-grandson of Timur through the Miranshah line, emerged victorious. He ruled from Samarqand over Transoxiana, west Turkestan, and parts of Afghanistan, but lost the whole of central and southern Persia, to the Qara Qoyunlu in 1452, who pushed up as far as Herat in 1458. Abu Said brought his lands great improvements, fostering agriculture and building up irrigation systems. When the Qara Qoyunlu were defeated by their rivals the Aq Qoyunlu in 1467, Abu Said advanced west in order to win back his territories. In February 1469 he suffered a crushing defeat at the hands of the Aq Qoyunlu ruler Uzun Hasan, and was taken prisoner and then executed. His son Sultan Ahmad (1469–1494) continued to govern from Samarqand, but his rule was continually threatened by the Uzbek Shaybanids. In 1497 Sultan Ahmad's nephew, Babur, later to be the first Great Moghul, managed to occupy Samarqand temporarily, before it finally fell to the Shaybanids. From Kabul, Babur was to conquer India in the years up to 1526.

In Herat, the last Timurid Husain Baiqara (1469–1506), a great-grandson of Timur through the Umar Sheikh line of descent, led the empire into a final golden age. As a brave military leader and skillful diplomat, he held on to Khorasan under competition from the Aq Qoyunlu and rival Timurid princes and managed to bring about a long period of peace. At his court he gathered together capable statesmen as well as poets and artists, wrote poetry and scientific treatises himself, and above all promoted Persian and Turkish literature. The traditions of his court were later continued by the Moghuls in India. Timur was now seen as the great, almost mythical founding figure of modern Persian-Turkish and Mongolian Islam. Soon after Husain Baqara died, during a military campaign against the Shaybanids in May 1506, the Shaybanids occupied Herat, and the Timurid era came to an end.

Reconstruction of Ulugh Beg's observatory, in Samarqand, painting by Nilsen, Samarkand, Observatory Museum Timur's grandson, Ulugh Beg (1394–1449), who ruled in Samarqand from 1409, was one of the most important scholars and astronomers of his time, and made some of the most accurate astronomical calculations of the Middle Ages. To this end, he had a mighty observatory containing a sextant built in Samarqand in 1428/29, of which only the parts set into the ground have survived.

Timur's tomb in the Gur-i Mir Mausoleum in Samarqand, beginning of the 14th century After Timur's death, in February 1405, in Utrar during a military campaign against China, his corpse was transported back to Samarqand and laid to rest in the Gur-i Mur Mausoleum, which was built specially for him and where other members of his family also lie. During an investigation of his bones in 1941, Soviet scientists were able confirm the existence of a deformed right knee and right shoulder, which had earned him the nickname "Lenk" or "lame one."

Architecture

Sergej Chmelnizkij

Characteristics of Timurid architecture

The development, and peculiarities, of Central Asian architecture between the middle of the 14th and the middle of the 15th centuries were determined by the existence of the world empire created by the military commander Timur, who was as cruel as he was capable. His enormous empire stretched from Asia Minor to India – taking in Delhi on its way – and from the Caucasus and the Kazakh steppes all the way to the Arabian Sea. Timur decided upon Samarqand in present-day Uzbekistan as the capital of this huge empire and made it dazzle with the splendor and radiance of its monumental and magnificent buildings. The building activity of this period was dominated by Timur's own passion for construction and his efforts to give his limitless power the architecture it deserved. Architects and artists from all of the lands he had conquered, from Asia Minor, Azerbaijan, the Caucasus, India, Iran, and elsewhere, were forced to contribute to the construction of often colossal state buildings of both a sacred and secular nature. In this fashion, completely different artistic schools and traditions were fused together, united by Timur's determination to achieve monumentality and splendor, and a characteristic international style was developed – what is now known as the style of the Timurid Empire.

The imposing external appearance of the monumental buildings now became the number one priority. These majestic structures were topped with domes, the enormous portals developed into a virtually free-standing architectural form and kind of status symbol, and proportions became more slender. High drums and external domes, stabilized by projecting brick ribs and wooden struts, were placed over the structural inner domes. These were merely external, decorative additions, not affecting the interior space. This idea originated as far back as the 11th century, but did not become widespread until the 14th and 15th centuries, when it gave these monumental buildings their characteristic appearance.

One structural innovation of the 15th century was to set the dome on two pairs of overlapping arches rather than on the traditional octagonal squinch. For this, two brick arches were built over a square chamber at an equal distance from the walls, and another two at right angles to them. Overlapping at the top, they formed a square base for the dome. A dome of this type was significantly smaller than one that sat on corner squinches, whose diameter was equivalent to the length of the room's sides. The spaces between the vertices of the arches were filled in with shield-shaped spandrels – rhombus-like concave in-filling between the overlapping ribs of the arches. This type of spandrel was also used between the squinches of the traditional, octagonal, lower part of a dome.

This construction method, which was extremely successful despite the seismic conditions that prevailed in Central Asia, changed the character of the interior space radically. Whereas previously the vertical progression of square hall and octagonal squinch area had made it seem static, it was now given a dynamic plasticity. This technique had originated in the Middle East, probably in Armenia, where it had been known since the 12th century. In the 14th

Details of facade coverings in the Shah-i Zinda necropolis near Samarqand, from left to right: Tilla Kari Madrasa 1660; Usto Ali Nesefi Mausoleum, 1380s; Turkan-aka Mausoleum, 1372
The most striking characteristic of Timurid architecture is the radiant tile mosaic and carved, glazed terracotta decoration that covers its surfaces. The usual facade coverings of the previous period, the 11th and 12th centuries, consisting of double brick bonds of a natural, yellowish color, were now only used on the back or side facades. The decoration displays geometric designs such as the unusual pattern formed of large, 16-point stars (middle), vegetal motifs, and inscriptions of a poetic con- tent or of Koran suras. On the left is a late example of a portal arch decorated with continuous, rope-like twisted ribbons of painted tile resting on a sort of column base.

century it started being used in Russian church architecture, and it is possible that Armenian building masters, who had fled from the lands conquered by Timur to their brothers in faith in Russia, were responsible for this.

An even more striking feature of the architecture of the Timurid Empire is its multicolored, sparkling tile mosaic facings, which covered the brickwork like a glistening skin. For the architecture of the preceding era, the 11th and 12th centuries, the very opposite had been the case: the aestheticizing of brickwork and construction itself, the natural, yellowish color of the bricks and terracotta, and the retention of clear architectonics even in the decoration. The buildings erected by Timur, however, were "dressed," in such a way that their structural organization was no longer visible. The interiors of the imperial buildings of the 14th and 15th centuries are dominated by wall paintings, the inside of the domes by gilt papier-mâché relief ornament, and also frequently encountered are wall coverings consisting of paneling of glazed, finely painted individual sections. Stalactite decorations or *muqarnas*, which coated and disguised brick vaulting and domes, were also widespread.

The striving for monumentality produced buildings of proportions not previously known and not achieved since. Even in the memorial architecture of the time, along with small mausoleums of the traditional type, that is to say domed buildings of square design, there arose magnificently decorated tombs of generous proportions which looked more like palaces. Their central chambers (*gurkhanas*) were surrounded by rooms of different shapes and functions. That this architecture was commissioned by the state, and developed in the service of the empire, is also evident in the construction of larger ensembles of sacred, memorial, and secular buildings regular in their design.

Khoja Ahmad Yasawi Mausoleum Complex, Turkestan (Jassy), 1389–1399
This ensemble, which is unique in its proportions, is typical of Timur's imperial style. The massive construction embraces a mausoleum over a venerated tomb, an enormous hall (*khanqa*) for the ritual gatherings of the Sufi dervishes, a mosque, as well as a library, and living accommodation, among other rooms. Characteristic of Timur's monumental buildings is the large-scale geometric pattern that covers wide areas of the walls like a carpet. The materials used for this were dark blue, turquoise, and white glazed bricks, set in place against the background of the natural, yellowish brick.

Architecture under Timur

Timur built the Aq Saray palace ("White, i.e. beautiful, Palace") in his home city Shahr-i Sabz, of which only the ruins of the enormous, richly decorated entrance portal survive. This was around 165 feet (50 meters) high, the span of its arch was 72 feet (22 meters), and it was flanked by massive corner pillars with polygonal bases and round shafts. Behind the portal extended a spacious courtyard with a water basin, enclosed by two-story buildings incorporating a multitude of columns and living accommodation. The portal inscription reads: "If you doubt our power, just take a look at our buildings!" and thus encapsulated the social function of architecture under Timur.

The colossal memorial and shrine complex built between 1389 and 1399 over the tomb of local saint Khoja Ahmad Yasawi in Jassy, the present-day town of Turkestan in Kazakhstan, has also been subordinated to this central idea. The building's complicated design, which involved the various types of room being fitted into a rectangular "pouch," indicates extremely rational and effective planning. It is remarkable that the enormous dome of the central chamber, lavishly decorated with *muqarnas*, rests not on spandrels or squinches, but merely on a structure of a type already described, consisting of wooden beams placed diagonally across the corners of the room.

General view and detail of a domed side chamber of the Bibi Khanum Friday Mosque, Samarqand, 1399–1404
In contrast to the palaces and Friday mosques that usually have vaulted *iwans* on their cross-axes, the gigantic Timurid Bibi Khanum mosque was given "little mosques" in this position in the middle of the courtyard side arcades. They resembled the enormous, domed main building at the end of the longitudinal axis but were simply smaller in scale.

The high outer dome of the building, which covers a structural inner dome, is stabilized by projecting brick ribs and is remarkable primarily for its splendid polychrome tile covering, which displays ornamental features and inscriptive bands.

Only a few impressive fragments remain of what was a similar and just as grandiose sacred and memorial complex from the end of the 14th century. This construction stood in Shahr-i Sabz, Timur's home city, and was apparently supposed to be his last resting place. This mighty building 300 × 165 feet (70 × 50 meters) bore the name Dar al-Sadat ("House of Power") and was located in the southeastern part of the city. From the point of view of its design it resembled the Turkestan building: behind the high entrance niche between the two massive corner pillars there would probably have been a large, domed chamber, and behind this in turn, positioned on the same axis, the mausoleum. Each of these areas would have been enclosed by two groups of rooms of various sorts. Only the left corner pillar of the portal remains, into which is integrated the unusually high mausoleum of Timur's son Jahangir, and which has then been made even higher by the addition of a pyramid roof. The tomb of another of Timur's sons, Umar Sheikh, is supposed to have been located in the right-hand corner pillar, which has now disappeared. The mausoleum Timur built for himself was never used. Of this, a marble-paneled vault with a shallow dome of unusual construction and a marble sarcophagus have survived. In 1404 a reception held in honor of the Spanish ambassador de Clavijo, who left an enthusiastic and vivid description of the event, took place in one of the rooms of this palace-like mausoleum.

The mosques of Samarqand and Bukhara

After his campaign of pillage to India, Timur, between 1399 and 1404, had one of the biggest mosques in the world built in Samarqand. Entry to this enormous edifice 460 × 325 feet (140.2 × 99.15 meters), known as the Bibi Khanum

Friday Mosque, was through a high portal with round corner towers, whose arches had a span of nearly 62 feet (19 meters). Behind the portal lay a spacious courtyard enclosed by domed galleries resting on carved marble columns, at the back of which stood the dome-covered main building of the mosque, towering up to a height of 144 feet (44 meters). Its gigantic portal was flanked by towers of polygonal design, whose decoration consisted of mosaic panels covering each of their sides and reaching right up to the top. Two smaller domed chambers stood on the cross-axis of the courtyard, and at each of the four outer corners stood a high, slender minaret. Glazed, polychrome linings covered the facades, and the portal facades in particular were decorated with an especially rich and complex mosaic and carved marble design. Decorative gold-blue paintwork covered the surfaces of all the inner rooms, leaving no free spaces. Building masters from various lands conquered by Timur, among them Azerbaijan, worked on the construction of the Bibi Khanum Mosque. Only its ruins now remain, but in fact the building started to decay before it could be completed. The pressure of the huge quantity of bricks was too great, and the excessively high and heavy dome was incapable of withstanding the tremors caused by frequent earthquakes as the arcades on their slender marble columns. What this showed was that the old construction techniques could not simply be transferred to a building of such gigantic proportions, and additionally that the foreign building masters were not acquainted with the natural conditions that prevailed in this region. During the Soviet period the decision was made to restore the mosque; this work has been continuing now for almost 30 years. Unfortunately, the authentic, majestic ruins of this mighty building have consequently been immured within a sham brick and concrete case and therefore to all intents and purposes destroyed.

The Kalan Friday Mosque in Bukhara was built during the first half of the 15th century, possibly over the remains of an old mosque that dated from the 12th century, whose minaret survives, but definitely following the model of the enormous mosque in Samarqand. Here, however, there are no small domed structures on the cross-axis, but relatively low portals serving exclusively decorative purposes. The 288 domes of the galleries that enclose the courtyard are not supported by slender, frail columns, but by solid pillars. Probably for the first time, the usual entrance portal niche was here given a polygonal design – a compositional feature that became widely used in the architecture of Bukhara in the 16th and 17th centuries. Entrance from the courtyard to the ruler's section of the building (*maqsura*) is through a wide, high portal niche. The focus of the square hall is a very deep niche containing a *mihrab* decorated with wonderful tile mosaics. The hall is covered by a dome, on the outside of which rises a turquoise exterior dome on a round drum covered with ornament. After the minaret, this is Bukhara's second most important landmark. The courtyard's flat galleries, stretching out lengthwise, provide an impressive contrast with the monumental *maqsura* and the symmetry of its entrance portal, which directly faces the portal of the Mir-i Arab Madrasa.

Mausoleums

At a distance of 655 feet (200 meters) southeast of the entrance to the Bibi Khanum Mosque in Samarqand, the ruins are visible of the mausoleum of the same name. This was probably part of the Bibi Khanum Madrasa, which disappeared a long time ago, but was aligned with the massive mosque opposite according to the *kosh* system. Beneath the floor of the mausoleum is the burial chamber, which consists of a central square space with a ruined dome and four deep, low, vaulted niches. A primitively constructed octagon leads up from the

square chamber of the upper room into the drum. It rests not on squinches or spandrels, but on diagonal beams set into the brickwork, which as usual were covered with a stucco stalactite decoration. This type of decoration also fills the upper halves of the narrow interior niches. The drum is decorated with a large-format Kufic inscription in glazed brick, and is crowned by the remains of a dome. Setting aside the splendidly decorated burial chamber, the building stands out strongly from the overloaded memorial architecture of this period due to the unusual harmony of its proportions and its restrained decoration. The wall covering above the stone dado of the burial chamber walls consists of small, polished bricks interspersed with blue and light blue panels. Mosaic paneling featuring a *gerich* (geometric star) design runs around the lower edge of the upper chamber, with the niches having a different star-shaped pattern to that of the walls of the square room. The paneling is divided up into individual tablets interwoven with gold, each framed by a mosaic border. On the walls above the paneling, traces remain of blue-on-white wall painting with the occasional use of green, yellow, brown, and other colors. Especially remarkable are the stylized and freely painted landscapes.

Similar decorative motifs, among them some mosaic paneling with a *gerich* design, decorate the interior of the Tuman-aka Mausoleum (1405) in the Shah-i Zinda necropolis in Samarqand. It would appear that the two buildings were built and decorated by the same craftsmen.

At the end of the 14th century, a complex of buildings was constructed in Samarqand, consisting of a *madrasa* and a *khanqa*, which offered shelter to pilgrims. The two buildings stand opposite each other on either side of an enclosed, square courtyard in such a way that each entrance portal is highlighted by the other. When Timur's favorite grandson, Muhammad, died, on the remaining side, opposite the courtyard entrance, a mausoleum was built in his honor, which is known as the Gur-i Mir ("Emir's Tomb"). It later became

Ruins of the prayer hall of the Bibi Khanum Mosque, Samarqand, 1394–1404
Timur began building his Friday mosque, the proportions of which were supposed to surpass those of all comparable buildings in the world, after returning from his victorious campaign to India. Thus the arch of the main building has a span of more than 18 meters, and the arch of the entrance portal measures nearly 19 meters across. The building masters retained the traditional schema, of domed hall with an inner dome resting on squinches and an outer dome sitting on a high drum, without making any adjustments other than a general increase in dimensions, and without taking into account the frequency of earthquakes in the region or the massive weight of the brickwork. As a consequence, the enormous building, with a height of 44 meters, began to crumble under its own weight. This process of decay had already started before the building work was finished, and the remains that have survived until the present day cannot really be restored.

Complex of buildings including the Gur-i Mir Mausoleum,
Samarqand, late 14th–early 15th century
The Muhammad Sultan Madrasa (2), named after Timur's favorite
grandson, a *khanqa* (3), and the courtyard between them with axial
iwans and portal (4) were all built at the end of the 14th century,
before the construction of the mausoleum that was later integrated
into the complex. The Gur-i Mir Mausoleum (1), which was designed
for Muhammad Sultan, was soon to become the final resting place
of Timur and his descendants.

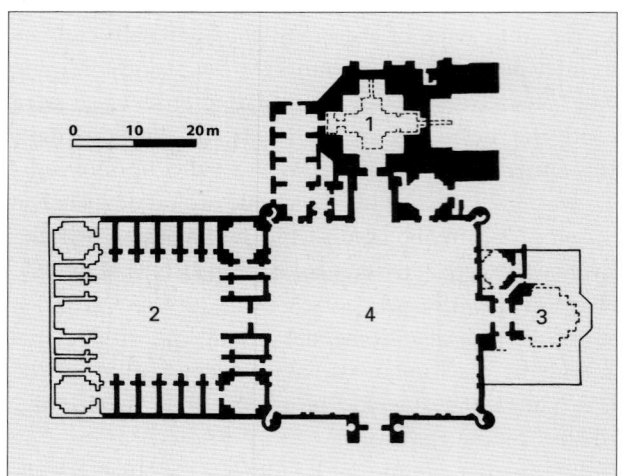

the final resting place of Timur and his descendants. The mausoleum's
architecture is extremely unusual: a high, solid-looking cylindrical drum, which
is crowned by a ribbed dome whose cross section has the shape of a pointed
arch, sits on an octagonal base. The cylinder, covered by an ornamental facing,
and azure dome dominate the building completely and give it a tower-like
appearance that still distinguishes the face of the old city. The square chamber of the mausoleum and its deep axial niches are decorated with paneling of
expensive onyx and painted ornament, while the interior of the dome is covered
by a blue-gold papier-mâché reliefwork decoration. The cruciform burial vault,
covered by a very shallow dome, is hidden away beneath this chamber. Close to
the Gur-i Mir stand the remains of a mausoleum of the new palace-like type,
known as the Aq Saray. This is a relatively small building from the middle of the
15th century, whose surviving portion comprises the central domed chamber,
the corner rooms, and a long, three-part gallery-like hall on the north side.

It is not really possible to ascertain what the building may have looked like
from the outside, but the remains of the interior architecture are breathtakingly
exquisite. Extremely fine tile mosaics and painted blue-gold *kundal* reliefwork
combine here with the elegance of the vaulting, which is supported by overlapping transverse arches. The small dome of the central chamber sits on paired
overlapping arches, with the spaces between them filled with a network of
delicate ribs.

The Ishrat Khana Mausoleum, built somewhat earlier, is larger than the Aq
Saray and has also been fortunate in managing to escape comprehensive restoration. Here, too, the large central chamber with deep axial niches is covered by
a shallow dome supported by overlapping arches. Two stories high in places, it
is surrounded by a multitude of impressively designed rooms of a variety of
forms and function decorated with mosaic panels and *kundal* paintwork.
This large building 92 × 75 feet (28 × 23) meters has survived in relatively good
condition. While even the large, exquisitely decorated portal still stands,
unfortunately nothing remains of the external dome and its drum, which would
have towered high above the inner dome of the middle chamber – a feature
characteristic of Timurid architecture. The Ishrat Khana's design, unusually

complicated for a mausoleum, has even given rise to some conjecture that this
building was not a tomb building at all, but a palace standing outside the city,
an idea apparently confirmed by the building's name – Ishrat Khana means
"Home of Joy." But the octagonal burial chamber with its shallow dome and
characteristic passage leading down to it leave no room for doubt regarding the
function of this wonderful building. Of the palaces built by Timur and his
descendants, incidentally, other than a portal of the Shahr-i Sabz palace and
some small archaeological finds, nothing has survived except the descriptions set
down by enthusiastic contemporaries.

Shah-i Zinda

Alongside the palace-like mausoleums, mausoleums of the traditional type were
also built by Timur and his descendants. They were small by comparison, and
designed for the relatives of the ruler and his dignitaries. Particularly impressive
examples can still be admired today in the Samarqand Shah-i Zinda ("Living
Shah") necropolis. The necropolis came into being over the alleged tomb of
Muhammad Qutham ibn Abbas, a cousin of Prophet Muhammad, who, according to legend, managed to escape down a crevice, where he can still supposedly
be found, while fighting the unbelievers. The mausoleums of Shah-i Zinda
developed along a narrow path that climbs northwards from the old city walls.
They are predominantly single-room buildings with the obligatory portal forming the main facade and a dome over which – except in the case of the oldest
mausoleums, which were still built in the old traditional way – rose a decorative
outer dome resting on a drum. The later the mausoleums were built, the larger
and more slender their decorative upper portions.

The decoration of the Shah-i Zinda mausoleum portals captivates with its
splendor and rich diversity, which stem from exquisite and no doubt very expensive techniques. Painted ceramic panels, carved, glazed terracotta, delicate tile
mosaics and decorative glazed brick bonds combine with the superb calligraphy
of Arabic and Persian inscriptions which quote not only from the Koran, but
also from elegiac poetry, and intermingle with floral and geometric patterns.

Inner dome of the Gur-i Mir Mausoleum,
Samarqand, from 1404
Covering a relatively small surface area, the
Gur-i Mir's dome rises majestically to an
internal height of 26 meters. The inside of the
dome is decorated with gilded papier-mâché
reliefwork. Pictured here are the results of
restoration work based on actual surviving
elements and impression marks left by
features that have been lost. This impressive
decorative technique was used in some very
important buildings in the 14th century, such
as the dome of the Bibi Khanum Mosque.
The square chamber of the mausoleum, along
with its deep axial niches, is decorated with
paneling of expensive onyx and painted
ornament. Hidden beneath its floor lies the
cruciform burial chamber, which is covered by
a very shallow dome.

Shah-i Zinda necropolis, Samarqand, end of the 14th to the beginning of the 15th centuries

The Shah-i Zinda necropolis, through which a narrow pathway runs, comprises some particularly impressive mausoleums. Pictured on the left of the path (see right) is a side facade of the mausoleum built by architect Ali Nesefi in the 1380s. The portal arch tympana of the Turkan-aka Mausoleum (below), built in 1372, are filled with a blue-and-white floral ornament. This exquisite and harmonious decoration sets a wonderfully elegiac tone for the tomb of a woman who died young, and is a good example of the opulent and lyrical decorative arts of the court under Timur.

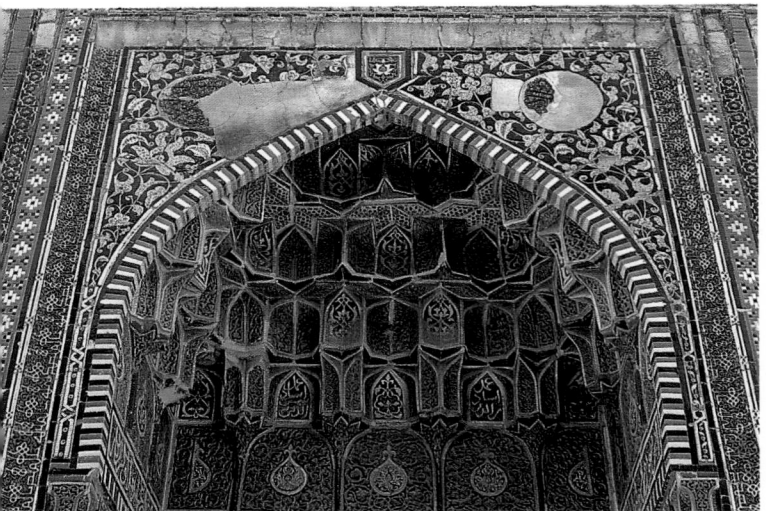

The decoration of each mausoleum has been individually crafted from precious materials in such a way that there is no repetition.

Since the entrance portals of the mausoleums represent a kind of final flourish of decoration within the empire, it is all the more remarkable that brickwork typical of pre-Mongol times (the 11th and 12th centuries), with its modest three-dimensional detail, has been used on the sides and not directly in the line of the onlooker's gaze. This attests to the fact that the "old style" had not been definitively forgotten, but simply hidden away. The magnificence of the interior decoration of the Shah-i Zinda mausoleums hardly corresponds at all to European expectations. In the mausoleum of Timur's sister Shirin-biki-aka (1385), for example, the walls are covered with ornamental paintings and decorated with a paneling of tiles across the glaze of which fine gold patterns have been traced. Stylized landscapes with very realistic magpies decorate one wall panel. The windows underneath the dome have been closed up with elaborately worked stucco grilles in which pieces of red, blue, orange, and green glass have been inlaid, giving them the appearance of stained-glass windows. A particularly impressive example is a two-room mausoleum built in the 1430s, which was thought to be the tomb of the astronomer Qadi Zada Rumi until the skeletons of two women were found there. Each of the rooms is crowned by a high, slender, tower-like dome structure and the inner domes are covered with complex stalactite work. Whereas one room would normally be the mausoleum and the other a mosque, the larger of the two rooms, which has four

The facade of the Ali Nesef Mausoleum, Shah-i Zinda, Samarqand

The mausoleums in Shah-i-Zinda all follow the same construction plan: an interior room with an almost square ground plan, usually topped by a two-staged dome, lies behind a superimposed facade. The fascination of the necropolis lies not in the architecture, but in the decoration of the facades. The master builder from Karchi (formerly Nesefi) adorned this mausoleum with a repeated eight-pointed star, symbolizing the eye of God observing the world.

axial entrances, had no *mihrab*, obligatory in a mosque, and so it is assumed that it was used as a small *khanqa*.

One piece of evidence for the fact that foreign building masters also contributed to the work carried out at Shah-i Zinda is the mausoleum known as the "octagon." This is a dome-roofed pavilion, open on each side, which stands on eight pillars connected by wide arches. A polygonal mausoleum like this was not typical of the memorial architecture of Central Asia, but was characteristic of Azerbaijan and Khorasan in Iran. The decoration of the "octagon," on the other hand, fits into the local tradition.

Architecture under Timur's heirs

Typical of Timur's imperial architecture, which, like that of all totalitarian states from all periods, regardless of its style, to some extent carries the stamp of work being carried out by command, are the gigantic proportions and the excessive splendor of decoration, which is not related to the construction of the building, but simply applied afterwards. These buildings were brought into being by the personal will of the "client," and made possible by the limitless resources pillaged during the campaigns of conquest. The automatic scaling-up of the dimensions led, however, to technical complications, as the example of the Bibi Khanum Mosque clearly shows. The fact that artists and building masters from various countries, with their own different traditions, contributed to the work resulted in a curiously international style, that resembled the future European Baroque, in spirit if not in form.

Timur's heirs, who ruled from Herat and Samarqand, won fewer victories, and brought back fewer spoils, but clearly had better taste. The monumental architecture of the first half of the 15th century generally impresses not because of its enormous dimensions, but because of its balanced proportions and the exquisite nature of its external and internal decoration. Tile mosaics (sometimes with carved marble insertions) dominate the facade coverings, the use of gold disappears from the wall painting, and the ornamentation becomes more refined.

The Ulugh Beg Madrasas

The three oldest surviving *madrasas* in Central Asia date back to the beginning of the 15th century, and were built by Timur's grandson, Ulugh Beg. An earlier one, built under Timur, formed part of the complex surrounding the Gur-i Mir Mausoleum. There, a *khanqa* and a small *madrasa* stood face to face on either side of a courtyard in a *kosh* arrangement. But too little remains of this *madrasa* to gain a proper impression of its original design. The good state of preservation of the three Ulugh Beg Madrasas, on the other hand, allow a clear assessment to be made – despite some lost features and a quantity of ill-advised and not always justifiable restoration work from recent and also earlier times.

The Central Asian type of *madrasa* came into being at the beginning of the 15th century. The *madrasas* were theological colleges in which the material sciences, including mathematics and astronomy, an area in which Ulugh Beg was an expert, were also taught.

All three of the Ulugh Beg Madrasas, in Bukhara (1418), Samarqand (1417–1420), and Gishduwan (1437) were, with certain small deviations, built using the same schema. The special feature of the *madrasa* in Bukhara is its main facade. Extending to the right and left of the high, slender portal, with its pointed entrance niche arch, are two sections of two-story pointed arch arcades – an architectural idea that became very widespread in the 16th and 17th centuries. On the carved door an inscription was legible until recently that according to legend referred to a ruling by Ulugh Beg: "To strive for knowledge is the duty of each and every Muslim man and woman." In the courtyard there are no side *iwans*, which may be a consequence of alterations carried out in the 16th century, a hypothesis supported by the existence of Abdullah Khanid wall coverings on the side courtyard facades.

The largest of the three Ulugh Beg Madrasas, which is the one in Samarqand, opens via an enormous portal onto the city's main Registan Square. In terms of its dimensions, it is comparable with Timur's buildings, but is not as heavy looking as the majority of them. Although the upper floor of cells surrounding the courtyard has disappeared, along with the arched loggias that

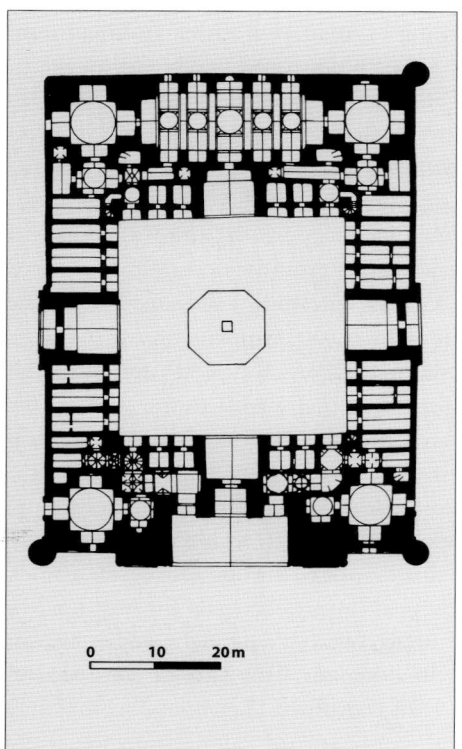

Facade and ground plan of the Ulugh Beg Madrasa, in Samarqand, 1417–1420

This *madrasa* on Registan Square is one of the largest in Central Asia. With its enormous portal and rich tile decoration it was the model for the Shir Dor Madrasa, built in the 17th century on the opposite side of the square. Its high entrance niche set into the portal and dome-covered lecture halls in the corners on either side, along with the square inner courtyard, which has deep, domed, axial *iwans*, make this a classic example of the Central Asian *madrasa*. Unusual are the passageways in the side *iwans*, the large hall mosque behind the rear *iwan*, and the additional lecture halls to its right and left, which have the same shape as those at the front. The entrances to the students' rooms, which run around the courtyard on two floors, occupy the courtyard facades on either side of the *iwans*. A slender, tower-shaped minaret rises up at each corner of the main facade.

Ulugh Beg Madrasa, in Bukhara, 1418
This building, which differs from the one in Samarqand in its more modest proportions and less lavish, but nevertheless very fine, decoration, served as an example for many *madrasas* in Bukhara and other cities in the

16th century. The technique employed here, for the first time, of fashioning the main facade from two-story arcading that reflected the shape of the rooms that lay behind it, was soon widespread.

contained their entrances and the upper portion of the portal too, the building nevertheless makes an unforgettable impression: the design of the *madrasa* is distinguished by certain special features. It has a dome-covered lecture hall with four axial niches at each of its four corners, not just to the left and right of the entrance portal, and an unusual mosque that has been placed between the back two of these. It consists of a lateral rectangular hall subdivided by four transverse arches, with a dome above each of the five sections. Along with those by the main entrance, there are also two further rooms in the side *iwans* which were used as lecture halls (*darskhans*). These peculiarities did not prevent the Ulugh Beg Madrasa in Samarqand from becoming the prototype for many *madrasas* in the future.

The single-story Ulugh Beg Madrasa in Gishduwan, with just four cells on either side of its courtyard, is the smallest of the three. The traditionally symmetrical main facade is richly decorated with tiles, and the wings on either side of the high portal take their shape from a pair of narrow arched panels that form the entrances to the halls that lie behind them. In contrast to the usual square plan of the two halls to the right and left of the portal, the hall of the mosque and the lecture hall here are rectangular and, like the mosque in the Samarqand *madrasa*, covered by vaulting supported by transverse arches. The one *iwan* on the rear wall projects with sloping corners from the rear facade, as does the rear *iwan* of the Ulugh Beg Madrasa in Bukhara.

Mausoleums

In the first half of the 15th century, a series of tomb and shrine buildings was built in Shahr-i Sabz, not far from the Dar al-Siadat, forming an original architectural ensemble. At its heart is the tomb of the renowned Sufi, Shams al-Din Kulal, the spiritual master of Timur's father Emir Taragai, over which Ulugh Beg had a dome-covered mausoleum built, decorated with blue and turquoise glazed brick mosaics. Not even fragments survive of the dome that must have once existed here, as it was replaced, probably a long time ago, by a flat ceiling with wooden beams, supported by two wooden columns. In 1435 the Gok Gumbad ("Blue Dome") Mosque was built directly opposite the Kulal Mausoleum, and served as the city's Friday mosque. Only its main building still stands, a square domed hall with axial niches, the length of whose sides is 39 feet (12 meters). On three of its axis points are entrances, the east one forming a portal that occupies the entire width of the building. The surfaces to the right and left of the entrance niche are each decorated with three arched panels positioned one above the other. Beneath the corner squinches underneath the dome are shield-shaped spandrels, which are typical of the time. Of the blue outer dome, from which the building takes its name, only the massive drum remains. Traces of polychrome tile decoration have survived, but only on the corner pillars of the portal and on the drum.

In 1437/38 a so-called *maqbara* was built on to the Kulal Mausoleum, a tomb building for Ulugh Beg's relatives and descendants. The elegantly proportioned building consists of a cube-shaped body and a high drum with an outer dome that has now been restored. The remains of the portal decoration consist of blue, light blue, and white glazed bricks on a background of the usual yellowish brickwork. The mosque and the two tomb buildings each occupy a side of the courtyard that lies between them, and thus form an impressive ensemble.

The Mosque of Anau

In 1456/57, at an astonishingly great distance from the cultural centers of the time, a large and unusual mosque was built in Anau in southern Turkmenistan, which stood for about 500 years before being destroyed by an earthquake in 1948. A dome-covered main building and two asymmetrical wings, which also had domed rooms in the middle of them, enclosed the small courtyard that lies between them in such a way that it formed a "pouch" shape, opening with its entire width to the northeast. The main building, which is the mosque itself, also opened to the northeast with almost its entire width, and was actually a dome-covered *iwan* with a high portal facade. Its exquisite decoration consisted of tile ornament and mosaic carving on a background of polished brick. The most striking portal decoration was located in the tympana above the wide central portal arch: a tile mosaic depicted two dragons of typical Chinese design snaking their way through apple blossom from the outside to the center. This Chinese subject was, however, adapted to fit the mode of representation typical for Central Asian miniature painting of the 14th and 15th centuries.

The square hall of the mosque, whose sides were 34 feet (10.5 meters) long, was covered by a dome of unusually stocky form, which would apparently have been covered by an outer dome. The dome appeared to be resting on a thick layer of stalactite decoration, which occupied the area between the four shallow arched niches; the stalactites, however, were covering diagonal wooden beams, which formed the real base on which the dome sat. This kind of construction was not uncommon in the 14th and 15th centuries. The *mihrab*, completely covered in radiant mosaics, provided the only area of color within the white interior of the hall. The hall was surrounded on three sides – all except the portal side – by a platform. This was occupied by groups of small cells similar to those of a *madrasa*. The design of the wings – a central domed hall surrounded by two-story galleries – has not been encountered anywhere else and its function is not known. Perhaps the central rooms were the lecture halls of a *madrasa* whose students lived in the cells, or else halls used for the gatherings of Sufi dervishes, thus forming part of a *khanqa*. One possible explanation for the curious design features of the Anau Mosque is that it was fairly close to the tomb of a certain Jamal al-Din, who was revered by the faithful. The combination of mosque, *madrasa*, tomb, and *khanqa* in the same complex did occur in Middle Eastern architecture, a fact that can be illustrated by numerous examples. There are no parallels, not even distant ones, however, for the Anau Mosque.

Ulugh Beg's Observatory

At the beginning of the 20th century, the remains of a building were discovered that is unique in the architecture of the 14th and 15th centuries due to the particular function it served. It was ascertained that the excavated parts of its foundations were those of an observatory that was built to the north of Samarqand in 1428/29 on the orders of Ulugh Beg. Ulugh Beg may not have been a successful military commander, but he was a famous scholar who compiled astronomical tables that were used right up to modern times, and who contributed to the spread of secular knowledge. Soon after his violent death the neglected observatory was razed to the ground.

The most important instrument of the observatory, the sextant, used for measuring the angular elevation of celestial bodies, was positioned along the north-south axis of this circular building, which had a diameter of 157 feet (48 meters). A quarter-circle segment, made of smooth, polished stone with notches marking the degrees and signs of the zodiac, was cut deep into the stony ground below the observatory. On either side of the sextant were various rooms of different, and in some cases, due to the round design of the building,

Above and below: **Ulugh Beg's Observatory**, Samarqand, 1st half of the 15th century
All that remains of Timur's learned grandson's observatory is a segment of circle, made of polished stone, which was cut into the ground: the lower part of a sextant that was used to measure the angular elevation of celestial bodies. After Ulugh Beg's assassination, the observatory was destroyed because of disapproval from religious scholars.

truly remarkable, shapes, which probably served as storage rooms for smaller instruments and workrooms for the scientists. Several hypotheses exist concerning the external appearance of the observatory and its internal organization. If one accepts the most recent and most convincing, it took the form of an enormous, three-story cylinder. Its two upper floors were designed as a continuous arcade, and large-scale geometric patterns in the style of the time decorated the ground floor, entrances, and windows. Unfortunately, no comparable buildings are known to us from the same period, only the observatories built later in Delhi and Jaipur, which were probably modeled on the Samarqand one.

In the monumental architecture of the first half of the 15th century it is possible to detect a certain turning away from the Timurid love of things big and the excessive use of polychrome decoration that permitted no surface to be left unadorned. The different buildings and different building types of this period stand in more of a harmonious relationship with each other, their proportions are better balanced, and their decoration is refined rather that resplendent. During this period, the old methods of dome construction were perfected and new ones discovered, even though the traditional engineering techniques also continued to be employed. A large number of the features of Timurid architecture – compositional, structural, and artistic – were also used and developed further in the following period, the 16th and 17th centuries.

The Arts of the Book
Mukkadima Ashrafi

The miniature during the Timurid period

The Timurid 15th century is one of the most glorious periods in the development of the miniature. A steady perfecting of the artistic vocabulary of the miniature can be followed throughout the whole of the century, culminating in a veritable blossoming of painting towards its end.

Whereas in the 14th century there had only been limited contact between the different centers of painting, during the 15th century more varied contacts developed. The migration of the craftsmen, which began with Timur's conquests of Baghdad (1393 and 1401) and Tabriz (1402), where there had been painting schools during the 14th century, was a contributory factor in this. Timur transported the best masters from the conquered lands to his capital Samarqand in Transoxiana, where they were enlisted to work on the adornment of his palaces and the production of artistic manuscripts. The Head of the Samarqand *kitabkhana* (library) and manuscript workshop was the renowned miniaturist Abd al-Hayy from Baghdad, whose work, according to Dust Muhammad, a 16th-century historian, was used as a model by all the Samarqand masters. Despite the fact that none of his work has survived, and nor have any Samarqand miniatures from the beginning of the 15th century, we can gain an idea of what the early painting was like, and of Abd al-Hayy's style in particular, from the work of the Baghdad master Junaid Sultani, who had studied alongside Abd al-Hayy with the teacher Shams al-Din. In the Middle Ages, artists of the same school worked in a uniform idiom despite their own individual styles. The principles of landscape and architectural representation and the compositional schemata found in Junaid Sultani's work also formed the basis of the work produced at the Timurid schools that were developing in Samarqand, Shiraz, and Herat during the first few decades of the 15th century. Characteristic of the painting being produced around Junaid Sultani in Baghdad were a multilayered picture construction and the technique of creating depth by means of an oval and diagonal arrangement of the picture's compositional elements. Frequent use of diagonal lines and a particularly poetic radiance are also typical.

The development of this style can be followed through the miniatures produced in Shiraz in the *kitabkhana* of Timur's grandsons Iskandar Sultan (1409–1415) and Ibrahim Sultan (1415–1435) during the early decades of the 15th century. The illustrations in the two manuscripts of the *Anthology of Poetry* (1410/11) are representative of the Shiraz style of this time. A synthesis has been achieved here between the three-dimensionality of the Baghdad school and the flatness of the Shiraz school of the 14th century. But in the Shiraz illustrations of the 1420s, a gradual rejection of the artistic principles of the Baghdad school is already noticeable. A new Shiraz style developed – based on the older Shiraz tradition – which, in the years 1420–1430, was dominated by a strict, flat system, and a form of composition that used few figures. Written sources document a migration of the Baghdad painters meanwhile to the new artistic center of Herat. A workshop was established at this time in the Herat *kitabkhana* of Timur's grandson Baisunqur (d. 1433), where a great number of outstanding craftsmen worked – calligraphers and artists – who had previously been active in Baghdad, Tabriz, Shiraz, and Samarqand. Thus the emerging Herat style was influenced by the styles of these artistic centers. In the work produced in Herat in the 1420s there is an unmistakable similarity with the

Bahram discovers the hall with the seven portraits, Shiraz, 1410/11, Lisbon, Fundação Calouste Gulbenkian
The poet Nizami describes in *Haft Paikar* (Seven Pictures) how Prince Bahram Gur discovers the seven pictures of his future wives in a room, normally kept locked, in the palace where he is being brought up. The unknown artist of this miniature knew how to portray the breadth of the round hall by grouping the elegantly elongated figures in pairs at the sides and leaving the center free.

depictions of landscape and architecture produced by Junaid and those found in the Shiraz miniatures of 1410/11. At the same time, however, new, independent features were already appearing: a certain precision, a suppleness of line, a richness of color, and less elongated figures than were typical of Junaid's work. The reduction in size of the figures had an impact on the relationships in scale between the different elements of the composition. This meant the room or space in which the characters were set, as depicted in the miniature, became larger, which was the important main achievement of the Herat school.

The work produced in the 1430s, such as the *Shahname* of 1430 and *Kalila and Dimna* of the same year, represented a new stage in the development of

painting in Herat. Miniatures of the *Shahname* from 1430 are therefore of great art-historical importance, as they created the prototypes for particular scenes that went on to be among the most popular – the lovers' meetings in the palace and in the countryside, the audience with the ruler, the hunt, and the battle. The Herat artists wanted to present the viewer of the miniature with a performance, just like the theatrical director does on the stage, and his mastery was judged according to his ability to build up the action. As a general rule, the main scene of the action has been cleared of trees, rocks, and peripheral figures. The latter take on the role of extras who have been pushed to the edges of the miniature.

The miniatures produced in Herat during this time are distinctive for their rich, rhythmical drawing, which stems from the strong lines given to the colorful figures, the multiplicity of details of differing sizes, and the spatial focal points. This rhythm was beginning to be adapted to the subject of the illustration: in the audience scenes, for example, the drawing is measured and slow; in the hunting and battle scenes, it is more dynamic. The elaboration of rhythm in the miniature is another of the important achievements of the Herat school of the 15th century. Also remarkable is its use of color, the richness, purity, and harmony of which are particularly captivating, as is the perfection of the lines which outline every detail and give each one a sense of completeness and independence.

Another center of intensive cultural activity was Samarqand, which was under the rule of Timur's grandson Ulugh Beg (1409–1449). While the few surviving Samarqand works from the 15th century do not give a complete picture of the development of the miniature there, they do demonstrate the high standard achieved by the art of the miniature in this region, its originality, its magnificent execution, and its pronounced decorative construction. It is characterized by three special features. Firstly, its space is only sparsely filled – in complete contrast to the Herat compositions, in which every available space is used and everything worked out in great detail. Secondly, its composition has a strong sense of order and clarity, based on clear vertical and horizontal lines and, thirdly, Samarqand miniatures feature a relatively small number of figures, which in turn are so self-contained that not even a hand movement is able to dissipate this sense of self-containment. All the miniatures radiate a sense of complete peace, and the use of large areas of color gives them a special painterly beauty.

During the first half of the 15th century, contact was established between the cultural centers of Samarqand, Shiraz, and Herat, which explains why similar characteristics are evident in the miniatures of each school. Because they developed within the Timurid Empire, which embraced a large number of different countries, they were able to gather in a wide variety of experience of the most diverse styles, and this was the basis for the glorious flourishing of painting that took place in Herat in the second half of the 15th century under Sultan Husain Baiqaras (1468–1506).

The multiplicity of painting genres and the individual stamp of the artists are both features of Herat miniatures from this time. Mirak, Bihzad, Khoja Muhammad, Shah Muzaffar, and Qasim Ali all belonged to the group of great miniaturists active there. The most famous of them was Kamal al-Din Bihzad, whom the Swedish scholar F. Martin called a "Raphael of the East."

Bihzad (1460–1535) was closely associated with the circle surrounding the poets Jami and Nawai, whose claim that their work was an artistic interpretation of daily life was a strong influence on his painting. In each of Bihzad's miniatures an interest in people and their lives and the attempt to depict these as fully as possible can be seen for the first time. In particular he extended the boundaries of the "representable" world: the limited space of the miniature now took in not only a multiplicity of individually characterized men and women, whose positions were precisely calculated, but also architecture and gardens, streams, reservoirs, and mountain landscapes. Bihzad worked out an ideal relationship between all the different elements of the composition by subordinating them to a unifying rhythm and making everything geometrically self-contained. He gives the representation of the

room a greater depth and sense of reality than it had before. His architecture is more three-dimensional and varied, the architectural decoration fascinates with its delicacy and the splendor of its details, its richness of color and the sparkling of its liberally applied gold. Bihzad and his circle were especially fond of light pavilions and tiled courtyards, separated from gardens by red wooden fences and gates with open carving. In landscapes, plane trees in their spring foliage (seldom their summer one), slender cypresses, blossoming spring trees, and young poplars, were all characteristic of their work. Also frequently encountered are tree stumps springing new shoots, bushes of dried twigs, irises, green glades, small watercourses with stones on their banks from under which flowers are growing, large-leafed plants, and rocks of various colors with fine, jagged contours.

Whereas the artists of previous periods had not set themselves the task of giving their figures individual characteristics and differentiating them from one another, in the middle of the 15th century the Herat school took a step in this direction. Bihzad strove to achieve a living, true-to-life portrayal of movements, poses, gestures, and faces, and in his portraits he succeeded in representing an individual's features, such as skin color, shape of face, and facial hair to such an extent that the individual whose portrait it was would be recognized by the viewer. He created a gallery of diverse figures at work and in their everyday life that had not been depicted before: *yurt*-dwellers, women cooking meals, men washing their feet before entering the mosque, a shepherd

playing a shawm, people carrying loads, workers kneading clay, stonemasons, bath attendants, barbers, woodcutters, gravediggers, inebriated dignitaries, and so on are all to be found in his miniatures. The artist also breathed life into character types already developed by others before him.

During the whole of his creative life he was constantly searching for new techniques that would enable him to depict people's movements in a more life like and accurate way, and strove to correctly depict the proportions of the human body. Bihzad's work represents the high point of the miniature during the Timurid period. By building on the achievements of his predecessors, he was able to perfect the already relatively well-developed artistic expression of the miniature and take it to new heights. His work astonishes with the perfection of its composition, the life like quality of its figures, its comprehensive depiction of life, and its spiritual depth.

When the Timurid Empire collapsed at the beginning of the 16th century, new dynasties came to power, such as the Safavids in Persia and the Shaybanids in Mawarannahr. The artists, once more, had to move to new patrons and to the new artistic centers that were emerging in Tabriz and Bukhara.

But the Timurid arts of the book, whose high standards were achieved as a result of the cross-fertilization that took place between the different schools and the development of new artistic challenges, lived on in the influence they were to exert over the art of the miniature in the 16th century.

Opposite far left: Humay reaches Humayun's castle,

Baghdad, 1396, London, British Library

This miniature is from a copy of the poem by Kwaju Kirmani, which was produced for the Jalayirid sultan Ahrnad (1328--1410) in Baghdad a few decades after the poet's death. Sultan Ahrnad promoted painters such as Abd al-Hayy and Junaid, whose style is distinctive for its freshness and keenness of detail and pointed the way for the miniature painting of the 15th century. Junaid, who has signed one of the nine miniatures, was probably also responsible for painting this elegant palace architecture and its idyllic garden, which had to be an appropriate setting for Humay and Humayun's first meeting. While he waits on horseback in front of the palace gates, she appears, in the expectation of her prince's arrival, on the palace's roof terrace. A whole book page is used for this illustration.

Opposite right: The construction of the palace of Khawarnaq, Herat, 1494/95, book illustration from Nizami's *Haft Paikar*, London, British Library

The artist Bihzad opened up a new perspective for Islamic miniature painting with this depiction of the building process, in which there is no reference to the royal client and the manual work itself provides the focal point. This unusual illustration disregards the traditional rules of composition and thus achieves an astonishing liveliness. Bihzad worked at the court of the last Timurid sultan Husain Baiqara. The individual who commissioned this copy of the *Khamsa* poem by Nizami, which was completed in 1494/95, was, however, not a member of the dynasty but Amir Farsi Barlas.

An older man watches girls bathing,

Herat, 1494/95, London, British Library

This miniature is an illustration taken from Nizami's *Khamsa* poem. Its subject, young girls being secretly watched by their master while bathing, was clearly popular during the Timurid period, because it gave the painters an opportunity, against the usual Islamic custom, to depict half-naked women in a light-hearted setting. The leading artists of this time, in particular Bihzad, disregarded the formalities of courtly art and took a more unconventional route instead. The new style is also apparent in the sweeping gestures of the bathers, while the peaceful architecture is a more traditional element.

The Shaybanids and the Khan Princedoms

History
Wolfgang Holzwarth

Outline of the region's history (1500–1900)

The map of the eastern Islamic world was completely redrawn between 1500 and 1530. Three new empires, with their centers far apart, developed out of the inheritance left by the Timurid Empire: the Shaybanid Uzbek Empire in Central Asia, the Safavid Empire in Iran, and the Indian Mughal Empire, with their emergent capitals in Bukhara, Isfahan, and Delhi respectively. This new regional order remained remarkably stable for over two hundred years and led to a second flowering of Islamic civilization in all three empires. Its buds had first appeared after the Mongol invasion, one of the most robust being Herat, the cultural capital at the heart of the Timurid Empire and a melting pot of an advanced Islamic "Turko-Persian" civilization which continued to exert its influence for a long time afterwards.

Around 1700, there were growing signs of a far-reaching crisis in the early modern regional empires. The influence of non-Muslim powers (among them the European powers) seems to have been increasing in tandem with a decline in the power held by the established political centers. Rival power blocs that could no longer be integrated into the imperial order were forming around their edges, such as Kokand and Afghanistan, and were demanding and achieving political autonomy. Regional diversity was emerging even more strongly from beneath the sophisticated and all-embracing, even cosmopolitan, late Timurid civilization. In about 1900, after two hundred years of political and cultural "provincialization," eastern Islam was forced into the modern world system dominated by Europe.

The rise and golden age of the Uzbek Empire (1500–c.1700)

The Uzbeks were Islamized Turko-Mongolian nomads from the steppes, made up of around 30 different tribes who had formed themselves into a confederation under the leadership of a member of the Genghis Khan dynasty. They led a nomadic existence on the Kipchak steppes, roughly the area occupied by present-day Kazakhstan. The Shaybanid Uzbeks, under Muhammad Shaybani Khan (1500–1510), conquered cultivated regions further south, lying in areas occupied by present-day Uzbekistan and northern Afghanistan: Mawarannahr, as it was then called, between the Syr Darya and Amu Darya Rivers, and parts of the old Khorasan region. The Kazakhs had pulled back out of the confederation of tribes and remained "freely roaming" (*qazaq*) lords of the steppes. Between three and four million people may have lived in the conquered regions, and these can be roughly divided (leaving aside a bilingual upper strata) into two main population groups: the Tajiks, Persian-speaking city dwellers and farmers in the fertile, irrigated oases, and the Turkomans, Turkish-speaking nomads in the rest of the hinterland. The army of the Uzbek conquerors numbered 50–100,000 men, while the tribal confederation itself amounted to perhaps 200–400,000 individuals. Once more, and for the last time on such a large scale, the people of the steppes had succeeded in exploiting the military potential of their tribal organization and turning the mobility and strike power of their nomadic horsemen, which had been repeatedly tested in smaller pillage-and-plunder raids, into a large-scale assault on the main centers, the cities.

Detail of the tilework of the Tilla Kari Madrasa, Samarqand, 1646–1660
The Tilla Kari Madrasa is one of the buildings enclosing Registan Square in Samarqand, the others being the Ulugh Beg and Shir Dar Madrasas. It not only serves as a *madrasa*, but is also the city's Friday mosque. In contrast to the Timurid buildings, with their tile cladding that covered the walls completely, this building displays a combination of decorative brick bonds and ornamental tile areas. It owes its name "The Gilded One" to the decorations on its interior walls.

Portal of the Bukhara Citadel, 18th century
On the other side of the gateway, which is fortified with twin towers and a dark entrance lined with dungeons, the path steeply leads up to the Citadel, which rises up on an artificial hill filled with the rubble of fortresses that previously stood on this historical site. In the 16th century, the Shaybanids made this former manor house the center of their empire. The 18th-century west gate is its oldest surviving part. In front of the portal there was once a market square and fairground.

Cultivated conquerors

Despite the competition that existed between them for power and pasture land, the Uzbeks were in fact quite close to the nomadic population groups of the conquered territories in terms of language and culture. The urbane nature of Timurid civilization, on the other hand, would initially have been quite alien to the migrant nomads from the steppes. This distance did not result in the malicious devastation of arable land and the cities, however, especially as the Uzbek khans were apparently quite open to the benefits of urban civilization from the very beginning, and quickly tried to shake off the stigma, which became attached to the Uzbek in his new surroundings, of being a barbaric backwoodsman.

The great conqueror Muhammad Shaybani had already lived in the cities of Astrakhan and Bukhara for periods as a child, and had later had contact with Timurid princely courts. Even one of his enemies, in trying to represent the capture of Herat (1507) as a catastrophe, stops far short of depicting him as a crazed annihilator. What was upsetting was that this half-educated man from the steppes behaved like a connoisseur of refined city culture, had the extreme arrogance to lecture the religious scholars on the Koran, attempted to create an image of himself as a poet, and took it upon himself to "improve" out and out masterpieces of miniature painting and calligraphy with his own hand.

In the second generation of Shaybanid khans, this adoption of the city-courtly cultural ideal, originally regarded as crude and foolish, was accompanied by tutoring and polishing from experienced local masters. These spiritual masters, recruited from the Naqshbandiya order, also continued to maintain the closest of relationships with the ruling dynasties from this time on. Alongside them was a throng of artists and intellectuals from Herat circles who had lost their positions and were now engaged at various Uzbek courts as princely tutors, "cultural representatives," and "image consultants." They were so successful in imparting the culture of the vanquished to the social elite of the conquering nation that one contemporary observer, who was under no obligation to eulogize, compared the level of culture surrounding Ubaydallah Khan (1533–1540), a second generation Shaybanid, favorably with its Timurid (Herat) model.

The organizing power of the Sufi orders

With their origins in ancient Islamic mysticism, a number of Sufi orders had formed since the time of the Mongols, and had increasingly seen it as part of their mission to try to shape the world and worldly rule in accordance with their own beliefs. One of these was the Naqshbandiya order, with its roots in the urban centers of Central Asia. This was a part of Timurid civilization that lived on in the Uzbek Empire. The order's leaders, who managed to preserve and consolidate their spiritual influence in the Uzbek Empire, came from highly respected and very wealthy Khoja ("master") families, which had become established in various different cities. The rules of the order by no means prescribed a hermit-like existence in a "dervish monastery." The hand turned to work and the heart turned to God," the order's brothers were able to go about their daily

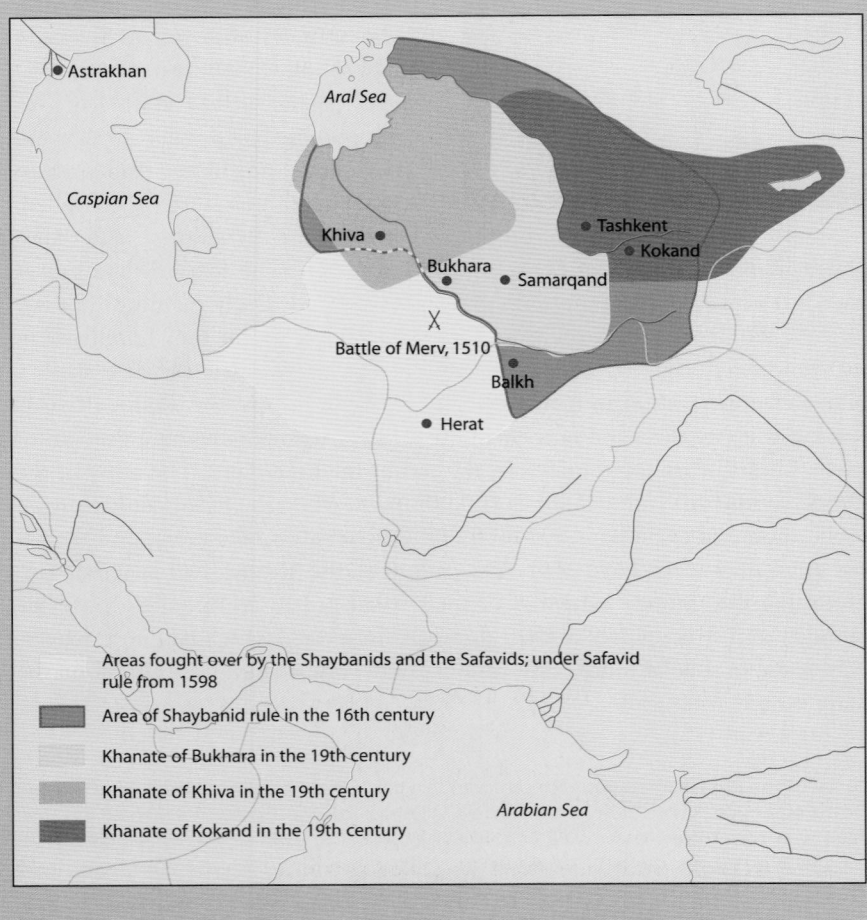

1500–1510	Rule of Muhammad Shaybani Khan		1737–1742	Balkh, Khiva, and Bukhara conquered by the Afsharid Nadir Shah
1507	The Shaybanids drive the Timurids out of their territory; eastern Khorasan, Transoxiana, Khwarazmia, Turkestan, and the Fergana Valley are all under Shaybanid sovereignty		1742–1770	Khiva occupied by the Persians and Iomud Turkomans
			from 1753	Rule of the Mangits in Bukhara (initially as viziers)
1510	Battle of Merv: Shaybanids defeated by the Persian Safavids; Muhammad Shaybani is killed		1785	The Mangit Murad Shah takes the ruling title "Prince of the Faithful" and establishes the Mangit khanate (1785–1921)
1533–1540	Rule of Ubaydallah Khan in Bukhara		1800–1809	Rule of Alim Khan in Kokand
1584–1596	Abdallah Khan (1583–1598) tries to increase his territory through several military campaigns		1809	Tashkent becomes part of the Kokand khanate
			1826–1860	The Mangit Nasrallah rules in Bukhara
1599–1605	Baqi Muhammad founds the Janid/Ashtarkhanid dynasty (1599–1785) in Bukhara		1860–1885	Emirate of Mazaffar al-Din, the last independent emir in Bukhara
1610–1640/42	Rule of the Ashtarkhanid imam Quli Khan		1868	Bukhara taken by Russia, in 1873 Russian troops conquer Khiva, and in 1876 the Kokand. which is annexed by Russia and renamed Fergana
1647–1680	Bukhara comes under the rule of Abdulaziz Khan			

lives as craftsmen, tradesmen, scholars, or administrators, and lead a normal family life. They met together regularly, however, at their "inn" (*khanqa*) or in an assembly house or prayer hall (*dhikr-khana*) in order to participate in communal ceremonies such as prayers, sermons, devotional drills, and night vigils.

Under the influence of the Naqshbandiya order, which was of Sunni orientation, and as a result of the dispute with its most bitter enemy – Safavid Iran, where the Twelvers branch of the Shia had been made the state religion – the increasingly militant Uzbek Empire saw itself as a refuge for Sunni orthodoxy. Thus it was thanks to the organizing, social power of the Sufi orders that Central Asia under the Uzbeks developed once more into a region that was able to define itself clearly in terms of culture to the outside world.

Brief outline of dynastic history: Shaybanids and Ashtarkhanids

The Uzbeks had brought Turko-Mongol traditions with them from the steppes that continued to have an influence on their political history. They retained the code of law and honor (*yasa*) sanctioned by Genghis Khan, which as an unwritten constitution or political ideal, formed a distinctly decentralized character between tribe and state. Actual power and decision-making authority lay with a council of state, in which members of the Khan dynasty as well as leaders of the most important tribal groups participated. This was presided over as the first among equals by the Great Khan.

Since sons, brothers, and to a certain extent, cousins, of the Great Khan could all claim an appropriate share of the patrimony, reigning princes carrying the title sultan or even khan sat in all the various regions of the Uzbek Empire. Supported by their respective local following and shifting alliances, these princes competed partly with one another, and partly with the Great Khan. Wars were therefore as frequently fought between dynastic rivals as they were against outside enemies. Abdallah Khan II, who set about strengthening central power particularly energetically, had killed nearly all his close relatives by the time he died in 1598, and in the end extinguished his own dynastic line. This is how the title khan came to pass to the Ashtarkhanid clan, who held it until 1748, ultimately without fulfilling any political function. Only in Khwarazmia, an oasis in the Amu Darya delta south of the Aral Sea, surrounded by (semi) desert, was a minor branch of the Shaybanid dynasty, which had ruled over an autonomous khanate since the Uzbek conquest, able to hold on to power, which it did until 1727.

Economic and cultural aspects of the development of the cities

While the tribal masses continued to cling to nomadic or seminomadic life-styles and formed the military backbone of the Uzbek khanate, the cities, as the seat of the political elite, experienced a remarkable upturn, which expressed itself, among other ways, in the architectural monuments of the time. Only the smallest circle of the city-based state elite had sufficient power and financial resources at their disposal to be able to initiate and influence the city's development. This circle consisted of members of the Khan dynasty, military commanders from the Uzbek tribes, and the highest spiritual office holders from the leading Naqshbandiya master families. It was this group of individuals who profited most from the revival of the cities, as they owned the majority of the commercial property (bazaar passages and halls, caravanserais, offices, baths, hot food stalls, and so on), and in turn spent a considerable proportion

Bazaar scene, miniature from the *Lisan al-Tair* by Nawai, Tabriz or Qazvin, c. 1550, Paris, Bibliothèque Nationale
Textile and ceramics salesmen serve customers from their shop compartments in a bazaar alley, and a traveling hawker offers his wares for sale. The illustration is part of a double-page picture. The alley continues on the opposite side with a butcher's shop and a bakery. Central Asian illustrators – not just of this story, but generally – chose not to take up everyday subjects such as the bazaar. The clothing indicates that the miniature has Safavid origins.

of their wealth on noncommercial buildings and foundations (mosques, colleges and so forth) through which their names would live on.

A certain lack of simultaneity in the (building) booms of the individual cities – in Bukhara it peaked in the 16th century, in Balkh and Samarqand in the 17th century – resulted from the political history of the khanate. One reason is that the Shaybanids were particularly interested in Bukhara because of its special reputation among Central Asian cities as an ancient center of Muslim scholarship and because it was the stronghold of the Naqshbandiya order. In 1560 Bukhara became the principal capital. A high level of building activity and an economic upturn prepared the way for the development of the capital and also accompanied it.

Under the Shaybanids, Bukhara was given the necessary infrastructure to replace Samarqand as the mercantile center of Central Asia and become an important junction in the widely extended trading network that now took in Siberia, China, India, Iran, the Ottoman Empire, and Moscow. The assumption frequently made, that the discovery of the sea route to India and China had immediately robbed Central Asia of its importance as a transit station for trade, is not really tenable in the light of recent research. Until about 1700, the long-distance trade that passed through Bukhara was thriving, any loss in east-west traffic being compensated for by an increase in north-south business. Traders from the subcontinent, offering white turban fabric, spices, perfume, and indigo, to name just a few of the goods being traded, were always on the lookout for horses for the cavalry of the Mughal Empire. The nomads of Central Asia and the people of the northern steppes sent animals to the horse market that took place in front of the northern city wall. Along with exotic rarities like walrus teeth, furs also found their way from the north to Bukhara, where they were used, for example, to make fur-trimmed caps (*tilpaks*). Trading relations with China were concealed as tribute missions – a condition imposed by imperial protocol. In this way Bukhar traders brought in horses, aprecious stones, metalware, and decorative weapons to the Chinese imperial

Man's coat, Bukhara, 19th century, silk ikat, 140 cm long. Berlin, Ethnologisches Museum
Magnificent silk coats often served as robes of office or honor for formal occasions. A ruler would decorate his confidants and trusted deputies with them, thus clothing them according to their rank. Ikat is a method of fabric patterning which involves the yarns being dyed in accordance with the required pattern before weaving takes place. The large-format pattern combines the "flowering plant" and "tree" designs with stylized almonds, pomegranates, and flower crowns.

court, which honored the goods submitted with gifts of silk fabrics (Atlas) and porcelain in return. Often, comparable examples of Central Asian handcrafts (for example local silk and ceramics) were to be found alongside imported luxury goods at the bazaar. Commercial building projects formed one aspect of the activities undertaken in Bukhara and other cities by the circle of individuals described above. The other consisted of endowments (*waqf*) concentrating on building projects and institutions designed to benefit the Muslim community: mosques and colleges (*madrasas*) predominantly, but also Sufi meeting houses and mausoleums. In a linguistically and ethnically pluralistic society, divided by extreme social inequality, the endowment system was a way of eliminating social tensions. The buildings and institutions it created for the public good – having a unifying effect – embodied the ideal of religious community (*millat*), providing sacred and public spaces to which different groups of Muslims from different sections of society all had equal access.

Times of unrest and radical change in the 18th century

The khanate had already undergone phases of weakness during the 17th century. Balkh had been temporarily occupied by the Mughal army, and Bukhara had been attacked and plundered by Khiva. The golden age of the Uzbek Empire came to an end with the rule of the last powerful Ashtarkhanid, Subhan Quli Khan, who once again ruled over the whole of the patrimony (Bukhara and Balkh) between 1681 and 1702. Its decline was ultimately precipitated by the expansionary activity of three powers that upset the whole inner Asian balance of power.

Memories of the Mongol global empire motivated the expansionist campaigns of the west Mongolian Oirats (Dzungars), who controlled so much of the Kazakh region (1718–1725) that they were able to join up with their tribal relatives, the Kalmuck Horde on the Volga. Under pressure from the west Mongols, defeated Kazakh groups moved south. Initially they were made welcome as reinforcements in a trial of strength that had broken out between rival khanates in Bukhara and Samarqand (1722), but they then stayed on in the war zone for seven years. By the end of this time the farmland was laid to waste, Samarqand had been completely depopulated, and only two of Bukhara's residential districts were still inhabited. Central Asia was then directly affected by the power politics of the Persian king Nadir Shah (1688–1748). Nadir's troops conquered not only Balkh, but also the two capitals (Khiva and Bukhara) of the former Uzbek Empire, which now fell apart at the seams and came to an end in the ensuing fighting between factions. Russia then finally prepared to assume its new role of dominant regional power, initially without direct confrontation with Central Asia. It acted politically, as a European protecting power, by forming an alliance with the Kazhaks, and economically in initiating direct trade links with China via Siberia (1728) and through the increasing importance of the Russian trading station Astrakhan to the north-south axis.

The deep economic and political crisis lasted for half a century (1720–1770), during which time Central Asia came to be bypassed by the main flow of trade, fell prey to the confusion of war, and experienced the deterioration of its cities. During this time of unrest, the khans lost all their authority and the Uzbek military commanders and tribal princes took over power. The Uzbek Empire fragmented into a number of princedoms, of which two (south of the Amu Darya) fell into the political orbit of Afghanistan. In the north, three new Uzbek dynasties emerged from the confusion of war: the Ming dynasty in Kokand, the Mangits in Bukhara, and the Qungrat dynasty in Khiva. The tribal princes (*amirs, beys/begs*) hesitated for awhile before taking the title khan, which strictly speaking was reserved for descendants of the Genghis Khan dynasty (now deprived of power).

The khan princedoms up to the Russian conquest

The period from 1700 up to the Russian conquest of Central Asia (1862–1884) could appear to be one of gradual decline. In actual fact, though, political stabilization took place from the end of the 17th century, accompanied by a revival of trade and the cities. The new khanates developed into more strongly centralized states. One measure that contributed to this, undertaken by all three, was the reform of their armies. As soon as the security of the caravan routes was restored, trade started to thrive once more. But here too the emphasis had changed, in terms of both the main routes for trade and the type of goods involved.

Kokand

The tribal princes of the Uzbek Ming clan founded their own capital, Kokand, in the Fergana valley, somewhat isolated from the devastated plains, back in 1740. In its founding phase, the Kokand princedom had less of an argument with Bukhara (the center from which it broke away) than with the neighboring Kirgiz tribes to the east and the Dzungars. Its most glorious period came after China had conquered the Dzungar territory and the oasis towns of the Tarim basin and integrated them into its new Sinkiang province between 1755 and 1759. Kokand tradesmen received Chinese trading privileges and were permitted to enter the city of Kashi, which neighbored the Fergana Valley and now lay in the extreme west of China. Kokand, whose princes took the title khan around 1800, was able to profit to an extraordinary extent from its relationship and direct trading contact with China. With its limited resources and a total population of three-quarters of a million, the khanate developed into an expanding trading city, which along with Tashkent also became an important center for trade with Russia (1809). Large-scale irrigation canals and a significant number of endowments (mosques and colleges) from the 19th century bear witness to the considerable prosperity of Kokand and the nurturing of its own city culture. Following bitter battles for its independent statehood, the Kokand khanate was annexed by Russia in 1876 and given the name Fergana.

Bukhara

When the Mangits took over rule in Bukhara in 1750, city life was still completely depressed; only from about 1770 did the capital start to recover slowly from the aftermath of war. The Mangits also carried the title of prince, but in the sense, adopted proudly in 1785, of "prince of the faithful" in emulation of the first four caliphs. The emphasis on this religious claim to leadership and the religious responsibilities of leadership dominated the political views of the emirs of Bukhara, who endeavoured to set the Muslim community a good example with their devout and disciplined way of life. "Dervish kings," such as Shah Murad and Emir Haidar, indicated through their dress and manner that they occupied the throne primarily as trustees of the Naqshbandiya order, and that any pomp or grandeur was repugnant to them. This was perhaps one of the reasons practically no new monumental buildings were erected under the Mangits, in stark contrast to commercial buildings. The rapidly growing number of caravanserais in Bukhara is evidence of the revival of long-distance trade, in which Russia became the khanate's biggest partner. The largest of the Central Asian khanates in terms of its population, which stood at two and a half million, Bukhara exhausted its strength fighting wars of expansion against Kokand and Khiva, aiming to restore the Uzbek Empire to its former territorial borders. It was certainly no match for the military offensive of the czar's empire. Following a series of military defeats, Bukhara surrendered to the Russian army, which had already occupied Samarqand, in 1868.

Kaltar Minar (Kok Minar), Khiva, 1852–1855
With a diameter of 46 ft (14 m) at its base, this tower "the color of the heavens" (*kok minar*) was designed to be 70 m high. Since the call to prayer would have been inaudible from this height, it would have been an object of pure prestige that put all comparable towers in the shade. The construction of the tower was undertaken by Muhammad Amin Khan between 1845 and 1855. Work ceased when the individual who commissioned it was killed during a military campaign. At a height of just 92 ft (28 m), the monument is now known as the "short tower" (*kalta minar*).

Khiva

In Khwarazmia, with its capital Khiva, the nomadic element of the population was particularly large relative to the farming and city-dwelling elements. Following the Persian occupation, bitter power struggles raged between the Turkoman and Uzbek populations (1742–1770): after this only 40 families lived on in Khiva. The Uzbek Qungrat princes (khans from 1804), who held the upper hand in these wars, managed to bind the beaten Turkomans to the khanate as allies and auxiliary troops. The urban development miracle of a resurrected Khiva was essentially due to the symbiosis that existed between the small agricultural oases and the nomads specializing in the "economy of pillage." Turkoman tribes made up roughly a quarter of the khanate's total population. They regularly undertook campaigns of pillage and slaving expeditions into the north of Persia, and approximately 40,000 slaves were working in Khiva, which had become the largest slave market and consumer of slave labor in Central Asia. The Turkomans offered convoy and caravan services, and Khiva developed into a trade center on the trans-Caspian Russian route which ran through Astrakhan. In 1855 the Turkoman tribes broke away once more from Khiva, in order to finally merge with fellow tribesmen and form the independent Tekke confederation. Khiva itself was captured by Russian troops in 1873 without offering any significant resistance, and the Tekke Turkomans were defeated in 1881 during heavy fighting with great loss of life.

Architecture

Sergej Chmelnizkij

The architecture of Bukhara and Samarqand in the 16–17th centuries and Khiva in the 18–19th centuries

On the threshold of the 16th century, the Timurid Empire fell victim to the invading Uzbeks under the leadership of Khan Shaybani. These steppe nomads, who invaded from the northeast, settled in Central Asia, became established there, and took over the Timurid state organization without any cultural discontinuity. The most famous of Shaybani's successors on the throne was Abdallah Khan II. During his reign, Bukhara was given the appearance it still retains by and large today: large secular buildings were constructed, caravanserais, *madrasas*, baths, market passageways (*tims*), and domed market halls (*taqs*), as well as *khanqas*, the meeting houses of the dervishes. It was not unusual for a mausoleum to be integrated into the design of a *khanqa*, but free-standing mausoleums from this period are almost unknown. Also dating from the 16th century are the first residential district mosques, which later became the most widespread type of sacred building.

The unique, expensively clad, and often enormous structures characteristic of the Timurids were replaced by buildings that, from the point of view of both their design and their markedly more modest decoration and construction technique, were more strongly focused on functionality.

During the first half of the 16th century, costly decorative techniques with complex manufacturing procedures were still used, such as tile mosaics consisting of cut ceramic pieces, which were later superseded by painted blue-and-white tiles with seemingly casual patterns. While the walls of earlier eras had been monolithic, the inner and outer skins were now constructed of brick with stucco mortar and the spaces between them filled with brick rubble and loam. This is the reason why the arches of many buildings have settled and lost their original shape.

The colorful tile decoration was now usually concentrated on the facades, and the interiors, even of large buildings, were rendered with white stucco, which gave the complicated three-dimensional finish of these interiors their impressive appearance. This was especially true for domed halls of any function, whose roof coverings frequently no longer rested on the earlier octagonal squinch structure, but on pairs of overlapping arches – a system that had emerged in Central Asia in the 15th century and was now very widespread.

Either a dome of modest diameter or – more frequently – a lantern sat on the central square formed by these arches. These new constructions represented an advance in terms of stability and durability. They were reliable and allowed large rooms to be covered. In addition they gave the domed hall a new, dynamic shape. The architectural ideal of this age was not the grandiose and luxurious, as under Timur and his successors, but a large number of buildings combined with functionality. It is not by chance that many more were built during this period than previously, and that important buildings were constructed everywhere, not just in the large cities.

Bukhara

It is the capital Bukhara, however, that dominates the face of Central Asian architecture of the 16th and 17th centuries right up to today. The city had spread southwest during the 16th century, and was surrounded by a 6-mile (10-kilometer) long compressed mud wall, protected by towers and punctuated by 11 fortified gates. Above the city rose the high artificial hill of Bukhara's citadel, called the Ark, as it still does today. The Pa-yi Kalan ("Foot of Sublimity") complex, the city center's most important ensemble of buildings, was constructed on slightly raised foundations to its east. The largest building of this group is the Kalan Friday mosque, the "Great Mosque," built in the 15th century, the interior furnishing of which was completed only in 1514. It was built on the site, and possibly followed the same ground plan, of a 12th-century mosque whose famous large minaret has survived. With an area of 426 × 262 ft (130 × 80 meters), the Kalan mosque is the largest after Timur's Bibi Khanum Mosque in Samarqand and the Friday mosque in Heart. Opposite the east portal of the mosque rises the portal of the Mir-i Arab Madrasa, to the same height. This placing of two monumental buildings opposite each other is known as the *kosh* (pair) system and is not uncommon in the architecture of the 16th and 17th centuries. In terms of its layout, the Mir-i Arab is a typical example of a *madrasa* from this period. Its complicated design has been carefully planned out, and the details as well as the decoration of the *madrasa* are extremely refined. The tympana of its portals and main facade are decorated by tile mosaics of a high quality, and tile incrustations have been set into the domes, which are filled with stucco stalactites, of the cross-*iwans*. Even the main portal, whose high arch is flanked on each side by six smaller arched panels, was covered with mosaics. As the earliest of Bukhara's *madrasas*, dating from the time of Abdallah Khan, the Mir-i Arab Madrasa became the model for most of those that followed.

The two *madrasas* standing opposite one another, the Madar-i Khan (1566/67) and the Abdallah Khan (1588/90) to the west of the Pa-yi Kalan

Pa-yi Kalan, Bukhara
The Pa-yi Kalan ("Foot of Sublimity") is the city's central architectural complex. The portals of the Mir-i Arab Madrasa (completed in 1535/36) on the left, and the Great Mosque, built on the site of a 12th-century mosque, on the right, stand face to face. Behind them towers the architectonic focal point of the city, the Kalan ("Great") minaret of 1127, a part of the original mosque that has survived.

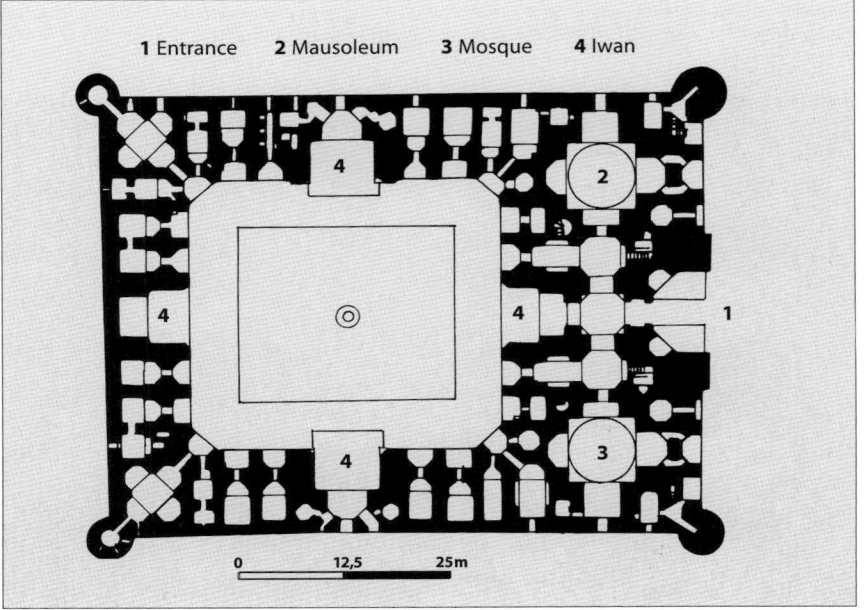

group, are a further example of a *kosh* schema. The facade of the small and modestly decorated Madar-i Khan Madrasa lies out of parallel with its inner courtyard facade, so its group of most important buildings – the vestibule and two cruciform domed chambers to either side of it, form part of a trapezium-shaped solid. The rectangular courtyard has no side *iwans*. Far more impressive and complex is the Abdallah Khan Madrasa opposite. Its main facade is typical of the shape of Central Asian *madrasas* of this time and later. At the center is a high portal with a domed entrance niche set in a rectangular framework. A horizontal inscription panel has been positioned over the arch. The outer edges of the portal appear to be rounded off due to the existence of small corner towers. To the left and right of the portal run two-story loggia-like arcades containing entrances to the living cells. The massive corner towers are the same height as the facade, which is decorated with delicate brick mosaics and white, dark blue, and light blue glazed panels of likewise delicate design. The courtyard has been furnished with cross-axial *iwans* set within impressive portal frames. Behind the right hand *iwan* (looking from the entrance) lie small cells that jut out from the side facade at rectangles. In a large, projecting part of the building behind the rear *iwan* there is a high domed room like a small, covered interior courtyard onto which the two-story cells surrounding it open in the style of loggias. The domed roofs of the two rooms on either side of the vestibule are particularly impressive. They rest on overlapping arches, are decorated with stalactites and "shield-shaped" spandrels, and have lanterns at their points. The axes of the right hand room are aligned with the four points of the compass, which does not correspond to the building's orientation: it may have been planned as a mausoleum for Abdallah Khan.

The largest of Bukhara's *madrasas* is the Kukaltash Madrasa (1568/69), which forms part of the Lab-i Khauz ensemble. A *khauz* is an urban water pool,

Main facade and ground plan of the Mir-i Arab Madrasa, Bukhara, 1535/36
This large building, which stands directly opposite the portal of the Kalan Mosque, is a classic example of a Bukhara *madrasa*. The building's lush, bright decoration is reminiscent of the splendor of the late Timurid period. The *madrasa's* founder was Sheikh Mir-i Arab from Yemen, the spiritual master of Ubaidallah Khan, who ruled at the time. To the sides of the entrance area were a mosque and a mausoleum, above whose small inner domes rose the massive drums of the blue outer domes. Four *iwans*, which served as lecture halls in summer, open onto the inner courtyard, and to the left and right of the *iwans* are the students' cells, arranged over two floors.

necessary given the lack of running water in the Middle Ages. Public buildings were frequently built around them, and areas developed which had a very pleasant atmosphere due to the water, trees, and shade. In Bukhara there were several ensembles of this type, just as there were in other Central Asian cities at the time. Along with the Kukaltash Madrasa, the other buildings in this particular ensemble were the Nadir Diwan Begi Khanqa (completed 1620) and Madrasa (1622). The Diwan Begi Madrasa was originally built as a caravanserai, which is why the obligatory domed chambers to the left and right of the vestibule are missing. The tympana of its portals are decorated with mosaics of fantastic birds. In the Kukaltash Madrasa, unusual techniques go hand in hand with a certain stereotyped design and badly preserved tile decoration.

The last of Bukhara's large *madrasas* was built in 1651/52 by Abdul Aziz Khan, and stands opposite the Ulugh Beg Madrasa, which dates from the 15th century. The building was supposed to surpass the old *madrasa*, but the intended comparison reveals signs of an artistic decline in which a certain loss of skillfulness and good taste can be detected. A disharmony between the component parts of the building, its rather casual proportions, the absence of homogeneity between main facade and courtyard facades, and the brightness of the exterior wall coverings, in which a garish yellow predominates, all contribute to this impression.

Its portal, however, is worthy of attention. Its polygonal niche is covered with a complex system of painted stalactites fastened to wooden batons. The courtyard has a marble paneling border running around it, and in many places the wall covering, in addition to the use of glazed panels, consists of tile mosaics, which had almost dropped out of use by this time. The interiors of both mosques, the winter mosque situated to the right of the portal and vestibule and the summer mosque within the rear *iwan*, are of fabulous magnificence. Ornamental *kundal* painting – a gold relief pattern on a blue ground, which imitates the local brocade (*kundal*) interwoven with gold – covers its walls and vaults. The vaults themselves, though, consist of complex stalactite structures that give the various spaces a wonderful, almost unreal effect like a fairy-tale stage set. This is especially true of the high hall of the winter mosque, whose four walls are shaped like portals, topped off with fantastic, stalactite domes not found anywhere else. In the large, domed lecture hall, the *kundal* patterning frames a panel depicting a building which stands between trees in dark blue on a white ground. Buildings with this appearance are not to be found in Central Asia, but remarkably, it bears a great resemblance to the Torre del Oro in Islamic Seville. One can only speculate as to the origins of the picture.

Among the 16th-century buildings of Bukhara are the first examples of a mosque type that later became very widespread, known as the residential district mosque. These not particularly large buildings not only served a sacred purpose, but were also the public centers of the residential districts and, in terms of the character of their architecture, stand somewhere between monumental, ceremonial buildings and simple domestic buildings.

The Balyand Mosque ("The High One") is a cube-shaped building standing on a high stone platform. The mosque has a wooden portico running along its north and east sides, which is closed off by elongated south and west walls. Its only room is covered by a wooden ceiling with star-shaped reliefwork decoration and stalactite cornices that, together with its central decorative dome, is suspended on chains. Even in its present form, the interior of this mosque, the oldest of the residential district mosques, has the appearance of a sumptuously encrusted box.

The Khoja Zain al-Din Mosque, hidden away in a residential district close to a water basin, has a complex, asymmetrical ground plan rare for a mosque. This is because it houses a tomb revered by the faithful, surrounded by several cells, in a loggia opening onto a lane. Of particular interest are the mosque's

Portal of the Nadir Diwan Begi Madrasa, Bukhara, 1622
This *madrasa*, built by Nadir Diwan Begi, stands opposite a *khanqa* on the same axis, which was also built by him. The two are separated by the expanse of water known as the Lab-i Khauz. Originally built as a caravan, its purpose was changed as the result of a misunderstanding. The emir invited to the opening of the caravanserai had had a lot to drink and bade farewell to his minister with the words: "I thank you for this beautiful *madrasa*." It is a well-known fact that an emir is never wrong. This detail of the tile mosaic shows flying herons among a stylized vegetal pattern and a sun with a human face.

square prayer hall and the portico supported by wooden columns that borders it on the northern and eastern sides. The hall's rich furnishings consist of mosaic paneling, polychrome wall decoration, and patterned *kundal* wall painting. The dome sits on squinches that combine with a system of complex shield-shaped spandrels. Its ribbed surface is supported by a magnificent stalactite cornice. All the niches – including the *mihrab* – are finished off with half-dome shaped stalactite structures. The white walls of the portico provide a contrast with the elegant blaze of color of the interior. The asymmetrical design is indicative of the affinity between this richly decorated mosque and the private urban houses that surround it.

Khanqas, the meeting houses of the Sufi dervish brotherhood regarded as holy places, are also to be found among the monumental 16th- and 17th-century buildings that have shaped Bukhara's appearance. This is where the dervishes lived, prayed, and received pilgrims. One such *khanqa,* near Bukhara stands by the tomb of Baha al-Din, the founder of the Naqshbandiya order; it was considered a second Mecca and attracted many pilgrims. The *khanqa* consists of a large, austere central building with four axial portals and a square, domed hall. Numerous cells of differing shapes, organized over two floors in a complex and elaborate way, and opening outwards through vaulted loggias, occupy the corners of the large square building. The tomb honored by the faithful, a garden, a water basin, and a caravanserai compose a picturesque ensemble surrounding the building. The slightly smaller Qasim Sheikh *khanqa* (1558/59) in Kermine, west of Bukhara, is also a centrally planned building. Its design, featuring a cruciform hall, impresses with its clarity and symmetry. Entrance portals are positioned on three of its sides, and possibly originally on the fourth, too. The main east portal is accentuated by its greater height and a border in the form of a frieze of blind arches. An exterior dome on a high drum rises up over an interior dome resting on overlapping arches – a design typical of Timurid architecture, but relatively rare in the 16th century.

Central Asian *khanqas* are always compact, are generally cube-shaped, and always incorporate a central domed hall in which, unlike in a mosque, there is no *mihrab*. The *mihrab* in the *khanqa* in Faizabad (1598/99) was probably

added later in the place of the west entrance. This impressive building is distinctive for its two multidomed galleries resting on heavy pillars, which border the hall on its southern and northern sides. The hall is impressive for the complex and unusual structure of the lower part of its dome. The dome itself is completely covered with a very delicate floral design of more unusually expressive coloration – white flowers on a black ground – that is not encountered anywhere else. Also unusual is the composition of the main facade, which climbs up towards the center in three stages: the outside, relatively low arcading of the side galleries is followed on either side by a higher wall containing two loggia-like cells placed one above the other, and in the middle rises the high, rectangular portal containing the elegant arch of its entrance niche. Visible behind is the pointed-arch silhouette of the dome.

The main facade of the small Diwan Begi Khanqa (1619/20) looks onto a pool of water that lies in front of it on the same axis. The rectangle of the portal, which has a pointed entrance niche arch, does not project out beyond

Above: Faizabad Khanqa, Bukhara, 1598/99
The domed side galleries, the high portal, and the two-story dividing walls between them, give this expressive Sufi monastery a rapid, upwardly thrusting dynamic focusing on its middle portion. The large, square hall used for the dervishes' mystic rituals is crowned by a dome that seems to hang in the air, supported by delicate, net-like pendentives – a multiplicity of overlapping ribbed arches.

Chor-Bakr, 5 km west of Bukhara, 1560–1563
The center of this necropolis built by Abdallah Khan consists of two domed buildings – a *khanqa* and a mosque – built parallel to each other and connected at the back by a narrow cell area. A relatively low minaret, constructed considerably later, stands on the same axis as this effectively open courtyard. Pictured here is the mosque building, whose long hall has vaulting of unusual design and construction which incorporates two half-domes between which rises an extremely small dome on top of a high support.

the wall, but rises high above the roof. Round towers occupy the corners of the facade, and the narrow portions of facade between the towers and the portal consist of four flat niches in rectangular frames arranged one above the other. The rectangular framework of the portal, its wide tympana, and the tympana of the small niches are all decorated with tile mosaics of mediocre quality. The side facades of the *khanqa*, which has the traditional domed hall at its center, also contain entrances which do not rise above roof level and do not have decorative coverings. A stereotypical assemblage of traditional techniques and designs can be detected in this *khanqa*, indicative of a certain creative decline in the architecture of Bukhara.

Bukhara's rulers did not build any monumental mausoleums, but instead created a unique memorial complex close to the city. In this unusual necropolis a multiplicity of smaller family tombs, surrounded by walls with entrance niches set into them, encircles the majestic central group of buildings. The complex, situated 3 miles (5 kilometers) from the city, is called Chor Bakr and came into being in the years 1560–1563 next to the tomb of local saint Abu Bakr Saad. The monumental center consists of three parts. A *khanqa* and a mosque stand on a shared platform parallel to one another, with their portals facing south. They are connected at the back by a two-story "wing" consisting of living cells and a central domed *iwan*. A small minaret was built on the same axis as this "pouch-shaped" courtyard. There is a certain asymmetry between the different buildings and facades making up this ensemble – the portal of the mosque is narrower than that of the *khanqa* – but the overall impression is one of equilibrium between the two buildings faced with arched loggias. The double-shell dome of the cruciform *khanqa* is supported by overlapping arches and net-like spandrels, which was a common technique at the time. Far more unusual is the internal layout of the mosque, whose long hall lies at right angles to the portal axis and is divided up by two transverse arches at its center. These in turn are spanned by two further arches which support a small dome. Above it rises

the external dome on its drum. The two half-domes on either side of the arches are finished off with a network of bent ribs that meet to form a star shape at the top. This unusual spatial organization, not featured anywhere else, gives the interior a surprising, incorporeal lightness. As the Chor Bakr complex has not been obstructed by dense urban development, it can be viewed from every angle. Its architecture can be seen as forming part and parcel of the landscape, originally a wide, lush, green area of parks and gardens.

The large amount of building activity in Bukhara in the 16th century was not confined to buildings of a sacred function. Central Asia's oldest surviving commercial buildings are also to be found here, and their architecture is no less impressive than that of the sacred buildings. Domed market halls (*taqs*), which brought together traders of similar types of goods, were built at the intersections of the central bazaar streets. The design and appearance of the market halls were determined by the concrete requirements of each one, but the central domed hall was common to all. The domed and vaulted rooms of the shops and workshops were arranged in one, two, or three rows between the streets. The domed market halls that have survived in Bukhara still carry their original names. The smallest of them is the Taq-i Sarrafan ("Moneychangers' Dome"). Its octagonal hall with four entrances and four niches is covered by a dome supported by two pairs of massive, overlapping arches. This construction is visible in the external architecture and gives the building, which can be seen from far around, a rare and unusual appearance. The Taq-i Telpak Furushan ("Hatsellers' Dome") was built further north at a point where three streets met, and is correspondingly hexagonal. The central hall is surrounded by galleries of domed cells and three-sided rooms, and its dome is supported by six heavy pillars, between which arched windows on the axes let the daylight in. The Taq-i Zargaran ("Goldsmiths' Dome") was built over the intersection between two streets in the old city center and has a square ground plan. In total it housed over 30 jewelers' shops and workshops in the niches of its central hall, its

Opposite: **Taq-i Sarrafan**, domed market hall in Bukhara, 16th century
This "Moneychangers' Dome" was built at the intersection of two streets. The octagonal room is covered by a dome that rests on two pairs of crossed arches. This type of construction, which was developed in the 14th or 15th century, has here been given an interesting variation: instead of being disguised on the outside, the crossed arches have deliberately been given prominence, thus giving the building an unusual external appearance.

Left: **Taq-i Zargaran**, domed market hall in Bukhara, 16th century
The "Goldsmiths' Dome" is one of three domed market halls that have survived in the city center. It consists of a large, octagonal, domed hall and numerous small rooms serving as shops and workshops, which are themselves domed, arranged around it in a square. The niches of the large hall, the galleries, and the annexes formerly accommodated over 30 goldsmiths' workshops. The central dome, which consists of eight crossed arches and a system of pendentives, sits on a squat lower portion that has pointed arches around its edges.

galleries, and its annexes. If the domed and vaulted labyrinths of the *taq* are impressive, so, too, is its external appearance, with small domes clustered around the large central dome in a complicated arrangement. Even the streets between the market halls were once vaulted. They were known as *tims*, which approximates to "passages." The Tim Abdallah Khan, built in 1577 for the silk trade, is similar to the domed market halls in form and function. This building, whose street facade has three projecting portals, has an almost square ground plan. In the center of the building, on the axis of the middle portal, wide double supports form a large, octagonal room. These carry the eight overlapping arches on which the dome rests. The high, domed room is surrounded by galleries of domed cells of varying sizes: together with the arched entrances, the interior loggias, and niches, they form a picturesque system of suites. The Tim Abdallah Khan is without doubt an excellent building and one that is characteristic of its time, even though the polychrome wall coverings customary for its period are missing.

Samarqand

Seventeenth-century Samarqand was dominated by the construction of important buildings. New monumental buildings appeared on Registan Square to replace damaged and dilapidated structures from the Timurid period, and gave it its definitive appearance. This is when the square acquired its "pouch" shape, opening across its entire width to the south. On the eastern side, the mighty Shir Dar Madrasa ("The One with Lions") was built opposite the Ulugh Beg Madrasa from the 15th century, which had remained undamaged, using a *kosh* schema. Constructed in the years 1619–1635/36, it obtained its name from the beasts of prey depicted on its tympana. The new *madrasa*, was intended by the city's ruler who commissioned it, Yalangtush, to be a mirror-image twin to complement the famous Ulugh Beg Madrasa opposite. The main facade is dominated by an enormous, projecting portal with a large pointed-arch niche that is edged with twisting ribbons of rope-like tilework.

Tile mosaics and tile patterns cover all the exterior surfaces of the building. By comparison with the immense portal with its depictions of animals in tile mosaics, the two-story wings of the main facade seem rather small. They are flanked by an elegantly proportioned minaret or tower at each corner, which have a cornice of stalactite garlands and an all-over decoration consisting of large-scale geometric patterns in glazed brick, just like the minarets of the Ulugh Beg Madrasa opposite. With its two rooms left and right of the portal, and the two-story arcading of the courtyard loggias, which is interrupted by four axial *iwans*, the building clearly takes its cue from its neighbor. As usual, decorative exterior domes are mounted eye-catchingly on drums. The dimensions of the building are impressive, but by comparison with its over-insistent multicolored decoration, its model seems to enjoy a perfect classical harmony. Like so often in the history of architecture, this attempt to outdo a predecessor, or even just to equal its achievement, was unsuccessful. Building work on the Tilla Kari Madrasa ("The Gilded One"), which borders the square on the north, lasted from 1646 to 1660 and was not ultimately completed. This large structure united the two functions of a *madrasa* and Samarqand's Friday mosque, which explains its extraordinary design. The usual domed rooms of mosque and auditorium flanking the portal are missing here, as are the high exterior domes which would normally rise above them behind the main facade.

Used early on in its history as a market square, the Registan, due to its
central location, eventually became the city's main square, serving an
official function, in the 15th century. This is when Ulugh Beg built the
largest of three *madrasas* (left) and a large *khanqa* opposite it. In the
17th century, Samarqand's ruler, Yalangtush, had the dilapidated
khanqa demolished and the Shir Dar Madrasa ("The One with Lions,"
right), which was supposed to mirror or even outdo the Ulugh Beg
Madrasa, built in its place. Ten years later the large caravanserai at the
end of the square was converted into a *madrasa* (middle, back) and
given the name Tilla Kari ("The Gilded One").

Portal tympana of the Shir Dar Madrasa
The portal tympana display a rare (for Islam)
example of figurative art, with the depiction
of beasts of prey (more like tigers than lions)
chasing a fallow deer and a sun in the form of
a human face rising behind one of them.

**View of the courtyard of the Shir Dar
Madrasa in Samarqand**, 1619–1635/36
The *madrasa's* courtyard facades consist of
two-story galleries of vaulted niches containing the entrances to the living cells. These
galleries are broken up by vaulted, axial *iwans*.

The whole of the west side of the courtyard is taken up by the city mosque,
whose center is formed by a domed hall with axial niches. Connected to it are
two further wings in the form of triple-aisled halls with domes supported by
octagonal pillars. The unusually heavy-looking exterior drum that covers the
internal dome of the *maqsura* remained without an external dome for 300 years;
it was only built a few years ago. The Bukhara influence is noticeable in the
polygonal border of the portal niche and low towers at the corners of the main
facade. The all-over decoration of the facade consists of glazed bricks, tiled
panels, and tile mosaics, just like that of the Shir Dar Madrasa, but its quality,
even by comparison with the Shir Dar, shows a marked decline. Samarqand's
Registan Square, whose buildings are subordinated to its majestic overall
proportions, is a rare example of a complete, self-contained architectural ensemble. Resembling an enormous stage open to the south, the square corresponds
spiritually, if not formally, to the idea of the forum of classical antiquity.

Located in southwest Samarqand is a complex of buildings constructed in
the 17th century next to the tomb of the renowned Sufi sheikh Khoja Ahrar.
The parts of it that have survived consist of a *madrasa* with mosque oriented
precisely towards Mecca, a summer mosque of the loggia type with a mosaic
mihrab, and a few buildings of later date. The *madrasa*, whose construction has
been attributed to the minister Nadir Diwan Begi, who built the *madrasa* and
khanqa named after him in Bukhara, features a simplified plan. The domed
halls to the left and right of the entrance portal are missing. The ends of the

courtyard's transverse axis are accentuated by portals. There is a summer mosque
on the western side of the asymmetrical courtyard, which has a polygonal water
basin, and the winter mosque borders the *madrasa's* longitudinal axis. The
winter mosque consists of a cruciform domed hall flanked by side chambers,
each of these having a portal niche that opens onto the courtyard. The building
was previously badly dilapidated, but a full restoration has now been carried out
which included the ornamental wall coverings of its courtyard facade. There are
several indications that it is older than the *madrasa*, but the decoration of both
parts of the building and its bright coloring, with predominant tones of yellow
and green, date without doubt from the 17th century. The summer mosque, a
loggia supported by columns with a mosaic *mihrab* in the middle of its back

wall, also dates from this time. The outer courtyard is bordered on the south by an old necropolis with marble stelae that are decorated with impressive patterning and calligraphy.

Khiva

Khiva, the capital of Khwarazmia in the late Middle Ages, can look back on a history spanning many centuries, yet its earliest surviving buildings date from the 14th century. The many monumental buildings that give this attractive city its characteristic medieval appearance were not in fact built until the 18th and 19th centuries, when Khiva rose out of its ashes once more, after a period of economic and political decline, and started to become powerful again.

The result of this late renaissance was a multitude of impressive buildings which together constitute a unique city center ensemble, the Ichan Qala, whose rectangular area, enclosed by a wall, is divided up by two streets which bisect each other to form the shape of a cross. The city's most important buildings are located on and around the street forming the horizontal bar of the cross, which connects the east and west gates. Here, for example, one finds *madrasas* standing close by one another and minarets of characteristic local design: a strongly tapering shaft ringed with bands of tiles that ends, without the customary "neck," in a small lantern. No other place in Central Asia has this many monumental buildings standing so close to each other as Khiva's Ichan Qala.

Khiva's numerous *madrasas* and several mausoleums were based on old models. The city's isolation from the other cultural centers of Central Asia is evident in this, and resulted in the preservation of older building techniques and

Above: **Left wing of the main facade of the Tilla Kari Madrasa**, Samarqand, 1646–1660
Both the courtyard facades and those that give onto Registan Square take the form of two-story arcades with loggia-style niches, of which the lower level houses the entrances to the students' cells and the upper level provides balconies for them.

Below: **Interior of the mosque's central domed hall**, Tilla Kari Madrasa, Samarqand
The entire west side of the *madrasa* is taken up by a large Friday mosque, at the center of which is a high domed hall with a deep *mihrab* niche splendidly decorated using the *kundal* technique, which consists of golden reliefs on a blue background.

forms. The specific local character of Khiva's architecture is to be seen primarily in its decoration, particularly in the glazed panel wall coverings with their delicate, mainly floral patterns. The dark blue, white and black color scheme gives the surfaces completely clad in it a metallic appearance. Alongside this, other decorative techniques carried over from the pre-Mongol times, and which had been almost forgotten in other cultural centers since the 14th century, were given a new lease on life, for example the double brick bonds with vertical decorative insertions, which had been characteristic of buildings of the Qarakhanid and Seljuk eras. Perhaps this curious historicism was meant to underline the fact that the Khiva khanate was the legitimate successor – culturally as well as politically – of these powers. Another individual feature is Khiva's wood carving, which was famous throughout the whole of Central Asia. The carved wooden doors and slender wooden columns with their characteristic narrow necks between base and shaft adorn both public buildings and well-appointed private houses, with their high, single-column loggias that open northwards.

Khiva retained the gently tapering portal design found in the architecture of the Khwarazm-Shahs and Sufis (12–14th centuries), which is not encountered anywhere else. The arched niches of Khiva's portals, which do not have the framework, consisting of arched panels arranged one above the other, typical of those of Bukhara and Samarqand, are all enclosed by recessed rectangular frames. Overall, however, a certain sobriety and the stereotypical application of tried-and-tested techniques can be detected in the architecture of Khiva's *madrasas* but is not present in its commercial buildings, indoor bazaars, palaces, and private houses.

For reasons not known, Khiva's building masters did not use pairs of overlapping arches as the supporting structure for their domes, even though this technology had been around since the 14th century. Here the domes rest on the

Muhammad Rakhim Khan Madrasa, in Khiva, 1871
This *madrasa* is one of the largest of the local, traditional type. Old techniques reminiscent of the decoration of the pre-Mongol era, such as the use of paired brickwork with vertical carved and glazed insertions, have been used in the design of the main facade in addition to the use of painted tilework. One of the *madrasa*'s most unusual features is its outer courtyard in front of the main facade, which is enclosed by single-story, domed buildings that open onto the courtyard with *iwans* like market passages.

traditional octagons with corner squinches, with lanterns sometimes placed at the point of the domes.

On entering the Ichan Qala through the west gate, visitors immediately see the high compressed mud walls of the Kuna Ark, the old citadel of the Khans, with the Kurinysh Khan Palace, the arsenal, and the mint on their left. On the right-hand side stands Khiva's largest *madrasa*, the two-story Muhammad Amin Khan (1852–1855). The spacious mosque on the left of its entrance is balanced by a modest lecture hall on the right, which can barely have accommodated the quantity of students indicated by the number of accommodation cells; as in Khiva's other *madrasas*, there are no *iwans*, which were elsewhere used as lecture halls, on the courtyard's cross-axis. The enormous Kalta Minar minaret (1855), not even half completed, rises up in the *madrasa*'s northeastern corner. Continuing along the street, the sizable Friday mosque building, which has a minaret integrated into its facade, can be seen a little further up on a small square on the right. This mosque was built in 1789 and consists of an enormous hall with a flat roof supported by 12 wooden columns. Many of the columns are very old: they originated in another building and were used here for a second time. The room is lit by two octagonal air shafts. From the outside, the mosque appears to be a closed, windowless solid but, on the inside, the seemingly infinite rows of columns create an impression of limitlessness.

To the south of the mosque, surrounded by the burial chambers of an old cemetery, is Khiva's most important shrine, the mausoleum complex of Pakhlawan Mahmud, a legendary poet and fighter from the end of the 13th and beginning of the 14th centuries. The overall effect of the ensemble, which has a large, domed *khanqa*, and forms a stylistic whole despite the different construction dates of its component parts, is one of solemnity.

The Kutlugh Murad Inak Madrasa (beginning of the 19th century), with its slender portal and wall covering of unglazed terracotta in relief, runs along the right-hand side of the main street, which narrows off very quickly, and the large Tash Kauli Palace Complex (1830–1838), the residence of Khiva's khans, runs along the left hand side. The extensive palace compound, which is surrounded by high walls fortified with towers, is subdivided into several distinct areas each arranged around their own courtyard and each with their own well-defined function, either official/state or private/domestic. The northern half, which is occupied by living accommodation, is separated from the southern, official half by a corridor. It consists of groups of either two or four uniformly shaped rooms opening onto a courtyard through a high loggia supported by very slender, carved columns. This rather sober design contrasts strongly with the southern, official half in which small adjoining rooms and large audience chambers are grouped picturesquely around small inner courtyards. These include throne rooms that open with loggias to the north. Tile coverings and double bonds of polished brick with carved, green ornamental insertions decorate the walls. *Yurts* (round tents for living) for nomadic guests unacquainted with the ways of the city, once stood on round, raised areas in the courtyards, and living accommodation for relatives and servants ran along the courtyard walls of both parts of the palace.

The narrow street between the palace walls and the Kutlugh Murad Inak Madrasa leads to the close-knit Pakhlawan Darwasa group of buildings at the east gate of the Ichan Qala. The present gatehouse building, a multidomed gallery containing market niches and a small bathhouse at its western entrance, was built at the beginning of the 19th century on the site of an older structure. It projects forward from the city wall, and its east portal has angular towers faced with double bonds and carved, green decorative insertions. Adjoining the domed gallery on the north side is the Allah Quli Khan Madrasa, which was built in 1882/83 in a *kosh* arrangement with the Kutlugh Murad Inak Madrasa, in other words the portals of the two buildings face each other on either side of a square. In front of the Allah Quli Khan's traditional facade, with its high central portal and symmetrical wings with loggia-like arcading, the remains of the old Khurjum Madrasa (1688) can be seen. This was divided into two halves when the Allah Quli Khan was built, partly covered with earth, and reorganized in such a way that its roof became the base of the new portal. The Allah Quli Khan Madrasa has a very attractive appearance that stems from the decoration, dominated by "Khwarazmian" tiling, with its dark blue, white, and light blue tones and black outlines to its patterns, of its main and courtyard facades.

To the north the *madrasa* is bordered directly by the long, monumental market building known as the Tim Allah Quli Khan (1835–1838) or Saray ("Palace") Bazaar. A row of heavy, cross-shaped pillars divides the room into two rows of dome-covered cells with a hexagonal, domed hall in the middle. Another broad room with a wide entrance to the Ichan Qala lies on the west side. The building has no decoration, but impresses with the harmony of its architectonic forms, its arched dome structures, the emphatic three-dimensionality of its construction, and its balanced proportions. The exteriors of both

Detail of the tile border on the back wall of the portal niche, Mausoleum of Najm al-Din Kubra, Kuna Urgench (1321–1333)
This carved ceramic tile forms part of the lower portion of the rectangular, inscription-bearing border that beautifully frames the entrance to the mausoleum.

Carved wooden column from the Tash Khauli Palace in Khiva, 1830–1832
Khiva has always been famous for its architectural wood carving. The best examples to be found are columns and doors, where the carving is often extremely intricate and masterfully executed.

View of the interior of Khiva's Friday Mosque, 1789
Khiva's large Friday mosque takes the form of a gigantic hypostyle hall with 13 rows of 17 columns, lit by two openings in its roof. Many of the columns are older than the mosque, and were removed from older buildings that were pulled down. Judging from the style of their decoration and the techniques employed, many of them date from the 14–15th and even from the 10-11th centuries. Hypostyle mosques of this type are extremely rare in Central Asia, and there is no other building comparable with this one.

Below: **Harem court of the Tash Khauli Palace in Khiva**, 1830–1838
The inner facades, with their alternating vertical end walls and square, shaded *iwans* is effective, if rather theatrical. The flat end walls between the *iwans*, with their small entrances and arched windows above, are decorated by relief ribbons of archaic, "pre-Mongol" design, consisting of pairs of polished bricks between which small carved, blue "bows" have been inserted.

of its end walls form city gates, whose corner towers are decorated with figurative bands. The *tim* (bazaar passage) building, incidentally, wedged in between two other large structures, can hardly be seen from the outside – the effect of its domed galleries and high rooms covered with pure white stucco can only be appreciated from the inside.

Further north, the extensive Allah Quli Khan Caravanserai (1832/33) follows on directly from the group of buildings around the Ichan Qala's east gate. It can be entered only from the hexagonal hall of the neighboring *tim*, which lies on the same axis as the caravanserai, thus underlining the unity of the two commercial buildings. The courtyard of the caravanserai is surrounded by a series of rooms on two floors. Goods would once have been stored underneath, and accommodation for the traders was situated upstairs. The upper rooms of its south side, however, were demolished when the *tim* was built and its dome repositioned on the caravanserai wall. The shop compartments of the lower floor retained their earlier function and were integrated into the *tim*. There is no internal decoration in this purely functional building.

Against a background of general decline in the architecture of Central Asia, the 18–19th-century architecture of Khiva is distinctive for its use of classical traditions. It is only here that a relatively original school of monumental building, albeit one that also looked to the past, was maintained. The architectonic procedures it uses connect it to the important Khwarazmian buildings of the 11th and 12th centuries. Its tile decoration is beautiful and unusual, and the wood carving of Khiva's late period is unique in the rich variety of its ornamental motifs.

Allah Quli Khan *Madrasa* in Khiva, 1834/35
In order to build this large *madrasa*, part of the eastern city wall had to be demolished, and a small, old *madrasa* dating from 1688, which then became a sort of ramp in front of the main facade of the new building, was more or less destroyed as well. Traditionally, the facade of a *madrasa* consists of a large central portal and wings of two-story arched loggias with corner towers that serve as minarets. The main and side facades, and even the backs of the facades, are richly decorated with tilework, which is unique in Khiva.

Opposite: ***Pakhlawan Mahmud Mausoleum, in Khiva***
The building of the tomb complex of poet and fighter Pakhlawan Mahmud lasted from the 14th century to the beginning of the 20th. The central building, the mausoleum pictured here, consists of a square, domed hall surrounded by a number of buildings added at various times. Externally, the building is remarkable for its courtyard-facing portal and high, blue dome. The interior furnishing of the chamber, which is completely covered in tiles, including the dome, is also extremely effective.

Tiles as Architectural Decoration

Sheila Blair, Jonathan Bloom

Buildings enveloped within a web of colored decoration are one of the most distinctive features of Islamic art, and throughout the centuries, glazed ceramic tiles have been one of the most popular means of achieving such chromatic effects. In the eastern Islamic lands, tiles arranged in geometric, vegetal, and epigraphic motifs were used to decorate interior and exterior walls, vaults, and domes: in the western Islamic lands geometric motifs predominated and tiles were used to decorate lower walls and floors.

Glazed bricks arranged in figural panels had been used in Assyrian, Babylonian, and Achaemenid architecture, but the use of wall tiles in Islamic architecture began only in the 9th century since Umayyad builders continued to prefer the Byzantine colored glass mosaic technique for decorating walls. The development of glazed tiles in the Abbasid period went hand in hand with the flowering of the ceramic industry, as potters developed a range of brilliantly colored glazes.

The first Islamic tiles were overglaze-painted with polychrome luster: in this technique, designs were painted on the glazed surface in various metallic oxides and then fired in a reducing (low-oxygen) kiln. Several fragments of polychrome luster tiles were excavated at Samarra, the Abbasid capital in Iraq, but the only group of such tiles to survive in situ are those installed around the year 862 around the *mihrab* of the Great Mosque at Kairouan in Tunisia. Decorated in several shades of green, brown, and yellow luster, these tiles were probably imported from Iraq and must have been extremely expensive, for the mosque's decorators did not set them side by side, the typical arrangement to cover a surface completely, but arranged them in a pattern to double the surface area covered.

By the late 11th century the technique of arranging tiles in geometric patterns, commonly known as tile mosaic, had developed in North Africa, for examples have been found decorating the floors of several palaces dating to that period. By the second half of the 12th century bands and panels of tiles were used to decorate the minarets attached to several mosques erected under the patronage of the

Dado frieze in the Hall of the Ambassadors, the Alhambra, Granada, 14th-century

Luster tile decoration on the *mihrab* of the Great Mosque of Kairouan, 862

Almohads, rulers of Morocco and southern Spain. The use of tile mosaic reached its apogee in the western Islamic world in the 14th century under the Merinids, who ruled Morocco 1196–1549, and the Nasrids, who ruled southern Spain 1230–1492, when builders covered the lower walls of buildings such as *madrasas* and palaces with intricate strapwork patterns made up from pieces of colored tile, laid side by side in an unbroken surface. The compositions were predominantly green, light brown, and white, but smaller amounts of yellow, blue, and black were also included. Epigraphic tile friezes, in which the black letters were formed by scraping through the glaze to the bisque body of the tile, were often used to separate and differentiate the lower walls, covered by geometric tile patterns, from the upper walls, covered with carved stucco in vegetal patterns. Tile was also used on such other surfaces as piers and columns and the spandrels of arches, where vegetal decoration is often found.

In the eastern Islamic lands, the use of tile developed differently from the 11th century. After exploiting brick patterns and stucco to create surface texture on their buildings, builders began to experiment cautiously with glazed elements to provide strong color and sharp contrast to the typical buff-colored brick walls. At first, these elements were just small brick end-plugs or molded tiles glazed in turquoise blue, but eventually other colors, such as white and dark (cobalt) blue, were used and the surfaces covered with tile were larger. Many Iranian minarets – such as the one at Sin dated 1129, or that at Nigar, built in the early 13th century – were girdled by inscription bands in glazed tile that increased the legibility and prominence of the text.

Other approaches were used for tiles intended for the protected interiors of buildings. In the 12th century, Iranian potters had perfected the art of making thin vessels from a fritted or stone-paste ceramic body and decorating them with several overglaze techniques, such as enamel or luster painting. Lusterware, which was produced continuously from the 12th century to the 14th in the city of Kashan in central Iran, was one of the most expensive ceramic techniques used in medieval Iran because of the additional cost of the materials and the double firing each piece required. The technique was particularly favored for star-shaped tiles, which were arranged with monochrome (usually turquoise) tiles in dadoes, and for square or rectangular plaques put together to form long inscription friezes. The potters' finest efforts, however, were reserved for large *mihrab* ensembles and multipartite panels which were intended to cover cenotaphs. Over 30 of these multipartite compositions survive. The largest, such as the *mihrab* made by the potter al-Hasan ibn Arabshah in 623 (1226) and once installed in the Maidan Mosque in Kashan, are more than 6.5 feet (2 meters) high and contain more than 40 individual tiles molded to shape. These glittering ensembles were the *pièces de résistance* of the medieval structures they adorned.

Rectangular tiles could be simply arranged in colored friezes to enliven an otherwise dull surface, but to make more complex patterns, such as arabesques, strapwork, or inscriptions, potters had to fit small pieces together in the technique known as tile mosaic. The large colored tiles are cut into small shapes, which are laid face down on a prepared design, covered with a layer of plaster, and formed into large plaques, which are then attached to

Luster decoration on the *mihrab* of the Maidan Mosque in Kashan, al-Hasan ibn Arabshah, 1226, Berlin, Museum für Islamische Kunst

the wall. This labor-intensive and expensive technique, which took full advantage of the glowing intensity of each individual color of tile, allowed artists an extraordinary freedom of design. The development of this technique, which began in the Seljuk period, was temporarily interrupted by the Mongol conquests in the 13th century, but by the end of the 14th century Iranian artisans had perfected the technique of completely covering a wall surface, whether flat, convex, or concave, with a mosaic of tile fragments executed in a range of seven brilliant colors including white, light and dark blue, black, ocher, green, and the tan of the bisque-fired tile itself. Designs became increasingly complex, employing naturalistic and floral arabesques and inscriptions. The apogee of the Iranian tile tradition may be viewed as the panels decorating the portal of Aq Saray, Timur's palace at Shar-i sabz, now in southern Uzbekistan.

The extraordinary intricacy (and expense) of the tile mosaic technique encouraged artists to develop quicker and cheaper ways of achieving similar multicolored effects. One popular method was the *cuerda seca* ("dry thread") technique, in which large tiles were painted with different colors of glaze. To prevent the glazes from running together during firing, they were separated by a greasy substance mixed with manganese that left a mat black line between the colors after firing. The *cuerda seca* technique, which is known in Iran as *haft rang* ("seven colors"), is much faster and cheaper than tile mosaic, but the colors are not as brilliant as they are all fired at the same temperature. Despite these limitations, the results achieved are often impressive, creating some of the most memorable ensembles found in Iranian Islamic architecture.

The high-status tile mosaic technique continued to be used for important parts of prestigious Iranian buildings well into the 17th century, such as the splendid dome over the Mosque of Sheikh Lutfallah in Isfahan, but large expanses in less-prominent areas were covered with *cuerda seca* tiles imitating the patterns developed for tile mosaic. Some of the most original *cuerda seca* tiles, however, were made not for mosques but for the palaces of 17th-

Tile panels with pictures of maidservants, Iran, 1st half of the 17th century, Berlin, Museum für Islamische Kunst

Ornamental tiles from the palace of Takht-i Sulaiman, Iran, 13th or 14th century

Sheikh Lutfallah Mosque in Isfahan, 1603–1619

in one technique or another, and while the individual elements may be less than perfect in themselves, the whole effect is memorable.

By the early 15th century, itinerant Central Asian or Iranian craftsmen had brought the *cuerda seca* technique to the Ottoman Empire. At the Yesil Cami ("Green Mosque") in Bursa, built by Mehmed I (1403–1421), the royal balcony overlooking the central hall is lavishly paneled with *cuerda seca* tiles, and has a dado of hexagonal monochrome tiles with stenciled gold patterns, as well as an elaborate 33-foot 10-meter) high *mihrab* executed in a combination of tile mosaic and *cuerda seca*. This extraordinary ensemble was proudly signed by tile makers from Tabriz, indicating their Iranian origin.

Another approach to achieving a multicolored tile surface was the use of underglaze painting, a technique that potters had developed for use on ceramic vessels from the late 12th century. The technique was widely adopted in the 13th and 14th centuries, when it was used to make individual tiles which were then laid in friezes. Although it was occasionally used in Timurid Central Asia, the technique became particularly popular in the Ottoman lands. Some of the first attempts decorated hexagonal tiles in cobalt blue with designs copying Chinese blue-and-white wares, but eventually the tiles were made square or rectangular and the palette was expanded to include turquoise blue, green, purple, and eventually the distinctive red associated with the city of Iznik, in southwestern Turkey.

Perhaps the largest and most spectacular tiles ever made were the five large 50 × 19 inches (127 × 48 centimeters) blue-and-white panels now installed on the walls of the Sunnet Odasi (Circumcision Room) of the Topkapi Palace, in Istanbul. Probably made in the Ottoman royal workshop in Istanbul during the early years of the reign of Suleyman the Magnificent (1520–1566), these extraordinary tiles depict birds and dragons amid chinoiserie leaves and blossoms. They are painted in two shades of blue on a luminous white ground and show an extraordinary command of all the tile maker's techniques.

Most of the tiles produced at Iznik to decorate the 16th-century royal mosques in Istanbul and Edirne were much smaller but were fired with the same brilliance and intensity. They were prepared in large compositions formed of many smaller tiles, employing the full range of colors and decorative motifs found on contem-

century Iranian noblemen in Isfahan. Several sets of these tiles are known: most of them have been removed from their original sites and are now preserved in European and American collections. The sets were all made to fit specific architectural spaces, either rectangular panels or the spandrels above arches, and most show male and female figures in garden settings. The compositions have been assembled from stock figures, accessories, and landscape elements, and rendered in six colors (green, light

and dark blue, black, yellow, and white).

The various tile techniques developed in Iran and Central Asia over the preceding centuries were available to artisans in 17th-century Samarqand. Buildings such as the Tila Kari Madrasa present a stunning combination of tile mosaic, *cuerda seca*, and the *bannai* technique, in which rectangular pieces of glazed tile alternate with unglazed brick to create woven patterns which sometimes spell out sacred names. Almost every exterior surface is covered

TILES AS ARCHITECTURAL DECORATION

porary tablewares. As the century progressed, however, the Iznik tile makers were unable to produce work of the same quality for the fixed rates the sultans paid.

Furthermore, the absence of imperial commissions during the late 16th century had greatly reduced the level of tile production. For example, by the early 17th century, those decorating the Mosque of Ahmed I in Istanbul had to procure new tiles at old prices or rely on available stock. The somewhat fussy decoration of the interior of the mosque is dominated by large expanses of blue tile (and paint), which has given the building its popular epithet, the "Blue Mosque."

On close examination, many of the tiles have runny colors and dull glazes, especially when compared to the finest work of the mid-16th century. The best tiles used in the mosque were recycled products made for the Topkapi Palace in the 1570s and 1580s. The Ottomans carried their taste for tiled interiors throughout their empire, and underglaze-painted square tiles assembled in large compositions became popular from the Levant to Tunisia, Algeria, and the Balkans.

In Egypt, the Mamluk Mosque of Aqsunqur (1347), for example, was redecorated in 1652 when the Janissary Ibrahim Aga Mustahfizan built his mausoleum next to the entrance. To replace the traditional revetment of multi-

Mihrab with tile mosaic and *cuerda seca* tiles in the Yesil Cami in Bursa, 1st half of the 15th century

Detail of the tile decoration in the Rustem Pasha Mosque in Istanbul, 1561

colored marble strips, which by then must have looked very old-fashioned, the *qibla* wall of the mosque and the mausoleum were revetted with large compositions of blue and green tiles, which have given the building its common sobriquet – as in Istanbul – the "Blue Mosque."

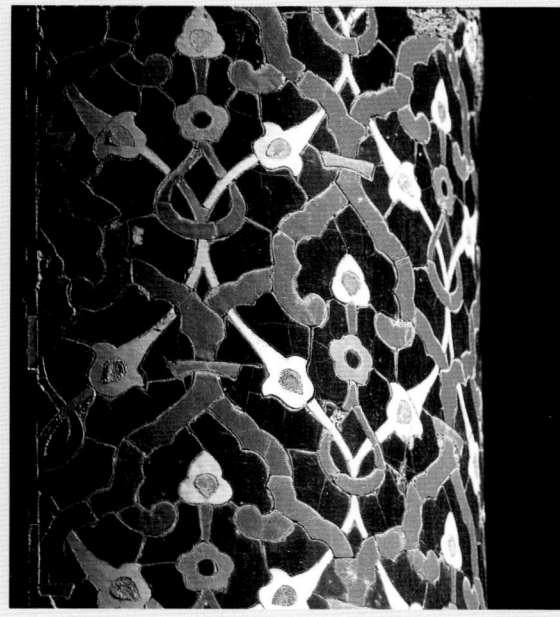

Above: **Detail of a column in the Tuman-aka Mausoleum in the Shah-i Zinda necropolis**, Samarqand, 1405

Right: **Portal of the Sheik-Lutfallah Mosque**, Isfahan, 1603–1619

Indian Subcontinent: from Sultanate to Mughal Empire

Shalimar Garden Lahore, created 1642/43
The Koran describes the eternal gardens of Paradise with deep shade, running water, fountains, and such fruit as the heart desires. The Mughals, like their ancestors in central Asia, loved gardens, also a symbol of royal authority, and developed sophisticated hydraulic systems to create "paradise on earth." Gardens thus served also as a setting for imperial ceremonials, as the lower terraces known as the Bagh-i Faiz Baksh seen here.

History
Philippa Vaughan

The Indian subcontinent (that is the area covered by present-day Pakistan, India, Bangladesh, parts of Afghanistan, Ladakh, Assam and Kashmir) has produced some of the finest expressions of Islamic art and architecture. Muslim dynasties and mystics from the Islamic heartlands formed and nurtured the development of Islamic states in which non-Muslim cultures represented the majority, yet retained their intellectual and artistic vigor. Mutual exchange was a constant feature of life at all levels, and non-Muslim ideas and motifs were absorbed to create a unique dimension in the Islamic visual arts.

The development of Indo-Islamic Culture

The development of Indo-Islamic culture began with the arrival of Arab armies in Sind in the years 711–712. The first phase of conquest absorbed the area roughly corresponding to Pakistan, where Arabic was the court language and Baghdad and Damascus were the mainsprings of cultural and commercial life. Arab communities settled at important centers along the major trade routes to China and in the principal ports along the coast as far as the Bay of Bengal.

During the 11th and 12th centuries, invasions from the northwest opened the Punjab to the influences of Persia and Central Asia. This orientation predominated during the 13th and 14th centuries when Turko-Iranian elites ruled the sultanate of Delhi, which at that time extended from the Punjab and Gujarat to Bengal, and the Deccan as far south as Madurai. Persian became the language of courtly culture and administration.

That a small elite could establish and retain control over such a vast and populous area while remaining a religious minority reflected a flexible attitude to religion on all sides. The early Muslim invaders were pragmatic, being primarily concerned with political and commercial control at minimal cost to themselves. The subsequent extension of political control in the early 13th century coincided with intensive missionary activity by the mystical orders. Working in the vernacular languages as well as the classical Persian and Arabic, they did not make conversion to Islam an essential prerequisite for participating in their form of religious experience. The development of Muslim society and spiritual life thus took place at all levels of society and did not create a

***Mihrab* in the tomb of Sultan Iltutmish,** Delhi, 1236
The *mihrab* in the tomb of Iltutmish, who turned the sultanate into an independent state, is distinguished by its exquisite decoration. Several styles of calligraphy are used for the bands of Koranic verses and the central panel is in intricate plaited Kufic script. The use of corbelling for the arch facilitated carving of the spandrels.

permanent sectarian divide from non-Muslims. Respect for saints regardless of denomination was an important cultural catalyst.

The sultans of Delhi welcomed the mystical orders and members of the court were counted among their followers. Many cultural practices specific to the subcontinent, such as music and poetry at Sufi shrines, received official sanction and remain part of contemporary practice. The caliph was far away or reduced to a figurehead after the Mongol invasions of the 11th century. Acceptance by the local elites of the ruler's right to rule was of greater importance, and the blessing of a Sufi sheikh had its own political weight in the recognition of sovereignty.

It was expected of the monarch to support and develop Islamic society and charitable institutions such as mosques and *madrasas*, markets and caravanserais, palaces for administration of government and the law, provision of water and drainage, urban planning and civic amenities, and to encourage intellectual and cultural life by attracting scholars and literati from all over the Islamic world. Patronage of architecture and the arts thus was not simply the fulfillment of personal artistic ambitions. Form and style were a dynastic statement, the language of power and identity both political and religious.

Arab traders had been in contact with Asia since at least Greek times. Soon after the first Muslim foray in 636 Caliph Umar (634–644) enquired about the area. The Arab historian Baladhuri (d. 892) reported the response: "Water scarce; fruit inferior; robbers impudent; the army if small, likely to be lost, if numerous likely to perish from hunger and thirst..." During the following 75 years the Makran was gradually annexed, until a large Arab army entered the Indus valley led by the 17-year-old Muhammad ibn Qasim, nephew of al-Hajjaj, governor of Iraq. Within three years he gained control of the entire area up to and beyond the city of Multan in the Punjab.

The principal cities established in the Indus delta were Bambhore and al-Mansura. Both were well planned. At Bambhore the Great Mosque dated 727 was the earliest in the subcontinent. Similar in plan to the Friday (congregational) mosques of Kufa (670) and of Wasit (702) constructed on the orders of al Hajjaj, the prayer hall, like its models, had no formal *mihrab*. A hierarchy of materials was used corresponding to the function of the structure: the dressed stone for the mosque and the palace standing out in an area where brick architecture predominated. The houses of notables nearby were in semidressed stone with, on the interior, lime-plastered walls and floors.

Right: **Arhai-din-ka-Jhompera Mosque, Ajmer,** 1200–1206

When the Muslim conquerors began to establish themselves on the Indian subcontinent, they first constructed mosques in major centers as a symbol of victory, and often built them very quickly. The name of the mosque shown here means that it was built in twelve and a half days. On the occasion of a visit by the caliph in 1229, Sultan Iltutmish added a monumental facade with seven arches in front of the prayer hall.

Below: **The Qutb Minar, inside the Quwwat al-Islam complex**, Delhi, begun 1199

This "Tower of Victory," erected by Qutb al-Din Aibak following the model of the minaret of Jam (1191–1198) was designed to symbolize the power of the new dynasty. Its red and yellow sandstone is carved with monumental Arabic inscriptions in *Naskhi* calligraphy. The Alai Darwaza, the great domed portal, alone survives of the grandiose additions by Sultan Ala al-Din Khalji. The innovations in construction and design suggest an experienced Seljuk architect. The practice of alternating stone courses of wide and narrow bands to strengthen the bonding was adapted later by the Mughals.

Below: **Tomb of Sultan Iltutmish in the Quwwat al-Islam complex,** Delhi, 1236

The ulama, the Islamic religious authorities, did not oppose the construction of this magnificent sandstone tomb with the sarcophagus of Sultan Iltumish's in the center, nor the accession to the throne of Iltutmish's daughter Raziya, who was described as a wise and capable regent.

The lower town, laid out in blocks with well-oriented streets, has simpler dwellings in line and plaster.

Al-Mansura, the Friday mosque of which had a formal *mihrab*, became a metropolis celebrated for its palaces, gardens, mosques and *madrasas*. Some Arab geographers of the 9th century compared Al-Mansura with Damascus.

The city of Multan to the north, with commercial and civic amenities comparable to those of al-Mansura, was the center of another province which by the 9th century had become independent. The city's great Sun Temple was not destroyed in these early years. In 985 the Arab geographer Maqdisi remarked upon its pre-eminent position in the center of the marketplace attracting pilgrims from throughout the subcontinent. Travellers described how the Arab court, which in the 10th century was of the Ismaili Shiite persuasion owing allegiance to the Fatimid caliphs of Egypt (after 965), had assimilated local dress and language.

Such blending of social customs was prompted by necessity, but it was not hindered by sectarian or caste considerations, for particular local reasons. The result was a cultural pluralism which continued for centuries. Arab and Hindu administrators and merchants were in constant contact. Hindus were predominantly devotees of the Lingayata sect whose acceptance of theism was not antipathetic to Muslim religious sentiment. Moreover, Hinduism had already developed flexible legal procedures for dealing with invaders, of whom the Arabs were but the most recent, integrating them into the Hindu world view as "non-Aryans," i.e. impure. A legal text, the *Devala-smrti* (c. 800–1000), concerned

with repurification, facilitated interaction between the communities provided that caste principles and procedures were followed, and penances for transgression were light. The return to the Hindu community after 20 years' profession of Islam, for example, carried the same penalty as eating garlic.

As part of yet another raid on Multan in 1010, Mahmud of Ghazna (998–1030) destroyed the Sun Temple and annexed the province to the Ghaznavid Empire. Ghazna was the most important islamic city of its time apart from Baghdad, and Hindustan was regarded as an almost inexhaustible source of treasure and slaves. It was also a recruitment area for troops, who were not required to convert to Islam as a condition of employment. By the 12th century Lahore, where Persian was the language of the court and administration, was its most brilliant outpost in the Muslim subcontinent. Ghaznavid innovations in architectural forms and techniques thus reached the Indian provinces: the new form of minaret with a tall and slender shaft; domes and pure arches in mosques and mausoleums, and the use of lime mortar.

The sultanate of Delhi

In 1181 Muizz al-Din Ghuri replaced the Gahznavid rule in Lahore and began a series of dramatic conquests which brought Hindustan under Muslim rule. Delhi and Ajmer fell in 1192, the kingdoms of Benares and Kannauj in 1194, and soon after Bihar and Bengal with its capital at Gaur. The Ghurid governor of Lahore assumed control of these dominions after Muizz al-Din died in 1206,

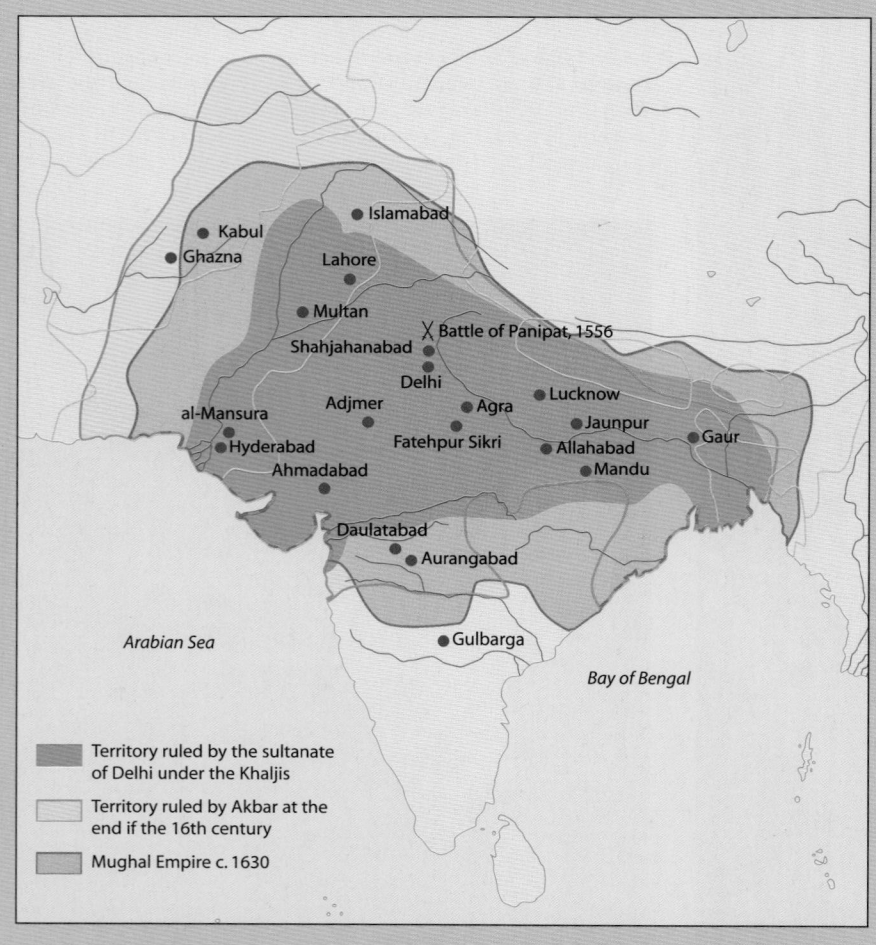

711–712	First campaigns by Arab-Muslim armies in the Indus delta
1001–1024	Mahmud of Ghazna (998–1030) conquers the Punjab
1186/87	Muizz al-Din Ghuri seizes Lahore from the Ghaznavids; the Ghurids extend their rule to Hindustan
1191–1192	First and second Battles of Tarain against the Rajput Confederacy; the Ghurids conquer Delhi
1206	Qutb al-Din Aibak founds the sultanate of Delhi
1210–1236	Reign of Iltutmish, during which the sultanate of Delhi achieves de facto independence from the Ghurids
1245/46	Beginning of Mongol campaigns in the Punjab
1296–1316	Gujarat, the Deccan, and southern India were conquered by the armies of Ala al-Din Khalji
1320	Ghiyath al-Din Tughluq founds the Tughluq dynasty
1325–1351	Reign of Muhammad ibn Tughluq, who failed in his

Territory ruled by the sultanate of Delhi under the Khaljis

Territory ruled by Akbar at the end if the 16th century

Mughal Empire c. 1630

separating them from Ghazna and Khorasan, and established what became known as the sultanate of Delhi. This his successor Iltutmish (1210–1236) molded into a truly independent state. The sultanate of Delhi comprised five successive dynasties, the first of which was the "Slave Sultans" (1206–1290), followed by the Khaljis (1290–1320), the Tughluqs (1320–1414), the Sayyids (1414–1451), the Lodi dynasty (1451–1526) and the Suris (1540–1555).

Victories were celebrated by the construction of monumental architecture declaring the new dynasty. First was the Friday mosque in Delhi, the Quwwat al-Islam. It was begun in 1193, with materials rescued from Hindu temples which had been demolished. Six years later the combined skills of Turko-Persian architects and calligraphers, and indigenous stonemasons, produced a great screen of finely dressed sandstone erected in front of the prayer hall. Also started was the Qutb Minar, a victory tower to spread the shadow of God to the east and west, as the inscriptions proclaimed. The technique of salvaging temples was followed at Ajmer, where the Arhai-din-ka-jhonpra Mosque was

Quwwat-al-Islam Mosque, Delhi
begun 1193
Qutb al-Din Aibak, the Turkish general who conquered Delhi for the Ghurid sultan of Lahore in 1193 began construction of this Friday mosque on Indian soil. The sandstone facade raised in front of the prayer hall in 1199 was finely carved with reliefs demonstrating the many traditions contributing to the Indo-Islamic repertoire. Bands of Kufic and Naskhi calligraphy alternate with undulating patterns of Buddhist origin and Hindu-inspired roundels of geometric design in the spandrels.

	attempt to move the capital to Daulatabad		
1329–1347	Individual provinces gain autonomy: Warangal (1329), Madura (1334), Bengal (1338), Daulatabad (1347)		
1345–1358	Reign of Shams al-Din Ilyas in Bengal, with Pandua as capital		
1347–1358	Reign of Ala al-Din Hasan Bahman Shah in Daulatabad; he founds a Bahmanid dynasty in the Deccan (1347–1527)		
1351–1388	Reign of Sultan Firoz Shah in Delhi		
1391	Gujarat becomes an autonomous sultanate		
1398	The Mongols under Timur invade India; Delhi is destroyed		
1402–1440	Jaunpur becomes a center of Islamic culture under Shams al-Din Ibrahim Shah, founder of the Sharqid dynasty		
1411	Foundation of the capital Ahmadabad by Ahmad Shah I (1411–1442) of Gujarat		
1436–1469	Reign of Mahmud Shah Khalji in Malwa		
1451–1526	The Afghan Lodi dynasty rules Delhi		

1526	Battle of Panipat: victory of Babur over the Lodi ruler of Delhi, Ibrahim II (1517–1526); beginning of the Mughal era
1527	End of the Bahmanid kingdom in northern Deccan; the provincial governors in Berar, Bijapur, Ahmednagar, Golconda, and Bidar gain autonomy
1540	Defeat of the Mughal ruler Himayun (1530–1540, 1555/56) by the Afghans under Sher Shah Suri. Humayun in exile in Persia and Kabul; in 1555 he regains his territories
1540–1555	Delhi is ruled by the Afghan Suri dynasty
1556–1605	Under the Mughal leader Akbar the empire extends over Afghanistan and north and central India, with capitals at Agra, Fatehpur, Sikri, and Lahore. He abolishes the *jizya* tax an non-Muslims (1564) and in 1582 founded a syncretic order (with 19 members). The new *Ilaki* era began in March 1584
1582	A league of Muslim dynasties in the Deccan region defeats the Hindu Vijayanagar kingdom
1605–1627	Reign of the Mughal Jahangir

1628–1658	Reign of the Mughal Shah Jahan; he builds the new capital, in Dehli Shahjahanabad
1658	Shah Jahan is overthrown by his son Aurangzeb (1658–1707)
1681–1707	Aurangzeb made his second capital at Aurangabad to pursue campaigns against the Muslim states of the Deccan and the Hindu Marathas
1738–1739	The Afghan Nadir Shah of Persia plunders Delhi and takes the Peacock Throne. The Mughal Emprie is threatened from all sides
1757	Battle of Plassey: the British East India Company gains effective control over Bengal
1761	Second Battle of Panipat: victory of the Afghans under Ahmad Shah over the Marathas
1765	Mughal emperor Shah Alam II grants financial authority over Bengal to the British East India Company
1799	Final defeat and death of Tipu Sultan of Mysore by the British East india Company
1803	Control of Delhi and the Mughal Empire is taken from the Marathas by the British

1857–1858	The rebellion against the British, its suppression, and the sack of Delhi
1858	The last Mughal emperor, Bahadur Shah II, is exiled to Rangoon; the British East India Company is dissolved. India becomes a British viceroyship

Portal of the Atala Djami Mosque, Djaunpur, 1408

Shams al-Din Ibrahim, governor of Jaupur, declared independence soon after Timur's sack of Delhi in 1399, founding the Sharqi dynasty. In 1408 he had the Atala Jami Mosque built, influenced by the traditions of the Tughluqs, who had ruled Delhi in the 14th century. The *pishtaq*, the monumental projecting portal, is characteristic for the new style.

built (1200–1206). A monumental screen of seven arches was added by Iltutmish in 1229, when the Abbasid caliph al-Mustansir came to Delhi and invested Iltutmish. By this time the city had been extended to new townships with gardens, bazaars, and mosques near the river Jumna, built by the nobility in response to royal command.

The Chaghatai Mongols played a major role in the decline of the Delhi sultanate through their numerous attacks on the Punjab beginning 1245/46. By 1296, when Ala al-Din Khalji (1296–1316) succeeded, the army had doubled in size and Delhi was effectively a vast armed camp. The need for new sources of revenue added an immediate practical purpose to Ala al-Din's ambitions to be a second Alexander. In 1298 he conquered Gujarat, and his general, the former slave Malik Kafur, conquered the Deccan and the south as far as Madurai. The kingdoms at first yielded booty and tribute, and were annexed in 1316.

These resources enabled Ala al-Din to embark upon a grandiose building program, which included expanding the Quwwat al-Islam and constructing nearby the Alai Minar, a tower which was to be twice the height of the Qutb Minar. It remained incomplete, however, and the Alai Darwaza, alone of the monumental domed portals, stands witness to the intended magnificence. The innovative construction and design suggests it was the work of an experienced architect from the Seljuk dominions. His legacy was the materials of red sandstone and white marble associated with royalty, the stone coursing, and the extensive calligraphic friezes in Persian extolling the ruler (rather than the traditonal verses from the Koran), features later adopted by the Mughals for their dynastic architecture.

In 1320 Ghiyath al-Din Tughluq established a new dynasty. Little survives of Tughluqabad, the huge fort he built in Delhi 1321–1325, but his tomb, probably constructed by his son Muhammad (1325–1351) showed a continuation of Khalji techniques and materials. Muhammad ibn Tughluq's visions were bold, and included invading Khorasan to end the Mongol menace, for which he raised a special contingent of 475,000 troops. To provide the space and food they required, in 1327 the officials and intelligentsia of the old city of Delhi were forcibly transferred to Daulatabad ("City of Prosperity") in the Deccan, which was the second capital until 1335–36.

The empire was well ordered, but was weakening under the strain and various provinces declared independence: Warangal (Deccan) 1329, Madura 1334, Bengal 1338, and Daulatabad (Deccan) 1347. Muhammad's successor Feroz Shah (1351–1388) was the last of the Delhi sultans to be invested by the Abbasid caliph, in Cairo in 1355. His magnificent palace citadel of Firuzabad in Delhi, with a Friday mosque, residences, gardens, and *hammams* marked the last flowering of Tughluq architecture, although the materials of construction were not the finely dressed sandstone of earlier buildings but random rubble and stucco, a style continued by the Lodi dynasty in the 15th century.

Timur's devastating invasion of India and sack of Delhi in 1399, slaughtering Hindus and Muslims alike, left the capital like a graveyard. In 1414 Sayid Khizr Khan, governor of Multan, took control of Delhi in the name of the Timurid Shah Rukh.

Regional sultanates

The early 15th century marked a watershed in the evolution of Indo-Muslim art and culture. After Timur's invasion Delhi lost its pre-eminence as a political and cultural center. A series of new, independent regional states developed. As new elites emerged, cultural affiliations were reorientated. The growth of vernacular languages as a medium of Islamic culture alongside classical Arabic and Persian, and the interaction of Muslim and non-Muslim mystics and

scholars, led to the flowering of Islamic art and culture of extraordinary originality. The Sufi orders, the open-minded Chishtiya in particular, played a vital role in this process.

Bengal evolved a unique blend of Perso-Sanskritic culture in which indigenous traditions often predominated. Large-scale missionary activity in the mid-14th century coincided with the establishment of a new dynasty by Shams al-Din Ilyas (1345–1358). The Adina Jami Mosque, begun in 1364, proclaimed the status of the new capital at Pandua. Although the form was typical of the sultanate, with a tall portal (*pishtaq*) marking position of the prayer hall, structural and decorative elements were in the style of Bengali temples, reflecting the court's reorientation towards the non-Islamic east. In the 15th century Bengali-Muslim architecture reflected vernacular forms of temple design, of which the tomb of Jalal al-Din Muhammad Shah (1414–1432), son of the Hindu rajah Ganesh of Pandua, was the prototype.

After Bengal broke away, the neighboring state of Jaunpur, founded in 1359, became the eastern bulwark of the Delhi sultanate. The governor received the title "King of the East"(Malik-al Sharq) from Feroz Shah Tughluq, hence the title of the Sharqi dynasty of Shams al-Din Ibrahim Shah (1402–1440), who declared independence soon after Timur's sack of Delhi. Jaunpur replaced Delhi as the center of Islamic culture in Hindustan, and mosques, *madrasas*, palaces and the great Atala Jami Mosque were constructed in the distinctive regional style. When Jaunpur was reabsorbed into the Delhi sultanate in 1479 the Lodi sultans destroyed much of its architectural heritage.

Malwa followed suit and in 1406 the capital was moved to Mandu. The new city was constructed in local dressed sandstone, echoing the earlier Tughluq style in its sober grandeur; but under Mahmud Shah Khalji (1436–1469), who was officially invested by the Abbasid caliph in Cairo, an exuberant style developed in which color was introduced by the use of different stones and glazed tiles. The kingdom fell to Gujarat in 1531 and finally to the Mughals in 1583.

In the Deccan Ala al-Din Hasan Bahman Shah (1347–1358) celebrated independence by constructing the central section of the Chand Minar at Daulatabad in 1347. The cylindrical shaft of this victory tower recalled the

Jahaz Mahal, part of the main palace complex in Mandu, c. 1440/50
After the governor of Malwa made himself independent of the sultan of Delhi, from 1406 he continued construction of the capital, Mandu. The Jahaz Mahal exemplifies the splendid building style developed by Sultan Mahmud Khalji. Mandu was beloved by the Mughal emperors Jahangir and Shah Jahan, who spent much time there.

Qutb Minar but details such as the pendant lotus supports of the three circular balconies were in the regional idiom. This reliance on earlier forms of the Delhi sultanate characterized Bahmanid religious architecture at the new capital of Gulbarga. It is particularly evident in tombs, which evolved from the squat domed cube with sloping walls similar to Ghyath al-Din Tughluq's to double-tiered cubes with high domes and straight walls similar to the Alai Darwaza at the Quwwat al-Islam. The Bahmanid territories were divided by Hasan's successor, and to mark the special status of Gulbarga in the province of Daulatabad a remarkable Friday mosque was built.

Between 1422 and 1427 the capitals were moved to Bidar. As a result of the influx of Shiites from Persia, tensions developed a court with the Dakhnis. They were muslims who descended from the early invaders from the north, Arabic mercantile communities, fromer Abyssinian slaves, and Hindu converts who were of the Sunni rite. The prime minister Mahmud Gawan balanced the factions but his magnificent *madrasa* built in 1472 was designed in the Persian cultural tradition.

In the early 16th century the Bahmani kingdom fragmented into smaller states ruled by their former governors. The most powerful were Ahmadnagar, Bijapur and Golconda, all of the Shiite tendency. The architectural and cultural style of their courts reflected the absorption of a regional idiom characterized by a sculptural approach to decorative detail.

In Gujarat, the evolution of Islamic art and culture was dominated by regional influences from the beginning. As in Bengal, Muslims of Gujerat did not invariably use Perso-Arabic language or script, preferring instead their own Gujarati language. Gujarat was independent by 1391, and in 1411 Ahmad Shah I (1411–1442) established the new capital of Ahmadabad. The style of the magnificent Friday mosque completed in 1424, with its prayer hall of 260 columns and sculpted minarets, was derived from temple architecture. It was situated as a focal point on the royal processional route running from the palace citadel by the river along the Maidan-i Shah (now obliterated by modern development) to the monumental gateway the Tin Darwaza, an aspect of city planning found in 17th century Shahjahanabad. The style reached its zenith under Mahmud Shah Begra (1458–1511), who founded cities at Junagadh, Champaner, and Mahmudabad, and added to Sarkhej and Ahmadabad. A late example was the mosque built by the Abyssinian Siddi Sayid in 1572, the year of the Mughal conquest.

The Mughal era

In the year 1526, Babur, a descendant of Timur Lenk, won the Battle of Panipat, northwest of Delhi, defeating the Lodi ruler. This marked the beginning of Mughal rule in India.

The dynasty's name, Mughal (meaning "Mongol" in Persian and Arabic), refers to the Chaghatai Mongol branch ruling in India. Having twice failed to retain control of Samarqand, former capital of the Timurid Empire, Babur turned his attention to India, which had formed part of Timur's great empire. By the time of his death at Agra in 1530, his position was still insecure, as Humayun, his son and successor, realised, for Babur's body was taken to Kabul for burial.

Above: **Prayer hall of the Friday Mosque of Gulbarga,** Deccan, c. 1365–1370
The Friday Mosque of Gulbarga was probably constructed in the late 1360s by Muhammad Bahman Shah, ruler of the first independent sultanate of the Deccan. The immense prayer hall, which is covered with 75 domes, is unique in India.

INDIA: FROM SULTANATE TO MUGHAL EMPIRE

Below: **Screens in the Siddi Sayid Mosque in Ahmadabad**, 1572, from the exterior (left) and interior (right)
These perforated sandstone screens are located in the prayer hall of the Friday Mosque of Ahmadabad, the capital of the sultanate of Gujarat. They feature variations of the Tree of Life design, whose sinuous tendrils extending through floral arabesques exhibit the brilliance of Gujarati sculptors.

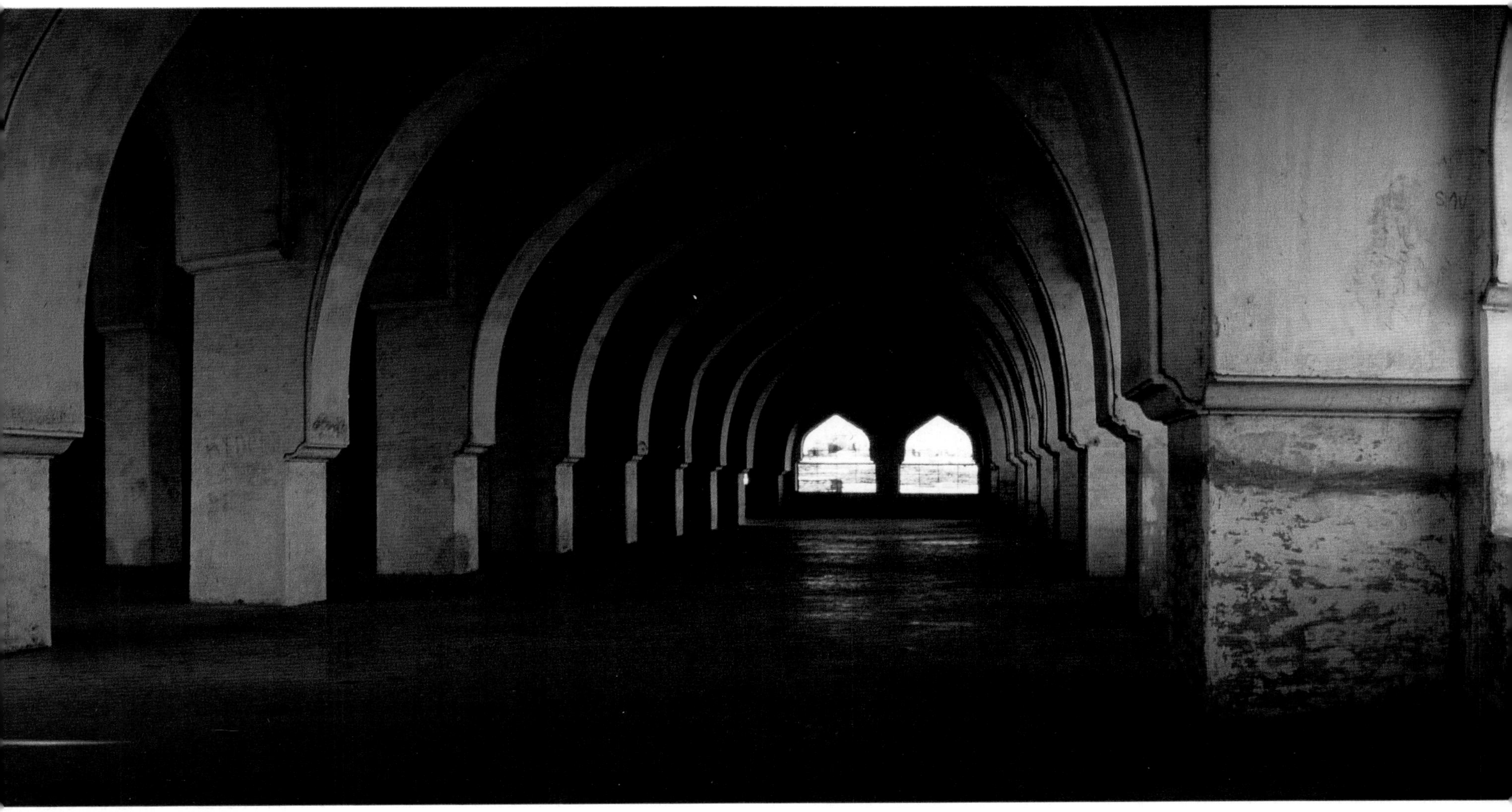

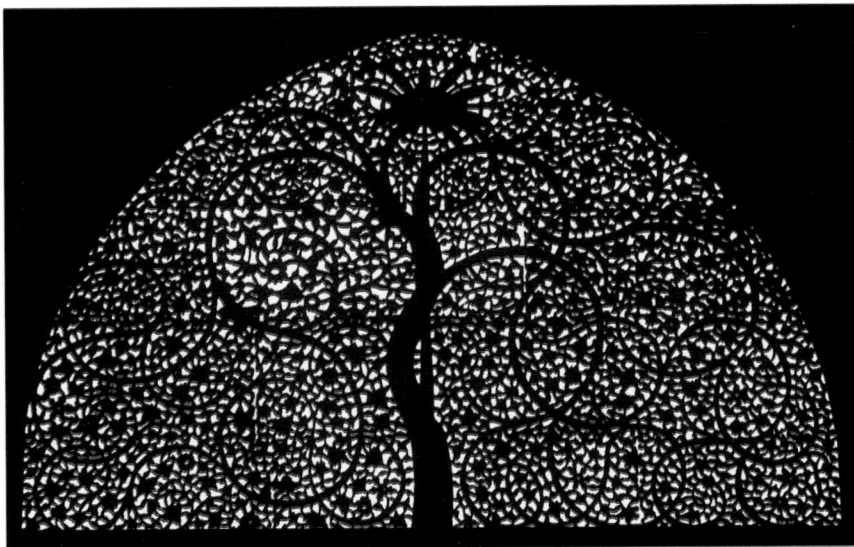

Humayun's efforts to consolidate his rule were thwarted by the Afghan Sher Shah Suri, based in Bihar. After a series of defeats, he escaped with a few loyal retainers through the deserts of Sind where Akbar, his son and heir, was born. For 18 months Humayun was given refuge in Persia by the Safavid shah Tahmasp, who also provided him with the means to regain Kabul, where his son was held hostage, and to reconquer the kingdom of Delhi. His premature death only a year later in 1556 left the kingdom in the hands of his 14-year-old heir.

Yet by the end of the 16th century Akbar had expanded control over territories stretching from Kabul and Kashmir to Bengal, extending through Khandesh, Malwa, the Rajput states of Rajasthan, and Gujerat, to the northern borders of the Deccan. An aristocracy established through military rank was created from among the Mughals of Central Asia, the Afghans, Persians and Hindu Rajputs, who constituted the nobility of the new empire, the chain of loyalty also consolidated through a policy of marriage alliances. Administrative, fiscal and commercial reforms were implemented.

The variety of cultural traditions was reflected in architecture and the arts, and the ceremonies and festivals which became part of imperial ritual. Akbar embarked upon a series of experiments in an attempt to weld the disparate cultural and religious elements of the court into a united whole, and temporarily introduced a new syncretic religion, of which he was the living god. In this way the emperor hoped to overcome religious schisms within the Muslim

Jahangir with a portrait of his father, Akbar, Hashim and Abu l-Hasan, Mughal style, c. 1615, Paris, Musée Guimet
The image of father and son together was intended as a statement of the legitimacy of Jahangir's succession, particularly relevant in view of his rebellion and establishment of an alternative court at Allahabad when crown prince. Akbar, on his deathbed, forgave him and recognized him as rightful heir. The Mughals consciously developed such imperial imagery and iconography.

Shah Jahan on the Peacock Throne
Govardhan, Mughal style, c. 1635. Cambridge, Massachusetts, Harvard University Arts Museum
The stylized, almost abstract portrait shows Shah Jahan on the Peacock Throne, first used for the New Year celebrations at the Agra Fort in 1635, was transferred to the new capital Shahjahanabad in 1648, and carried off to Persia by Nadir Shah in 1739. Shah Jahan greatly valued ceremonial and the symbolic significance of art.

nobility and divisions between Muslims and non-Muslims, and above all to destroy the power base of the religious elite.

Under Akbar's successors, Jahangir and Shah Jahan, the empire reached the apogee of its power and splendor. Jahangir (1605–1627) encouraged the construction of gardens, and developed garden suburbs in Agra and in Kashmir, which was the court's summer residence. As Jahangir's addiction to opium increased, his wife Nur Jahan assumed responsibilities of government. Her father, Itimad al-Daula and her brother, Asaf Khan, held the highest positions in the empire, and her niece Mumtaz Mahal ("Chosen One of the Palace"), for whom the Taj Mahal was built, was married to the heir apparent, later Shah Jahan (1628–1658). The aesthetic sensibilities of these Persian nobility from Khurasan was a major contribution to the emeregnet court style as well as a vital political support for the dynasty.

Asaf Khan's intervention in the dynastic struggle ensured Shah Jahan's succession to the throne in 1628, several months after his father's death.

Almost immediately he began major building projects which were to become the hallmark of his reign. In the palaces at Lahore and Agra public areas and private apartments were rebuilt, and the cities embellished with gardens. After the premature death of his beloved wife Mumtaz Mahal in 1631 he constructed her monumental tomb, the Taj Mahal, at Agra. In 1646 he began the fortified palace in the new capital at Delhi called Shahjahanabad, and encouraged extensive urban development by the nobility and by his daughter Jahanara ("World Adornment") who had filled her mother's position as first lady of the realm. At the same time Shah Jahan' armies campaigned beyond the northwest frontier of Kabul to regain the lands in Balkh and Badakhshan claimed as part of the Mughal dynastic inheritance.

Aurangzeb (1658–1707), his son and successor, who seized the throne in the year 1658, keeping his father imprisoned in the Agra Fort until his death, finally abandoned these ambitions. He reorientated the dynastic focus to the subcontinent, campaigning in the Deccan until he finally subdued Bijapur and

Goldconda in 1686–1687. Austere in temperament and religious practice, he was less interested in the arts and connoisseurship than his predecessors and tended to ignore the link between art and power.

The flowering of Mughal culture from the mid-16th to the mid-17th century is among the greatest manifestations of Islamic art and architecture. In an age when art and power were intertwined, it was self-consciously imperial, and aesthetics was made an aspect of sovereignty.

Acknowledging their debt to the heritage of Transoxiana and Khorasan in the sphere of architecture bequeathed by the first two dynasts, Timurid principles were applied to new forms, executed in indigenous materials to create a unique expression. In the arts, the royal workshops provided the catalyst for a fusion of indigenous and new techniques, responding to the demands of court patronage. The independent sultanates of the Deccan fostered artistic traditions distinct from the Mughals in orientation and aesthetics. Architecture was influenced initially by Turko-Iranian forms, but by the 17th century was more deeply rooted in indigenous traditions molded by contact through the sea routes with the Middle East. Similarly, the arts in general had achieved a unique identity remarkable in both refinement and execution, a synthesis of the indigenous with the traditions of Isfahan and Tabriz. The Mughal conquest of the Deccan was a devastating but brief interlude as the Asaf Shahs of Hyderabad were effectively autonomous and fostered the distinct styles of the region.

The succession of weak Mughal rulers in Delhi in the 18th century resulted in a dramatic contraction of the empire under pressure from various invaders. Independent states emerged, which evolved new styles. At Lucknow, capital of the province of Oudh, the king welcomed artists from the Mughal court and offered patronage to Europeans. Agra and Lahore fell to non-Muslim rulers, whose courts absorbed many features of Mughal artistic expression. In 1803 the British East India Company took control of Delhi from the Marathas and ruled through the Mughal emperors until 1858, when Bahadur Shah II was imprisoned in Rangoon and the East India Company was dissolved. Thereafter the subcontinent was ruled as a British Viceroyalty until 1877, when Queen Victoria was declared Empress.

Babur's victory at the Battle of Panipat in 1526, miniature from the *Baburname*, Lahore, 1597/98. New Delhi, National Museum
Babur kept a diary written in Chaghatai Turkish, the mother tongue of the Mughuls, in which he described the flora, fauna, and customs of the lands through which he campaigned, as well as political events and personal anecdotes. In 1589 the Khan-i Khanan, one of the highest imperial officials and a renowned arts patron, presented a Persian translation of the text to Akbar. At least four illustrated versions were prepared in Akbar's painting studios.

Architecture
Philippa Vaughan

Architecture of the Great Mughals

The Mughal emperors accorded great importance to architecture as a symbol of kingship. "A good name for kings is achieved through lofty buildings … that is to say, the standard of the measure of men is assessed by the worth of their building and from their high-mindedness is estimated the state of their house," wrote Akbar's historian Qandahari at the end of the 16th century. Form and style were perceived as a reflection of dynastic identity. Moreover, style was linked to notions of legitimacy, for a claimant to the throne could not rely upon force alone to achieve lasting loyalty from his subjects, particularly when the ruling group was such a small minority among the Muslim population, quite apart from the many millions of non-Muslims in the realm.

Such ideas were current in the sultanate courts and the architectural vocabulary of the Mughals would have been understood for the symbolism it was intended to establish. Mughal theories of kingship further developed the link between legitimacy and architectural style by emphasizing not only the Timurid and Genghisid heritage on which they based their claims to India (Babur was related to Timur on his mother's side and to Genghis Khan through his father), but also ideas of semidivine origin. The ruler as God's vicegerent on earth was percieved as a manifestation of the perfect man reflecting the divine quality of cosmic architect.

Architecture under the first Mughal emperors, Babur (1526–1530) and Humayun (1530–1543 and 1555–1556)

Babur won the sultanate of Delhi in 1526 when his army of 12,000 defeated the 100,000 troops fielded by Ibrahim Lodi at Panipat. His first act on entering Delhi was to circumambulate the tombs of the Chishti Sufi saints Nizam al-Din Auliya (d. 1324) and Khoja Qutb al-Din Bakhtyar Kaki (d. 1236), acknowledging their spiritual status through this ritual and receiving by association a form of religious sanction for his authority. He then visited the tombs of the Sultans Ghiyath al-Din Balban and Ala al-Din Khalji, and the Qutb Minar, symbolically establishing his line as successor to the great Muslim dynasties of Delhi. The route, adapted to include Humayun's tomb, was incorporated into Mughal processional ritual.

Baburs described his architectural ambitions, but little remains beyond a few wells, garden pools, and three mosques including one at Panipat. In his memoirs, Babur wrote that the qualities he sought in architecture were harmony and symmetry – the most important aspects of the Timurid aesthetic – and recorded his yearning for flowing water. Gardens were his great interest, both as a source of pleasure and for ceremonial where public audiences, distribution of honours to the nobility, celebrations and feasting took place. Thethrone was placed in the open air on magnificent carpets beneath richly ornamented canopies.

The Mughal hold on Hindustan was still tenuous when Babur died in 1530. The problem for Humayun, Babur's eldest son and successor, was to weld the diverse groups among the nobility and fief holders into a cohesive court owing unquestioned allegiance to the Mughal sovereign. Despite continuous efforts he was unable to retain their loyalty after his final defeat by

Musamman Burj in the Agra Fort, 1637
The Agra Fort was constructed for Akbar by Qasim Khan in 1565–1573. The red sandstone structure replaced the brick fortress built by the Lodis. This view from the east beyond the moat shows the Musamman Burj apartments built by Shah Jahan and completed in 1637. Here he spent his final years under house arrest gazing at the Taj Mahal, the tomb of his favorite wife.

Veranda of the Musamman Burj in the Agra Fort, 1637

Shah Jahan destroyed many structures erected by his father Jahangir and rebuilt them in white marble. The Musamman Burj is among the most magnificent: its dadoes are exquisitely carved with floral motifs also found in miniature painting, and the border designs, similar to the Taj Mahal, are inlaid with semiprecious stones.

Sher Shah Suri of Bihar in 1543, and an entourage of 30 persons followed him to self-imposed exile in Persia. During this time he spent many months in Herat admiring his Timurid heritage and made a "grand tour" of the shrines and monuments of Persia. These were formative years, when Humayun, who was renowned for his learning, had the opportunity to appreciate Ilkhanid, Timurid, and early Safavid architecture.

There is little surviving of Humayun's buildings. His first architectural symbol was a mosque whose tall portal (*pishtaq*) and high, domed prayer hall declared their Timurid origins. The Kachpura Mosque at Agra, now ruined, was built near Babur's garden, demonstrating the importance of the garden as a center of court life. In 1533 he began construction of the palace citadel Purana Qila in Delhi, called Dinpanah ("Asylum of the Faith"), built in the red sandstone which became associated with imperial Mughal architecture.

The architecture of Akbar (1556–1605)

When Akbar succeeded to the throne in 1556 the Mughal Empire was still in the making. The context of the artistic developments of the following 50 years was the conquest and control of territory from Kabul, Kashmir, and Bengal to Gujarat, Sind, and Malwa; and the need to establish a unified fiscal, military, and administrative structure. The creation of a cohesive court focused on the emperor was an imperative underlying Akbar's cultural policy and its artistic and architectural expression.

The first major project of the reign was the construction, not of a mosque, but of his father's tomb in Delhi (1562–1571) designed following Timurid concepts. Akbar also built the great palace citadel at his capital of Agra, begun in 1565 and completed in 1573 under the supervision of Qasim Khan, Amir al-Bahr ("Commander of the Seas"). The contemporary chronicler Abu l Fazl recorded that it contained more than 500 stone buildings. Few structures from

Akbar's time remain, however, either at Agra or in the other forts he built – at Ajmer, gateway to Rajasthan (1570), Lahore, guarding the northwest frontier (1575), and Allahabad (1583), one of the most sacred non-Muslim sites in India.

Of particular interest, therefore, is the Jahangiri Mahal, a residential palace for ladies of the royal household, situated within the Agra Fort. The Timurid principles of symmetry were observed for both the facade and the interior courtyards, which were built in red sandstone. The inner courtyard was characteristic of the Subcontinent, with low-eaved pillared halls to the north and south with walls and brackets adorned with ornate relief carving. The courtyard overlooking the river echoed the palace architecture of Transoxiana, with an *iwan* (an open vaulted hall) on the east side, a veranda with tall slender, richly faceted columns, and a cusped pool in the center fed by a single channel, as in Timurid courtyards and gardens. The different styles reflected the variety of cultural traditions within the royal household, for Akbar's marriage alliances included the hindu Rajput nobility as well as Muslim aristocracy from the subcontinent, Persia, and Central Asia.

The architecture of Fatehpur Sikri, the city constructed on the rocky ridge south of Agra, manifested Akbar's syncretic ambitions. Concerned at the lack of an heir, Akbar had sought the intervention of a Sufi saint, Sheikh Salim Chishti, at Sikri, where, in 1569, his son the future Emperor Jahangir, was born to one of his Rajput wives. In thanksgiving, Akbar called his son Salim and established a walled city and imperial palace, of which the focus was the the shrine of Sheikh Salim (d. 1572), located in the courtyard of the Friday (congregational) mosque. Just as Humayun's tomb in Delhi was associated with the Chishti shrine of Nizam al-Din Auliya, Akbar associated his new city with the area's Chishti shrine. In this way, he aimed to popularize his rule at a time when, following the conquest of Gujarat, Mandu, and Khandesh, the Mughal domains were growing into an empire.

The Jahangiri Mahal was constructed by Akbar as a residential palace for ladies of the royal household. The co-existence of different styles reflected the cultural diversity of the early Mughal court. The courtyard's pillared halls correspond to Indian models built from wood, while the *iwan* designs are taken from Transoxianan architecture.

The Pearl Mosque was constructed by Shah Jahan after the capital had been moved to the new city of Shahjahanabad, at Delhi. The facade of the prayer hall, which is not articulated by a central *pishtaq*, is similar to the mosque Shah Jahan constructed at the Chishti shrine in Ajmer.

The dynastic architecture of Fatehpur Sikri was modeled on Timurid forms and styles. Pre-eminent were the mosque, constructed 1571–1574, and the triumphal gateway called the Buland Darwaza ("Lofty Gate"), built 1568–1578, whose height (180 feet, 54 meters) and span surpassed Timur's great *iwan* at Shahr-i Sabz.

The mosque, the largest in the empire, whose inscription states that it was built by Sheikh Salim, was distinguished by the high central *pishtaq*, the Mughal interpretation of a classic Timurid feature which acts as the dominant stylistic reference in a facade owing much to the pre-Mughal traditions of Mandu. The interior of the prayer hall is richly embellished with geometric patterns in white marble inlaid in the red sandstone, with arabesques and floral motifs based on Timurid prototypes painted in polychrome and gilt. The shrine of Sheikh Salim was established as another focal point in the courtyard through the use of white marble. The square domed chamber with elaborate porch was modeled on the tomb at Sarkhej, Gujarat, conquered in 1572.

The architectural styles of the sultanate of Gujarat, a synthesis of the pre-Islamic Jain and Hindu traditions, were the dominant influence in the imperial palaces. The general layout and the variety of building types and decoration reflect Akbar's experiments in architectural forms and court ceremony. Centers of artistic production for the court were developed: illustrated manuscript studios, a translation academy, and workshops for textiles, carpets, jewelry, and metalwork, which were essential accoutrements of sovereignty.

In the year 1584 Akbar moved the capital to Lahore as a more suitable base from which to defend the northwest frontier against attacks from Persia, but members of the court, including Akbar's mother, Maryam Makani, continued to use Fatehpur Sikri as a major residence. Jahangir stayed several months in 1619.

An architectural style associated with imperial authority had been established by 1584. Governors of the provinces were encouraged, indeed commanded, to construct their major administrative centers to reflect the imperial Mughal style. The Rajput raja Man Singh of Amber, Akbar's brother-in-law and principal emir of the realm, constructed the palaces and administrative centers of Bihar and Bengal, which both reflected the general plan and style of the capital city of Fatehpur Sikri. At Jaunpur a magnificent bridge was constructed by the governor.

During the last years of his reign, Akbar was preoccupied with the revolt of his son, Prince Salim, who established his own independent court at Allahabad, but on his deathbed in 1605 he recognized him as his rightful heir.

Architecture under Jahangir (1605–1627)

Salim took the titles Jahangir ("World Seizer") and Nur-al Din ("Light of the Faith"), continuing the light imagery used so frequently in Akbar's metaphors of sovereignty. He also followed the tradition of linking Mughal rule to roots in both Timurid ancestry and ancient dynasties on the subcontinent. He thus ordered a Mauryan monolithic pillar bearing the edicts of the renowned emperor Ashoka (d. 231), which had fallen to the ground, to be inscribed with his own lineage interspersed with invocations to God and re-erected in his fort at Allahabad.

Jahangir's most significant architectural project was his father's tomb at Sikandra whose Timurid-style gateway, completed in 1612–1614, reconfirmed the artistic and political orientation of the dynasty. This magnificent monument revealed Jahangir's abilities as a patron of architecture; so too did his gardens, at Agra and in the summer capital of Kashmir. In his memoirs (*Tuzuk-i Jahangiri*) he expressed great interest in architecture, and with pride showed his son, the future Shah Jahan, around Akbar's palace at Fatehpur Sikri while staying there to avoid the plague in Agra. Yet there is little left of the edifices built for him by Khwaja Jahan Muhammad Dust in the palace citadels of Agra and Lahore as they were largely replaced by Shah Jahan.

Contemporary accounts of Jahangir's palaces convey their magnificence and his concern with imperial symbols. At Agra he constructed a turret overlooking the Jumna known as the Shah Burj ("King's Tower"). Palaces at

Fort and palace areas of Fatehpur Sikri,
1569–1571
Situated 38 km west of Agra, Fatehpur Sikri served as capital, together with Agra, until the court moved to Lahore in 1584. Akbar chose this location out of gratitude to a Sufi sheikh who had predicted the birth of an heir to the throne and who was buried here. In the foreground is the caravanserai, where the Jesuit Fathers, who stayed at the Mughal court, lodged. In the background are the Friday mosque and the Buland Darwaza gateway. The chronicler Qandahari described Fatehpur Sikri as "Paradise on the brink of a precipice."

Below: **Shrine of Sheikh Salim Chishti**,
Fatehpur Sikri, 1580/81
Situated in the courtyard of the Friday Mosque, the shrine is similar to earlier tombs in Gujarat an Mandu, a single-story square chamber surrounded by an enclosed corridor for circumambulation.

Below: **Buland Darwaza, Fatehpur Sikri**,
1568–1578
The monumental gateway leading into the courtyard of the Friday mosque, was constructed subsequent to the other buildings of the mosque. The height and span of the arch were greater than those of Timur's entrance *iwan* at his palace in Shahr-i Sabz, a reference to the Mughal's dynastic heritage inscriptions commemorate Akbar's conquest of Gujarat in the year 1572.

Agra and Lahore were decorated with wall paintings based on Islamic and Christian sources. The Jesuits, who attended the Mughal court and participated in religious discussions, presented Christian images to the emperors, and Mughal versions were prepared for albums. At Lahore, Jahangir embellished his most important additions to the fort with images associated with King Solomon, presented in the Koran as the ideal ruler. Indeed the sole inscription on the fort described Jahangir as "a Solomon in dignity." The outer walls, constructed in brick, were faced with polychrome tile mosaic panels depicting aspects of the legend of Solomon: angels leading jinns by a chain, alluding to Solomon's wisdom and ability to control the invisible world as well as the visible. The theme was continued in the Kala Burj, a tower serving as an informal audience chamber. The use of a domed ceiling, redolent with metaphors of the dome of heaven, was itself unique in Mughal residential architecture and the message was reinforced in the vaulting by Solomonic imagery of angels and phoenix.

Despite his connoisseurship of mosque architecture – well attested in his memoirs – Jahangir did not build any mosques. He granted this privilege to his Hindu Rajput mother, called Maryam al-Zamani ("Mary of the Age"), who constructed the Begam Shahi Mosque in Lahore in 1611/12. Situated just beyond the Masti gate of the fort through which the public audience hall was reached, the three entrances to the walled courtyard each bore an inscription identifying her as the patron. The prayer hall had a tall *pishtaq* flanked on each side by two smaller arches, and was exquisitely embellished with polychrome floral and geometric motifs. Innovative features which were to become part of the Mughal repertoire included the intricate squinch netting of the dome (as in Kala Burj), whose radiating stellate forms each bore a name of God; and the depiction of the cypress tree and wine vessels, visual allusions to the divine, which appeared in the tombs of Prince Khusrau and Sultan Nisar Begam in Allahabad (1624/25) and the tomb of Itimad al-Daula at Agra completed in 1627/28.

Like Maryam al-Zamani, Nur Jahan, who married Jahangir in 1611, had extensive financial resources based on trading activities. With other great notables, she responded to Jahangir's call for caravanserais on the great trade routes from Bengal to the Punjab, along which he had established public wells and towers (*kos minars*) to mark distances. Nur Jahan's caravanserai outside Agra, which reputedly could house 2,000–3,000 people and 500 horses, was at the end of the lucrative trade route with Patna on which she controlled the tariffs. She shared Jahangir's interests in architecture, gardens, and the arts, and participated wholeheartedly in his patronage.

As Jahangir's addiction to opium increased so did her power, which by the early 1620s extended even to minting coinage in her name. Nur Jahan bore Jahangir no children, and during the succession crisis following Jahangir's death in 1627, she backed Shahriyar, her own leprosy-smitten son by her first husband. It was her own brother, Asaf Khan, who intervened to establish Shah Jahan as the rightful heir. Nur Jahan retired to her garden properties at

View from the Panch Mahal into the inner palace area of Fatehpur Sikri, to 1574

The palace city, an area of numerous courtyards and gardens, had three main functional areas. Here a residential pavilion in the foreground formed part of the *zanana* and beyond is the building traditionally known as "Jodh Bai's Palace." It has a symmetrical courtyard, four-*iwan* plan in which a temple was included, probably for Akbar's Rajput wives.

Shahdara in Lahore where she constructed her own tomb and died in the year 1645.

The buildings of Shah Jahan (1628–1658)

The coronation of Shah Jahan took place at Agra on February 14, 1628. The coinage of the realm, imperial edicts, and sermons thereafter incorporated his titles, Sahib-i-Qiran-i-Sani ("Lord of the Fortunate Conjunction"), in which he followed Timur, and Shah Jahan Padishah Gazi.

Shah Jahan's appreciation of the symbolic importance of architecture and the role of ceremonial in statecraft was expressed by the court historian Salih Kambo: "It is evident that an increase in such things (buildings and ceremonial) creates esteem for the rulers in the eyes of the people and increases respect for the dignity of rulers in the people's hearts." Shah Jahan, like his predecessors, was a munificent patron of architecture, and pursued his interests with even greater vigour as emperor, having already shown his abilities as a prince in additions to the Kabul Fort, the Shalimar Park in Srinagar, Kashmir, the Shahi Bagh in Ahmadabad, and palaces and gardens in Burhanpur.

His first act of patronage as emperor, in January 1628, a month before the coronation, was the construction of a mosque at the shrine of the saint Mu'in al-Din Chishti in Ajmer. He thereby followed the earlier Timurid tradition, rather than that of his two immediate predecessors, whose first monuments after accession were dynastic tombs. The inscription along the facade compares the shrine to the Kaaba in Mecca and explains that it was constructed without a dome to ensure that the saint's tomb remained pre-eminent. The unusal length of the inscription, in Persian rather than Arabic, presaged similar epigraphs on mosques built later in the reign.

Shah Jahan's attention to ceremonial was evident in his orders, issued immediately after the coronation, for renovating the Halls of Public Audience (*diwan-i amm*) in the forts of Agra and Lahore. Forty-pillared halls were built, called "Chihil Sutun" by chroniclers, intentionally alluded to Sassanian models. They were similar in shape to the prayer halls of Mughal mosques, but with the focal point of the *mihrab* replaced by the place where the emperor appeared in public (known by the Sanskrit word *jharoka*). The parallel imagery was deliberate, for Shah Jahan maintained the Mughal aspirations to unite spiritual and temporal authority on earth, his eulogists describing him as the *qibla* (direction of prayer) of his subjects. The metaphor was reinforced by the inclusion of a mosque on the western side of the courtyard directly opposite the *jharoka*.

In Lahore, the imperial apartments reserved for the emperor and the imperial family were rebuilt in white marble, Shah Jahan's preferred material, with coffered ceilings richly gilded and studded with Aleppo glass. Lahore, already renowned as a garden city, was further embellished by the magnificent imperial park which came to be known as the Shalimar Bagh.

At Agra the ceremonial of the Hall of Public Audience was formalized and enriched by the installation of silver balustrades within the hall to distinguish the upper hierarchy of nobility. Those of lower rank stood in the galleries around the perimeter of the huge quadrangle, which they were ordered to embellish at their own expense with fine brocades and carpets. The Hall of Private Audience (*diwan-i khass*), overlooking the river, was constructed in white marble exquisitely decorated with floral motifs inlaid in semiprecious stones. The ceiling within was covered with gold and silver, and a long Persian inscription dated 1637 compared the room to the highest heavens and likened the emperor to the sun. Opposite was the imperial *hammam* (bath), where private audiences were also held. The emperor's private residential quarters were in another quadrangle, overlooking the river.

Agra had become a sizable city beyond the palace fortresses, and Shah Jahan, together with his eldest daughter Princess Jahanara, initiated its embellishment as an imperial capital. In front of the fort, a large public area was built in the shape of an irregular octagon, with pillared arcades, and space for merchants.

Jahanara requested the privilege of providing the city with a Friday mosque. This was a notable development in Mughal civic architecture, for it was the first imperial Friday mosque constructed outside the palace citadel (except for Fatehpur Sikri, a special situation). The inscription on the facade

states that the mosque was begun in 1643 and completed in 1648. The mosque was part of a large complex, the courtyard having chambers for a *madrasa* (still used today), while outside there were a bazaar, a caravanserai, an inn for travelers, a communal kitchen for the poor, a well, and a *hammam*.

The imposing mosque was raised on a high platform and the three bulbous domes, decorated in an unusual chevron pattern of red sandstone and white marble, were a landmark throughout the city. The high *pishtaq* in the center of the facade was framed by a wide band of black calligraphy inlaid in white marble, proclaiming the Persian titles of the benefactress: "Protector of the World, Princess of the Women of the Age, Queen of the World, Mistress of the Universe," together with praises for the emperor and the building's cost, 500,000 rupees. In view of this, it is curious that Shah Jahan later constructed the large Pearl Mosque within the Agra Fort completed in 1653, five years after the court had moved to the new capital, at Delhi.

At Agra and Lahore public space was too limited for the proper observance of new ceremonial. Designing the new capital named Shahjahanabad thus involved extensive urban planning and the layout of processional routes, as well as the construction of a palace citadel. At an astrologically auspicious time in 1639 the foundations of the the Red Fort were laid, designed by the architects Ustad Hamid and Ustad Ahmad, who had worked on the Taj Mahal. Shah Jahan himself played an active part, checking and adapting the plans, and making periodic visits to the building site.

The essential features of the forts at Agra and Lahore were repeated at Shahjahanabad. The Hall of Public Audience was similarly laid out, the magnificent marble throne decorated with symbols of kingship. The scenes of Orpheus playing the lute to the animals, inlaid in the marble placed directly over the emperor's head, clearly established the analogy with Solomon, the ideal ruler. In the Hall of Private Audience was the renowned, gem-encrusted

Above: Gateway to the Red Fort of Shahjahanabad, Delhi, 1639–1648
Between 1639 and 1648 Shah Jahan constructed Shahjahanabad as his new seat of government in Delhi. The majestic impact of the two principal gateways was diminished by emperor Aurangzeb's later addition to each of an outer barbican. Both the Akbarabadi Darwaza (today the Delhi Darwaza) and the Lahori Darwaza formed part of the processional routes used in the splendid court ceremonies.

Below: Sawan Pavilion in the Red Fort, completed in 1648
The fort developed into a city within a city, with a large bazaar and workshops, to satisfy the requirements of the court. The private areas of the royal family's palace apartments included gardens with pavilions cooled by flowing water and cascades.

Stone elephants, Delhi Darwaza
The Indian war elephants were awesome for Alexander the Great, who invaded Punjab in 326 B.C., as they were for Babur. Here they stand in stone – quite peacefully – between the inner and outer gates of the fort of Shahjahanabad, demonstrating the size and strength of the Mughal Empire. These were reinstated by Lord Curzon, viceroy 1899–1905.

Peacock Throne (Takht-i Shahi), seized by Nadir Shah in 1739 and taken to Persia. The white marble hall was richly embellished on the interior with floral sprays inlaid in semiprecious stones and gilt, and on the walls of the central chamber was inscribed the oft-quoted Persian verse: "If there be a paradise on earth, it is here, it is here, it is here."

The fort was a city within a city, housing over 50,000 persons and with a huge covered bazaar and workshops supplying the needs of the court, from textiles and swords to paintings and perfume. Its massive walls dominated the city of Shahjahanabad, which was laid out in carefully planned sectors where members of the court constructed mosques, bazaars, and gardens. Dara Shukoh, the heir apparent, and many great nobles built their residences along the riverbank.

Ladies of the imperial household played a significant role in developing the city, constructing mosques, markets and caravanserais in the imperial red sandstone. Princess Jahanara built the great arcaded bazaar known as Chandni Chauk stretching west from the Lahore Gate on each side of the canal. In the center, halfway along, was a huge octagonal caravanserai, and parallel, but behind the avenue, she laid out the extensive Sahibabad Gardens. The focal point at the end of the avenue was the red sandstone mosque built by Fatehpuri Begam, the third wife of Shah Jahan. To the south of the Akbarabad (Agra) Gateway, the second entrance to the fort, Shah Jahan's first wife, known as Akbarabadi Begam, built a mosque and caravanserai. There Shah Jahan attended the Friday prayers, processing with the court in full splendor until his own Friday mosque was ready in 1656. This, commissioned in 1650 and which he called the Masjid-i Jahannuma ("World Displaying Mosque"), was the most magnificent in terms of scale, design, and decoration.

In 1657, soon after it was completed, Shah Jahan developed a severe illness which appeared to presage his death and sparked a succession crisis. His third surviving son, Aurangzeb, emerged the victor, imprisoning his father in the Agra Fort until his death in 1666.

Detail of the Khass Mahal in the Red Fort, Shahjahanabad, Delhi, 1639–1648
The Khass Mahal served as the imperial private apartments. The River of Paradise flowed through the central chamber.

Ground plan of the Red Fort of Shahjahanabad, Delhi
The Red Fort was designed on a geometric grid. The central vertical axis aligned the gateway with the huge Hall of Public Audience (*Chihil Sutun*) and the imperial apartments.

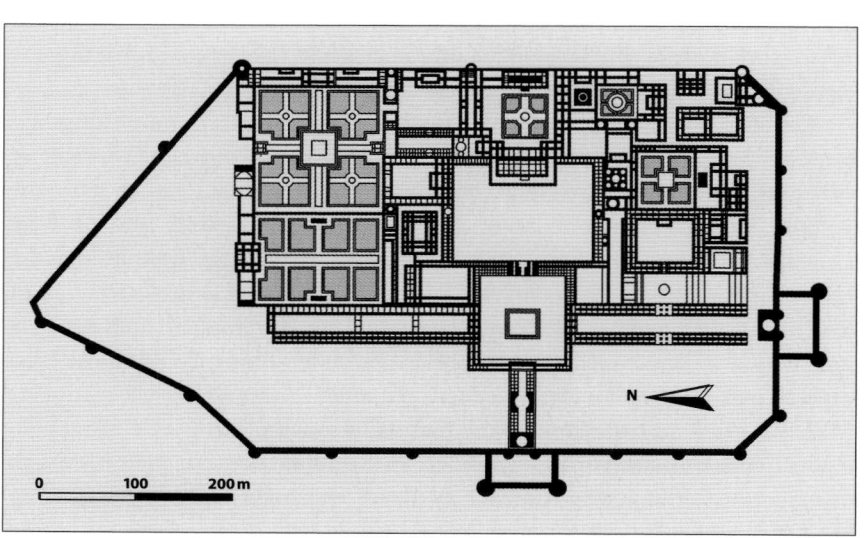

Architecture under Aurangzeb (1658–1707)

Following his two coronations in 1658, first in the Shalimar Bagh outside Delhi and later in the Red Fort, Aurangzeb's first act was the construction of the Pearl Mosque in the Shahjahanabad fort. Built entirely of white marble, it was near the private apartments, and was completed, after five years of building, in 1662/63. Decorative features, such as the elaborately carved marble of the courtyard and foliate arabesques reserved for palaces under Shah Jahan, were here used for religious architecture. They are also found in the great Badshahi Mosque in Lahore, the last expression in the grand tradition of imperial Mughal architecture. Mosques and gardens, the principal forms of architecture built by the imperial family during the final years of Aurangzeb's reign, were variations on the established theme.

Aurangzeb himself did not share his predecessors' perception of kingship, rejecting the semidivine element and the association of duties of sovereignty with patronage of the arts. He emphasised the functional rather than the symbolic aspects of architecture, believing that palaces and gardens were necessary for kings, the first for accommodating the huge retinue and the second for reviving energies depleted by administration. He declined a life of luxury, and dispensed with many aspects of royal ceremonial such as daily presentation of the emperor to the public and entertainment with musicians. Imperial patronage of the arts also decreased under Auranzeb.

As an excellent commander who had spent much of his life on campaign, he was impatient with what he considered self-indulgence. His piety also took on a rigorous form. It was consistent with his approach that equally as much emphasis should be placed upon conservation and maintenance of earlier

Badshahi Mosque, Lahore, 1673–1674
The Badshahi Mosque, constructed in the reign of Aurangzeb, is the largest Mughal mosque and the last great flowering of Mughal architecture. Lahore suffered many devastating invasions in the 18th century, finally becoming the capital of the Sikhs who adapted the Mughal style. In the foreground is the Hazuri Bagh Badari, the pavilion built in 1818 by Ranjit Singh, Sikh ruler of the Punjab. Beyond is the gateway to the mosque, approached by monumental steps similar to those at the Friday mosque at Shahjahanabad.

mosques as on the development of civic amenities such as wells and roads.

Moreover, financial resources had become over-extended by Shah Jahan's campaigns in the 1650s to regain the ancestral lands of Balkh, Badakhshan, and Samarqand. Aurangzeb's decision finally to abandon these ambitions thereafter defined the Mughals in the context of the subcontinent and, without the association with political legitimacy, the Timurid aesthetic ceased to dominate. In 1693 he moved the capital from Shahjahanabad to Aurangabad, following the conquest of the Deccan, and, although he ensured the maintenance of the Red Fort during his absence, the lack of an active patron led artists in the imperial workshops to seek patronage elsewhere.

After Aurangzeb's death in the year 1707, the Mughal Empire contracted continuously. The sack of Delhi in 1739 by Nadir Shah Afghan of Persia, followed by numerous further raids over the next half-century, left the city stripped of all portable valuables. Those who could sought refuge elsewhere. Provincial governors declared independence and established courts that extended patronage to former imperial artists.

In the province of Awadh the Mughal governors were effectively autonomous after 1754, and the evolution of architecture and the arts in the capitals of Lucknow and Faizabad show the transition from Mughal to regional forms. Moreover, during the late 18th century, the growth of British and French influence, particularly in northern and eastern India following the transformation of the East India Company into a British administrative agency with a governor-general, provided a new fund of images associating power with style. European elements, such as Palladian-style columns and Adam-style fanlights, were used in palatial architecture and interiors were often decorated with European-style furniture.

In the sphere of religious architecture Shia forms were emphasized, defining an identity distinct from the Sunni Mughals. An enormous hall (*imambara*) for the Shia celebrations of Muharram and for storing the standards (*alam*) and shrines (*taziya*) was constructed in 1784 by Nawab Asaf al-Daula, together with a mosque, a well, and an enormous gateway. Elements from the Deccan, where *imambaras* were built for the Shia dynasties, were evident, as they were in tombs such as that of his mother, Bahu Begam, completed at Faizabad around 1816. The extravagant hybrid style was quite different from the controlled exuberance and sheer beauty of Deccani architecture, which produced some of the finest expressions of Islamic art.

Ahmadnagar, Bijapur, Golconda, and Hyderabad in the Deccan

The sultanates of the Deccan emerged as states independent of the Delhi Sultanate in the course of the 14th and 15th centuries. Despite various realignments within the region, and numerous Mughal campaigns intended to exact tribute as much as to aquire direct control, they were not absorbed into the Mughal Empire until Aurangzeb's conquest of Bijapur and Golconda in 1686/87. However, central Mughal control was but a brief interlude for in 1724 the Mughal governor Nizam al-Mulk Asaf Jah with his capital at Hyderabad was effectively autonomous, and there was thus an essential continuity in the cultural and artistic evolution of the Deccan.

The long-established indigenous Muslims (Dakhnis) were linked through the network of trading relationships through the sea routes with the Arabian Peninsula, Africa, southern Iran, the Ottoman Empire and Europe. To these

Imambara, Lucknow, 1784
This *imambara*, a monumental hall for great festivals, was constructed for Nawab Asaf al-Daula. The rulers of Awadh, with their capital at Lucknow, were effectively autonomous after 1754 and emphasized their identity through Shia forms of religious architecture, often showing Deccani influence thus distinguishing themselves from the Sunni Mughals. In secular buildings, European elements provided images associating style with power, as well as new technology – bridges were actually imported and assembled in Lucknow. In this *imambara* they began the celebrations of Muharram, which commemorates the death of Husain, the third imam and son of Ali, who perished in the Battle of Kerbela in 680.

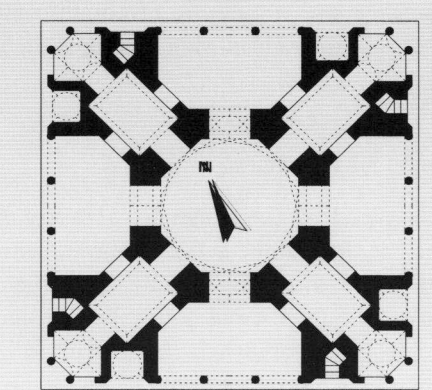

Ground plan of Farah Bagh,
Ahmadnagar, Deccan, 1576–1583
Built for Sultan Murtaza Nizam Shah I, this palace was constructed in the middle of a large tank. It is an irregular octagon on a *hasht bihisht* ("eight paradises") plan around a central domed chamber, similar to Humayun's tomb and the Taj Mahal showing how, in Indian architecture, secular and religious forms were interchangeable.

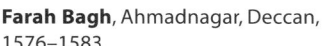

Farah Bagh, Ahmadnagar, Deccan, 1576–1583
The Deccan established its independence from the Delhi Sultanate in the 14th century, and during the 15th and 16th centuries it was subdivided into smaller states, where the architectural forms introduced by the Turko-Persian elites were modified by indigenous traditions. This monumental palace in the center of a large tank, built as an irregular octagon on the *hasht bihisht* plan, reflected Timurid prototypes in its scale and the deep ogee arches.

exotic sources of cultural influence on Deccani art were added the non-Islamic traditions of the Jains, Hindus, and the Lingayata sect, which flourished in the southern peninsula, transmitted through the close relationships between the communities and patronage of non-Muslim artists and craftsmen by Muslim rulers. Their artistic influence was manifested in decorative detail and in the volumetric approach to form so distinctive of Deccani art.

In the kingdom of Ahmadnagar, founded in 1496, the contrast between Persian models and indigenous forms was evident in architecture of the reign of Sultan Murtaza I (1565–1588), as in the Farah Bagh, completed in the year 1583, a monumental octagonal palace outside the city built in the center of a large tank.

The impact of Persian urban traditions can be seen in the axial alignments of audience halls with ceremonial portals, commercial streets, and defensive gateways at Golconda, where the Qutb Shahs first established their capital. However, indigenous traditions were established in their new capital of Hyderabad, built a few kilometers to the south in 1591.

A committee for urban planning was formed at court to include architects, builders, and surveyors from Persia and Iraq, as well as Brahmin specialists from south India. The design agreed upon followed the Brahmin principles of Vastu-shastras, and the shape of the city, for which there were several possible classical forms, was the swastika. The center, which in a Hindu city would be a temple, was marked by the monumental Char Minar. This ceremonial gateway had four entrances, each aligned to a cardinal point. Built in the Shia form of a *taziya*, a model for small-scale gateways in Bukhara and Isfahan, the faceted stucco was wrought in the Deccani style with arcades, pierced balconies, and lotus petal supports for each tier of the minarets and the domes. As a statement of cultural identity, it was a clear contrast to the great gateways of the Sunni Mughals, such as the Buland Darwaza at Fatehpur Sikri, and to the tradition of urban planning exemplified by Shahjahanabad built 50 years later.

The development of the city of Hyderabad in the 19th century by the Asaf Jahs was again characterized by an international search for sources of inspiration throughout the subcontinent, Japan, and Europe. In the context of Islamic architecture, an innovation of symbolic importance was the acceptance of the dome in secular buildings such as the Law Courts and the Osmania Hospital, where it was associated with the duties of kingship and worldly power but distanced from the traditional allusion to the vault of heaven.

Tombs and gardens as images of Paradise

Two of the greatest monuments constructed by the Mughals – Humayun's tomb and the Taj Mahal – were domed tomb chambers of such monumental magnificence that they came to symbolize the architectural achievements of the dynasty. The paradisal imagery of gardens and heavenly mansions developed in Mughal funerary architecture paralleled the metaphor of creating paradise on earth found in epigraphy on imperial palaces.

The High Court, Hyderabad, 19th century
Golconda fell to the Mughals in 1687, but from 1724 the local governor, Nizam al-Mulk Asaf Jah ruled in *de facto* independence. After 1858 Hyderabad was the most powerful state in the subcontinent. Although the artistic continuity was hardly disturbed, some elements of Mughal architecture, such as the monumental *pishtaq* associated with regal authority, were absorbed into Hyderabadi forms. The use of the dome in secular architecture reflected European models.

Char Minar, Hyderabad, 1591
This monumental ceremonial gateway with openings in the four cardinal directions was constructed for Sultan Muhammad Quli Qutb of Golconda and later marked the center of his new capital at Hyderabad. The city plan, drawn up by a committee assembled for the purpose, followed Brahmin principles as well as Persian influences.

The Tomb of Humayun

Akbar's first major architectural project was the construction of his father's tomb in Delhi, an innovative statement in form and execution, which established the cultural identity of the dynasty. A dynastic tomb was a break with custom, for Babur and Humayun built mosques at Panipat and Agra, respectively, as symbols of their authority. In this they followed the Timurid tradition of dynastic architecture in the forms of great mosques and *madrasas*. Indeed, Akbar perhaps consciously revived the Ghenghisid tradition of monumental tombs for the grandiose scale and octagonal form of Humayun's echoed the mausoleum at Sultaniya in Persia built by the Ilkhanid sultan Üljaitü. Sher Shah Suri's great tomb at Sassaram in Bihar, completed in 1545, was also a symbol to counteract, for it was the Suris who had challenged the dynasty by expelling Humayun for 12 years and whom it was necessary to show as vanquished.

The architects of Humayun's tomb, Mirak Sayid Ghiyath and his son Sayid Muhammad, were trained in the Timurid idiom. They had worked for Husain Baiqara at the former Timurid capital Herat and for the Uzbek ruler of Bukhara laying out gardens in the Timurid style. Begun in 1562, the work on the tomb was supervised by Akbar's mother from 1565 when the capital

was moved to Agra, and completed in 1571. The administration of the complex, which included 300 Koran reciters (*hafiz*), a *madrasa* and a communal kitchen for distributing food to the poor (*langar*), was entrusted to Akbar's favorite stepmother until her death in 1582.

The mausoleum, set on a high platform analogous to a throne (*takht*) was a vast irregular octagon (called *muthamman baghdadi* by the Mughals) with a tall drum and slightly bulbous dome. The radial ground plan forming eight rooms around the central domed chamber was known as the *hasht bihisht* ("eight paradises"), an allusion to the eight gates of Paradise in the Koran.

The symmetry of the plan, which was reflected in elevation, was indebted to Timurid concepts, but the construction methods were indigenous. The brick core was clad in finely dressed red sandstone, the stone courses alternately broad and narrow. Key elements were articulated in white marble, with which

View and ground plan of the Tomb of Humayun, Delhi, Mirak Sayid Ghiyath and Sayid Muhammad, 1562–1571
The tomb of the second Mughal ruler, Humayun, was the first of the great Mughal mausoleums. The scale and principles of design show Timurid influence, and reflect the dynastic origins and aspirations of the Mughals. Humayun appreciated the Timurid architecture of Herat which he visited in exile. The architects – father and son

– had worked in the former Timurid capital at Herat and later for the Uzbek ruler of Bukhara. At the tomb of Humayun Timurid architectural concepts were expressed through the craftsmanship of the subcontinent.

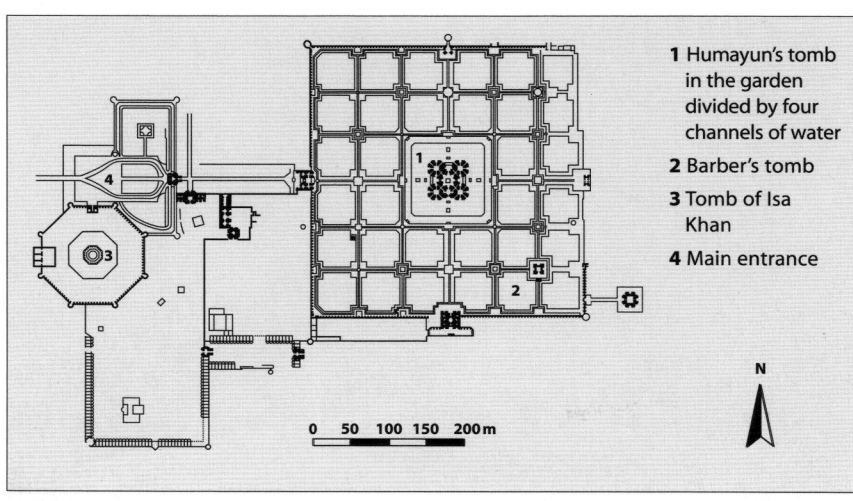

1 Humayun's tomb in the garden divided by four channels of water

2 Barber's tomb

3 Tomb of Isa Khan

4 Main entrance

0   50 100 150 200m

N

View from the Tomb of Humayun into the park, Delhi, 1564
The Tomb of Humayun is situated in the middle of an extensive garden. Gardens recalled the Koranic images of Paradise whose shade, fountains, flowing rivers and heavenly mansions offered a blissful life in the next world. The idea of the gatekeepers of Paradise implied an enclosure. Mughal dynastic tombs embodied these metaphors.

Below: **Tomb of Humayun**, Delhi, 1562–1571
The cenotaph lies in the center of the octagonal domed chamber, marking the position of the sarcophagus in the crypt below.

the dome was entirely faced. The only decoration was the six-pointed star prominently placed in the spandrels, an auspicious symbol in Islamic astrology and alchemy of the union of opposing elements. It alludes to Humayun's interests in these areas, for his biographer recorded that he wore different-colored robes for each day of the week according to that day's planet.

Situating the mausoleum in the center of a large garden was a remarkable innovation in the design of both tombs and gardens which was adopted for subsequent Mughal tombs. Babur was buried in a garden, yet he did not have a tomb, only a headstone; and while the Timurids were renowned for their love of gardens, they did not associate them with their tombs. The garden was designed on a grid, being divided by broad walkways to form a *chahar bagh* ("Fourfold Garden"). The channels recalled the rivers of Paradise – water, milk, honey, and wine – which fed pools where believers quenched their thirst, surrounding platforms ready for the carpets lined with rich brocade where the righteous could recline, plucking the readily accessible fruit, their hearts refreshed by the clear-flowing water.

The *chahar bagh* around the Tomb of Humayun and its further development in later dynastic tombs and pleasure gardens was unique to the Indian subcontinent. Its distinct form evolved in response to topography and owed more to indigenous concepts found in early medieval Islamic sites than to Persian models.

When the "heart-delighting, Paradise-like" tomb described by Akbar's historian Badaoni was completed, the emperor peformed the rite of circumambulation, also visiting the tomb of Nizam al-Din Auliya nearby. It was the first of five such formal visits associated with Akbar's search for spiritual enlightenment at this and other holy monuments of Delhi. He thereby instituted an imperial ritual, continued by Jahangir and Shah Jahan, in which dynastic sovereignty and legitimacy were associated with spiritual authority.

Opposite: **Tomb of Akbar**, Sikandra, completed in 1614
When Jahangir visited his father's tomb soon after his accession he was displeased and ordered parts of it to be rebuilt, suggesting that it was begun during his father's lifetime. It is situated in the center of a "four-fold" garden with water channels and pools set in the broad walkways. The vestibule behind the great *pishtaq* on the south side is richly decorated with floral arabesques in polychrome stucco and Koranic verses in gold on a blue ground, recalling Paradise.

INDIA: FROM SULTANATE TO MUGHAL EMPIRE

Gateway to the Tomb of Akbar, Sikandra, 1612–1614
The highly decorated surfaces were characteristic of Jahangiri architecture, and new vaulting systems were introduced based on Safavid and Timurid prototypes. The minarets, which fell during an earthquake, were reinstated by Lord Curzon, viceroy of India 1899–1905.

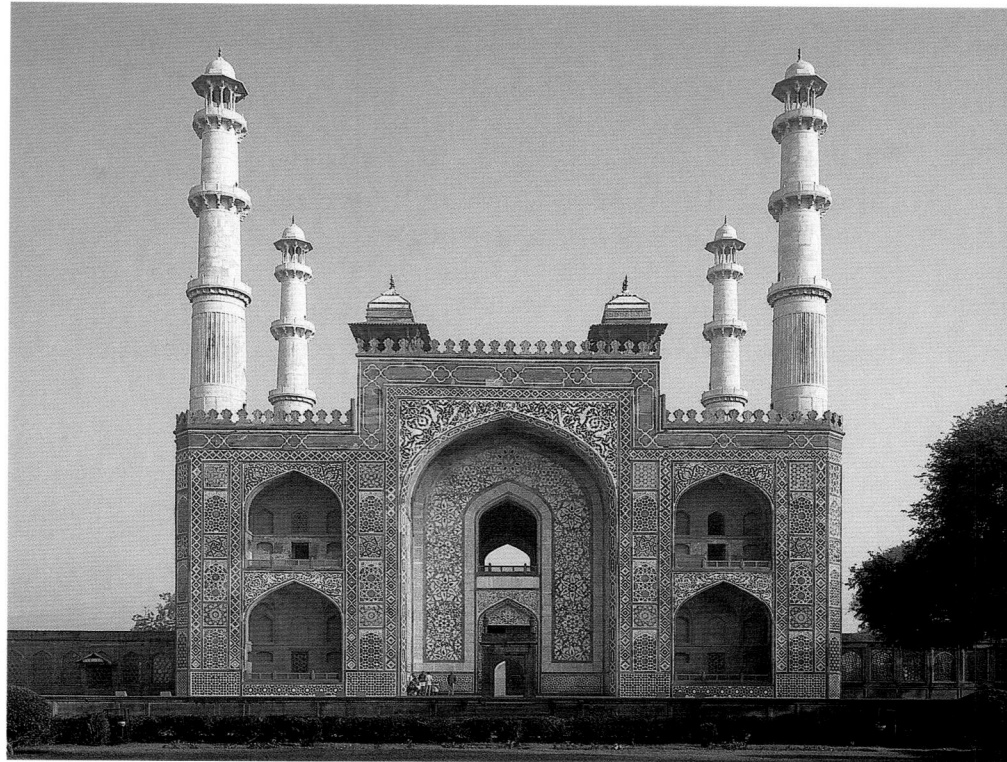

Tomb of Akbar

Akbar's mausoleum and garden at Bihishtabad ("Abode of Paradise") in Sikandra, near Agra, was the first major architectural project undertaken by Jahangir. The paradisal imagery was elaborated in different forms. While the garden setting was similar to Humayun's tomb – situated beside the river Jamuna in the center of a large walled garden – the structure was quite different. The five tiered stories were without a dome, the topmost having a courtyard where the Timurid-style cenotaph in white marble lay open to the sky according to Koranic precepts. In style it resembeld contemporary palace architecture, a grandiose version of the five-tiered Panch Mahal at Fatehpur Sikri. It recalled the Koranic vision of "beautiful mansions in the gardens of everlasting bliss" where "lofty mansions one above the other have been built" and beneath which flow "rivers of delight."

Persian poetic inscriptions dated 1612 and 1614 around the main gateway, an innovation in religious architecture, eulogized the deceased emperor and Jahangir as patron. The verses proclaimed the paradisal imagery of the visual metaphor: "Hail, blessed space happier than the garden of Paradise/Hail lofty buildings higher than the divine throne/A paradise, the garden of which has thousands of Rizwans as servants/A garden which has thousands of paradises for its land/The pen of the mason of the Divine Decree has written on its court/These are the gardens of Eden, enter them and live forever."

Other gardens of the Mughal emperors

The Mughal interest in garden design was not limited to funereal architecture. Babur, a great horticulturalist who described in his memoirs (the *Baburname*) the many gardens he had laid out, detested the heat and dust of the Indian climate and so included baths (*hammam*) in his garden design. At Agra he laid out the Hasht Bihisht ("Eight Paradises") garden, which served as a court and residence. The site, later developed by Nur Jahan as a pleasure garden known as as the Bagh-i Nur Afshan was one of 33 residential gardens along the riverfront, which were remodeled by members of the court at this time. Among these courtiers was Itimad al-Daula, Nur Jahan's father and vizier to Jahangir, who laid out a garden with a pavilion in the center. It was entered via an orchard, continuing a Timurid custom whereby the sale of the produce contributed to

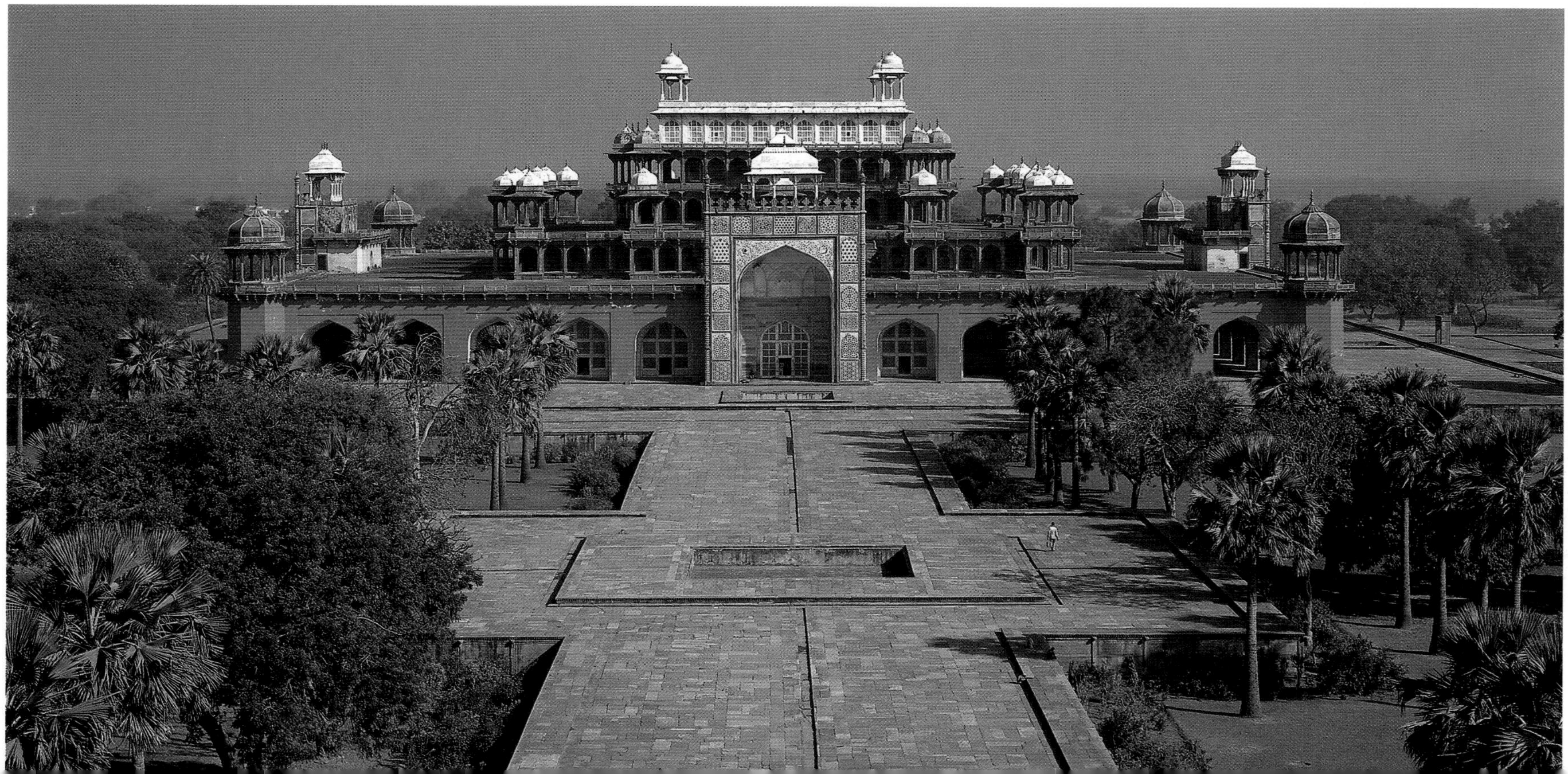

Imparting" garden (*Bagh-i Farah Bakhsh*) for imperial audiences; and an upper garden "Bestower of Plenty" (*Bagh-i Faiz Bakhsh*) for private use where the higher section was reserved for the ladies of the court and inner family circle. Nur Jahan herself, and also Shah Jahan's eldest daughter and first lady of the realm, Princess Jahanara, laid out several gardens.

Jahangir also developed gardens as resting places along the arduous route to Srinagar from Lahore. Their different purpose was reflected in their design. Hasan Abdal (near Islamabad), where the prolific springs could provide water for an army of 50,000, was the last *manzil*, (resting place), before Srinagar capable of quartering the entire court. The garden plan was curiously asymmetrical on account of the topography. Hydraulic engineering had so evolved at the court of Shah Jahan that the emperor could commission a garden at his capital of Lahore laid out on the Kashmiri linear model with terraces and cascades, despite the lack of gradient in the site and absence of fast-flowing water. This was achieved by the architect and engineer Ali Mardan Khan, who built a canal 100 miles,(160 km) in length fed by the river Ravi where it leaves the mountains. The hydraulics at first proved inadequate for the garden design and were perfected by Mullah Alam Alahi Tuni. When completed, water was supplied at uniform pressure to 410 fountains and five cascades, the level of the canals and pools being constantly regulated to remain full without

the upkeep of the garden. The Tomb of Itimad al-Daula, designed on a *hasht bihisht* plan was located in a classic Mughal form of *chahar bagh*.

It was probably first used as a pleasure garden since according to the Mughal fiscal system land reverted to the emperor on the death of the owner, an exception being the establishment of an endowment for religious purposes (*waqf*). Consequently it was a frequent practice among the nobility to develop gardens with pavilions which ultimately became family tombs.

The gardens of Kashmir, which Jahangir used as the summer residence of the court, most faithfully realized the poetic vision of Paradise. In the *Tuzuk-i Jahangiri* he gave a detailed account of Kashmir, that "garden of eternal spring… with enchanting cascades beyond all description," where even the roofs of houses and mosques were planted with tulips. Although the first garden in Kashmir, the Nasim Bagh, laid out by Akbar, was a plantation of trees in which the design element of water was absent, it was the channels, pools, and fountains which provided the main feature of parks laid out in the time of Jahangir. On the banks of Lake Dal at Srinagar the springs and rippling streams descending into the lake were harnessed to create a main channel (*nahr*) flowing through the center of the garden with occasional cross-axial canals (*jadwal*) in the Persian form of *chahar bagh*. A series of terraces (*martabas*) provided cascades between each level, often with a platform above; the main feature consisted of the large pools where fountains played around the central pavilion.

In the Shalimar ("Abode of Love") Park, begun in 1620, whose construction was initially undertaken by Prince Khurram and further extended by him in 1634 after his accession to the throne as Shah Jahan, there were three: a small fore-garden serving as an "antechamber" for the public; a lower "Joy

Taj Mahal, Agra, 1632–1643
This, the world's most famous tomb, was built by Shah Jahan for his beloved wife Arjum and Banu Begam, known as Mumtaz Mahal. The construction was supervised by Makramat Khan, who later supervised the building of the Red Fort at Shahjahanabad and Abd al-Karim, a master architect under Jahangir, and took altogether 11 years to complete. Shah Jahan claimed close involvement with the design, perhaps accounting for the ommission from the official chronicle of the actual architect's name, which is believed to be Ustad Ama.

overflowing. A similar canal was later built to supply Shahjahanabad and its gardens.

The park was known as the Bagh-i Faiz Bakhsh and the Bagh-i Farah Bakhsh, but from 1654 was referred to in contemporary accounts as the Shalimar Bagh. The lower terrace was for members of the court, and on the upper level were imperial residences and audience halls, and a *hammam* accessible to the women's apartments. The supervision of Khalil Allah Khan ensured that this enormous project, begun in 1641, was completed in one year, four months, and five days at a total cost of 600,000 rupees, a little more than the tomb Shah Jahan constructed for his father and completed a few years earlier.

Chroniclers hardly referred to the construction of Jahangir's tomb. He was buried in Nur Jahan's garden at Shahdara, Lahore, whose design followed the Mughal funerary *chahar bagh* plan. The mausoleum, situated in the center, was in the form of a throne (*takht*), with a minaret at each corner. There is no dome or upper story as on his deathbed Jahangir had expressed the wish that his tomb should be open to the air like Babur's. While the structure was relatively simple, the red sandstone articulated in white marble, similar to Nur Jahan's which she built for herself nearby, the cenotaph is of white marble exquisitely decorated with inlaid semiprecious stones in the manner of the Taj Mahal.

The Taj Mahal

The most perfect visual metaphor for the Paradise garden created by the Mughals is the Taj Mahal, the tomb built for Shah Jahan's beloved wife Mumtaz Mahal. The Persian couplets inscribed on the entrance gateway make the imagery explicit: "Hail, blessed space happier than the garden of Paradise!/Hail, lofty building higher than the divine throne!"

So great was the emperor's grief that his hair turned white in a few days, and he needed to wear spectacles to hide the effects of weeping. The poet laureate Abu Talib Hamadani (d. 1652) known as Kalim expressed the emperor's distress in Persain couplets in his *Padshahnameh*: "the King of Kings cried out with grief/ Like an ocean raging with storm … the aggrieved heart lost its control/ How can wine remain when the goblet is broken? …His two eyes competed with each other,/ Each claiming to shed a larger share of the heart's blood."

Mumtaz Mahal died at Burhanpur on June 17, 1631 giving birth to her 14th child. Six months later her body was brought to Agra, escorted by Prince Shah Shuja and her principal lady-in-waiting Satti al-Nisa Khanam, and laid

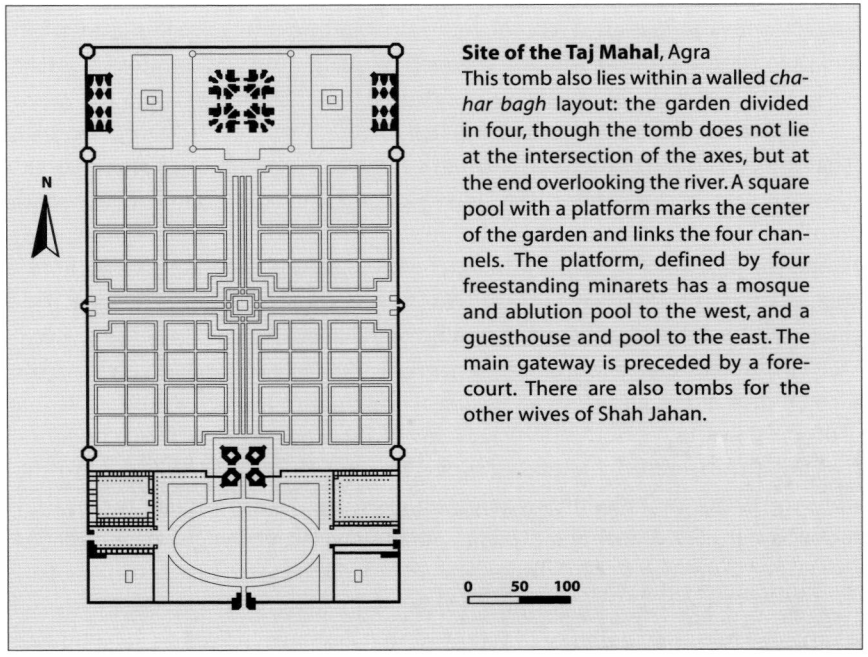

Site of the Taj Mahal, Agra
This tomb also lies within a walled *chahar bagh* layout: the garden divided in four, though the tomb does not lie at the intersection of the axes, but at the end overlooking the river. A square pool with a platform marks the center of the garden and links the four channels. The platform, defined by four freestanding minarets has a mosque and ablution pool to the west, and a guesthouse and pool to the east. The main gateway is preceded by a forecourt. There are also tombs for the other wives of Shah Jahan.

0   50   100

Cenotaphs of Mumtaz Mahal and Shah Jahan, Taj Mahal, Agra, 1632–1643
The interior of the central chamber is decorated with translucent floral sprays of semiprecious stones inlaid into the white marble.

The original gold screen was removed soon after installation to pre-empt looting and replaced by the present carved marble screen.

Detail of the decoration on an exterior dado, Taj Mahal, Agra, 1632–1643
The profuse and accurately detailed floral decoration of the Taj Mahal demonstrates the intense interest taken in nature during the

Mughal era. Similar plant motifs are found – as decorative bands or complete panels – in Shah Jahan's albums of paintings, on carpets, and on other textiles.

to rest in the garden. The chronicler Muhammad Salih (d. after 1660) described the setting in the *Shah Jahanname* as "the honor of the terrestrial world … (in) a garden having the marks of Paradise … (with) no like and equal on the surface of the earth in spaciousness of area and novelty of design…"

The layout was indeed unique. The mausoleum was situated overlooking the river rather than in the center of the garden, from which it was separated by a high plinth. A mosque and guesthouse (*mihman khana*) were placed in mirror image to each side of the mausoleum. This feature was entirely new in the sepulchral architecture of the subcontinent, for, while a mosque was often included in a tomb complex, albeit not in Mughal royal tombs, a guesthouse was an innovation, as also were the four free standing minarets. The garden was laid out according to the Mughal *chahar bagh* plan – divided into four quarters – but with a pool at the central intersection.

The main gateway was approached through a great square, the Jilau Khana, a feature introduced at Jahangir's tomb but here much more elaborate. On each side were residential facilities for tomb attendants, and to the south are platforms with subsidiary tombs. It was an enormous complex, including further to the south a township named Mumtazabad with intersecting bazaar streets and four caravanserais; still further south was another square, two caravanserais, and houses constructed by merchants.

The annual income of 200,000 rupees from the bazaars and caravanserais formed part of the endowment (*waqf*) of the tomb, together with the income (100,000 rupees) from 30 villages for associated expenses: maintenance; stipends for overseers, attendants, reciters of the Koran and so on; contributions to charity; and commemoration expenditure. The subsidiary tombs were probably intended for Shah Jahan's other wives, although they bear no epigraphic inscriptions. The tombs were a mirror image of each other, being situated at the end of a small square garden with a guesthouse to the north and south. Beyond the perimeter wall was the Fathpuri Mosque, its building

attributed to Fathpuri Begam, Shah Jahan's third wife. Built in red sandstone, the prayer hall was on a high plinth at the same level as the tombs. Outside the perimeter wall and on the same north-south axis was the octagonal tomb in red sandstone believed to have been constructed for Sati al-Nisa Khanam (d.1647), teacher and confidante first to Mumtaz Mahal and then to Princess Jahanara, for whom she held the Great Seal used to solemnize imperial documents.

The whole complex was associated with ladies of the imperial household. Indeed, it was a monument to womankind, an aspect enhanced by certain ceremonies performed at the time of the anniversary of death, which were particular to the Taj Mahal.

The observance of the first anniversary of death took place according to precise royal orders, establishing the future pattern of ceremonial. The site, where the tomb foundations were already laid, was prepared with carpets and canopied tents of velvet and brocade. A full day and night were spent in prayers, almsgiving, feeding the poor, and the fulfilment of further religious duties. Those present were the nobles of the court, scholars, saintly persons, the important religious leaders, as well as ordinary citizens. A feast was provided for rich and poor alike, and 50,000 rupees was distributed among the deserving. The unusual feature was the repetition of the ceremonies for the ladies of the royal household and of the court the following day, performed with equal maginficence and in the same manner. This second day of rituals,

Opposite: **Taj Mahal**, Agra, 1632–1643
The Taj Mahal, an image of true love surviving beyond death, is reflected in the central water channels, enhancing the mystical metaphor of reflection and the veils of reality. Koranic verses inlaid in black marble frame the four high portals (*pishtaq*) recalling Paradise and

the after life. Although the slightly bulbous dome betrays a Deccani influence, the mausoleum, with its harmonious proportions, is above all the highest expression of Timurid architecture.

INDIA: FROM SULTANATE TO MUGHAL EMPIRE

Herat and moved to Lahore under Jahangir. He received the title Nadir al-Asr ("Wonder of the Age") for his achievements, which included the royal apartments in the Red Fort at Shahjahanabad. His three sons all followed in his footsteps. His eldest son, Ata Allah, designed the tomb (Bibi ka Maqbara) of Aurangzeb's wife Rabia Daurani in Aurangabad, a city which became the capital of the Mughal Empire in 1693 after the conquest of the Deccan. This was the last of the monumental imperial tombs as Aurangzeb himself, like his sister Jahanara, buried near the shrine of Nizam al-Din in Delhi, preferred a simple open grave within the precint of a Sufi shrine; he was buried at Khuldabad, near Daulatabad, by the tomb of Sheikh Zain al-Din Shirazi. With the return of the capital to Delhi, Humayun's tomb became the dynastic mausoleum. The last Mughal emperor was captured in its gardens in 1857 and taken to Rangoon, where he was imprisoned and died in 1862.

Tombs in Deccan

Quite different from the Taj Mahal in concept and design was the almost contemporary tomb in Bijapur, Deccan, built in 1626 by Ibrahim Adil Shah II (1580–1627) – the Ibrahim Rauza. Originally intended for his queen, Taj Sultana, it was used as a mausoleum for the sultan and his family. In Bijapur, and in Ahmadnagar (of which Bijapur was once a part), Timurid elements were evident in the funerary and palace architecture of the 16th century. After Bijapur's independence from Ahmadnagar during the reign of Ibrahim Adil Shah II, a regional style evolved, of which the Ibrahim Rauza was the supreme example.

The layout was harmoniously asymmetrical. The mausoleum, in a garden enclosure, was not situated in the center but adjacent to one side of the perimeter wall. In front was an ablution pool and beyond, on the east-west axis, an associated mosque. The garden was not laid out as a Mughal *chahar bagh*: indeed, there was no trace of water channels, and their absence must be assumed as intentional, for Bijapur had a sophisticated system of water management based on Iranian models.

The structure, a single square chamber placed on a square plinth, is constructed of black basalt, a material characteristic of the Deccan. It has a bulbous dome resting on a circular drum framed by a frieze of lotus petals, a form echoed on top of the minarets and the small decorative towers of the roof gallery. The intricate brackets supporting the overhanging eaves (*chajjas*) end in lotus buds. Architectural details are emphasized through exquisite sculpting, whether of the friezes of Koranic verses around doorways, windows, and pierced screens in monumental *Naskhi* calligraphy, the geometric designs of dadoes and pillars, or the interior carving of the single square chamber.

If finesse of design and execution defined the Ibrahim Rauza, grandeur was the mark of the Gol Gumbad, the mausoleum built in the year 1656 for Muhammad Adil Shah (1627–1656). The hemispherical dome rising on a lotus-petalled drum measured 144 feet (44 meters) in external diameter and was second in size only to St. Peter's in Rome. The chamber was not built on the *hasht bihisht* plan but was a simple cube with octagonal minarets at each corner constructed in brick and finished in stucco.

which was not a practice associated with other roal tombs, required the associated guesthouse and mosque. The woman's assembly was open to all and especially the needy, and another sum of 50,000 rupees was distributed.

Shah Jahan's chroniclers claimed that the design for the layout of the Taj Mahal was suggested by the emperor. It is also likely that he selected the calligrapher, Amanat Khan, renowned for the inscriptions on the gateway to Akbar's tomb at Sikandra, for the extensive program of Koranic inscriptions on the mausoleum and cenotaphs.

The architect was not mentioned in the official chronicles but only the supervisors Makramat Khan, minister of public works, and Mir Abd al-Karim. However, a poetic manuscript published in the 20th century revealed his identity as Ustadh (Master) Ahmad Lahori (born c.1570–1575, d. 1649), a building engineer practised in astronomy, geometry, and mathematics, who came from a Khorasani family in the former Timurid capital of

In the kingdom of Golconda a distinct Deccani style also appeared in sepulchral architecture after the mid-16th century. Whereas in Bijapur royal tombs were distributed throughout the city, in Golconda there was a royal necropolis where numerous tombs of varying sizes were constructed in an extensive planted area. Neither formal gardens nor water appear to have been an integral part of the overall scheme, although gardens and huge artificial lakes formed part of the urban design of nearby Hyerabad. The typical form of a Golconda tomb was a cubic chamber with a bulbous dome resting on a frieze of lotus petals springing from a high drum. The structure was set on a high, square, arcaded plinth. Built in brick and plaster, they were sometimes faced with glazed tiles, although only a few isolated traces survive; travelers described gilded domes. It is the elaborate plasterwork friezes, the crenellated parapets deeply modelled, and the pierced geometric plasterwork of screens and minarets which are so striking today.

The sculptural qualities of Qutb Shah funerary architecture was especially apparent in the tomb of Hayat Bakshi Begam, a powerful queen who played an active role in the kingdom during the reigns of her husband, Muhammad Qutb Shah of Golconda (1611–1626) and her son Abdullah (1626–1672). The tomb was completed in 1666, together with the associated mosque, a year before her death.

Unlike the Mughals, the Qutb Shahs of Golconda did not perceive individual royal tombs as a focus for court ritual. Indeed, nowhere in Deccan was there an equivalent of the imperial Mughal dynastic tomb. The Mughal *chahar bagh* funereal enclosure was not imitated, nor an equivalent visual metaphor offered for the gardens of Paradise. The worlds beyond and the link between this world and the next were left to the imagination, or conjured as a Bijypur through the rhythms of Koranic verses in exquisitely sculpted calligraphy.

Above: **Tomb of Muhammad Qutb Shah,** Golconda, completed in 1626
The style reveals the sculptural approach to architecture so characteristic of the Deccan – the tiered structure articulated by turrets and finials, the bulbous dome supported on lotus petals which once was covered in brillantly colored ceramic tiles.

Ibrahim Rauza Mausoleum, Bijapur, Deccan, 1626
The tomb of Ibrahim Adil Shah II, originally intended for his wife, Taj Sultana, was used as a family mausoleum. The tomb and the mosque each have bulbous domes which – typical for Deccan – are supported on lotus petals, and have turrets and finials. The outer walls of the structure, built in black schist, are richly embellished with panels of calligraphy and geometric designs carved in low relief.

Decorative Arts

Philippa Vaughan

Calligraphy and painting under the Mughals

The Timurid court of Herat was one of the greatest centers of book production. The early Mughal emperors revered the Timurid standards of excellence until Akbar questioned the idea of accepting earlier models blindly.

Babur himself was a calligrapher and poet in Chaghatai Turki, the Mughals' native language, and devised his own script using it to copy a Koran, which he sent to Mecca. However, he did not have the resources, nor perhaps the inclination, to develop a painting atelier, unlike Humayun, who retained a painter among his small entourage in exile. During his time in the Safavid dominions Humayun met calligraphers and artists, persuading several to join his court. Abdus Samad and Mir Sayid Ali established the court atelier, drawing to it painters from non-Muslim as well as Muslim courts, including Persia and Bukhara. Under their early supervision and Akbar's patronage, the Mughal arts of the book were transformed for almost a century. Akbar himself could hardly write and probably suffered from dyslexia – his choniclers described him as *ummi*, literally "unlettered" – but he had an excellent eye and a good memory for the books which were read to him daily. As his chronicler

Abu'l Fazl noted: "there are no historical facts of the past ages, or couriosities of science, or interesting points of philosophy with which His Majesty … is unacquainted."

An extensive library was an essential requisite of sovereignty and by 1605 Akbar had amassed 24,000 volumes. They were cataloged and stored according to content, author, calligrapher, and language – Hindi, Persian, Greek, Kashmiri, Arabic – as well as the monetary value of the manuscript. Among them were Timurid masterpieces inherited from Babur and Humayun, and libraries acquired through conquest of the sultanates of Gujarat, Malwa, and Kashmir. Books were received as gifts, such as the Polyglot Bible prepared for Philip II of Spain, which the Jesuits brought when visiting the Mughal court in 1580, the largest in a growing corpus of European works. Literati presented their manuscripts: the Persian translation of Babur's memoirs (*Baburname*) was received from the translator Abdur-Rahim Khan Khanan in 1589.

The library was expanded by the many volumes copied, translated, and illustrated by the imperial workshops. Project directors planned each manuscript and assigned the work to the papermakers, calligraphers, illuminators, gilders, burnishers, apprentices who prepared the pigments, and the painters. Akbar guided the choice of subject and selected new cycles of illustrations for the repertoire of Persian poetic texts familiar at the Timurid courts and had a weekly inspection of output conferring rewards according to the excellence of paainting.

Mary sura, illuminated doublepage from a Koran manuscript, Lahore 1573/74, London, British Library
Only a few Koran manuscripts of this quality have survived from the Mughal era. This manuscript is written in *Muhaqqaq* and *Naskhi* calligraphy and its colophon reads: "Copied by Hibatullah al-Husayni for the use of the Sultan, Lahore, 981."

Right: **The Prophet Elias rescuing Nur al-Dahr from the sea**, Mir Sayid Ali, miniature from the *Hamzaname* manuscript, Mughal, c. 1570. London, British Museum
The *Hamzaname*, was the first major project undertaken by Akbar's painting studio. A total of 1,400 large-format folios were produced in 12 or 14 volumes between 1562 and 1577. The Persian artist Mir Sayid Ali, who left the court of Shah Tahmasp to work for the Mughals, was in charge of planning the illustrations.

Babur approaching the fort in Andijan on receiving news of his father's accident, miniature from the *Baburname*, 1595–1602, New Delhi, National Museum
During the Mughal era a new literary genre developed – the illustrated history recounting the deeds of the ruler to forge a new dynastic identity. Babur recorded his memories in his own hand.

Akbar speaks to his people, miniature from the *Akbarname* of Abu l-Fadl, 17th century, Tehran, Reza Abbasi Museum
Akbar commissioned the court chronicler Abu l-Fadl to write an account of his reign. The emperor was presented as a heroic ruler in whom were united the arts of peace and war. This scene shows the ruler on a white horse listening to the appeals of his subjects in the presence of his army.

Virgin and Child, miniature from a *muraqqa* album, Basawan, Mughal, c. 1590–1600, San Diego, Museum of Art
The Jesuits accepted Akbar's invitation to visit the court at Fatehpur Sikri and arrived in 1580, bringing with them gifts including paintings, prints, altarpieces, and seven volumes of the Polyglot Bible. Many images were copied by Mughal painters, some directly, while others, as here, were adapted to a Mughal setting.

Persian master calligraphers were welcomed, continuing an earlier tradition of migration to the sultanate courts where native-born calligraphers were trained by expert practitioners. Mir Masum Nami, a poet, physician, historian of Sind, and Mughal ambassador at the court of Safavid Shah Abbas provided the chronograms and *nastaliq* inscriptions on the Buland Darwaza at Agra. Mir Dauri Katib al-Mulk of Herat worked on the *Hamzaname*. Akbar's favorite calligrapher was Muhammad Husain Kashmiri, called Zarin Qalam ("Golden Pen"), who copied the classical Persian poetic texts essential to a Timurid king for illustration by his finest artists.

Akbar believed in the power of the image and the didactic role of painting. The first major project of his reign was the *Hamzaname*, tales of chivalry and exotic adventures featuring the Prophet's Uncle Hamza. Then came Persian translations of Hindu epics such as the *Razmname* ("Book of Wars") or the *Ramayana*. One could see the choice of works as a form of public relations to facilitate mutual cultural understanding, particularly in the harem, for Akbar's marriages with Rajput princesses brought non-Muslim customs into the heart of the imperial residence.

A new genre was developed: illustrated histories and chronicles of the dynasty with the emperor as hero. The memoirs of Babur (*Baburname*) and the history of Akbar (*Akbarname*) placed new demands upon the artists, requiring for credibility a realistic presentation of the principal personalities, material culture, and landscape involved. Akbar sat for his likeness and ordered the nobility to do the same. He rejected criticism from the orthodox with their own argument: "It seems to me that a painter is better than most in gaining a knowledge of God. Each time he draws a living being he must draw each and every limb to it, but seeing that he cannot bring it to life must perforce give thought to the miracle wrought by the Creator and thus obtain knowledge of Him."

Through his exposure to the works of European painters, Akbar discovered new ways of seeing and encouraged his artists to adopt their techniques. As the chronicler Abu l-Fadl observed, "Although in general a picture represents a material form … the painters of Europe quite often express, by using rare forms, our mental states, and thus they lead those who consider only the outside of things to the place of inner meaning." He explained their approach in metaphysical terms such as "perceiving the links between the visible and invisible worlds."

Jahangir continued the transformation of painting regarding both subject matter and style. Although not a visionary like Akbar, he was sympathetic to mystics regardless of sect, and as a prince commissioned an illustrated translation of a Sanskrit philosophical work on Vedanta, advocating that the absolute

Detail of a pictorial carpet, 1580/90 Mughal, Boston, Musuem of Fine Arts
The phoenix, which is attacking the *rukh*, a composite beast, and the hunting cheetah were symbols associated with royal power. Their use reflects Akbar's interest in adapting images from secular and non-Muslim sources to enhance the imperial iconography and to integrate all the population groups in the empire.

Begam enjoying a performance by actors in Portuguese costume, Mir Kalan Khan, Mughal, Delhi, 1742, San Diego, Museum of Art
Life in the *zenana* (the women's quarters, or harem, as it was known in Indian and Persian) had many pleasures. This picture shows a scene from a theatrical performance in costume, given for the entertainment of the princess and her retinue.

could be attained without physical separation from the world. He was fascinated by natural phenomena and, following the Koranic injunction to know the Signs of God, commissioned natural history studies of flora and fauna, which were of extraordinary quality. These were bound in large albums (*muraqqa*), along with other works which aroused his interest, such as Deccani and Persian paintings, European prints, Mughal interpretations of European themes, and imperial allegorical portraits, thus introducing European themes to the Mughal style.

Portraiture and the depiction of personality was developed by Jahangir to new heights of brilliance. Concern for modeling, spacial depth, and the uniqueness of individual physical form was a radical departure of perception as well as technique and the artists' response to imperial demands was a testament to their abilities as well as his inspiration as patron. He claimed to recognize individual artists' styles, even if several worked on a single painting. "And if there be a picture containing many portraits, and each face be the work of a different master, I can discover which face is the work of each of them", he wrote in his memoirs (*Tuzuk-i Jahangiri*).

The *Tuzuk* (begun before 1612) was the only large-scale illustrated manuscript of his reign, since his preference was for smaller manuscripts or individual folios worked by a single artist. A new genre of imperial portraiture reflecting the allegory and symbolism of English models followed the visit of

Sir Thomas Roe, sent by James I to negotiate trading concessions for the East India Company in the year 1615.

Folios of calligraphy were also bound in the albums with borders decorated with vignettes of court or country life or floral motifs. Jahangir particularly liked *Nastaliq* script and collected folios with pious sayings or pithy Persian quatrains by the calligraphy masters Sultan Ali Mashhadi (d. 1519) — the Sultan al-Khattatin ("King of Calligraphers"), and Mir Ali Haravi of Herat (d. 1556). Contemporary masters were commissioned to execute manuscripts or monumental calligraphy, for example Abd al-Haqq Shirazi, designer of the *Naskhi* and *Nastaliq* inscriptions on Akbar's gateway and mausoleum at Sikandra. He also designed the extensive Koranic inscriptions in *Naskhi* on the Taj Mahal for Shah Jahan.

Shah Jahan, whose hand was even less accomplished than Jahangir's, nonetheless appreciated calligraphy. Folios of Persian quatrains, or verses in the Mughals' native Chaghatai Turki which Shah Jahan's grandmother complained that he could hardly understand, were bound in the *muraqqa* albums. So too was fine calligraphy by the heir apparent, Dara Shukoh, who was taught by a Persian master, Abdur-Rashid Daylami along with his Hindu secretary Chandar-Bhan Brahman. Prince Aurangzeb, an accomplished calligrapher who copied several Korans, and his brother Shah Shuja were each instructed by Persian masters.

Velvet floorspread, late 17th century, Mughal, 203 × 116 cm, London, Victoria and Albert Museum
The stylized flowering plant became a dominant motif of Mughal art during the 17th century, and was depicted with realistic detail. Velvets such as the one shown here decorated the imperial court.

Paintings in the albums, and the magnificent illustrated chronicle of the reign (*Padshahname*) displayed a new orientation under Shah Jahan. His concern with the effect of majesty and the role of ceremonial as a cohesive element for the court was reflected in the desire to create an immediate visual impact. "Realism" and "naturalism" ceded place to technical perfection in depicting material culture; and a different spatial sense led to the massing of figures, which emphasized the whole rather than individual personalities. Re-establishing detail as part of a boundless eternity marked a re-establishment of the Indian perception shared by Muslim and non-Muslim alike.

At the Deccani courts miniature painting was without a didactic purpose. Its aim was to refresh the mind and spirit by conjuring a lyrical atmosphere via depicting the joys of poetry and poetic fantasy, of love and music, or recalling the ultimate end of life through contemplation of ascetics both male and female. It reflected a private world rather than historical events or the clash of armies. The styles of Ahmadnagar, Bijapur, and Golconda, each of exquisite refinement and technical brilliance, combined in their own way the sensuality of south Indian art with the rhythms of Persia, remaining abstract and with a certain mystical quality. The "naturalism" of European paintings evoked little response, although examples were known several decades before they reached the Mughal court.

Most remarkable was the output of Bijapur under Sultan Ibrahim Adil Shah II (1579–1627), one of the greatest patrons of his time. Himself a musician and poet, and a mystic inclined to the essence of both Muslim and Hindu thought, he sought to attract to his court the most creative artists, writers, and thinkers from throughout the Muslim world. Calligraphers included the master Mir Khalilullah Shah, who had left the Safavid court and was rewarded for his work by the title Padishah-i qalam ("King of the Pen") and the right to sit on a throne. Ibrahim's mausoleum exhibited an extraordinary range of calligraphic styles, including Kufic, square Kufic, Thuluth, Naskhi and Nastalig, all superbly sculpted in hard black basalt.

The calligraphy of the Deccan surpassed that in all other areas of Hindustan, and the sarcophagi of the Qutb Shahs at Golconda show a similarly amazing quality and variety of inscriptions as at Bijapur. Painting in Golconda was also rich, the several coexistent styles retaining their vitality well into the 17th century. After the sultanate had to recognize the authority of the Mughals in 1635, it absorbed their influence creatively. Following Aurangzeb's conquest in 1686 and 1687, Mughal influence became more dominant for a while, but by this time it was combined with the Rajput idiom of Bikaner and Jaipur, which at Hyderabad evolved into a charming courtly style until the turn of the 19th century, when British art and architecture became the fashion.

Textiles and metalwork

Imperial patronage of the arts was intended to enhance the image of sovereignty and provide the symbols of kingship. Principal state occasions, such as succession to the throne, military victory, dynastic marriages, or the birth of a child to the ruling family, were celebrated with festivities lasting days or weeks. Babur's peripatetic life and minimal resources cramped his style until his arrival in India, although he regularly bestowed robes of honor, continuing a custom followed by earlier Indian rulers including the Tughluqs. Humayun's accession feast in 1531, however, was on a grand scale. In the Hall of Public Audience and other rooms constructed for the event emblems of royalty were laid out – military accessories such as jeweled scimitars, gilded armor, a gilt quiver; manuscripts, pen boxes and albums with paintings and calligraphy; brocade coverlets, cushions, European velvet, and Portuguese cloth, and a gilded bed; the floors were spread with Persian carpets. Over 12,000 robes of honor were distributed, the recipients including more than a hundred begams (princesses) who had traveled from Central Asia to attend.

Akbar expanded the number of festivals – an instrument of policy to weld the diverse cultural and religious groups at court into a cohesive whole. To the feast days of the Muslim lunar calendar were added those sacred to Hindus (especially the Rajputs) such as Dahehra and Diwali. The Hindu ceremony of weightment was included in the celebrations of the regnal year (calculated according to the Hindu solar calendar) as an occasion for public charity. Twice a year the monarch was publicly weighed on gilded scales against different types of objects, from gold, silk, and perfumes to vegetables and salt, which were then distributed to the needy. With the growing importance of the Khorasani nobility the Persian New Year (*nauruz*) was also adopted and courtiers competed to entertain the emperor in their houses and gardens. The host offered numerous gifts, which were laid out for the emperor to peruse, keeping what pleased him and returning the rest.

Abu l-Fadl, Akbar's chronicler, described in detail the imperial workshops (*karkhanas*) developed at Fatehpur Sikri. Near the palace was the House of Perfume and "the studios and workrooms for the finer and more reputable arts such as painting, goldsmith work, tapestry making, carpet and curtain making, and the manufacture of arms." Akbar himself both observed and participated "because he is very dextrous in all jobs … I have seen him making ribbons like a lace-maker, and filing and sawing and working very hard … (for he) does not shrink from the minutiae of business, but regards the performance as an act of Divine Worship." The workshops were organized as part of the emperor's household, and the objects were carefully inventoried before being stored.

Textiles were among the most highly prized means of displaying the range of his power during festivals and welcoming ceremonies for distinguished guests. The most valuable, which were the awnings, carpets, screens, and panels for imperial tents, were kept in the emperor's private storehouse (*farras-khana*). Abu l-Fadl recorded the scale of the losses in the devastating fire at Fatehpur Sikri in 1579: "Approximately one crore (10,000,000) pieces of awnings (*shamiyana*), tents (*kargah, khayama*), and screens (*sarpada*) made from gold cloth, European velvet, woollen cloth, damask silk, satin and brocade, brocaded carpets, and embroidery of an amount beyond description were burnt."

As well as importing the fabrics – velvets from Europe, Iran, and Gujarat, broadcloth from Turkey and Portugal, silk from Yazd, Mashhad, and Herat, – to be copied in his workshops, Akbar also imported the weavers, principally from Persia, to direct the studios. Carpet weaving was probably introduced to India at this time, and by the end of Akbar's reign centers existed in many towns beyond the imperial capitals of Agra, Fatehpur Sikri, and Lahore. While motifs such as animals and arabesques reflected Persian models, they were rendered with a greater sense of naturalism already evident in painting. The close relationship between the artists and craftsmen in developing new designs, whether for carpets, textiles and shawls, monumental calligraphy, metalwork, or hardstone carving, was a feature of Mughal art facilitated by the development of the *karkhanas* within the precincts of the imperial palaces.

While an Indian provenance is sometimes difficult to establish for carpets and other craft objects produced in the 16th century, the Mughal style became clearly defined under Jahangir. The trend to naturalism in depicting plants, animals, and the human figure was felt in all media. The flowering plant motif, which was indebted to European herbals as well as to natural history painters, crystalized in the 1620s and reached its zenith under Shah Jahan. It was appreciated by Aurangzeb, who commissioned chintzes from Golconda and further south for his army camp. The cloth was called "Masulipatan" after the port from which it was exported to Europe and where the flowering tree textile motif was developed. Absorbed into the repertoire of workshops among both Muslim and Hindu communities, this motif continued to dominate textile design in the 18th century.

Box, north India, 17th century, enamel set with ruby, Washington, Freer Gallery of Art
This box, probably used to store betel leaves, is characterized by a striking, multicolored floral decoration, whereby all its elements are trimmed in fine gold wire.

Water pipe stand, Bidar, Deccan, c. 1650, inlaid with brass and silver, 8 in (21 cm)
Water pipes were introduced to the Mughal court in the early 17th century. The designs on this pipe stand are based on traditional Hindu fertility motifs: the lotus pool and the "overflowing vase."

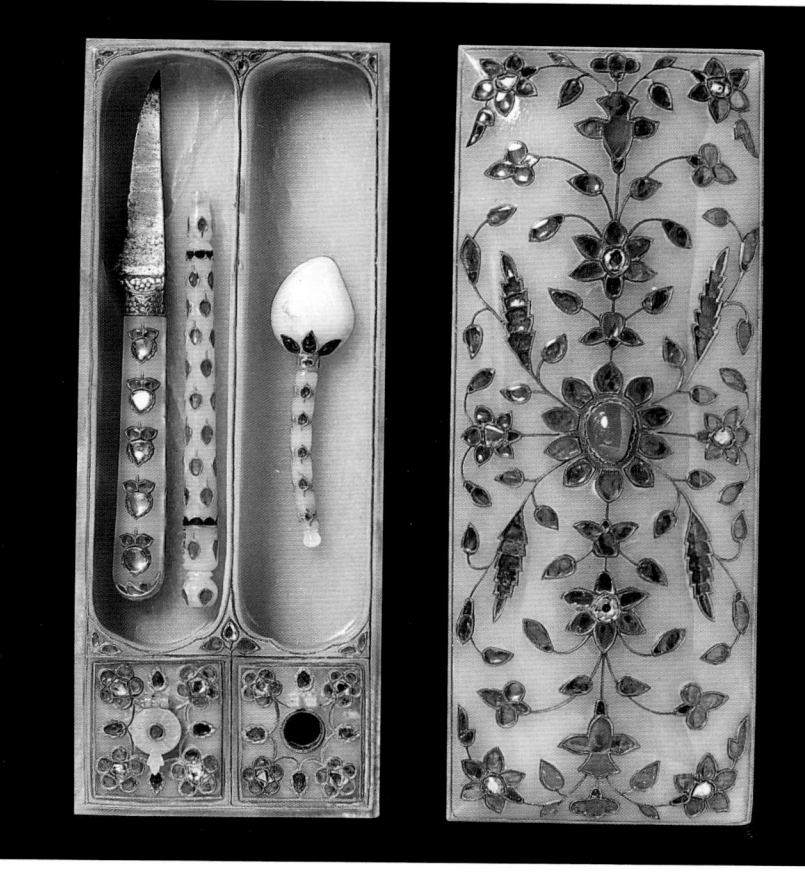

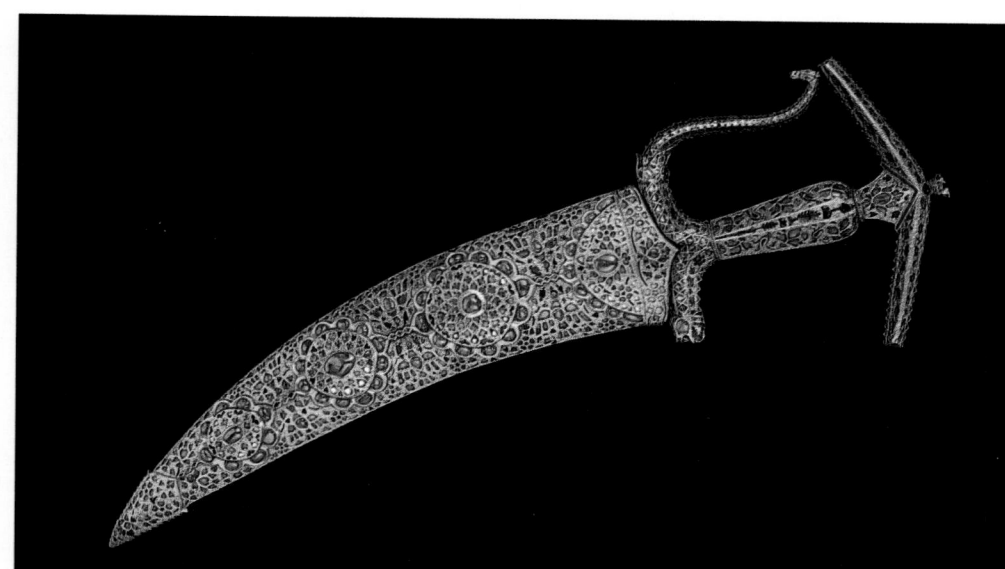

Pen box, c. 1650, Mughal, jade set with rubies, London, Victoria and Albert Museum
This magnificent jewel-encrusted pen box contains a knife to cut in the reed, a stylus handle and a spoon to measure the ingredients for ink.

Jeweled dagger and sheath
Mughal, c. 1619, length 14 in (36 cm), Kuwait, al-Salah Collection
The gold hilt and scabbard of this dagger are engraved and set with rubies, emeralds, diamonds, agate, enamel, glass, and ivory. This is most probably the dagger commissioned by Jahangir in 1619 and described in his memoirs.

The manufacture and import of luxury items were further developed through Jahangir's connoisseurship and aesthetic sensibilities. He continued the principal festivals evolved by Akbar as a feature of court life and added his own weekly celebration, called in his memoirs the "party of cups" (*bazm-i piyala*). The English ambassador Sir Thomas Roe attended the *nauruz* festival and the emperor's birthday party in 1616, leaving us a description of the cup of gold set with rubies, turquoises, and emeralds from which he drank.

Shah Jahan brought state occasions to new heights of grandeur. The marriages of his sons had been planned before the death of Mumtaz Mahal. After the mourning period, the task of commissioning and assembling gifts was continued by Princess Jahanara, Shah Jahan's daughter. Jewelry, gem-encrusted utensils, and textiles were prepared for the bride, and robes of honor for the imperial princes and princesses, and the wives and daughters of the nobility, each of whom received seven or nine pieces of rich fabric accompanied by jewelry. The principal nobles each received nine suits of clothes with a gold embroidered waistcoat and jeweled daggers or scimitars. The gifts were laid out for viewing in the Hall of Public Audience before being delivered in a magnificent procession to the bride's home. The total cost of the festivities, which included firework displays, was 1.6 million rupees.

By the time of Aurangzeb's wedding, a few years later, Jahanara pleaded fatigue with making wedding arrangements and her younger brother was given one million rupees to arrange his own. Whether as a result of this early humiliation or through natural temperament, during his reign Aurangzeb discouraged display of power and wealth, which he considered "unnecessary." Artists and craftsmen sought patronage elsewhere during the 18th century. Regional traditions were refreshed by new talent and indigenous aesthetics reasserted.

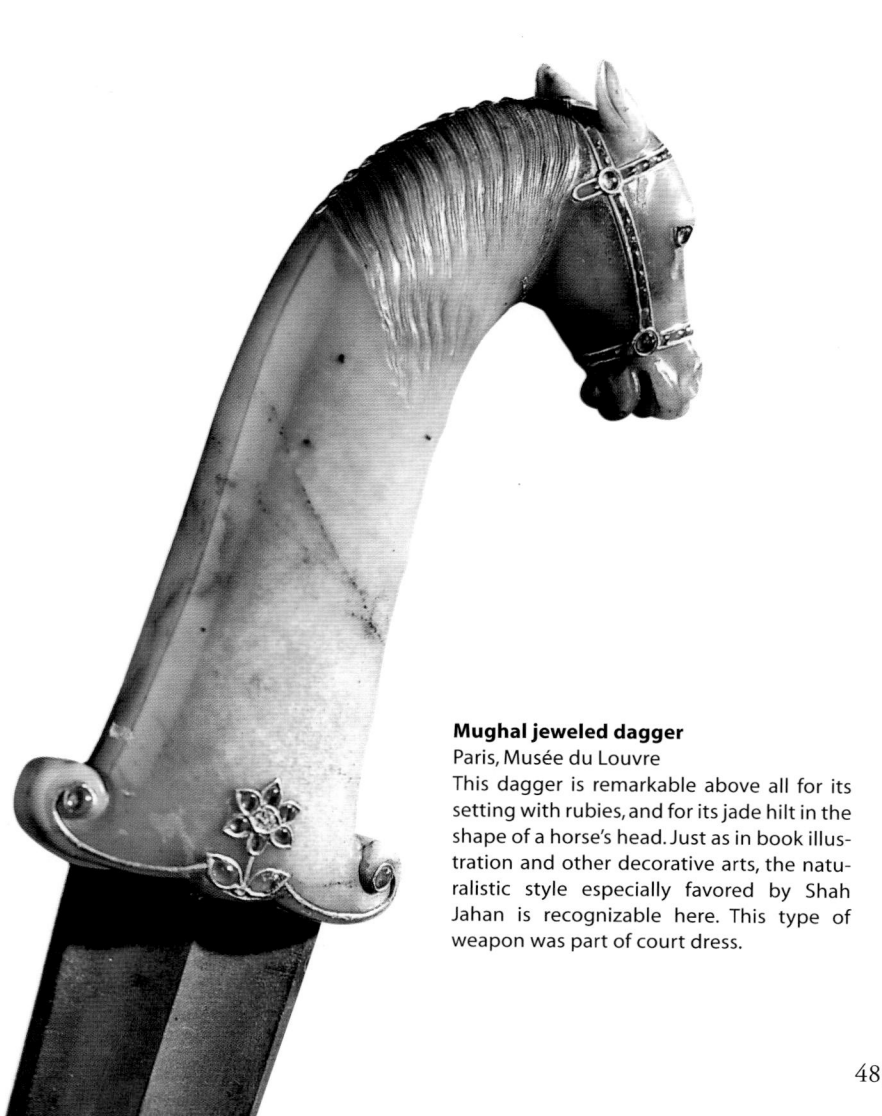

Mughal jeweled dagger
Paris, Musée du Louvre
This dagger is remarkable above all for its setting with rubies, and for its jade hilt in the shape of a horse's head. Just as in book illustration and other decorative arts, the naturalistic style especially favored by Shah Jahan is recognizable here. This type of weapon was part of court dress.

The Garden as a Reflection of Paradise

Marianne Barrucand

There are gardens at both the beginning and the end of mankind's destiny – the Garden of Eden and Paradise – and this is equally true for Muslims, Christians, and Jews alike. The Koran gives detailed descriptions of the eternal garden, which is "as large as heaven and earth" and "in whose hollows brooks flow." In it stand "thornless trees that spread their shade" with "fruits hanging low in clusters," and it is where the "Blessed, richly clothed, lie on couches lined with thick brocade." It is a garden of many springs, with rivers flowing with water, milk, honey, and wine ("that does not intoxicate"). Many of its springs are spiced with camphor or ginger, and their water, mixed with wine, is handed to the faithful by "boys graced with eternal youth" and "large-eyed, chaste houris," the Paradise virgins with "swelling breasts," comparable to "hidden pearls."

Paradise appears to be a garden landscape enclosed by a wall, since both gates and gatekeepers are mentioned. Sura 55 tells of two similar gardens beside which lie another two, different gardens. All four of them possess flowing springs, shady trees, exquisite fruits, and beautiful houris. There are also tents and buildings in the heavenly garden: dwellings, houses, castles, and chambers among which are "rooms in which streams flow." But all these buildings are scattered throughout the garden and in no way resemble a city. The concept of a "heavenly Jerusalem" (or here, Mecca) is alien to Islam.

Among the terms used by the Koran to denote Paradise, *janna* ("garden," pl. *jannat*) is the most common. Eden is called either *adn* or *jannat adn*, and there is frequent mention of a garden of delights (*jannat naim*), a garden of refuge (*jannat al-mawa*), and a garden of immortality (*jannat al-khuld*). The word *raud* is also used to denote the heavenly garden, but only a little later, in connection with Muhammad's grave. "Garden" has also been etymologically linked with "cemetery," almost from the beginning. Our word "Paradise" derives from the Persian term *firdaus* (*pairi*, "around" and *daiza*, "wall") via the Greek *paradeisos*.

The relationship between garden and Paradise in the Koran is very clear and well formulated. However, it would be wrong to consider the very real Islam art of the garden

Fantastic landscape, anthology of literary and mystical texts, Iran, late 14th century, Istanbul, Museum of Turkish and Islamic Art

exclusively – as often happens – in a religious and literary context. Between heaven and earth there is a multitude of diverse and beautiful gardens.

The Koran gives no precise guidelines for the creation of a garden. All that can be inferred from the sacred text is the importance of shady trees, flowing water, a protective outer wall, the scattered, richly decorated buildings that adorn

the landscape, and the absence of flowers, grottoes, and ponds. All in all, the Barada mosaic in the Great Mosque in Damascus probably comes very close to this picture. This idea of Paradise and the garden has been shaped by the dreams of Arabia's desert-dwellers, who knew of the Persian *paradeison* parks if only from the accounts of others. In the Maghreb and on the Iberian Peninsula, the Roman traditions prevailed, in the Punjab, the ancient Indian ones. The important question here is whether these different local traditions are able to account for the various garden forms of the Islamic world, or whether they really do all have the religious basis as their common denominator.

Since the majority of Islamic countries are located in hot, dry regions with an oasis culture, one of the main problems of the art of the garden has always been irrigation. Both the western and eastern parts of the Islamic world had inherited the *qanawat* system from Persia. Underground canals (thus protected from evaporation caused by the sun) carried water from raised headwaters over large distances, making use of gentle gradients. Covered access points were built at regular intervals in order to allow for their rather laborious maintenance. These *qanawat* installations, which stretched through the desert landscape like long strings of pearls, could be recognized from a long way off. Where

Watercourse in the Nilkanth Pavilion, Mandu, 2nd half of the 16th century

Fountain in the Court of the Lions in the Alhambra, Granada, 2nd half of the 14th century

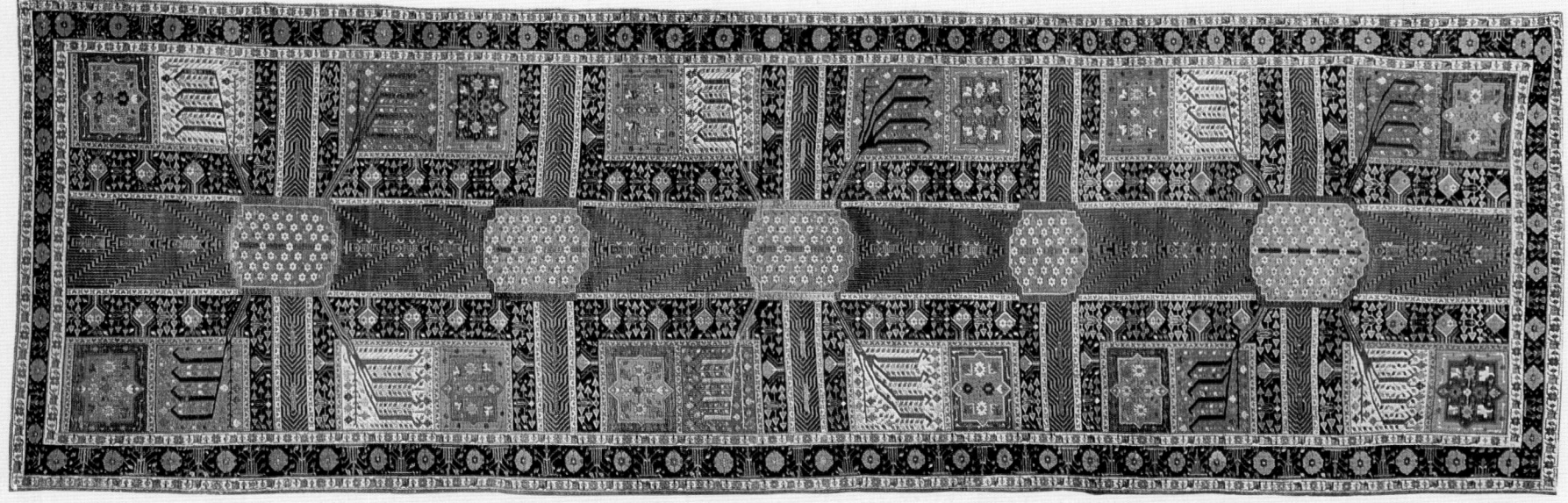

Garden carpet, northwestern Persia, 18th century, Berlin, Museum für Islamische Kunst

the climate allowed it, open canals were built, which diverted water from rivers and carried it through the country over considerable distances. The distribution systems in the case of both the *qanawat* and the canals were very cleverly worked out and controlled. In the princely gardens, the water flowed through channels decorated with tiles right into the rooms of the palace. It welled from marble basins, poured over staircase waterfalls and terraced areas, and ran over colorfully tiled walls. Lions were a popular motif on fountains, not only in the Alhambra.

A wide variety of gardens exists, from the barely structured parklands to the *hortus conclusus*. The large, walled parklands, which embody the fundamental idea of the Koranic Paradise, are to be found – or more accurately were to be found, since these belts of greenery which circle the cities have often fallen prey to modern urban development – everywhere from India to Morocco and Andalusia. In the Maghreb, the Berber word *agdal* is commonly used to refer to an "unwatered meadow," while *buhaira*, on the other hand (from Arabic: *bahr*, "sea"), denotes an artificially irrigated park. Although *agdal* usually refers to unwatered green areas, the famous palm groves of the Marrakech Agdal are in fact irrigated. Hunts and equestrian contests were held in this kind of park, as shown in a picture from the Qasr al-Hair al-Gharbi.

Garden of the Alcázar, Seville, 12th century

The other type consists of the enclosed, protected pleasances, in which blossoming and fragrant shrubs and trees were surrounded by galleries with pillars or columns. In extensive parts of the Islamic world, this type of garden was represented in its most modest form by the water fountain surrounded by pots of flowers that well-appointed townhouses had at their center for the enjoyment of visitors and guests. These gardens, that were generally known as *riyad* (a plural form of *rauda*), were always laid out orthogonally, either square or rectangular, whether they belonged to princes or ordinary citizens. In the royal gardens, sumptuous rooms

in the middle of a facade opened onto the garden, and were connected with each other by means of raised pathways. This type of garden, divided up into four parts, is very widespread in the Islamic world. The pathways, covered with tile or marble, cross the plant beds, laid out like ponds, at a height of up to 7 feet (2 meters). Their walls are decorated with tiles or paintwork. The visitor to the garden trod on neither earth nor grass, picked no flowers, but simply breathed in the scent of the ornamental shrubs – citrus plants were especially popular – and admired their blooms. There was often a water fountain or pavilion at the center of the cross formed by

the two axes. This garden model was adopted for the political capital of Andalusia, Medina al-Zahra, back in the 10th century; it has been shown to have existed in Seville in the 11th and 12th centuries, and was still being used in Morocco in the 19th century. There are similar internal gardens in the Near East, but such high, raised paths seem to be characteristic of western Islam. While the cross-axial design certainly dates back to Roman garden practice, the origins of the raised paths are not, however, clear.

The widely used term *chahar bagh* ("four gardens" or the "garden divided into four"), however, is Persian and does not actually have an Arabic equivalent. Literature concerning the Islamic garden is happy to claim that the expression "garden divided into four" derives from the Koran (etymologically, this is not the case), as sura 55 mentions two sets of two gardens. It cannot be assumed that this unclear description of four gardens is the only basis for the cross-axial garden. Physical models, as well as practical considerations, are in all likelihood

View of the Portal Palace in the park of the Taj Mahal, Agra, 1632–1643

Palace garden in Fez, 17th century (restored)

equally important factors. While the famous royal Persian gardens – known as Chahar Bagh – which were built all the way into Moghul India, always have a strict geometric layout, they are often divided up by paths and water channels into more than four parts. So really the term "four" ultimately serves only to express the idea of a strict geometrical schema. Many of these gardens are laid out in the form of overlapping terraces, which allows the gradients thus created to be used in the play of water. Tiled pathways, water gullies, and flower beds all feature in these gardens, which served as the model for the Persian "garden carpets." Between the princely parklands outside the cities, used for riding and hunting, and the equally princely, "pleasure" garden, which is exclusively for passive enjoyment, there was a whole series of gardens that combined the functional with the pleasurable: the *munya*, rich country estates whose owners, as well as building sumptuous rooms and columned walkways, also planted vegetable gardens, vines, and fruit trees. This type of "crafted" landscape also had its roots in Roman traditions.

Gardens also served as final resting-places for the dead. These could be near-natural landscapes, carefully laid out and well-tended parks, "four-part" gardens, or *riyad*. In Rabat (Morocco), the large cemetery by the sea is a near-natural, green landscape with anonymous tombstones and no other attempts to embellish the area. The royal Ottoman burial complexes are situated in park landscapes, such as in Bursa, which are like romantic parks in which symmetry gives way to nature (it is tempting here to think of the difference between "English" and "French" gardens). The burial sites of the Indian rulers, however – the most famous being the Taj Mahal – consist of rich, cross-axial designs with watercourses, elaborate fountains, and splendid monuments. The view of the landscape beyond was supposed to enhance the beauty of the buildings. In Andalusia and Morocco, many of the dynastic burial sites were designed as buildings with internal gardens, although in Marrakech the burial pavilions of the Sadites are located in gardens, and the graves of the Merinids in Fez and Rabat are situated in garden landscapes.

In terms of typical garden architecture, on the one hand there are the galleries and rooms which enclose the inner gardens and, on the other, free standing garden pavilions, which can sometimes be quite large. The rooms were sometimes built into massive towers – as for example in the case of the Comares tower in the Alhambra – but they could just as equally be open, light halls like the buildings on the narrow side of the Acequia courtyard in the Generalife. The free standing pavilions can be tremendously heavy, such as the Manzah in the royal garden of Meknes, or delicate and stylish, like the kiosks in the gardens of the Topkapi Palace in Istanbul.

These buildings were always products of the architectural traditions of their respective regions and can only be properly understood as such. Their common denominator is their function as garden architecture: they are always open buildings, as the view of the gardens in front of them or surrounding them is forever important. In the case of the Alhambra and the Taj Mahal, this requirement also includes the view of the landscape beyond the complexes. It appears that the sumptuous rooms in the wings that enclose the gardens were usually reception rooms, in which beauty and harmony were indicators of the owner's status. By contrast, the freestanding pavilions seem to have been designed for relaxation, either in the

Patio de la Sultana in the Generalife, country estate near the Alhambra Palace, Granada, beginning of the 15th century

form of social gatherings or even for the final slumber of death.

What is certain is that the literary theme of Paradise as garden and garden as Paradise is timeless in Islam, although strictly speaking the real gardens of Islam have relatively little in common with the Koranic notion of Paradise. It is easier to see them as the continuation of pre-Islamic traditions of garden design, which led to the park landscapes of the Ottomans and the large, intricate, repeatedly subdivided gardens of Persia, which in Islamic India were adopted with even more expense and with the addition of elaborate fountains. Common to all these gardens is a basic geometric schema.

Axial symmetry seems to be the fundamental rule, even though the various axes are sometimes subtly displaced (for example in the Court of the Lions in the Alhambra). In this respect these gardens all correspond to the important defining principle of so much Islamic art, that of the abstraction of motifs originating in nature: nature itself becomes the work of art – in the arabesque as well as in the art of the garden.

Garden in the fortress palace of Amber, Rajastan, 17th century

Iran: Safavids and Qajars

Dome of the Shah Mosque in Isfahan, begun 1611
The construction of the Shah Mosque in the main square, the Maidan, was intended by Shah Abbas the Great to emphasize Isfahan's role as the religious center of his empire. The huge dome and four *iwans* are clad in glazed green and blue tiles, while the geometric and plant motifs and the surrounding bands of calligraphy are gold and white.

History

Markus Hattstein

Shah Ismail and the beginnings of the Safavids

The coming to power of the Safavids in 1501 marked the beginning of the modern era in Persia. They created a well-organized and durable state which ended some 250 years of continual political fragmentation and foreign rule by Mongols, Timurids, and Turkomans. The Safavid dynasty also brought increasing uniformity to the population structure, creating a kind of Iranian national state, and its decisive adoption of Twelver Shia laid the foundations for Iran's specific religious development, which has continued until the present day.

The beginnings of the Safavids date back to the destruction of central religious authority by the Mongol invasions in the mid-13th century, which gave added impetus to a mystical, regional form of "popular Islam" and to various Sufi sects. Around 1300, Sheikh Safi (1252–1334) founded his own order, the Safawiya, in Ardabil in eastern Azerbaijan. This rapidly increased in popularity and became the focus of a mass religious movement and yearnings for social and revolutionary salvation. Safi and his direct successors were strict Sunnites until the order adopted the principles of Twelver

Iskandar doing battle against Darius, Persian miniature from the work of Mir Ali Shir Nawai, 16th century, Paris, Bibliothèque Nationale
During the rule of the Safavids, Iran developed its own special form of Islamic culture. This trend also favored the realization of the old Iranian heritage in art. In this miniature, for example, we see Alexander the Great fighting against the Persian king Darius III.

Shia in the mid-15th century and became increasingly militant in its doctrine.

Sheikh Junaid (1447–1460) sent missionaries to various neighboring countries and established a Turkoman military leadership within the Safawiya, whom he subjected to his religious authority. His son, Sheikh Haidar (1460–1488) wanted to create his own state, based on an order of knights, in Azerbaijan, and created a uniformed troop known as the Qizilbash ("redheads" or "red caps"), because they wore red turbans with 12 folds representing the 12 imams.

When Haidar invaded neighboring Circassia in 1488, his son Ismail was one year old. He was brought up in the strict spirit of the Shia, and soon became master of the order. As a boy, he developed a strong sense of his vocation and an imposing presence that would distinguish him as a ruler. Throughout his life, he sought to convey his religious enthusiasm to others, and was a passionate poet and brilliant propagandist of his own cause. In 1499, at the age of 12, he decided to seize power in Iran. He and his fanatical followers advanced from the province of Gilan on the Caspian Sea across eastern Anatolia to Tabriz. After Ismail's victory against the Circassians, the Turkoman Aq Qoyunlu ruling in Iran fled as he advanced. In August 1501 he arrived in Tabriz and established

Safavid rule. By the year 1507 he had also conquered Iraq and defeated the Uzbeks to the east; in 1512, the whole territory of the Aq Qoyunlu and the rest of Persia were under Safavid rule.

In his domestic policy, Ismail ignored the advice of his closest followers and the opposition of much of the population by imposing Twelver Shia as the state religion. He summoned Shiite scholars from throughout the Islamic world and drove the Sunnites out of Persia, at the same time providing generous promotion opportunities to those who converted to Shia. In this way, he created a theocratically legitimized absolute monarchy, but as the shah he also remained the master of the Safawiya order. Like the previous Turkoman dynasties, the Safavids were confronted with the problem of reconciling two population groups within the empire. The military elite of the Turkoman Qizilbash emirs (the "Lords of the Sword"), which was organized into tribal federations, demanded a share of power in return for its previous support for the Safawiya. The shah was increasingly dependent on the domestic Persian administrative elite in the chancelleries (the "Lords of the Pen") to maintain the new state. Shah Ismail and his successors operated an active policy of maintaining the balance of power, but it took them a long time to limit the dominance of the Qizilbash emirs. They therefore increasingly favored the old Iranian elite of officials and large landowners, and thus the "nationally resident" element,

against the tribalism of the Turkomans.

The Safavid victory had created unrest among both the Uzbeks to the east and the Ottomans to the west. Although Ismail avoided provoking the Turks during his conquests, the Turks engaged in bloodthirsty persecution of all those in Anatolia with Safawiya sympathies. The warlike Sultan Selim I (1512–1520) invaded Persia and his superior troops inflicted a devastating defeat on the Persians at Caldiran in August 1514. As a result, eastern Anatolia finally fell to the Ottoman Empire. After this date, relations between the Safavids and the Ottomans ranged from lasting mistrust to open hostility, but the Persians had to recognize the superiority of Turkish weapons. When Shah Ismail died in Tabriz in May 1524, he left a difficult inheritance to his successors, not all of whom possessed his religious charisma.

His son Shah Tahmasp (1524–1576) was still a child, so the Qizilbash emirs initially ruled on his behalf. However, their violent mutual hostility played into the hands of their external enemies; 1524–1537 battle raged with the Uzbeks to the east over the province of Khorasan, and 1530–1555 with the Ottomans to the west over Azerbaijan. As the Ottomans steadily advanced, Tabriz, which was occupied for a time, became an exposed border city. Shah

Tahmasp, who in 1533 took over the reins of power himself, therefore in 1548 made Qazvin in the Iranian highlands the new capital of the empire.

In 1537, the shah forced the Uzbeks to make a peaceful withdrawal from Khorasan, and a peace treaty with the Ottomans in 1555 gave Azerbaijan to the Safavids but resulted in the loss of Iraq. He created buffer states in the border regions and then gradually incorporated these into the empire. Tahmasp also made successful expeditions to Georgia, which he occupied in 1554 and turned into a Safavid province. From this point onwards, he increasingly recruited Georgians and other Caucasians to lead his army, beginning the military reform which would be completed by his grandson, Abbas I. The loss of Anatolia favored the nationalization and Iranization of the Safavid culture which occurred under his government. Tahmasp was prudent but had a tendency to bigotry. He cleansed the official Shia of the revolutionary and eschatological elements introduced by his father, and encouraged Persian book painting, which reached its first high point during his reign.

After Tahmasp died, in May 1576, the empire was ruled by his sons, the bloodthirsty Ismail II (1576–1577) and Muhammad Khudabanda (1578–1587), who was almost blind and was unable to rule. It came to the

Dovecotes near Isfahan
The dove is revered as the bird which Muhammad took with him on his *hegra* to Medina; it was also regarded as an erotic symbol in Islam, as in ancient Greece. Dove breeding was very popular among the more culturally sophisti- cated elements of Safavid society, and was often practised in great style. Large tower-shaped dovecotes were built near towns and cities, and the birds were looked after by specially trained workers.

brink of the abyss when the Ottomans occupied Georgia and Kurdistan in 1578 and various provinces declared their autonomy from central government. The court was governed by the Qizilbash emirs, whose murderous violence claimed the lives of the shah's wife, the grand vizier, and the crown prince. Major reforms were long overdue when the governor of Mashhad appointed one of Muhammad Khudabanda's younger sons, the ten-year-old Prince Abbas, as shah in 1581, replacing his father. Abbas was under the protection of the governor, who eventually, in 1587, marched on Qazvin with his troops.

Shah Abbas the Great

When Prince Abbas arrived in Qazvin with his patron in October 1587, his father immediately handed over the reins of power to him. He took to the task enthusiastically and, as Abbas I, known as "the Great" (1587–1629), he became Persia's most important shah. Despite some setbacks, he unswervingly held to his goal of giving Iran a new face. In 1590, he ended the war against the Ottomans which had been raging since 1578, and gave them Azerbaijan, Iraq, parts of Kurdistan, and Tabriz in order to have a free hand domestically and reorganize the Persian army. By 1598 he was able to reconquer the whole of Khorasan from the Uzbeks, and then he turned on the Ottomans. He annexed the island of Bahrain in 1601, occupied Azerbaijan in 1603, and by 1608 had reconquered Shirvan, Armenia, and Georgia. After a victory near Tabriz in 1623/24, he was finally able to annex Kurdistan and Iraq to the Safavid Empire once more.

Despite these brilliant military victories, Abbas the Great's real successes were in domestic policy, and particularly in his consistent centralization of all areas of public life, which led to a huge increase in royal power. The first aim of his thorough military and administrative reforms was to neutralize the Qizilbash emirs; following the Ottoman example of the Janissaries, he created a cavalry and a standing army consisting of the sons of Christian Georgians, Circassians, and other Caucasians. These were effectively military slaves (*ghulam*), who as *shahisawani* ("men loyal to the king") personally served the ruler and were paid direct from the royal treasury. Most of the later provincial governors and military commanders came from their ranks, as the shah was able to build on their loyalty.

Abbas I wanted to bring together all the available productive energies in Persia, and following his campaigns he settled over 70,000 Armenians and 100,000 Georgians in Iran. As a result the Caucasians, and particularly the Georgians, became the third ethnic component of the Safavid Empire, which lessened the differences between Turkomans and Persians and created a new basis for the political elite. By giving newly created government posts to Caucasians, the shah was emphasizing that rank was no longer determined by origin, but was his to award. Abbas also subjected the more distant provinces of the empire to central control, made a number of them direct possessions of the crown, and incorporated the last remaining buffer states from the time of his grandfather into the empire. The court of the king was now the sole center of the empire.

In 1598, in order to demonstrate the new importance of the court, Abbas made Isfahan the capital of the Safavid Empire and turned the city centered on its great square, the Maidan, into one of the most imposing metropolises of the Islamic world, and described as the "Pearl of Islam" or "Half of the World." He created economic prosperity by settling Caucasian craftsmen and artists in their own districts or suburbs, and by bringing Jewish and Christian merchants and artisans into the country and granting them wide-ranging cultural autonomy, in order to make use of their economic power. His court workshops produced crafts of all kinds for export, significantly increasing the wealth of the court. In addition, he developed excellent economic and diplomatic relations with other countries, particularly Mughal India, the Crimean Tartars, and the court of the Russian czars. Abbas created a single coinage, reformed the leasehold and tax systems, and in 1622 seized the trading port of Hormuz in the Persian Gulf from the Portuguese, replacing it with the mainland port of Bander Abbas, from where he controlled trade in the Gulf.

Abbas's political foresight, religious tolerance, and spiritual openness freed trade, business, and the arts from all religious restrictions; at the same time he presented himself as a fervent Shiite, both in his public appearances and numerous religious endowments. He also allowed the clergy great freedoms, though these were clearly subordinated to his political goals. When Abbas the Great died in his summer residence of Ashraf in January 1629, Iran was a modern and firmly established empire which was at its economic and political apogee.

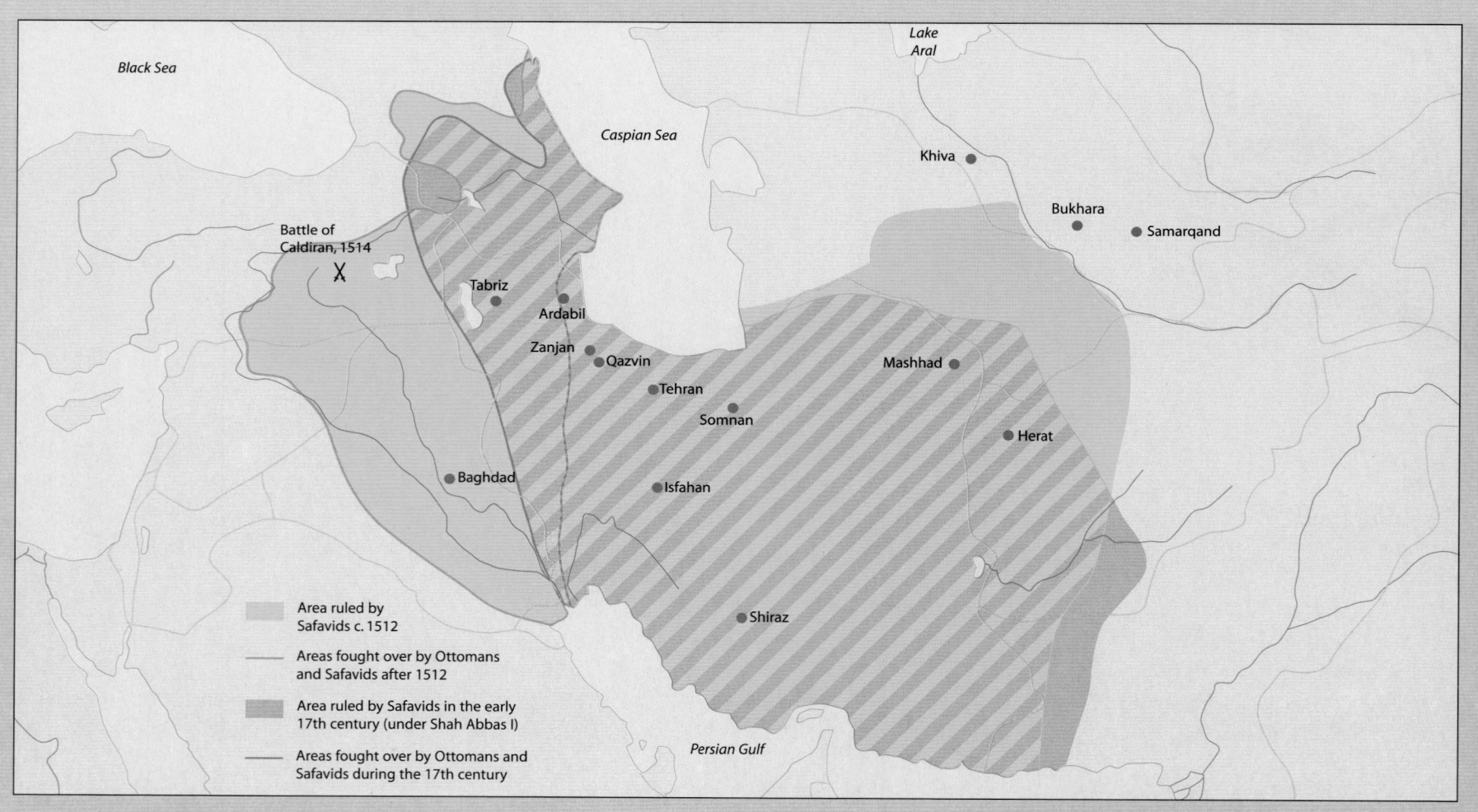

Area ruled by Safavids c. 1512

Areas fought over by Ottomans and Safavids after 1512

Area ruled by Safavids in the early 17th century (under Shah Abbas I)

Areas fought over by Ottomans and Safavids during the 17th century

The later Safavids

Abbas I fighting the Uzbeks, 1597 Fresco, Isfahan, Chihil Sutun Palace
The main enemies of the Safavids were the Ottoman Empire to the west and the Uzbeks to the east. After Shah Abbas I had consolidated his power internally, he led a number of successful campaigns against the Uzbeks, during which he expelled them from Khorasan and occupied this area.

In his dealings with his family, however, Abbas the Great made serious mistakes. Filled with mistrust, he had his sons brought up in the harem in a state of virtual imprisonment, and did not allow them any political education or preparation for the role of sovereign; he also had several of his sons and grandsons executed or blinded. From that time onwards, Safavid princes were either raised in an atmosphere of terror, intrigue, and rumor, or simply neglected so that most of them ended up as outcasts or suffering from severe mental disturbance. This was ultimately one of the reasons for the decline of the Safavid Empire.

Shah Safi I (1629–1642), Abbas the Great's grandson and successor, was one such personality. He had grown up under constant threat, and when he came to the throne he behaved with an extravagance verging on profligacy. His paranoia led him, by 1634, to have the remainder of his family, the military and administrative leaders, and the provincial governors removed. He withdrew himself completely from the public eye, took no part in government, and drowned his sorrows in wine, while the country was governed from 1634 onwards by the grand vizier Mirza Taqi, an administrator of great integrity and experience. The Ottomans, who had exploited the change of government in 1629 to attack and occupy Armenia, took Baghdad in 1638; this city remained occupied by the Turks until the First World War. In 1639, Mirza Taqi signed a peace treaty which finally brought the war between the Safavids and the

1301	Safawiya order founded by Sheikh Safi	1598	Khorasan recaptured; Isfahan becomes the new capital of the Safavid Empire
1501–1512	Shah Ismail (1501–1524) drives the Turkoman Aq Qoyunlu out of Iran and establishes Safavid rule; Twelver Shia becomes the state religion	1601–1624	Safavid territory expanded westwards to include Bahrain, Azerbaijan, Shirvan, Armenia, Georgia, Kurdistan, and Iraq
1514	Battle of Caldiran: the Safavids defeat the Ottomans	1629–1642	Reign of Shah Safi I
1524–1576	Reign of Shah Tahmasp	1638	The Ottomans capture Baghdad
1548	Capital of the empire is moved from Tabriz to Qazvin	1639	New peace treaty between Ottomans and Safavids
1554	Georgia becomes a Safavid province	1642–1666	Reign of Shah Abbas II
1555	End of the Ottoman–Safavid war (Peace of Amasya)	1648	Safavid Empire is extended to include Afghanistan
	Azerbaijan falls to the Safavids, and Iraq to the Ottomans	1666–1694	Reign of Shah Safi II, under the name of Sulaiman from 1668 onwards
1578–1587	Reign of Shah Muhammad Khudabanda	1694–1722	Reign of the last Safavid shah, Sultan Husain
1578	The Ottomans capture Georgia and Kurdistan from the Safavids	1722	The Afghan Ghalzai tribe capture Isfahan; their leader, Mahmud, becomes the new shah
1581	Khorasan becomes autonomous. Governor of Mashhad proclaims Prince Abbas as shah	1736–1796	Reign of the Afsharid Nadir (1736–1747) and Shah-Rukh (1748–1796)
1585	Ottomans take Tabriz	1750–1779	Karim Khan Zand rules central and southern Iran under the title of *wakil* (regent)
1587–1629	Reign of Shah Abbas I		

1779	The Qajar Agha Muhammad takes control of northern Persia	1890	Tobacco riots: the population rebels against exploitation of Persia by the European powers
1786	Tehran becomes the Qajar capital	1906	Persia becomes a constitutional monarchy
1796	Agha Muhammad Khan becomes shah of Persia	1907	Treaty between Britain and Russia: Persia divided into zones of influence
1797–1834	Reign of Fath Ali Shah		
1813	Treaty of Golestan: end of the war between Tehran and Russia over the Caucasus region (1804–1813). The Caucasus falls to Russia	1908–1909	Civil war in Tehran, Shah Muhammad Ali (1907–1909) deposed
1828	Treaty of Turkmanchai: end of hostilities between Tehran and Russia (1826–1828); further areas fall to Russia	1909–1925	Reign of the last Qajar Shah, Ahmed Mirza Shah (in exile from 1923 onwards)
1834–1848	Reign of Muhammad Shah	1914–1917	Persia occupied by the British and Russians during the First World War
1848–1851	Efforts at modernization made by Nasir al-Din Shah (1848–1896) and the grand emir Mirza Taqi Khan	1921	Coup by Reza Khan, officer in the Cossack Brigade
1848–1852	Riots by the Babi movement, whose leader, Ali Muhammad Bab, is executed (1850)	1925	Reza Khan appoints himself as shah of Persia under the name of Reza Shah Pahlavi
1856–1857	British prevent the Qajars' attempt to capture Herat; Persia recognizes Afghanistan's independence in the Treaty of Paris (1857)		

Ottomans to an end. The vizier followed Abbas the Great's policy of increasing integration for the Georgians, who were resettled and encouraged to operate businesses.

Safi's son Abbas II (1642–1666) had been brought up in a similarly harsh manner to his father, but was a strong and active personality who displayed his power through elaborate courtly ceremonial and magnificent receptions. He ran the government himself, increased the crown's possessions, and secured roads and trading routes. He also encouraged economic exchanges with the European trading companies, particularly the British East India Company, which were allowed to set up branches and given their own jurisdiction. His battle against corruption and cronyism and for greater prosperity meant that improving the legal system was one of his particular concerns. Under Abbas, the Safavid cult of the king and the state evolved until the role of the shah as supreme head of the Safawiya order was completely overtaken by that of the absolutist ruler legitimized by God. Abbas promoted the more apolitical philosophers, mystics, and Sufis, partly to create a counterweight to the political influence of orthodox Shiite legal scholars.

As the second most important political official, the grand vizier was also responsible for supervising the court's factories, which gradually took over the administration of all the crown's assets. The shah deliberately maintained the balance of power through this dual administrative function. The last few years of this able leader's reign were overshadowed by increasing mental disability caused by inherited syphilis, which led him to pursue a bloodthirsty persecution of his family.

His son Safi II (1666–1694) was another victim of a harem upbringing: although pious, peace-loving, and a connoisseur of the arts, he was also ostentatious, lazy, and cut off from those around him. Although destroyed by drugtaking, he returned to the throne in March 1668 in response to an astrological prediction, taking the name Shah Sulaiman and leaving the job of government to the eunuchs of the harem, who formed a kind of secret council. Essential political reforms were not carried out, and the Uzbeks and other neighboring peoples were able to conduct raids on Persian territory unhindered.

The reign of his son Sultan Husain (1694–1722), the last ruling Safavid, was marked by continued mismanagement, but for different reasons. The shah was a peaceable, friendly and restrained leader, but he was also fanatically religious. The senior Shiite clergy, who had already acquired significant influence during his father's reign, now became all-powerful. Under their domination, the

Shah Abbas the Great receiving a legation, c. 1650, Fresco, Isfahan, Chihil Sutun Palace Abbas I's skilled economic policy created prosperity. The European powers and Indian Mughals developed good business relationships with the Safavids. The painting shows the shah at a magnificent banquet in honor of a legation, with musicians and dancers as entertainment

shah persecuted the philosophers, mystics, and Sufis who had been promoted by his grandfather, and unleashed fanatical campaigns of forcible conversion on Sunnis, Jews, Christians, and other religious minorities. The result was a climate of religious intolerance which was untypical of the Safavid Empire, and soon made the government unpopular. This was not helped by huge tax increases and the creation of new taxes intended to stem the country's economic decline and boost falling government revenues.

The Shiites' forcible conversions were particularly opposed by the Sunnis of the new Afghan part of the empire, the province of Qandahar. This had been annexed in 1648, and had previously enjoyed wide-ranging cultural autonomy. After the shah had his Georgian troops quash a revolt, the Afghans, led by the Ghalzai tribe, deposed all of the shah's officials and soldiers stationed in Afghanistan and regained *de facto* autonomy in 1709. In 1719, the Ghalzai, under their leader Mahmud, attacked Persia and took one city after another, eventually laying siege to Isfahan in April 1722. The city was starved into surrender the following October. Sultan Husain was forced to hand over power to Mahmud, who named himself shah before being executed in 1726.

Troubled times: Nadir Shah and Karim Khan Zand

The Ghalzai became involved in factional infighting, and the territory descended into chaos, providing the Ottomans with an opportunity to capture the western part. They divided this between themselves and Russia. From 1722 onwards, the rest of the empire was ruled by ambitious army commanders who installed various Safavid princes, mostly children, as puppet rulers.

It was against this background that General Nadir, who came from the Turkoman Qizilbash tribe of the Afshar, rose to power as one of the greatest conquerors in the history of Iran. He drove the Afghans out of Isfahan in 1726, and from the whole of Persia in 1730, in the name of a Safavid puppet, and recaptured Azerbaijan and the Caucasus from the Ottomans. In 1736 he deposed the shah and ascended the throne himself as Nadir Shah (1736–1747). He then moved the capital to Mashhad.

In 1738 Nadir Shah occupied Afghanistan, and in the following year he reached Delhi, where he plundered the vast treasures of the Mughals, seizing the "Peacock Throne," which became the symbol of the shah of Persia. He then went on to subjugate Khiva and Bukhara. Unlike his aggressive political expansion, his religious policy aimed to achieve reconciliation with the Shiites of his empire, which inevitably involved a move away from radical Shia. In 1741, towards the end of Nadir Shah's reign, a conspiracy by his closest advisers was uncovered. He was already a cruel figure, but the discovery led to outbreaks of senseless violence, and in June 1747 he was assassinated by his own Afshar emirs. The empire immediately collapsed; Afghanistan and Azerbaijan became independent, and Nadir's blind grandson Shah-Rukh (1748–1796) had to limit himself to his own Afshar state in Khorasan, with Mashhad as its center.

In central and southern Iran, the military leader Karim Khan Zand (1750–1779) established the Kurdish dynasty of the Zand, based in Shiraz. This was the first domestic Persian dynasty after nearly 1,000 years of foreign rule. Instead of usurping the title of shah, Karim Khan officially became the "regent" (*wakil*) of a Safavid puppet ruler. His was a successful and peaceful period of government, and as a gifted statesman he developed closer trading ties with India via the Persian Gulf, granted tax cuts to the peasants, and constructed factories and irrigation canals. The period of peace ended with his death in 1779, when his successors began making war on one another and in 1794 fell victim to the Qajars.

Butcher's shop in the Isfahan bazaar, miniature from a manuscript by Sultan Husain, Iran, 1590. Berlin, Museum für Islamische Kunst Shah Abbas made Isfahan his capital in 1598 and, through the judicious settlement of merchants and craftsmen, made it one of the most important cities in the Islamic world. The bazaar in Isfahan became the principal trading center of the empire, particularly for carpets and textiles.

The rule of the Qajars

The Qajars were originally Turkoman nomads who controlled the northwest of Iran, but their military aggression eventually brought the whole country under their control. Their leader, Agha Muhammad Khan, had been castrated as a child by Nadir Shah's successor; hence the eunuch's title, "Agha." He had then been held as a political hostage by Karim Khan Zand, but escaped in the year 1779 after the latter's death. He gradually broke down the domination of the Zands, and in 1786 made Tehran the capital of his rapidly expanding empire. After the removal of the last Zand ruler in 1794 and successful campaigns in Azerbaijan and Armenia in the following year, he made himself shah of Persia in 1796. He used harsh means to establish centralized power, and bequeathed a united Persia to his successors when he was murdered in 1797. However, along with his successors, he failed to achieve control over the country's severely damaged economy, which was increasingly falling into European hands.

Nadir Shah

painting, c. 1740, London, Victoria and Albert Museum
Nadir Shah (1736–1747), from the Turkoman Qizilbash tribe of
the Afshar, was a successful army commander who drove the
Afghans out of Persia before ascending the throne himself in
1736 and becoming the most important Persian conqueror
of the modern era. In 1738/39 he occupied Afghanistan and
parts of Transoxiana and penetrated into India as far as Delhi.
Unpopular for his cruel and mistrustful nature, in 1747 he fell
victim to a conspiracy by his emirs.

Karim Khan Zand

Persian miniature, 19th century, Paris, Musée du Louvre
The Kurdish tribal leader Karim Khan Zand (1750–1779)
established a peaceful government in the south of Iran, based
in Shiraz. He did not adopt the title of shah, but functioned
officially as the "regent" of a Safavid puppet ruler. Karim Khan
developed closer trading links with India and made Shiraz into
an important center of culture and commerce. After his death
in 1779, his successors became involved in bitter power
struggles which destroyed the empire they had inherited.

Fath Ali Shah, painting, 19th century, London, British Library
The Qajar Fath Ali Shah (1797–1834) was politically dominated
by the European powers, particularly Britain.

Agha Muhammad's nephew and successor Fath Ali Shah
(1797–1834) developed close diplomatic ties with the European powers and
began creating a greater awareness of Persia's pre-Islamic past. He also built
a particularly close political relationship with the British, who regarded
their involvement in India as being endangered by an increasingly strong
independent Afghanistan. Despite British support, after military defeats Persia
lost the Caucasus to Russia in the treaties of Golestan (1813) and
Turkmanchai (1828); Russian influence and funds were competing with
the British in Iran. The guiding force behind the Persian policy was the enlightened heir to the throne, Abbas Mirza, who was determined to modernize the
country but died in 1833.

His son Muhammad Shah (1834–1848), who followed his grandfather
onto the throne, turned his attention eastwards. With Russian support
he became militarily involved in Afghanistan and Central Asia, but was forced
by the British to withdraw. His attempts to revive the country's economy and
create a counterweight to Britain and Russia by signing treaties with smaller
European powers such as Belgium and Spain enjoyed little success. At home,
since 1840 the shah had been using harsh measures to suppress the Babi
movement, the forerunner of the Baha'i religion; in 1852, after a failed assassination attempt on the shah, its adherents were almost completely wiped out.

During the long reign of Nasir al-Din Shah (1848–1896), the economy
came wholly under European control. This placed the shah at odds both with
the powerful liberal merchant classes, who sought an end to autocracy and a
greater say in politics and the economy, and also with the Shiite clergy, who
accused the shah of being dependent on Europe. After long hesitation, he
awarded the British the concession to build a railway and industrialize the
country, but was then forced to withdraw this under pressure from the
merchant classes. The Islamic reformer Jamal al-Din al-Afghani (1838–1897)
was in Persia 1886–1890, and his opposition to the Europeanization of the
Islamic rulers and the selling out of the country made the mood even more
volatile. The awarding of the tobacco monopoly to Britain's Major Talbot in
1890 lead to localized riots and lasting opposition to the shah from intellectuals, merchants, and religious leaders. The shah was eventually assassinated by
supporters of Afghani in 1896.

The government of his son Muzaffar al-Din Shah (1896–1907) was very
much affected by the "tobacco riots" and the struggle by the Persian upper
classes for a modern constitution. The exploitation of the country's natural
resources by the European powers and a general increase in bread prices led to
further unrest, while the government was ruining the country by obtaining
loans from Russia, which in return received various monopolies and Persia's

Nasir al-Din Shah on a European chair, painting, 19th century, Paris, Musée du Louvre
Nasir al-Din Shah (1848–1896) became increasingly unpopular at home due to his admiration for Europe and his awarding of trading monopolies and concessions to European powers. Accused of selling out Persian interests, he was assassinated in 1896.

Ahmad Mirza Shah, early 20th century, Tehran, J. Sonstil collection
The last Qajar ruler, Ahmad Mirza Shah (1909–1925), came to the throne when he was a child, but was kept away from any political influence by parliament and by the British occupation of Persia. In 1925 he was deposed by Reza Khan, who made himself shah, and went into exile in France, where he died in 1940.

customs revenue. In October 1906, the newly elected parliament (*majlis*) forced the shah to accept a constitution, making the country a constitutional monarchy. In 1907 Britain and Russia ended their struggle for influence in Persia with a treaty which divided it into a British zone in the southeast, a Russian zone in the northwest, and a neutral area.

In 1908, Shah Muhammad Ali (1907–1909) ordered his Russian Cossack brigades to attack the elected parliament, which caused riots in Tehran. These grew into a civil war and forced the shah to flee the country. As his son Ahmad Mirza Shah (1909–1925) was still a child, the parliament assumed power. During the First World War, Persia became a pawn of the European great powers. Large sections of the country were occupied by the British and Russians in 1918, and there were revolts by the Shiites in the south of the country. In 1919, the British forced Persia to adopt the status of a British protectorate, though this was diluted down in 1921.

Since 1921, the commander of the Cossack Brigade, Reza Khan, had been preparing a coup. The brigade was the country's most important military unit, so he also had the function of war minister. Using an energetic policy of reform modeled on that of Ataturk, in 1925 he caused parliament to depose the last Qajars and send them into exile, and made himself shah of Persia.

Architecture

Sheila Blair, Jonathan Bloom

The Safavid Empire through the eyes of travelers

From the 17th century on, a succession of European travelers visited Iran. They came for several reasons. Perhaps the most important was the new European interest in trade with the East. For example, the East India Company of London was chartered on December 31, 1600, and the Dutch East India Company followed within two years. In addition to Persia's commercial advantages, Europeans thought of the country as a natural ally against their common enemy, the Turks, for Persian rulers, especially Shah Abbas (1587–1629), were perceived as tolerant of Christians. As more travelers reached Persia, reports filtered back to Europe about the wonders of the country and its new capital Isfahan. People in Elizabethan England, for example, regarded Persia as a land of great pomp and luxury. These reports encouraged more Europeans who had the financial means to travel in this age of prosperity to make the long and arduous journey there.

European travelers to Safavid Persia were a motley band, ranging from ambassadors to adventurers. Most were young, and many came under their own steam. They came from various countries by different routes: over the Zagros Mountains from Baghdad or across Anatolia, up from the Gulf or down from Russia. The writers and illustrators are the ones we know the best and care about the most, for they offer a wealth of information about Safavid Persia and its arts.

The first European to reach Persia in this period was Sir Anthony Sherley, a self-appointed emissary from Queen Elizabeth of England to Shah Abbas. He arrived in Qazvin in December 1598 with a party of 26. Sir Anthony received a royal reception and struck up a warm friendship with Shah Abbas. This splendid treatment was the exception, however, and many other foreigners were ignored. When Charles I of England sent a return embassy to Iran, including Sir Anthony's younger brother Robert, they became embroiled in a diplomatic incident over credentials and were received coldly by Shah Abbas.

Shah Mosque in Isfahan, from Pascal Coste, *Monuments modernes de la Perse*, c. 1841
The French architect Pascal Coste published his impressions of a visit to Persia in 1839 with detailed documentation. Here he shows the inner courtyard of the Friday mosque that Shah Abbas had built on the edge of the Maidan. On the left is the main *iwan* and the dome over the *mihrab*; on the right is the west *iwan*, crowned by an aedicule, from which the muezzin issued the call to prayer.

Robert Sherley died in Persia, and the leaderless embassy found its way back home, where one member, Thomas Herbert, wrote a vivid account of life at the Safavid court.

The next to arrive was the Roman nobleman Pietro della Valle, a scholar and romantic, who was seeking solace from a broken heart in travel. He went first to Istanbul and then to the Holy Land, where he married. He brought his wife to Persia in 1616, struck up a friendship with Shah Abbas, and lived there for seven years. He wrote voluminous letters home to a friend in Naples describing his experiences; these, first published in 1650 as his *Viaggi*, fill seven volumes.

Other travelers were equally informative. Jean Baptiste Tavernier, son of an engraver from Antwerp, was an inveterate traveler who, between 1632 and 1668, made six journeys to or through Persia. Tavernier's *Six Voyages* reads like a modern-day tour guide: in addition to detailed descriptions of various routes, he includes chapters on currency, camels, caravans, and the like. Good on commerce, he was somewhat weak on antiquities. On his journey in 1644, he was accompanied by Father Raphael du Mans, a Capuchin father and mathematician who studied Persian and gathered information on the country and its people. This he published as *Estat de la Perse* in 1660, with the idea of helping the French minister Colbert form the French India Company. There were many religious missions from Europe to Iran: French Capuchins, Spanish and Italian Carmelites, and Portuguese Augustinians. Their respective governments often underwrote these religious missions since they formed part of the burgeoning interest in establishing trade links with the East.

The embassy sent by Frederick II Duke of Holstein, which arrived in Isfahan in 1637, was secretly commissioned to wrest the silk monopoly from the Dutch East India Company by diverting it through Russia. Since the Russian terms were unfavorable and the high duties made Persian silk too expensive, the mission was unsuccessful. The leaders tried to turn their secret rade mission into a political one and spent nine months in the Safavid capital. The mission's official chronicler, Adam Olearius, left an account of the journey and thorough descriptions of Isfahan's buildings and the ceremonies held in them.

The doyen of 17th-century travelers to Persia was Jean Chardin. Son of a wealthy Huguenot jeweler in Paris, Chardin went to Persia to make money selling jewels. He lived in Isfahan for 18 months (1666–1667) and again for four years (1672–77). During this time, he learned Persian thoroughly and recorded what he saw systematically, so that he is the most reliable and accurate of all the European travelers. He set out, for example, to compile a complete record of every quarter of Isfahan. To do so, he formed a research team comprising the Dutch agent in the city, two mullahs (who were charged with recording mosques, off-limits to foreigners), and various friends. Chardin also hired an artist to draw sketches. The ten-volume journal of these travels

Men's costume, engraving from Sir John Chardin, *Travels in Persia*, 17th century
Sir John Chardin, the son of a Huguenot jeweler, spent over five years in Iran and recorded many details of daily life in the report of his travels, which was illustrated with engravings. The chapter on clothes includes several pictures of men and women dressed in Persian costume. Men, he recounted, wore a pair of long underpants which hung to the ankles but had no feet, a long shirt, a waistcoat, and a robe. Various styles of dress are depicted in this engraving.

was initially a popular failure but has since become the major European source for life in Isfahan at the time.

The Swedes became interested in Iran at the end of the 17th century. The most important mission was that sent by Charles XII in 1682, which reached Isfahan in March 1683. It was led by the Dutchman Ludwich Fabritius, the German physician Engelbert Kaempfer served as a secretary. The mission made no headway with Shah Sulaiman (1666–1694), so the mission returned to Sweden. Kaempfer, remained and, at the suggestion of Father Raphael, the doctor entered the service of the Dutch East India company and served in the Gulf for four years before departing for Japan. Kaempfer's book, *Amoenitatum Exoticarum* (On Exotic Delights), published in his native Lemgo in 1712, gives a portrait of Shah Sulaiman and detailed descriptions of the Persian system of government and the duties of court functionaries. It also includes a remarkable bird's-eye-view drawing of the palace grounds in Isfahan.

Cornelius le Bruyn, another inveterate traveler to the Orient, arrived in Isfahan in 1704, and became friendly with the agent for the Dutch East India Company, who had lived there for 21 years. Consequently, le Bruyn's account is generally reliable and is supplemented by plates made from his own drawings.

Many of the travelers repeatedly cover the same ground, with descriptions of topography, flora, and fauna. They often speak about the Armenians, no doubt because of their relative accessibility to European Christians. Most, although not all, travelers were tolerant toward, but not very interested in, Islam. In terms of art and architecture, the accounts of European travelers are most important for their descriptions of the new capital, Isfahan. They speak little about mosques, which were closed to foreigners, and their accounts of palaces, parts of which were private, are rather confusing. By contrast, they provide much information about public architecture.

The most impressive sight for foreigners in Isfahan was the city's great new public square or Maidan, and many travelers give vivid accounts of the parades, polo matches, and other activities that took place there. At the north end of the Maidan near the entrance to the bazaar was a coffeehouse, which is still in operation. Coffeehouses became widespread in Persia at this time as places where well-to-do men and intellectuals could meet and talk. The one in Isfahan was no exception, and many travelers came there to learn the latest news. The foreigners were also fascinated by the layout and neatness of the bazaars, where certain industries or trades were concentrated in specific areas. In general, they praised local artistic achievements, such as carpet making, tilework, and metalwork, although they have little to say about the local art of painting, which was being transformed as artists began to adopt unfamiliar European pictorial conventions.

European travelers also mention caravanserais, public baths, bridges, monasteries, the now-vanished gardens along the main avenue known as the Chahar Bagh, and the Hazar Jarib, the park that lay at the end of it on the other side of the river. Similarly, travelers' accounts are useful in reconstructing now-destroyed houses. Chardin, for example, rented a house on the east side of the Maidan (great square) that had belonged to a rich courtier and Tavernier describes the bird-and-flower paintings that decorated the interiors. The accounts of some European travelers are sometimes verbose and gossipy, but they provide a good corrective to those of the Safavid court chroniclers, who were paid to put forward the official position.

The tomb complex at Ardabil and the development of Safavid architecture

With its abundant grasslands, Azerbaijan in northwestern Iran had become the leading province of Iran in the Mongol period. Ardabil was a regional center in the northeast, located some 110 miles (180 kilometers) east of Tabriz on the slopes of an extinct volcano. It was the home of a local Sufi order, which Sheikh Safi al-Din (1252–1334) transformed into an international religious movement whose propaganda (*dawa*) extended as far abroad as Ceylon. Safi al-Din himself wielded some political influence at the Mongol court, and by the beginning of the 16th century his lineal descendants and successors as heads of the Safaviya order had increased their political power and authority to the extent that they ruled over a theocratic state whose territories matched the borders of modern-day Iran. To mark their claims of sovereignty and establish their legitimacy as rulers, the Safavids expanded and rebuilt the family tomb complex at Ardabil, making it one of the largest in the realm, matched only by the shrine around the tomb of the eighth Imam Reza at Mashhad in the northeast of Iran.

The tomb complex at Ardabil has as its focus the Haram Khana, the cylindrical tomb tower erected over the grave of Sheikh Safi by his son Sadr al-Din. Adjacent, to the east, is the Dome of the Princes, the tomb of Muhyi al-Din (d. c. 1324–1325), Safi al-Din's eldest son who predeceased his father. These two buildings served as the nucleus of the tomb complex, with several service structures to the north, such as a rectangular hall known as the Dar al-Huffaz and a large octagonal building. Under Safavid patronage, the tomb complex was enlarged until it contained some 30 structures, loosely strung out around a garden and a paved courtyard in front of the two tombs.

Safavid work on the dynastic tomb complex at Ardabil began in the early 16th century. The dynasty's founder, Ismail (1501–1524) visited the site three times, beginning in the spring of 1500, to seek the assistance of his ancestors before launching his bid to seize power. The first building added to the site in Safavid times was the small domed tomb that marks Ismail's grave. The tiny building 7.5 × 8.5 feet (2.4 × 2.65 meters) was squeezed between the Haram Khana and the adjacent Dome of the Princes; the tomb's location, and its form and decoration, which echo those of Safi al-Din's tomb, emphasize Ismail's connection to his ancestors. The Safavid tomb, with a fine cenotaph marking the grave, may have been ordered by Ismail himself or, more likely, by his son and successor Tahmasp (1524–1576), who was responsible for the first major expansion of the tomb complex.

Tahmasp visited Ardabil twice, first in 1535 and again the following summer. The official reason, according to the ruler's own memoirs, was that he did so in response to a vision of Ali, the first Shiite imam. In the six years following the second visit, Tahmasp acquired major properties around the earlier tombs. The main building constructed on this land was the huge Jannat Sarai. An octagonally shaped building about 20 times the area of Ismail's tomb, it occupies a commanding position at the east end of the great inner courtyard. It was probably intended as the ruler's tomb, though, in the confusion and rivalry following Tahmasp's sudden death in 1576, he was hastily buried in the palace at Qazvin and his body was moved several times. The large octagonal tomb would have been a fitting culmination to the series of large imperial mausoleums built by the rulers of Iran, most notably the tomb of the Mongol sultan Üljaitü at Sultaniya. Tahmasp also ordered fine fittings for the tomb complex at Ardabil. The most famous was the magnificent matched pair of medallion carpets dated year 946 of the *hegira* (1539/40). The Jannat Sarai is the only space at the tomb complex large enough to house

these gigantic carpets, which, when laid side by side, formed a square 35 feet (10.67 meters) each side.

The tomb complex at Ardabil was expanded for a second time by Shah Abbas I. The monarch visited it three times in the opening decade of his reign, in the context of battles against the Ottomans in Azerbaijan. In the last years of the 17th century, however, his interests turned elsewhere. Not only was he occupied with his new capital Isfahan but his attentions were also directed eastward against the Uzbeks. In 1596/97, in the face of the Uzbek threat, Abbas ordered his grandfather Tahmasp's bones dug up from where they had been reinterred in Mashhad and reburied at the shrine of Ali Zain al-'Abidin in Isfahan.

At the beginning of the 17th century Abbas transferred his attentions back to Azerbaijan. Between 1604 and 1608, in the course of several military campaigns against the Ottomans, Abbas visited the tomb complex at Ardabil repeatedly, combining these trips with the bestowal of major gifts and renovations to the tomb complex and also to that at Mashhad. The bequests included the estates and personal property, as well as tax revenues. Ardabil received many items of jewelry, weapons, horses, sheep, and goats, but the gifts that are best known, at least to art historians, are the manuscripts and the porcelains.

Aerial view of the Maidan at Isfahan
The centerpiece of the new capital laid out by Shah Abbas at Isfahan was the large public square or Maidan. On the north side (top) is the portal to the bazaar that connected the new city with the old. On the west (left) is the Ali Qapu, the entrance to the palace precinct. Facing it on the east (right) is the small Sheikh Lutfallah Mosque. The largest building lies on the south: the great Friday mosque known as the Shah or Imam Mosque.

According to the endowment deed (*waqf*), the library at Ardabil received histories, poetry anthologies, and Persian literature in general, whereas Mashhad was given copies of the Koran and scientific works in Arabic. The different endowments show the esteem in which the Safavids held the two shrines: the former dedicated to a member of the Safavid family and the latter to a member of the Prophet's line. The books gifted to Ardabil include many of the most famous illustrated manuscripts from the Safavid period, such as the copy of Jami's *Haft Aurang* (Seven Thrones), transcribed for Tahmasp's nephew Ibrahim Mirza between 1556 and 1563 and a copy of Attar's *Mantiq al-Tair* (Language of the Birds).

Abbas's gift to the tomb complex at Ardabil also included a huge collection of Chinese porcelain, amounting to a staggering 1162 pieces, many of them very large. The collection included 58 celadons, 80 white wares, as well as other monochrome and polychrome wares, but the most important objects in the collection were the 400 or so pieces of blue-and-white porcelain. Most pieces bear an inscription in a rectangular cartouche, which was engraved into the glaze and names the donor. To house the objects deeded to the tomb complex, Abbas also ordered restorations to several of the buildings there. For the porcelain, he rebuilt the large octagonal building that had been constructed on the east side of the complex. Befitting its new function, it became known as the "Chini Khana" (Porcelain House). According to Jalal al-Munajjim, chief astronomer at Shah Abbas's court, the porcelain was transferred to Ardabil in September 1611. The interior of the building, which is richly decorated in gold and blue with multiple niches, tilework, and fine plasterwork, dates from this period.

Abbas also renovated the Dar al-Huffaz, the large rectangular hall where the Koran was read and which also served as a library. On the southern side of the hall, next to the cylindrical tomb tower of Sheikh Safi, Abbas had the raised platform known as a *shahnishin* enlarged, and also had new gold and silver fittings made for the doors and windows. He also had the interior of the hall redecorated with new gilding, painting, and plasterwork. An inscription running around the hall and *shahnishin* dates the work to 1627/28.

Further renovations by Abbas to the tomb complex centered on the Jannat Sarai, which had been badly neglected in the years since its construction. Water had seeped through the roof and so blackened the walls that the giant carpets may have been damaged. At the same time as the necessary renovations were carried out, the outer courtyard at the tomb complex was paved to serve as a walkway to the inner parts. Ranges of arches on both sides once contained the tombs of emirs, close companions, and the children of the sheikhs. The arches were originally decorated with some of

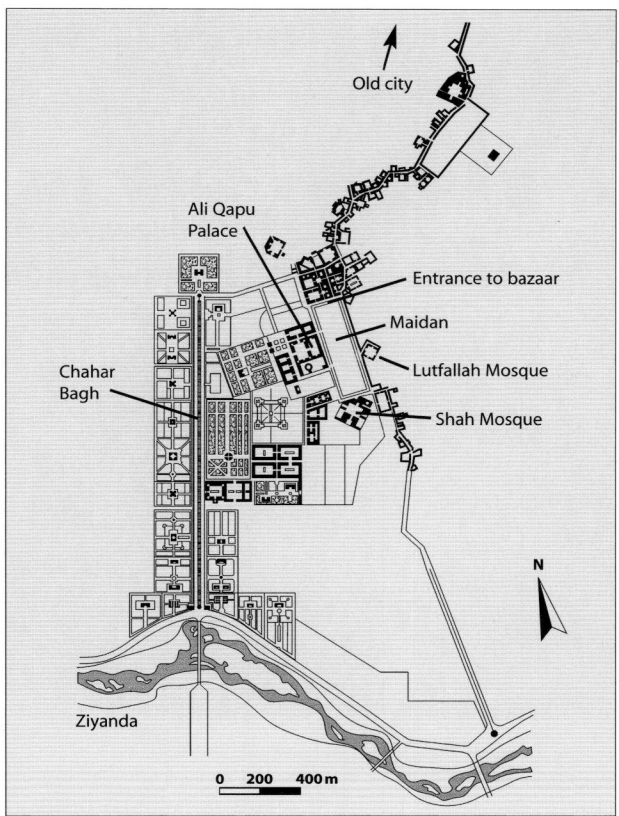

Map of Safavid building in Isfahan, from 1590
When Shah Abbas moved his capital from Qazvin to Isfahan c. 1590, he laid out a new city quarter to the south of the old city. A long bazaar connected the old city with the new maidan, or royal square. To the west (left) lay the palace precinct, which stretched westward to the Chahar Bagh, an avenue that ran north-south to the river.

the finest tile mosaic from the Safavid period, although little of it remains intact today.

The nearby tomb of Sheikh Safi's father, Sheikh Jibrail (d. 1358/59) was also restored by Abbas. Located one and a half miles (3 kilometers) north of Ardabil in the nearby village of Kalkhuran, the tomb has a pentagonal entrance and square tomb chamber surmounted by a tall, bulbous dome. Although it owes its form and function to Timurid tombs in Central Asia, it probably dates from the early 16th century. It was redecorated under Abbas in 1620/21. Like the shrine of Safi al-Din, the tomb for his father was famed for its costly carpets, gold and silver lamps, and fine inlaid work.

All the repairs undertaken by Abbas at Ardabil had symbolic as well as practical motivations. He consciously used endowments as political instruments to shore up his two main claims to legitimacy. By restoring the tomb of Imam Reza at Mashhad, he championed the Alid cause; by renovating the complex at Ardabil, he strengthened his own family line.

Arcades in the Maidan in Isfahan, from 1600
Trade was the economic foundation of Safavid life, and its importance is clear from the refitting of the great square in the new capital at Isfahan. The Maidan was originally intended for state ceremonies and sports but, within a decade of its construction, two stories of shops were added around the perimeter and let at low rents to attract reluctant merchants to relocate from the old city center.

Isfahan: the Pearl of Islam

The greatest act of architectural patronage undertaken by Abbas was his relocation of the capital to Isfahan. This was not the first time that the Safavids had moved the capital. Tabriz had been the Safavids' original capital, but in 1555, under the threat of an Ottoman invasion, Tahmasp had moved the capital 250 miles (400 kilometers) away from the frontier to Qazvin. Constant pressure from the Ottomans on the west frontier, as well as from the Shaybanids on the east, led Abbas to relocate it again in the 1590s. Transferring the capital away from the insecure borderlands to the center of the country was part of Abbas's policy to consolidate Safavid political and religious authority, develop state capitalism, and establish Safavid Iran as a world power.

Isfahan had already been capital of Iran in the 11th and 12th centuries under the Seljuks, and many buildings from that period survive in the north of the city. As part of his city planning program, Abbas relocated the commercial, religious, and political center of the city south-southwest toward

Lutfallah Mosque in Isfahan, 1603–1619
The main building on the east side of the Maidan takes it name from the Sufi sheikh Maisi al-Amili. It is called a mosque in its foundation inscription over the doorway, but its exact function is unclear. The illustration below shows a detail of the dome cladding, one of the most beautiful of its era, which is decorated with a spiral arabesque in blue and white.

Dome of the Lutfallah Mosque in Isfahan, 1603–1619
Although the portal was restored in the 20th century, the interior of the mosque is virtually untouched and shows the splendors of Safavid tilework. At the apex of the dome is a sunburst, from which descend tiers of ogive-shaped medallions, which swell in size with the curve of the dome. The medallions are decorated with floral motifs which play against the monochrome ground. The scattered light makes the composition invoke the whirling firmament.

the Ziyanda River. The heart of the new city was the large rectangular maidan (1700 × 520 feet 512 x 159 meters), known as Naqsh-i Jahan (Design of the World). Conceived, planned, and constructed between 1590 and 1595, the new public square was originally intended for state ceremonies and sports but, in a second phase completed by 1602, the Maidan was redeveloped for commercial purposes. Two stories of shops were added around the perimeter and let at low rents to persuade reluctant merchants to relocate from the premises in the old city center.

The Maidan was the feature of the new city that most impressed foreign travelers. Covering 20 acres (8 hectares), it was far larger than contemporary plazas in Europe. They praised it for its sheer size and its architectural homogenity and described it as a great square overflowing with life, from the bazaars and a backdrop of pageantry and ceremonial splendor. A stone channel ran around the perimeter of the square at a short distance from the arcade and separated the space for walking from the central area, which was originally unpaved and covered with gravel. The covered walkway and the outer arcades served as a bazaar. The great central space housed the stalls of merchants, craftsmen, barbers, and entertainers, but it could be cleared for military parades, drill by the shah's personal militia, archery contests, polo matches, and festivals. At night 50,000 earthenware lamps hung from thin poles in front of the buildings to illuminate the square.

The bazaar portal

The entrances to four buildings are set around the Maidan, rather like the four-*iwan* plan writ large. On the north sits the majestic portal to the bazaar, consisting of a high *iwan* flanked by two stories of vaulted galleries, which housed the *naqqara-khana*, or music pavilion, where a court orchestra played daily on trumpets and drums. The decoration on the portal reflects Abbas's preoccupations in founding the new city. The spandrels of the *iwan* are covered with tile mosaic depicting Sagittarius, under whose astrological sign Isfahan was founded, set on a ground of floral arabesques. The interior faces of the *iwan* have faded frescoes showing Abbas's victories over the Shaybanids.

The portal leads to a two-storied bazaar, the *qaisariya*, the selling place for fine textiles, which were the mainstay of the Safavid economy. Behind the portal lay a domed node, known in Persian as a *chaharsu* ("four directions," or "four bazaars"). To the east lay the royal mint; to the west, the royal caravanserai, with 140 rooms, was the largest in the city. It had space for cloth merchants on the ground floor, and workshops and stores for jewelers, goldsmiths, and engravers above. To the north and east, a grid of lanes intersecting under domed spaces led to more caravanserais, baths, and a hospital. The covered bazaar stretched for over a mile (nearly 2 kilometers), linking the new Maidan with the old one near the Friday Mosque.

The Lutfallah Mosque

Soon after the Maidan was completed, Abbas ordered a new building erected on the east side. The Lutfallah Mosque, which is dated by an inscription from 1603–1619, takes it name from Sheikh Lutfallah Maisi al-Amili, the distinguished scholar and teacher who came to Isfahan at Abbas's request and took up residence on the site; the mosque was only named after him later, after his death in 1622/23. In plan, the mosque comprises a single domed room 63 feet (19 meters) each side. The basement contains another room of almost the same dimensions covered with low vaults resting on four octagonal piers. Since it

contains a *mihrab*, the domed room is aligned with the *qibla* and set at an angle approximately 45 degrees from that of the main facade. When viewed from the Maidan, the dome is to the right of the main portal. The exterior of the dome is covered in a spiraling arabesque set against an unusual tan ground. It contrasts with the portal *iwan*, ablaze with blue glittering tile – most of it added in the mid-20th century during restoration under Reza Shah Pahlavi.

The portal of the Lutfallah Mosque gives access to a corridor which passes around two sides of the sanctuary, so that one enters the main room opposite the *mihrab*. Emerging from such a dark, twisting corridor, the interior of the mosque is a huge contrast, for the vast, glowing room is probably the most perfectly balanced interior in all Persian architecture. In elevation, the room consists of the standard tripartite arrangement of square base, octagonal zone of transition, and dome, but the two lower stories have been integrated by arches outlined with a cable binding executed in light blue tile and a magnificent inscription band in white on a dark blue ground. The only other example of such vertical integration is the north dome added to the Friday Mosque in Isfahan in 1088, and Safavid architects may have taken their cues from their Seljuk predecessors. As in the earlier example, the dome of the Lutfallah Mosque is a single shell, one of the very few in Safavid architecture.

What sets the interior of the Lutfallah Mosque apart from its Seljuk prototype – and from all other interiors in Safavid architecture – is the exquisite tile decoration. The apex of the dome is filled with a giant sunburst, from which descend tiers of ogival medallions filled with floral motifs, which swell in size with the curve of the dome. Light streaming through the screened windows flickers across the glazed surfaces. The dado and some of the upper wall surfaces are revetted with tiles painted in carpet patterns; their flat surfaces are distinguished from the tile mosaics, whose uneven surfaces scatter light. The architecture and decoration are so fine that the craftsmen are credited in

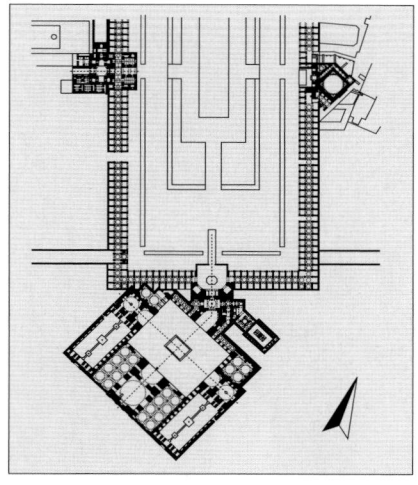

View and ground plan of the Shah Mosque in Isfahan, from 1611
The largest building on Shah Abbas's new Maidan in Isfahan was a Friday mosque. Its large portal, flanked by minarets, was set in the middle of the south side on the Maidan. The mosque itself had to face Mecca, so it is set at a 45° angle to the portal, so that the *mihrab* can correctly mark the *qibla*, the direction of prayer. The mosque uses the four-*iwan* scheme, with a central courtyard surrounded by two-story arcades linking four *iwans*.

the inscriptions. The architect was Muhammad Riza, son of the master Husain, the builder from Isfahan; the inscriptions were designed by the royal calligrapher Ali Riza-yi Abbasi. The exact function of the building is rather puzzling. In the foundation inscription over the entrance portal, it is called a mosque (*masjid*), but the building lacks the standard accoutrements such as a courtyard, side galleries, *iwans*, or minarets. The plan fits better within the long-established Iranian tradition of large domed mausoleums, but no one is known to have been buried there. Some scholars have called it a royal chapel, but this type of building is unknown in Iranian architecture and the mosque is across the Maidan from the palaces of the royal family.

The Shah Mosque

On the south side of the Maidan, opposite the bazaar portal, sits another similar portal, also comprising an *iwan* flanked by two stories of galleries. It gives access to a monumental mosque, which was founded by Abbas to replace the Friday Mosque in the center of the Seljuk city. It was known for centuries as the Shah Mosque but has recently been renamed the Imam Mosque. Begun in the spring of 1611, construction of the new Friday (congregational) mosque was not finished until about 1630 under Abbas's successor Safi (1629–1642), and the alabaster dadoes were not installed until 1638. The building was endowed by the shah with agricultural and commercial properties in and around the city, and both the building and its generous endowment were another aspect of Abbas's plan to shift the city's commercial and religious center away from the old area near the Friday Mosque and to the newly constructed district.

Winter prayer hall of the Shah Mosque in Isfahan
The congregation had covered prayer halls for inclement weather. The *iwan* and domed room on the *qibla* side were flanked by rectangular prayer halls, each with eight small domes carried on piers. Whereas the portal of the mosque is covered in the expensive technique of tile mosaic, the upper surfaces of the prayer halls are clad in *haft rang* (*cuerda seca*) tiles (above), a method used to cover large surfaces.

The entrance vestibule of the Shah Mosque is aligned with the Maidan, but the rest of the building, like the Lutfallah Mosque, is turned approximately 45 degrees to face Mecca. The large building 330 × 430 feet (100 × 130 meters) is laid out along the lines of the typical plan used for Friday mosques in Iran: it has a central courtyard 230 feet (70 meters) each side surrounded by arcades, with an *iwan* in the middle of each of the four sides and a domed prayer hall beyond the *iwan* on the *qibla* side. The plan is distinguished from many by its unusual concern for symmetry, possible only because the shah could acquire as much land as needed for his royal construction.

The plan of the Shah Mosque has several other noteworthy features, which reflect Abbas's concerns in founding a new Friday mosque. As in several mosques built by the Timurids — most notably the Bibi Khanum Mosque, erected by Timur in Samarqand — the lateral *iwans* in the Shah Mosque also lead to domed chambers. In addition, the domed prayer hall in Isfahan is flanked by vaulted rectangular chambers that serve as winter prayer halls, while on either side of the central court are arcaded rectangular courts that function as *madrasas*. By controlling the appointments to teaching positions in the new Friday mosque, Abbas was able to control the clergy, just as his Seljuk predecessors had done in building new *madrasas* throughout the realm. In the Shah Mosque, as in the Bibi Khanum Mosque, paired minarets soar from both entrance portal and sanctuary *iwan*, but in Isfahan the call to prayer was given from an aedicule, known in Persian as a *guldasta* ("bouquet"), over the west *iwan*. Such an aedicule is common in later mosques and shows that such tall minarets were unsuitable for the call to prayer. To the left of the vestibule is a domed quincunx and another arcaded courtyard containing latrines. The presence of such large areas devoted to ablution and personal hygiene suggests that Abbas anticipated large crowds visiting the mosque.

The entrance portal of the Shah Mosque displays the finest tile decoration in the building. It is entirely executed in tile mosaic in a full palette of seven colors (dark blue, light blue, white, black, yellow, green, and biscuit). A wide inscription band with religious texts written in white *thuluth* script on a dark blue ground frames the *iwan*, and a cable binding in light blue springing from alabaster vases frames the arch. Glittering tiers of *muqarnas* fill the half-dome, some panels of which are decorated with stars and vines scrolling from vases, while other panels, in the balcony over the doorway, are decorated with facing peacocks. Below, magnificent panels laid out like prayer mats flank the doorway, which is revetted with alabaster panels. Another inscription, with the foundation text, runs around the *iwan* over the doorway and below the half-dome; like the framing band, it is executed in white *thuluth* letters on a dark blue ground, but the patron's name in the center, directly above the doorway, is highlighted in light blue. The inscription ends with the name of the master calligrapher who designed it, Ali Riza, who also designed the inscriptions for the Lutfallah Mosque, and the date, year 1025 of the *hegira*, corresponding to 1616.

The rest of the Shah Mosque is decorated with tiles of poorer quality, probably because money was short and the spaces to be covered were vast. Above the continuous alabaster dado, all vertical surfaces on both exterior and interior are clad in polychrome glazed tiles, most of which were replaced in the 1930s on the basis of extant remains. The tile revetment is predominantly blue, except in the covered halls, which were later revetted in tiles of cooler, yellowy-green shades. In this technique of polychrome glazing, called in Persian *haft rang* ("seven colors"), and known elsewhere in the Islamic world as *cuerda seca*, a tile is painted with colors separated by a thin line of a greasy black substance which burns off in firing. The polychrome technique is much faster than tile mosaic, in which tiny pieces are cut from monochrome tiles and assembled to make designs, but the effects are not as dramatic. The colors are muted since they are all fired at the same temperature, and the tiles do not reflect light as variously as the small pieces in tile mosaic.

The crowning feature of the Shah Mosque is the enormous dome over the prayer hall. Rising 170 feet (52 meters), the dome is set on a 16-sided zone of transition and a tall drum. Unlike the dome over the Lutfallah Mosque, the one in the Shah Mosque has a double shell, with the exterior bulbous dome rising about 46 feet (14 meters) above the interior hemisphere. Derived from Timurid prototypes, this arrangement is best known from the tall dome used over the tomb of Timur in Samarqand. The dome, the exterior of which is tiled with a spiraling beige arabesque on a light blue ground, seems to float, despite its large size, above the other domed roofs of the mosque, which are left plain.

The Ali Qapu

The fourth building, set on the west side of the Maidan, is the entrance to the palace complex, the Ali Qapu ("Lofty Gate" or "Sublime Portal"). Unlike the three other buildings, it does not have a monumental portal since it was not a public building. Rather, it was begun by Abbas as a modest atrium for the royal gardens. Over the next 60 years, however, it was repeatedly modified and extended and the final building consists of a block 66 × 60 × 108 feet (20 × 20 × 33 meters) preceded by an entrance complex, itself surmounted by a columned veranda. This veranda (*talar* in Persian), is a traditional Persian form found already in the Achaemenid audience hall, or *apadana*, at Persepolis. Extending the Ali Qapu in front brought the building into alignment with the arcades added around the Maidan by 1602; adding the porch provided an elevated viewing stand for royalty and guests. The ingenuity and playfulness of Safavid court architects can be seen in the way they transformed the *talar* from a ground-level veranda into one towering two stories above the ground.

The complex and almost haphazard plan and elevation of the Ali Qapu reveals the additive nature of the structure. The main block is subdivided into five main stories and an intermediate one, and all differ markedly in plan. Many of the supporting elements do not continue from floor to floor. The main supports, which are massive on the lower floors, become lighter and thinner at the top. From the third floor they turn into hollow pilasters. On the fifth floor they are a network of thin arches from which a fantastic plaster shell is suspended. The shell is composed of *muqarnas* niches painted with geometric and arabesque designs and pierced with the shapes of the Chinese porcelain and Safavid lusterware that the shahs collected. The shell played an acoustic as well as a decorative role in distributing sound, as the room was used for evening entertainments and is now called the "music room." The functions of other rooms in the building, such as the reception hall with water tank and fountain on the level of the *talar*, can be easily determined, but it is unclear how many of the smaller rooms were used. They were once richly decorated with wall paintings, most of which, only faintly visible today, show scenes of a mildly erotic nature.

The Ali Qapu served as a gateway to a 17-acre (7-hectare) park dotted with small courtyards, walled gardens, and pavilions. The area adjacent to the royal Maidan housed the royal workshops, service quarters, administrative offices, and residential facilities for gatekeepers and eunuchs. Behind it was a more private area with several gardens and residences for the shah, his wives, and other members of the royal family.

View and section of the Ali Qapu in Isfahan, from 1590
The Ali Qapu ("Lofty Gate") sits on the west side of the new Maidan in Isfahan. It was originally designed as a modest entrance to the palace precinct. After the Maidan was remodeled at the beginning of the 17th century, the Ali Qapu was transformed into a royal viewing stand in the form of a *talar*, or columned veranda. Many of the supporting elements do not continue from floor to floor.

The Safavid garden palaces in Isfahan

The largest building in the palace precinct is the Chihil Sutun Palace, which was set in a walled garden aligned with the axis of the Maidan, so the nucleus of the building may have been part of the original urban design laid out by Abbas. The palace itself, however, was built under Abbas II (1642–1666) in 1647 and reconstructed in 1706, after it had been damaged in a fire the previous year. The palace is set behind a long reflecting pool 425 × 65 feet (110 × 20 meters) filled by water from fountains and jets. The building itself consists of three discrete parts. The front section is a *talar*, with 20 columns supporting a flat wooden roof. The name of the palace, Chihil Sutun ("Forty Columns"), is popularly thought to derive from the combined total of the 20 columns of the *talar* and their reflection in the long pool, but this interpretation is probably inaccurate, for the word "forty" in Persian simply means "very many." The *talar* leads to a deep porch flanked by rectangular halls, and at the back of the building is the main reception room, a large hall 75 × 36 feet (23 × 11 meters) covered with transverse vaults supporting domes. Shallow porches on the four sides open to the exterior. The intermingling of interior and exterior spaces was enhanced by the extensive use of glass, which dissolved the wall surfaces. The *muqarnas* vault in the entrance *iwan* was covered with small pieces of glass that deflected the light, and other panels were filled with larger expanses of full-length Venetian glass mirrors presented by the Doge.

Most of the interior surfaces in the Chihil Sutun are painted with murals. The small rooms flanking the entrance *iwan* have panel-like paintings so similar to those found in contemporary manuscripts and albums that some of the murals are attributed to Muhammad Qasim, who was one of the court painters of Abbas II. Some scenes are taken from literature, such as the well-known story of Yusuf and Zulaika. Others show languid youths, both Persian and foreign, picnicking in the country, drinking, pouring wine, chat-ting with cup and bottle in hand, reclining on cushions, or seated side by side under trees in open landscapes. Although set in an idealized landscape, these paintings depict activities that would have taken place in the gardens around the palace. By contrast, the main rectangular hall is decorated with four large historical murals showing a battle scene and three receptions for eastern rulers. In addition to the contrast in subject matter, the large murals differ dramatically in style from the small paintings. The large historical paintings are in a more Europeanized manner, with modulated light, shading, and perspective, whereas the small ones are in a traditional Persian style.

View from east and interior decoration in the Chihil Sutun Palace in Isfahan, from 1647
The Chihil Sutun ("Forty Columns") is the largest palace remaining in the royal precinct at Isfahan and is set in front of a reflecting pool in a walled garden. The reflection in the pool appears to double the 20 columns of the high veranda, which leads to an *iwan* and a great hall. Many interior rooms are decorated with splendid murals; those in the smaller rooms are similar to miniatures in contemporary manuscripts. The illustration on the left shows one of these paintings, in which young people are drinking together at a picnic in the country, pouring wine, and gossiping with cup and bottle in hand. Although the landscape is idealized, this doubtless portrays life in the palace gardens.

Right: **Detail of vault in Hasht Bihisht**,
Isfahan, from 1669

As in many palaces in Isfahan from the Safavid era, in the Hasht Bihisht a magnificent stucco *muqarnas* vault has been installed under the roof. The niches of the vault feature pierced ornamentation and painting. In the 19th century many were restored and decorated with mirrored glass. The vaults reflect light and sound, thus forming a connection between the interior of the palace and the outside world. This transparency effect was further amplified by a pool of water.

Below: **View from east of Hasht Bihisht**,
Isfahan, from 1669

This pavilion was added to the western section of the royal precinct at Isfahan under Shah Sulaiman. It comprises a central domed hall surrounded by four lateral *iwans* and rooms on the four diagonal axes. This plan, with eight rooms arranged around a central domed hall, gave rise to the name Hasht Bihisht ("Eight Paradises"), a pun on the eight heavens in Islamic cosmography. Already known in the 15th century, this plan was popular for many secular buildings erected in later times throughout the eastern Islamic lands, ranging from the pavilion known as the Cinili Kiosk in the Topkapi Palace, Istanbul, to the Taj Mahal in Agra.

Some scholars have attributed the different styles of paintings in the Chihil Sutun to different dates, but more recent research suggests that the two styles reflect the two different contexts and audiences for the paintings. The small paintings in Persian style were mainly in the private rooms, whereas the large murals decorated the audience hall which was used for festivities to celebrate Nauruz, the Persian New Year, and the formal reception of foreign dignitaries.

The choice of subjects for the large murals – the Safavid shah in discussion with his eastern neighbours – reflects Abbas II's preoccupations at the time with the eastern frontier of his empire. The large murals also reflect the complex and ceremonial audiences that had developed after the death of Abbas I. Visitors commented on the three-tiered hierarchy of seating, with the shah furthest from the entrance, governors, foreigners, and mid-rank officials in a second tier, and dancers and musicians at the bottom. These murals, then, give us an idea of contemporary audiences in the mid-17th century, but they also belong to a long tradition of official triumphs and embassies known in Iran and Central Asia from pre-Islamic times, ranging from Persepolis to the palace at Afrasiyab (Old Samarqand).

Hasht Bihisht

The other Safavid pavilion to survive in the palace precinct at Isfahan, the Hasht Bihisht ("Eight Paradises"), set in the Bagh-i Bulbul ("Garden of the Nightingale"), was erected in 1669 by Abbas III's successor, Sulaiman I. Located across the covered way, or hippodrome, that bisected the precinct diagonally, the garden is aligned not with the Maidan but with the axis of the Chahar Bagh avenue on the far side. The two-storied pavilion, measuring some 30 meters (100 feet) each side, consists of a central hall roofed with a *muqarnas* vault crowned by a lantern structure over the central basin. Large openings on four sides lead to porches facing the gardens, and small doors in the corners lead to groups of chambers on two stories. This plan, with eight rooms arranged around a central domed hall, gave rise to the name Hasht Bihisht, a pun on the eight levels of heaven in Islamic cosmography. Texts indicate that the Timurids and Turkomans had already built this type of palace in Herat and Tabriz in the 15th century, and the plan was also developed by the Mughals in India for imperial tombs such as the Taj Mahal.

Even more than its precursors, the Ali Qapu and the Chihil Sutun, the Hasht Bihisht palace exemplifies the intermingling of interior and exterior typical of Safavid palaces. From within, one can always see the garden outside, and from the gardens one can always see into the spaces within. Hydraulic systems fed a fountain in the central basin and cascades in the south *iwan* and beyond the north side, so that running water enhanced the interpenetration of volumes. So did light: the interior is lit from several sources, and light would have reflected off the shimmering water and the mirror mosaic in the ceilings.

Like the other buildings in the palace precinct, the Hasht Bihisht pavilion was richly decorated. A few tile panels with birds and animals survive in the spandrels on the exterior, and originally there must have been other, more elaborate scenes like the sets of seven-color tiles now removed to museums. Composed of multiple tiles, the large panels show male and female figures in garden settings. The languid youths offering food and drink are tile equivalents of the paintings on the interior of the Chihil Sutun. Much of the interior decoration in the Hasht Bihisht was redone in the 19th century, probably along the lines of the original work. Ceilings, like those at the Ali Qapu, were painted and covered with mirrorwork, and the Qajar ruler Fath Ali Shah (1797–1834) added large tiles showing himself enthroned between his sons.

The western edge of the palace precinct was marked by the long Chahar Bagh ("Four-fold Garden") avenue. This elegant boulevard, some 2.5 miles (4 kilometers) in length, was flanked by the palaces of the nobles, whom the shah encouraged to add fine buildings in the new capital. Water enhanced the garden effect, for the avenue was bisected by a canal punctuated by fountains and cascades and planted with flowers and trees – a three-dimensional realization on an enormous scale of a typical garden-design carpet.

Safavid bridges and the Armenian district of New Julfa

To the south, the Chahar Bagh avenue opens onto the Si-o Se Pol ("Bridge of Thirty-three Arches"), erected by Abbas's general Allahvardi Khan in 1602. A remarkable 985 feet (300 meters) in length, it has a passage for beasts of burden flanked by raised lanes for pedestrians. Projecting pavilions allow pedestrians to stop and enjoy the splendid view of the river. Though twice as long, it is not as complicated as the Khwaju Bridge, which crosses the river downstream. As with the Chahar Bagh avenue itself, the Si-o Se Pol combined aesthetic pleasure with practical functions, for the bridge linked the city to the important areas

Khwaju Bridge in Isfahan, 1650
Downstream from the Si-o Se Pol is the imposing Khwaju Bridge, which is set on a stone platform divided by sluices which allow the water to stream through the bridge. On the west, or upstream, side, the platform is divided into spear-shaped contreforts which break the river's flow. The two-storied bridge is wide enough for laden caravans to cross on the road in the center, while pedestrians can stroll through the arcades on the sides.

on the south side of the river. These included not only the great pleasure gardens on the slopes of Takht-i Rustam, Hazar Jarib ("Thousand Acres") or the Bagh-i Abbasabad ("Garden of the Abode of Abbas"), but also New Julfa, the economically important Armenian quarter.

In 1603, during his campaigns against the Ottomans, Abbas had encountered the Armenian community of Julfa on the left bank of the Araxes River. He was much impressed by the merchants and their city, which had emerged in the late 16th century as a major commercial center with an estimated population of 10,000–12,000, some 2,000 houses and seven churches, as well as mercantile connections stretching from Venice to India. In establishing his new capital at Isfahan, Abbas wanted to use the Armenians as intermediaries to control the silk industry, which was a state monopoly. Hence, in 1604, he ordered the Armenians to move from the valley of Ararat, on the war-torn borderlands of the northwestern frontier, to Isfahan, where he had a small township built for them on the south bank of the river. To gain the loyalty of these industrious merchants, Abbas allowed the Armenians of New Julfa their religious liberty under their own mayor and judges. In 1606, along with construction of the new town, they established Our Savior's Cathedral, which served as the center of Georgian Christianity in Persia. The prosperity of the Armenian population is reflected in the rebuilding of the cathedral between 1655 and 1664, when the original small church was turned into a monumental structure, with a magnificent altar preserving the relics of St. Joseph of Arimathea.

Buildings under Abbas's successors

Most of the new capital of Isfahan was planned during the time of Abbas, and only a few other buildings were added by later patrons. In 1656, for example,

Madar-i Shah Madrasa, Isfahan,
early 18th century
The theological school known as Madar-i Shah ("Mother of the Shah"), erected under Shah Husain in the early 18th century, was one of the few monuments built in Isfahan after its golden age under Shah Abbas. Set on the main thoroughfare of the Chahar Bagh, the complex included a caravanserai, stables, and a bazaar. The secluded courtyard, shaded walkways, and whitewashed plaster with the vaulting lines picked out in blue (below), evoke the quiet contemplative life that is still carried on in the *madrasa*.

Interior view of the vestibule dome in the Madar-i Shah Madrasa, Isfahan, early 18th century
The monumental portal of the Madar-i Shah Madrasa leads from the Chahar Bagh, the most important north-south street in Isfahan, into a domed octagonal vestibule. The Dome and walls are clad in glowing yellow, glazed bricks, which form the background for a geometrical linear decoration, which runs from the arch spandrels and from the center of the dome. The half-domes are decorated with kite-shaped shields, and the dome itself with a sunburst, whose rays end in 16 medallions.

the Hakim Mosque was built with funds sent from India by the court physician of Abbas II, who had fled to Mughal territory. Following the traditional four-*iwan* plan, this Friday mosque is notable for its size and its inscriptions, designed by the most famous calligrapher of the time, Ali Riza.

Most of Abbas I's successors had neither the interest nor the money to build major constructions in Isfahan, and only one major complex is associated with the patronage of later shahs: the ensemble known as the Madar-i Shah ("Mother of the Shah"), built by Shah Husain (1694–1722). Located just off the Chahar Bagh avenue, the complex included a large *madrasa*, as well as a caravanserai, stables, and a bazaar, whose combined revenues supported the charitable foundation. The buildings are set out on a rigidly symmetrical and axial plan. The *madrasa*, caravanserai, and stables are set in a row and connected by the bazaar, which runs along their north sides. The bazaar is a broad corridor 720 feet (220 meters) long bordered on both sides by arcades: the 260-foot (80-meter) stretch on the west lying against the back of the *madrasa* has deep recesses for shops, while the central and eastern parts have shallower booths.

The *madrasa* follows the traditional plan of four *iwans* grouped around an open courtyard. Like the Chahar Bagh itself, the courtyard is intersected by pools and pathways. It is surrounded by two stories of rooms for students. The domed chamber, set at right angles to the entrance and therefore not accurately aligned with the *qibla*, copies that of the Shah Mosque, although the tilework shows a notable decline from that of the previous building. There are large bands of simple checkerwork and almost no tile mosaic; the geometric designs are often coarse, and the palette includes a caustic yellow. Nevertheless, the courtyard of the Madar-i Shah Madrasa, with its shaded walkways, white-washed plaster with the vaulting lines picked out in blue, and shimmering tilework reflected in the pool, bestows an air of grace and serenity on the building far greater than its architecture might otherwise merit. The expansive scale, logical planning, and confident massing of forms in the complex returns to the precedent established by Abbas I in his layout of the city a century earlier.

Decorative Arts

Elke Niewöhner

The most beautiful Safavid works of art were book illustrations, and the finest examples of these were the miniatures produced under royal patronage in Persia during the first half of the 16th century.

This was before the development of the uniform style which dominated all art in Iran during the 17th century, evolving in the capital, Isfahan under Shah Abbas I (1588–1629). In the first few decades of Safavid rule, the established painting schools in Herat, Shiraz, and Tabriz continued to operate. But the influence of the capital, first Tabriz and then Qazvin, resulted in the creation of the very finest examples of this art. These included works such as the *Shahname* and Nizami's *Khamsa*, both produced for Shah Tahmasp I.

In 1501, during the conquest of Tabriz, the Safavids under Shah Ismail captured a painting workshop which had flourished during the Turkoman period, together with the works that were in progress there at the time. Manuscripts with exceptional calligraphy and illustrations were coveted treasures which were passed on not only from generation to generation, but also from one royal house to another.

Three surviving manuscripts contain miniatures from the time of Shah Ismail I (1501–1524). The history of one of these, a *Khamsa* (a collection of five epic poems) by the great Persian poet Nizami (1141–1209), demonstrates how much these beautiful books were coveted. It was begun in Herat for Abu l-Qasim Babur (1422–1457), the son of the great Timurid bibliophile Baisungur, but came into Turkoman hands and was continued under the aegis

Bahram hunting a lion, miniature from Nizami's *Khamsa*, Sultan Muhammad, Tabriz, 1539–1543, gouache, gold and silver on paper, 36.5 × 25.1 cm, London, British Library

The painter has portrayed the landscape in the new, more formal style, but the hunters and their prey are much excitingly alive.

Shirin's suicide, miniature from Nizami's *Khamsa*, Tabriz, c.1505, gouache, gold on paper, 29.5 × 19 cm, London, Keir Collection
The final scene from the epic of Khusrau and Shirin was added to the manuscript, which came from the Turkoman royal collection, during the first few years of the reign of Shah Ismail I. Women are shown mourning the dead Shirin inside the palace, while children and men with horses wait outside the gate.

of several princes. It then passed to an emir of Shah Ismail I, during whose reign a number of illustrations were added to the unfinished work. These are recognizable by the typical Safavid headdress, a pointed red cap usually wrapped in a turban cloth; but the painting style is no different to that of the earlier Turkoman style, with its strong sense of movement, luxuriant vegetation, elaborate architecture, and brilliant colors.

One of the best painters in this style was Sultan Muhammad, who worked on a *Shahname* (King's Book) produced during the reign of Shah Tahmasp between 1525 and 1535. The *Shahname*, an epic poem of approximately 60,000 verses written by Firdausi (c. 940–1020), is still today honored as the Persian national epic. The *Shahname* of Shah Tahmasp I was probably the largest book project of the 16th century. It comprised 742 large folios measuring 18.5 × 12.5 inches (47 × 31.8 centimeters), in which the generously illuminated text is surrounded by a broad, dotted gold frame. Of the folios, 258 have large, whole-page illustrations.

The Shah's personal interest in calligraphy and painting probably created the impetus for this project. While he was still a child, he was sent to Herat as governor, where he was taught by the masters of the famous, formerly Timurid painting school. When he returned to Tabriz at the age of 12, the celebrated painter Bihzad is reputed to have been in his entourage and to have been appointed as director of the royal studio there. Tahmasp himself enjoyed writing calligraphy, and was no mean proponent of this form of art, as one surviving manuscript shows.

It is not certain whether Bihzad actually came to Tabriz, but the influence of his rather more formal style began to appear in the exuberant paintings produced there around this time, as well as in the work of Sultan Muhammad. In Shah Tahmasp's *Shahname*, Sultan Muhammad depicts rocks, seemingly growing like crystal, and foaming like waves. In some cases, he painted imps and faces onto rocks and included animals.

The great *Shahname* was presented as a gift to the Ottoman sultan Selim II (1566–1574), and probably remained in the Ottoman collections in Istanbul until the beginning of the 20th century. In 1903 it came into the possession of Baron Edmond de Rothschild, and in 1959 it was sold to an American collector who had it taken apart and sold the individual illustrations at auction, thereby destroying the unity of an Islamic work of art which had remained intact for over 400 years.

Until the second half of the 16th century a whole book was regarded as a work of art, but not the individual miniatures. Individual painters therefore took a background role and only rarely signed their names elaborately within the picture. Only later did art lovers and connoisseurs begin ascribing the miniatures in a book to particular painters, for example in Nizami's *Khamsa*, a work originally intended for Shah Tahmasp I, dating from the years 1539–1543.

The text of this *Khamsa* was written by the most famous calligrapher of Shah Tahmasp I's era, Shah Mahmud al-Nishapuri, whose magnificent script earned him the epithet Zarin Qalam ("Golden Pen"). The artists were stated as being the masters Aqa Mirak, Muzaffar Ali, Sultan Muhammad, and Mir Musawwir, but only the name of Mir Musawwir appears as a signature on a wall in the miniature "Nushirwan in the ruins of a palace." The pictures ascribed to Sultan Muhammad show the influence of the Bihzad school of Herat; the rocks are more simplified and the composition more balanced than in earlier works.

This *Khamsa* was not completed during the reign of Shah Tahmasp I, and the manuscript was kept in the royal library as a highly valuable work of art. Eventually, more than 130 years later, the painter Muhammad Zaman (active 1649–1704) was commissioned to complete it. He added four of his own

Sam retrieving his son Zal from Mount Alburz, miniature from Firdausi's *Shahname*, Sultan Muhammad or one of his pupils, Tabriz, c. 1522–1525, gouache, gold and silver on paper, 28.2 × 18.5 cm Berlin, Museum für Islamische Kunst
The hero Sam has left his son Zal (who was born with white hair) out in the wilderness to die, but is ordered in a dream to ride into the mountains and find him. The mythical bird Simurg has saved Zal and placed him in its nest, and now persuades him to return to his father, who is approaching from the plains. The contrast between the wildness of the mountains and civilization embodied by the rider is emphasized by the composition and coloring of the painting.

miniatures in his typically modern, European-influenced style, and these look odd within the context of the whole work.

The reason why this magnificent production was not completed during Shah Tahmasp's reign was probably the fact that his interest in book art began to decline around 1545. He himself stopped writing and painting, and dismissed the artists working in his studio. One of these, the famous

The *aziz* (prime minister) and Zulaikha being greeted by the people as they arrive outside the Egyptian capital, Miniature from Jami's *Haft Aurang*, the story of Yusuf and Zulaikha, Iran, 1556–1565, gouache and gold on paper, 34.5 × 23.4 cm, Washington, Freer Gallery of Art

The beautiful Zulaikha, seated in a litter on the back of a camel and accompanied by elegantly dressed horsemen and maidservants, waits to be showered in gold coins in accordance with the traditional custom. The *aziz* is on horseback, and turns to receive a dish full of coins and precious stones.

blocks within the text in which the painter could then add a miniature. For the other 26 illustrations, the writers left out a few verses at the beginning of a new page and at the same time left a whole page for the miniature, which was painted separately on a different sheet. Then all the pages with text on both sides were inserted in double-layered colored frames, while those which were written on one side only had the appropriate miniature glued onto their backs. Only then were the remaining and still missing lines of text written onto the illustrations, and then the artists painted thousands of framing lines, lines between the columns of text, and triangular corner markings. After that the colophons, or formulas at the end stating the identity of the writer, were written, and the broad frame papers were then painted in gold with animal and plant motifs. Finally, all the pages were placed together in the right order, bound together with thread, and inserted in the cover of the book.

The process of producing a miniature also involved several stages. In most cases, the painter was given a sheet of paper which had already been written on, and with space left for a miniature. The theme of the illustration was evident from the lines of text on the page, which the painter could presumably read for himself, but it was agreed upon before hand, as most miniatures were usually based on existing examples illustrating the same themes in the same way.

Next, the painter designed the composition with a brush and thin black ink. The outlines were drawn using finely perforated templates which were placed on the blank page, and the design was either pricked out through the perforations or transferred to the page using powdered charcoal. Next, the painter inked in the final design using stronger black lines; errors were corrected using white pigment. Once the design had been fixed, the colors were added. Gold and silver were added first, as they contained a substance which dissolved the other colors if they came into contact with them while still wet. Next came the basic colors of the landscape and figures, details of vegetation and architecture, clouds, details of objects and of human and animal figures, and finally the faces of the people.

In most cases, it is not known whether a single artist carried out all these steps on his own, or whether the page was handed on from one specialist to another. The latter may very well have been the case in a large studio such as that of Shah Tahmasp's court. In the smaller centers of book production which continued to operate under the patronage of local nobles during the 16th century in provincial cities such as Shiraz, Mashhad, and Herat, and, of course, in independent workshops in the bazaar, a single artist would have carried out all the work and also made the cover at the end.

Research on Jami's *Haft Aurang*, which was produced for the provincial governor Ibrahim Mirza, shows just how long and difficult the creation of such a large work could be. Calligraphers who had already been recruited left Mashhad, where Ibrahim Mirza had his residence, because they had more important commitments elsewhere. They took with them the work they had started, and finished it in other cities. In other cases, such as that of Shah Mahmud al-Nishapuri, the writer was old when he accepted the commission and was unable or unwilling to complete part of the task, so new artists had to be found.

However, the role of artists was not simply confined to producing books. Both in commercial workshops in the bazaars and in studios at the court, they also designed patterns for other types of art including carpets and textiles.

Carpets were made in the Near East at a very early stage, but the first complete, dated examples produced in Tehran date from the 16th century. We know from pictures of carpets in miniatures that, at least from the 15th century onwards, they were professionally knotted based on patterns, since they include similar decorations to those in book illuminations and on book

calligrapher Shah Mahmud al-Nishapuri, was commissioned in Mashhad by Shah Tahmasp's nephew, Ibrahim Mirza (1540–1577), the royal house's greatest connoisseur and patron of the arts, to produce a work which is now in the Freer Gallery of Art in Washington. This was the *Haft Aurang* (Seven Thrones), seven verse epics by the poet Jami (1414–1492). Detailed examination has revealed that the book was produced in stages, and many different artists and craftsmen must have worked together to create an artwork of this quality.

Five different authors in three cities (Mashhad, Qazvin, and Herat) wrote the 304-page text. Only two of the 28 miniatures were produced in the manner generally used in illustrated books: the writers left empty rectangular

Ardabil carpet, signed by Maqsud Kashani, northwest Iran, 1539/40, silk and wool, 10.51 × 5.34 m London, Victoria and Albert Museum

This is regarded as the most famous of all Persian carpets. Together with an almost identical one in the Los Angeles County Museum of Art, it forms a pair which was probably made for the family shrine of the Safavids in Ardabil. Apart from the outstanding quality of the woollen knots on a silk warp, these two earliest surviving Persian knotted carpets bear their date of production knotted into a cartouche and the master's signature, and therefore play a key role in historical research.

covers. As the rectangular shape of a book is very similar to that of a carpet, it is not surprising that similar compositions and ornamentation were chosen. Usually, the surface was divided into a center area and a border, sometimes consisting of several bands of various widths. It was common for the center section to be divided into a central medallion and four corner sections. The surfaces were filled with intricate patterns, with the corner pieces often appearing as part of the medallion, thus creating the impression that the

latter had been divided into four quarters and one quarter placed in each corner.

Shah Tahmasp I established royal carpet and textile factories in a number of cities, including Tabriz, Kashan, Isfahan, and Kerman. It was in these, for example, that the famous pair known as the Ardabil carpets were produced. Unusually for textiles, these have the date, year 946 of the *hegira* (1539/40) woven into them. Their extraordinarily fine patterning could be created only by using very fine materials: silk for the warp and woof, and wool for the knots.

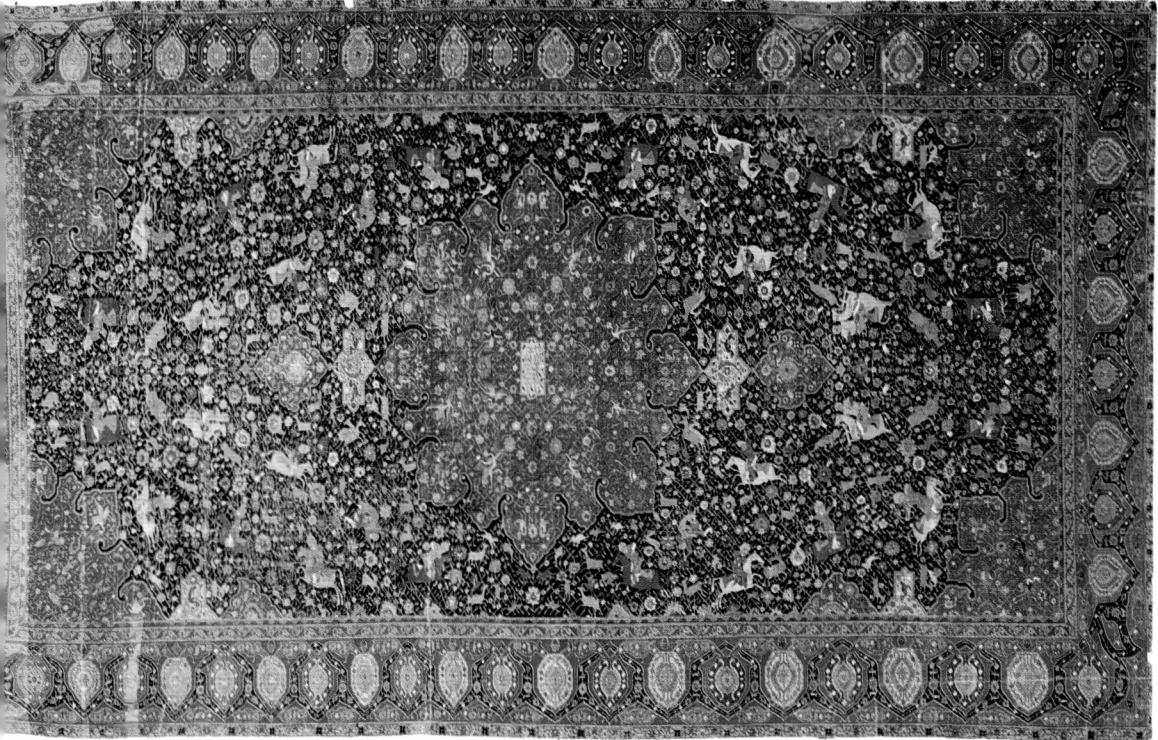

Hunting carpet, Giyath al-Din Jami, northwest Iran, 1542/43, wool, silk, and cotton, 3.35 × 6.82 m Milan, Museo Poldi Pezzoli

This carpet has a central medallion and four corner pieces with a symmetrical pattern of flying cranes and bands of cloud. The surrounding field is peopled with huntsmen on horseback and their prey, a very ancient motif in Iranian art. A cartouche contains the artist's name and the date.

Left: **Nasir al-Din Shah standing beside a cannon**, portrait by Mirza Baba al-Husaini, Tehran, c. 1850, gouache on paper, 72.8 × 23.3 cm London, British Library
The painter Mirza Baba came from the Imami family of Isfahan, which produced a number of lacquer and enamel painters during the 19th century. His work contains many elements of European painting. For example, he shows Nasir al-Din Shah in a short, European uniform tunic, while keeping the Persian Astrakhan' hat with its bejeweled plume, armbands, belt, and the sword just visible at his side.

Right: **Shahzada Muhammad Beg of Georgia**, portrait by Riza-yi Abbasi, Isfahan, c. 1620, Indian ink and watercolor on paper Berlin, Museum für Islamische Kunst
This young man gazing dreamily into the distance is identified by an inscription on the lower edge as a Georgian prince. His fur-trimmed robe appears to confirm his high rank. He is standing expectantly with one foot slightly raised and his hands folded over a knotted scarf in front of his body. During the reign of Shah Abbas I, many Georgians worked in royal service, and the best-trained formed an elite corps that was also used for administrative functions. Shahzada Muhammad may have been one of these.

The third dated 16th-century Safavid carpet is decorated with hunting scenes, has a cotton warp, and was made in 1542/43. It is now in the Museo Poldi Pezzoli in Milan. The piece depicts animals and humans in the same styles as miniatures of the time, and there is therefore no doubt that the design was based on examples from book studios.

Both the Ardabil and hunting carpets are medallion carpets. According to recent research, they were produced only three years apart, but they are very different. The Ardabil carpets are elegant and covered in color so that they are almost dark; the hunting carpet is brilliantly colored, but the angular tendrils in the background are less attractive than the spiral ones of the Ardabil carpets.

Shah Tahmasp's interest in book art suddenly declined in the second half of his long reign, which lasted from 1524 to 1576. He took some painters to his new capital city of Qazvin, where he finally settled in 1555, so that they could paint the interior of his new palace. However, the other artists were dismissed. Some found jobs with Ibrahim Mirza in Mashhad; others worked freelance in the bazaar, and others still went west to work for the Ottomans or east to the court of the Moghul rulers in India.

This emigration intensified after the death of Shah Tahmasp I. His son Ismail II took power for 18 months between 1576 and 1578, and had the art lover Ibrahim Mirza murdered along with most of the royal princes. During this short period, Ismail attempted to have a large *Shahname* made, but he no longer had access to such outstanding artists as his father had. A few pages of this uncompleted *Shahname* are now dispersed in various locations.

In the meantime, painters and calligraphers had discovered a new source of income. It was only a small step from producing individual pictures for books, and scenes or figures for carpets, silks, metal containers, and ceramics, to painting single sheets for sale. These could be produced relatively easily,

without the backing of a large studio, and sold on the open market, where there were always art lovers who could not afford to maintain a whole studio but were willing to buy pages by well-known artists. Connoisseurs could distinguish between the individual styles, but it became common for artists to sign their work.

During this period, for the first time in Safavid history, artists and scholars began considering the aesthetic aspects and content of painting. Until then, only calligraphy had been recognized as an art form; since it involved writing God's word, the Koran, it was regarded as having God's approval. Now, two artists and a scholar began supporting figurative painting, which had until this point always been condemned by orthodox religion. They cited the fact that Imam Ali, who had been revered by the Shiites, had been both a calligrapher *and* a painter. This happened in a state which had been founded with a Shiite emphasis, and in which one might have expected figurative representations to be condemned on religious grounds. Yet nonetheless it was precisely the highest political leaders who were the most enthusiastic supporters of painting.

The three proponents of figurative painting were Dust Muhammad, a painter and calligrapher during the reign of Shah Tahmasp I; Sadiqi Beg, a painter and poet under Shah Abbas I, and his contemporary Qazi Ahmad, a historian. They believed that figurative painting should be respected just as much as calligraphy. Sadiqi Beg was particularly interested in the practical aspects of painting; he divided art into different areas, and made a distinction between decorative and figurative painting. He believed that the former should confine itself to inanimate things such as tendrils, flowers, and geometric patterns; it should be used for such purposes as marginal painting, and should be based on the finest examples of work by earlier artists. Figurative

painting should depict animals on the basis of earlier examples too, but humans – and this was revolutionary in Safavid art – should be painted using direct observation from life. The aim should be to reproduce the inner nature of the individual, so that someone looking at the painting would have the same impression as the artist seeing the living person.

This statement indicates the direction which Safavid painting had taken during the second half of the 16th century, and which became the general mode during the subsequent period under Shah Abbas I (1588–1629). The shah was not simply another great patron of the arts. He used art to make political statements and in pursuit of economic objectives, encouraging the export of carpets and silk weaving to Europe as well as the production of blue-and-white Chinese-style ceramics, because this style was greatly sought after in Europe and Persian imitations could be sold at high prices. He reportedly recruited Chinese potters because, although Persian ones had been using Chinese motifs for a long time, they had transformed these into their own style and could not really compete with Chinese ware.

In 1599, Shah Abbas I moved the capital further inland from Qazvin to Isfahan, where he began a carefully planned and politically motivated construction program. Isfahan became not only the new political focus, but also a cultural center which influenced the styles of smaller provincial cities.

The reign of Shah Abbas I is particularly associated with the group of so-called "Polonaise" carpets, which were made in the royal factories. The shah liked to give them to European guests as gifts, and they were also commissioned directly by members of the European nobility. Some of them even had their coats of arms knotted in to the carpets; one document from 1602 states that Sigismund III Wasa, king of Poland, commissioned an Armenian to buy silk carpets for him in Kashan. He reportedly acquired six carpets, and then paid an additional five crowns to have the royal coat of arms added.

The term "Polonaise" was coined at the Paris World's Fair of 1878, and was actually based on a misunderstanding: a carpet was sent from Krakow bearing the coat of arms of a local family, and was therefore assumed to be Polish. Not until later was it realized that the carpet had been knotted in Safavid Persia.

Nearly all Polonaise carpets use a similar pattern of geometrically arranged, spiral tendrils with leaves and flowers. The patterns came from the royal studio in Isfahan, where the leading artist was now Riza, who called himself "Riza-yi Abbasi" to emphasize his close relationship with Shah Abbas I. At the beginning of the shah's reign, Riza was still working for the director of the royal studio, the painter Sadiqi Beg, on a *Shahname* which Shah Abbas had commissioned in the tradition of his forefathers. Riza then began specializing in portraits and small scenes on single sheets, for which he became famous. He introduced a new style distinguished by its very confident and fine brush-strokes and its inclusion of voluminous ribbons and turbans. Riza signed his works, in accordance with what was now common practice, and they can therefore definitely be attributed to him; although there were also some copies, these cannot have been intended as fakes but rather as copies in the modern sense. Since artists were now respected for their personalities, we can trace the path of Riza's life from historical sources, which is not the case with any earlier artists.

Like many Iranian painters, Riza came from a family of artists. His father Ali Asghar was a painter at the court of Shah Tahmasp I, and went to Mashhad when the shah dismissed his artists. Riza appears to have trained there, possibly even in the studio of the great patron of the arts Ibrahim Mirza. In 1595, when the *Shahname* he had been working on with Sadiqi Beg was completed, Riza must have been a member of the royal studio. The earliest known work bearing the signature "Riza-yi Abbasi" dates from 1603. He must have suffered some kind of crisis not long after this date, because he gave up his post at the court and began associating with some distinctly shady characters, whom he portrayed instead of the attractive young men and women from courtly society who had previously been his main subjects.

These courtly figures in the style of Riza-yi Abbasi soon became very widespread; no artist appears to have been untouched by his influence. They were used as patterns for other types of art on fabrics, metal containers, and ceramics. The art of silk weaving deserves special mention, because both the technique itself and the designs it used reached their zenith under Shah Abbas I. The fabrics combined figures in the style of Riza-yi Abbas with very finely drawn flowering plants and vignettes from courtly circles. There were silk-weaving mills in a number of Persian cities, and the shah sought to place them all under direct royal supervision so that he could maintain the trading monopoly; silk trading was one of the most important sources of income for the state, which, in practice, meant the royal house. For the same reason,

Women surrounded by flowering plants, Iran, first quarter of the 17th century, silk, gold, and silver threads with silver core, 207 × 103 cm, Leipzig, Grassi-Museum
The repeated female figure worked in velvet on this fabric is just about to make a movement; hence the position of her feet and the way in which she is grasping the cloth hanging down her back. This fragment, composed of six parts, is one of the finest examples of Safavid textile art; no other motif was woven in this selection of colors.

European trading companies, of which the best known was probably the British East India Company, were interested in silk trading. Their representatives and other European travelers were attracted to the country by an economic policy which deliberately encouraged exports, and the Europeans described Kashan and Isfahan as particularly important centers of silk manufacturing.

Ceramics were another medium for these pictures of often idealized courtly individuals. Motifs depicting dreamy-looking youths with wine bottles and elegantly clad women appear on plates, bowls, and bottles, as well as wall tiles. The latter were particularly suited for the representation of whole scenes in prosperous courtly settings, preferably amid a garden landscape.

The new style also appears on metal containers in the form of endlessly repeated systems of tendrils, animal friezes, and human portraits in medallions. Instead of the artists' signatures, which were usual on valuable metal containers even before the time of the Safavids, Persian poems became popular as inscriptions. These were placed in cartouches, together with the name of the container's owner. In some cases the space for the owner's name was left blank, which shows that these containers were made not only to commission but also for the open market, but that for some practical reason the name was never inserted. New types of containers also appeared that were very different from those of previous eras: large-bellied bowls with lids, pails with broadly spreading centers on narrow bases, and tall candlesticks with vertical patterning that were particularly typical of Safavid metalwork.

The first contacts with European painting occurred during the 16th century; for example, Shah Ismail I reportedly commissioned an Italian artist to paint the interior of a palace in Shiraz. Closer contacts developed during the reign of Shah Abbas I as a result of his very active trading policy. Missions from Europe brought paintings as gifts for the shah and other senior dignitaries, and a Dutch painter was appointed to the royal studio in Isfahan. This provided an opportunity for Iranian artists to become familiar with the European style of painting, with its use of central perspective and light and shade that was so different from the flatness of traditional miniature painting.

The first major painter in Persia to adopt these European influences in his work was Muhammad Zuman, who was active from 1649 to 1704. He was so respected as a painter that he was commissioned to paint the missing miniatures from the Nizami *Khamsa* which had been started during the reign of Shah Tahmasp I but not completed.

During the reign of Abbas I's successor, his grandson Safi I (1629–1642), the court studio continued to produce patterns for the factories which technically and stylistically were little different from those of the time of Abbas I. The painter Riza worked until his death in 1635, while his son Safi was the leading textile pattern designer during the reign of Shah Safi I's son, Abbas II. Riza's most prominent pupil, Muin Musawwir, distinguished himself by his skill at drawing and the themes of his pictures; some of his surviving drawings depict scenes from everyday life in Isfahan in an almost journalistic way. This was unusual in miniature painting, and may have been inspired by a knowledge of European pictures.

Ali Quli Jabbadar, a contemporary of Muhammad Zaman, also combined traditional miniature painting with clear European elements. He was mainly active during the reign of Shah Sulaiman (1666–1694), an eccentric man who was not interested in affairs of state but was a patron of the arts. The artist produced many portraits of him, since the European fashion for portrait painting had also arrived in Persia. The latest dated work by Ali Quli Jabbadar is a portrait of the Russian emissary to the Safavid court from 1716, during the reign of the last Safavid shah, the bigoted Sultan Husain. Although his

Tile picture, Isfahan, first quarter of the 17th century, quartz frit ceramic, painted and glazed, 198.1 × 101.6 cm, London, Victoria and Albert Museum
During the reign of Shah Abbas I, the royal palaces in Isfahan, and also many houses, had their walls decorated with painted tiles. This one shows a typical garden scene in the style of Riza-yi Abbasi: a courtly couple resting amid flowering bushes and trees and being served with food and drink by servants. The irregular shape of the top edge shows that this tile picture was made for a very specific place on a wall.

religious beliefs should have prevented him from having anything to do with figurative paintings, the shah commissioned a portrait of himself and the whole of his court.

Ali Quli Jabbadar appears to have been the founder of a whole dynasty of court painters. Both his son Abdal Beg and his grandson Ali Beg were appointed as heads of the court studio, the latter after the Safavid era, under Nadir Shah (1736–1747). The royal studio survived even during the political and economic crises of the 18th century when the rulers were no longer great patrons of the arts.

One painter active during this period was Sadiq, who received commissions both from Nadir Shah and later from Karim Khan Zand (1751–1779). The pictures he painted for the latter in his capital, Shiraz, during the peaceful years of his government are still preserved there in a pavilion sometimes known as the Pars Museum. Some of these oil paintings depict Karim Khan and his court. Sadiq was also a painter of miniatures and lacquerwork and in the buildings constructed by Karim Khan in Shiraz, the walls and facades were decorated by stonemasons and stucco and ceramic artists. All of these techniques survived throughout the political and economic chaos that dominated most of the 18th century. But Persian art did not receive a truly new impetus until the arrival of the Qajars, a new dynasty of rulers and patrons of the arts.

Fath Ali Shah, the second Qajar to ascend the throne (1797–1834), was the dynasty's first patron of the arts. He was a good-looking but vain man who commissioned many portraits of himself, both in the form of large oil paintings, which had largely replaced miniatures in the royal studio, and using other techniques. Lacquer and enamel painting in particular flourished during the rule of the Qajars in the 19th century. Lacquer painting was closely related to miniatures, since it too used water-based colors and was applied mainly to relatively small objects such as pen boxes, book covers, mirror and spectacle cases, and other small containers. These objects were made from papier mâché, coated in a plaster-like substance, painted in watercolors, and then sealed with a transparent coat of lacquer. They displayed the great variety of forms and colors typical of Qajar painting, with flowers (roses and irises were particularly popular), foliage, and fruits being used both as central and background motifs. The style of painting at this time is distinguished by lively, elaborate forms, bright colors, very detailed drawing and careful shading, which, as a European element, had become universal by the 19th century.

Because of its size, enamel painting is very similar to lacquerwork, and many artists worked in both media. Enameled gold, silver and copper containers were objects of great luxury. Plates, bowls, small boxes, vases and the metal parts of waterpipes were painted with similar motifs to the lacquerwork, but used a different range of colors: their pale pinks, yellows, greens, blues, and rich blacks and whites made them much clearer than lacquerwork, almost slightly gaudy.

During the 19th century, the motifs used in enamel painting were increasingly influenced by European style and subject matter. European clothing appeared alongside Persian costumes, and landscapes were close imitations of European versions, often at the expense of artistic composition. Often the

Left: **Brass ewer**, Iran, c. 1600, cast, engraved the ground filled with black composition, Düsseldorf, Kunstmuseum
The form of this ewer, covered in dense tendril decoration and with an onion-shaped body, narrow neck, and funnel-shaped opening, is more like one of the ceramic bottles of the time.

Below: **Plate with lion and sun decoration**, Muhammad Jafar, Tehran, 1817/18, enameled gold, diameter 32.1 cm, weight 2.2 kg, London, Victoria and Albert Museum
The Persian ambassador Mirza Abu l-Hasan gave this plate bearing the emblem of the Iranian royal household to the British East India Company in London in 1819.

existing models were poor-quality prints of second-rate works or cheap postcards with dubious themes. The Persian productions included romantic landscapes and European buildings shown in perspective, and also traditional scenes from Persian history, for example from the *Shahname*, which had already inspired so many miniature painters. These historical and mythological scenes appeared on small lacquer containers and also large tile pictures covering entire walls of buildings. The tile decoration on the city gate of Semnan, for example, shows the great Persian hero Rustam engaged in battle with a white *div*, a mythical figure.

Recent events from the new Iranian, that is Qajar history were also recorded as subject matter in pictures, and the sovereign was frequently portrayed. Many of these portraits were painted by the heads of the court art studio in the new Qajar capital, Tehran. The two Naqqash-Bashi, or head court painters, Mirza Baba and Mihr Ali, who worked under Fath Ali Shah,

painted impressive oil portraits of him. During the reign of Nasir al-Din Shah (1848–1896), Muhammad Ismail was appointed as head court painter. He came from a family of painters in Isfahan who specialized mainly in lacquerwork. During the first two thirds of the 19th century, five members of this family made a major contribution to lacquer painting until the Imami family of painters, also from Isfahan, came to prominence. Riza Imami, for example, painted a mirror case for the Paris World's Fair of 1867. This is now in the Victoria and Albert Museum in London, where it is regarded as the museum's finest piece of lacquerwork.

One of the pupils of the court painter Mihr Ali was Abu l-Hasan Khan Ghaffari (1812–1866), who came from a respected family in Kashan that produced numerous artists. During the reign of Muhammad Shah (1834–1848) he was given a position in the court studio and was then sent on a royal mission in 1846–1850 to study painting in Rome and other Italian

Pen box with a portrait of Manuchihr Khan Mutamid al-Daula, Muhammad Ismail, Isfahan, 1847, papier-mâché with lacquer painting, length 24.1 cm, London, Victoria and Albert Museum
This box bears a depiction of the former Georgian slave Manuchihr Khan, who around 1840 was one of the most powerful men in Iran. He is accompanied by a retinue of 26 men, many of them with long beards and Astrakhan' hats in the Qajar style. This is the earliest known work of Muhammad Ismail, who later became head court painter.

IRAN: SAFAVIDS AND QAJARS

cities. After he returned to Persia, Nasir al-Din Shah appointed him as head of the court studio and gave him a number of important commissions. As a painter, he designed over a thousand miniatures for a six-volume Persian translation of *The Thousand and One Nights* and also supervised their production, which sometimes involved as many as 34 painters working at the same time. He was also responsible for the large murals which are now in the Iran Bastan Museum in Tehran, and was involved in the establishment of the Dar al-Funun, the first educational institution in Iran to be influenced by Western ideas and one of the forerunners of the present-day Tehran University. In 1861, he was appointed manager of the state printing press and the official government newspaper, for which he created a number of masterly lithograph portraits of princes and senior dignitaries. In the same year he received the title Sani al-Mulk ("Artist of the Kingdom"), by which he is best known.

In the years that followed, Abu l-Hasan Khan Ghaffari acquired even more administrative responsibilities in the printing industry, but he also continued to teach painting at the Dar al-Funun. One pupil was his nephew Muhammad Ghaffari (1852–1940), who bore the honorary title "*Kamal al-Mulk*" ("Perfection of the kingdom"). He became the last court painter of the Qajars, during whose era the transition to a purely European style of painting took place. While Abu l-Hasan Khan's studies in Italy had influenced only his own style, Muhammad Ghaffari's studies of painting in France and Italy around 1900 made its mark on the whole of Persian art. But as a master of portraiture, a genre which had developed out of miniature painting, Abu l-Hasan Khan had fulfilled Sadiqi Beg's requirement that a picture should create the same associations in the viewer as if the viewer were standing face to face with the living person depicted in the painting.

Prince Ardashir Mirzas, governor of Tehran, portrait by Abu l-Hasan Ghaffari, Tehran, 1854, gouache on paper, 31.6 × 20.4 cm, Paris, Musée du Louvre
Prince Ardashir Mirza, a grandson of Fath Ali Shah, held numerous military and administrative posts during his life. The painter, who is famous for his detailed portraits, has sensitively depicted the marks these responsibilities have left on the thickset prince's face. A European-looking tree appears through the window on the left.

Islamic Carpets

Sheila Blair, Jonathan Bloom

Carpets are one of the most accessible forms of Islamic art. For millennia, well before the rise of Islam, the sheep-raising nomads of western Asia produced such textiles, whose upper surfaces were usually knotted. Since they were in daily use textiles generally had a fairly short life-span and only very few pieces have survived from the premodern period. Consequently, it is only from the late 19th century that a relatively large number of nomadic and tribal carpets have survived.

The oldest surviving carpet is believed to be the one discovered in the 1940s in ice at Pazyryk in southern Siberia, which dates from before the Christian era. Measuring 6 × 6.5 feet (1.8 × 2 meters), the Pazyryk carpet is made of wool. The field of 24 squares containing stylized flowers is framed with a border displaying fallow deer, horses, and lions. It is impossible to determine where the carpet was made, but the sophistication of the technique and design indicate that such textiles had been produced for centuries. Excavations at several Near Eastern archeological sites have produced fragments of pile carpets dating to the Sassanian and early Islamic periods, but otherwise our knowledge of carpets before the late 15th century is largely based on literary sources. Perhaps the most splendid carpet described in the sources was the "Spring of Khusrau," a huge carpet, some 290 square feet (27 square meters), which covered the floor of the Sassanian palace at Ctesiphon when the Arabs conquered it in the year 637.

Isolated carpet fragments of varying size and dating before the 12th century have been found in such extremely dry locations as the rubbish heaps of Old Cairo, but the oldest surviving group of carpets dates from the first half of the 14th century. They are known as "Konya" carpets because some 20 examples were discovered in 1903 in the Ala al-Din Mosque at Konya in central Anatolia, where they had been hidden under successive layers of carpets laid on the floor of the prayer hall. These carpets are coarse, and knotted with symmetrical knots in a limited range of strong colors, such as medium and dark red, medium and dark blue, yellow, brown, and ivory. Scholars had initially attributed them to the patronage of the Seljuk sultans, who ruled Konya in the 12th and 13th centuries, but as some of the motifs used on the carpets derive from Chinese silks dating to the Yuan dynasty (1279–1368), the group is now assigned an early 14th-century date.

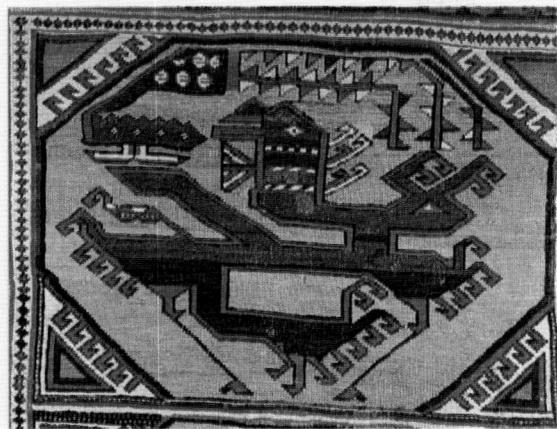

Animal carpet (detail), Anatolia, 15th century, 172 × 90 cm
Design shows a dragon and phoenix fighting; discovered in central Italy, Berlin, Museum für Islamische Kunst

Holbein carpet, Turkey, 16th century

Opposite: **Parzyryk carpet**, southern Siberia, 4–5th century
B.C., 1.8 × 2 m, wool, Leningrad, Hermitage

A second small group of carpets, known as "animal carpets" because the field is dominated by a stylized representation of one or more animals, is slightly later. Only three examples are known to survive: one found in a church in central Italy in 1886; one in the Swedish village of Marby in 1925; and a third reportedly found in Tibet and acquired by the Metropolitan Museum of Art in New York in 1990. Like the Konya carpets, animal carpets have symmetrical knots but they are much smaller, measuring only about 3–4.5 feet (1–1.5 meters) each side. They vary in color and show such creatures as birds or dragons. Animal carpets must have already been in production in the early 14th century, as they are depicted in two paintings from the Great Mongol *Shahname*, which was illustrated at Tabriz c. 1335. By the late 14th and early 15th centuries, these carpets must have been exported to Europe, for several are depicted in Italian paintings. In contrast, Konya carpets were made only for local use, and only a few fragments of this type have been found outside Anatolia.

By the middle of the 15th century, Anatolian weavers were producing large-pattern "Holbein" carpets, many intended for export to Europe. The typical example, knotted in brightly colored wool in a variety of colors, primarily brick-red with white, yellow, blue, green, brown, and black, has a rectangular field containing several large octagons inscribed in square frames. These are usually decorated with stapwork patterns and separated and enclosed by bands of smaller octagons. Several borders of varying width usually include an elegant band of pseudo-inscription in which the stems of the letters appear to be twisted together. These carpets get their name because many are depicted in paintings by Hans Holbein the Younger (1497–1543), such as his *Ambassadors* of the year 1533 in the National Gallery in London. They first appear in European paintings dated to the 1450s, where they are shown on floors in patrician settings or as luxury table coverings.

Another early group are the "Mamluk" carpets, which have intricate centralized designs in red, green, blue, and yellow revolving around one or more large octagonal medallions. The entire field is densely decorated with geometrical motifs composed of more or less regular octagons, hexagons, and triangles that produce an almost kaleidoscopic effect. Warp, weft and pile are S-spun, a technique normally associated with Egypt, and the carpets are all knotted with an assymetrical knot open to the left. Mamluk carpets are normally made of wool but one extraordinary example with three medallions was knotted in silk, giving a lustrous and radiant effect. This group, of which many examples were exported to Italy, has been attributed to several centers on the eastern and southern shores of the Mediterranean between the 15 and 17th century, when either the Mamluk (until 1517) or Ottoman sultans ruled the region.

In the 16th century – under the Safavids – the production of carpets became a state enterprise, and the first signed and dated carpets survive from this period, indicating that carpets had achieved new importance as works of art. Unlike traditional nomadic carpets, which were woven from memory, the designs for these factory-made carpets were carefully prepared on paper. One particularly fine example is asymmetrically knotted in many brilliant colors of wool on silk warps and cotton wefts with approximately 265 knots per square inch (41 knots per square centimeter). The lobed central medallion, depicting 40 flying cranes, is surrounded by a lively hunting scene on a deep blue ground. The huntsmen – some mounted, others on foot – fight ferocious lions, cavorting deer and other animals. The hunters wear the distinctive early Safavid turban wrapped around a tall red cap. An inscription in the center of the carpet states that Ghiyathal-Din Jami made (presumably designed) it in year 949 of the *hegira* (1542/43). The central location of the signature in the medallion, combined with the radiating design, indicate that this carpet was designed to be spread under and around a royal throne, presumably that of the reigning shah, Tahmasp. The hunting scenes would then be oriented properly to the ruler's gaze, and the designer's signature would have been literally under the ruler's feet, which was a traditional metaphor of humility.

The production of carpets was transformed under Abbas I when they became a commercial commodity for domestic and foreign consumption. He had the Armenian population of Julfa on the Araxes River in Azerbaijan relocated to New Julfa, a new suburb to the south of Isfahan. Their monopoly of the silk trade became their main source of wealth and a crucial source of revenue for the Safavid state. The figural designs popular in court carpets and textiles of the 16th century were increasingly superseded by floral patterns. The new type of carpet is exemplified by the "Polonaise" carpets, of which

Mamluk wool carpet, Cairo, c. 1500, 3.34 × 5 m, Vienna, Austrian Museum for Applied Art

"Polonaise" carpet, Kashan, Iran, 1601, Residenz München, East Asia Collection

some 300 examples are known, many of them gifts to Europeans in Iran or commissions by the noble houses of Europe.

Although most examples have now faded to a dusky rose tonality, they were knotted in bright green, blue, yellow, and pink silk on silk or cotton warps and enriched with silver and gold brocading. They were first called "Polonaise" when exhibited in the Paris Exhibition of 1878, for one example from Krakow bears the coat of arms then believed to be that of the Polish Czartoryski family. A flatwoven rug (*kelim*), now in Munich, with a similar design, bears the arms of Sigismund Wasa III, King of Poland. A document dated September 12, 1602 records that Sigismund sent an Armenian, Sefer Muratowicz, to buy silk carpets in Kashan. There he bought six pairs of carpets and paid five extra crowns to have the king's arms put on the carpets. Almost all Polonaise carpets share a similar arrangement, with several borders and guard bands of varying width enclosing a rectangular field. The field contains one or more central medallions and quarter-medallions in the corners. The ground features arabesques of flowers and leaves spiraling in a stately rhythm over the field.

Another group of carpets attributed to the time of Abbas are the so-called "vase carpets." Their one-directional design is characterized by a lattice on three planes, one system composed of an ivory spiralling vine, the others of thicker red and blue stems. The stems issue from vases (hence the name) and bear an abundance of large and small blossoms, sprays, and leaves.

In addition to these knotted carpets, Safavid craftsmen also produced extraordinary flatweaves (*kelim*), such as a fragmentary example made in the 16th century and one in the Rothschild collection. Measuring 86 × 58 inches (219 × 148 centimeters), it has the traditional format of pile carpets, with a rectangular field and several borders, but is flatwoven in several colors of silk – white, yellow, green, red, light blue, dark blue, brown, black against an ivory silk ground. The fine technique allowed the transfer of a linear drawing from paper to textile. Four houris in the center are surrounded by picknickers in the four corner panels and a swirling design of trees and fighting animals in the field. The border contains cartouches with single or paired animals.

The origins of pile carpets in India are considered to be obscure. Woollen floor coverings, perhaps piled, may have been manufactured as early as the 14th century, but

ISLAMIC CARPET MAKING

production increased under the patronage of the Moghuls in the 16th century, when Indian craftsmen adopted Persian techniques and designs.

Although the carpets of western Asia are better known, there was also a long tradition of knotting rugs in Islamic Spain. Made at least from the 12th century, Spanish carpets were traded into Europe from the 13th century. The growing popularity of Turkish carpets in Europe only encouraged Spanish production, and Spanish weavers adopted several Turkish design motifs, although they continued to use a distinctive type of knot, tied on only one warp thread. A particularly noteworthy example of an early Spanish carpet is the "Synagogue" rug, knotted in reddish-brown, black, blue, and yellow wool and probably dating from the 14th century. Jews used rugs for seating and hanging beside the Torah ark as decoration.

North Africa was another region in which carpets had been woven for centuries. Written sources tell us of North African carpets being sent as tribute to the Abbasid caliphs of Baghdad in the 9th century, but the earliest carpets to survive from the region date from no earlier than the 19th century. In Moroccan cities, for example, some pile carpets were produced, copying and reinterpreting Turkish imports. Elsewhere, however, the nomadic Berber tribes of the Atlas Mountains continued to produce traditional types of rugs and carpets.

In Iran, after 1860, village weavers quickly adapted through economic necessity to a market which preferred room-sized carpets, runners, and area rugs. Large numbers were woven in a stronger, coarser technique, able to withstand wear from Europeans accustomed to wearing shoes inside the house and bringing outside dirt inside.

In southwestern Iran many rugs were made by non-Persian nomadic groups and marketed mainly in the city of Shiraz, capital of the Fars region. One of the best-known types was produced by the Qashqai tribesmen. These small tribal rugs from southwestern Iran can be contrasted to the large dragon carpets from the central and southern Caucasus. The oldest type of pile-woven rug from the area, they date back as far as the 17th century. These large rugs, often as long as 20 feet (6 meters) and relatively narrow, were made as commercial products. Knotted in bright colors on a woollen foundation, dragon carpets are characterized by lattices of sawtooth leaves which form rhomboidal compartments filled with simplified and stylized dragons fighting phoenixes, or lions with flames springing from their shoulders.

Safavid _kelim_, Kashan or Yazd, 3rd quarter of the 16th century, silk and metallic thread, London, Christie's Images

The emerging empire

Mehmed's son, Murad II (1421–1451), besieged Constantinople and forced the Anatolian princes to pay tribute. His annexation of Serbia in 1439 as a province of the Ottoman Empire provoked the last "Crusade" of the European powers, which were utterly defeated by Murad at the Battle of Varna in November 1444.

At home the sultan weakened the traditional *ghazi* elite by developing the *devsirme* system, a periodic levy of the most talented Christian youths in the Balkan countries, whom he had converted to Islam and trained for leading positions in the army and the administration. For a long time they formed the political elite of the Ottoman Empire as exponents of Ottoman engagement in Europe. Ottoman possessions in the Balkans had been secured through victory in the Second Battle of Kosovo in 1448, when Murad died in February 1451.

His son, Mehmed II Fatih (the Conqueror; 1451–1481), was the most distinguished ruler of the Ottomans. He began the siege of Constantinople in April 1453 and took the city on May 29, 1453, by which triumph he became the most famous and acknowledged leader of the Islamic world. He made the city the imperial capital with the name Istanbul and settled there large colonies of different peoples from all the imperial provinces, granting tax privileges to traders and craftsmen. He also started the reconstruction of the city, which since 1204 had become dilapidated. Christians and Jews were settled there under his special protection and he granted them far-reaching cultural autonomy, which gave the capital its "multicultural" atmosphere. He saw himself as the future ruler of the world ("Ghazi of the Muslims, Khan of the Turks, and Emperor of the Christians").

After the victory over Byzantium, the sultan pushed ahead with further expansion of the empire, both in the west and the east. He conquered the new

principality of Serbia in 1454, occupied the Peloponnese from 1458, annexed the Genoese trading colonies on the Black Sea, and in 1463 occupied Bosnia. In the east he conquered the Turkmen principality of Qaraman in 1468 and Little Armenia in 1474. He landed in southern Italy in 1480, occupied Otranto and advanced further north. He seems to have been considering the idea of advancing towards Rome, into the "Heart of Christianity," and eliminating the power of the pope, when he suddenly died in May 1481.

At home, Mehmed II laid the foundations of a new Ottoman social order. By taking over Byzantine imperial ceremonies the sultan set himself further apart from his people. The *devsirme* elite and the Janissary officers gained the greatest influence and filled the most important government offices. By giving preferential treatment to the non-Muslim sections of the population Mehmed secured their loyalty for himself. He established the principle of the indivisibility of the realm, by advocating fratricide when a new ruler assumes power. With his own compendium of laws he created the basis for the corpus of law of Suleyman the Magnificent.

The reign of Mehmed II's pious son, Bayazid II (1481–1512), was a period when these changes were consolidated. Bayazid concerned himself with internal problems, limiting the power of the *devsirme* elite in order to reassure the Turkish parts of the empire and putting the economy, which had been hard hit under his father's administration, back on its feet. Because of the piety of the sultan, the *ulama*, an Islamic religious council, achieved considerable influence and halted the advancing cultural "Europeanization."

Bayazid still felt compelled to wage war. In 1483 he completed the conquest of the Balkans with the occupation of Herzegovina and controlled the North European trade routes via the Danube and the Black Sea. However, he was unable to snatch Belgrade away from the Hungarians. War with Venice (1499–1503) led

Left: **Sultan Suleyman the Magnificent**, Ottoman miniature, 16th century, Istanbul, University Library
Under Suleyman the Magnificent (1520–1566) the Ottoman Empire stood at the zenith of its power and display of splendor. After successful campaigns in the Balkans and in the Maghreb, Sultan Suleyman devoted himself to internal consolidation of the empire and erected a series of superb buildings, such as the Topkapi Palace in Istanbul. In the last years of his life harem officials were already dominant, which was to spell the political decline of the power of the ruler under his successors.

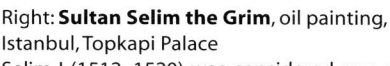

Right: **Sultan Selim the Grim**, oil painting, Istanbul, Topkapi Palace
Selim I (1512–1520) was considered one of the most successful Ottoman rulers. He secured power at home using great severity and occupied Syria and Egypt (1516/17) as well as parts of the Arabian Peninsula, including Mecca and Medina. He thus increased the territories of the Ottoman Empire, doubling their size. Selim, who is regarded as a hero of Turkish historiography, later adopted the title of caliph for the Ottoman sultans.

to the conquest of all the Venetian bases in the Peloponnese, which gave the Ottomans important naval bases in the Mediterranean. From 1503 the sultan had to intervene on many occasions in eastern Anatolia, where various local rulers took advantage of the ascendancy of the Safavid dynasty in Persia to seize their independence. In the end Bayazid found himself confronted with a revolt led by his warrior son, Selim, who in 1512 forced his father to abdicate.

The empire at its zenith

Selim I Yavuz (the Grim; 1512–1520) had boundless ambition and on coming to the throne he put down in writing that he wanted to become ruler of the whole civilized world and thus the first legitimate successor to Alexander the Great. He eliminated all his brothers and nephews, and of his own five sons only Suleyman was allowed to live.

His attention was directed towards the east and south of the empire. After concluding peace treaties with the Europeans, he pursued with vigor the extermination of all the Sufis and followers of the Safavids in Anatolia, called for a "Holy War" against the Shiites and invaded Persia. Following his victory over the Safavids at the Battle of Chaldiran in August 1514, Selim occupied Azerbaijan and eastern Anatolia and deported all craftsmen and traders from Istanbul. After that he conquered Kurdistan and thus controlled the eastern trade with Persia. In 1516 the sultan used the appeal from the weak Mamluks for help against the Portuguese as an excuse to march on Aleppo and defeat the Mamluk

army. He occupied Syria and Egypt, which henceforth came within the Ottoman sphere of influence. Once again the prestige of the sultan grew considerably with his sovereignty over the holy places of Mecca and Medina. In addition, Selim assumed the traditional title of caliph.

In his short reign, Selim I, who witnessed the decline of Venice and prepared to make the Ottomans the dominant power in the Mediterranean, doubled the size of the empire as well as the national treasury and is regarded as a hero of Turkish historiography.

His son, Suleyman II (1520–1566), whom Europeans call "the Magnificent" and the Turks "the Law-giver," was on the throne during the cultural zenith of the empire. After his father had secured the east and south, Suleyman concentrated once again on the west: in 1521 he took Belgrade as his main base in the Balkans, advanced along the Danube, and in August 1526 he defeated the Hungarians at the Battle of Mohacs. The king fell in the battle and had no heir, so a power vacuum developed in Hungary. This buffer state between the great empires was occupied by the Hapsburgs in the northwest and by the Ottomans in the southeast and so they confronted each other for a considerable period of time. When the Hapsburgs occupied central Hungary in 1528, they were driven out by Suleyman, who then besieged Vienna in a countermove in 1529. A peace treaty was arranged in 1533, but the conflict broke out again and again for some time after. Suleyman and the Hapsburg emperor Charles V also confronted each other as enemies in the Mediterranean. In 1533 the sultan engaged the corsair Khair al-Din Barbarossa, who opened up

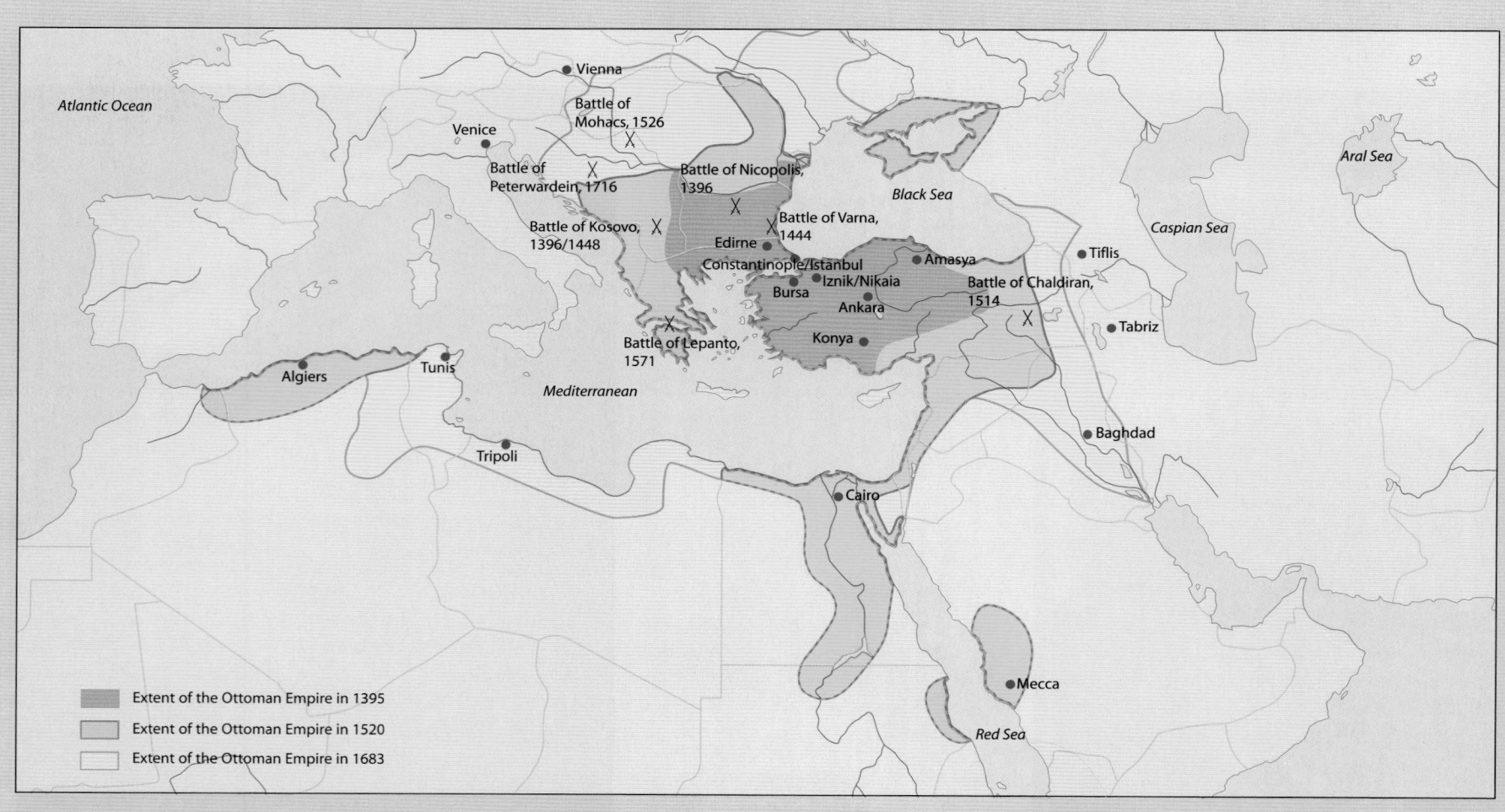

THE OTTOMAN EMPIRE

Janissary band

The Janissaries formed the much-feared elite troops of the Ottoman army. From about 1360 they were recruited from among the boys of the occupied Christian Balkan territories, were strictly quartered in barracks, militarily trained, and totally committed to the ruler. They originally consisted of some 15,000 men, but in the 17th century their numbers were built up to 100,000. In battle, the Janissaries were held back at first and only intervened to seize victory when the enemy was already exhausted. From the beginning of the 18th century they constituted a sort of "state within a state," which is why they were disbanded as an organization after an attempted coup in 1826.

Algeria and Tunisia to the Ottomans and in 1540 won a massive victory over the combined European fleet at the Battle of Prevesa. Until the Christian victory at Lepanto (1571) the Ottoman fleet remained the dominant force in the Mediterranean.

The time of Suleyman the Magnificent was a unique epoch when culture and the arts blossomed. Through the *devsirme* system there was a certain mobility among the elite and enormous prospects for advancement. However, the converts to Islam believed that loyalty to the ruler and the state, together with a proper understanding of the correct behavior and speech used in the upper strata of society, should be prerequisites for such advancement. The various religious communities enjoyed a large degree of cultural and judicial autonomy and were under the direct protection of the ruler. The legal system displayed a considerable flexibility: compared with traditional Islamic law, which embraced different aspects of private and social life, public law tended to work in favor of the organization and power of the state. Suleyman gained special credit for himself through the codification and compilation of this system.

In the last years of his reign Suleyman withdrew more and more from everyday politics, which he left to his grand vizier, and abandoned himself to the sensual pleasures and joys of the harem. When he died in September 1566 he had thus planted the seeds of disastrous developments under his successors.

c.1300–1326	Reign of Osman I, founder of the Ottoman Empire	1514	Battle of Chaldiran: the Ottomans defeat the Persian Safavids and conquer Mesopotamia and Kurdistan	and the Peloponnese go to Austria, Poland, and Venice	international debt law is established
1354	The Ottomans begin their conquest of the Balkans			1717–1730	"Tulip Time": the grand vizier Nevsehirli Ibrahim Pasha opens up the empire to European culture
1363-65	Under Murad I (1359–1389), the first Ottoman sultan, Edirne becomes capital of the empire	1516–1517	The Ottomans take Syria and Egypt from Mamluk control and bring to an end the Abbasid shadow caliphate in Cairo		1876–1909 Sultanate of Abdul Hamid II
1389	First Battle of Kosovo: Serbia becomes a vassal state of the Ottoman Empire	1520–1566	Sultanate of Suleyman II	1718	Peace of Passarowitz: further Ottoman territories are lost to the Hapsburgs
1396	The Ottomans under Bayazid I (1389–1402) defeat the Crusaders at Nicopolis	1529	Failure of the first Ottoman siege of Vienna		1876–1877 Proclamation of an Ottoman constitution by Midhat Pasha
		1534–1574	The Ottomans extend their power into North Africa	1774	Treaty of Kuchuk Kainarji ends the Russo-Ottoman War (1768–1774). With the Peace of Jassy (1792) the Crimea finally falls to Russia
1402	Defeat of the Ottomans by the Mongols under Timur near Ankara	1555	Ottoman-Safavid peace treaty (Peace of Amasya): Iraq and eastern Anatolia are ceded to the Ottomans		1908–1909 The Young Turks seize power: new parliamentary elections, liberal constitutional reform: Mehmed V (1909–1918) becomes constitutional sultan
1413–1421	Sultanate of Mehmed I			1789–1807	Selim III forms the Nizam-i-jadid army and embassies are established in Europe
1422	The Ottomans under Murad II (1421–1451) besiege Constantinople	1566–1574	Sultanate of Selim II		
		1571	Naval Battle of Lepanto		1914–1918 First World War: the Ottomans fight on the side of the Central Powers
1444	Victory of the Ottomans over the Hungarians (Battle of Varna)	1638	Ottoman-Persian War (1623–1638) ends with the Peace Treaty of Qasr-i Shirin: Iraq comes under Ottoman sovereignty while Azerbaijan and the Caucasus come under Safavid sovereignty	1789–1801	French expedition to Egypt: through the expulsion of the French by Muhammad Ali, Egypt achieves *de facto* autonomy; in 1841 the sultan bestows on him the hereditary title of Viceroy of Egypt
1448	The Ottomans overcome the Hungarian army under Hunyadi at the Second Battle of Kosovo				1918–1922 Reign of the last Ottoman sultan, Mehmed VI
1451–1481	Sultanate of Mehmed II				1923 The Republic of Turkey is proclaimed: Mustafa Kemal (Ataturk) becomes president
1453	The Ottomans take Constantinople	1683	Failure of the second Ottoman siege of Vienna	1826	Destruction of the Janissaries by Mahmud II (1808–1839)
1512–1520	Sultanate of Selim I	1699	Peace of Karlowitz: parts of the Ottoman territories in the Balkans	1839–1876	Period of the Tanzimat reforms: the army, judiciary, law and educational system are all radically reformed
				1875	Financial collapse of the empire;

The decline of the Ottoman Empire

Since much of the immense power of the sultan depended on his personality, the decline began immediately with Suleyman's successors. Brought up in the closed world of the harem, which was characterized by boredom, sensual pleasures, and intrigue, many sultans developed into insecure, unworldly despots, who had no interest in the affairs of state. The grand vizier became the most important political force, but he still regularly had to give reassurance to the Janissaries, who demanded more money and new privileges at the accession of each sultan, and he was generally involved in a dangerous power struggle with the forces of the harem. A succession of capable grand viziers protected the empire from evil forces. The often complete withdrawal of the ruler from public life led to total domination by the *devsirme* elite and to the ruling classes being able to avoid any kind of government control. Corruption and nepotism flourished throughout.

Naval Battle of Lepanto on October 7, 1571, painting by Giorgio Vasari, 16th century, Vatican, Sala Regia
From the beginning of the 16th century, the Ottomans held sway in the Mediterranean and inflicted serious damage on the trade of the Christian sea powers of Spain and Italy. After the sultan had taken possession of the important trading post of Cyprus in 1570, the confrontation culminated in a violent naval battle between galleys in the Gulf of Lepanto (Greece) in 1571. With heavy losses on both sides, the Christian fleet of Papal, Spanish, and Venetian forces under the leadership of the Spanish prince Don Juan of Austria was victorious over the Ottomans. The west celebrated this victory as the triumph of Christianity over its enemies.

Suleyman's son, Selim II (1566–1574), who was already given the epithet "the Sot" during his lifetime and did finally succumb to drink, devoted himself entirely to the pleasures of the senses and distanced himself from governmental affairs. In 1570/71 the Ottoman fleet took possession of Cyprus, but in October 1571 it was still forced to suffer a devastating defeat by the combined Christian

Ottoman parade helmet,
16th century, Istanbul,
Topkapi Palace Museum
This helmet from the reign of Suley-man the Magnificent shows that artistic refinement and ennoblement also extended to the skilled armorer. Weaponry for the court was made exclusively for show. The time when the sultans used to lead their armies against their enemies came to an end in the middle of the 16th century.

The Ottoman army lays siege to Vienna 1529,
Ottoman miniature, a page from the *Huner-name*, 1588, Istanbul, Topkapi Palace Museum
After the Ottomans had defeated the Hungarians at Mohacs (1526), the Ottomans and the Hapsburg empire confronted each other in Hungary. When King Ferdinand occupied central Hungary in 1528, he was driven out by Sultan Suleyman, who in a counterattack advanced towards Vienna and in vain laid siege to the capital.

fleets in the Gulf of Lepanto. With Selim's son, Murad III (1574–1595), an epileptic with a fear of people, there began the ill-fated rule by the women of the harem (mainly the sultan's mother or the favorite wife of the ruler) and the palace eunuchs, as well as the leading Janissary officers (Aghas). This followed the assassination of the able grand vizier Mehmed Sokollu (1565–1579). The empire suffered economic collapse in the central provinces. At the beginning of the 17th century competent and energetic sultans like Osman II (1618–1622) and Murad IV (1623–1640) were once again in control of the state and above all they were successful in their struggle against the Persian Safavids.

The 17th century witnessed various state crises: the famous grand viziers from the House of Koprulu, Mehmed (1656–1661) and Ahmed (1661–1676), attempted to combat general stagnation with far-reaching reforms, but they were only partially able to win through in their battle against corruption. After succeeding in strengthening central power, the ambitious grand vizier Kara Mustafa (1676–1683) decided to advance into Hungary and in 1683 to lay siege to Vienna, but the Turks were defeated at Kahlenberg by the Hapsburg imperial army and troops under the Polish king John Sobieski and were driven back. The imperial commander Prince Eugene of Savoy, who strove for a political alliance between Western and Central Europe against the Ottomans, drove the Turks out of Hungary and beat them several times (1697 at the Battle of Zenta, and 1716 at the Battle of Peterwardein). In 1717 he was also able to occupy Belgrade for the Hapsburgs.

In the 18th century Ottoman rule in the Balkans got into increasing difficulties through an alliance between the Hapsburg empire and a strengthened Russia. Between 1683 and 1718 the Ottomans (with varying degrees of success) waged three wars against the Hapsburgs (which ended in the Peace of Passarowitz 1718) and between 1736 and 1792 three wars against Russia (which ended in the Treaty of Jassy 1792). The result was the loss of a greater part of the Balkans to the Hapsburgs – the Danube now formed the frontier – as well as the Crimea, Bessarabia, and Podolia to Russia. The Ottomans also had to accept significant interference by both powers within the empire, which led to stronger "Europeanization" of the Ottoman culture, particularly during the so-called "Tulip Time" of the europhile Sultan Ahmed III (1703–1730).

Political reform, modernization and the end of the empire

Selim III (1789–1807) was the first of the two great reformers to occupy the sultan's throne. Influenced by the philosophical movement known as the Enlightenment and recognizing political decline, he began an energetic fight against corruption, restructured the state treasury, and ordered sweeping reform legislation. Recognizing the military superiority of Europe, he reorganized his forces on the European model as the "New System" and began instructing both officers and officials in technology and the natural sciences. His actions provoked the opposition of the old elite and in particular the Janissaries, who deposed him in 1807 and, a year later, when the victorious forces of reform wanted to restore him to the throne, they put him to death.

His successor, Mahmud II (1808–1839), put himself resolutely at the head of the reformers. Continuing Selim's policy towards the army, he assembled new troops and finally broke the power of the Janissaries, all of whom he had massacred during a rebellion in June 1826. Politically, he set up a cabinet on the European model, changed the Turkish national dress (abolition of the caftan and the baggy trousers, replacement of the turban with the fez), improved the position of civil servants, and promoted technology, the natural sciences, and medicine by establishing special state schools.

The era of the reforming sultans was marked by the fragmentation of the Ottoman Empire and by military engagements resulting in heavy losses. In 1798

Napoleon temporarily occupied Egypt and Syria. From 1804 Egypt became increasingly independent under Muhammad Ali and involved the Sublime Porte in various wars. After a large part of Bulgaria had declared independence in 1797, wars and rebellions followed between 1804 and 1815 for the autonomy and independence of Serbia. Between 1821 and 1830 a war was fought for the independence of Greece, supported by the European powers. In 1828/29 the empire lost Romania and was able to suppress revolts in Albania and Bosnia only with some difficulty. In 1839 the Ottomans finally suffered a catastrophic defeat

Sultan Selim III receives the court, painting, late 18th century, Istanbul, Topkapi Palace
The regular receptions of the imperial household in the courtyard of the Topkapi Palace with its polished 16th-century ceremonial were meant to underline the claim of the sultan to be both religious and political leader of the Islamic world. In practical terms, however, power had passed to the harem and the particular governing elite, so most of the 18th-century sultans were purely symbolic figures. Selim III, attempted to change this situation.

Sultan Murad IV (1623–1640), watercolor, 19th century, Istanbul, Museum of Turkish and Islamic Art
This sultan, notorious for his atrocities at home, reconquered Azerbaijan and Iraq as the last Ottoman warrior ruler to ride at the head of his troops.

Sultan Selim III (1789–1807), painting, end of the 18th-century, Istanbul, Topkapi Palace
Influenced by the ideas of the European Enlightenment, Selim III, as the first great reforming sultan, established the governmental power of the ruler and opened up his empire to European technological and scientific influences.

Sultan Abdulhamid II (1876–1909), portrait, end of the 19th century, Istanbul, Topkapi Palace
Abdulhamid II completed the reform program energetically but paternalistically so that in 1909 his autocratic regime provoked the revolt of the Young Turks, who overthrew him and restored the suspended constitution of 1877.

by the Egyptian Muhammad Ali and they were saved only by the timely intervention of the European powers.

The political reforms known as Tanzimat left their mark on the reigns of Mahmud's two sons, Abdulmecid (1839–1861) and Abdulaziz (1861–1876). The Tanzimat was a reform program instituted by the sultan and his government, which could be seen as a late variant of "enlightened absolutism." The reformers brought in a centralist legal system based on the French model, which extended the influence of the government into every area of social life through decrees and acts. Basic legal reform had as its objective the judicial standardization of the empire. Muslim and non-Muslim subjects became equal under the law. In 1839 the military was reorganized as a regular army. The training and education system finally ended the monopoly of the Islamic *madrasas* in favor of state schools with training in technology and natural science.

The Tanzimat reforms soon came under pressure, however. Besides resistance from the traditional *ulama*, the members of the new technical elite also formed themselves into an opposition as they were familiar with democratic ways of thinking through their training, and called for nothing less than an end to autocracy and for political participation. In 1871 there was a rapid decline in the number of reforms following the death of the leading reformer. Through corruption, poor administration, and the outrageous extravagance of the sultan, the empire was virtually bankrupt by 1875. When Abdulaziz showed increasing signs of mental illness, forces of reform from the provinces seized power and persuaded the sultan that he should abdicate.

The new sultan, Abdulhamid II (1876–1909), established a constitution and reorganized the government authorities. A new voting system made it possible for all the political forces within the empire to gain some influence in parliament. Individual rights such as religious and press freedom were also guaranteed and

compulsory school attendance was introduced. But Abdulhamid used the state crisis of 1877 to suspend parliament and to bring to an end the Tanzimat reforms. The efficient state bureaucracy was restructured along strictly hierarchical lines and the system of state schools was extended to give a state monopoly of education (foundation of the University of Istanbul, and schools for women).

Abdulhamid was an able organizer but his autocratic and reactionary regime increasingly provoked resistance. The Turkish-nationalist aligned "Young Turk Movement" became the leading body of opposition. They seized power in 1908 with support of the army leadership, forced the re-establishment of the constitution and parliament and in 1909 replaced the sultan, who was planning a counter-coup, with his brother, Mehmed V (1909–1918). Power lay with the Young Turks in this new constitutional monarchy. They took part in the Balkan Wars of 1912/3, when European provinces of the empire strove for independence and in 1914 pushed through the entry of Turkey into the war on the side of Germany and Austria. Internally the country was ideologically torn between the various political trends of Pan-Islamism or Ottomanism, Turkish nationalism, and modern democratic movements.

The defeat of 1918 sealed the fate of the empire, which was dismantled by the Western Allies and confined to Anatolia. The last sultan, Mehmed VI (1918–1922) had to recognize this arrangement in the 1920 Treaty of Sèvres. At that same time, the Greeks occupied Izmir and Smyrna. In Turkey, opposition groups, primarily nationalist in outlook, were formed against the harsh conditions imposed by the Allies. The leader of these groups in 1919 was Mustafa Kemal, who soon became popularly known as Ataturk ("Father of the Turks"). He turned the empire into a republic and through a policy of modernization and Europeanization transformeded the country into a Turkish national state. In 1922 he deposed Sultan Mehmed V and finally abolished the caliphate in March 1924.

Architecture

Almut von Gladiss

Ottoman art has developed its own particular form of expression in architecture, ceramic tiles and vases, textiles, and last but not least, the art of the book. It set new standards of quality in many fields. The unrestrained enthusiasm of the ruler for ceremonial, the immense financial strength of the empire, an appreciation of planning and precision, as well as an inexhaustible source of ideas which flowed from the master builders, artists, and craftsmen from both Islamic and Christian backgrounds, all helped Ottoman art to flourish over a long period of time.

The origins of Ottoman architecture – Bursa and Edirne

The source of Ottoman architectural development was the traditional pillared mosque after the Seljuk model, which stands out in the cityscape simply because of its size. The Ulu Cami ("Great Mosque") founded in 1396 in Bursa and the Eski Cami ("Old Mosque") founded in 1403 in Edirne, both of which lie in close proximity to the business quarter and occupy sites of 207 × 164 feet (63 × 50 meters) and 161 × 151 feet (49 × 46 meters) respectively have dome vaults resting on massive stone pillars. Bursa has twenty such domes and Edirne has nine. The size and shape of the domes accentuate the central axis with its definitive prayer niches. The oblong design of the room meet the needs of prayer, when the believers line up in rows opposite the *qibla* wall. However, in spite of its undeniable monumentality, the multidomed mosque proved to be the model that underlay the tendency already evident in early Ottoman times, toward standardization of rooms and prestigious dome architecture.

Above: **Ulu Cami in Bursa**, founded in 1396
With its numerous domes and the minarets flanking the facade, the Ulu Cami of Bursa is a simply monumental edifice, standing out from the modest single-dome mosques of the early Ottoman era.

Below: **Prayer hall of the Ulu Cami in Bursa**
Massive pillars divide the spacious hall. The name of Allah appears with various decorative symbols in the large-scale calligraphy on the walls and pillars. The reflection of the writing on the central axis achieves decorative symmetry in the hall.

Mausoleum of Mehmed I in Bursa, after 1421
Above the Green Mosque of Mehmed I in Bursa rises the sultan's mausoleum. It is built on an octagonal ground plan and vaulted over with a dome of flat bricks. The walls are subdivided by a series of marble ogives and decorated in between with tiles that replaced the original tile cladding after an earthquake. The interior (below) is tiled to a height of a good three meters. The prayer niche, which is twice that height, looks particularly magnificent with the curved palmette crown and the multicolored *cuerda seca* tile decoration. On the podium is displayed the tiled sarcophagus of the sultan.

The former Byzantine settlements of Bursa and Edirne, which the Ottomans chose as their first capitals, opened up interesting perspectives to the new rulers for their own building projects. Against a background of traditional building deeply rooted in the lands of the eastern Mediterranean, they began to combine mosque buildings with religious and social facilities in *kulliyes* (foundation complexes), which became the focal points of official life. With spacious foundation buildings they underlined the legitimacy of the ruler and bore witness to their commitment to undertake religious and social tasks for the well-being of the Islamic community. So they acquired a high reputation and respect for themselves and for members of their dynasty and laid claim to a reward in the life hereafter. Generally, the ruler's mausoleum was built into the foundation complex.

Murad I (1360–1389) founded a mosque in Bursa, which had been the imperial capital since 1326. This mosque had a central domed room which had an upper floor used as a *madrasa* and is situated outside the town enjoying an inspiring view over the plain, with a Koran school, a kitchen for the poor, a pump room, and the mausoleum, which Murad I intended to be his last resting place. The exposed situation on the edge of this historic town also characterizes the foundation complex of the next ruler. Murad's son and successor, Bayazid I (1389–1402), who was to receive the title of sultan from the caliphs of Cairo for his military success against the unbelievers, constructed separate buildings, one mosque, and two *madrasas*, which, together with a kitchen for the poor, a bath house, a small pavilion, and the mausoleum lay within a walled compound. This mosque, in contrast to the one built by Murad of mixed house stone and brick, is a massive cube of marble blocks. On the main axis it has two large domed rooms,

connected in the middle by a wide arch. Smaller vaulted rooms, side rooms and the entrance hall surround these domed rooms on three sides. The rear part, with the *mihrab* bay extending over the whole rectangular building, is raised above the entrance hall floor level. A gallery, presumably suggested by Byzantine buildings, which can be reached by some steps from the entrance portal, enabled the sultan, who generally had a podium on the left side of the prayer niche, to have a view over the 66-foot (20-meter) long room with the *qibla* wall at the end.

The next foundation complex in Bursa dates back to Sultan Mehmed I (1413–1421), son of Bayazid. The mosque (Yesil Cami), which also has a *madrasa*, a kitchen for the poor, and the mausoleum of its founder, is redolent of the twin-domed prayer hall of the mosque of Bayazid I, built 20 years before. Its decor and interior furnishings follow Seljuk traditions. The blocks of masonry show extensive relief decoration alongside clearly defined molded edges. This gives a magical attraction above all to the monumental main portal, which has intertwined arabesques at the gable end, callipraphic friezes on the doorframe, and traditional *muqarnas* vaulting over the entrance. The decor of the inner rooms consists of green- and blue-glazed hexagonal tiles, giving rise to the name of the building – "Green Mosque" (Yesil Cami) – and it is intensified in the prayer niche and the sultan's enclosure, where these two pillars of the whole concept of the Ottoman state are suitably emphasized by a particular star and tendril ornamentation in vivid colors. While in the time of the Seljuks tile mosaic was usual in Anatolia, here for the first time the *cuerda seca* technique was used, in which the different glazing colors are applied next to one another and prevented from running together while firing by separating lines of fat. From the evidence of their signatures, the master craftsmen came from the northwest Persian city

Europe. Edirne already had a number of mosques when Sultan Murad II (1421–1451) built the Uc Serefeli Cami between 1438 and 1447. The mosque is named after the three ambulatories of the biggest of its four minarets, which is 223 feet (68 meters) high. For the first time, it combined a rectangular prayer hall extended in width, by a wide rectangular forecourt at right angles to it, into a unified building structure on a roughly square ground plan with dimensions of 216 × 210 feet (66 × 64 meters). The dome space rises on a hexagon of wall sections and pillars, so that the dome, with the hitherto unachieved breadth of 79 feet (24 meters), allows the prayer niche to reach an impressive height. With the flanking pairs of domes, which rank in the same order of magnitude as the domes of the sultan's mosques at Bursa, it has the typical appearance of a building of standard square limestone block construction. Also for the first time, four minarets, which rise from the corners of the courtyard, were included in the plan. In combination with the powerful dome they signaled the new superpower's claim to leadership after 100 years of following a successful policy of expansion. With the height of its minarets, the size of its dome, and the breadth of its fountain courtyard, the Uc Serefeli Mosque served as a model for later sultans' mosques.

Istanbul – Islam takes possession of the old imperial city

Ottoman rule in Anatolia and southwest Europe had been consolidated when Mehmed II, son of Murad II, came to the throne in Edirne with the firm objective in mind of capturing Constantinople. Two years later the imperial Byzantine capital fell, and after three days of plunder the sultan went to Hagia Sophia to say his prayers in the fascinating atmosphere of this Byzantine house of God and to take possession of the brilliant domed building for Islam. This principal church of Constantinople, built by Anthemios of Tralles and Isidore of Miletus and officially consecrated in 537, towered above the whole city, with its powerful 184-foot (56.2-meter) high ribbed dome. Henceforward, the central dome construction held good as a model and as a challenge to the Ottoman master builders, causing a change of direction from the traditional spatial arrangement in buildings toward a heightened effect of space. With its conversion to a mosque under Mehmed the Conqueror (Fatih) and Bayazid II, Hagia Sophia – Ayasofya – was given two minarets as a visible sign of victorious Islam.

Mehmed Fatih Kulliyesi

In the last decades of Byzantine rule, however, Constantinople had become run down to the point of being an architectural desert. The first major contribution to the renovation of the city was carried out by Mehmed II (1444–1481) with his mosque complex, the Mehmed Fatih Kulliyesi, which was started ten years after he captured the city. It replaced the Byzantine Apostles' Church, which was the second largest church in Constantinople, with university buildings attached to it, and occupied a hill near the ancient Valens Aqueduct. In the foundation inscription the sultan refers with unbridled self-confidence to his objective of recreating the desolate and dilapidated city, where, he emphasized, many commanders had already failed before him. Completed in seven years, the mosque complex was financed from the spoils of campaigns against the unbelievers and from a poll tax required of all non-Muslim subjects. This domed edifice is over 130 feet (40 meters) high and with its wide forecourt formed the focal point of a spacious park. The sultan's intention to show himself to be the successor to the Byzantine emperor and to give important public works their proper place is reflected in the monumental symmetry of the complex. It is lined on each side with 656-foot (200-meter) long rows of *madrasas*, whose more

Uc Serefeli in Edirne, 1438–1447
The Uc Serefeli Cami in Edirne is the largest building of the early Ottoman era. For the first time a large forecourt was laid out in front of the prayer hall, where there were fountains for ritual ablution. The domed hypostyle halls, which stand along the edge of the courtyard axis, have alternate gray and red stones in the arcade arches. One of the four minarets, which tower above the corners of the courtyard, has a diagonally ribbed shaft, which is reminiscent of Seljuk building styles.

of Tabriz. They also created the tile cladding for the mausoleum, completed only after the death of Mehmed, which, as a domed octagon 89 feet (27 meters) in height, was a monument of a size hitherto unknown in Anatolia. This building style and tile decoration were to point the way ahead for building the mausoleums of future rulers in Istanbul.

Since the victories of Sultan Murad I (1359–1389) the Ottomans had pressed forward the expansion of the empire into the Balkans with all their might. The Thracian city of Edirne served as imperial residence and gateway to

modest style of building emphasizes the dominance of the mosque. In the area of the prayer niche the dome was enlarged with a half-dome reminiscent of Hagia Sophia. After it was damaged by earthquakes in 1509 and 1766, and then collapsed, the minaret was renovated by the architect Mehmed Tahir Agha, and refelcts the influence of mosques built by later sultans.

Mehmed the Conqueror was not, however, altogether satisfied with the building work after completion and had the architect Sinan the Elder executed in prison. It is not known whether he was disappointed with the building, which turned out to be too small in comparison with Hagia Sophia, or whether he did not agree with the reuse of some ancient columns. Two colossal porphyritic columns of Byzantine origin set between the new crossing pillars and wall pillars and the columns of pink granite and verd antique which lead to the forecourt perhaps make the older culture appear all too vivid.

The 16 *madrasas* that line the courtyard in two rows on both sides are more modest in appearance, though with their 230 rooms they take up more than twice the area of the mosque and the courtyard. They were intended to make the new capital the focus of science, as is stated in the foundation charter, and to help towards strengthening Sunni Islam. Judges and scholars of jurisprudence, who kept watch on adherence to religious laws, were trained here, prayer leaders and preachers for the mosques received instruction, and secretaries were prepared for their careers in the state administration. The foundation made a substantial contribution towards the economic recovery of this whole quarter of the city. In addition to this one-off investment in construction, the supply of materials for maintenance was worth well in excess of 1.5 million akce (a contemporary silver coin), into which revenues were poured from 12 bathhouses in Istanbul and Galata as well as from 50 villages in Thrace. This enormous sum paid the workers and financed all the associated institutions – a hospital, a hostel and a kitchen for the poor, where every day 3,300 loaves were distributed and meals provided for over 1,000 people.

Bayazid II Kulliyesi

Mehmed the Conqueror required the rich and powerful to take the initiative in having buildings erected and to build not only houses of prayer but also market halls, workshops, guesthouses, and baths. When the government of his successor, Bayazid II (1481–1512), took office, the city had several newly erected groups of buildings belonging to the viziers, while the sultan himself, as governor of Amasya, had founded mosque complexes in that city as well as in Manisa and Edirne. He had already been ruling on the Bosphorus for 20 years when he commissioned the architect Yaqub Sah ibn Sultansah to build a mosque complex in Istanbul, which was erected between 1501 and 1506 on the site of the ancient Forum of Theodosius near the Eski Saray ("Old Palace") which had been founded by Mehmed and towered above the bazaar quarter.

Following the model of Hagia Sophia, the half-dome is flanked on the longitudinal axis by two secondary half-domes, which arch over the *mihrab* and the entrance. The galleries, like side aisles, give extra breadth to the prayer hall. They are closely connected to the central area through a double arcade with granite columns between the transverse pillars. Having wings at the sides extends the entrance hall and the minarets are built on the outer ends of these wings. This extraordinary length of almost 328 feet (100 meters), which is crossed by the entrance to the domed building, is obviously caused by the rigid geometry of the whole site. So the length of the entrance hall corresponds to the total length of the mosque and mosque courtyard, both of which are based on squares of almost equal dimensions. Clear proportions of space and openness are obviously part of

Bayazid Cami, Istanbul, 1501–1506
The Bayazid Cami is made up of many groups of buildings: the courtyard with its domed hypostyle halls, the central domed building, which, like Hagia Sophia, was enlarged by means of a half-dome on an east-west axis and the domed *tabhane* wings (with travelers' accommodation) connecting the minarets on both sides. By extending the buildings both in length and breadth the architect has striven for balance. To the left is the kitchen for distributing food to the poor.

the architect's concepts. The rich decor of the building with its traditional Islamic subjects stands in complete contrast to this clear geometry. There are marble tablets with colorfully encrusted interlace and square Kufic script set into the bases of the minarets, in the arcade arches gray limestone alternates with red sandstone, and the marble rows of pinnacles on the ledges show cloud scroll formations. *Muqarnas* decoration is found both in the vaults over the deep portal niches as well as on the slender minarets, whose balconies are underpinned with rings of niches. The remarkably precise masonry work is also evident in the marble fittings in the inner room, the large *mihrab* with a border of *muqarnas* and the *minbar* (pulpit), which has braid and arabesque decoration on its side walls and on its staircase archway. While the *minbar* of the Ulu Cami in Bursa, built in the previous century, was crafted in wood in the Seljuk tradition, work was now in marble, thus continuing an old Byzantine specialty.

Near the mausoleums of its founder and his daughter, Sultan Bayazid's complex incorporated a *madrasa*, a kitchen for the poor, and a bathhouse. These provided a focal point for that part of the city, which had in the meantime become densely populated. The *madrasa* is impressive because of its open plan with a wide, columned courtyard, off which lie the domed rooms for the students. Opposite the entrance portal protrudes the large lecture hall, in which the Seihulislam, the senior judge and reporter on legal matters, would give lectures.

Sultan Selim Cami

Sultan Selim I (1512–1520) chose a terrace above the Golden Horn for his mosque. This building was erected posthumously and opens out from a wide forecourt. It is a plain cubic space connected to a massive dome, for which the mosque built by Bayazid II in Edirne between 1484 and 1488 was the model. With a diameter of 80 feet (24.5 meters) and a height of 107 feet (32.5 meters), the comparatively low-set dome, which blends with the square building below by having pendentives underneath it, surpasses in size all domes built previously. Its overwhelming massiveness reflects the tremendous drive of the builder, who had doubled the size of the empire in a few years through his policy of expansion.

The conquests of Mehmed, Bayazid, and Selim were the prerequisites for the great building complexes of the capital city. By the acquisition of land they provided the state with new regions for taxation, which paid the running costs of these establishments. In these foundation complexes, looting from the magnificent Byzantine buildings meant the irreversible subjection of the Eastern Roman Empire. Later, after the conquest of Syria and Egypt, building materials from Islamic countries were included in the plans, as when Selim I had the marble incrustations of buildings in Cairo confiscated and had a complete building dismantled and moved from Cairo to Istanbul so as to speed up progress with the building of the Topkapi Saray ("New Palace").

The concentration of remarkably large and magnificent mosques and foundation complexes in Istanbul, which demonstrated the absolute power of the dynasty, also fulfilled the needs of the Muslim population, which had doubled in number in a few decades, mainly through the arrival of Muslims from Anatolia. The new organization of the state had clearly improved the quality of life, as attested by multifaceted points of reference, when in the year 1537 Matraqi Nasuh produced the first city plan. The illustrated maps of Istanbul and Galata stretch over a double page of 12 × 18 inches (31 × 45 centimeters) in the work of this chronicler of the victorious campaign of Sultan Suleyman against Iraq, which set out from Istanbul.

It is a work of amazing topographical and architectural precision. Near the Byzantine sea wall is the wide square where the ancient hippodrome had been, with all the typical ancient monuments, such as obelisks and spiral columns. At the end rises the massive domed edifice of Hagia Sophia with its minarets, added as a sign of victorious Islam. The walled palace compound of the Topkapi Palace with its pavilions and gardens occupies the end of the city peninsula, and the Old Palace, which no longer exists, appears in the middle of the map as a walled park enclosing the palace itself and more pavilions. The principal mosques are situated on the central axis of the city. The Bayazid II Mosque is drawn with its mausoleums in the immediate neighborhood of the Old Palace and the market halls of the Great Bazaar. Below rises the enormous domed edifice of the Mehmed Fatih Mosque, which is represented on the same scale as Hagia Sophia, its counterpart, and is shown detached from the bustle of the city by a walled courtyard. The next piece of land facing the Golden Horn shows the small Selim I Mosque right on the edge. During the decades of renovation, near the variously designed large buildings there had been erected numerous small mosques with foundation complexes attached and among them rows of shops and bathhouses, which with their characteristic hypostyle halls and domes covered in gray lead completely filled the area. On the other side of the Golden Horn, which served as Istanbul's harbor, is shown the district of Galata with its Galata Tower, the highest point on the fortifications of the old Genoese trading settlement.

Sinan's principal works

The maps of Istanbul were produced at a time when the greatest Ottoman builder, Sinan, was just beginning his career. He was to give the city a breathtaking appearance in an unusually long creative period, which would include nearly 200 building projects. In a brilliant achievement of urbanization, he created the fabulous silhouette characterized by mighty domes and slender minarets – a magnificent architectural landscape – which at least from the distance has no sense of being overcrowded. The exotic appeal of the array of buildings dominating the Golden Horn, where Hagia Sophia, the Bayazid II Kulliyesi, and the Suleymaniye Complex built by Sinan break majestically through the sea of houses of the Old City, filled the large number of visitors from Europe with enthusiasm. It has attracted artists such as Melchior Lorich, the painter and engraver from Flensburg, member of the German Embassy from 1555, who by 1559 had already completed a pen-and-ink drawing more than 36 feet (11 meters) long, and later in 1590 Heinrich Hendorfski, painter to the German ambassador, who was to produce atmospheric colored drawings of the city.

Sinan (1491–1588), who had been brought to Istanbul from central Anatolia through the "boy harvest" (*devsirme*) and converted to Islam, had acquired

Sultan Selim Cami in Istanbul, 1522
The Sultan Selim Cami was completed two years after the death of Selim I by his son Suleyman the Magnificent. It is a domed cubic building with a nine-domed *tabhane*, with lodgings for dervishes and other travelers, running along both sides. The wide forecourt extends over the whole width of the prayer hall and a part of the *tabhane*. The two minarets of the mosque rise from the corners of the *tabhane* and the forecourt.

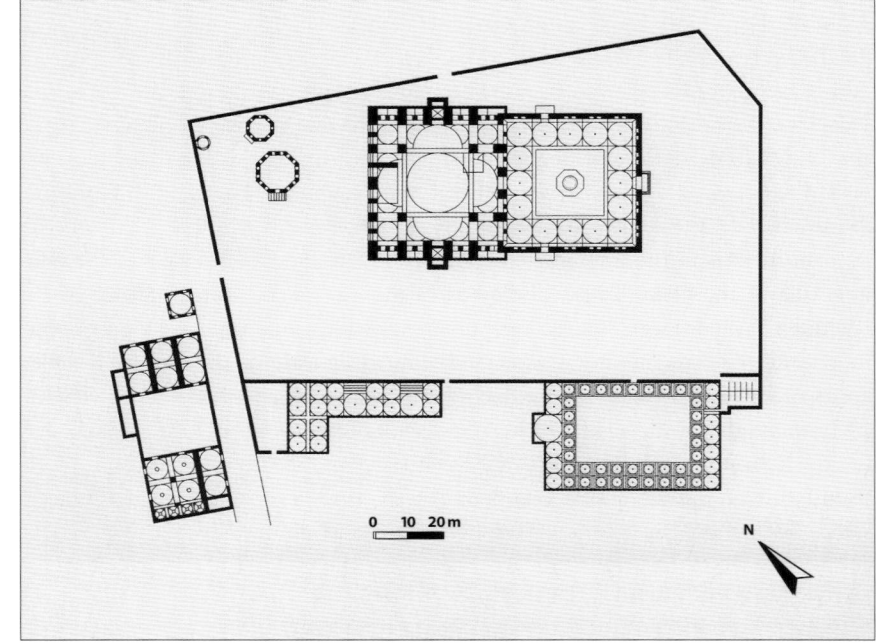

various technical skills through his service with the pioneers on the campaigns of Suleyman the Magnificent and in 1538 was appointed head of the Ottoman building authority, where at that time there were a good dozen master builders employed. As chief architect of the court, he was the first to have the building plans from the sultan and his family, who built not only in Istanbul and the core Ottoman territories but also in the provinces. Building styles developed in Istanbul served as models for the whole Ottoman Empire.

Sinan's strengths lay in his planning. His brilliant creative power was fired by the vision of a domed building in the style of Hagia Sophia. His first job was the conversion of a foundation for Hurrem, Suleyman's favorite concubine, who was from Russia, which included not only a mosque but *madrasas*, Koran schools, and kitchens for the poor in Istanbul – the Haseki Hurrem Kulliyesi – but also guesthouses and kitchens for the poor in Mecca, Medina, and Jerusalem. The establishment of a religious foundation was possible for free men and also for women, who were now beginning to emerge more and more from the isolation of the women's chambers and showing philanthropic commitment. Mihrimah, the daughter of Suleyman and Hurrem, even commissioned Sinan to build two large foundation complexes, which were built over a period of 15 years. The Harbor Mosque in Uskudar on the Asiatic coast of the Bosphorus, which he completed in 1548, had a very popular belvedere, which offered an uninterrupted view across the sea to the gardens of Galata. Henceforth the female members of the dynasty, primarily the mothers of the sultans, preferred to establish their foundation complexes amid the still comparatively untouched landscape of Uskudar, particularly renowned for its gardens.

View and ground plan of the Sehzade Complex in Istanbul, 1544–1548
The Sehzade Complex was the first important building of the court architect Sinan. Its main dome is flanked on four sides by half-domes as on Byzantine cross-dome churches, and is in addition supported by smaller half-domes on the diagonals. In the ground plan the standardization of the layout of the prayer hall becomes apparent. The diameter of the dome is half the measurement of that of the sides of the square room. The forecourt, which lies in front of the minarets at the corners of the mosque, occupies virtually the same surface area. To the rear lies the mausoleum of the prince and other tombs. A *madrasa*, a lodging house, and a kitchen for the poor make up the rest of the foundation complex.

The Sehzade Complex

Mehmed, son of Suleyman and Hurrem and chosen successor to the throne, died of smallpox at Manisa. Sinan was subsequently instructed to erect a large complex in his memory between the Mehmed Fatih Kulliyesi and the Bayazid II Kulliyesi, which was completed in 1548 after a period of four years. The institution known as the Sehzade Cami ("Prince's Mosque"), which besides the mosque and its forecourt also included mausoleums, a *madrasa*, an elementary school, a hospital, and a kitchen for the poor, was later described by Sinan as the work of his apprenticeship, while he saw the Suleymaniye Complex, built ten years later, as his work as a journeyman, and the Selimiye Complex of Edirne, which was officially opened in 1574, as his masterpiece. Within the mosque, there are two equally large square areas – the prayer hall and forecourt joined together into one unit – after the model of Bayazid II's Mosque. The transept – as in Byzantine churches – has been extended to create a central room of enormous width through the addition of four half-domes on the axes of the main dome. The diameter of the dome, at 62 feet (19 meters) amounts to half the length of the side of the building, giving well-balanced proportions. The elegant design of the facade stands in contrast to the simple, straightforward interior. On the exterior several loggias hide the walls, the bases of both the minarets on the corners of the building between the prayer hall and the forecourt, the corner domes resting on square tambours, and the tower-like buttresses with false domes, which connect the central building to the half-dome. The rich structure of the exterior of the building matches the high-quality decor, which not only includes ledges and *muqarnas* portals topped with battlements but is also evident on the minarets, where a band of decoration with braid and knotwork motifs

Courtyard and interior view of the Sehzade Mosque in Istanbul, 1544–1548
In the middle of the courtyard (above) is a fountain used for ritual ablutions which has a canopy of later date. The hypostyle hall around the courtyard has been built higher to accommodate the mosque portal. The interior (below) is broken only by the four pillars supporting the dome, which set off the central vault from the four half-domes, with the broad transverse arches and the pendentives in between them. A wall with many windows accentuates the setting of the modern prayer niche.

Below: **Suleymaniye Complex in Istanbul**, 1550–1557
This view is from the south side of the Suleymaniye Complex over the roofs of the *madrasas*, where the curtain wall with its windows breaks the line of the dome structure. The graded wall arch, which stretches between the towering pillars with their false domes, carries the weight of the principal dome. This arch is accentuated just like the fenestrated walls of the side dome rooms below. The openings to the loggias can be seen between the pillars that support the half-domes.

The Suleymaniye Complex in Istanbul, 1550–1557

This aerial photograph conveys some idea of the enormous extent of the Suleymaniye Complex. The mosque alone with its forecourt surrounded by four minarets is 110 meters in length. It forms the focal point of a walled compound. On the same side as the courtyard are the foundation buildings arranged at right angles. These buildings with their rows of domes are aligned with the plan of the mosque forecourt and have their rooms grouped around internal courtyards. The foundation complex thus conveys a balanced and uniform appearance, in spite of the variety of buildings.

matching the facets reaches as far as the first ambulatory. The octagonal mausoleum, in a walled garden behind the mosque, is decorated with tiles like the mausoleum of Selim I. The coloring and technique is reminiscent of the tile cladding in the mausoleum of the prince's ancestor and namesake Mehmed I in Bursa.

The Suleymaniye Complex

As an architectural statement by the ruler, in the form of superb architecture, the Suleymaniye Complex, which Sinan began to build in 1550, was to surpass all previous sultans' mosques. After the military successes of his father Selim in Syria, Egypt, and West Iran and his own victorious campaigns in Iraq and the Balkans, Suleyman the Magnificent (1520–1566) ruled over a global empire – and world-level architecture was to bestow a visible expression of his power. In the late 16th century, the Ottoman historian Mustafa Ali described Suleyman's buildings almost as important as his conquests as a mark of his unequalled greatness. The sultan personally selected a site on a slope above the Golden Horn, where there was an extensive piece of land available after the fire at the Old Palace. The building was to rise on this site to be as striking as the Dome of the Rock on the Temple Mount in Jerusalem. After prolonged work in planning and terracing, the laying of the foundation stone took place in the presence of the sultan on June 13, 1550, an auspicious date according to the court astrologer.

The mosque is almost twice the size of the Sehzade Mosque and lies in the middle of a walled compound 708 feet (216 meters) in length and 472 feet (144 meters) wide. The architect adopted the dome system, with two flanking half-domes, small corner domes, and lateral curtain walls, from Hagia Sophia. Characterized by the massive quadrate pillars, the interior is extended to the entrance and the prayer niche and is given more width on the transverse axis through the addition of galleries on the other side of the lateral triple arcades.

On the exterior there are two-storied hypostyle halls with curtain walls, whose massive masonry is broken by rows of windows. The forecourt with a fountain for ritual washing in the middle has a colossal portal with a tympanum framed by half-columns and four minarets at the corners, which accompany the rise of the dome with their graded heights of around 230 feet (70 meters). The mass of buildings rises gradually in a characteristic style, starting with the prominent central dome of the entrance hall over the half-domes and the corner domes of the strengthening pillars, right up to the principal dome with the clearly visible buttresses. This dome boasts a diameter of 87 feet (26.5 meters) and an apex height of nearly 157 feet (48 meters). Gilded crests with

Interior of the Suleymaniye Mosque in Istanbul 1550–1557

Square-edged dome pillars dominate the interior of the mosque. The longitudinal dimension is accentuated by the fenestrated curtain wall, which rests on a row of columns and connects to the sides of the building, and by the *mihrab* area, which extends under the half-dome. The fenestrated *qibla* wall shows the tripartite structure of the building, which can be seen throughout. A tiled area here for the first time surrounds the marble prayer niche. On the right are the marble pulpit for sermons and the platform for the singers.

the Islamic symbol of the crescent moon sparkle from the peaks of the domes and the minarets.

The identification of the sultan as world ruler and his role as protector of orthodox Islam is emphasized in the foundation inscription over the main portal of the mosque, which is accentuated by a *muqarnas* vault. It was written by Suleyman's senior judge and legal scholar, the *Seyhulislam*, who had the sixth Sura read out each day, which begins with praising the absolute power of God and ends with divine authorization of worldly power: "And it is He who has appointed you viceroys in the earth ..." The Suleymaniye Mosque forms a visible symbol of Ottoman worldly rule. During festivities, the model of the mosque, which was as big as the famous architectural models of the Italian Renaissance, was carried by a dozen powerful men in procession for the edification of the masses, as is shown in a miniature from the *Surname* (Feast Book) written in 1582.

Incorporated in the Suleymaniye Complex are the mausoleums of Suleyman and his wife Hurrem, which were built in the years 1556 and 1558 directly behind the *qibla* wall of the mosque, which had been strengthened with powerful buttresses. There are also many *madrasas*, which according to the foundation charter had to serve the glory of religion and religious sciences as well as strengthening worldly rule. The scholars of the *madrasas* were actually

Dome of Hagia Sophia in Istanbul, 532–537 Forty windows light the ribbed dome of Hagia Sophia. Its apex is 56 meters above floor level, and running around the dome, in place of the original mosaic, is a text from the Koran in the striking Sulus calligraphy of the 16th century.

Following the *bismillah* ("In the name of God, the Merciful, the Compassionate") is the so-called "light verse," sura 24. 35, which commends the whole building to the control of Allah: "God is the Light of the heavens and the earth ..."

summoned into the palace for regular discussions. In addition to the religious schools, there was a corresponding medical high school, which along with its hospital was the leading establishment of its kind in the Ottoman Empire. A kitchen for the poor and a guesthouse run along the narrow side of the mosque compound opposite the main door. The foundation buildings, repeating the plan of the mosque courtyard, are lined with domed hypostyle halls, emphasizing the sense of belonging and achieving uniformity.

The services supplied by the foundation complex corresponded to the needs and the expectations of a rapidly growing population. The Ottoman metropolis, with its population of several hundred thousand, had developed into the greatest city in the whole of the Mediterranean area. Every quarter of the city had its own foundation complex, on which official life was focused, but none was as big as the Suleymaniye Complex. It had some 800 employees, some of whom dealt with education and research while others were fully occupied in caring work

Dome of the Suleymaniye Mosque,
Istanbul, 1550–1557

The vaulting arrangement of the Suleymaniye Mosque is borrowed from Hagia Sophia, and yet the massive two-colored arches that lift the dome above the open space create bright conditions. These arches rest on a system of protruding corbels, which surrounds the whole space and separates the sphere of the vault from the lower depths. With the original blue finish within the dome, Sinan allowed himself a view of the infinity of the firmament.

in the hospital, the kitchen for the poor, or the guesthouse. The annual income of the foundation was close to 1 million akce (a silver coin). This money was to be raised from the 217 villages and 30 communal fields, which the foundation owned, among other sources.

While the building of this vast construction dragged on, doubts about the competence of the architect arose. The sultan required Sinan to complete the mosque in the shortest time, hinting at the fate of Sinan the Elder. After a period of strained day and night working and summoning all the forces available, Sinan opened it for worship when he handed over the key in October 1557.

In its proportions, it surpassed all previous major Islamic edifices and formed a counterbalance to Hagia Sophia in the cityscape, even though it did not reach the size of the latter (dome diameter 107 feet, 31.9 meters, height 184 feet, 56.2 meters). While the Byzantine building had a mysterious effect with light streaming into the vaulted area over a gloomy central space, the Ottoman building, lit from floor to dome in equal measure, is convincing in its clarity and logic.

The economic power of the Ottoman Empire permitted major construction projects to a hitherto unknown extent. The court maintained a building management office, which, in consultation with the sultan, planned and oversaw various building projects, drew up estimates of costs, knew how to calculate labor and materials costs, procured building materials, and organized the work. This mammoth operation was controlled at great bureaucratic expense and progressed at speed. In the case of the Suleymaniye Complex, the building processes are documented in account books, which record in detail all the various aspects of the building up to the fitting-out with 30 new manuscripts for the recitation of the Koran.

The manual workers, Muslim and Christian in roughly equal numbers, were recruited from Istanbul and other areas and organized into qualified master craftsmen and unskilled labor. In the summer there were often more than 3,000 workers employed on the site, above all stonemasons and wallbuilders, who worked in small groups on particular tasks. The military, with young Janissaries from the campaigns or from the "boy harvest," was organized to do all kinds of supporting jobs: guarding, transporting heavy loads, and working in the quarries.

The procurement of materials fills the greater part of the account books. While porphyritic, granite and marble columns coming from old Byzantine buildings were reused and columns were even brought from Roman temples in Alexandria (Egypt) and Baalbek (Lebanon), the beige-colored limestone came substantially from the quarries on the Sea of Marmara. Shipping the loads weighing many tons – the 30-foot (9-meter) high granite columns of the arcade arches inside the Suleymaniye Mosque weigh some 30 tons (28 tonnes) – was an adventure in itself. Iron for the window lattices and for locking together the blocks of stone, and lead for the roofs and domes were mainly brought in from the Balkans. The colored window glass, which has survived in the *qibla* wall, was presumably imported from Venice and assembled on site by local glaziers. The carpets came from the west Anatolian knotting centers and from Cairo, the grass mats from Egypt and Sudan.

The tile decoration of the mosque was supplied from the northwestern Anatolian city of Iznik, whose pottery workshops had become well known for their ceramic vessels with underglaze painting. This process imitated the hard white ceramic and the cobalt blue underglaze painting of Chinese export porcelain and had enriched the traditional leaf tendril patterns with eastern floral and cloud motifs. The 12-inch (30-centimeter) hanging lamps from the foundation complex of Bayazid II are among their most remarkable creations. Decorative tiles in the Suleymaniye Mosque are evident only, apart from on the window lunettes, on the *qibla* wall, where polychrome panels complement the marble *mihrab*. While the surmounting frieze shows the Islamic creed, the medallions on the side carry the opening suras of the Koran, which call for daily prayers in majestic script with overlength strokes. The expressive calligraphy goes back to a design by the leading calligrapher Ahmed Karahisari. These medallions from the studio in Iznik demanded the highest skill, as each field of script included 64 square tiles, each showing only one a tiny part of the radial script. For the first time these compositions also show, besides the familiar subtle blue tones, a bright tomato red, which was obtained from the iron-rich Armenian bole and provides stunning splashes of color on the white background. In the mausoleums of Suleyman and Hurrem, the tile decoration, with floral tendrils spreading over the surface, gives a sense of splendor. This is a drawing style cultivated in the court studio of the Topkapi Palace, which draws its elegance from the long serrated and curved leaves (*saz*) that are incorporated into the pattern structure.

The sketches from the court studio encouraged the tile painters, who had started out with blue-and-white tiles for buildings in Edirne, to produce ornate compositions, which – assembled from numerous 10 inch (26 centimeter) square tiles – created a fascinating effect. With them there appear such flowers as were cultivated in the Ottoman gardens – tulips, carnations, roses, ranunculi, and hyacinths, as well as invented pinnate and palmate leaves – which, arranged symmetrically, form the background for the magnificent patterns. The partly

Rustem Pasha Mosque in Istanbul, 1561
In the mosque of Rustem Pasha, a particular sponsor of craftwork, Iznik tile manufacture, with its boundless possibilities, reached its apogee. While the flower fields of the prayer niche are composed of differently painted tiles, the rest of the tiled walls are made up of standard tiles with border motifs, which can be joined together in the continual repetition of an elegant pattern. The dome pillar is clad with similar tiles in vast numbers.

Sokollu Mehmed Pasha is known as the builder of several complexes. In Istanbul he founded a mosque on a slope facing the Sea of Marmara for his wife, Esmahan, daughter of Selim II, after he had destroyed, according to a building inscription, a church of the unbelievers, "to create a place of prayer, where unbelief and darkness once ruled." The mosque complex occupies a spacious courtyard with a triangular columned hall and connecting rows of rooms, which serve as *madrasas*. The prayer hall, marked by its towering dome, has rich tile decoration around the stone prayer niche, which is connected to an arch extending up as far as the window area of the dome. The motif on the arch is repeated by the tiled area at the side of the *mihrab* and filled in with foliage work. The restriction of tile decoration to the important parts of the building and the matching of designs help to achieve a balanced effect.

natural, partly fantastic plant decoration, whose brightness is enhanced by means of clear glazes, was capable of transporting the believers, momentarily, into another world – into the heavenly paradise garden, which is constantly promised to them in the Koran and in the Koranic inscriptions in mosques such as in the Suleymaniye.

Mosques of the grand viziers

Many of Sinan's mosque buildings are remarkable for their splendid tiled walls. These are exemplified above all in three buildings erected for clients from the upper strata of society who came from the "boy harvest": Grand Viziers Rustem Pasha and Piyale Pasha from Croatia and Grand Vizier Sokollu Mehmed Pasha from Bosnia.

Rustem Pasha, who had the best connections at court through his marriage to Suleyman's daughter Mirimah, invested his wealth in many building projects. The mosque founded in 1561, for which he acquired a choice building plot below the Suleymaniye Complex, is situated in a confined position in the middle of the bazaar, so that the special fountains for ritual washing had to be set directly on the street. The prayer hall is raised up on a platform, under which there are shops and workshops, and from a double entrance hall it opens out as an octagon with dome and diagonal half-domes. The light coming in through narrow rows of high windows and extensively glazed arched walls bathes the areas of tiles, which cover the walls up to the dome pendentives and the pillars up to the impost ledges, in a strange brightness. The squared prayer niche shows the niche motif repeated and filled with floral bouquets. Corresponding rows of niches also appear on the rows of contemporary prayer mats, which have not in fact been preserved from the Rustem Pasha Mosque, but from the slightly later mosque of Selim II.

Selimiye Mosque in Edirne, 1574

The bazaar, which lies in front of the Selimiye Complex, is totally dominated by this celebrated late work of Sinan and acts as a base to enhance the height of the construction. The central room is vaulted, with a 43-meter-high dome. On the left stretches the forecourt with the gradually rising system of domes of the hypostyle halls. In the interior, the immense width is supported by the spacious diagonal half-domes and the accompanying vault architecture, which go right up to the dome space. The effect of space is increased by the ample light coming in, which penetrates through the rows of windows in the dome, the curtain walls, and the half-domes.

The Selimiye Complex

Within 20 years Sinan had established himself as the most important architect of his time. He knew how to demonstrate the absolute power of the sultan and his family in the cityscape of Istanbul. By planning, he knew how to make use of the often difficult sloping sites and confined conditions in densely populated quarters of the city for his buildings and how to compensate for the disadvantages of a building site through inspired solutions. At an advanced age he began his "master work" for Selim II (1566–1574), the sole surviving son and successor of Suleyman, who was in the habit of using the old palace at Edirne, the former capital city, for official functions. The mosque was constructed on a site of 623 × 426 feet (190 × 130 meters) in the middle of what was a small city in relation to Istanbul. It was completed in 1574, a few months before the sultan's death. Its dome is 138 feet (42 meters) high and it has four slender minarets, which, with a height of almost 233 feet (71 meters) surpass all Islamic prayer towers. Sinan looked with enormous pride on the crowning of his life's work. In the biography recorded by Mustafa Sai shortly before his death, he refers to the minarets, with their separate spiral staircases to the ambulatories, which could scarcely be accommodated in the slender towers, and, in contrast, to the dome, which with a diameter of 103 feet (31.28 meters) is in fact the largest of all Ottoman buildings. He boasted that he had achieved the enormous proportions of the dome of Hagia Sophia, which in the opinion of Christians demanded too much of Muslim architects, and that with God's help and the support of the sultan he had considerably surpassed them. Actually, Sinan must have been very familiar with Hagia Sophia, for he had made a meticulous study of its spatial proportions when repairing the 1,000-year-old Byzantine building.

THE OTTOMAN EMPIRE

The dome of the Selimiye Mosque rests on an octagonal arrangement of pillars, whose tower-like construction on the exterior marks the corners of the high drum. The arches extending from the pillars open out alternately onto the fenestrated curtain walls at the sides and onto the corner domes, which are also illuminated by windows. Together with a second, lower row of arches, which integrates the gallery architecture and is also illuminated by the fenestrated curtain walls, they provide the 197 × 144 foot (60 × 44 meter) interior with an enormous breadth and lightness. In the center on a system of open arches stands the marble rostrum of the muezzins, which covers a small well, bearing a resemblance to the washing well of the Ulu Cami at Bursa. The original wells for ritual cleansing lie in the middle of the forecourt, which occupies the same surface area as the domed room and is surrounded by domed and hypostyle halls.

The windows of the ambulatories are surmounted by tiled lunettes, which are repeated in the interior of the domed room. The tile decoration is richer than that of the Suleymaniye Mosque and goes right up to the area of the marble prayer niche, which, connected to a pair of pillars through the side walls, reveals a separate room. While the text decoration was designed by a well-known Istanbul calligrapher in consultation with the sultan, the floral work appearing on the walls of the prayer niche represents the usual high quality of products from Iznik. The magnificent painted tiles of the sultan's loge form the frame for another *mihrab* with *muqarnas* vaulting and a window covered by a wooden shutter, which allows a view of the sky. The floral decoration is picked up from the prayer rugs, which belong to the sumptuous initial furnishing of the mosque and are kept in fragments of up to 26 feet (8 meters) in length in the Istanbul Museum of Turkish and Islamic Art.

The mosque forms the focal point, within the Istanbul foundation, complex for institutions serving the general public over a wide area. The Selimiye Complex includes only a *madrasa* and a house for the Koran readers, whose square ground plans occupy the corners of the mosque compound behind the *qibla* wall. At the wish of the builder, Selim II's mausoleum was not erected here but near Hagia Sophia in Istanbul.

When Sinan died in 1588, he had developed convincing formulae for the layout of mosques and the accompanying educational and social complexes. He was celebrated as the Euclid not only of his century but of all time, as it says in the foundation document for his mausoleum, which lies near the Suleymaniye Complex. From this comparison with the famous Greek mathematician we must assume that in his constructions he laid down the basic cast-iron rules of geometrical figures and proportions and that this task was seen as the work of a lifetime, which replaced all that had gone before and could in no way be surpassed. None of the later great Ottoman buildings could succeed without his inspired spatial concepts.

Both the sultan's mosques in Istanbul constructed by Sinan's immediate successors in the office of chief architect – the Yeni Valide Cami on the Golden Horn, begun by Davud Agha in 1598 and completed by Mustafa Agha in 1663, and the mosque of Sultan Ahmed I at the Hippodrome, built by Sedefkar Mehmed Agha between 1605 and 1617 – show the 'four-leafed clover' plan first applied at the Sehzade Mosque, in which the central dome is supported on four sides by half-domes.

The Blue Mosque

Sultan Murad III built a foundation complex in Manisa, following plans by the venerable Sinan and carried out by the architects Mahmud and Mehmed Agha. Like his son, Mehmed III, he had handed over the building work in Istanbul to his energetic mother. Sultan Ahmed I acquired one of the coveted sites in the city at the Hippodrome opposite Hagia Sophia, where any edifice towering above the

Selimiye Mosque in Edirne, 1574
The central space with its massive angular dome pillars is bounded by triple arcades with galleries on the sides of the rectangular transept, which make use of the depth of the buttresses; because of their windows, they are visible over the arcades of the exterior galleries. The gallery at the same time serves to conceal the great supporting arches, which divert the load of the double skin of the dome from the dome pillars. Thanks to these subtle techniques, the ambitious impression of space is not spoilt by numerous heavy supporting pillars and buttresses. The mighty dome just seems to float over lightweight exterior walls.

Sea of Marmara could have the greatest effect. Little more than half the size of the Byzantine building, the mosque asserts itself by having six minarets, of which two pairs surround the dome building, as at the Selimiye Mosque at Edirne, while the third pair flank the entrance to the forecourt. Altogether, they provide 16 ambulatories for the muezzins, whose call to prayer would ring out like a choir of many voices across the peninsula.

The prayer hall is scarcely any smaller than that in the Suleymaniye Mosque and yet it is covered with a comparatively small dome of 75 feet (23 meters) diameter and 140 feet (43 meters) total height. The sultan demanded by decree the same Iznik tiling for his building and in addition had complete tile walls from the Topkapi Palace reused, resulting in a magnificent and boundless display, a bewildering abundance of 21,000 tiles. The court, however, was prepared to pay only the original price for the tiles, which had been fixed under Sultan Suleyman but completely overtaken by inflation in the meantime, so that many of the 300 workshops in Iznik were unable to maintain the level of quality and went over to offering their products for sale on the open market.

During the planning of the Sultan Ahmed Cami, also known as the "Blue Mosque" because of its blue paintwork, the high clergy were critical of the sultan since he could not refer to any glorious victories. In his writings for the Ottoman court the historian Mustafa Ali explains that only the rulers who returned from holy wars with booty and new territories had the right to build charitable buildings such as hospitals, soup kitchens, or schools. Tax revenues should not be used for such projects that were, in the end, unnecessary, even if they involved the construction of additional mosques. According to the author's estimate, the building of a sultan's mosque cost at least 50 million akce, which

corresponded to half the Egyptian tribute payment. Historically, though, many Islamic rulers had taken substantially more money from well-filled state coffers for their building projects.

Mustafa Ali saw the incessant building activity in the great cities as exhibitionism by the mighty and a strategy for improving their reputation. He was critical that thousands of small towns had neither a mosque nor a monastery, and certainly had no kitchen for the poor. In fact, the building projects carried out in the names of the ruling dynasty, high dignitaries, and provincial governors had been concentrated on the cities, on the ancient capitals of Bursa and Edirne, on the temporary princely residences of Amasya and Manisa, and on places with more than 10,000 inhabitants such as Konya, Kayseri, Ankara, Tokat, Sivas, Maras, Gaziantep, Kastamonu, Diyarbakir, Aleppo, Damascus, and Cairo. In addition, the old feudal families that had survived were active as builders in their home cities.

Commercial buildings

Besides the mosques that were also founded in less urbanized areas such as the Balkans or the Arabian Peninsula, it was commercial buildings that attracted the business-minded upper classes: multidomed market halls (*bedestans*) in central locations, which served as secure transshipment centers for quality goods. In the Istanbul Kapali Carsi ("Covered Bazaar") the two market halls going back to the times of Mehmed II and Suleyman the Magnificent are connected by numerous shopping alleys and khans covering an area of 74 acres (30 hectares). In addition to the royal facilities in the city, with businesses on the ground floor and rooms

for the traders on the upper floor, caravanserais were built in the trade routes, some of which offered a vast range of services. The complex of Sokollu Mehmed Pasha in Luleburgaz on the road from Istanbul to Edirne contained, on an enormous site, a small mosque, a spacious *madrasa*, a Koran school, a bathhouse and a bazaar, all combined in an axisymmetric plan. At the caravanserai of Selim II at Payas, a Mediterranean port and starting point of the road to Aleppo, a courtyard lined with sleeping quarters complete with kitchens, meal rooms, and gardens stretches over an area of 21,500 square feet (2,000 square meters) near the mosque. Baths (*hammam*) and a bazaar complete the complex, which again was planned on strictly geometrically lines. As in the time of the Seljuks, whose caravanserais were more widely used, the new facilities were established at set distances one from another in line with the state plan for the safety of trade and pilgrim routes. Pilgrim caravans could be based at particular service stations, such as can be seen at the pilgrimage center built under Suleyman and Selim II at Damascus, which has a mosque, *madrasa*, kitchen wing, and a designated area for tents.

Ottoman palace architecture – the Topkapi Palace

In contrast to the mighty mosque architecture supporting such enormous domes, comparable to the buildings of the European Renaissance, no such colossal image on the scale of European structures was created for this palace. Small residences already existed outside the historic city in Bursa and Edirne, when Sultan Mehmed II, two years after the conquest of Constantinople, built his first palace in the center of the city. This palace was known as the Old Palace ("Eski Saray")

Above: **Dome of the Sultan Ahmed Cami (Blue Mosque) in Istanbul**
The interior of the Sultan Ahmed Cami has four round columns five meters in diameter, which are fluted like the contemporary minarets and covered in decoration above the lines of the Koranic text. A corbel ledge underpinned with *muqarnas* work carries the arch architecture of the vault. From it extend the massive top arches, which carry the dome. This colossal space is illuminated by 260 windows, which originally contained colored glass imported from Venice. The building structure is softened by a proliferation of tile cladding and blue paintwork. The architect of the Blue Mosque, Mehmed Agha, had already made the throne for Sultan Ahmed, a rather cluttered composition of mother-of-pearl, tortoiseshell, and precious stones on walnut, and was well known for his theatrical taste when he was appointed chief court architect in 1606.

Opposite: **The Sultan Ahmed Cami (Blue Mosque) in Istanbul**, 1610–1617
The Sultan Ahmed Cami overlooks the Sea of Marmara. As in the Sehzade Mosque, the main dome is extended on four sides with half-domes, which transfer the load onto the bearing wall and an arrangement of pillars. The side view of the central building, flanked by four minarets, shows the loggia halls in between the pillars. Two further minarets on the forecourt accentuate the angles of the main entrance facade. In front is the *madrasa* belonging to the mosque.

Baghdad Koshk (Kiosk) in the Topkapi Palace in Istanbul, 1638–39
On the viewing terrace on the northwest corner of the Topkapi Palace rises the very elegant Baghdad Koshk, which Sultan Murad IV had erected to commemorate his success-
ful Baghdad campaign of 1638. Behind the slender marble columns of the entrance hall opens out a low building with windows reaching almost to the floor, which afford views onto the park and the architecture of the city.

Cinili Koshk in the Topkapi Palace in Istanbul, 1473
The remarkable features of the Cinili Koshk, constructed together with three further pavilions by Mehmed the Conqueror, are the open hypostyle hall at the front and the
functions room at the rear, with a view over the palace gardens. The two-story building has a cruciform arrangement of rooms with a dome over the center. It owes its name ("Tiled Kiosk") to its rich interior decoration.

and included several pavilion-type buildings, which lay in a park and were screened by a double surrounding wall. The sultan also built the fortress of Yedikule near the Sea of Marmara, making use of the fortified towers of the old wall of Byzantium. This fortress was able to serve as a treasure chamber and, in case of attack, as a refuge.

The buildings were hardly complete when the sultan decided on an area of more than 150 acres (60 hectares) on the point of the city peninsula, whose elevated position with the Byzantine sea wall behind it met his security require- ments as a site for his palace. On a sightseeing tour of the conquered city, the extensive ruined landscape of the Byzantine palaces at the Hippodrome had made a lasting impression on him. They had been left to decay after being plundered by the Crusaders in 1204. Building work began in 1459 and lasted throughout the sultan's reign. From that time onward, the Yeni Saray ("New Palace"), later known as the Topkapi Saray, was for centuries the showplace of the unrestrained royal desire to build. The complex, whose exterior was finished off with a surrounding wall complete with towers and gates, is of modest height as a palace, with numerous pavilions, laid out in a scattered formation and with the spacious gardens which reflect the closeness to nature of Islamic culture, imbued with illusions of paradise. The Mediterranean enthusiasm for garden landscapes, which had been recorded ever since the age of Roman palaces and country villas, was revived in the 14th century in the Nasrid palace city of the Alhambra. The Ottomans also loved views over luxuriant gardens with geometrically designed

flower and vegetable beds, in which streams and fountains provide coolness and cypresses and plane trees afford some shade. On the Saray headland stretched terrace gardens lined with rows of cypresses as far as the Byzantine sea wall. In the seclusion and peace of this park landscape – with an absolute ban on talking in the presence of the sultan – the courtly ceremonial could develop, which only served to accentuate the distance between the sultan, persisting in solemn inaccessibility, and ordinary mortals.

The palace city consisted of three groups of buildings, lying behind one another, which were adapted to different functions. The complex is approached

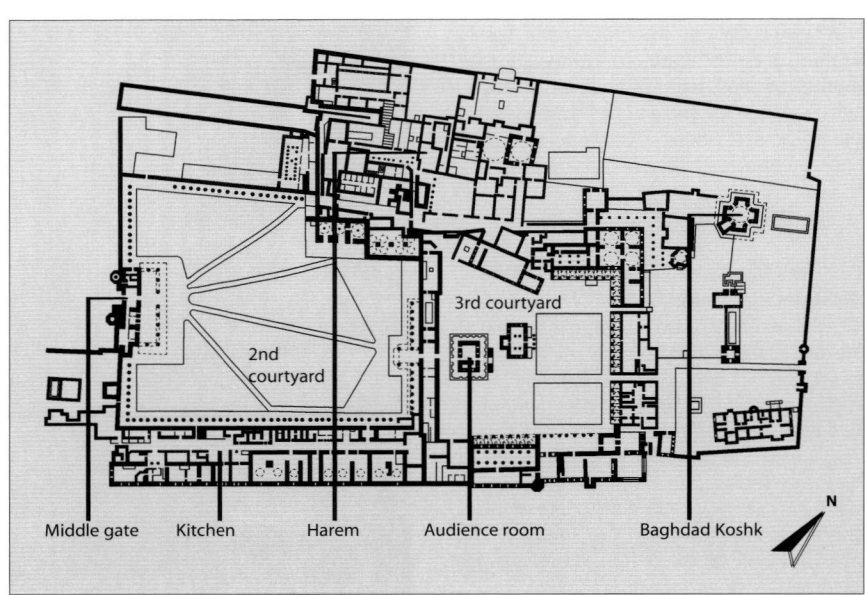

Topkapi Palace ground plan, 1459 and later
This plan shows the three courtyards of the Ottoman residence one behind another. The second and third courtyards can be seen, and the tulip garden, which is fenced off in the northern part of the viewing terrace. In the
northern corner of the second courtyard are the divan room, the state chancellery, and the financial administration. Behind the third courtyard's gate is the audience room. In the north are the sultan's private chambers, living quarters for the state court and the harem.

through the Bab-i Humayun ("Sovereign's Gate") which was built near Hagia Sophia by Mehmed II. Behind this is the first courtyard, with the Byzantine church of St. Irenaeus used as an arsenal and various pavilions in different styles. Of these only the Cinili Koshk summer pavilion, which covers an area of 92 × 118 feet (28 × 36 meters), has been preserved, its name ("Tiled Kiosk") referring to the rich tile decoration. Behind the entrance hall, whose timber pillars were replaced with stone columns after a fire, there is a hall with a cruciform ground plan and a domed central area, which opens into a reception room with a view over the gardens. The room design makes use of ideas from the palace of the Aq-Qoyunlu rulers at Tabriz, the fiercest adversaries of the Ottomans in the east, who were utterly defeated in the year building began.

The second courtyard can be approached through the gatehouse of the Orta Kapi ("Middle Gate"), which is surmounted with battlements and flanked with towers. On the east side of the courtyard is a long kitchen wing with enormous places for cookers and dome-shaped chimney hoods. In the adjacent rooms not only were the tin-plated cooking utensils stored but also the fine dinner services, mainly unbelievable quantities of Chinese porcelain. On the side of the courtyard opposite the kitchen wing and at a somewhat lower level were the stables. In a corner of the courtyard stands the domed Kubbe Alti, in which the viziers, under the supervision of the grand vizier, had meetings with the high-level financial officials and the military as well as the head of the state chancellery, during which the sultan followed the proceedings from a box with a grill in front. The magnificent decoration, with heavy silks and satins, bejeweled cushions as well as exquisite carpets, is emphasized in contemporary chronicles. In the adjacent domed rooms were accommodated the state chancellery, the treasury, and the financial administration.

Behind a wide gate stretches the third courtyard with the audience hall (Arz Odasi) built by Selim I, which is surrounded on all four sides by hypostyle halls. On a bejeweled throne the sultan received the respect of embassies from all parts of the empire and from Persia and Europe. Gifts from the embassies were transferred to a treasure room in a corner of the courtyard, which in addition was stacked with precious war booty from the various campaigns and held the state vestments and precious jewelry of the royal family. Separated by the palace school, which occupies one whole side of the courtyard, in the opposite corner lie the domed rooms containing the relics of the Prophet Muhammad and the Rightly Guided Caliphs, which Selim I had acquired through his defeat of the Mamluks. The Ottomans took great pleasure in their new role as protectors of the holy cities of Mecca and Medina and custodians of the holy relics, and thereby justified their claim to leadership of the Islamic world.

The adjacent rooms include the sultan's private chambers, which were regularly enlarged, especially when the sultan's wife Hurrem insisted that the harem moved into the New Palace after a fire in the Old Palace. After another devastating fire, which broke out in the Topkapi Palace in 1574, Sultan Murad III, who left the business of politics to his grand vizier in order to devote himself to the fine arts, began the improvement of the harem complex. Apart from the

View over the harem at the Topkapi Palace in Istanbul, end of the 16th century
This view over the harem conveys an impression of the unique situation of the Topkapi Palace on the peninsula of the ancient acropolis overlooking the Golden Horn, the Bosphorus, and the Sea of Marmara. The lead-covered roofs, with the softly curved domes and the unexpectedly elevated chimney towers form a confusing and yet harmonious composition of forms. The great twin domes in the center of the picture cover the Saloon of Sultan Murad III and the later Throne Room.

Above: **The Saloon of Sultan Murad III in the Topkapi Palace in Istanbul**, late 16th century
Situated on the edge of the harem, the Saloon of Sultan Murad III is a square hall with pendentive dome, whose construction dates from the time of Sinan. The golden dome painting and the surrounding tile cladding – which is broken up by glass windows – the fountain, and wall niches, are all examples of sumptuous magnificence.

Below: **The Throne Room in the Topkapi Palace in Istanbul**, mid-17th century
On the right-hand side of the Throne Room, which is situated immediately next to the Saloon, is the throne sofa with its wooden canopy under a tiled Koranic inscription. The platform under the balcony for the court musicians was reserved for the ladies of the harem. The Throne Room was redesigned in the 18th century with rococo décor.

sultan's mother and his four principal wives, hundreds of concubines, and at least as many servant girls were accommodated here, as well as an army of black eunuchs, who were responsible for the protection and control of the ladies of the harem. A tiled panel, whose inscription refers to the completion of a pavilion next to the sultan's bathhouse in the year 1574/75, dates from the beginning of this phase of renovation. A blossoming plum tree, which controls the symmetry of the decoration, and floral compositions of tulips, carnations, ranunculi, and hyacinths transfer the splendor of the flowers that blossomed in the palace gardens into the interior of the palace. The entrance to the Saloon of Sultan Murad III is bordered with almost identical tiled panels. This room, which goes back to Sinan, is vaulted with a pendentive dome decorated with graceful arabesque paintings, in whose top medallions appear the beneficent Koran sura 112, while, round the base of the dome runs a band of tiles bearing the "throne verse" (sura 2. 255). These significant inscriptions give rise to the assumption that the room was not only used as a private chamber but also as a reception room. A marble fountain set into a wall niche was designed to prevent the overhearing of state secrets with the noise of its splashing. The adjoining Throne Room (Hunkar Sofasi) was completed in the middle of the 17th century. It houses the throne sofa, which stands prominently on a platform and is surmounted by a wooden canopy, and was used to receive the ladies of the harem and for festive occasions.

The greatest festival at court was the Festival of Circumcision, for which there was a separate pavilion (Sunnet Odasi) available, renovated by Sultan Ibrahim (1640–1648). The entrance facade, screened by a hypostyle hall standing in front of it, is renowned for its tiled walls, where tiles from the golden age of Ottoman tile production had been reused. In a magnificent blue-and-white composition are combined a rectangular panel with densely packed bands of cloud and a tripartite arch wall, with little blossoming plum trees in the middle and flowering tendrils at the side, together producing a balanced composition, in which the bands of cloud motif recurring in the arch spandrels joins it all together. In the dense tendrils with pinnate leaves and full peony flowers appear pheasants and fabulous Chinese beasts, which come from designs from the court studio. Contrary to Ottoman tradition some of the buildings arranged around atria or alleyways, for example the princes' chambers, have tile-clad exterior walls.

The Sunnet Odasi occupies a terrace in the Tulip Garden, which was laid out on top of the old fortifications, together with the Golden Canopy (of gilded copper) – also constructed by Ibrahim and offering a unique view over the park and the massive royal mosque buildings – and two further pavilions. Both the Revan Koshk and the Baghdad Koshk, which were built on the occasion of the victories of Murad IV (1623–1640) at Erevan and Baghdad, have three or four fenestrated alcoves furnished with low sofas, eminently suitable for meditative contemplation of the stunning landscape. In the Baghdad Koshk the walls are decorated with tiles up to the base of the dome, where tiles from older palace buildings were also reused alongside new tiles. The wooden doors, window shutters, and wall cupboards show the usual interlace with inlaid mother-of-pearl, ivory, and tortoiseshell, which together produce a surface with a sumptuous effect. The dome carries subtle paintwork with gold stars on a red background and the flat ceilings over the bays bear painted arabesques.

With the decline of tile production painted wooden wall panels came into fashion. Sultan Ahmed III (1703–1730), whose enthusiasm for the tulip gave its name to a whole period, had a room in his private chambers paneled and converted to a dining room by the addition of a magnificently colored still-life painting of floral bouquets arranged in vases and baskets of fruit. This kind of interior decoration had reached its peak in the 17th century in townhouses in the Syrian province. The oldest surviving wall paneling, inscribed with the dates 1600/01 and 1603, comes from the reception room of a grand house in Aleppo.

Tile decoration in the Sunnet Odasi (Circumcision Pavilion),
Istanbul, Topkapi Saray, 1640–1648 restored
Older tile panels were used in the cladding on the facade of the Sunnet Odasi. This triptych, which is designed as a mirror image, illustrates the high standard of the tile painting from Iznik, with blossoming plum trees in the center and arabesques enlivened up with birds and fabulous creatures at the sides. The tiles date from the middle of the 16th century. The central panel, inspired by the plum trees of the palace garden, already shows the bright clay red, which appears for the first time in the tile decoration of the Suleymaniye and on the vases in the mosque there.

The head of the household was an important merchant who bore a name with Christian references, Isa ibn Butrus (Jesus, son of Petrus). He commissioned for the painting prominent artists, who were not only the masters of floral painting enriched by the addition of birds and fabulous creatures, but also dared to include scenes of figures in the style of contemporary book illumination. Most of these are entwined in arabesques, which are interspersed with carnations, tulips, roses, hyacinths, bellflowers, and lilies as well as peonies and curved pinnate leaves. Both the large panels in the main alcove have prominent representations of figures, which are concerned with two particular themes. On one side there are two throne scenes: in the first the ruler receives the severed head of his enemy on a plate; in the second he goes off for a ride with his falcon,

The Aleppo Room, 1600–1603 Berlin, Museum of Islamic Art
The painted wooden paneling was installed in the villa of a rich Aleppo merchant at the beginning of the 17th century. The walls of this reception hall, are covered with high-quality painting over a length of 35 meters up to the height of the cornices. Contemporary book illumination and tile painting are reflected in the arabesque work, enlivened by birds and fabulous creatures, and in detailed scenes with figures.

for which a magnificently bridled and saddled horse stands ready. Hunting and banquet motifs allude to the privileges of the ruling class. On the other side the painting is devoted to religious themes. The New Testament is represented by portrayals of Mary and Jesus as well as the Last Supper, where Jesus appears in a circle with his disciples, his hands raised in a blessing. The Old Testament is represented by a portrayal of the Sacrifice of Isaac. Abraham is in the process of putting the knife to the throat of his son who is kneeling before him, while the delivering angel hovers nearby with the sacrificial beast.

Abraham and Jesus were, like many biblical prophets, also honored in Islam. The genre of stories about prophets had won a large readership amongst the urban upper class in the second half of the 16th century, for whom illustrated editions were for the first time being produced. Sultan Murad III eventually commissioned the court studio in Istanbul to produce the histories of the prophets (*Siyer-i Nabi*) by the blind poet from Erzurum, Darir, in a magnificent edition. The six-volume work, which honors the descent and life of the prophet Muhammad and has more than 700 miniatures illustrations, could not be finished until the last years of the reign of his son and successor Mehmed III. Since it had never been illustrated before because of the reservation prevailing at the time regarding the representation of figures in the religious domain, hundreds of new types of illustration were demanded from the painters. They succeeded in their task by producing the impression of festive rapture through soft lines, light, bright colors, and the playful use of clouds and little angels, so that the prophet is transfigured with a white facial veil and a golden halo of flame.

Mosque lamp, Iznik 1549, height 38 cm, London, British Museum
This mosque lamp was produced by a master craftsman by the name of Musli in Iznik and was donated to the Dome of the Rock in Jerusalem in the course of the restoration work on the harem complex undertaken by Suleyman the Magnificent. Besides the religious inscriptions it shows dainty ornamental cloud scrolls, which are framed by delicate arabesque painting. While the decoration looks back to earlier models, the coloring is typical of Iznik pottery of the 1540s. Quality ceramic from Iznik, a city some 100 km from Istanbul, had no competition in the whole of the Ottoman Empire.

Decorative Arts

Almut von Gladiss

With the conquest of Constantinople the Ottomans saw themselves as the heirs of Byzantium, of the former cultural counterweight to the caliph's metropolis of Baghdad. Mehmed the Conqueror, more of a Renaissance prince than strict religious champion, reflected on bygone displays of magnificence and on his new position in the ranks of world leaders. He summoned painters and medallists from Europe to come to his court, among them Gentile Bellini from Venice and Costanzo de Ferrara. Portraits by the Italian masters created the foundation for the development of Ottoman portrait painting. Costanzo's bronze medallion inspired the leading court painter Sinan to produce a 15 × 11 inch (39 × 27 centimeter) portrait study of the Sultan. Such mastery of portrayal, where individual psychological characterization combined with a well-developed sense of reality, was never again achieved. While the skillfully executed portrait of the 50-year-old, painted in private, represented the claim to power of a successful ruler, later portraits of the Ottomans generally mirror the ideal of a timeless existence, a life led according to the rules of courtly etiquette.

The art of the book

Besides painters, Mehmed employed numerous writers, who worked on the copying of Turkish, Persian, and Arabic manuscripts at the newly established libraries. In the center of this artistic creativity was the production of magnificently illuminated Koranic manuscripts for the newly established mosque complexes. Mehmed's son, Bayazid, had, as governor of Amasya, learnt the art of calligraphy with the venerable Sheikh Hamdullah and persuaded the latter to follow him to Istanbul and to place his abilities at the service of this flourishing capital city. However, the court studio, established within the first courtyard of the Topkapi Palace, took in not only native masters but also numerous Persian artists, who had an unsurpassed wealth of experience based on the long unbroken tradition of Persian book arts. The *Book of Solomon* by the poet Uzun Firdevsi from Bursa (15th century) and dedicated to Bayazid II shows as a miniature frontispiece an unconventional composition with seven horizontally arranged picture cycles, which are devoted to the legendary royal city of the biblical king, who himself appears as ruler of the world, surrounded by angels and birds, in a tower building of the same style as the Orta Kapi in the Topkapi Palace. The mysteries of the cosmos are explained as a reality through connection with real pieces of architecture, which is an indication of the basically functional character of the Ottoman painter.

After the conquest of the Safavid residence Tabriz by Selim I, the Ottomans made further artists move to Istanbul, where the classical literary works were copied on a major scale. By the time Suleyman the Magnificent came to the throne the court studio had increased to 41 painters and a number of bookbinders through the incorporation of capable artists from all parts of the empire. With the intention of creating within a short period of time a cultural base for this still young world power that would match its political importance, extensive stocks of books were also either purchased or seized, such as the private libraries of the last Aq-Qoyunlu and Timurid rulers, parts of the Safavid court library from Tabriz, and of the Bibliotheca Corviniana from Buda. In the course of the 16th century the court also received hundreds of valuable books as embassy gifts from the Safavids: In1576, 18 Korans alone, together with 61 volumes of Persian poetry and numerous albums of paintings.

The Battle of Caldiran, miniature from the *Selimname* of Sukru Bitlisi, 1525 Istanbul, Topkapi Palace Museum
The *Selimname*, commissioned by Suleyman the Magnificent immediately after the death of his father Selim, glorifying the deeds of his predecessor, comes at the beginning of this illustrated history of the Ottomans. After Selim had defeated the Persian army in 1514, he took the Persian capital of Tabriz and returned to Istanbul with rich booty of war. This miniature painting shows the armies confronting each other at Caldiran. On the right are the superior Ottoman forces that won the victory.

Suleyman the Magnificent on the throne, Ahmed Feridun Pasha, 1569, Istanbul, Topkapi Palace Museum
The chronicle of Suleyman's last Hungarian campaign shows the Sultan receiving his vassal Johann Sigismund Zapolya at his camp. The ruler is seated on an enormous throne in front of a magnificent tent, whose dome-like canopy indicates the ruler's status. This historical work reaches its peak with the death of Suleyman in Szigetvar and the ensuing conquest of the city by Grand Vizier Sokollu Mehmed Pasha.

Mehmed the Conqueror, Sinan Vey, c. 1480, 39 × 27 cm, Istanbul, Topkapi Palace Museum

This portrait of Mehmed the Conqueror from one of the palace albums records the influence of the Italian portrait art of Gentile Bellini. The sultan, shown sitting cross-legged in typical Turkish style, has the cruel aura of an army commander. The handkerchief in his left hand is a traditional ruler's accessory, while the rose in his right hand testifies to his closeness to nature. "No one takes more pleasure in carrying flowers than the Turk," emphasized the French botanist Pierre Belon du Mans in his *Description of the Flower Market in Istanbul* (1546–1549).

Selim II at archery
Nigari, second half of the 16th century,
Istanbul, Topkapi Palace Museum
This unconventional portrait by the court
painter Nigari shows Selim II practicing archery. The disproportionate size and the
energetic movements convey strength of
leadership and conceal the weakness of will
and alcoholism of this sole surviving son of
Suleyman the Magnificent.

Suleyman lays siege to Rhodes, from the
Suleymanname of Arifi, 1558, Istanbul, Topkapi
Palace Museum
After a five-month siege in January 1523, Sul-
tan Suleyman took the Mediterranean island of Rhodes. In the foreground the sultan
appears astride his steed to encourage his
troops, who, under the protection of the Janissaries, are attempting to sap the fortifications.

However, the court studio no longer saw its task as merely to copy classical
Persian and Turkish works but also to prepare sumptuous editions of the poems
of its rulers, the anthologies of Selim I and Suleyman the Magnificent, and to
develop historical painting to the glory of the dynasty. Historical works on the
Ottomans having appeared since the 14th century, illustrated accounts of their
deeds were first produced through cooperation between leading scholars and the
royal artistic studio. The historian Matraqi Nasuh had accompanied Sultan
Suleyman on his campaigns and immediately did the illustrations, with his staff
of assistants, for both of his written works on the campaign of 1537 in Iraq and
Iran and the campaign of 1543 in Hungary. There are clear portrayals of the
cities, villages, fortresses, castles, and harbors that the army had passed.

The Ottomans had created the office of *Shahnameci*, whose duty was to use
the events of the time to create a history of the reign, following the model of the
famous *Shahname* of the Persian poet Firdausi (c.935–c.1005). In this work the
sultan was to be honored not as a mythical hero but as an illustrious head of state
who was above all criticism. These works glorified the deeds of the Ottoman
armies and those of their ancestors. The triumphal scene and the fairy-tale display
of splendor, which the bare, if exuberant, text could not convey in a sufficiently
impressive way, were portrayed by the artists in fairly realistic paintings, which
bolstered the edifying effect of the text. The miniatures stressed dramatic
incidents in the life of a ruler and elaborated the events, in which the central
figure's presence proved crucial for the quality of the picture over and above the
episode portrayed.

Sultan Suleyman had already had his father's life recorded in a chronicle
when he appointed Arifi as *Shahnameci* in the middle of the 16th century. He
was an experienced chancellery official, who, with Elkas Mirza, a brother to the
Safavid Shah Tahmasp, had fled Shirwan for Istanbul after a failed rebellion. The
sultan was so moved by the first 30,000 verses of the *Shahname-i Al-i Osman* that
he seconded a group of calligraphers and artists solely to produce this work. This
first Ottoman history with illustrations of figures is made up of five volumes, the
largest of which is the *Suleymanname*. It has 617 pages and 69 miniatures covering the events of the period from 1520 to 1555 and was completed three years
after Suleyman's death. The artists were familiar with court ceremonial, which is
evident in the festive scenes at the accession and in the reception of ambassadors.
From their own experience they were also familiar with the principal rooms
of the palace, as the magnificent double-page paintings indicate. With palace,

battle, siege and execution scenes, the *Suleymanname* by Arifi served as a handbook for all later historical works.

Suleyman's last years were described by Ahmed Feridun Pasha in a work about the campaign at Szigetvar. In the miniature painting showing the taking of the city, which takes up a double page, there is the portrayal of figures combined with a sensitive representation of the topography. Suleyman died at Szigetvar in 1566 and this historical work ends with the accession to the throne of Selim II and the first years of his reign. The accompanying 20 miniatures are by the court artist Osman, who laid great store by the documentary aspect of his work and who also strove for a fairly realistic portrayal, which is evident in a comparison between the frail Suleyman and the youthful Selim. A further portrait by the court painter Nigari conveys the impetuous energy of the successor to the throne, who is shown practising archery.

In his cooperation over many years with the *Shahnameci* Lokman, who was appointed by Selim II in 1569 and worked at court under Murad III for 20 more years, Osman displayed an unsurpassed skill in historical painting, which was expressed in a strongly self-confident style. In the *Shahname-i Selim Khan* completed in 1581 he used the first miniature for a self-portrait, which shows him together with the painter Ali, the author Lokman, the scholar Semseddin Ahmed Karabagi, and the calligrapher Ilyas Katib. In the background there are piles of reference books, writing and painting patterns as well as a pencil box and other working materials. These people had privileged positions that were the envy of many. However, they were at the same time subjected to strict control by the court. In one of his works Lokman relates that his literary abilities had been examined by experts from the court and by the *Seihulislam* before he could start work and that the calligraphers, illustrators, and miniature painters involved also had to submit samples of their art. The *Shahname-i Selim Khan* comprises 43 miniatures, which prominently display glorious land and sea battles. The infamous Battle of Lepanto in the Gulf of Patras, where the Ottomans lost almost their whole fleet in 1571, is absent however.

Lokman's two-volume *Shahinshahname* covers the reign of his patron Murad III from 1574 to 1588, representing the high points of his rule in 153 miniatures. Apart from the usual throne and battle pictures there are also several references to the achievements of his time, such as the new observatory, which started operation in Galatasaray. The magnificent volumes were intended in the first place for the edification of the Ottoman family, who knew how to appreciate that type of stimulating material and were always able to find new ways to glorify the head of their dynasty or their ancestors. In the two-volume historical work *Hunername* were described the lives of all the Ottoman sultans from Osman, the founder of the dynasty, to Suleyman the Magnificent. Typical of the illustrations is the contrast between intimate scenes, which show the sultan hunting or in the company of his closest advisers, and the battle scenes, with their panoramic landscapes, in which the army divisions are clearly arrayed and which illustrate the superior might of the Ottomans with their highly-organized masses of troops.

Finally, in the *Surname* there is but one single event: the 52-day Circumcision Festival, which was arranged in 1582 for the son of Murad III in Istanbul, who later came to the throne as Mehmed III. The stimulus was the legendary Circumcision Festivals of the court of the caliph in Baghdad, at which according to established tradition the guests were showered in coins as gifts.

The Festival was celebrated near the palace gate at the ancient Hippodrome, which is marked by monuments, spiral columns, and two obelisks. While the sultan, princes, and high dignitaries surveyed the events from a terrace at the Ibrahim Pasha Palace, the invited guests and below them the ambassadors of foreign powers all sat on a nearby wooden grandstand. The festivities were opened by the religious leaders with a prayer for the dynasty and reached their climax in

The Procession of the Guilds: Acrobats, from the *Surname* by Vehbi and Levni, 1720 Istanbul, Topkapi Palace Museum
The most important hand-painted miniature of the later Ottoman period is the *Festival Book* of Sultan Ahmed III. It refers to the festivities on the occasion of the circumcision of his four sons in 1720 and records the 15 days of mass entertainment for the people of the capital.

the 21-day procession of the guilds, which demonstrated their products and services. Since there was no previous model for the portrayal of such processional displays, Osman and his studio had to summon up all their skills of fantasy and creativity for the 437 (surviving) miniatures. These did not concentrate on the sultan, who always remains in the same position, but on events in the arena, a varied show with numerous surprises. Festive floats are drawn across the square and platforms are carried along, on which craftsmen and traders represent their organizations and with great pride draw attention to the high standard of the goods and services that made life in the Ottoman capital worth living. Textile workers appear with heavy bolts of material, glass blowers with a glass kiln, *hammam* operators with customers in portable bathtubs, butchers with chopped mutton, and bakers with an oven. Stallholders selling hot food and coffee show how they prepare their specialties and serve their customers. The gardeners file past with magnificently colored floral arrangements. A further group attracts attention with a gigantic yellow tulip. Garden tulips were an absolute triumph in Europe at that time, after the German emperor's ambassador had brought back to Vienna plants and bulbs from his Turkish travels.

While the guilds displayed their services, musicians, dancers, tightrope walkers, actors, magicians, clowns, and wrestlers took part in the public event, followed by a firework display at the end of an eventful day. Despite the wealth of figures in the pictures, the faces occasionally showing some variation, and the overextravagant hustle and bustle, the end result is uniformity, as if it were a parade of soldiers where everything works as it would in a well-run puppet theatre. Below the honored guests were numerous Europeans, who, recognizable by their broad-brimmed hats and their short cloaks with lace scarves, follow the performance from chairs especially placed in front of the marquees. Sultan Ahmed III was the first to dispatch ambassadors to Paris and Vienna. He also sent landscape gardeners on study trips to Europe to give some stimulus to art, which had begun to stagnate. All of this led to an eclectic culture.

Ottoman luxury goods

Ever since its foundation in the late 15th century the court studio at the Topkapi Palace had not only been the center for bibliographic art but also an enthusiastic experimental workshop for incomparable luxury goods. Through their exquisite clothes and expensive jewelry, especially the grandiose brooches with precious stones that they wore in their turbans, the Ottomans put themselves at the pinnacle of contemporary potentates, who in turn became transfixed in admiration, like mere underlings, in the face of this overwhelming display of splendor. Items of booty from campaigns and exquisite gifts from neighboring states, as well as those from state servants devoted to the sultan, formed the core of the contents of the treasure room. The masters of the court studio took as inspiration the treasures plundered from the Safavid palace in Tabriz by the soldiers of Selim I in 1514, among them a dark green nephrite pitcher with fine gold wire ornamentation surrounding the names of the first Safavid ruler, Ismail. A black obsidian pitcher in the same form, naturally somewhat larger, shows comparatively thick arabesques and in addition a sumptuous border of rubies, which sparkle in golden floral wreaths. The tankard with boiled drinking water, which was kept ready for Suleyman and his successors for official occasions, was a striking golden showpiece, set with emeralds, rubies, and jade plaques. The candelabras, almost 3 feet (90 centimeters) high, from the foundation complex of Ahmed I, were so thickly encrusted in jewels that the modest base metal of

A further festival book was commissioned from the court poet Vehbi by the Sultan Ahmed III (1703–1730) on the occasion of the circumcision of his four sons in 1720. The 137 miniatures are by the painter Levni from Edirne, whose leadership helped the court studio to flourish once again and who staged the lavish mass entertainment with remarkable realism. The Hippodrome had become too small for the crowds of spectators because of the building of the mosque of Ahmed I. The procession therefore started from a festival site by the Golden Horn, where the sultan and the state court were assembled in marquees, via the decorated streets to the Topkapi Palace, where the circumcision took place. The closing ceremony took place in the third courtyard with the Sunner Odasi and the new library building of Ahmed III.

gilded copper was hardly visible. Porcelain was also decorated with inlays of jewels, for which monochrome Chinese pottery was used in particular, since the Iznik ceramics were not suitable for further color effects because of their multicolored painting.

This combination of the choicest materials characterized numerous products from the court workshop, which was like a great storehouse of expensive raw materials mostly coming from foreign trade, expenditure on which was tightly controlled. In order to fashion the items so that they would appear as brilliant as possible, many original artistic tricks were employed. For example, they underlaid the pieces of tortoiseshell on book covers with shiny metal foil, or the rock crystal covering of gold vessels with delicately painted paper. Rich trimming with turquoises is remarkable on turban and belt jewelry, mirrors, and weapons. The sword of Suleyman the Magnificent, identifiable by the dedication inscription running along the steel blade, has an ivory hilt with golden loops of clouds and on the blade the fabulous phoenix and dragon with sparkling ruby eyes, heraldic symbols from the Central Asian homeland of the Turks. The sword was manufactured according to the signature on the spine of the blade by a Tekke-Turkmen craftsmen, which contributed as much to the reputation of the court workshop as did the craftsmen from the Balkans.

Ottoman silk weaving was at first concentrated within the old capital of Bursa, where up to the end of the 16th century raw materials from Iran were used exclusively. The early silks show restful compositions with strings of rosettes, emphasized with gold and silver embroidery on a deep red background, reminiscent of the crimson red of the Byzantine court. The Cintamani motif, with tiger stripes and three leopard heads, was used as a symbol of power in memory of the legendary kings and heroes of the distant past, whom they imagined in animal skins. A velvet caftan in the Topkapi Palace believed to belong to Mehmed the Conqueror has dark red versions of the Cintamani design on a golden background, while a monumental throne bench in walnut, which dates back to the time of Bayazid II and is also kept in the Topkapi Palace, carries tiger stripes on the seat and mother-of-pearl dots carefully arranged on the backrest, which together with the ivory cloud formations clearly display the eastern tradition.

The silk weaving industry, which flourished in Istanbul in the 16th century favored for luxury material a regular pointed oval net as a web structure, into which are set strings of medallions. Tulips and carnations or whole bouquets of flowers serve as a filling motif. Curved garlands of palm leaves, or single contrarotating or parallel climbing sheaves of tendrils with flowering twigs and fruit, all bring movement into the design. The width of the weave was generally 26 inches (68 centimeters), while the pattern repeat could be extended as far as the length required. With the finest silk brocades, which were prepared for Suleyman's sons Mustafa and Bayazid (who died in 1553 and 1561, respectively), the pattern repeat exceeds the total length of the 4.1 or 4.8 foot1 (26 or 1.47 meter) caftans. The extremely rich palette of color matches the lavishness of the compositions. Since the production of such magnificent patterns involved great expenditure, the princely caftans remain unique items. Some of the numerous Ottoman garments held in the Topkapi Palace Museum come from the treasure chamber and others from the family mausoleums. Apart from single colored material, they frequently use materials with two or three colors, which produce beguiling color tones of bright red and shimmering gold and green.

The caftan is a straight-cut, occasionally loose-fitting and generally floor-length robe, which in front is either loosely overlapped or fastened with buttons and loops of ornamental braid running across the chest. It is lined with cotton or silk and faced on the hems with silk or fur. The sultan and the high officers of state often wore three caftans one over another, a short-armed garment over a long-armed garment, and then over that one a caftan with long false arms, which

Medallion ushak, Turkey, 1573, 670 × 350 cm, Istanbul, Museum of Turkish and Islamic Art

This medallion ushak comes from the mosque of the Vizier Piyale Pasha, which was completed in 1573. Carpets made in western Anatolia ever since the late 15th century following designs from the Istanbul court studio are noted not only for their large size but also for their elegant arabesque patterns. The structural scheme is of a central medallion and half-medallions that start in the corners on both sides. The rippled and serrated contours are just as typical as the precise inner pattern.

Caftan, Turkey, late 16th century, silk, Istanbul, Topkapi Palace Museum
The pattern of this silk caftan, trimmed with fur at the neck, is characterized by the pointed oval net popular in the 16th century. The intersection points of the climbing tendrils are overlaid with medallions filled with flowers, from which rise tulips and pomegranates. In the portrait by the court painter Nigari, Sultan Selim II wears a robe with a similar pattern.

were just as much symbols of luxurious lifestyle as the lavish garments one on top of the other. The talisman shirts possessed by the Ottoman princes display some exceptional features. They are embroidered and labeled with Koranic verses, prayers, numerological squares, and magic symbols.

The quantity of both the garments and the decorative materials suggest a large number of experienced weavers in Istanbul and Bursa. State quality control ensured a comparatively high standard and in the case of irregularities the state could close down whole sectors. So in 1564 more than half the Istanbul brocade weavers had to stop work on the orders of the court because of fraud involving gold and silver thread.

In western Anatolia there were already numerous carpet workshops in operation, when the building boom which began under Mehmed II and Bayazid II triggered a growing demand for essential products for furnishing the mosques and residences. The first carpets commissioned by the court, the large format medallion and star ushaks, show a large-scale web structure with pointed oval or star-shaped fields, which have a rare expressiveness with their clear blue and red color tones. The medallion ushaks are up to 33 feet (10 meters) in length, which

required perfectly organized workshops with plenty of master craftsmen, large looms, and considerable stocks of different colored wool. Such financial investment could only be made by the court, which also put at their disposal the graphic design for the strikingly fine pattern inspired by the art of the book. The pattern consists of a central pointed medallion with rippled border and serrated quarter-medallions in the corners and in the large sizes the pattern is enlarged in the repeat scheme. A fork-leafed quatrefoil serves as the principal ornament, while leaves and floral stems run around the outside.

In competition with the ushaks were carpets with horizontally and vertically sewn octagons, whose borderlines show typical interweaving, where the main borders repeat the interlacing motif in a decoration suggesting Kufic script. This tendency towards geometric stylization can lead to the complete dissolution of forms, so that the entire surface presents itself as well-ordered arabesque work. The types of carpet are named after the western painters Hans Holbein and Lorenzo Lotto, who meticulously reproduced the patterns and the vividness of these carpets in their paintings. From the 15th century Italy was a profitable market for carpet sales. Buyers of these magnificent carpets came from the nobility and even the church, since St. Peter's in Rome numbered four Ottoman carpets among its treasures according to an inventory of 1489.

After the conquest of Cairo by Selim I, the Ottomans made use of the technical perfection of the Mamluk manufacturers, whose carpets could be knotted more closely using much finer wool than the Turkish and therefore could more easily create those gracefully turbulent motifs. Drawings of patterns from the Istanbul court studio supplied just the basis for the arrangements of plants with curved pinnate leaves, palmette and rosette blooms, carnations, pointed tulips, and hyacinths. Apart from the shiny Egyptian wool, cotton could be used for the white floral sections and silk for the basic weave. When in 1585 Murad III summoned to Istanbul 11 master carpet makers from Cairo with a large quantity of Egyptian wool, he presumably planned to enlarge the industry in the capital, which was struggling to fulfil orders from the court with its 16 master craftsmen. Small prayer mats were actually manufactured in Istanbul with the typical Egyptian cherry red and green colors, as several examples show, including a piece from the mausoleum of Selim II.

The essential element of the prayer mat is the niche motif, which like the prayer niche in the mosque is meant to point towards Mecca, the direction the believer has to face in the ritual prayers. Besides the individual prayer mat, the long prayer carpet with horizontal and vertical rows of niches was introduced for communal prayer in the mosque. The examples held in the Istanbul Museum of Turkish and Islamic Art, which come from mosques in both Istanbul and Edirne and were part of their original furnishings, still reach to a length of 26 feet (8 meters), even in their fragmentary state, which gives some indication of how impressive they once were.

Cooperation with the tent makers, who provided enormous marquees for festivals and military campaigns, posed a particular challenge for the art of textiles. In the *Suleymanname* by Arifi there are pictures of circular and rectangular tents with magnificent canopies, often trimmed with metals, and with walls of floral materials, which create an illusion of a garden pavilion. Ahmed Feridun's chronicle of Suleyman's last Hungarian campaign shows a sea of white tents in front of the gates of the fortress city of Szigetvar on the River Drava, where the sultan died in 1566. These tents are grouped in hundreds around the enormous tent of the sultan, erected on the riverbank, and a group of large tents for meetings between the grand vizier and other army commanders. Preserved from the 17th century, these commanders' tents reach an impressive 30 feet (9 meters) in length with a ridge height of 13 feet (4 meters), which is occasionally extended by a protective textile roof. The timber framework carries a textile covering with lavish additions of satin and gilded leather, which emulate pavilion architecture

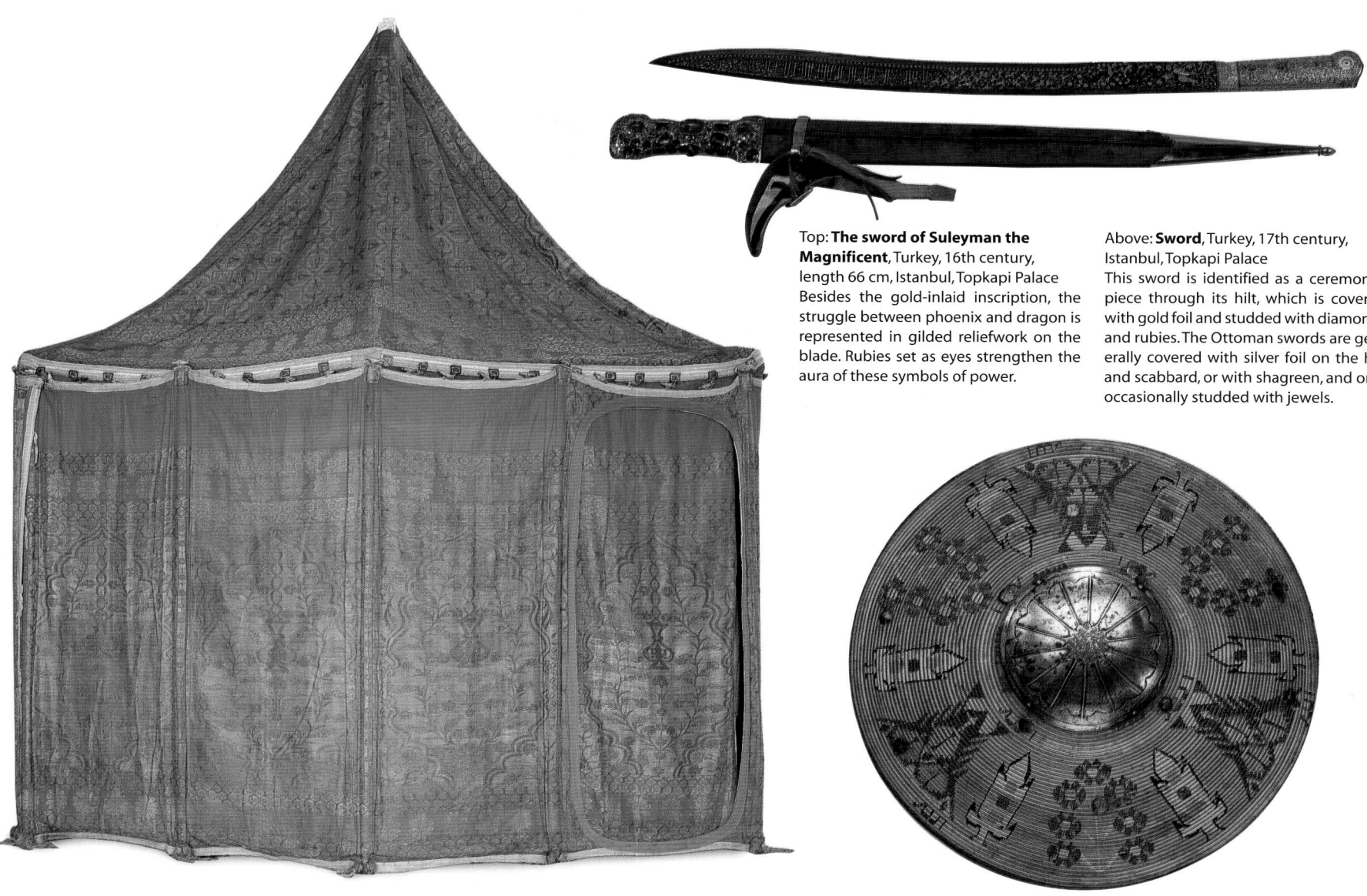

Top: **The sword of Suleyman the Magnificent**, Turkey, 16th century, length 66 cm, Istanbul, Topkapi Palace
Besides the gold-inlaid inscription, the struggle between phoenix and dragon is represented in gilded reliefwork on the blade. Rubies set as eyes strengthen the aura of these symbols of power.

Above: **Sword**, Turkey, 17th century, Istanbul, Topkapi Palace
This sword is identified as a ceremonial piece through its hilt, which is covered with gold foil and studded with diamonds and rubies. The Ottoman swords are generally covered with silver foil on the hilt and scabbard, or with shagreen, and only occasionally studded with jewels.

Magnificent tent, Turkey, 2nd half of the 17th century, silk, ridge height 5.1 m, ridge length 4 m, Vienna, Kunsthistorischesmuseum
This magnificent tent was part of the booty taken at the battles near Vienna in 1683. It consists of two wall-pieces and a roof. The wine-red silk material, strengthened with canvas and an inner lining, shows rich arabesques in gold, silver, green, and light red.

Shield, rattan, Karlsruhe, Badisches Landesmuseum
This shield consists of canes from the rattan palm which run in 45 concentric spirals around a wooden center covered with an iron boss. Besides the calls on Allah, which are woven into the edge in silver wire, there appear cypresses, flowering trees, and decorative triangles in various colors of silk.

with their flower-filled archways. The Ottoman tents aroused great admiration in Europe because of their beauty, their well-thought-out construction and their practical operation. As a result, they were carefully preserved, along with other items of plunder from the Turkish wars, and today, together with flags, riding tack, and weapons, provide a record of the magnificent and technically perfect Ottoman field equipment in museums in Budapest, Vienna, Munich, Karlsruhe, Dresden, and Krakow.

Following the defeat of Grand Vizier Kara Mustafa at Vienna in September 1683 the Ottomans had left behind war materials in enormous quantities, among which were numerous showpieces distinguished by their expensive materials and outstanding workmanship. The battle clubs, which had developed from ancient weapons of war into status symbols, have silver heads with wavy blades decorated with tendrils. The javelins have handles of gilded silver with turquoise inlay. The bow and arrow, a particularly fearsome weapon ever since the distant Asiatic past of the Turks, are painted and have decorative rings of precious metals. The leather quivers, occasionally covered with velvet, are embroidered with silver wire or studded with little silver plates. Scimitars and daggers have blades of Damascus steel and hilts of ivory, horn, or wood studded with precious stones or metals. The shields often consist of rattan and willow canes, which are coiled in concentric spirals around a central wooden disc with an iron boss nailed onto it. Silk or silver wire was used to embellish the woven shields with motifs of colored leaves or clouds, or with the name of Allah, whose protection the religious warrior expected.

Contemporaries like Busbeck, envoy of Emperor Ferdinand I, who left a glowing description of a parade of troops at the court of Suleyman the Magnificent, were enchanted by the regular display of sumptuousness, which they held to be a fundamental trait of Ottoman society.

Islamic Calligraphy

Elke Niewöhner

Calligraphy has a very special place in the art of Islam, because it is tightly bound up with the Koranic revelation in two ways. Firstly, God's word in the form of the Koran represents unique evidence of divine revelation, which was actually conveyed orally to Muhammad, but was then recorded in writing by his companions and circulated in writing. Secondly, this revelation is described in the Koran itself as an "elegantly proportioned script," which is preserved with God on "spotless sheets of paper," and which is "beautiful" and "unsurpassable."

Right up to the present day these words are an inspiration to all copyists of the Koran to be guided in their art by the heavenly beauty of the divine word; and they have supplied a motivation to perform calligraphy, which can be compared with the forces that brought forth religious and secular painting, as well as sculpture, and music in the Western world.

There is Arabic calligraphy in all sizes and in all modes of artistic expression, but those which have become the most important are the works written, from the 8th century onwards, on paper with a simple quill pen. The calligrapher would sit on the floor, hold the page supported on one knee, and write with firm, sure strokes, which demanded his full physical and intellectual control over the quill. It was necessary to practice for years to master this art and the masterpieces of calligraphy created in this way aroused admiration everywhere, were collected, protected, highly valued, and traded at collectors' prices.

Originally, the dissemination of the Koran was in a clear ceremonial script. The Arabic alphabet used in Mecca and Medina in the first half of the 7th century is, like all Semitic scripts, a consonantal script.

It has 28 phonemes and is written from right to left, allowing all letters to be joined up from the right. Some phonemes, however, cannot be joined to the left so this can leave gaps within words. Three of the phonemes are semivowels, i.e., consonants which simultaneously serve as long vowels in writing, e.g., "w" is also a long "u." Short vowels had to be inferred from the context, but before long the necessity arose to indicate these short vowels by means of auxiliary signs. The same goes for the system of one to three points used for distinguishing those letters

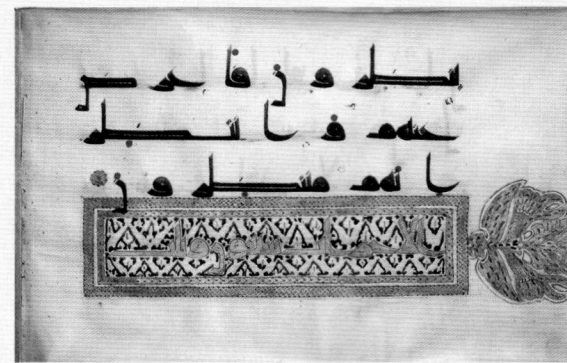

A page of a Kufic Koranic manuscript, Iraq or Syria, 9th or 10th century, parchment with ink and gold illumination, Berlin, Museum für Islamische Kunst

Grave stela with Kufic inscription, Egypt, 872, limestone, Berlin, Museum für Islamische Kunst

whose basic form is similar, e.g. "s" and "sh" or "b" and "t."

In this early period, still in the 7th century, Kufic developed as a Koranic script; this is an angular script with exceedingly clear contours, which appears monumental also in small format; with its impressive symmetry it expresses the self-assurance with which Islam in its classical period disseminated its holy scripture.

Kufic was, in spite of its name, which derives from the city of Kufa in Iraq, a script which spread over the whole Islamic world, from Spain in the west to beyond Iran in the east, a universal script for a universal civilization. In specially established calligraphy studios Korans were written on parchment in oblong format, and inscriptions were designed that were later chiseled into stone for buildings, or woven or embroidered into materials as ornamentation.

Until the 12th century Kufic was preserved as the Koranic script. However, as Islam spread to countries and regions where languages other than Arabic were spoken, and as these local languages adopted the Arabic script (the most important are Persian and Ottoman Turkish), new demands had since arisen and new forces were being felt.

From the beginning there had been a more rounded form of the script for everyday writing in business and administration, in culture and science, and in private correspondence. It is believed that from this rounded script developed the "the six styles," which the vizier Ibn Muqla (d. 939) codified as the beginning of the 10th century in Baghdad, and which since then, even up to the present day, have served as a guide for all Islamic calligraphers and were further developed in very different directions: Naskhi, Muhaqqaq, Raihani, Tauqi, Riqa, and Thuluth. Ibn Muqla devised a system by which the relationship of single letters to each other can be judged by points made with the quill. In this way a clear definition of proportions was set up within a style of writing.

The Arabic script has simple basic shapes but is irregular in its proportions, because small rounded shapes stand beside long, thin, vertical strokes, and round curves extend downwards. In a line of writing there is always an imbalance between an upper part that is too empty and a

Obverse and reverse of a gold coin with a Kufic inscription, Granada, 1125, Berlin, Museum für Islamische Kunst

lower part with a large number of small shapes. Here the calligraphers endeavored again and again to create a balance.

For example, they enlarged the upper ends of letters into leaf shapes or took the lower ends up into elegant curves and let them "blossom" into plant shapes.

Alternatively, they allowed the letters themselves to wind, curve, and twine around each other. Thus "blossoming" or "decorated" Kufic developed, a script where the writing bearly stands out against a background of floral and leaf motifs. The ends of the letters were even extended to become human or animal heads, yet these never appear in Korans, only in inscriptions on buildings or on vessels, particularly metal ones.

The script had quickly become an art form that could be used everywhere, particularly on buildings for decoration, because the representation of figures still met with reservation. Within Kufic there appeared local styles such as the "slanting Persian" script or the style used in Spain and northwest Africa, from which emerged the later "Maghrebi" script.

The introduction of paper, which came into the Islamic world from China via Central Asia in the 8th century, was particularly important for the development of calligraphy. To be sure, one continued to write Korans on parchment, because it kept better and was more prestigious – the same also holding true for documents. But with the introduction of paper, everyday business writing, and particularly literary works, received a boost comparable with that which was initiated by the invention of movable characters in printing.

As long as the Koran was written on parchment Kufic was preserved, but by the 12th century paper was generally accepted here, too, and Kufic was given up as the Koranic script. Instead, three of the styles codified by Ibn Muqla came into use for Korans: Naskhi, Muhaqqaq, and Raihani, while the three other styles were retained for writing in offices, in the administration, and in correspondence.

The earliest preserved Koran on paper in Naskhi was written by Ibn al-Bawwab in Bagh-

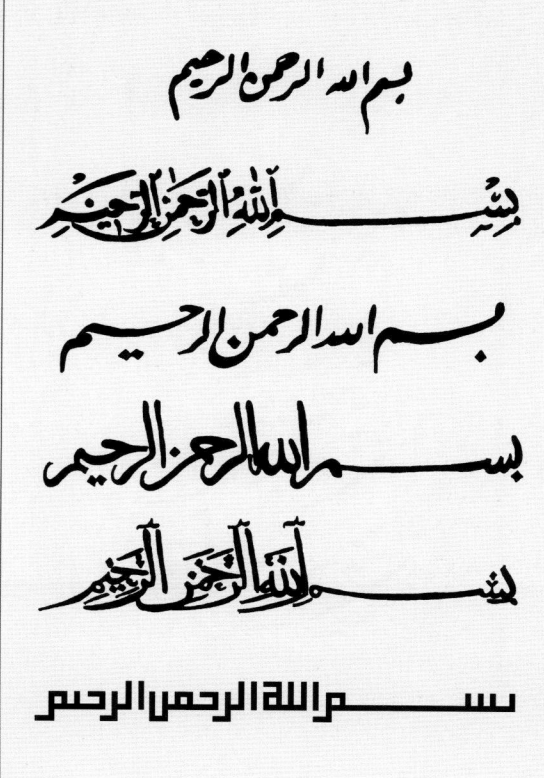

Introductory phrase "In the Name of God" in the six different styles (from top to bottom): Riqa, Naskhi, Nastaliq, Thuluth, Muhaqqaq, Square Kufic

dad in the year 1001. A pupil of Ibn Muqla and the most celebrated calligrapher of his time, he is second only to Ibn Muqlai as a theoretician of calligraphy. His work was perfected in the 13th century by Yaqut al-Mustasimi (d. 1298), whom both Persian and Ottoman calligraphers use as a model. They themselves have made fundamental contributions ever since to the further development of calligraphy beyond the "six styles."

In Persia, it was above all the development of Nastaliq, a characteristic style which was used preferentially for texts in the Persian language. With Islam, the Persians had also adopted the Arabic script for their language and now found a writing style that suited them, which is still in use even today. In the 17th century there developed from Nastaliq a style called Shikaste, a script characterized by contractions and exaggerated curves, which only the practiced reader can decipher.

Around 1500, in the Ottoman Empire, Sheikh Hamdullah, in an attempt to achieve unambigu-

Detail from the facade of the mausoleum of Ahmad Yasawi, Turkestan (today Kazakhstan), 1391–1399, brick mosaic with a Kufic inscription

Persian calligraphy in the Nastaliq style, signed by Ahmad al-Husaini, c.1575, Berlin, Museum für Islamische Kunst

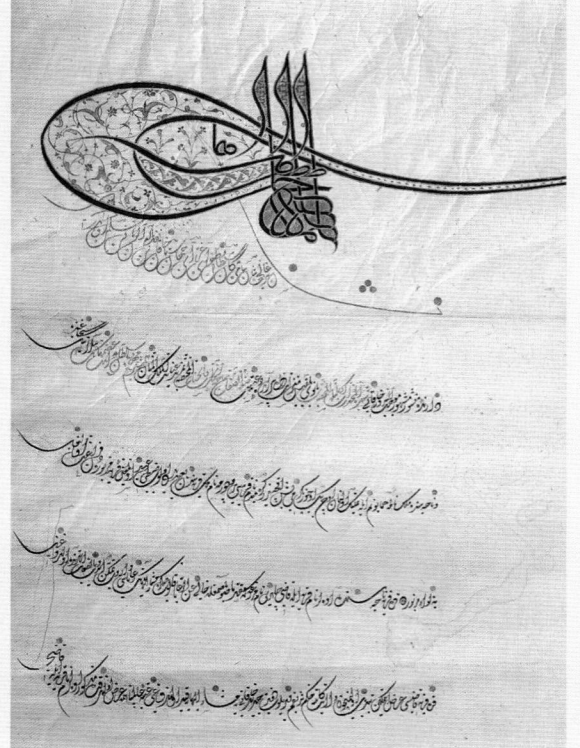

Sultan's Tughra of Selim III and decree of December 30 to January 8, 1569, Istanbul, Museum of Turkish and Islamic Art

had to be carefully planned if it were to be aesthetically balanced, and the relationship of the lines to each other had also to be taken into consideration, so that curves swinging down would not come into conflict with strokes coming up from the line below. Finally, facing pages had to be included jointly in the planning process, in order to avoid imbalance.

These considerations applied to books as well as to calligraphic compositions, which consisted of just a few lines, often just one sentence or even one word. From very early times such compositions were found written on essential commodities; later they were written on signed single sheets, which were gathered together, glued onto boards, and bound into albums. Persian poetry in Nastaliq, frequently written diagonally across the page, was as popular in India as in Iran, whereas in the Ottoman Empire short religious texts in scripts of different sizes on oblong pages were preferred. Tenth-century ceramics from Samarkand are among the most impressive examples of the use of script on objects in daily use. The innumerable inscriptions in architecture also had to be planned meticulously, and in Turkey and Persia, when drawn by well-known calligraphers, they were often signed.

Calligraphy is an art which is not merely learned by memorizing the rules; it requires a special talent if real mastery is to be achieved. Modern-day artists try hard to gain this mastery wherever Arabic script is cultivated as part of their tradition.

ous legibility gave still more clarity to the Naskhi script, stylized by Yaqut al-Mustasimi. Almost 200 years later Hafiz Osman enhanced this quality with further simplifications. Most modern calligraphers in Turkey follow this tradition. With the Diwani style, Ottoman calligraphers also developed a few variations of calligraphy, to be used in all official documents. Diwani is almost as difficult to read as Shikaste, but gives documents a special form that sets them apart from all other writings. At their beginning stands the Tughra, one of the most impressive inventions of Ottoman calligraphers: the name of the sultan is written in a most elaborate, ornamental form.

For any calligrapher in training it was always normal at least to attempt to become really proficient in the "six styles." This involved not only learning the theoretical basis of each style but first and foremost practicing as well as developing an eye for the proportions of the surface that had to be filled with writing. In the case of the Kufic Korans on parchment it was a horizontal surface, on which the lines were not arranged according to words but groups of

letters, which made fluent reading difficult. With Korans written on paper came the upright size, and now every line had to end with a complete word. It was not permissable, however, to write the words too cramped together nor to spread them too far over the set margins. Thus every line

"God is Our Help to Success", album page by Hafiz Osman, in Thuluth and Naskhi, 17th century, 21 × 15 cm, Berlin, Museum für Islamische Kunst

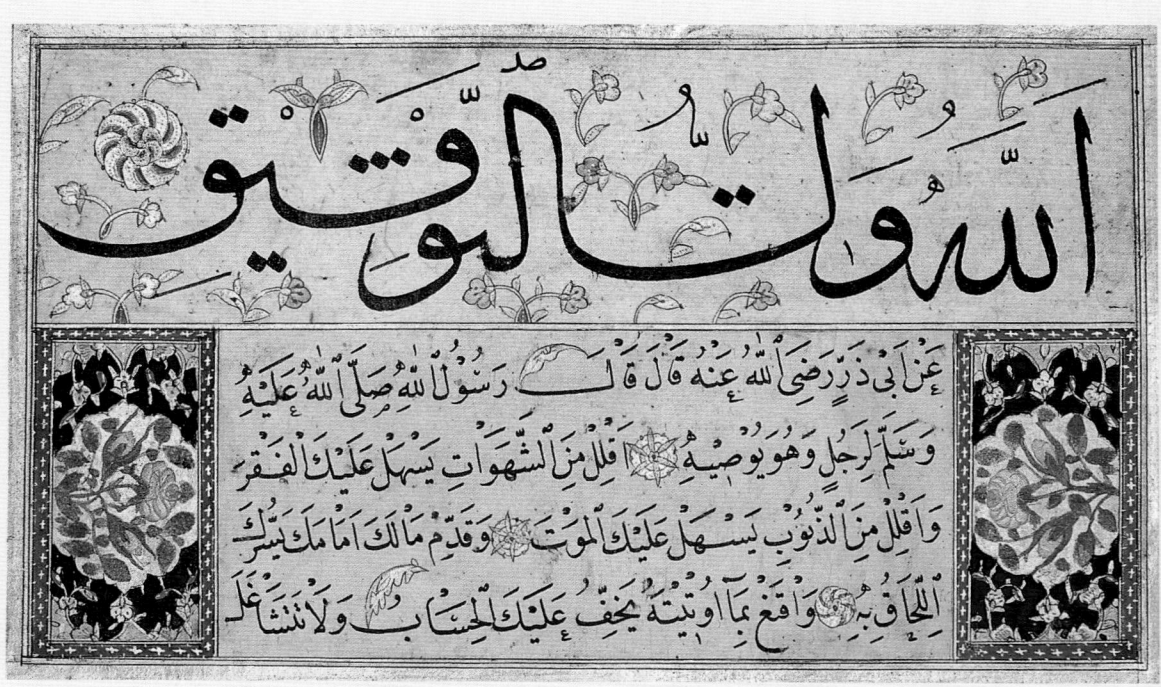

Decorative page with a religious text in Naskhi in the form of a bird, Iran, 17th century, Berlin, Museum für Islamische Kunst

Islam in the Modern Age

Friday Mosque at N'Jamena, Chad, 1986
This building has clearly borrowed from Moghul architecture of the 17th century. The mosque repeats on a smaller scale the pattern of the Badshahi Mosque in Lahore built in 1673/74, with the facade stretching between two monumental minarets, the use of copper-covered onion domes, and the forecourt. Externally, however, the arcades surrounding the courtyard suggest a reference to the Dome of the Rock in Jerusalem. With its quotations from the history of Islamic building, the mosque is a typical example of modern Islamic architecture, which is often characterized by the attempt to combine the historical heritage with present-day trends.

History

Markus Hattstein

Developments between 1800 and 1914 – European colonialism and political reform

The rapid social change that took place in Europe in the period of the French Revolution and Napoleon (1789–1815) led in foreign politics to a commercially motivated expansion of European influences into other regions: European colonialism. By the 18th century European powers and commercial companies had already gained important footholds in the countries of the Maghreb, the Near East, and Asia. With Napoleon's invasion of Egypt (1798), however, there began a new chapter in relations between East and West. In the Near East, in the wake of the conquerors came the administrators, explorers, and archaeologists, and with the technological revolution of the 19th century (steamships, railways, telegraph) great distances were covered more quickly and connections made to distant lands.

From the beginning of the 19th century the world empire of the Ottomans was severely weakened and lost its non-Turkish provinces in quick succession: Greece

and the Balkans became independent, while in the eastern provinces the British and the French supported local efforts to gain independence in order to secure political and commercial influence. France pursued its interests most directly in the Maghreb: in 1830 it took possession of Algeria and put the neighboring countries of Morocco and Tunisia under commercial pressure, both of them coming to the verge of state bankruptcy through European loans and finally having to accept official French protection. In these countries France pushed ahead aggressively with the settlement of French colonists (*colons*), who took the best land. European colonists dominated not only agriculture and most of the overseas trade, but also the exploitation of mineral resources, discovered after 1880. The Italians in Libya and the Spanish in North Morocco followed their example.

Britain took possession of India in 1857 and intervened massively in Persia and Afghanistan to promote its commercial interests. In Egypt, the British supported the attempts by Muhammad Ali and his successor to gain independence (1805–1849). When the heirs of Muhammad Ali got into debt with various prestige projects (*inter alia* the Suez Canal, 1869), the British took possession of Egypt in 1882. After initial difficulties the British also brought the Sudan under their control and made protectorate agreements with the southeastern Gulf States of the Arabian Peninsula. By the beginning of the 19th century Indonesia and Malaysia were firmly in the hands of the Dutch and the British, respectively. Circumstances deteriorated in the regions of Syria, Iraq, Palestine, and the Lebanon. They were

Right: **King Faisal of Iraq** (1883–1933)
Prince Faisal, son of Sharif Hussein of Mecca, was the upholder of hope at the Arab National Congress, which after the First World War strove for self-government for the Arabs. Chosen as king of Syria, Lebanon, Jordan, and Palestine by the National Congress in 1920, he was expelled by the French, who claimed the region as their mandated territory, and in 1921, with British help, he was chosen as King of Iraq. He founded the Hashemite dynasty of Iraq, which was removed in 1958 by Iraqi officers in a bloody coup.

Left: **King Abdullah of Jordan** (1882–1951)
Faisal's brother Abdallah became emir of Transjordan (from 1946 the Kingdom of Jordan) in 1921 with British help. He had to agree to the establishment of a Jewish state of Israel and then receive the exodus of Palestinians into Jordan. Because of his policy of reconciliation within the region he was assassinated by an Islamic fanatic in 1951 in al-Aqsa Mosque. He founded the currently ruling Hashemite dynasty in Jordan.

still, for the time being, part of the Ottoman Empire, but they found themselves abandoned to a massive struggle for influence between the British and the French.

European influence led to great changes in all of these countries. A cabinet system on the European model was established almost everywhere, and in 1861 Tunisia became the first Islamic country to introduce a constitution. The colonial powers enforced a free-trade policy, under which they secured many concessions and monopolies for themselves, and pressed ahead with far-reaching schemes for removing the jurisdiction of *sharia* law by secularizing and centralizing the justice system. European technology and military training, along with a network of European residents and consuls, dominated official life in these countries. The systems of education and training were reformed in the European ethos, slavery was abolished, and traditional clan rule repressed. Through improved medical care and preventive hygiene measures many countries experienced a population explosion and a drift from the countryside into the cities.

The Europeans placed great weight on training a domestic elite, who often followed their careers in the colonial motherland, which led to exile from their people at home and from traditional Islam. Training objectives were the technological and military subjects, yet the colonial powers were unable to prevent the emergence of a small intellectual circle in the colonies and protectorates. The export of European nationalism seriously undermined the traditional communal spirit of Islam but it led to a new self-confidence in many countries and to the rediscovery of their own history. One obvious indication of this was the *coup d'état* in the Ottoman Empire by the nationalist "Young Turks" in 1908. The colonies and the protectorates were involved to different extents in the First World War.

Opposite: **Napoleon's Battle of the Pyramids**, 1798, Louis Lejeune, 19th century, Versailles, Royal Palace
In 1798 Napoleon Bonaparte annexed Egypt, at that time a province of the Ottoman Empire, in order to contain British influence in the region and to create a French base in that part of Africa. Despite many victories, such as the Battle of the Pyramids, Napoleon's attempt to advance via Egypt and Syria into the heart of the Ottoman Empire failed and furthered the growing independence of Egypt under Muhammad Ali and his successors.

The role of Islam: cultural self-contemplation and political movements

In the eyes of Europeans, Islam was an antiquated religion and an obsolete social system, which stood in the way of a disciplined and centralized administration; even the native champion of Islamic culture, too, recognized the need for fundamental change. The development of national literature and the triumphal march of the European educational and training system from the second half of the 19th century encouraged the growth of a small elite, who became very sophisticated and took a stance that was as critical of their own traditions as it was of the European advance.

The leaders of this tendency to reflection on cultural matters, known as "*salafiya*," were prepared to accept the military and technological superiority of Europe but refused to recognize any European spiritual, moral, or cultural superiority. They did not simply conjure up the past heyday of Islam, but saw Islam as the keystone of a future cultural identity for their people. Through their ideas and appeals they became the spiritual fathers of modern Islam, yet they were the godfathers of some positions taken by the later Islamists (or "Fundamentalists"), above all with regard to the scope of *sharia* law.

The European powers could see with their own eyes the strength of reform movements in Islam. The most obvious was the rebellion of Muhammad Ahmad (1844–1885), the "Mahdi," in the Sudan, who expelled the Egyptians and the British from the country and took Khartoum in 1885. The British and the Egyptians could not defeat the Islamic regime of his successor until 1898/99. Still more successful was the strictly puritanical reform movement of the Wahabis in the Arabian Peninsula, in whose name the al-Saud family became the dominant power in the region. From 1902 Abd al-Aziz, known as Ibn Saud (1880–1953), conquered the Hejaz together with most of the Arabian Peninsula including Mecca and Medina, and in 1932 proclaimed the Kingdom of Saudi Arabia. The Senussi movement in Libya, which finally took over leadership of the struggle against Italian occupation and installed the emir or king of Libya in 1922, also had a similarly puritanical orientation. Nowhere did the European powers consult the Islamic authorities in order to cooperate with them, so almost everywhere the latter took an aggressive stance on the side of the anticolonial freedom movements.

The 20th century: the road to national independence

The end of the First World War marked for the time being the zenith of political power for Britain and France, since the Ottoman Empire had fought on the side of Germany and Austria and was now one of the defeated nations. Territorially, it had to confine itself to Turkey and to give up its Arabian provinces. The two great powers (the Entente) had in the Sykes-Picot Agreement of 1916 already reached agreement on their spheres of influence, which led to the French mandate over Syria and Lebanon and to the British mandate over Palestine (and later Israel), Jordan, and Iraq. Both powers were allied to the Hashemite family of Sharif Hussein of Mecca (1856–1931), who had made himself king of the Hejaz in 1916 (though he was expelled from there in 1924 by Ibn Saud). The Entente powers permitted the installation in 1920/21 of Hussein's sons Abdullah (1882–1951) and Faisal (1883–1933) as emirs or kings of Transjordan (Palestine and Jordan) and of Iraq, respectively. Abdullah, however, was committed to the authorization of a Jewish state (guaranteed in the Balfour Declaration of 1917). In 1922 the British recognized the independence of Egypt, where Fuad I (1868–1936), a descendant of Muhammad Ali, took the title of king. Britain was able, by and large, to secure for itself the lion's share of trade with the countries of the east and to extend further its position as a world naval power.

France got into a precarious position in the Maghreb, since it found itself confronted by well-organized and European-trained liberation movements, which

also gained a considerable hearing internationally. Britain faced similar difficulties in India after Afghanistan had expelled all British influence in 1919. In the Indian National Congress, Hindus (under Mahatma Gandhi and Pandit Nehru) and Muslims (under Muhammad Ali Jinnah) demanded both the withdrawal of the British and national independence, energizing their demands with well-thought-out actions. In Turkey, the nationalist government under Mustafa Kemal Ataturk (1881–1938), who deposed the last Ottoman sultan in 1922, undertook radical modernization, secularization, and Europeanization of the country. Prompted by these reforms, Reza Khan (1878–1944) overthrew the Kajars in Persia in 1925 and made himself shah. His authoritarian modernization and secularization led to an ongoing conflict with the Shiite clergy, which finally ended in 1978 with the overthrow of the Pahlavi dynasty and the establishment of the Islamic Republic of Iran.

In the Second World War, the Islamic countries took varied positions, yet there were clear sympathies in some liberation movements for Nazi Germany because of its struggle against the British and the French. With the end of the war, the time was ripe for national independence. France gave Syria and Lebanon their independence in 1945, but conditions remained difficult there because of the complicated ethnic and religious mix. In 1947 the Italians finally had to withdraw from Libya. In the same year India achieved its independence, yet the Muslim leader Muhammad Ali Jinnah (1867–1948), who feared the numerical inferiority of the Muslims in India, engineered the creation of a purely Islamic state of

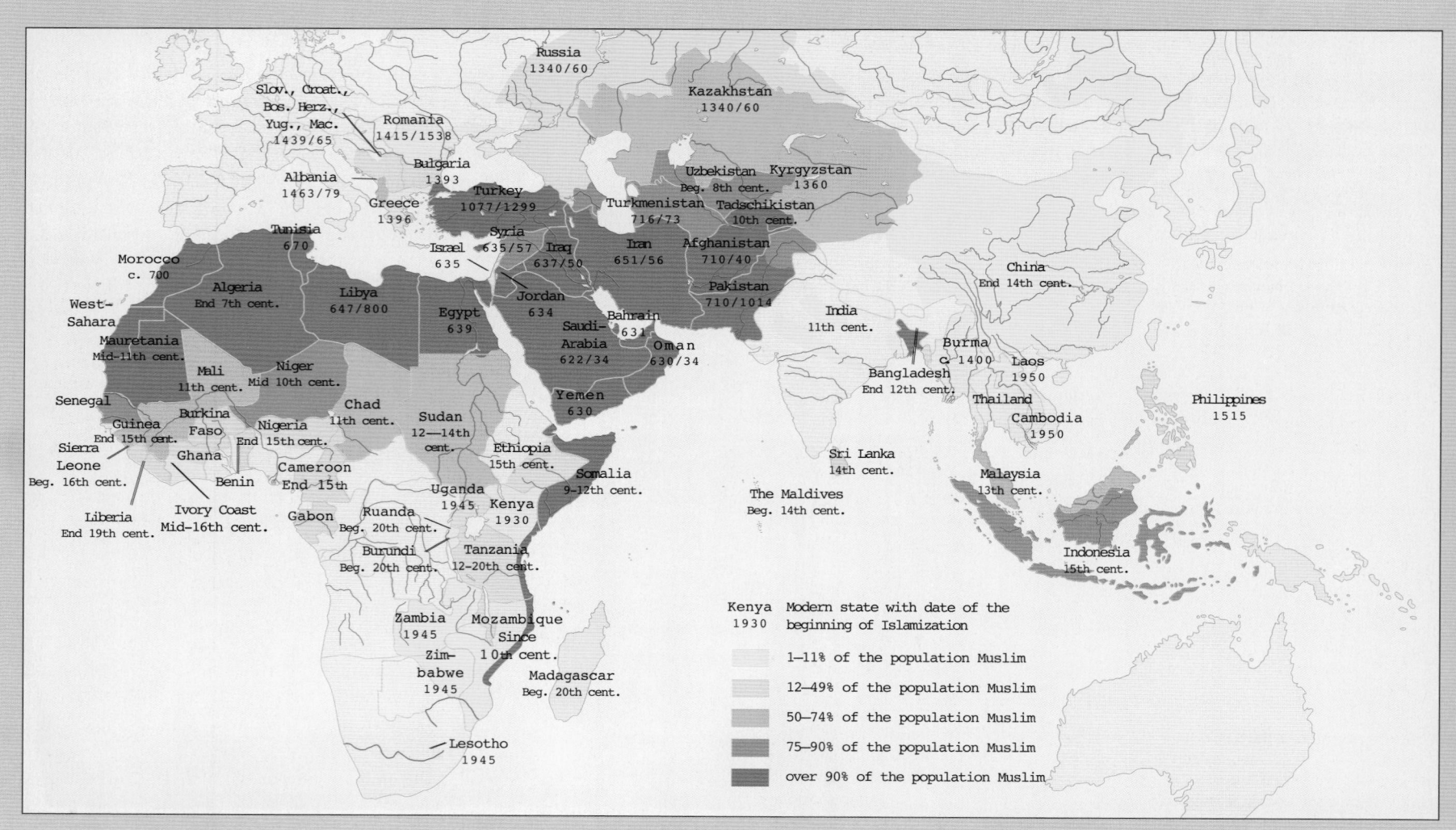

ISLAM IN THE MODERN AGE

Mustafa Kemal "Ataturk" (1881–1938)
The army officer Mustafa Kemal Pasha, who was involved in the Young Turk rebellion of 1908, used his position as president of the Turkish National Assembly to depose the last Ottoman sultan in 1922 and to force Greece to evacuate Asia Minor. As state president from 1923, he carried out a thorough program of secularization and modernization of the country and brought Turkey closer to Europe in its script, dress, and education system. As creator of the modern Turkish nation state, he was given the title of "Father of the Turks" (Ataturk) by parliament in 1934.

Pakistan in the west. After a bloody civil war there was an exchange of populations according to their religious allegiance, so that another Islamic state in the east of India came into being: East Pakistan, which later became Bangladesh (from 1972). Indonesia had already declared itself independent under Ahmed Sukarno (1901–1970) in 1945 and Malaysia followed in 1957. In both countries the many religious and ethnic minorities have equal civil rights.

The situation developed particularly seriously in Palestine, where mainly Zionist Jews settled from 1917. When the flow of Jewish settlers from Europe intensified after 1945, the attempt by the British to limit the number of Jewish immigrants, in accordance with their earlier commitments on Jordan and Palestine, led after bloody clashes to the foundation of the State of Israel and the division of Jerusalem between Israel and Jordan. The majority of the Palestinians were either exiled to Jordan or brought under Israeli authority, whereby the region became a prime flashpoint. An attempt by the Arab states to push Israel back led in 1967 to the defeat of the Egyptian-led Arab troops. After another defeat of the Arabs in 1973, Egypt and Jordan changed their political stance, and peace talks began, into which were also drawn the Palestinians under their leader Yasser Arafat (b. 1929).

Serious problems also arose in the Maghreb. After a period of reprisals against the local independence movements, France had to bow to international pressure. In 1956 Morocco declared itself independent, and the sultan, who had become the leader of the campaign for national independence, assumed the title of King

1798–1801	Egyptian expedition by the French: after the expulsion of the French, Muhammad Ali leads the Egyptians to *de facto* independence, from 1841 a viceroyalty
1832–1847	Independence struggle under Emir Abd al-Qadir against French occupation of Algeria (begun in 1830)
1839–1876	Period of reform in the Ottoman Empire (Tanzimat reforms): the army, judiciary, administration, and educational system all overhauled
1857–1861	Tunisia adopts a constitution and becomes a constitutional monarchy
1858	India becomes a British viceroyalty
1863	Béclard Convention: Morocco becomes a French protectorate
1881	The Mahdi Rebellion in the Sudan
1881–1883	Tunisia becomes a French protectorate (Conventions of Bardo and La Marsa)
1882–1936	Egypt is occupied by the British
1898–1954	Anglo-Egyptian condominium in the Sudan
1914–1918	First World War: the Ottoman Empire sides with the Central Powers
1916	Sykes-Picot Agreement: Britain and France divide the Near East into British and French spheres of influence
1917	Balfour Declaration: the British promise the Zionist movement support for the establishment of a Jewish "national homeland" in Palestine
1920	Britain is granted Palestine, Iraq, and Transjordan; France, Syria and Lebanon as League of Nations mandated territories
1922–1924	Formation of the Republic of Turkey: sultanate (1922) and caliphate (1924) abolished; 1923 republic declared, Mustafa Kemal becomes president
1925	End of Kajar rule in Persia; Reza Khan becomes shah of Persia
1928	Hasan al-Banna founds the Muslim Brotherhood in Egypt
1932	Foundation of the state of Saudi Arabia
1945–1947	After the Second World War (1939–1945) India, Transjordan, Syria, and Lebanon become independent (1946), Pakistan is established (1947), the Republic of Indonesia proclaimed (1945), and the Arab League founded (1945)
1948	Foundation of the State of Israel and the first Arab-Israeli war; further wars follow (1956 Sinai campaign, 1967 the Six-Day War, 1973 Yom Kippur War)
1952	Military coup in Egypt led by General Neguib and Gamal Abd el-Nasser, end of the monarchy (1922-1952)
1956–57	Morocco, Tunisia, and Malaysia achieve autonomy
1958	Coup in Iraq ends the monarchy there (1921-1958), declaration of the Republic of Iraq
1958–1961	Egypt and Syria form the United Arab Republic
1962	End of the struggle for independence in Algeria (1954–1962); fall of Imam Ahmad (1948–1962) in Yemen, proclamation of the Arab Republic of Yemen
1967	Proclamation of the People's Republic of South Yemen (later the People's Democratic Republic of Yemen)
1968	General Suharto becomes president of Indonesia
1969	Military coup led by Muammer al-Gaddafi in Libya
1972	East Pakistan becomes the newly independent state of Bangladesh
1975–1990	Civil war in Lebanon
1978–1979	Islamic revolution in Iran: foundation of the Islamic Republic of Iran under Ayatollah Ruhollah Khomeini
1978–1979	Camp David Agreement: the peace treaty between Israel and Egypt leads to the isolation of Egypt in the Arab world
1979–1988	Soviet occupation of Afghanistan
1980–1988	Iran-Iraq War
1990	Union of North and South Yemen as the Republic of Yemen
1990–1991	The Persian Gulf War: an international alliance under the leadership of the USA forces Iraq to withdraw from Kuwait which it had occupied. The Madrid Conference initiates new direct negotiations between Israel, its neighbors, and, most significantly, the Palestinians
1991–1992	Algerian parliamentary elections: the military prevent the election victory of the "Islamic Salvation Front"

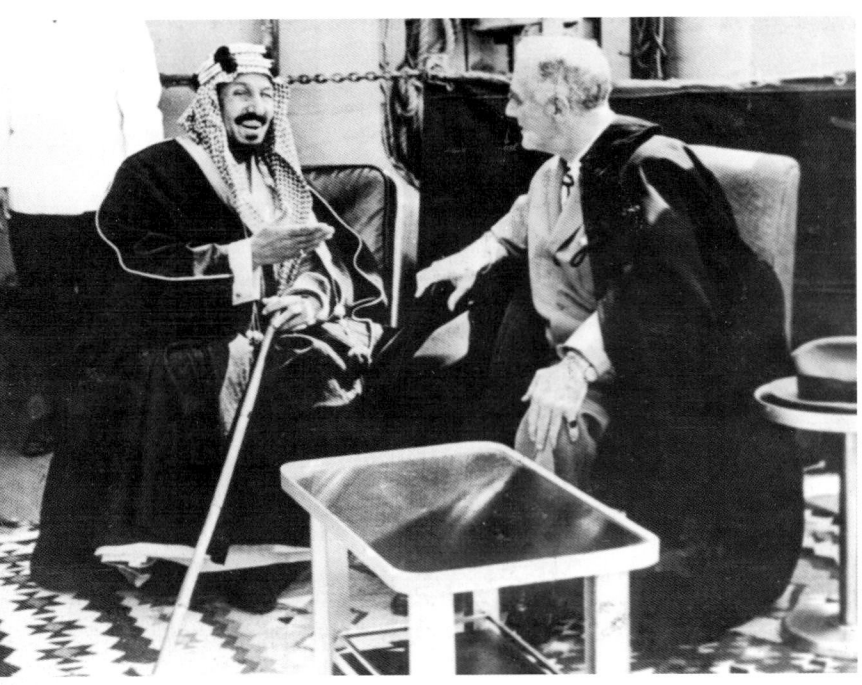

Left: **King Ibn Saud (1880–1953) with US President Franklin D. Roosevelt**, 1945
Abd al-Aziz, dubbed Ibn Saud (1880–1953), conquered the central Arabian Peninsula from 1902, expelled the Hashemites from the Hejaz in 1924, and in 1932 proclaimed the Kingdom of Saudi Arabia. By means of several shrewd agreements, above all over the Arab oil claim, Ibn Saud came to an understanding early on with the USA under which he recognized this coming world power of the postwar order. This picture shows the two statesmen on board the US cruiser *Quincy*.

Right: **Muhammad Ali Jinnah and Pandit Nehru**
The lawyer Muhammad Ali Jinnah (1867–1948), leader of the Muslims in India since 1916 (right), fought side by side with the Hindu leaders Mahatma Gandhi and Pandit Nehru (left) against British rule in India, but from 1940 called for the partition of the country into Hindu and Muslim states. In the bloody civil war that followed Indian independence, he brought about the creation of an Islamic Pakistan, and in 1947 became its first governor-general.

Muhammad V (1909–1961). In Tunisia, the charismatic lawyer Habib Bourguiba (b. 1903) negotiated independence in 1956 and set in train a radical modernization of the country. In Algeria, which officially belonged to France, the struggle for independence became particularly bloody. After peaceful liberation movements, which argued for an autonomous republic within a union with France, had been suppressed with great severity in the years following 1945, the Algerian Liberation Front (FLN) radicalized itself and went over to open rebellion in 1954, while the military organization of French-Algerians (OAS) terrorized the Muslim population. A spiral of terror and counter-terror with bloody attacks and bombings shook mainly the coastal cities and finally crossed over to the French mainland, where the population was deeply split on the Algerian question. Finally President de Gaulle stood up to the military chiefs and to the French-Algerians and granted the country independence in 1962.

Present-day areas of conflict

Particularly in the mainly secular states such as Turkey, Tunisia, Algeria, Indonesia, Syria, Lebanon, Egypt (after 1952), and Iraq (after 1958), major modernization programs in education, technology, the armed forces, medicine, and science were undertaken at governmental level and there were developments in the vocational training of women. *Sharia* law was generally limited to local or family problems and a thoroughly secular and European-style system of state courts predominated. Those countries which were ruled in a more traditional way, such as Morocco, Jordan, the Gulf States, and Malaysia, also undertook significant modernization programs, while the influence of traditional Islamic structures in official life remained more strongly entrenched in countries such as Saudi Arabia, Pakistan, Sudan, and Libya.

From 1954 Egypt under President Gamal Abd el-Nasser (1918–1970) played a very significant role within the Islamic world at a time when the Arab region in particular was conscious of the politico-economic dominance of the USA and of attempts by the USSR to extend its political influence. Nasser pursued an active policy of neutrality ("nonalignment") in relation to the two superpowers but with political support at home for socialism and the USSR. When he nationalized the Suez Canal in 1956, British, French, and Israeli forces took possession of the Canal Zone but were compelled to withdraw by the USA and the USSR, who saw their interests in Egypt in peril. Nasser, who initiated important campaigns for modernization, social reform, and major technical projects, was regarded in the Arab world as a hero of new Arab self-confidence, who by populist methods propagated the idea of pan-Arabism (especially through Egypt's union with Syria 1958–1961) and made himself leader of the struggle against Israel. His example had an effect on various countries: Iraq, where in 1958 a group of officers removed the Hashemite ruling family; Yemen, where in 1962 the ruling imam was deposed; and Libya, where Colonel Muammer al-Gaddafi (b. 1942) deposed the king in 1969 and ever since has combined revolutionary zeal with a modernist but strict Islam. Even in Saudi Arabia there was in 1962 a modernist revolt by several princes. The "Nasserist" system was also for many people the sponsor of the coups by the Baath Party in Syria and Iraq, which formulated an "Arab Socialism." In many countries, such as the Gulf States, this new self-confidence forced a final withdrawal of the former protectorate powers.

In the 1970s, in most of the countries, such as Egypt, Syria, Iraq, and Indonesia, there was widespread renunciation of socialist principles and an emphasis on national unity. Since the political differences between Arab countries also became clear, the concept of pan-Arabism declined in favor of a strong pan-Islamism with the emphasis on cultural exchanges and economic aid. The more populous countries of Asia, such as Pakistan, Bangladesh, and Indonesia, also played an important part in the Organization of Islamic Conferences, which was revived in 1974. The 1970s were overshadowed politically by religious civil war in Lebanon.

An event that had seismic repercussions throughout the Islamic world was the deposition of the shah of Persia in 1978 and the proclamation of the Islamic Republic of Iran by Ayatollah Ruhollah Khomeini (1902–1989). This new form of government had an immediate effect on the Islamic movements in Lebanon, Sudan, Pakistan, and Afghanistan, and also strengthened the activities of other Islamic groups. Until then, radical Islamic movements, such as the Muslim Brotherhood in Egypt and Syria, had been largely suppressed and kept away from political power. Aims and methods of Islamic groups range from parliamentary participation in Jordan to terrorist actions in Algeria and Afghanistan, yet on the whole they demand a radicalization of political Islam in the struggle against developments in the modern world, such as secularism, liberalism, and religious freedom. Although they are kept under control in most Islamic states, as before, they generate their energy from discontent, lack of prospects, and major social problems that exist in many countries. In several states they have political influence, such as in Pakistan, where the religious scholar Abu l-Ala al Maududi (1903–1979) formulated the principles of an Islamic system of governance, or their activities lead to divisions in society, as in Turkey and to a certain extent in Egypt.

The Islamic struggle in Algeria became particularly violent. In 1991 the Islamic Salvation Front (FIS), at that time a legal organization, was on the point of winning the election. A coup by military leaders took place at the beginning of 1992 and supporters of the FIS responded with a series of acts of terrorism and sabotage, which plunged the country into a bloody civil war that still continues. The struggle in Afghanistan is also a violent one. Radical Islamists, the Mujahedin, who had been supplied with weapons and know-how by the West during the Soviet occupation of the country (1979–1988), afterwards seized power and are prepared to take up arms against all "Western" and "un-Islamic" forces. It should, however, be stressed that most Islamic countries today steer a cautious but self-confident course between, on the one hand, keeping to the Islamic way of life and strengthening their Islamic identity and, on the other hand, being part of the international community of states, with the attendant prospects and risks of global technology and communication.

Demonstrators in Iran with pictures of Ayatollah Khomeini
The removal of the shah in 1978 and the declaration of the Islamic Republic of Iran in 1979 under the leadership of Ayatollah Ruhollah Khomeini (1902–1989) led to a radical change in the social order. The Islamic Revolution gave impetus to the Islamic movements in other countries, which led to serious conflicts with the more modernist and secular governments.

Left: **Yasser Arafat and Yitzhak Rabin with US President Bill Clinton in Washington DC**
The picture shows the Palestinian leader, the Israeli prime minister Rabin and the president of the USA in September 1993 in the garden of the White House after the signing of a treaty on Palestinian self-government in the West Bank territories.

Right: **Gamal Abd el-Nasser**
Gamal Abd el-Nasser (1918–1970), president of Egypt from 1954, became leader of the pan-Arabist movement in 1956. His system of government, which combined internal modernization with an external policy of allegiance to the "non-aligned movement," led to sub-versive movements in many Arab states and gave Arab self-confidence new impetus.

In Search of the Exotic East

Annette Hagedorn

A preoccupation with the art of the Islamic world is a European phenomenon that has been observed in different forms since the time of the Crusades. It is marked by contacts with the Islamic world that were sometimes hostile but also often stimulating.

In the 19th century, however, this phenomenon became more significant after the upheaval in intellectual life caused by the Enlightenment. It developed in the middle and the second half of the 19th century to reach a peak that was characterized more by the amount of discussion about the East (i.e., the Islamic world) than by its depth. This phenomenon became known as "Orientalism." On the one hand, there had been since the 18th century those who, mindful of the Turkish wars, condemned Islamic peoples as barbarous enemies, this attitude finding particular expression in operatic characters. On the other, there were those who idealized them as representatives of the "Noble Savage," of man in his noble, natural state, as popularized by the novels of Voltaire, for example. The 19th-century approach is quite different, as much factual information and actual knowledge of the Islamic world started to reach Europe. Many painters and creative artists were able to gain an idea of Islamic art on the spot or from the great Euro-

Above left: **The mosque in the castle garden at Schwetzingen**, 1750

Above right: **The mosque at Potsdam**, 1841–1843, Ludering Perius

pean collections. It is characteristic of the division in ideologies during this period that a series of different theoretical approaches led to the study of Islamic art. They had an effect well into the 20th century, and in some areas had a marked influence on the development of new artistic movements in Europe.

First of all there arises the question about contact with form and content in Islamic art, the roots of which lie in the 18th century, because then a division could already be observed between the two areas of "external form" and "intellectual content." One example that expresses this tense relationship particularly well is the mosque building in the castle garden at Schwetzingen (1750), whose exterior design imitates not only different Islamic architectural forms but European ones as well.

Both the domed building and the form of the minarets are derived from Ottoman mosques, the whole complex being reminiscent of Indian buildings, and yet clearly classical forms of European architecture have been

The Royal Pavilion, Brighton, 1815, designed by John Nash

integrated into the hypostyle halls facing the lake in front of the mosque. On the one hand, as a building in a pleasure garden of the late rococo period, this mosque was used for events at royal festivals, which shows the division of formal architectural quotations and contextual structures particularly clearly. On the other hand, during the conception of this building the architect had still endeavored, at least subliminally, to make some reference to the way of thinking of the Islamic East. The epigrams fixed to many internal and external walls clearly carry quotations of Islamic sayings. But then it is certainly not a matter of using actual quotations from Islamic authors but more one of using the recreations of European authors. The misunderstanding of such examples of Islamic art becomes perfectly obvious in a building like this or at the numerous Ottoman and Moorish style cafes, smoking rooms, and bathhouses of the 19th century, so one ought not to underestimate the impact it had on the positive, creative development of European art in the 19th and 20th centuries.

This is obviously particularly impressive in the field of applied art. The fascination here was both with the technical quality and skilled perfection of the products of oriental craftsmanship and with the fact that the artists could not understand most of the inscriptions and symbols they frequently came across (and so it

Glass vessel in the form of an Arab mosque lamp, Philippe J. Brocard, yellow-green glass with red, blue, and white enamel paint and gilding, Art collection of the City of Coburg

Ceramic plate in the Ottoman style, manufacturer Vilmos Zsolnay, Pécs, Mettlach, Keramikmuseum

was the perfect middle way between cultures). Here there are only isolated attempts to fill the shapes with contexts (such as, for instance, repeated comments and tips on Ottoman symbolism). In the main, however, it can be seen that European arts and crafts were influenced almost exclusively by the formal aspects of Islamic art.

One obvious example of this is the work of the French glass artist Philippe J. Brocard (producing in Paris from 1869), various of whose works looked back to Mamluk glass objects, for example, to the model of the inscribed medallion often featured. He replaced these inscriptions, however, with floral ornamentation or – as in the case of a mosque lamp in the Musée des Beaux Arts in Nancy, for instance – instead of the original inscription he showed a pseudo-Islamic flourish, which on closer examination seems to indicate the Latin word *lux*. The approach really consisted of reviving, for Europe as well, the significance of written flourishes in Islamic art, though this flourish had to be replaced by European intellectual content because of a lack of knowledge (on the part of the artist, the viewer, or the purchaser). Beyond this Brocard clearly shared the prevailing interest in Islamic artistic techniques and in the fantastically formed vessels and decorative patterns, which Islamic art had well in advance of the European traditions and which were thus particularly valued by European craftsmen.

Firing and glazing techniques were therefore tried out in the field of ceramic art. In particular Turkish-Ottoman Iznik ceramics and Moorish luster ceramics were studied and revived. People found the possibilities so fascinating that they wanted nothing more to do with the naturalistic Biedermeier and Victorian

Tile in the Ottoman style, manufacturer Villeroy und Boch, Mettlach, Ceramics Keramikmuseum

decoration. So, from the middle of the 19th century, increasing numbers in the European art and craftwork movement, with backgrounds in English architectural and artistic theory, sought a new style which would be suitable for applied art. The first opportunity in this connection that presented itself to European artists and craftspeople was the variable geometrical decoration found in the Islamic world. This was primarily the stylized two-dimensional floral decoration of Ottoman ceramics, which exerted a dominating influence in the second half of the century. As the interest in this decoration spread through very different European countries, the products of 60 European firms and manufacturers clearly came to reflect the intensive analysis of Ottoman examples. Particularly in the field of German arts and crafts there was discussion on the principles of what was the proper and ideal art for decorating everyday articles, a debate which was kindled by Islamic art and was to make a decisive contribution to new directions in applied art at the end of the 19th and the beginning of the 20th centuries.

Examples from the 19th century provide an impressive demonstration of how conceptual and decorative features of Islamic art were used in patterns and how principles for decoration in applied art were developed. On tiles made by the Villeroy & Boch company an Ottoman motif style is combined with a clear coloration, arranged quite intentionally with plenty of contrast in carefully measured two-dimensional colored surfaces with a flat floral decoration. The subsequent development of these ideas ultimately led in the 20th century to the total removal of all representational decoration. Working from the geometric decoration on

IN SEARCH OF THE EXOTIC EAST

western Islamic ceramics, as well as fabrics and carpet designs from the Islamic world, adherents of the Bauhaus school of design, who held intense and varied discussions about Islamic art (Richard Riemerschmid and Margarete Willers, for example), succeeded in developing an everyday art using abstract decoration.

A totally separate story unfolded in the development of European painting. Unlike arts and crafts, the study of the style of Islamic painters, i.e., the two-dimensional style of Islamic miniaturists, began at the turn of the 20th century.

Works of 19th-century painters who chose Islamic subjects still almost completely retained the old traditions of European academic painting. They represent the European artist's fascination with a strange world, which was both a place that fulfilled a longing for freedom of ideas and also provided the opportunity to express wishes, desires, and feelings in exotic garb. This is noticeable in the paintings of the French artist Eugène Delacroix, which vigorously portray the violent confrontations in the French North African colonies and yet equally convey a romantic image of freedom and readiness for battle. However, this approach is mainly exemplified through the large number of orientalist paintings of bazaar,

Opposite: Jean Léon Gérôme (1824–1904), **Men at prayer in the Amr Mosque in Cairo**, oil on canvas, New York, Metropolitan Museum of Art

John Frederick Lewis (1805–1876), **Harem scene**, Constantinople, Newcastle upon Tyne, The Laing Art Gallery

harem and slave scenes, which offered European painters a welcome opportunity to depict erotically colored subject matter. Even in the work of an artist like John Frederick Lewis, whose paintings remain more restrained and disguised, there predominates an interest in representing a strange and incomprehensible world, one that allows the European observer an almost voyeuristic peep into a forbidden realm. It is clear from the paintings of Jean Léon Gérôme that only an apparently realistic picture can represent both aspects of contact with foreign lands. In his painting of men praying, Gérôme shows, in an entirely European style, which has an almost photographic feel in its realistic reproduction of detail, a group of people at prayer in a hall, which the knowledgeable observer would recognize as the Amr Mosque in Cairo. He also attempts to retain this realism in his portrayal of figures. While this definitely succeeds for the details of clothing and faces, in comparison the realism of the whole picture is called into question. To the European observer the picture of an exotically-clad barbaric warrior, which fascinated and

shocked in equal measure, was painted in an apparently realistic setting at a strange prayer ritual. This offered the opportunity not only for distance and identification, but also for the projection of the observer's own imagined desire and repressed feelings.

This admiration of foreign lands clearly distinguishes European contact with the Islamic East in the 19th century from the previous period. To an extent previously unknown, culturally aware Europeans and European artists were able to travel and gain authentic practical knowledge of the Islamic world and its culture.

An extremely large number of them traveled in the East to make direct contact on the spot with this foreign world. Ever since the Middle Ages, through the Crusades and pilgrimages, there had been continuous interest in the lands of the Bible. Many educational visitors, scientists, and artists also traveled to the eastern Mediterranean area to gain their own impressions of these genuine cultural sights. On account of their geographical position the western Islamic countries were, in addition,

Eugène Delacroix, **The Ladies of Algiers**, oil on canvas, Paris, 1834, Boston, Museum of Fine Arts

Louis Comfort Tiffany, **Shops in Algeria**, gouache on paper, 1895,
Baltimore, Museum of Art

considerably easier to reach than other exotic destinations.

The late 19th century as a whole is characterized by an urge to visit far-off countries, which were linked to illusions of paradise. This process, however, also served to give Europe a separate identity from these foreign lands. Here we may call to mind the travel literature of Karl Mays or the journeys of Paul Gauguin, who quite deliberately set off on that kind of journey. Artists who were looking for such a strange world found it with the most modest financial outlay in the lands of the Islamic East. For that reason, it is not too surprising to note that particular countries, places, and routes became popular and thus were able to develop into a sort of 19th-century "Grand Tour." What travelers sought or hoped to discover on these journeys found particularly full expression the impressive accounts of the American painter R. Swain Gifford, who in 1870/71, with L.C. Tiffany, toured the countries of Europe and the Maghreb. He wrote in detail to his family that Tangiers was the most beautiful city he had seen on his travels. This account was intended for publication, and it matched so precisely the illusions that European artists and painters had had from the outset about the Islamic world that it appeared almost as a commentary to the

paintings of his friend L.C. Tiffany, who on the same tour produced works that captured exactly these aspects of Eastern life in gouache and in oil.

In spite of all the interest in and fascination with the foreign country, it was in the end experienced only superficially and it remained strange and fascinating above all because of its totally different character. This kind of preoccupation with Islamic art could only occur in a period when in Europe the content and form of its own art no longer came together into a unity. This was because painting had forfeited to photography its illustrative, interpretative function and architecture could quite freely use ostentatious quotations from times past separated from their original functions and then put these quotations together to form new compositions. In such a historical period, examining the external form of any foreign art informs the viewer how far it is removed from the content of his own art. It was perhaps in this period that the art of Islamic countries had the greatest and most enduring influence on the wider development of the Modern Movement in Europe. Here, the works of modern architecture offer an impressive example. In the first decades of the 20th century, architects like Walter Gropius or Le Corbusier succeeded in

developing a form of expression that broke radically with familiar traditions and directed itself towards completely new principles of form. Both architects had studied Islamic art: Gropius spent almost a year in 1907/08 studying Moorish art in Spain, while Le Corbusier traveled to Turkey in 1911 for an intensive period of architectural study. Ottoman architecture provided him with a treasury of shapes and ideas from which he could draw for the structuring of space and gave him lessons in proportion.

There was also, however, a comparable development in arts and crafts. The theoretical artistic analysis of two-dimensional decoration that developed into abstract decoration, at the beginning of the 20th century, strongly coincided with the study of Islamic art. Here, Moorish and western Islamic art, with their abstract, complex geometric decoration and color schemes, set the style. The designs of Johannes Itten make it crystal clear that adherents of the Bauhaus School paid close attention to the principles of Islamic applied art and also Islamic painting.

It was Itten who, in 1921, analyzed the color composition and formal construction of Islamic miniatures and on this basis developed new principles for classical themes in European painting. However, those artists who at the beginning of the 20th century were totally committed to modern painting turned in the first decades of the century towards Islamic art and its stylistic features. The famous exhibition "Masterworks of Muslim Art" was held in Munich in 1910 at the peak of this trend. It had a far-reaching national and international impact and provoked a major response in painting (from Robert Delaunay, August Macke, Edvard Munch, and Wassily Kandinsky, for example). These painters were no more preoccupied with the exotic content of Islamic art than were their predecessors of the 19th century. However, they were very attracted by the two-dimensional effect of Islamic painting, particularly in the representation of figures, which corresponded to their own attempts to find a new kind of painting. From then on, the picture was, above all, a perceptibly two-dimensional object. Besides that, the shapes and colors of Islamic countries, their buildings, materials, and artistic objects, fascinated these artists. So works such as Macke's Tunisia watercolors, with their vividly colored surfaces reduced to geometrical shapes and two-dimensional figures, thus breaking with previous traditions, or Matisse's and

Kandinsky's North African paintings, cannot be explained except by the preceding intense examination of the principles of Islamic art, all of which can be verified from the records kept in diaries and letters by these painters. While in the first decades of the 20th century Islamic art contributed quite decisively in this way to finding a new, really modern European artistic language, there was a second, parallel aspect to this preoccupation with the Islamic East, which can be observed almost unbroken up to the end of the 20th century. The European obsession with Islamic art was indeed decisively influenced by the pleasure people got from souvenirs and the possibility of combining the most varied of stylistic elements. Here was the opportunity to collect, as a witness to one's own travel experience, independent of the stylistic norms of modern aesthetics, something that was bizarre, colorful, unusual, and strange. Characteristic of such contact with foreign parts is, for instance, the Arab Room in the villa in Potsdam of Berlin banker Herbert Gutmann, which dates from the 1920s. In this room, in a totally oriental atmosphere with wall decoration in the most varied Islamic styles, artistic objects from both the Islamic East and from China and Southeast Asia were brought together.

So European art's preoccupation with the Islamic East from the 19th century onwards is marked by the quest for its own path, one in which it could set itself apart from all things foreign, by means of the opportunity to study foreign art and culture to a depth and to an extent hitherto never experienced. All that artists judged worthy of study was whatever supplied an answer to the difficulties found in their own cultural circle. In spite of all the fascination they have attracted, Islamic art and culture still leave an impression of a strange exotic world, about which people could teach themselves but whose innermost feelings they could never truly understand.

August Macke, **Turkish cafe 1**, oil on plywood, 1914, Bonn, Städtisches Kunstmuseum

The Arab Room in the villa of Herbert Gutmann, Potsdam, 1920s

Architecture and Art

Annette Hagedorn

The variety of artistic developments in the 19th and 20th centuries

In the 19th century deep-seated sociopolitical changes within the Islamic world led in all spheres of art to a rupture with older artistic traditions. This was particularly affected by the intensified contact of artists working in the East with the culture and art of Europe. As a consequence, there was both a greater openness of Islamic artists to European styles and also varied and distinctive new approaches to the analysis of their own traditions. Over and above that, European artists were working in many Islamic countries, some of whom became teachers, transmitting European architectural theories at universities and newly founded art schools. These teachers had, *inter alia*, developed new approaches towards the proportioning of buildings as well as the application of building decoration. Adoption of a European building style was viewed in many Islamic countries as an opportunity to progress in a more "modern" direction. One typical example of this was the intention of the Egyptian khedive Ismael to Europeanize Cairo, following the precedent of the city plan for Paris by Baron Georges-Eugène Haussmann (1809–1891).

Through this admiration for European art and the influence of European companies Islamic traditions almost came to a point of collapse and the infrastructure of older craft industries was almost annihilated by the European industrial system. Only when, from 1870, certain rulers gave their support for new construction was there a rise in production figures and in craft quality. The number of students of architecture also increased with state support, but they were sent to Europe to learn practical skills. Universities that carried out this training were in Rome, Milan, London, Glasgow, Berlin, Nuremberg and, particularly, Paris.

Architecture

In the Islamic world it was now possible to see the development of a limited combination of Eastern and Western styles. The whole of Islamic secular architecture from the middle of the 19th century was therefore strongly influenced by models from Western colonial states. Conversely, in the early 20th century, building styles and formal elements from the Islamic world provided stimulus for architectural development in Europe and North America. Architects such as Walter Gropius and Le Corbusier then discovered the attraction of applying Eastern form reduction (as in the buildings of Sinan or the medieval architecture of the Maghreb) to their concept of modern architecture.

This international integration was also pushed forward in the 20th century through the centralism of the USSR, which had a global effect. Then, in place of regional, ethnically-orientated artistic styles in the various Islamic republics of their own confederation and in the Islamic world in general, there now emerged a unifying style oriented towards the modern world in the service of ideology. As a result of this artistic policy, the unusual features of individual Islamic regions temporarily disappeared almost completely, but became even more strongly and widely emphasized in periods of nostalgia for their own traditions. This latter trend became obvious, for example, when the Ottoman type of central dome mosque with pencil-slim minarets spread into various countries as a leitmotif and since the 19th century has become the international symbol of the "mosque" building type.

Even if, because of international economic and political uniformity, 20th-century Islamic architecture can no longer be conclusively viewed in isolation, there remains in existence one typically Islamic building: the mosque. That is why the following remarks are limited to this special type of building, including

a range of the most important examples and trends within 20th-century mosque architecture.

One of the essential criteria for the assessment of modern mosque architecture is the relationship of a building to its physical and ecological context as well as to its landscape environment. From this point of view, the designs of the Iranian architect Kamran Diba are the most instructive, for instance his Namaz-Khaneh garden mosque in Teheran, but also the Friday Mosque in Shushtar, designed in 1977. Here he returns to classical formal elements, such as the *ziyada*, which surrounds the original inner area of the mosque. He copies this and combines it with concepts of space interpreted in a modern way, like in the structuring of the minaret.

Opposite: **The King Faisal Mosque in Islamabad**, Pakistan, Vedat Delakoy (Turkey), 1966–1986
This mosque was designed for 10,000 believers within the prayer hall and a further 80,000 on the adjacent site also belonging to the mosque. The mosque is named after King Faisal of Saudi Arabia who promised to finance the project when on a visit in 1966. Affiliated to the mosque are the Institute for Islamic Research and, since 1982, parts of the International Islamic University. The interior was decorated by the Turkish artist Menga Ertel in ceramic tiles with some imposing calligraphic decoration.

Right: **Istiqlal, or Freedom Mosque, the state mosque of the Republic of Indonesia**, Jakarta, F. Silaban, 1955–1984
The tradition of the state mosque was developed in Indonesia, the country with the largest Muslim population in the world. Only Indonesians were allowed to enter the competition for its design and construction. Materials used had to be long-lasting and available within the country. Silaban chose concrete and steel for manufacturing the building components. The decorative fittings of the prayer hall, with an area of 36,980 sq. m., are of marble, ceramic, and steel.

The Great Mosque of Niono, Mali, Mali, 1948–1973
Built of clay, sun-baked clay bricks, and wooden beams for the roof and facade consruction, the mosque has been enlarged to its present size in three stages since 1948. The original 126 sq m prayer hall, a hypostele hall with 68 columns, now extends over 726 sq m, and almost fills the whole area within the Mosque. Inside the courtyard further buildings and a washing area are to be found.

The King Abdallah Mosque, Amman, Rasem Badran, 1989
This mosque has a regular octagonal ground plan, which is oriented towards the symmetrically positioned dome in the center. A pupil of the Egyptian architect Hassan Fathy, Rasem Badran, like his teacher, carefully studied older architectural models. That way he developed his own architectural style, in which building forms adopted from older models are integrated into the design in a purified form.

Another important element in the erection of mosques is the representation of the relationship of the building to its cultural context. This factor becomes increasingly important for mosques and cultural centers built in non-Islamic countries. With the strong internationalization of modern society in the last third of the 20th century, Islamic religious communities spread throughout the Western world. These communities often finance the building of mosques and schools from their own resources. An example is the Yavush Sultan Selim Mosque of the Islamic community in Mannheim. In this building modern formal elements are combined with the classical leitmotifs of the Turkish spindle minaret and the dome; inside there is very traditional architecture with an ambulatory around a fountain. At the same time a relationship is created between the modern outside world and, in the arrangement of the interior, the intrinsically religious building elements and traditions of Islamic architecture. This interplay between modern form and Islamic tradition is also found in other buildings of Islamic communities in Western industrialized states, above all where mosque buildings are integrated into larger Islamic cultural institutions. The great variety of communities for which these buildings have been developed can in the more successful cases be seen in the buildings themselves. So it is in London, where several Islamic cultural centers with accompanying mosque buildings have been established which are quite different in form although situated within just a few miles of one another.

The cultural context has an entirely different significance for the great state mosques, which are constructed in young newly independent states and make a deliberate connection to the ideology of the older, established states. The mosque in Jakarta (Indonesia) provides one of the most telling examples. The building harks back to old architectural styles such as the originally Ottoman spindle minaret, but transforms them into an abstract symbol, and then refers to forms from modern office buildings and large-scale mid-20th-century complexes. Here, the mosque, which principally serves as a prayer hall for the assembly of believers, has to enable the people to identify with the modern state promoting itself with Islam as its state religion.

Since the first third of the 20th century, two important trends can be discerned in the development of form in mosque buildings: the study of existing local tradition and the strong influence stemming from the international use of modernistic forms. Typical of the continued existence of local forms of architecture and of a kind of ethnographic mosque style are the buildings erected in the region of West Africa where clay is the principal material. The mosques in Djénné and Niono in Mali are separated in time by over 100 years and yet still show a very similar sort of ambulatory with matching building techniques and materials as well as some elements of form.

A certain tension between modern building forms and materials used and traditional architectural forms can be seen again and again in the mosque designs in the eastern Mediterranean area and the Near East. In Turkey especially, local traditions in architecture, together with the Ottoman building traditions among the successors to Sinan, are being studied more and more often. The story of the construction of the King Abdallah Mosque in Amman (Jordan) is almost equal in this sense to a political declaration. In 1979 Rasem Badran presented a modernist plan, which referred to the Islamic building traditions of the region only in the basic shape of the great dome and the smaller half-domes on the annex, but otherwise was visibly inspired by the modern concrete architecture of Europe and the USA. In the end, the completed building, to a large degree, actually reflected Badran's concept. And yet the details of form, such as the fenestration of the upper dome area, the shape of the *sherefes* (minaret balconies), the external decoration of the dome with large-scale ornamentation, and the classical calligraphy and star braid patterns, all of these at least quote from, and even consciously hark back to, the tradition of Ottoman mosque building. The adoption of individual elements of classical Islamic architecture and their transfer into a modern form with modern materials is an approach that can also

King Saud Mosque in Jedda, Saudi Arabia, Abdel al-Wakil, 1989
Al-Wakil is a pupil of Hassan Fathy who, for his buildings, made a study of classical architectural forms and materials from Nubian art of the Islamic period. In constructing the King Saud Mosque, al-Wakil refers, both with the entrance area and with the minaret, to the Sultan Hasan Mosque of 1356–63 in Cairo. In addition, some other elements of the building (the shape of the dome, the *iwan*) make visible reference to Mamluk architecture.

King Hassan II Mosque in Casablanca, Morocco, Michel Pinseau, 1986–93
The prayer hall of the mosque was designed for 25,000 believers. The minaret that dominates the building is 200 meters high and in its design follows traditional tower minarets of the Maghreb. The roof over the prayer hall is remarkable: an area of 25 × 70 meters can be rolled back if required. The building also houses a Koran school, a library, and exhibition space.

be recognized in the King Saud Mosque in Jedda. Here, the architecture works through its simple Cubist forms, through the smooth upper surfaces, devoid of decoration, and yet at the same time it plays around with the classical elements of Mamluk architecture, such as, for instance, the shape of the minaret, the footbridge to the dome with fenestrated triangles, and a row of windows in the drum area.

Buildings such as the Sultan's Mosque in Singapore (1924–1928) or the Mosque of Hassan II in Casablanca (1986–1993) testify for a widespread unbroken relationship with tradition. The Singapore mosque, with the form of its dome and minaret and also with such details as the shape of the windows and the exterior decoration, clearly refers back to the Moghul architecture of the 16–19th centuries and via these features qualifies as a building from the past. For its part, the King Hassan Mosque in Casablanca looks to classical elements of North African mosque buildings. The minaret precisely follows the tradition of tower minarets in the Maghreb. The layout of the interior, too, consisting of many walkway arches, *muqarnas* column heads and vaulting as well as multicolored painted ceilings, revives the traditions of old Moroccan art, which was a matter of particular concern to the builder, King Hassan II.

A similarly recent high regard for old traditional crafts can also be seen in Iran and Turkey, where the ceramic decoration of mosques in Isfahan and Istanbul was restored with the use of old techniques. The King Hassan Mosque, however, at the same time also adopted new approaches. The roof of the prayer hall can be opened with the help of modern technology and the *qibla* is indicated with a laser beam. It is indicative that the design of this building was by a French architect, while local craftsmen carried out the decoration.

The difficulty in finding a design that combines tradition and the modern world and yet is also acceptable to the general public is demonstrated by the failed efforts of the distinguished Egyptian architect Hassan Fathy. With his designs for New Gorma at Luxor he wanted to go back to the traditional clay brick architecture of the region and at the same time create a modern building that would respond to the functional requirements of a mosque. His ideas were indeed well received in the international art world, but they were felt by the general public to be "not rich enough" and "lacking decoration" and for the most part were rejected.

The architect Jahangir Mazlum tried to follow a rather different path in 1977–1987 with the al-Ghadir Mosque in Tehran, in which he used consistently modern forms, such as in the dome, which was formed like a prism from angular overlapping segments, but the whole design combined with a traditional Persian decorative technique. So lines of calligraphy in relief brickwork or in blue-glazed tiles were integrated into this monumental building, thus making reference to Seljuk and Timurid decorative styles. This mosque, whose 12-sided shape recalls the 12 imams of Shia, is a very successful attempt to combine old traditions, religious ideas and modern approaches into a harmonious whole.

A series of radical new approaches to the layout of mosques is particularly evident in Bangladesh, Pakistan, and Saudi Arabia. These countries attempted to follow a quite separate path in Islamic architecture. Bangladesh and Pakistan in the 1960s and 1970s were strongly under the influence of the American architect Louis Kahn (1901–1974). The mosque in Islamabad was constructed 1970–1986 by Vedat Delakoy and actually the design still plays with classical forms, but these are rendered by modern techniques and in modern building forms. The great dome was turned into a tent-like folded roof that spans the wide prayer hall. The minarets, with an educated reference to the Ottoman spindle minaret, appear refined, sharp, and needlelike, and have no *sherefes*. The structure of the exterior is plain exposed concrete with the surfaces decorated with textured concrete, so that this mosque has its effect via the main block and the wings of the building, not through any surface decoration superimposed on the structure. To that extent the architect here has answered the main European point of criticism of Islamic architecture, namely that bearing and loading elements are not distinguishable one from another, but are hidden under a covering of ornamentation that spreads over the whole structure.

The buildings of the London-based architect Basil al-Bayati should be viewed against the background of the postmodernist trends of the 1980s. Using all available technology, he achieved some extremely unusual building forms. For his design for the "Mosque of the Books" he simply used the familiar formal elements of dome and minaret. However, the side walls of the prayer hall were themselves fragmented and arranged like the pages of an open book. For al-Bayati knowledge and belief are two sides of the process of discovery, and his design interprets the purpose of the building complex through the external structure.

The modern mosque, which is constructed by Islamic as well as non-Islamic architects in the many different parts of the world, always includes an interpretation and a message that reaches far beyond the original purpose of the building as a prayer room. For that reason, over the last 150 years building forms have been drawn, as if by a pendulum swinging to and fro, between a separate tradition and influences from outside, where the quest for a modern Islamic identity, especially over the last 30 years, has left its mark on architectural design.

always been compelled to avoid natural, imitative representation of people. The three-dimensional naturalistic sculptures of the 19th century also demonstrate the Europeanization of the Islamic world and the renunciation of religious dogma. The ban on images was strictly obeyed only in sacred areas. In the 20th century, as the former European colonies established themselves as independent states, the erection of freestanding statues always had to be combined with a political message. And yet, especially in the first half of the 20th century, the influences of European movements in monumental sculpture like Art Nouveau and Art Deco were predominant in many Islamic countries, as, for instance, with Mahmud Muhtar's statue *Egyptian Awakening*, which used the well-known visual element of the sphinx in a composition of images oriented towards European forms. The trend towards monumental sculpture became stronger in the course of the 20th century and often came under the influence of official communist-socialist art, as propagated by the USSR and adopted more and more in allied states. For that reason, a new sculptural art was developed against an explicitly political background and deliberately advanced as a counterbalance to the classical Islamic view of the world, in order simultaneously to promote an image of national identity.

Sculpture

In the course of the 20th century a far-reaching break with Islamic tradition took place in the genre of monumental sculpture, examples of which can be found in very different regions of the Islamic world. With their three-dimensional subjects, sculptors in exceptional numbers confronted the Islamic ban on images, which is derived from Koranic traditions. Since the early days of Islam, artists had

Mahmud Muhtar, **Egyptian Awakening**, Cairo, 1919–1928, granite
This monumental sculpture was produced at the time of the struggles for independence after the First World War, towards the end of the British protectorate in 1922. In art there was also a search for typical Egyptian traditions, in which the Pharaonic era was interpreted as the last real Egyptian culture before domination by a succession of foreign powers. The combination of a recumbent sphinx, referring to that Pharaonic era, with the representation of a woman, who removes the veil from her face, vividly refers to the emergence of a new era of radical change.

Ismail Fattah, **The Martyrs' Monument** (Saheed Monument), Baghdad, 1983, height 40 meters
These onion domes, cut open and clad in blue-turquoise tiles, and set on an artificial island, were erected on the orders of state president Saddam Hussein to the memory of the Iraqi dead of the first years of the Iran-Iraq War (1980–1988). The monumental architectural sculpture is equally impressive and frightening in its simplicity.

Muhammad Shah, 1846/[?], oil on canvas, 220 × 125 cm, Berlin, Ethnographic Museum
This oil painting is a portrait of the Kajar prince Muhammad Shah (1834–1848). Under his regency, a large number of reproduction techniques were introduced into Persia, which also influenced the style of Persian painting. In this transitional period, many European artists traveled to Persia, some of whom were asked by the shah to paint portraits of him. Even if Persian artists presumably did paint this portrait, it is an attempt to paint a seated subject with the use of perspective and thus shows European influence.

Chaïba Tallal, **Untitled**, 1986, oil on canvas, 114 × 91 cm, Collection of La Société Générale Marocaine de Banques
Chaïba Tallal is today one of the best-known women painters of the Maghreb. She has no art school qualification and worked first as an embroideress before turning to painting. Her work was first exhibited in Paris. An independent expressive mixture of modern naïve painting and Moroccan folk art has brought Tallal success in these tremendously effective compositions. She takes her subjects from life in the villages, which she visits repeatedly from her home in Casablanca.

It is possible, in addition, to ascertain other developments in those states which had had a stronger exchange between artists from Europe and from the Islamic world. These developments are obviously discernible in the works of the numerous Turkish and North African artists who live, often for long periods, in Western Europe and then return once again to their native lands. Behind their designs is a view of sculpture that is oriented towards modern international art in its use of form and its concept of context. It was possible to create large abstract sculptures or wooden carvings of figures for which ideological orientation and religious bans were no longer relevant. So in the 19th and especially the 20th centuries a glaring split with Islamic tradition can be observed in the field of sculpture. This sort of art is subject to modernistic international trends, especially within the Islamic world, so that in this sphere it is only possible to promote the revival of traditions in a small way.

Painting

As in architecture, it is possible to recognize a state of creative tension between the exertion of European influence on painting and the maintenance of eastern Islamic tradition. In the 19th century, under European influence, there developed for the first time in the history of Islamic culture a free style of painting. Particularly receptive at first to this artistic trend was Iran, which has always been inclined towards painting, so large-scale portraits of Persian rulers and members of the Kajar court were produced in the royal studio (*naqqashane*), but also, after 1798, as wall decoration in over 40 newly built castles. These representations are oriented towards the Western portrait, which emulates the natural model, but the old traditions of Islamic miniature painting can be detected through the tendency towards two-dimensionalism and decorative internal drawing of individual color surfaces. This attempt to find a middle way between

the tradition of Islamic miniature painting and the contemporary Western art of portraiture has parallels in the later painting of the Mughal dynasty in India and also in Ottoman landscape painting of the 19th century.

At the end of the 19th century and in the first decade of the 20th century, art was molded in numerous Islamic countries by artists who had studied in Europe and who – after returning home – strove for an independent synthesis between the modern world of the West and domestic feelings about art. Because of this, associations of artists sprang up, which diligently sought to find fashionable new approaches that would gain acceptance against the established forms of their predecessors, which they saw as antiquated. So, for instance, in Turkey the Society of Free Artists and Painters, which had appeared in the 1920s, fought the predominance of the Late Impressionist style and promoted against it an abstract artistic ideal. One of the chief advocates of this new development is Sabri Berkel, whose compositions show a strong European Cubist influence. He combines Cubist formal elements with the two-dimensional surface and very color-intensive traditions of Ottoman miniature painting. Because of that, Berkel's series of works in the first half of the 20th century, which attempted to find a way towards calligraphy-oriented abstract composition via examination of European Cubism, are exemplary of this genre.

Besides this style of painting strongly affected by academic art teaching from Western European art colleges, there developed from the middle of the 20th century, principally in the North African states, an original style of painting independent of academic training methods, based primarily on the folk art of the individual region. In these pictures there occurs again and again an intensive study of everyday life in the East, which now for the first time appears to be worthy of painting on a larger scale. Compositions of this kind adopt older traditions of folk art frequently classed as naïve painting or primitivism, such as for instance the vivid arrangement of color, the filling of picture surfaces right to

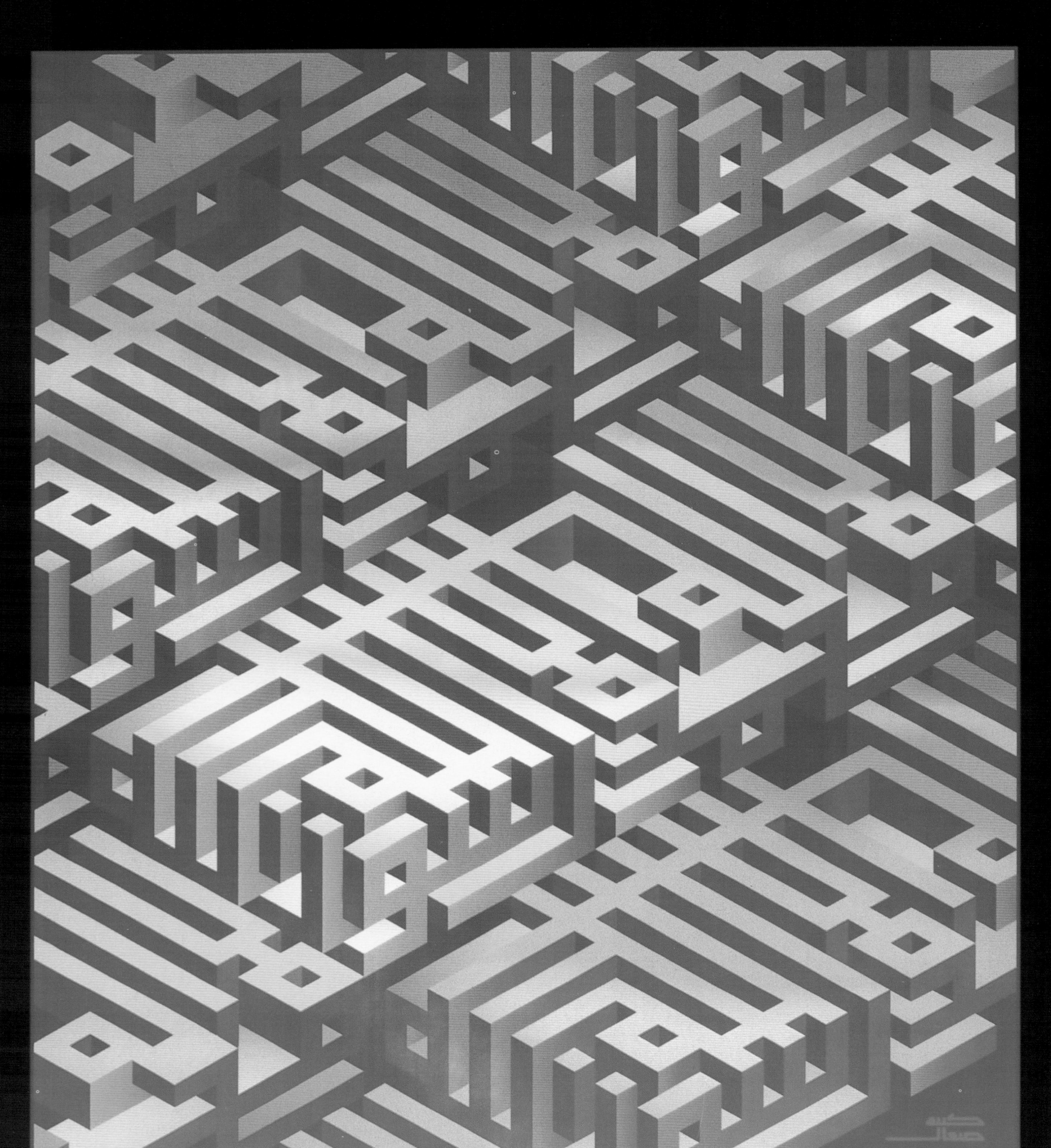

Wijdan Ali, **Calligraphic Abstraction**, 1993, acrylic on paper, 70 × 50 cm, in private ownership

Wijdan Ali studied history in Amman and in 1962 was Jordan's ambassador to the United Nations. Since the early 1980s she has fought a campaign via art exhibitions and publications to make an international public familiar with the present-day illustrative art of the Islamic world. This picture shows part of the letter "T," which in Arabic stands for the first part of the oath "by" (God). Wijdan Ali deals with the calligraphy as modern design in the form of an abstract composition, in which the chosen letter can refer indirectly to historical events or religious ideas.

Opposite: Mamoun Sakkal, **Steps and Shadows**, 1994, computer-assisted graphics, in private ownership

Sakkal is an architect, town planner, and designer and also teaches these subjects in Washington D.C. In the design shown here, the artist shows in three-dimensional Kufic script the Islamic creed (shahada): "There is no god but God and Muhammad is the messenger of God." The wording is to be read from three directions, of which the first part is contained in the vertical surface of the picture, the second part in the horizontal. The strong color scheme emphasizes the liveliness of the composition and also refers to the great variety of Islamic religious ideas.

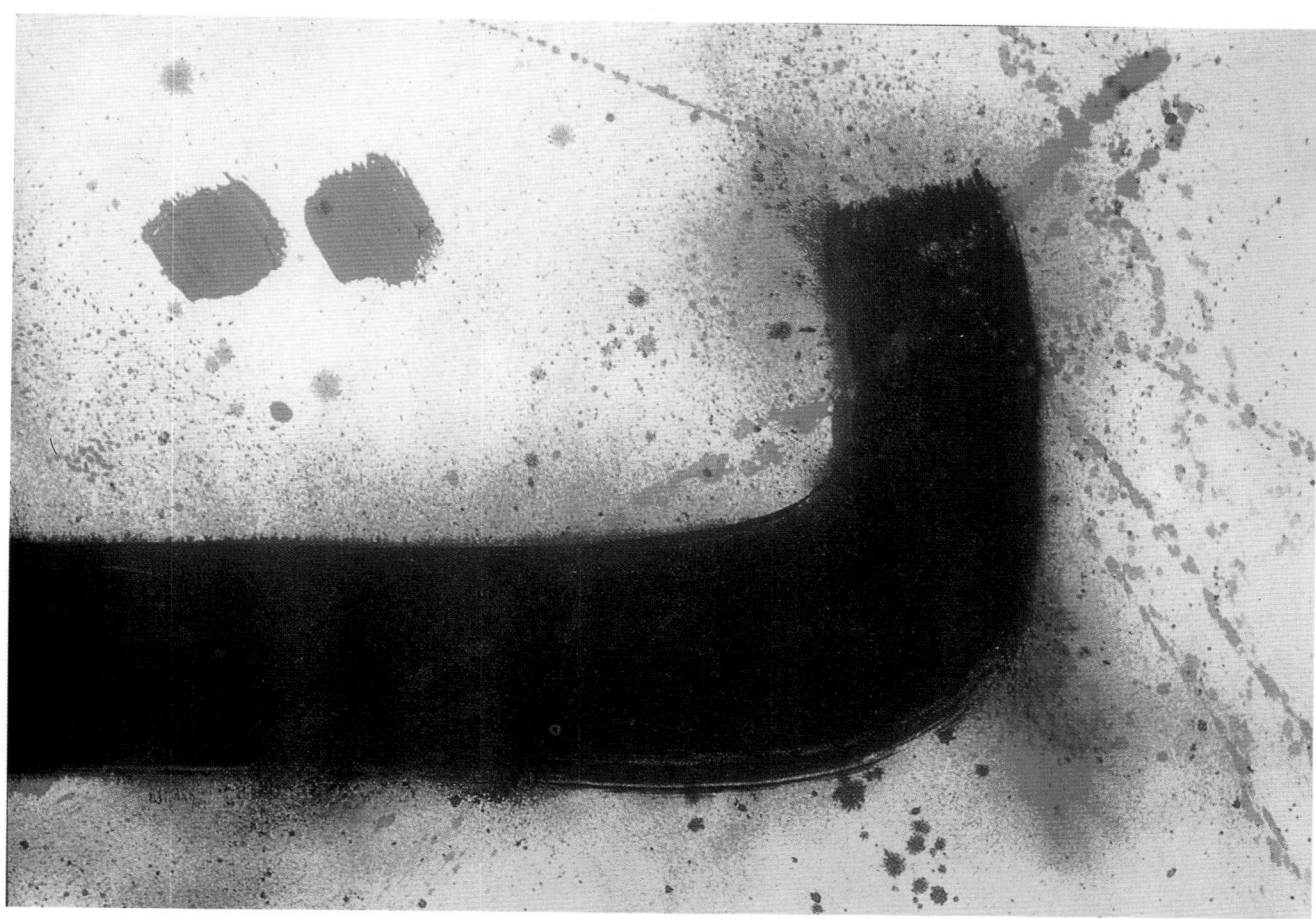

the edge (the *horror vacui*, "fear of emptiness"), and the purely two-dimensional perception. The heavily stylized, frequently almost stereotyped representation of natural subjects that is found again and again to different degrees in the work of North African artists, is also linked to this same aesthetic sense.

In the last quarter of the 20th century there developed in various Islamic countries a painting style which endeavored to rediscover and revive the "Islamic" element in art, so largely returned to the traditions of calligraphy. For, in spite of the evolution towards independent easel pictures taking place from the 19th century onwards throughout the Islamic world, traditional bibliographic art still remained important as it was looked upon as the principal characteristic achievement of Islamic art.

Such moves to combine easel painting and calligraphic art are found in the works of a fairly large number of artists. Among them, for instance, is Ahmed Mustafa, who in his pictures combines natural elements with decorative script that completely fills the surfaces. The inscriptions – mainly extracts from the Koran – are arranged in such a way that they suggest a surreal three-dimensionality in the picture.

With these pictures Ahmed Mustafa alludes to the Islamic ban on reproducing nature and at the same time adopts approaches which combine calligraphy as the original art form of the Islamic world with the artistic media and stylistic trends of the 20th century.

The Jordanian artist Wijdan Ali also frequently refers to Arabic script in her works. She deals as well with religious themes and creates a combination of past and present, for instance when she portrays the assassination of Husain, a descendent of the Prophet, at Kerbela in the 7th century, which for her stands for injustice in general, which has always existed.

These different approaches make it easier to understand the efforts made in the late 20th century to develop a modern, but still Islamic, easel painting, and to position this alongside Western art.

The basic problem with a descriptive overview of art in the Islamic world over the last 150 years is that it not only embraces an area that stretches from the Western Sahara to Indonesia, which naturally comprises a wealth of regions and states each with its own separate traditions, but also covers a long period of time. So by the very nature of things we are dealing with extremely heterogeneous art, and in the end only extreme openness to international Modernism can be considered a unifying element. It is problematic to speak of the specific art of individual countries, because the trend towards globalization felt everywhere since the 19th century has also led to a more intense artistic dialog between cultures. Consequently, the definition of the term "Islamic art" becomes increasingly difficult. Until now this referred to the religious background that united cultures over an enormous geographical area. For the present-day, however, as Ernst Grube suggested in 1978, first of all we have to define certain observable essential features of artistic works, which can be ascribed only by the content and cultural traditions of the Islamic religion. Such a definition is, however, yet to be found.

Appendix

Authors

Mukaddima Aschrafi

Prof. Dr. Mukaddima Aschrafi was born on July 5, 1936 in Tashkent and lives today in Dushanbe, Tajikistan. After graduating in art history from Moscow University (1959), she worked as a research assistant at the Institute for Oriental Studies of the USSR Academy of Science between 1959 and 1961 and later in the Manuscript Department of the Institute for Oriental Studies of the Tajikistan Academy of Science (1961–1965) and from 1965 to 1972 in the Department for the History of Central Asian Culture at the Institute for Oriental Studies of the USSR Academy of Science. Since 1972 she has held senior positions at the Institute for Cultural History of the Tajikistan Academy of Science and in 1997 she became professor of art history at the Technical University of Tajikistan. Prof. Aschrafi has spent time lecturing in France, Britain, and Ireland, and at Harvard and Oxford. She is a member of the Societas Iranologicae Europae (European Society for Central Asian Studies) and of the Tajikistan Society for Oriental Studies, as well as being author of the Tajikistan Encyclopedia of Literature and Art History.

Marianne Barrucand

Prof. Dr. Marianne Barrucand was born in 1941 in Freiburg (Saxony), gained her doctorate from Strasbourg in 1969, spent some years living in Rabat, where she was involved in research work, and since 1976 has taught Islamic art history and archeology at the Sorbonne in Paris. After qualifying as a lecturer in 1979 she gained her professorship there in 1985 and was director of the Arabic and Islamic Studies Department at the Sorbonne between 1989 and 1993. Prof. Barrucand has held visiting professorships at various German universities and was the driving force behind the ERASMUS network for Arabic and Oriental studies. Between 1987 and 1991 she was a member of the Commission Nationale de Centre National de la Recherche Scientifique (CNRS), and in 1997 became a member of the European Science Foundation. In 1989 she was commissioned by the CNRS to compile the international photographic archive entitled "Mashreq-Maghreb. Archives photographiques du monde islamique," was scientific adviser to the "Les trésors du Caire fatimide" exhibition at the Institut du Monde Arabe in Paris in 1996 and conducted an international colloquium, "L'Egypt fatimide. Son art et son histoire," at the Sorbonne in 1998. In 1999 Prof. Barrucand was created a member of the Légion d'Honneur.

Jesús Bermúdez López

Jesús Bermúdez López was born in 1959 in Granada, and studied philology, geography, and history, also graduating from the Arabic-Islamic Department of the University of Granada in Semitic Philology. As a specialist in Islamic art and archeology, he was involved in the creation of the "Special plan for the Alhambra and Alijares." He has taught at various institutions, including the University of La Sapienza in Rome, the Academia de Egipto in Italy, and as a guest lecturer on Mashreq-Maghreb courses, and was involved in the photographic archive of the Islamic world at the Otto-Friedrich University, Bamberg. He is currently head of the Department for Cultural Development of the Patronato del Alhambra, the management committee for the historical monuments of the Alhambra and the Generalife. He is a member of the Center for Historical Studies on Granada and its Kingdom and honorary member of the Friends of the Alhambra cultural association.

Sheila Blair

Dr. Sheila Blair was born in 1948 in Montreal, studied art history and sociology and gained a doctorate in art history and Near Eastern studies at Harvard. She has taught at various institutions, including the Pahlavi University in Shiraz (Iran), Harvard University, and the University of Pennsylvania, and has traveled widely through the Near East and Central Asia in pursuit of her research work. In addition to her own publications, she has co-authored numerous books and essays on Islamic art and architecture with her husband, Jonathan Bloom. Dr. Blair is now at Boston College where she and her husband are the Norma Jean Calderwood University Professors of Islamic and Asian Art.

Jonathan Bloom

Dr. Jonathan Bloom was born in 1950 in New York, studied art history, specializing in Islamic art, and gained a doctorate from Harvard on early Fatimid architecture in North Africa and Egypt. He was assistant lecturer at the Institute for Art History in Harvard between 1981 and 1987 and taught as guest lecturer at such institutions as the University of California in Los Angeles, at Yale University, and in Geneva and Bamberg. Dr. Bloom ist now at Boston College where she and her husband are the Norma Jean Calderwood University Professors for Islamic and Asian Art. He has spent a number of years traveling, researching and publishing works with his wife, Sheila Blair.

Sergej Chmelnizkij

Prof. Dr. Sergej Chmelnizkij was born in 1925 in Dnepropetrovsk (Ukraine), studied at the University of Architecture in Moscow and then worked as an architect in Bukhara and in the central restoration works in Moscow, before gaining a doctorate in Central Asian architecture from the Institute of Art History of the USSR Academy of Science. He worked at the Institute of History of the Tajikistan Academy of Science and at the same time held a professorship in planning and art history at the Polytechnic University in Dushanbe. His comprehensive scientific work is based on regular excavations, in Central Asia and Tajikistan in particular. Prof. Chmelnizkij has lived in Germany since 1980. He has worked for the Museum of Islamic Art, the German Archeological Institute, the Berlin Landeskonservator (administrative office for the preservation of works of art), and the government of Berlin, and has taught at various German universities.

Volkmar Enderlein

Dr. Volkmar Enderlein studied classical archeology, art history, and ancient history at the Friedrich-Schiller University, Jena, working on the Sassanid coins in the University's coin collection. In 1959 he became the scientific member of staff at the Islamic Museum of the State Museums of Berlin and has been director there since 1979. Dr. Enderlein has taught at Humboldt University, made numerous study trips to Syria, Jordan, Central Asia, India, and Pakistan, and published works on various aspects of Islamic art and on the history of the collection at the Islamic Museum.

Joachim Gierlichs

Dr. Joachim Gierlichs was born in 1959 in Munich, studied classical archeology, Christian archeology, Byzantine, and Islamic art history in Bonn, Munich, Erlangen and Heidelberg. He gained a doctorate in Islamic art history in 1991 with the thesis "Medieval animal reliefs in Anatolia and northern Mesopotamia." He has taken part in excavations in Syria and has been a frequent traveler to Mediterranean countries, the Middle East, and Central Asia. Apart from his work as scientific assistant at the Museum of Islamic Art in Berlin, he has had teaching contracts at the Free University of Berlin, the Martin Luther University, Halle, and the Rhineland Friedrich Wilhelm University. Dr. Gierlichs has been co-director of the Islamic Arts Society in London since 1999.

Almut von Gladiss

Dr. Almut von Gladiss was born on May 29, 1943, studied classical archeology, art history, and history in Münster, Rome, and Cologne, and in 1970 gained a doctorate from Cologne on Roman triumphal arch architecture in Provence. She spent many years on excavations and research work in Turkey and received a one-year travel fellowship from the German Archeological Institute which involved her traveling through Mediterranean countries, and the Near and Middle East. Apart from her work as consultant to the German Archeological Institute in Berlin, she has been involved in numerous exhibition and publication projects and since 1987 has been the scientific assistant at the Museum of Islamic Art in Berlin.

Julia Gonnella

Dr. Julia Gonnella was born in 1963, studied Islamic archeology and art history, oriental studies, and ethnology in London and Tübingen. She has taken part in excavations in Syria and Egypt, and gained a doctorate in 1995 on the Islamic veneration of saints in Aleppo. Between 1994 and 1996 she worked as a scientific museum assistant at the Museum of Islamic Art in Berlin and on the "Aleppo Room" exhibition. Since the fall of 1996 Dr. Gonnella has been in charge of the Islamic section of Syrian/German excavations at the citadel of Aleppo and researching the medieval fortification.

Oleg Grabar

Prof. Dr. Oleg Grabar was born in 1929 in Strasbourg, studied history, art history, and oriental languages at the Sorbonne and Harvard and gained a doctorate from Princeton in 1955. He began by teaching at the University of Michigan, where he became professor of art history in 1964, then taught from 1969 at Harvard University and from 1990 to 1998 at the Institute for Advanced Study at Princeton University. He has also taught as guest professor at Columbia University, New York University, the Institut du Monde, the Ecole des Hautes Etudes en Sciences Sociales, and the Collège de France. From 1964 to 1972 he led excavations of Qasr al-Hair al-Sharqi in Syria. Prof. Grabar was a member of the management committees of the Aga Khan Program for Islamic Art and Architecture, the Max van Berchem Foundation in Geneva, and the American Academy of Arts and Sciences. He is a member of the College Art Association, the Medieval Academy of America, the American Oriental Society, the American Research Center in Egypt, the Middle East Studies Association, the American Academy of Arts and Sciences, and the American Philosophical Society, and is also an honorary member of the German Archeological Institute, the Istituto per gli studi del Medio e Estremo Oriente in Rome, the British Academy and the Austrian Academy of Science. Prof. Grabar has set out the results of his research work on Islamic art history in numerous publications.

Annette Hagedorn

Dr. Annette Hagedorn gained her doctorate in Islamic art history on medieval metalwork before devoting herself to the study of the reciprocal relationships in the visual arts between the Islamic world and Europe. Her special area of interest is the Orientalist style of applied art in the 19th and 20th centuries. Since 1991 she has undertaken teaching contracts at the universities of Bonn, Mainz, and Utrecht on Islamic art and its interaction with European and North American art and has been involved in exhibitions and publications on Orientalism.

Markus Hattstein

Markus Hattstein was born in 1961 and has lived in Berlin since 1982. He has studied philosophy, sociology, Catholic theology, comparative religion, and Islam. Today he works as a freelance writer and publisher's reader.

Wolfgang Holzwarth

Dr. Wolfgang Holzwarth is an ethnologist, with Iranian studies as a minor. His area of work is the cultural history of Central and Southern Asia from early modern times. He has conducted field research in Afghanistan and Pakistan, and has spent time in Uzbekistan, Tajikistan, and other Asiatic countries in connection with research projects on archives and sources for the Free University and the University of Bamberg. Dr. Holzwarth is currently associate at the Central Asian Seminar at Humboldt University Berlin. He has published works on various aspects of Islamic regional history and historiography.

Natasha Kubisch

Dr. Natasha Kubisch studied art history, communications science, and theater science at Münster, Munich, Granada, and Madrid. In 1991 she gained a doctorate from Ludwig-Maximilians University in Munich on the Islamic-inspired building decoration of Santa María la Blanca, the oldest synagogue in Spain. She was then commissioned by the German Archeological Institute to work on the building decoration of the caliphal residence Medina al-Zahra in Spain and has since then published works on Spanish-Islamic and Judaic art.

Sibylle Mazot

Dr. Sibylle Mazot was born in 1962 in Paris, studied history and art history at the Sorbonne, and in 1995 gained her doctorate from there on the Islamic influence on architecture in the Norman kingdom of Sicily. She has been involved in several excavations in Sicily and Tunisia, written articles on Muslim influences on the medieval architecture of Palermo, and taken part in several international scientific conferences.

Viktoria Meinecke-Berg

Dr. Viktoria Meinecke-Berg is an art historian and has spent almost twenty years working in the Middle East, initially as a freelance employee of the German Archeological Institute in Cairo and later in Damascus. Today she lives in Hamburg and publishes works on various aspects of Islamic art, particularly Ottoman ceramics, the topography and building history of Cairo, and Fatimid art.

Elke Niewöhner-Eberhard

Dr. Elke Niewöhner-Eberhard was born in 1942 in Giessen and gained her doctorate in 1970 from the University of Freiburg im Breisgau in the fields of Islamic, Arabic-Islamic, and Persian-Turkish studies on Ottoman polemics against the Safavids. She has taught at the Ruhr University, Bochum, at the Asia Institute and the Goethe Institute of the Pahlavi University in Shiraz (Iran) and has had long research residences in Yemen and other parts of the Islamic world. Dr. Niewöhner-Eberhard has worked at the Museum of Islamic Art in Berlin and the Kestner Museum in Hanover, and has been scientific assistant at the Lower Saxony State Archive in Wolfenbüttel since 1996.

Peter W. Schienerl

Dr. Peter W. Schienerl was commissioned by the Austrian Academy of Science to conduct ethnological research projects in Egypt and other parts of the Islamic world. He later became a university lecturer (Munich, Vienna) and has since 1994 been head of the Documentation Office for Islamic Art and Architecture (DIKK) in Munich. In 1984 he was elected as the correspondent member of the Institut d'Egypte and has published the results of his cultural anthropological research work in a number of books and technical journals.

Philippa Vaughan

Dr. Philippa Vaughan is an art historian specializing in Mughal art and architecture. She is currently vice-president of the Royal Asiatic Society in London and consultant to the Aga Khan Trust for Culture in Geneva. A central aspect of her publications on Mughal art and architecture has been the role of women in art.

Bibliography

Islam – World Religion and Cultural Power

Arberry, A. J. trans. *The Koran – Interpreted.* Oxford, 1998.

Azzam, H. M. *Der Islam. Geschichte, Lehre und Wirkung.* Bindlach, 1989.

al-Buhari, Sahih. *Nachrichten von Taten und Aussprüchen des Propheten Muhammad.* Stuttgart, 1991.

Eliade, M. "Mohammed und der Aufstieg des Islam," in M. Eliade, *Geschichte der religiösen Ideen,* Vol. 3/1. Freiburg, 1983.

Glassé, C. *Concise Encyclopaedia of Islam.* London, 1989.

Glubb, J. B. *A Short History of the Arab Peoples.* London, 1978.

Haarmann, U., ed. *Geschichte der arabischen Welt.* Munich, 1987.

Halm, H. *Die Schia.* Darmstadt, 1988.

Halm, H. *Der schiitische Islam. Von der Religion zur Revolte.* Munich, 1994.

Hartmann, R. *Die Religion des Islam.* Darmstadt, 1992.

Ibn Ishaq. *Das Leben des Propheten.* Stuttgart/Vienna, 1986.

Kermani, N. *Gott ist schön. Das ästhetische Erleben des Koran.* Munich, 1999.

Le Gai Eaton, C. *Der Islam und die Bestimmung des Menschen.* Munich, 1994.

Nagel, T. *Geschichte der islamischen Theologie. Von Mohammed bis zur Gegenwart.* Munich, 1994.

Nagel, T. *Staat und Glaubensgemeinschaft im Islam,* 2 vols. Zurich/Munich, 1981.

Netton, I. R. *A Popular Dictionary of Islam.* London/New Jersey, 1992.

Paret, R. *Mohammed und der Koran,* 6th ed. Stuttgart, 1985.

Robbe, M. *Welt des Islam. Geschichte und Alltag einer Religion.* Leipzig, 1989.

Robinson, F. *Atlas of the Islamic World.* Amsterdam, 1991.

Robinson, F., ed. *Cambridge Illustrated History of the Islamic World.* Cambridge/New York, 1996.

Schimmel, A. *Der Islam. Eine Einführung.* Stuttgart, 1990.

Waines, D. *An Introduction to Islam.* Cambridge, UK, 1995.

Watt, W. M., and A. T. Welch. *Der Islam,* 3 vols. Stuttgart, 1980.

Wittfogel, K. A. *Die Orientalische Despotie.* Frankfurt am Main, 1977.

Art and Culture in the Islamic World

Abu-Deeb, M. *Al-Jutjanis's Theory of Poetic Imagination.* Warminster, 1979.

Ahsam, M. M. *Social Life under the Abbasids.* London, 1979.

Blair, S., and J. Bloom. *The Art and Architecture of Islam 1250–1800.* New Haven/London, 1994.

Bloom, J., and S. Blair. *Islamic Arts.* London, 1997.

Bürgel, C. *The Feather of the Simurgh.* New York, 1988.

Ettinghausen, R., and O. Grabar. *The Art and Architecture of Islam 650–1250.* New Haven/London, 1987/1994.

Grabar, O. *The Formation of Islamic Art.* New Haven/London, 1973/1988.

Grabar, O. *The Mediation of Ornament.* A. W. Mellon Lectures in the Fine Arts, 1989. Princeton, 1992.

Hillenbrand, R. *Islamic Architecture.* Edinburgh, 1994.

Hillenbrand, R. *Islamic Art and Architecture.* London, 1999.

Michell, G., ed. *Architecture of the Islamic World. Its History and Social Meaning.* London, 1995.

Nasr, S. H. *Islamic Art and Spirituality.* Alberg, 1987.

Necipoglu, G. *The Topkapi Scroll. Geometry and Ornament in Islamic Art.* Los Angeles, 1995.

Petersen, A. *Dictionary of Islamic Architecture.* London, 1999.

Sabra, A. I. *The Optics of Ibn al Haytham.* London, 1989.

Schimmel, A. *A Two-Colored Brocade.* Chapel Hill, 1992.

Soucek, P. "Nizami on Painters and Poets," in R. Ettinghausen, ed., *Islamic Art at the Metropolitan Museum.* New York, 1972.

Syria and Palestine

Almagro Gorbea, A. "El Palacio Omeya de Amman," in *La Arquitectur.* Madrid, 1983.

Creswell, K. A. C. *A Short Account of Early Muslim Architecture.* J. W. Allan, rev./ed., The American University in Cairo. Cairo, 1989.

Creswell, K. A. C. *Early Muslim Architecture. Vol. I, 1–2, Umayyads, A.D. 622–750.* 2nd ed. Oxford, 1969.

Creswell, K. A. C., R. Holod, J. Knustad, and W. Trousdale. *City in the Desert. Qasr al-Hayr East.* Cambridge, Mass., 1978.

Grabar, O. *The Formation of Islamic Art.* New Haven/London, 1973/1988.

Hamilton, R. W. *Khirbat al Maffar. An Arabian Mansion in the Jordan Valley.* Oxford, 1959.

Hamilton, R. W. *Walid and his Friends. An Umayyad Tragedy.* Oxford Studies in Islamic Art VI. Oxford, 1988.

Iraq, Iran, and Egypt

Bloom, J. "The Qubbat al-Khadra in Early Islamic Palaces," in *Ars Orientalis* 23 (1993), pp. 131–137.

Creswell, K. A. C. *Early Muslim Architecture,* 2 vols. Oxford, 1969.

Dimand, M. S. "Studies in Islamic ornament," in *Ars Islamica* 4 (1937), pp. 293ff.

Ettinghausen, R., and O. Grabar. *The Art and Architecture of Islam 650–1250.* New Haven/London, 1987/1994.

Grabar, O. *The Formation of Islamic Art.* New Haven/London, 1973/1988.

Grabar, O. *The Mediation of the Ornament.* A. W. Mellon Lectures in the Fine Arts, 1989. Princeton, 1992.

Hodges, R., and D. Whitehouse, *Mohammed, Charlemagne and the Origins of Europe.* Ithaca, NY, 1983.

Hutt, A. *Islamic Architecture. Iran I.* London, 1977.

Kühnel, E. *Die Arabeske. Sinn und Wandlung eines Ornaments.* Wiesbaden, 1949.

Lassner, J. *The Shaping of Abbasid Rule.* Princeton, 1980.

Lassner, J. *The Topography of Baghdad in the Early Middle Ages.* Detroit, 1970.

al-Masudi. *The Meadows of Gold. The Abbasids.* P. Lunde, and C. Stone, ed./trans. London, 1984.

Rogers, J. M. "Samarra. A Study in Medieval Town-Planning," in A. H. and S. M. Stern Hourani, *The Islamic City.* Oxford/Philadelphia, 1970, pp. 119–156.

Tunisia and Egypt

Amari, M. *Storia degli Musulmani di Sicilia,* new ed. Florence, 1954/1972.

Behrens-Abousif, D. *Islamic Architecture in Cairo. An Introduction.* Leiden, 1989.

el-Bekri. *Description de l'Afrique septentrionnale par Abou Obeïd-el-Bekri.* Mac Guckin de Slane, trans. Paris, 1965.

Bellafiore, G. *Architettura in Sicilia nelle età araba e normanna (827–1194).* Palermo, 1990.

Bianquis, T. "La prise du pouvoir par les Fatimides en Égypte (357–363/968–974)," in *Annales Islamologiques* II (1972), pp. 49–108.

Creswell, K. A. C. *The Muslim Architecture of Egypt, Vol. 1. Ikhshîds and Fâtimids (939–1171).* New York, 1978.

Dachraou, F. *Le califat fatimide au Maghreb (296–365/909–975). Histoire, politique et institutions.* Tunis, 1981.

L'Égypte fatimide. Son art et son histoire. Report from the colloquium held in Paris 28–30 May 1998. Paris, 1999.

Eredità dell'Islam. Arte islamica in Italia. Catalog of the exhibition in the Palazzo Ducale, Venice, 30 October 1993 – 30 April 1994. Milan, 1993.

Ettinghausen, R., and O. Grabar. *The Art and Architecture of Islam 650–1250.* New York, 1991.

Federico II, immagine e potere. Catalog of the exhibition in the Castello Svevo, Bari, 4 February – 17 April 1995. Venice, 1995.

Golvin, L. *Le Magrib Central à l'époque des Zirides. Recherches d'archéologie et d'histoire.* Paris, 1957.

Golvin, L. *Recherches archéologiques à la Qal'a des Banu Hammad.* Paris, 1965.

Halm, H. *Die Schia.* Darmstadt, 1988.

Lézine, A. *Architecture de l'Ifriqiya. Recherches sur les monuments aghlabides.* Paris, 1966.

Lézine, A. *Deux villes d'Ifriqiya. Études d'archéologie, d'urbanisme, de démographie. Sousse, Tunis.* Paris, 1971.

Lézine, A. *Mahdiya. Recherches d'archéologie islamique.* Paris, 1965.

Lézine, A. *Sousse. Les monuments musulmans.* Tunis, 1968.

Marçais, G. *L'architecture musulmane d'Occident (Tunisie, Algérie, Maroc, Espagne et Sicile). Arts et Métiers Graphiques.* Paris, 1954.

Marçais, G. *La Berbérie musulmane et l'Orient au Moyen-Age.* Paris, 1946.

Raymond, A. *Le Caire.* Paris, 1993.

Sanders, P. *Ritual, Politics, and the City in Fatimid Cairo.* Albany, 1994.

Sourdel, D. and J. *La civilisation de l'Islam classique.* Paris, 1983.

Staacke, U. *La Ziza. Un palazzo normanno a Palermo. La cultura musulmana negli edifici dei Re.* Palermo, 1992.

di Stefano, G. *Monumenti della Sicilia normanna,* new ed. Palermo, 1972.

Talbi, M. *L'émirat aghlabide 184–296/800–909. Histoire politique.* Paris, 1966.

Trésors fatimides du Caire. Catalog of the exhibition at the Institut du Monde Arabe, 28 April – 30 August 1998. Paris, 1998.

Tronzo, W. *The Cultures of his Kingdom. Roger II and the Cappella Palatina.* Princeton, 1997.

Williams, C. *Islamic Monuments of Cairo.* Cairo, 1993.

Syria, Palestine, and Egypt

Allan, J. W. *Persian Metal Technology 700–1300 AD.* London, 1979.

Allen, T. *Ayyubid Architecture.* 6th ed.(Solipsist Press, Occidental, California: Electronic Publication) 1996–1999.

Ashtor, E. *East-West Trade in the Medieval Mediterranean.* Hampshire, 1986.

Atil, E. *Renaissance of Islam, Art of the Mamluks.* Washington, 1981.

Atil, E., and P. J. Chase. *Islamic Metalwork in the Freer Gallery of Art.* Washington, 1985.

Baer, E. *Ayyubid Metalwork with Christian Images.* Cologne, 1989.

Baer, E. *Metalwork in Medieval Islamic Art.* Albany, 1983.

Burgoyne, M. H. *Mamluk Jerusalem. An Architectural Study.* Jerusalem, 1987.

Constable, O. R. *Trade and Traders in Muslim Spain.* Cambridge, 1995.

Creswell, K. A. C. *The Muslim Architecture of Egypt,* 2 vols. Oxford, 1952/1959.

Fuglestad-Aumeunier, V., ed. *Alep et la Syrie du Nord.* Aix en Provence, 1992 (*Revue du Monde Musulman et de la Méditerranée* 62).

Gabrieli, F., and U. Scerrato. *Gli Arabi in Italia. Cultura, contatti e tradizioni.* Milan, 1979.

Gaube, H. and E. Wirth. *Aleppo. Historische und geographische Beiträge zur baulichen Gestaltung, zur sozialen Organisation und zur wirtschaftlichen Dynamik einer vorderasiatischen Fernhandelsmetropole.* Beiträge zum Tübingen Atlas des Vorderen Orients, No. 58. Wiesbaden, 1984.

von Gladiss, A. "Zur Geschichte der Tauschierkunst im islamischen Mittelalter," in *Acta Praehistorica et Archaeologica* 28, Berlin (1996), pp. 117–145.

Goitein, S. D. *Letters of Medieval Jewish Traders.* Princeton, 1973.

Gonnella, J. *Das Aleppo-Zimmer. Ein christlich-orientalisches Wohnhaus des 17. Jahrhunderts aus Aleppo (Syrien).* Mainz, 1996.

Gonnella, J., W. Khayata, and K. Kohlmeyer, "Die Zitadelle von Aleppo," in M. Fansa, H. Gaube, and J. Windelberg eds, *Damaskus-Aleppo. 5000 Jahre Stadtentwicklung.* Mainz, 2000, pp. 250–258.

Herzfeld, E. *Matériaux pour un corpus inscriptionum arabicarum. Deuxième partie: Syrie du Nord. Inscriptions et monuments d'Alep.* Cairo, 1954–1955.

Hill, D. R., and Ibn al-Razzaz al-Jazari. *The Book of Knowledge of Ingenious Mechanical Devices.* Dordrecht, 1974.

Hillenbrand, C. *The Crusades. Islamic Perspectives.* Edinburgh, 1999.

Humphreys, R. S. *From Saladin to the Mongols. The Ayyubids of Damascus 1193–1260.* New York, 1977.

Jackson, D. E. P., and M. C. Lyons. *Saladin. The Politics of the Holy War.* Cambridge, 1981.

James, D. *Qur'ans of the Mamluks.* London, 1988.

Kessler, C. "Funerary Architecture within the City," in *Colloque International sur l'Histoire du Caire,* Gräfenhainichen, 1974, pp. 257–267.

Kessler, C. *The Carved Masonry Domes of Mediaeval Cairo.* London, 1976.

Khayata, W., and K. Kohlmeyer. "Die Zitadelle von Aleppo – Vorläufiger Bericht über die Untersuchungen 1996 und 1997," in *Damaszener Mitteilungen* X (1998), pp. 69–96.

Klengel, H. "Die historische Rolle der Stadt Aleppo im vorantiken Syrien," in Gernot Wilhelm, ed., *Die orientalische Stadt. Kontinuität, Wandel, Bruch.* 1. international Colloquium der Deutschen Orient-Gesellschaft, 9.–10 Mai 1996 in Halle/Saale. Saarbrücken, 1997.

Komaroff, L. *The Golden Disk of Heaven. Metalwork of Timurid Iran.* New York, 1992.

Korn, L. *Ayyubidische Architektur in Ägypten und Syrien. Bautätigkeit im Kontext von Politik und Gesellschaft.* Tübingen University dissertation, 1999.

Lamm, C. J. *Mittelalterliche Gläser und Steinschnittarbeiten aus dem Nahen Orient.* Berlin, 1929–1930.

Lapidus, I. M. *Muslim Cities in the Middle Ages.* Cambridge, Mass., 1967.

Masters, B. *The Origins of Western Economic Dominance in the Middle East. Mercantilism and the Islamic Economy in Aleppo, 1600–1750.* New York, 1988.

Meinecke, M. *Die mamlukische Architektur in Ägypten und Syrien (648/1250 bis 923/1517).* Glückstadt, 1992.

Melikian-Chirvani, A. S. *Islamic Metalwork from the Iranian World 8th–18th centuries.* London, 1982.

Porter, V. *Medieval Syrian Pottery.* Oxford, 1981.

Raby, J., ed., *The Art of Syria and the Jazira 1100–1250.* Oxford, 1985.

Raymond, A. *Le Caire.* Paris, 1993.

Raymond, A. "Les grands waqfs et l'organisation de l'espace urbain à Alep et au Caire à l'époque ottomane (XVIe–XVIIe siècles)," in *Bulletin d'Études Orientales* XXXI (1980), pp. 113–128.

Sack, D. *Damaskus. Entwicklung und Struktur einer orientalisch islamischen Stadt.* (Damaszener Forschungen, Vol. I.) Mainz, 1989.

Sauvaget, J. *Alep. Essai sur le développement d'une grande ville syrienne des origines au milieu du XIXe siècle.* (Bibliothèque Archéologique et Historique No. 34), 2 vols. Paris, 1941.

Scerrato, U. *Metalli islamici.* Milan, 1996.

Spallanzani, M. *Ceramiche orientali a Firenzi nel Rinascimento.* Florence, 1978.

Tabbaa, Y. *Constructions of Power and Piety in Mediaeval Aleppo.* Pennsylvania, 1997.

Ward, R. *Islamic Metalwork.* London, 1993.

Spain and Morocco

Acien Almansa, M. "Madinat al-Zahra en el urbanismo musulmán," in *Cuadernos de Madinat al-Zahra* 1, Cordoba (1987), pp. 7–26.

Almagro Corbea, A., and A. Jiménez Martin. *Giralda.* Madrid, 1985.

Arié, R. *El Reino nasrí de Granada.* Madrid, 1992.

Arié, R. *L'Espagne musulmane au temps des Nasrides.* Paris, 1973.

Azuar Ruiz, R., M. Bevia, M. Borrego Colomer, and R. Saranova Zozaya. "La rábita de Guardamar (Alicante). Su arquitectura," in *Cuadernos de Madinat al-Zahra* 2, Cordoba (1988–90), pp. 55–67.

Barrucand, M., and A. Bednorz. *Maurische Architektur in Andalusien.* Cologne, 1992.

Basset, H., and H. Terrasse. *Sanctuaires et forteresses almohades.* Paris, 1936.

Beckwith, J. *Caskets from Cordoba.* London, 1960.

Bermúdez López, J. and P. Galera Andreu. *Guía Oficial de visita al Conjunto Monumental de la Alhambra.* Granada, 1998.

Bermúdez Pareja, J. *Pinturas sobre piel en la Alhambra de Granada.* Granada, 1987.

Brentjes, B. *Die Mauren.* Leipzig, 1989.

Brisch, K. *Die Fenstergitter und verwandte Ornamente der Hauptmoschee von Córdoba.* (Madrid Forschungen 4.) Berlin, 1966.

Brisch, K. "Madinat az-Zahra in der modernen archäologischen Literatur Spaniens," in *Kunst des Orients,* Wiesbaden (1963), pp. 5–41.

Brisch, K. "Zu einer Gruppe von islamischen Kapitellen und Basen des 11. Jahrhunderts in Toledo," in *Madrider Mitteilungen* 2 (1961), pp. 205–212.

Cabanelas Rodríguez, D. *El techo del Salón de Comares en la Alhambra.* Granada, 1988.

Cabanelas Rodríguez, D. *Literatura, Arte y Religión en los Palacios de la Alhambra.* Granada, 1984.

Caille, J. *La mosquée de Hassan à Rabat.* (Publications de l'institut des hautes études marocaines LVII.) Paris, 1954.

Casamar, M. "Almoravides y Almohades. Introdución," in *Al-Andalus. Las artes islámicas en España.* Exhibition catalog, Madrid, 1992, pp. 75–83.

Cressier, P. "Les chapiteaux de la grande mosquée de Cordoue (oratoires d' Abd ar-Rahman I. et d'Abd ar-Rahman II) et la sculpture de chapiteaux à l'époque émirale," Parts 1 and 2, in *Madrider Mitteilungen* 25 (1984), pp. 212–281 and 26 (1985), pp. 257–313.

Cressier, P., P. Marinetto Sánchez, "Les chapiteaux islamiques de la péninsule ibérique et du maroc de la renaissance émirale aux almohades," in *L'Acanthe (dans la sculpture monumentale de l'Antiquité à la Renaissance),* Paris, 1993, pp. 211–246.

Creswell, K. A. C. *Early Muslim Architecture. II Abbasids, Umayyads of Cordova, Aghlabids, Tulunids and Samanids A. D. 751–905.* Oxford, 1950.

Cuadernos de la Alhambra, Granada. Vol.1 (1965). Vols 33–34 (1997–1998).

Delgado Valero, C. *Toledo islámico. Ciudad, arte e historia.* Toledo, 1987.

Dodds, J. D., ed. *Al-Andalus. The Art of Islamic Spain.* New York, 1992.

Dozy, R. P. A. *Geschichte der Mauren,* 2 vols. Leipzig, 1874 (reprint 1965).

Eguaras Ibáñez, J. *Ibn Luyun. Tratado de Agricultura.* Granada, 1988.

Ewert, C. "Baudekor-Werkstätten im Kalifat von Córdoba und ihre Dispersion in nachkalifaler Zeit," in A. J. Gail, ed., *Künstler und Werkstatt in den orientalischen Gesellschaften.* Graz, 1982, pp. 47–57.

Ewert, C. "Die Moschee am Bab al-Mardum in Toledo. Eine 'Kopie' der Moschee von Córdoba," in *Madrider Mitteilungen* 18 (1977), pp. 287–354.

Ewert, C. *Forschungen zur almohadischen Moschee. Lieferung 4: Die Kapitelle der Kutubiya-Moschee in Marrakesch und der Moschee von Tinmal.* (Madrider Beiträge 16). Mainz, 1991.

Ewert, C. *Spanisch-Islamische Systeme sich kreuzender Bögen. I. Die senkrechten, ebenen Systeme sich kreuzender Bögen als Stützkonstruktionen der vier Rippenkuppeln in der ehemaligen Hauptmoschee von Córdoba.* (Madrider Forschungen 2). Berlin, 1968.

Ewert, C. "Spanisch-Islamische Systeme sich kreuzender Bögen. II. Die Arkaturen eines offenen Pavillons auf der Alcazaba de Málaga," in *Madrider Mitteilungen* 7 (1966), pp. 232–254.

Ewert, C. *Spanisch-Islamische Systeme sich kreuzender Bögen. III. Die Aljafería in Zaragoza.* (Madrider Forschungen 12/1). Berlin, 1978.

Ewert, C. "Tipología de la mezquita en Occidente. De los omeyas a los almohades," in *Actas del II. congreso de arqueólogia medieval española I.* Madrid, 1987, pp. 180–204.

Ewert, C., A. von Gladiss, K.-H. Golzio, and J. Wisshak. *Denkmäler des Islam. Von den Anfängen bis zum 12. Jahrhundert.* Mainz, 1997.

Ewert, C., and M. Gomez-Moreno. *El arte arabe español hasta los Almohades, arte mozarabe.* (Ars Hispaniae III.) Madrid, 1951.

Ewert, C., and J.-P. Wisshak. *Forschungen zur almohadischen Moschee. Lieferung 1: Vorstufen. Hierarchische Gliederung westislamischer Betsäle des 8. bis 11. Jahrhunderts. Die Hauptmoscheen von Qairawan und Córdoba und ihr Bannkreis.* (Madrider Beiträge 9). Mainz, 1981.

Ewert, C., and J.-P. Wisshak. *Forschungen zur almohadischen Moschee. Lieferung 2: Die Moschee von Tinmal (Marokko).* (Madrider Beiträge 10). Mainz, 1984.

Fernández Puertas, A. *La fachada del Palacio de Comares. (The Facade of the Palace of Comares.)* Granada, 1980.

Fernández Puertas, A. *The Alhambra.* London, 1997.

Forkl, H., ed. *Die Gärten von Islam.* Stuttgart, 1993.

Galera Andreu, P. *La imagen romántica de la Alhambra.* Madrid, 1992.

Gallego y Burín, A. *La Alhambra.* Granada, 1963.

García Gómez, E. *Foco de antigua luz sobre la Alhambra.* Madrid, 1988.

García Gómez, E. *Poemas árabes en los muros y fuentes de la Alhambra.* Madrid, 1985.

von Gladiss, A., ed. *Schätze der Alhambra. Islamische Kunst aus Andalusien.* Berlin, 1995.

von Gladiss, A., K. H. Golzio, and J. P. Wisshak. *Denkmäler des Islam. Von den Anfängen bis zum 12. Jahrhundert.* Mainz, 1997.

Glick, T. F. *Islamic and Christian Spain in the early Middle Ages.* Princeton, N.J., 1979.

Golvin, L. *Essais sur l'architecture religieuse musulmane I-III.* Paris, 1970/71, 1974, 1979.

Golzio, K.-H. *Geschichte Islamisch-Spaniens vom 8. bis zum 13. Jahrhundert* (Madrider Mitteilungen).

Golzio, K.-H. *Guía de Granada.* Granada, 1892.

Grabar, O. *La Alhambra. Íconografía, formas y valores.* Madrid, 1980.

von Grunebaum, G. E. "Die Almorawiden. Die Almohaden," in G.E. von Grunebaum, *Der Islam in seiner klassischen Epoche.* Zurich/Stuttgart, 1966.

Hernández Jiménez, F. *Madinat al-Zahra. Arquitectura y decoración.* Granada, 1985.

Kress, H. J. *Die islamische Kulturepoche auf der iberischen Halbinsel.* Marburg/Lahn, 1968.

Kubisch, N. *Die Synagoge Santa María la Blanca in Toledo. Eine Untersuchung zur maurischen Ornamentik.* Frankfurt am Main/Berlin/Bern and others, 1995.

Kühnel, E. *Die islamischen Elfenbeinskulpturen VIII.–XIII. Jahrhundert.* Berlin, 1971.

Kühnel, E. *Granada.* Leipzig, 1908.

Les jardins de l'Islam. Islamic Gardens. Granada, 1976.

Le Tourneau, R. *The Almohad Movement in North Africa.* Princeton, N.J., 1969.

Lomax, D. W. *Die Reconquista.* Munich, 1978.

López-Cuervo, S. *Medina az-Zahara. Ingenería y forma.* León, 1986.

Manzano Martos, R. *Casas y palacios en la Sevilla almohade. Sus antecedentes hispánicos. Casas y palacios de Al-Andalus. Siglos XII y XIII.* Barcelona, 1995.

Manzano Martos, R. *La Alhambra.* Madrid, 1992.

Marçais, G. *L'Architecture Musulmane d'Occident I–II.* Paris, 1954.

Marçais, G. *Les monuments de Tlemcen.* Paris, 1903.

Marçais, G. *Manuel d'art musulmán I–II.* Paris, 1954.

Martínez Caviró, B. *Céramica hispanomusulmana.* Madrid, 1991.

May, F. Lewis. *Silk Textiles of Spain: Eighth to Fifteenth Century.* New York, 1957.

Muñoz Molina, A. *Stadt der Kalifen. Córdoba.* Reinbek bei Hamburg, 1994.

Navarro Palazón, J. ed. *Casa y palacios de Al-Andalus. Siglos XII y XIII.* Barcelona/Madrid, 1995.

O'Callaghan, J. F. *A History of Medieval Spain.* Ithaca, NY, 1975.

Ocaña Jiménez, M. *El cúfico hispano y su evolución.* Madrid, 1979.

Ocaña Jiménez, M. "Panorámica sobre el arte almohade en España," in *Cuadernos de la Alhambra* 26 (1990), pp. 91–111.

Pérez, J. *Ferdinand und Isabella.* Munich, 1989.

Rubiera Mata, M. J. *Ibn al-Yayyab. El otro poeta de la Alhambra.* Granada, 1994.

Schreiber, H. *Halbmond über Granada.* Bergisch Gladbach, 1980.

Souto, J. A. "El capitel andalusi en los tiempo de la fitna. Los capiteles de la mezquita aljama de Zaragoza (1018–1021/2)," in *Coloquio Internacional de capiteles corintios prerománicos e islámicos (ss. VI–XII d. C.).* Madrid, 1990, pp. 119–144.

Terrasse, H. *L'art hispano-mauresque des origines au XIIIe siécle.* Paris, 1932.

Terrasse, H. *Islam d'Espagne. Une rencontre de l'Orient et de l'Occident.* Paris, 1958.

Terrasse, H. *La mosquée al-Qarauiyin à Fes.* Paris, 1968.

Terrasse, H. *Nouvelles recherches archéologiques à Marrakech.* Paris, 1957.

Terrasse, H., G. Deverdun, and J. Meunie. *Recherches archéologiques à Marrakech.* Paris, 1952.

Torres-Balbás, L. *Arte almohade. Arte nazarí. Arte mudéjar.* (Ars Hispaniae IV.) Madrid, 1949.

Torres-Balbás, L. *Ciudades hispano-musulmanes.* Madrid, n.d.

Torres-Balbás, L. *La Alhambra y el Generalife de Granada.* Madrid, 1949

Valdés Fernández, F. *La Alcazaba de Badajoz. I. Hallazgos islámicos (1977–1982) y testar de la puerta de Pilar.* Madrid, 1985.

Vallejo Triano, A. "Madinat al-Zahra. El triumfo des estado islámico," *Al-Andalus. Las artes islámicas en España.* Exhibition catalog. Madrid, 1992, pp. 27–39.

Valor Piechotta, M. *El último siglo de la Sevilla islámica (1147–1248).* Seville, 1995.

Vernet, J. *Die spanisch-arabische Kultur in Orient und Okzident.* Zurich, 1984.

Vílchez, C. *La Alhambra de Leopoldo Torres Balbás (obras de restauración y conservación. 1923–1936).* Granada, 1988.

Viñes Millet, C. *La Alhambra de Granada. Tres siglos de Historia.* Cordoba, 1982.

Wördemann, F. *Die Beute gehört Allah.* Munich, 1985.

Yanes, B. *Spanien. Auf den Spuren der Mauren.* 1990.

The Maghreb

Abun-Nasr, J. Miri. *A History of the Maghrib.* Cambridge, 1975.

Barrucand, M. *Urbanisme princier en Islam. Meknès et les villes royales islamiques post-médiévales.* Paris, 1985.

Caillé, J. *La Ville de Rabat jusqu'au protectorat français.* Vol. I–II. Paris, 1949.

Cambridge History of Islam. Vol. 2. Cambridge, 1990.

Chiauzzi, G., F. Gabrieli, C. Sarnelli Cerqua, et al. *Maghreb médiéval. L'apogée de la civilisation islamique dans l'Occident árabe.* Aix-en-Provence, 1991.

Daoulati, A. *Tunis sous les Hafsides. Evolution urbaine et active architecturale.* Tunis, 1976.

Dokali, R. *Les mosquées a la période turque à Alger.* Algier, 1974.

Duri, A. *Arabische Wirtschaftsgeschichte.* Zurich/Munich, 1979.

Golvin, L. *La madrasa médiévale.* Aix-en-Provence, 1995.

Golvin, L. *Palais et demeures d'Alger à la période ottomane.* Aix-en-Provence, 1988.

Gonzalez, V. *Émaux d'al-Andalus et du Maghreb.* Aix-en-Provence, 1994.

Haarmann, U., ed. *Geschichte der arabischen Welt.* Munich, 1987.

Hajenkos, B. *Marokkanische Keramik.* Stuttgart, 1988.

Hassar-Benslimane, J. *Le passé de la ville de Salé dans tous ses états. Histoire, Archéologie, Archives.* Paris, 1992.

Hill, D., and L. Golvin, *Islamic Architecture in North Africa.* London, 1976.

Hourani, A. *Die Geschichte der arabischen Völker.* Frankfurt am Main, 1992.

Hourani, G. Fadlo. *Arab Seafaring in the Indian Ocean in Ancient and Early Medieval Times.* Beirut, 1963 (reprint by Princeton Oriental Studies, Vol. 13. Princeton, 1951).

Klimkeit, H.-J. *Die Seidenstrasse. Handelsweg und Kulturbrücke zwischen Morgen- und Abendland.* 2nd ed. Cologne, 1990

Marçais, G. *Algérie médiévale.* Paris, 1957.

Marçais, G. *Manuel d'art musulman I–II.* Paris, 1954.

Marçais, G. *Tunis et Kairouan.* Paris, 1937.

Maroc: les trésors du royaume. Exhibition catalog from the Petit Palais, Musée des Beaux-Arts de la Ville de Paris, 15.04. – 18.07.1999). Paris, 1999.

Maslow, B. *Les Mosquées du Fes et du Nord du Maroc.* Paris, 1937.

Meissner, M. *Die Welt der Sieben Meere. Auf den Spuren arabischer Kaufleute und Piraten.* Leipzig/Weimar, 1980.

Revault, J. *Palais, demeures et maisons de plaisance à Tunis et dans ses environs.* Aix-en-Provence, n.d.

Santelli, S. *Tunis*. Saint Germain du Puy, 1995.

Seddon, D. *Stamm und Staat. Ansätze zu einer Geschichte des Maghreb*. Berlin, 1980.

Sijelmassi, M. *Les enluminures des manuscrits royaux au Maroc*. Paris, 1987.

Terrasse, H. *L'Art Hispano-Mauresque (des origines au XIIIe siecles)*. Paris, 1932.

Terrasse, H., and J. Hainaut. *Les Arts Décoratifs au Maroc*. Paris, 1925.

Triki, H., and A. Dovifat. *Medersa de Marrakech*. Paris, 1990.

Early Empires of the East

Bombaci, A. *Kufic Inscription in Persian Verses in the Court of the Royal Palace of Masud III. at Ghazni*. Rome, 1966.

Brown, P. *Indian Architecture. The Islamic Period*. 5th ed. Bombay, 1968.

Maricq, A., and G. Wiet, *Le minaret de Djam*. Paris, 1959.

Melikian-Chirvani, A. S. "Eastern Iranian Architecture. Apropos of the Ghurid parts of the Great Mosque of Herat," in *Bulletin of the School of Oriental and African Studies* 33 (1970), pp. 322–327.

Schlumberger, D., and J. Sourdel-Thomine, *Lashkari Bazar. Une résidence royale ghaznévide et ghoride*. Paris, 1978. Stark, F. *The minaret of Djam. An excursion in Afghanistan*. London, 1970.

Central Asia and Asia Minor

Albaum, L. I., and B. Brentjes. *Herren der Steppe*. Berlin, 1978.

Altun, A. *An Outline of Turkish Architecture in the Middle Ages*. Istanbul, 1990.

Aslanapa, O. *Turkish Art and Architecture*. London, 1971/Turk Sanati Istanbul, 1984.

Bausani, A. "Religion in the Saljuq Period," in *The Cambridge History of Iran*. Vol. 5. Cambridge, 1968.

Chmelnizkij, S. *Construction and Ornament. Artistic Form and Decoration in the Art of Asia and Africa*. Moscow, 1969 (in Russian).

Chmelnizkij, S. *Die antike Ordnung in der mittelalterlichen Architektur Mittelasiens*. (Akten des XIII. internationalen Kongresses für klassische Archäologie.) 1990.

Chmelnizkij, S. "Petschak und Michrab. Zur Frage der Herkunft der Portalformen in der zentralasiatischen Architektur," in ANNALI, Instituto Universario Orientale 47 (1987).

Crane, H. "Bericht über die Grabung in Kobadabad 1966," in *Archäologischer Anzeiger* 1969 (1970), pp. 438–506.

Crane, H. "Notes on Saljuq Architectural Patronage in Thirteenth Century Anatolia," in *Journal of the Economic and Social History of the Orient* 36 (1993), pp. 1–57.

Duda, H. W. *Die Seltschukengeschichte des Ibn Bibi*. Copenhagen, 1959.

Erdmann, K.-H. *Das anatolische Karavansaray des 13. Jahrhunderts. 1. Teil*. (Istanbuler Forschungen 21.) Berlin, 1961.

Gabriel, A. *Monuments turcs d'Anatolie*. 2 vols. Paris, 1931–34.

Gabriel, A. *Voyages archéologiques dans la Turquie Orientale*. Paris, 1940.

Gierlichs, J. *Mittelalterliche Tierreliefs in Anatolien und Nordmesopotamien. Untersuchungen zur figürlichen Baudekoration der Seldschuken, Artuqiden und ihrer Nachfolger bis ins 15. Jahrhunderts*. (Istanbuler Forschungen 42.) Tübingen, 1996.

Grabar, O. *The Great Mosque of Isfahan*. London, 1990.

Hillenbrand, R. (ed). *The Art of the Seljuqs in Iran and Anatolia*. Costa Mesa, CA, 1994.

Kuran, A. "Die anatolisch-seldschukische Architektur," in E. Akurgal, ed., *Kunst in der Türkei*. Fribourg/Würzburg, 1980, pp. 85–116.

Lambton, A. K. S. "The Internal Structure of the Saljuq Empire," in *The Cambridge History of Iran*. Vol. 5. Cambridge, 1968.

Meinecke, M. *Fayancedekorationen seldschukischer Sakralbauten in Kleinasien*. (Istanbuler Mitteilungen, Suppl. 13.) Tübingen, 1976.

Nagel, T. *Die islamische Welt bis 1500*. Munich, 1998.

Nizam al-Mulk, *Das Buch der Staatskunst. Siyasatnama*. Zurich, 1959.

Öney, G. *Anadolu Selçuklu mimarisinde süsleme ve el sanatlari. Architectural Decoration and Minor Arts in Seljuk Anatolia*. 2nd ed. Ankara, 1988.

Öney, G. "Baukunst und Kleinkunst," in E. Akurgal, ed., *Kunst in der Türkei*. Fribourg/Würzburg, 1980, pp. 85–116.

Otto-Dorn, K. "Figural Stone Reliefs on Seljuk Sacred Architecture in Anatolia," in *Kunst des Orients* 12 (1978/79), pp. 103–149.

Otto-Dorn, K. "Kunst der Seldschuken," in K. Otto-Dorn, *Kunst des Islam*. Baden-Baden, 1964/2nd ed. 1980, pp. 126ff.

Redford, S. "The Seljuqs of Rum and the Antique," in *Muqarnas* 10 (1993), pp. 148–156.

Rice, T. Talbot. *Die Seldschuken*. Cologne, 1963.

Schneider, G. *Geometrische Bauornamente der Seldschuken in Kleinasien*. Wiesbaden, 1980.

Schneider, G. *Pflanzliche Bauornamente der Seldschuken in Kleinasien*. Wiesbaden, 1989.

Yavuz, A. T. "The Concepts that Shape Anatolian Seljuq Caravanserais," in *Muqarnas* 14 (1997), pp. 80–95.

Islamic Mongols

Blair, S. "The Mongol Capital of Sultaniyya, 'the Imperial'," in *Iran* 24 (1986), pp. 139–151.

Blair, S., and J. Bloom. *The Art and Architecture of Islam 1250–1800*. London, 1994.

Grabar, O., and S. Blair, *Epic Images and Contemporary History. The Illustrations of the Great Mongol Shah-nama*. Chicago, 1980.

Naumann, R. *Die Ruinen von Tacht-e Suleiman und Zendan-e Suleiman*. Berlin, 1977.

Paone, R. "The Mongol Colonization of the Isfahan Region," in *Isfahan. Quaderni del Seminario di Iranistica, Uralo-Altaistica e Caucasologia dell'Universitá degli studi di Venezia* 10 (1981), pp. 1–30.

Wilber, D. M. *The Architecture of Islamic Iran. The Il-Khanid Period*. Princeton, 1955/reprinted, New York, 1969.

Central Asia

Allan, J. *Islamic Ceramics*. Oxford, 1991.

Allen, T. *A Catalogue of Toponyms and Monuments of Timurid Herat*. Cambridge, Mass., 1991.

Allen, T. *Timurid Herat*. Wiesbaden, 1983.

Ashrafi, M. "Central Asian Miniature Painting," in *Macmillan's Dictionary of Art*. London, 1996.

Ashrafi, M. *Khangamii naqqashi ba adabiyat dar Iran*. Tehran, 1989.

Ashrafi, M. *The Bukhara Miniature School of the 40–70s of the 16 c.* Duschanbe, 1974.

Ashrafi, M. *The Samarkand Miniature Paintings of the 15 c.* Tashkent, 1996.

Atil, E. *Ceramics from the World of Islam*. Washington, DC, 1973.

Barthold, W. *Ulug Beg und seine Zeit*. Nendeln i. Liechtenstein, 1966.

Beaupertuis-Bressand, F. *L'Or bleu de Samarkand*. Paris, 1997.

Binder, F. *Ayshen Delemen, Samarkand – Chiwa – Buchara. Islamische Hochkultur in Mittelasien*. Freiburg im Breisgau, 1990.

Burton, A. *The Bukharans. A Dynastic, Diplomatic and Commercial History 1550–1702*. Surrey, 1997.

Denny, W. B. *The Ceramics of the Mosque of Rüstem Pasha and the Environment of Change*. New York, 1977.

Golombek, L., and M. Subtelny, eds. *Timurid Art and Culture. Iran and Central Asia in the Fifteenth Century*. Leiden, 1992.

Golombek, L., and D. Wilber *The Timurid Architecture of Iran and Turan.* 2 vols. Princeton, 1988. *L'Héritage timouride. Iran – Asie centrale – Inde, XVe–XVIIIe siècles.* (Cahiers d'Asie centrale, No. 3–4), Tashkent/Aix-en-Provence, 1997.

Kalter, J., and M. Pavaloi, eds. *Erben der Seidenstrasse. Usbekistan.* Stuttgart, 1995.

Lentz, T., and G. D. Lowry. *Timur and the Princely Vision.* Washington, DC, 1989.

Manz, B. Forbes. *The Rise and Rule of Tamerlane.* Cambridge, 1989.

Masson, M. E., and G. A. Pugachenkova. "Shakhri Syabz pri Timure I Ulug Beke. Shahr-i Sabz from Timur to Ulugh Beg," J. M. Rogers, trans., in *Iran* 18 (1980), pp. 121–143.

McChesney, R. D. "Economic and Social Aspects of the Public Architecture of Bukhara in the 1560's," in *Oriental Art* 2 (1987), pp. 217–242.

Nagel, T. *Timur der Eroberer und die islamische Welt des späten Mittelalters.* Munich, 1993.

Porter, V. *Islamic Tiles.* London, 1995.

Pugatschenkowa, G. A. *Samarkand – Buchara.* Berlin, 1979.

Pugatschenkowa, G. A. *Termes – Shahr-i Sabz – Chiwa.* Berlin, 1981.

Subtelny, M. E. "Arts and Politics in Early 16th Century Central Asia," in *Central Asiatic Journal* 27 (1983), pp. 217–148.

India

Aijazuddin, F. S. *Historical Images of Pakistan.* Lahore, 1992.

Asher, C. B. *Islamic Monuments of Eastern India and Bangladesh.* Leiden, 1991.

Asher, C. B. *The New Cambridge History of India. Architecture of Mughal India.* Cambridge, 1992.

Baridon, M. "Jardins des horizons lointains. L'Islam," in *Les Jardins,* 3rd ed. Paris, 1999, pp. 209–345.

Barrucand, M. "Gärten und gestaltete Landschaft als irdisches Paradies. Gärten im westlichen Islam," in *Der Islam* 65 (1988, 2), pp. 244–267.

Beach, M. C., E. Koch, and W. Thackston. *King of the World. The Padshahnama. An Imperial Mughal manuscript from the Royal Library, Windsor Castle.* London, 1997.

Begley, W. E. *Monumental Islamic Calligraphy from India.* Villa Park, Illinois, 1985.

Begley, W. E., and Z. A. Desai. *Taj Mahal. The Illumined Tomb. An Anthology of Seventeenth-Century Mughal and European Documentary Sources.* (Aga Khan Program for Islamic Architecture). Cambridge, Mass., 1989.

Brand, M., and G. Lowry. *Akbar's India. Art from the Mughal City of Victory.* New York, 1985.

Brooks, J. *Gardens of Paradise. The History and Design of the Great Islamic Gardens.* London, 1987.

Brown, P. *Indian Architecture. Islamic Period.* Bombay, 1956/reprinted 1975.

Crowe, S., and S. Haywood. *The Gardens of Mughal India.* London, 1972.

Ettinghausen, R., and E. B. Macdougall, eds. *The Islamic Garden.* Dumbarton Oaks Colloquium on the History of Landscape Architecture IV. Washington DC, 1976.

Frykenberg, R. E. *Delhi Through the Ages. Essays in Urban History, Culture and Society.* Delhi, 1986.

Gardet, L. "Djanna," in *Encyclopédie d'Islam.* Vol. 2, 2nd ed. Leiden/Paris, 1977, pp. 459–464.

Hambly, G. *Cities of Mughal India. Delhi, Agra and Fatehpur Sikri.* New York, 1968.

Horovitz, J. *Das koranische Paradies.* Jerusalem, 1923.

Hussain, M., A. Rehman, and J. L. Wescoat Jr, eds. *The Mughal Garden. Interpretation, Conservation and Implications.* Lahore, 1996.

Jones, D., ed. *A Mirror of Princes. The Mughals and the Medici.* Bombay, 1987.

Koch, E. *Mughal Architecture. An Outline of its History and Development. 1526–1858.* Munich, 1991.

Lehrman, J. *Earthly Paradise. Garden and Courtyard in Islam.* Berkeley, Los Angeles, 1980.

Michell, G., ed. *Ahmadabad.* Bombay, 1988.

Michell, G., and M. Zebrowski. *The New Cambridge History of India. Architecture and Art of the Deccan Sultanates.* Cambridge, 1999.

Merklinger, E. S. *Indian Islamic Architecture. The Deccan 1347–1686.* Warminster, 1981.

Moynihan, E. B. *Paradise as a Garden in Persia and Moghol India.* New York, 1979.

Mumtaz, K. Khan. *Architecture in Pakistan.* (Aga Khan Program for Islamic Architecture). Singapore, 1985.

Pal, P. *Master Artists of the Imperial Mughal Court.* Bombay, 1991.

Pal, P., J. Leoshko, et al. *Romance of the Taj Mahal.* Los Angeles/London, 1989.

Petruccioli, A., ed. *Der islamische Garten.* Stuttgart, 1995.

Petruccioli, A. *Mughal Architecture. Pomp and Ceremonies.* Journal of the Islamic Environmental Design Research Centre, Carucci Editore, IX Year, No. 11.

Rani, A. *Tugluq Architecture.* Delhi, 1991.

Schimmel, A. *A Two-Colored Brocade. The Imagery of Persian Poetry.* Chapel Hill/London, 1992.

Schimmel, A. *Islam in the Indian Subcontinent.* Leiden/Cologne, 1980.

Skelton, R., ed. *The Indian Heritage. Court Life and Arts under Mughal Rule.* Victoria & Albert Museum, London, 1982.

Soudavar, A. *Art of the Persian Courts.* New York, 1992.

Stoler Miller, B., ed. *The Powers of Art. Patronage in Indian Culture.* New Delhi, 1992.

Volwahsen, A. *Islamisches Indien.* Munich, 1969.

Walker, D. *Flowers Underfoot. Indian Carpets of the Mughal Era.* The Metropolitan Museum of Art. New York, 1997.

Welch, S. C. *India! Indian Art and Culture 1300–1900.* The Metropolitan Museum of Art. New York, 1985.

Yamamoto, T., M. Ara, and T. Tsukinowa. *Delhi. Architectural Remains of the Delhi Sultanate Period.* 3 vols. Tokyo, 1967–1970.

Zebrowski, M. *Gold, Silver and Bronze from Mughal India.* London, 1997.

Zebrowski, M. *Deccani Painting.* London, 1983.

Iran

Bausani, A. *Die Perser. Von den Anfängen bis zur Gegenwart.* Stuttgart, 1965.

Beattie, M. "Ardabil Carpet," in *Encyclopaedia Iranica.* Vol. II. London/New York, 1987.

Bérinstain, V., S. Day, É. Floret, et al. *Teppiche. Tradition und Kunst in Orient und Okzident.* Cologne, 1997.

Black, D. ed. *The Macmillan Atlas of Rugs and Carpets.* New York, 1985.

Blair, S., and J. Bloom. *The Art and Architecture of Islam, 1250–1800.* New Haven/London, 1994.

Blunt, W. *Isfahan. Pearl of Persia.* Reprint, London, 1974.

Brentjes, B. *Chane – Sultane – Emire.* Leipzig, 1974.

Canby, S. R. *The Golden Age of Persian Art 1501–1722.* London, 1999.

Canby, S. R. *The Rebellious Reformer. The Drawings and Paintings of Riza-yi Abbasi of Isfahan.* London, 1996.

Diba, L. S., ed. *Royal Persian Paintings. The Qajar Epoch 1785–1925.* Exhibition catalog, Brooklyn Museum of Art. New York, 1998.

Dickson, M. B., and S. C. Welch. *The Houghton Shahnameh.* 2 vols. Cambridge, Mass., 1981.

Enderlein, V., and W. Sundermann, eds. *Schahname. Das persische Königsbuch. Miniaturen und Texte der Berliner Handschrift von 1605.* Leipzig/Weimar, 1988.

Erdmann, K. *Der orientalische Knüpfteppich. Versuch einer Darstellung seiner Geschichte.* Tübingen, 1955/1960/1965/1975.

Ettinghausen, R. "New Light on Early Animal Carpets," in R. Ettinghausen, ed. *Aus der Welt der Islamischen Kunst. Festschrift für Ernst Kühnel.* Berlin, 1959, pp. 93–116.

Falk, S. J. *Qajar Paintings. Persian Oil Paintings of the 18th and 19th centuries.* London, 1972.

Glassen, E. "Schah Ismail I. und die Theologen seiner Zeit," in *Der Islam.* 48 (1972).

Glaube, H. *Iranian Cities.* New York, 1979.

Hillenbrand, R. "Safavid Architecture," in P. Jackson, and L. Lockhart, ed. *The Timurid and Safavid Periods. The Cambridge History of Iran.* Vol. 6. Cambridge, 1986, pp. 789–792.

Kühnel, E. "Der Maler Muin," in *Pantheon* 29 (1942), pp. 108–114.

Lane, A. *Later Islamic Pottery.* London, 1957.

Luft, P. "Gottesstaat und höfische Gesellschaft. Iran im Zeitalter der Safawiden," in J. Osterhammel, ed., *Asien in der Neuzeit 1500–1950.* Frankfurt am Main, 1994.

Luschey-Schmeisser, I. *The Pictorial Tile Cycles of Hast Behest in Isfahan and its Iconographic Tradition.* Rome, 1978.

McChesney, R. "Four Sources on Shah Abbas's Building of Isfahan," in *Muqarnas* 5 (1988), pp. 103–134.

Melikian-Chirvani, A. "Safavid Metalwork: A Study in Continuity," in *Studies on Isfahan, Iranian Studies* 8 (1974), pp. 543–585.

Neumann, R., and G. Murza. *Persische Seiden. Die Gewebekunst der Safawiden und ihrer Nachfolger.* Leipzig, 1988.

Pope, A. U. *Persian Architecture. The Triumph of Form and Colour.* New York, 1965.

Robinson, B. W. *Studies in Persian Art.* 2 vols. London, 1993.

Roemer, H. R. *Persien auf dem Weg in die Neuzeit.* Beirut, 1989.
Savory, R. *Iran under the Safavids.* Cambridge, 1980.

Schweizer, G. *Iran. Drehscheibe zwischen Ost und West.* Stuttgart, 1991.

Shreve Simpson, M. *Sultan Ibrahim Mirza's Haft Aurang.* New Haven/London, 1997.

Spuhler, F. *Seidene Repräsentationsteppiche der mittleren bis späten Safawidenzeit. Die sog. Polenteppiche.* Dissertation. Berlin, 1968.

Stchoukine, I. *Les peintures des manuscrits Safavis de 1502 à 1587.* Paris, 1959.

Stchoukine, I. *Les peintures des manuscrits de Shah Abbas I à la fin des Safavis.* Paris, 1964.

Stevens, R. "European Visitors to the Safavid Court," in *Iranian Studies 7* (1974), pp. 427–457.

Welch, A. *Artists for the Shah. Late Sixteenth-Century Painting at the Imperial Court of Iran.* New Haven, 1976.

Welch, A. *Shah Abbas and the Arts of Isfahan.* New York, 1979.

The Ottoman Empire

Atasoy, N., and F. Çagman. *Turkish Miniature Painting.* Istanbul, 1972.

Atasoy, N., and J. Raby. *The Pottery of Ottoman Turkey.* London, 1989.

Atil, E. *The Age of Süleyman the Magnificent.* Washington/New York, 1987.

Atil, E. *Turkish Art.* Washington/New York, 1980.

Atil, E. *Turkish Art of the Ottoman Period.* Washington, 1973.

Babinger, F. *Mehmed der Eroberer.* Munich, 1987.

Bartoli, L., E. Galdieri, F. Gurrieri, et al. *Mimar Sinan. Architettura tra oriente e occidente.* Florence, 1992.

Bayram, S., ed. *Mimarbasi Koca Sinan yasadigi çag ve eserleri.* Istanbul, 1988.

Deroche, F. *The Abbasid Tradition. Qur'ans of the 8th to the 10th centuries AD.* (The Nasser D. Khalili Collection of Islamic Art, Vol. 1.) London, 1992.

Fada'ili, H. *Atlas-i Khatt.* Isfahan, 1391/1971.

Frank, G. *Die Herrscher der Osmanen.* Vienna/Düsseldorf, 1980.

Goodwin, G. *A History of Ottoman Architecture.* Baltimore/London, 1971.

Goodwin, G. *Sinan.* London, 1993.

Huart, C. *Les calligraphes et les miniaturistes de l'Orient Musulmane.* Paris, 1908.

James, D. *Das arabische Buch. Eine Ausstellung arabischer Handschriften der Chester Beatty Library im Museum für Kunst und Gewerbe.* Hamburg/Dublin, 1983.

Jorga, N. *Geschichte des Osmanischen Reiches.* 5 vols. Frankfurt am Main, 1990.

Khatibi, A., and M. Sijelmassi. *Die Kunst der islamischen Kalligrafie.* Rev. from the French trans. by W. Höck, and B. Kassimi-Alaoui. New ed. Cologne, 1995.

Klever, U. *Das Weltreich der Türken.* Bayreuth, 1978.

Kreutel, R. F., ed. *Kara Mustafa vor Wien.* Munich, 1967.

Kühnel, E. *Islamische Schriftkunst.* Rev. and suppl. reprint of the 1942 ed. Graz, 1986.

Kuran, A. *The Mosque in Early Ottoman Architecture.* Chicago/London, 1968.

Kuran, A. *Sinan.* Washington/Istanbul, 1987.

Ölçer, N., ed. *Turkish Carpets from the 13th–18th centuries.* Istanbul, 1996.

Orientalische Buchkunst in Gotha. Ausstellung zum 350 jährigen Jubiläum der Forschungs- und Landesbibliothek Gotha, 11.9. – 4.12.1997. Gotha, 1997.

Peters, R. *Geschichte der Türken.* Stuttgart, 1961.

Petrasch, E., R. Sänger, E. Zimmermann, and H. G. Majer. *Die Karlsruher Türkenbeute.* Munich, 1991.

Petsopoulos, Y. *Kunst und Kunsthandwerk unter den Osmanen.* Munich, 1982.

Rogers, J. M., ed. *Topkapi Sarayi-Museum. Architektur.* Herrsching am Ammersee, 1988.

Rogers, J. M. *Topkapi Sarayi-Museum. Manuskripte.* Herrsching am Ammersee, 1986.

Rogers, J. M. *Topkapi Sarayi-Museum. Kleinodien.* Herrsching am Ammersee, 1987.

Rogers, J. M. *Topkapi Sarayi-Museum. Textilien.* Herrsching am Ammersee, 1986.

Safadi, Y. H. *Islamic Calligraphy.* London, 1978.

Sauermost, H. J., and W.-C. von der Mülbe. *Istanbuler Moscheen.* Munich, 1981.

Schweizer, G. *Die Janitscharen. Geheime Macht des Türkenreichs.* Salzburg, 1984.

Sözen, M., and S. Güner. *Turkish Decorative Arts.* Istanbul, 1999.

Vogt-Göknil, U. *Sinan.* Tübingen/Berlin, 1993.

Welch, A. *Calligraphy and the Arts of the Muslim World.* New York, 1979.

Yetkin, S. *Historical Turkish Carpets.* Istanbul, 1981.

Islam in the Modern Age

Abdel-Malek, A. *Ägypten. Militärgesellschaft (Nasser).* Frankfurt am Main, 1971.

Ali, W. *Contemporary Art from the Islamic World.* London, 1989.

Ali, W. *Modern Islamic Art. Development and Continuity.* Gainesville, Fl., 1997.

Antes, P. "Islam," in P. Antes, ed., *Die Religionen der Gegenwart.* Munich, 1996.

Asher, M., et al. *Die Geschichte der türkischen Malerei.* Istanbul, 1989.

el-Attar, H. *Al Fann. Die Kunst. Zeitgenössische Kunst aus islamischen und vom Islam geprägten Ländern.* Kassel, 1995.

al-Bayati, B. *Basil al-Bayati. Architect.* London, 1988.

Bozdogan, S., et al. *Sedad Eldem. Architect in Turkey.* London, 1987.

Frank, G. *Allahs grosse Söhne.* Frankfurt am Main, 1990.

Haus der Kulturen der Welt. *Die andere Moderne. Zeitgenössische Kunst aus Afrika, Asien und Lateinamerika.* Berlin, 1997.

Heine, P. *Konflikt der Kulturen oder Feindbild Islam.* Freiburg, 1996.

Holod, R. *Hasan-uddin Khan. The Mosque and the Modern World.* London, 1997.

Holod, R., and D. Rastorfer, eds. *Architecture and Community. Building in the Islamic World Today.* (The Aga Khan Award for Architecture 1). Millerton/Oxford, 1983.

Jencks, C. *Die Postmoderne. Der neue Klassizismus in Kunst und Architektur.* Stuttgart, 1987.

Karnouk, L. *Contemporary Egyptian Art.* Cairo, 1995.

al-Khalil, S. *The Monument. Art, Vulgarity and Responsibility in Iraq.* London, 1991.

Khatibi, A. *Mohamed Sijelmassi. Islamische Kalligraphie.* Cologne, 1995.

Lerch, W. G. *Mohammeds Erben. Die unbekannte Vielfalt des Islam.* Düsseldorf, 1999.

Meier, A. *Der politische Auftrag des Islam.* Wuppertal, 1994.

Meyer, T., ed. *Fundamentalismus in der modernen Welt.* Frankfurt am Main, 1989.

Sakr, T. *Mahamed Refaat. Early Twentieth-Century Islamic Architecture in Cairo.* Cairo, 1992.

Scharabi, M. *Industrie und Industriebau in Ägypten. Eine Einführung in die Geschichte der Industrie im Nahen Osten.* Berlin, 1992.

Schreiber, F. *Die Saudis.* Vienna, 1981.

Serageldin, I., and J. Steele. *Architecture of the Contemporary Mosque.* London, 1996.

Steele, J. *Architecture for Islamic Societies Today.* London, 1994.

Steele, J. *Hassan Fathy.* London, 1988.

Taeschner, F. *Geschichte der arabischen Welt.* Stuttgart, 1964.

Theophilus, J. "Ahmed Moustafa. Expressing the Essential," in *Arts in the Islamic World* 24 (1994), pp. 21–24.

Tibi, B. *Der religiöse Fundamentalismus im Übergang zum 21. Jahrhundert.* Mannheim, 1995.

The Islamic calendar

The migration of the Prophet Muhammad from Mecca to Medina (the *hegira*) marks the start of the Islamic calendar. This is still the case today, although the Islamic calendar is being increasingly supplanted by the West's Gregorian calendar, which dictates world trade and politics.

While the Prophet's precise date of birth is not known, the date of the *hegira* (July 16, 622 A.D.) represents the first precise date in Islam. Furthermore, the actual molding of Islam by Muhammad as leader of the Muslim community began in Medina, so this date was of great significance to the early religion. The Islamic calendar was introduced under the second legally constituted caliph, Umar (634–644 A.D.) – over 900 years earlier than the Gregorian calendar of Pope Gregory XIII used today in Christian countries. It replaced the lunisolar calendar customary in ancient Arabia, a lunar calendar that periodically added a month, in order to balance the discrepancy with the solar year.

However, the Islamic calendar is also based on the lunar year. It comprises 12 months (from new moon to new moon in each case), each with 29.5306 days, producing a year of 354.367 days. 30- and 29-day months alternate and an extra day is added 11 times over the course of 30 years. Because the lunar year is roughly 11 days shorter than the solar year, the start of the Islamic year does not fall on the same date as the solar calendar again for 33 years; 33 lunar years therefore correspond to 32 solar years. Shifts in the lunar year relative to the seasons meant that the calendar was problematic for trade and administration from the very outset, because the dates of harvests and taxes constantly had to be recalculated. Consequently, the stage was set for calendar reform right from the Middle Ages.

The precise conversion of years according to the *hegira* (**H**) into years after the birth of Christ (**C**) is only possible using the following formulae:

$$\mathbf{H} \times 32/33 + 622 = \mathbf{C} \quad \text{or} \quad (\mathbf{C} - 622) \times 33/32 = \mathbf{H}$$

This book is essentially based on the Christian calendar. However, where dates in the Islamic calendar are quoted from historical documents or inscriptions these are marked as *hegira* years.

Transliteration

This book contains names and terms in many different languages of the Islamic world. On grounds of readability, it was not possible to use a precise, scientific transliteration system. A consistent method of spelling is used where possible and appropriate, though there are exceptions. The English form of the Middle Eastern words should enable the reader to pronounce them with some degree of accuracy. However, where names and terms have common English spellings, these are used (e.g. Acre, sheikh, souk, Umayyad, etc.).

In general, no account is taken of local language usage, such as those of Persia or India: formal Arabic is used throughout. An exception is Turkish, which has its original spelling (minus diacritics on vowels).

With some deviations, this is the basis of the Arabic transliteration system:

dj   is a voiced sibilant (j)
ch   is the voiceless variant (ch)
th   is a voiceless th
dh   is a voiced th
sh   is pronounced sh
s   is a voiceless s, **z** a voiced s
kh   is pronounced k
Turkish: ç = ch, ş = sh

Glossary of dynasties

Markus Hattstein

Abbadids *Taifa* rulers of Seville 1013–1091. The Banu Abbad were a Hispano-Arab dynasty tracing their descent from the ancient Arab Lakhmids. Following the downfall of the caliphate of Cordoba, the kadi of Seville, Abu l-Qasim Muhammad ibn Abbad (1013–1042) seized power in Seville, initially in the name of the Hammadids. Under his son, Abu Amr al-Mutadid (1042–1069) and grandson, Muhammad al-Mutamid (1069–1091), major patrons of the arts and science, Seville grew to be the center of the refined culture of the *taifa* kingdom and the most powerful state; large parts of al-Andalus came under their authority: Huelva in 1052, Algeciras in 1058, and Cordoba in 1069/78. Al-Mutamid was the driving force behind the appeal for help made to the Almoravids following the Christian capture of Toledo (1085), yet his vacillation between 1089/90 led to the conquest of al-Andalus by the Almoravids, who ousted him in 1091.

Abbasids Second dynasty of caliphs 750–1258. Main capital: Baghdad from 762, Samarra 836–883/892. The Arab tribe of Banu l-Abbas, whose lineage was said to descend from the Prophet's uncle, al-Abbas ibn Abd al-Muttalib. With the cooperation of Shiite groups, Abu l-Abbas al-Saffah (749/50–754) removed the leadership of the Umayyads in a bloody campaign. He and his brother, Abu Jafar al-Mansur (754–775), introduced harsh measures to consolidate their power; in 762 Baghdad was founded. The political and cultural zenith came under Harun al-Rashid (786–809) with the help of the Barmakids (until 803) and his son, al-Mamun (813–833), who made Baghdad the center of science and raised Mutazilite rationalism to the state doctrine. From 800 onwards, various provinces sought independence from the empire under their own dynasties. Following the assassination of al-Mutawakkil (847–861), political power dissipated and the Abbasids finally came under the supreme control of various military dynasties: the Buyids (945–1055), the Great Seljuks (1055–1194), and the Khwarazm-Shahs (1192–1220), so that the caliph was reduced to a religious figurehead. Caliphal sovereignty was largely restored to Caliph al-Nasir (1180–1225), but his great-grandson, al-Mutasim (1242–1258), who had refused to join the Mongol "peace federation," fell victim to the Mongol invasions in 1258. An Abbasid shadow caliphate was established (1260–1517) under the tutelage of the Mamluks in Cairo.

Abd al-Wadids or Zayanids. Berber dynasty in western Algeria 1236–1554. Main capital: Tlemcen. From the Banu Abd al-Wad, also known as the Banu Zayad, which belonged to the Zanata tribal group on the northern edge of the Sahara and migrated to northern Algeria in the 11th century. The Abd al-Wadids were clients of the Almohads, who assigned to them the governorship of Tlemcen. When the Almohads fell from power, Abu Yahya Yaghmurasan (1236–1283) gained independence and established a rigid state structure; under him and his successors, Tlemcen grew into a cultural and trading center. They pursued a tricky seesaw policy between the stronger Merinids (Morocco) and the Hafsids (eastern Algeria/Tunisia), who drove them out several times during the 13th and 14th centuries. Finally, they fell under the sovereignty of the Merinids, but then experienced a public restoration and cultural heyday under the learned Abu Hammu II Musa (1359–1389), before succumbing to the authority of the Hafsids. As a result of the military incursions of Spain from 1510 onwards, the Abd al-Wadids placed themselves under the protection of the Ottomans (in 1516/17 Algiers and Tlemcen were captured by the Ottoman corsair Aruj Barbarossa). In 1552–1554 the Ottomans finally occupied western Algeria and overthrew the last Abd al-Wadid ruler.

Afsharids Afghan dynasty in Persia and Afghanistan 1736–1796. Main capital: Mashhad. The dynasty was founded by General Nadir from the Afghan Qizilbash tribe, part of the Afshars. Nadir advanced as the military leader of a Safavid shadow shah (see Safavids), expelled the Afghans (Ghalzai) from Persia in 1730 with the conquest of Isfahan, and finally rose to the throne himself as Nadir Shah (1736–1747). Modern Iran's most prominent expansionist, he occupied Afghanistan and parts of the Central Asian khanate (Khiva) in 1737, then led a military campaign to India in 1738/39. Assassinated by his own emirs in 1747, his successors were unable to maintain the empire; his blind grandson, Shah-Rukh (1748–1796), continued to rule in Khorasan only until 1796, when he was removed by the Qajars.

Aghlabids Arab dynasty in Ifriqiya (eastern Algeria, Tunisia, western Libya), as well as Lower Italy and Sicily 800–909. Main capital: Kairouan. The dynasty was named after the Abbasid army commander al-Aghlab, whose son, Ibrahim I (800–812), became governor of Ifriqiya in 787 and gained independence in 800. After quashing several Berber uprisings, the dynasty experienced its political zenith under Abdallah I (812–817) and Ziyadat Allah I (817–838). After 827 the Aghlabids conquered Sicily (Palermo in 831), occupied Bari in 841, plundered Rome in 846, conquered Malta in 868, and made the Italian coastal towns pay taxes. Internally, they constantly had to battle against religious uprisings and Berber groups. The political decline began after Ibrahim II (875–902) with the loss of territory to the Byzantines (Calabrians), Tulunids, and rebellious tribes; in 909 they were ousted by the Fatimids.

Alawids Ruling Sharif dynasty in Morocco since 1666. Main capital: Fez, 1672–1727 Meknes, from 1912 Rabat. The Alawids, descendants of the Prophet's grandson al-Hasan, came to Morocco at the end of the 13th century and settled to the south of the Haut Atlas and in the oases of Tafilelt. With the help of religious brotherhoods, rulers of the Tafilelt region from 1631, Mulai al-Rashid (1664–1672) conquered Fez and the sultanate in 1666. His son, Mulai Ismail (1672–1727), reorganized the country, created economic prosperity, developed the "dynastic town" of Meknes as a stage for the most important festivals of the Maghreb, and won back Moroccan towns from Europeans (Tangier in 1684, Arzila in 1691). The ensuing political anarchy was ended by his grandson Sidi Muhammad (1757–1790), who stabilized the country's economy, via trading agreements with Western powers. From the start of the 19th century, its economy became increasingly dependent on European powers and it suffered military defeats against the French and Spaniards; in 1863 a protection treaty was signed with France (the Béclard Convention). Mulai Hasan (1873–1894) implemented reforms based on the European example; young sultans then reigned until 1927 under the tutelage of France, which imposed a French and Spanish protectorate on Morocco in 1912. The growing nationalist forces gathered around Sultan Sidi Muhammad (1927–1961), who proclaimed Morocco's independence in March 1956 and assumed the title of king as Muhammad V. The authoritarian government of his son, Hassan II (1961–1999), completed the decolonization process with partially democratic institutions and great foreign policy flexibility but had to defend itself against a number of attempted coups. In 1975/76 Hassan occupied the Spanish Sahara and in 1979 the western Sahara (the "Green Marsh"). In July 1999 he was succeeded by his son, Muhammad VI.

Almohads Berber dynasty in North Africa (Morocco, Algeria, Tunisia, Libya) and Spain (al-Andalus) 1130–1269. Main capitals: Marrakech and Seville. The name is derived from the Arabic *al-muwahhidun* ("believers in the unity of God") and reflects the attitude of the strictly puritanical reform movement led by Ibn Tumart (c. 1080–1130), from which the dynasty emerged. Ibn Tumart declared war on the Almoravids after 1118 and resided in Tinmal (High Atlas) from 1124. His successor, Abd al-Mumin (1130/33–1163), managed to seize power in Morocco (capture of Marrakech in 1147) and the whole of northern Africa (Tunisia and Libya by 1160), as well as Islamic Spain (1146–1154). The cultural zenith came under Abu Yaqub Yusuf (1163–1184) and Yusuf Yaqub al-Mansur (1184–1199) with the development of towns and promotion of spiritual life (Averroes and Ibn Tufail were prominent scholars); a decisive victory over the Christians came in 1195 at Alarcos. Under al-Nasir (1199–1213) uprisings in northern Africa were quashed, but the Almohads suffered a heavy defeat against the Christians at Las Navas de Tolosa in 1212. Their power wilted after 1213 with the loss of Spain to the rulers of the *taifa* states and the Christians (after 1228), Tunisia to the Hafsids, and Algeria to the Abd al-Wadids (1229/36). Between 1224 and 1236 two rival branches ruled in Morocco and Spain. Driven back into Morocco by the Merinids in 1244, the Almohads gradually lost power and were removed by them in 1269.

Almoravids Berber dynasty in Morocco, Mauritania, western Algeria, and Spain (al-Andalus) 1056/60–1147. Main capital: Fez, from 1086 Marrakech. The dynasty, originally a puritanical reform movement, derived its name from the Arabic *al-murabitun* ("the men of Ribat"). The Almoravids first moved south, where they succeeded in conquering Gana and converting northern Africa to Islam; under Yusuf ibn Tashfin (1060–1106) they seized power in Morocco and western Algeria, founding Marrakech in 1062. In 1086 they conducted their first campaigns in Spain (with victory at Zallaqa), before they conquered Islamic Spain from the *taifa* rulers (1089–1094). Under Ali ibn Yusuf (1106–1143) they suffered losses against the Christian Reconquista and after 1130 were forced back to northern Africa by the Almohads, to whom they succumbed in 1147: the last Almoravid ruler was ousted during the capture of Marrakech.

Amirids Viceroys of the Spanish caliphate 978–1009 and rulers of the *taifa* kingdom of Valencia 1016/21–1085. Hispano-Arabic dynasty of Yemeni origins; family of the viceroy, Muhammad ibn Abu Amir, known as al-Mansur (978–1002), and his eldest son, Abd al-Malik (1002–1008), who led the Spanish caliphate to a final period of prosperity through successful military engagement in Spain (capture of Barcelona in 985 and Santiago de Compostela in 997) and in the Maghreb (capture of Fez in 986). Following the murder in 1009 of al-Mansur's younger son, Abd al-Rahman, who had sought the rank of caliph, his son, Abd al-Aziz (1021–1061), moved to Valencia (administered by client lords since 1016), where he and his descendants were recognized as rulers. After being expelled from Toledo (1065–1076) by the Dhun-Nunids, they were then ousted by them in 1085. Amirid client rulers established several fiefdoms in southeastern Spain, including Almeria (1012–1041), Murcia and Denia (1019–1076), Tortosa (1038–1061), and on the Balearics (1019–1114).

Anatolian Seljuks also known as the Rum Seljuks. Turkish dynasty in Anatolia 1077–1308. Main capital: Iznik (Nicaea), from 1116 Konya. The Anatolian Seljuks are a branch of the Great Seljuks, who occupied Anatolian territory after the victory of Malazgirt (1071); their founding father, Kutalmish, was a cousin of the Seljuk rulers Tughril and Chaghri. His son, Suleyman I (1077–1086), conquered Iznik in 1078. Initially under the formal authority of the Great Seljuks, the Anatolian Seljuks acquired far-reaching autonomy during the conflicts of the Crusades. The first period of prosperity came under Kilic Arslan II (1156–1188/92), who until 1178 had control of the Danishmends' territory. The fragmentation of the empire resulting from its division between his 12 sons in 1192 was consolidated only after 1204 under Giyath al-Din Kaikhusrau I (1204–1211). Following a period of political and cultural prosperity under Izz al-Din Kaikavus I (1211–1219) and Ala al-Din Kaiqubad I (1219–1237), the political decline began. After 1240 there came territorial losses, a defeat by the Mongols (at Kose Dagi near Ankara, 1243), and the plundering of the Anatolian Seljuk lands, after which they retreated to Antalya. From 1279 they were under the supreme authority of the Persian Ilkhanids, who made the Anatolian Seljuk territory a province of their empire in 1308.

Aqqoyunlu Turkoman federation of the "Tribes of the White Sheep," rulers of eastern Anatolia, Azerbaijan, Persia, Iraq, Afghanistan, and Turkestan (1467–1502). Main capital: Amid, from 1468 Tabriz. Named after their original totem animal, they were Oghuz Turks; in around 1340 they began to carry out raids against Byzantium, Mesopotamia, and Syria, took control shortly after of Diyarbakir with its center at Amid, and intermarried with the Christian Comnenes of Trabezond (later emperors of Byzantium). Their first advance came under Qara Yuluk Uthman (1389–1435), who as an ally of Timur Lenk was appointed emir of Diyarbakir in 1402 and expanded its territory. After 1435, the Aqqoyunlu found themselves squeezed (territorial losses) by the rival Qaraqoyunlu. The empire experienced its political zenith under Uzun Hasan (1453–1478), who annihilated the Qaraqoyunlu in 1467 and had seized their territories by 1469; in 1469 he achieved a convincing victory over the Timurids. After 1459 he conducted campaigns in Georgia, and conquered Hasankeyf (1462), and Harput (1465); in 1471 he advanced into Karman (Anatolia) and fought against the Ottomans in an alliance with European powers (1473 defeat). The Turkoman culture flourished under Uzun Hasan and his son Yaqub (1478–1490); 1490 marked the start of the struggle against the up-and-coming Safavids, who drove the Aqqoyunlu out of Tabriz in 1501 and finally stripped them of their political power in 1502. In 1507 the last Aqqoyunlu ruler was expelled from Mardin.

Artuqids Turkish dynasty in southeast Anatolia and northern Mesopotamia (Diyarbakir province) 1098–1232 and 1408. Following the victory at Malazgirt (1071) as a consequence of the Seljuks' drive westward, the founder of the dynasty, Artuq ibn Ekseb, became the Seljuk governor of Jerusalem and Palestine in 1086. His sons, who succeeded him in 1091, were driven from Jerusalem by the Fatimids in 1098 and set up dominions in northern Mesopotamia: Sokman I (1098–1104) established the branch of Diyarbakir and Hasankeyf (1098–1232), his brother al-Ghazi I (1104–1122), prefect of Baghdad from 1101, the branch of Mardin and Maiyafariqin (1104–1408); another branch ruled in Harput (1185–1233). Initially under the Seljuks, then the Zangids and the Khwarazm-Shahs, the Artuqids achieved large-scale autonomy during the Crusades. Under Nasir al-Din Mahmud (1201–1222) there was an active building program in Diyarbakir, which reached its cultural zenith. The Diyarbakir and Harput branches of the dynasty were removed by the Ayyubids in 1232/33 and the Mardin branch by the Qaraqoyunlu in 1408.

Assassins Own name: Nizarites. Extreme Shiite (Ismaili) sects with their own states established in Iran and Syria 1090–1256/70. Their popular name was derived from the Arabic *hashishiyun* ("hashish-eater"). A religious splinter group (Nizarites) of the Fatimids, their grand master Hasan-i Sabbah (d. 1124) conquered the mountain strongholds of Alamut and the surrounding mountains around 1090 and began an aggressive mission in northern Iran, as well as battles with the Seljuks. After 1092, a number of religious fanatics launched a series of spectacular attempts on the lives of leading Sunnis and other opponents. The Assassins developed an esoteric doctrine and at the start of the 12th century began to extend themselves, even into the Syria of the Crusade era, under an independent grand master, the "Old Man of the Mountains." Whether or not their murderous commando unit was actually under the influence of narcotics is questionable. In 1256 the Assassins were destroyed in Persia by the Mongols under Hülägü and by 1270 in Syria by the Mamluk sultan Baibars.

Ayyubids Kurdish dynasty in Egypt, Syria, and Iraq 1171–1250/60. Main capitals: Damascus and Cairo. Named after the Kurdish military leader Ayyub from Armenia, who entered the service of the Zangids as Abbasid governor of Taktrit near Baghdad and became governor of Damascus. His brother, Shirkuh, and his son, Salah al-Din (Saladin), became military leaders of the Fatimids in Egypt; Saladin (1138–1193), the greatest Islamic hero of the Crusades, became vizier of Cairo in 1169, removed the Fatimids in 1171, and united Egypt and Syria under his rule (under the formal sovereignty of the caliph of Baghdad). In 1175 he adopted the title of sultan, occupied Aleppo in 1181, and gained sovereignty of northern Mesopotamia; he led the battle against the Crusaders and was able to win Jerusalem back from them in 1187 (with a victory at Hattin). Following his death, the empire was divided between his five sons and his brother, al-Adil (1193/1200–1218), who by 1200 had restored the unity of the realm. In 1218 the empire was once again divided: a main dynastic branch with the sultanate under al-Kamil (1218–1238) in Cairo and secondary branches in Damascus, Aleppo, and Hims. The main branch in Cairo ended in 1250 with the assassination of the sultan al-Muazzam by the Mamluks, the secondary branches of Damascus and Aleppo were removed in 1260 by the Ilkhanids, and the Hims branch by the Mamluks in 1262; one branch remained in Hama until 1341. The Ayyubids of Yemen constitute an independent branch.

Sultan Abdul Hasan of Golconda, Deccan, San Diego Museum of Art

Bahmanids Afghan dynasty in the Deccan (peninsular India) 1347–1526. Main capital: Kulbarga. Following the conquest of the Deccan by the sultans of Delhi in 1322, the Afghan Hasan Gangu Bahmani (1347–1358), who had advanced in the court of the sultans in Delhi and been given the honorary title Zafar Khan, seized power during a revolt in Kulbarga and founded the Bahmanid dynasty, which first ruled in the northern Deccan. His successors, particularly Muhammad Shah II (1463–1482), who seized Orissa in 1471 and advanced south, extended their rule to the whole Deccan, so that their empire stretched from one coast to the other. When at the end of the 15th century the empire was divided up into different provinces the rulers there gained autonomy; the Bahmanid Empire broke up into eight successor states and in 1526 ceased to exist.

Barakzai Afghan dynasty of the emirs or kings of Afghanistan 1826–1973. Main capital: Kabul. As the foremost tribe of Afghanistan, the Barakzai were the country's viziers from 1747. They were largely removed from power by the ruling Durrani at the end of the 18th century, but the Barakzai leader, Dust Muhammad (1826–1839 and 1842–1863), ousted the Durrani from the throne in 1826. In 1834 he assumed the title of emir, became ruler in Kandahar, and later also first ruler of the united Afghanistan in 1863, thanks to British help. His successors, Shir Ali Khan (1863–1879) and Abd al-Rahman (1880–1901), had to defend themselves against other pretenders. In the state of tension that existed between the British, Russians, and Persians, the Barakzai took the side of the British, who occupied their country in 1879/80. In 1893 British sovereignty was secured in return for payments under the Durrand treaty with Britain. In 1919 Aman Ullah (1919–1929) led a war against the British, achieved foreign policy independence and assumed the title of king (padishah) in 1926; he implemented reforms based on the Ataturk model. Following disturbances, Nadir Shah (1929–1933) transformed the country into a constitutional monarchy in 1931 by means of a progressive constitution. His son, Zahir Shah (1933–1973), steered a careful course after 1945 between the USSR and the Western powers. Following restrictions on the rights of the monarch under a new constitution in 1964, he was deposed following a coup by Afghan officers in July 1973.

Bengalis Governors and sultans of Indian dynasties in northeast India and Bangladesh 1202–1576. Main capital: Gaur (Lakhnawti), later Firuzabad, from 1564 Tandah. The conqueror of Bengal, Muhammad Bakhtiyar Khalji (1202–1205), and his descendants began as governors of the Ghurids, the sultans of Delhi. The great cultural independence of the region, which until 1202 represented the last Buddhist state on Indian soil, made it easier for them to assert their independence as sultans in 1338; they began by ruling as two dynastic branches in west and east Bengal. The Ilyas dynasty, which ruled west Bengal from 1339, extended its rule throughout Bengal in 1352, but was expelled by the Raja-Khan dynasty (1409–1442). After the demise of the Ilyas dynasty in 1486, another four dynasties followed; having already been occupied by the Moguls (1537–1552), in 1576 Bengal was occupied by Emperor Akbar and added to the Mughal empire.

Buyids also known as the Buwaihids, a Dailamite (Iranian) dynasty in western Iran and Mesopotamia 932/945–1056/62. The Banu Bayah or Banu Buwaih originated in the highlands of Dailam and traced their origins back to the ancient Iranian kings. Their name comes from Abu Shudya Buyah, who rose to power under the Samanids and Ziyarids; his three sons conquered territory for themselves and were given honorary caliphal titles: Ali Imad al-Daula (932–949) conquered Fars (his dynastic branch ruled up to 1055, from 1012 also in Iraq), Hasan Rukn al-Daula (932–976) Rayy, Hamadan, and Isfahan (his branch ruled up to 1023), and Ahmad Muizz al-Daula (932–967) Iraq, Ahwaz, and Kerman (his branch ruled up to 1012). Ahmad occupied Baghdad in 945 and established the protectorate over the Abbasid caliphate (up to 1055). The most important Buyid ruler was Ali's son, Khusrau Adud al-Daula (943–983), who became head of the dynasty, then in 977 gained control over Iraqi territories, extending his power base still further. The Buyids particularly stimulated the Iranian element of Islam. Eventually came instability and a division in the Iraqi branch in Iraq (1020–1055) and Kerman (1012–1056). The Rayy branch was removed in 1023 by the Ghaznavids, the remaining branch in 1055/56 by the Seljuks, who also took over the protectorate of the caliphate; the last Buyid pretenders remained in Kerman until 1062.

Danishmends Turkish dynasty in Asia Minor 1085–1173. Main capital: Danishmand. The founder of the dynasty was Shams al-Din Ahmad (1085–1104), who during the course of the Seljuk invasion set up his own dominion to the west in Cappadocia (Sivas/Sebaste, Kayseri/Caesarea, Malatya/Melitene, Tuqat), which was fortified by his son Gumushtegin (1104–1134). His successors maintained their position against the Crusaders until 1173, when their territories were absorbed into the empire of the Anatolian Seljuks.

Delhi, sultans of. Members of the major Islamic dynasties of India 1206–1526/56. The sultans of Delhi were the successors of the Ghaznavids and Ghurids in the Punjab and northern India. During the decline of the Ghurids, their Turkish general Qutb al-Din Aibak (1206–1210) declared his independence and established the realm of the so-called "slave sultans" of Delhi. Among these, Iltutmish (1210–1236) was the most prominent: the conquest of Sind earned him a reputation as the main architect of Islamic rule in India. In 1290 the "slave sultans" were toppled by the Khalji dynasty (1290–1320); Ala al-Din Khalji (1296–1316) repelled the Mongols and conquered the Deccan (central India) for Islam. From the Tugluq dynasty that followed (1320–1414), Firuz (1351–1388) was able to consolidate its rule in northern India, yet following his death various sultanates defected from Delhi (Bengal, Deccan, Gujarat, Jaunpur, Malwa). In 1398 Delhi was occupied by Timur Lenk. The Sayid dynasty (1414–1451) was followed by the Afghan Lodis (1451–1526), who were removed in 1526 by the first Great Mughal, Babur. With the expulsion of his son, Humayun, by Sher Shah Suri (1540–1545) and his successors (up to 1556), the sultanate of Delhi was reestablished for a short period.

Dhun-Nunids Rulers of the *taifa* kingdoms of Toledo, 1028/29–1085, and Valencia, 1065–1076 and 1085–1092. The Banu Dhun-Nun, an arabized Hispano-Berber dynasty, already had control over Toledo (852–930), before it became subject to the caliph of Cordoba. In 1028/29 Ismail al-Zafir (1028/29–1043) was able to regain power over Toledo; his successors, Yahya I al-Mamun (1043–1075) and Yahya II al-Qadir (1075–1085) expanded the realm and occupied Valencia from 1065 to 1076, but paid taxes to Castile. When Alfonso VI conquered Toledo in 1085, he helped his vassal, al-Qadir, to regain control over Valencia, where he was murdered in 1092. Valencia fell to "El

Cid," Rodrigo de Vivar, and was not conquered by the Almoravids until 1102.

Durrani Afghan dynasty of the shahs of Afghanistan 1747–1826. Main capital: Kandahar, Kabul from 1772. The Durrani tribe in Afghanistan gained independence under its chief, Ahmad Shah Durrani (1747–1772), following the murder in 1747 of Nadir Shah of Persia, who had occupied the country. Durrani founded Afghanistan's most powerful emirate, assuming the title of shah. In 1750 he conquered Herat. Stable rule was set up by Taimur Shah (1772–1793), before it was endangered by internal power struggles after 1801. In 1816 the Durrani had to defend Herat against the Persians; in 1817 they were divided into two ruling branches in Kabul and Peshawar/Kashmir. Conflicts with the viziers of the Barakzai house marked the start of their decline. After being removed from the throne by the Barakzai in 1826, the last Durrani ruler was finally expelled in 1842.

Fatimids Shiite counter-caliphate in Tunisia, Egypt, Syria, and for a while in northern Africa between Morocco and the Arabian Peninsula 909–1171. Main capital: Kairouan, 920 Mahdiya, from 973 Cairo. The Fatimids derived their name from the Prophet's daughter, Fatima, and could trace their roots back through nine generations to the last imam, Ismail of the Seveners branch of the Shia. Their founder, Ubaydallah al-Mahdi, (909–934), was helped to power by the Ismaili missionary Abu Abdallah al-Shii as the future Mahdi and, following the annihilation of the Aghlabid Empire, conquered Tunisia, Libya, eastern Algeria, and Sicily, which remained under the rule of the Fatimids until 1061. In 969 al-Muizz (953–975) conquered Egypt and founded Cairo; ongoing conflicts emerged with the Abbasids in relation to Syria and with the Spanish Umayyads over northern Africa; between 965 and 1070 the Fatimids had authority over Mecca. They achieved their political and cultural zenith under al-Aziz (975–996) and al-Hakim (996–1021), whose eccentricities, however, led to religious unrest (including the emergence of the religious community of the Druze). The long caliphate of al-Mustansir (1036–1094) was followed by religious division (Nizarites and Mustalites). Under al-Hafiz (1131–1149) the Fatimid rule was limited to Egypt. The last caliphs were under the influence of various military rulers; the Ayyubid Saladin, vizier in Cairo from 1169, abolished Fatimid rule in 1171 and returned Egypt to Sunna control.

Ghaznavids Turkish dynasty in Afghanistan, Khorasan (Persia), and northern India 977–1150, in the Punjab until 1186. Main capital: Ghazna, from 1156 Lahore. Following the conquest of the town of Ghazna by the Samanid army commander Alptegin in 962, his successor Sebuktegin (977–997) became governor of the Samanids in the Ghazna region, where he enjoyed *de facto* independent rule and conquered lands in Khorasan. His son, Mahmud of Ghazna (998–1030), the most important early Islamic conqueror, eliminated the Samanid rule over Khorasan in 999, conquered Baluchistan and Khwarazmia, neutralized the Qarakhanids and fought as a strict Sunnite against the Buyids (Rayy was captured in 1029). Mahmud was acknowledged by the caliph and given an honorary title; from 1001 his Indian conquests proceeded as far as Gujarat, Sind, and Kanauj in the centrer of the subcontinent, and paved the way for Islam in India. His son, Masud I (1030–1040), concentrated on India but was defeated in 1040 by the Seljuks at Dandanqan, who expelled the Ghaznavids from Khorasan, driving them eastward. Ibrahim I (1059–1099) relinquished all territories in the Oxus region; his rule was limited to eastern Afghanistan and northern India. Bahram Shah (1118–1152) enforced his rule in the Punjab under the authority of the Seljuks. In 1161 the Ghaznavids were driven back further by the Ghurids, who captured Ghazna, and in 1186 removed the Ghaznavids at the conquest of Lahore.

Ghurids Afghan dynasty in Afghanistan and northern India 1150–1206/12. Main capital: Firuzkuh, also Lahore in 1186. The Shansabani tribe from the mountains of central Afghanistan in the Ghur region, who only came to Islam in the 11th century and had been under the authority of the Ghaznavids since 1010. In 1099 the Ghurids were ruled from Ghazna by Ghaznavid governors, but from 1146 enjoyed self-rule in Firuzkuh; they plundered Ghazna in 1150 under Ala al-Din Husain (1149–1161) and by 1161 had taken possession of the Afghan land held by the Ghaznavids. From 1178 they made conquests in India: from Peshawar to the Sind coast (1182); in 1186 they conquered Lahore and removed the Ghaznavids. There followed dual rule by the elder Ghiyath al-Din (1163–1203) in Firuzkuh and Herat and his brother, Muizz

The Mughal shah Jahangir, 1605 miniature, St. Petersburg, Institute for Oriental Studies

al-Din (1173–1206), from 1203 overall ruler in Ghazna, from 1186 in Lahore. In 1193 the Ghurids captured Delhi and extended their empire to Gujarat in the south and Bengal in the east (1202). The empire disintegrated rapidly following the assassination of Muizz al-Din: Afghanistan had fallen to the Khwarazm-Shahs by 1212 and India in 1206 to the Turkish general Aibak, who established the sultanate of Delhi.

Golconda Qutb-Shahs of. Indian (actually Turkoman) dynasty in the Deccan (peninsular India) 1512–1687. Main capital: Muhammadnagar (Golconda), from 1590 Hyderabad. The dynasty was founded by a nephew of the last ruler of the Qaraqoyunlu, who fled to India when their empire collapsed in 1478. His son, Sultan Quli (1512–1543), governor for the Bahmanids in Telingana from 1493, broke free following the fall of the Bahmanid Empire in 1512 and established the Qutb-Shah state, which secured great independence under the stable government of his successors: the governments of Muhammad Quli (1581–1612) and Abd-Allah (1626–1672) marked the cultural zenith. The last ruler, Abu l-Hasan (1672–1687), is remembered primarily as a poet. In 1687 the Qutb-Shah state was conquered by the Mughal ruler Aurangzeb, who proceeded to annex the entire Deccan to the Mughal Empire.

Hafsids Berber dynasty in Tunisia, eastern Algeria, and Tripoli 1229/36–1574. Main capital: Tunis. The Banu Hafs, Masmuda tribe in the High Atlas. They were named after Abu Hafs Umar (1090–1175), one of the first supporters of and a close adviser to the founding father of the Almohads, Ibn Tumart; his son became the hereditary governor of the Almohads in Tunisia. His son Abu Zakariya Yahya I (1228–1249), gained independence in 1229/36 and set up the largest empire to succeed the Almohads. His son, Muhammad I al-Mustansir (1249–1277), fended off the Seventh Crusade in 1270 and adopted the title of caliph. His death was followed by bloody power struggles at the end of the 13th century between pretenders and the branches of the dynasty in Bougie and Constantine, and occupation of territory by the Merinids from Morocco in the mid-14th century. The recovery and greatest political advance came under the rulers Abu l-Abbas Ahmad (1370–1394; from 1357 joint-ruler of Constantine), Abu Faris Azzuz (1394–1434), and Abu Amr Uthman (1435–1488). During this period of peace and prosperity, Tunis became the most important center of the Levant trade. After 1494 there came a rapid decline in the power and independence of different towns and regions. Under the political dominance of the Ottoman corsairs (Aruj and Khair al-Din Barbarossa) from 1505, they were forced to accept the occupation of Tunis by Emperor Charles V in 1535. The last Hafsids struggled to maintain their position between the resident Ottoman authorities and the attacking Spaniards; in 1574 the Ottomans finally occupied Tunis and deposed the Hafsids.

Hamdanids Arab dynasty in Mesopotamia and Syria 904/29–1003. Main capitals: Mosul and Aleppo. Belonging to the Taghlib tribe, their ascent began with the founder of the dynasty, Hamdan ibn Hamdun, who became Abbasid governor in the area of Mardin in 890. His son, Abdallah (904–929), became governor of Mosul in 906 and ruled Baghdad from 914; as governors of Mosul and Aleppo with honorary caliphal titles, his sons, Hasan and Ali, became rulers of the Syria-Mesopotamia region. The brutal Hasan Nasir al-Daula (929–968) gained increasing independence from the Buyids as ruler of Mosul and Diyarbakir. He founded the Mosul branch of the dynasty, which ruled until 991. As ruler of Aleppo, his brother, Ali Saif al-Daula (945–967), was an important combatant against Byzantium and patron of the arts; he established the Aleppo branch, which converted to Shiism in 969 and became subordinate to the Fatimids. These ousted the Hamdanids in 1003.

Hammadids Berber dynasty in Algeria 1007/15–1152. Main capital: al-Qala, from 1090 Bougie. The Banu Hammad, branch of the Zirids of North Africa. Their founder, Hammad ibn Buluggin (1007/15–1028), was given the town of Ashir near Algiers by his nephew, the controlling Zirid in al-Mansuriya. In 1007 he founded the main capital of al-Qala and gained independence in 1015 by accepting the authority of the caliphs of Baghdad. Following various battles, his son, al-Qaid (1028–1054), gained from the Zirids acknowledgment as the independent ruler of Algeria. Under Buluggin (1055–1062) the Hammadids extended their empire to Morocco (temporary occupation of Fez), under al-Nasir (1062–1088) to Tunisia (as far as Tunis and Kairouan), and advanced into the Sahara. Under growing pressure from the Bedouins after 1104, the last ruler, Yahya (1121–1152), had to limit his territory to the Algerian coast and in 1152 Bougie passed to the Almohads.

Hammudids Rulers of the *taifa* kingdoms of Malaga and Algeciras 1016/18–1058, rulers of Cordoba 1016–1027. The Banu Hammud, arabized Hispano-Berber dynasty, branch of the Idrisids. Their leader, Ali ibn Hammud (1016–1018), governor of Ceuta in 1013 and leader of the African contingent of the Spanish caliphate, rose to power in Malaga in 1016 and became caliph of Cordoba after the removal of the Umayyads. Following his murder, his brother al-Qasim (1018–1021 and 1023–1025), governor of Algeciras, Tangier, and Arzila, and his son Yahya (1021–1023 and 1025–1027/35) ruled in dispute with each other in Cordoba and Malaga. Driven out of Cordoba in 1027, Yahya (d. 1035) and his successors ruled briefly in Malaga and Algeciras, maintaining their position until Malaga fell to the Zirids of Granada and Algeciras to the Abbadids of Seville in 1058.

Hashimites Arab dynasty of the Sharifs of Mecca; kings of Hijaz 1916–1925, kings of Iraq 1921–1958, and ruling kings of Jordan from 1921. They claimed descent from the Prophet's grandson, al-Hasan. Emir Hussain I ibn Ali (1856–1931), sharif of Mecca from 1908 under Ottoman sovereignty, conducted negotiations with the British in 1915 over an Arab kingdom under British mandate. Following the Sykes-Picot Agreement, under which the Arab provinces of the Ottoman Empire were divided into British and French zones of influence, he became king of the Hijaz (central Arabia with Mecca and Medina) in 1916. In 1924 he was expelled by Ibn Saud; his eldest son, Ali, who assumed the title of king in 1924, also had to yield in 1925. Of his younger sons, Faisal I (1883–1933), was elected king of Syria in 1920 by the Arab National Congress (Syria, Lebanon, Jordan, Israel); driven out by the French, he became King of Iraq in 1921 at the initiative of the British. The Iraqi Hashimite branch was brutally removed by Iraqi officers in 1958 with the assassination of his grandson, Faisal II. His brother, Abdallah I (1882–1951), became emir of Transjordania and Palestine under British sovereignty in 1921/23 (in return for assurances of an Israeli state for the Jews) and in 1946 king of the independent Jordan. Following his assassination, his grandson, Hussain II (1952–1999), steered a tricky course between national independence, support for the Palestinians expelled to Jordan, foreign and economic policy dependence on the USA, resistance to Egyptian influence (President Nassar's pan-Arabism), and reconciliation with

Israel, while fending off several attempted coups. In February 1999 he was succeeded to the throne by his son, Abdallah II.

Hudids Rulers of the *taifa* kingdom of Zaragoza (1039–1110). The Banu Hud, Hispano-Arabic dynasty. Its leader, Sulaiman ibn Muhammad (1039–1046) took over Zaragoza from the Banu Tujib. His successors, Ahmad I al-Muqtadir (1046–1081) and Ahmad II al-Mustain (1085–1110), were keen patrons of the arts, initiating an active building program (Aljafería), and led Spanish resistance to the Almoravids. When the latter conquered Zaragoza in 1110, Abd al-Malik (1110–1136) was able to escape to Rueda, where the last of the Hudids held out until 1146.

Husainids Last dynasty of the Beys of Tunisia (1705–1957). Main capital: Tunis (Bardo). Founded by the Turkish cavalry commander Husain ibn Ali (1705–1735), who in the confusion that followed the removal of the Muradids seized power in Tunisia and gained large-scale independence from the Ottomans. Family strife under his nephew, Ali Pasha (1735–1756), led to the plundering of Tunis in 1756 and Algeria's hegemony in the region. There followed a period of reconstruction and economic prosperity with the restoration of full sovereignty (1807) under Ali Bey (1759–1782) and Hammuda Bey (1782–1814) (the "Golden Age"), as well as cultural arabization of the country and creation of a national state. Facing increased economic pressure from Europe following the French occupation of Algeria (1830), Ahmed Bey (1837–1855) and Muhammad al-Sadiq (1859–1882) carried out reforms based on the European model. In 1869 there was an international financial inspectorate overseeing Tunisia and national reforms were prevented. In 1881 Tunisia became a French protectorate (via the Bardo Convention). The rule of subsequent beys stood between French tutelage and the support of national endeavors to gain independence (by the Destour party); in 1943 the French deposed the nationalist bey Muhammad al-Munsif. In 1957 the last Husainid, Muhammad al-Amin, known as Bey Lamine (1943–1957), was ousted when the Republic was proclaimed by Habib Bourguiba.

Ibadites Branch of the first religious division of Islam, the Kharajites ("Rebels"), with their own state structures. The Ibadites first waged war against the Umayyad caliphs from Basra and established several theocratic republics under the leadership of their own imams. In the mid-8th century they ruled various towns in Libya, Tunisia, and Algeria. The Ibadites then migrated to the Algerian Sahara. Ibadite imams ruled from 751 until the end of the 18th century in Muscat and Oman, and during the 18th century in Bahrain and Zanzibar too. Ibadite communities still exist today in Libya, Tunisia, and Algeria, and are particularly strong in Oman.

Idrisids First independent dynasty in Morocco 788–974. Main capital: Walila, from 807 Fez. Founded by Idris I ibn Abdallah (788–793), a descendant of the Prophet's grandson, al-Hasan, who survived the massacre of the Abbasids following a revolt in Ali's family in 786 and fled to Walila (Morocco). Proclaimed imam by Berber tribes in northern Morocco, he extended his territory as far as Tlemcen in 789 and founded Fez. Poisoned in 793, probably at the instigation of Harun al-Rashid, he is regarded as the national saint of Morocco. His son, Idris II (793–828, ruling imam from 804) settled more and more Andalusians and Tunisians, developed Fez into the capital, and consolidated political power. When his son, Muhammad (828–836), divided the realm between his eight brothers in 836, the dynasty fell apart, and was destroyed by internal power struggles. After 917 the Idrisids fell first under the sovereignty of the Fatimids and from 932 of the Spanish Umayyads, who attacked Morocco on numerous occasions and forced the Idrisids from power. After various attempts at retrieving political freedom, the last Idrisids were captured by the troops of the Spanish Umayyads in the Rif and northwest Morocco in 974 and then deported to Cordoba, where the last ruler died in 985. A branch of the dynasty, the Idrisids of Asir, descendants of the founder of the puritanical Idrisiya brotherhood, Ahmad al-Idrisi, ruled 1911–1934 over the highlands of Asir (on the Red Sea coast between the Hijaz and Yemen), until they were annexed by Saudi Arabia.

Ilkhanids Mongolian dynasty in Persia, Iraq, parts of Syria, eastern Anatolia, and the Caucasus 1252/56–1335. Main capital: Tabriz, from 1307 Sultaniya. Hülägü (1252/56–1265), a grandson of Ghengis Khan, conquered Iran in 1256 on behalf of his brother, the Great Khan Möngke, and launched the Mongol attack on Baghdad in 1258. He assumed the title Ilkhan ("subordinate or peaceful khan") in recognition of the leadership aspirations of the Great Khan of the Mongols. In 1260 he was defeated by the Mamluks under Sultan Baibars at Ain Jalut (in Palestine), hindering the expansion westward. Hülägü's son, Abaqa (1265–1282), consolidated his authority via the battle against the Mamluks and subdued the Caucasus; a political alliance with Christian Europe failed. During the short-lasting governments that followed, the economic and financial systems went into decline. Under Khan Ghazan (1295–1304), who made Islam the state religion, and his brother, Üljaitü (1304–1316), who converted to Shiism in 1310, the empire experienced its political and cultural zenith. The last Ilkhanid, Abu Said (1316–1335), a Sunnite, declared peace with the Mamluks (1323), restored Mongol sovereignty over Anatolia, and successfully advanced into the Caucasus. After this the empire broke up into different dominions, which developed separately.

Islamic Mongols Following the death of Ghengis Khan (1227), his vast empire was divided up among his four sons, Jöchi, Chaghatai, Ügedei (successor as Great Khan), and Tolui, who thereby became founding fathers of the Mongol tribal organizations (*ulus*). Once Tolui's son, Möngke (1251–1260), had become Great Khan of Mongolia, he entrusted his brothers Kubilai and Hülägü with the conquest of China and Persia; Hülägü conquered Iranian territory in 1256, launched the Mongol assault on Baghdad in 1258, and founded the empire of the Ilkhanids, who converted to Islam in 1295 (dissolved in 1335). The Chaghatai *ulus* converted to Islam in 1326 (under Khan Tarmashirin), leading to the split between Islamic Transoxiana and "heathen" Mongolistan. In the name of the Chaghatai *ulus*, Timur Lenk (1370–1405) conquered vast territories in the west and claimed the inheritance of the Ilkhanids. The Jöchi *ulus* (in Russia, the western part of the empire) partially converted to Islam in 1258 (under Berke Khan) and finally in 1313 (under Khan Uzbek). The Jöchi tribes were united as the Golden Horde in 1378 (under Khan Toqtamish), but were defeated by Timur Lenk (1495/96) in the battle for the leadership of the Islamic Mongols.

Jalayirids Mongol dynasty in Iraq (Mesopotamia), western Iran, and Azerbaijan 1336–1432. Main capital: Baghdad, also Tabriz (1358–1388). The important Mongol tribe of Jalayir (of the founding father Ilka) in Transoxiana did not belong to Genghis Khan's federation. Having arrived in Iran in 1256, they rose to high office under the Ilkhanids and, following their downfall (1335), constituted the major power in Iraq and parts of Persia. Sheikh Hasan Buzurg the Great (1336–1356) seized power in Baghdad in 1336 and ruled from 1340 as an independent ruler. His son, Sheikh Uwais (1356–1374), conquered northwest Iran in 1358 (Tabriz-Sultaniya area) and Azerbaijan in 1360 from the Golden Horde and occupied Mosul and Diyar Bakr in 1365; he was a leading patron of the arts with a splendid household. His son, Husain (1374–1382), fought violent battles against the Muzaffarids in Iran and the Qaraqoyunlu in Diyar Bakr; his brother, Ahmad (1382–1410), fought against Timur Lenk, who expelled him from Baghdad in 1393. His return in 1395 led to the destruction of Baghdad by Timur Lenk in 1401. Back in Baghdad from 1406, the Jalayirids were finally driven out by the Qaraqoyunlu in 1411. The last Jalayirids stayed in Basra and Khuzistan until 1432, when they were once again ousted by the Qaraqoyunlu.

Janids also known as the Astrakhanids. Uzbek dynasty of the khans of Bukhara 1599–1785. These descendants of the Golden Horde were driven out of the khanate of Astrakhan into Transoxiana by the Russians in 1554. Baqi Muhammad (1599–1605) succeeded in deposing his cousin, the last Shaybanid, in 1599 and seized power in part of the khanate (area of Bukhara, Samarkand, Fergana, and Balkh), consolidated under Imam Quli (1610–1642). In 1732 the Janids had to accept the secession of the khanate of Kokand and in 1752 the loss of further territories. Following the rule of Abd al-Faiz (1707–1747) there ensued a large-scale loss of power: having been ousted from their position (1753–1758), they were under a regent from 1758, and finally subject to the related Mangits, who deposed them in 1785.

Khans of Khiva Uzbek (Mongol) dynasties in Khwarazmia (1511/15–1919). Main capital: Kuna Urgench, from the year 1615, Khiva. Descendants of the Jöchi *ulus* (Ghengisids), also known as the Golden Horde. Under Shaybanid sovereignty from 1500, Ilbars I (1511/15–1525) established his own princedom (from 1804 a khanate), which was occupied several times in the 16th and 17th centuries by Bukhara, in 1740/41 by Nadir Shah of Persia, and 1764–1770 by the Iomund Turkomans. Under Muhammed Rahim II (1864–1910) there was a period of Russian occupation in 1873. The last khans existed under a Russian protectorate, were politically unimportant, and were deposed by the Soviets in 1919.

Khans of Kokand Uzbek (Mongol) dynasty in Uzbekistan 1700/32–1876. Main capital: from 1732, Kokand. Descendants of the Jöchi *ulus* (Ghengisids), also known as the Golden Horde. Initially under Bukharan sovereignty, Shah Rukh Beg I (d. 1694) managed to gain substantial independence, which his successors, Shah Rukh Beg II (1700–1721) and Abu Rahim Beg (1721–1739/40), developed into complete autonomy. From the time of Alim Khan (1799–1809/16), who also annexed Tashkent in 1809, the dynasty used the title Khan and, from the time of Muhammad Umar (1809/16–1822), the title Amir al-Muslimin ("Prince of Believers"). In 1841/42 and 1852/53 their territory was occupied by Bukhara and in 1876 by Russia. The last khan, Nasir al-Din (1875/76), was driven out to Afghanistan.

Khedives Dynasty of the viceroys of Egypt (under Ottoman rule) 1867–1914. Main capital: Cairo. Having inherited from Muhammad Ali (1805–1849) and his successors extensive cultural independence in Egypt, his grandson, Khedive Ismail (1863–1879), was able to enforce *de facto* autonomy in 1867, developed by his son Taufiq (1879–1892) and his grandson Abbas Hilmi (1892–1914). From 1876, financial risk-taking and involvement in prestigious projects e.g. the Suez Canal, were supported by loans from the major European powers. Egypt was occupied by the British in 1882 and became a British protectorate in 1914, leading to the deposition of the Khedive following national uprisings. His successors were his uncle (Taufiq's brother), Husain Kamil (1914–1917), and Ahmed Fuad (1917–1922), until the latter assumed the title of king in 1922 as Fuad I (1922–1936). The rule of the monarchy in Egypt ended with his son Faruk (1936–1952).

Khwarazm-Shahs Turkish dynasty in Khwarazmia (Transoxiana), later also in Turkestan, Afghanistan, Iran, and parts of Iraq 1077–1220/31. Main capital: Kuna Urgench, 1212 Samarqand. The dynasty's founder, Anushtegin (1077–1097), came to prominence under the Seljuks, who appointed him governor of Khwarazmia. Under Qutb al-Din Muhammad (1097–1128) and Ala al-Din Aziz (1128–1156) the empire achieved substantial autonomy, expanded into Khorasan, and fell into conflict with the Seljuks from 1135. Il-Arslan (1156–1172) appropriated the eastern Seljuk Empire in 1157; Ala al-Din Tekish (1172–1200) prevailed as the Seljuks' successor in Iran and became the new protector of the caliph in Baghdad. The greatest expansion took place under Ala al-Din Muhammad (1200–1220). After 1206 he took possession of the Ghurid Empire in Afghanistan, moved through Transoxania, and out towards Mongolia in the east, removing the Qarakhanids from Samarqand in 1212. In 1218 he provoked the invasion of the hordes of Ghenghis Khan and during his escape witnessed the collapse of his empire. His son, Jalal al-Din (1220–1231) was murdered after a hazardous life as a fugitive; the empire fell to the Mongols.

Mamluks Military slave dynasty in Egypt, Syria, and Iraq 1250–1517. Main capital: Cairo. Their name is derived from the Arabic *mamluk* ("taken into possession"). In 1250 the predominantly Turkish military slaves of the Ayyubids seized power in Cairo and recruited non-Muslim boys, whose loyalty was guaranteed through strict quartering in barracks and isolation from the population; the system became less severe later, but established an exceptional degree of political stability. Under the outstanding Sultan Baibars (1260–1277), the Mamluks stopped the Mongol expansion westwards and successfully fought against the Crusaders; in 1291 they drove the last of the Crusaders out of Acre. Cairo became the most important center for trade between the East, India, and Europe, and the economy flourished. Sultan Barquq (1382–1399) successfully resisted Timur Lenk's advance to the southwest and organized the new state. Sultan Barsbai (1422–1438) pursued an unfortunate economic policy based on state monopolies, but led a successful expedition to Cyprus. After 1450 there came a period of economic decline, which coincided with the obsolescence of the dynasty's war machinery. In 1517 the Mamluks were ousted by the Ottomans under Selim I and their territories annexed. For reasons of religious legitimation, the Mamluks had had Abbasid shadow caliphs under their charge in Cairo since 1260.

Mangits Uzbek dynasty of the khans of Bukhara 1785–1921. A tribe of the Nogai federation; originally settlers in the territory of the Golden Horde, they later moved to Transoxiana with the Shaybanids at the start of the 16th century. Their rise came under the related Jalayirids. In power firstly as regent (1707–1717) and then as ruler (1753–1758), Mir Masum Shah (1785–1800), regent in Bukhara from 1770, deposed the last Jalayirids and seized power for himself. Following unrest during the early days, Mangit rule stabilized under Nasrullah Bahadur (1826–1860); in 1873, under Sayid Muzaffar (1860–1885), Russia occupied their territory. The last khans were ousted by the Soviets in 1921.

Merinids Berber dynasty in Morocco 1244–1465. Main capital: Fez. The Banu Marin, a nomadic Zanata tribe from the eastern border territories of the Sahara, settled in eastern and southeastern Morocco from the start of the 12th century. After increasing tension with the ruling Almohads, the Merinids, under the brothers Abu Yahya Abd al-Haqq (1244–1258) and Abu Yusuf Yaqub (1258–1286) took Meknes (1244), Fez (1248), and other important towns in Morocco. They deposed the last Almohads in Marrakech in 1269 and extended their power until they were the most important military force in the Maghreb; on several occasions they launched military attacks in Spain. Under Abu Yaqub Yusuf (1286–1307) they spread as far as Algeria. A period of political success followed under Abu l-Hasan Ali (1331–1351) and Abu Inan Faris (1351–1358), who also drove out the Abdalwadids and occupied Tlemcen, even advancing as far as Tunisia for a short time. A rapid decline came after 1358: child sultans ruled 1358–1374 and 1393–1458 under the tutelage of the related Wattasids and between 1374 and 1393, the Nasrids of Granada. The last Merinid ruler, Abd al-Haqq (1421–1465), temporarily ended the rule of the Wattasids with a massacre in 1458, but died shortly afterwards during a popular uprising in Fez; Morocco fell to the Wattasids.

Mughals (Great Mughals) (Timurid)-Mongolian dynasty of Turkish origin in India 1526–1857. Main capital: Agra. The first Mughal, Babur, was a descendant of Timur Lenk on his father's side, and of Ghengis Khan on his mother's side. As ruler of Samarqand in 1497, he conquered Kabul in 1504 and advanced from Afghanistan to India. Following a victory over the Lodi, he became shah of India (northern and central India; 1526–1530). His son, Humayun (1530–1556), was driven to Persia by Shir Shah Suri in 1540 and was able to win back his father's territory only in 1555. The political high point came with the reign of Akbar the Great (1556–1605), who consolidated rule over Hindustan and expanded as far as Bengal in the east, exercising sovereignty over all the Muslim states in India; he operated a policy of tolerance and religious reconciliation between Muslims and Hindus and reorganised the state administration. Under Jahangir (1605–1627) and Shah Jahan (1628–1658) the Mughal territories grew, trade relations with Europe intensified, and immense splendor and sumptuousness was enjoyed. Aurangzeb (1658–1707), the last Great Mughal of significance, conquered Bijapur (1686) and Golconda (1687), but gave up the policy of religious reconciliation in favor of a strictly Sunnite Islam. From the 17th century, there was political and, above all, economic pressure from the trading companies of Portugal and England. After 1707 the Mughals became increasingly insignificant; in 1739 Delhi was occupied by Nadir Shah of Persia and in 1803 by the British. The last Mughal was deposed by the British in 1857; in 1877 Queen Victoria assumed the title Empress of India.

Muzaffarids Arab dynasty in southern Iran (Fars, Kerman), Kurdistan, and for a time throughout Persia 1314–1393. Main capital: 1319 Yazd, from 1353 Shiraz. The dynasty is named from Sharaf al-Din Muzaffar, grandson of a ruler in Khorasan, who advanced in the court of the Ilkhanids and became governor of Maibod near Isfahan. His brutal son, Mubariz al-Din Muhammad (1314–1358), succeeded his father in 1314 and occupied Yazd in 1318, where he was acknowledged as governor. When the Ilkhanids fell (1335) he became independent, conquered Kerman in 1341 and Fars with Shiraz in 1353, and occupied Isfahan and Tabriz in 1357, making the Muzaffarids the most important political power in Iran; subsequently there were battles with the Jalayirids for dominance over the Iran-Iraq region. Cultural achievement and wealth arrived under Shah Shuja (1358–1384). From 1387 the Muzaffarids became absorbed in a battle between pretenders, until they were removed by Timur Lenk in 1393.

Nasrids Last Islamic dynasty in Spain (al-Andalus) 1232/38–1492. Main capital: Granada. The Banu Nasr or the Banu l-Ahmar, Khazraji tribe, Hispano-Arabs in the area to the north of Jaén. Taking advantage of the fall from power of the Almohads in Spain, in 1232 Muhammad ibn Nasr (Ibn al-Ahmar) proclaimed himself Sultan Muhammad I in Arjona (1232–1273) and conquered vast territories in southern Spain (in 1238 Granada and Malaga). He and his son, Muhammad II (1273–1302), consolidated their rule, acknowledging the formal sovereignty of Castile, and were able to maintain their position using a skillful policy of changing alliances with the Merinids of Morocco and the Christian kings of Spain. The cultural zenith of Granada as the refuge of Muslims in Andalusia was achieved in the reign of Yusuf I (1333–1354) and Muhammad V (1354–1359 and 1362–1391). After 1408/17 there was a period of rapid political decline, due to the warring between different pretenders and family branches, and dependence on Castile. A final political consolidation came under Mulai Hasan (1464–1482 and 1483–1485) and his brother, al-Zaghal. Hasan's son, Muhammad XII, known as Boabdil (1482–1483 and 1485–1492), could no longer withstand the advancing forces of the Catholic Monarchs, Ferdinand and Isabella, and was forced to cede the beleaguered Granada in January 1492.

Ottomans Turkish dynasty in Turkey (Balkans to Anatolia), sultans of the Ottoman Empire 1280/1300–1922. Main capital: 1280 Yenisehir, 1326 Bursa, 1366 Edirne, from 1453 Istanbul/Constantinople. As an association of Ghuzz Turks, in the 13th century they were driven out of central Asia by the Mongols towards the west, where they formed a belligerent frontier emirate in Bithynia (from 1237) and later drove back the Anatolian Seljuks. Under the first sultan, Osman (1280/1300–1326) and his successors came a period of successful self-assertion and expansion, achieved to the cost of the Byzantine Empire (conquest of Bursa in 1326 and Edirne in 1361). In 1354 the Ottomans established their first strongholds in the Balkans (Gallipoli) and assembled the elite Janissary corps, which enabled them to expand rapidly though the Balkans and into Anatolia (with victories in the battles of Kosovo in 1389 and Nicopolis in 1396). In 1402 they suffered defeat by the troops of Timur Lenk at Ankara, which was followed by political confusion. A reorganization of the state and further expansion followed under Murad II (1421–1451) and Mehmed II (1451–1481), who conquered Constantinople in 1453 and destroyed the Christian Byzantine Empire. The Ottomans became the leading power in the Islamic world and landed in Lower Italy in 1480/81. Selim I (1512–1520) conquered the whole of the Near East (Syria and Palestine in 1516, Egypt in 1517, followed by the Arabian Peninsula), emerged victorious against the Safavids at Chaldiran in 1514, and took over Azerbaijan; he assumed the title of caliph. The cultural zenith was the rule of his son, Suleyman II the Magnificent (1520–1566), who conquered the Balkans (as far as Hungary, siege of Vienna in 1529) and expanded control of the Mediterranean (occupation of the entire Maghreb coast from 1552, rule over Algeria, Tunisia, Libya). After 1566, with a few exceptions, weak or incapable sultans ruled, so that the period from 1656 saw the supremacy of the great viziers and Janissary officers, as well as cultural refinement and political decadence. In the ongoing conflict with the Hapsburg Empire (Vienna was besieged again in 1683), the Ottomans were on the defensive after 1700. The state structure was reorganized under the reforming sultans, Selim III (1789–1807) and Mahmud II (1808–1839), which coincided with the collapse of the Ottoman Empire; 1839 saw the beginning of the Tanzimat reforms based on the European model. Abdulhamid II (1876–1909) implemented the Tanzimat policy by authoritarian means and fell into lasting conflict with bourgeois-liberal and nationalist opposition groups. In 1922 the last Ottoman sultan, Mehmed VI (1918–1922), was deposed and in 1924 the caliphate was disbanded by Mustafa Kemal Ataturk.

Pahlavi Iranian dynasty of the Shahs of Persia 1925–1979. Main capital: Tehran. The dynasty's founder, Reza Khan (1878–1944), was a commander of the Cossack brigade under the Qajars, toppled the government in 1921, was prime minister 1923–1925 and had himself elected shah by the National Assembly in 1925, following the removal of the Qajars. With the support of the military, he conducted an authoritarian modernization and secularization program based on the Ataturk example, which resulted in ongoing conflict with the Shiite clergy; in 1934 he introduced the name "Iran" (rather than "Persia") as the country's official designation. Due to his sympathies with Hitler, he was deposed by the British and Soviets in 1941 during their occupation of the country. His son, Muhammed Reza Pahlavi (1919–1980), ruled under the supervision of the British and Soviets until 1946 and thereafter depended on the USA and the West for his foreign policy. Following a conflict with Prime Minister Mossadegh and a brief departure (1953), he eliminated the opposition with the help of the USA (using the SAVAK secret police) and from 1964 forced an authoritarian modernization of the country along Western lines (the "White Revolution"). As part of the ongoing conflict with the bourgeois opposition, the socialists, and the Shiite clergy, he was forced to leave the Iran in January 1979, escaping the "Islamic Revolution" inspired by Ayatollah Khomeini.

Qajars Turkoman dynasty of the shahs of Persia 1779/96–1925. Main capital: Tehran from 1786. Originally Turkoman nomads descended from Qizilbash emirs, the Qajars ruled over Astarabad in northwest Iran from 1750. Their leader, Agha Muhammad Khan (1779–1797), took over power in Persia (with the bloody removal of the Zand in Kerman in 1794, and of the Afsharids in Mashhad in 1796), united the nation, and adopted the title of shah in 1796. His nephew, Fath Ali Shah (1797–1834), was already under enormous pressure from the British following military defeats by Russia (1813 and 1828, involving loss of the Caucasus); Persia became the object of opposing British and Russian interests. Under Nasir al-Din Shah (1848–1896) the economy was controlled by British monopolies and concessions (railways, telegraph), which led to an ongoing conflict with the bourgeois opposition and a call for a reduction in the ruler's power. The British tobacco monopoly led to unrest in 1890 and a parliamentary battle for a modernistic constitution, which was enforced in 1906 against Shah Muzaffar al-Din (1896–1907). In 1908 there was a popular uprising in Tehran due to the storming of the parliament by the Shah's Cossack brigade. The powerless last Qajar, Ahmed Mirza (1909–1925), had to accept the occupation of further parts of Persia by the British and Russians (leading to a British protectorate in 1919), as well as revolts by the Shiites in the south. In 1925 he was deposed by the powerful prime minister Reza Khan Pahlawi, who made himself Shah of Persia.

Qarakhanids Turkish (Uiguric) dynasty in Transoxiana 840–1212. Main capitals: Qara Ordu, Kashgar, Bukhara in 992, also Samarqand in 1042. The Qarluq tribe, which belonged to the Uiguric tribal federation in Mongolia and had been settled in Kashgaria since the 8th century; initially vassals of the Uiguric Empire, they gained independence as rulers of the steppe in 840. There was a double kaganate (rule) under a Great Kagan (eastern section, main capital: Qara Ordu) and an assistant kagan (western part, main capitals: Taraz and Kashgar). In the 10th century came the Islamization of the empire. Abu Musa Harun I (982–993) conquered Bukhara in 992 and his successors had taken over the Samanid Empire by 999. The Ghaznavids became the opponents of the Qarakhanids after 1008 and, after 1040, notably, the Seljuks. The final division between east and west kaganates came in 1041/42. The east kaganate was under the stable rule of Abu Shuja Arslan (1032–1056/57) and Tughril I (1057–1074/75), but Harun II (1074/75–1102) had to recognize the sovereignty of the Seljuks. Having been subjected to invasions by the Mongol Qara Khitai since 1130, the last east kagan in Kashgar was removed by the Khwarazm-Shahs in 1210/11. The west kaganate prospered under Ibrahim I (1038–1067), who resided in Samarqand from 1042, and Nasr II (1067–1080). Ahmad I (1081–1089/95) was dominated by the Seljuks after the occupation of Bukhara and Samarqand and his successors were installed and deposed by them. Under Qara-Khitai sovereignty from 1141 and that of the Khwarazm-Shahs after 1180, the last Qarakhanid ruler was removed by the latter in 1212.

Qaraqoyunlu Turkoman federation of the "Tribes of the Black Sheep," rulers over eastern Anatolia, Azerbaijan, the Caucasus, large parts of Iran, and Iraq 1380/90–1469. Main capital: Tabriz in 1391, also Baghdad in 1411. Belonging to the Oghuz Turks, they were named after their original totem animal. As allies of the Jalayirids, they ruled under Qara Muhammad (1380–1390) from the area to the south of Lake Van (eastern Anatolia, center: Ardshish) through Armenia and Azabaijan. His successor, Qara Yusuf (1390–1420), declared his independence and occupied northwest Iran with Tabriz. Expelled by Timur Lenk on numerous occasions, he was able to prevail against the Timurids in 1405, adopted the title of sultan in 1408, and drove the Jalayirids out of Baghdad in 1411, appropriating their territories; by 1419 he had conquered Diyarbakir, parts of Georgia, and Shirvan. Under Qara Yusuf and Qara Iskandar (1420–1435) there were victories and defeats in battles in Kurdistan and against the Timurids in Transcaucasus. The greatest expansion and the political zenith came under Jahanshah (1435–1467), who finally cast off the supreme authority of the Timurids in 1447, conquered central and southern Iran with Isfahan in 1452, Fars and Kerman in 1453, and even occupied Herat in 1458. In 1467 he was defeated by the rival Aqqoyunlu dynasty, who removed the last Qaraqoyunlu ruler in 1469. A nephew of Jahanshah fled to India in 1478, where he established the dynasty of the Qutb-Shahs of Golkonda (which lasted until 1687).

Qaramita Ultra-Shiite, social-revolutionary movement with its own state on the Persian Gulf (Bahrain) 899 – c. 1030. Center: al-Muminiya (today: al-Hufuf). Influenced by the slave rebellion of Zanj in southern Iraq (with social-revolutionary motives; quashed in 883), as well as eschatological Ismaili movements, the founder, Hamdan Qarmat, wanted actively to bring about the arrival of the Mahdi and in 892 established a stronghold in southern Iraq (an "emigrating area"); he achieved a great following among farmers, craftsmen, the urban proletariat, and the socially disenchanted. In 899 the Qaramita set up an independent state with "communist" elements (community of property, freedom from taxation, interest-free state loans, leadership under a committee of six, etc.) and introduced a counter-caliph. In the struggle against the Abbasids, they occupied trading routes and attacked pilgrim caravans, laying siege to Damascus in 901 and ruling over Oman and Hadramawt after 904. In 930 they took over Mecca and stole the Black Stone from the Kaaba, which was only returned in 951; they disseminated intensive religious propaganda in Syria, Yemen, and Khorasan, and also influenced the thinking of the Fatimids. It was not until 1030 that the Qaramita state was eliminated by troops of the caliph in Baghdad.

Reyes de Taifa (*taifa kingdoms*) Small kingdoms in Spain (al-Andalus) 1010/31–1091/1110. With the decline of the Spanish caliphate after 1010 and its collapse in 1031, the *taifa* kingdoms emerged as regional powers. Of the 23–26 small kingdoms, the most important were the Abbadids of Seville, the Aftasids of Badajoz, the Amirids of Valencia, the Dhun-Nunids of Toledo, the Hammudids of Malaga and Algeciras, the Hudids of Zaragoza, and the Zirids of Granada. The in-fighting between these states assisted the advance of the Christian Reconquista in the north and, after 1090/91, the conquest of al-Andalus by the Almoravids, who eliminated the *taifa* kingdoms. *Taifa* states reemerged in Spain during the decline of the Almoravids (1143–1172) and that of the Almohads (1224–1238).

Rustamids Dynasty of Ibadite imams in the city-state of Tahart (Algeria) 776–908. The dynasty's founder, Abd al-Rahman ibn Rustam, was briefly governor of Kairouan in 758 and, following his escape to Tahart, was chosen as imam (776–784). A claim to political authority over parts of Algeria was made by his son, Abd al-Wahhab (784–823), who yielded to the protection of the Spanish Umayyads, with whom he always had an excellent relationship. Internal peace and prosperity under Abu Said al-Aflah (823–868) and Abu Hatim Yusuf (868–894/906) transformed Tahart into the intellectual and religious center of the Kharijites in northern Africa. Ousted and expelled in 908 by the Shiite leader, Abu Abdallah al-Shii, in the name of the aspiring Fatimids, the Ibadites migrated to southern Algeria, where they still live today in Wadi M'Zab (and are known as Mozabites).

Sadites (Saadis) Sharif dynasty in Morocco 1554–1659. Main capitals: Marrakech and Fez. The Banu Sad, who migrated from the Hijaz to the Daratal (southern Morocco) at the start of the 14th century. After 1505, they extended through southern Morocco with the help of religious brotherhoods, fought against the ruling Wattasids, and became leaders in the defensive action against the Portuguese (occupation of Marrakech in 1525, conquest of Agadir in 1541 by the Portuguese, capture of Fez in 1549). In 1554 Muhammad al-Sheikh (1549/54–1557) toppled the Wattasids, secured Sadite rule with great harshness, and captured Tlemcen; his son, Mulai Abdallah (1557–1574), successfully averted the controlling influence of the Ottomans. Next came conflicts between the pretenders. In 1578 the Sadites annihilated the Portuguese at al-Qasr al-Kabir. The political zenith came under the rule of Ahmad al-Mansur (1578–1603), who secured economic prosperity and organized a state administration that would endure for centuries (the Makhzan system). In 1603 division of the territory led to a decline in power and the off-shoot of an independent dynastic branch in Fez (1610–1626). In 1659 the last Sadite ruler was murdered and Morocco fell to the Alawids.

Safavids Turkoman dynasty of the shahs of Persia 1501–1722/36. Main capital: Tabriz, Qazvin in 1548, and Isfahan from 1598. The Sufi order founded around 1300 by Sheik Safi (1252–1334) in Ardabil (eastern Azerbaijan) soon acquired significance as a religious and political focus. In the mid-15th century, the Safavids became converts to Shiism. Their rise to power came under the spiritual sheikhs Junaid (1447–1460) and Haidar (1460–1488), who created a rigid political organization and gathered together their own troops (named "Qizilbash" or "Red Heads/Caps" after their headgear) to spread their doctrine. Shah Ismail I (1501–1524), successor to Haidar after 1494 and fervent Shiite propagandist, seized power in Iran (1499–1501), starting with the province of Gilan, by driving out the related dynasty of the Qaraqoyunlu. In 1507 he occupied Iraq, immediately elevated Twelver Shiism to the national religion, and sought political reconciliation between the Turkomans (the Qizilbash, the military) and the Iranian population (the administration). A defeat by the Ottomans at Chaldiran in 1514 was followed by ongoing conflict with the Ottomans in the west and the Uzbeks in the east. Under Tahmasp (1524–1576) there was substantial diplomatic neutralization of the enemy, normalization of religious policy, and the beginning of patronage of the arts. Following subsequent troubles, there was a reconsolidation of the state under Abbas I the Great (1587–1629). He annexed Bahrain in 1601, occupied Azerbaijan in 1603, and conquered Shirwan, Armenia, Georgia, and parts of Afghanistan in 1608. In 1623/24 he was able to reannex Kurdistan and Iraq to the Safavid empire. Internally, he undertook army reform with Christian military slaves, developed Isfahan into the "Pearl of the World," and generated prosperity through skillful economic policy and control of the Persian Gulf. His successors were often weak personalities, yet complicated court rituals were developed and a shah cult. The last high point was the rule of Abbas II (1642–1666) through an intensive exchange of goods with European trading partners and internal political reforms; in 1648 he annexed parts of Afghanistan. A rapid economic decline began under the last Safavid, Sultan Husain (1694–1722), who, through religious intolerance and compulsory conversion to the Shiite faith, provoked the Sunnite parts of the empire. As a result, the Sunnite Afghans (the Ghalzai) moved into Persia from 1719, beleaguered and conquered Isfahan in 1722 and deposed Husain, who was executed in 1726. Up until 1736 (in some provinces 1773) Safavid shadow rulers were installed. Power was transferred to the Afsharids and Zand, and finally to the Qajars.

The Qajar shah Nasir al-Din Shah, miniature, Paris, Musée du Louvre

Saffarids Ruling dynasty in Persia, Afghanistan, and parts of Transoxiana 861/867–903. Main capital: Merv. The adventurer Yaqub ibn Lait (861–878), known as al-Saffar ("The Coppersmith"), built strong troop units from urban self-defense groups and gangs of robbers from the local region and made himself lord of his home town of Sistan (in eastern Persia). From 867 onwards he took possession of the territory of the Tahirids (Herat and Fars with Shiraz in 868, then Balkh and Tokharistan), whom he finally drove out of Khorasan in 873, as well as Afghanistan. Recognized in 871 by the caliph as governor of the entire eastern half of the Abbasid Empire, he conducted a campaign against Baghdad in 876. His brother, Amr (878–900), was initially able to hold onto power and was even recognized as governor of Transoxiana in 895, but he was defeated by the Samanids in 900 and taken prisoner. An attempt made by his grandson, Tahir (900–903), to win back power from Sistan proved unsuccessful. His descendants ruled Sistan as governors from 921 (main capital: Nimruz), under Seljuk sovereignty from 1068, until removed by Timur Lenk in 1383.

Samanids Iranian dynasty in Transoxiana, parts of Persia, and Afghanistan 819/874–999. Main capital: Bukhara. Their founding father and namesake, Saman Khudat, descended from an old Iranian priestly family; after 819 his four grandsons became Tahirid governors in Samarqand, Fergana, Shash, and Herat. Nasr I ibn Ahmad (874–892), son of the governor of Samarqand, took over his office in 864, became Abbasid governor of Transoxiana after the collapse of the Tahirids in 874, and claimed *de facto* independence. His brother, Ismail (892–907), had destroyed the Saffarid Empire by 903 and taken possession of Afghanistan and large parts of Persia with Khorasan. The empire underwent its greatest expansion under Nasr II (914–943): from Baghdad, Kerman, and Mazandaran (Persian Gulf) to Turkestan and the Indian border. From 945 onwards the Buyids drove the Samanids back to Transoxiana and Khorasan. Under Mansur I (961–976) and Nuh II (976–997), the flourishing court constituted the focal point of spiritual life in Persia and Persian Islamic literature. Having for many years guarded the border against the Turkish peoples attacking from the east, in 994 the Samanids lost Khorasan to the Ghaznavids and in 999 Transoxiana to the Qarakhanids, who finally drove them out; in 1005 the last Samanid was murdered while fleeing.

Sanussiya (Sanussi movement) Religious brotherhood, part rulers in Libya from 1840, emirs in 1922, 1951–1969 kings of Libya. Main capital: Jaghbub in 1855, Kufra in 1895, Tripoli from 1909. The founder of this puritanical religious reform movement, Muhammad ibn Ali al-Sanussi (1787–1859), preached from 1840 in Cyrenaica and spread his mission throughout Libya. When he was driven out by the Ottoman regents, in 1855 he moved his center to the oasis of al-Jaghbub. His son and successor, Muhammad al-Mahdi (1859–1902), gave the order a permanent organization based in the oasis of Kufra. His cousin, Ahmad al-Sharif (1902–1916), had been fighting, on the Turkish side, against the Italian invaders since 1911. Al-Mahdi's son, Muhammad Idris (1916–1969), had been secular ruler of Cyrenaica from 1918 (under Italian sovereignty) and became emir of Tripolitania in 1922. Driven to Cairo by the Italian fascists (1923–1942), the Sanussi movement waged war against the Italians under Umar Mukhtar (executed in 1931). The emir was returned to Libya in 1947 (followed by the 1949 constitution and national independence) and became king of Libya in 1951 as Idris I; in 1969 he was ousted by Libyan officers under the leadership of Colonel Gaddafi.

al-Saud Arab ruling family in central Arabia up to 1735, reigning kings of Saudi Arabia from 1932. Main capital: Riyadh. Their roots lie in the Dariya oasis in Najd. Under Sheikh Muhammad ibn Saud (1735–1765) the family established a relationship with the strictly puritanical reform movement of the Wahhabis, which remains the state religion of Saudi Arabia today. Under Abd al-Aziz (1765–1803) they spread as far as Kuwait in 1788. The first occupation of Mecca and Medina came between 1803 and 1811, and, under Turki (1820–1832) they took Riyadh; in the 19th century they achieved a gradual expansion, but there were serious conflicts within the family. Their advance came under Abd al-Aziz, known as Ibn Saud (1880–1953), who subdued the whole of Najd and Hijaz with his soldiers from 1902 onwards, drove the Hashimites out of Mecca in 1924/25, assumed the title of king in 1926, and joined the entire Arabian Peninsula between Najd and Yemen to the kingdom of Saudi Arabia in 1932. By means of advantageous treaties with Western powers and the exploitation of its oil resources, the family acquired great wealth, with Ibn Saud as head of a patriarchal clanship. Upon his death, the country was ruled by his sons. Following the deposal of the profligate Saud

(1953–1964), Faisal initiated a period of careful modernization and cultural enlightenment. Thanks to its rich oil reserves and religious traditionalism, Saudi Arabia holds an important position among the Islamic nations. Under King Khalid (1975–1982) and Fahd (from 1982) there has been a period of political dependence on the USA and the West, and technological modernization, coupled with a retention of the traditional, authoritarian ruling structures.

Seljuks also known as the Great Seljuks. Turkish dynasty in Afghanistan, Persia, eastern Anatolia, Iraq, Syria, and on the Arabian Peninsula 1038–1157 or 1194. Main capitals: Merv and Isfahan. Belonging to the leading tribe of the Oghuz Turk group, the Seljuks adopted Islam in around 960 under the tribal leader Seljuk; they were initially in the service of the Qarakhanids of Transoxiana. Seljuk's grandsons, Tughril (1038–1063) and Chaghri (1038–1060), divided the territory into a western half (later Isfahan) and an eastern half (Merv). Following his victory over the Ghaznavids (1040 at Dandanqan), the elder Tughril extended the empire to the west, conquered Persia, parts of Anatolia, and Iraq after 1042, and replaced the Buyids as protector of the caliph in Baghdad in 1055 (becoming an honorary caliph and a sultan). The political and cultural zenith of the Seljuks came with the overall rulers Alp Arslan (1060/63–1072) and Malik Shah (1072–1092), as well as their prominent vizier, Nizam al-Mulk (1060/65–1092), who enforced Sunnism as the state religion with the help of the *madrasa* system. In 1064 the Seljuks occupied Armenia, gained sovereignty over Mecca in 1070, defeated Byzantium in 1071 at Malazgirt, and conquered the Arabian Peninsula. Signs of disintegration began to emerge after 1092, due to a power struggle between pretenders, and a new empire finally emerged under Sultan Mahmud (1105–1118) with a subsequent division. A weakening regime in the west (Iran/Iraq) existed until 1194, while a final period of prosperity came under Sultan Sanjar in the east (1118–1157). Finding itself constantly harassed by its neighbors from 1135 onwards, the eastern empire fell to Turkish tribes and Khwarazm-Shahs in 1157 and the remainder of the western empire also to the Khwarazm-Shahs in 1194. Breakaway dynasties resulted in the Shaybanids' own branches in Kerman (1041–1187; main capital: Bardashir) and Syria (1094–1117; main capitals: Damascus and Aleppo), as well as the Anatolian Seljuks.

Shaybanids Uzbek (Mongol) dynasty in Transoxiana and Afghanistan 1500–1599. Main capital: Samarqand. The Shaybanids were descendants of Shayban (grandson of Ghenghis Khan and brother of Batu Khan), to whom the latter granted Hungary. His line (1226–1659) comprised the khans or zars of Tiumen and, for a while, the khans of the Golden Horde. Muhammad Shaybani Khan (1500–1510), founder of the Transoxianan khanate, ruled Turkestan from 1487/93, bringing an end to Timurid rule by conquering Samarqand (1497, finally in 1501) and Herat (1507), occupied Tashkent in 1503, and advanced as far as Kuna Urgench in 1505; he died trying to seize Khorasan from the Safavids. His successors stabilized the empire. His line ruled in Bukhara from 1540, experiencing its cultural and political apogee under Abdallah II (1556/83–1598). Abdallah was khan of Bukhara from 1556 and in 1583 he reunited the empire. In the confusion that followed his death, the main Shaybanid dynastic line collapsed and was inherited by the related Jalayirids (Astrakhanids) in 1599.

Spanish Umayyads Emirs or caliphs (929) of Cordoba, rulers of Islamic Spain (al-Andalus) 756–1031. The Spanish Umayyads were founded by Abd al-Rahman I (756–788), a grandson of the Umayyad caliph Hisham, the only survivor of the Abbasid massacre of the Umayyads (750), who fled to Spain and seized power there. He and his successors, Hisham I (788–796) and al-Hakam I (796–822), created a stable state structure, brought political conciliation to the country and conducted successful border battles against the Christians in the north. The first cultural flowering came under Abd al-Rahman II (822–852) through the patronage of literature and science and the refinement of customs and traditions: Al-Andalus became the center of western Islam. Next, central power was relinquished in favor of regional government, which led to the successes of the Christian Reconquista. After government was recentralized and the political zenith achieved under the rule of Abd al-Rahman III (912–961), who assumed the title of caliph in 929 and restored sovereignty in Spain. He was able to expand the Umayyad territory towards the Fatimids in North Africa (becoming overlord of Fez and Mauretania in 932) and ruled over the Idrisid state. Al-Andalus experienced another period of cultural creativity under his learned son, al-Hakam II (961–976), who

The Ottoman sultan Bayazid II, miniature, 16th century. Istanbul, University Library

was able to continue his father's policy. During the subsequent decline of the caliph's office under his young son Hisham II (976–1013), power was transferred to the victorious Amirids under the regent al-Mansur (978–1002). The period after 1009 saw civil war and anarchy in the warring between different pretenders and also against the Hammudids of Malaga. In 1031 the last caliph, Hisham III (1027–1031), resigned his position and al-Andalus split into *taifa* kingdoms.

Tahirids Arab dynasty in Khorasan and western Turkestan 820–873. Main capital: Nishapur. In 820 Caliph al-Mamun made his general Tahir ibn al-Husain (820–823; who had appointed al-Mamum as caliph in 811 in preference to his brother) governor of Khorasan, where Tahir gained independence in 821 (under the formal sovereignty of the caliph), but remained commander of the Baghdad garrison, as did his successors. His sons, Talha (823–828) and Abdallah (828–845), increased this independence and made their court a center of Arabic art and science, but also led expeditions for the caliph into Egypt (with the conquest of Alexandria in 827). From 867 the Tahirids lost their neighboring countries to the Saffarids, who finally drove them from power in 873.

Timurids Dynasty of Turkish origin in Transoxiana and Afghanistan, and (until 1405) northern India, Iran, Iraq, Syria, eastern Anatolia, and parts of the Caucasus 1363/70–1506. Main capitals: Samarqand, also Herat from 1405. The founder of the dynasty was Timur Lenk (1328–1405) from the Transoxianan Turkish tribe of the Barlas. Emir of Kesh (Shahr-i Sabz) from 1360, he conquered large parts of Transoxiana from 1363 onwards with various alliances (Samarqand in 1366, Balkh in 1369), and was recognized as ruler over them in 1370. Acting officially in the name of the Mongolian Chaghatai *ulus*, he subjugated Mongolistan and Khwarazmia in the years that followed and began a campaign westwards in 1380. By 1389 he had removed the Kartids from Afghanistan (Herat) and advanced into Iran and Iraq from 1382 (capture of Isfahan in 1387, removal of the Muzaffarids from Shiraz in 1393, and expulsion of the Jalayirids from Baghdad). In 1394/95 he tri-

umphed over the Golden Horde and enforced his sovereignty in the Caucasus; in 1398 subjugated northern India and occupied Delhi; in 1400/01 conquered Aleppo, Damascus and eastern Anatolia; in 1401 destroyed Baghdad; and in 1402 triumphed over the Ottomans at Ankara. In addition, he transformed Samarqand into the "Center of the World." In 1405 Timur died in Utrar during a campaign to conquer China. Following attempts by several grandsons to seize power, his son Shah-Rukh (1405/09–1447) won through, maintaining sovereignty in most of Timur's territories from Herat, although Anatolia and Iran/Iraq were lost to the Qaraqoyunlu. Various cultural centers emerged under Timur's grandsons, with Samarqand remaining important under the learned astronomer Ulugh Beg (1409–1449). Internal power struggles followed after 1447/49, but the government in Samarqand remained stable under Abu Said (1451–1469). His son, Sultan Ahmad (1469–1494), was oppressed by the Shaybanids, who captured Samarqand in 1497/1500. The last chapter of cultural fecundity was opened in Herat under Husain Baiqara (1469–1506), whose court was an important artistic center. In 1506/07 Timurid rule was ended by the Shaybanids with the capture of Herat. A fifth-generation descendant of Timur, Babur, became the first Mughal of India.

Tulunids Arabized Turkish dynasty in Egypt, Syria, and Palestine 868–905. Main capital: Fustat. Founder of the dynasty was the Turkish military slave Tulun, who rose to the office of commander of the household troops at the court of the Abbasids. His son, Ahmad (868–884), inherited this office in 854, and in 868 became deputy governor and resident of the caliph in Egypt, where he immediately gained independence; in 877 he occupied Syria and Palestine with the help of mercenary armies. His son, Khumavaraih (884–895), gained recognition as governor of Egypt, Syria, and northern Mesopotamia, marrying his daughter to Caliph al-Mutadid. Under his son, Harun (896–904), there was a fall from power and battle against the Qaramita. In 905 the Tulunid territory was reconquered by the caliph's troops in Baghdad.

Umayyads First caliphal dynasty 661–750. Main capital: Damascus. Named after its founding father, Umayya, a member of the Prophet's tribe. The founder of the dynasty was Muawiya I ibn Abu Sufyan (661–680) who, as governor of Syria, emerged in 657 as an opponent of Caliph Ali and, following his murder, seized power, which he made inheritable. There followed ongoing conflicts with various Arab tribes and religious movements in early Islam. Political successes were the rule of Abd al-Malik (685–705), who reorganized the state administration (including monetary reform) and developed Jerusalem as a religious center, and also that of al-Walid I (705–715), who advanced Islamic conquests (in 711 as far as Spain in the west and Industal in the east, with Bukhara and Samarqand conquered in 715). There then followed rulers whose reigns were short-lived, as well as an increase in the number of rebellions among conquered populations protesting at the privileges enjoyed by the Arabs. Under Hisham (724–743) there was consolidation, but this was followed by political instability and uprisings by Kharijite and Shiite groups, who helped the Abbasids rise to power. These expelled the last Umayyad caliph, Marvan II (744–750) in 750 and removed the Umayyad family. One of Hisham's grandsons who had fled established the rule of the Spanish Umayyads in Cordoba in 756.

Uqaylids Arab dynasty in northern Syria and northern Iraq 990/996–1096. Main capital: Mosul. The Banu Uqayl, of the Qays tribal group, with possessions throughout North Africa. Initially under Hamdanid sovereignty, their leader, Abu Dhawwad, conquered Balad in 990 and Mosul in 992, but was driven out by the Buyids; his brother, Mukallad (996–1000), gained recognition as governor of Mosul, Kufa, and other towns. Following a consolidation of power under his son, Karvash (1000–1050), Abu l-Makarim Muslim (1061–1085) extended his rule from Baghdad to Aleppo (capturing Raqqas in 1070, Aleppo in 1079). The Uqaylids were subject to Fatimid sovereignty from 1011 and helped them to conquer Baghdad in 1058/59. After Muslim had fallen in battle against the Great Seljuks in 1085, their authority went into decline and in 1096 the Seljuks drove them into an area to the north of the Persian Gulf.

Wattasids Berber dynasty in Morocco 1472–1554. Main capital: Fez. Descendants of a branch of the nomadic Zanata on the northern edge of the Sahara, who settled in eastern Morocco and the Rif from the 13th century. Having come to prominence under their relatives, the Merinids, as viziers and governors they took over the regency for the Merinid child sultans (1358–1374 and 1393–1458); in 1458 all but two brothers were slaughtered during the massacre that killed the last Merinid ruler. The surviving Muhammad al-Sheikh al-Mahdi (1472–1505), in Arzila since 1465, from his base there seized power in Fez in 1472 and installed his family's rule. There followed a harsh battle against religious brotherhoods and rebellious towns. His successors, Muhammad al-Burtugali (1505–1524) and Abu l-Abbas Ahmad (1524–1550), had to struggle against the invading Portuguese and Spanish, to whom they lost broad coastal territories, and also against the advancing Sadites in the south. The last Wattasid ruler fell in 1554 during the fight against the Sadites.

Zand Kurdish dynasty in southern Iran and Azerbaijan 1750–1794. Main capital: Shiraz. Tribe of the southern Iranian group of Kurds known as the Lak. Exiled to Khorasan by Nadir Shah in 1731, it retreated under its leader, Karim Khan Zand, into the southwest in 1747. Karim Khan (1750–1779) occupied the whole of southern Iran and assumed the title Wakil ("representative"). Following the conquest of Mazandaran (1759) and Azerbaijan (1762), he developed a successful regime, led the country into great economic prosperity (involving trade with India, construction of irrigation channels, a fair tax policy), and made his court a cultural center. Following his death, the state disintegrated in the power struggle waged by pretenders, until the last Zand ruler was violently eliminated by the Qajars in Kerman in 1794.

Zangids Turkish dynasty in northern Syria and Iraq 1127–1174 or 1262). Main capital: Aleppo, Damascus in 1154. The founder of the dynasty was Aqsunqur, a Seljuk military slave and *atabeg* (tutor) to the Seljuk Tutush of Aleppo. His son, Imad al-Din Zangi (1127–1146),

became governor of Iraq (with Baghdad) in 1127 and conquered Mosul (1127), Aleppo (1128), and other Syrian towns. Through political skill and successful battles against the crusading nations, he acquired authority over Mesopotamia and large parts of Syria. While his son, Nur al-Din (1146–1174), conquered Syria and occupied Damascus in 1154, his brother, Saif al-Din (1146–1149), inherited Mesopotamia and established the Mosul dynastic branch (1146–1262). Nur al-Din led Zangid rule to its apogee and was able to extend his sovereignty as far as Egypt (under the Fatimids) and over all branches of the family. His son, Ismail, was defeated in 1174 by the Ayyubids, under Saladin, who had risen in the service of the Zangids; the secondary dynastic branches in Sinjar (1170–1220) and Jazira (1180–1250) were also removed by the Ayyubids, the Mosul branch by the Ilkhanids in 1262.

Zaydites Official name of the Fiver Shiites (named after their fifth imam, Zayd ibn Ali), who established their own state structures. A Zaydite dynasty (also named the Alids after the founding father of the Shiites) established by Hasan ibn Zayd (864–883), ruled in Mazandaran, Tabaristan, and Dailam (Iran, to the south of the Caspian Sea) 864–1126. The most important Zaydite state was Yemen. In 893 the well-respected commander of the Zaydites, Yahya ibn Husain (859–911), was invited to Yemen as mediator by the tribes there and established a Zaydite imamate in Sada in 901. He and his successors brought substantial areas of Yemen (including Sanaa) under their control and ruled as Rassids (of the Banu Rassi tribe); following the Ottoman occupation of Sanaa (1547), they were vassals of the Ottomans. The related line of the Banu Kasim, ruling imams since 1592, ruled in Sanaa from 1635 and was able to persuade the Ottomans to make a peaceful exit from Yemen. The Zaydite imams ruled with Fiver Shiism as state religion until 1962. The most important imam of modern times, Yahya ibn Hammidaddin (1904–1948),

concluded beneficial treaties with the European powers, modernized Yemen, and assumed the title of king in 1926. In 1962 the last Zaydite imam was ousted by Yemeni officers.

Zirids of North Africa. Berber dynasty in Tunisia and northern Algeria 971–1152. Main capitals: al-Mansuriya in 971, Kairouan in 1048, Mahdiya from 1057. Banu Ziri. Clients of the Fatimids, from 935 they were resident in the stronghold of Ashir near Algiers under Ziri ibn Manad, who fell in the service of the Fatimids in 971. His son, Buluggin (971–984), became the largely independent governor of Tunisia and northern Algeria (Constantine region) and conquered territories in the west stretching as far as Ceuta; under his successors there followed violent battles against rival Berber tribes. In 995 what were later to be the Zirids of Granada, and in 1007/15 the Hammadids, broke away. Al-Muizz (1016–1062) became subject to the caliph of Baghdad in 1045, whereupon the Fatimids started the Banu Hilal invasion of North Africa in 1057/58. Under Tamim (1062–1108), Zirid rule became restricted to the coastal towns of Tunisia. Under the sovereignty of Roger II of Sicily from 1148, the last Zirid ruler, al-Hasan (1121–1148/52), finally surrendered Algiers, their last city, to the Almohads in 1152.

Zirids of Granada. Rulers of the *taifa* kingdoms of Granada (1012–1090) and Malaga (1058–1090). Berber tribe of Banu Ziri, secondary branch of the Zirids of North Africa. Their leader, Zavi ibn Ziri (1012–1019), from 995 hostile pretender to the Zirids of North Africa and leader of the Berber contingents in southern Spain, seized power in Granada following the collapse of the caliphate of Cordoba in 1012. Under his successors, Habbus (1019–1038), Badis (1038–1073), and Abdallah (1073–1090) Granada became the most important cultural center of southern Spain; in 1058 he also acquired authority over Malaga but was finally ousted by the Almoravids in 1090.

Time chart of Islamic dynasties

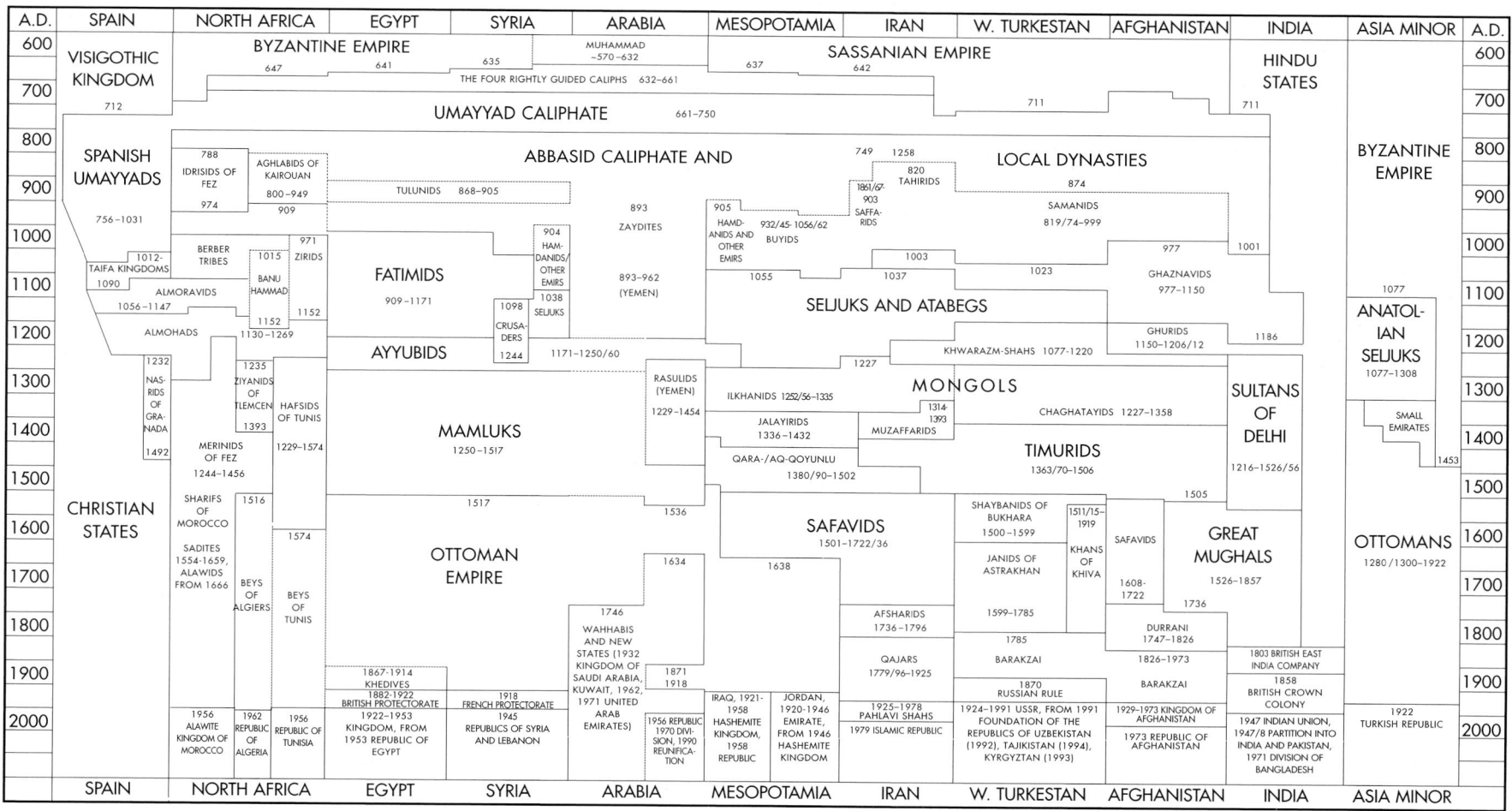

Glossary

Dr. Annette Hagedorn (art) and Bernadette Schenk (religion and cultural history)

A word appearing in italics indicates further information on the term in another glossary entry.

A

Acanthus (Gr.: akanthos) A variety of thistle commonly found in the Mediterranean. The leaf of the plant has a serrated or sinuated edge and is slightly involuted. The leaf was used as a decorative shape on Greek funerary steles from 500 B.C. and has become one of the main symbols of Greek and Roman art. In the Islamic world, the acanthus leaf has been an essential decorative motif in architecture and crafts since the 7th century. Even in those early times, finely detailed artistic images were produced, which could be both naturalistic and also highly abstract in their representation. The most important examples came from the art of the Persian Sassanid dynasty (224–651) and also eastern Byzantine art.

Aedicule (L.: aedicula, Engl.: small house) A framing of portals, windows, and niches created by means of two columns, pillars, or pilasters, which support timbers and a triangular or segmental arch gable.

Aggiornamento (It.) Postponement for an indefinite period.

Alabaster (Gr.: name of the ancient Egyptian town of Alabastron) A naturally occurring, fine-grained, pure white gypsum compound. Alabaster is easy to shape and has therefore been used for decorative architecture, cladding, and sculpture since Greek and Roman times (including alabaster *paneling*). It can easily be ground down to a fine dust, which can then be mixed with water and used to create various shapes. The term *gach* is used to denote this in East European art history.

Alcove (Ar.: al-qubba) A small, windowless recess connected to the main room.

Alfiz (Sp.: alfeizar, Ar.: al-fasha) The rectangular embrasure of an arch. The opening beneath the arch remains unframed.

Alicatado (Sp.) *Mosaic* with geometrical decorative motifs made from glazed ceramic.

Ancon, also *console* (Fr.: console, Engl.: ancon, base) Projecting, load-bearing truss.

Apse (L.; Gr.: hapsis) A semicircular or polygonal recess with an arched half-dome in which an altar can stand. When annexed to a church's main choir or that reserved for clerics, it is also called the exedra. There are often small side apses at the ambulatory, transept, or side aisles (*transept* or side rooms).

Aquamanile (from L.: aqua, Engl.: water, and manus, Engl.: hand) The term has its origins in the Middle Ages when it was used to denote a

Archivolt

basin in which the clergy washed their hands during liturgy. In the literature on Islamic art the term is applied to water vessels in animal form worked in metal, which had originated in pre-Islamic Iran. Aquamaniles are either individual objects or water spouts in a fountain. Just as with the free standing, animal-shaped censers, these are attributed great importance in Islamic art, since they are the only figural sculptures, except for individual examples of architectural sculpture.

Arabesque (from It.: arabesco) A form of ornamentation dating back to Hellenistic times based on intertwined vegetal forms in which the individual elements are largely detached from nature and heavily stylized. This unrealistic representation of creepers and tendrils that is at odds with nature itself is consistent with Islamic beliefs, according to which man should not imitate God's work. Arabesque ornament is well ordered and composed of intertwined leaf stems, which are interlaced in a geometric, two-dimensional system.

Arcade (L.: arch) Arches supported on columns or piers. *Riwaqs* were constructed as covered arcades in Ummayad architecture, which turned the mosque's courtyard (sahn) into an arcaded courtyard. Arcades can also be found built on top of one another on several levels. In addition, there are also *blind arcades*, i.e., arcades set against a wall to enliven the design. They have no load-bearing function.

Arch A curved structure in a wall opening, which bears the load or transfers it to pillars or columns and is used to span quite large distances between walls. The summit of the arch, bearing the keystone, is the crown. The underside is called the intrados, the front face the head or capital. The free triangular forms between the arch and the adjacent wall are called the *spandrel*. Different forms of arch are created based on the circle or segments of it. Forms (selected paying particular attention to the Islamic world): 1. Round arch: a semicircular arch. 2. Horseshoe arch: a three-quarter arch on a rectangular wall opening, particularly typical of the architecture of the Maghreb and Spain. 3. *Ogee* arch: the line of the arch starts by forming a semicircle, but the middle portion of the line is broken at the top and ends in a convex projection pointing upwards. 4. Pointed arch: an arch tapering to a point. The form is constructed from two circular arches, the centers of which lie on the *springing* or capstones of the arch. 5. Multicentered arch: an arch composed of several circle segments, between which are "nosings." Depending on the number of circle segments, these are referred to as three-center arches, four-center arches, etc. 6. Stalactite arch: an arch decorated with stalactite or *muqarnas* elements.

Arch spandrel (*Arch*)

Archivolt (It.: archivolto, Engl.: facing arch; from Gr.: archein, Engl.: to start, rule and L.: volutus, Engl.: rolled, turned) A molded or decorated arch, like an architrave (main beam supporting the load of the superstructure) arched to the semicircle above the supports of a soffit (perpendicular cut surface of a wall opening).

Ark (Pers.: arg, Engl.: *citadel*, fortification)

Artesonado or coffered ceiling In architecture, the name given to a ceiling made up of a number of sunken sections (square or rounded). The panels may be part of a supporting system or purely decorative (painted, stucco, wood). These ceilings appear in the Islamic world during the early period under the influence of Hellenistic art and during the late period under European influence.

Atabeg (Turk.) Title held by a senior dignitary among the Seljuks (11–13th centuries) and their successors.

Ataurique (Sp., from Ar.: tawrik) The use of decorative motifs, as used in *stucco* work and in Spanish ceramic art, based on stylized vegetal motifs in a wide variety of compositions. The perfectly two-dimensional ataurique motifs have their origins in the pre-Islamic Persian art of the Sassanids and were constantly adapted to changing contemporary styles over the following centuries. Ornamentation to which the term ataurique is applied largely corresponds to the *arabesque* repertoire of motifs.

Attic (L.L.) A free standing low wall or balustrade above the principal cornice of the column order of a structure's facade. The attic often

Horseshoe arches in the Ornate Hall of Medina al-Zahra

serves to conceal the roof and create more aesthetically pleasing proportions.

Azulejo (Sp., Ar.: al-zullaig) The name given to Spanish and Portuguese ceramic tiles with tin glazing. These tiles were used mainly for geometrical wall decoration. However, by adding lime to the glazes resistant floor tiles could be produced. Important production sites included Paterna, Valencia, Seville (main production center since the 14th century). Azulejos are still produced today using a variety of techniques.

B

Baghdad paper format Although parchment had first been used for Arabic handwriting, it was replaced by paper in 751, after this was introduced by Chinese prisoners of war. The first high point in terms of quality came in the 14th century, when particularly large editions of the *Koran* were published by royal commission. The term "full Baghdadi format" was used to denote this size.

Balustrade (It.: balaustrata) A row of balusters supporting a coping, which was used mainly during the Renaissance and Baroque periods for banisters, balconies, terraces, and at the base of roofs.

Barrel vault (*Vault*, 1.)

Basin (It.: bacino) Ceramic bowl or basin set into a wall as a means of decoration, frequently used in the architecture of post-Islamic Spain (Mudejar). Clear evidence of the high esteem in which Egyptian and Spanish ceramic art was held is the fact that ceramics from Egypt dating back to the 11–12th centuries and Spanish ceramics from the 14–15th centuries were often used to decorate the outsides of Italian palaces.

Bauhaus The school of art and design in Weimar. It was founded in 1919 following the amalgamation of the already disbanded school of arts and crafts, opened by Henry van de Velde in Weimar, and the school of fine arts. The school's first principal was Walter Gropius. Bauhaus had a lasting influence on new designs worldwide in every area of art. Famous artists of the day taught at the Bauhaus, to enable a connection to be made between craft and technique, thereby helping to make the world of art into an integral whole. In 1925 the school moved to Dessau before it was closed in 1933.

Bazaar (Pers.: basar, Ar.: souk) A business district in towns in the Islamic world. The bazaar is not only a marketplace, but the town's entire business center. It is open each day, except for public holidays, and is made up of permanent, covered buildings, which can be constantly extended as required. Preliminary forms of similar marketplaces were already around in Greek and Roman times.

Berber The collective name used to denote races of different ethnic backgrounds living in North Africa, probably of European-

Mediterranean origin, who speak Berber dialects. With the Arab invasion in the 8th century the majority converted to Islam.

Bey (Turk., Engl.: gentleman) A general title of rank, originating from the old Turkish word beg. It became synonymous with the Arab title *emir*.

Blind arcade (*Arcade*)

Boss capital A capital made from roughly hewn stone without fine sculpting. A *boss* capital is usually any capital left in an unfinished state.

Boss work Masonry using *boss* ashlars.

Boss (O.H.G. bozan, Engl.: to strike) An ashlar, the front of which is only roughly worked.

Brahmins (Sans.) Members of the highest caste in Hindu society, originally made up only of priests. Nowadays, they also include poets, scholars, and politicians, and occupy a prominent position of high standing in society.

Brocading (Fr. brocher, Engl: to brocade) A technique involved in the art of carpet-making whereby silver threads are worked into the weave, thereby emphasizing the pattern. The technique is mainly used in the weaving of silk carpets. The brocading is made up of silk threads wound from ultrafine threads of beaten out gold or silver. This technique is still used today in the production of carpets in Turkey.

C

Caftan (Ar.: qaftan or quftan) A collarless, ankle- or calf-length robe, open at the front from top to bottom and made from various different fabrics. The caftan is buttoned and tied with a girdle. It may be worn either as an undertunic or an overgarment, but can be adapted to the situation in which it is worn. The caftan originated in Persia in the 9th and 10th centuries and has since spread to all parts of the Islamic world.

Caldarium (L.: caldus, Engl: hot) The hot bath in public bathhouses in Greek and Roman times. In Islamic bathhouses, the caldarium was turned into a magnificently decorated room. The ruler could even invite guests here on festive occasions.

Caliph/caliphate (Ar.: successor, representative or succession, representation) An Islamic title for a ruler. According to the mainstream Sunni view, the caliph was a successor to the Prophet Muhammad. However, Umayyad and subsequent caliphs were regarded as God's representatives or God's shadows on earth. Their claim to comprehensive religious authority could not, however, be enforced in practice. The problem of the Imitation of the Prophet, who had not laid down any prescriptions for this himself, produced the greatest rift in Islam – mainly between the two most important strands of the *Muslim* faith, the Sunnis (*sunna*) and the Shiites (*Shia*).

Calligraphy (Gr.: kalos, Engl.: beautiful, and grapheme, Engl.: writing; hence the art of fine writing) The Arab script has a special significance in the Islamic world, since it is the means of communicating the *Koran*. The formation of the different scripts is therefore regarded as almost a religious act, since they translate the once proclaimed text. The oldest Arabic script is the Mashq, a script developed in the 7th century, but replaced by Kufic since the 8th century. Types of script: 1. Kufic: Arabic script named after the city of Kufa; due to its age, it was attributed an almost holy significance as the only script used to record the *Koran*. Kufic is a square, geometric script characterized by strong, vertical elements and horizontal parts of letters. Cursive scripts also developed, which were subjected to certain rules by the calligrapher Ibn Muqla (886–940); they were used from the 10th century. 2. Thuluth. 3. Naskhi. 4. Muhaqqaq. 5. Rayani (lowercase letters of Muhaqqaq). 6. Riqa (lowercase letters of Tauqi). 7. Tauqi. Nastaliq (8.) emerged in the 14th century. As a writing script, Naskhi has come to be generally accepted, as it is relatively easy to read and write. Decorative calligraphy is present in all art forms. Sometimes the letters are linked to animal or vegetal motifs. The script is described as either flowery or speaking, respectively, depending on whether vegetal embellishments or figurative elements are used.

Calotte (Fr.: calotte, Engl.: skull-cap) In architecture, a spherical section such as, for example, the vaulted part of a niche.

Cannelures (from Fr. canneler, Engl.: to channel; from Lat. canna, Engl.: reed) Concave grooves running vertically down the shaft of a column, pillar, or pilaster. They may abut one another with sharp ridges (edges) or be separated by webs.

Cantilever vault (*Vault*, 7.)

Caravanserai (Pers.) A lodging for travelers and traders with facilities for the safe storage of their goods and stalls for their packhorses. The enclosures were often well fortified, since they were located as free standing structures roughly every 20 miles (30 kilometers) along the main trading routes. Their designs became increasingly impressive, with large entrance portals and rich architectural decoration. The zenith of caravanserai architecture came during the time of the Seljuks in the 12–13th centuries.

Cartouche (Fr.: cartouche, Engl.: ornamental frame) A smooth area of wall enclosed in an ornamental frame in which inscriptions or heraldic devices can be inserted.

Caldarium in the Alhambra *Caldarium*

Casbah (Ar.: qasaba) A castle or fortress (*citadel*) in the towns of the Maghreb (i.e., North Africa).

Casemate (L., Fr.: case) Bomb-proof vaulted chamber within a fortress.

Celadon (from Fr.) A term denoting the glazing technique, light green and reminiscent of jade, used on East Asian earthenware or porcelain. The technique was first developed in East Asia for ceramics and was then adopted by porcelain producers at the time of the Ming dynasty (1279–1664). Celadon is a ceramic glaze fired in a reducing atmosphere at high temperatures (1200–1250°C). The green coloring is produced through the addition of ferrous oxides. The glaze consists of nine coats that are sprayed on and painted, in order to achieve an even shade. In centers of ceramic art throughout the Islamic world, pottery similar to celadon in color and, in some cases, shape was produced during the late 12th and early 13th centuries. In the early 16th century, pottery (*Iznik*) was produced in Turkey with the insides painted in celadon colors.

Cenotaph (Gr.: kenotaphion, Engl.: empty tomb) A tomb for a person whose body is buried elsewhere (in Ottoman tomb architecture, in a basement story) or is missing.

Champlevé and cloisonné enamel (Fr.: raised field, compartmentalized) The main difficulty in the manufacture of *enameled* objects is preventing the different colors from running together. Two different techniques can be used in metalwork: 1. Champlevé: Depressions are engraved in the surface of the metal, in which the glass powder is fired. 2. Cloisonné: Thin plates are set on edge on the metal. The colors are fired in the resulting compartments. Smoothing and polishing gives the enameled objects an extremely colorful, elegant appearance.

Citadel (from It.: città, Engl.: town) A fortress in the safest part of a town, consisting of several buildings and fortified walls, which turned the citadel into a town (within a town). There is no generally applicable design for fortresses, since they are heavily dependent on local conditions. Fortress construction led to the development of many new techniques (walls, towers, *vaults*, moats, fountains, weapons). The structure may be on an elevated site or protected by moats. The building complex is surrounded by several walls. These were not only extremely strong, but also built with sections projecting forward (bastions), to allow the positioning of more weapons. The entrance in the outer wall is created by a portal with a path running at an angle through the wall, so that the enemy could be held off until the very last minute in the event of an attack.

Cloud band A decorative motif from Ottoman art that was primarily used on *Iznik* pottery in the 14th and 15th centuries. The motif

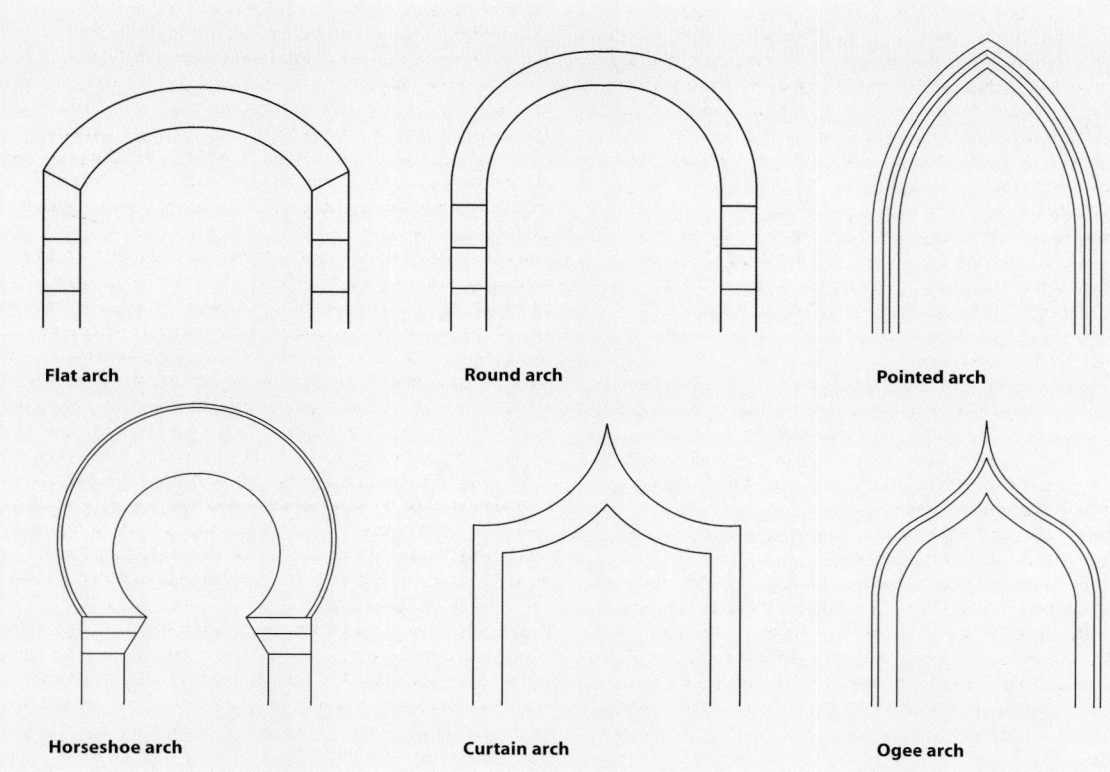

Flat arch

Round arch

Pointed arch

Horseshoe arch

Curtain arch

Ogee arch

originated in Chinese art and appears in Ottoman art as the successor of stylized clouds.

Clover-leaf (triconch) arrangement In religious architecture, the transept arms end in apses that correspond to the apse of the main aisle, giving the impression of a clover-leaf shape. The design was first developed in the Byzantine era; similar structural forms in the Islamic world are therefore denoted using this term.

Coffered vault (*Vault*, 3.)

Colophon In manuscripts, the final inscription containing details of the nature and origins of a text, as well as the writer's name and the date and place of writing. In many cases, only some of this information is given, which means it is often difficult to assign a manuscript accurately.

Compartment (L.) In Islamic *mosque* architecture, the multicompartment mosque appears as a supporting hall with a ground plan divided up into regular sections comprising a number of quadratic zones.

Composite capital In this form of column capital, developed in Roman times, Corinthian and Ionic decorative forms are combined.

Console (Fr.: console; Engl.: *ancon*, base; from the L.: solidus, Engl.: solid) A bracket projecting from the wall, usually profiled or figured, which acts as a support for, among other things, *arches, cornices* (horizontally projecting strips on walls), balconies, or figures.

Copts The Coptic church is the national church of Egypt. It rejected the resolutions laid down by the Council of Chalcedon (451), according to which Christ was a single person but had two natures – one divine and one human. In contrast to this, the Copts continued to profess monophysitism, i.e. the view that Christ is not only a single person, but also has only one nature. Following the Arab conquest of Egypt in 640, the Copts were extensively Arabized, but have still been able to retain their characteristic individuality to the present day.

Cornice A horizontal strip projecting from the wall and linking the horizontal sections of a building.

Cross/groined vault (*Vault*, 2.)

Crossing That part of a religious building at which the longitudinal and transverse elements intersect. The reinforced corners produced at this intersection are converted into pillars, known as crossing pillars. In what is known as a concealed crossing, this part of the space is hidden from view from the rest of the building by four *arches*. In the Ottoman tradition a domed structure is built over the crossing, so this architectural form is found at the center of Ottoman domed *mosques*.

Crypt (Gr.: kryptein, Engl.: to conceal) Originally large, underground burial chambers in ancient catacombs, later the underground burial vault in churches, located beneath the choir and altar. In Islamic art, underground chambers are found in mausoleums, where they are also used as burial vaults.

Cube/cubic (from Gr., L.: cubus) A cubic structural form has a cube-shaped outline. Cubic forms of different sizes can also occur in rhythmic graduations above or alongside one another. The medieval architecture of the Maghreb dabbles with cubic forms. European architects in the late 19th and early 20th centuries admired not only Ottoman

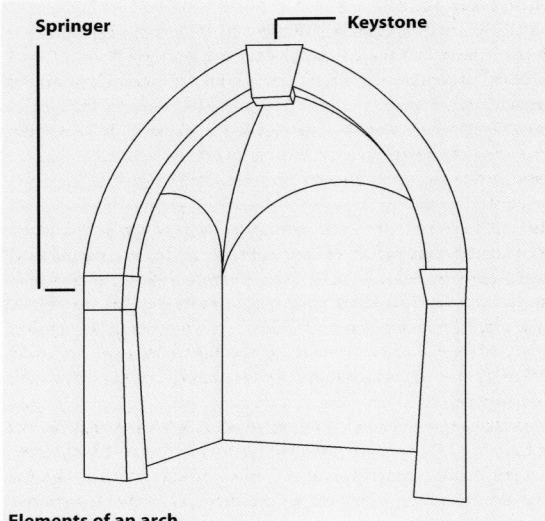

Elements of an arch

architecture but also local adobe architecture and its principles became the inspiration for their own work.

Cuerda seca (Sp., Eng.: dry thread) A glazing technique used in ceramics whereby the different parts of the decoration are separated from one another by a line of oily manganese dioxide powder. After firing, these lines are dark and lusterless and divide the different colored glazes. Developed in the mid-15th century in Seville (Spain).

Curtain wall (L.: curtina, Fr.: courtine) A wall between two bastions in the boundary walls of fortresses (*citadel*).

D

Dervish (Pers., Engl.: poor) Dervish is the name used to denote a member of an Islamic order (tariqa), who lives a life of poverty under the leadership of a sheikh (leader) and endeavors to minimize their bodily functions through religious exercises, in order to release their souls of all physical compulsions. This includes 40-day periods of meditation with fasting and little sleep and, in some orders, listening to music and the dhikr, a combination of prayers and invocations of God with physical movements.

Devsirme (Turk.) The gathering of boys practised in the Ottoman Empire since the 15th century, i.e. the periodic recruitment of the most suitable Christian adolescents from the Balkan provinces for conversion to Islam and lifetime service as soldiers of the *sultan*. Many of the adolescents recruited in this way, who were predominantly of farming stock, were able to climb the social ladder and gain political influence.

Dey (Turk.: dayi, Engl.: maternal uncle) Originally an honorary title in Turkey. This term was later used (1671–1830) to denote the rulers of Algiers, who came from the Turkish military aristocracy and lived mainly from piracy.

Dhimmi (Ar., Engl.: charge) In Islam the "peoples of the book" (ahl al-kitab) are regarded as protected peoples, and originally, according to the *Koran*, included Christians, Jews, Sabaeans, and followers of Zoroastrianism (Ar. majus). Hindus and Buddhists also fell into this category later. Although dhimmis, unlike idolators, could not be forced to convert to Islam, they were exposed to a series of discriminating measures. So, for instance, they had to pay a poll tax (jizya) and distinguish themselves from *Muslims* in their dress and the way they wore their hair.

Dialectics (Gr., Engl.: expert in disputation) A philosophical ideal involving the uncovering of contradictions through dialogue and identification of the true state of affairs. The term is generally used to denote the art of discussion. The word discourse (L.: discurrere, Engl.: to run around), which is often used in a similar context today, corresponds to the term dialectic, but only insofar as discourse involves a lively discussion and debate that contributes to the formation of ideas. The standard of truth required by dialectics therefore takes on a secondary importance. Dialectics is part of Arabic philosophy (falsafa), which had evolved from Greek tradition.

Dome The convex section of a building covering a round (or sometimes oval) base. The dome's external silhouette may be hemispherical, pointed, or onion-shaped, in addition to which there are also shallow domes. The dome may be constructed in a variety of ways. The Islamic world includes examples of ribbed domes (1), folded domes (2), parachute or umbrella domes (3), double shell or double domes (4). The transitional area may contain windows and domes may also contain a limited number of points where light is admitted. Three-dimensional decorative forms are often found on the dome and above the crown opening or *lantern* (5), designed as a raised structure containing windows. 1: Ribbed dome: a dome made up of load-bearing ribs between which non-load-bearing filling is inserted. 2. Folded dome: a dome with a folded surface made up of convex, bead-like, walled ribs only separated from one another by flutes. A design particularly typical of Central Asia. 3. Parachute (or umbrella) dome: a round dome in which the *vault* is made up of several segments that cover a building in the manner of a parachute. 4. Doubleshell (or double) dome: a twin-shell dome *vault*. Although the two shells making up the dome can be interconnected by fins, they are usually constructed quite separately for formal aesthetic reasons. The inner dome closes the building to the interior, while the outer dome is intended to add height; it is of a lighter weight construction than the inner shell. Double shell (or double) dome (*Dome*, 4.).

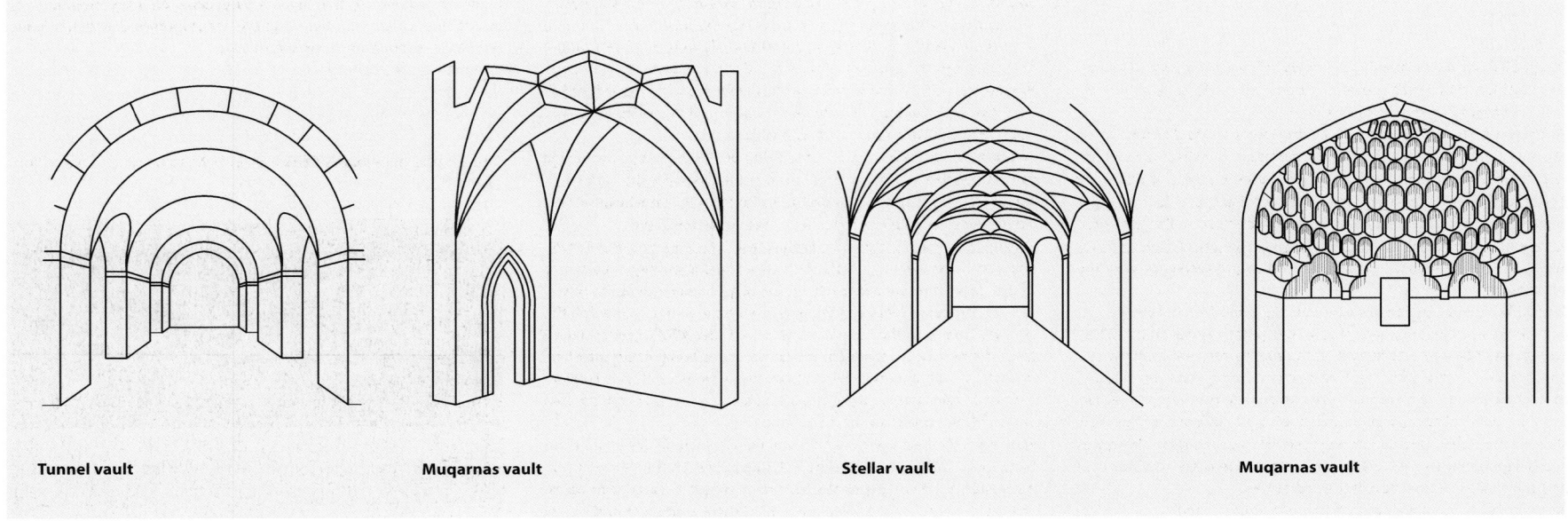

| **Tunnel vault** | **Muqarnas vault** | **Stellar vault** | **Muqarnas vault** |

Hammam in Kerman

E

Egg tempera (*Tempera painting*)
Embossed work A metalwork technique in which a thin plate of metal is beaten into a hollow body using differently shaped hammers. This is a sort of cold metal forging process.
Emir (Ar.: amir, Engl.: commander, governor) In the early days of Islam, this was a title held by the commanders of Muslim troops and governors of newly conquered lands. Later, provincial governors were referred to as emirs and enjoyed full administrative and fiscal powers – irrespective of whether they were appointed by the *caliph* or were only acknowledged in this office subsequently, since they had gained power in a particular area and were the *de facto* sovereign ruler there.
Enamel (Fr.: émaille) Variously colored liquid glass applied by fusion to metal or glass. In Islamic metalwork the enameling technique was used to decorate handles and knife or dagger sheaths. In glasswork, the enameling technique had been in use since the 12th century, reaching its zenith in the 13th and 14th centuries and then its finale in the 15th century. The main centers of production were in Syria (Aleppo, Raqqa, Damascus) and Egypt (Cairo). When using the enameling technique on glass, the ornamentation was first marked out in red lines, leaving lines free between the individual color blocks, later defined in gold leaf.
Enchasing (L., Fr.: ciseau, Engl.: chisel) A form of metalworking in which the decoration is beaten into the metal using differently shaped hammers.
Engobe (Fr.: colored clay) The engobe technique involves coating the surface of a ceramic vessel with clay previously diluted with water, producing a mat finish after firing. The engobe may be applied to the vessel by dipping or it may be painted on with a brush.
Esplanade (L.: planus, Engl.: level) An open space or particularly wide promenade. Wide promenades resulted from the demolition of medieval city walls. The term esplanade can also be applied to wide parade areas within castle grounds.

F

Face wall A flat wall containing windows beneath a wide *arch*, creating the transition to the *vault*. The term is used for the side walls in the main space of Ottoman domed *mosques*.
Faience (after the Italian town of Faenza) Term used to describe a type of pottery with a porous body and white tin glaze, which influences pottery found in the Islamic world. The term denotes a type of quartz *frit* pottery with multicolored motifs created from fireproof colors using the *in-glaze* technique. The decoration is painted on the dry glaze and fired at very high temperatures (fireproof colors). The term is also used for Spain's Moorish tin-glazed pottery, which was produced between the 14th and 16th centuries.
Fatwa (Ar.) A legal opinion given by an expert (mufti) on individual matters. It helps a judge (sing.: qadi, pl.: qudat) to pass judgment, but can also be requested by a private individual, in order to determine whether or not an action is compatible with Islamic law. Through the ages, numerous fatwa gatherings have taken place to provide the basis for new fatwas. The political and social influence of legal opinions, which were always a means of adapting *Muslim* society to the changing times, was and is dependent on the credibility and reputation of the mufti concerned and also on the reaction of the authorities.
Ferman (Pers.) Command or edict of the Ottoman *sultan*.
Folded dome (*Dome*, 2.)
Folio (L.: folium, folio, Engl.: leaf, abbrev. fol.) A sheet in a manuscript in which the pages are numbered consecutively, while the front and back covers are distinguished by the letters a) and b) (also r and v for recto and verso).
Freestone A natural stone regularly worked on all sides. The freestone is the opposite of the roughly cut quarry stone.
Fresco (Ital.: fresco, Engl.: fresh) A mural painted on plaster that is not quite dry.
Frieze In architecture this is a continuous band of figural or abstract ornamentation, used to decorate the exterior or interior of a building. Friezes can also be used as linking elements, if they divide stories visually, or as the final decorative element at the top. In architectural applications, friezes made from stucco, marble, or ceramic were applied to walls. They could also be painted, particularly when used indoors. In the figurative sense, friezes are also used as decorative elements in many forms of applied art.
Frit pottery (quartz frit pottery) Pottery with a body produced from a mixture of white clay, quartz, and glass dust or from ground, fired, glazed ceramics. This technique was used in many periods of Islamic art. The most famous pottery made using this technique is the Turkish *Iznik* pottery of the 15–17th centuries.
Frontispiece 1. The first page of a manuscript. 2. The pediment over doors and windows and the gable over the middle part of a building.

G

Gach (Pers.: gadj, Engl.: stucco) (*Alabaster* or *stucco*)
Gerich (Pers.: gereh, Engl.: knot) A gerich ornament is the term used to describe the often frequently intersecting lines in the abstract geometrical decorative motifs of Islamic art. These woven or knotted patterns are never random or unstructured, having their roots in stellar or *calligraphy* motifs, and are to be found in all genres of Islamic art.
Ghazi (Ar.) A champion who takes part in a raid (Ar.: ghazwa), i.e., a foray against infidels. The term later became a title of honor for Turkish-Oghuz *emirs* in Asia Minor and also for Ottoman *sultans*.
Gnostics (gnosis, Gr., Engl.: knowledge, information) Adherents to a doctrinal system whereby knowledge of spiritual mysteries is available only to certain individuals. Such beliefs gave rise to the development of various small sects from 2 A.D. onwards. These were based on Jewish wisdom and Iranian dualist principles by which the world is composed of good and evil, light and dark, hero and villain.
Grand tour An expression from the 18th century used to denote a trip by educated art-lovers to Italy. In the 19th century, the term was used to denote any journeys serving to promote artistic refinement or education in general. Destinations included oriental countries, as well as Italy and France, and also Greece and Spain.
Guldast (Pers.: gol-dasteh, Engl.: *minaret*, tower) Square tower in Persian fortification and castle architecture.

H

Hadiths (Ar., Engl.: story) The record of the Prophet's words and deeds, i.e., the *sunna*. A hadith consists of two parts - the subject matter (matn) and the chain of those passing on the tradition (isnad), which returns the entire content through eye witnesses and recounters right back to the Prophet himself. Canonical credence has been accorded to the hHadith collections of al-Bukhari (d. 870) and Muslim (d. 875), which are called sahih or "sound" (term for a perfect isnad).
Hajib (Ar.: hadjaba, Engl.: to protect) Title of a court attendant, whose functions varied according to region and time. Originally the hajib was a sort of chamberlain, who guarded access to the ruler. Later he often presided over palace staff or acted as an overseer of the guard.
Hajj (Ar., Engl.: pilgrimage) The pilgrimage to Mecca is one of the Five Pillars of Islam, i.e., every *Muslim* is bound to make this journey at least once in their life, if they are able to do so. The pilgrimage requires the observance of precisely defined rituals and ceremonies and is valid only if the pilgrim adheres to the conditions of a particular form of consecration (ihram). Ihram means that pilgrims cannot shave, comb or cut their hair, or cut their nails, and must refrain from sexual relations. It is also obligatory for certain clothing to be worn, consisting of two pieces of unsewn white cotton and sandals at most.
Hammam (Ar.: hammam, Engl.: to heat up) A structural design for a hot bathhouse dating back to Greek and Roman times. The bathhouse could be erected as an independent structure or as part of a palace complex. The main rooms are the frigidarium (cold bath), *caldarium*, and harara (sweating room). There is usually a central domed room, which is surrounded by smaller domed rooms. The bathhouse is still an essential part of the Islamic way of life today.
Hanif (Ar., Engl.: one who seeks God) In Islam, the term hanif is used to denote one who follows the true and original, i.e. monotheistic, religion. It is said that the occasional monotheistic follower could already be found among "pagan" Arabs. In the *Koran* the term hanif is mainly applied to Abraham, who embodies the ideal of religious ascetics and supporters of the pure monotheistic religion corrupted by Jews and Christians.
Hegira (Ar.) The migration of Muhammad from Mecca to Yathrib, later to become Medina, in 622. The "migrators" from Mecca (muhajirs) and "helpers" (ansar), i.e. believers in Medina, became the nucleus from which Islam was born. The hegira marks the beginning of the Islamic era.
Hellenism The last era in Greek art. It covers, roughly, the period from Alexander the Great to Augustus (whose reign lasted until 14 A.D.). During this phase, the balance and uniformity of the classical period was abandoned in favor of various stylistic formulations (such as, for example, strong expression and movement of forms). This culminated in a classicistic attitude of mind, also affecting the visual arts. Hellenism was not a phenomenon of the visual arts alone, but a basic approach that found its expression in a wide variety of cultural spheres throughout the Greek world.
Hippodrome (Gr., Engl.: horse-racing course) Horse-racing courses existed as early as Greek and Roman times, when they were initially U-shaped, later changing into a stadium form. Hippodromes were also part of palaces and municipal facilities in the Islamic world. Equestrian games and horseraces were held there. In public hippodromes pageants of a non-sporting nature could also be held.
Horseshoe arch (*Arch*, 2.)
Hypocaust (Gr. hypo, Engl.: beneath; Gr. kausis, Engl.: heat) Underground heating system from Greek and Roman times. More closely defined, hypocausts were the spaces between the floor and the ground in which warm air circulated in Roman spas, villas, and palaces. At one end of the heated floor, there was also an underground boiler room. In the Islamic world, such underfloor heating was used in castles and bathhouses.
Hypostyle (Gr.) The Greek structural form of the hypostyle refers to a hall in which the roof is supported by columns. In Islamic architecture, the term hypostyle is particularly used to denote the holy area in front of the *qibla* wall in the courtyard *mosque*.

I

Iconography (Gr., Engl.: pictorial representation) The word relates to a school of art history that concerns itself with explaining and establishing the content of pictures. This tradition grew up in the Middle Ages, when collections of paintings and objects were acquired on a scientific basis and the interpretation of ancient representations became important. Today, identifying the iconographic significance of Islamic pictorial art is often fraught with problems. It can often be explained only in part and may vary, due to uncertainty over origins. It is often found that motifs from the repertoire known since classical times were rejected, their significance changed over time, or was completely replaced by meanings inherent in a corresponding Islamic repertoire of motifs and symbolic content.

Calligraphy of a verse of the *Koran*, 1423, Istanbul, University library

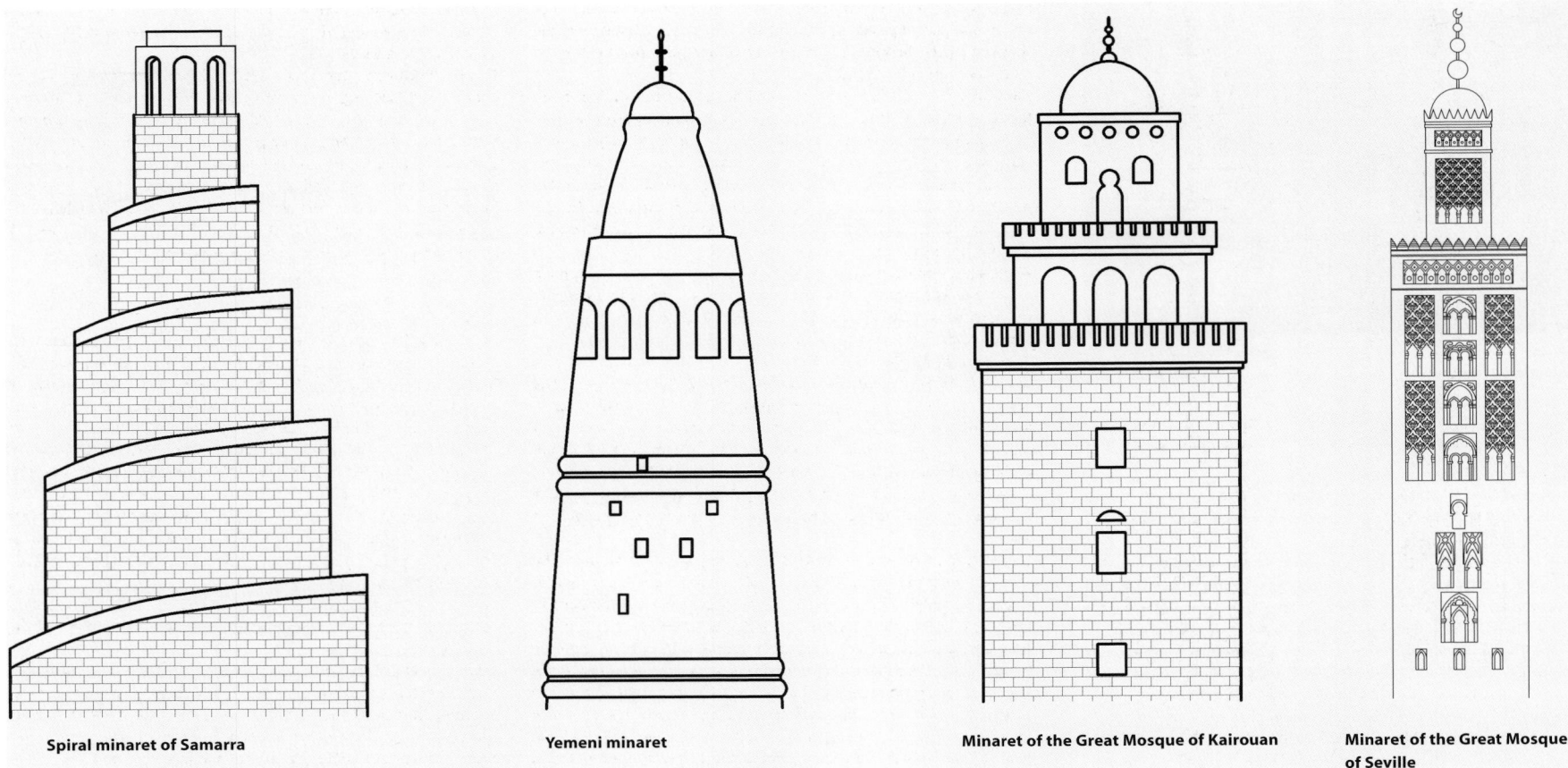

Spiral minaret of Samarra

Yemeni minaret

Minaret of the Great Mosque of Kairouan

Minaret of the Great Mosque of Seville

Ifriqiya (Ar., Engl.: Africa) Following North Africa's conversion to Islam, the name given to the territory covered today by Tunisia, eastern Algeria and parts of Libya.

Ijtihad (Ar., Engl.: utmost effort) Independent, reasoned jurisprudence based on the *Koran* and the *sunna*. At the end of the 9th century, Islamic law and jurisprudence had largely completed its development and the notion that the "gate of ijtihad" was closed became widespread. However, a few outstanding religious and legal scholars, like al-Ghazzali, have continually claimed for themselves the law of ijtihad. Above all, the Islamic reformers of the 19th and 20th centuries called for the "gate of ijtihad" to be reopened, in order for Islamic law to be adapted to modern ways of life.

Illumination (L.: illuminare, Engl.: to illuminate, embellish) From the 7th century A.D. books and manuscripts were being embellished by illumination in the Islamic world also, not only with figural motifs, but additionally with a wealth of vegetal, epigraphic, and abstract motifs. Consequently, manuscripts of the *Koran* could be lavishly decorated. The artist who creates the illuminations is called the illuminator. Calligrapher and illuminator must work hand-in-hand in the production of manuscripts, to divide up the pages appropriately. The calligraphers often started work first, setting the tone for the page design with their script.

Imam (Ar.) The imam is 1. the prayer leader in ritual communal worship; 2. the most senior leader of the *Muslim* community, comparable with the *caliph*. While the term imam emphasizes the religious function of the Muslim leader, the title *caliph* indicates his function as a community leader in succession to Muhammad. The office of imam (the imamate) holds a special significance among the Shiites (*Shia*), for whom belief in the imamate and the infallibility of the imam is a constitutive dogma.

Imambara (Ar./Pers.: magbarah, Engl.: grave) A great hall used on high religious feast days. The graves of revered Shiite (*Shia*) saints were also referred to as imambara.

Incrustation (L.: incrustare, Engl.: to apply hard coating) A wall facing or floor covering of colored, polished slabs of either marble or *porphyry*, which are assembled in patterns, thereby dividing up areas and embellishing them.

Incrustations (L.: incrustare) Since ancient times incrustations have been inlaid in large stone wall or floor areas. To produce these, different colored stones are placed in indentations made in the base stone. The term is also generally used in applied arts to methods in which hard decorative materials (e.g. glass, pearls, precious stones) are inlaid in a soft base (e.g. putty, cement). Other techniques producing the same results are also described using special terms (*inlaying*, Bidri technique).

In-glaze painting A technique in which paint is applied to dry but unfired pottery that has either been glazed or coated with slip. The color of the paint sinks into the glaze during firing and is thereby fixed.

Inlaying A metalworking technique in which a soft precious metal (gold, silver, also copper) is worked into the harder metal wall of a vessel made from bronze or brass. This involves the decorative motifs being engraved into the surface up to a depth of one millimeter using etched contours. The thin plates of precious metal are then hammered into these depressions. A costly variant of this method of inlaying is the undercutting technique, whereby the edges of the depressions are undercut and the precious metal plates pressed beneath the edges. The metal inlays are also enriched with engraved decorations once in place in the vessel.

Insula (L., Engl.: island) The term is derived from Roman municipal architecture, at that time denoting rented blocks made up of several buildings, which were located in a section of the road system made up of roads running perpendicular to one another. Such insulae have been retained in some towns dating back to Roman times. The ancient road system was often adopted, but the buildings within the insula itself were replaced.

Intarsia (L., Ar.) Ornamental work created from colored woods, ivory, tortoise-shell, metal, or mother-of-pearl inlaid in wood. The intarsia technique reached its peak during the Renaissance, when figural decoration also emerged. Within the sphere of Islamic culture, the technique was used on *minbars* and wooden doors, for ceiling and wall decoration, on furniture and in the applied arts.

Intrados Inner or outer surface of an arch. Intrados also exist in square window or wall openings. The word also describes the perpendicular, cut face of the wall opening.

Isocephaly The depiction of different people and also animals in a work of art with the heads on one plane. This originates from the ordered work of relief art and drawing in ancient Greece.

Iwan (Pers.) A *vaulted* hall opening onto a courtyard. The principal form of the iwan developed in the house and palace architecture of the Near East during the late classical period. The iwan's design satisfied many functions in Islamic architecture and was therefore used both in religious and also secular buildings. An iwan may, for example, take the shape of a monumental entrance, in which case it is referred to using the Persian term *pishtaq*. In Persian architecture, the "four-iwan scheme" was developed for the *mosque*, involving four iwans opening opposite one another onto a central courtyard. This scheme also influenced a series of early Ottoman buildings, although in these examples the central courtyard does not remain open but has a vaulted ceiling. The iwan was also used in the grounds of *madrasas* to create a structure set out around a courtyard, in this case the students' living accommodation, which was spread over several stories. The iwan is principally of importance in Persian architecture and only occasional examples of it appear in the art of the Mediterranean region (Egypt, Turkey).

Iznik A town in the west of present-day Turkey (ancient name: Nicaea). During the days of the Ottoman Empire, pottery (vessels and tiles) known as Iznikware was produced from the 15th century onwards using the quartz *frit* method with colored paint applied beneath a transparent tin glaze (*faience*). There are several style groups in Iznik faience, although some of these were produced in parallel. Around 1480 the most significant period began, with blue-and-white painting based on the Chinese example; from 1560 pieces were increasingly developed with highly colorful decoration, some of it involving distinctly realistic plant motifs. This period of success came to an end around 1700 when large orders from the Ottoman court began to dry up and the quality of both the bodies and glazes diminished. Pottery from the towns of Damascus and Kutahya was similar to the ware produced in the town of Iznik, but failed to match its outstanding quality. In certain instances, when the pottery is not inscribed, it is difficult to attribute it to one of the three centers of production, as a result of which the term Iznikware is generally applied today to all pottery from these three towns.

J

Jain (from Sans.: Jina, Engl.: victor, after the honorary title of the religion's founder) Follower of Jainism, an Indian religion that emerged at

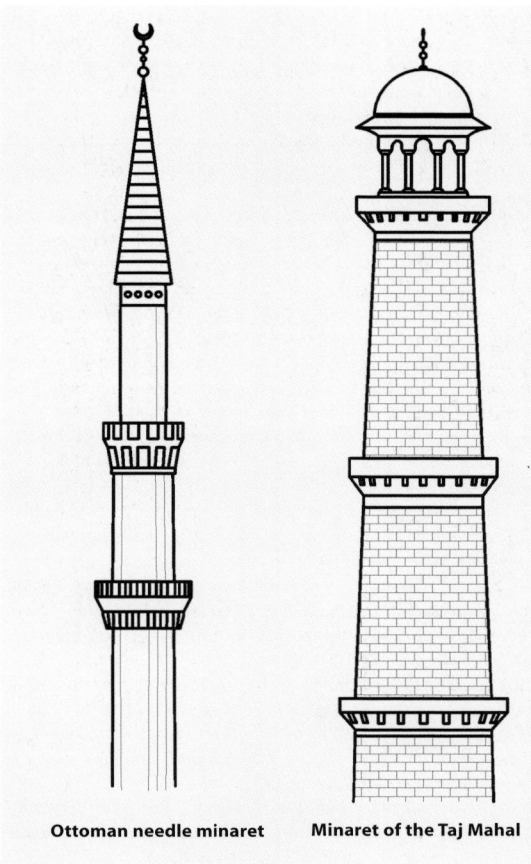

Ottoman needle minaret **Minaret of the Taj Mahal**

the same time as Buddhism. Its founder was Vardhamana or Mahavira (d. c. 477 B.C.), who is regarded as the last of 24 tirthankaras or "makers of the ford," i.e., discoverers of a ford to release the individual from the flow of the birth cycle. Jainism is based on a strictly ascetic doctrine of redemption; the supreme ethical principle is the killing of any living being is absolutely forbidden. With the development of Hinduism and the advance of Islam, since 1200 Jainism has become less and less prominent, but still has a large number of followers today.

Janissaries (deriv. from Turk.: yeni ceri, Engl.: new troop) Janissaries was the title given to the infantry troops of the Ottoman army, who were made up of the capicullari or "slaves of the gate" and formed an elite unit. They were recruited solely from *Muslim* proselytes and were directly answerable to the *sultan*. It was only at the start of the 19th century, when a European-style army was created during the *Tanzimat* reforms, that the Janissaries were disbanded.

Jharoka (Ind.; Pers. from jar, Engl.: shout, cry, call) The name given to a window or balcony at which the ruler appeared. Also the Indian name for the prince's throne.

Jihad (Ar.: jahada, Engl.: struggle) The name given to the duty incumbent on the *Muslim* community to wage war against unbelievers, i.e. non-Muslims or those who, although calling themselves Muslims, had actually fallen away from Islam. However, the Jihad not only includes military action to expand and defend the borders of Islamic territory, but also the individual striving for moral and religious perfection. According to the *Koran*, the jihad is a creditable undertaking for which the reward is paradise.

Jinn (Ar.) Under Koranic tradition the jinn are an intermediate creation between mankind and the angels. They were originally created from fire, can assume a variety of forms and are capable of reason. As with humans, they are called to account at the Last Judgment.

K

Kaaba (Ar.: al-Kaba) The most holy shrine of Islam, a rectangular building in the middle of the Great Mosque at Mecca, housing the Black Stone. In pre-Islamic times, the Kaaba was a place used for the worship of idols, until Muhammad "cleansed" it in 630 and had all the images of idols removed. Since 632 the Kaaba has been a purely Islamic shrine. This

religious reinterpretation dates back to the construction of a religion by Abraham as one of pre-Judaic monotheism, the center of which was the shrine at Mecca. According to this, Abraham and his son Ismail laid the foundation stone of the Kaaba.

Karkhana (Pers.: kar khana, Engl.: workshop) In literature on Indian art, this term is used to denote the princely workshops of the Mughal rulers of India. It is the same as the kitabkhana of the Persian princely courts. It was here that both the decorative designs for the princes' art (architectural decoration, book *illumination*, ceramics, and other products of applied art), as well as art objects, were produced, thereby enabling a uniform dynastic style to develop. The same objectives were also pursued by the Ottoman Nakkashkhans.

Khadra (Ar.) The word literally means "private room," but is also used in art-historical literature to denote the throne room in Islamic palaces. In the early days of Islamic art, the sovereign sitting on the throne was concealed from the view of visitors by a curtain. This ceremonial dates back to the traditions of Sassanian court life.

Khan 1. (Pers., Engl.: nest, shelter) (*Caravanserai*). 2. (Turk.) A title used by Turkish nobility and most common among the Seljuks and Mongols.

Khanqa (Pers.: khanagah, Engl.: "cloister," monastery) A *dervish* cloister or monastery, often also with accommodation for pilgrims. The building of such complexes was often facilitated by foundations. The Sufis (*Sufism*) could live here in a community observing their religious practices. Some khanqas with a mausoleum became the focus for the veneration of a saint.

Kharijism (Ar., deriv. from kharaja, Engl.: to remove, draw out) The Kharijites were the group of followers of Ali, the Prophet's cousin, who disapproved of his authorizing the convening of a court of arbitration at the end of the Battle of Siffin in 657 against Muawiya. The court of arbitration was to resolve the dispute surrounding the legitimacy of the murder of the third *caliph*, Uthman, and his successors. In protest at this readiness to compromise, the Kharijites left Ali, because they believed only God could settle the dispute between Ali and his adversary Muawiya. Unlike the Sunnis (*sunna*) and Shiites (*Shia*), they did not restrict the *caliphate* to the line of the *quraish*, but to the best-qualified Muslim, irrespective of social standing.

Khauz (Pers., Engl.: water vessel, cistern, pool, small pond) The term khauz can be used to refer to a huge variety of water reservoirs. There are metal bowls in applied art, too, that are large enough to be referred to using this term. An example of this is the large metal bowls produced during the Timurid period in the late 14th century. In the (*miniatures*) of Persian book *illumination* from the same period, these bowls are frequently seen in court scenes.

Khedive (Pers., Engl.: sovereign) From 1867 to1914 the title of the viceroys of Egypt under the command of the Ottoman *sultan* Ismail (1863–1879), Taufiq (1879–1892), and Abbas Hilmi (1892–1914). This title had been bestowed upon Ismail in 1867 to emphasize his special status and the largely autonomous position of Egypt within the Ottoman Empire.

Kiosk (Pers.: kushk, Turk.:kosk, Engl.: kiosk) A small, open-sided or partially closed pavilion within gardens and courtyards in the Islamic world. The design was also adopted in Europe and the word "kiosk" has survived until today.

Koran (Ar.: qur'an, from qara'a, Engl.: to read) The sacred book of Islam, which was revealed to the Prophet Muhammad in the Arabic language. For *Muslims*, the Koran is the direct word of God (kalam Allah). It is neither in chronological nor subject order, but divided into 114 chapters (*suras*) of increasing length, which contain different numbers of verses (aya, pl. ayat) and are written in rhymed prose. Among scholars of Islamic law, the Koran is regarded as the first source of jurisprudence, although it contains only a limited number of legally relevant prescriptions. Apart from general ethical/moral principles, it mainly consists of glorification and praise of God as the almighty and benevolent ruler, admonitions, parables, and warnings of the Last Judgment.

Kosh system (Pers.: khoush, Engl.: courtyard, enclosed in a courtyard) Two related structures standing opposite one another on a large square or in a fairly large castle area. The term is mainly applied to Central Asian architecture. The best-known example of the kosh system is Registan Square in Samarqand.

Kufic (*Calligraphy*)

Kulliye (Turk.) A religious building complex made up of school, living accommodation, bath, and kitchen for the poor, also in some cases with a hospital, built particularly during the Ottoman era, with the largest of these complexes originating in the 16th century. Kulliyes were usually built in conjunction with a *mosque* and were not founded by the *sultan* himself, but by other wealthy individuals.

Kumbet (Turk., Pers.: gunbad, Engl.: *dome*) The term kumbet is used to denote free standing, domed graves. These could also be built as standard funerary steles.

Kundal (from Pers.: gun, Engl.: color, and Pers.: del, Engl.: heart, soul) Multicolored painting on a relief base. This painting technique is particularly sumptuous when gold paints are used. It is used both in architectural decoration (on *stucco* or *gach*) and also in arts and crafts.

Kundekari (Turk.: kandagari, Engl.: to cut, engrave) A carving technique for ivory or mother-of-pearl, enabling these forms to be inlaid in wood for decorative purposes. The word kundekari is also used to denote the wood carvers who use this technique. The term is also used for woodwork in which different-colored woods are combined.

L

Lajvardina (Pers.: sang-i lajvard, Engl.: lapis lazuli) A type of stone found in Russia, Afghanistan, Iran, and Chile that is usually dark blue (sometimes also turquoise). The term lajvardina was adopted to denote a particular technique used in Iranian ceramics from Sultanabad and Kashan, which were characterized by their intense blue or turquoise color, achieved using cobalt constituents in the glaze (the glaze was not made from the lajvardina stone). This technique was only used in the late 13th and 14th centuries. The ceramics were first coated with a very thick layer of blue glaze and fired. The design was then painted onto this glaze in iron red and particularly also black-and-white paint and the pottery fired for a second time at a lower temperature. Gold leaf was applied to the design as a finishing touch.

Lantern (L.: la(n)terna and Gr.: lamptera, Engl.: light, lamp) A round or polygonal structure containing windows raised above a *dome* or vault opening (*Dome*, 5.).

Law schools In Sunni Islam (*Sunna*), four schools of law (madhab, pl. madhahib) have been recognized as equally authoritative and the focus for interpretations of the canonical texts (*Koran* and *Hadiths*). Although there are no fundamental differences in dogma between them, they occasionally adopt a different position and teachings on a few practical matters, such as inheritance and family law. They are each named after an outstanding legal scholar: the Hanafites after the scholar Abu Hanifa (d. 767), the *Malikites* after Malik ibn Anas (d. 795), the Shafiites after Muhammad ibn Idris al-Shafi (d. 820), and the Hanbalites after their teacher, Ahmad ibn Hanbal (d. 855). The Shiites (*Shia*) follow their own Jafarite law school (named after Imam Jafar al-Sadiq, d. 765). Each individual *Muslim* is in theory free to choose one of these law schools.

Lazo (Sp., Engl.: bow, knot) A star-shaped, interlaced pattern used in mosaics in Spanish architectural decoration. In the ceramic decoration of the Alhambra, star-shaped, interlaced patterns are composed of many individual parts, with the white strips of the star pattern requiring the greatest possible precision from the tile manufacturer, due to their overlaps. The areas lying between the star-shaped, interlaced pattern are filled with multicolored elements. Since the 15th century this extremely time-consuming technique has been replaced by tiles (*azulejos*) made using the *cuerda seca* process.

Levant (L., Ital. from levarsi, Engl.: to stand up, rise [sun]) Countries in the eastern part of the Mediterranean (Turkey, Syria, Lebanon, Israel, Egypt, Cyprus). As a passageway for the main trading routes, the Levant was a fiercely contested area. During the Crusades, Crusader nation states were established in parts of the territory, which were only able to withstand the superior strength of the *Muslims* (Mamluks, Ayyubids, and others) for a few years. The last areas of occupation were Antioch, which survived until 1268, Tarabulus (Lebanon) until 1289, and Acre, which fell in 1291.

Liturgical system (Gr.) In the liturgical system, craftsmen and builders had, since early oriental times and then also in Islamic times, been summoned to complete great building works in individual provinces or towns. For each building assignment specialists were called in for their particular construction or decorative skills (*stucco, mosaic*, vaulting, etc.). The development of the great residential towns (Samarra, Damascus, Baghdad, Cordoba, Cairo), in particular, required teams of craftsmen.

Loggia (Ital.) An open vestibule on the ground floor of a building or a room on an upper story open on one or more sides. It is not attached to the building like a balcony, but incorporated in the structure itself. There also exists a free standing loggia or arcade in which the structure is open on three sides and covered by a multiyoke *vault*.

Lunette (Fr.: lunette, Engl.: little moon) A semicircular panel above doors or windows, usually with a pictorial decoration.

Luster A technique developed in the 7–8th centuries for glass decoration in Iraq and Egypt. In the 9th century it was adopted for use on ceramics in Mesopotamia. Luster is made from metal alloys that are applied as *on-glaze* colors at a low temperature to ceramics that have already been fired in a reducing atmosphere. The paint is fixed during a second low-temperature firing (600–900°C). Copper, gold, silver, and platinum are the color components, which are pulverized, mixed with various additives, and fired for three days. Luster ceramics are characterized by their iridescent surface. They were created throughout the Islamic world in all periods. They reached their zenith in the 9–10th centuries in Mesopotamia, the 9–11th centuries in Egypt, and the 12–14th centuries in Iran, as well as the 13–17th centuries in Spain.

M

Madhab (pl. madhabib) (*Law schools*)

Madrasa (Turk., Ar.: madrasa, Engl.: a place of reading, learning) The madrasa is a public school for teaching the doctrine of the *Koran* and Islamic law. However, mathematics, medicine, literature and language were also taught as part of a four-year course. The madrasas were initially attached to *mosques*; from the 11th century, an arrangement developed in Iran that enabled teachers and pupils to live and work together. They frequently enabled orthodox dogma to be promoted. The founder of this school system was the Seljuk vizier Nizam al-Mulk (1018–1092).

Maghribi Form of Kufic script (*calligraphy*) developed in western Islamic countries.

Mahdi (Ar., Engl.: "divinely guided one") Originally an honorable epithet for Abraham or Muhammad, for example. In the eschatological sense, this term is mainly used among Shiites (*Shia*), for whom the figure of the mahdi is a fundamental element of their faith. They identify the mahdi with the lost *imam*, who will rule by divine prescription and free mankind from wrongdoing and sin. The longing for a mahdi as a savior in times of need was particularly strong in times of political, social and economic strife and regularly produced mahdis who surrounded themselves with supporters and opposed the existing order. Such expectations are most sharply characterized in popular belief.

Maidan (Ar., Pers.: maidan, Engl.: square) An open area without buildings (usually in a town center) that served as a congregating point. Squares could be used for cultural, legal, and sporting (*hippodrome*) events.

Malikites (*Law schools*)

Maqsura (Ar.) A prayer room in Friday *mosques* separated off by a wooden partition and intended for the ruler or his governor. It isolated the ruler from the community and ensured his safety.

Marabout (Ar.: murabit, Engl.: inhabitant of a cloister) In North Africa this term originally referred to a pious *Muslim* who combined the exercise of religious duties with the observance of military functions in a cloister-like settlement (*ribat*). From these marabouts came the Almoravids, a Berber dynasty (1061–1147) that formally acknowledged the Abbasid rule of Baghdad. Local healers and mystics are still called marabouts in North and elsewhere in Africa today.

Masjid (*Mosque*)

Medallion (Fr.: médaillon) A picture or relief (raised, three-dimensional presentation on a flat surface) in a round or elliptical frame.

Medina (Ar., Engl.: town) The word medina designates whole towns or parts of towns and is incorporated in castle names, since as self-contained buildings castles had the character of a town.

Mescit (*Mosque*)

Mexuar (Sp., Ar.: meshwar) In the original sense, a conference room. In palaces, the mexuar was the room in which law was discussed in public on several days of the week.

Midha (Ar.) Ritual cleansing bath.

Mihrab (Ar.) A niche in the wall of the *mosque* oriented towards Mecca to indicate the direction of prayer (*qibla*). The first niche-shaped mihrab is said to have been in the mosque at Medina, dating back to 705/706. The prayer niche was regarded as a sacred symbol. In many mosques there are several mihrab niches in the *qibla* wall, which were often donated. The mihrab comes in different shapes: semicircular, polygonal, rectangular. It was often richly finished using a vast array of decorative techniques (*tile mosaic*, *mosaic*, marble, decorated columns, *stucco ornamentation*).

Minai (Pers.: mina, Engl.: *enamel*) A type of Persian ceramic produced in the late 12th and 13th centuries. The pieces were usually coated with a light-colored, almost white glaze. Details of the highly colorful painting were then applied in blue and green using the *in-glaze* technique, before the piece was fired at a high temperature. The painting was then supplemented by *on-glaze* painting, producing a very colorful decoration almost reminiscent of book illumination (*miniature*). The motifs in

Column capitals in Mudejar style in the church of Santa María la Blanca in Toledo

this case were sometimes applied so symmetrically around the axis that the luxurious fabrics of the time would also have served as a model. The ceramics were fired for a second time at a very low temperature to fix the colored painting.

Minaret (from Ar.: manara, Engl.: "place of fire or light") A tower-shaped structure belonging to the Friday *mosque*, used to give the call to prayer. In Arab territory, the idea for such a place probably arose from the house of Muhammad in Medina in 624, where there was a raised area for the call to prayer. It is thought that the design partly developed in western Mediterranean lands from the lighthouses of Greek and Roman times. But the reinforced square towers of the Umayyad Mosque at Medina are also believed to have provided a model. Apart from the odd exception, minarets stand right next to mosques or are part of the structures themselves.

Minaret crown A rod-shaped or concave crown affixed to the roof or top of the minaret.

Minbar (or mimbar, Ar., Engl.: armchair, seat, throne) A pulpit reached via a stepped substructure in Friday mosques, usually to the right of the *mihrab*. Originally the *caliph's* seat as a ruler or judge,or that of their representative, during Friday prayer, the khutba.

Miniature (Lat.: minium, Engl.: minium or cinnabar painting) In the original meaning, a small, figural composition in manuscripts, which was added to the page of a book or inserted in the text as an individual illustration. However, the term can also be used for compositions on the surface of applied art (metal, glass, ivory, ceramics). Although figural miniature painting has been well rooted in the Islamic world since the 11th century, fragments of the *Koran* with architectural illustrations to be found today in Sanaa in Yemen prove that representational book illustrations, although without figures, had been created at least as far back as the early 8th century. As a consequence, illustrated manuscripts emerged in all centers of the Islamic world. The themes related both to religion and court life, even reflecting everyday life in some cases.

Moiré (Ital., Fr.) Changing (rippling) effects in fabric and paper decoration.

Moors (Sp.: moriscos) The Muslims in Spain forcibly converted to Christianity after 1492 who, although baptized as Christians, still usually observed their *Muslim* beliefs in secret. At the start of the 17th century they were finally expelled from Spain – mostly to North Africa, but also to the Ottoman Empire and France.

Mosaic (origin of the word unclear; possibly Ar.: muzauwaq, Engl.: decorated, or Gr.: mousika, Engl.: art, or museion, Engl.: dedicated to the Muses) Pictures or patterns (scenic or ornamental) composed of colorful elements of stone, marble, glass, or glazed, fired clay, set in a bed of wet mortar. Mosaics could be used to decorate floors, walls, *vaults*, and *domes*. The basic idea of decorating surfaces by cementing together colorful elements was one that actually emerged very early. The Roman and Byzantine period is regarded as marking the zenith of mosaic art. It was very highly valued in the Islamic world, to the extent that artists from the Byzantine Empire were repeatedly commissioned to produce mosaics.

Mosque (Ar.: masjid, Turk.: cami, Engl.: "place of prostration") The general term masjid refers to mosques that could be used every day. The particularly important Friday (or congregational) mosques, where the communal Friday worship is held, are called masjid-i jami or -i juma. Even before the mosques were built, following the death of the Prophet in 632, there was already a place where the religious community attached to Muhammad could congregate. The meaning of the word masjid as a place where one prostrates oneself in prayer leaves worshippers free to choose where they pray and is not linked to any particular building; even the *Koran* leaves no instructions on any given form of place for praying. Muhammad's house in Medina became the starting point for the development of the Arab courtyard mosque. This house resembled in design houses from the Arabian Peninsula, with an open, rectangular, walled courtyard within a square ground plan. The courtyard mosque that grew from this included some elements of the original type. In front of the *qibla* wall, indicating the direction of prayer, a prayer hall (haram) was built with many pillars (*hypostyle*) and aisles. In front of this there was an open area (sahn) surrounded by *riwaqs*. Each mosque was supplemented by one or several *minarets*.

Mosque hanging lamp Lamps made from glass, ceramic, or metal that were used to illuminate *mosques* and in many instances were hung in large numbers just in front of the *qibla* wall. The most famous examples were created in Mamluk Egypt in the 13th and 14th centuries; the enameling techniques used and quality of the inscriptions make them some of the most outstanding Islamic objects. They were frequently imitated in Venice in the 15th century and Europe in the 19th century.

Mozarab (deriv. from Ar.: mustarib, Engl.: "would-be Arab") Christians of Roman-Visigothic origin in medieval Spain, who after the Arab conquest in 711 lived under Islamic rule and enjoyed *dhimmi* status.

Mudejars (Sp., Ar.: mudajjan, Engl.: tamed, domesticated) The term used for *Muslims* who, following the reconquest of the Iberian Peninsula by the Christians, were allowed to remain in Spain in return for payment of a tribute.

Muezzin (Ar.: muadhdhin) The prayer caller who summons believers to prayer from the *minaret* of the *mosque* before the five daily acts of worship.

Muhaqqaq (*Calligraphy*, 4.)

Muharram (Ar.) The first month of the Muslim calendar. For Shiites (*Shia*), this is a month of mourning, during which commemorations are held for Husain, one of the two sons of Ali. The first nine days are devoted to contemplating the suffering of Husain and his companions at Karbala, on the 10th his death in battle against Yazid I, the son of Muawiya, is commemorated, and on the 13th his burial. The 10th day of Muharram is the most important day of mourning for Shiites and is marked each year by passion plays and pilgrimages.

Mulai (Ar., Engl.: Sir) A customary title of honor in different parts of the *Muslim* world. In the Maghreb and Andalusia, it is principally used for saints and Sufis (*Sufism*), as well as dynasties who are able to trace back their genealogy to the Prophet Muhammad.

Mullah (Pers., from Ar.: maula, Engl.: master, gentleman) Since the time of the Safavids (1145–1722), a title used for a religious scholar in Iran.

Multicentered arch (*Arch*, 5.)

Muqarnas (Ar.) The graduated division of a *squinch* into a number of niches/miniature squinches, producing a sort of cellular structure. The muqarnas decoration can have a vast array of geometrical divisions and can assume various three-dimensional decorative forms. The muqarnas *vault* is purely decorative and has no load-bearing function. A subgroup of the muqarnas vault is the stalactite *vault*, which gives the impression of stalactite ornamentation because here muqarnas forms are shaped into freely hanging, icicle-like structures made from *stucco* or stone. Muqarnas ornamentation was freely used in architecture, on *domes*, entrance portals, niches, capitals, and decorative surfaces, but also in art and crafts, employing a vast array of materials.

Musalla (Ar., Pers.: namaz-gah) An enclosed area with a *qibla* wall, where large groups of worshippers can pray, usually outside settlements.

Muslim (Ar., of Islam, Engl.: devotion to God) Anyone who devotes himself or herself to God is a Muslim. The acceptance of Islam is completed with the profession of the faith (shahada). The shahada is the first of the Five Pillars of Islam – then worship (salat), alms-giving (zakat), fasting (saum), and pilgrimage to Mecca (hajj).

Mutazilites (Ar., from itazala, Engl.: to separate, isolate oneself) Founders and followers of speculative dogmatism in Islam, which had its apogee in the 9th century. They believed that religious dogma was to be understood, explained, and justified by means of rational argument – unlike the doctrine of traditional followers, for which it was only the wording of the revelation and not the basic reason that was crucial. At the center of the Mutazilite doctrine was the strictly monotheistic declaration of the unity of God and, associated with this, the rejection of any anthropomorphic description of God, faith in his justice, the doctrine of creation of the Koran, man's freedom of will, and the rejection of all doctrines of predestination.

Muwallad (Ar., Engl.: born) In Muslim Spain, the children of Christians of Spanish origin whose parents were converted to Islam.

N

Naqshbandi order A Sufi order (Sufism) dating back to Baha al-Din Naqshband (d. 1389) and disseminated from China through Turkestan and into Turkey.

Naskhi (Calligraphy)

Nastaliq (Calligraphy)

Necropolis (Gr.) A large area of graves or mausoleums. Despite Islam's original rejection of the cult of the dead and elaborate architectural design of graves, saints' tombs date from as early as the 7th century A.D. The building of tombs became an established ritual in the Islamic world by the 12th century. Vast necropolises grew up, often close to cities. As the cities expanded, these then became graveyards for that city zone. The best-known Islamic necropolises contain the graves of the Mamluk rulers of the 14–16th centuries.

Niello (L. nigellus, Engl. blackish) A decoration is etched onto a metal plate (e.g. silver, brass), which is filled with a mixture of lead, borax, copper, sulfur and silver. The work is then polished. This is a technique that has been utilized since ancient times. In Islamic art it is primarily used to supplement metalwork decoration.

Nimbus A disk-shaped background or halo surrounding the head of individuals in painting or sculpture. Nimbi are often also referred to as haloes because the nimbus developed in early Christian art from the 4th century in the depiction of Christ. In Islamic art, nimbi were absorbed into Arabic book illumination from Byzantine art and possibly also from Buddhist examples from Central Asia in the late 12th century. They were used in the same period in a wide variety of areas in the Islamic world in illustrations of people on objects from every field of art and crafts. The function of the nimbus, therefore, was always to emphasize the head (also animal heads), without this having any religious significance.

Nisba An element of oriental names that either indicates the place of origin of the artist or his family or the artistic genre or role of the artist in the production of works of art. The nisba provides important information on the production of applied art based on the division of labor, since the details given are in some cases precise occupational titles.

O

Ogee An S-shaped, three-dimensional decorative form, consisting of a concave and a convex section. Ogees are usually integral parts of cornices.

Ogee arch (Arch, 3.)

Ogee arch niche A wall niche sunk into the wall beneath an ogee arch (Arch, 3.).

On-glaze decoration Paint is applied to a fired glaze and then refired at a low temperature.

Ornament A form of surface decoration. The ornament may be nonrepresentational, vegetal, figural, or calligraphic (calligraphy). Ornaments are incorporated into a decoration that systematizes and classifies the area to be embellished. All forms of ornament occur in Islamic art, with the calligraphic form clearly predominating and figural forms being of less importance.

P

Palmette (L., Fr.) An ornamental form made up of palm leaf motifs in a symmetrical configuration. The origins of this motif lie in the Greek art of the archaic period. During Islamic times, unique forms of palmette were created following the Mongol invasion of the 13th century. The

conflict and fusion with Chinese lotus motifs became increasingly important in this form.

Paneling A wooden wall lining made up of several sheets.

Panneau (deriv. from Fr.) A wooden panel or a board made from another material for painting with epigraphic, geometric, figural, or floral decorations.

Papyrus (Gr.) The stem pulp of a plant growing in the Nile delta was used to produce a writing material for documenting speeches made by the Egyptian rulers. Strips of the plant were placed in layers running crosswise on top of one another and then pressed together. The resulting surface was finally polished. Papyrus is yellow-white in color. The resulting material was sometimes dyed for particularly precious manuscripts and rolls of parchment. Papyrus was increasingly replaced by paper from late ancient times on.

Parachute (or umbrella) dome (Dome, 3.)

Parrying stick The parrying stick on the sword was used to guarantee absolute obedience from horses.

Pasha (Pers., probably from padishah, Engl.: great ruler) The title given to a senior Ottoman dignitary. Only under the Turkish Republic was it replaced by the rank of general.

Paten (Lat.: patina, Engl.: bowl) A shallow, formerly large, dish on which the Host is presented at Mass. During the service, the large patens were placed on the wine chalice until the offertory (distribution of the Host). Today, small dishes are more common. In the Middle Ages patens were made of metal (usually gold or gold-plated silver, with precious stones and ornaments) and richly decorated.

Patio (Sp., Engl.: inner courtyard) An inner courtyard open to the sky representing an important element of Spanish and Spanish-American architecture. Such courtyards are to be found both in house and palace architecture. The atrium of private houses in Roman times had the same function as the patio in Spanish architecture, because here, too, the different living areas are assembled around the courtyard.

Pendentive A spherical triangle (corner spandrel) that links the quadratic structure below and the round shape of the dome.

Peony (Gr.) The peony was taken up as a motif in Chinese art of the 6th century, although it experienced its zenith in terms of representational quality and quantity in the 14th century with the decoration of Chinese porcelain. Chinese decorative motifs like the peony or lotus have been used in the art of Islamic countries since the late 15th century. Sometimes used very freely and in stylized form, these motifs have therefore found constant applications. The peony may occur as an individual motif or rows of peonies may also be used to create strips in which the flowers are connected at the pedicels to create waves of tendrils or circular forms.

Pier hall (Hypostyle, Mosque)

Pilaster (L., Ital.: pila) Pillar engaged in the wall or a pillar-like projecting strip on the wall with the outline contour of a pillar. The pilaster has a supporting function: it strengthens and divides the wall, supporting the timberwork, i.e. the area between the wall or column and the roof.

Pishtaq (Pers.) Monumental main entrance of castle or mosque. Such portals are characterized by a high arch in front of an iwan.

Pitch nose An outlet for hot pitch or oil in castle walls, mostly on the projecting battlements. Oriel-like forms are also known.

Pointed arch (Arch, 4.)

Polychrome (Gr.: polychromia) This term is still used in art today to denote the use of many colors, as opposed to monochromy or the use of a single color. It can be applied to works of every artistic genre.

Porphyry (Gr.: porphyreos) All stones of a vitreous composition with phenocrysts of large crystals. Porphyry was regarded as an imperial material for construction and decoration and was used both in the ancient world and during the Byzantine period as a material for making human busts, sarcophagi, and architectural parts. A shiny finish could be achieved by polishing the porphyry. Spoils (e.g. columns) made from this were reused in the Islamic architecture of the Mediterranean region.

Portico (Lat.: porticus, Engl.: porch) A covered colonnade forming the entrance to a building. In European architecture the top of the portico is usually finished with a gable.

Pyx (Gr.) A box or tin for the storage of church relics, hosts, perfumes or other precious objects. The materials for pyxes were wood, ivory, or precious metals.

Q

Qalansuwa Pointed head covering for men.

Qibla (Ar.) The direction of prayer, oriented towards Mecca. In the early days of the Islamic faith, followers prayed towards Jerusalem, but in 624

the town of Mecca was proclaimed the direction of prayer, in order to strengthen the new faith. The mihrab is also to be found in the qibla wall of mosques, although this has no special ritual significance other than to indicate the direction of prayer as part of this wall.

Qizilbash (Turk., Engl.: redhead) The Turkoman followers of the Safavid dynasty in Persia (1501–1722), dating back to Safi al-Din Ishak (d. 1334), the leader of a Sufi order (Sufism) in Ardabil. Although the Qizilbash were Ottoman citizens, they did not profess the Sunni (sunna) branch of Islam, but instead supported the Shiite (Shia) Safavids. They were nicknamed "redheads" because of the red caps they wore.

Quraish (Ar.) The name of the Meccan tribe to which the Prophet Muhammad belonged. Under Sunni (sunna) law, all his successors, i.e. the caliphs, also had to be able to trace their genealogy back to the quraish.

R

Rahle (Ar.) A free standing, folding stand made from wood and shaped like a pair of scissors, for holding the Koran or other precious books. These bookstands could be decorated with ivory or metal. The wood could be enriched with carved ornamentation.

Rajah (Sans., Engl.: king, prince) The title given to Indian Hindu princes prior to Indian independence.

Rajputs (Sans.) Members of a warring caste that originated in northern India, later spreading throughout northern India and Nepal. In the 10th century Rajput princes established a number of kingdoms, which dictated the history and culture of northern India. During the zenith of the Mughal empires (1715–1707), they remained largely faithful to the Mughal rulers and served as generals and provincial governors.

Rayhani (Calligraphy)

Reconquista (Sp.) The Christian reconquest of the Iberian Peninsula from the Arabs, who had occupied it since 711. This ended in 1492 with the fall of Granada to Isabella I of Castile and Ferdinand II of Aragon.

Repoussoir (Fr., Engl.: contrast) A dark motif placed in the foreground of paintings to reinforce the impression of depth in the picture.

Ribat (Ar.) Fortified monastery-like building located close to the frontiers of the Islamic world. It was from these foundations that the holy war was launched. In this respect, they provided soldiers with the opportunity of exercising their religion and undertaking religious mediation.

Ribbed dome (Dome, 1.)

Ribbing Facade design in central and eastern Iranian architecture. Half-columns or half-cylinders were placed close together on the facade, highlighting the well-fortified nature of the building and lessening the impact of battering rams in the event of attack. However, ribbing was also used for decorative effect on facades, as its depth created special light and shade effects. Ribbed facades have been used in Central Asia since 200 B.C. Ribbing was also used on domes and minarets.

Riwaq (Ar.) Arcades on four sides of the courtyard (sahn) in Arabic courtyard mosques. There is often a main riwaq that is particularly accentuated as the entrance to the actual prayer hall in front of the mihrab.

Rococo (Fr., from rocaille, Engl.: rock work, shell work) A style of European art from the 18th century, in which the characteristic decorative forms are profusely elaborate, asymmetrical and rich. The main decorative colors are gold, a mat light blue, and pale pink.

Round arch (Arch, 1.)

S

Safavid order A Sufi order (Sufism) dating back to Safi al-Din Ishak (1252–1334), mainly popular among Turkoman tribes living in Azerbaijan, eastern Anatolia, and Syria. This grew into the Persian ruling dynasty of the Safavids (1501–1722), after Ismail (d. 1524), the then master of the order, became Shah of Persia in 1501.

Salafis (Ar. from salaf, Engl.: move forward, presage) Members of the Islamic reform movement of the 18th and 19th centuries, which propagated a return to the pure origins of Islam and the traditions and principles of the forefathers (salaf), in order to renew or "purify" religion, state, and society by having direct recourse to the authoritative sources – the Koran and the sunna. The veneration of saints, mystical practices, and belief in miracles and magic were regarded as corruptive influences and inadmissible innovations. Among the best-known representatives of the Salafis were Jamal al-Din al-Afghani (1839–1897) of Persia and the Egyptian religious scholar Muhammad Abduh (1849–1905).

Salsabil (Ar.: sabil, Engl.: path, road, way; and selsal, Engl.: cool, precious; Engl: drinking fountain) In terraced gardens, marble slabs into which abstract, stepped patterns are carved and across which water flows. The

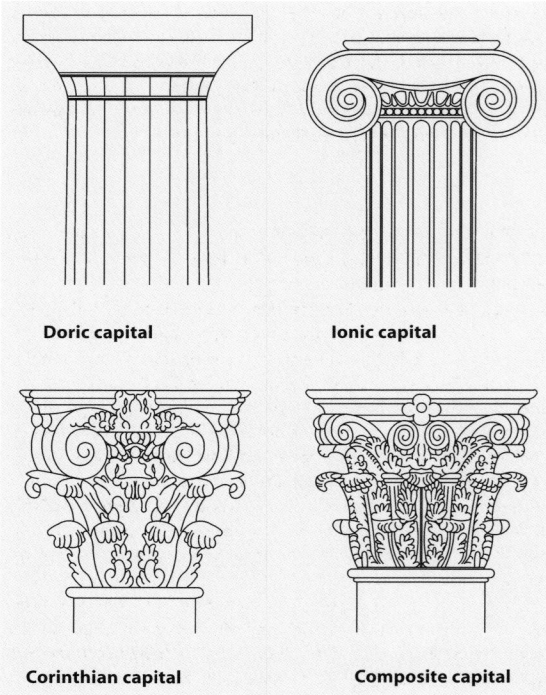

Doric capital   Ionic capital

Corinthian capital   Composite capital

solidity of the decoration made the water move more vigorously, producing a pleasant murmuring and babbling. In Turkish the word is generally used for public fountains. In Islamic mythology, salsabil is the name given to one of the rivers in Paradise (Koran 76. 18).

Sarai (Ar., Turk.: saray, Engl.: seraglio, palace) A palace building in the Islamic world, later used to refer to the women's apartments within the palace.

Sayid (Ar., Engl.: Lord) An honorary title for the descendants of the Prophet Muhammad, more narrowly defined as the Hasanids and Husainids, the descendants of the two sons of Ali and Fatima. But the title was and is also bestowed upon Sufi authorities (*Sufism*), saints, and notable theologians.

Sculpture The art form resulting in the creation of three dimensional images. As well as depicting a figure or object, a sculpture may also be non-representational, translating abstract shapes into three dimensional form. Sculptures do not always reproduce the entire body of the object being depicted. In the case of figural representations, a distinction is therefore made between full or free sculpture, semi-sculpture and relief. Any free standing sculpture is a full sculpture. A relief or semi-sculpture provides only a view of a body or object and is flatter. Although the front of the body or object need not necessarily be the subject matter, the parts shown are completely sculpted. Semi-sculptures are connected to a base area or a column, from which they actually appear to grow. Despite the problematic relationship with depiction of images, all types of sculptures exist in the Islamic world. Within palace architecture, free sculptures have survived from the early Islamic period along with a wide variety of semi-sculptures. Seljuk palaces also had a wealth of figural ornamentation. If the sculptural depiction remains connected to the wall, it can no longer be regarded as an independent being, due to the body's dependence on the ground. It therefore conforms to Islamic dogma, according to which man may not create a living being, as this is the preserve of Allah. After a long period during which no sculptures were created, the Islamic rulers who, from the early 19th century, had been subject to European influence, , began to commission free standing sculptures as a symbol of their power.

Sebka (Ar.) Ornamental surfaces composed of adjacent rhombuses and used to decorate Spanish architecture.

Shabrack A saddlecloth used on horses or also a magnificently decorated cover for horses, illustrated particularly widely in Ottoman and Indian art. The horses adorned in this way are very accurately depicted in the miniature paintings of the 16–19th centuries, thereby providing an impressive record of the splendor of the armies.

Shadirwan (Pers.: sardi, Engl.: coolness, freshness, and wand, Engl.: vessel, dish) A fountain or well in a *mosque* courtyard or the main room of a palace or villa.

Shah (Pers.: shah, Engl.: king) The ancient Persian title of king, already used by Achaemenid and Sassanid rulers.

Shahname (Pers., Engl.: king's book, literally: *shah* letter/document) An epic poem by the Persian Abu i-Qasim Firdausi. In his work, which was written c. A.D. 1000 in Ghazna at the court of the Ghaznavid ruler Mahmud (998–1013), the poet relates the lifetimes and deeds of the Persian rulers of mythological and historical times in an often glorifying or romantically transfigured style. The Shahname is of outstanding significance above all as an historical literary monument to the Modern Persian language. The work was based on old written sources, some of which, however, were only passed down by word of mouth even at that time. Since the 12th century motifs from the epic cycle have been used to decorate Persian ceramics and since the 14th century precious Shahname manuscripts have been created containing numerous *miniatures*, which have become the embodiment of Persian court art. The most precious manuscripts were created during the time of the Safavids. Metalwork, fabrics, carpets, and even architectural decoration also constantly refer to the epic.

Sharia (Ar., Engl.: clear path) The totality of the Islamic legal and moral order, which is based on the prescriptions of the *Koran* and the *sunna*, and is not uniformly codified. It guides and determines all aspects and areas of the lives of *Muslims* – from individual religious acts, through hygiene and family life, to the structure of the state and society. The sharia is regarded as divine law and is therefore untouchable and incontrovertible in its basic tenets, unlike human legislation (fiqh).

Sharif (Ar., Engl.: noble, majestic) In pre-Islamic times, a term used to denote those of noble descent and distinguished character. In Islam, sharif became a title of honor for a man able to trace his genealogy back to Muhammad and his family (ahl al-bait).

Sherefe (Ar.) A balcony on the *minaret* used for the call to prayer. A striking structural feature, particularly in Ottoman architecture, when sherefes were attached to many *minarets* on several levels.

Shia (Ar., Engl.: party) The party of Ali, Muhammad's cousin and son-in-law. Its supporters, the Shiites, narrowed down the Prophet's successors to chosen descendants of Ali as a member of Muhammad's family (ahl al-bait). Following the series of recognized *imams*, the last of whom retreated into "occultation" (ghalba), but remains present on earth, a distinction is made between the Fiver Shia (Zaydites), the Sevener Shia (Ismailis), and the *Twelver Shia* (Imamites).

Simat A covered street with shops on it.

Snipe A species of bird found mainly in the woods and marshlands of Europe and Asia and in North and South America. Among princes of the Islamic world, all types of hunting were regarded not only as a welcome distraction, but also as proof of their strength. This ideal was a hangover from old oriental times. In around 1000 A.D. Firdausi described hunting in his *King's Book* (*Shahname*) as a princely virtue. Snipe, like quail, were regarded as a real delicacy.

Souk (Ar.) Market (bazaar) The word souk can also be an element of the names of towns and cities.

Spandrel In architecture, the spandrel generally denotes the triangular surfaces at the side of an *arch*. In arcades the area between two arches is also called the spandrel. Suspended spandrels are partial vaults that lead to the *dome*.

Spoils (Lat.: spolia, Engl.: weapons or booty taken from the enemy) Recycled structural elements, such as columns, capitals, *arches*, and also stones. The use of spoils had a variety of motives. Spoils were firstly used due to a shortage of building materials and, secondly, reusing parts of buildings in conquered regions was an expression of victory (e.g. the use of what had previously been religiously significant stones as doorsteps).

Springing The stone course between the wall, pier or column, and *arch* or *vault*, which is frequently accentuated by the profiled, projecting springing plate.

Springing cornice A *cornice* finishing the springing (abutment of an *arch* or *vault*).

Squinch An *arch* with niches built over the corners of a square base to transform it into an octagon, so that the transition can be made to the round *dome*.

Stalactite A cone-shaped keystone in open roof timbering or at the intersection of timber ceilings. In Islamic architecture an element of the *muqarnas vault*.

Stalactite arch (*Arch*, 6.)

Stalactite vault (*Muqarnas*)

Stucco A material made of gypsum, lime, sand, and water used while still wet for architectural decoration. Stucco dries very quickly in the sun, but is not waterproof. It could either be applied straight onto the building or used in prefabricated *panels*, which were then fixed to the building. The

ornamentation was carved into the wet plaster (chip-carving technique). Stucco could even be used to make three-dimensional figures by pouring it into a mold.

Sublime Porte Originally the residence of the grand vizier of the Ottoman Empire. The term was later generally used as a synonym for the Ottoman government.

Sufism (Ar. tasawwuf, from suf, Engl.: woolen garment) Islamic mysticism dating back to the 7–8th century that seeks a spiritual path to God. Although the overwhelming majority of the mystics (Sufis) recognize the *sharia* and the Five Pillars of Islam, they regard inner purification, the means to inner knowledge (marifa), as more important than the observance of "external" commandments.

Sultan (Ar., Engl.: authority, government) An Islamic title of authority, which as early as the 10th century was the customary form of address for independent rulers who were no longer under the central control of the *caliph*. This title was not officially recognized until the 11th century, when it was adopted by the Turkish dynasty of the Seljuks, in order to emphasize their claim to universal dominion. All the Ottoman rulers were also called sultans.

Sunna (Ar., Engl.: custom, code of behavior) The practice, i.e., the actions and messages of the Prophet, as passed down in the *Hadiths*. According to the *Koran*, the sunna are the second source of Islamic law. Sunnis, i.e., "people of the Prophet's tradition and the community" (ahl al-sunna wa l-jamaa), is the name given to the majority of *Muslims* who first formed the mainstream of Islam in around 800 in opposition to the Kharijites (*Kharijism*) and Shiites (*Shia*). They limit the *caliphate* to qualified members of the *quraish*, but place the main emphasis not so much on selecting the correct *imam* as on the unity of society.

Sura (*Koran*).

T

Talar (Pers., Engl.: hall, reception room) A hall constructed with columns and open on four sides, which may also be located in front of a reception room. This architectural design used in palace architecture has its origins in Persian or Near Eastern house construction.

Tambour The drum-shaped base of a *dome*.

Tanzimat (Ar., Engl.: orders, reforms) The Ottoman reforms of the 19th century, the main aims of which were administrative centralization and efficiency. Through the selective adoption of European principles and knowledge, the army, administration, law, and education were to be reformed. The high point of the Tanzimat was marked by the two edicts of 1839 and 1856 and the introduction of a constitution in 1876.

Taziya (Ar., Engl.: consolation) A theater genre of the Shiite (*Shia*) religious community. It relates to the massacre of Karbala in 680, when Husain (Muhammad's son-in-law) and other relatives of the Prophet were rescued by Umayyad soldiers. Since the 16th century, there has

Squinch dome with *muqarnas stucco*

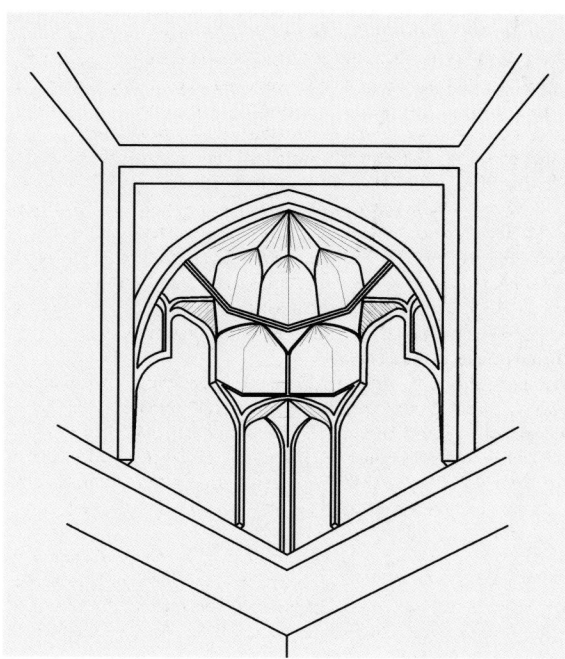

Multicentered arches in the Alcazar in Saragossa

been public mourning in Iran, Afghanistan, and India during the month of *Muharram*. The processions, often stretching for miles, influenced different artistic genres (fabrics, jewelry, painting, music, and the cinema).

Tectonic (Gr.) This term actually pertains to the study of the structure and movement of the earth's crust. In its figurative sense, the word is used in the structural analysis of works of art, particularly architecture. In this case it relates to the construction of non-moving individual parts to produce a complete work. In the same sense, the word is also used in applied art to the assembly of works of art.

Tempera painting (Ital.: temperare, Engl.: to mix) Use of paints that are mixed with water but are not water-soluble, due to the binding agents added (oil, egg, honey, glue). Using egg yolk to bind the pigments produces particularly lustrous color effects. Egg tempera can also be used on smooth bases.

Theocracy (Gr.: theokratia) A form of government in which religion or the church set the standards for social order. The ruler in this case is regarded as God or God's representative.

Thuluth (*Calligraphy*, 2.)

Tile mosaic The most sumptuous building decoration of the Islamic Middle Ages, consisting of geometric, floral, and *calligraphic* patterns assembled as a *mosaic* from multicolored ceramic elements. Internal and external walls were decorated with ceramics using this technique. Fired, color-glazed tiles are worked in, based on the predefined pattern of the area to be decorated. To prepare the wall or *dome*, the glazed decorative parts are laid in a bed of mortar and, once this has dried, the panels containing the mosaic elements, with the glazed surface outermost, are placed on the wall.

Tiraz (Pers.: tarazidan, Engl.: to embroider) An embroidered decorative band on fabrics up to a yard wide, but usually narrow strips that can be found at upper arm level on special robes; since the 8th century, the name of the *caliph* or prince who donated the memorial garments would be indicated in the decoration. However, texts from the *Koran* could also be used. In countries of the Islamic world, tiraz production was regulated by the court and was often centered on workshops within the prince's court. Since several thousands of garments were being repeatedly given away, a regular court tiraz industry developed.

Transept (Fr.) In architecture, the main aisle intersecting the multiplicity of smaller aisles. In Christian churches, the transverse aisle between the nave and the choir. In Islamic mosque architecture, transverse aisles are particularly common in North African *mosques*, which follow the *T-shaped scheme*. Here, the transept is immediately in front of the *qibla* wall, running at right angles to the aisles leading up to the wall. In the Great Mosque at Damascus, by contrast, the transept aisle is the center aisle leading to the *qibla* wall, since the other three aisles in the prayer hall run parallel to the *qibla* wall.

T-shaped scheme/layout The emphasis placed on the depth axis of the prayer hall leading up to the *mihrab*, particularly in Syrian, North African, and Spanish *mosque* architecture. A *transept* running parallel to the *qibla* wall and a center aisle running perpendicular to this create a T, in which the center aisle is higher than the other aisles and often accentuated by additional *domes* and decoration, with the *mihrab* being especially emphasized.

Tughra (Turk.) An artistic signature indicating the name of the ruling Ottoman *sultan*. The name was accompanied by a victory phrase. This rich, personal seal was used to certify state documents. It followed the style of Nakkaskhanid (*karkhana*) models. The *calligraphy* is enriched with intertwined, vegetal motifs.

Turbe (Turk., Ar.: turba, Engl.: dust) A Turkish grave or mausoleum. The turbe is usually part of a religious foundation. The founder of the building complex and members of his direct family would be buried in it.

Turkish triangle Folded, projecting, and receding triangles in diamond cut form at the transition from the square base to the *dome* (only found in early Ottoman architecture).

Twelver Shia The Twelver Shiites, or Imamites, are the most important branch of the *Shia*. They revere a series of twelve *imams*, of whom the last, Muhammad al-Mahdi, disappeared and, it is believed, will return at the end of time, to proclaim the Last Judgment and establish a kingdom of justice on earth. Twelver Shia doctrine is the state religion in Iran.

Tympanum (Gr., Engl.: drumskin, kettledrum) The segmental space above a portal or on a gable.

U

Ulama (Ar. pl., sing. alim, Engl.: sages, scholars) Religious and legal scholars within whose circles Islamic knowledge and faith are preserved. Their knowledge of traditions makes them responsible for guaranteeing the observance and application of religious principles, thereby embodying the consent of the *Muslim* community – irrespective of the current ruler.

Umbrella leaf A leaf whose outer contour is the shape of an open umbrella. The leaf dates back to the ancient Egyptian motif repertoire of the papyrus. The motif occurs in Islamic art only in Egyptian carpet design of the Mamluk era, thereby indicating here too the continued existence of pre-Islamic decorative ornaments in a narrow local environment.

Umma (Heb./Aram., Koranic, Engl.: people, community) The term umma dates back to the "municipal code" of Medina (623), which under the leadership of Muhammad brought together both *Muslims* and Jewish tribes and clans to create a political association for protection and solidarity. With the Prophet's break from Judaism and Christianity and the military successes of the Muslims, however, the umma became a community exclusively for (Muslim) believers, who were bound together by religious ties, recognized God alone as their leader, and subjugated themselves to his laws.

Underglaze painting The painting of a ceramic object on the unfired, unglazed pottery. A colored but transparent glaze is then applied.

V

Valide (Turk., Ar.: walida, Engl.: mother) The mother of the Ottoman *sultan*, who had the highest status in the harem.

Vault An arched ceiling of a room usually composed of wedge-shaped stones or voussoirs. Unlike *domes*, vaults are also built over long rooms. The abutments – walls or piers, for example – support the thrust of the arch. The following are selected forms, paying particular attention to the Islamic world: 1. Barrel (or tunnel) vault: a ceiling with a semicircular or pointed arch section. 2. Cross or groined vault: a cross vault is formed by the intersection of two barrel vaults. The intersecting edges produce groins. 3. Coffered vault: a barrel vault finished at the narrow ends by concave cheeks. 4. *Muqarnas* vault. 5. Stalactite vault. (Muqarnas) 6. Cantilever vault (also: artificial vault): A vault created from courses of projecting stones placed on top of one another, with horizontal joints. The application of a load (building heavy stones on top) prevents the walled structure from collapsing.

Verde antico (It.) A green marble with a vivid color, due to the angular fragments of stone contained in it. Objects made from this material look even more precious when polished.

Vignette (Fr.: vigne, Engl.: vine) A decorative design consisting of vine tendril motifs added to the edge of manuscripts. Generally used in book *illumination* as small, decorative embellishments often also containing figural representations.

Vizier (Ar. from wazara, Engl.: to bear a load) An important administrative title that emerged for the first time in Abbasid times. The vizier was responsible for administering and governing a vast empire. Originally acting as adviser to the *caliph*, he was granted ever-increasing powers as time went by, although these were never uniformly established.

Votive gift (L.) A votive gift is an expression of request or thanks to a revered saint. This ritual is not known in the Islamic world, where saints are not revered in the Christian sense.

W

Wahhabis Supporters of the teachings of Muhammad ibn Adb al-Wahhab (1703–1792), who preached strict monotheism and a return to

the original, unadulterated Islam. All "innovations," which also included numerous practices involved in popular Islam, such as the veneration of saints, were rejected. The teachings spread throughout the Arabian Peninsula. Through his alliance with the Saudi dynasty, Ibn Abd al-Wahhab also came to be regarded as the spiritual father of what was later to become modern-day Saudi Arabia (from 1932).

Y

Yasa (Turk., Engl.: law) The law of Mongol leader Ghenghis Khan (1155–1227), which probably dates back to the start of the 13th century and is a collection of behavioral codes.

Yoke Section within a uniform sequence of vaulted zones or spatial units. Two main beams support the structural section in each case.

Young Turks The collective name given to the opposition movement in the Ottoman Empire, which covered a vast diversity of objectives. It was formed during the second half of the 19th century in opposition to the despotism of Sultan Abdul Hamid II (1876–1909). The Committee of Union and Progress was to emerge as the most important group, which took power in 1908 and forced the sultan to reinstate the 1876 constitution and reopen parliament. However, the era of the Young Turks (1908–1918) ended in a military dictatorship, which pursued a strict policy of Turkism and secularization and was unable to prevent the collapse of the Ottoman Empire (1918).

Yurt (Turk.) A round tent used by the nomads of Central Asia. Yurts are constructed from timber frames covered with felting (koshmas), so that they are habitable even in winter. They could be finely decorated with carpets and works of art. Carpets were used to divide them up into several rooms, as in an ordinary house. Yurts were still used by the Turkish peoples of Central Asia into the 20th century.

Z

Zawiya (Ar.: corner) This term was used to denote small *dervish* monasteries. A religious man could live in one and be buried there too. As a result, zawiyas often became memorials or shrines.

Ziggurat (Akkadian: as far as can be determined, a temple tower) A form of ancient oriental tower dating back to around 2050 B.C. It has several levels, ascending in tiers. These structures are cited as a possible early forms of the two spiral-shaped *minarets* of the *mosques* in Samarra from the time of *Caliph* al-Mutawakkil in 847/861. However, due to the great differences both in the formal structure and in the proportions of the individual elements, it is questionable whether the Abbasid spiral minarets were not simply inventions of their own time.

Ziyada (Ar., Engl: an addition) A courtyard between the actual structure of a *mosque* and the outer walls surrounding it.

Turbe of Hasan Padisha, Turkey

Index

Picture credits

The publishers would like to express their thanks to the museums, archives, and photographers for kindly agreeing to allow the reproduction of their works and for their friendly support with the compilation of this book.

The publisher has endeavored to obtain and fulfill the copyright for all the works depicted in the pictures. However, should further claims arise, the individuals concerned are asked to contact the publisher.

(a.=above; b.=below; l.=left; r.=right; c.=center)

© **Aga Khan Trust for Culture**, Geneva: 45 c., 594 a.l.; (photograph: J. Betant) 594 r.; (photograph: A. W. El Wakil) 595 l.; (photograph: G.Tsahson) 593 b.
© **Agence Rapho**, Paris: (photograph: Georg Gerster) 31; (photographs: Roland and Sabrina Michaud) 12 b., 14, 15 a./b.l., 16, 17, 19 r., 21, 22 a.l./a.r./b.l./b.r, 24, 25 l./c., 28l./r., 30, 32 a.l., 39, 40, 44 b., 45 a.r., 46 r./l., 48 b.r./l., 51 r./l., 53 r., 54 b., 55b., 56 l., 57 a.l., 60, 69 l., 82 r., 110, 112, 114, 121 b.r./b.c., 125 a., 132 a., 133 r., 141, 143, 157 c., 176, 188 a.l., 190 c., 208, 245, 258 a./b., 261, 262, 272, 273, 285 l., 286 b., 291 a.r., 294, 298–299, 300, 301 b., 310, 311, 312 r., 313 c./r., 314 l., 330, 331 a./b., 335, 336 a./b., 337 l./r., 338 a./b.l., 339 a./b., 340, 349 a., 368, 369 a.r., 372 a./b., 373 r., 375 r., 386(387, 389 a., 391, 394 a./b.r/l., 395 b., 396 a./b., 409, 414 l., 415 a., 416 r./l., 419, 442 a.r./b., 451 b.l., 455 a., 460 b., 461 b., 462 l., 464 a., 466 r./l., 469, 470 a./b.r., 472, 473 a., 474 b., 475, 478 b., 483 a., 485 c., 486 l., 490 a./b.l., 493 b., 502 c., 503 r., 508, 514, 518 a.l., 534–535, 537 l., 545 l., 551 b., 557 b., 558 a./b., 561 b., 563, 569, 592, 600; (photographs: Christian Sappa) 10, 131
© **Agentur Artur**, Cologne: (photograph: Klaus Frahm) 586 a. r.
© **Agentur Anne Hamann**, Munich: 42 (photograph: Georg Gerster)
© **Agentur Schuster**, Oberursel: (photograph: Yann Arthus Bertrand) 244
© **The Ancient Art and Architecture Collection**, London: 41, 148 a., 157 b.r., 301 a., 308 b., 316 b.
© **Arcaid**, London: (photograph: Nick Meers) 595 r.
© **Archiv für Kunst und Geschichte**, Berlin: 20, 25 r., 27, 91 a., 173 a., 591 a.; (photograph: Werner Forman) 19 l.; (photographs: Jean-Louis Nou) 68 a./b., 221 r., 252 r.
© **Archives Mashreq-Maghreb**, Paris: (photograph: Marianne Barrucand) 146
© **Archivo Oronoz**, Madrid: 206–207, 212, 214 l., 215, 216 a./b., 220, 238 l., 239 a.r./b.r./l., 240 a., 243, 247, 248, 251 a./b., 252 l., 253, 268, 280 r./l., 282, 312 l.
© **The Ashmolean Museum**, Oxford: 200 a.r.
© **Badisches Landesmuseum**, Karlsruhe: 573 b.r.
© **The Baltimore Museum of Art**, Baltimore: (Contribution from Mrs. Alvin Thalheimer for the Fanny Thalheimer Memorial Fund, BMA 1973.14) 590
© **Markus Bassler**, Dosquers: 45 b., 219, 225 a./b., 228 a., 233 a.r./l., 234, 236 a./b., 237 r./l., 264, 266 l., 267 b.
© **Bayerische Staatsbibliothek**, Munich: (signature: 14563 Cod. arab) 270 a., (signature: 14809, Cod. arab 3, fol.34) 322 r., (signature: 14847, Cod. arab. 2603 fol. 1v.) 343 r.
© **Frédérique Beaupertuis-Bressand**, Paris: 362 b., 363 b., 364, 406–407, 418 r./l., 423, 425 a., 445 c., 575 b.
© **Achim Bednorz**, Cologne: 48 a., 209 a./b., 221 l., 223, 227, 228 b.r., 229, 231 a., 233 b., 250 b.r./l., 265, 275, 281, 283 b., 286 a.r./l., 289 a./b.l., 291 a.l., 293 a./b.r., 297 b.
© **Biblioteca Apostolica Vaticana**, Rome: 270 b.
© **Bibliothèque Nationale**, Paris: 53 l., 325 a./b., 327, 342, 351, 402 r., 414 r., 433, 496
© **Bildarchiv Steffens**, Mainz: (photograph: Abdelaziz Frikhar) 8; (photograph: Archeophoto) 457; (photographs: Rudolf Bauer) 167 a.r., 178, 316 a.; (photographs: Heike & Helmut Hahn) 438 b.; (photograph: Werner Heidt) 161 l.; (photographs: Ladislav Janicek) 65, 455 b.l., 564 b.; (photographs: Henri Stierlin) 43, 44 c., 60, 65 a., 81 l., 95, 98, 100, 103 b., 104, 105 b., 111, 124 a., 126, 133 l., 138 b., 147 b., 151, 159, 160 r., 164–165, 378 a., 398 l., 399 a.r./b., 451 b.r., 452(453, 465, 480 l., 494–495, 500, 511, 515 a., 557 a.; (photograph: Günther Wagner) 464 b.
© **Bildarchiv Preußischer Kulturbesitz**, Berlin: 13, 15 b.r., 74 b.r., 121 a.l., 170, 199 r., 202 a., 210, 353 r., 449 b.l., 491 a., 521, 524 r., 544 a., 577; (photographs: Jörg P. Anders) 307 l., 531 b.; (photographs: Katz) 271, 388, 389 b.r./l., 412 r.; (photograph: Hans Kräftner) 47 a.r.; (photographs: J. Liepe) 119 b., 163 a.r./b.l., 200 a.l., 204 b.r., 576 b.; (photographs: G. Niedermeiser) 47 a.l., 74 b.l., 82 a., 107 a.l./a.r/b.r., 123, 154 r., 155 a., 205 a.r., 352, 384, 501, 565 a.r., 573 a./b., 575 a. l., 576 a.l.; (photograph: Obrocki) 434; (photograph: Oeberg) 121 b.l.; (photograph: Gisela Oesterreich) 597 l.; (photograph: Arno Psille) 199 l.; (photograph: R. Saczewski) 531 a.; (photograph: Wolfgang Selbach) 29; (photograph: G. Stenzel) 449 a.
© **Jonathan Bloom**, Richmond, New Hampshire: 125 b., 127 a.l., 255 r., 379, 397
© **Michael Braune**, Hanover: 193
© **The Bridgeman Art Library**, London: (Christie's Images) 276; (Bulloz) 588 b.
© by permission of **The British Library**, London: 50 r., 412 l., 426, 428 l., 429, 484 l., 502 r., 520 l., 524 l.
© **The British Museum**, London: 204 a., 205 b., 484 r., 565 b.
© **Siegfried Büker**, Berlin: 107 b.l., 109, 170 l., 222, 257, 269, 334, 338 b.r., 393 b., 596 r.
© **Cabildo de la Catedral de Girona**, Girona: (photograph: Josep Maria Oliveras) 241 l.
© **Centro de Arte Moderna de Fundacao Calouste** Gulbenkian, Lisbon: 428 r.
© **Sergej Chmelnizkij**, Berlin: 355 a.r/l./b.r./l., 356 a., 357 b.l., 358, 360 a., 361 r., 363 a., 365, 367
© **Christie's Images**, London: 533
© **The Cleveland Museum of Art**, Cleveland: (1999, Purchase from the J. H. Wade Fund, 1989.50) 405
© **Collection Société Générale Marrocaine de Banques**, Casablanca: 597 r.
© **Conjunto Arqueológico Madinat al-Zahra**, Córdoba: (photographs: Manuel Pijuan) 232 r./l.
© **Copyfoto**, Madrid: 211
© **G. Dagli Orti**, Paris: 12 a., 18, 32 b., 54 a., 56 a.r., 57 a.r., 113 r., 188 b.l., 348, 353 l., 376, 499, 515 b., 536, 537 r., 539, 542, 543 r./c./l., 561 a., 567, 576 a.r., 580
© **The David Collection**, Copenhagen: (photographs: Ole Woldbye) 122, 196 r., 197 r./l., 214 r.
© **Deutsches Archäologisches Institut Madrid**: (photographs: Reinhard Friedrich, Neg. R 163-67-12, R167-67-7) 222 c./r.
© **Thomas Dix, Grenzach-Wyhlen**: 127 b., 341 a./b., 454, 455 b.r., 467 a./ c./b., 468 a./b., 470 b., 471, 476 b., 477 a./b., 478 a., 479, 480 r., 481, 482, 492 a.
© **Erzbischöfliches Dom- und Diözesanmuseum**, Vienna: 400
© **Karin Fischer**, Berlin: 408, 416 c., 422 a.r.
© **Courtesy of the Freer Gallery of Art, Smithsonian Institution**, Washington D.C.: 34, 203 c., 205 a.l., 345, 382 r./l., 383, 401 a.r., 403 r., 488 l., 522
© **Christine-Anne Gaillard**, Paris: 115 a.r./a.l./b., 440
© **Georg Gerster**, Zumikon: 102
© **Joachim Gierlichs**, London: 9, 359, 360 b.r./l., 362 a., 370, 373 l., 378 b.r./c./l., 381 a./b., 385 a.r/c./l., 398 r., 422 a.l./b., 431, 439 a., 445 r., 516 b., 519
© **Giraudon**, Paris: 307 r.
© **Julia Gonella**, Berlin: 167 b., 177 a., 180 r./l., 181 r./l.
© **Grassimuseum Leipzig**: (photograph: Matthias Hildebrand) 526
© **Manfred und Markus Hattstein**, Krefeld/Berlin: 11 a., 32 a.r., 135 a., 136 a.l., 137, 138 a., 144 b.r./l., 145, 319 b., 321 a./b.
© **Hoa-Qui**, Paris: (photographs: Xavier Richer) 254, 303, 304, 318, 322 l.
© **Hulton Getty Picture Collection**, London: 581 a.r./l., 583, 584 a.r./l., 585 a./b.r./l.
© **Institut Amatller D'Art Hispànic**, Barcelona: 235
© **The Institute of Oriental Studies of the Russian Academy of Science**, St. Petersburg: 525
© **The Israel Museum**, Jerusalem: 82 b.l.
© **Olivier Jaubert**, Paris: 346–347
© **The Keir Collection**, Ham, Surrey: (photographs: A. C. Cooper) 204 b.c., 401 b., 520 r.
© **Keramikmuseum**, Mettlach: 587 a.r./l.
© **Kharbine-Tapabor**, Paris: 169
© **Khuda Bakhsh Oriental Public Library**, Patna: 411
© **W. A. Klenko**: 357 a.
© **Koninklijke Bibliotheek**, The Hague: 166 (75 F 5, fol. 1r)
© **Natascha Kubisch**, Berlin: 35, 76 b.l., 77, 84 a., 148 b., 149, 152 a.r/b.r., 249, 259, 260, 262 a./b., 266 r., 267 a.r./l., 421, 430, 439, 443 a./b., 491 b.
© **Kunsthistorisches Museum**, Vienna: 158, 162 a./b., 173 b., 573 l.
© **Kunstmuseum Düsseldorf**: 528 a.l.
© **Kunstsammlungen der Veste Coburg**: 587 b.
© **The Laing Art Gallery**, Newcastle upon Tyne: 588 a.
© **Landesbildstelle Berlin**: 591 b.
© **Laurent Lecat**, Paris: 323 b.
© **Legatum Warnerianum**, University Library Leiden: 341 l.
© **Jürgen Liepe**, Berlin: 595 a.
© **Los Angeles County Museum of Art**: (Shinji Shumeikal Acquisition Fund) 392, (The Nasli and Alice Heeramaneck Collection, Gift of Joan Palevsky) 401 a.r., 449 b.r.; (photograph: Peter Brenner) 415 b.
© **Philippe Maillard**, Paris: 155 b.r., 156 a./b., 157 b.l.
© **Sibylle Mazot**, Paris: 144 a., 161 r.
© **Michael Meinecke**: 190 l., 192 a.
© **Victoria Meinecke-Berg**, Hamburg: 182, 183 b.l., 184 r./l., 327 a.
© **Mengès**, Paris: 45 c.r., 568 a.l.; (photographs: Winnie Denker) 451 a.l., 545 r., 547 a., 552 r., 562 l., 564 a.; (photographs: Reha Günay) 44 a., 451 a.r., 549, 551 a., 562 r., 570 a./b., 572; (photograph: Aras Nefeçi) 548
© **The Metropolitan Museum of Art**, New York: (1986, Edward C. Moore Collection, Bequest of Edward C. Moore, 1891, 91.1.1538) 196 l.; (1986, Rogers Fund, 1951, 51.56, photograph: Shecter Lee) 202 b.; (1985, Fletcher Fund, 1947, 47.100.90) 203 l.; (1995, Purchase, Lila Acheson Wallace Gift, 1992, 1992.54) 390; (Rogers Fund, 1955, 55.44) 402 l.; (1980, Catharine Lorillard Wolfe Collection, Bequest of Catherine Lorillard Wolfe, 1887, 87.15.130) 589
© **José Morón Borrego**, Seville: 213, 285, 292, 305, 306, 317
© **Wolf-Christian von der Mülbe**: 547 b., 550, 553, 556
© **Museo Arqueológico Provincial de Córdoba**, Córdoba: 239 a.l. (photograph: Alvaro Holgado)
© **Museo Arqueológico Nacional**, Madrid: 238 r., 250 a.
© **Museo de Burgos**, Burgos: 241 r.
© **Museo Poldi Pezzoli**, Milan: 523 b.r./b.l.
© **Museo Provincial de Lugo**, Lugo: 242 l.
© **Museo Provincial de Teruel**, Teruel: 242 r.
© **Museum für Türkische und Islamische Kunst**, Istanbul: 571
© **Namikawa Foundation**, Shimane: 55 a., 57 b., 195 a.l., 200 b., 203 r., 385 b.r./c./l., 541 r./l., 565 a.l., 566 l., 573 a.r.
© **Alastair Northedge**, Paris: 106, 108
© **Courtesy of the Oriental Institute of the University of Chicago**: 96
© **Alexandre Orloff**, Paris/New York: 134 a./b., 255 l., 308 a., 309, 313 l., 314 r., 315, 319 a., 320, 357 b.r., 361 l., 366, 417, 437, 438, 442 a.r., 445 l., 446 r./l., 447, 492 b.
© **MAK – Österreichisches Museum für Angewandte Kunst**, Vienna: 201
© **Österreichische Nationalbibliothek**, Vienna: 195 a.r., 198 r./l., 427
© **Paisajes Españoles**, S. A., Madrid: 230
© **Basilio Pavón Maldonado**, Madrid: 136 a.r./b.
© **Deborah Phillips**, Braunschweig: 256
© **Planet**, Paris: (photographs: Robert Polidori) 11 b., 49, 58/59, 61 a./b., 66 a.r./b., 70, 71, 72 a./b., 73 a./b., 74 a., 75, 76 a./b.r., 78, 80, 81 r., 84 b., 85, 97 a./b.l., 167 a.l., 174, 175, 192 b., 476 a.
© **Jaroslav Poncar**, Cologne: 460 a.(461 a.
© **Luke Powell**, Middlebury, Vermont: 328–329
© **Residenzmuseum**, Munich: 532 b.
© **RMN**, Paris: 38, 172 a./b., 195 b., 240 b.; (photographs: Hervé Lewandowski) 120, 413, 503 l., 529 (photographs: Arnaudet) 323 a.r./l.
© **Mohammad al-Roumi**, Paris/Damascus: 67
© **The Royal Asiatic Society**, London: 50 l.
© **The Royal Coin Cabinet**, Stockholm: 324
© **The Russian Author's Society**, Moscow: (photographs: Vadim Gippenreiter) 420, 424, 425 b., 435, 436, 438 a., 441, 444
© **The al-Sabah Collection**, Dar al-Athar al-Islamiyyah, Kuwait: 127 a.r., 489 a.r.
© **Courtesy of the Arthur C. Sackler Museum**, Harvard University Art Museums, Cambridge, Mass.: (Gift of Edward W. Forbes) 403 l.; (Private Collection) 462 r.
© **Mamoun Sakkal**, Bothell, Washington: 599
© **Collection Société Générale Marrocaine de Banques**, Casablanca: 597 r.
© **San Diego Museum of Art**, San Diego: (Edward Binney 3rd Collection) 485 r., 486 r.
© **Scala**, Florence: 47 b., 79, 83, 87, 103 a., 117 a.l., 140, 163 b.r., 217, 287 r./l., 296, 540, 596 l.
© **Schatkamer van de Sint-Servaasbasiliek**, Maastricht: 194
© **Sipa Press**, Paris: (photograph: Reha Günay) 552 l.; (photograph: J. Nicolas) 578(79
© **Staatliche Museen Kassel**: (photograph: Arno Hensmanns) 277
© **Staatliches Museum für Völkerkunde**, Munich: (photographs: S. Autrum-Mulzer) 121 a.r. (Neg. Nr. 28-8-2), 163 a.l.; (photograph: c. Weidner-El Salamouny) 204 b.l.
© **The State Hermitage Museum**, St. Petersburg: 344, 404 a./b.r./l., 530
© **Anne und Henri Stierlin**, Geneva: 33, 36, 37 a., 45 a.l., 52, 66 a.l., 69 r., 90, 91 b., 94, 99, 101, 105 a., 113 l., 116 a./b., 117 a.r./l., 124 b., 128, 132 b., 135 b., 139, 147 a. 150, 152 l., 153, 160 l., 170 r., 171, 177 b., 179 b., 183 a./b.r., 185, 186 r./l., 187, 188 b.r., 189, 190 r., 191 r./l., 226, 278 a./b., 283 a., 284, 288, 289 b.r., 290, 291 b.r./l., 292 a.r./b.r., 293 b.l., 295, 297 a., 326, 349 b., 369 a.l./b., 371 a./b., 374, 375 l., 380, 395 a., 399 a.l., 448 a./b., 450, 463, 485 l., 489 b.r., 490 b.r., 493 a., 497, 504, 507, 509, 510 a.r./a.l./b., 512 a./b., 513, 516 a., 517, 518 a./b.r., 527, 544 b., 546, 554, 555, 559, 560, 566 r., 568 r.
© **The Textile Museum**, Washington D.C.: (na. 73.368) 119 a.
© **Courtesy of the Trustees of the Victoria and Albert Museum**, London: (photograph: Daniel McGrath) 154 l.; (photograph: Ian Thomas) 155 b.l.; (V&A Picture Library, London) 487, 489 a.l., 502 l., 523 a., 528 a.r./b.
© **Universitat de Barcelona**, Barcelona: 231 b.
© **University Library**, Leiden: 343 l.
© **Philippa Vaughan**, London: 458, 459, 473 b., 474 a., 483 b., 488 r.
© **Verwaltung Schlösser und Gärten Schwetzingen**: (photograph: Foto-Thome) 586 a.l.
© **Donald Wilber**, Photo courtesy of Asian Art Archives, University of Michigan: 393

Acknowledgments

The publishers would like thank Dr. Almut von Gladiß of the Museum für Islamische Kunst, Berlin, for her constant willingness to support the project throughout its various stages with advice and assistance and also for her various special lectureships; Dr. Julia Gonnella, Berlin, for her special lectureship on India; Dr. Christiane Kothe, Cologne, for her specialist editing on the Alhambra; Dr. Natascha Kubisch, Berlin, for commitment over and above her contributions to the text; Mrs. Christa Kienapfel of the Museum für Islamische Kunst, Berlin, for her constant willingness to help; Mrs. Heidrun Klein of the Bildarchiv Preußischer Kulturbesitz for her help with the procurement of pictures; Mr. Henri Stierlin, Geneva, for his help with the picture research.

Publishing and art direction: Peter Feierabend
Editing: Juliane Stollreiter
Design: Erill Vinzenz Fritz (manager), Kathrin Jacobsen
Map editing: Monika Schrimpf
Picture editing: Katleen Krause, Dennis Riffel, Florence Baret
Chronological tables: Melanie Kamp, Christine Diefenbacher,
Barbara Konrad-Lütt
Index : Julia Niehaus, Torsten Kölzsch, Jutta Fischer
Plans and outlines: Florian Glowatz/TOPOS, Berlin;
Sergej Chmelnizkij, Berlin
Cartography: Rolf Krause, Essen;
Studio für Landkartentechnik Maiwald, Norderstedt

Original title: Islam – Kunst und Architektur
ISBN 3-8331-1036-8

Translation from German: George Ansell, Anthe Bell, Richard Elliott, Phil Goddard,
Harriet Horsfield, Michele McMeekin, Martin Pearce and Anthony Vivis
in association with First Edition Translations Ltd, Cambridge, UK
Editing: Kay Hyman in association with First Edition Translations Ltd, Cambridge, UK
Typesetting: The Write Idea in association with First Edition Translations Ltd, Cambridge, UK
Project coordination: Andrew R. Davidson for First Edition Translations Ltd, Cambridge, UK
Project Manager: Kristin Zeier
Revision of the English text: Jardi Mullinax and Russell Cennydd

Printed in Italy

ISBN 3-8331-1178-X

10 9 8 7 6 5 4 3 2 1
X IX VIII VII VI V IV III II I